Handbook
of Debt
Management

PUBLIC ADMINISTRATION AND PUBLIC POLICY

A Comprehensive Publication Program

Executive Editor

JACK RABIN
Professor of Public Administration and Public Policy
Division of Public Affairs
The Capital College
The Pennsylvania State University—Harrisburg
Middletown, Pennsylvania

1. *Public Administration as a Developing Discipline* (in two parts), Robert T. Golembiewski
2. *Comparative National Policies on Health Care*, Milton I. Roemer, M.D.
3. *Exclusionary Injustice: The Problem of Illegally Obtained Evidence*, Steven R. Schlesinger
4. *Personnel Management in Government: Politics and Process*, Jay M. Shafritz, Walter L. Balk, Albert C. Hyde, and David H. Rosenbloom
5. *Organization Development in Public Administration* (in two parts), edited by Robert T. Golembiewski and William B. Eddy
6. *Public Administration: A Comparative Perspective, Second Edition, Revised and Expanded*, Ferrel Heady
7. *Approaches to Planned Change* (in two parts), Robert T. Golembiewski
8. *Program Evaluation at HEW* (in three parts), edited by James G. Abert
9. *The States and the Metropolis*, Patricia S. Florestano and Vincent L. Marando
10. *Personnel Management in Government: Politics and Process, Second Edition, Revised and Expanded*, Jay M. Shafritz, Albert C. Hyde, and David H. Rosenbloom
11. *Changing Bureaucracies: Understanding the Organization Before Selecting the Approach*, William A. Medina
12. *Handbook on Public Budgeting and Financial Management*, edited by Jack Rabin and Thomas D. Lynch
13. *Encyclopedia of Policy Studies*, edited by Stuart S. Nagel
14. *Public Administration and Law: Bench v. Bureau in the United States*, David H. Rosenbloom
15. *Handbook on Public Personnel Administration and Labor Relations*, edited by Jack Rabin, Thomas Vocino, W. Bartley Hildreth, and Gerald J. Miller
16. *Public Budgeting and Finance: Behavioral, Theoretical, and Technical Perspectives*, edited by Robert T. Golembiewski and Jack Rabin
17. *Organizational Behavior and Public Management*, Debra W. Stewart and G. David Garson
18. *The Politics of Terrorism: Second Edition, Revised and Expanded*, edited by Michael Stohl
19. *Handbook of Organization Management*, edited by William B. Eddy
20. *Organization Theory and Management*, edited by Thomas D. Lynch
21. *Labor Relations in the Public Sector*, Richard C. Kearney
22. *Politics and Administration: Woodrow Wilson and American Public Administration*, edited by Jack Rabin and James S. Bowman
23. *Making and Managing Policy: Formulation, Analysis, Evaluation*, edited by G. Ronald Gilbert
24. *Public Administration: A Comparative Perspective, Third Edition, Revised*, Ferrel Heady
25. *Decision Making in the Public Sector*, edited by Lloyd G. Nigro
26. *Managing Administration*, edited by Jack Rabin, Samuel Humes, and Brian S. Morgan
27. *Public Personnel Update*, edited by Michael Cohen and Robert T. Golembiewski
28. *State and Local Government Administration*, edited by Jack Rabin and Don Dodd

Additional Volumes in Preparation

ANNALS OF PUBLIC ADMINISTRATION

Handbook
of Debt
Management

edited by
Gerald J. Miller
Rutgers University at Newark
Newark, New Jersey

Marcel Dekker, Inc.   New York • Basel • Hong Kong

Library of Congress Cataloging-in-Publication Data

Handbook of debt management / edited by Gerald J. Miller.
    p. cm. — (Public administration and public policy ; 60)
    Includes index.
    ISBN 0- 8247- 9388- 9 (alk. paper)
    1. Finance, Public—United States—Handbooks, manuals, etc.
2. Debts, Public—United States—Handbooks, manuals, etc. 3. Local
finance—United States—Handbooks, manuals, etc. I. Miller,
Gerald. II. Series.
HJ257.2.H356   1996
336.3'6'0973—dc20

95- 49763
CIP

The publisher offers discounts on this book when ordered in bulk quantities. For more information, write to Special Sales/Professional Marketing at the address below.

This book is printed on acid-free paper.

MARCEL DEKKER, INC.
270 Madison Avenue, New York, New York 10016

Current printing (last digit):
10 9 8 7 6 5 4 3 2 1

PRINTED IN THE UNITED STATES OF AMERICA

To my mother,
Reba S. Miller

Preface

The *Handbook of Debt Management* has two purposes. The first is to provide materials for the academic and corporate trainer whose responsibility is to teach government managers and securities industry professionals the basics of debt management.

The second purpose is to help prepare securities industry professionals seeking licenses through the Municipal Securities Rulemaking Board Principal Qualification Examination (Test Series 53, administered by the National Association of Securities Dealers), the Municipal Securities Representative Qualification Examination (Test Series 52, also administered by NASD), and the General Securities Registered Representative Examination (Test Series 7, jointly sponsored and required by the New York Stock Exchange, the American Stock Exchange, the Chicago Board Options Exchange, the Philadelphia Stock Exchange, the National Association of Securities Dealers, and the Municipal Securities Rulemaking Board).

None of the licensing or testing organizations has sponsored or approved this handbook. However, we feel that the material provided will assist meaningfully in preparing both the licensing candidate and the academic and corporate student with specific information and skills. Upon study and reflection, candidates and students should more easily prove their competence to perform their jobs.

This handbook deals with the practice of government debt management in the United States. The first part covers the "municipal" market, the market generally encompassing state and local governments. The second part describes the "treasury" market and practices prescribed for and followed by the U.S. government.

STATE AND LOCAL GOVERNMENT DEBT MANAGEMENT

The debt management process among municipal issuers substantially relates to law. Tax laws, state constitution, and statutory prescriptions, as well as local structure preference, dictate what shall be done to sell municipal securities and, usually, how that sale shall be done. Part I starts with a broad background for municipal securities sales by surveying legal, policy, economic, and structural presumptions bearing on what government managers must do. This is followed by a description of the general steps in the process of selling securities.

Setting Policy for State and Local Debt Management

State and local debt management is done within various frameworks, each limiting or exploiting the purposes of debt. Debt policies often confound tax policies and vice versa, not only at the local and state level of government borrowing, but at the federal level as well. Federal law, in fact, provides what many consider an overly generous subsidy to state and local capital asset expansion. Still, the generosity of federal laws is a very political gesture, one that may be forced to work differently as the political winds change. Moreover, state and local governments exploit structural opportunities, through the public authority, to gain greater leverage over, if not an absolute increase in, borrowing power.

We start with the landmark U.S. Supreme Court decision in *South Carolina* v. *Baker*, in which the court holds that state and local bond issuers have no constitutional right to immunity from federal taxation on the interest paid by their securities; that tax preference exists solely because of Congress's decision to grant it. Clearly then, the municipal market is in part a creation of federal law. The intergovernmental cooperation required led a panel, the Anthony Commission (Chapter 1), to take a long look at the market and recommend improvements. This commission's study is a clear and thoughtful discussion of the issues that have been decided and those still requiring action; thus, the study will have a substantial impact throughout the 1990s on legislation passed by Congress, and even more on the debate over the direction the market's development will take. Just as clearly, Chapters 3–5 examine the economic justification for the tax-exempt status of municipal bond interest payments. In a different way, Chapter 6 looks at the economic trade-off in financing capital assets; if there is an economic argument for taxes or for borrowing. Finally, Chapter 7 examines the impact of structural differentiation on borrowing, especially the use of public authorities to finance capital assets.

Capital Budgeting

The budget for purchasing or constructing capital assets usually sparks the beginning of the process resulting in the sale of securities to finance these projects. This section discusses why we need separate capital budgets and presents three contrasting approaches to capital budgeting, defining that form of budgeting, and justifying its use. Understanding this material will enable the reader to distinguish infrastructure finance from pork barrel political spending.

Chapter 8 describes the rational exercises of planning by outlining the process of cost-benefit analysis. Chapter 9 looks at the different schools of thought regarding capital budgeting, especially the contrasting schools called "good government, " "intercommunity competition, " and "opportunistic politics." Chapter 10 elaborates on the relationship between capital budgeting, organization strategic planning, community capital improvement plans, and economic development. Finally, Chapter 11 tells the story of the institutionalization of capital budgeting in New Jersey state government.

Formulating Debt Policy

Determining affordability and applying such limits to capital budgets rounds out debt policy making; that is, the number and type of projects financed is a function of not only capital plans but also debt policy: what the community can afford, what the community can afford to finance out of current revenues, and the debt-financing structures that the law and the voters allow. Chapter 12 outlines the elements of policy required of state and local governments if comprehensive planning is a goal, while Chapter 13 presents a more normative model, based on analysis of specific financial condition variables. Then, in three case studies, we look at the substance of debt policies at the state and local level. At the state level, Chapter 14 shows Maryland's policy and reflects on how well the state has achieved its past goals. At the city level, Chapter 15 provides a statement of Dallas's goals and objectives in great detail. Finally, at the intergovernmental level, Chapter 16 considers the cooperation among governments necessary to produce a genuinely workable debt policy.

New Issue Financing

Once the capital budget is fixed and debt policy set, the financial manager has several choices as to the method of financing and whom to choose as advisors. Paying for capital projects out of current revenues seems sensible to many since the government does not have to go into debt. However, as Chapter 17 illustrates, the analysis underlying this choice is rigorous. Current revenues being only one choice, the U.S. General Accounting Office (Chapter 18) surveys others at the state level, briefly outlining the decision process in choosing among various debt-financing methods.

The advisors chosen to help a government financial manager plan and then borrow the funds necessary to finance a capital project get detailed scrutiny in Miller's description of debt networks (Chapter 19). He argues that advisors act less as agents hired to perform a specific task than as equal players in the decisions about what, when, and how to borrow. With controversy raging over the merits and drawbacks of negotiated bond sales (as opposed to competitively bid bond sales), Chapter 20 provides a decision sequence that managers may follow in making the best use of this method of hiring advice.

Issue Structure

Of acute interest today is the issue of whether bonds should be competitively bid or negotiated with an underwriter. The structure and sizing of bond issues get attention in the next section, which answers the question: What strategy should the financial advisor and the issuer follow in order to achieve their goals? Chapter 21 elaborates the various methods of designing bond issues and the methods used to achieve the issuer's goals.

Disclosure

Disclosure is defined as the informing of prospective bond buyers and present bond owners of facts relevant to understanding the value of their investments. In the early 1990s, no hotter topic concerned those participating in the municipal market. This section asks the key questions about disclosure: what disclosure means, what standards control disclosure; the offering statement's connection with disclosure, getting information for the offering statement, and publishing these data. Chapter 22 looks at disclosure in terms of informing the public about risks. The excerpts from the U.S. Securities and Exchange Commission's rules on disclosure (Chapter 23) show efforts now made to improve the process of getting information from the issuer to the bond buyer.

Rating Debt

To the prospective and present bond owner, financial data lie somewhere within the saying that there are "lies, damn lies, and statistics." Despite efforts by financial advisors and government managers to capture a clear picture of the issuer in the offering statement, by the bond counsel to allay legal and tax fears, and by the organization's auditor to verify financial statements, bond buyers tend to rely on the credit-rating agencies for comfort. What do rating agencies do and how do they do it? In a phrase, rating agencies classify or categorize issuers and the debt they are issuing based on information the issuers present as well as information that the issuers have provided over time.

Rating agencies ask simply: What is the likelihood of timely repayment of principal and interest? The answer is a categorical one, called a rating symbol; thus the ever-present metaphor: AAA or excellent. How do the rating agencies work? Chapter 24 describes the rating agencies' work and analyzes the underlying correspondences within the ratings.

The ratings do matter, because the difference in interest costs between highly rated and less highly rated debt is substantial. Despite these important distinctions for issuers, the information the ratings convey to bond buyers suffers from lack of timeliness. Richard Y. Roberts, one of the current (1995) members of the U.S. Securities and Exchange Commission, argues in Chapters 25 and 26 that the ratings agencies must undergo tougher scrutiny, if for no other reason than for the legal role they play in investment managers' work. Following these arguments, Chapter 27 presents the checklists that a major rating agency uses to ensure the adequacy and completeness of information its staff needs to assess the likelihood of a bond issuer's timely repayment of principal with interest. This section closes with a series originally published by Moody's Investors Service on the five major sets of factors bearing on a debt rating: economic, financial, administrative, debt, and legal.

Marketing, Sale, and Underwriting

Although competitive versus negotiated bond issues are dealt with in a previous section, Section H describes the technical analysis done to judge bids or establish a negotiated award. Implicit in the discussion in this section is a view of how the secondary municipal bond market works. Chapter 33 looks at the two most common methods of determining the lowest bid in a competitive sale. Chapter 34 examines two additional methods while Chapter 35 shows the relevance of the method Harold Bierman advocates in the previous chapter. Finally, an issue brief from the California Debt Advisory Commission explains the components of the coupon and price of a bond in a negotiated bond sale (Chapter 36).

Managing Accumulated Debt

After the debt sale comes the apparently routine work of paying off the debt. Part of this routine is refunding bonds as interest rates fall. Since the Internal Revenue Service and Congress control much of the structure and limits of refunding, Chapter 37 presents calculations involved in assuring that excess earnings do not jeopardize the tax exemption on the interest that bond buyers receive.

A more serious issue arises after the bond sale when, in the otherwise routine world of management, a default occurs; that is, what happens when the issuer cannot or will not make timely repayment of principal with interest. Chapter 38 examines one such default and its lessons.

NATIONAL DEBT MANAGEMENT

The second part of the handbook deals with U.S. government debt management issues. Three issues concern us first. First, should borrowing/debt finance only capital assets, and how should we categorize those assets? Second, what is wrong (or not so wrong) with a nation running an operating budget deficit? And, third, how should we look at, or feel about, the burden of the debt our nation has accumulated?

On the issue of debt for capital assets, Chapters 39 and 40 take somewhat opposing views. Premchand (Chapter 39) argues the common-sense separation of operations from investment in budgeting with investment having a long-term horizon and assets financed by debt. Mikesell (Chapter 40), on the other hand, sees capital assets as merely a playful term that could cover anything Congress might want to fund with debt, regardless of whether it is a "true" investment.

On the subject of the deficit that Mikesell alludes to, Macia Lynn Whicker (Chapter 41) examines the issue of revenues and debt from a historical perspective. She admits that the set of problems that have developed over time cannot be solved easily; nevertheless, she surveys the revenue and other solutions to provoke debate and, ultimately offer a solution.

On the issue of debt burden, John B. Carlson (Chapter 42) asks whether we realize what might happen if we do not take control of the accumulated debt. He hazards a guess as to what would happen if foreign investors stopped financing our deficits; warns against hastily reducing the debt.

These topical questions beg for broader explanation. Thus, principles of debt management appear regularly as they have for decades. A survey of the development of these principles is provided in Section B of Part II. The Organization for Economic Cooperation and Development, an organization created by the major developed countries in the world to promote sound, sustainable economic growth and employment as well as expanded world trade, brought together a group of experts in the early 1980s to assess debt management from various national perspectives. Their report (Chapter 43) represents broad international consensus about these matters. James Tobin, the Nobel prize–winning economist, whose paper is still among those most cited in the study of debt management at the national level, reflects the important aspects of the practice from the 1960s (Chapter 44). Chapter 45 represents the 1950s, a period that had generally, if not always, balanced budgets and low deficits but that had to deal with low inflation and the debt from Chapters 46–50 bring together views of prominent economists who comment on the immediate postwar period of the late 1940s, a time of massive lending to Europe.

Bringing the discussion back to the present, Chapter 51 looks at the debt situation and the "principles" of the early 1990s. Finally, Chapter 52 revives a proposal to index bonds (zero-coupon bond appreciation, specifically) to the inflation rate. The feature would make treasury instruments more attractive to investors and would aid the Federal Reserve in its goal of maintaining price stability.

Selling debt issues at the national level has unique interest paralleling the process outlined and discussed in Part I, on municipal issues. Chapter 53 looks at issues brought to a head by an attempt by a primary dealer in U.S. debt securities or "treasuries" to corner the market in the early 1990s. In the report, a joint committee of the U.S. Department of the Treasury, the U.S. Securities and Exchange Commission, and the Board of Governors of the Federal Reserve System outlines a course of action that will affect treasuries sales for the remainder of the twentieth century.

Taking slightly different tacks, three other chapters, published more or less contemporaneously, take on the issue of U.S. Treasury auctions from a technical perspective. V. V. Chari and Robert J. Weber in Chapter 54 opt for a "uniform-price, sealed-bid" auction. Vincent Reinhart (Chapter 55) looks at a popular proposal—the second-price, sealed-bid auction—in terms of the events prompting the joint committee's work, and he critiques an open-outcry system as well. Next, E. J. Stevens and Diana Dumitru (Chapter 56) offer changes to current practice that might eliminate many problems and reduce the need to formulate a policy arbitrary of auction rules.

Finally, we ask whether even hypothetically a government's debt ever gets repaid. If not, can it simply roll over the debt forever? Andrew B. Abel (Chapter 57) takes the question, one at the frontiers of economic research, under study. He uses the interest rate/growth rate in gross national product, the comparison of treasuries with other securities, and national fiscal policy as issues bearing on the question.

Gerald J. Miller

Contents

Contributors

Charles C. Abbott[†]

Andrew B. Abel   Department of Finance, The Wharton School, University of Pennsylvania, Philadelphia, Pennsylvania

Anthony Commission on Public Finance   Washington, D.C.

Harold Bierman, Jr., Ph.D.   Nicholas H. Noyes Professor of Finance, Samuel Curtis Johnson Graduate School of Management, Cornell University, Ithaca, New York

Greg Blees   Department of Finance, City of Saint Paul, Saint Paul, Minnesota

Board of Governors of the Federal Reserve System   Washington, D.C.

Steven Bocamazo   Moody's Investors Service, New York, New York

James H. Burr, M.A., J.D., M.B.A.   Public Finance Department, Legal Analysis Group, Moody's Investors Service, New York, New York

California Debt Advisory Commission   Sacramento, California

Capital Debt Affordability Committee, State of Maryland   Annapolis, Maryland

John B. Carlson, Ph.D.   Economist, Research Department, Federal Reserve Bank of Cleveland, Cleveland, Ohio

V. V. Chari   Advisor, Research Department, Federal Reserve Bank of Minneapolis, Minneapolis, Minnesota, and Harold H. Hines Professor of Risk Management, J. L. Kellogg Graduate School of Management, Northwestern University, Chicago, Illinois

G. Marc Choate   Professor of Finance, Atkinson School of Management, Willamette University, Salem, Oregon

City of Dallas Department of Budget and Management Services   Dallas, Texas

Frederick D. Crowley, Ph.D.   Associate Professor Department of Accounting and Finance, Indiana University/Purdue University-Fort Wayne, Fort Wayne, Indiana

Paul Devine   Moody's Investors Service, New York, New York

[†]Deceased

Thomas A. Dorsey, J.D., Ph.D.   Senior Vice President and Managing Director, Public Finance Underwriting Division, AMBAC Indemnity Corporation, New York, New York

Diana Dumitru   Senior Research Assistant, Federal Reserve Bank of Cleveland, Cleveland, Ohio

William H. Eldridge, J.D., M.B.A.   Associate Professor, Department of Management Science, Kean College, Union, New Jersey

Peter Fortune, Ph.D.   Professor, Department of Economics, Tufts University, Medford, and Economist, Research Department, Federal Reserve Bank of Boston, Boston, Massachusetts

Gerasimos A. Gianakis, Ph.D.   Assistant Professor, Department of Political Science, Kent State University, Kent, Ohio

Roger H. Gordon, Ph.D.   Professor, Department of Economics, University of Michigan, Ann Arbor, Michigan and the National Bureau of Economic Research, Cambridge, Massachusetts

Merl Hackbart, Ph.D.   Professor of Finance and Public Administration, Department of Finance, School of Management, College of Business and Economics, University of Kentucky, Lexington, Kentucky

Arie Halachmi, Ph.D.   Professor, Management and Policy Analysis, Institute of Government, Tennessee State University, Nashville, Tennessee, and Fellow, The Netherlands Interuniversity Institute of Government (NIG), University of Twente, Enchende, The Netherlands

Seymour E. Harris[†]

Alvin H. Hansen[†]

Robert L. Hetzel, Ph.D.   Vice President, Research Department, Federal Reserve Bank of Richmond, Richmond, Virginia

W. Bartley Hildreth, M.P.A., D.P.A.   Professor, Hugo Wall School of Urban and Public Affairs, and F. Frank Barton School of Business, Wichita State University, Wichita, Kansas

Michael Johnston   Moody's Investors Service, New York, New York

James C. Joseph   Assistant Director, Government Finance Research Center, Government Finance Officers Association, Chicago, Illinois

Edward Krauss   Moody's Investors Service, New York, New York

Richard Larkin   Managing Director, Standard & Poor's Corporation, New York, New York

Anthony L. Loviscek, Ph.D.   Assistant Professor, Department of Economics, W. Paul Stillman School of Business, Seton Hall University, South Orange, New Jersey

Tom McLoughlin   Government Finance Research Center, Government Finance Officers Association, Chicago, Illinois

Katherine McManus   Moody's Investors Service, New York, New York

Alfred Medioli   Moody's Investors Service, New York, New York

Gilbert E. Metcalf, Ph.D.   Professor, Department of Economics, Tufts University, Medford, and the National Bureau of Economic Research, Cambridge, Massachusetts

John L. Mikesell   Professor, School of Public and Environmental Affairs, Indiana University, Bloomington, Indiana

Gerald J. Miller, Ph.D.   Associate Professor, Department of Public Administration, Rutgers University at Newark, Newark, New Jersey

---

[†]Deceased

Jerry Mitchell, Ph.D. Associate Professor, School of Public Affairs, Baruch College, City University of New York, New York, New York

Moody's Investors Service New York, New York

Municipal Securities Rulemaking Board Washington, D.C.

Richard A. Musgrave* Santa Cruz, California

Gary Norstrem Department of Finance, City of Saint Paul, Saint Paul, Minnesota

Organization for Economic Cooperation and Development Paris, France

Michele M. Patrick, M.G.A. Assistant Managing Director, Office of the Managing Director, City of Philadelphia, Philadelphia, Pennsylvania

A. Premchand Assistant Director, Fiscal Affairs Department, International Monetary Fund, Washington, D.C.

Amy v. Puelz, Ph.D. Assistant Professor, Department of Management Information Sciences, Edwin L. Cox School of Business, Southern Methodist University, Dallas, Texas

James R. Ramsey, Ph.D. Vice President of Finance and Administration, and Professor of Economics, Western Kentucky University, Bowling Green, Kentucky

Vincent R. Reinhart Assistant Director, Division of Monetary Affairs, Board of Governors of the Federal Reserve, Washington, D.C.

Richard Y. Roberts Commissioner, United States Securities and Exchange Commission, Washington, D.C.

Earl R. Rolph Professor, Department of Economics, University of California at Berkeley, Berkeley, California

Eugene Schiller Department of Finance, City of Saint Paul, Saint Paul, Minnesota

Lawrence H. Seltzer[†]

D. Keith Sill, Ph.D. Economist, Research Department, Federal Reserve Bank of Philadelphia, Philadelphia, Pennsylvania

Bernard Smith Director, Department of Finance, City of Halifax, Halifax, Nova Scotia, Canada

Robert W. Stanley Vice President and Assistant Director, Department of Public Finance, Moody's Investors Service, New York, New York

E. J. Stevens, Ph.D. Consultant and Economist, Research Department, Federal Reserve Bank of Cleveland, Cleveland, Ohio

Fred Thompson, Ph.D. Grace and Elmer Goudy Professor of Public Management, Atkinson School of Management, Willamette University, Salem, Oregon

James Tobin, Ph.D. Sterling Professor of Economics Emeritus, Cowles Foundation for Research in Economics, Yale University, New Haven, Connecticut

United States Department of Treasury Washington, D.C.

United States General Accounting Office Washington, D.C.

United States Securities and Exchange Commission Washington, D.C.

Robert J. Weber Professor of Decision Sciences, J. L. Kellogg Graduate School of Management, Northwestern University, Chicago, Illinois

---

**Former affiliation*: Harvard University, Cambridge, Massachusetts
[†]Deceased

George J. Whelan, M.A.   Administrative Officer, Commerce Department, City of Philadelphia, Philadelphia, Pennsylvania

Marcia Lynn Whicker, Ph.D.   Professor, Department of Public Administration, Rutgers University at Newark, Newark, New Jersey

Robert W. Zinn, C.P.A.*   Assistant County Administrator, Pinellas County Government, Clearwater, Florida

---

**Current affiliation*: Consultant, Indian Rocks Beach, Florida

Handbook
of Debt
Management

1

South Carolina *v.* Baker

SUPREME COURT OF THE UNITED STATES: SYLLABUS

South Carolina *v.* Baker, Secretary of the Treasury

On Exceptions to Report of Special Master

No. 94, Orig. Argued December 7, 1987—Decided April 20, 1988

Section 310(b)(1) of the Tax Equity and Fiscal Responsibility Act of 1982 removes the federal income tax exemption for interest earned on publicly offered long-term bonds (hereinafter referred to as bonds) issued by state and local governments (hereinafter referred to collectively as States) unless those bonds are issued in registered (as opposed to bearer) form. South Carolina invoked this Court's original jurisdiction, contending that § 310(b)(1) is constitutionally invalid under the Tenth Amendment and the doctrine of intergovernmental tax immunity. A Special Master was appointed. After conducting hearings and taking evidence, he concluded that § 310(b)(1) is constitutional and recommended entering judgment for the defendant. South Carolina and the National Governors' Association (NGA), as an intervenor, filed exceptions to various factual findings of the Master and to his legal conclusions concerning their constitutional challenges.

Held:

1. Section 310(b)(1) does not violate the Tenth Amendment or constitutional principles of federalism by effectively compelling States to issue bonds in registered form. Pp. 4–9.

(a) The Tenth Amendment limits on Congress' authority to regulate state activities are structural, not substantive—that is, the States must find their protection from congressional regulation through the national political process, not through judicially defined spheres of unregulable state activity. In this case, South Carolina has not even alleged that it was deprived of any right to participate in the national political process or that it was singled out in a way that left it politically isolated and powerless. The allegations South Carolina does make—that Congress was uninformed and chose an ineffective remedy—do not amount to an allegation that the political process operated in a defective manner. Pp. 5–7.

(b) NGA's contention that § 310 is invalid because it commandeers the state legislative and administrative process by coercing States into enacting legislation authorizing bond registration and into administering the registration scheme finds no support in the claim left open by *FERC* v. *Mississippi*, 456 U.S. 742. Section 310 regulates state activities; it does not, as did the statute in *FERC*, seek to control or influence the manner in which States regulate private parties. That a State wishing to engage in certain activity must take administrative and sometimes legislative action to comply with federal standards regulating that activity is a commonplace that presents no constitutional defect. Moreover, under NGA's theory, any State could immunize its activities from federal regulation by simply codifying the manner in which it engages in those activities. Pp. 7–9.

2. Section 310(b)(1) does not violate the doctrine of intergovernmental tax immunity by taxing the interest earned on unregistered state bonds. Section 310(b)(1) is inconsistent with this Court's holding in *Pollock* v. *Farmers' Loan & Trust Co.*, 157 U.S. 429, that state bond interest was immune from a nondiscriminatory federal tax, but that decision has been effectively overruled by subsequent case law. Under the intergovernmental tax immunity jurisprudence prevailing at *Pollock*'s time, neither the Federal nor the State Governments

Note: Where it is feasible, a syllabus (headnote) will be released, as is being done in connection with this case, at the time the opinion is issued. The syllabus constitutes no part of the opinion of the Court but has been prepared by the Reporter of Decisions for the convenience of the reader. See *United States* v. *Detroit Lumber Co.*, 200 U.S. 321. 337.

could tax income that an individual directly derived from *any* contract with the other government. This general rule was based on the rationale that any tax on income a party received under a contract with the government was a tax on the contract and thus a tax "on" the government because it burdened the government's power to enter into the contract. That rationale has been repudiated by modern intergovernmental tax immunity case law, and the government contract immunities have been, one by one, overruled. The owners of state bonds have no constitutional entitlement not to pay taxes on income they earn from the bonds, and States have no constitutional entitlement to issue bonds paying lower interest rates than other issuers. The nondiscriminatory tax under § 310 is imposed on and collected from bondholders, not States, and any increased administrative costs incurred by States in implementing the registration system are not "taxes" within the meaning of the tax immunity doctrine. Moreover, the provisions of § 310 seek to assure that *all* publicly offered long-term bonds are issued in registered form, whether issued by state or local governments, the Federal Government, or private corporations. Pp. 9–20.

Exceptions to Special Master's Report overruled, and judgment entered for defendant.

Brennan, J., delivered the opinion of the Court, in which White, Marshall, Blackmun, and Stevens, JJ., joined, and in which Scalia, J., joined except for Part II. Stevens, J., filed a concurring opinion. Scalia, J., filed an opinion concurring in part and concurring in the judgment. Rehnquist, C. J., filed an opinion concurring in the judgment. O'Connor, J., filed a dissenting opinion. Kennedy, J., took no part in the consideration or decision of the case.

SUPREME COURT OF THE UNITED STATES: NO. 94, ORIG.

State of South Carolina, Plaintiff *v.* James A. Baker, III, Secretary of the Treasury of the United States

On Bill of Complaint [April 20, 1988]

Justice Brennan Delivered the Opinion of the Court

Section 310(b)(1) of the Tax Equity and Fiscal Responsibility Act of 1982 (TEFRA), Pub. L. 97-248, 96 Stat. 596, 26 U.S.C. § 103(j)(1), removes the federal income tax exemption for interest earned on publicly offered long-term bonds issued by state and local governments unless those bonds are issued in registered form.* This original jurisdiction case presents the issues whether § 310(b)(1) of TEFRA either (1) violates the Tenth Amendment and constitutional principles of federalism by compelling States to issue bonds in registered form or (2) violates the doctrine of intergovernmental tax immunity by taxing the interest earned on unregistered state bonds.

I

Historically, bonds have been issued as either registered bonds or bearer bonds. These two types of bonds differ in the mechanisms used for transferring ownership and making payments. Ownership of a registered bond is recorded on a central list, and a transfer of record ownership requires entering the change on that list.† The record owner automatically receives interest payments by check or electronic transfer of funds from the issuer's paying agent. Ownership of a bearer bond, in contrast, is presumed from possession and is transferred by physically handing over the bond. The bondowner obtains interest payments by presenting bond coupons to a bank that in turn presents the coupons to the issuer's paying agent.

In 1982, Congress enacted TEFRA, which contains a variety of provisions, including § 310, designed to reduce the federal deficit by promoting compliance with the tax laws. Congress had become concerned about the growing magnitude of tax evasion; Internal Revenue Service (IRS) studies indicated that unreported income had grown from an estimated range of $31.1 billion to $32.2 billion in 1973 to a range of $93.3 billion

---

Notice: This opinion is subject to formal revision before publication in the preliminary print of the United States Reports. Readers are requested to notify the Reporter of Decisions, Supreme Court of the United States. Washington, D.C. 20543, of any typographical or other formal errors, in order that corrections may be made before the preliminary print goes to press.

*For simplicity, we will refer to state and local governments collectively as "States" and will refer to publicly offered long-term bonds as "bonds."

†The record owner of a registered bond may sometimes differ, however, from the beneficial owners, and sellers can transfer beneficial ownership of most types of registered bonds without entering a change on the central list.

to $97 billion in 1981. Compliance Gap: Hearing before the Subcommittee on Oversight of the Internal Revenue Service of the Senate Committee on Finance, 97th Cong., 2d Sess., 126 (1982). Unregistered bonds apparently became a focus of attention because they left no paper trail and thus facilitated tax evasion. Then Assistant Secretary of the Treasury for Tax Policy John Chapoton testified before the House Ways and Means Committee that a registration requirement would help prevent tax evasion because bearer bonds often represent unreported and untaxed income that, without a system of recorded ownership, the IRS has difficulty reconstructing. Hearings on H. R. 6300 before the House Committee on Ways and Means, 97th Cong., 2d Sess., 35 (1982). He also expressed concern that bearer bonds were being used to avoid estate and gift taxes and as a medium of exchange in the illegal sector. *Ibid.* In reporting out the bill containing the provision that eventually became § 310 of TEFRA, the Senate Finance Committee Report expressed the same concerns

> The committee believes that a fair and efficient system of information reporting and withholding cannot be achieved with respect to interest-bearing obligations as long as a significant volume of long-term bearer instruments is issued. A system of book-entry registration will preserve the liquidity of obligations while requiring the creation of ownership records that can produce useful information reports with respect to both the payment of interest and the sale of obligations prior to maturity through brokers. Furthermore, registration will reduce the ability of noncompliant taxpayers to conceal income and property from the reach of the income, estate, and gift taxes. Finally, the registration requirement may reduce the volume of readily negotiable substitutes for cash available to persons engaged in illegal activities. S. Rep. No. 97-494, Vol. 1, p. 242 (1982).

Section 310 was designed to meet these concerns by providing powerful incentives to issue bonds in registered form.

Because § 310 aims to address the tax evasion concerns posed generally by unregistered bonds, it covers not only state bonds but also bonds issued by the United States and private corporations. Section 310(a) requires the United States to issue publicly offered bonds with a maturity of one year or more in registered form.* With respect to similar bonds issued by private corporations, §§ 310(b)(2)–(6) impose a series of tax penalties on nonregistration. Corporations declining to issue the covered bonds in registered form lose tax deductions and adjustments for interest paid on the bonds, §§ 310(b)(2) and (3), and must pay a special excise tax on the bond principal, § 310(b)(4). Holders of these unregistered corporate bonds generally cannot deduct capital losses or claim capital-gain treatment for any losses or gains sustained on the bonds. §§ 310(b)(5) and (6). Section 310(b)(1) completes this statutory scheme by denying the federal income tax exemption for interest earned on state bonds to owners of long-term publicly offered state bonds that are not issued in registered form.

South Carolina invoked the original jurisdiction of this Court, contending that § 310(b)(1) is constitutionally invalid under the Tenth Amendment and the doctrine of intergovernmental tax immunity. We granted South Carolina leave to file the instant complaint against the Secretary of the Treasury of the United States, *South Carolina* v. *Regan*, 465 U.S. 367 (1984), and appointed as Special Master the Honorable Samuel J. Roberts, 466 U.S. 948 (1984). The National Governors' Association (NGA) intervened. After conducting hearings and taking evidence, the Special Master concluded that § 310(b)(1) was constitutional and recommended entering judgment for the defendant. South Carolina and the NGA filed exceptions to various factual findings of the Special Master and to the Master's legal conclusions concerning their constitutional challenges.

II

We address the claim that § 310(b)(1) violates the Tenth Amendment first.† South Carolina and the NGA contend, and the Master found, that § 310 effectively requires States to issue bonds in registered form, noting that if States issued bonds in unregistered form, competition from other nonexempt bonds would force States to increase the interest paid on state bonds by 28–35%, and that even though almost all state bonds were issued in bearer form before § 310 became effective, since then no State has issued a bearer bond.

---

*Section 310 also provides various special exceptions to the registration requirements and incentives provided under subsections (a) and (b) for long-term publicly offered bonds issued by private corporations and federal and state governments, but those exceptions are not relevant here.

†We use "the Tenth Amendment" to encompass any implied constitutional limitation on Congress' authority to regulate state activities, whether grounded in the Tenth Amendment itself or in principles of federalism derived generally from the Constitution.

Report of Special Master pp. 2, 23–24. South Carolina and the NGA thus argue that, for purposes of Tenth Amendment analysis, we must treat § 310 as if it simply banned bearer bonds altogether without giving States the option to issue nonexempt bearer bonds. The Secretary does not dispute the finding that § 310 effectively requires registration, see Brief for Defendant, p. 19 (urging the Court to adopt all the Master's findings), preferring to argue that § 310 survives Tenth Amendment scrutiny because a blanket prohibition by Congress on the issuance of bearer bonds can apply to States without violating the Tenth Amendment. For the purposes of Tenth Amendment analysis, then, we treat § 310 as if it directly regulated States by prohibiting outright the issuance of bearer bonds.*

A

The Tenth Amendment limits on Congress' authority to regulate state activities are set out in *Garcia* v. *San Antonio Metropolitan Transit Authority*, 469 U.S. 528 (1985). *Garcia* holds that the limits are structural, not substantive—*i.e.*, that States must find their protection from congressional regulation through the national political process, not through judicially defined spheres of unregulable state activity. *Id.*, at 537–554. South Carolina contends that the political process failed here because Congress had no concrete evidence quantifying the tax evasion attributable to unregistered state bonds and relied instead on anecdotal evidence that taxpayers have concealed taxable income using bearer bonds. It also argues that Congress chose an ineffective remedy by requiring registration because most bond sales are handled by brokers who must file information reports regardless of the form of the bond and because beneficial ownership of registered bonds need not necessarily be recorded.

Although *Garcia* left open the possibility that some extraordinary defects in the national political process might render congressional regulation of state activities invalid under the Tenth Amendment, the Court in *Garcia* had no occasion to identify or define the defects that might lead to such invalidation. See *id.*, at 556. Nor do we attempt any definitive articulation here. It suffices to observe that South Carolina has not even alleged that it was deprived of any right to participate in the national political process or that it was singled out in a way that left it politically isolated and powerless. Cf. *United States* v. *Carolene Products Co.*, 304 U.S. 144, 152, n. 4 (1938). Rather, South Carolina argues that the political process failed here because § 310(b)(1) was "imposed by the vote of an uninformed Congress relying upon incomplete information." Brief for Plaintiff 101.† But nothing in *Garcia* or the Tenth Amendment authorizes courts to second- guess the substantive basis for congressional legislation. Cf. *Minnesota* v. *Clover Leaf Creamery Co.*, 449 U.S. 456, 464 (1981). Where, as here, the national political *process* did not operate in a defective manner, the Tenth Amendment is not implicated.

B

The NGA argues that § 310 is invalid because it commandeers the state legislative and administrative process by coercing States into enacting legislation authorizing bond registration and into administering the registration scheme. They cite *FERC* v. *Mississippi*, 456 U.S. 742 (1982), which left open the possibility that the Tenth Amendment might set some limits on Congress' power to compel States to regulate on behalf of federal interests, *id.*, at 761–764. The extent to which the Tenth Amendment claim left open in *FERC* survives *Garcia* or poses constitutional limitations independent of those discussed in *Garcia* is far from clear. We need not, however, address that issue because we find the claim discussed in *FERC* inapplicable to § 310.

The federal statute at issue in *FERC* required state utility commissions to do the following: (1) adjudicate

*Given our holding *infra*, at ——, that a federal tax on the interest paid on state bonds does not violate the intergovernmental tax immunity doctrine, one could argue that any law exempting state bond interest from the tax applicable to interest on other bonds is, in effect, a subsidy, and that Congress' decision to subsidize only registered state bonds must be judged under our Spending Clause cases. See generally *South Dakota* v. *Dole*, 483 U.S. ——, —— (1987) (stating that "a perceived Tenth Amendment limitation on congressional regulation of state affairs did not concomitantly limit the range of conditions legitimately placed on federal grants," but that at some point "the financial inducement offered by Congress might be so coercive" as to be unconstitutional). The parties have not, however, chosen to attack or defend § 310(b)(1) based on a Spending Clause theory, and we decline to address the unlitigated issues of whether Spending Clause analysis applies or what its import would be in this case.
†South Carolina also filed a number of exceptions to the Master's findings that the registration requirement imposed little financial or administrative burden on States and had little effect on States' ability to raise capital. These exceptions, and the NGA's exception to the Master's failure to find an interest rate differential between registered and bearer bonds, raise no issue concerning the operation of the national political process, and we need not address them here.

and enforce federal standards, (2) either consider adopting certain federal standards or cease regulating public utilities, and (3) follow certain procedures. The Court in *FERC* first distinguished *National League of Cities* v. *Usery*, 426 U.S. 833 (1976), noting that the statute in *National League of Cities* presented questions concerning "the extent to which state sovereignty shields the States from generally applicable federal regulations," whereas the statute in *FERC* "attempts to use state regulatory machinery to advance federal goals." *FERC*, 456 U.S., at 759. The Court in *FERC* then concluded that, whatever constitutional limitations might exist on the federal power to compel state regulatory activity, Congress had the power to require that state adjudicative bodies adjudicate federal issues and to require that States regulating in a pre-emptible field consider suggested federal standards and follow federally mandated procedures. *Id.*, at 759–767.

Because, by hypothesis, § 310 effectively prohibits issuing unregistered bonds, it presents the very situation *FERC* distinguished from a commandeering of state regulatory machinery: the extent to which the Tenth Amendment "shields the States from generally applicable federal regulations." 456 U.S., at 759. Section 310 regulates state activities; it does not, as did the statute in *FERC*, seek to control or influence the manner in which States regulate private parties. The NGA nonetheless contends that § 310 has commandeered the state legislative and administrative process because many state legislatures had to amend a substantial number of statutes in order to issue bonds in registered form and because state officials had to devote substantial effort to determine how best to implement a registered bond system. Such "commandeering" is, however, an inevitable consequence of regulating a state activity. Any federal regulation demands compliance. That a State wishing to engage in certain activity must take administrative and sometimes legislative action to comply with federal standards regulating that activity is a commonplace that presents no constitutional defect. After *Garcia*, for example, several States and municipalities had to take administrative and legislative action to alter the employment practices or raise the funds necessary to comply with the wage and overtime provisions of the Federal Labor Standards Act.* Indeed, even the pre-*Garcia* line of Tenth Amendment cases recognized that Congress could constitutionally impose federal requirements on States that States could meet only by amending their statutes. See *EEOC* v. *Wyoming*, 460 U.S. 226, 253–254, and n. 2 (1983) (Burger, C. J., dissenting) (citing state statutes from over half the States that did not comply with the federal statute upheld by the Court). Under the NGA's theory, moreover, any State could immunize its activities from federal regulation by simply codifying the manner in which it engages in those activities. In short, the NGA's theory of "commandeering" would not only render *Garcia* a nullity, but would restrict congressional regulation of state activities even more tightly than it was restricted under the now overruled *National League of Cities* line of cases. We find the theory foreclosed by precedent, and uphold the constitutionality of § 310 under the Tenth Amendment.

III

South Carolina contends that even if a statute banning state bearer bonds entirely would be constitutional, § 310 unconstitutionally violates the doctrine of intergovernmental tax immunity because it imposes a tax on the interest earned on a state bond. We agree with South Carolina that § 310 is inconsistent with *Pollock* v. *Farmers' Loan & Trust Co.*, 157 U.S. 429 (1895), which held that any interest earned on a state bond was immune from federal taxation.

The Secretary and the Master, however, suggest that we should uphold the constitutionality of § 310 without explicitly overruling *Pollock* because § 310 does not abolish the tax exemption for state bond interest entirely but rather taxes the interest on state bonds only if the bonds are not issued in the form Congress requires. In our view, however, this suggestion implicitly rests on a rather mischievous proposition of law. If, for example, Congress imposed a tax that applied exclusively to South Carolina and levied the tax directly on the South Carolina treasury, we would be obligated to adjudicate the constitutionality of that tax even if Congress allowed South Carolina to escape the tax by restructuring its state government in a way Congress found more to its liking. The United States cannot convert an unconstitutional tax into a constitutional one simply by making the tax conditional. Whether Congress could have imposed the condition by direct regulation is irrelevant; Congress cannot employ unconstitutional means to reach a constitutional end. Under *Pollock*, a tax on the interest income derived from any state bond was considered a direct tax on the State and thus unconstitutional. 157 U.S., at

---

*See generally Hearings on S. 1570 before the Subcommittee on Labor of the Senate Committee on Labor and Human Resources, 99th Cong., 1st Sess. (1985); The Impact of the Supreme Court's Garcia Decision Upon States and Their Political Subdivisions: Hearing before the Subcommittee on Economic Goals and Intergovernmental Policy of the Joint Economic Committee Congress of the United States, 99th Cong., 1st Sess. (1985).

585–586. If this constitutional rule still applies, Congress cannot threaten to tax the interest on state bonds that do not conform to congressional dictates. We thus decline to follow a suggestion that would force us to embrace implicitly a proposition of law far more controversial than the current validity of *Pollock*'s ban on taxing state bond interest, and proceed to address whether *Pollock* should be explicitly overruled.*

Under the intergovernmental tax immunity jurisprudence prevailing at the time, *Pollock* did not represent a unique immunity limited to income derived from state bonds. Rather, *Pollock* merely represented one application of the more general rule that neither the federal nor the state governments could tax income an individual directly derived from *any* contract with another government.[†] Not only was it unconstitutional for the Federal Government to tax a bondowner on the interest she received on any state bond, but it was also unconstitutional to tax a state employee on the income earned from his employment contract, *Collector* v. *Day*, 11 Wall. 113 (1871), to tax a lessee on income derived from lands leased from a State, *Burnet* v. *Coronado Oil* 285 U.S. 393 (1932), or to impose a sales tax on proceeds a vendor derived from selling a product to a state agency, *Indian Motocycle Co.* v. *United States*, 283 U.S. 570 (1931). Income derived from the same kinds of contracts with the Federal Government were likewise immune from taxation by the States. See *Weston* v. *City Council of Charleston*, 2 Pet. 449 (1829) (federal bond interest immune from state taxation); *Dobbins* v. *Commissioners of Erie County*, 16 Pet. 435 (1842) (federal employee immune from state tax on salary); *Gillespie* v. *Oklahoma*, 257 U.S. 501 (1922) (income derived from federal lease immune from state tax); *Panhandle Oil Co.* v. *Knox*, 277 U.S. 218 (1928) (vendor immune from sales tax on vendor's proceeds from sale to the United States). Cases concerning the tax immunity of income derived from state contracts freely cited principles established in federal tax immunity cases, and vice versa. See, *e.g.*, *Coronado Oil*, *supra*, at 398; *Indian Motocycle*, *supra*, at 575–579; *Pollock*, *supra*, at 586. See generally *Indian Motocycle*, *supra*, at 575 (immunity of States from federal tax equal to immunity of Federal Government from state tax); *Metcalf & Eddy* v. *Mitchell*, 269 U.S. 514, 521–522 (1926); *Collector* v. *Day*, *supra*, at 127.

This general rule was based on the rationale that any tax on income a party received under a contract with the government was a tax on the contract and thus a tax "on" the government because it burdened the government's power to enter into the contract. The Court in *Pollock* borrowed its reasoning directly from the decision in *Weston* exempting federal bond interest from state taxation

> 'The right to tax the contract to any extent, when made, must operate upon the power to borrow before it is exercised, and have a sensible influence on the contract. The extent of this influence depends upon the will of a distinct government. To any extent, however inconsiderable, it is a burthen on the operations of government. ... The tax on government stock is thought by this court to be a tax on the contract, a tax on the [government's] power to borrow money ... and consequently to be repugnant to the Constitution.' *Pollock*, *supra*, at 586, quoting *Weston*, *supra*, at 467, 468.

Thus, although a tax was collected from an independent private party, the tax was considered to be "on" the government because the tax burden might be passed on to it through the contract. This reasoning was used to define the basic scope of both federal and state tax immunities with respect to all types of government contracts.[‡] See,

---

*The Secretary also argues that we need not reach the tax immunity issue on the ground that, because all state bonds have been issued in registered form since § 310 became effective, no federal tax on state bearer bond interest has ever actually been imposed. We see no reason, however, why South Carolina cannot bring a facial challenge to § 310 rather than an as applied challenge.

[†]Income indirectly derived from a contract with the government was treated differently. See, *e.g.*, *Willcuts* v. *Bunn*, 282 U.S. 216, 227–230 (1931) (constitutional to tax capital gain on sale of state bond because State not a party to the sale contract); see also *Greiner* v. *Lewellyn*, 258 U.S. 384 (1922) (constitutional to tax transfer of estate even though state bonds are included in determining the value of the estate).

[‡]The sources of the state and federal immunities are, of course, different: the state immunity arises from the constitutional structure and a concern for protecting state sovereignty whereas the federal immunity arises from the Supremacy Clause. The immunities have also differed somewhat in their underlying political theory and in their doctrinal contours. Many of this Court's opinions have suggested that the Constitution should be interpreted to confer a greater tax immunity on the Federal Government than on States because all the people of the States are represented in the Federal Government whereas all the people of the Federal Government are not represented in individual States. *Helvering* v. *Gerhardt*, 304 U.S. 405, 412 (1938); *McCulloch* v. *Maryland*, 4 Wheat. 316, 435–436 (1819); *New York* v. *United States*, 326 U.S. 572, 577, and n. 3 (1946) (Opinion of Frankfurter, J.). In fact, the federal tax immunity has always been greater than the States' immunity. The Federal Government, for example, possesses the power to enact statutes immunizing those with whom it deals from state taxation even if intergovernmental tax immunity doctrine would not otherwise confer an immunity. See, *e.g.*, *Graves* v. *New York ex rel. O'Keefe*, 306 U.S. 466, 478 (1939). The States lack any such power. Also, although the Federal Government has always enjoyed blanket immunity from any state tax considered to be

e.g., *Coronado Oil*, *supra*, at 400–401 ("Here the lease . . . was an instrumentality of the State. . . . To tax the income of the lessee arising therefrom would amount to an imposition upon the lease itself"); *Panhandle Oil*, *supra*, at 222 ("It is immaterial that the seller and not the purchaser is required to report and make payment to the State. Sale and purchase constitute a transaction by which the tax is measured and on which the burden rests"); *Gillespie*, *supra*, at 505–506 ("'A tax upon the leases is a tax upon the power to make them. . . .'" (quoting *Indian Territory Illuminating Oil Co.* v. *Oklahoma*, 240 U.S. 522, 530 (1916))). The commonality of the rationale underlying all these immunities for government contracts was highlighted by *Indian Motocycle*, *supra*. In that case, the Court reviewed the then current status of intergovernmental tax immunity doctrine, observing that a tax on interest earned on a state or federal bond was unconstitutional because it would burden the exercise of the government's power to borrow money and that a tax on the salary of state or Federal Government employee was unconstitutional because it would burden the government's power to obtain the employee's services. *Id.*, at 576–578. It then concluded that under the same principle a sales tax imposed on a vendor for a sale to a state agency was unconstitutional because it would burden the sale transaction. *Id.*, at 579.

The rationale underlying *Pollock* and the general immunity for government contract income has been thoroughly repudiated by modern intergovernmental immunity caselaw. In *Graves* v. *New York ex rel. O'Keefe*, 306 U.S. 466 (1939), the Court announced, "The theory . . . that a tax on income is legally or economically a tax on its source, is no longer tenable." *Id.*, at 480. The Court explained

> So much of the burden of a non-discriminatory general tax upon the incomes of employees of a government, state or national, as may be passed on economically to that government, through the effect of the tax on the price level of labor or materials, is but the normal incident of the organization within the same territory of two governments, each possessing the taxing power. The burden, so far as it can be said to exist or to affect the government in any indirect or incidental way, is one which the Constitution presupposes. . . . *Id.*, at 487.

See also *James* v. *Dravo Contracting Co.*, 302 U.S. 134, 160 (1937) (the fact that a tax on a government contractor "may increase the cost to the Government . . . would not invalidate the tax"); *Helvering* v. *Gerhardt*, 304 U.S. 405, 424 (1938). The thoroughness with which the Court abandoned the burden theory was demonstrated most emphatically when the Court upheld a state sales tax imposed on a government contractor even though the financial burden of the tax was entirely passed on, through a cost-plus contract, to the Federal Government. *Alabama* v. *King & Boozer*, 314 U.S. 1 (1941). The Court stated

> The Government, rightly we think, disclaims any contention that the Constitution, unaided by Congressional legislation, prohibits a tax exacted from the contractors merely because it is passed on economically, by the terms of the contract or otherwise, as part of the construction cost to the Government. So far as such a nondiscriminatory state tax upon the contractor enters into the cost of the materials to the Government, that is but a normal incident of the organization within the same territory of two independent taxing sovereignties. The asserted right of the one to be free of taxation by the other does not spell immunity from paying the added costs, attributable to the taxation of those who furnish supplies to the Government and who have been granted no tax immunity. So far as a different view has prevailed, we think it no longer tenable. *Id.*, at 8–9 (citations omitted).

King & Boozer thus completely foreclosed any claim that the nondiscriminatory imposition of costs on private entities that pass them on to States or the Federal Government unconstitutionally burdens state or federal functions. Subsequent cases have consistently reaffirmed the principle that a nondiscriminatory tax collected from private parties contracting with another government is constitutional even though part or all of the financial burden falls on the other government. See *Washington* v. *United States*, 460 U.S. 536, 540 (1983); *United States* v. *New Mexico*, 455 U.S. 720, 734 (1982); *United States* v. *County of Fresno*, 429 U.S. 452, 460–462, and n. 9 (1977); *United States* v. *City of Detroit*, 355 U.S. 466, 469 (1958).

---

considered to be "on" the government under the prevailing methodology, the States have never enjoyed immunity from all federal taxes considered to be "on" a State. See *infra*, at——, and n. 13. To some, *Garcia* v. *San Antonio Metropolitan Transit Authority*, 469 U.S. 528 (1985), may suggest further limitations on state tax immunity. We need not, however, decide here the extent to which the scope of the federal and state immunities differ or the extent, if any, to which States are currently immune from direct nondiscriminatory federal taxation. It is enough for our purposes that federal and state tax immunity cases have always shared the identical methodology for determining whether a tax is "on" a government, and that this identity has persisted even though the methodology for both federal and state immunities has changed as intergovernmental tax immunity doctrine shifted into the modern era. See *Graves*, *supra*, at 485.

With the rationale for conferring a tax immunity on parties dealing with another government rejected, the government contract immunities recognized under prior doctrine were, one by one, eliminated. Overruling *Burnet* v. *Coronado Oil*, 285 U.S. 393 (1932), and *Gillespie* v. *Oklahoma*, 257 U.S. 501 (1922), the Court upheld the constitutionality of a federal tax on net income a corporation derived from a state lease in *Helvering* v. *Mountain Producers Corp.*, 303 U.S. 376 (1938). See also *Oklahoma Tax Comm'n* v. *Texas Co.*, 336 U.S. 342 (1949) (upholding constitutionality of federal tax on gross income derived from state lease). Later, the Court explicitly overruled *Collector* v. *Day*, 11 Wall. 113 (1871), and upheld the constitutionality of a nondiscriminatory state tax on the salary of a federal employee. *Graves* v. *New York ex rel. O'Keefe*, 306 U.S. 466 (1939).* And in the course of upholding a sales tax on a cost-plus government contractor, the Court in *King & Boozer* overruled *Panhandle Oil Co.* v. *Knox*, 277 U.S. 218 (1928). See also *James, supra* (upholding state tax on gross income independent contractor received from Federal Government). The only premodern tax immunity for parties to government contracts that has so far avoided being explicitly overruled is the immunity for recipients of governmental bond interest.[†] That this Court has yet to overrule *Pollock* explicitly, however, is explained not by any distinction between the income derived from government bonds and the income derived from other government contracts, but by the historical fact that Congress has always exempted state bond interest from taxation by statute, beginning with the very first federal income tax statute. Act of Oct. 3, 1913, ch. 6, § II(B), 38 Stat. 168.

In sum, then, under current intergovernmental tax immunity doctrine the States can never tax the United States directly but can tax any private parties with whom it does business, even though the financial burden falls on the United States, as long as the tax does not discriminate against the United States or those with whom it deals. See *Washington, supra,* at 540; *County of Fresno, spura,* at 460–463; *City of Detroit, spura,* at 473; *Oklahoma Tax Comm'n, spura,* at 359–364. A tax is considered to be directly on the Federal Government only "when the levy falls on the United States itself, or on an agency or instrumentality so closely connected to the Government that the two cannot realistically be viewed as separate entities." *New Mexico, supra,* at 735. The rule with respect to state tax immunity is essentially the same, see, *e.g., Graves, supra,* at 485; *Mountain Producers Corp., supra,* at 386–387, except that at least some nondiscriminatory federal taxes can be collected directly from the States even though a parallel state tax could not be collected directly from the Federal Government.[‡] See generally *supra,* at ——, n. 10.

---

*Prior to that the Court had already confined *Collector* v. *Day*, 11 Wall. 113 (1871), to its facts in *Helvering* v. *Gerhardt*, 304 U.S. 405 (1938), which upheld the constitutionality of a federal tax on the salaries of state employees involved in state construction projects.

[†]South Carolina and the Government Finance Officers Association as *amicus curiae* argue that the legislative history of the Sixteenth Amendment, which authorizes Congress to "collect taxes on incomes, from whatever source derived, without apportionment," manifests an intent to freeze into the Constitution the tax immunity for state bond interest that existed in 1913. We disagree. The legislative history merely shows that the words "from whatever source derived" of the Sixteenth Amendment were not affirmatively intended to authorize Congress to tax state bond interest or to have any other effect on which incomes were subject to federal taxation, and that the sole purpose of the Sixteenth Amendment was to remove the apportionment requirement for whichever incomes were otherwise taxable. 45 Cong. Rec. 2245–2246 (1910); *id.*, at 2539; see also *Brushaber* v. *Union Pacific R. Co.*, 240 U.S. 1, 17–18 (1916). Indeed, if the Sixteenth Amendment had frozen into the Constitution all the tax immunities that existed in 1913, then most of modern intergovernmental tax immunity doctrine would be invalid.

[‡]All federal activities are immune from direct state taxation, see *Graves*, 306 U.S., at 477, but at least some state activities have always been subject to direct federal taxation. For a time, only the States' governmental, as opposed to proprietary, activities enjoyed tax immunity, see *e.g., Helvering* v. *Powers*, 293 U.S. 214, 227 (1934); *South Carolina* v. *United States*, 199 U.S. 437, 454–463 (1905), but this distinction was subsequently abandoned as untenable by all eight justices participating in *New York* v. *United States*, 326 U.S. 572 (1945). See *id.*, at 579–581, 583 (opinion of Frankfurter, J., joined by Rutledge, J.); *id.*, at 586 (Stone, C. J., concurring, joined by Reed, Murphy and Burton, JJ.); *id.*, at 591 (Douglas, J., dissenting, joined by Black, J.)). Two justices reasoned that any nondiscriminatory tax on a State was constitutional, even if directly collected from the State. See *id.*, at 582–584 (Frankfurter, J., joined by Rutledge, J.). Four other justices declined to hold that every nondiscriminatory tax levied directly on a State would be constitutional because "there may be non-discriminatory taxes which, *when laid on a State*, would nevertheless impair the sovereign status of the State quite as much as a like tax imposed by a State on property or activities of the national government. *Mayo* v. *United States*, 319 U.S. 441, 447–448. This is not because the tax can be regarded as discriminatory but because a *sovereign government is the taxpayer*, and the tax, even though non-discriminatory, may be regarded as infringing its sovereignty." 326 U.S., at 587 (Stone, C. J., concurring, joined by Reed, Murphy and Burton, JJ.) (emphasis added) (the cited discussion from *Mayo* stressed the difference between levying a tax on a government and on those with whom the government deals); see also *id.*, at 588 ("Only when and because the subject of taxation is State property or a State activity must we consider whether such a non-discriminatory tax unduly interferes with the performance of the State's functions of government"). The four justices then concluded that the tax at issue was constitutional even though directly levied on the State because recognizing an immunity would

We thus confirm that subsequent caselaw has overruled the holding in *Pollock* that state bond interest is immune from a nondiscriminatory federal tax. We see no constitutional reason for treating persons who receive interest on government bonds differently than persons who receive income from other types of contracts with the government, and no tenable rationale for distinguishing the costs imposed on States by a tax on state bond interest from the costs imposed by a tax on the income from any other state contract. We stated in *Graves*, "as applied to the taxation of salaries of the employees of one government, the purpose of the immunity was not to confer benefits on the employees by relieving them from contributing their share of the financial support of the other government, whose benefits they enjoy, or to give an advantage to a government by enabling it to engage employees at salaries lower than those paid for like services by other employers, public or private. . . ." 306 U.S., at 483. Likewise, the owners of state bonds have no constitutional entitlement not to pay taxes on income they earn from state bonds, and States have no constitutional entitlement to issue bonds paying lower interest rates than other issuers.*

Indeed, this Court has in effect acknowledged that a holder of a government bond could constitutionally be taxed on bond interest in *Memphis Bank & Trust Co.* v. *Garner*, 459 U.S. 392 (1983), which involved a state tax on federal bond interest. Although that case involved an interpretation of 31 U.S.C. § 742, we premised our statutory interpretation on the observation that "[o]ur decisions have treated § 742 as principally a restatement of the constitutional rule." 459 U.S., at 397. We then stated: "Where, *as here*, the economic but not the legal incidence of the tax falls upon the Federal Government, such a tax generally does not violate the constitutional immunity if it does not discriminate against holders of federal property or those with whom the Federal Government deals." *Ibid.* (emphasis added).

TEFRA § 310 thus clearly imposes no direct tax on the States. The tax is imposed on and collected from bondholders, not States, and any increased administrative costs incurred by States in implementing the registration system are not "taxes" within the meaning of the tax immunity doctrine. See generally *United States* v. *Mississippi Taxc Comm'n.*, 421 U.S. 599, 606 (1975) (describing tax as an enforced contribution to provide for the support of government). Nor does § 310 discriminate against States. The provisions of § 310 seek to assure that *all* publicly offered long-term bonds are issued in registered form, whether issued by state or local governments, the Federal Government, or private corporations. See *supra*, at ——. Accordingly, the Federal Government has directly imposed the same registration requirement on itself that it has effectively imposed on States. The incentives States have to switch to registered bonds are necessarily different than those of corporate bond issuers because only state bonds enjoy any exemption from the federal tax on bond

---

immunity would "accomplish a withdrawal from the taxing power of the nation a subject of taxation of a nature which has been traditionally within that power from the beginning." *Ibid.* We need not concern ourselves here, however, with the extent to which, if any, States are currently immune from direct federal taxation. See *supra*, at ——, n. 10. For our purposes, the important principle *New York* reaffirms is that the issue whether a nondiscriminatory federal tax might nonetheless violate state tax immunity does not even arise unless the Federal Government seeks to collect the tax directly from a State.

*South Carolina distinguishes the taxes by arguing that the interest paid to a State's bondholders is more essential to the maintenance of a state government than the salaries paid to employees. This strikes us as counterintuitive in fact. More importantly, the essential/nonessential distinction it invokes is exactly the type of distinction we concluded was unworkable in *Garcia*, 469 U.S., at 542–547 (rejecting rules of state immunity turning on whether a governmental function is "essential," "governmental" versus "proprietary," "traditional," "uniquely governmental," "necessary," or "integral").

"'There is not, and there cannot be, any unchanging line of demarcation between essential and non-essential governmental functions. Many governmental functions of today have at some time in the past been nongovernmental. The genius of our government provides that, within the sphere of constitutional action, the people—acting not through the courts but through their elected legislative representatives—have the power to determine as conditions demand, what services and functions the public welfare requires.'" *Id.*, at 546, quoting *Gerhardt*, 304 U.S., at 427 (Black, J., concurring).

Similarly, Justice O'Connor would have us judge the constitutionality of each tax imposing an indirect burden on state and local governments by determining whether the tax had "substantial" adverse effects on those governments. *Post*, at 2–4. We fail to see how this substantiality test distinguishes taxes on state bond interest from taxes on state employees' salaries. More importantly, we disagree with Justice O'Connor's apparent assumption that if this Court does not undertake the open-ended and administratively daunting inquiry required by her test, we leave States at the mercy of a congressional power to destroy them via excessive taxation. *Post*, at 4–5. The nondiscrimination principle at the heart of modern intergovernmental tax immunity caselaw does not leave States unprotected from excessive federal taxation—it merely recognizes that the best safeguard against excessive taxation (and the most judicially manageable) is the requirement that the government tax in a nondiscriminatory fashion. For where a government imposes a nondiscriminatory tax, judges can term the tax "excessive" only by second-guessing the extent to which the taxing government and its people have taxed themselves, and the threat of destroying another government can be realized only if the taxing government is willing to impose taxes that will also destroy itself or its constituents.

interest, but the sanctions for issuing unregistered corporate bonds are comparably severe. See *ibid.* Removing the tax exemption for interest earned on state bonds would not, moreover, create a discrimination between state and corporate bonds since corporate bond interest is already subject to federal tax.

IV

Because the federal imposition of a bond registration requirement on States does not violate the Tenth Amendment and because a nondiscriminatory federal tax on the interest earned on state bonds does not violate the intergovernmental tax immunity doctrine, we uphold the constitutionality of § 310,* overrule the exceptions to the Special Master's Report, and approve his recommendation to enter judgment for the defendant.

It is so ordered.

Justice Kennedy took no part in the consideration or decision of this case.

Justice Stevens, Concurring

Although the Court properly finds support for its holding in *Garcia* v. *San Antonio Metropolitan Transit Authority*, 469 U.S. 528 (1985), the outcome of this case was equally clear well before that case was decided. See *South Carolina* v. *Regan*, 465 U.S. 367, 403–419 (1984) (Stevens, J., concurring in part and dissenting in part). It should be emphasized, however, that neither the Court's decision today, nor what I have written in the past, expresses any opinion about the wisdom of taxing the interest on bonds issued by state or local governments.

Justice Scalia, Concurring in Part and Concurring in the Judgment

I join in the Court's judgment, and in its opinion except for Part II. I do not join the latter because, as observed by The Chief Justice, *post*, at 2, it unnecessarily casts doubt upon *FERC* v. *Mississippi*, 456 U.S. 742 (1982), and because it misdescribes the holding in *Garcia* v. *San Antonio Metropolitan Transit Authority*, 469 U.S. 528 (1985). I do not read *Garcia* as adopting—in fact I read it as explicitly disclaiming—the proposition attributed to it in today's opinion, *ante*, at 5–6, that the "national political process" is the States' only constitutional protection, and that nothing except the demonstration of "some extraordinary defects" in the operation of that process can justify judicial relief. We said in *Garcia*: "These cases do not require us to identify or define what affirmative limits *the constitutional structure* might impose on federal action affecting the States under the Commerce Clause. See *Coyle* v. *Oklahoma*, 221 U.S. 559 (1911)." See 469 U.S., at 556 (emphasis added). I agree only that that structure does not prohibit what the Federal Government has done here.

Chief Justice Rehnquist, Concurring in the Judgment

Today the Court reaches two results regarding § 310(b)(1) of TEFRA that I believe are analytically distinct. First, the Court finds that § 310(b)(1) does not violate the Tenth Amendment by compelling States to issue bonds in registered form. Second, the majority concludes that the statute also does not contravene the doctrine of intergovernmental tax immunity; in doing so, the majority overrules our decision in *Pollock* v. *Farmers' Loan & Trust Co.*, 157 U.S. 429 (1895). While I agree that the principles of intergovernmental tax immunity are not threatened in this case, in my view the Court unnecessarily casts doubt on the protective scope of the Tenth Amendment in the course of upholding § 310(b)(1).

The Special Master appointed by the Court made a number of factual determinations about the impact that the TEFRA registration requirements would have upon the States. Most notably, the Special Master found that the registration requirements have had no substantive effect on the abilities of States to raise debt capital, on the political processes by which States decide to issue debt, or on the power of the States to choose the purpose to which they will dedicate the proceeds of their tax-exempt borrowing. After an exhaustive investigation, the Special Master summarized: "TEFRA has not changed how much the States borrow, for what purposes they borrow, how they decide to borrow, or any other obviously important aspect of the borrowing process." Report of Special Master 118.

This well-supported conclusion that § 310(b)(1) has had a *deminimis* impact on the States should end, rather than begin, the Court's constitutional inquiry. Even the more expansive conception of the Tenth

---

*Because we hold that Congress could have prohibited States from issuing any unregistered bonds by direct regulation, we necessarily reject South Carolina's argument that § 310(b)(1) is an impermissible regulatory tax because it imposes a tax on activities not subject to federal regulatory power. That § 310(b) is purely regulatory in purpose and effect and was never intended to raise any federal revenue does not alone render it unconstitutional. See *Minor* v. *United States*, 396 U.S. 87, 98 n. 13 (1969).

Amendment espoused in *National League of Cities* v. *Usery*, 426 U.S. 833 (1976), recognized that only congressional action that "operate[s] to directly displace the States' freedom to structure integral operations in areas of traditional governmental functions," runs afoul of the authority granted Congress. *Id.*, at 852. The Special Master determined that no such displacement has occurred through the implementation of the TEFRA requirements; I see no need to go further, as the majority does, to discuss the possibility of defects in the national political process that spawned TEFRA, nor to hypothesize that the Tenth Amendment concerns voiced in *FERC* v. *Mississippi*, 456 U.S. 742 (1982), may not have survived *Garcia* v. *San Antonio Metropolitan Transit Authority*, 469, U.S. 528 (1985). Those issues, intriguing as they may be, are of no moment in the present case and are best left unaddressed until clearly presented.

Justice O'Connor, Dissenting

The Court today overrules a precedent that it has honored for nearly a hundred years and expresses a willingness to cancel the constitutional immunity that traditionally has shielded the interest paid on state and local bonds from federal taxation. Henceforth the ability of state and local governments to finance their activities will depend in part on whether Congress voluntarily abstains from tapping this permissible source of additional income tax revenue. I believe that state autonomy is an important factor to be considered in reviewing the National Government's exercise of its enumerated powers. *Garcia* v. *San Antonio Metropolitan Transit Authority*, 469 U.S. 528, 581 (1985) (O'Connor, J., joined by Powell and Rehnquist, JJ., dissenting). I dissent from the decision to overrule *Pollock* v. *Farmers' Loan & Trust Co.*, 157 U.S. 429 (1895), and I would invalidate Congress' attempt to regulate the sovereign States by threatening to deprive them of this tax immunity, which would increase their dependence on the National Government.

Section 310(b)(1) of the Tax Equity and Fiscal Responsibility Act of 1982 (TEFRA), 26 U.S.C. § 103(j)(1), provides that the interest paid on state and local bonds will be subject to federal income tax unless the bonds are issued in registered form. The Court readily concludes that Congress could have prohibited outright the issuance of bearer bonds without violating the Tenth Amendment. *Ante*, at 5–7. But regardless of whether Congress could have required registration of the bonds directly under its commerce power, I agree with the Court that Congress may not accomplish the same end by an unconstitutional means. *Ante*, at 9-10. In my view, the Tenth Amendment and principles of federalism inherent in the Constitution prohibit Congress from taxing or threatening to tax the interest paid on state and municipal bonds. It is also arguable that the States' autonomy is protected from substantial federal incursions by virtue of the Guarantee Clause of the Constitution, Art. IV, § 4. See Merritt, The Guarantee Clause and State Autonomy: Federalism for a Third Century, 88 Colum. L. Rev. 1, 70–78 (1988) (arguing that judicial enforcement of the Guarantee Clause is proper).

The Court never expressly considers whether federal taxation of state and local bond interest violates the Constitution. Instead, the majority characterizes the federal tax exemption for state and local bond interest as an aspect of intergovernmental tax immunity, and it describes the decline of the intergovernmental tax immunity doctrine in this century. But constitutional principles do not depend upon the rise or fall of particular legal doctrines. This Court has a continuing responsibility "to oversee the Federal Government's compliance with its duty to respect the legitimate interests of the States." *Garcia, supra*, at 581 (O'Connor, J., joined by Powell and Rehnquist, JJ., dissenting). In my view, the Court shirks its responsibility because it fails to inquire into the substantial adverse effects on state and local governments that would follow from federal taxation of the interest on state and local bonds.

Long-term debt obligations are an essential source of funding for state and local governments. In 1974, state and local governments issued approximately $23 billion of new municipal bonds; in 1984, they issued $102 billion of new bonds. Report of Special Master 20. State and local governments rely heavily on borrowed funds to finance education, road construction, and utilities, among other purposes. As the Court recognizes, States will have to increase the interest rates they pay on bonds by 28–35% if the interest is subject to the federal income tax. *Ante*, at 4. Governmental operations will be hindered severely if the cost of capital rises by one-third. If Congress may tax the interest paid on state and local bonds, it may strike at the very heart of state and local government activities.

In the pivotal cases which first set limits to intergovernmental tax immunity, this Court paid close attention to the practical effects of its decisions. The Court limited the government's immunity only after it determined that application of a tax would not substantially affect government operations. Thus in the first case to uphold federal income taxation of revenue earned by a state contractor, this Court observed that "neither government may destroy the other nor curtail in any substantial manner the exercise of its powers." *Metcalf & Eddy* v. *Mitchell*, 269 U.S. 514, 523–524 (1926). When this Court extended its holding to the case of a state tax on a federal contractor, it expressly noted that the tax "does not interfere in any substantial way with the performance of federal functions." *James* v. *Dravo Contracting Co.*, 302 U.S. 134, 161 (1937). In upholding the application of the federal income tax to income derived from a state lease, this Court decided that mere theoretical concerns about interference with the functions of government did not justify immunity, but that "[r]egard must be had to substance and direct effects." *Helvering* v. *Mountain Producers Corp.*, 303 U.S. 376, 386 (1938). In *Helvering* v. *Gerhardt*, 304 U.S. 405 (1938), this Court upheld the application of the federal income tax to income earned by a state employee, because there is "[no] immunity when the burden on the state is so speculative and uncertain that if allowed it would restrict the federal taxing power without affording any corresponding tangible protection to the state government." *Id.*, at 419–420.

The instant case differs critically from the cases quoted above because the Special Master found that, if the interest on state and local bonds is taxed, the cost of borrowing by state and local governments would rise substantially. This certainly would affect seriously state and local government operations. The majority is unconcerned with this difference because it is satisfied with the formal test of intergovernmental tax immunity that can be distilled from later cases. Under this test, if a tax is not imposed directly on the government, and does not discriminate against the government, then it does not violate intergovernmental tax immunity. See *ante*, at 16–17.

I do not think the Court's bipartite test adequately accommodates the constitutional concerns raised by the prospect of applying the federal income tax to the interest paid on state and local bonds. This Court has a duty to inquire into the devastating effects that such an innovation would have on state and local governments. Although Congress has taken a relatively less burdensome step in subjecting only income from bearer bonds to federal taxation, the erosion of state sovereignty is likely to occur a step at a time. "If there is any danger, it lies in the tyranny of small decisions—in the prospect that Congress will nibble away at state sovereignty, bit by bit, until someday essentially nothing is left but a gutted shell." L. Tribe, American Constitutional Law 381 (2d ed. 1988).

Federal taxation of state activities is inherently a threat to state sovereignty. As Chief Justice Marshall observed long ago, "the power to tax involves the power to destroy." *McCulloch* v. *Maryland*, 4 Wheat. 316, 431 (1819). Justice Holmes later qualified this principle, observing that "[t]he power to tax is not the power to destroy while this Court sits." *Panhandle Oil Co.* v. *Mississippi ex rel. Knox*, 277 U.S. 218, 223 (1928) (Holmes, J., joined by Brandeis and Stone, JJ., dissenting). If this Court is the States' sole protector against the threat of crushing taxation, it must take seriously its responsibility to sit in judgment of federal tax initiatives. I do not think that the Court has lived up to its constitutional role in this case. The Court has failed to enforce the constitutional safeguards of state autonomy and self-sufficiency that may be found in the Tenth Amendment and the Guarantee Clause, as well as in the principles of federalism implicit in the Constitution. I respectfully dissent.

2

Preserving the Federal–State–Local Partnership: The Role of Tax-Exempt Financing

Anthony Commission on Public Finance
Washington, D.C.

I. INTRODUCTION

Hardly a day goes by when a tax-exempt municipal bond has not affected each American's life. Municipal bonds issued by state and local governments are used to finance public facilities as diverse as roads, bridges, schools, courtrooms, airports, water filtration plants, hazardous waste facilities, hospitals, wastewater treatment facilities, ports, and housing. Tax-exempt municipal financing benefits individuals, communities, and the nation by supporting education, commerce, transportation, health, justice, and many other public services that facilitate the economic growth and development of the United States and the well-being of its citizens.

Municipal bonds are sold by cities, counties, towns, states, and other governmental units to raise funds to provide basic public services to their citizens. Borrowing by state and local governments is not a sign of financial imprudence; indeed it is the most appropriate way of financing long-term capital improvements so that current taxpayers are not required to bear a disproportionate share of the cost of public improvements to be used over many years. Like private corporations, state and local governments must rely on private investors to lend them money, which is repaid along with interest.

The ability to sell debt with interest exempt from federal income taxes has been a significant benefit to state and local governmental borrowers, reducing their borrowing costs by 20 to 50%. The practical effect of this lower borrowing cost is a direct reduction of the tax burdens that citizens would otherwise have to shoulder to finance essential public services. This interest rate savings to state and local taxpayers has long stood as a symbol of the partnership between the federal government and state and local governments in our federal system.

In recent years state and local governments' ability to raise funds in the municipal bond market has been significantly restricted by the federal government for two principal reasons. First, the federal government has limited the uses for which bond proceeds could be spent. These limitations were imposed in response to tax-exempt financing for a wide variety of private facilities providing only indirect public benefit. Second, the federal government decided to limit the total volume of tax-exempt financing in response to the effect its substantial growth was perceived to have on the federal deficit.

All too often, however, restrictions were implemented without sufficient consideration of the effects they would have on appropriate public borrowings or the establishment of a broad public policy for the financing and provision of public services. Furthermore, broad general restrictions were adopted in response to

---

Adapted from a report to Beryl F. Anthony, Jr. (Oct. 1989).

sometimes inaccurate and often exaggerated reports of the issuance of billions of dollars of bonds of dubious public benefit.

The Anthony Commission on Public Finance was created by Representative Beryl F. Anthony Jr. of Arkansas to (1) consider the effect of the current federal tax law on the ability of state and local governments to carry out their responsibilities to their citizens and (2) recommend appropriate changes in that law consistent with both financial prudence and the respective rights of the national, state, and local governments in our federal system.

The commission has reviewed the recent history of tax-exempt finance and related federal legislation over the last two decades, has considered both the rights and obligations of state and local governments and has determined that the continued ability of state and local governments to finance the projects needed by their citizens is critical to the economic growth of the United States and the health and welfare of its citizens. In particular, the commission makes a number of recommendations for improvements in federal law that will materially assist state and local governments in meeting their financial needs without permitting abusive transactions that serve no legitimate public purpose.

This report of the Anthony Commission on Public Finance (1) presents an overview of the current public finance system, (2) analyzes the effect of recent changes in the ability of state and local governments to carry out their increasing responsibilities to their citizens, and (3) makes recommendations aimed at improving federal public policy toward state and local government financing.

The commission is aware of an expressed concern that it seeks a "rollback" of federal tax policies culminating in the Tax Reform Act of 1986. The reasonableness and appropriateness of the recommendations made by the commission speak for themselves. The commission recognizes that a number of types of financing that proliferated over the last two decades were appropriate matters of concern to the federal government. Its report supports the continued prevention of abusive transactions while strongly recommending the elimination of significant and often unnecessary problems recent federal tax provisions have created for legitimate borrowings by state and local governments. The recommendations carefully balance the federal interest in both precluding abusive transactions and achieving tax equity with the right and responsibility of state and local governments to provide public services and projects in the most efficient and cost-effective manner.

A.   Background on the Anthony Commission on Public Finance

In January 1988, Congressman Beryl F. Anthony Jr., responding to concerns expressed by Arkansas Governor William Clinton and other public officials about the increasing level of federal restrictions on public finance, invited a panel of individuals to share their collective experience in analyzing the cumulative effects of federal tax policy toward state and local governments over the last two decades and to determine if improvements could be made. The members of the commission are primarily representatives of issuers of tax-exempt bonds, including six elected officials.

The commission divided itself into five task forces with each assigned to study particular questions. Over a 15-month period, it examined the current tax law provisions affecting tax-exempt bonds, analyzed the congressional revenue-estimating process and, in particular, focused on the proper relationship between the federal, state, and local governments in encouraging responsible and effective governmental borrowing.

This report (1) provides an assessment of recent changes in the treatment of tax-exempt debt under the federal tax law, (2) offers a statement of appropriate public policy, taking into account the legitimate interest of federal, state, and local governments, and (3) concludes with a series of recommendations, which have been set off in boldface print, for improvements in the internal revenue code (the "tax code" or the "code").

In its discussions the commission established that its recommendations would be guided by two important principles: (1) recommended changes should represent improvements in public policy and (2) the suggestions must be reasonable from a revenue perspective and not distort the equities of the current income tax system.

B.   The Changing Face of Federalism: More Needs, Less Money

The commission's recommendations reflect the frustrating dilemma facing state and local governments today. They find themselves at the end of a cycle, beginning in the 1930s, that produced an increasing federal role, both in supplying services directly to citizens and in assisting state and local governments in meeting their needs. Ironically, that cycle is ending and the flow of funds from Washington has been dramatically reduced at the very time when the national infrastructure desperately needs a major—and very expensive—upgrading.

During the past few years, the federal government has begun to relinquish responsibility for meeting many national social and economic priorities.[1] This trend has included mandates on state and local governments to assume responsibility for both new programs and programs previously receiving federal dollars. Unfortunately, this return of responsibility to state and local governments has been accompanied by neither new federal financial assistance nor new revenue sources to fund the programs. Indeed, it has come at the same time that many federal assistance programs were reduced.[2]

The changes in federal spending for infrastructure programs since 1980 noted below illustrate the substantial reduction of federal assistance programs.

- In fiscal year (FY) 1981, general revenue sharing budget authority was $4.6 billion. In 1986, the program was eliminated.
- In FY 1981, community development block grant (CDBG) and urban development action grant (UDAG) budget authority totalled $4.4 billion. In FY 1989, UDAGs have been eliminated and the CDBG program is estimated to be $3.0 billion.
- In FY 1980, funding for the Environmental Protection Agency's wastewater construction grant program was $3.4 billon. This fell to $1.95 billion in FY 1989.
- Public transportation funding in FY 1981 was $3.53 billion, while in FY 1989 it was estimated to be $1.5 billion.
- In housing, federal financial support in FY 1981 was $26.7 billion in budget authority. In FY 1989, the federal contribution had fallen to $7.5 billion.

State and local governments have reacted to these dramatic declines in federal assistance by increasing their own revenues from taxes, user charges, and fees; by reducing services to their citizens; and by otherwise reducing expenses.[3] Currently 41 states are considering or have enacted a variety of tax increases for the coming fiscal year (not including Louisiana and Massachusetts, which face severe budget deficits but have had their tax increase proposals defeated). See Appendix A for a list of current state tax increase proposals.

Yet new revenues have not even come close to solving the nation's infrastructure financing problem. Figure 1 demonstrates the steady decline in annual investment in the nation's infrastructure between 1968 and 1984. Despite increasing public awareness and concern over deterioration of infrastructure, spending levels on public structures and equipment are still at historically low levels.[4]

This decline inhibits national economic growth and international competitiveness. A report by the Federal Reserve Bank of Chicago points out that countries with high public investment in infrastructure have

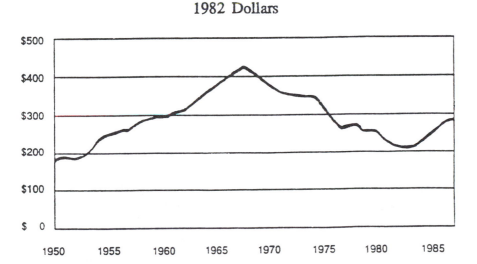

Figure 1   Annual per capita expenditures on gross fixed investment (1950–1987).

higher productivity growth. The report concludes that "a root cause of the decline in the competitiveness of the United States in the international economy may be found in the low rate at which our country has chosen to add to its stock of highways, ports, airports, and other facilities which aid in the production and distribution of goods and services."[5]

The evidence that our nation's infrastructure has not received adequate attention is not merely anecdotal. During the past 20 years, infrastructure spending has dropped from 2.3% of gross national product to 1.0%. In 1988, the National Council on Public Works Improvement reported to the president and Congress that as a nation we have far outgrown the infrastructure capacity built during the 1950s and 1960s and now face restricted economic growth unless we repair and expand that capacity.[6] Some signs of strain are

- The Federal Highway Administration estimates that over 60% of the United States, paved roads and 25% of the interstate highway system need resurfacing or reconstruction.
- The U.S. Environmental Protection Agency estimates that 400 cities and towns have not met the secondary treatment standards currently required by the federal Clean Water Act.
- Shortages of affordable housing are reaching crisis proportions throughout the country. The Neighborhood Reinvestment Corporation estimates that by the year 2003, 19 million Americans could be homeless. Nevertheless, federal funding for housing programs has been cut drastically and the ability of state and local governments to provide affordable housing has been severely restricted.

If state and local governments are going to have any chance of meeting the pressing needs for more infrastructure and other capital improvements, they must borrow more money, and they must do so on a cost-effective basis.

II. HISTORY OF TAX EXEMPTION: ACTION AND REACTION

The current restrictions on tax-exempt borrowings by state and local governments can only be understood in the context of (1) the general history of the tax exemption of municipal bonds under the tax code and (2) the complex and often confusing legislative changes made by Congress over the last 20 years. These changes were in response to an "institutional resistance" by the federal government to state and local financing and a perception by some members of Congress that state and local governments had issued bonds for improper purposes or otherwise had taken undue advantage of the general right to issue tax-exempt bonds. The last two decades have increasingly created a distressing adversarial relationship between the federal government and state and local governments, a relationship that has made each side unduly suspicious of the other; has undermined the federal, state, and local cooperation essential to sound public policy; and often has produced legislation that harms state and local governments far more than it benefits the federal government.

The legislative history summarized below illustrates an alarming breakdown of comity in the federal system. From the broad general framework of workable legislation adopted in 1968 and 1969, the adversarial relationship between Washington and the statehouses and city halls has, in the last decade, produced an increasingly complicated and unnecessarily burdensome legislative framework.

A. Legislative History

Municipal bonds came into widespread use in the 1820s and 1830s as a growing nation financed internal improvements. Much of this financing was for projects that today might fall into the category of "private-activity bonds," including railroads, canals, and turnpikes. In 1817, bonds were issued to finance the construction of the Erie Canal. Bonds also were issued to finance water supply systems, boardwalks, wooden pavements, and public schools. New York City financed its first municipal water system with a bond issuance in 1837. By 1840, there were an estimated $200 million worth of municipal bonds outstanding—$175 million issued by states and $25 million by localities.

During the depression of the early 1870s, a number of transportation projects failed to generate anticipated revenues. As a result, defaults were numerous. It is estimated that one-fifth of all municipal bonds were in default in some fashion by the middle of the 1870s. In response to these troubled financings, many state constitutions and otherwise to impose severe restrictions on government borrowings.

The modern federal income tax was introduced shortly after the ratification of the Sixteenth Amendment to the U.S. Constitution.[7] The legislative history of the Sixteenth Amendment suggests that a substantial number of its supporters did not believe it gave the federal government the right to tax the interest on state and local government bonds, and the original version of the code specifically excluded such interest from taxation.[8]

From time to time over the following decades, certain federal officials recommended elimination of the exemption. Significantly, such a recommendation by Andrew J. Mellon, Secretary of the Treasury under Presidents Harding and Coolidge, led to the proposal of a constitutional amendment permitting Congress to tax municipal bonds, which was adopted by the House but defeated in the Senate.

By 1950, the uses of municipal bonds had expanded, and the volume of outstanding municipal securities reached $24 billion. This growth reflected not only a continued need to finance schools, roads, and public buildings, but also a newfound ability to utilize revenue bonds to finance a variety of public needs without pledging the credit of the government issuers through general obligations.

In the 1950s, revenue bonds were being issued for highways, turnpikes, airports, and public utilities. By the 1970s and 1980s, they were also financing housing, nonprofit hospitals, pollution control equipment for private industry, sports stadiums, convention centers, and public power projects. As late as the latter half of the 1960s, general obligation bonds still accounted for 65% of new bond issues. Today, they represent only about 30% of municipal bond volume.

With the development of conduit financing, Congress began to consider restrictions on tax-exempt borrowing.[9] During debate on the internal revenue code of 1954, a proposal to deny tax exemption for bonds financing facilities leased to private companies was included in the House version of the bill but dropped by the conference committee.

The continued growth of such financing, however, made congressional response inevitable. By 1968, many states had authorized conduit financings to stimulate economic growth. *The Revenue and Expenditure Control Act of 1968* (the "1968 act") contained the first restrictions on the use of tax-exempt debt by issuers and was the first of a long list of legislative provisions reflecting Congressional reaction to the expanding use of municipal bonds.

The 1968 act created the modern concept of "private-activity bonds," then called "industrial development bonds" or IDBs.[10] In the 1968 act, Congress (1) eliminated bonds for projects primarily for the benefit of private persons; (2) created two major exceptions, one based on the type of use (exempt facilities) and the other based on amount (exempt small issues) with no requirements as to use other than that substantially all the proceeds be used for land or depreciable property; and (3) treated 501(c)(3) organizations in a manner parallel to governmental entities so long as these organizations were acting exclusively in their charitable capacity. This permitted such organizations to incur debt on essentially the same terms as local governments through bonds issued by governmental conduit issuers. This basic pattern survived legislative changes over the next 20 years.

The Tax Reform Act of 1969 addressed another major perceived abuse in the tax-exempt area, arbitrage.[11] Congress was concerned about issuance of debt by state and local governments for the *primary* purpose of investing the proceeds in taxable securities to yield a profit, a practice generally referred to as arbitrage. Over the next 20 years, primarily through increasingly complex legislation and regulations, the Treasury Department attempted to close what it saw as loopholes in the original arbitrage rules. The continued creativity of the financial community in producing financing vehicles that would maximize permitted arbitrage profit was matched by increasingly sweeping legislation and regulations. As discussed below, this process culminated in 1986 with the virtual elimination of all arbitrage earnings.

From 1971 to 1978, various tax acts eased restrictions placed on IDBs by the 1968 act. These acts expanded the list of exempt facilities to include bonds issued for water treatment and distribution systems and for electrical generating systems, amended the small-issue exception so that certain expenditures would not count against the small-issue IDB limit and raised the small-issue IDB exception from $5 million to $10 million.

The Mortgage Subsidy Bond Act of 1980 restricted the use of tax-exempt bonds issued to finance single-family home mortgages. These bonds are known as mortgage revenue bonds (MRBs). Limits were placed on the prices of the homes financed, and purchasers had to be first-time homebuyers. In addition, the law placed state-by-state limits on the amount of tax-exempt MRBs that could be issued, the first "volume cap," and placed arbitrage restrictions on investment of bond proceeds, including the first "rebate" requirement, which required payment to the federal government of interest income on bond proceeds in excess of the rate on the bonds. Restrictions were also imposed on the use of IDBs for the purpose of multifamily housing construction. Use of the housing so financed was restricted to families of low-to-moderate income.

The Tax Equity and Fiscal Responsibility Act of 1982 (TEFRA) preserved the general structure of the code but provided substantial new restrictions on private-activity bonds. TEFRA required that informational reports be submitted to the federal government on all new private-activity bond issues, introduced the first restrictions on the types of projects eligible for financing by small-issue IDBs, prohibited the use of small-issue IDBs in conjunction with other financings, restricted the average maturity of IDBs and restricted the issuance of multiple lots of small-issue IDBs. In addition, TEFRA required that IDBs be approved by referendum or by state or local elected officials after a public hearing.

TEFRA also restricted the accelerated cost recovery system allowances for property financed with tax-exempt bonds, eased certain restrictions governing the tax exemption of MRBs, and reduced the deductibility by banks for federal income tax purposes of the cost of purchasing or carrying municipal bonds from 100% to 85%. Finally, TEFRA required, as a condition of tax exemption, that all bonds be issued in registered form.

The Social Security Amendments of 1983 indirectly subjected tax-exempt interest to income taxation by including it in the calculations of a Social Security recipient's income and then taxing a portion of Social Security payments under a formula tied to that income.

The Deficit Reduction Act of 1984 (DEFRA) included additional restrictions on IDBs. Extensive arbitrage restrictions were added, including a rebate provision similar to that applied to MRBs in 1980. The total nationwide use of small-issue IDBs by a single entity was limited; a volume cap limited the issuance of certain IDBs and student loan bonds within a state; and the list of prohibited uses was extended to include gambling and liquor facilities, airplanes, and health clubs. Small-issue IDBs were restricted to "manufacturing facilities" after 1986. DEFRA also restricted the issuance tax-exempt municipal bonds if the bonds were federally guaranteed. The tax exemption for MRBs was extended through 1987. Finally, the deductibility by banks of the costs of purchasing or carrying tax-exempt securities was reduced further, from 85 to 80%.

The Tax Reform Act of 1986 (the 1986 act) imposed the most comprehensive restrictions to date on the use of tax-exempt financing. Tax exemption was eliminated for private-activity bonds issued to finance sports facilities, convention centers, air and water pollution control facilities, industrial parks, and privately owned transportation facilities. In addition, the definition of private-activity bonds was tightened. Before 1986, a bond was categorized as a private-activity bond if more than 25% of the bond proceeds was used by a nongovernmental entity and more than 25% of the principal or interest was secured by property used by or revenues derived from a private concern. The 1986 act generally reduced these thresholds to 10%.[12]

In addition, existing separate volume caps on student loan bonds and IDBs and on MRBs were replaced by a unified volume cap, which applied on a state-by-state basis to bonds issued to finance certain mass commuting facilities, facilities for the furnishing of water, sewage facilities, privately owned solid waste facilities, multifamily housing projects, facilities for the local furnishing of electric energy or gas, local district heating or cooling facilities, and hazardous waste facilities, as well as to MRBs, small-issue IDBs, student loan bonds, and redevelopment bonds. For the first time, bonds for 501(c)(3) organizations were defined as private-activity bonds. Such bonds were not included in the volume cap, but they were subjected to certain preexisting restrictions on private-activity bonds, and a limit of $150 million was imposed on the total amount of outstanding tax-exempt debt that could be issued for "nonhospital" projects undertaken by a 501(c)(3) organization. Additionally, limits were placed on the incomes of homeowners benefiting from the MRB program.

Moreover, interest on newly issued private-activity bonds [except qualified 501(c)(3) bonds] was included as a specified preference item in computing the individual and corporate alternative minimum tax (AMT). Fifty percent of the interest on all tax-exempt municipal bonds also was included in the corporate AMT calculation of book income.[13] In addition, the 1986 act expanded the rebate requirement to substantially all issues of tax-exempt obligations. Advance refunding bonds, which are bonds issued to refund outstanding bonds before they are redeemed or paid, were limited to one for each issue of governmental bonds, and bank deductibility of the cost of purchasing or carrying municipal bonds was totally eliminated, except for certain small governmental issues. Issuers were restricted to using only 2% of the proceeds of private-activity bonds to pay the costs of issuing such bonds (except for MRBs of less than $20 million, in which case the limit was 3.5%).

Just 1 year after the enactment of the 1986 act, the *Omnibus Budget Reconciliation Act of 1987* (the 1987 act) defined bonds issued to finance the acquisition of nongovernmental electric and gas output property as private-activity bonds, subject to state volume caps. Exceptions were granted for governmental units that issued bonds to purchase output facilities to meet increased demand within their service areas or to meet the additional demand of service areas acquired through general-purpose annexations. Transition rules allowed existing public power authorities to qualify for the exceptions.

The Technical and Miscellaneous Revenue Act of 1988 (the 1988 act) further restricted the use of tax-exempt debt by imposing low-income tenant requirements on multifamily housing projects financed with certain tax-exempt bonds issued on behalf of 501(c)(3) organizations. The act also proscribed tax-exempt bonds for the purchase by an issuer of multifamily housing units outside its jurisdiction unless such purchase occurred in connection with a federal or state court-ordered or court-approved housing desegregation plan.

The 1988 act also prevented issuers from investing proceeds of non-AMT bonds in AMT bonds to obtain the interest rate differential, and it restricted certain pooled financing restrictive. At the urging of the Anthony Commission, a modified approach was adopted to effective compliance by state and local governments with the federal mandates that in many cases created the need for "pool bonds." It required that issuers have a "reasonable date of issuance of the bonds, stipulated that an anticipated increase in interest rates could not be the basis for these "reasonable expectations," and required that the costs of issuance of these bonds be substantially paid within 6 months of the date of their issuance.[14]

The 1988 act extended the sunset of the MRB program until December 31, 1989, but added new targeting provisions, including a provision to recapture some of the subsidy received by MRB mortgagees for loans made after December 31, 1990. It also expanded tax-exempt financing by allowing bonds to be issued to finance high-speed rail transit but subjected 25% of the proceeds of such bonds to the state volume cap.

Finally, at the urging of the Anthony Commission, the 1988 act clarified the U.S. Treasury Department's existing authority to draft broad safe harbors in the arbitrage rebate regulations and expressed a congressional intent that the regulations as proposed by workable and understandable.[15]

The foregoing legislative history dramatically demonstrates increasing restrictions on state and local governments' ability to provide capital projects, the breakdown of comity in the federal system, and a distressing absence of coherent consideration of appropriate public policy toward state and local government.

B. Judicial History

On April 20, 1988, in *South Carolina v. Baker*, The U.S. Supreme Court ruled that the U.S. Constitution does not prohibit the federal government from taxing the interest on state and local government bonds. The decision specifically overturned the Court's 1895 decision in *Pollock v. Farmers' Loan & Trust Co.* In *Pollock*, the Court had ruled that a tax on the interest on state and local government bonds was ultimately a tax on the state that issued the bonds and was unconstitutional under the doctrine of intergovernmental tax immunity because such taxation would restrict the state's borrowing power, and therefore its ability to operate.

Pollock was consistent with the Court's holding in the landmark case *McCulloch v. the State of Maryland*, decided in 1819. In that case, the Court held that, because the federal government had the power to incorporate a bank, it had the implied power to preserve such a bank. Because "the power to tax involves the power to destroy," the federal bank was immune from the potentially destructive taxing power of the state of Maryland.

The decision in *McCulloch* subsequently led to the parallel doctrine that, just as the federal government and its instrumentalities were constitutionally immune from state taxation, the states and their instrumentalities were constitutionally immune from federal taxation.

Prior to the adoption of the Sixteenth Amendment in 1913, permitting a federal income tax, Congress and the states carefully balanced state and federal government powers and responsibilities between the enumerated powers of the national government contained in the Constitution and the reservation of power to the states under the Tenth Amendment.

The question then arose as to whether the reciprocal immunity doctrine of *Pollock* continued to be good law. Both the legislative history of the Sixteenth Amendment and Supreme Court decisions after its passage implied that the doctrine was not altered. At the time of passage of the proposed amendment by Congress, and during the process of ratification by the states, the amendment was challenged as potentially allowing the federal taxation of states' debt obligations. The Congress reacted strongly against this challenge, and members of both the Senate and the House went on record denying that the amendment affected the immunity of state obligations from federal taxation.

The Supreme Court's landmark decision in *South Carolina v. Baker* addressed more than the particular legislative provision that triggered the case. South Carolina's challenge was to the provision in TEFRA requiring the issuance of tax-exempt bonds in registered form. Despite the position of both the Treasury

Department and the special master in the case that such provision was not a tax and therefore could be upheld without reversing *Pollock*, the Court issued a decision sweeping in scope. It held that state and local governments do not have protection against congressional provisions restricting their right to issue tax-exempt bonds other than through the political process, that is, by appealing to Congress and the administration.

Thus, the *South Carolina* decision places squarely on Congress the responsibility to protect, within the federal system, the legitimate right of state and local governments to finance their needed capital improvements. *South Carolina* raises serious concerns about the willingness of the federal government, under severe deficit pressure, to recognize and protect the rights of state and local governments in a federal system.[16] If Congress is to fulfill its constitutional responsibilities, it must recognize its duty to look at the effect on all levels of government of the tax-writing process and to accept its obligation to treat state and local governments as a coequal in the process of serving citizens. *South Carolina* has given Congress, at least in the area of tax policy, unlimited power to help or hinder the effective development of state and local government finance.

In contrast, the *South Carolina* decision did not alter the federal statutory prohibition on state and local governments' ability to tax the interest income from federal securities. In 1986, it was estimated that this benefit to the federal government cost states and localities $4.0 billion annually. It appears only fair that if the federal government considers taxing interest on state and local government bonds, it should also consider according to state and local governments reciprocal treatment, permitting them to tax the interest received by taxpayers on federal bonds.[17]

South Carolina has stimulated efforts to educate the Congress about the importance of tax exemption. Concurrent resolutions have been introduced in both houses of Congress and resolutions have been adopted by several state legislatures calling on Congress to propose a constitutional amendment to protect tax exemption for governmental bonds. In January 1989, a constitutional amendment was introduced in the U.S. Senate, the purpose and effect of which would be to preserve the tax exemption for governmental bonds for public purposes while preserving the right of the federal government to prevent abuses.[18]

III. STATEMENT OF PUBLIC POLICY: TOWARD A FEDERAL-STATE-LOCAL PARTNERSHIP

In seeking federal support for important public projects and services, state and local governments increasingly have been treated like "just another special interest group" rather than as a partner in a federal system of government. This is fundamentally, conceptually, and historically wrong. It also reflects the increasingly adversarial relationship spawned by a perception of "abuses" in the issuance of tax-exempt bonds and the increasing and sometimes short-sighted preoccupation of the national government with its own deficit problem.

The Anthony Commission believes the federal government should establish a policy to work with state and local governments in a partnership to provide public services. The federal government must recognize that its judicially unfettered power to control the tax exemption of state and local government bonds must be exercised with the full recognition of the impact on state and local taxpayers as well as on the federal Treasury.

State and local governments cannot fulfill their responsibilities to provide public services and meet federal standards and mandates without the cooperation of the Congress and the administration. Specifically, the federal government should preserve tax exemption so that public services and projects can be provided at the lowest possible cost. Although the federal government may curb abuses, it should not overregulate the public finance system generally and impose restrictions that burden state and local governments with both financial inflexibility and increased costs. State and local governments should have broad freedom to carry out their responsibilities to their citizens. One of the strengths of our federal system has been the varying approaches taken by state legislatures and local governments to enhance the economic and social well-being of their residents.[19]

The rules under which municipal bonds can be issued should therefore be as flexible as possible consistent with carefully drawn restrictions to prevent specific abuses, including overissuance, early issuance, and other practices that are driven by exploitation of interest rate differentials rather than public borrowing needs.[20] Where rules already exist, they should be enforced, and civil penalties for tax law violations should be reviewed to determine their effectiveness and modified as needed. Penalties, however, should be realistic. If bonds are issued with soundly based legal opinions as to tax exemption, the private purchaser of the securities should not be penalized if an issuer thereafter purposely or inadvertently acts improperly.[21]

Fundamental fairness rather than expediency or retribution should guide the process of congressional policy. The Anthony Commission does not believe it was—or is—the intent of Congress to undermine the ability of state and local governments to meet the needs of their citizens. It is confident that the overwhelming majority of members of Congress are sympathetic to the needs of state and local governments and wish to promote their ability to borrow on an effective and efficient low-cost basis.

The commission believes, however, that the Congress has overreacted to a number of perceived abuses and has enacted far-reaching proposals without the appropriate level of investigation and consideration. The problem in large part reflects the complexity and political demands on the federal tax-writing process. This process often is subject to political pressures from every major interest group in the United States, it is unduly driven by a questionable process of revenue estimates, and it is often accomplished in an atmosphere that discourages careful consideration and thoughtful legislative drafting.

The commission also is concerned that in recent years the tax-writing process has become so constrained by deficit concerns that it has prevented Congress from careful consideration of important policy questions. There has emerged from the tax-writing process in recent years a clear, if unwritten, rule that no public finance proposal that is, by any calculation, "revenue negative" will be even considered unless its proponent offers a companion proposal that is at least as "revenue positive." Furthermore, no attention is given to the fact that a proposal may impose substantial costs on state and local governments. This approach stifles serious discussion of public policy considerations in tax law affecting state and local government bonds. It falsely implies that encouraging one type of state or local government financing is only properly considered if another is discouraged; it focuses the debate on the tax exemption mechanism rather than the policy objectives served by that mechanism; and at its extreme it prevents Congress from exercising its legislative sovereignty in adopting policies that serve the public good.

The Anthony Commission believes that Congress can and will respond positively to evidence that the modification of certain provisions is an appropriate way to carry out the original purposes of the 1986 act, while recognizing the special rights and responsibilities of state and local governments. It is in this spirit that the commission makes its recommendations.

The commission's specific recommendations reflect a strong belief in the desirability of a public policy that

- Recognizes the right of state and local governments to utilize tax-exempt debt when financing their basic governmental facilities and services
- Accepts the right of Congress to protect against abuses of the use of tax-exempt bonds, both in the extension of tax-exempt financing for nongovernmental projects and in the use of bond proceeds by governmental entities primarily to exploit interest rate differentials
- Promotes cooperation between Congress and state and local governments in encouraging the use of tax-exempt financing to solve the immense need for infrastructure expansion and replacement and the extension of needed governmental services
- Does not require that public projects be financed in any particular way, but recognizes the continuing need for state and local governments to adopt individual approaches, including public/private partnerships
- Encourages (1) the reexamination by Congress of provisions in the tax code that go far beyond their stated purpose of preventing abuses and (2) the application of a truly federal cost-benefit analysis that recognizes that it is unsound policy to adopt legislation that increases the cost to citizens as state and local government taxpayers over and above any savings to them as federal taxpayers

The commission's suggested legislative classification of public-purpose and private-activity bonds reflects the strong belief that

- State and local governments should be free from federal interference generally when issuing bonds, the sole purpose of which is to finance appropriate governmental activities not involving private parties
- Congress should continue to recognize the desirability of controlled use of tax-exempt financing to solve particular problems even when private use occurs

The commission's recommendations with respect to the alternative minimum tax and bank deductibility are based on abundant evidence that the existing provisions, however well intended, take far more out of the treasuries of state and local governments than they put into the Treasury of the United States.

The recommended amendment of the current arbitrage rebate requirement reflects the common-sense conclusion that the current provisions go far beyond the original stated purpose to eliminate "arbitrage-driven" transactions and impose needless and costly restrictions on state and local governments. Implementation of the provisions has proven to be even more difficult and complicated than expected, and appropriate modifications are entirely consistent with the original congressional purpose.

Finally, the commission recommends the alteration or elimination of a number of particular provisions that do not meaningfully or in a cost-effective manner promote any significant federal policy.

IV. AVAILABILITY OF TAX-EXEMPT FINANCING: RECOMMENDATIONS FOR MORE CAREFULLY DEFINING PUBLIC PURPOSES

Recent federal legislation restricting tax-exempt financing has stimulated considerable debate as to what types of facilities and activities are entitled to such financing. The commission strongly believes that state and local governments are entitled to issue bonds with a minimum of restrictions to finance their essential governmental purposes. The commission does not believe that state and local governments have the unfettered right to pass the benefits of tax-exempt financing to projects not serving a public purpose; the commission emphatically believes, however, that federal legislation should reflect careful decision making in Washington that will, in appropriate cases, encourage the limited and effective use of private participation in appropriate public projects financed with tax-exempt debt. Accordingly, it recommends certain changes that will encourage such use.

Federal tax law has evolved over several decades from a time when interest on all obligations of state and local governments was exempt from federal income taxation to the current structure under which federal tax law classifies tax-exempt obligations into two broad categories: (1) governmental bonds and (2) private-activity bonds.[22]

Over the years, federal law has effectively precluded the use of tax-exempt bonds for purposes that do not serve a public purpose through governmental activity. Much of the federal government's motivation in restricting the issuance of state and local government bonds is attributable to transactions that violated the intent of the original federal public policy toward such obligations.

The commission believes that federal policy with respect to the issuance of tax-exempt bonds should reflect the twin goals of (1) premitting state and local governments maximum freedom in financing governmental projects and (2) recognizing and encouraging financings in which appropriate private use can materially assist the efficiency of providing public services.

A. Definitions of Tax-Exempt Bonds

Sound public policy must recognize the need for flexibility in responding to the needs of a dynamic society. As conditions change, the role of state and local governments in delivering a particular service should also change. For example, at one time, mass transit was predominantly private in ownership; today mass transit is a public function. It is simply not good public policy to constrain local flexibility through a narrow list of approved purposes or functions when community needs, practices, and resources vary as much as they do.

Generally, under current law "governmental bonds" (i.e., tax-exempt bonds that are not private-activity bonds) are those that finance publicly owned and operated facilities. These include publicly owned schools, roads, health facilities, water and sewer systems, gas and electric systems, parks, and other governmental buildings or facilities. Current law, however, contains a number of inconsistencies and restrictions that label as private-activity bonds debt issued to finance governmental facilities and activities clearly serving a public purpose—such as airports, public docks and wharves, public solid waste disposal facilities, public mass commuting facilities, public parking garages, and local public water and sewer facilities. These restrictions inhibit the ability of state and local governments to respond to the legitimate needs of their constituents in the most cost-effective way.

The current rules contain counterproductive restrictions that exclude projects that are truly public in both benefit and control and fail to distinguish between material private benefit and private involvement that does not undermine the public purpose of the project. They unnecessarily hamper effective provision of public services by restricting management agreements with private parties, thereby discouraging the most efficient operation of facilities benefiting the general public, such as solid waste disposal, health care, and public parking. These arrangements are severely constrained if a government wants to protect the "governmental" status of the bond, even though a management contract might be the most efficient and lowest-cost alternative for delivering a public service.

The current rules similarly miscategorize as private-activity bonds those bonds issued to finance facilities owned or operated by charitable 501(c)(3) organizations, even when they are used exclusively in furtherance of charitable public purposes.

The Anthony Commission proposes the continued application of the current "private-activity tests" for differentiating public and private activities, refined to permit private involvement that does not undermine the essential public nature of the financing or pass to the private party the benefits of tax exemption. The two broad general categories of tax-exempt bonds in the commission's proposal are *public-purpose bonds* and *private-activity bonds.*

B. Public-Purpose Bonds

In general, bonds should be treated as tax-exempt public-purpose bonds if the facility financed is publicly owned and operated or the primary benefits from a privately provided–privately managed facility accrue to the community as a whole rather than to private parties. In so defining public-purpose bonds, the commission recognizes that exclusively public operation is not always the best or even a practical way to further the public interest. If a facility serves a public use, the public sector should be free to implement the activity through whatever means are most efficient, economically advantageous, and consistent with local policy concerns, *so long as* the economic benefit of the tax exemption is not transferred from the public entity to a private entity.

The proposed subcategories of public-purpose bonds are

- Governmental bonds
- Public-activity bonds
- Exempt-purpose—501(c)(3)—bonds

1.   Governmental Bonds
Governmental bonds are those that finance governmentally owned and operated facilities with only limited private involvement and benefit. The rules to determine whether that is limited or substantial private involvement and benefit would be based primarily on the continued application of the current private business tests (trade or business and security interest tests) and the private loan financing test, modified to permit private involvement that does not produce inappropriate private benefit.

Under current law, a private use of a facility arises from any of the following arrangements with a private person: (1) a lease, (2) an output purchase contract, (3) a management or operating contract lasting longer than 5 years, generally, or (4) an ownership interest. This mechanical test results in the classification as private-activity bonds of debt indisputably financing public rather than private facilities.

The commission suggests that use of a governmentally owned and operated facility by a private person should not affect its qualification for tax-exempt financing if such use is pursuant to contractual or other arrangements that

- Are entered into pursuant to arm's-length negotiations
- Provide for the payment of fair market prices with respect to the use and operation of the facility
- Do not pass on to the private user the benefits of the lower interest rate on the bonds due to the federal income tax exemption unless the benefit of the lower interest rate is completely shared with the general public through regulatory, contractual, or other mechanisms[23]

For example, renting surplus space in a municipal office building to a private entity would not jeopardize the tax-exempt status of the bonds if the space is leased at a fair rental value negotiated on an arm's-length basis. Similarly, publicly owned and operated airports and sewer facilities should not be categorized as private activities merely because private entities utilize such facilities or their services at market rates. Utilization of private parties to manage governmentally financed and owned facilities should be permitted when such management is both directly beneficial to the governmental entity and does not pass the benefits of tax exemption to the private party. Such arrangements are particularly useful in developing technologies to solve some of our most pressing problems, such as solid waste and hazardous waste disposal.

Workable rules to implement the three standards suggested above require careful development. We believe, however, that the above principles can be applied fairly and consistently and with a reasonable degree of certainly without the kind of abuses that have previously tainted certain types of financings. We can think of no better opportunity for an appropriate partnership between the levels of government in our federal system than developing the statutory and regulatory provisions necessary to permit such creative problem solving.

2. Public-Activity Bonds

Certain facilities should be eligible for tax-exempt financing because of their unquestioned public nature. Current tests distinguishing governmental from private-activity bonds simply should not apply to such facilities. Instead, subject to appropriate limitation, such facilities should be eligible for tax-exempt financing, whether owned and operated publicly or privately.

Examples of such activities and services include solid waste disposal facilities, hazardous waste disposal facilities, wastewater treatment and collection facilities, community development, and certain multifamily rental housing projects. The list of such public activities would have to be carefully defined to ensure that they provide important and meaningful benefits to the public and follow the limits relating to ownership and operation listed below.

To ensure that public-activity facilities primarily benefit the general public, the following limitations would apply:

- Any private party owning or managing the facility would not be entitled to take cost recovery deductions or investment tax credits.
- A private person managing the facility could purchase the facility only at fair market value, determined at the time of purchase.
- Management contracts or similar arrangements would be allowed, but only for a period no longer than the economically useful life of the facility.
- Any public-activity project or facility must be designed and operated so as to serve the general public, and for this purpose, the current tax-law criteria would apply.
- The average maturity of the bond issue must not exceed 120% of the expected economic life of the facility.
- The state or local unit of government issuing the bonds must retain a significant level of control over the operation of the facility.
- All such financings would be subject to the public hearing and public approval requirements that currently apply to private-activity bonds.

3. Exempt-Purpose Bonds

Congress's original structuring of the "industrial development bond" test treated 501(c)(3) organizations as "exempt persons" along with state and local government entities, rather than as private persons, such as individuals and for-profit corporations. This distinction, which remained in the code until the 1986 act, reflected both the public purposes of such organizations and the extensive regulations developed by the Treasury Department under section 501(c)(3) of the code, ensuring that such organizations act only for public rather than private benefit. The statutes and regulations governing tax-exempt bonds therefore appropriately limit 501(c)(3) organizations' use of tax-exempt bonds to the financing of facilities used *exclusively* for charitable "exempt activities."

The 1986 act treated "qualified 501(c)(3) bonds" as private-activity bonds but exempted them from several of the more onerous provisions affecting private-activity bonds, including the volume cap, the prohibition against advance refundings, and the alternative minimum tax.[24]

Bonds issued for 501(c)(3) organizations should be classified as public-purpose bonds. The existing rules governing the use of tax-exempt bonds by 501(c)(3) organizations unnecessarily restrict the use of bond proceeds to finance facilities exclusively used in charitable activities for a public benefit.

Although 501(c)(3) organizations do not literally satisfy the governmental ownership and operation criteria, where they provide public services that are broad-based in nature that would otherwise have to be provided directly by a governmental entity, such as health care and education, the commission supports classifying these bonds as public-purpose bonds, subject, however, to the present public hearing and voter or governmental approval requirements.

Concerns about the general qualifications of certain 501(c)(3) organizations for tax exemption and about the treatment of "unrelated trade or business activities" of tax-exempt organizations are now being addressed by Congress in connection with a review of appropriate sections of the code. The tax law has long reflected a distinction between the charitable activities of 501(c)(3) organizations and appropriate but incidental unrelated activities that are subject to income taxation and that may not, therefore, be financed with tax-exempt bonds. Access to the benefits of tax exemption by 501(c)(3) organizations can and should be regulated by the proper application of rules relating to the tax-exempt status of 501(c)(3) organizations and their activities.

To the extent that there is congressional concern with the scope and manner of the operation of certain exempt-purpose organizations, Congress should impose restrictions directly on such activities rather than amend the tax-exempt bond provisions. In connection with its current review of section 501(c)(3) issues, Congress should satisfy itself that the criteria under section 501(c)(3) are appropriate to assure that qualifying organizations operate in a manner consistent with Congress's view of proper public purposes. There is no practical reason to distinguish between activities that are found to be exclusively in furtherance of charitable exempt purposes under section 501(c)(3) and those qualifying for tax-exempt financing.

C. Private-Acitivty Bonds

Under current law, bonds are defined as private-activity bonds as a result of the use by and financial involvement of private persons. As pointed out above, this definition has incorrectly categorized a number of indisputably public purposes as private. In the system being proposed by the commission, the private-activity characterization applies when a financed facility is owned and operated by a private person who realizes any of the tax benefits of ownership of such facility (i.e., cost recovery deductions or tax credits), or the facility financed does not provide a public activity or service. Both the purpose and effect of such a rule are simple. The benefits of tax-exempt financing should pass directly to the taxpayers; private participation should not be discouraged as long as such benefits are passed directly to the taxpayers.

No change is proposed in the current code treatment whereby certain private-activity bonds for "exempt" activities are eligible for tax exemption. No expansion of this list is advocated, and the current tests defining each of the exempt activities would be retained. Additionally, no change is suggested in the current prohibition on the use of tax-exempt bonds to finance certain facilities including, among others, airplanes, skyboxes, or other private luxury boxes; health club facilities; gambling facilities; and liquor stores.[25] Other current restrictions on private-activity bonds such as the volume cap, the requirement for public hearings, and the 120% maturity limit, also would remain unchanged.

Under the definitions of public-purpose and private-activity bonds proposed by the commission, certain facilities eligible to be financed with private-activity bonds may also be financed with public-purpose bonds. To summarize, the categorization of exempt private-activity bonds is distinguishable from public-purpose bonds by virtue of the ownership and operation of the facility by private persons entitled to and who take cost recovery deductions and tax credits. For example, a solid waste disposal facility may be financed by either public-purpose bonds or private-activity bonds, depending upon the ownership and operating arrangements. If the facility is governmentally owned and governmentally operated, it is eligible to be financed with a tax-exempt public-purpose bond. If the same facility is governmentally owned, but operated by a private party subject to the standards enumerated above for governmental bonds, it would still be eligible for tax-exempt financing with public-purpose bonds. If privately owned and operated, such a facility would still be eligible to be financed with tax-exempt public-purpose bonds as long as the fundamental limitations identified above for public-activity bonds are not violated. For example, the private owner could not depreciate the facility for tax purposes. Finally, if the same solid waste facility was privately owned and operated and the owner took depreciation, the facility would be eligible to be financed with private-activity bonds, subject to the state volume cap and other restrictions, because solid waste disposal facilities are on the list of exempt activities.

Figure 2 shows the proposed system for categorizing tax-exempt bonds, which includes tax-exempt governmental, public-activity, exempt-purpose, and private-activity bonds.

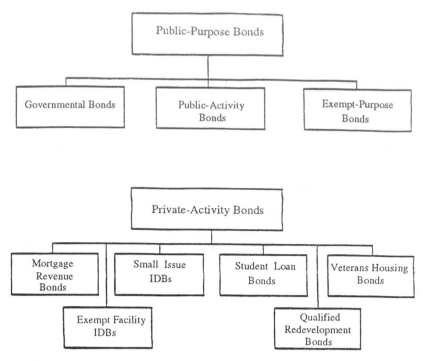

Figure 2   Proposed system for categorizing tax-exempt bonds.

V. PRESERVING THE MARKET FOR TAX-EXEMPT DEBT: RECOMMENDATIONS FOR BROADENING THE MARKET

The benefit of tax-exempt bonds to the local taxpayer is a direct reflection of the willingness of investors to accept lower interest rates in return for the tax exemption on interest. The leadership in Congress has repeatedly stated that it has no wish to abolish the issuance of tax-exempt bonds for legitimate public purposes. Such sentiments should be supported by policies that also enhance the market for such bonds. These policies should reflect a long-term commitment of the Congress, which though not legally binding, would provide much needed comfort and stability to the municipal bond market.

Historically, the three major groups purchasing tax-exempt bonds have been commercial banks, property and casualty insurance companies, and the household sector, which includes individuals, trusts, and mutual funds. Each sector's demand for tax-exempt investments has been influenced by changes in marginal tax rates and "bracket creep" due to inflation. The varying profitability of banks and insurance companies has influenced institutional demand over time.

Broadening the market for tax-exempt debt is essential. The continuous imposition of new restrictions has reduced incentives to purchase tax-exempt debt, causing higher interest rates and greater volatility in the marketplace, making state and local financing—and financial planning—more expensive and difficult. In the absence of a well-functioning tax-exempt bond market, many projects would not be feasible and the financing capacity of state and local issuers would be sharply curtailed. Some examples of recent tax law changes that have reduced investor demand are

- The inclusion of tax-exempt debt in the income base of Social Security recipients to determine the taxability of their Social Security benefits (1983 Social Security amendments)
- Reductions in the bank interest deduction for interest costs incurred to purchase and carry tax-exempt debt, first from 100% to 85%, then to 80% and then to zero—except for certain small governmental issues (TEFRA, DEFRA, and the 1986 act)
- Inclusion of tax-exempt debt in the calculation of taxation of foreign branch profits of corporations (the 1986 act)

- Reductions in insurance company loss reserves equal to 15% of tax-exempt interest on newly purchased bonds (the 1986 act)
- Inclusion of tax-exempt interest earned on private-activity bonds issued after August 7, 1986, in the calculation of the individual and corporate alternative minimum tax (the 1986 act)
- Inclusion of 50% of tax-exempt interest earned on all bonds in the calculation of corporate book income (75% of adjusted current earnings starting in 1990) for purposes of the corporate alternative minimum tax (the 1986 act)
- Taxation of book income, which includes tax-exempt interest, under the Superfund Tax (the Superfund Amendments and Reauthorization Act of 1986)[26]

Some recent proposals that, if enacted, would increase state and local borrowing costs by reducing the number of possible purchasers of tax-exempt bonds, include those to

- Limit the amount of tax-exempt interest an individual could earn in any given tax year
- Reduce the *de minimis* deduction corporations are able to take for costs they incur to purchase or hold tax-exempt debt
- Preclude certain corporations from deducting interest costs incurred in connection with certain tax-exempt leases
- Tax the market discount investors receive when purchasing bonds in the secondary market on a current basis rather than when the bonds are sold
- Include interest on all bonds, rather than just private-activity bonds, in the alternative minimum tax (AMT) calculation
- Include tax-exempt interest in the definition of adjusted gross income for the purpose of phasing out the earned income credit or determining eligibility for the medical disallowance or other exemptions and deductions
- Modify the adjusted current earnings (ACE) provision of the corporate AMT and increase the tax on tax-exempt interest[27]

While none of the recent enactments or any of the proposals would alone destroy the market for tax-exempt debt, their cumulative effect is to erode gradually such market by introducing unparalleled uncertainty, greater interest rate volatility and extreme complexity, all of which ultimately result in substantially higher borrowing costs.

The Anthony Commission urges Congress not to take any action that would directly or indirectly reduce market demand. The commission also recommends reconsideration of the following four current law provisions that have had a substantial adverse impact on state and local governments and provide no significant benefit to the federal government:

- Inclusion of tax-exempt interest on private-activity bonds as a tax preference item under the individual AMT
- Inclusion of tax-exempt interest on private-activity bonds as a tax preference item under the corporate AMT
- Inclusion of tax-exempt interest in the book income (or adjusted current earnings) of a corporation for purposes of the calculation of the corporate AMT
- Elimination of the bank interest deduction

A. The Threat to the Municipal Bond Market

Relative to the after-tax return on taxable securities such as Treasury obligations of similar maturity, municipal bond yields are near historical lows. Underwriting spreads have declined, and spreads in the secondary market are quite narrow. By these standards, the municipal bond market is a liquid, well-functioning provider of investment capital. However, the net purchases of municipal bonds over the period of 1976 through 1988, shown in Fig. 3, reveal a market increasingly dominated by individual purchasers and therefore vulnerable to extreme interest rate volatility because of external factors unrelated to either the credit of the issuers or general economic conditions.[28]

The present market composition should be contrasted with the historic market, where demand for municipal bonds came almost exclusively from three sectors—commercial banks, property and casualty

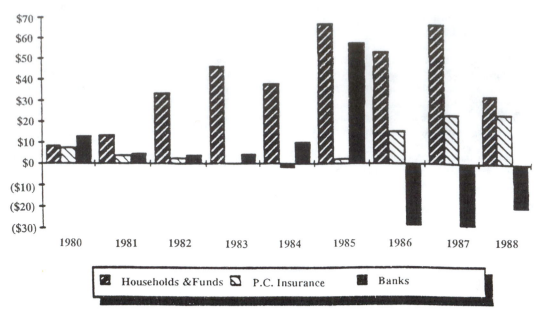

Figure 3   Buyers of tax-exempt bonds, 1980–1988 (net flows in billions of dollars).

insurers, and households (including mutual funds). Furthermore, Fig. 3 does not show that the demand from property and casualty insurers (P&Cs) is expected to decline, sharply and permanently.

The principal reason for the projected decline in P&C demand is the change after 1989 in the calculation of the corporate AMT. Under the 1986 act, 50% of a corporation's tax-exempt income is included in book income in the calculation of the corporate AMT. The 1986 act also provided that, in 1990, book income will be replaced by ACE, with the ACE preference equal to 75% of the amount by which ACE exceeds what otherwise would be alternative minimum taxable income. The change from 50% of book income to 75% of ACE will dramatically reduce the desire of P&Cs to own tax-exempt bonds. Furthermore, the proposed change in the recently introduced H.R. 1761, increasing the amount of tax-exempt interest taxed from 75% to 100%, would exacerbate the problem significantly. In addition, since some banks are affected by the current book income provision, the scheduled and proposed changes discussed above would further reduce bank demand for bank-eligible small issues.[29]

The net result of these changes would be a municipal bond market almost exclusively dependent on individuals. Demand from individuals has been strong enough to support the market so far, but overreliance on one sector to support the municipal market can cause serious problems. In the spring of 1987, for example, a sharp decline in demand from individuals and open-end funds in a weak market environment caused long-term bond prices to decline sharply. The increase in rates in the municipal market was substantially greater than the increase in the taxable market. If P&Cs, who were major purchasers of municipal bonds in 1987, no longer purchase tax-exempt bonds, the decline in the market will be far more severe during future periods of bond market weakness.[30]

B.   Alternative Minimum Tax

In 1986, Congress included interest on tax-exempt bonds in the calculation of the individual and corporate AMT. There were three separate AMT provisions affecting the tax-exempt debt of states and localities.

Although the federal government had previously refrained from directly taxing the interest on state and local government securities, the 1986 act included tax-exempt bond interest in the AMT calculation.[31] The press reported congressional concern that corporations were able to avoid paying any federal income tax because of numerous tax law provisions. To remedy this situation, a plan emerged from the Senate Finance Committee to subject all tax-exempt interest to the alternative minimum tax. The market, stunned by the proposal and especially its retroactive application to interest on bonds already in the portfolios of individuals and corporations, shut down, and at least one major public bond issue was delayed.

The proposal to tax state and local bond interest was ultimately altered significantly, restoring the market for the debt, but not without imposing some hardship on issuers.[32] A new AMT system emerged that created a multitiered and multifaceted market for tax-exempt debt.

Although the precise effect of the AMT is unknown, there is general agreement that private-activity bonds subject to AMT pay roughly 25 more basis points (or one-quarter of 1%) of interest than similar bonds not subject to the tax. For a city financing a $10 million sewer facility with a private-activity bond, the resulting additional cost over 20 years would be $368,000.

There is no evidence that anything approaching the cost of AMT to state and local governments actually reaches the federal Treasury. This is because the AMT provision has separated investors in municipal bonds into two distinct categories: (1) those who are sure they will pay the regular tax and therefore may buy some private-activity bonds, and (2) those who are uncertain, or who clearly fall into the AMT category. Investors in the second category (either individuals or corporations) simply will not buy, or continue to own, private-activity bonds that are subject to the AMT.[33]

The commission makes the following recommendations:

- Eliminate the tax-exempt interest preference item for private-activity bonds under the individual AMT.
- Eliminate the tax-exempt interest preference item for private-activity bonds under the corporate AMT.
- Eliminate tax-exempt interest from ACE (or any alternative to ACE).[34]

The major reasons for these recommendations are

- It is in the national interest to provide state and local governments with the ability to obtain low-cost financing for infrastructure and other improvements that benefit the nation as a whole by strengthening the national economy and improving the competitiveness of the United States.
- Available research does not cite tax-exempt interest as a major factor contributing to the corporate tax avoidance problem.[35]
- For the vast majority of purchasers, investments in tax-exempt securities are not tax shelters. Tax-exempt bonds are purchased with after-tax income and the investor is taxed indirectly by the governmental issuer because the investment pays a below-market return.
- Tax-exempt interest is an efficient incentive because financing is provided for desirable projects at little cost to the federal government. There is no bureaucracy required to manage the program as is the case with direct grant programs, and state and local governments have more flexibility to be responsive to state and local policy processes.
- The taxation of tax-exempt private-activity bond interest under the AMT results in a two-tiered market, which includes individuals and corporations who are subject to the AMT and those who are not. Taxpayers who are subject to the AMT do not pay more tax; they change their buying pattern and only purchase bonds not subject to the tax. The additional cost to local governments goes directly to investors and does not benefit the federal government.
- State and local issuers have to pay higher interest rates to sell their private-activity bonds because of the loss of market liquidity associated with the imposition of the AMT.
- Taxpayers who know that they will never be subject to the AMT invest in the private-activity bonds that offer an interest premium and thereby receive an unjustified interest windfall.
- Data recently collected from a sample of individual taxpayer returns by the Internal Revenue Service reinforce earlier studies that show that people who own municipal bonds are in the middle-income as well as upper-income brackets, and that virtually all taxpayers in all income categories have taxable income. Thus, taxpayers do not totally eliminate their tax liability through tax-exempt bonds.[36]

While there may be a slight gain to the federal government from the inclusion of tax-exempt interest in the AMT, there is an unquestionably large cost imposed on states and localities. The interest rate on AMT bonds includes an amount that reflects the liquidity risk created by the smaller market for those bonds. Additional cost is created because purchasers fear they will be subject to the AMT in future years. This interest rate premium is borne by all issuers without any benefit to the federal government.

The AMT provisions affecting tax-exempt bonds are perhaps the most striking example of provisions in the 1986 act that were well-intentioned, do not accomplish their stated purpose, and impose costs on state and local governments far beyond any benefit to the federal government. Their repeal would be an important first step in redefining the partnership between the federal government and state and local governments. It would also reflect an appropriate application of a truly national cost-benefit analysis that measured the costs to state and local taxpayers as well as the benefits to them as national taxpayers.

C. Bank Deductibility

Since 1917, the tax code has contained provisions encouraging banks and other financial institutions to purchase the debt of state and local governments. These provisions recognized that (1) since banks are in the business of borrowing money to make loans, they should be exempt from the general requirement that borrowing costs associated with tax-exempt debt cannot be deducted from gross income, and (2) banks are uniquely suited to purchase the securities of state and local governments in communities in which they are doing business because they understand both the issuers' needs and creditworthiness. Until 1982, banks played a vital role in the tax-exempt market. In 1972, they held 51.1% of the outstanding municipal bonds.

In 1982, Congress began to limit the bank interest deduction for carrying costs associated with tax-exempt debt, reducing the deduction first to 85% in 1982 and then to 80% in 1984, and finally eliminating it for most issues in 1986. As a result of these provisions, by the end of 1988, banks held only 20% of outstanding municipal bonds.

The Federal Reserve Bank of San Francisco has found that the net effect of this change on banks is still difficult to predict but that it continues to produce a decline in tax-exempt debt as a percentage of bank portfolios. In 1986, tax-exempt securities represented 7.5% of bank assets. Just 1 year later, this percentage fell to 6.3%, a drop of almost 17%.[37] The Congressional Research Service not only has noted the adverse impact on tax-exempt issuers of the repeal of bank deductibility, but has raised the concern that as depository institutions switch from low-yielding tax-exempt assets to higher-yielding taxable assets, they may be assuming more risk. The Congressional Research Service warns that the bank deduction provision may need to be revisited in light of the responsibility of Congress to ensure the safety and soundness of the American financial system.[38]

An analysis prepared for the commission by First Tennessee Bank National Association has concluded that the 5-year cost for issuers due to the loss of the deduction ranges from $2.0 billion to $3.8 billion.[39] The range of this estimate reflects the uncertainty of such future variables as banks' general profitability, tax position, portfolio mix, and interest earnings on other investments, but even given this difficulty, it is evident that the additional interest paid by state and local governments because of the repeal of bank deductibility far exceeds any incremental federal benefit. When the provision was first proposed, an estimated $1.3 billion federal revenue increase was projected. Later that estimate was reduced to the $400–500 million range. The final estimate of the Joint Committee on Taxation forecasted a $55 million revenue increase over 5 years. The projected revenue gain is based on the assumptions that the volume of tax-exempt debt will not be reduced and the bonds will continue to be purchased, but by taxpayers with lower marginal tax rates.[40]

In 1986, Congress recognized the importance of banks as purchasers of small governmental issuers' debt and retained the deduction for them. The commission believes that banks, which have held more than 50% of the tax-exempt debt outstanding at various times, should be encouraged to remain buyers of such debt. The commission recognizes that legitimate congressional motivation, reflected in the 1986 act, to reform the tax treatment of banks. Accordingly, until a thorough analysis can be made of the effects of the 1986 act, the commission recommends that, at a minimum, the current $10 million small-issuer exemption should be increased to $25 million to facilitate the placement of tax-exempt debt with banks.[41]

The commission also recommends a change to eliminate the discrimination against states that utilize statewide entities to issue certain bonds that would otherwise qualify for the small-issuer exemption. A statewide issuing authority should be able to issue debt for facilities within a political subdivision that qualify for the small-issuer exemption if the political subdivision consents and if such bonds would qualify for the exemption if issued by the locality or a related issuer. Currently, a community hospital can utilize the small-issuer exemption for bonds issued for it by the local government or a conduit authority created by the local government, but not by a statewide authority.

The above recommendations are supported by the following:

- The 1986 policy decisions failed to address adequately traditional concerns about the preservation of the market for tax-exempt debt. Banks have curtailed their purchases of new-issue tax-exempt bonds and are selling their tax-exempt holdings. This threatens greater market volatility, less liquidity, and higher borrowing costs.

- Many states have laws requiring banks to pledge security for government deposits and in some states the required pledge is municipal debt. Declining bank portfolios of municipal debt have complicated compliance with these provisions.[42]

- The congressional goal of reducing tax avoidance by banks has been achieved through other tax law modifications, including the elimination of loan loss reserve deductions for large banks, elimination of the investment tax credit, and modifications to the corporate AMT.

- The potential revenue gain to the federal government of $55 million over 5 years is insignificant when compared with the higher borrowing costs being incurred every day by states and localities. Currently the demand for tax-exempt debt by individuals is brisk, but a slight downturn in this segment of the market will cause a sharp increase in borrowing costs to state and local governments.

- Banks are substituting higher yielding taxable debt for the tax-exempt debt they previously held. This development has introduced more risk into a banking system already experiencing financial difficulties.

The 1986 act focused more on the effect on banks than on the costs to state and local taxpayers. The commission suggests that this area needs to be carefully reconsidered, since the provision is substantially increasing state and local borrowing costs without any significant benefit to the federal government.

VI. ARBITRAGE REBATE REQUIREMENT: RECOMMENDATIONS FOR RELIEVING REGULATORY OVERKILL

The arbitrage rebate requirement was perhaps the most intrusive and ultimately costly provision for state and local governments included in the 1986 act. Although the concept of "rebating" earnings on the investment of bond proceeds to the federal government may seem simple, its implementation indisputably is not. The complexity of the problem is reflected by the fact that more than 2½ years passed before the Treasury Department was finally able to promulgate only a *portion* of the regulations regarding the rebate, 243 pages of extraordinarily complex and confusing provisions.[43]

The Commission believes that the rebate requirement represents substantial regulatory overkill and goes far beyond the original intent of Congress. It also believes that, in light of the overwhelming evidence as to how burdensome implementation of the rebate rules is going to be, Congress will embrace the commission's recommendations to modify the rebate requirement to reduce the burdens on state and local government without permitting arbitrage-driven transactions.

The clear purpose of the rebate requirement was to eliminate "arbitrage-driven" transactions. It is appropriate for the commission and the entire public finance community to recognize legitimate federal concern when tax-exempt bonds are issued under financing structures dependent upon the generation of substantial arbitrage profit or without clear evidence that bond proceeds would be promptly used for an appropriate governmental purpose.

For many years after enactment of the 1969 arbitrage provisions, Congress was satisfied with the adequacy of regulatory provisions allowing state and local governments to retain, without restriction, investment earnings on appropriately qualifying funds. The arbitrage "profit" on bond proceeds held and prudently invested before being spent, for example, did not (and does not) constitute a major threat to the federal Treasury justifying interference with such prudent investment and the use of investment earnings for public purposes. In fact, the original purpose of the arbitrage provisions was to prevent the issuance of obligations solely to invest proceeds to produce a higher yield than the interest to be paid on the issue. This permitted state and local governments to manage funds in a way to maximize the return to the public by reducing project costs.

It was only when the flexibility of such regulations was exploited (and in some cases the regulations were violated) that arbitrage became a major issue. The rebate requirement was first applied to MRBs in 1980, and then to IDBs in 1984 and to substantially all issues in 1986, including literally thousands of issues that could in no circumstances be described as arbitrage-driven.

Compliance with the rebate requirement imposes significant recordkeeping burdens related to the tracking of investment earnings and the expenditure of bond proceeds. It mandates a costly procedure that must be followed even in instances where no arbitrage is likely to be earned and no rebate is required. The

Joint Committee on Taxation estimate of a federal revenue gain of at most $150 million from all the arbitrage changes made in 1986 pales in comparison to a conservatively estimated compliance cost for states and localities of $1.1 billion.[44]

The arbitrage restrictions, including the rebate provision, are not revenue provisions, but are intended solely to eliminate arbitrage-driven transactions and to prevent the excessively early issuance of bonds. Maximizing earnings on bond proceeds before their prompt expenditure is sound financial policy for state and local government. Indeed, it is often dictated by state law. Yet federal tax law, misled by overreaction to abuses, has embraced a theory that all such earnings are in conflict with federal policy objectives. The ironic results have included not only a substantial increase in transaction costs, but the issuance of greater debt to cover the lost investment earnings.

Congress recognized the burdens of arbitrage rebate by creating a few limited exceptions; for example, for small issuers and in instances where all bond proceeds obtained from a bond sale are spent within 6 months after issuance. Even these limited exceptions are of no use to a large number of issuers, and they fail to recognize the thousands of bond issues not qualifying for such exceptions that are in no way abusive or deserving of the costs and burdens of the current rebate rules.

The recent publication of partial rebate regulations indicates what a monster the Congress has inadvertently created in the rebate requirements. The costs and burdens of rebate will begin to grow rapidly as more and more issuers are required to make actual calculations and payments. Congress should move promptly to remove those burdens from state and local governments that prudently invest and promptly spend the proceeds of their bonds for appropriate public purposes.

The Commission's recommendations reflect the following conclusions:

- Current arbitrage rebate restrictions are extraordinarily complicated, imposing substantial transaction costs on state and local governments and, if fully enforced, on the federal government itself.
- Arbitrage provisions should minimize burdens while preventing the recurrence of arbitrage-driven transactions.
- Enforcement of the current arbitrage regulations will cost citizens as state and local government taxpayers far more than any possible benefit to the federal government.
- The rebate requirement was not intended by Congress to be a revenue-enhancing measure, but instead an abuse-preventing measure. Therefore modifications and improvements to the requirements should not be rejected on the grounds of decreased federal revenue.
- So long as bond proceeds are promptly and appropriately spent for public purpses, the use of investment proceeds for similar public purposes is appropriate. To the extent that Congress may consider this a "subsidy" to the state and local governments, it is a desirable and efficient subsidy.

The Commission's basic recommendation is the creation of substantial exceptions to the overall rebate requirement that will (1) encourage the prompt expenditure of bond proceeds and (2) permit the great majority of state and local government financings, undertaken for public purposes and in no sense arbitrage driven, to proceed without the imposition of the requirement to calculate and pay rebate.

In particular, the commission recommends that no rebate be required if the issuer proceeds with due diligence to spend bond proceeds, and, in fact at least 25% of the proceeds are spent within 1 year, at least 50% within 2 years, and at least 95% within 3 years. Requirements similar to existing ones would require that any issuer initially claiming this exception would be reasonably expected to meet the spending targets, and if such expectations are not realized, a "penalty" would be imposed on the issuer, measured by a specified percentage per annum of the unspent proceeds.[45] As long as the spending targets are met, there would be no need to calculate the yield on the bonds or the yield on the investments; nor would issuers have to change their accounting systems to track and allocate investments.

This relatively simple solution, which could be adopted for either all bonds or all public-purpose bonds, would have eliminated virtually all of the abusive transactions that have received so much attention over the last several years. In addition, any proceeds of the penalty could be paid into a national trust fund for state and local infrastructure projects. The commission earnestly urges the Congress to pass promptly provisions that will relieve bond issues meeting these tests from the extraordinary burdens that rebate currently imposes.

VII. OTHER SUBSTANTIVE PROPOSALS: RECOMMENDATIONS FOR EASING BURDENS

In seeking to prevent abusive transactions, Congress has promulgated a number of restrictions that provide little or no benefit to the federal government, while substantially inhibiting the ability of state and local governments to shoulder their own responsibilities to their citizens. In this section, the commission recommends elimination and modification of a number of such requirements in a manner that recognizes the federal concern that motivated such provisions while eliminating needless burdens and maximizing the flexibility that each state and local government should have to meet the needs of its citizens.

A. Costs of Issuance Limits

Issuance expenses are legitimate costs for bond-financed projects, just as they are for private-debt financings. State laws, accounting principles, and common sense all reflect the appropriateness of treating the costs of undertaking a capital financing as part of the cost of the project financed.

Issuance expenses for bond issues vary widely, reflecting that complicated transactions will have higher issuance costs. Transaction costs as a percentage of the issue size obviously vary greatly.[46] The increased complexity of the federal tax law was directly increased legal expenses in tax-exempt transactions. The increased emphasis on disclosure in the municipal area has had a similar effect.[47]

The 1986 act limits the amount of proceeds of private-activity bonds that can be used to pay "issuance expenses" to 2% of the proceeds of the issue. The legislative history of this provision reflects a direct congressional response to transactions with unusually large reported fees.

An issuance expense limitation is not a necessary or effective way to prevent the payment of excessive fees. Furthermore, it is a burdensome provision, creating substantial unfairness for a number of legitimate issues and, ironically, actually increasing issuance expenses by requiring issuers and their counsel to struggle with the identification and calculation of such expenses. Issuance expense limitations also reflect an unwarranted paternalistic approach to state and local government. Specific cases of overreaching on the state, local, or, indeed, federal level can be dealt with without all-embracing controls.

Nevertheless, there have been proposals to extend the provision to cover all tax-exempt bonds, to reduce the 2% limit to 1%, and even to prohibit the use by state and local governments of other available funds to pay issuance costs in excess of these limits, a punitive proposal of dubious constitutionality.

The current 2% rule creates special burdens on state and local governments issuing bonds for public activities such as airport runways and terminals and solid waste disposal facilities that are private-activity bonds under the code. No proper public policy is served by creating artificial limits to the amount of legitimate expenses for government undertakings. There is no evidence that, outside of the now-ended arbitrage-driven transactions, there have been any abuses to justify this kind of inflexible restriction.

The commission strongly opposes any extension or intensification of the current rule. It also proposes repeal of the existing provision, which not only has caused substantial transaction costs but also has discouraged the appropriate level of professional assistance to state and local governments on legal, economic, and disclosure matters.

B. Definitional Changes

The following three specific provisions in the Tax code related to the definition of governmental bonds are singled out by the commission for revision:

- The 10% threshold
- The $15 million public power limit
- The related-use restriction

1. Ten-Percent Threshold

From 1968 to 1986, the code provided a 25% threshold for applying the trade or business and security interest tests. Although there is no a priori basis for saying that the 25% test is correct and the current law 10% or any other number is wrong, the 10% test imposed by the 1986 act creates important disadvantages as compared with a 25% test.

The reduced test was premised upon a concern expressed in the legislative history of the 1986 act that "abuses" were prevalent where governmental bonds were structured to maximize the amount of private use of the bond proceeds without violating the 25% test. There does not appear to have been any attempt to substantiate the existence of these alleged abuses. To the contrary, the vast majority of bond issues did not entail the alleged abuse.

The 10% test results in further complication—and therefore expense—for each governmental financing. Significant effort is often required to substantiate compliance with the 10% rule. These problems rarely arose during the nearly 20 years that a 25% standard applied.

The 10% test seriously impairs the ability of municipal governments to plan for future governmental needs through limited and temporary private use of government facilities. Examples include the lease of surplus space in a municipal office building and the sale of surplus generating capacity of a municipal power plant. In these cases the 10% test would limit a city to building facilities that have less than 10% excess capacity in the early years until municipal needs increase. The 10% limitation presents the city with the following options:

- Build the facility with such limited excess capacity.
- Include greater than 10% excess capacity, permit only 10% to be used by a nongovernmental entity, and leave the remainder unused.
- Allow use of surplus capacity over 10% and finance the facility through the issuance of higher-cost taxable debt.

The commission recognizes that many of the problems created by the 10% threshold would be ameliorated if Congress enacts the commission's recommendations set forth above regarding the application of the private business use test where the benefit of the financing does not inure to private parties. The 10% threshold, however, should be continued only if there is evidence of widespread abuse. If such evidence exists, alternative means of eliminating the abuse should be considered, while restoring the threshold to 25%. The commission recommends that, in the interim, the 10% limitation be increased to 25% for bond issues with a principal amount that is not in excess of $25 million. For these issues the 10% limitation is the most onerous, compliance is the most difficult, and the possibility of abuse is most remote. Further, the commission recommends that the 10% and 25% limitations be applied by comparing the amount of such private use to the total available space or capacity of the facility over the reasonably expected useful life of the facility.

2. $15 Million Public Power Limit

The commission is unaware of a valid public policy reason to apply the private-business tests differently for different types of facilities. To limit the private use portion of bonds issued to finance public power and other output facilities to $15 million appears to be totally without merit. In an era when central station power plants routinely cost hundreds of millions of dollars, this $15 million restriction effectively eliminates the private use percentage threshold. The commission recommends the elimination of the $15 million public power limit.

3. Related-Use Requirement

The impact of the 1986 act's strict private-business tests is significantly greater when applied in conjunction with the related-use requirement of current law. This requirement apparently stems from congressional concern that significant amounts of bond proceeds from governmental issues were being used to finance private activities unrelated to the public activity being financed and for which Congress had not specifically authorized tax-exempt financing. Under current law not more than 5% of bond proceeds may be used for facilities "unrelated" to the financed public facility. Additionally, the related use must also be proportionate to the governmental or public use financed with the bond proceeds.

Problems arise in applying this test because of (1) the unavoidable vagueness inherent in the concept of "relatedness" and the application of a "facts and circumstances" standard, (2) the infinite number of factual situations that arise, and (3) the problems of attempting to allocate mixed-use facilities between related and unrelated uses and governmental and private uses. There is also no demonstrable need for the imposition of the related-use requirement particularly in light of the fact that the private loan financing test imposes a 5% limit on the loan of bond proceeds to a nongovernmental person.

The commission proposes the elimination of the related-use requirement because its complexity and vagueness have effectively reduced the 10% private use test to a 5% test for many issues.

C. Volume Caps and Related Provisions

As a result of the 1986 act, the code currently contains a unified volume cap restricting the dollar amount of bonds of particular types that can be issued in each state to the greater of $50 per capita of $150 million. Any private-use portion of governmental bonds in excess of $15 million must be included under the state private-activity bond volume cap.

Although the commission is not making recommendations with respect to the volume cap in general or discussing the substantial public policy and legal questions inherent in any such system of federal controls of state and local activity, the commission finds that including any portion of a governmental bond under the volume cap to be administratively burdensome and inconsistent with the appropriate treatment of public-purpose governmental bonds.

This provision has proved to be administratively burdensome because it is often impossible to determine the precise dollar amount of proceeds of a very large issue that are allocable to a private use. Further, a local government may find that the full annual state volume cap has already been allocated to private-activity bonds and that no cap amount is available at year-end for allocation to the governmental public-purpose bonds.

D. Sunset Provisions

Under current law, the issuance of tax-exempt qualified small-issue bonds and qualified mortgage bonds (including mortgage credit certificates) would be prohibited after December 31, 1989. These sunset provisions, which have been extended several times in the 1980s, cause considerable disruption in the planning and marketing of these types of bonds. Furthermore, such sunsets are inappropriate and unnecessary for bonds subject to the state volume limitations. Having controlled the volume of such bonds and eliminated financings for particular types of facilities, Congress should leave the states free to utilize their allocation in the manner they determine will best serve their citizens. These sunset provisions should be eliminated and the bonds treated the same as all other private-activity bonds, so that each state may target such use in a manner consistent with its own economic development strategy.[48]

E. Advance Refundings

The commission recognizes a legitimate congressional interest in restricting advance refundings, but it reminds Congress that the ability to undertake such financings is frequently essential for prudent financial planning. States and localities use advance refundings of bonds to take advantage of interest rate savings and efficiently manage debt, thereby lowering their cost of borrowing. Municipal bonds cannot generally be sold at attractive interest rates to the public without providing substantial "call protection," ensuring that the bonds will not be redeemed for a specified period of time. The existence of such call protection and the frequent need for local governments to alter existing financing documents or to take advantage of lower interest rates often require the use of advance refundings. Prudent use of advance refundings should continue to be permitted.

The 1986 act generally allows governmental bonds issued after December 31, 1985, to be advance refunded once, permits two advance refundings of pre-1986 governmental bonds, and prohibits advance refundings for all private-activity bonds [other than qualified 501(c)(3) bonds] and of all governmental bonds that do not satisfy the related-use requirement. The commission recommends that all public-purpose bonds be eligible for an unlimited number of advance refundings, subject to the current restrictions on structuring such refundings.

F. State and Local Governmental Series (SLGS) Program

The 1986 act mandated certain modifications to the State and Local Government Series (SLGS) program to provide a viable alternative to arbitrage rebate.[49] Congress instructed the Treasury to create a new demand-deposit SLGS program to complement the existing time-deposit program; however, the current program is ineffective and unused by issuers because the regulations require that the time-deposit and demand-deposit programs cannot be utilized simultaneously. This inflexible requirement effectively precludes issuers from using the program because expenditures cannot be planned with sufficient accuracy. In addition, in spite of changes effective August 1, 1989, the demand-deposit program still provides a rate of return on the investment too low to make the program attractive to issuers, even for short-term investments for which the program should be workable.

The rate of return on the demand-deposit SLGS results in a rate of return below the bond yield, resulting in an actual monetary loss to issuers. The congressional purpose of providing a workable alternative to rebate is simply not being served when issuers are forced to lose money on the investment in demand-deposit SLGS and then additionally cannot mix time-deposit investments with part of their proceeds to minimize the resulting loss.

New "zero-interest" SLGS available September 1, 1989, may be used only for investment of proceeds originally entitled to unrestricted yield. Outside of the limited case of investment of unexpected proceeds when a temporary period expires, this new class of SLGS cannot be used to lower yield when other proceeds simultaneously are invested in market obligations. Thus, the new class will not be very useful in complying with arbitrage restrictions.

The improvements recommended by the commission to make the program workable are to (1) provide an adequate return to state and local governments, (2) permit the Treasury Department to enter into a contract with a private business to run the program, and (3) permit investments by the issuer to be divided between time-deposit and demand-deposit obligations and between zero-interest SLGS and open-market obligations to lower yield to meet arbitrage restrictions.

G. $150 Million Limitation on Outstanding Nonhospital Bonds

The commission recommends repeal of the provision in section 145(b) of the code that limits the outstanding principal amount of tax-exempt nonhospital bonds for any 501(c)(3) organization to $150 million.

The commission does not believe that the artificial limitation of $150 million is appropriate.[50] It discriminates against larger 501(c)(3) organizations and is inconsistent with the general principle of the code that activates by 501(c)(3) organizations exclusively in promotion of charitable purposes are activities of clear public benefit qualifying for tax-exempt financing.

The cap similarly discriminates against multifacility health care organizations, often with religious affiliations, that operate hospitals, nursing homes, and facilities for the elderly. The limitation of the exception to "hospitals" also creates substantial transaction costs and, more importantly, fails to recognize the increasing importance of health care provided other than in traditional acute-care beds. Ironically this rather pointlessly discourages the financing of new facilities and new modes of health care delivery at a time when the federal government itself is encouraging the development of such health care.[51]

H. Miscellaneous Arbitrage Restrictions

Several technical recommendations in the arbitrage area are made by the commission.

1. Tax and Revenue Anticipation Notes (TRANs)

Tax and revenue anticipation notes (TRANs) are short-term borrowings used to provide state and local governments with cash to pay bills while awaiting the receipt of taxes and other revenues. TRANs have traditionally been sized based on an issuer's cumulative projected cash-flow deficit plus its next 30 days' general fund operating expenses. The 30-day cushion guarded against unforeseen cash-flow problems. In 1983, the Treasury Department proposed capping TRAN issue size at 105% of an issuer's projected cash-flow deficit but withdraw its proposal following widespread criticism.

In August 1986, however, the summary of the Senate-House conference agreement on the 1986 act resurrected the issue as part of the discussion of the arbitrage "six-month expenditure test." A "safe harbor" for TRANs issuers wishing to avoid the arbitrage rebate provided that, if during the 6-month period after the date of issuance, the "actual cumulative cash-flow deficit" of the governmental unit exceeded 90% of the face amount of the borrowing, the proceeds were "deemed" spent for the purpose of meeting the 6-month expenditure test and the rebate could be avoided. The narrowness of the safe harbor prompted substantial opposition, but no modification was made. The commission believes that the restrictions of the current safe harbor for TRANs prevent state and local issuers from meeting their cash-flow needs. The reasons for modifying the safe harbor are as follows:

- The "test" to determine whether the expenditure of TRAN proceeds is occurring expeditiously should be based on a time standard rather than the size of the issue.

- The original way of sizing a TRAN issue was reviewed by Treasury in 1983 and deemed to be reasonable and prudent.
- As noted by Senator Moynihan in a letter to Senator Packwood dated September 17, 1986, the issue was not discussed by any member of the Senate or the House prior to the appearance of the summary in the conference agreement.
- Fourth, prior to the 1986 act, issuers sized TRANs based on a *projected* cumulative cash-flow deficit. The current safe harbor changed the rules by basing the 6-month expenditure analysis on *actual* cumulative cash-flow deficits. This change forces an issuer to be extremely conservative in estimating its deficit. By borrowing so conservatively, an issuer may be forced to borrow twice thereby, among other things, paying twice the costs of issuance.

The commission urges that the projected deficit standard replace the actual deficit standard as it now exists in the safe harbor and that there be additional ways to meet the 6-month expenditure test. Specifically, if an issuer can definitively account for the expenditure of TRAN proceeds through separate accounting or through tracing of funds, it should be deemed to have met the test and not be subject to the rebate requirement.

Footnote 173 of the tax-exempt bond provisions in the *General Explanation of the Tax Reform Act of 1986*, which dealt with the TRANs safe harbor, required Treasury to develop rules that define cumulative cash-flow deficits as having occurred

only if no amounts other than bond proceeds are available to the governmental units to pay the expenses for which bond proceeds are to be used. In determining whether an amount is available to a governmental unit, these rules may provide that the fact that the amount is deposited in special purpose accounts or otherwise earmarked is to be disregarded if the governmental unit using the TRAN proceeds either (i) established the restrictions on the use of the other funds, or (ii) has the power to alter the use of the other funds.[52]

During consideration of the 1987 Omnibus Budget Reconciliation Act, language was included in Title III to deal with problems created by footnote 173. The definition of "available revenue" included in footnote 173 by the joint tax committee staff was a significant expansion of the existing Treasury regulations and caused severe problems for localities that have committed funds for a special purpose such as employee retirement benefits. It is inappropriate to require issuers to include such funds in the determination of their "available revenues" when calculating the cumulative cash-flow deficit merely because they have the technical legal authority to divert such committed funds to other purposes.

If the current law safe harbor is not modified, the commission recommends that any regulations determining when governmental funds are available to meet a cumulative cash-flow deficit shall be prospective in effect and shall not be issued as temporary regulations. This will provide the municipal finance community with the opportunity to develop a reasonable definition with the Treasury that will not retroactively affect transactions done in good faith.[53]

2. *Treatment of Cash Contributions to 4-R Funds*

Bond issuers are frequently required by rating agencies or lenders to establish reserve funds to protect against interruptions in anticipated revenue streams or to maintain or replace equipment needed in the production of the revenue stream. The code provides that no more than 10% of the proceeds of an issue of bonds can be held in such a "reasonably required reserve or replacement fund" ("4-R fund"). Prior to the 1986 act, the arbitrage earned on a qualified 4-R fund benefited the issuer. Presently, amounts held in the 4-R fund are not required to be yield-restricted, but a rebate must be paid if the yield on the securities in the 4-R fund is higher than the bond yield.

If the issuer has sufficient monies on hand to fund the reserve without borrowing for it, it may deposit these monies in the 4-R fund rather than borrowing the funds. However, the code requires that even money provided by the issuer not from bond proceeds is subject to the rebate requirement and thus subjects taxes and other revenues of the issuer to the rebate. This obviously discourages issuers from using their own revenues to fund the 4-R fund and therefore encourages an increase in tax-exempt borrowing.

The commission recommends amending the code to provide that gross proceeds shall not include amounts other than original proceeds or investment earnings thereon that are part of, or invested in, a 4-R fund.

3.   Rebate Exemption for 4-R Funds

As mentioned above, many issuers are required to have a reserve fund if they are to be able to borrow at attractive rates. Such a fund should not preclude an issuer's ability to utilize the 6-month exception to the rebate exemption currently existing in the code. The Internal Revenue Service has recognized this point in the preamble to its recently promulgated rebate regulations. The commission urges the service to promulgate promptly specific regulations on this subject so that issuers may begin to use the exception as soon as possible.

I.   Small-Issuer Exemptions

Several changes in the 1986 act were viewed by Congress to be too onerous for state and local issuers of relatively small amounts of tax-exempt bonds, so exceptions were created. In this section several changes in the small-issuer exemptions are recommended.

1.   Need for Consistency in Small-Issuer Exemptions

The code denies a deduction to financial institutions for that portion of their interest expense attributable to the recepit of tax-exempt interest and provides an exception for obligations sold by an issuer that reasonably expects to issue no more than $10 million of bonds during the calendar year. This provision was regarded as imperative because small issuers often do not have access to the public capital markets due to the infrequency with which they borrow, the small amounts that they borrow at one time, and other factors limiting access to the general bond market, including the necessary high cost of entry relative to the amount of the financing. The traditional market for these small issuers was local or regional banks that understood their creditworthiness and wanted to support local institutions. The elimination of the bank interest deduction for such small issuers would have driven banks from the market for such bonds, at best raising interest rates for issuers often least able to afford such increases and at worst denying such borrowers access to any meaningful market.

Likewise, the code provides an exception from the rebate requirement for small issuers. This provision is important because there is little opportunity for small issuers to earn arbitrage while the complexity and cost associated with compliance with the rebate were deemed onerous. The rebate exception applies to small governmental units that reasonably expect to issue no more than $5 million of bonds per calendar year.

These two provisions provide important relief from the special burdens for the small issuers of tax-exempt bonds. There is little consistency between the terms of the two exceptions, which makes them complicated and compliance more costly.

The commission recommends that the current law arbitrage rebate exemption, which is $5 million, be amended to be the same amount as the bank interest deduction exemption for small issuers. H.R. 3807, which passed the House Public Works Committee in 1988, increased the rebate limit from $5 to $25 million. The commission supports raising both small-issuer exemptions to $25 million.

2.   Determining Eligibility for Small-Issuer Exemptions

Under the code, to qualify for the small-issuer rebate exemption, the issuer must count the aggregate face amount of all tax-exempt bonds issued by such unit (and all subordinate entities thereof) during the calendar year in which such issue is sold to determine if the $5 million annual rebate limit is exceeded. If an issuer advance refunds an earlier issue, both the old bonds (which have been replaced by the new bonds, typically at an interest savings to the issuer) and the new bonds must count towards the $5 million annual limit.

The bank deductibility exemption does not contain the restriction requiring the double counting of the refunded and refunding bonds. These rules should be consistent, and the less restrictive rules should be adopted. As Congress recognized in the bank deductibility provision, it is unfair to double count the bonds, since the exception is based on expected issuance of bonds during the year, not cumulative issuance of bonds over several years.

The commission recommends that (1) any private-activity bond, (2) the amount of a refunding bond that does not exceed the outstanding amount of the bond to be refunded, and (3) certain other bonds of subordinate entities that are allocated to the issuer should not be taken into account in determining qualified issuer status, making the small-issuer rebate exemption consistent with the bank deductibility exemption.

J.   Voter Referendum/State Legislature Approval Option

While the commission does not advocate change in the current list of qualifying exempt private-activity bonds, the commission also recognizes that a federally created list of approved facilities restricts the rights of state and local governments to select those private activities that are appropriate beneficiaries of tax-exempt financing. Thus, in certain jurisdictions, it may be more important to encourage the construction of facilities, which though not specifically prohibited by Congress, simply may not be enumerated on the list of exempt facilities or otherwise found within the categories of tax-exempt bonds.

Accordingly, the commission recommends that a mechanism be created under which tax-exempt private-activity bonds, subject to the volume cap, may be utilized for a project that is not for a prohibited purpose and is specifically approved by either a statewide referendum of the state legislature. Under this procedure, the ultimate decision regarding the eligibility for tax-exempt private-activity bond financing will be left to each state government and its constituents, subject to specific prohibitions by the federal government. Such a provision would simultaneously preserve the federal policies expressed both in the volume cap and in the list of strictly prohibited facilities while maximizing the ability of state and local governments to do tax-exempt financings for those activities that they have determined to be most important to their citizens.

The implementation of such a voter approval/state legislature approval process should be established after only careful consideration of the differing state referenda and legislative procedures to assure that adequate consideration will be given to the involvement of local government officials in such approval. Such local officials will, of course, be involved in the approval of private-activity bonds through the public hearing and government approval process as under current law.

K.   Miscellaneous Corrections

The code now contains a number of provisions affecting private-activity bonds that serve no significant federal purpose in light of the volume cap on such bonds. Many of these reflect attempts by Congress, prior to the 1986 Act, either to restrict the volume of bonds or to ensure that appropriate governmental decision making was reflected in their issuance.

Under the volume cap, each state is allocating a valuable resource, the availability of tax-exempt financing. Common sense and experience since 1986 indicate that state and local governments act carefully to allocate such a scarce resource in accordance with their public purposes.

Accordingly, a number of the restrictions currently existing in the code serve no purpose. They frequently create substantial transaction costs, causing issuers and their lawyers much time and expense in compliance and creating the constant risk of unfair and uneven treatment that is inherent in complicated tax provisions interpreted by a wide variety of private lawyers reaching different conclusions and requiring different levels of certainty in approving transactions. More importantly, they fail to recognize that for transactions subject to a volume cap, there is rarely any compelling reason for Washington to restrict the right of states to make certain fundamental choices as to types of financings and procedures permitted.

The recommendations as to these provisions are contained in Appendix B and will serve the goals of promoting tax simplification and equitable treatment for all issuers and ending restrictions whose only effect is to complicate and harass.

VIII.   FAIR PLAY FOR STATE AND LOCAL GOVERNMENT: THE NEED FOR CONGRESSIONAL ACTION

The commission is deeply disturbed by the increasing introduction of legislative provisions restricting state and local government bonds that purport to be effective, not when they are passed into law by the full legislative process, but on the date of their introduction. The unfairness of this is obvious to anyone familiar with the reality of the municipal bond market. Such legislation casts a cloud over the sale of bonds that are perfectly legal and appropriate under existing federal law, in many cases preventing such sale or resulting in higher interest rates.

Such provisions, in fact, often amount to de facto legislation and ultimately deny Congress its legislative power. State and local government issuers and those who buy their bonds should be entitled to rely on current law until it is changed. No individual member of Congress should be able, even for a temporary period, to deny state and local governments their rights under existing law merely by introducing legislation.

The commission condemns the use of retroactive effective dates and strongly urges the leadership of Congress to adopt policy statements and procedures that will stop it. Such procedures should include the refusal to schedule hearings on any legislation that is introduced with a retroactive effective date. Committees should, of course, still have the flexibility to approve legislation with effective dates other than final enactment, after public hearings and opportunities for affected parties to be heard, when there is substantial evidence that the failure to utilize such dates will result in the issuance of abusive transactions.[54]

If Congress is to carry out its responsibility to state and local governments, a responsibility made all the more important by the Supreme Court's decision in *South Carolina*, it must recognize the need for fundamental fairness in dealing with state and local government issuers. The commission strongly urges Congress to take action in this area in the name of fairness and to recognize the fundamental right of state and local governments to rely on the provisions that Congress has enacted into law until Congress itself changes them.

IX. CONCLUSION

During the past few years, state and local officials have had to face a new and painful reality: substantial federal support for many state and local projects has come to an end. Compounding this problem, the ability of state and local governments to access the tax-exempt bond market to finance important public projects has been reduced and made more costly by the federal government. These changes have occurred during a period when federal mandates on state and local governments and the backlog of deferred infrastructure projects were continuing to expand. The result has been a severe strain on federal, state, and local relations.

Unfortunately, as the reduction in federal support has occurred, little consideration has been given to the overall impact of federal policy at the state and local level. Critical questions that have not been addressed include

- What is the proper federal role in funding state and local projects? For example, should there be a national infrastructure capital budget, as suggested in *America in Ruins*?[55] In the absence of direct federal funding, what leadership role can or should the federal government play?
- How should federal resources available for state and local projects be targeted? Possible areas of increased emphasis include: (1) projects mandated under federal law, such as clean water, hazardous waste cleanup, and other environmental priorities; (2) projects related to long-term economic growth; (3) projects with a national or regional impact; and (4) critical projects that might not get funded at all in the absence of federal support, as a result of inadequate financial capacity at the state or local level.
- How can various sectors of the federal government work together to assure maximum flexibility for state and local funding? Often, little attention has been given as to how tax-law changes interact with other policy mandates, such as clean water and waste disposal.

One of the most disturbing trends in the area of governmental finance has been the reduced perception of a partnership between the federal governmental and state and local governments. Important components of the transition from partners to adversaries include

- State and local governments are increasingly perceived as "just another special interest group." Often, input from state and local officials has been neither sought nor accepted.
- Little or no attention is given to the aggregate impact of federal tax initiatives at the state or local level. In this context, a provision that saves $1 billion at the federal level, but costs state and local governments $2 billion, may seem attractive in Washington when the state and local component is ignored. No consideration is given to the fact that federal, state, and local expenditures are all paid for from the same source—the taxpayers of the United States.

We now have "one-way federalism." More responsibility for capital projects is being passed from the federal level to the state and local levels, while methods for helping state and local governments finance their increased share of the burden have been withheld and in fact removed by Congress. For even as this shift in responsibility was reaching a crescendo accompanied by lowered federal aid, the 1986 act produced a simultaneous assault on tax-exempt bonds.

The commission believes that tax-exempt financing for state and local governments is a keystone of the federal-state-local partnership that must be preserved and enhanced. If that partnership is to grow stronger and succeed in supporting future economic growth, Congress must examine the current public finance system and address the following important questions:

- What is the role of the federal tax exemption in supporting the financing of state and local projects?
- How can input from state and local officials be given a sufficient hearing as changes in the tax code are developed?

At the same time, the commission recognizes that Congress can legitimately restrict tax-exempt financing to

- Minimize or eliminate tax-exempt financings for projects with little or no public benefit
- Minimize financing beyond an amount legitimately needed for the actual costs of the project
- Minimize the amount of time bonds are outstanding for a given project before construction begins

The problem, however, is the recent changes to the tax code have created burdens for *all* issuers, including those who have supported congressional efforts to prevent tax-exempt financings that do not serve the public. Unfortunately, the tax-writing process has itself become generally insensitive to the broader concerns of our federal system. One of the goals of the Anthony Commission on Public Finance is to identify ways to make the code provisions on municipal bonds less complex and burdensome while still meeting legitimate federal goals in a comprehensive fashion.

This report of the Anthony Commission on Public Finance and the recommendations contained herein are intended to promote congressional debate and action that will improve the public finance system and strengthen the federal-state-local partnership. The importance of this partnership is more critical than ever if our citizens are to be effectively and efficiently served by all the governments that their tax dollars support.

NOTES

1. For a thoughtful discussion of the current state of federalism, see *To Form a More Perfect Union*, The Report of the Committee on Federalism and National Purpose, Daniel J. Evans and Charles S. Robb, chairmen, National Conference on Social Welfare, Washington, D.C., 1985.
2. Rymarowicz, L. and Zimmerman, D. *Federal Budget and Tax Policy and the State-Local Sector: Retrenchment in the 1980s*, Congressional Research Service Report, Report 88-600E, Washington, D.C., Sept. 9, 1988. This report outlines the scope of the federal budget retrenchment policies in the 1980s.
3. State and local tax levels have increased roughly in proportion to the growth of the economy in the 1980s, but at a lower rate than in previous years. See Gold, S. and Zelis, J. "Interstate Tax Comparisons and How They Have Changed Over Time," *Tax Notes*, 42 (12), March 20, 1989; 1501–1518.
4. In real per capita terms, state and local government annual new investment peaked in 1968 and was in decline up until the last several years. By 1979, the real per capita amount of publicly owned capital stock (the stock of all existing government equipment and structures) began to decline, indicating that investment was not sufficient to offset the depreciation and retirement of facilities and to add to the total capital stock per person. For a more in-depth discussion of these data and the infrastructure financing challenge, see Petersen, J. E. with Holstein, C. and Weiss, B. *The Future of Infrastructure Needs and Financing*, Government Finance Research Center, Government Finance Officers Association, Washington, D.C., Dec. 1988.
5. For example, Japan invested 5.1% of its annual output in public facilities while the United States invested 0.3%. See Aschauer, D. A., "Rx for Productivity: Build Infrastructure," *Chicago Fed Letter*, Federal Reserve Bank of Chicago, Sept. 1988, Number 13.
6. National Council on Public Works Improvement. *Fragile Foundations: A Report on America's Public Works*, *Final Report to the President and Congress*, Washington, D.C., Feb. 1988.
7. The Sixteenth Amendment, permitting a federal income tax not apportioned among the states by population, was adopted in response to the Supreme Court's determination in *Pollock* v. *Farmer's Loan & Trust Co.* that such a tax was unconstitutional.
8. This legislative history is discussed in both the Supreme Court decison in *South Carolina* v. *Baker* and in the amicus brief filed by the Government Finance Officers Association. The original code did not specify whether the exemption was constitutionally required or merely a legislative decision.
9. Conduit bonds are issued by governmental units for the benefit of private concerns where the governmenta is not liable for the payment of debt service on the bonds and is not involved in the operation of the project financed. These bonds were customarily payable, not from any tax or other governmental revenues, but solely from the payments made by the benefiting private company. These bonds were generally issued under legislatively authorized programs undertaken to stimulate economic growth and were, in effect, a limited form of government assistance, passing on

the benefits of tax-exempt financing to private business undertakings found by the government issuer to benefit substantially the local economy.

10. Alarmed by the rapidly growing volume of industrial development bonds, the U.S. Treasury in 1967 ruled that the interest earned on these bonds was subject to taxation. The ruling was withdrawn in 1968 because the legislation enacted that year eliminated the need for it. The 1968 act put into the law a definition of IDBs and attempted to clarify their tax-exempt status. Essentially, IDBs were defined to be securities issued by state and local governments where

- A major portion (more than 25%) of the bond proceeds is used by a nonexempt entity in a trade or business
- Debt service on the debt is secured in whole or in major part (more than 25%) by property used in or payments derived from a business, regardless of whether the bonds are also obligations of the issuer.

These "tests" are known as the trade or business test and the security interest test.

The 1968 legislation denied tax exemption for IDBs, excepting (1) those IDBs issued to finance certain types of facilities that were designated in a list of "exempt activities" or "exempt facilities" as they are sometimes called, (2) small-issue IDBs, and (3) those issued to finance industrial parks.

11. The bill that became the Tax Reform Act of 1969 also originally contained a provision by which an issuer could choose to issue taxable or tax-exempt bonds. If an issuer chose the taxable option, the issuer would receive from the federal government a direct payment equal to the interest cost of the borrowing in excess of the tax-exempt interest cost. Because of fierce opposition from groups representing state and local officials, who were concerned that such a proposal contained the seeds of federal control over local expenditure, the provision was dropped by the House Ways and Means Committee. It surfaced again a number of times in various forms but was never seriously considered by Congress.

12. The term *private-activity bond* was introduced by TEFRA, which defined private-activity bonds as industrial development bonds and student loan bonds and lumped them together for the purpose of the state volume cap. It was in the 1986 act that the term private-activity bond replaced *industrial development bond* in connection with the tightening of the trade or business and security interest tests from 25% to 10%.

13. The AMT is, in effect, a separate income tax system that parallels the regular income tax system and levies a flat federal tax (21% for individuals, 20% for corporations) on a broader base of taxable income. The broader base of income, known as alternative minimum taxable income, is calculated according to complex rules set out in the code. In general, the AMT operates by comparing the amount of tax owed under the AMT with the amount of "regular tax" owed by the taxpayer. If the AMT tax is greater than the regular tax, the excess amount is added to the regular tax, and the sum is the amount owed the federal government.

14. The "reasonable expectations test" has existed for many years in the arbitrage regulations in that issuers must have reasonable expectations of spending the proceeds within certain temporary periods if they are to take advantage of those temporary periods. The provision in the 1988 act was the first extension of this principle to the broader general qualification for tax exemption.

15. In September 1987, the Government Finance Officers Association proposed various safe-harbor provisions to the U.S. Treasury Department for inclusion in the arbitrage rebate regulations, including a recommendation providing that

An issuer of long-term fixed debt would not be deemed to have earned arbitrage subject to the rebate calculation if (a) the average maturity on the issue was no less than a specified number of years such as 10 years, and (b) the issuer invested the bond proceeds in market securities or of guaranteed by the federal government (or similar securities offering the same yield) with an average maturity less than a specified number of months, such as 24 months.

Treasury responded that it lacked legislative authority to draft such a broad safe harbor, so legislative clarification was obtained to permit, though not require, the federal government to simplify the regulations for issuers not earning any material arbitrage profit.

16. The *South Carolina* decision, 99 L Ed 2d 592, 108 S Ct. 1355 (1988), relies heavily on *Garcia* v. *San Antonio Metropolitan Transit Authority*, 469 U.S. 529 (1985). The majority in *South Carolina* found that *Garcia* holds that the states "must find their protection from congressional regulation through the national political process, not through judicially defined spheres of unregulable state activity." The treatment of state and local government in the 1986 act and in other tax legislation in recent years brings to mind the special concerns expressed by Mr. Justice Powell in his dissent to *Garcia.* He quoted the conclusion of the Advisory Commission on Intergovernmental Relations that "a variety of structural and political changes occurring in this century have combined to make Congress particularly *insensitive* to state and local values" (emphasis added). Justice Powell continued

Federal legislation is drafted primarily by the staffs of the Congressional committees. In view of the hundreds of bills introduced at each session of Congress and the complexity of many of them, it is virtually impossible for even the most conscientious legislators to be truly familiar with any of the statutes enacted. Federal departments and agencies customarily are authorized to write regulations. Often these are more important than the text of the statutes. As is true of the original legislation, these are drafted largely by staff personnel. The administrative enforcement of federal laws and regulations necessarily is largely in the hands of the staff and civil service employees. These employees may have little or no knowledge of the states and localities that will be affected by the statutes and regulations for which they are responsible. 469 U.S., 529, 576 (1985).

17. In 1986, with the introduction of S. 2166, Senator Durenberger's staff estimated that approximately $80 billion in interest income earned by private investors in 1985 from federal securities would be exempt from state and local income taxes, amounting to a $4.0 billion revenue loss for states and localities. This estimate was made employing the same methodology used by the U.S. Treasury Department when it calculated the state-local revenue loss for 1982 to be $2.0 billion. See U.S. Treasury, Office of State and Local Finance, "State-Local Tax Expenditures Relating to the Federal Government," *State-Local Fiscal Relations: Report to the President and Congress*, Washington, D.C., Sept. 1985, p. 327.

     In addition to federal borrowing being exempt from state and local taxation, much federally assisted borrowing, which includes the debt of government-sponsored enterprises, is also exempt. The Office of Management and Budget predicts that by 1990 there will be $259.3 billion in government-sponsored enterprise debt outstanding, which is typically for private purposes. The recent savings and loan bailout legislation authorizes the Resolution Refunding Corporation to sell $50 billion in debt that will, by law, be exempt from state and local taxes.

18. Since the *South Carolina* decision, (1) seven states—Utah, South Carolina, Oklahoma, North Dakota, Texas, New Mexico, and Idaho—have called for a constitutional amendment protecting the tax-exempt status of municipal bonds; (2) more than 35 public interest groups have formed a public finance network representing state and local officials interested in preserving tax-exempt finance; (3) Senator William V. Roth Jr. and Representative Larry Combest have introduced identical concurrent resolutions, (Senate Con. Res. 18 and House Con. Res. 39, respectively) expressing the sense of the Congress that "Federal laws regarding the taxation of State and local government bonds should not be changed in order to increase Federal revenues;" and (4) Senator Roth, along with Senators Thurmond, Pell, and Symms, has introduced Senate Joint Resolution 28 (S. J. Res. 28).

     S. J. Res 28 proposes an amendment to the U.S. Constitution providing that "Congress shall not have the power to lay and collect taxes on income representing interest on obligations issued by or on behalf of the several States and their political subdivisions to raise revenues for governmental undertakings and operations for a public purpose or to finance property owned and operated by governmental entities for public purposes." The resolution also permits Congress to exclude from taxation income or other amounts derived from other obligations issued by or on behalf of state and local governments.

19. It is useful to recall Justice Brandeis' famous comment that the states serve as laboratories. Justice Bandeis wrote

     To stay experimentation in things social and economic is a grave responsibility. Denial of the right to experiment may be fraught with serious consequences to the Nation. It is one of the happy incidents of the federal system that a single courageous State may, if its citizens choose, serve as a laboratory; and try novel social and economic experiments without risk to the rest of the country. *New State Ice Co.* v. *Liebmann*, 285 U.S. 262, 311 (1932).

20. The commission recognizes that the implementation of workable and flexible rules requires major changes in the process of adopting Treasury regulations. The commission believes that Treasury should be authorized to cooperate with states and local government officials in the drafting of future regulations affecting the issuance of tax-exempt bonds and agrees with the recommendations of the Regulation Simplification Task Force.

21. The commission takes note of the work currently under way studying the need for revisions to the penalty provisions of the Internal Revenue Code. Senator Pryor has formed the Private Sector Penalty Task Force to consider and report on penalty reform, and the Internal Revenue Service itself has formed an internal study group to address the penalty structure in an attempt to develop an underlying philosophy of penalties and to provide guidance to administrative and legislative reform. The commission supports provisions encouraging compliance but does not favor penalizing innocent bondholders. The enforcement of tax-exempt bond provisions should be reviewed to take into account that threats to take away tax exemption is not always the best public policy because the risk of loss of tax exemption imposes a yield penalty on all issuers—whether in compliance or not.

22. Under current law, exempt-activity bonds, small-issue industrial development bonds, mortgage revenue bonds, veterans' mortgage bonds, student loan bonds, and qualified redevelopment bonds are all considered private-activity bonds, and activities of 501(c)(3) organizations and the United States government are treated as private trades or businesses and are, therefore, also categorized as private activities.

23. Under current law the federal government is not a "governmental unit" for purposes of determining private use but rather a "private person" treated like a for-profit corporation. Acceptance of the above recommendations of the commission would eliminate the anomalous result that bonds financing a water system for a rural county may be "private-activity bonds" merely because a local military base purchases 11% of the water. Such a change, however, may not eliminate problems under the broad and vague provisions of section 149(b) of the code, which denies the tax exemption to any "federally guaranteed" bond. The commission recognizes the legitimate federal concern behind section 149(b) and recommends that Congress amend or clarify this provision to permit tax-exempt financing where the only involvement of the federal government is as a consumer, at fair market price, of services and utilities supplied by local governments.

24. Reflecting a compromise between the Senate and the House, the conference report accompanying the 1986 tax reform act states

The use of the term private-activity bond to classify the obligations of Section 501(c)(3) organizations in the Internal Revenue Code of 1986 in no way connotes any absence of public purpose associated with their issuance. Thus, the conferees intend, and the statute requires, that any future change in legislation applicable to private-activity bonds generally shall apply to qualified 501(c)(3) bonds only if expressly provided in such legislation.

See *Conference Report to Accompany H.R. 3838*, 99th Congress, 2nd Session, Report Number 99-841, Volume II, Washington, D.C., Sept. 1986, Volume II, p. 687.

25. Sports facilities, convention or trade show facilities, and air or water pollution control facilities would not generally be eligible for financing with the proceeds of tax-exempt bonds. See, however, the discussion of the voter referendum/state legislative procedure in Section VII of this report. This procedure, if adopted into law, would permit the limited financing of such facilities with tax-exempt bonds in individual states but would not permit the financing of specifically prohibited facilities.

26. Corporations are subject to an "environmental tax" of 0.12% of the excess of their alternative minimum taxable income over $2,000,000.

27. On April 14, 1989, House Ways and Means Committee Chairman Dan Rostenkowski introduced H.R. 1761. Its purpose was to begin an informed discussion about possible modifications in the corporate alternative minimum tax. This new plan would, in effect, subject *100%* of a corporation's tax-exempt interest income (regardless of when the bonds were issued or for what purpose) to the 20% AMT.

28. The household sector consists of direct purchases of municipal bonds by individuals, as well as surrogates who buy bonds on behalf of individuals, such as open and close-end bond funds, unit trusts, and bank trust departments. See Board of Governors, Federal Reserve System, *Flow of Funds Accounts, Fourth Quarter 1988*, Washington, D.C., March 10, 1989.

29. An analysis by Smith Barney indicates that, under the provisions of the 1986 act, net demand for municipal bonds from P&Cs will decline from about $24 billion in 1988 to $0–$10 billion in 1989. If the tax on ACE increased from 75 to 100% as was proposed, P&Cs would, in all likelihood, sell many of the tax-exempt bonds that they hold, resulting in negative net demand from P&Cs. This reduction in demand is likely to be permanent, although the magnitude of the decline will vary from year to year.

30. The Anthony Commission notes the existence and encourages further discussion of various proposals to address market inefficiencies and broaden demand for tax-exempt debt, including the "Proposal for Uniform Taxation of Municipal Bond Interest" by Professor Henry Aaron of the University of Maryland and the Brookings Institution.

31. A provision of the Social Security Amendments Act of 1983 (Public Law 98-21), known as section 86 of the internal revenue code, required taxpayers to pay income tax on Social Security benefits if their total income exceeded certain amounts. One of the income items that had to be included in the income base of the taxpayers was tax-exempt interest income. There were several constitutional challenges to this provision. In general, federal courts found that the inclusion of tax-exempt interest in determining the taxpayer's gross income under code section 86 was not a direct tax on exempt interest and did not violate the principle of intergovernmental tax immunity. See *Peter Shapiro, Essex County Executive* v. *James A. Baker, III, Secretary of the Treasury*, U.S. District Court, Dist. N.J., 84-2492, Nov. 5, 1986.

32. The commission notes that H.R. 1761 discussed in Note 27, above, is similar to the Senate Finance Committee plan with respect to the corporate alternative minimum tax.

33. A few investors in bond funds might inadvertently end up receiving interest subject to the AMT but most of them will not be in the AMT category. Some revenue might also be gained from the corporate book income provision. The additional revenue to the federal government from the AMT has never been separately estimated by the Joint Committee on Taxation because its estimates do not provide a breakdown by tax preference item.

34. The House Ways and Means Committee has approved adjustments in the current tax law provisions governing the corporate alternative minimum tax that are intended to simplify the corporate AMT. A recent report on the ACE adjustment to the alternative minimum tax scheduled for 1990 under the 1986 act concludes that ACE needs to be modified to make it workable and that a delay in the effective date of the current law is needed so that corporations will have adequate time to begin their preparations for making the transition to ACE. See Starr, S. P., and Solether, R. A., "The Corporate AMT: Is Adjusted Current Earnings an Ace in the Hole?" *Tax Notes*, March 20, 1989, pp. 1489–1500.

35. Citizens for Tax Justice, a Washington-based public interest group, has prepared four reports on corporate tax avoidance: *130 Reasons Why We Need Tax Reform* (1986); *Corporate Taxpayers & Corporate Freeloaders* (1985); *Money for Nothing: The Failure of Corporate Tax Incentives, 1981–84* (1985); and *The Corporate Tax Comeback: Corporate Income Tax After Tax Reform* (1988). The major problem areas identified in the group's 1986 report were accelerated depreciation, the investment tax credit, tax preferences for special industries, and the completed contract method of accounting.

The most recent report finds that tax reform created a more level playing field for all businesses by putting tax avoiders on the tax rolls and providing relief to corporations unable to exploit tax loopholes. Although tax-exempt interest is to identify as a cause of low tax rates for some firms in the financial services industry, in fact, their effective tax rates in 1987 generally range from 12.5 to 24.5%, with only one firm below at 2.5%.

No indication is given as to whether these firms have continued to purchase tax-exempt bonds after 1986, when the bank interest deduction was eliminated and the book income provision adopted. These top rates were paid even though the bank interest deduction was prospective as to bonds in the portfolios of corporations prior to the effective date of the 1985 act and such bonds continue to be eligible for an interest deduction.

36. See, U.S. Department of the Treasury, Internal Revenue Service, *Statistics of Income Bulletin*, Volume 8, Number 1, Summer 1988, Washington, D.C., p. 13.

37. Neuberger, J. A. "Tax Reform and Bank Behavior, *Federal Reserve Bank of San Francisco Weekly Letter*, San Francisco, Dec. 16, 1988.

38. Eubanks, W. W., *Bank Soundness in Light of the Tax Reform Act of 1986 and Possible Glass-Steagall Act Repeal*, Congressional Research Service Report, Report 88–118 E, Washington, D.C., Feb. 1, 1987, p. 18.

39. To arrive at this conclusion, it was necessary to estimate (1) how many bonds the banks might buy if more qualified tax-exempt obligations were available, and (2) how much additional interest local governments are paying because banks generally no longer purchase their debt. Historically, banks have had an annual demand for $30.0 to $37.5 billion of tax-exempt debt. In 1987, only $6.0 billion in bank qualified debt (small governmental issues less than $10 million) was purchased by banks.

The current interest rate differential between bonds that qualify for the bank deduction and those that do not is approximately 50 basis points (one-half percentage point). Since 1986, when this two-tiered market was created, the spread between rates has ranged from 30 basis points to 110 points.

The $2.0 to $3.8 billion estimates were derived by assuming the higher costs of borrowing for nonbank eligible bonds and applying them to the unmet demand figures to produce a projection of the additional borrowing costs for issuers. See Horn, R. "Comments to the Anthony Commission on Public Finance," First Tennessee Bank, Memphis, April 1988.

40. Joint Committee on Taxation, *General Explanation of the Tax Reform Act of 1986* (the "*Blue Book*"), JCS-10-87, Washington, D.C., May 4, 1987, p. 1368.

41. The original—and quite appropriate—justification for the current small-issuer exception was that local banks were the obvious purchasers of bonds for smaller communities that do not regularly sell debt in regional or national markets. Similar reasons would apply to a $25 million issue for, e.g., a local sewer authority that has never previously issued publicly sold bonds or a community hospital building a replacement facility.

42. A provision in the 1986 act "grandfathers" bonds acquired prior to August 8, 1986, and accordingly encourages banks to retain such bonds in their portfolio. The problem of securing deposits is likely to increase as such grandfathered bonds mature or are redeemed.

43. Congress in the Technical and Miscellaneous Revenue Act of 1988, in recognition of the complexity of the arbitrage rebate, directed the Treasury Department to write regulations that were "workable and understandable" and authorized the inclusion of safe harbors to simplify compliance with the arbitrage requirement. The regulations are neither "workable" nor "understandable" and fail to include such safe harbors. Instead, they are complex and confusing and grossly underestimate the administrative burdens and compliance costs to be incurred by state and local governments.

44. In 1987, the Government Finance Officers Association estimated that 4,000 issues would be sold each year during the 5-year period used to estimate revenues. The annual calculation cost, assuming the use of a firm specializing in arbitrage rebate services, was $3,000 per issue. This meant the total annual cost was $12 million ($3,000 × 4,000 issues). This amount only accounted for the calculation cost and not the cost of assembling the needed data on an ongoing basis.

It was assumed that 50% of the issues sold annually would use all bond proceeds in 3 years, so no calculation costs would be incurred beyond that period for those bonds. The other 50% were assumed to have to be tracked and calculations made each of the 5 years because proceeds, other than the original proceeds, existed. The estimate of total calculation costs for bonds issued in an annual period came to $138 million and, for 5 years, $690 million.

The second part of the calculation attempted to estimate the fixed costs per issue, including needed staff, accounting refinements, and special fees. The estimate was $21,000 per issue. For the 4,000 issues sold each year for the 5-year period, this totaled $420 million. This added to the $690 million calculation costs produces a total estimate of $1.1 billion.

The actual cost of compliance with the proposed arbitrage rebate regulations will be extraordinary. The commission suggests that Treasury's estimates do not take into account significant compliance burdens and that its estimate of approximately 90 minutes for issuers to comply with the regulations is not credible.

45. To avoid any possibility of unnecessary bond issuances, the IRS could be authorized to adjust temporarily the penalty if an abnormal yield curve or an abnormal differential between taxable and tax-exempt rates made this necessary in order to deter arbitrage-driven transactions.

46. An April 1989 preliminary report underscored the wide range in variation of total costs of issuance. For small issues ($5 million or less) they range from a high of 10.59% to a low of 0.89%. For large issues ($75 million or more), the range is substantially narrower, from 1.61% to 0.64%. The differences in reported costs depend on the method of

sale (competitive or negotiated), type of security (general obligation or revenue bond), the average maturity of the debt, and other factors. See Forbes, R., Flanagan, D., and Fairclough, S. "Costs of Issuance on Tax-Exempt Debt," Financial Markets Research Center, State University of New York at Albany School of Business, 1989.

47.   The Securities and Exchange Commission in the September 28, 1988, *Federal Register* published a staff report containing three initiatives regarding the municipal securities market: a legal interpretation of municipal underwriter disclosure responsibilities, a proposed rule governing the timing and distribution of disclosure documents, and a proposal for a central repository for disclosure documents. On June 28, 1989, the SEC approved a modified version of this rule.

48.   The commission is aware that the "recapture" provision applicable to facilities financed with MRBs, added to section 143 of the code by the Technical and Miscellaneous Revenue Act of 1988, is controversial. The General Accounting Office is studying the probable effect of the recapture provision and organizations representing issuers of MRBs (the National Council of State Housing Agencies and the Association of Local Housing Finance Agencies) are cooperating with cosponsors of MRB extension legislation to develop a less onerous approach than the recapture provision of current law.

49.   The SLGS program was established in 1972 to provide investment opportunities for state and local government issuers of tax-exempt debt permitting compliance with arbitrage rules. SLGS are a special series of U.S. Treasury certificates of indebtedness, notes, and bonds. If an issuer invests bond proceeds in these securities, the issuer does not have to comply with the current law arbitrage restrictions, including the arbitrage rebate requirement.

50.   The prime motivation for this provision was apparently the issuance of large amounts of bonds by private not-for-profit colleges.

51.   Modification of the $150 million provision to introduce the concept of the "qualified health care bond" rather than a "qualified hospital bond" would reduce transaction costs and promote public policy in the delivery of health care. The recommended change in such provision by the commission is set forth in Appendix B.

52.   Joint Committee on Taxation, *General Explanation of the Tax Reform Act of 1986*, p. 1211.

53.   A proposal to revise the safe harbor has also been made by New York City. Under this proposal, the TRANs safe harbor would be revised to allow a minimum of 10 days' funds. For some governments the current law safe harbor may be a small proportion of the government's actual expenditures, requiring great precision in estimating the pattern of expenditures. The suggested alternative would lmit the amount of the TRANs issuance while at the same time allowing a cushion for the government to make expenditures. The commission believes that it should be considered as a minimal change in the right direction.

54.   The commission recognizes that in rare circumstances, there may be justification for action that utilizes dates effective prior to the date of enactment to prevent a "rush to market." For example, the leadership of Congress, in August 1986, proposed an immediate restriction on blind pool transactions. That case stands in marked contrast to recent uses of retroactive effective dates. In that case, the leadership of *both parties* in *both houses* acted in concert with the Treasury Department only after there was, in fact, a rush to market of questionable transactions.

55.   Choate, P. and Walter, S. *America in Ruins: Beyond the Public Works Pork Barrel*, Council of State Planning Agencies, Washington, D.C., 1981.

APPENDIX A: STATE TAX DEVELOPMENTS (AS OF 10/06/89)

Alabama

Increase in out-of-state hazardous waste fee $8 in 1990, up to $16 in 1991.

*   Revenue to be used for waste cleanup.

Alaska

Bill passed to increase tax on cigarettes by $.04 per pack (from $.16 to $.20); bill passed that allows the Bristol Bay aquaculture association to impose a 1% salmon enhancement tax on the value of raw fish caught by association members; $.08 increase in gas tax; oil price increased to $15.65 per barrel; 1% sales tax increase.

*   Revenue to pay for municipal assistance programs.

An oil company may not deduct transportation costs when connected with an oil spill. (Exxon will reimburse the state for the $40 million appropriation for the oil spill response.)

*   These funds earmarked for oil and hazardous release response fund.

1990

Proposed 10% city excise tax on tobacco products. (Voters will decide on the tax which would amount to $.12 per pack on cigarettes.)

Arizona

Governor signed bill to cut budget and provide a supplemental appropriations shift of $19 million from special accounts to general fund; governor signed a bill which will add federal excise taxes to list of nondeductable taxes including estate and gift taxes, taxes imposed on employee contributions to retirement plans and self-employment taxes, and taxes on motor and aviation fuel. (This bill applies retroactively to taxable years beginning 12/31/88.)

Arkansas

2% tax on tourist attraction admissions; 2% tax on lodging imposed.

- Revenue to be used to promote tourism.

$.07 increase in gas tax.

- Revenue to be used for highway repair.

California

Cigarette tax increased $.25.

- Revenue used for programs to reduce and prevent smoking among children; support research in tobacco-related disease, and pay physicians and hospitals that render care to uninsured, indigent patients.

Bill approved which would double the state excise tax on liquor; 6% tax imposed on legal fees.

- Funds used for poor and mid-income people for greater access to legal system.

Governor signed bill to raise the current gas tax of $.09/gal. to $.14 in 1990–91, and then $.01 each year thereafter, for 5 years; 30% increase in commercial trucking weight fees.

- Funds earmarked for roadways and mass transit systems.

1990

Proposal to add a $.25 per barrel fee on oil.

- Funds to be used to pay for spill prevention and cleanup.

Colorado

Bill passed to increase the state excise tax on gasoline $.06/ga. (from $.12 to $.18) and up to $.22/gal. in 1991; increase driver's license fees from $6.50 to $12.00; increase vehicle registration fees to $7 and $12 (depending on the age of the vehicle).

1990

Proposed imposition of the 3% sales tax on food purchases; proposed increase in state tax on cigarettes of $.12 per pack (to $.32).

Connecticut

The following tax package was adopted at the close of legislative sesson on 6/7: sales tax from 7.5% to 8%; capital gains tax treatment changed to parallel the federal government's treatment at the flat rate of 7%; sales tax extension to radio and television repair, surveying, maintenance, electrical, plumbing, carpentry work, architectural and engineering work, health and athletic clubs, business utilities (excepting manufacturing and energy generation and with an exemption on the first $150 for electricity bills); increase in the surcharge on the corporation tax from 15% to 20%; disallowance of the deduction for corporate income taxes paid in other states; elimination of the sales tax exemption for meals.

Delaware

House committees have approved two bills to raise tax on hotel and motel room rates by 2% (to 8%).

- Funds generated by this tax would be divided evenly between the state Department of Natural Resources and Environmental Controls' Beach Preservation Program and the county in which the tax was collected. One bill stipulates that each county must use its portion to promote tourism.

Distrit of Columbia

6% district sales tax extended to services such as pest control, surveying, data processing, janitorial service, private garbage hauling, landscaping and tax information services; 1% tax increase on restaurant meals and lodging; 6–8% tax on liquor; $.025/gal. gas tax increase.

Florida

Legislative session closed without imposing any new taxes.

1990

Proposed boost in taxes for homeowners to offset the decrease in commercial property assessments. Proposed increase in gas tax of $.10/gal. (currently $.097/gal.).

- Funds earmarked for public transportation, local road repair, and new highways.

Georgia

1% sales tax increase; 3% tax imposed on video rentals.

- Funds for highways.

Idaho

Bill signed to bring into law a 5% sales tax on mail and telephone sales by out-of-state firms. .05% tax increase on cigarettes (per pack); 1% tax increase on chewing tobacco.

- Funds for tobacco educational programs.

Illinois

Bill passed for a 0.5% increase in state individual income tax for the next 2 years; $.10 per pack tax increase on cigarettes.

- Funds earmarked for an attack on drugs as follows: $14 million for education and prevention; $19 million for enforcement; $17 million for treatment; $65 million for job training; and $65 million for schools.

$.06/gal. increase in gas and diesel fuel excise tax (currently $.13 and $.145/gal. respectively).

- These funds would be used for highway improvements.

Extend the 5% sales tax to computer software, sales by retailers soliciting orders by mail order catalogs, telephone sales, cable television advertisements, and shopping systems.

- The revenue would be used for funding the state program to pay a portion of the utility bills of persons living on fixed incomes.

Indiana

Bill to create a state lottery passed; parimutuel wagering on horse races.

- Funds for "Build Indiana" capital improvement plan.

Tax on hazardous waste increased $2.00 per ton in 1989 up to $6.00 by 1991; surcharge of 3.5% (from 3%) on state income tax and a 0.8% surcharge on the corporate tax approved; proposed $.18 increase in cigarette excise tax.

1990

Proposed $.06 increase in gas and diesel fuel excise taxes (currently $.16/gal.).

Iowa

Imposition of 1% tax per container on soft drinks.

- Funds used for environmental cleanup.

Kansas

2% tax on the sale price of fertilizer and pesticides.

- Funds earmarked for cleanup expense.

$.04 tax increase in gas and fuel in 1989, up to $.07 by 1992 (currently $.11 for gas and $.13 for diesel); increase in state sales tax of 0.25% (to 4.25%).

- Funds to be used for highway funding plan.

30% tax increase in vehicle registration fees.

Kentucky

Property tax increase from $.25 to $.30 per $100 of valuation.

- Funds to be used for school reform.

Louisiana

Voters rejected all state tax revisions.

1990

Louisiana lawmakers have decided to continue a 3% state sales tax from July through December 31 then reduce it to 2%.
The trust fund initiative asks voters to approve a $.04 gasoline tax for financing a four-lane highway to New Orleans airport and port facilities.

Maine

On July 12, a bill was signed into law increasing cigarette excise tax to $.09 a pack (currently $.28) over the next 2 years; taxes on smokeless tobacco and other products are increased; the tax on alcoholic beverages sold in bars rises from 5% to 10%; and new taxes are imposed on the resale of boats of nonresidential vacation rentals.

- Funds to be used for health insurance subsidy.

The governor signed a landmark solid waste bill July 12, extending the $.05/bottle deposit law to all nonalcoholic beverages except dairy products sold in plastic, glass, or metal containers of one gal. or less.

Wine and liquor bottles will have a $.15 deposit. The new law also imposes disposal fees on consumer products ranging from $1 for tires and batteries to $15 for major appliances.

Maryland

Taxpayers are asked to make deductible contributions to the Chesapeake Bay Trust and the state's endangered species program; proposal of new property settlement charges; proposal announced for light-rail projects which would lead to gas tax increase.

Massachusetts

Job cuts and salary and wage freeze initiated. Over 300 amendments have been proposed for the budget for fiscal 1990 which began July 1, 1989.

1990

A supplemental budget was signed into law July 26 that includes a temporary 15% increase in the state tax on wages and salaries.
Petition filed to increase the sales tax from 5% to 6%.

- Revenue from this proposed tax to be used solely for education: 3/4 to K-12 and 1/4 for higher education.

Michigan

1% increase in state sales tax (from 4% to 5%).
- Funds to be used for schools, higher education, corrections, drug prevention programs, and mental health.

Governor proposes $28 million in user fees be imposed in a wide array of groups.

Minnesota

Committee approved lottery bill with prize payback at 70%; 1% increase in gas tax; 6% sales tax will be applied to the sale of lottery tickets.

- Funds used for highway improvement.

10% tax on net proceeds from bingo; other charitable gambling will be 2% of gross proceeds, with a 4% rate on earnings over $500,000, up to a 12% rate on earnings over $900,000; 2% increase in property tax.

1990

Governor proposes imposing a 6% sales tax on garbage collections.

- Funds used to finance recycling.

Mississippi

Imposition of 6% sales tax on garbage collections; $9 tax per ton for garbage taken to landfills; $1 per ton for garbage burned in incinerators; plus $4 per ton for incinerator ash which must be taken to landfills.

- Funds to be used to finance recycling programs for the state.

Missouri

Governor signed a bill to increase state sales tax from 4.225% to 4.425% for a 9-month period and impose a tax increase of 1% for both individual and corporate income taxes for a 2-year period.

- Funds used for higher education.

Elimination of most of the exemptions to the state sales tax.

Proposed state tax imposition on long distance interstate calls. (Tax proposal would have to go to voter approval.)

- Funds to finance low-income housing.

Montana

$.02 per pack excise tax on cigarettes (to $.16); 3% sales tax imposed (food and drugs exempt); 10% increase on net income from video gaming machines (to 25%); reapportionment of property tax to equalize funding to schools.

Nebraska

Bill approved imposing $.003/gal. on gas and $.001/gal. on diesel fuel.

- Funds to be used to pay for the cleanup of leakage from underground storage tanks (LUST).

Nevada

Property tax increased by assessing all property yearly at 100% of full market value; repeal the Supplemental City-County Relief Tax (1.7% of sales tax collections); put annual gaming tax to general fund use and replace the slot machine tax with gross receipts tax; Nevada-based carriers to pay mileage fees the same as out-of-state carriers; registration and motor carrier fees were increased; $5 diesel fuel taxes were increased by 2 cents; and a .5% insurance premium tax was approved; property tax rate increased from $0.06 to $.09 per $100 assessed valuation; increase tax on net mining proceeds to 5%; mining operations would no longer be able to deduct development cost, depreciation, repairs, or insurance premiums; 0.25% increase in state sales tax; $.15 increase in cigarette tax; 0.5% increase in tax on insurance premiums.

New Hampshire

Real estate transfer tax from $3.50 to $4.75 per $1,000. of assessed value; 4% increase in tobacco tax (from $.17 to $.21).

New Jersey

$.10 increase on tolls.

- Would enable the state to issue new bonds to finance parkway repairs.

Bill passed to collect 6% sales tax on leased cars and office equipment up front rather than over the term of the lease; 6% sales tax extended to the retail sale and lease of telephones and telephone equipment effective 4/1/89.

- Funds to be used to pay for a statewide 911 number to summon police, firefighters, or an ambulance.

A corporate income tax surcharge which raises the rate to 9.375% from 9% for 1 year was passed.

- These funds would be used to fund hazardous waste cleanup.

1990

6% sales tax imposed on all telephone/mail orders by New Jersey residents.

New York

Tax on the interest used to finance mergers and acquisitions; new tax imposed on smokeless tobacco products; state sales tax extended to floor coverings, mail order, and teleshopping sales; $.03/gal. tax on refined petroleum products; $.02/gal. tax on residual petroleum products; gov. transferring $400 million from various state trust funds to close portion of the state deficit; refinancing the debt on the Empire State Plaza complex generating $39 million.

North Carolina

Bill approved to increase motor fuel tax by $.0525/gal. raise sales taxes on boats and aircraft and add a 3% vehicle use tax; increase in sales tax on rental cars from 2% to 8% percent in October 1989.

- Funds will pay for state infrastructure.

1990

Agreement signed to impose a 5% use tax on merchandise residents purchase from out-of-state retailers.

North Dakota

Individual income tax rate increased from 14 to 17%; tax imposed on bingo cards; removal of sales tax exemption for coffee, tea, and cocoa.
$.03 increase in gas tax; and $.02 increase in diesel fuel to be effective July 1 were passed. However, a petition requesting referral was submitted to the secretary of state before they took effect. Thus, the state continues to collect at the old rate.

- Funds to be used to clean up leaks from service stations and for the state's road system.

Sales tax increased from 5.5% to 6%; tax illegal drugs @ $3.50/gram of marijuana, $200/gram of controlled substance, and $2,000/50-dose unit of controlled substances not sold by weight. Increase of $.03/pack in cigarette tax; raise tax on cigars and smokeless tobacco from 25% to 30% of wholesale price; insurance premium tax increased from 1.25 to 1.75%; proposed imposition of sales tax on all out-of-state catalog sales.

1990

Proposed 10% surtax on 1990 state income tax returns.

Ohio

Bill signed to increase gas tax by $.052 (currently $.148/gal.) over the next 2 years.

- Funds designated for the Department of Transportation.

1990

Bill proposed permitting of parimutuel sports wagering.

- Funds would be earmarked for the elderly.

Oklahoma

Bill passed to charge $1.00/tire on sale of new and used tires.

- Funds earmarked for a scrap-tire recycling fund.

Bill passed to increase tax by $.01/gal. on all sales of motor and deisel fuels and blending materials sold to state fuel distributors.

- Tax collections will be used to create and maintain a $10 million environmental indemnity fund.

Oregon

Proposal of service tax to tax out-of-state business including broadcasting and advertising; increase in cigarette tax of $.01 (from $.27 to $.28) per pack.

- Funds used for transportation programs for elderly and disabled.

Increase in gas tax of $.02/gal; property tax assessment charge of $20 recording fee in changes in property ownership and an increase in delinquent tax from 12% to 16%; increase in the state automobile registration fee from $10 to $15/year; truck will be subject to higher weight-mile taxes in 1990 and 1991.

Proposal to add an advisory measure on the fall ballot asking voters how best to pay for the state's schools, i.e., increase the state personal income tax, creation of a state sales tax, statewide property tax, etc.

Pennsylvania

Legislative session closed without incresing any taxes.

Rhode Island

Legislative session closed without increasing taxes. (State enjoying a surplus.)

South Carolina

Proposal for counties to impose a 1% local option sales tax based on voter approval; balance of tax hikes scrapped by senate leaders.

South Dakota

Legislative session closed without increasing taxes.

Tennessee

Sales tax extended to include interstate telephone calls; local communities to impose an additional 1.5% tax on interstate calls.

- Funds earmarked for schools.

  State has imposed 7 ¾% sales tax on out-of-state mail order purchases; proposed increase in gas tax from $.17 to $.21/gal. of gas and increase of diesel fuel by $.01.

1990

Proposal to increase state sales tax an additional 2.75% (from current 5.5%).

Texas

Increase in cigarette tax from $.26 to $.33 per pack; increase in sales tax with voter approval (currently $.06 with cities and transit authority assessing an additional $.01 on the dollar).

- Funds would pay for jail construction and other criminal justice needs.

Vermont

Bill approved to increase the state excise tax on gas from $.13 to $.15/gal. and the excise tax on diesel fuel from $.14 to $.22/gal. increase of 10% in vehicle registration fees and an additional 10% surcharge on truck registration fees.

- Funds to be used for highway maintenance.

Virginia

Local option tax allowing northern Virginia counties and cities to levy income taxes up to 10% of state taxable income if approved by local voters.

- Funds earmarked for transportation/road improvement.

.2% tax increase in diesel fuel.

- Funds to be used to pay for cleanup of leaky storage cites.

Washington

Imposition of new taxes on cigarettes, alcohol, and gambling devices.

* Funds would pay for antidrug efforts.

Increase in retail sales and use tax by .9%.

* Funds to be used to fund children's, youth, and family programs.

Impose corporate income tax of 4.2%; 2.06% tax on hospitals' net patient services revenue.
Impose a 25% tax on pornography retail sales price.

* Funds to be earmarked for crime victims' compensation for children who have been sexually abused.

West Virginia

Increase of 30% in employers' quarterly workers' comp premiums; increase gas tax from $.1535/gal. to $.2035; restore current 6% sales tax on food; increase business franchise tax rate from 0.55% to 0.75%; increase severance tax on minerals from 4% to 5%; eliminate sales tax exemption for contractors when they buy building materials; increase in kilowatt hour tax for out-of-state use to 4%; increase tax on natural gas stored underground.

Wisconsin

Legislative session closed without any new taxes.

1990

Proposed measure to increase payroll tax (5% on the first $20,000, 4% of the next $5,000, 3% of the next $5,000, 2% of the next $5,000, and 1% of the next $5,000 of wages per employee).

* These funds would finance statewide health insurance for the uninsured.

Wyoming

Increase cigarette tax from $.08 to $.12 per pack; $.02 increase in gas and fuel.

* Fund to be used to pay for cleanup of contamination from leaking underground storage tanks (LUST).

APPENDIX B: SUGGESTED TECHNICAL CHANGES TO THE INTERNAL REVENUE CODE OF 1986

The following proposals are designed to eliminate restrictions and complications in the law affecting tax-exempt bonds that no longer effectively serve any federal policy.

Small-issue provisions. Many of the tests imposed by section 144 require issuers and their lawyers to engage in extensive investigations to verify compliance. The proposal elimination of the so-called $40,000,000 limit provisions (Sections 144(a)(6) and 144(a)(10)) reflects the view that in utilizing their allocation under the volume cap, states should not be discouraged from providing assistance to corporations that have bond-financed activities in other areas if the particular undertaking best serves the economic interest of the state.

Manufacturing definition. The current definition of a manufacturing facility in section 144(a)(21)(c), modified in an unhelpful way in the 1988 act, restricts the freedom of the individual states to choose the type of nonretail activities that provide the most important economic stimulation. It also creates the need for an often expensive and complicated investigation to discover meaningless distinctions between direct and indirect ancillary facilities. An appropriate general manufacturing restriction would restrict financings to "industrial facilities," defined as follows:

The term *industrial facility* means any facility that is used in the manufacturing, warehousing, processing, or production of tangible personal property. Industrial facility shall include related office facilities and research and development facilities but shall not include retail facilities, the primary purpose of which is not functionally related and subordinate to the manufacturing, warehousing, processing, or production of tangible personal property.

Aggregation of issues. Substantial burdens, including large transaction costs, are created by the inability of governmental entities to issue simultaneously one or more issues, the components of which are qualified for tax exemption under different provisions of the code. For example, issuers should be able to combine small-issue and exempt-facility bonds.

The original motivation for these aggregation rules no longer exists. The result is often two issues separated by 30 days and therefore double issuance costs.

The commission therefore recommends that Congress adopt a provision permitting the simultaneous issuance of bonds qualifying under separate code sections so long as each component qualifies and is properly identified. The commission recognizes that it may be appropriate for such issues to be treated as a single issue for certain purposes, such as arbitrage yield, to prevent possible abuses. A provision permitting simultaneous issues obviously would reduce costs and would be consistent with provisions of the legislative history of the Tax Reform Act of 1986 recognizing, e.g., allocation of costs for a single multiuse facility between "government bonds" and 501(c)(3) bonds.

Additional recommendations. The following are additional recommendations for changes in the current code.

Provision	Proposed changes	Reason for change
§ 144(a)(4)(A) [election for $10,000,000 issue]	Remove concept of "election."	Unnecessary requirement. Policy served as well if issuer and beneficiary are simply required to follow other rules of § 144 (a)(4) whenever issue size is over $1,000,000.
§ 144(a)(7)	Eliminate prohibition on joint issues.	Unnecessary. Original policy was to prevent circumvention of limits placed on exempt-facility bonds. See discussion in text on aggregation.
§ 144(b)(3) [student loan residency requirement]	Eliminate.	Volume cap provides sufficient incentive to make states administer programs for benefit of residents and in-state students.
§ 145(b) [$150,000,000 volume cap]	Instead of loss of tax exemption, violation should result in unrelated taxable business income to 501(c)(3) in an amount equal to the interest on the unqualified bonds.	Shift risks of violation to beneficiary of bonds proceeds; remove uncertainty from market.
§ 145(b)(3) [$150,000,000 volume cap]	Eliminate "common control."	Standard is too vague. "Management" can be defined to include effective control as to financial decisions, which is only relevant control for bond purposes. Management should be defined not to include corporate structures or relationships necessary for religious rather than financial control.

Provision	Proposed changes	Reason for change
§145(c) [$150,000,000 volume cap exception]	Limit nonhealth care rather than nonhospital financings.	The definition of *hospital* is virtually unworkable in today's medical environment and is contrary to federal policy of encouraging more outpatient treatment and other less intensive forms of care. Hospital should become "health care."
§147(c) [limit on land acquisition]	Eliminate.	Volume cap and other require-ments eliminate potential abuses.
§147(d) [prohibition on financing existing property]	Eliminate or add exception where acquired property not currently in service or where prior owner is bankrupt.	Volume cap controls overall abuses of acquisition of existing property. The return to states of ability to alleviate distress situations to improve tax base, even if no rehabilitation, will not create abuses.
§147(f) [public hearing]	Eliminate.	Public hearing generally does not effectively inform public but simply provides another stage at which technical mistakes can be made. Transaction costs often increased. Volume cap is effec-tive political policeman.
§149(d)(5) [definition of advance refunding]	Change period to 180 days if issuer rebates all investment "profit" on escrow.	Current law 90-day rule artificially restricts "window" during which a "simple refunding" can be ndertaken for many issues that are redeemable only on semi-annual payment dates. Rebate or alternative proposed in this report should cure any abuses.

3

Municipal Debt Finance: Implications of Tax-Exempt Municipal Bonds

Peter Fortune
Tufts University, Medford, and Federal Reserve Bank of Boston, Boston, Massachusetts

I. INTRODUCTION

This chapter provides a broad overview of economic and public policy issues arising from the use of tax-exempt debt to finance activities of state and local ("municipal") governments. The goals of the chapter are to explain changes in the structure of the municipal bond market in recent years, to examine the effects of tax policy on municipal bond yields, to reflect on the problems created by tax exemption as well as on proposed reforms of the market for municipal bonds, to examine the connection between the market for municipal bonds and the volume of municipal capital investment, and to analyze the extent to which tax exemption alters the economywide allocation of resources.

Section II is an overview of the key features of municipal bonds, of the most significant changes in the structure of the market in recent years, of the constitutional and legislative basis for tax exemption, and of the yields and ownership of municipal bonds. Section III focuses on significant features of the income tax code affecting the municipal bond market. Section IV presents an economic and econometric analysis of the determinants of municipal bond yields. Section V addresses some prominent issues in the debate about the viability and effects of tax exemption. Section VI assesses the nature of the subsidy associated with tax exemption and the implications for resource allocation. Section VII is a summary of the chapter.

II. AN OVERVIEW OF THE MUNICIPAL BOND MARKET

This section provides an extensive overview of the characteristics of municipal debt, the statutory requirements for eligibility for tax exemption, the constitutional history of the exemption, the recent history of municipal bond yields and ownership, and recent innovations in the municipal bond market.

A. Forms of Municipal Debt

Municipalities issue debt in a variety of forms, subject to both state and federal legislation. State constitutions and statutes typically restrict short-term debt to purposes related to working capital, bridging the gap between expenditures and receipts, while long-term debt is limited primarily to the financing of capital outlays.

A significant portion of this work was done while I served as a visiting scholar at the Federal Reserve Bank of Boston. I am grateful to the bank, and to Eric Rosengren, Richard Kopcke, and Joe Peek for advice and constructive comments.

The most prominent forms of short-term debt, or notes,* are tax anticipation notes (TANs), revenue anticipation notes (RANs), grant anticipation notes (GANs), and bond anticipation notes (BANs). TANs, RANs, and GANs are used to provide funds for operating expenses, such as payments for wages, salaries, utilities, and materials. TANs are repaid from anticipated tax revenues, GANs are repaid from federal or state grants, and RANs are repaid from nongrant, nontax revenues. BANs, used to provide temporary financing of capital outlays, such as purchase of equipment and construction of schools and roads, are repaid from the permanent long-term bond financing.

Long-term bonds are issued for permanent financing of capital outlays, such as construction of bridges and roads, water and sewage systems, and schools. The purpose of long-term debt is to smooth out the path of tax revenues required to finance capital outlays and to distribute those revenues over time in conformity with the stream of benefits resulting from the project. For example, a solid waste disposal system is "too expensive" to be financed out of tax revenues in a single year, and the benefits of the disposal system occur over a long period. Therefore, financing from tax revenues would place a high burden on the current generation of taxpayers but no financial burden on future beneficiaries. Long-term bonds provide a way of addressing these problems of the lumpiness of capital spending and of the intergenerational nature of benefits.†

There are two broad classes of long-term municipal debt, which differ according to the source of debt service payments (coupons plus principal). General obligations (GOs) are backed by the "full faith and credit" of the community, meaning that debt service is to be paid from general tax revenues. GOs are, other things being equal, a safe form of investment for individuals and financial institutions, particularly when there are no limits on the ability of the issuer to raise the money via taxes.‡ Only a few defaults of GOs have occurred since the Great Depression, the most prominent being New York City in 1975 (on $2.4 billion of notes) and Cleveland in 1978 (on $15.5 million of notes).

Revenue bonds have less secure backing—the revenues from specific projects. These bonds are issued by governmental agencies established to finance, construct, and manage specific facilities. Examples of the hundreds of revenue authorities around the United States are the Massachusetts Turnpike Authority, the Massachusetts Port Authority, the Massachusetts Water Resource Authority and—for a national flavor—the Washington Public Power Supply System (WPPSS). If the revenues from the project (e.g., auto tolls, airplane landing fees, and water and electricity billings) are not sufficient to meet debt service payments, defaults occur, and in extreme circumstances, the agency seeks protection under chapter 9 of the federal bankruptcy code. In this case the courts decide which claimants—employees, suppliers, or bondholders—will get paid. The bulk of municipal bond defaults have been revenue bonds, the most prominent in recent history being the 1983 default by WPPSS on $2.25 billion of bonds issued to finance nuclear generating facilities.§

Revenue bonds are the most rapidly growing form of bond indebtedness for states and local governments. This is due in part to restrictions in state constitutions that limit the ability of municipalities and states to issue GO bonds. While revenue bonds carry higher interest rates than GO bonds, the use of revenue bonds is the result of a mutually beneficial arrangement between issuers and investors: issuers can finance projects with revenue bonds without ransoming their taxing authority, paying the higher interest rates with fees and user charges borne by the beneficiaries of the projects, while investors can get higher rates of return in the form of a risk premium on municipal bonds.

Recent years have seen a rapid expansion of municipal bonds issued for purposes other than the traditional financing of infrastructure constructed by states and local governments. Among these are "private-activity" municipal bonds, advanced refundings, and arbitrage bonds.

---

*The term *notes* is usually applied when the maturity of the instrument is 13 months or less. *Bonds* refer to instruments with more than 13 months to maturity.

†This assumes that there is not full capitalization of tax liabilities into property values. If full capitalization does exist, in which case the tax liability associated with borrowing by a state or local government is fully reflected in the value of residential and commercial property, the residents at the time of the bond issue will pay the full costs of the debt service, regardless of maturity.

‡The most default-free securities are, of course, U.S. Treasury bonds, for the government can always print the money to meet debt service payments if tax revenues are insufficient.

§One innovation in the past twenty years has been municipal bond insurance. About ten percent of the WPPSS default was insured by a private company. The investors in the unit trusts which bought that insurance did not lose principal or coupons as a result of the default.

B. Eligibility for Tax Exemption

Section 103(a)(1) of the internal revenue code excludes from taxable income the obligations of a state, a territory, or a possession of the United States, or any political subdivision of any of the foregoing, or the District of Columbia. In many cases the determination of eligibility for tax exemption is straightforward. However, the right to issue tax-exempt bonds is not automatic. In order to be eligible for exemption, a bond must meet the standards imposed by law in section 103 of the internal revenue code as interpreted by the Internal Revenue Service (IRS). The purpose is, of course, to prevent municipalities from using tax-exempt debt to finance projects not judged to be for municipal purposes.

Until recently the IRS did not actively monitor newly issued municipal bonds to determine compliance with eligibility requirements. Instead, it reacted to complaints, often from underwriters who were concerned about a competitor's activities. However, the rapid growth in private-activity municipal bonds in the last two decades, particularly in the mid-1980s, has led to increased monitoring of tax-exempt bonds. Indeed, in 1988 the IRS established an information gathering programs unit with the responsibility of gathering information on matters of concern to the chief counsel's office; among these were questions of disputed use of tax exemption (Zimmerman, 1991). Even so, there is no systematic analysis by the IRS of form 8038 submissions.*

The first serious questions about eligibility coincided with the use of tax exemption for private purposes. This began on a significant scale in the 1960s, when municipalities began to use their favored access to credit markets to induce businesses to locate within their jurisdiction. The device employed was the industrial development bond (IDB), issued by a municipality to finance construction of structures that were then leased to the private business, the lease payments providing the funds to meet debt service payments. In this way a business could finance its construction of factories and office space at municipal interest rates rather than at corporate bond rates.

The success of tax-exempt IDBs led to a plethora of similar revenue bonds, each designed to serve a specific constituency. Examples are mortgage revenue bonds, issued to finance loans at below-market interest rates to households to purchase homes; student loan bonds, issued to make loans to students at favorable rates; and pollution control bonds, issued to provide low-cost funds to corporations to acquire equipment for reduction of water and air pollution.

By the early 1980s the issuance of private-activity bonds was out of control. This can be seen in Fig. 1, which shows the share of all long-term debt outstanding (corporate and foreign bonds, municipal bonds, and mortgages) that is tax exempt, whether for public or private purposes. The figure shows that total tax-exempt bonds declined as a share of all bonds and mortgages from 1960 through 1990, with a brief surge in the early 1980s. The state and local government share for public purposes declined throughout the period, while the private-activity share (issued on behalf of households and corporations) grew to almost one-third of outstanding tax-exempt bonds by 1985.

The rapid growth of private-activity tax-exempt bonds led to the realization that those issues were having effects not intended by Congress. First, the federal taxpayer was underwriting a capital-cost subsidy for households and corporations, a subsidy never intended by Congress. (The nature of the subsidy is discussed in Section VI.) Second, the competition for tax-exempt credit from private-activity bonds was forcing interest rates up for the intended beneficiaries of tax exemption—issuers of public purpose bonds.

While limits on private-purpose municipal bonds had existed since 1969, they were tightened considerably by the Tax Reform Act of 1986. Section 103(c), under which the private-activity definition is established, now allows several tests to determine whether or not a bond is private-activity. The first test—which is the most widely applied—is a joint test of uses of funds and of security interest; if more than 10% of a bond's proceeds are used for a business or trade *and* if more than 10% of the debt service is derived, directly or indirectly, from a private use, the bond is deemed a private-activity bond.†

In order to be tax-exempt a private-activity bond must, with some exceptions, satisfy certain maturity restrictions and must be within the volume limit established for each state in 1986. A state's volume limit is now set at the greater of $50 per capita or $150 million. While tax exemption is automatically extended to private-activity bonds within that limit, there are seven categories of private-activity bonds excluded from the volume limit; these are "exempt facility bonds" (airports, docks and wharves, solid waste, etc.), qualified mortgage bonds, qualified veteran's mortgage bonds, qualified small issue industrial development bonds,

---

*Form 8038 must be submitted to the IRS by an issuer of municipal bonds.
†Prior to 1986 these tests had established a 25% threshhold.

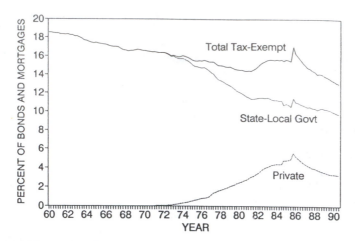

Figure 1   Tax-exempt share of outstanding bonds and mortgages.

qualified student loan bonds, qualified redevelopment bonds, and qualified section 501(c)(3) nonprofit organization bonds.

Figure 1 shows that there was a dramatic reversal of the earlier trends after the 1986 tax reform act. Following a brief surge in private-activity issues in 1985 in anticipation of the limitations imposed in the 1986 act, the outstanding amount of tax-exempt bonds for private purposes declined sharply in spite of the numerous exemptions built into the limits.

Another problem category of bonds is arbitrage bonds. In the 1960s state and local governments became aware that tax exemption was a money machine: by issuing tax-exempt bonds at favored interest rates and investing the proceeds in taxable bonds, a municipality could earn a spread equal to the difference between the taxable and tax-exempt rates. If a bond is deemed to be an arbitrage bond, the issuer must rebate to the federal government any arbitrage profits made or the bond will retroactively lose its tax exemption and become taxable to the holder.

In 1969, section 103(c) of the internal revenue code was changed to define arbitrage bonds as bonds whose proceeds, beyond a "reasonably required" reserve, were used to invest in securities with a "materially higher yield" for more than a "temporary period." The problem of arbitrage bonds is presented most clearly when a bond is issued with the sole purpose of investing the proceeds at a higher interest rate and earning the spread over the period until the bond is repaid; this blatant use of tax exemption was clearly eliminated by the 1969 legislation. However, over the intervening 25 years the interpretation of section 103(c) has changed frequently.

The frequent change in arbitrage restrictions is the result of two conflicting goals, the first being to close off the arbitrage opportunities still being employed despite the regulation, and the second being to allow tax exemption for bonds issued for "reasonable" uses, when the proceeds are "temporarily" invested in earning assets. Because municipalities often find themselves in the situation of issuing a bond before the proceeds are expended, temporarily holding the proceeds, the difficulty in the arbitrage restrictions is setting standards that allow this to happen for reasonable purposes while eliminating the abuses of tax exemption.*

An example of the problematic nature of arbitrage restrictions is advanced refunding, the issuance of a new municipal bond to pay off an outstanding bond. The proceeds of the new issue are typically placed in an escrow account that holds U.S. Treasury securities, whose income is sufficient to pay the debt service on the advance refunding bonds and to yield net income. The amount of the proceeds of the advance refunding issue, plus accumulated net income, is designed to be sufficient to pay off the original bond. Clearly this must be done before the retirement of the original issue at either maturity or a call date.

---

*For much of the life of the arbitrage regulations, a municipality could avoid the arbitrage bond limitations by investing no more than 15% of the bond's proceeds in a reserve fund, and by showing "due diligence" in completing the project that the bond is intended to finance, with an upper limit of 5 years on the "temporary holding period (Buschman and Winterer, 1983). This still allowed considerable leeway for earning arbitrage profits, and the 1986 tax reform act further tightened the restrictions.

The optimal timing for an advanced refunding is when interest rates are low, and the advance refunding is often done well before the actual retirement of the outstanding issue. If the delay arouses the interest of the IRS, the new issue can be interpreted as an arbitrage bond and, in order to maintain the tax-exempt status of the advance refunding issue, the municipality must rebate to the Treasury the spread between the interest earned on the Treasury securities and the interest paid on the newly issued municipal bond. If this rebate is not made, the investor will lose the tax exemption even if he or she had every reason to believe that the exemption was allowed when the bond was purchased.

C. The Question of Constitutionality

The exemption of state and local interest payments on municipal bonds from federal income taxation has a long history, originating in a question about the legality of taxation of activities of one level of government by another level of government. During the years immediately following the American Revolution, power rested in the states, and the federal government was weak. Concern for the financial fragility of the new federal government, combined with several attempts by states to tax the activities of the federal government, led to a series of Supreme Court decisions under Chief Justice Marshall that protected the central government from the taxing powers of the states.

Marshall's well-known dictum that "the power to tax is the power to destroy" was, in fact, a statement designed to protect the central government, although in modern times it has been used to support protection of the states from federal taxing powers. One of the most important of these cases was *McCulloch* v. *Maryland* (1819),* in which Marshall's court struck down a tax levied by the state of Maryland on the Bank of the United States. This was the origin of the exemption of federal activities from state taxation.

The first federal income tax was enacted during the Civil War. It taxed both salaries and interest payments by states and local governments, but in *Collector* v. *Day* (1871),† the Supreme Court ruled that the application of the tax to the salary of a state judge was unconstitutional. This decision established the doctrine of reciprocal immunity, in which the federal government and state and local governments were protected from the tax powers of the other. The expiration of the federal income tax in 1872 meant that this decision had a limited effect, but enactment of a new federal income tax in 1894 revived the issue. The 1894 federal income tax explicitly recognized *Collector* v. *Day* by exempting salaries paid by state and local governments, but included interest payments by states and local governments in the tax base.

The federal taxation of state and local interest payments was struck down in *Pollock* v. *Farmer's Loan and Trust Company* (1895) , ‡ when the Supreme Court held that interest on a state bond should also be exempted from federal taxation. This case has been central to the argument that the exemption is protected by the Constitution.

The modern federal income tax was ushered in with the Sixteenth Amendment to the Constitution in 1913. The Sixteenth Amendment gave Congress the power "to lay and collect taxes on income, from whatever source derived." In the new income tax enacted after the Sixteenth Amendment the question of reciprocal immunity was avoided by explicitly exempting both interest *and* salaries paid by states and local governments, thus adhering to both *Collector* v. *Day* and *Pollock* v. *Farmer's Trust*. It is important to note that the basis of the exemption was not in the Sixteenth Amendment itself, but was in the congressional legislation establishing the income tax. Even so, the force of earlier Supreme Court decisions reinforced those who adhered to the view that the exemption was grounded in the Constitution.

Because the initial tax rates were very low, the effect of this exemption of municipal interest income on the state and local cost of capital was small. However, as federal income tax rates rose, the exemption of municipal interest became an economic issue. The 1920s and 1930s were a period of considerable debate about the interest exemption, with parties lined up on the basis of economic self-interest. On one side business organizations (such as the U.S. Chamber of Commerce), private utility companies (which opposed a subsidy to their public competitors), and many state governments in the industrial North joined to oppose tax exemption. On the other side, many state governments in the nonindustrial South strongly supported the exemption because of the subsidy it conferred and because they had little industrial base to be harmed by the competition for funds.

---

*4 Wheat. 316.
†11 Wall. 113.
‡157 U.S. 429.

A constitutional amendment to eliminate the exemption failed in 1922, but it continued to be urged by the Coolidge, Harding, and Hoover administrations. Gradually the scope of the exemption was narrowed by judicial decision rather than legislation. In *Helvering* v. *Gerhardt* (1938)* the Court upheld a federal tax on the salary of New York Port Authority employees, and in *Graves* v. *New York ex rel. O'Keefe* (1939)† the Court upheld a state tax on a federal salary that Congress had not explicitly exempted from the tax. The effect of these decisions was to overturn *Collector* v. *Day.* While this ultimately paved the way for the elimination of the intergovernmental exemption for salaries, the exemption continued for interest payments, primarily as a result of the efforts of states and local governments.

Proponents of the view that the exemption is protected by the Constitution have appealed to early Supreme Court decisions, such as *Pollock* v. *Farmer's Loan and Trust Company,* and to the proposals in the 1920s to eliminate the exemption through a constitutional amendment. A significant minority of the legal profession continued to assert that taxation of state and local interest was barred by the Constitution. Whatever one's views of the constitutionality issue, however, legislation has clearly conferred tax exemption; the Internal Revenue Code of 1954, which is the basis for the present tax code, specifically exempted municipal interest income from the federal income tax.

The uncertainty about the constitutionality of the exemption was eliminated in a series of Supreme Court decisions in the 1980s. The first important decision involved the Social Security Act amendments of 1983, which imposed a tax on 50% of social security benefits if the taxpayer's income was above a specified level. For the purposes of this computation, "income" was defined as including interest from municipal bonds. As a result, the amendments indirectly imposed a tax on municipal interest if municipal interest income was sufficient to result in payment of taxes on social security benefits. The Supreme Court refused to hear cases charging that this was unconstitutional, thereby allowing continuation of the indirect taxation of municipal interest.

The second important piece of legislation weakening tax exemption was the 1982 Tax Equity and Fiscal Responsibility Act, which limited the exemption to municipal bonds issued in registered form, forcing all bearer bonds into the taxable category.* The purpose of this was to allow the federal government to track municipal interest income, an objective not implemented until 1987, when federal income tax forms required taxpayers to report municipal interest income even though it was not subject to tax.

Just when Congress was weakening the exemption, the Supreme Court clearly rejected any constitutional foundation for it. In *Garcia* v. *San Antonio Metropolitan Transit Authority* (1985),† addressing the question of the applicability of federal overtime rules to state and local government employees, the Court expressed the view that the taxation of state and local interest payments was a matter of legislation, not a constitutional issue; if Congress wished to tax municipal interest, it was free to do so. This was upheld and clarified in *South Carolina* v. *Baker* (1988),* which upheld the 1982 TEFRA removal of tax exemption for state and local bonds not held in registered form. In his majority opinion on *South Carolina* v. *Baker,* Justice Brennan argued that "states must find their protection from Congressional regulation through the national political process, not through judicially defined spheres of unregulated state activities."

Thus, at present there is no constitutional protection for the exemption of municipal interest income. However, Congress has given no indication that it is interested in including municipal interest in the federal income tax base. The reason is that tax exemption has become a very valuable subsidy for states and local governments, and states and local governments have formed a powerful lobby to protect their preferred access to credit markets.

D. Special Aspects of Municipal Bonds

1. The Serial Form of Municipal Debt

Municipal bonds differ from corporate, U.S. Treasury, and other taxable bonds in ways other than tax exemption. Perhaps the most prominent is the serial form of municipal bond issues, which affects both the liquidity and trading costs of municipal bonds.

---

*304 U.S. 405.

†306 U.S. 466.

*A bond is held in registered form if the owner's name is recorded by a transfer agent—usually a bank—whose function is to keep ownership records. The other form is a bearer bond, which is deemed to be owned by whoever holds it and for which there is no record of ownership.

†469 U.S. 528.

*485 U.S. 505.

Corporate and Treasury bonds typically originate as a single issue in which each certificate carries the same coupon rate, call date, and maturity data. While retirement schedules typically differ—some corporate bonds are retired in a lump sum, while others are retired gradually through sinking funds—the essential feature of a taxable security is a single issue broken up into a large number of certificates, each with the same characteristics.

Municipal bonds, on the other hand, are typically sold in a "serial" form in which each "strip" is a separate bond. This means that instead of a single large issue, the bond consists of a series of smaller issues, each with its own maturity. For example, suppose that Dubuque, Iowa, wants to borrow $100 million to construct a sewage system. Instead of issuing one 20-year bond, which trades as a unit, it might issue twenty bonds, each having a different maturity: the first "strip" has a 1-year maturity, the second strip has 2 years to maturity, and so on until the twentieth strip, which has 20 years to maturity. The distribution of the total amount between strips is a financial decision that the city must make at the time of the issue; for example, the city might want to retire an equal amount in each year, so each strip would have a par value of $5 million.

The municipal bond is sold as a block to the winning underwriting syndicate. But when the syndicate sells the issue, it splits it into the individual strips, and the individual strips into separate certificates, which are marketed separately.

The advantage of the serial form is that the underwriter can typically get a higher price for the entire issue by selling each strip to those investors who most want that maturity, and the issuer can tailor the retirement schedule to its needs by deciding how much of the issue will be allocated to each strip. If each strip is small, however, the cost of secondary market trading in individual strips might be higher than if the issue were traded as a unit, and this higher transaction cost will be reflected in a lower price paid by the investor.

2. *Underwriting and Net Interest Cost*

Municipal bonds are marketed by underwriters, who buy the issue from the municipality. There are two methods of selecting the underwriter. The first is through direct negotiation, typically with an underwriter who has handled previous issues. The second is through competitive bidding, in which an issuer advertises its intent to borrow and solicits bids. The solicitation specifies in detail the characteristics of the bond issue (term, serial structure, coupon restrictions). The winning underwriter is typically selected as the low-interest-rate bidder. Negotiated underwriting has become the dominant form, representing approximately 80% of bond issues in 1992, up from 60% in 1980.

The process of issuing municipal bonds is complex, involving several parties. Bond counsel establishes the legitimacy of tax exemption and determines that the issue does not violate state statutes and constitutional restrictions, financial advisers help to structure the specific characteristics of the issue, credit rating agencies provide information on credit quality, underwriters provide the marketing and distribution service, transfer agents maintain records on ownership of registered bonds, and printers print the prospectus (called the Official Statement). Recent estimates of the expense of a bond issue are reported in Table 1. These range from 2.5% of bond proceeds for small issues ($5 million or less) to 1% of proceeds for large issues ($75 million or more).

Selection of the winning bidder in competitive bidding is typically based on the "interest rate." The conventional measure of the interest rate on a security is the "true interest cost" (TIC), also called the yield to maturity or, in the jargon of economics, the internal rate of return. This is defined as the interest rate that makes the present value of the cash flows equal to the price of the bond. For a serial bond issue with N strips $(n = 1, 2, \ldots, N)$, coupon rate c_n and face value F_n for the nth strip, and price P, the TIC is the solution for r in the equation

$$P = \sum_{n=1}^{N} \left\{ \sum_{t=1}^{n} [c_n F_n (1 + r)^{-t}] + F_n (1 + r)^{-n} \right\} \tag{1}$$

While the TIC is the appropriate measure of yield for evaluating municipal bonds, the underwriting of municipal bonds has traditionally been based on the concept of net interest cost (NIC), which differs in important ways from TIC.

NIC is constructed as a weighted average of coupon rates, where the weight on a strip's coupon rate is greater the longer the strip's term and the larger the proportion of total face value attributable to that strip. Thus, unlike TIC, NIC is derived from the undiscounted sum of cash flows, and therefore ignores the time value of money.

Table 1 Costs of Issuing Municipal Bonds

	Size of issue (millions of dollars)					
	0–5	5–10	10–25	25–50	50–75	≥75
Underwriter's spread						
Thousands ($)	35.4	83.4	180.9	362.5	560.2	1962.5
Bond proceeds (%)	1.31	1.25	1.06	1.03	0.92	0.90
Financial adviser						
Thousands ($)	14.3	21.8	32.9	29.9	32.1	63.5
Bond proceeds (%)	0.63	0.31	0.02	0.09	0.05	0.04
Bond counsel						
Thousands ($)	11.5	17.9	37.2	59.2	56.6	81.9
Bond proceeds (%)	0.47	0.24	0.04	0.16	0.09	0.06
Credit rating						
(Moody's or S&P)						
Thousands ($)	4.3	5.7	6.9	9.4	11.5	15.8
Bond proceeds (%)	0.16	0.08	0.04	0.03	0.02	0.01
Average Size ($000)	2,550	6,850	22,200	35,200	61,200	210,300
Average cost						
Thousands ($)	65.5	128.8	257.9	461.0	660.4	2,123.7
Bond proceeds (%)	2.57	1.88	1.16	1.31	1.08	1.01

Source: Financial Markets Research Center (1989), Exhibit 3, as reported in Zimmerman (1991). Numbers for credit rating cost are the highest of Moody's or Standard and Poor's. The major excluded costs are audit, notice of sale, and official statement.

Formally, NIC is defined as

$$NIC = \sum_{n=1}^{N} \left\{ [nF_n c_n - S] / \Sigma nF_n \right\} \qquad (2)$$

where S is the excess of price bid over par value. The numerator is the total amount of cash payments made by the issuer over the life of the entire issue, $nF_n c_n$ being the total payments associated with the nth strip. The denominator is called the number of "bond years" in the issue. Note that if the price premium is ignored (i.e., S = 0) NIC is simply a weighted average of the coupon rate on each strip, with the weights being the proportion of bond years attributable to the strip.

NIC was developed as a criterion for underwriter selection in the days before high-speed computers. The advantage of NIC is that it is easily calculated directly from the information on the bond issue. TIC, on the other hand, is quite difficult to calculate since it is the solution to a high-order polynomial equation. In addition, there can be multiple TICs if the coupon structure of the bond issue is complicated.

There are two disadvantages to NIC. First, it can give incorrect signals about who is the low bidder—a bid with the lowest NIC might not be the bid with the lowest TIC. Second, because underwriters who bid on the issue also set the coupon structure of the issue, they can reduce the NIC by front-loading the coupons; that is, by structuring the issue with higher coupon rates in the shorter strips and lower coupon rates in the longer strips. While this can reduce the NIC, hence increasing the underwriter's probability of winning the issue, it does so by creating discounts on the longer-term strips. Because investors are averse to these discounts, they require a higher yield to maturity on the long-term end of the bond issue, and this can raise the overall TIC of the issue.*

These problems with NIC have been discussed at some length. One of the seminal articles was by Hopewell and Kaufman (1974), who concluded that use of NIC as a bid-selection criterion did create substantial costs for the issuer. While there has been some dispute about the magnitude of the problem, time has reduced it in several ways. First, awareness of the problems of NIC bidding has led to restrictions on

---

*The potential for NIC to create additional costs to the issuer is greater the higher the slope of the yield curve. As we shall see in the next section, the municipal bond yield curve tends to have an even greater slope than the yield curve for taxable bonds.

coupon structure that mitigate the problem. For example, the problem is greatest when the municipal yield curve has a high slope, and adoption of a restriction that coupon rates be nondecreasing with term can force the coupon rate structure to more closely approximate the "true" yield curve. Second, there is much more widespread use of TIC bidding than in the early 1970s, when it was very rare.

3. Municipal Bond Duration and the Yield Curve

Investors in bonds experience two types of interest rate risks arising from interest rate variability. The first is capital value risk—if interest rates change, the price of an asset sold before maturity will change, making the holding of long-term assets risky for investors with short-term needs. The second risk is reinvestment rate risk—a change in interest rates will alter the accumulated value of the reinvested income from the bond.

For example, suppose that an investor wanting to accumulate $100,000 at the end of 10 years invests in a 20-year bond. The value of that bond at the end of 10 years consists of two parts: the price of the bond and the accumulated value of the reinvested coupons received during the first 10 years. A rise in interest rates will reduce the price in the tenth year, but increase the value of the reinvested coupons. Thus, capital value risk and reinvestment rate risk move in opposite directions when interest rates change.

The concept of duration was developed in order to manage interest rate risk. If the duration of a bond is equal to the investor's holding period, the value at the end of the holding period is "immunized" from interest rate changes. Thus, in the example just given, if the investor had invested in a bond with a 10-year duration, he would know precisely how much money he would have at the end of 10 years; it would not be affected by any interest rate changes.

The duration of a security is a weighted average of the period until each payment, where the weight for each payment is the proportion of the present value of the security due to that payment. If C_t is the cash payment in the tth period, and r is the rate of interest, the "present value factor" (PVF) for the tth payment is $PVF_t = C_t(1 + r)^{-t}$. For the final payment (at time t = N) the present value factor is $PVF_N = (C_N + F)(1 + r)^{-N}$. Duration is calculated as

$$D = \sum_{t=1}^{N} [PVF_t/\Sigma PVF_t]\, t \qquad\qquad (3)$$

Thus, the weights used in calculating duration are the proportion of the total present value due to the payment in the tth period. This formulation shows that duration is greater the lower the coupon rate paid in each year. The reason is that a lower coupon rate means that a larger portion of present value is due to the final payment, hence the duration is closer to the term to maturity. In addition, duration is inversely related to the rate of interest; the higher the interest rate, the lower the PVF for distant payments relative to near-term payments, and the shorter the duration.

The proper measure of the "longevity" of a security is its duration, not its term. Bonds with the same terms can have very different durations, depending on the pattern of the cash flows over the life of the bond. This requires a reinterpretation of the concept of the yield curve.

As normally defined, the yield curve shows the relationship between the yield to maturity and the term to maturity. Yield curves are normally upward sloping because bonds with longer terms have greater interest rate risk. However, bonds with equal terms can have different durations, and duration is the proper measure of interest rate risk. Thus, the slope of the yield curve is affected by differences in duration: for any term, say 20 years, a bond will have a higher yield the longer its duration.

Other things being equal, municipal bonds have longer durations than taxable bonds because the tax advantages are reflected in lower coupons, hence a larger portion of total cash flow comes from the distant payment of face value at maturity. Thus, the yield curve for municipal bonds should normally slope upward more rapidly than the yield curve for taxable bonds, reflecting the greater interest rate risk for each term to maturity.

Figure 2 shows the interest rate ratio—the ratio of yields on Treasury bonds to yields on prime grade municipal bonds—for 1-year, 5-year, 10-year, and 20-year terms. The interest rate ratio clearly increases with the term to maturity, meaning that the yield curve for municipal bonds slopes upward more rapidly than the Treasury yield curve. This is particularly true before the Tax Reform Act of 1986, as shown in the yield curve for 1985.

Thus, municipal bonds have a greater slope to the yield curve. This is due in part to the longer durations

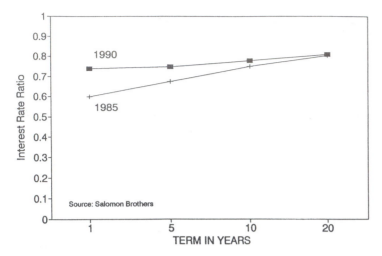

Figure 2   Treasury and municipal bond yield curve.

associated with each term. As we shall see later, it is also a consequence of the structure of the municipal bond market.

4.   Assessing Credit Quality

During the 1930s about 7% of municipal bonds—issued by 4,770 municipal units—defaulted, typically with permanent loss to investors. Most of these were GOs, and most of them were highly rated by Moody's, the only rating agency until the entry of Standard and Poor's in 1950.* Since World War II, there have been very few defaults of GOs, and those few have involved small permanent losses to investors. Revenue bond defaults, while more frequent, are still rare.

Until the 1960s the two ratings agencies provided ratings for a municipality's debt if the market was sufficiently broad to interest subscribers in the service. In the 1960s the agencies adopted a fee structure, requiring that issuers pay directly for their rating. Because numerous statistical studies have concluded that the average unrated municipal bond trades at rates equivalent to Moody's Baa, the lowest "investment-grade" rating, issuers do not pay for ratings unless they are confident of an investment grade result.

The assessment of municipal credit quality, while an essential activity, is more difficult than corporate credit for several reasons. The first is that there is so little default experience among municipal issuers, particularly GOs. As a result, ratings are based more on a priori conceptions of quality than on actual evidence.

A second factor affecting credit quality assessment is that there is no federal legislation requiring disclosure of material information. Indeed, municipal securities were explicitly exempted from most provisions of the Securities Act of 1933 (which focused on underwriting) and from the Securities Exchange Act of 1934 (which focused on broker/dealer activities). Thus, while the Securities Exchange Commission (SEC) can investigate cases of outright fraud under sections 10 and 17 of the 1933 act, there are no federal restrictions on the disclosure of material information and practices in marketing and distribution of municipal securities.

The 1975 amendments to the Securities Exchange Act of 1934 required municipal brokers and dealers to register with the SEC, and created the Municipal Securities Rulemaking Board (MSRB) as an independent, self-regulatory body to establish rules for broker/dealer behavior. The exemption of issuers and underwriters from disclosure requirements was not affected, and remains in effect.

Thus, disclosure of relevant information is a matter both of state law and of custom and practice. The ability of individual investors to ferret out information is limited, creating a greater emphasis on the rating agencies and on financial institutions with information-gathering resources.

There has been some debate about the role of credit ratings as determinants of yields on municipal bonds. Part of this debate focuses on the question of whether or not rating agencies provide independent information of value to investors. The question is whether or not ratings assigned by Moody's or Standard and Poor's

---

*Petersen (1974) reports that 78% of rated bonds that defaulted had ratings of Aa or Aaa.

merely mimic the markets' assessment of risks rather than provide new information. A seminal study by Jantscher (1970) straddled both positions, concluding that the variation of yields on bonds within a single rating category was consistent with the direction of future changes in rating—a bond with a yield at the high end of the distribution for its rating class was likely to be downgraded—and that a change in a published rating triggered an adjustment in market prices.* Rubinfeld (1973) also finds that published ratings have an independent influence on bond yields.

Regardless of the direction of causality between published ratings and bond yields, there is abundant evidence that bond yields are associated with ratings. Table 2 reports the ratings differentials, holding other variables constant, derived in two well-known studies (Kessel, 1971; Capeci, 1991). The differential between Aaa and Aa rated bonds was roughly 20 basis points (bp) in both studies, 20 years apart. There appears to be a decline in the Aaa-Aa differential, perhaps due to the increase in bonds deriving the Aaa rating from bond insurance. The differential between A and Baa appears to have increased.

5. Regional vs. National Markets

Most analyses of the municipal bond market maintain the convenient fiction that there is a single national market. While little can be done to remedy this, and indeed, the national model does apply to some large issuers (e.g., New York City), we should remember that the market for many municipal bonds is local or regional. This occurs for several reasons.

First, as noted above, there is no standardized information on the characteristics of borrowers. This means that assessing credit quality requires some effort that is likely to be geographically restricted. For example, Weston, Massachusetts, is a small—but highly rated—community with less than $10 million in outstanding long-term debt. While Boston banks and investors have an incentive to learn about Weston's credit characteristics, California banks do not. Thus, Weston, like most smaller communities, faces a local market.

A second factor contributing to regional or local markets is taxation. Most states exempt the interest paid by their own political jurisdictions from state income taxes. Thus, investors in states with income taxes have an incentive to invest in bonds issued within their state. As we shall see later, this is reflected in bond yields; states with high income taxes have lower borrowing costs, other things being equal.

Thus, there is undoubtedly a payoff to learning about the unique characteristics of each state, and using those in assessing the determination of prices and quantities. The precise magnitude of that payoff is probably better known to bond traders than to public policy analysts.

E. Yields and Ownership of Tax-Exempt Debt

1. Recent History of Yields

Exemption from federal income taxes confers an advantage upon the holder of municipal bonds. That advantage leads investors to require lower before-tax yields on municipal bonds than for taxable bonds of equivalent maturity and risk. The result is that the yield to maturity on tax-exempt bonds is less than the yield on taxable bonds with equivalent maturity and quality.

This advantage is shown in Figure 3, which reports the ratio of the yield on prime-grade municipal bonds to the yield on U.S. Treasury bonds. This "interest rate ratio" is shown for 1-year, 5-year, and 20-year bonds.

---

*Of course, this does not fully resolve the debate. It is consistent with the notion that the market makes sophisticated assessments of risk and that the rating agencies provide additional information. It is also consistent with the hypothesis that the rating agencies merely assign a rating according to the observed yields on a community's bonds.

Table 2 Yield Differentials by Credit Rating

Rating difference	Kessel (1971)	Benson (1979)	Capeci (1991)
Aaa-Aa	0.15	0.25	0.08
Aa-A	0.22	0.16	0.27
A-Baa	0.24	0.21	0.80

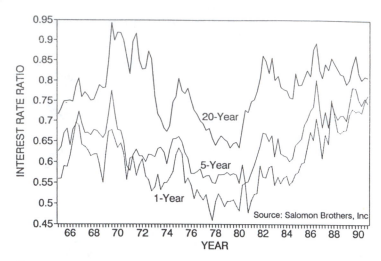

Figure 3   Interest rate ratios for selected terms (municipal bonds vs. U.S. treasury bonds) .

Prime-grade municipal and U.S. Treasury bonds are not precisely equivalent: Treasuries are of higher credit quality because the federal government can print the money necessary to repay its debt; Treasuries trade at lower transactions costs because they have a single issuer, while municipals are issued by a variety of states, local governments, and authorities whose quality is difficult to determine and whose issue sizes can be small; Treasuries are traded in a thick market, while municipals have a lower level of liquidity; and Treasuries have a shorter duration for each term to maturity, and therefore sell at a lower yield. But these differences are (arguably) sufficiently small to allow us to use the interest rate ratio as a measure of the influence of tax exemption on municipal bond yields.

Several important observations can be drawn from Figure 3. First, for each of the three maturities shown, the interest rate ratio is less than unity, reflecting the tax advantages of municipal bonds. Second, for each maturity the interest rate ratio is highly variable; at times the advantage of tax exemption to the issuer appears to be quite small, as in 1969 and the mid-1980s, when 20-year municipal bonds carried yields almost equal to 20-year Treasury bonds, while at other times the advantage is very great, as in the late 1970s when the interest rate ratio for 20-year bonds was about 0.65.*

Finally, as noted above, the yield curve for municipal interest rates rises more rapidly than the yield curve for Treasury securities. This is evident from the fact that the interest rate ratio is higher for 5-year bonds than for 1-year bonds, and higher for 20 years than for 5 years. This phenomenon almost disappeared in the late 1980s, especially for short- to intermediate-term bonds. Both the more rapidly rising yield curve (relative to Treasuries) of 1966 to 1985, and the elimination of the differential for short- to intermediate-term bonds, are primarily due to the role of commercial banks in the municipal bond market. These changes—which mean that municipal bonds appear to trade more like taxable bonds—have been particularly marked since the Tax Reform Act of 1986.

2.   *Municipal Bond Ownership*

Figure 4 shows that prior to the mid-1980s the largest holders of tax-exempt debt were financial institutions, primarily commercial banks and property and casualty insurance companies.† Indeed, from 1960 through 1980 the share held by households declined from over 40% to about 25%, with most of the market share moving

---

*The 1969 experience is an anomaly that is probably due to the debate surrounding the 1969 tax reform act. The House proposals included state and local interest in the new alternative minimum tax (AMT). While the AMT was adopted, state and local interest income was not subject to the AMT. However, the prospect that these proposals would be adopted led to very high interest rate ratios in that year. For a discussion of the debate, see Huefner (1971), p. 100 ff.

†Property and casuality insurance companies were by far the most important insurance companies in the municipal bond market. Until recently, life insurance companies faced relatively low tax rates, limiting their interest in municipal bonds.

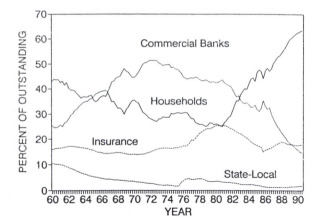

Figure 4   Share of outstanding state and local bonds held by selected sectors.

toward commercial banks. State and local governments (primarily retirement funds) were significant holders of municipal bonds in the early 1960s, with about 10% of the outstanding stock, but this share declined thereafter. Insurance companies (primarily property and casualty insurers) have maintained a 15 to 20% share of outstanding state and local bonds, with a brief surge from 1975 to 1980 and a return to the normal share by 1985.

Beginning in the mid-1980s the ownserhip pattern of tax-exempt bonds changed dramatically, with commercial banks sharply reducing their share from almost 55% in 1980 to about 25% by 1990. The withdrawal of commercial banks from the market was matched by an increase in the share held by households, from about 25% in 1980 to over 60% in 1990. The nature of household ownership also changed, with unit investment trusts and mutual funds acting as conduits and providing both diversification opportunities and liquidity services not available to most households prior to the 1980s.

The tax structure provides some explanation of these changes in ownership. Until the 1981 Economic Recovery Tax Act (ERTA), households faced tax rates as high as 70%, while commercial banks and property and casualty insurance companies faced a tax rate of 46 to 52%. Furthermore, until 1982 commercial banks could deduct from their taxable income all interest paid to carry municipal securities, a tax advantage that gave them a strong incentive to hold tax-exempt debt. Thus, high-income households, commercial banks, and property and casualty insurance companies had the greatest incentives to hold tax-exempt bonds and were the dominant holders.*

The 1982 Tax Equity and Fiscal Responsibility Act (TEFRA) reduced the deductibility of interest expense for carrying tax-exempt securities to 85% of the interest paid. The advantage was further reduced by the 1984 Deficit Reduction Act to 80% of carrying costs. Finally, with some exceptions,† the 1986 tax reform act completely eliminated any deduction by banks of interest paid to carry municipal bonds, virtually extinguishing the advantages for banks of tax-exempt securities. Figure 4 shows the banks' share of the market stabilizing in the early 1980s and falling sharply after 1985. The plunge after 1985 is the result of the sharp decline in corporate income tax rates and the elimination of banks' deduction of interest paid to carry municipal bonds.

F.   Recent Innovations in the Municipal Bond Market

In the last decade there has been a great deal of innovation in the market for municipal debt. This has been stimulated by the increasing importance of households as investors, either directly or indirectly, as well as by the tide of innovation experienced in all security markets.

---

*The property and casualty insurance sector's share of the market remained low in spite of high statutory tax rates because those companies experience a strong cycle in profitability. Thus, the tax advantages of municipals were enjoyed only during profitable years. This reduced the effective tax advantages.

†Municipal bonds acquired before August 16, 1986, still had deductible carrying costs. This led to a surge in bank purchases of private-purpose bonds in anticipation of grandfathering of the exemption. Also, deductibility was continued for bank purchases of small local issues.

This section, which draws on Petersen (1991), will address three main forms of innovations: private credit enhancements, designed to ease the fear of default; changes in the municipal debt instrument, designed to shift the distribution of interest rate risk; and development of derivative securities.

1. Private Credit Enhancements

In recent years the quality of municipal bonds—both GO and revenue—has been increasingly supported by privately provided credit enhancements. The three main types of enhancements are bank lines of credit, bank standby letters of credit, and municipal bond insurance.

Bank lines of credit are typically used to ensure that short-term municipal debt will be paid on time; they have been used most frequently for tax-exempt commericial paper. The line of credit agreement stipulates the term of the line, the conditions under which it can be used, the commitment fee, and the "drawdown rate" that is charged if the line is actually used. Lines of credit are a relatively weak form of support designed to ensure liquidity but not to protect against default. Indeed, credit lines specifically state that the line can not be drawn on if the issuer is in default.

Standby letters of credit (LOCs) are negotiated by a municipal bond issuer with a commercial bank. Typically, these LOCs promise to pay any principal and interest "on time" for a period of 5 to 10 years. Unlike lines of credit, LOCs are irrevocable and can be drawn on to provide funds for defaulted obligations. Thus, they are a credit enhancement, not merely a source of liquidity. At the end of the 1980s over 20% of newly issued municipal bonds were supported by standby LOCs.

The third form of private enhancement—municipal bond insurance—began with the formation of the American Municipal Bond Assurance Indemnity Corporation (AMBAC) in 1971. At present there are two additional major municipal bond insurers: the Municipal Bond Insurance Association (MBIA), formed in 1973, and Financial Guaranty Insurance Company (FGIC), started in 1983. These three companies provided about 90% of municipal bond insurance in 1990.

Municipal bond insurance involves a one-time premium reported to average about 0.3% of the undiscounted sum of payments (principal and interest) over the life of the bond.* The actual premium is reported to range from a low of 0.1% to a high of 2.0% (Quigley and Rubinfeld, 1991), depending on the underlying credit quality of the issuer, the size of the issue, and other considerations.

Moody's and Standard and Poor's assign insured municipal bonds the credit rating of the insurance company, not the rating of the issuer. At present, the three major insurance companies are Aaa-rated. However, Bland and Yu (1987) found that insured municipal bonds tend to trade at yields between Moody's A and Baa-1 ratings. Thus, the expansion of insured municipal bonds—to over 30% of new issues in 1990—has adulterated the meaning of the Aaa rating. This proliferation of "artificial" Aaa-rated bonds accounts in part for the decreasing interest rate differential between Aaa- and Baa-rated municipal bonds.

Several studies have attempted to quantify the advantage of municipal bond insurance to the issuer. This task is difficult because of the problem of disentangling two effects of bond insurance. The first is that it increases the credit rating, and the second is a direct effect of insurance; it acts as a quality signal to bond buyers that would affect yields even in the absence of a credit rating effect. These difficulties were overcome in a recent study by Quigley and Rubinstein (1991).

About 30% of municipal bond insurance is bought by bond buyers, not by issuers. This "aftermarket" insurance does not cover the entire issue, but only the portion of interest due to the insurance buyer. For example, a unit investment trust might purchase insurance for municipal bonds in its portfolio. As a result, data exist for the same bond issue on both an insured and uninsured basis. Since the creditworthiness of the issuer and all other characteristics of the bond issue are the same, the data on "twins" can be used to infer the direct effect of bond insurance. Quigley and Rubinfeld report that the TIC on insured bonds is about 14 to 28 bp below the TIC for the uninsured twin. This translates to a 1.9% to 3.8% increase in the price at which a newly issued insured municipal bond comes to market, a result consistent with other studies using less appropriate data.†

Perhaps the best-known instance of municipal bond insurance occurred in 1983, when WPPSS defaulted on $2.25 billion of bonds issued to construct uncompleted nuclear power plant. About 10% of those bonds

---

*Norris, F. (March 13, 1991). "Nagging Question in Bond Insurance," *New York Times*, p. C8.

†For example, Kidwell et al. (1987) found that bond insurance reduced the NIC by 34 bp, while the premium paid was equivalent to 11.7 bp.

were held by a unit investment trust that purchased aftermarket insurance and, therefore, experienced no loss of interest or principal.

2. *New Municipal Debt Instruments*

As noted above, one strategy for protection from interest rate risk is to hold securities with a duration equal to the investor's holding period. One innovation that has allowed this strategy to be pursued is the development of zero-coupon municipal bonds, in which there are no cash payments until maturity. Sold at a significant original issue discount, zeros have a duration equal to the term to maturity, hence are easily integrated into an interest rate immunization strategy. For the myopic borrower focused only on the near-term tax levy effects of debt service, zeros have the advantage of requiring no cash outlay until maturity. One drawback to the zero exists in states with debt limitations, which are specified in terms of the face value of the debt. Because zeros have a high face value relative to bond proceeds, they artificially "use up" debt limits. Zeros tend to be issued more heavily in periods of high interest rates, reflecting the sizable cash savings they allow. In 1990 zeros accounted for about 4% of newly issued municipal bonds.

A second innovation is the use of variable rate municipal bonds (VRMBs), which have been used primarily for revenue bonds. VRMBs accounted for 20% of new issues in 1985, before the 1986 tax reform act tightened the issue of tax-exempt private activity municipal bonds. In 1990 VRMBs accounted for 7% of new issues.

VRMBs have long terms but coupons that adjust according to short-term interest rates. Because VRMBs have limitations on the frequency of rate adjustment, and often have lifetime caps on the rate that is paid, they do have capital value risk. This risk can be further reduced by inclusion of put options, requiring the issuer to buy the bond back at a fixed price at the investor's option. They also can be convertible into fixed-rate debt, a feature valued by investors if interest rates fall.

Uncertainty about future cash requirements, arising from both rate variability and putability, leads issuers of VRMBs to use credit facilities, such as bank lines of credit, to ensure that the issuer can obtain the cash needed to make required payments. VRMBs do expose the issuer to uncertainty about the tax levy consequences of its debt.

Yet another innovation is the certificate of participation (COP). This is analogous to an industrial revenue bond with the state or local government leasing the facility. A recent example is the Brevard County, Florida, government center. This was financed by COPs issued by Brevard County, secured by the lease payments made by Brevard County under a leasing agreement. The use of COPs has increased in recent years, with an estimated $65 billion outstanding in 1993. One advantage of the COP for the municipality is that because it is not technically long-term debt, it does not require the voter approval often associated with municipal bonds. However, the Brevard County example reveals a significant drawback for investors: the lease agreement can be canceled.*

Innovative ways are being found to circumvent restrictions on the use of tax-exempt financing. An example is the refunding escrow deposit (RED) used as a substitute for advanced refunding issues, which were made difficult by the arbitrage provisions of the Tax Reform Act of 1986. Under an RED, investors simultaneously deposit an amount into an escrow account and enter into a forward purchase agreement to buy a new bond issue at a predetermined rate at the time that the outstanding bonds become callable. The escrow account is invested in Treasury securities and the interest is paid to the investors. At the first call date the escrowed amount is exchanged for newly issued bonds, and the proceeds of the new issues are used by the municipality to retire its outstanding bonds.

Wall Street has also become involved in municipal finance innovations in the secondary markets. Following the lead of the Treasury security market, outstanding municipal bonds are packaged into pools that are then sold in a variety of forms, similar to the collateralized mortgage obligation. Some investors buy Interest-Only certificates, others buy Principal-Only certificates. In addition, some certificates have variable rates. Among the most exotic are "inverse floaters," which pay a higher rate when interest rates decline.

3. *Hedging with Derivative Securities*

The 1980s witnessed an explosion of options and futures markets designed to allow investors to hedge against price changes in underlying securities. These innovative opportunities were extended to the municipal bond market as well.

---

*Citizen opposition to Brevard's "palace in a cow pasture" led to lease approval being placed on a ballot after the COP had been sold. A concerted effort by the MBIA, which has insured the COP, led to its approval by a small margin.

Currently one futures contract for municipal bonds, the muni bond index (MBI), is traded on the Chicago Board of Trade (CBT). This contract is for future delivery of cash equivalent to $1000 times the bond buyer index (BBI), an index of 40 GO and revenue bonds meeting a number of criteria: bonds included in the BBI must be rated A or higher, must be actively traded, must be outstanding in amounts $50 million or greater, must have at least 19 years to maturity, must have at least one at-par call date prior to maturity, and must have a first call date of between 7 and 16 years. The price of a bond is based on the middle three quotes from five dealers, with the average price adjusted by a conversion factor to be equivalent to an 8% coupon rate. The BBI is the simple average of the 40 prices.

For example, on June 14, 1993, this contract was traded for June and September delivery. The closing price for the September contract was 100 and 22/32, or 100.6875, so a single contract purchased at the close was for September delivery of $100,687.50. If the BBI is $101 at delivery the holder of a contract would make a gross profit of $312.50; the seller of the contract would lose that amount. This contract allows an individual or financial institution to hedge against unanticipated changes in municipal bond yields and prices.*

In addition to this futures contract, an option contract for the MBI futures contract is also traded on the CBT. This is traded for a range of strike prices, with each option allowing the holder to buy (if a call) or sell (if a put) $100,000 of a futures contract at the specified strike price. For example, at the close of June 14, 1993, one could buy a December 1993 call on the MBI futures contract with a strike price of 100 for a premium of $1,703. If the futures price at the December delivery date exceeds the strike price the holder could realize a profit by exercising the option and simultaneously selling the futures contract.

III. THE INCOME TAX CODE AND MUNICIPAL BOND YIELDS

Section II touched on some aspects of recent tax legislation to explain major changes in the municipal bond market. This section reviews key features of the income tax code that influence the demand for tax-exempt debt, and therefore help to explain municipal bond yields. This journey through the income tax code provides background essential to the formal analysis of the determination of municipal bond yields in Section IV.

A. The Federal Income Tax Code

1. *Federal Taxation of Ordinary Income*

The internal revenue code identifies two forms of taxable income. The first is "ordinary income," which consists of cash payments such as coupons, interest paid, cash dividends, and original issue discounts. The second is "capital gains," defined as the difference between the price at which an asset is sold and its "cost basis" at the time of sale. The code allows the holder of a tax-exempt bond to exclude ordinary income but not capital gains from taxable income. Coupons, interest, and cash dividends are, with some exceptions, defined as ordinary income and included in a taxpayer's taxable income in the year they are received unless they are explicitly excluded, as in the case of a tax-exempt bond.[†]

Original issue discount (OID) is the difference between the par value of the bond—the amount paid at maturity—and the initial price at which the bond came to market. For example, suppose a bond has a par value of $1000 and was originally issued at a price of $900. The difference of $100 occurs because the coupon rate on the bond is less than the interest rate prevailing on similar securities at the time of issue. The tax code treats this as cash income even though it gives rise to no cash payment until the bond matures. If the bond is taxable, the OID is included in taxable income as it accrues; if the bond is tax-exempt, it is not included in taxable income.

The tax code does not allow the investor to wait until the bond matures before he or she "earns" the original issue discount. Instead, investors must amortize it over the life of the bond. If the bond's income is taxable, the amortized value is added to each year's taxable income; if the bond is tax-exempt, it is not added to taxable income. In either case, the amortized value of the original issue discount is added to the cost basis of the bond, and becomes relevant to the calculation of capital gains.

---

*Because an investor's municipal bond portfolio will not precisely match the portfolio assumed by the bond buyer, buyers and sellers of municipal bond futures contracts will not normally be able to create perfect hedges; that is, they will experience "basis risk."

[†]Among the other exceptions are return of capital dividends and a major portion of dividends received by financial institutions.

As noted above, the amortization of the original issue discount also affects the cost basis of the bond. The amount of OID assigned to each year is added to the cost basis of the bond, so that accumulated OID is not treated as capital gains when the bond matures or is sold. The logic is straightforward: if you have "earned" OID in the past, it was either taxed if the bond was taxable or treated as tax-exempt if the bond is tax-exempt. If the cost basis is not adjusted upward to reflect the accumulated OID, when the bond is sold that amount would be treated as capital gains—and capital gains are taxed whether the bond is tax-exempt or not!

The tax treatment of OID has become important since the introduction of zero-coupon bonds in both corporate and municipal bond markets. Prior to the 1982 TEFRA, OID was amortized at a linear rate. Thus, if the bond used as an example above has a 10-year period to maturity, one-tenth of the OID, or $10, would be added to taxable income in each year. After TEFRA, OID was amortized as accrued interest; the investor calculated the interest rate that would accumulate the initial price to be equal to the price at maturity, and an amount equal to that interest rate times the cost basis was treated as ordinary income in each year.

The effect of tax treatment of OID was to distort the interest rate ratio prior to 1982. The linear amortization gave corporations an excessive deduction in the early years of the debt issue, thereby encouraging corporate debt issues. At the same time, the linear amortization inhibited investors from investing in zero-coupon bonds. As a result, the corporate bond yield tended to be higher, and the interest rate ratio lower, until the correction embodied in the 1982 TEFRA.

2.   Federal Taxation of Capital Gains

The internal revenue code taxes capital gains on a cash basis rather than on an accrual basis. This means that gains are taxed only when realized upon the sale of the asset, not as they accrue "on paper" over the holding period. The amount of capital gains is defined as the difference between the price at which the asset was sold and the "cost basis" of the asset. The cost basis is usually the price (including brokerage commissions) at which the asset was purchased, but, as noted above, the cost basis can also reflect certain adjustments such as original issue discount.

The effect of the opportunity to defer capital gains taxes is to reduce the effective tax rate on accrued gains. For example, suppose that during 1993 a stock in your portfolio increases by $10 per share. If capital gains were taxed on an accrual basis, you would have to include that $10 in your 1993 taxable income even though you had not sold the asset. But suppose that you do not sell the stock until 1998. Assuming a capital gains tax rate of 28%, you will pay a tax of $2.80 per share in 1998, but (assuming an interest rate of 5%), the value in 1993 of your 1998 capital gains tax liability was only $2.19. Thus, your effective capital gains tax rate in the year of accrual is 21.9%, not the statutory 28%. The advantage is greater the higher the interest rate and the longer the deferral.

Indeed, capital gains taxes can be avoided completely by holding assets until death because the cost basis of assets is adjusted to the market price at the time of death, effectively eliminating any taxation of the capital gains when heirs sell the assets. Note that even though an estate tax exists, so that capital gains might appear to be taxed, two estates of equal size will pay the same tax even though one might have a considerably greater appreciation component than the other. Thus, the estate with the greater capital gains will not pay any additional taxes.

Except for brief periods in U.S. history, capital gains have been taxed at a lower rate than ordinary income. For example, from 1942 to 1978 the tax code allowed an investor to exclude 50% of capital gains from taxable income, thus setting the capital gains rate at 50% of the ordinary income tax rate. Furthermore, during much of that time the maximum capital gains tax rate was set at 25%. From 1978 to 1986 the code allowed 60% of gains to be excluded, which, because of the 50% maximum tax rate on ordinary income, had the effect of reducing the maximum tax rate on capital gains to 20%. Thus, an individual taxpayer in the highest bracket would pay 50% on ordinary income but only 20% on capital gains.*

The Tax Reform Act of 1986 eliminated this differential. Under that law, 100% of capital gains are included in taxable income and, with a 33% maximum tax rate on ordinary income, the maximum capital gains tax rate was also 33%. The Revenue Reconciliation Act of 1990 restored a slight differential in favor of capital gains by setting a maximum capital gains tax rate of 28%. This remains in effect.

---

*Since 1969 there has been an AMT, which applies in unusual circumstances and can have the effect of increasing the tax rate on capital gains. This does not have a substantial effect on the tax positions of most investors, and has not been considered in our overview of capital gains taxation.

Note that capital gains taxation makes municipal bonds selling at a discount less attractive because the investor is taxed on part of the return. On the other hand, the desirability of discounted taxable bonds is not affected if capital gains are taxed as ordinary income, and it is enhanced if the capital gains tax rate is less than the ordinary income tax rate (as it was prior to 1986). Thus, discounted municipal bonds will have higher yields relative to taxable bonds (because part of the return is taxable), and this effect will be more prominent if capital gains are taxed at a lower rate than ordinary income.

To see this, assume that an investor is choosing between a newly issued taxable bond and a newly issued tax-exempt bond, each priced at par. She knows that if interest rates rise, the price of each bond will fall, and that if, she sells the bond at a loss, the capital loss is deductible regardless of whether the bond is taxable or tax-exempt. But the market discount at the time of sale will expose the new buyer to capital gains taxes. Because part of the return to the municipal bond will now be taxable, the new buyer will pay a still lower price to compensate her for the capital gains taxes.

While taxation of capital gains adversely affects the price of a municipal bond, it is not disadvantageous for the taxable bond since the new buyer will pay taxes whether his income is in the form of coupons or capital gains. Therefore, the prospect of interest rate increases (bond price decreases) should make municipal bonds less desirable than taxable bonds, inducing a higher interest rate ratio. This effect should have been greater prior to the 1986 tax reform act, when capital gains were taxed at lower rates than ordinary income. Furthermore, the effect of the taxation of capital gains on municipal bonds should also be greater when interest rates and asset prices are more volatile. The econometric analysis in Section IV will employ a measure of price variability to determine whether or not this hypothesis is supported.

3.   Federal Taxation of Capital Losses

The tax treatment of capital losses is not symmetrical with the treatment of gains. While 100% of realized gains are included in taxable income, the tax code might not allow full deduction of losses from taxable income if losses exceed capital gains: for a married couple filing jointly, losses can be fully deducted up to the amount of capital gains plus $3,000, but any losses above that amount must be carried over to future years. Thus, while a taxpayer can ultimately deduct all losses as long as taxable income is sufficient to take the deduction, the ceiling on the loss deduction allowed in a single year means that the present value of the tax saving is reduced by the requirement to defer the deduction to future years.

For example, consider a married person filing jointly who has taxable ordinary income of $20,000. Suppose that this person has a capital gain of $2,000 and a capital loss of $10,000. In the current tax year she can deduct $5,000 of capital losses—$2,000 against the capital gain plus the $3,000 maximum loss offset. The remaining $5,000 of capital losses can be carried over to future years; $3,000 can be deducted in the next year, and the remaining $2,000 in the second year.

The absence of full-loss offsets leads investors to alter their portfolios to reduce their exposure to price risk. This does not mean that they should avoid risky assets, only that the absence of full-loss offset provides an incentive to reduce investments in risky assets below the level that would prevail with full-loss offset.

B.   State Income Taxes

The focus of this chapter is the federal income tax code, but no survey of the connection between taxation and the municipal bond market is complete without reference to state income taxation. Forty-two states levy an income tax on interest and dividends, with tax rates ranging from very low levels to a high of 12% in Massachusetts and North Dakota.* In addition, 36 of the states with an income tax exempt some or all interest paid by government agencies within their own jurisdiction, and tax all out-of-state municipal interest income. Thus, in most states in-state municipal bonds offer a tax advantage.

If the marginal investor in a state's bonds is a resident of that state, jurisdictions in the state will pay lower municipal bond rates than those paid in states with lower tax rates. This will occur because the intrastate investors will pay a higher price for those bonds than will investors in other states.

However, if the marginal investor is out of state, high state income tax rates will not affect the municipal

---

*These rates are for 1990 income. Connecticut has a 14% maximum rate on interest and dividends; the Connecticut tax is levied only if 1990 federal adjusted gross income exceeds $54,000.

bond yields paid by jurisdictions within the state. In this case, the advantages of within-state tax-exempt bonds accrue as a windfall to within-state investors.

The importance of this segmentation has been examined by Kidwell et al. (1984), who conclude that—as a generalization—a state's residents are the marginal investors in that state's local bonds. Therefore, they find that high state income taxes do (other things being equal) confer lower borrowing costs on the state and its political subdivisions.

C.   Recent Tax Legislation

The key events in legislation in recent years are summarized in Table 3. The most prominent change has been a radical revision of tax rate schedules with both a general reduction in tax rates and a reduction in the degree of progressivity. As we shall see in the next section, the rate reductions should lead to an increase in interest rate ratios, while the decline in progressivity should reduce the rate ratios. In addition, since 1985 the tax rate schedule has been indexed, thereby reducing the "bracket creep" that slowly pushed tax rates up and reduced the interest rate ratio. Finally, there have been specific changes that limit the desirability of municipal bonds to financial institutions.

1.   Changes in Tax Rates

Federal taxation of corporate income establishes a lower tax bracket for corporations with very low net incomes, but most corporate income is taxed at the maximum statutory tax rate. That rate changed very little until 1987; the maximum tax rate on corporate income was 52% in the early 1960s, 50% in 1964, 48% in 1965, 46% in 1979, and the present 34% in 1987. Thus, the corporate tax rate has not varied sufficiently to account for the significant variation in the interest rate ratio.

Changes in the personal income tax rate schedule have been more dramatic. The 1981 ERTA reduced the maximum personal income tax rate to 50%, and reduced other personal income tax rates by 25% over a 3-year period. The Tax Reform Act of 1986 dramatically reduced tax rates for most income levels. The maximum tax rate on personal income was reduced from 50% to 38.5% in 1987 and 33% for 1988 and later years. The 1986 act also simplified the individual income tax rate schedule by cutting the number of brackets from fourteen to only four (15%, 28%, 33%, and 28%), widening the income levels associated with each bracket and thus reducing the problem of bracket creep.

The most recent change—the Revenue Reconciliation Act of 1990—further reduced the number of tax brackets to three (15%, 28%, and 31%) for 1991 and later years, thereby eliminating the "bubble" for upper-income levels. In addition, the amount of itemized deductions was reduced by 3% of income over $100,000; for example, if a taxpayer's income is $110,000, his itemized deductions are reduced by $300, effectively raising his marginal tax rate from 31% to about 32%.

The maximum statutory tax rate on personal income was 91% in the early 1960s, then fell to 70% in 1965 where it stayed through 1981 with a brief period (1968–1970) of increase because of a surtax levied to finance the Vietnam War. In 1982 the maximum rate was reduced to 50%, then to 33% in 1987.

The marginal tax rates for four levels of real income, measured in 1980 dollars, are shown in Fig. 5. For all real income levels except the top one ($100,000) the marginal tax bracket increased from 1962 through 1981; this increase was due to bracket creep. It is clear that the changes in tax rates initiated by ERTA in 1981 and followed by the 1986 tax reform act have been more generous for high levels of income than for low; the marginal tax rate at the $25,000 real income level was actually higher in 1990 than in 1962. Thus, to the extent that tax rates affect investment decisions, small effects, if any, should be seen for securities held by lower-income groups (bank deposits, corporate bonds) and the effects should be more dramatic for securities held by upper-income groups (common stocks, municipal bonds).

2.   Indexation of the Tax System

Prior to the 1980s the tax system was based solely on nominal income levels. This meant that the depreciation allowed businesses for plant and equipment was based on original cost, not replacement cost, and the tax rate schedule was based on the money value of taxable income. This clearly presented a problem in an inflationary environment such as that prevailing in the 1970s and early 1980s.

One effect of inflation is that the cost of replacing physical assets, such as vehicles, equipment, and structures, exceeds the original cost of the assets. As a result, historical cost depreciation—based on the

Table 3 Important Tax Legislation in Recent Years

1976	Tax Reform Act	• Lengthened holding periods for long-term capital gains from 6 months to one year. • Created tax-sheltered Individual Retirement Accounts (IRA).
1978	Revenue Act	• Widened personal income tax brackets. • Reduced maximum corporate income tax rate from 48% to 46%
1981	Economic Recovery Tax Act (ERTA)	• Cut maximum personal income tax rates from 70% to 50%. • Reduced personal income tax rates at all levels by 25% over a 3-year period. • Initiated indexation of tax brackets beginning in 1985. • Introduced superaccelerated depreciation of business assets (ACRS). • Expanded tax-sheltered investment opportunities. —Introduced all savers certificates. —Expanded eligibility for IRAs. —Introduced net interest exclusion.
1982	Tax Equity and Fiscal Responsibility Act (TEFRA)	• Allowed deduction of only 85% of interest paid to carry municipal bonds. • Established 10% withholding tax on interest and dividends.
1983	Social Security Act amendments	• Subjected 50% of social security benefits to federal income tax. (Led to indirect taxation of municipal interest.)
1984	Deficit Reduction Act	• Allowed deduction of only 80% of interest paid to carry municipal bonds. • Postponed ERTA's interest exclusion. • Extended tax exemption for mortgage revenue bonds to 1987. • Reduced holding period for long-term capital gains to 6 months. • Limited depreciation on assets leased to tax-exempt entities.
1986	Tax Reform Act	• Replaced 14 personal income tax brackets with only four (15%, 28%, 33%, 28%). • Increased corporate income tax rate to 34%. • Eliminated deduction of interest paid by commercial banks to carry municipal bonds. • Placed limits on eligibility of "private-purpose" municipal bonds for tax exemption. • Dramatically reduced the tax advantages of many tax shelters, such as real estate.
1990	Revenue Reconciliation Act	• Established three tax brackets (15%, 28%, 31%). • Set maximum capital gains tax rate at 28%. • Reduced itemized deductions by 3% of income over $100,000.
1993	act (in progress)	• Establishes six tax brackets (15%, 28%, 31%, 36%, 39.6%). • Eliminates income ceiling on 1.45% Medicare tax. • Includes 80% of social security benefits in taxable income if income exceeds threshold level.

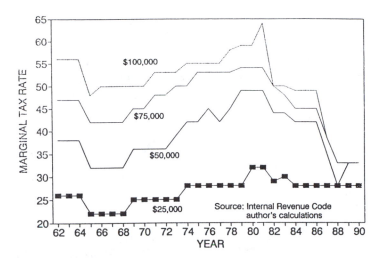

Figure 5   Marginal personal income tax rates.

original cost of the depreciable asset—means that businesses cannot fully recognize the cost of replacing equipment as a deductible cost of business. The effect is to overstate business income by including in it the difference between "economic" depreciation on a replacement cost basis and historical cost depreciation. This overstatement of business profits results in higher tax payments and a deterioration of the firm's financial position.

A second effect of an inflationary environment is that it results in higher tax rates on real income. This has been particularly important for personal income taxes, which, for much of this century, had a complex set of tax brackets. For example, in 1986, before the Tax Reform Act of 1986 became effective, there were fourteen tax brackets: for a married taxpayer filing jointly these ranged from 11% for income between $3,670 and $5,940 to 50% for taxable income over $175,2505.

Because the income levels at which tax brackets changed were tied to money income rather than real income, an inflationary environment meant that individuals moved into higher tax brackets when their money income rose, even though their real incomes remained unchanged or even declined. This phenomenon, called bracket creep, raised the effective tax rate on real income over time as inflation continued.

The 1981 ERTA introduced indexation of the personal income tax brackets, beginning in 1985. With indexation, the break points between tax brackets are increased according to a general price index. For example, in 1985 the tax rate was 28% for taxable income in the range of $31,120 to $36,630, but in 1986 the 28% rate was applied to taxable personal income between $32,270 and $37,980, reflecting an inflation of about 3.7% between 1985 and 1986.

Indexation has eliminated the problem of bracket creep, at least for taxpayers whose consumption bundle mimics the composition of expenditures that the general price index represents. For other taxpayers a weak connection between real tax rates and inflation might remain, but this has been reduced by the movement toward a flat-rate tax system in the 1986 and 1990 tax laws.

3.   Other Aspects of the 1986 Act

As discussed in Section II, the 1986 tax reform act imposed restrictions on private-activity use of tax-exempt bonds. This favored the tax-exempt bond market, forcing private borrowers back into the taxable bond market and, to the extent that relative supplies of taxable and tax-exempt debt affect relative yields, raising the spread between taxable and tax-exempt yields.

A second piece of the 1986 legislation restricted the tax advantages of a wide range of "tax shelters." For example, depreciation of real estate was dramatically reduced, raising the effective tax rate on real estate investments. This elimination of tax shelters was used as a selling point by the municipal bond industry, the claim being that municipal bonds were the sole remaining tax shelter. If this claim were true, the municipal bond rate should have fallen relative to taxable bond yields, reinforcing the effect of private-activity bond limitations.

A third nontax rate feature, also noted above, was the elimination of the commercial bank deduction for costs of carrying municipal bonds. The effect of this change offsets to some extent the effect of the other two legislative changes; municipal bond yields would rise relative to taxable bond yields as nonbank sectors were induced to increase their holdings of municipal bonds.

Thus, the 1986 legislation not only dramatically changed the tax rate structure, it also introduced important nontax rate changes that could have, in principle, either favored or harmed the municipal bond market.

4. Post-1986 Tax Legislation

The sweeping changes in the tax code adopted in 1986 were designed to "rationalize" the federal income tax by inhibiting adverse tax incentives to invest in low-productivity "loopholes" while reducing the progressivity of the federal income tax. This reform appears to be on the path to reversal. As noted above, the effect of the 1986 act was to reduce the tax incentives to hold municipal bonds for both households and financial institutions, while at the same time reducing the range of alternative sources of tax shelters.

The first departure was 1990's Revenue Reconciliation Act. This changed the structure of tax brackets by establishing only three brackets (15%, 28%, and 31%) instead of the four brackets in the 1986 act. This eliminated the bubble bracket while raising the tax rate on the highest incomes from 28% to 31%. The 1990 act also established a maximum capital gains tax rate of 28%, thereby restoring the preferred status of capital gains. Finally, it introduced a creative way of reducing the average value of itemized deductions while not affecting the value at the margin. This had the effect of increasing the effective marginal tax rate for itemizers by about 1% (to 32%) while maintaining the incentive of taxpayers to engage in activities that generated deductions (e.g., charitable contributions).*

The election of President Clinton in November 1992 promises more significant revisions of the income tax code. At the time of this writing, the House Ways and Means Committee has passed legislation that increased the corporate income tax rate from 34% to 35%, established five personal income tax brackets (15%, 28%, 31%, 36%, and 39.6%), and eliminated the income ceiling on the 1.45% Medicare tax. Combined with the 3% reduction in itemized deductions, this increased the effective maximum personal income tax rate to over 42%.

This bill, which was passed by the House by only a three-vote margin, is now being debated in the Senate, where it is expected to face an even tougher battle. However, most analysts expect the tax increases on high-income taxpayers to be adopted in 1993.

IV. THE DETERMINANTS OF MUNICIPAL BOND YIELDS

In this section we use the insights developed in the previous sections as the basis for a statistical analysis of municipal bond yields. The primary purpose is to test whether the recent experience for the yields on municipal bonds is, in fact, consistent with the propositions developed in the previous section. Our analysis will focus on interest rate ratios, as defined in the Section II and shown in Fig. 3.

A. Explanations of the Interest Rate Ratio

1. The Traditional Explanation

Why do interest rate ratios vary so much over time? Why has the ratio been higher for long maturities than for short maturities? Why has the difference between the long and short maturities almost disappeared in recent years? This section presents a simple model of the municipal bond market that addresses these questions.

We assume that municipal bonds and taxable bonds are substitutes in investors' portfolios. Each investor will choose an amount of municipal bonds based on her tax rate and on her assessments of the relative liquidity of municipal bonds. For each investor, the optimal holding of municipal bonds will be that quantity for which $(R_M/R_T) = l + (1 - t)$, where t is her tax rate and l is the liquidity premium required by the investor. While the tax rate is exogenous to the investor's decision, the liquidity premium is endogenous; as an investor

---

*The 1990 act reduced the amount of itemized deductions that could be taken by 3% of taxable income in excess of $100,000. Thus, a taxpayer with $200,000 of taxable income and $30,000 of deductions could only take $27,000 of deductions.

contemplates increasing the amount she invests in municipal bonds, she will require a higher interest rate ratio to compensate for the increased risk and lower liquidity.

The liquidity premium is due to several sources of risk inherent in municipal bond ownership. The first is lower liquidity and higher transactions costs caused by the serial form of municipal bonds; because each bond is traded in separate strips, the average size of transaction is often small, which leads to increased transactions costs, and investors often can not sell their municipal bonds as quickly as Treasury or corporate bonds can be sold. In addition, we have seen that the tax code penalizes municipal bonds relative to taxable bonds when bond prices fall. Finally, investors are uncertain about future income tax rates, and will require some premium to compensate them for this uncertainty. While the nature of each of these risks is quite different, we will use the term *liquidity premium* for the additional interest rate ratio required by investors to compensate for the extra risks.

We assume that the liquidity premium is zero for the first dollar of municipal bonds held by an investor; if an investor holds no municipals, he considers the first dollar of municipals to be equivalent to a dollar of taxable bonds. This means that for intramarginal investors, the interest rate ratio will exceed the value $(1 - t)$ by the liquidity premium required to induce them to hold municipal bonds. But for the marginal investor, who holds a small amount of municipal bonds, the interest rate ratio is $(1 - t_m)$, where t_m is the marginal investor's tax rate.

Figure 6 shows the demand functions for municipal bonds of two investors, the "first investor," whose tax rate, t_{max}, is the highest, and the "marginal investor," with tax rate t_m. The quantity of municipal bonds acquired is along the horizontal axis. The vertical axis shows the interest rate ratio. The horizontal lines at interest rate ratios $(1 - t_{max})$ and $(1 - t_m)$, respectively, show each investor's demand function for municipal bonds *if* tax-exempt and taxable bonds are perfect substitutes. In that case, investors do not require a liquidity premium and only tax rates matter in determining whether to buy a tax-exempt or a taxable bond. The upward-sloping solid lines labeled D_1 and D_m are the actual demand functions, with the vertical distance to the broken line representing the liquidity premium required to induce the investor to hold each quantity of municipal bonds.

Figure 6 assumes that the bond markets have settled into an equilibrium in which the interest rate ratio is just sufficient to induce a marginal investor with tax rate t_m to buy a small amount of tax-exempt bonds. The equilibrium interest rate ratio is $(1 - t_m)$, which is high enough to induce the first investor to hold Q_1^* in tax-exempt bonds. For each investor, the interest rate ratio is composed of two parts. The first is the ratio required to give tax-exempts the same after-tax return as taxable bonds; for the first investor this is $(1 - t_{max})$. The second part is the liquidity premium required to compensate intramarginal investors for the extra risks they attach, at the margin, to tax-exempt bonds. For the first investor the liquidity component is $l(Q_1^*)$. For the marginal investor the liquidity component is (by assumption) zero.

Following an unfortunate convention, we will use the term *windfall income* to designate any income from tax-exempts in excess of the income required to break even on an after-tax basis. For the first investor the dollar value of windfall income is measured by R_T^* (area A + area B).* But R_T^* area B is not really a windfall,

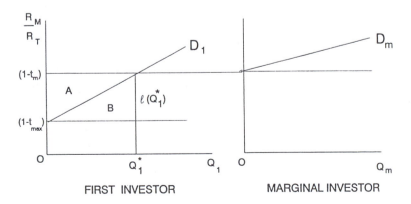

Figure 6   Individual investors in the municipal bond market.

for it is the amount of extra income required to induce the investor to hold Q_1^* of municipal bonds. The only true excess income is measured by R_T^* area A. This is the "investor's surplus," which exists because the investor earns interest on her intramarginal investment in excess of the amount required. Note that in the case of a linear demand function, the investor's surplus will be 50% of the investor's windfall income.

Figure 7 shows the municipal bond market under these conditions. The vertical axis represents the interest rate ratio while the horizontal axis shows the quantity of municipal bonds outstanding. The upward-sloping schedule, marked DD, is the demand function for municipal bonds; as the interest rate ratio rises, more investors are induced by tax considerations to hold municipal bonds. As the market travels up the demand schedule, the marginal tax rate of investors is falling because new investors drawn into the market have lower tax rates.

The bond supply schedule, SS, is assumed to be moderately sensitive to the municipal bond rate, hence it is downward-sloping but with a steep slope. The bond supply function will also shift with the level of the taxable bond rate. To understand this, note that while the supply of municipal bonds is affected by the interest rate on municipal bonds, the vertical axis in Figure 7 is the interest rate *ratio*, which depends on both interest rates. As a result, the position of the supply schedule will depend upon the level of the taxable bond rate; at any given rate ratio, a higher R_T implies a higher municipal bond rate, and a lower quantity of tax-exempt bonds issued. Thus, SS will shift leftward (rightward) when R_T rises (falls). For expository purposes, we will assume that R_T is at its equilibrium level and is not changing.

This model suggests that there are two basic demand-side determinants of the municipal bond yield. The first is the maximum tax rate t_{max}. A fall in t_{max} will make municipal bonds less attractive to the first investor, encouraging him to buy less municipals and shifting DD to the left.* The second factor is the progressivity of the federal income tax schedule; a less progressive tax rate schedule will create a flatter slope of the DD schedule so that it rotates clockwise at the rate ratio $(1 - t_{max})$. This creates a lower rate ratio. Thus, the interest rate ratio should be inversely related to the maximum tax rate and directly related to the degree of progressivity in income tax rates. We shall see that our econometric analysis supports these hypotheses.

2. The "New View" of Municipal Bond Yields

Before proceeding, we note that in recent years another school of thought on municipal bond yield determination has arisen. This school, associated with Fama (1977) and Miller (1977), argues that the personal income tax rate schedule—the focal point of the traditional explanation—is irrelevant, and that the interest rate ratio is determined by the corporate income tax rate (t_c).

The "new view" can be understood in two ways. Fama argued that corporations, primarily commercial

---

*Because the vertical axis is in units of taxable interest, any area in Fig. 7 is measured in units of the taxable interest rate. To convert an area to a dollar value we must multiply it by R_T. This is why the dollar value of windfall income is R_T^* (area A + area B), rather than simply area A plus area B.

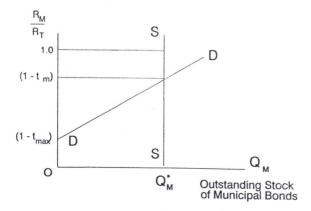

Figure 7   Determination of the interest rate ratio.

banks, are the marginal investors in municipal bonds. Thus, the DD schedule follows the personal tax rate schedule for low quantities of municipal bonds outstanding; for these quantities, individuals with tax rates between t_{max} and t_c will provide the funds. However, the DD schedule becomes horizontal at a ratio of $(1 - t_c)$; any tendency for the ratio to go above that level will induce banks to enter the market in sufficient volume to restore the ratio to $(1 - t_c)$. Because the volume of municipal bonds outstanding is great enough to fully absorb the funds of high-bracket investors, commercial banks become the marginal investors and the equilibrium rate ratio will be $R_M/R_T = (1 - t_c)$.

Miller's explanation of the new view is slightly more exotic. According to the stripped-down Miller version, individual investors—and the personal tax rate schedule—determine the demand function, so DD remains the effective demand schedule. But Miller argues that the effective supply schedule for municipal bonds is horizontal at the interest rate ratio $(1 - t_c)$.

In Miller's view, common stocks and municipal bonds are perfect substitutes in investors' portfolios, and common stocks are virtually tax-exempt.* As a result, in equilibrium the equality $R_M = R_S$ will hold, where R_S is the yield on common stocks. Because a corporation will choose its debt-equity ratio so as to minimize its cost of capital, if the required return on stocks (R_S) exceeds the after-tax cost of debt (R_T), the corporation will sell bonds; this occurs when $R_S/R_T > (1 - t_c)$. On the other hand, if the cost of equity is less than the after-tax cost of debt, corporations will sell equity; this occurs when $R_S/R_T < (1 - t_c)$. Since all corporations face the same tax rate, all will either finance themselves with debt or with equity unless $R_S/R_T = (1 - t_c)$, in which case each firm will be indifferent; some firms will choose debt, others will choose equity and still others will finance themselves with both debt and equity. This describes the equilibrium.

Because equity and municipal bonds are (by assumption) perfect substitutes in investor's portfolios, $R_S = R_M$, and the debt-equity decisions of corporations will ensure that $R_M/R_T = (1 - t_c)$; the interest rate ratio is determined by the corporate income tax rate. In effect, the supply schedule SS is horizontal at the interest rate ratio $(1 - t_c)$. At any higher ratio municipalities will not alter their debt decision, but corporations will sell less equity that, under the Miller assumptions, is equivalent to less tax-exempt debt.

The new view received some empirical support in its early years, a prominent example being the work of Trczinka (1982). However, it fails to fit the 1980s data, as shown by Fortune (1988) who used Trczinka's method, and by Peek and Wilcox (1986), who used a different method. Furthermore, the event analyses by Poterba (1986; 1989) have demonstrated the importance of the personal income tax.

In addition, recent changes in the structure of the market clearly have weakened any validity of the new view. For example, Fama's explanation is based on high commercial bank participation in the municipal bond market, but banks were notoriously absent from the market for municipal bonds in the 1980s. Also, Miller's explanation is less convincing in the 1980s, when corporations clearly were not balancing debt and equity at the margin, but were apparently at a corner solution: issuing debt in large quantities and retiring equity.

3. The Term Structure of Municipal Bond Yields

The analysis of the previous sections assumes a single type of municipal bond, and does not allow us to analyze such issues as the term structure of municipal bond yields. We have seen that the interest rate ratio rose sharply after 1986 for 1-year and 5-year terms, while it changed little for 20-year bonds. Figures 1 and 3 show clearly that this happened, and also show that after 1986 the 1-year ratio was almost equal to the 5-year ratio.

The most widely held explanation of these changes in the term structure of municipal bond yields appeals to the notion of "market segmentation." For much of this century commercial banks have been important investors in the market for tax-exempt debt, and banks prefer (other things being equal) to invest in securities with short-to-intermediate maturities. Households, on the other hand, have traditionally preferred longer-term bonds. This description of the municipal bond market certainly fit the data over the years when it was formed—the 1960s and 1970s.

However, as noted above, this picture changed dramatically in the mid-1980s, when banks withdrew from investments in municipal securities. Because banks typically hold shorter maturities, the primary impact of this withdrawal was in those maturities. This meant that one or both of two things had to happen. First, municipalities had to reduce their issue of short-to-intermediate debt; this could be accomplished by reducing

---

*Note that if taxables and tax-exempts were perfect substitutes, this would not be true. High-bracket investors would invest all of their available funds in tax-exempts. A change in the tax rate they face will alter the windfall income they receive, but not alter the amount invested.

capital outlays, by increasing use of tax revenues to finance capital outlays, or by substituting longer-term debt for short-to-intermediate bonds. Second, some nonbank sectors had to be induced to acquire short-to-intermediate debt when they would not otherwise have done so. Both of these adjustments require a rise in short-to-intermediate municipal bond yields relative to long-term yields.

The primary adjustment was of the second form; households responded by increasing their ownership of municipal bonds, much of this in the short-to-intermediate maturities. The shortening of average maturities in the household sector was aided by several financial innovations that reduced the risks (and increased the liquidity) of municipal bonds. Chief among these were the formation of mutual funds specializing in municipal debt of all maturities, but, particularly of short-to-intermediate maturities. These allowed households with small portfolios to diversify their holdings as well as to gain liquidity by check-writing privileges and by redemption of shares at net asset value. A second innovation was the development of private firms providing municipal bond insurance. While bond insurance had been first provided in the early 1970s, the explosion of the market in the 1980s was induced by the growing dominance of households in the municipal bond market.

4. The Effect of Future Tax Rates

The bond yields that prevail at any moment will be affected by anticipations of future tax rates; if investors believe that tax rates will rise (fall) in the future, they will require a lower (higher) yield on newly issued municipal bonds, relative to the yield on newly issued taxable bonds.

It is difficult to quantify the role played by anticipations of tax rates; nobody keeps a record of what "the market" thinks tax rates will be in the future. One approach is to use "event analysis" to infer the influence of anticipated taxes. Poterba (1986) and Fortune (1988) have investigated the behavior of interest rates at times of tax policy changes, and find that the behavior of interest rates is consistent with the influence of anticipated tax rates on municipal bond yields.

Another approach is to assume that the market correctly anticipates the future. In this case, actual future tax rates can be used to infer the effect of tax rate anticipations at any moment. However, the notion that—on average—the market is correct has received considerable attention, and very little support, from academics. For example, Fortune (1991) surveys the evidence from the stock market, concluding that "the efficient market" is a concept worth selling short.

A third approach, adopted here, is to use market data to infer tax rate anticipations. Suppose that an estimate is sought for the tax rate anticipated by the marginal investor in municipal bonds between 5 and 10 years from now, denoted by t_{5-10}. If $R_{M,5,10}$ as the yield on a municipal bond bought 5 years from now that matures 10 years from now, and $R_{T,5,10}$ is the yield on an equivalent taxable bond, the implied future tax rate is $t_{5-10} = 1 - (R_{M,5,10}/R_{T,5,10})$.

Unfortunately, no direct information on future interest rates is available. While there is a futures market in municipal bonds, it does not extend very far into the future and it is based on a bond yield index, not on yields for specific securities. However, indirect information can be found in the term structure of interest rates. According to the expectations hypothesis, the most widely held theory of the term structure, the yield to maturity on a 10- year municipal bond bought now ($R_{M,0,10}$) is mathematically related to the yield on a 5-year bond bought now ($R_{M,0,5}$) and to the expected yield on a 5-year bond bought in 5 years ($R_{M,5,10}$). The relationship is

$$(1 + R_{M,0,10})^{10} = (1 + R_{M,0,5})^5(1 + R_{M,5,10})^5 \tag{4}$$

According to this relationship, a dollar invested now in a 10-year bond will have an accumulated value equal to the accumulated value in 10 years of a sequence of two investments: a dollar invested now in a 5-year bond, followed by investment of the accumulated value in a second 5-year bond maturing 5 years from that date of purchase.

If the relationship did not hold, investors would not diversify their portfolios by holding both 5-year and 10-year bonds. Consider investors with a 10-year horizon. If the left side of Eq. (4) exceeds the right side, those investors would hold only 10-year bonds because the terminal value would exceed the terminal value from buying 5-year bonds and reinvesting the proceeds at maturity in 5-year bonds. If, on the other hand, the left side is less than the right side, the investors would buy 5-year bonds and reinvest in 5-year bonds at maturity. Only when the equality in Eq. (4) holds will investors hold both 5-year and 10-year bonds.

This relationship allows us to derive an estimate of the anticipated yield on 5-year municipal bonds in 5 years. Solving Eq. (4) for $R_{M,5,10}$ gives

$$R_{M,5,10} = [(1 + R_{M,0,10})^2/(1 + R_{M,0,5})] - 1 \qquad (5)$$

Because the values of $R_{M,0,10}$ and $R_{M,0,5}$ are known right now, Eq. (5) can be used to calculate the value of $R_{M,5,10}$ which is implicit in the yield curve. This can also be done for taxable securities. An estimate of the tax rate that is expected to prevail between 5 and 10 years in the future can then be obtained as

$$t_{5-10} = 1 - (R_{M,0,10}/R_{T,5,10}) \qquad (6)$$

This approach is subject to a number of criticisms. First, it assumes that the taxable and tax-exempt yields used in the calculations are for securities that are equivalent in all respects except tax exemption. This is unlikely, because the issuers of taxable and tax-exempt bonds are inherently different in terms of default risk, because call features or other special features might make the bonds different, and because transactions costs can differ, with municipal bonds generally less liquid and traded in a thinner market than taxable bonds.

Second, this approach assumes that investors are indifferent to the maturity structure of their portfolio; no "market segmentation" exists, all investors care about is the expected yield on their portfolios, and market risks are irrelevant to portfolio decisions.

Using Salomon Brothers data for 5-year and 10-year prime municipal bonds and U.S. Treasury bonds, estimates of t_{5-10} have been derived. These are shown in Fig. 8. The implied future tax rate shows a good bit of noise in it, as one would expect because of the potential for factors such as call features to distort the yield curve relationships, but the general outlines of the series seem to fit reasonable well; the implied future tax rate fell sharply after 1979 in apparent anticipation of the tax rate reductions in the 1981 ERTA. Furthermore, after 1982 the implied future tax rate is about 15 to 20%, consistent with the low tax rates introduced in the 1981 ERTA and subsequent tax acts. Also, the mid-to-late 1970s show a high anticipated future tax rate, a result consistent with the discussions of the times, an example being President Carter's statement that "the tax system is a disgrace to the human race." It is no surprise that this period of high anticipated tax rates was also a period of low interest rate ratios.

B.   Econometric Analysis

In this section we estimate a model of interest rate ratios. The variables to be explained are four rate ratios, the three shown in Fig. 3 plus the 10-year ratio, for the period from June 1970 through December 1989.

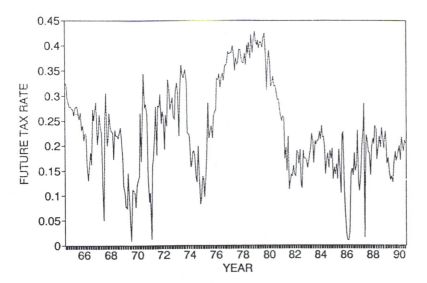

Figure 8   Future tax rate (5–10 years out). *Source*: Salomon Brothers, Inc. and author's calculations.

Our model uses several tax rate variables to capture the effect of changes in tax rate legislation. To represent the personal income tax rate schedule, we have used the *maximum personal income tax rate* (TMAX), and a measure of *tax rate progressivity* (PROGRSV), defined as the difference between the maximum personal tax rate and the tax rate for an individual with $25,000 of real taxable income (see Fig. 5). The maximum tax rate employed in defining these variables is the rate paid by those in the highest income bracket. Until 1987, this was also the highest rate levied, but the 1986 tax reform act introduced a bubble in the tax rate schedule so that the highest income taxpayers paid less than the maximum tax rate. Thus, for the period from 1988 to 1990 we use 28% as the maximum tax rate, not the 33% bubble rate.

The traditional view of municipal bond yields predicts that the first (TMAX) should have a negative coefficient, while the coefficient on the second (PROGRSV) should be positive; a more progressive tax rate schedule, given the maximum rate, should increase municipal bond yields relative to taxable bond yields. Note that because the tax rate data are available annually, we have assigned the same tax rate to each month in the year.

Our econometric model does not incorporate the new view for two reasons. First, as noted above, there is abundant evidence against the hypothesis that corporate income tax rates dominate the determination of the interest rate ratios. Second, an experiment in which we included the maximum corporate income tax rate did not support the new view; the corporate income tax rate had the wrong sign and was not statistically significant.

In order to capture the influence of *anticipated future tax rates*, we have constructed several measures of the implicit future tax rate: t_{2-5} is the implicit tax rate for 2 to 5 years in the future, t_{5-10} is the implicit tax rate 5 to 10 years out, and t_{5-20} is the implicit tax rate 5 to 20 years hence. Each is constructed from the yield curve data that were used to construct Fig. 3, using the method described above. These constructed variables are available for every month in the sample. Rather than include all three in the regression for each rate ratio, we included only the ones that seemed most relevant: t_{5-20} in the 20-year regression, t_{5-10} in the 10-year regression, and t_{2-5} in the 5-year regression. Anticipated future tax rates were excluded from the 1-year regression because the relevant tax rate is known at the time of purchase.

We have argued that the *anticipated variability of bond prices* should affect the interest rate ratio because market discounts on municipal bonds are subject to capital gains taxes, placing them at a disadvantage relative to taxable bonds if bond prices fall, but giving them no advantage if bond prices rise. In order to reflect this, we have used the Ibbotson Associates (1990) data on the monthly rate of change in prices of long-term Treasury bonds. These data have been used to construct a volatility index for each month. The result is a variable, called VOLATILE, available for each month.*

Three dummy variables were used to capture fixed effects. One, labeled NY, is for the New York City financial crisis, which is assumed to occur in the period from June 1975 to December 1976. During this period the yields on lower-rated municipal bonds rose relative to yields on prime grade bonds, but the New York City crisis could affect prime grade bonds as well, although the direction of effect is not clear; NY could have a positive coefficient because the quality of high-grade bonds was called into question, or it could have a negative coefficient because of a flight to quality that drives high-grade bond yields down.

A second dummy variable, named TRA86, applies to the period January 1987 through the end of the sample. We know that the 1986 tax reform act had a variety of effects on the municipal bond market other that those that operate through tax rates (which are already captured in TMAX and PROGRSV). The limits on private-activity bonds and the severe limits on other tax shelters should induce a negative coefficient on TRA86, but the elimination of commercial bank deductibility of municipal carrying costs should have a positive effect. While we can not specify the sign of the coefficient on TRA86 a priori, the common view is that the elimination of carrying cost deductibility dominated the effect.

The third dummy variable, labeled Y86, is for the 12 months of 1986. This is introduced to capture any effects of the active and often-changing debate about tax policy during 1986.

Estimation of the model was done with three stage least squares (3SLS), using a correction for first-order autocorrelation. Three stage least squares is a method of joint estimation of a system of equations combining seemingly unrelated regression (SURE) and two stage least squares (2SLS). The four interest rate ratios are

---

*The rate of change in bond prices is Ibbotson's total return on long-term government bonds in each month less the income return due to coupons. The monthly volatility index is the square of the deviation of the bond price change from its sample mean, divided by the sample variance. The variable VOLATILE is the simple average of the volatility measure in the past 3 months.

viewed as a four-equation system because of the potential for omitted variables common to interest rates at all four maturities. The SURE method employs this information on correlation between residuals to derive efficient estimates of the parameters.

The 2SLS aspect of 3SLS was necessary because the variables for anticipated future tax rates are endogenous; they are derived from the term structure of interest rates, and therefore use the same interest rates that are used in defining the interest rate ratios. In order to eliminate this problem of feedback from the dependent variables to the variables t_{2-5}, t_{5-10}, and t_{5-20} we used a rather long list of instruments.*

The estimation was done with a correction for first-order autocorrelation. The specific method of estimation involved two steps. First, we estimated each of the four equations separately using 2SLS with an autocorrelation correction. This gives four autocorrelation coefficients, one for each equation; the autocorrelation coefficients estimated at this stage are reported as the variable RHO. Second, the variables in each equation were transformed to partial differences using the autocorrelation coefficient estimated for that equation in the first stage, after which the transformed variables were employed in a 3SLS estimation of the four-equation system.

The results, reported in Table 4, provide strong support for the insights gained from our discussion of tax legislation. With respect to the fixed effects, we find that the New York City financial crisis played no role; the coefficient is negative in each equation, suggesting that this period was one of lower municipal bond yields, but it is not statistically significant.

The dummy variable Y86 is positive and statistically significant for all maturities. The very active debate about tax policy in 1986 increased the interest rate ratios because of the uncertainty about future tax rates. The implied increase in the rate ratios in 1986 was about 0.025 for 20-year bonds, 0.05 for 10-year bonds, 0.02 for 5-year bonds, and 0.08 for 1-year bonds. At the 1988 to 1990 averages of Treasury bond yields, these rate ratio increases imply an increase in municipal bond yields by 23 bp, 41 bp, 15 bp, and 62 bp, respectively.[†]

TRA86 tells us that the period of effectiveness of the 1986 TRA (1987 and after) was also a period of higher interest rate ratios. Like Y86, the impact appears to be greatest for 1-year bonds, which had a rate ratio 0.10 higher after 1986, but it was both statistically and economically significant (roughly 0.01 to 0.02) for other maturities. This is predicted from the elimination of the deduction for commercial bank carrying costs. The municipal bond yield effects of TRA86, evaluated at 1988 to 1990 Treasury bond yields, were 10 bp for 20-year bonds, 20 bp for 10-year bonds, 19 bp for 5-year bonds, and 82 bp for 1-year bonds.

The tax rate variables are all statistically significant with the signs predicted by our theory. According to the estimated coefficients, the reduction in the maximum tax rate (TMAX) was 22% (from 50% to 28%) after the 1986 tax reform act reduced the interest rate ratios by about 0.05 for 20-year bonds, 0.10 for 10-year bonds, 0.04 for 5- year bonds and 0.18 for 1- year bonds.[‡] The corresponding declines in municipal bond yields, evaluated at 1988 to 1990 Treasury bond yield levels, were 46 bp, 82 bp, 35 bp, and 146 bp, respectively.

The tax progressivity variable (PROGRSV) also is statistically and economically significant in each equation. The 1986 tax reform act reduced the progressivity variable by 22%, from 22% in 1985 to 0 in 1988. This reduced the rate ratios by 0.04 for 20-year bonds, 0.07 for 10-year bonds, 0.03 for 5-year bonds, and 0.15 for 1- year bonds.[§] The corresponding decreases in municipal bond yields are 32 bp, 57 bp, 27 bp, and 120 bp.

In each equation the coefficient on anticipated future tax rates is negative and statistically significant; when the market expects tax rates to be high, the interest rate ratio is reduced as tax-exempt bonds are substituted for taxable bonds. The very high t-statistics attest to the statistical importance of tax rate anticipations, and the size of the coefficients attests to their economic significance.

In order to assess the economic significance of the 1986 tax reform act we have calculated the change in the interest rate ratio between 1982 to 1985 and 1988 to 1990 attributable to changes in statutory tax rates

---

*The instruments were all of the exogenous variables in the system, including a constant term, as well as the following additional instruments, all available monthly: a time trend, the level of the CPI, the rate of inflation (CPI), the civilian unemployment rate, real personal income, the earnings-price ratio for the S&P500, and the 3-month Treasury bill rate.

[†]The 1988- 1990 averages for Treasury bond yields were 8.7% for 20 years, 8.6% for 10 years, 8.5% for 5 years, and 8.0% for 1 year.

[‡]The effects are calculated as the reported coefficients on TMAX times 22 (the decline in the maximum tax rate) .

[§]The effects are calculated as the reported coeffients on PROGRSV times 22(the decline in the progressivity variable) .

Table 4 Determinants of Interest Rate Ratios Three-Stage Least Squares Regression Results 1-, 5-, 10-, and 20-Year Maturities

(June 1970–Dec. 1989)

Independent variable	Dependent variable (R_M/R_T) maturity			
	Twenty-year	Ten-year	Five-year	One-year
Constant	0.3841	0.4636	0.3545	0.3275
	(42.53)	(28.81)	(44.35)	(8.57)
t_{5-20}	−0.7004	—	—	—
	(79.85)			
t_{5-10}	—	−0.4832	—	—
		(28.51)		
t_{2-5}	—	—	−0.7705	—
			(153.49)	
Volatile	0.0011	0.0019	0.0014	0.0070
	(1.46)	(1.54)	(1.96)	(2.17)
TMAX	−0.0024	−0.0043	−0.0019	−0.0083
	(3.27)	(4.01)	(2.69)	(2.73)
PROGRSV	0.0017	0.0031	0.0015	0.0071
	(2.42)	(3.10)	(2.38)	(2.47)
NY	−0.0010	−0.0031	−0.0018	−0.0089
	(0.22)	(0.49)	(0.43)	(0.48)
1986	0.0258	0.0475	0.0183	0.0780
	(4.60)	(5.74)	(3.44)	(3.30)
TRA86	0.0115	0.0226	0.0221	0.1019
	(1.86)	(2.50)	(3.75)	(3.92)
RHO	0.6088	0.5170	0.6310	0.6023
	(2.82)	(1.80)	(5.47)	(5.541)
$\overline{R}^2$	0.9514	0.8818	0.9526	0.3071
DW	2.1845	1.9849	2.1597	2.1134

Note: The method of estimation is 3SLS with correction for first-order autocorrelation; RHP is the autocorrelation coefficient. The $\overline{R}^2$ and DW are for the transformed equations. The instruments are used for the future tax rate variables; see footnote for instrument list. Numbers in parentheses are absolute values of t-statistics. The t-statistics are corrected for instrumental variables estimation.

(TMAX and PROGRSV), as well as the fixed effect captured in the dummy variable TRA86. We have also converted the changes in rate ratios to changes in municipal bond yields using the 1988–1990 average values of the four Treasury bond yields.

The results are reported in the top portion of Table 5. These three tax policy variables account for a rise in the municipal bond yield by 25 to 44 bp for the longer maturities, and by a large 107 bp for the 1-year maturity. The primary source of the large increase at the 1-year maturity is the TRA86 dummy variable. That this is most important at the short maturity is consistent with the withdrawal of a primary short-term lender—commercial banks—from the tax-exempt debt market.

Another avenue for tax policy is anticipated tax rates. The bottom portion of Table 5 assesses the effects of our anticipation variables after the 1986 tax reform act. The results suggest only a minor effect of tax rate anticipations for 20-year and 10-year bonds; the implied yield changes are −11 bp and −7 bp, respectively. However, we find a 52 bp *increase* in 5-year yields in the post-TRA86 period. This suggests that tax rates were expected to decline further in this period.

The combined effect of all four tax policy variables in Table 5 is to increase municipal bond yields after the 1986 tax reform act. The impacts are greater for shorter-term bonds, ranging from a mild 14-bp increase for 20-year bonds to a 107-bp increase for 1-year bonds.

Bond price volatility (VOLATILE) increases the rate ratios, as our discussion of capital gains taxation

Table 5   Effects of Tax Legislation on Interest Rate Ratios and Municipal
Bond Yields

(1982–1985/1988–1990)

Independent Variable	Maturity			
	Twenty-year	Ten-year	Five-year	One-year
	Tax policy variables			
TMAX	+0.0528	+0.0946	+0.0418	+0.1826
PROGRSV	−0.0361	−0.0659	−0.0319	−0.1509
TRA86	+0.0115	+0.0226	+0.0221	+0.1019
Subtotal ratio	+0.0282	+0.0513	+0.0320	+0.1336
R_M	+ 25 bp	+ 44 bp	+ 27 bp	+107 bp
	Anticipated tax rate variables			
T_{5-20}	−0.0123	na	na	na
T_{5-10}	na	−0.0076	na	na
T_{2-5}	na	na	+0.0616	na
Subtotal ratio	−0.0123	−0.0076	+0.0616	na
R_M	− 11 bp	− 7 bp	+ 52 bp	na
Total ratio	+0.0159	+0.0437	+0.0936	+0.1336
R_M	+ 14 bp	+ 37 bp	+ 79 bp	+107 bp

Source: Coefficients in Table 4 times average values of variables in 1982–1985 and
1988–1990. The conversion from interest rate ratios to municipal bond yields is done
at the 1988–1990 average for Treasury bond yields: 8.75%, 8.63%, 8.45%, and
8.01%, respectively. ("bp" denotes basis points. "na" denotes not applicable.)

suggests. While the t-statistics suggest that this effect is not as reliable as the effect of tax variables, the
evidence does support the hypothesis that the more volatile the bond prices (hence the higher the probability
of a price decrease) the less desirable the municipal bonds. Our explanation of this is the effect of capital
gains taxes on the relative desirability of tax-exempt and taxable bonds when market discounts exist.

We conclude that the data provide very strong support for the role of personal income tax legislation,
and of the elimination of bank deductibility of carrying costs, in affecting interest rate ratios.

V. PUBLIC POLICY ASPECTS OF TAX EXEMPTION

Fifty years ago Henry C. Simons challenged the concept of tax exemption, remarking that (Simons, 1938)

> The exemption of the interest payments on an enormous amount of government bonds . . . is a flaw of major
> importance. It opens the way to deliberate avoidance on a grand scale . . . the exemption not only undermines
> the program of progressive personal taxation but also introduces a large measure of differentiation in favor of
> those whose role in our economy is merely that of rentiers.

While the "program of progressive personal taxation" appeared to have been left behind by the 1986
tax reform act, Simons' criticism of the exemption is still widely held. The purpose of this section is to identify
the problems posed by tax exemption, and to assess some alternatives. Our analysis goes well beyond the
issue of equity, which is the heart of Simons's complaint. We ask whether the results of tax exemption represent
an appropriate outcome, and we question whether tax exemption is really necessary to achieve the benefits
that are stated in its favor. The first section addresses three major problems of municipal bond market
performance: market instability, vertical equity, and financial efficiency. These problems have driven the
debate about reform of the market. The second section discusses estimates of the effect of the exemption on
federal tax revenues, on the interest savings of state and local governments, and on financial efficiency. The

third section analyzes several proposals for reform that can mitigate the problems outlined in the previous sections.

A. Municipal Bond Market Performance

Why does Congress allow municipal interest to be exempted from federal taxes in the face of a very large chronic deficit in the federal budget, even though it is now clear that there is no constitutional requirement that this tax policy continue? The rhetoric of tax exemption is philosophical, appealing to notions of appropriate intergovernmental relations and, in particular, to the doctrine of reciprocal immunity: no level of government should use its taxing authority to impose harm on another level of government. But the true force behind tax exemption is that it provides states and local governments with a valuable subsidy that can be enjoyed at their discretion. The political support for the exemption is very strong, and it will continue unless a better way can be found to structure a subsidy to states and local governments.

An assessment of the economics of tax exemption, which is a subsidy of capital costs, suggests that the case for it is weak. The economic argument must rest on the view that, in the absence of a capital cost subsidy, states and local governments will produce an inadequate amount of public services with insufficient capital intensity. While the final word on this issue is not yet spoken, the debate continues in the current discussion about public infrastructure, such as highways, schools, and solid waste facilities. For example, Munnell (1990) finds a high marginal productivity of infrastructure, suggesting that there is an inadequate amount available, while Hulten and Schwab (1991) find no indication of inadequate infrastructure.

However, even if we believe that there is insufficient infrastructure, we argue that there are better methods than tax exemption to achieve these goals. Three fundamental criticisms of tax exemption have received the most attention. The first criticism is that tax exemption induces unnecessary volatility into municipal bond yields. According to this *market instability* argument, tax exemption narrows the market for municipal bonds and makes that market more sensitive to changes in the distribution of investible funds between individuals and financial institutions, as well as to other factors that affect financial markets. The result is that municipal bond yields are more volatile than yields on comparable taxable bonds, introducing cyclical variations in the cost of capital for states and local governments. This also introduces variability into the value of the capital-cost subsidy enjoyed by municipalities.

The second criticism, echoing Simons's complaint, is that tax exemption violates the concept of *distributional equity;* it confers upon the wealthy a valuable opportunity to increase their after-tax income, and it erodes the degree of vertical equity in our tax system by allowing the wealthy to avoid taxation in ways not available to the less affluent. This criticism is the most commonly heard in popular discussions of tax exemption.

The third criticism is that tax exemption is *financially inefficient* because it imposes greater costs on federal taxpapers than the benefits it confers upon state and local governments. Note that the word *efficiency* in this context is used quite differently from the engineering context (getting the most for any given amount of inputs) or the economic context (Pareto optimality, or making each person as well off as possible given the positions of all other people). The focus of financial efficiency is on the very narrow question of how much benefit is received by lower levels of government per dollar of cost to the federal treasury.

A fourth criticism is that tax exemption fails to encourage economic efficiency. Instead, it is argued, tax exemption encourages overproduction of public services as well as use of too much capital by the public sector. A corollary is that the private sector has inadequate capital with which to produce goods and services. This view is based on the assumption that a competitive market economy, unfettered by government intervention in prices, will induce an appropriate allocation of resources. We will discuss this issue in the third part of this section.

1. Market Instability

Figure 3, discussed in Section II, showed the interest rate ratio for municipal bonds of 1-year, 5-year, 10-year, and 20-year maturities. For each maturity, this is defined as the ratio of the yield-to-maturity on high-quality municipal bonds (Salomon Brothers prime grade) to the yield on U.S. Treasury bonds of the same maturity. We found in Section IV that much of the movement in these interest rate ratios can be explained by changes in the income tax code.

It is clear that the interest rate ratio is highly variable for each maturity. From high ratios in the early 1970s, the ratio declined sharply until the early 1980s, after which it rose again. Thus, municipal bond yields are more volatile than yields on U.S. Treasury bonds. It is interesting to note, however, that much of this volatility disappeared in the last half of the 1980s. In Section IV we concluded that the reduction in volatility in the 1980s was largely the result of the reduced progressivity of the tax system, as well as of tax policies that reduced commercial bank incentives to hold municipal bonds.

As we shall see, the interest rate ratio can be interpreted as determined by the tax rate of the marginal investor in tax-exempt bonds; indeed, this *implicit tax rate* can be inferred from interest rate data as $t_m = 1 - (R_M/R_T)$. The implicit tax rate is also the rate of subsidy of state and local capital costs due to tax exemption. For example, if the marginal investor's tax rate is 30%, then state and local governments face a cost of capital that is only 70% of the cost associated with issuing taxable bonds. Thus, the variation in the interest rate ratio translates into variation in the rate of subsidy.

2. *Financial Efficiency and Vertical Equity*

In order to assess the efficiency and equity problems, we use the model of the municipal bond market developed in Section IV. The next few paragraphs repeat some of that analysis for readers who might have missed it.

We assume that municipal bonds and taxable bonds are substitutes in investors' portfolios. Each investor will choose an amount of municipal bonds based on his tax rate and on his assessments of the nonpecuniary advantages or disadvantages of municipal bonds. Among these nonpecuniary factors are differences in call features, tax rate uncertainty, duration, and liquidity. The optimal holding of municipal bonds will be that quantity for which $(R_M/R_T) = l + (1 - t)$, where t is his tax rate and l is the "liquidity premium" required by the investor. The liquidity premium is the investor's compensation for nonpecuniary characteristics. While the tax rate is exogenous to the investor's decision, the liquidity premium is endogenous, as an investor contemplates increasing the amount he invests in municipal bonds, he will require a higher interest rate ratio to compensate for the increased risk and lower liquidity of municipal bonds.

We also assume that the liquidity premium is zero for the first dollar of municipal bonds held by an investor; if an investor holds no municipals, she considers the first dollar of municipals to be equivalent to a dollar of taxable bonds. This means that for intramarginal investors, the interest rate ratio will exceed the value $(1 - t)$ by the liquidity premium required to induce them to hold municipal bonds. But for the marginal investor, who holds a small amount of municipal bonds, the interest rate ratio is $(1 - t_m)$, where t_m is the marginal investor's tax rate.

Figure 6 shows the demand functions for municipal bonds of two investors: the "first investor," whose tax rate, t_{max}, is the highest, and the "marginal investor," with tax rate t_m. The quantity of municipal bonds acquired is along the horizontal axis, and the vertical axis shows the interest rate ratio. The broken lines that are horizontal at $(1 - t_{max})$ and $(1 - t_m)$, respectively, show each investor's demand function for municipal bonds *if* tax-exempt and taxable bonds are *perfect* substitutes. The upward-sloping solid lines labeled D_1 and D_m are the actual demand functions, with the vertical distance to the broken line representing the liquidity premium required to induce the investor to hold each quantity of municipal bonds.

Figure 6 assumes that the bond markets have settled into an equilibrium in which the interest rate ratio is just sufficient to induce a marginal investor with tax rate t_m to buy a small amount of tax-exempt bonds. The equilibrium interest rate ratio is $(1 - t_m)$, which is high enough to induce the first investor to hold Q_1^* in tax-exempt bonds. For each investor the interest rate ratio has two parts. The first is the ratio required to give tax-exempts the same after-tax return as taxable bonds; for the first investor this is $(1 - t_{max})$. The second part is the liquidity premium required to induce the first investor to hold the quantity of tax exempts he chooses. For the first investor the liquidity component is $l(Q_1^*)$, but for the marginal investor the liquidity component is (by assumption) zero.

Following an unfortunate convention, we will use the term *windfall income* to designate any income from tax-exempts that is in excess of the income required to break even on an after-tax basis. Thus, for the first investor the amount of windfall income is given by the sum of areas A and B, multiplied by the taxable interest rate, or area (A+B) $*R_T$. However, (area B) $*R_T$ is not really a windfall, for it is the amount of extra income required to induce the investor to hold Q_1^*. The only true excess income is measured by (area A) $*R_T$; this is the "investor's surplus," which exists because the investor earns interest on his intramarginal investment in excess of the amount required. Note that in the case of a linear demand function, the investor's surplus will be 50% of the investor's windfall income.

Figure 7 shows the municipal bond market. The vertical line labeled SS is the supply function, showing the quantity of municipal bonds outstanding at each interest rate ratio. We have assumed that this is not interest-elastic so as to focus our attention solely on the demand function.* The upward-sloping schedule DD shows the demand for municipal bonds as a function of the interest rate ratio; this is the horizontal summation of each investor's demand function.

DD rises because as the amount of bonds outstanding increases, the rate ratio must rise by enough to induce intramarginal investors to switch some portion of their portfolios from taxable to tax-exempt bonds, as well as to induce new marginal investors to enter the market as the original marginal investors become intramarginal investors. For each quantity of municipal bonds outstanding, the vertical distance to DD is $(1 - t')$, where t' is the tax rate of the investor who buys the last dollar of municipal bonds. Thus, for the quantity actually outstanding (Q_M^*), the tax rate of the marginal investor is t_m and, recalling the assumption that $l = 0$ for the marginal investor, the equilibrium interest rate ratio is $R_M/R_T = (1 - t_m)$. The marginal investor is receiving exactly the interest rate ratio she requires to be induced to hold municipal bonds, but all intramarginal investors are receiving windfall income, a portion of which is investors' surplus.

Consider the first few dollars of municipal bonds issued. These will be sold to the investors with the highest tax rate (t_{max}); these investors would be willing to buy municipal bonds if the interest rate ratio were as low as $(1 - t_{max})$, but because Q_M^* of municipal bonds are sold, the interest rate ratio must be $(1 - t_m)$. The windfall income for the highest-bracket investors—per unit of taxable interest paid—is, therefore, $R_M/R_T - (1 - t_{max}) = t_{max} - t_m$; the dollar amount of the windfall is this times the taxable interest rate, or $(t_{max} - t_m)*R_T$. Note again that this windfall is not all unearned; some portion of it (approximately half) is a necessary reward for risk.

If we extend this analysis to compute the total windfall income for investors with higher tax rates than the marginal investor, we see that it is represented (per unit of R_T) in Fig. 9 by area B; the dollar value of the total windfall is (area B) $*R_T$. In practice, one can estimate the total windfall income using the following formula:

$$\text{Windfall income} = (\bar{t} - t_m)R_TQ_M \qquad (7)$$
$$= (\bar{t} - t_m)[R_MQ_M]/(R_M/R_T)$$

In this formula $\bar{t}$ is the "average marginal tax rate," the average of tax rates paid by all investors in municipal bonds,[†] and t_m is the marginal investor's tax rate, calculated from the observed interest rate ratio as $t_m = 1 - (R_M/R_T)$. Windfall income is the difference $(\bar{t} - t_m)$ multiplied by total interest paid on municipal bonds R_MQ_M and divided by the interest rate ratio; in Fig. 9 this amount is shown as (area B) $*R_T$.

The equity problem is inextricably connected to the financial efficiency problem. In order to assess the degree of financial efficiency, we need to calculate the federal revenues lost because of tax exemption, and to compare that with the interest payments saved by state and local governments. Consider first the interest savings experienced by states and local governments. In the absence of tax exemption, municipalities would pay an interest rate ratio of 1.0, but because of tax exemption they pay a rate ratio of $(1 - t_m)$, thereby reducing the rate ratio by $[1 - (1 - t_m)] = t_m$.[‡] Interest savings is therefore measured by (area A) $*R_T$, which is

$$\text{Interest savings} = t_mR_TQ_M \qquad (8)$$

The revenue cost to the Treasury is the sum of two components: the windfall income received by high-bracket investors plus the interest savings of municipalities. The dollar value of revenue cost is (area A + area B) $*R_T$. Thus

$$\text{Revenue cost} = R_T*[t_m + (\bar{t} - t_m)]Q_M \qquad (9)$$
$$= \bar{t}R_TQ_M$$

---

*There is considerable evidence that, in the long run, the amount of debt issued to finance capital outlays is not interest-sensitive, though the timing of debt issue is influenced by the interest rate cycle. Recent evidence does suggest, however, that arbitrage activity does induce some interest sensitivity to the supply of municipal bonds (Metcalf, 1990; 1991).

[†]The average marginal tax rate would be the sum of each investor's marginal tax rate weighted by the proportion of total municipals bonds outstanding which he or she holds, or $\bar{t} = \sum t_i s_i$, where i is an index over investors, s_i is the share of municipal bonds owned by the ith investor, and t_i is the ith investor's tax rate.

[‡]For expository convenience, we assume that $l = 0$ if tax exemption is not allowed; i.e., that all nonpecuniary factors that lead to different pricing of municipal and private bonds are due to the exemption. This is clearly not true, and as a result our analysis tends to understate the interest savings of state and local governments.

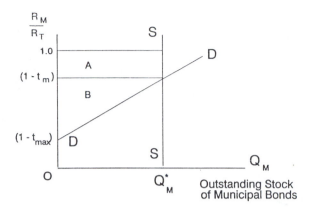

Figure 9 Costs and benefits of tax-exemption.

If, as has historically been true in the United States, there is progressive income taxation, the average marginal tax rate exceeds the marginal tax rate ($\bar{t} > t_m$) and area (A+B) > area A. Thus, the revenue cost must exceed the interest savings enjoyed by state and local governments by the amount of windfall income.

We see that the financial inefficiency of tax exemption exists because of the equity problem, so reduction of the equity problem implies progress on the efficiency problem. The degree of financial efficiency can be measured by the "efficiency index," defined as the proportion of revenue costs that accrues to state and local governments as interest savings. This efficiency index is the ratio of area A to area (A+B), or

$$\text{Efficiency index} = t_m/\bar{t} \tag{10}$$

B.　Estimates of Federal Tax Revenue Costs, Municipal Interest Savings, and Financial Efficiency

There have been several studies attempting to measure the revenue costs and efficiency of tax exemption. One approach, which we will call the *Meltzer-Ott method* (see Meltzer and Ott, 1963), is to estimate the average marginal tax rate from data on ownership of municipal bonds and on the tax rates of each sector, to estimate the marginal tax rate from the interest rate ratio, and to use Treasury or Federal Reserve Board flow-of-funds data on the outstanding stock of tax-exempt bonds. The second approach, which we call the *OMB method*, is to use the tax expenditure budget, reported annually by the Office of Management and Budget (OMB; Office of Management and Budget, 1990).

The Meltzer-Ott method was used by the Treasury Department in 1965 (Joint Economic Committee, 1966) to calculate the interest savings and revenue costs on state and local bonds sold in 1965 over the lifetime of those bonds. The Treasury Department estimated an average marginal tax rate of 42% and a marginal tax rate of 28%. The interest savings over the lifetime of gross state and local bonds newly issued in 1965 was $1.9 billion, with revenue cost of $2.9 billion. From (10) we see that these estimates imply an efficiency index of about 65%.

These early Treasury estimates are incorrect because they rest on a confusion between average and marginal analysis. The bonds sold in 1965 were incremental to the stock of outstanding municipal bonds, and the likely purchasers were the near-marginal investors in tax-exempts, for whom the windfall income would be very small. But the 1965 application of the Meltzer-Ott method assumes that the incremental supply of bonds is bought by the *average* investor, whose tax rate is measured by the average marginal tax rate. The result is a potentially serious exaggeration of the costs of new bond issues. The method employed is therefore more suitable to estimating the costs of eliminating tax exemption for all outstanding bonds; in this case the average marginal tax rate is relevant.

The Meltzer-Ott method also makes some strong assumptions about market adjustments that occur in response to tax exemption. First, the method infers tax rates from the existing pattern of ownership of municipal bonds, and assumes that in the absence of tax exemption those owners would simply have bought taxable bonds (including, of course, taxable municipals) to replace the no-longer-available tax-exempt bonds. Second, it assumes that the general level of interest rates on taxable securities is not affected by the existence of tax exemption. However, the adjustments that would occur if tax exemption did not exist are far more complex than these assumptions suggest.

Consider the second point first. The effect of tax exemption on the taxable bond rate depends on the elasticity of the supply of both taxable and tax-exempt bonds. The Meltzer-Ott method assumes that either the outstanding stock of municipal debt is independent of interest rates (as, for convenience, we assumed above), or that the private sector supply of debt is infinitely interest-elastic. In the first case, the introduction of tax exemption would induce governments to switch their issues from taxable to tax-exempt form, but investors would switch exactly that amount of their portfolios to tax-exempts and out of taxable bonds. Because the shift in demand for taxable bonds (as investors switch from taxables to tax-exempts) is exactly matched by the shift in the supply function (as governments issue tax-exempts rather than taxable bonds), the net result is no change in the taxable bond yield. In the second case, increased issues of municipal bonds in response to tax exemption "crowd out" an equal amount of taxable bonds, leaving the taxable bond yield unchanged.

If, in contrast to the assumption of the previous section, state and local governments respond to lower interest costs by issuing more bonds, the introduction of tax exemption will increase the quantity of loanable funds demanded and push up the general level of interest rates. As this happens, private borrowers will reduce their bond issues in response to the higher costs. Only if the supply of private taxable bonds is infinitely interest-sensitive will the taxable bond rate remain unchanged; if not, the taxable bond rate must go up.

Now consider the first point. The Meltzer-Ott method assumes that investors simply switch from tax-exempts to taxable bonds, so that the pattern of ownership of outstanding tax-exempt bonds tells us the relevant tax rates of those who would otherwise invest in taxable bonds. However, this need not be true. For example, suppose that tax exemption were eliminated for all outstanding municipal bonds and that current holders of tax-exempt bonds try to shift into the next best tax shelter—common stocks. In this case, portfolio changes might create no additional taxes apart from temporary capital gains tax revenues. The net effect on tax revenues will not depend on the tax rates of investors who switch from tax-exempts to equities, but upon the tax rates of those who sold the equities and switched into taxable bonds. Presumably these tax rates are lower than the rates of the former tax-exempt bondholders because the equity sellers gave up the tax shelter of municipal bonds. Thus, the method tends to overstate the relevant average marginal tax rate.

We have used the Meltzer-Ott method to estimate revenue losses and interest savings for 1990. We choose 1990 for two reasons: it is the most recent year for which data are available, and it is sufficiently long after the Tax Reform Act of 1986 to allow a new equilibrium in the ownership of municipal bonds to be reached. As discussed in Section I, the tax reform act created dramatic changes in the municipal bond market. First, the ownership of municipal bonds shifted sharply from financial institutions, particularly commercial banks, to households; while financial institutions and households each held about 50% of municipal bonds in 1985, the household share of outstanding tax-exempts rose to about 65% by the end of 1990. Second, there was a dramatic decline in the corporate income tax rate from 46% to 34%, and in the maximum personal income tax rate from 50% to 33%. Both acted to increase the interest rate ratio.

In order to derive estimates for 1990, we rely on Poterba and Feenburg (1991), who estimate that in 1988, after the tax reform act was fully implemented, the average marginal income tax rate for households was 28%. For financial institutions, which held about 35% of outstanding municipals, the tax rate was 34%. The weighted average of those tax rates is 30.1%; this is our estimate of the average marginal tax rate.

The marginal tax rate for 1990 is assumed to be 23%; this is based on the average interest rates for 1985 to 1990 of 8.77% for 10-year Treasury bonds and 6.78% for 10-year prime municipal bonds.* At the end of 1990 the outstanding stock of municipal bonds was $837 billion. Combined with the previous assumptions, the Meltzer-Ott estimates of 1990 interest savings for state and local governments is $16.9 billion, with revenue cost to the Treasury of $22.0 billion. The efficiency index is 77%.

The OMB method is based on the tax expenditure budget developed in 1968 by the Treasury Department under the direction of Stanley Surrey (Surrey, 1973). The tax expenditure budget reports the estimated cost to federal taxpayers of the loopholes in the internal revenue code during each fiscal year. Table 6 reports the revenue costs in the tax expenditure budget for FY1990 at $24.2 billion, close to the $22.0 billion derived

---

*Newly issued municipal bonds have (roughly) a 20-year average maturity. We have used 10-year bonds to allow for retirements. Indeed, if the retirement schedules are linear, the average maturity of municipal bonds would be about 10 years.

Table 6   Revenue Losses from Exclusion of Interest on
State-Local Debt, Fiscal Year 1990 (BILLIONS OF DOLLARS)

Total		$24.515
Public purpose debt		$10.730
Private purpose debt		10.785
IDBs for businesses[a]	4.310	
IDBs for authorities[b]	.720	
Mortgage revenue bonds	1.570	
Rental housing	1.180	
Student loans	.345	
Nonprofit education	.235	
Nonprofit health	2.190	
Veteran's housing	.235	

Source: *Special Analyses, Budget of the United States: FY 1990*,
Office of Management and Budget, Washington DC.
[a]Energy facilities, pollution control, sewage and water facilities,
small-issue IDBs
[b]Airports, docks, sports and convention facilities, mass commuting.

from the Meltzer-Ott method. Because these estimates are so close, we have some confidence in concluding that the costs to the federal taxpayer of tax exemption were in the range of $22 billion to $24 billion. Applying the 77% efficiency index found by the Ott-Meltzer methods, we estimate interest savings for states and local governments of $16.9 billion to $18.5 billion.

Note that in 1990 there was a large amount of private-purpose bonds receiving tax exemption, and only about 47% of the revenue losses were for public-purpose bonds. The use of tax-exempt bonds for private-activity purposes, particularly businesses, housing, and nonprofit hospitals, had been curtailed by the 1986 tax reform act, but still involves significant revenue losses on bonds issued prior to August 1986.

C. Proposals for Municipal Bond Market Reform

Several reforms of the municipal bond market have been proposed. As we shall see, none of them has been adopted. Instead, the market performance problems have been mitigated by a policy change that could not have been predicted 15 years ago: a dramatic reduction in the progressivity of personal income tax rates.

1. Elimination of the Exemption

One approach, which has little political support, is to eliminate tax exemption and to force municipalities to issue only taxable bonds. If this were done without grandfathering of outstanding bonds, the Treasury could recoup approximately $22 to $24 billion of tax revenues.

Because the efficiency, equity, and volatility problems are all due to the difference between taxable and tax-exempt bond yields, this would entirely eliminate those problems. It also would increase the cost of capital faced by states and local governments, as well as eliminate the human capital invested in underwriting tax-exempt bonds. The political power of the financial community and of state and local government officials is too great to make this a viable proposal.

2. Substitution of a Direct Subsidy

A more moderate proposal is to substitute a direct subsidy for tax exemption. In order to do this, Congress might eliminate tax exemption entirely, restricting state and local governments to issuing taxable bonds. It could then restore a capital cost subsidy by committing the Treasury to pay to each state or local government a direct subsidy related to the size of its interest payments. If the Treasury wrote a check to states and local governments in an amount equal to the proportion s of their interest payments on taxable bonds, the net interest cost of municipal borrowing would be $(1 - s)R_T$.

Elimination of tax exemption cuts the connection between tax rates and the demand for municipal bonds. In effect, the demand schedule for municipal bonds becomes horizontal at an interest rate ratio of 1.0; the interest rate ratio will be unity, or, stated differently, the municipal bond yield R_M will always equal the taxable bond rate. The total interest paid by municipalities will be $R_T Q_M$.

The payment of a direct subsidy equal to the proportion s of interest payments reduces the *net* interest paid by state and local governments on taxable bonds from R_T to $R_T(1 - s)$. Whether municipalities are better off under the direct subsidy plan than under tax exemption depends on the subsidy rate; if $s > t_m$, the direct subsidy will reduce interest costs by more than the value of tax exemption. If, in addition, $s < \bar{t}$ the direct subsidy will also reduce the costs to the Treasury. Thus, any value of the subsidy rate between $\bar{t}$ and t_m will make both levels of government better off while also eliminating the equity and efficiency problems.

Why has this reform not received much support? This seems especially surprising since, as we have seen, the subsidy rate could be set high enough to increase the capital cost subsidy to state and local governments *and* reduce the costs to federal taxpayers. The opposition comes from several sources. First high-income investors do not want to see their windfalls eliminated; this is particularly true after the 1986 tax reform act, which eliminated many other tax shelters. Second, states and local governments fear that a direct subsidy is the first step toward elimination of any subsidy; after adopting a direct subsidy, Congress might either eliminate it or drastically reduce the subsidy rate, leaving state and local governments with a much-reduced subsidy in the future. Finally, the securities industry—particularly that portion involved in underwriting and trading municipal hands—has lobbied vigorously against any changes in tax exemption because municipal bond underwriters, traders, and attorneys do not eagerly accept the consequences.

3. The Taxable Bond Option

A complete elimination of tax exemption, whether or not it is accompanied by a direct subsidy, is not in the political cards. This leads us to consider a reform that combines aspects of the current system and of taxable bonds with a direct subsidy. This is the taxable bond option (TBO), which was initially proposed in the 1940s as a method of eliminating tax-exempt securities (Seltzer, 1941), and which received considerable attention in the early 1970s (Galper and Petersen, 1971; Fortune, 1973a; 1973b; Huefner, 1971).

The TBO would give state and local governments the *option* to issue either taxable or tax-exempt bonds. In order to provide an incentive to issue bonds in the taxable form, a direct subsidy linked to the interest costs of taxable municipal bonds would be paid to the issuing government. In order to induce municipalities to issue taxable bonds, the subsidy rate must exceed the tax rate of the marginal investor in tax-exempts in the current regime; if $s < t_m$ the TBO would not be chosen because municipalities would be better off issuing tax-exempt bonds at a rate of $R_T(1 - t_m)$ than taxable bonds at a net rate of $R_T(1 - s)$. Only if s exceeds t_m would municipalities have an incentive to issue taxable bonds at the margin. But as municipalities substitute taxable bonds for tax-exempts, the volume of tax-exempt bonds would decline and the tax rate of the marginal investor in tax-exempts would increase. If the subsidy rate is less than the maximum tax rate (t_{max}), the market will settle down to a new equilibrium with municipal bonds issued in both taxable and tax-exempt forms. In this new equilibrium, the new marginal investor's tax rate will be equal to the subsidy rate ($t_m = s$), because municipalities will adjust the composition of their debt so that at the margin taxable and tax-exempt bonds carry equal net interest costs.

Consider Fig. 10, a replica of Fig. 9 with an important reinterpretation. The DD schedule is now the demand schedule for *tax-exempt* bonds, so the horizontal distance from the vertical axis to DD shows the amount of tax-exempt bonds that will be demanded at each interest rate ratio. The supply schedule SS shows the amount of total municipal debt—taxable *and* tax-exempt—that will be outstanding. Thus, at each rate ratio, the horizontal distance from DD to SS represents the amount of *taxable* bonds issued.

Figure 10 assumes a subsidy rate on taxable bonds exceeding the subsidy via tax exemption ($s > t_m$). The introduction of the TBO results in a kinked supply schedule for tax-exempt bonds. At any rate ratio less than $(1 - s)$, municipalities will issue only tax-exempts, so that SS is the supply schedule for tax-exempts when $R_M < (1 - s)R_T$. For any rate ratio greater than $(1 - s)$ there will be no tax-exempts issued, so when $R_M > (1 - s)R_T$ the supply schedule coincides with the vertical axis. Finally, at $R_M = (1 - s)R_T$ the supply schedule is horizontal between the vertical axis and SS. Thus, with a TBO the equilibrium interest rate ratio will be $(1 - s)$, the amount of tax-exempt bonds outstanding will be Q_{TE}^*, and the amount of taxable bonds will be $(Q_M^* - Q_{TE}^*)$.

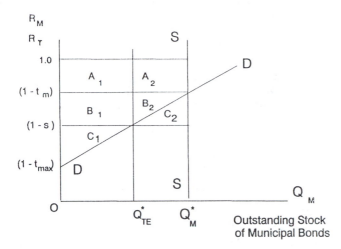

Figure 10   The taxable bond option.

The TBO will eliminate the volatility problem because the equilibrium ratio of tax-exempt to taxable interest rates will be set at $(1 - s)$; any shifts in DD or SS will alter the composition of municipal debt, but will not affect the equilibrium interest rate ratio. For example, a rightward shift in SS in Fig. 10 will lead to an increase in municipal bonds outstanding, all of which will be in the taxable form issued at the net cost of $R_T(1 - s)$. Thus, the interest rate ratio is unaffected by either supply or demand shifts because taxable bonds are the marginal form of debt.

The equity and efficiency problems are only partially eliminated by the TBO; they are totally eliminated for all taxable bonds issued, but they continue (though at a lower level) for tax-exempt bonds. To show this, Fig. 10 has been decomposed into six areas: A_1, B_1, and C_1 apply to the tax-exempt bonds sold, while A_2, B_2, and C_2 apply to taxable bonds. Table 7 shows the interpretation of each of these areas.

The TBO must cost the federal taxpayer more than reliance on tax exemption alone. This incremental cost arises because the TBO only has an effect if $s > t_m$; that is, if, at the margin, the direct subsidy exceeds the indirect subsidy of tax exemption. Because the federal costs of any tax-exempts issued will not change (being determined by the tax rates of the investors in tax-exempts), the total costs to the federal taxpayer must rise. The size of this additional cost is measured by R_T^* (area C_2).

The interest savings enjoyed by the states and by local governments will increase by R_T^*area $(B_1 + B_2 + C_2)$; R_T^*area B_1 is the value of increased interest savings on tax-exempt bonds that are still issued, while R_T^*area $(B_2 + C_2)$ is the increased savings on the volume of debt that shifts from the tax-exempt to the taxable form. Thus, a TBO will increase the interest savings enjoyed by state and local governments.

In summary, a TBO will eliminate the volatility problem and mitigate the equity and efficiency problems. The magnitude of the reduction in the equity and efficiency problems will depend upon the subsidy rate on taxable bond interest; the higher the subsidy rate the greater the share of municipal bonds issued in the taxable form, and the lower the equity and efficiency problems. Indeed, if the subsidy rate were set at t_{max}, all municipal debt would be issued in the taxable form, and we would have achieved the elimination of equity and efficiency problems. In this case we would have replicated the results achieved by legislative elimination of tax exemption and a direct subsidy rate of t_{max}.

The TBO is clearly a compromise that maintains tax exemption but gives municipalities a carrot to induce them to issue taxable bonds. It has been opposed by the same groups that have opposed the more extreme reform of completely eliminating tax exemption and replacing it with a direct subsidy on taxable municipal bonds. While the opposition has been a bit less monolithic—with, for example, less concerted opposition among municipal finance officials, it has been sufficiently vigorous to halt elimination of a TBO.

4.   A Flat Income Tax

A fourth approach is to adopt a flat-rate schedule for personal income taxes. Recall that the upward slope of the demand schedule in Fig. 7 occurs for two reasons. First, the progressivity of the income tax rate schedule

Table 7 Equity and Financial Efficiency of a Taxable Bond Option

	Before TBO	After TBO	Increment
1. U.S. Treasury cost	$A_1+A_2+B_1+B_2+C_1$	$A_1+A_2+B_1+B_2+C_1+C_2$	C_2
On tax-exempts	$A_1+A_2+B_1+B_2+C_1$	$A_1+B_1+C_1$	$-(A_2+B_2)$
On taxables	None	$A_2+B_2+C_2$	$A_2+B_2+C_2$
2. Interest savings of state-local governments	A_1+A_2	$A_1+A_2+B_1+B_2$	$B_1+B_2+C_2+C_2$
On tax-exempts	A_1+A_2	A_1+B_1	(B_1-A_2)
On taxables	None	$A_2+B_2+C_2$	$A_2+B_2+C_2$
3. Windfall income of investors	$B_1+B_2+C_1$	C_1	$-(B_1+B_2)$
On tax-exempts	$B_1+B_2+C_1$	C_1	$-(B_1+B_2)$
On taxables	None	None	None

Note: The areas in this table are defined in units of the taxable bond rate. To convert them to dollar values, each area should be multiplied by R_T.

means that additional bonds outstanding must induce a higher rate ratio to compensate investors with tax brackets lower than the initial marginal investor. Second, each investor requires a liquidity premium that increases with his holding of municipal bonds. With a flat tax rate schedule the progressivity component disappears, and the market demand function depends solely on the liquidity premium schedules of individual investors. The market demand schedule will therefore be flatter. This will reduce the instability, efficiency, and equity problems.

The Tax Reform Act of 1986 introduced a four-bracket personal tax rate schedule (15%, 28%, 33%, 28%), initiating a major step toward a flat-rate system. The 1990 Revenue Reconciliation Act, which adopted a 15%, 28%, and 31% schedule, was an additional step in this direction. While the move toward a flat-rate system was not due to any effort to mitigate the problems of tax exemption, it has had that effect. The major appeal of this approach is political. High-income investors are happy to trade the value of municipal bonds as a tax shelter for lower tax rates, state and local governments still receive a subsidy (although it is smaller) and do not face the uncertainty about continued payment of a direct subsidy, and municipal bond underwriters do not find the demand for their services is dramatically threatened.

VI. THE ECONOMICS OF TAX EXEMPTION: RESOURCE ALLOCATION AND ECONOMIC EFFICIENCY

In this section we examine the effect of tax exemption on municipal investment. In the first part we address the question of the nature of the tax subsidy to municipal investment, concluding that it is not through the direct effects of the exemption of municipal interest. Rather, it is due to the exclusion from taxable income of imputed income from municipal capital. Even so, the subsidy is equivalent to a pure capital-cost subsidy.

In the second part we formulate a simple model of the effects of a capital-cost subsidy on resource allocation. In the third part this model is applied to tax exemption of municipal activities, and explicit estimates of the resource allocation effects are computed.

A. The Nature of the Tax Subsidy to Municipal Investment

The traditional view of municipal finance, which we have espoused in previous sections, holds that tax exemption of municipal interest confers a capital-cost subsidy on state and local capital outlays. This subsidy, it is argued, arises because the tax advantages of municipal bonds are reflected in the interest rate, leading to a lower cost of debt for municipalities relative to private borrowers. In this view, the rate of subsidy—as a proportion of municipal interest costs—is equal to the tax rate of the marginal investor in municipal bonds (t_m).

In recent years a new view has emerged. This argues that tax exemption does not affect the cost of funds for a community, and therefore does not confer a subsidy to municipal investment. Examples of this new view are Southwick (1979), who found a "Modigliani-Miller theorem" for state and local government finance—the cost of capital for municipalities is independent of the means of finance—and Gordon and Metcalf (1991), who argue that there is no subsidy if the tax rate faced by a municipal resident is equal to the tax rate of the marginal investor in municipal bonds, and that

> In sum, the tax exempt status of municipal bonds should have little or no effect on capital investment by municipalities. Its main effect is to open up arbitrage opportunities for investors in extreme tax brackets (p. 78).

In this section we argue that the traditional view is valid, but with some minor modifications. This is essential to the validity of the next section, for if there were no tax subsidy to municipal investment, there would be no resource allocation effects to consider.

The new view is predicated on the assumption that municipal financial decisions are—and should be—made with a focus on the taxpayer's interests. Suppose that a municipality can borrow in the municipal bond market at the rate r_m or can finance investment by a tax levy. In the latter case, for each dollar of tax the taxpayer sacrifices an interest income of $(1-t)r$, where t is her tax rate and r is the interest rate on taxable bonds. Hence, if $r_m < (1-t)r$, the taxpayer would prefer that investment be financed by an issue of municipal bonds, while if $r_m > (1-t)r$ the taxpayer would be better served by tax finance.

The thrust of the modified traditional view is as follows: even if the new view is correct in its conclusion that tax exemption does not clearly and significantly favor debt finance over tax finance, the absence of a direct subsidy to debt finance does not imply the absence of a tax subsidy to municipal investment. While the new view does make a valid point, the traditional view can be rescued with two minor modifications.

First, the subsidy to municipal investment does not arise from tax exemption of municipal interest income. Rather, it occurs because income from the product of private-sector capital is subject to an income tax, while the product of a municipal capital is not. In this sense, municipal capital is analogous to owner-occupied housing, for which the interest costs are deductible while the imputed income is exempt from tax.

Second, and as a first approximation, the rate of subsidy to municipal capital costs is not the tax rate of the marginal investor in municipal bonds (t_m). Instead, this establishes a floor on the subsidy rate; if the "representative taxpayer" in the community has a tax rate (t) which exceed t_m, then the subsidy rate is t, not t_m. In this case, the use of municipal bonds at interest rate r_m is more expensive than tax finance, which requires the taxpayer to give up an income of $(1-t)r$. On the other hand, when $t < t_m$ the use of municipal bonds is less expensive than tax finance, and municipal investment should be financed by debt. When $t_m = t$ there is no advantage of one form of finance over another. The new view argues that as an approximation $t_m = t$.

The modified traditional view means that the relevant rate of subsidy is "usually" set by the municipal bond market, but that for affluent taxpayers it might be higher. In the modified traditional view the existence of a tax subsidy for municipal investment arises from two possible sources. The first is the direct avenue, in which affluent communities with $t_m > t$ find that debt finance is cheaper than tax finance. It is this avenue that the new view rejects.

The second avenue is that the imputed income from municipal capital (e.g., teachers' services, miles of road, sewage facilities) is not included in the definition of taxable income, while the income from private capital is subject to the federal income tax.

1. A Consumer-Theoretic Model of Taxpayer Financial Choice

Our model describes a consumer who inherits income from past decisions (Y_1) and chooses the utility-maximizing amounts of three goods: consumption in period 1 (C_1), consumption in period 2 (C_2), and services from municipal government capital (S). It is assumed that municipal capital is formed in period 1 but provides services in period 2, and that these services are related to the municipal capital stock and labor employed through the technology $S(K_m, L_m)$, which exhibits diminishing returns; the marginal products are S_K and S_L. The consumer's utility is described by $U(C_1, C_2, S)$.*

---

*While K_m is the consumer's share of municipal capital, her benefits depend upon *total* municipal capital. Because her share is constant, K_m can be used as an indicator of the total capital stock.

The consumer can produce income in the second period by accumulating business capital (K_b) in the first period and combining it with labor employed in the second period (L_b). Future income is generated according to the technology $F(K_b, L_b)$, which is subject to diminishing returns; the marginal products are F_K and F_L. She can finance current consumption or capital accumulation by issuing business debt (D_b) in any amount at the pretax interest rate (r). If $D_b < 0$ the firm is an investor in bonds. The consumer pays income taxes at the rate t. The interest cost of business debt is deductible from business income; business debt repayment is not deductible. The net cost of municipal debt to the consumer depends upon the tax deductibility of municipal taxes, which is reflected in the parameter δ, where $\delta = 1$ if the taxpayer takes a standard deduction and $\delta = (1 - t)$ if she itemizes.

The consumer also chooses a level of municipal debt, of which D_m is her own share. Note that the consumer will not want to pay taxes to have the money invested in municipal bonds because she could achieve the same result herself. Thus, $D_m \geq 0$.

Unlike business debt, which can take on any value, the volume of municipal debt issued is limited in several ways. First, arbitrage restrictions prohibit issuance of municipal debt to finance holding of business bonds. Second, most states require that municipalities issue long-term debt only to finance capital outlays, hence $D_m \leq K_m$. Third, we assume that municipalities are limited by state statute in their ability to levy taxes in order to finance holding of securities.

The utility maximization problem is

MAX $U(C_1,C_2, S(K_m, L_m))$
subject to
$C_1 = Y_1 - (K_b - D_b) - \delta(K_m - D_m)$
$C_2 = (1 - t)[F(K_b) - rD_b - wL_b] + tK_b - D_b - \delta(1 + r_m)D_m - \delta wL_m$
$K_m \geq D_m$ and $D_m \geq 0$ $\hspace{2cm}$ (11)

This model is essentially the one presented by Metcalf and Gordon (1991), with the addition of private production and financial opportunities to the consumer's choice set, and of labor as a factor of production. Current consumption is current income *less* business "retained earnings" (income required to finance business capital) and the after-tax value of municipal taxes levied to finance municipal capital. Future consumption is after-tax business income (incorporating the deductibility of interest and labor expenses) *less* principal repayments of business debt, after-tax municipal debt service, and the after-tax municipal wage bill *plus* the tax savings of depreciation.

Utility maximization involves two shadow prices. Let λ be the shadow price associated with the constraint $(K_m - D_m) \geq 0$, and let μ be the shadow price on the constraint $D_m \geq 0$. Note that each shadow price is zero unless the constraint is exactly satisfied, in which case the shadow price is positive.

The optimal amounts of capital and debt in both business and municipal sectors are described in the following first-order conditions:

a) $U_2[(1 - t)F_K + t] - U_1 = 0$
b) $-U_2[1 + (1 - t)r] + U_1 = 0$
c) $U_S S_K - \delta U_1 + \lambda = 0$
d) $-U_2[\delta(1 + r_m)] + \delta U_1 - \lambda + \mu = 0$
e) $U_2(1 - t)[F_L - w] = 0$
f) $-U_2\delta w + U_S S_L = 0$
g) $\lambda(K_m - D_m) = 0$
h) $\mu D_m = 0$ $\lambda, \mu \geq 0$ $\hspace{2cm}$ (12)

2. The Near-Irrelevance of the Debt vs. Tax Decision
This model yields the result, already shown by Gordon and Metcalf, that the municipal cost of capital is "almost" independent of the source of funds, so tax exemption does not provide a clear subsidy for municipal debt. Any subsidy arises only when the tax rate is less than the marginal bond investor's tax rate; that is, when $t < t_m$.

To see this, note that Eq. (12b) and Eq. (12d) imply the following relationship:

$U_2\delta[(1 - t)r - r_m] = \lambda - \mu$ $\hspace{2cm}$ (13)

Consider the case in which municipal debt is issued up to its constrained maximum ($D_m = K_m$), that is, when $\lambda > 0$ and $\mu = 0$. In this case we see that $\lambda = U_2\delta \cdot \max[(1 - t)r - r_m, 0]$. Thus, because $U_2\delta > 0$, this applies when $(1 - t)r > r_m$. The municipality is induced to use debt up to its "debt capacity" because debt is cheaper than tax finance.

A second case occurs when $\lambda = \mu = 0$. In this case the consumer chooses an intermediate municipal debt position; that is, $0 < D_m < K_m$. This occurs when $(1 - t)r = r_m$, so the marginal cost of funds is $(1 - t)r$ regardless of the source of funds.

The third case occurs when $D_m = 0$ so $\lambda = 0$ and $\mu > 0$. In this case no municipal debt is issued and we have $\mu = U_2\delta \cdot \max[r_m - (1 - t)r, 0]$. This occurs when $(1 - t)r < r_m$, so the cost of tax finance is less than the cost of municipal debt. In this case the consumer will choose to levy taxes to finance municipal capital. The marginal cost of funds is $(1 - t)r$.

Thus, the rate of subsidy associated with tax exemption depends upon the relationship between t and t_m. If $t_m > t$ there is a subsidy to municipal debt finance because taxpayers will prefer to use debt finance rather than tax finance; by doing so, they retain tax money that can be invested in private debt at a higher after-tax rate. If $t_m = t$ the taxpayer is indifferent between tax finance and debt finance, and if $t_m < t$ the taxpayer will prefer tax finance for municipal investment.

Table 8 shows an example of the case in which the taxpayer is indifferent between debt finance and tax finance. A proper evaluation of the decision about whether to finance the construction projects with taxes or debt rests on a consideration of the after-tax consequences for taxpayers. While such decisions are often made by simply summing coupon payments over the life of a bond issue, this is not an appropriate method of evaluation because it ignores the time value of money.

Table 8 is based on several assumptions about the municipal bond rate and the interest rate earned by the "typical" taxpayer. We assume that taxpayers itemize deductions, and are in a 31% federal income tax bracket. We also assume that taxpayers can invest in taxable bonds earning 9.4%, for an after-tax interest rate of 6.5%, and that the municipal bond rate for the town is also 6.5%, and that bonds issued by the

Table 8   Debt Finance vs. Tax Finance

| | Payment schedule for municipal bonds | | | | | |
Year	Outstanding balance (1)	Coupon (2)	Debt repaid (3)	Pretax levy (4)	After-tax levy (5)	Opportunity cost (6)
1	3,660	237.900	183	420.900	290.421	164.15
2	3,477	226.005	183	409.005	282.213	164.15
3	3,294	214.110	183	397.110	274.006	164.15
4	3,111	202.215	183	385.215	265.798	164.15
5	2,928	190.320	183	373.320	257.591	164.15
6	2,745	178.425	183	361.425	249.383	164.15
7	2,562	166.530	183	349.530	241.176	164.15
8	2,379	154.635	183	337.635	232.968	164.15
9	2,196	142.740	183	325.740	224.761	164.15
10	2,013	130.645	183	313.845	216.553	164.15
11	1,830	118.950	183	301.950	208.346	164.15
12	1,647	107.055	183	290.055	200.138	164.15
13	1,464	95.160	183	278.160	191.930	164.15
14	1,281	83.265	183	266.265	183.723	164.15
15	1,098	71.370	183	254.370	175.515	164.15
16	915	59.475	183	242.475	167.308	164.15
17	732	47.580	183	230.580	159.100	164.15
18	549	35.685	183	218.685	150.893	164.15
19	366	23.790	183	206.790	142.685	164.15
20	183	11.895	183	194.895	134.478	2689.55
21	0	0	0	0	0	0
Present value					2,525.40	2,525.40

municipality—or bought by the taxpayer—would have 20-year terms. Finally, we assume that if the municipal bonds are issued they will be in twenty equal strips, each with a face value of $183,000. The bondable portion of the construction project is assumed to be $3,660,000.

Columns 1 through 3 of Table 8 show the beginning-of-year outstanding balance, the annual coupon payment, and the annual debt repayment if the town issues a 20-year bond with a 6.5% coupon rate on each strip. The outstanding balance in each year shown in column 1, derived by taking the previous year's outstanding balance and deducting the principal repaid during the current year, is shown in column 3. For example, at the beginning of year 1 the outstanding amount of bonds is $3,660,000. If the bonds are 20-year bonds the debt repayment in year 1 is $183,000, so outstanding debt at the beginning of year 2 is $3,477,000.

Column 4 shows the pretax tax levy required to finance the debt service on the bonds; this is the sum of columns 2 and 3. Column 5 shows the after-tax tax levy, assuming the taxpayer itemizes at a 31% federal income tax rate. Note that the tax levy declines with the passage of time because of the retirement of earlier strips.

Column 6 shows the opportunity cost of the bond issue; that is, the cost of tax finance. If taxpayers pay the $3,660,000 immediately as a tax levy, the net cost to them after deduction of state and local taxes at 31% is $2525.40. The 6.5% after-tax yield on that amount invested in a 20-year taxable bond is $614,150 per year, and the repayment of principal at the end of 20 years is $2525.40. Thus, the taxpayers sacrifice income of $614,150 in each of the 19 years, as well as a payment of $2689.55 in the twentieth year.

The two choices, then, are debt finance, which generates a cost to taxpayers shown by column 5, or tax finance, which generates the costs shown by column 6. Each of these has a different time path of costs. Debt finance costs more in the first 17 years, but less in the last 3 years.

However, the two costs shown in columns 5 and 6 are identical in spite of the apparent difference in "tilt" of the payment stream. Because both have the same present value ($2,425.40), a taxpayer can choose one method of municipal finance and construct exactly the same costs implied by the other method. For example, if tax finance is chosen, the taxpayer can take the "savings" experienced in the first 17 years by foregoing debt finance, invest them in taxable bonds at a 6.5% after-tax rate of interest, and build up a fund that is just sufficient to pay the higher costs experienced in years 18 through 20.

This example assumes that the taxpayer's tax rate is identical to the implicit rate of subsidy of tax-exempt bonds; that is, that $t = t_m$. This is the basis for the conclusion that debt finance is irrelevant—it is equivalent to tax finance.

There are, of course, certain caveats about the irrelevance proposition. First, it assumes that the taxpayer's tax rate is equal to the tax rate of the marginal investor in municipal bonds. Second, it assumes that taxpayers are not "liquidity-constrained"; that is, that they can make their decisions solely on the basis of financial considerations and can choose an option independent of the tilt of costs involved. A liquidity-constrained taxpayer cannot choose the more expensive option because he has no liquid assets or private borrowing power available to finance it.

3. The Tax Subsidy to Municipal Investment

In spite of the near irrelevance of tax exemption to the choice of debt versus tax finance, the federal income tax code provides a significant subsidy to municipal investment. To see this, note that in the absence of differential taxation, the Pareto optimal allocation of resources will satisfy the condition $F_K/S_K = F_L/S_L$; that is, the marginal rate of transformation between capital and labor are the same in each sector.

The actual resource allocation will differ from the Pareto optimal allocation for two reasons. First, there is a direct capital-cost subsidy when $r_m < (1 - t)r$. Second, while income from private business activity is subject to federal income tax, the imputed income from municipal services is tax-exempt. The result is a tax subsidy that is primarily a subsidy to municipal capital.

This can be seen formally from an examination of first-order conditions. According to these, the consumer's optimal level of private and municipal factors is described by

a) $F_K = 1 + r$
b) $U_S S_K = \delta U_2[(1 + r) - \max(t, t_m)r]$
c) $F_L = w$
d) $U_S S_L = \delta w$ (14)

Equation (14b) states that the marginal municipal cost of funds is r_m when $r_m < (1-t)r$, and $(1-t)r$ when $r_m \geq (1-t)r$.* The remaining conditions are straightforward. Note that the cost of municipal capital is less than the cost of private capital by the amount $\max(t, t_m)$. This is the subsidy per unit of municipal capital. Note that it exists even if there is no subsidy to municipal debt finance.

Recall that in a Pareto optimal allocation the marginal rates of substitution between capital and labor will be equal in each sector, so $S_K/S_L - F_K/F_L = 0$. Our analysis reveals that the actual allocation of resources will satisfy

$$(S_K/S_L) = [F_K - \max(t, t_m)r]/F_L \tag{15}$$

Thus, tax exemption of municipal services and of municipal interest is equivalent to a reduction in the cost of municipal capital by the amount $t_m r$ or tr, whichever is higher.

In a Pareto optimal allocation, both sectors would face the same factor prices so the ratio of marginal products in each sector would be equalized. However, the subsidy creates a new equilibrium with a lower marginal product of capital relative to the marginal product of labor in the municipal sector than in the private sector.

Thus, the tax system creates a subsidy that is equivalent to a municipal capital-cost subsidy even though the mechanism is different from the tax exemption of municipal interest. And the subsidy is the same—or higher—than the amount predicted by the traditional view.

B.   The Microeconomics of Economic Efficiency

The equity and efficiency problems are not "social costs." Rather, they are "zero-sum" costs in the sense that one sector's gain is matched by another sector's loss. For example, the efficiency problem is zero-sum because it affects the distribution of income, not the aggregate amount of income received; the gains enjoyed by state and local government taxpayers through lower interest costs, and by affluent investors through windfall income, are matched by costs to federal taxpayers.

In this section we focus on the *social* costs of tax exemption. The problem of social costs, or economic inefficiency, is inherent in any capital-cost subsidy; it will occur even in the absence of market instability, efficiency, and equity problems.

The core of the social cost problem is the resource allocation effect of capital-cost subsidies. Because the tax system reduces the cost of capital of municipalities it alters the relative amounts of capital and labor that state and local governments use to produce public goods. In addition, by affecting the relative prices of public and private goods, it induces economic agents to demand more public goods and fewer private goods, thereby shifting the composition of aggregate production. The ultimate effect of a capital-cost subsidy enjoyed by the public sector (but not by the private sector) is to increase the share of output produced by the public sector, and to increase the relative capital intensity of public-sector production.

The effects on resource allocation can be examined using standard microeconomic analysis. In Fig. 11 we show an Edgeworth-Bowley box designed to illustrate this problem. There are two sectors in the economy: the private sector, designated by the subscript "p," and the state and local government sector, designated by the subscript "m." There are also two factors of production: capital, designated by K, and labor, designated by L. The box assumes that the total amount of each factor is fixed; the width of the box shows the total amount of capital $(\overline{K})$ and the height of the box is the total amount of labor $(\overline{L})$. Eastward movements represent a shift in capital from the private to the government sector (a rise in K_m and an equal decline in K_p), while northward movements are a shift in labor allocation from the private to the government sector (a rise in L_m and an equal decline in L_p).

The economy's allocation problem is to determine how each factor will be allocated between the private and public sectors. This also determines how much of each good is produced. The Pareto optimal allocation of resources will place the economy on the curve connecting the southwest corner of the box, labeled O_m, to the northeast corner, labeled O_p. Any allocation of resources that moves the economy off this curve is an inefficient allocation because it reduces the output of one sector without increasing the output of the other.

The southwest corner of the box is the origin from the vantage point of the government sector. At O_m the government sector uses no capital or labor and produces no output, while the private sector employs $K_p = \overline{K}$ and

---

*Conditions 3c and 3d imply $U_S S' = U_2 \delta(1 + r_m) - \mu$. We know that when $\mu > 0$, $\mu = U_2 \delta \cdot \max[r_m - (1-t)r, 0]$. Substitution of μ into the equilibrium condition yields (14b) after minor manipulation.

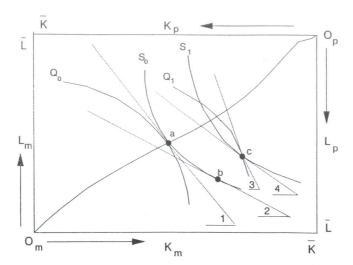

Figure 11   Tax-exemption and resource allocation.

$L_p = \bar{L}$, producing the largest possible output consistent with the economy's factor supplies. There are an infinite number of government-sector "isoquants," each convex to this origin and each showing the amounts of K_m and L_m which produce a given amount of public goods. For example, the curve labeled S_0 shows the combinations of government capital and labor that produce the amount S_0 of public goods, and the curve S_1 is the isoquant for a higher level of public goods. We know that $S_1 > S_0$ because there are some points on S_1 that employ more of one factor while employing the same amount of the other factor, hence S_1 must represent higher output. Thus, the further northeast a government sector isoquant, the higher the public good output it represents.

The northeast corner, O_p, is the origin for the private sector, at which no factors are employed by the private sector and no private output is produced. At O_p all of the economy's capital and labor is employed by the government sector, and public good output is maximized. There are an infinite number of private-sector isoquants, each convex to the origin O_p, and each representing the amounts of capital and labor necessary to produce a given level of private goods. Two of these isoquants are shown as Q_0 and Q_1, with Q_0 representing the higher level of private output.

The marginal product ratios for each sector are represented by the slope of the isoquant for that sector. Because—in the absence of taxes or subsidies—both sectors face the same factor prices, each sector will be induced to choose factor combinations that have the same marginal product ratios; that is, the same isoquant slopes. As noted above, the line connecting O_m and O_p is all the points that represent an efficient allocation of resources. This, it turns out, is all the points at which the isoquants are tangent and, therefore, have equal slopes.

For example, consider point "a," which we assume is the point at which the economy rests before introduction of tax exemption. At point a the isoquant S_0 is tangent to the isoquant Q_0. Any other point on S_0 will, because of the shapes of the isoquants, be on a lower (more northeasterly) private-sector isoquant than Q_0. Thus, any movement away from a gives lower private output for the same level of government output. The result is economic inefficiency because there is a lower level of private output than is necessary to produce S_0 of public output.

We are now in a position to investigate the effects of tax exemption. We assume that the economy is initially in a general equilibrium at point a and that both sectors pay the same user cost of capital and the same wage rate. At this initial general equilibrium, the economy is Pareto efficient.

Now suppose that tax exemption is introduced and the cost of capital in the government sector is below the capital cost of the private sector. The private section still faces the same factor price ratio, measured by $\angle 1$, but the relative factor costs for governments will be reduced to, say, the ratio measured by angle $\angle 2$. The private sector wishes to remain at point a, but the government sector would want to move to point b, which minimizes the cost of producing S_0 of output under the new factor cost ratio.

Tax exemption has thrown the economy into disequilibrium; the private sector wants to use the amount of capital and labor represented by point a, leaving the government sector only $\bar{K} - K_p$ of capital and $\bar{L} - L_m$ of labor. In the initial equilibrium that was precisely the amount of capital and labor that the government sector wanted to use, but now the government wants to use more capital and less labor. In short, the introduction of tax exemption creates an excess demand for capital and an excess supply of labor. Furthermore, tax exemption has driven a permanent wedge between the factor prices faced by the private and public sectors: the private sector faces a higher cost of capital relative to the cost of labor than does the government sector. Because of this wedge, the economy can never come to an equilibrium on the line $O_m O_p$; it can never be Pareto efficient.

Where is the new general equilibrium? Clearly the excess demand for capital must lead to a rise in the user cost of capital in the private sector as both sectors bid for the scarce capital stock. Also, the excess supply of labor must lead to a fall in the wage rate as labor becomes unemployed in the government sector and seeks employment in the private sector. The migration of capital to the government sector and of labor to the private sector and the rise in the cost of capital combined with a decline in the cost of labor will continue until the economy reaches a new point, such as point c.

At point c the factor choices of the two sectors are consistent; the private sector wants to employ factors in exactly the amounts necessary to maintain full employment. Also, each sector is once again minimizing its production costs because it is once again equating the relative marginal products (slope of isoquant) to the relative factor costs. However, the relative factor costs, which were equal at a, are not equal at c. At point c $\angle 3$ is the factor price ratio for the private sector, while $\angle 4$ is the price ratio for the public sector. Because $\angle 4 < \angle 3$, the government sector has a marginal product of capital less than that in the private sector and a marginal product of labor greater than in the private sector.

The public sector is now producing with a higher level of capital intensity, while the private sector is producing at a lower capital-labor ratio. Clearly, point c is not Pareto efficient because a Pareto improvement would occur if resources were reallocated to reach a point on $O_m O_p$; this would allow production of more of one good with no sacrifice in the production of the other good. But the price system will not induce that movement; there is a permanent incentive for government to produce with too much capital and too little labor.

How far apart will points a and c be? Will c be to the southeast of a (more capital employed but less labor in the public sector) or to the northeast of a (more capital and more labor in the government sector)? The answers depend on two important considerations: *technology*, which fixes the substitutability between factors and thereby affects the curvature of the isoquants, and *preferences*, which determine consumer's willingness to substitute private goods for public goods. As far as technology is concerned, the higher the "elasticity of substitution" between capital and labor in each sector, the more each sector will alter its capital-labor ratio in response to the change in relative factor prices. For each sector, the elasticity of substitution has a minimum of zero, which corresponds to a fixed-coefficients technology. If both sectors have zero elasticity, the curve $O_m O_p$ would represent the only possible points of equilibrium. Thus, if no factor substitutions can occur, there can be no misallocation of factors between sectors.

At the other extreme, the elasticities can be extremely high, approaching straight-line isoquants. In that case, very small changes in relative factor prices will induce extremely large changes in factor proportions, and the resource allocation effects of tax exemption will be large.

The final equilibrium will also be affected by preferences, which affect the substitutability between government and private goods. This is measured by the price elasticity of demand for government goods. Tax exemption will induce a fall in the relative price of government goods. If relative product prices have a very small effect on demand, tax exemption will have little effect on the relative quantities of each good; point c will be very close to point a. If, on the other hand, private and public goods are close substitutes, there will be larger shifts in the mix of products.

Except in the extreme case of zero substitution between factors and zero price elasticity of demand, it will always be the case that a capital-cost subsidy for the government sector will induce capital to move from the private sector to the public sector. However, the direction of labor movements will depend upon the price elasticity of demand for public goods. If this is sufficiently high, the capital-cost subsidy will induce consumers to switch from private to public goods so much that the public sector increases its employment of both capital *and* labor.

C. Measuring the Resource Allocation Effects of Tax Exemption

1. *An Economic Approach to Measuring Tax-Induced Inefficiency*

Arnold Harberger (1962) developed a simple general equilibrium analysis of the effects of taxation on the allocation of resources. In the intervening 30 years, there have been a number of extensions and refinements of the basic model, but the Harberger model has become the standard for analyzing the resource allocation effects of a wide range of taxes. In this section we outline the Harberger model. In the next section, we employ the model to derive estimates of the resource allocation effects of tax exemption.

The Harberger model is a formalization of the insights in Fig. 11. The model assumes two producing sectors in the economy, one sector producing a good in the quantity S and the other producing a good in quantity Q. Each sector employs two factors of production, capital K and labor L. The total amount of each factor is fixed in quantity, so that the factor allocation problem is simplified to the allocation of the total quantity of each factor between the two sectors. It is assumed that full employment of both factors prevails, so that no factor units of either factor fail to be allocated to production in the economy. Thus, if K_m and L_m are the capital and labor employed in the untaxed (government) sector that produces Y, and $\overline{K}$ and $\overline{L}$ are the total amounts of capital and labor, then $K_p = \overline{K} - K_g$ and $L_p = \overline{L} - L_g$ are the capital and labor employed by the taxed (private) sector.

Each sector has a production function, designated $Q = F(K_p, L_p)$ and $S = S(K_m, L_m)$, respectively. Each sector employs each factor up to the point where the marginal value product is equal to the factor price. The model assumes competitve factor markets, so that each factor is paid its marginal value product. Also, production functions each exhibit constant resturns to scale.

We assume, for convenience, that the private sector faces a tax on capital costs rather than that the government sector experiencing a capital-cost subsidy. If the factor price of capital in the government sector is C_m, then the factor price of capital in the private sector is $C_m + \theta$, where θ is the capital income tax per unit of capital. The value of θ is crucial to the resource allocation effects of tax policy.

There are three primary parameters that affect the size of resource allocations resulting from a tax on capital in one sector. The first two are the elasticity of substitution between capital and labor in the two sectors, denoted by σ_p and σ_m; the greater either σ_p or σ_m, the larger the changes in the capital labor ratios in the associated sector, and the smaller the changes in the relative factor prices. This follows the general principle that the closer the substitutability between any two commodities, the larger the response in the ratio of the quantities used in response to any relative price change. Thus, a given change in relative quantities can be achieved by a smaller relative price change when two commodities are close substitutes.

The third primary parameter is the price elasticity of demand for the public good, E_m. The higher this price elasticity, the larger the shift in the allocation of the consumers' consumption bundle in response to any change in relative prices; for any given change in relative prices, the shift in demand between the taxed and untaxed sector is greater when the goods are closer substitutes.

2. Applying the Economic Approach

To estimate the resource allocation effects of tax exemption, we must assume values for the primary parameters, discussed above, which describe the response of economic agents to changes in relative prices. In addition, values must be assigned to several secondary parameters, which describe the allocation of resources in the economy. Among these are the capital income shares in each sector (f_K and g_K), the ratio of government-sector capital to private-sector capital (λ_K), and the ratio of government labor to private labor (λ_L).

The appropriate values of these secondary parameters will depend upon the definition of the private sector. Is it defined as nonfinancial corporations, all corporations, or all businesses, including unincorporated enterprises? Does it include production of housing services? Of farm output? There is no single answer, and we have chosen a definition that includes all private nonagricultural production of goods and services except housing.

Using the BLS establishment surveys of nonagricultural payrolls, we find that from 1980 to 1985 there were 17.4 state and local sector employees for every 100 private-sector employees, hence $\lambda_L = 0.174$. The Commerce Department's capital stock estimates (Musgrave, 1990) indicate that in the period from 1982 to 1989 there was an average of \$40.50 of state and local sector capital for every \$100 of fixed nonresidential capital stock, hence $\lambda_K = 0.405$.

According to Hulten and Schwab (1987), from 1980 to 1985 about 24% of the value added in the state and local government sector was due to the services of the capital stock, hence $g_K = 0.24$. The National Income Accounts indicate that over the same period about 60% of private-sector value added was attributable to labor compensation, so we have used $f_K = 0.40$.

There has been a great deal of work on the elasticity of substitution between capital and labor in the private sector. We believe that the consensus puts this at somewhat less than unity; we have chosen $\sigma_p = 0.90$ (Beckman and Sato, 1969). There is considerably less agreement about the elasticity of substitution in the state and local sector. Fortune (1983) reports results consistent with a Cobb-Douglas technology, implying $\sigma_m = 1.0$.

However, there is a long-standing argument that public-sector activities are labor-driven and that the public sector does not have the same flexibility in the capital-labor ratio that the private sector enjoys (Baumol, 1967; Baumol et al., 1985). This, it is argued, means that new capital-intensive technologies are not easily introduced and that the ability to substitute between capital and labor when relative prices change is weak. The result is low productivity growth and rising production costs in the state and local sector. A recent paper by Blackley and DeBoer (1991) supports the Baumol hypothesis, finding that capital and labor are weak complements. In order to allow for a wide range of estimates, we have assumed two possible values of the state and local elasticity of substitution: $\sigma_m = 1.0$ and $\sigma_m = 0.25$.

The final parameter whose value must be assumed is the price elasticity of demand for state and local goods, E_m. A survey of the literature by Inman (1979) reported an average value of 0.50 for the uncompensated elasticity. DeBartolo and Fortune (1982) estimated the compensated elasticity at 0.15.* We will use both values.

The Harberger model calculates the effect of a tax imposed on each unit of capital in the private sector. As noted above, the parameter θ measures the additional tax levied on capital costs in the private sector. The analysis of the previous section on the nature of the tax subsidy shows that the size of this differential tax per dollar of private capital is $\max(t, t_m)r$. This is about 0.0265 using 1985 to 1990 data. From 1985 to 1990 the average Aaa corporate and Aaa municipal bond yields were $r = 0.1267$ and $r_m = 0.1002$. Thus, $t_m = 0.21$ and $t_m r = 0.0266$.

A more sophisticated approach, using full information on the U.S. income tax code, would be to use the difference between the corporate and municipal costs of capital using Jorgenson's definition of the cost of capital. For the corporate sector this is $C_p = (1 - t_c Z)\{[r(1 - t_c) - \pi + \Delta]/(1 - t_c)\}$, where Z is the present value of depreciation allowances, r is the nominal corporate bond rate, π is the expected rate of inflation, and Δ is the depreciation rate. The excess of this over the municipal cost of capital, $C_m = r_m - \pi + \Delta$, would be a more precise measure of θ. Reasonable values for these parameters for 1985 to 1990 are $t_c = 0.46$, $Z = 0.34$, $\pi = 0.05$, $\Delta = 0.08$, $r = 0.1267$, and $r_m = 0.1002$. (See Kopcke, 1981.) These numbers would give $C_p = .1538$ and $C_m = .1302$, yielding $\theta = 0.0236$, a result close to the value used in our calculations.

We have used $\theta = 0.03$ in our calculations to be on the conservation side.

3. The Magnitude of Resource Allocation Effects

The assumed parameter values are reported in Table 9. The results of our analysis are reported in Table 10. As expected, tax exemption reduces the net cost of capital for the public sector and raises the private-sector cost of capital. It also creates a rise in the public sector's capital-labor ratio ranging from 0.66% (if $\sigma_m = 0.25$) to 2.13% (if $\sigma_m = 1.00$). Furthermore, aggregate output is reduced by 0.07% to 0.23%, with private output falling and public output increasing. The magnitude of the decline in aggre- gate output depends upon the elasticity of substitution between capital and labor in the public sector; the greater σ_m, the larger the reallocation of capital and labor and the greater the decline in aggregate out- put.

The last two rows of Table 10 translate the proportional change in aggregate output to dollar values, using the 1980 to 1985 average level of nonfarm, nonfederal value added. The decrease in aggregate out- put ranges from $2.38 billion for low values of E_m and σ_m, to $7.63 billion for high values of those parameters. Translated to per capita values, tax exemption costs from $10.18 to $32.67 per person. The estimate using our preferred parameter values ($E_m = 0.50$, $\sigma_m = 0.25$) is a total of $3.43 billion, or $14.66 per capita.

These estimates indicate that tax exemption creates mild social costs in the form of output foregone. The amounts are not so dramatic as to make the exemption a serious problem on this score, but they are also not so small as to make the analysis of social costs irrelevant. The reader should be aware that these costs are measured against the alternative of a perfectly competitive economy without subsidies, and that for the imperfect world we face, the introduction of tax exemption could, in fact, improve resource allocation. Indeed, those who believe that there is insufficient public infrastructure in the U.S. economy argue that market outcomes do not efficiently allocate resources and that government should intervene to increase public infrastructure.

---

*The uncompensated price elasticity of demand includes the income effect of a relative price change, and is typically larger than the compensated elasticity, which is the substitution effect.

Table 9 Parameter Values Used in the Harberger Efficiency Model

Parameter	Definition		Values
f_K	Capital share of value added, private	(1980–1985)	0.40
g_K	Capital share of value added, public	(1980–1985)	0.24
γ_K	Ratio of public/private employment	(1980–1985)	0.174
γ_L	Ratio of public/private capital stock	(1982–1989)	0.405
σ_p	Elasticity of substitution, private	—	0.90
σ_m	Elasticity of substitution, public	—	0.25, 1.00
E_m	Price elasticity of demand, public goods	—	0.15, 0.50
θ	Added user cost of private capital	(1980–1985)	0.03

Note: The private sector is nonfarm. The public sector is all state and local government.

VII. SUMMARY

This chapter assesses the implications of tax exemption of municipal interest payments for the municipal bond market, for the capital costs faced by municipalities, and for the performance of the broader economy.

Section I provides an overview of the municipal bond market. It discusses the "traditional" forms of municipal debt, the statutory and constitutional issues in establishing eligibility for tax exemption, the recent

Table 10 Estimated Social Costs of Tax-Exemption for Selected Values of σ_m and E_m

	$E_m = 0.15$		$E_m = 0.50$	
	$\sigma_m = 0.25$	$\sigma_m = 1.00$	$\sigma_m = 0.25$	$\sigma_m = 1.00$
User cost of capital				
Private sector	+0.29%	+0.86%	+0.36%	+0.92%
Public sector	−2.71%	−2.14%	−2.64%	−2.08%
Product prices				
Private sector	+0.12%	+0.35%	+0.14%	+0.37%
Public sector	0.65%	−0.51%	−0.63%	−0.50%
Aggregate	+0.03%	+0.25%	+0.05%	+0.27%
Output				
Private sector	−0.10%	−0.24%	−0.17%	−0.32%
Public sector	+0.12%	+0.13%	+0.39%	+0.43%
Aggregate (%)	−0.07%	−0.20%	0.11%	−0.23%
Capital employed				
Private sector	−0.26%	−0.71%	−0.36%	−0.82%
Public sector	+0.63%	+1.75%	+0.89%	+2..01%
Labor employed				
Private sector	+0.00%	+0.07%	−0.04%	+0.01%
Public sector	−0.05%	−0.38%	+0.23%	−0.07%
Capital per employee				
Private sector	−0.26%	−0.78%	−0.32%	−0.83%
Public sector	+0.68%	+2.13%	+0.66%	+2.08%
Aggregate output				
Aggregate ($)	−$ 2.38b	−$ 6.56b	−$ 3.43b	−$ 7.63b
Per capita ($)	−$10.18	+$28.15	+$14.66	+$32.67

Note: The calculations are based on 1980-1985 data. The aggregate output index is a Divisia index of the proportional changes in public and private output, with a 12% share of value added in the public sector.

history of municipal bond yields and ownership, and recent innovations in the municipal bond market. This section dispels the notion that municipal bonds are a stodgy form of debt, with little innovation and with no significant structural changes. We conclude in this section that there is no longer a basis for viewing tax exemption as constitutionally protected, that there has been a significant change in ownership of municipal bonds—away from commercial banks and toward individual investors, often acting through mutual funds and unit trusts—and that the relationship between municipal bond and taxable bond yields has changed significantly in response to federal tax legislation.

Section II also finds that there has been considerable innovation in the way credit quality is assured (particularly through private bond insurance), in the form of the municipal bond (particularly through variable rate instruments) and in the opportunities available for individuals and financial institutions to hedge against interest rate risks (particularly through futures and futures option contracts).

Section III discusses some important features of the U.S. income tax code that influence municipal bonds. It also reports on major pieces of legislation affecting the municipal bond market, particularly the Economic Recovery Tax Act of 1981 and the Tax Reform Act of 1986.

Section IV presents the "traditional" economic view of the determination of municipal bond yields, which stresses a relationship between personal income taxes and bond yields. This is contrasted with the "new view," which focuses on corporate income taxes as a primary determinant of municipal bond yields. In this section we also present econometric evidence on the determinants of the relationship between tax-exempt and taxable bonds. This evidence reveals that the level and progressivity of the personal income tax structure is important, as are expectations of future personal income tax rates. In addition, we find that the level of municipal bond yields is directly related to the volatility of interest rates.

Section V discusses some public policy aspects of tax exemption. In this section we assess the performance of the municipal bond market, particularly the implications of tax exemption for market stability, for financial efficiency, and for vertical equity. We also pursue the financial efficiency issue by developing estimates of the costs of tax exemption to the U.S. Treasury, of the interest savings experienced by municipalities, and of the transfer of income from federal taxpayers to high-income investors. In this section we also discuss four reforms that would mitigate the public policy problems: complete elimination of the exemption, substitution of a direct subsidy, introduction of a taxable bond option, and implementation of a flat income tax.

The focus of Section V is on the "zero-sum" problems posed by tax exemption. These are in the form of transfers of income between groups without affecting the total income enjoyed by the economy. For example, the market instability problem affects the cost of debt finance for municipalities relative to the cost for the private sector, thus it affects the distribution of costs among borrowers but not necessarily the economywide cost of capital. Financial efficiency involves distribution of income between federal and state and local taxpayers, and vertical equity addresses the distribution of after-tax income among individuals.

Section VI also focuses on the problems created by tax exemption, but here we are concerned with its "social" costs. These are in the form of redirection of resource allocation from higher to lower productivity uses. In this section we discuss the true nature of the capital-cost subsidy associated with tax exemption, concluding that it is not really through the reduction in interest costs on municipal bonds. Rather, the subsidy arises because municipal services—such as services of owner-occupied housing and consumer durables—are exempt from federal taxes while services of private capital are taxed. Even so, we find that the effect of this modified form of exemption is equivalent to a direct municipal capital-cost subsidy.

Section VI lays out the microeconomics of the social costs of the exemption, discusses a simple model designed to measure these costs, and implements that model using reasonable values of the relevant parameters. We find that tax exemption creates a reallocation of resources from the high-tax sector (private firms) to the low-tax sector (state and local governments), and that this reallocation is equivalent to a loss of national income ranging from $2.4 billion ($10 per capita) to $7.6 billion ($33 per capita), depending on the assumptions.

REFERENCES

Baumol, W. J. (1967). *Amer. Econ. Rev.*, 57: 415–426.
Baumol, W. J., Batey, S. A., and Wolff, E. N. (1985). *Amer. Econ. Rev.*, 75: 806–817.
Beckman, M. J. and Sato, R. (1969). *Amer. Econ. Rev.*, 59: 88–101.
Benson, E. D. (1979). *J. Finance*, 34: 871–885.
Bland, R. L. and Yu, C. (1987). *Gov. Finance Rev.*, 3: 23–26.

Bushman, C. and Winterer, P. S. (1983). *The Municipal Bond Handbook* (F. J. Fabozzi, et al., eds.) vol. I, Ch. 15, Dow Jones-Irwin, pp. 204–227.

Capeci, J. (1991). *Nat. Tax J.*, *44*: 41–51.

Fama, E. (1977). "A Pricing Model for the Municipal Bond Market," unpublished working paper, University of Chicago.

Financial Markets Research Center (1989). "Cost of Issuance on Tax Exempt Debt: An Initial Report on the FMRC 1988 Survey," School of Business, State University of New York at Albany.

Fortune, P. (1973a). *New England Econ. Rev.*, 3–31.

Fortune, P. (1973b). *Nat. Tax J.*, *26*: 3–31.

Fortune, P. and G. DeBartolo (1982). *Nat. Tax J.*, *35*: 55–67.

Fortune, P. (1983). *Nat. Tax J.*, *36*: 233–236.

Fortune, P. (1984). *Pub. Finance Q.*, *12*: 347–354.

Fortune, P. (1988). *Nat. Tax J.*, *41*: 219–233.

Fortune, P. (1991). *New Eng. Econ. Rev.*, 17–39.

Fortune, P. (1993). "On the Nature of the Tax Subsidy to Municipal Investment," discussion paper 93–04, Tufts University Economics Department, Mass.

Galper, H. and Petersen, J. E. (1971). *Nat. Tax J.*, *24*: 205–234.

Gordon, R. H. and Metcalf, G. E. (1991). *Nat. Tax J.* *44*: 71–80.

Harberger, A. (1962). *J. Polit. Econ.*, *71*: 215–240.

Hopewell, M. and Kaufman, G. (1974). *Nat. Tax J.*, *27*: 531–541.

Huefner, R. (1971) *Taxable Alternatives to Municipal Bonds: An Analysis of the Issues*, research report no. 53, Federal Reserve Bank of Boston, Boston.

Hulten, C. R. and Schwab, R. M. (1987). "Income Originating in the State-Local Sector," NBER working paper 2314.

Hulten, C. R. (1991). *Nat. Tax J.*, *44*: 121–134.

Inman, R. P. (1979). *Current Issues in Urban Economics* (P. Mieszkowski and M. Strazheim, eds.), Johns Hopkins University Press, Baltimore, pp. 270–321.

Jantscher, G. (1970). "The Effects of Changes in Credit Rating on Municipal Borrowing Costs," IBA occasional paper/1, Investment Bankers Association of America, Washington, D.C.

Joint Economic Committee (1966). *State and Local Public Facility Needs and Financing*, 89th Congress, 2nd Session, vol. 2, U.S. Government Printing Office, Washington D.C., pp. 327–333.

Kenyon, D. (1991). *Nat. Tax J.*, *44*: 81–92.

Kessel, R. (1971). *J. Polit. Econ.*, *79*: 706–737.

Kidwell, D. S., Koch, T. W., and Stock, D. R. (1984). *Nat. Tax J.*, *37*: 551–561.

Kidwell, D. S., Sorenson, E. and Wachowicz, J. (1987). *J. Finan. Quant. Anal.*, *22*: 299–313.

Kopcke, R. W. (1981). *Public Policy and Capital Formation* (Board of Governors of the Federal Reserve System), Washington, D.C., 163–173.

Lamb, R. and Rappaport, S. P. (1980). *Municipal Bonds: The Comprehensive Review of Tax-Exempt Securities and Public Finance*, McGraw-Hill, New York.

Metcalf, G. (1990). *Rev. Econ. Stat.*, *72*: 390–396.

Metcalf, G. (1991). *Nat. Tax J.*, *44*: 57–70.

Miller, M. (1977). *J. Finance*, *32*: 261–275.

Munnell, A. (1990). *New Eng. Econ. Rev.*, 11–33.

Musgrave, J. (1990). *Surv. Current Bus.*, *70*: 51–75.

Office of Management and Budget (1990). *Special Analyses, Budget of the United States Government*, U.S. Government Printing Office, Washington D.C.

Ott, D. J. and Meltzer, A. H. (1963). *Federal Tax Treatment of State and Local Securities*, the Brookings Institution, Washington, D.C.

Pechman, J. A. (1987). *Federal Tax Policy*, the Brookings Institution, Washington, D.C.

Peek, J. and Wilcox, J. (1986). *New Eng. Econ. Rev.*, 29–41.

Petersen, J. E. (1991). *Nat. Tax J.*, *44*: 11–28.

Poterba, J. M. (1986). *Studies in State and Local Public Finance* (H. S. Rosen, ed.) University of Chicago Press, Chicago, pp. 5–49.

Poterba, J. M. (1989). *Reg. Sci. Urban Econ.*, *19*: 537–562.

Poterba, J. M. (1991). *Nat. Tax. J.*, *44*: 93–103.

Quigley, J. M. and Rubinfeld, D. L. (1991). *Nat. Tax J.*, *44*: 29–39.

Seltzer, L. (1941). *Bull. Nat. Tax Assoc.*, 189–199.

Simons, H. C. (1938). *Personal Income Taxation*, University of Chicago Press. Chicago.

Southwick, L. (1979). *Land Econ.*, *55*: 177–189.

Surrey, S. (1973). *Pathways to Tax Reform: The Concept of Tax Expenditures*, Harvard University Press, Cambridge, Mass.

Trczinka, C. (1982). *J. Finance*, *37*: 907–923.

Zimmerman, D. (1991). *The Private Use of Tax-Exempt Bonds: Controlling Public Subsidy of Private Activity*, the Urban Institute, Washington D.C.

4

The Role of Federal Taxation in the Supply of Municipal Bonds: Evidence from Municipal Governments

Gilbert E. Metcalf

Tufts University, Medford, and the National Bureau of Economic Research, Cambridge, Massachusetts

Over 50 years ago, the American economist Henry Simons argued that the federal tax exemption for municipal bond interest income was "a flaw of major importance" (1938; 172). Since then, economists have argued the merits of this tax expenditure; politicians for the most part have supported the subsidy, arguing that it is an important component of federal support to state and local governments. Additionally, most state and local politicians have argued that there is a constitutional right to the tax exemption. This latter argument was decisively rejected in 1988 when the U.S. Supreme Court ruled that state and local governments had no constitutional right to issue bonds free from federal taxation. For a brief period, municipal bond prices plunged before congressional leaders assured traders that Congress had no intention of taxing traditional municipal bonds [1].

This incident illustrates the sensitivity of municipal bond prices to federal taxation. It reflects in main the important influence of federal taxation on the demand for municipal bonds. There is an extensive literature on the influence of federal taxation on the demand for municipal bonds, and Poterba (1989) provides a good introduction to that literature. This chapter considers the role of federal taxation in affecting the supply of municipal bonds. There are two important ways in which federal taxation affects supply. First, the tax-exempt nature of most municipal debt creates opportunities for financial arbitrage as municipal governments can borrow at tax-exempt rates and reinvest at taxable rates, thereby earning an arbitrage spread. While this activity is illegal—and has been for over 20 years—enforcement is difficult and opportunities for evasion persist. Empirical evidence presented below suggests that prior to the Tax Reform Act of 1986 (TRA86), this activity occurred at the municipal level and corroborates evidence presented in Metcalf (1990a) for arbitrage activity at the state level.

Federal tax policy can affect the supply of debt on a second dimension by altering incentives to finance local spending by private versus public borrowing. Viewed in this light, the supply of municipal bonds increases with the spread between the after-tax rate of return on saving for individuals in a community and the municipal borrowing rate. Federal tax policy then has two effects: first, exempting municipal bond income from federal taxation reduces the municipal interest rate and second, taxing the return to savings of residents within a community affects the desired supply of that community's public debt.

In the next section, I review the various ways in which federal tax policy can affect the decision to issue tax-exempt debt at the state and local level. Two factors lead to increased levels of financial assets (and in one case debt also) in a community, while a third factor leads to an increase in debt. With respect to this third factor, I present a model of debt finance from which debt supply equations can be derived. In the second section I provide estimates of the parameters of the debt supply model from a panel data set of 185 cities and

Adapted from the National Tax Journal XLIV: 57–70 by permission of the National Tax Journal.

towns in the United States over an 11-year period from 1980 through 1988. The policy implications of these results are discussed in a concluding section.

I. FACTORS AFFECTING THE SUPPLY OF MUNICIPAL BONDS [2]

The tax-exempt nature of municipal debt creates a direct and obvious opportunity for abritrage activity by state and local governments. A municipal government can borrow at the tax-exempt rate (r_m) and invest the proceeds in taxable securities (earning r). Since municipal governments are not subject to federal taxation, the yield spread $r - r_m > 0$ is a pure tax arbitrage gain. Since 1969 this activity has been illegal. Federal regulations have been written, rewritten, and amended on a steady basis since 1972. As noted in Metcalf (1989), it has been difficult to write regulations which eliminate the arbitrage opportunity yet do not create undue burdens and limitations on the financial activities of state and local governments [3]. The major difficulty in enforcing regulations follows from the concept of "replacement." Consider a community which traditionally has paid for capital projects out of general tax revenues but which in a particular year decides to issue a tax-exempt bond for a capital project. Rather than reducing tax collections by the amount of the bond, the community can invest the extra tax revenues in taxable securities. From an accounting perspective, the bond proceeds are being spent on a capital project and no arbitrage is occurring. From an economic perspective, the community has engaged in tax arbitrage. The difficulty is that the bond proceeds have "replaced" the tax revenues which are now available for investment. While the IRS rules explicitly prohibit replacement as a means of evading the arbitrage rules, an accounting system with a multitude of fund accounts creates significant difficulties in linking specific debt proceeds to specific investments.

This difficulty will exist so long as communities both hold assets and issue debt. In FY 1988, cities and towns held \$139.8 billion in noninsurance financial assets and had \$139.4 billion in long-term debt outstanding, excluding public debt for private purposes. Of this \$65.7 billion is long-term full faith and credit debt. Even if governments act in completely good faith to avoid engaging in tax arbitrage, the very fact that financial assets are held while debt is outstanding means that arbitrage profits are being made [4].

Tax reform (TRA86) created two significant checks on arbitrage. First, volume caps on revenue bonds limit the amount of debt that may be issued and therefore limit arbitrage activity with revenue debt. However, no limits are placed on full faith and credit debt [5]. Second, more stringent arbitrage rules were enacted. However, the experience with previous arbitrage rules should make one cautious in assuming that the new rules will be more effective than previous ones. This view is buttressed by the evidence presented in Metcalf (1990a), where 40 state governments are followed over a 7-year period. In that paper, I find a significant marginal effect of changes in the yield spread ($r - r_m$) on the levels of noninsurance financial assets held by the state government, suggesting that arbitrage rules are not binding at the state level. Later in this chapter, I consider whether the rules bind for city governments over a 9-year period prior to TRA86.

A second form of arbitrage which leads to increased asset holdings (though not debt levels) is saving arbitrage. Communities can raise taxes and invest the proceeds in taxable securities. The interest from the investment is then returned in the future in the form of lower taxes. In effect, the community does the saving for the individual earning an additional return of $r - (1 - \tau)r$ or $r\tau$ where τ is the marginal tax rate on interest income to residents in the community. The greater this "interest tax wedge," the greater the incentives to engage in this type of "saving" arbitrage. There are two factors which reduce the likelihood of communities engaging in saving arbitrage. First, for residents to be willing to forego income today for future income, there must be some link between current fiscal activity and future activity in light of individual mobility. A necessary condition for the arbitrage to work is that there be complete capitalization of the future tax savings into property values (at the local level). Second, the agency problems which might lead to fiscal managers increasing spending rather than reducing future taxes must somehow be overcome. It is not surprising that neither Gordon and Slemrod (1986) nor Metcalf (1990a) found evidence for saving arbitrage in their data sets. When testing for tax arbitrage, I will also consider the possibility of saving arbitrage.

In the introduction, I argued that the supply of municipal debt should be related to the spread between the after-tax rate of return available to residents of the community and the tax-exempt rate that the community must pay on debt it issues. To show this, I present a very simple model in a two-period framework. Consider a community which is choosing to finance public expenditures through a combination of borrowing and taxes. To simplify, assume that the community is made up of N homogeneous individuals with identical preferences modeled by the utility function $U(C_1, C_2, G)$, where C_1 is consumption in the first period and C_2 consumption in the second period. All government spending occurs in the first period (G). Taxes are raised in a lump sum fashion in either period (T_1 or T_2) so that the individual budget constraint is given by

$$C_1 + \frac{C_2}{1 + \rho} = Y - T_1 - \frac{T_2}{1 + \rho},$$ (1)

where ρ is the taxpayer's after-tax rate of return on saving or borrowing. The government faces the budget constraint that all borrowing must be repaid out of second period taxes

$$G = B + NT_1$$ (2)

$$(1 + r_m)B = NT_2$$ (3)

where r_m is the municipal borrowing rate. This rate is endogenous and equals the risk-free net of tax return that investors can get elsewhere (v) plus a risk premium. The risk premium depends on the ratio of debt outstanding to some measure of the ability to repay debt in the future (V) along with other attributes (M) of a community which affect its ability to repay debt (e.g., broadness of tax base, scale economies in the production of goods and services)

$$r_m = v + \phi(B/V) + \xi(M).$$ (4)

Since individuals are identical, the community's choice comes down to maximizing $U(C_1, C_2, G)$ subject to (1)–(4) over the arguments C_1, C_2, G, B, T_1, and T_2. Assuming that there is positive taxation in both periods and positive borrowing in the first period, we can combine the first order conditions for taxes and borrowing to obtain the supply function for municipal bonds in implicit form [6]

$$\begin{aligned}1 + v + \phi(B/V) + \xi(M) \\ + (B/V)\phi' = 1 + \rho.\end{aligned}$$ (5)

The marginal cost of an increment of borrowing is the direct cost plus the indirect cost of raising the cost of any additional borrowing that the community might wish to engage in; this is set equal to the marginal benefit which is the decrease in private borrowing required to finance a given level of public spending through taxes. (Private borrowing can take the form of private dissaving.) Rewriting Eq. (5) slightly emphasizes the fact that the supply of bonds is dependent on the yield spread between the after-tax rate of return available to residents in the community and the municipal borrowing rate

$$\rho - r_m = (B/V)\phi' (B/V).$$ (6)

The after-tax yield spead is a function of the ratio of debt to the measure of the ability to repay. Assuming convexity of the function ϕ, this function can be inverted to yield the debt to tax base measure (B/V) as a function of the yield spread, $\rho - r_m$ [7].

The key role that federal tax policy plays on the supply side is in the after-tax yield spread and more particularly the specification of ρ. I assume that ρ equals $(1 - \tau)r$, where r is the before-tax return to saving (borrowing) by residents of the community and τ is the marginal tax rate on saving (borrowing) by residents. If residents are saving at the margin, public spending can be financed by public borrowing at rate r_m or by drawing down private saving with cost $(1 - \tau)r$. If residents are borrowing at the margin, the cost of private borrowing depends on the borrowing rate as well as the degree of deductibility for interest costs. Prior to the Tax Reform Act of 1986 (TRA86) all interest costs could be deducted, so that the appropriate tax rate would be $p\tau$ where p is an indicator variable equaling 1 when the taxpayer itemizes on her federal tax return and 0 otherwise. After 1986, most interest payments became nondeductible, with the important exception of mortgage and home equity interest. The deduction on home equity loans allowed many homeowners to repackage their consumer debt and continue to receive the deduction. Thus, one should not assume that ρ jumped to r after 1986 for all taxpayers [8].

Inverting Eq. (6) above leads to the estimating equation

$$b_{it} = \beta_0 + \beta_1(\rho - r_m)_{it} + \theta_i + \xi_t + \varepsilon_{it}.$$ (7)

To control for unobservable "taste" variables specific to each state, I allow for the possibilty of an individual (city) effect (θ_i), and to control for cyclical or macroeconomic influences common to all states, I add year dummies (ξ_t). I assume that the error term, ε, is independent and identically distributed with mean zero.

This formulation assumes that actual debt levels represent desired debt levels in each year. An alternative formulation would be a partial adjustment model (analogous to the models in the corporate sector, such as Auerbach's 1985 model). Unlike physical capital, however, where there is a cost of adjustment to accumulate or decumulate capital, there are fewer impediments to changes in financial capital. There are call provisions on municipal bonds, opportunities to buy bonds in the open market, and mechanisms for advance refunding of the debt.

This study differs from previous studies of municipal bond supply (e.g., Asefa et al., 1981; Gordon and Slemrod, 1986) in several ways. First, where previous studies have included a municipal borrowing rate as an explanatory variable, they have not accounted for the endogeneity of the borrowing rate. Second, I have a panel data set which allows me to control for city-specific influences on debt and asset levels (individual effects) if appropriate. Finally, I use the NBER TAXSIM tax calculator to compute marginal tax rates for different spread variables. In the next section, I discuss the data and estimation results in more detail.

II. DESCRIPTION OF THE DATA AND EMPIRICAL RESULTS

In this section, I describe a data set on 185 cities and towns in the United States used in this analysis. Financial data come from the *Annual Survey of Governments* conducted by the U.S. Bureau of the Census. Besides data on revenue and expenditures, the survey contains detailed data on financial assets and outstanding debt, as well as debt issued and retired each year. One advantage of this data set is that the Census Bureau makes considerable efforts to construct data records which are comparable across government units. While these data provide a wealth of information about fiscal decisions in a community, one must exercise some care when using them. In particular, the Government Division of the Bureau of the Census uses different data collection methods for large cities (cities with population greater than 300,000) than for smaller cities and towns. The large cities (so-called jacket cities) are given greater scrutiny by Census representatives who compile data directly from official accounts and records of the cities. Data from smaller communities are collected primarily by a mail canvass with some follow-up in the field to verify or question particular statistics. In the regressions which follow, I have data on 185 cities and towns, of which 42 are jacket cities [9].

One complication arising with local data is the existence of overlapping jurisdictions. Cities may have special districts within or across city limits carrying out activities for city residents or have services provided at the county level. Lacking detailed data with which I could allocate debt from other districts to particular communities, I have not corrected for this problem. Differences in allocation of responsibility may be well modeled as a component of an individual effect, however; in that case, I can control for differences across jurisdictions without explicitly measuring them. I can distinguish between traditional full faith and credit debt and revenue debt issued by the community. During the period of this sample, there was an increasing reliance on revenue debt until 1988 when the restrictions on revenue debt imposed by TRA86 began to bite. Below I analyze both full faith and credit debt and total long-term debt.

I examine data on local governments over an 11-year period (fiscal years 1978 through 1988) [10]. These data are supplemented by data from Moody's *Bond Record*. From this source, I obtain generalized credit ratings for general obligation (GO) debt for cities and towns in the data set [11]. I then impute to each community a borrowing cost (r_m) equal to the average borrowing cost for a 30-year GO bond of that rating at the beginning of the fiscal year. I use the rate on a 20-year Treasury bond at the beginning of the fiscal year as my measure of r [12].

My first analysis investigates the extent to which arbitrage activity occurred at the margin for city governments prior to TRA86. As shown in Table 1, noninsurance trust financial asset holdings averaged $466 per capita in constant dollars (1982) over the 9-year period from FY 1978 through FY 1988. The city and towns in this sample held roughly half as many financial assets as did state governments over this period [13]. The before-tax yield spread ($r - r_m$) averaged 238 basis points with a standard deviation of 63 basis points. This provides a measure of the return to the tax arbitrage which should result in higher financial asset (and debt) holdings.

I include a measure of the returns to saving arbitrage which I call the "interest tax wedge" ($r\tau$). For τ, I use the NBER TAXSIM tax calculator to compute the marginal tax rate on interest income for a hypothetical family of four filing a joint tax return and not itemizing. I impute to the family the median household effective buying income (EBI) for that community at the beginning of the fiscal year after adding the average of local tax collections. Effective buying income is a measure of disposable income (net of federal state and local

Table 1   Summary Statistics

Variable	Mean	Standard deviation	Minimum	Maximum
Noninsurance financial assets (real, per capita)	465.92	427.14	4.40	4900.00
Before-tax yield spread	2.38	.63	.89	3.67
Interest tax wedge	2.38	.73	.75	5.05
Tax collections (per capita)	296.95	179.48	43.06	1268.65
Long-term debt (per $1000 of income)	77.78	68.08	.96	700.41
Full faith and credit debt (per $1000 of income)	32.61	26.33	0.0	184.25
Revenue debt (per $1000 of income)	45.17	63.15	0.0	695.47
After-tax yield spread	−.17	.90	−2.20	1.36
Retail sales (per capita)	6692.77	2016.32	1529.77	16516.57
Population (× 1000)	245.1	311.3	62.5	3364.2

Note: Summary statistics are over 185 cities and towns for the fiscal years 1978 through 1986 for the first four variables (1665 observations) and for the fiscal years 1978 through 1988 for the remaining variables (2035 observations).

taxes). It is calculated by the market statistics division of Bill Communications and is published in the *Annual Survey of Buying Power*. This income concept has been used previously by Holtz-Eakin and Rosen (1988) in a different context. This gives a measure (albeit imperfect) of after-federal-tax income. I then program TAXSIM to determine the before-federal-tax income and marginal tax rate which yields that measure of income [14]. As discussed above, the tax wedge should be positively correlated with asset holdings if saving arbitrage is occurring. I also include long-term debt per capita on the right-hand side. Increasing debt increases the legal amount of financial assets a community can hold. A strong test of arbitrage activity, then, is whether communities increase their holdings of financial assets as the yield spread increases holding debt levels constant. The final variable included in the regression is per capita local tax collections (constant dollars) to capture scale effects in the data set. Cities differ in the amount of services they provide to their residents. Cities providing more services may have larger asset holdings unrelated to arbitrage activity (e.g., sinking funds and bond reserve funds). While I would like to include other fiscal and demographic variables in the analysis, they are simply not available for a time series-cross section analysis such as this one. Including individual effects (fixed effects) is an attempt to capture some of the information contained in these data; to the extent that the demographic data are slow-moving over time, there should not be significant bias.

As noted in Metcalf (1990a), the yield spread variable is likely to be negatively correlated with the residual in an asset regression. Unobserved factors which may induce higher holdings of financial assets are likely to be positively correlated with the credit rating of the community for a given level of debt. These include such factors as the strength of the local economy, its tax base diversity and employment levels, among other things. To correct for this, I run two-stage least squares (2SLS) regressions using population and retail sales per capita as instrumental variables for the credit rating (and thus r_m). Both variables are reported by the *Annual Survey of Buying Power*. Retail sales should be a valid instrument as it measures economic activity within the community and should be negatively correlated with the borrowing rate. Population is included to control for possible scale economies in the community which may affect borrowing costs. Alternatively, large cities typically have larger debt issues which may be more marketable and hence reduce borrowing costs for communities.

Table 2 presents regression results on asset holdings both for the full data set of 185 cities and the 42 largest cities. All regressions include year dummies. The first regression includes dummy variables for individual effects (a fixed effects regression). Including the fixed effects removes the variation in the data across communities. Even so, the results are striking: after controlling for debt, there is a strong reponse in asset holdings to changes in the yield spread. The coefficient estimate of 1412.5 suggests that a 10 basis

Table 2 Regressions with Real per Capita Noninsurance Trust Financial Assets as
Dependent Variable

	Variable				
	(1)	(2)	(3)	(4)	(5)
Before-tax	1412.49	1332.34	483.60	1054.88	289.82
yield spread	(419.67)	(370.18)	(189.22)	(451.47)	(217.56)
Interest tax	75.32	—	—	—	—
wedge	(46.80)				
Tax collections	−.64	−.63	−.10	.15	.47
(per capita)	(.28)	(.26)	(.08)	(.34)	(.18)
Debt (per capita)	.40	.40	.39	.41	.39
	(.02)	(.02)	(.01)	(.04)	(.03)
R^2	.688	.701	.424	.757	.611
T	10.16	10.40	—	9.13	—
	(.038)	(.015)		(.028)	
Number of	1665	1665	1665	378	378
observations					
Type of	FE	FE	FE	FE	FE
estimator					

Note: This table reports results of instrumental variable regressions of noninsurance asset holdings on the variables in the table plus dummy variables for the years. Standard errors are reported in parentheses. Instruments used are population and retail sales per capita. T is a test of the null hypothesis that individual effects are uncorrelated with exogenous variables. The designation FE stands for fixed effects estimator while RE stands for random effects estimator.

point increase in the yield spread leads to a $141 increase in asset holdings (roughly 30% of the mean value of asset holdings in the sample). The estimate implies an elasticity of asset holdings with respect to the yield spread of 7.2 (evaluated at the means) and suggests that the arbitrage rules do little to discourage or limit arbitrage activity.

The interest tax wedge coefficient, a measure of the degree of saving arbitrage, enters negatively and is statistically insignificant. (Remember, it should enter positively if saving arbitrage is occurring.) There is little support for saving arbitrage activity in this or other regressions. Hence, I drop this variable in further regressions. The coefficient on the tax collections variable enters negatively and is statistically significant. Cities with greater amounts of tax collection hold fewer financial assets. Finally, the coefficient on the debt variables is .40 and strongly significant. A dollar of additional debt leads to an increase in asset holdings of $.40 due to the reserve funds, temporary holding periods, and other legal mechanisms available for holding assets.

The second regression excludes the interest tax wedge variable. Results are little changed with the coefficient on the yield spread variable falling to 1332. Both these regressions suffer from the problem that cross-section variation in the data has been removed in the fixed effects estimation. Since considerable variation occurs across communities in asset holdings, it would be useful to estimate the regressions without fixed effects. I do this in the third column, where I report results from a random effects estimator. This estimator assumes that the individual effects are drawn from a distribution with mean zero and constant variance. Given this error structure, the random effects estimator is a generalized least squares estimator. While the random effects approach is more efficient in that I'm not estimating city-specific intercepts, it may lead to inconsistent parameter estimates if the individual effects are correlated with the yield spread variable. Before reporting the results, it should be noted that I tested for the presence of correlated individual effects. The test statistic, denoted T, is reported at the bottom of the fixed effects regressions in the first two columns. The statistic is a chi-square random variable with 4 degrees of freedom in the first regression and 3 in the second. In either test, one rejects the hypothesis that the individual effects are uncorrelated with the exogenous variables. This suggests that the random effects estimates are likely to be biased. Keeping that in mind, let us consider the estimates. The coefficient on the yield spread variable drops to 483.6 while the other coefficient estimates are largely unchanged [15]. The sharp fall in the coefficient estimate from that produced in the fixed effects regression is striking. Even if this smaller estimate is correct (and not subject to bias due to the left out individual effects), the arbitrage response is still very large, with an elasticity (estimated at the means) of 2.47.

The last two regressions limit the sample to the 42 jacket cities. The coefficients on the yield spread variables are similar to those in the full sample regressions and the debt variable coefficients still precisely estimated as .4. However, the tax collection coefficient now switches sign but is insignificant in the fixed effects regression. Again, the test for correlated individual effects rejects lack of correlation between the individual effects and the exogenous variables at the 5% level.

The regressions in Table 2 suggest the following. First, there is evidence of arbitrage activity even after controlling for debt. Using the fixed effects estimate for the full sample (the second regression), the elasticity of asset holdings with respect to the yield spread (measured at the mean values for the data set) is 6.8. Second, there is no evidence of saving arbitrage. Third, a dollar of additional debt leads to a $.40 increase in asset holdings reflecting the legal opportunities for arbitrage available. Finally, correlated individual effects are significant in the asset regressions.

I now move on to measuring debt supply regressions. My measure of b_{it} is outstanding long-term full faith and credit debt (book value) per $1000 of income in community i at the end of fiscal year t. The average amount of long-term debt outstanding for the 185 cities and towns for the 11-year period is $77.78 per $1,000 of income. The majority of this is revenue debt ($45.17) and the rest full faith and credit debt ($32.61).

The average after-tax yield spread is $-.17$ basis points across the sample with a standard deviation of 90 basis points. That the average after-tax yield spread is negative is troubling. In part this may reflect an upward bias in my estimates of marginal tax rates. On average in my sample, the computed marginal tax rate is 21%. But in part, this reflects the high cost of issuing tax-exempt debt in the middle and latter 1980s. Porterba (1989) reports implied marginal tax rates on tax-exempt bonds below 20% for the calendar years 1985 and on. There is also a sharp drop in calendar year 1982, which corresponds to my fiscal year 1983 when the after-tax spread fell sharply (Table 1 in Poterba, 1989).

Table 3 presents regressions with long-term full faith and credit debt outstanding per $1000 of income as the dependent variable. Regressions are presented both for the full data set as well as for the 42 jacket cities. Right-hand-side variables include the after-tax spread variable in all regressions and year dummies in the fixed effect and random effect regressions. All regressions include instrumental variables (population and retail sales per capita) for the spread variable as noted above. The first two regressions exploit the cross section variation in the data for the 185 cities. The first regression pools the entire data set and includes year dummies to control for supply shocks common to all cities, while the second regression is a cross section of the average observation for each city (averaged over time). In both regressions, the coefficient on the spread variable is roughly 60 and statistically significant. To the extent that cross section regressions measure long-run relationships, these regressions suggest that there is a large and important response of municipal debt supply to changes in the after-tax yield spread. A 10 basis point difference in yield spread leads to an 18% change in full faith and credit debt outstanding measured at the mean value of the debt variable in the sample. Regressions 6 and 7 replicate the first two regressions for the 42 large cities in the sample. The estimated coefficients are the wrong sign and have very large standard errors. This suggests that the smaller sample size may not allow precise estimates or that unobserved characteristics of the larger cities may be important.

Before controlling for individual unobserved characteristics, I present two time series regressions (regressions 3 and 8) which average the data for all cities in any year; this may yield insights about the short-run response of debt supply as tax laws have changed. In both the full data set and the smaller data set, the estimated coefficient is roughly 5.2 and is statistically significant to the full cities regression (regression 3). Note that these regressions have 11 observations. Now a 10 basis point change in the yield spread leads to a change in debt supply of nearly 2%.

However, neither the time series or cross section variation controls for any unobserved characteristics in the community. The last set of regressions assumes an individual effect for each city. The fourth and ninth regressions are fixed effects regressions, essentially treating the individual effects as city-specific intercepts while the fifth and tenth regressions treat the individual effects as random draws from a distribution with mean zero and unknown variance. Consider first the estimates using the entire sample (regressions 4 and 5). The fixed effects estimate is 20.9 with a two-sided p value of less than 5%. I ran a test for the hypothesis that the individual effects are uncorrelated with the instrumental variables and fail to reject uncorrelated individual effects at the 5% level. This is reported in the fourth column of Table 3. Given this result, I estimate

Table 3 Debt Regressions Using Full Faith and Credit Debt

	Coefficient on after-tax spread (standard error)	Type of estimator	R^2	T (P-value)	Number of observation
(1)	59.48 (6.68)	XS	.031	—	2035
(2)	63.67 (19.94)	B	.042	—	185
(3)	5.23 (2.32)	TS	.234	—	11[a]
(4)	20.90 (9.88)	FE	.783	3.69 (.055)	2035
(5)	25.99 (9.07)	RE	.037	—	2035
(6)	−143.37 (154.67)	XS	.005	—	462
(7)	−34.68 (141.21)	B	.005	—	42
(8)	5.15 (2.91)	TS	.061	—	11[b]
(9)	79.75 (31.15)	FE	.564	3.44 (.064)	462
(10)	78.13 (43.00)	RE	.011	—	462

Note: This table reports results of instrumental variable regressions of full faith and credit debt on the after-tax yield spread and dummy variables for the years. The instruments used are population and retail sales per capita ($1982). T is a test of the null hypothesis that individual effects are uncorrelated with the exogenous variables. It is distributed as a chi square random variable with 1 degree of freedom.

Under the heading "Type of Estimator," the codes stand for the following: XS—cross section over all states and time periods; B—cross section over the cities using the average of observations across time; TS—time series over the 11 years using the average of the observations across cities in any year; FE—fixed effects regressions; and RE—random effects.

[a]Each observation is an average over the 185 cities.

[b]Each observation is an average over the 42 jacket cities.

a random effects model and obtain a slightly higher coefficient estimate of 26.0 which is significant at the 1% level. Using the 42 jacket cities only, I also fail to reject uncorrelated individual effects and obtain a coefficient estimate of roughly 78 using the random effects estimator. However, this is a less precisely estimated coefficient than is the random effects estimate from the full sample.

What estimate of a supply response should we use given this array of estimates? The two time series estimates give a sense of the short-run response of debt supply to changes in the yield spread. While one must be cautious in interpreting regressions with 11 observations, it is not surprising that the coefficient estimates are much smaller than those estimated using the cross section variation in the data. But even with only 11 observations, the estimates are fairly precisely measured. The best estimate of the supply response to changes in the after-tax yield spread is probably the random effects estimator using the full data set. The coefficient estimate is statistically significant, and the estimator does not remove much of the cross section variation as does the fixed effects estimator yet does account for the fact that there are unobserved differences across cities. That estimate of 26.0 suggests that a 10 basis point change in the yield spread leads to an 8% change in full faith and credit debt based on the mean value of full faith and credit debt in my sample.

However, if the random effects estimate from the tenth regression is to be believed, large cities respond with greater change in debt holdings to changes in the after-tax yield spread [16]. Whether this difference (if true) is the result of more sophisticated financial management or of a political and bureaucratic difference between large and small cities is beyond the scope of this chapter.

Finally, in Table 4 I run the same regressions as in Table 3 with total long-term debt (full faith and credit and revenue) as the dependent variable. The percentage of debt issued as full faith and credit in the sample has fallen from a peak of 63% in 1978 to a low of 45% in 1987 [17]. If revenue debt is substituting for full faith and credit debt, a natural question is whether the after-tax yield spread affects total debt as it does full faith and credit. The regressions in Table 4 suggest that the answer is yes. As in Table 3, both the fixed effects and random effects estimates are statistically significant in the full sample and there is no evidence in support of correlated fixed effects in either the full or restricted sample. Based on the coefficient estimate of 95.6 from the full sample random effects model, a 10 basis point increase in the after-tax yield spread leads to a 12.3% increase in total long-term debt. While the mix of debt may be changing over time, the levels of debt respond to changes in yield spread across communities and time. That the supply of municipal bonds responds to changes in the after-tax yield spread has policy implications that I discuss in the last section.

III.   IMPLICATIONS AND CONCLUSIONS

In summary, the data on municipal governments for the period of the late 1970s and most of the 1980s suggest the following: first, that the arbitrage rules prior to TRA86 have not been effective in eliminating tax arbitrage at the margin. Second, there is little evidence that saving arbitrage is occurring, whereby residents save through their community to earn a before market rate of return. Finally, there is evidence that federal tax policy influences the desired supply of tax-exempt bonds in communities as well as affecting the demand for those bonds by investors. For full faith and credit debt, I estimate a semielasticity of bond supply with respect to the after-tax yield spread of .80. For total long-term debt, the semielasticity estimate is 1.23.

In a federal system such as that found in the United States, the justification for a subsidy of the form given by municipal bonds should arise from efficiency or distributional concerns. With respect to efficiency, there may be some concern that there is a suboptimal amount of real investment in the state or locality due to beneficial spillovers on other communities or states. With respect to distributional concerns, there may be efforts to redistribute income among communities or states. The research reported above suggests that the exemption from federal taxation of municipal bond interest income is likely to improve neither of these objectives. Efficiency won't be enhanced if the bonds are simply being used to finance private borrowing and saving at preferential rates.

The municipal bond subsidy also has a perverse distributional effect. With a progressive income tax system, the implicit tax on municipal bonds is typically less than the marginal tax rate on interest income of

Table 4   Debt Regression Using Total Long-Term Debt

	Coefficient on after-tax spread (standard error)	Type of estimator	R^2	T (P-value)	Number of observations
(1)	87.13 (30.42)	FE	.697	.35 (.554)	2035
(2)	95.60 (25.53)	RE	.023	—	2035
(3)	155.78 (76.89)	FE	.634	.08 (.777)	462
(4)	137.49 (86.31)	RE	.096	—	462

Note: This table reports results of instrumental variable regressions of long-term debt on the after-tax yield spread and dummy variables for the years. See Table 3 for list of instruments and other details of regression output.

the holders of the bulk of municipal bonds. Therefore, a substantial fraction of the subsidy is diverted from communities to high tax rate holders of the bonds. This is likely to be a problem even after the substantial flattening of the U.S. rate structure after TRA86. While top marginal tax rates are currently 28% (or 33%), the implicit tax rate on municipal bonds has hovered around 17 or 18% over the past few years [18].

Any plan to alter the subsidy to state and local governments through the exemption of municipal bond interest income from federal taxation must take into account the behavioral response of local governments implied by the statistical findings above. Inelastic supply of bonds means that reducing the yield spread toward zero will not change the stock of municipal bonds—for supply reasons. The coefficient estimates reported here suggest that there would be a substantial decrease in the desired supply of tax-exempt bonds if the spread were driven toward zero.

What this chapter does not provide is a political economy explanation for the strong support for tax-exempt municipal bonds despite their efficiency and equity deficiencies. One possible explanation which deserves investigation is that the tax exemption is a form of precommitment from the federal government to state and local governments that other subsidies do not provide. The challenge for policy makers is to construct some other subsidy instrument which yields the same level of subsidy protection while reducing the efficiency and equity costs of the existing system.

NOTES

1. For an analysis of the market's reaction to *South Carolina* v. *Baker*, see Poterba (1989). An historical summary of the erosion of the tax exemption of certain types of municipal bonds is given in Davie and Zimmerman (1988).
2. This section draws on my previous papers (Metcalf, 1989; 1990b), as well as an important paper by Gordon and Slemrod (1986).
3. Of course, arbitrage could be eliminated either by allowing state and local governments to invest only in tax-exempt securities or by eliminating the tax exemption for municipal debt. To date, Congress has not chosen to attempt either of these solutions to the arbitrage problem.
4. However, some of the holdings are in special federal securities called SLUGs, which are specifically designed below market rate Treasury bonds created to allow state and local governments to bank bond proceeds without earning arbitrage profits. Unfortunately, I am not able to obtain data on municipal holdings of SLUGs in the empirical analysis which follows.
5. Revenue debt is debt backed by the revenues of particular projects (e.g., ticket sales from a sports arena). General obligation debt is debt backed by the full taxing authority of the issuing jurisdiction. This is typically the safest debt issued by a government. Full faith and credit debt (FFC) is a slightly broader category than general obligation debt. It includes G.O. debt but also includes any debt payable from nontax sources but which represents liabilities to the community if the nontax sources are insufficient to cover required debt payments.
6. To be precise, this is the equilibrium relationship between r_m and B.
7. Alternatively, (5) can be inverted to yield B/V as a function of $\rho - v$ and M. The advantage to this approach is that $\rho - v$ is exogenous whereas $\rho - r_m$ is not. However, the other measures that affect the credit quality of debt (M) must be included in the regression explicitly. The credit rating, though, is a useful summary measure of these other factors affecting credit quality and I proceed by using the credit rating explicitly and using an instrumental variable approach to control for the feedback from B/V to r_m.
8. Even if consumer debt repackaging had not occurred, there would not have been a discontinuous jump in any case as the interest deduction was phased out over time.
9. For the 11-year period of my sample, I had data for 230 cities and towns. There were 45 communities for which data were either missing or inaccurate, leaving me with 185 communities.
10. For the arbitrage regressions, I have 9 years of data. Data on noninsurance financial assets were not available for fiscal years 1987 and 1988 as of yet.
11. The ratings I use to impute borrowing costs are ratings on overall city or town credit as opposed to a rating on a specific bond issue.
12. I use a 20-year rate rather than a 30-year rate to control in part for the callable nature of most municipal debt.
13. In what follows, financial assets will refer to noninsurance trust financial assets. The insurance trust assets are primarily held for pension funds. As noted in Metcalf (1990a), it is difficult to disentangle arbitrage activity in the pension funds from shifts in the timing of wage payments through over- and underfunding. However, one should note that prior to TRA86, it was legal to issue tax-exempt bonds and use the proceeds to purchase nontaxable annuities for pension funds. Hence any evidence in this data set of arbitrage probably understates the true extent of the activity prior to tax reform.
14. This measure ignores important heterogeneity across families in family size, home ownership status, etc. It also underestimates before-tax income by ignoring state tax collections. On the other hand, it also overestimates before-tax income by imputing all local taxes to the resident.

15. I get very similar estimates from running the regression without random effects. I also considered the time series variation in the data, running regressions on the means of the observations for each of the 9 years. However, with so few observations, I get extremely imprecise estimates. Hence I do not report them here.
16. This is also true in percentage terms. A 10 basis point change in the yield spread is associated with 19% change in debt (measured at the mean of the sample).
17. In 1988, the fraction of debt issued as full faith and credit rose by slightly more than one percentage point in my sample.
18. Note, though, the findings of Feenberg and Poterba (1991). They find that the subsidy diversion has been substantially reduced since TRA86.

REFERENCES

Adams, R. D. (1977). *Pub. Finance Q.*, 5: 175–202.
Asefa, S. A., Adams, R. D., and Starleaf, D. R. (1981). *Pub. Finance Q.*, 9: 271–280.
Auerbach, A. J. (1985). *Corporate Capital Structures in the United States* (B. Friedman, ed.), National Bureau of Economic Research, Chicago, pp. 301–324.
Davie, B. and Zimmerman, D. (1988). *Tax Notes*, June 27: 1573–1580.
Feenberg, D. and Poterba, J. (1991). *Nat. Tax J.*, 44: 57–70.
Gordon, R. H. and Slemrod, J. (1986). *Studies in State and Local Public Finance* (H. Rosen, ed.) National Bureau of Economic Research, Chicago: pp. 53–78.
Holtz-Eakin, D. and Rosen, H. (1988). *Fiscal Federalism: Quantitative Studies* (H. Rosen, ed.) University of Chicago Press, Chicago, pp. 107–136.
Leeds, P. (1983). *The Municipal Money Chase* (A. M. Sbragia, ed.), Westview Press Inc., Boulder, Colo., pp. 113–144.
Metcalf, G. E. (1989). *Proceedings of the Eighty-First Annual Conference*, National Tax Association-Tax Institute of America, Des Moines Iowa, pp. 109–114.
Metcalf, G. E. (1990a). *Rev. Econ. Stat.*, 390–396.
Metcalf, G. E. (1990b). "Federal Taxation and the Supply of State Debt," NBER Working Paper No. 3255. Moody's Investors Service. *Moody's Bond Record*, various issues and years, 1977–1984.
Poterba, J. (1989). *Reg. Sci. Urban Econ.*, 19: 537–562.
Sales and Marketing Management Magazine. Annual Survey of Buying Power, various years.
Sbragia, A. M. (1983). *The Municipal Money Chase* (A. M. Sbragia, ed.), Westview Press, Boulder, Colo., pp. 67–112.
Simons, H. (1938). *Personal Income Taxation*, University of Chicago Press, Chicago,
U.S. Bureau of the Census. *City Government Finances*, U.S. Government Printing Office, Washington D.C., various years.

5

Do Tax-Exempt Bonds Really Subsidize Municipal Capital?

Roger H. Gordon
University of Michigan, Ann Arbor, Michigan, and the National Bureau of Economic Research, Cambridge, Massachusetts

Gilbert E. Metcalf
Tufts University, Medford, and the National Bureau of Economic Research, Cambridge, Massachusetts

Many writers have claimed in the past that the tax-exempt status of interest on municipal bonds provides a subsidy to municipal expenditures, and more particularly to municipal investment. For example, Musgrave and Musgrave (1989, p. 562) claim that "[w]ith state and local borrowing used for capital expenditure, such support is equivalent to a matching grant for capital outlays." Similarly, Pechman (1987, pp. 125–126) claims that taxing municipal bond interest income "would discourage borrowing by some localities and thereby reduce capital expenditures for public purposes." The objective of this note is to argue that the theory underlying such claims is highly deficient. Municipal investment is subsidized by the tax-exempt status of municipal bonds only if increasing capital investment by an extra dollar enables a community to borrow more, and thereby gain more from its right to borrow at this low rate. If the community could borrow as much as it wants anyway, then no subsidy exists. But just as wealthy investors in municipal bonds buy tax-exempt bonds until risk-bearing costs make further investment in them unattractive, low-tax-bracket individuals can engage in the reverse arbitrage by borrowing through their municipalities at the tax-exempt rate until nontax costs make further borrowing unattractive. [1] If these nontax costs, rather than the amount of capital investment undertaken by the municipality, limit the amount of municipal borrowing, then there is no subsidy to capital investment. We also argue, however, that the revenue costs of the tax-exempt status of municipal bonds have been substantially overestimated in the past.

What then underlies the claims that the tax-exempt status of municipal bonds subsidizes municipal capital expenditures? The argument goes as follows: When municipal bonds are tax-exempt, the interest rate on these bonds is reduced, allowing municipalities to borrow at this lower interest rate when they raise the same funds. If municipal bonds were instead made taxable, municipalities would have to pay the higher taxable interest rate when they raise the same funds. If r denotes the taxable interest rate and r_m denotes the tax-exempt interest rate, then the subsidy to municipal capital expenditures due to the tax-exempt status of municipal bonds is measured by $r - r_m$ times the amount of funds the community needs to raise to finance capital projects. This amount, $r - r_m$, would be received each year the bonds are outstanding. [2]

The same intuition underlies the Treasury's calculation of the revenue cost of the tax-exempt status of municipal bonds. As noted in Toder and Neubig (1985), the Treasury's calculations of the revenue cost assume that if municipal bonds were made taxable, municipal borrowing would remain unchanged, and those who

Adapted from *National Tax Journal* XLIV: 71–79 by permission of the *National Tax Journal*. We would like to thank the editors and a referee for comments on a previous draft.

previously purchased the tax-exempt bonds would now purchase the taxable bonds. If all those who had purchased the tax-exempt bonds were in the tax bracket t* such that $r(1-t^*)=r_m$, then the calculated revenue cost of the tax-exempt status of municipal bonds is simply $rt^* = r - r_m$ times the amount of municipal bonds issued. This just equals the size of the subsidy to municipal capital expenditures, calculated under the above assumptions. If municipal bonds were in part purchased by investors facing tax rates higher than t^*, then the revenue cost would exceed the subsidy to municipal capital expenditures, making this approach to subsidizing municipal capital expenditures less "efficient." This logic is implicit in virtually all papers in the area, most recently Feenberg and Poterba (1991).

I. PROBLEMS WITH THE TRADITIONAL VIEW

A. Ignores Availability of Tax as Well as Debt Financing

What is wrong with this line of reasoning? To begin with, would municipalities continue to borrow to finance capital expenditures if municipal bonds were made taxable? Rather than borrowing initially to finance the capital expenditures and then raising municipal taxes in each future period to pay the interest charges on the municipal debt, a community could instead raise taxes initially to finance the capital expenditures. Which alternative is more attractive? Assume if taxes are used initially to finance a capital project that municipal residents would finance these one-time taxes by withdrawing funds from their savings. If these savings had been in taxable bonds/bank deposits, then these savings had been earning a net-of-tax rate of return of $r(1 - t)$, where t is the marginal tax rate faced by the typical (median) resident. [3] If taxes were used to finance the project, residents would therefore find their income reduced in each future period by $r(1 - t)$ times the cost of the capital project. But if the project had instead been financed entirely with debt, then future taxes would be r times the cost of the capital project. As long as $t > 0$, then residents would prefer to finance the project with taxes rather than with debt. [4] Therefore, the cost of funds for a municipal capital project is $r(1 - t)$ rather than r. When municipal bonds are tax-exempt, municipalities can finance capital projects either with taxes where the foregone rate of return on savings is $r(1 - t)$ or with municipal bonds where the interest rate is r_m. They should prefer whichever alternative is cheaper. If this were the only problem, then we would measure the size of the subsidy to municipal investment from making municipal bonds tax-exempt by the reduction in the cost of funds from $r(1 - t)$ to $\min(r(1 - t), r_m)$. This contrasts with the traditional view that the cost of funds would be reduced from r to r_m.

Given this revised story about municipal behavior, what is the revenue cost of making municipal bonds tax-exempt? Assume for simplicity that when municipal bonds are tax-exempt, all municipal capital projects are financed with debt. When the tax-exempt status of municipal bonds is eliminated, the above reasoning suggests that all capital projects should instead be tax financed. If so, then municipal bonds would disappear. If municipal capital investment remains unchanged, then residents reduce their savings by the same amount. Financial markets would still balance if those who previously purchased the municipal bonds now buy the securities no longer purchased by municipal residents. Would the traditional revenue estimate still be right if these residents had saved entirely in taxable bonds? In this case, eliminating the tax-exempt status of municipal bonds causes taxable bonds to shift from the portfolios of residents to the portfolios of those who previously purchased municipal bonds. Tax revenue increases only to the degree to which the typical purchaser of a municipal bond is in a higher tax bracket than the typical resident of a community undertaking a capital investment project. Since those now holding municipal bonds are typically the very wealthy, revenue would still be forecast to rise, but by less than in the traditional view since the traditional view ignores the taxes previously paid on the taxable bonds by municipal residents.

B. Ignores Portfolio Rebalancing in Revenue Estimation

This revised view still overestimates the revenue gain from eliminating the tax-exempt status of municipal bonds for at least two reasons. First, the typical resident will finance the capital project in more diverse ways than just by reducing investments in taxable bonds. For example, residents may reduce their savings in less heavily taxed financial assets, in which case shifting the ownership of these assets to those who are in higher tax brackets raises less revenue.

Second, even if residents did finance capital spending entirely by reducing their purchases of taxable bonds, those who previously purchased the municipal bonds will not likely shift to investing in taxable bonds.

Instead there should be a broader rebalancing of portfolios, so that the most lightly taxed assets continue to be owned primarily by those in the highest tax brackets, and conversely. For example, those who previously owned municipal bonds could invest instead in corporate equity, real property, or other lightly taxed assets. These assets would be purchased from those in somewhat lower tax brackets. At the end of this chain, the lowest tax bracket investors (e.g., pension funds) would purchase the taxable bonds no longer purchased by municipal residents. On net, this rearrangement of portfolios is driven by an attempt to minimize tax liabilities, and results in a smaller increase in tax revenue than was forecasted previously. Therefore, even though the tax-exempt status of municipal bonds provides less of a subsidy to municipal capital than is traditionally thought, the revenue cost of this tax-exempt status is also less than traditionally thought.

C. Ignores Risk Costs of Financial Arbitrage

Problems with the traditional view do not end here. So far, the tax-exempt status of municipal bonds still reduces the cost of municipal expenditures from $r(1 - t)$ to $\min(r(1 - t), r_m)$. But this presumes that there are no other cost differences between tax and debt finance of municipal investment. But when communities borrow, they always face the risk that unexpected changes in their tax revenue or in interest rates may make it difficult for them to repay the debt. Default on existing debt can be very costly, as shown for example by Leeds (1983) who documented the reorganization costs faced by New York City during its fiscal crisis in 1975. In addition, when lenders recognize ex ante the possibility of default, they will monitor the activity of the municipality more closely, charging implicitly for the costs of this monitoring by raising the interest rate r_m at which they are willing to lend to the municipality. The municipality may be able to reassure lenders by purchasing insurance which guarantees repayment of the debt, [5], but the cost of this insurance rises the more borrowing the municipality does. Even if default never occurred, borrowing heavily puts municipal residents in a highly leveraged position, which has its own risk-bearing costs. Just as we normally presume that wealthy investors in municipal bonds purchase enough of these bonds so that at the margin they are indifferent between purchasing yet more vs. investing instead in other assets (or borrowing yet more), it is equally natural to presume that municipalities issue municipal bonds until their residents are indifferent between issuing yet more bonds and financing capital expenditures instead through taxes. But what if the costs of municipal debt have risen to the point that the community is indifferent between further issues of debt and increased municipal taxes? Then the marginal cost of funds for municipal expenditures equals $r(1 - t)$, which also equals r_m plus the extra costs at the margin of more municipal debt, whether these extra costs are due to extra risk-bearing costs, extra monitoring costs which are charged to the borrower, or a higher probability of paying the costs brought on by default. But if the marginal cost of funds for municipal investment equals $r(1 - t)$ even when municipal bonds are tax-exempt, there is *no* resulting subsidy to municipal investment, since as argued above the cost of funds is also $r(1 - t)$ when municipal bonds are taxable.

II. A FORMAL MODEL OF MUNICIPAL BORROWING

In order to make these arguments more formally, consider a simple two-period economy, in which residents consume C_i in period i, and benefit from municipal investment K undertaken in the first period. Their utility function can be expressed by $U(C_1, C_2, K)$. Residents receive exogenous income of Y_i and pay lump-sum taxes to the municipality of T_i in each period i. In the first period, their income can be consumed, saved, or paid in taxes to the community. If savings are denoted by S, then budget balance in the first period implies that $Y_1 = C_1 + S + T_1$. If residents earn some net-of-tax rate of return ρ on their savings, then budget balance in the second period implies that $Y_2 + S(1 + \rho) = C_2 + T_2$. If for simplicity the only two assets available to savers are municipal bonds and U.S. government bonds, and if the typical (median) tax bracket of residents is t, then $\rho = \max(r(1 - t), r_m)$.

The community in the first period invests K, financing it through some combination of taxes and debt. If T_1 represents taxes in the first period and D measures the size of the debt issue, then the community's budget balance in the first period implies that $K = T_1 + D$. However, most states impose the constraint on communities that debt can be issued only to finance capital expenditures, so that $D \leq K$. [6]. In the second period, the community raises taxes to repay the debt. The expected rate of return investors require on this debt, net of any costs they face, is equal to r_m. However, we also assume that the community ex ante pays additional expected costs $c(D/Y_2)$ per dollar of debt issued, where $c(0) = 0$, $c' > 0$, and $c'' > 0$. This function captures implicitly any costs of risk-bearing, expected costs of default, or monitoring costs (paid by the community through a higher coupon), all of which should increase as D rises relative to the income level of the community. [7] Given these costs, the community's budget balance in the second period implies that $T_2 = D(1 + r_m + c(D/Y_2))$.

If the community chooses K and D so as to maximize the utility of the typical resident, where T_1 and T_2 follow from the budget constraints in each period, what should it do? If we let λ represent the Lagrangian on the constraint that $K \geq D$, and make use of the condition characterizing the individual's optimal savings, then the first-order condition characterizing the optimal policy can be expressed by

$$\frac{\partial U}{\partial C_1} = \frac{\partial U}{\partial K} + \lambda \tag{1}$$

where

$$\lambda = \max\left(\rho - r_m - c - \left(\frac{D}{Y_2}\right) c', 0\right) \frac{\partial U}{\partial C_2}. \tag{2}$$

As is seen in Eq (1), municipal investment is subsidized only to the degree to which $\lambda > 0$. In interpreting λ, consider first the situation in which $c = 0$ always. Since $\rho = \max(r_m, r(1 - t))$, we find that $\lambda = \max(r(1 - t) - r_m, 0)$. Therefore, $\lambda > 0$ only in communities in which $r(1 - t) > r_m$. Since, by definition, $r_m = r(1 - t^*)$, we find that municipal investment is subsidized only in communities in which $t < t^*$, and the size of the subsidy is proportional to $r(1 - t) - r_m$, rather than to $r - r_m$ as presumed in the traditional view. Here, K is subsidized because investing a dollar more allows the community to issue a dollar more municipal bonds, where the gain from issuing a dollar more bonds is proportional to $r(1 - t) - r_m$.

When the function c can differ from zero, then the size of the subsidy is reduced or eliminated even in these communities. If communities stop borrowing because the value of c has risen to the point that $r(1 - t) = r_m + c + (D/Y_2)c'$, rather than because $D = K$, than $\lambda = 0$ and there is no subsidy to municipal investment. Even if borrowing continues until the constraint $D \leq K$ is binding, the size of the subsidy to municipal investment is now proportional to $r(1 - t) - r_m - c - (D/Y_2)c'$, rather than to $r - r_m$.

We therefore find that the tax-exempt status of municipal bonds provides a subsidy to municipal investment only to the degree to which the constraint $D \leq K$ is binding. But this constraint, when it exists, comes from state rather than from federal legislation [8]. But why should states impose restrictions on the amount of debt municipalities can issue, thereby limiting their ability to take advantage of the tax-exempt status of municipal bonds? One possible reason is offered by Epple and Spatt (1986), who argue that states hope to create a reputation for debt enforcement in order to reduce the cost of borrowing for all communities in the state. However, that reputation is only credible if communities within the state rarely default. A default by one community produces a negative externality on other communities in the state by increasing the perceived likelihood of default by these other communities. One way a state can correct for such externalities is to impose a limitation on municipal borrowing; for example, by requiring that borrowing be done only to finance capital expenditures. Since the state as a whole faces no federal constraints on municipal debt issues, however, the optimal constraints would imply that the state is indifferent at the margin to new debt issues. From the state's perspective, therefore, municipal investment is not subsidized by the tax-exempt status of municipal bonds even if each community individually would prefer to issue more debt than the state allows. As a result, if municipalities respond to a binding constraint that $D \leq K$ by investing more, the state would want to offset this distortion to municipal investment incentives by reducing any subsidy it provides to municipal investment. These subsidies are often provided to internalize benefit spillovers across communities, so reducing them is straightforward.

The above story must be changed when residents are renters rather than owners. In aggregate, according to the *Statistical Abstract of the U.S., 1990*, 36% of occupied housing units (occupied primarily by poorer households) are rented. Renters are affected by how municipal investments are financed only to the degree to which their rents are affected. But do their rents depend on whether debt issues or taxes are used to finance municipal investments? Rents ultimately depend on the supply and demand for housing. In the short run, the supply of housing is relatively fixed, so that rents depend only on demand. Extra municipal investment can make the community more attractive, so increase demand and therefore equilibrium rents. But the method of financing this investment does not affect demand. Will it eventually affect supply? When comparing current property taxes with taxes in future periods to repay municipal debt, apartment owners will compare the two using their own net-of-tax discount rate. Since landowners are normally in high tax brackets, given the favorable tax treatment of apartment buildings, their discount rate will normally equal r_m. As a result, they will be indifferent to the form of finance. Therefore, even in the long run, rents will be unaffected by the form of municipal finance. If the tax-exempt status of municipal bonds were eliminated and communities shifted to using only tax finance, then equilibrium rents remain unchanged [9]. Therefore, renters gain nothing from the tax-exempt status of municipal bonds, not even arbitrage profits from the municipality's ability to borrow at the tax-exempt rate. In particular, municipal investment is not subsidized in communities in which the median voter is a renter, regardless of the tax rate t in these communities.

While the analysis above must be altered when there are renters, it is not likely to be affected if taxes can be exported, whether they are exported to nonresidents or to the federal government through deductibility. If the fraction of taxes exported remains constant over time, then there are no changes in the story at all. If a fraction p of taxes is exported, then the cost to a resident of raising a dollar in taxes is $1 - p$, whether it is raised today to finance a capital project or raised tomorrow to repay a bond issued to finance the project. If the fraction of taxes exported is rising over time, then there are incentives to increase debt financing of capital projects. But this incentive exists regardless of the tax treatment of municipal bonds.

Our analysis has also made the simplifying assumption that communities are homogeneous so that tax rates do not vary across individuals within a community. At the community level, sorting works to increase homogeneity; low-tax-rate individuals will prefer communities with higher amounts of municipal borrowing, while high-tax-rate individuals will prefer communities with lower amounts of municipal borrowing. With heterogeneity in tax rates within a community, our argument is not altered, though the measurement of the subsidy is made more complicated. Assuming a decisive voter framework, the appropriate tax rate used to determine the mix of tax and debt financing is that of the decisive voter. Given the mix of financing chosen, the correct tax rate for measuring the size of the subsidy is a weighted average marginal tax rate, with local tax shares as weights.

III. DISCUSSION AND CONCLUSIONS

Why are these results so different from the effects of the tax deductibility of corporate interest payments on corporate investment rates? Many papers argue that corporate investment incentives increase due to the favorable tax treatment of corporate interest, so how can we argue that municipal investment is unaffected by the favorable treatment of municipal bonds? The key difference is that when corporations invest more, this enables them to borrow more so allows them to increase their interest deductions. Not only does the extra capital generate more income to help repay new debt, but the extra capital can be used as security for the new debt. Therefore, lenders are willing to lend more if corporations invest more. In contrast, municipal investment rarely generates any cash flow and it cannot be used effectively as security for municipal debt. Lenders' "security" is simply the property tax base of the community, which is unchanged by municipal investment. When a municipality invests more, it therefore does not change its ability to borrow.

If the tax-exempt status of municipal bonds does not provide a subsidy to municipal investment, what role does it play in the economy? The effects on wealthy investors are easy to describe. Consider, for example, the diagram in Fig. 1 describing the net-of-tax rate of return on taxable (line TT) and tax-exempt (line MM) bonds, as a function of the tax rate of the investor. As seen in the diagram, any investor in a tax bracket above t* earns more after tax by investing in municipal bonds than in taxable bonds. In fact, such investors have an incentive to borrow at the taxable rate, deduct the interest, and use the proceeds to invest further in municipal bonds [10]. Standard portfolio theory forecasts that they will engage in this arbitrage until they face enough risk from unexpected changes in the value of r relative to that of r_m that at the margin the risk-bearing costs of further arbitrage just outweigh the tax benefits. But the same story can be told in reverse for those investors in tax brackets below t*. These investors prefer to invest in taxable rather than municipal bonds, and would gain from borrowing at the tax-exempt rate to invest further at the taxable rate. While such investors cannot as individuals borrow at the tax-exempt rate, they can do so collectively through their municipal government. By the same logic as is used for wealthy investors, they should engage in this reverse arbitrage until the risk-bearing costs or other nontax costs of further arbitrage just offset the tax gain. These two arguments are entirely symmetric. The municipality serves as a financial intermediary for low-bracket investors, just as a stockbroker serves as a financial intermediary for high-bracket investors. In each case, intermediaries may charge some for their services [11], but intermediaries are not subsidized by the asymmetric tax treatment of the two assets. On net, those in extreme tax brackets at both ends gain from the tax-exempt status of municipal bonds, while those in intermediate tax brackets are basically left unaffected [12].

Making interest on municipal bonds taxable would eliminate the above arbitrage possibilities for both low-tax-bracket and high-tax-bracket investors. However, it would not eliminate all the arbitrage possibilities

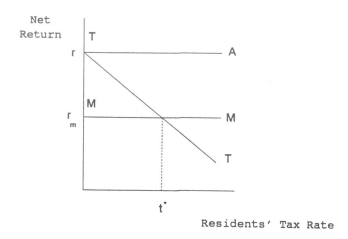

Figure 1   Net Return for Bondholders.

municipalities have available. If municipalities invest surplus funds in taxable bonds, the resulting interest income is received free of tax. Therefore, investors can receive a rate of return (r), line TA in Fig. 1 if they invest in taxable bonds through their municipality. The higher the tax bracket of the individual, the greater the gain from this possibility [13]. Section 148 of the IRS code currently restricts the degree to which communities can borrow at r_m to invest at the taxable rate r. It does not limit, however, the degree to which a community can raise taxes now, invest the funds in taxable bonds, then use the resulting interest income to reduce taxes in the future [14]. If communities were to stop issuing municipal bonds if these bonds become taxable, however, then section 148 would no longer limit their ability to invest in taxable bonds. If anything, therefore, municipal investment in taxable bonds should increase as a result of making interest on municipal debt taxable [15].

The only way to eliminate the arbitrage possibilities available to municipalities would be to pass through any interest income received by the municipality, and interest payments made by the municipality, to individual residents for tax purposes. The logic is the same as that underlying schemes to integrate the corporate and the personal income tax [16]. In each case, under current law, income owned by an individual is taxed at one rate if the individual receives it directly, but at a different rate if it is received to begin with by a corporation or a municipality "owned" by the individual. The distortions created by these differences in tax rates would be eliminated if all income owned by the individual, regardless of whether it is received directly or indirectly, is taxed at the same rate. The easiest way to do this would be to include in each individual's taxable income his share of the taxable income received by a corporation he owns shares in, and his share of the taxable income or tax deductions of a municipality he lives in. Then, even if the municipality earns a rate of return r on investments in taxable bonds, residents would receive a net rate of return $r(1-t)$. Similarly, even if the municipality has to pay a rate of return r on any debt it issues, the net-of-tax costs of this debt to residents would become $r(1-t)$.

In sum, the tax-exempt status of municipal bonds should have little or no effect on capital investment by municipalities. Its main effect is to open up arbitrage opportunities for investors in extreme tax brackets. When municipal bonds are tax-exempt, those in the highest tax brackets can earn a more attractive rate of return, while those in the lowest tax brackets can borrow through their municipalities at a lower interest rate. Renters, however, cannot gain from their municipality's ability to borrow at this low rate. Since many low-tax-bracket individuals are also renters, the gains from the tax-exempt status of municipal bonds go primarily to those in the highest tax brackets.

NOTES

1. These nontax costs can include not only risk-bearing costs, but also increased risk of municipal default, with all the costs that involves.
2. If bonds are retired at the same rate that the capital financed by them depreciates, then the figure $r - r_m$ measures

the reduction in the required rate of return on municipal investment arising from the tax-exempt status of these bonds. Normally, however, new debt issues are retired more quickly than the capital depreciates, leading to a smaller reduction in the required rate of return on new investment than $r - r_m$.

3. Of course, the residents may not finance the initial taxes by withdrawing the funds from their savings (i.e., private consumption might fall), and the savings may not have been entirely in taxable bonds. But as long as each resident were doing some savings, then the alternative sources of funds would have the same cost as foregone savings at the margin. Similarly, as long as each resident had some savings in taxable bonds (or had borrowed some at this interest rate), then the alternative investments would earn a rate of return equivalent in utility terms to $r(1 - t)$.

4. If individuals itemize, so that they can deduct any municipal taxes they pay, then the costs of financing with either alternative would be reduced by the same proportion. If, however, individuals itemize in some periods and not others, then they would want to structure the financing so that all of the taxes are paid in those periods in which they itemize.

5. See Quigley and Rubinfeld (1991) for a discussion of municipal use of insurance.

6. While it would have been equivalent here to assume that $T_1 > 0$, this equivalence would no longer hold if we allowed for noncapital expenditures by the municipality.

7. While the coupon on the debt can rise as the community borrows more to compensate lenders for any losses they may incur in the event of default, if it does so simply to offset underpayments in the event of default, leaving the expected receipts of lenders the same, then it also leaves the expected payments by the community the same. This effect of extra borrowing therefore does not appear in the function $c(.)$.

8. If no such state-imposed constraint exists, then the above model implies that municipal capital investment cannot be subsidized by the tax-exempt status of municipal bonds. According to Hill (1978), four states do not have any limits on municipal debt levels.

9. The argument that only tax finance will be used is a bit weaker here. While landlords would prefer tax finance, tenants would be indifferent unless they recognized the unfavorable effects of debt finance on rents in the long run.

10. This form of arbitrage is in principle prevented by section 265 of the IRS code, though enforcement of this section is extremely difficult.

11. Competitive pressure, due to mobility in the municipal context, should cause these charges to equal the resource cost of engaging in this financial activity. Stories about a "flypaper effect" presume that these competitive pressures on a municipality are weak, however.

12. To the extent that those in low tax brackets are renters, however, they do not gain from their community's ability to borrow at the tax-exempt interest rate. Given how commonly those in low tax brackets rent, the gains from the tax-exempt status of municipal bonds should go primarily to those in high tax brackets.

13. See Gordon and Slemrod (1986) for further discussion.

14. Some states, for example, have enacted tuition prepayment programs, in order to take advantage of this tax-exempt form of savings. In this particular case, however, the IRS has moved to tax the income accruing within these plans to the participating individuals. (See *The New York Times*, Aug. 29, 1988).

15. Since municipal borrowing would become very expensive if interest on municipal debt were taxable, communities would want to avoid any debt issues. One way to avoid sharp fluctuations in municipal tax rates over time is to raise taxes in anticipation of future capital investments, putting the funds in the interim in taxable bonds. For this reason as well, municipal investments in taxable bonds should increase.

16. Such schemes are described, for example, in McLure (1979).

REFERENCES

Epple, D. and Spatt, C. (1986). *J. Pub. Econ., 29*: 199–221.

Feenberg, D. and Poterba, J. (1991). *Nat. Tax J., 44*.

Gordon, R. H. and Slemrod, J. (1986). *State and Local Public Finance* (H. Rosen, ed.), University of Chicago Press/N.B.E.R., Chicago.

Hill, M. (1978). *State Laws Governing Local Government Structure and Administration*, Institute of Government, University of Georgia, Athens.

Leeds, P. (1983). *The Municipal Money Chase* (A. Sbragia, ed.), Westview Press, Boulder, Colo.

McLure, C. (1979). *Must Corporate Income Be Taxed Twice?* Brookings Institution, Washington, D.C.

Musgrave, R. and Musgrave, P. (1989). *Public Finance in Theory and Practice*, McGraw-Hill, New York.

Pechman, J. (1987). *Federal Tax Policy*, Brookings Institution, Washington, D.C.

Quigley, J. and Rubinfeld, D. (1991). *Nat. Tax J., 44*.

Toder, E. and Neubig, T. (1985). *Nat. Tax J., 38*: 395–414.

6

Nothing Is Certain but Death and Taxes: The Conditional Irrelevance of Municipal Capital Structure

G. Marc Choate and Fred Thompson
Atkinson School of Management, Willamette University, Salem, Oregon

The conventional wisdom says that municipal finance has a lot in common with personal finance:

> local governments should live within their income (revenues): they [should] borrow [only] to finance extraordinary, major capital projects . . . they [should] try to save for a rainy day; and they should use budgets to make both ends meet. . . . Capital budgets should be separately established for the purpose of controlling expenditures of individual, extraordinary, major capital projects (Bordner, 1982:14).

This is much the same as saying municipalities cannot or should not borrow and must therefore ration capital. Even sophisticated financial analysts often endorse pay-as-you-go financing for local governments and assign a distinctly subordinate role to capital budgeting in public-sector financial management (Mikesell, 1991:168–70, 408–409). Furthermore, many financial analysts implicitly presume that local governments are liquidity constrained. A. J. Keown and J. D. Martin, for example, assert that "budgeting in the public sector means satisfying as many conflicting goals as possible by distributing the dollars of a limited budget" (1974:22).

Yet, given the existence of a capital market in which municipalities can borrow, these notions are flatly contradicted by the principles of corporate finance taught in most business schools (Baesel et al., 1981:23–32). Capital budgeting is the backbone of private-sector finance. It is concerned with all decisions that have future consequences. Its time horizon is the life of the decision; its focus is the discounted net present value of the decision alternative. Corporate theory teaches that in the presence of a capital market in which funds can be obtained at a price, the welfare of a firm's shareholders will be maximized by the implementation of all projects offering positive net-present values. This conclusion follows from the separation principle, often called Fisher separation after its formulator, Irving Fisher. This principle states that a firm's operating decisions are separate from the personal consumption decisions of its owners. Normatively speaking, this means that firm's financial decisions should be guided by a single goal: maximization of the wealth of its shareholders. Depending upon the individual shareholder's time preference for consumption, he or she can then borrow against this wealth or lend it to maximize personal satisfaction or utility.

Many students of corporate finance further argue that a firm's capital budgeting decisions should also be independent of the financing or capital-structure question. This view is associated with the work of Nobel laureates Franco Modigliani and Merton Miller, who adumbrated it in their germinal article "The Cost of Capital, Corporate Finance and the Theory of Investment" (1958). This article made two distinct conceptual breakthroughs. First, it established a new method of proof for economics, the law of one price, which says that owing to the possibility of "homemade leverage" or "arbitrage" by investors, two similar assets must have the same price (i.e., must be priced to yield the same expected rate of return). This methodology has since become central to financial economics. Second, Modigliani and Miller proved that under certain conditions, a firm's value will be the same regardless of whether it finances its activities with debt or equity.

I. DOES CAPITAL STRUCTURE MATTER?

The purpose of this chapter is to show that municipal finance may be more like corporate finance than is usually appreciated. More precisely, we show that under reasonable conditions municipal capital structure is irrelevant. Of course, as Jerome Baesel, D. T. Methé, and David Shulman (1981:26) have observed, "In public-sector finance, the issue that corresponds to the capital-structure question in corporate finance is whether the tax policy (bonds versus current assessment) of the community matters." Hence, what we show in this chapter is that the value of a municipality does not depend on the way it chooses to finance public spending.[*] Our argument begins with a simple model. We use this model to show that under fairly general conditions municipal borrowing does not matter, that it neither helps nor harms the individuals who live in the municipality. This means that benefits to citizens from community-provided services will be the same regardless of whether they are financed by debt or taxes. Given the conventional wisdom about municipal finance, the implications of this conclusion are somewhat surprising; it suggests that public officials who agonize over balancing municipal budgets are actually wasting their time. So long as *municipal borrowing does not affect individual consumption levels or choices*, municipal debt is irrelevant.

We then show that the irrelevancy of municipal debt may be contingent upon symmetrical income-tax treatment. It appears that America's income-tax system favors debt over pay-as-you-go municipal financing; that is, some municipalities could actually increase the welfare of at least some of their citizens by using debt to reduce local taxes. If this observation is valid, then public officials who agonize over balanced budgets are not only wasting their time, in some cases they may actually injure the citizenry.

Our point is not that public officials are indifferent to the harm they might do to the citizenry. Quite the contrary. If public officials fail to maximize citizen welfare, their failure is probably due to a misunderstanding of how to do so, not to lethargy or disregard. Frankly, we believe that most public-sector managers and budgeters are ill-served by their training. First of all, the teaching materials on public financial management are not very good. We think that public financial managers should have a solid understanding of financial accounting and the use of accounting ratios to evaluate financial conditions, of cost-benefit analysis, and of the use of operating budgets as managerial control devices. They should also know about revenue, debt, and cash administration. Unfortunately, most public financial management texts either omit these topics or cover them superficially, in part because they try to cover everything in one course.

Second, corporate finance has undergone a revolution in the last 30 years, a revolution that has largely passed public financial management by. At one time, corporate finance was mainly concerned with evaluating the effects of operations on financial statements, computing financial ratios, and analyzing accounting rules. The new corporate finance is mathematically rigorous; its theorems are deduced from first principles and proven by econometric models. More important, it works. Wall Street may be firing economists, but the economists that are being fired are not the ones who price options, calculate betas, and design portfolios. We believe that many of the central concepts of the new corporate finance could be useful in public financial management. For example, the capital-asset pricing model could help to integrate a variety of topics—discount rates, borrowing costs, cash management, and the like. However, using these concepts presumes that public finance is fundamentally like corporate finance. We are inclined to accept this presumption, but are still not entirely comfortable with it. One of our purposes in writing this chapter is to try it on for size.

II. A SIMPLIFIED MODEL OF MUNICIPAL FINANCE

Our model rests on the following assumptions:

Individuals in our model live in a single-period world spanning two points in time. We will call the first point or moment the present and the second the future ($t = 0$ and $t = 1$).

Individuals maximize their utility by making choices about present and future levels of consumption [i.e., the ith individual seeks to maximize his or her utility (U_i) where utility is a function of two moment consumption (C_{i0}, C_{i1}). Consumption comprehends the consumption of municipally supplied services and amenities and residential services, as well as the consumption of all other goods and services.

---

[*]Robert Barro (1974) makes a similar claim with respect to the national debt in his now justly famous article, "Are Government Bonds Net Wealth," in which he argues that both the case for and the case against public borrowing are flawed. While he acknowledges that wasteful spending is imprudent, he demonstrates that changes in the size of the federal budget deficit have no effect upon economic activity. It makes no difference, he concludes whether federal government spending is financed by borrowing (i.e., by selling bonds) or by raising taxes.

Further, the isoutility maps (indifference maps) of the individuals in our model are presumed to be convex to the origin.].

Each individual has an income endowment or wealth constraint (Y_{i0}, Y_{i1}), that is net of income and property taxes. Individual behavior is governed by the magnitude of these endowments. Further, this income endowment is presumed to have two components, residential property income—which is just equal in magnitude to the consumption value of the residential services provided by the property to its owner—and all other income. Only the latter is subject to income taxes.

Each individual makes decisions about both present and future consumption levels (C_{i0}, C_{i1}). These decisions are ultimately constrained by the individual's income endowment (Y_{i0}, Y_{i1}), but, if present income is not initially equal to the individual's optimal level of current consumption $(C_{i0} \neq Y_{i0})$, current consumption (C_{i0}) can be adjusted by borrowing (lending) at the private rate of interest (R_p) against future income (Y_{i1}).

There are no alternative productive opportunities available to individuals of this model; they can neither buy nor sell real property and taxes cannot be shifted from one individual to the next.

Only individuals pay taxes. They pay two kinds of taxes, income and property. Property taxes per moment for the ith individual are initially equal to T_i, which means that T_{i0} is assumed to be equal to T_{i1}. The municipality provides the same level of services to each individual in both the present and the future. For the sake of convenience the cost of this service is assumed to be equal to T_i and to have zero consumption value to the ith individual.

Consumption, endowments, and taxes are certain and the market rate of interest, R_p, is risk-free.

We use this basic model to evaluate the consequences of a variety of scenarios or cases. The first case looks at the debt equilibrium in the absence of municipal debt.

A. Case I: No Municipal Borrowing—Interest Payments Are Neither Taxable as Income when Earned nor Deductible from Taxable Income When Paid

In the absence of municipal debt, it should be obvious that, given our assumptions, the quantity of debt produced will be determined by demand (on the part of lenders) and supply (on the part of borrowers). The private interest rate will be the equilibrium price for debt. Hence, $R_p = R_a$, which is the equilibrium risk-free rate of interest in the absence of municipal debt. This case is shown in Fig 1.

To reach equilibrium, the ith individual will adjust his or her endowments so as to maximize $U_i(C_{i0}, C_{i1})$ by borrowing or lending at the market rate of interest, $R_p = R_a$, as shown in Figs. 2(A) and 2(B). Fig. 2(A) illustrates the borrower's equilibrium, while (B) the lender's. In both figures, the ith individual is endowed with Y_{i0}, Y_{i1}, which implies the consumption possibilities schedule (or budget line) labeled C_{i0}, C_{i1}, since by definition $C_{i0} + C_{i1}/(1 + R_a) = Y_{i0} + Y_{i1}/(1 + R_a)$. The formula for the budget line is of course $C_{i1} = Y_{i0}(1+R_a) + Y_{i1} - C_{i0}(1 + R_a)$, and its slope is dC_{i1}/dC_{i0} or $-(1 + R_a)$. And in both figures, borrowing/lending permits the

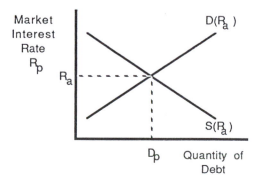

Figure 1 Debt in equilibrium.

ith individual to increase utility from isoutility line U to >U, with max. $U_i(C_{i0}, C_{i1})$ at the point of tangency of the isoutility line (>U) and the budget line (C_{i0}, C_{i1}).

In our simplified model, borrowing and lending can take place for a variety of reasons—for example, mismatches between initial endowments and consumption preferences (as depicted in Figs. 2(A) and (B); one such reason could be the prior imposition of taxes. The critical point is that the market affords the individuals in our model the opportunity to borrow or lend and thereby optimize their consumption levels. Hence, each individual can be presumed to be at his or her optimum prior to the decision of the municipality to borrow.

1. Case 1A: Municipal Borrowing—Where Interest Payments Are Neither Taxable as Income when Earned nor Deductible from Taxable Income when Paid

Now let us assume that in the initial moment the municipality borrows at rate R_a an amount equal to T_i on behalf of the ith individual and $\sum T_i$ in the aggregate. This has the result of reducing the ith individual's property taxes in moment one from T_i to zero and of increasing his or her property taxes in the future moments to $T_i(2 + R_a)$, and in the aggregate, reducing $\sum T_{i0}$ to zero and increasing $\sum T_{i1}$ from $\sum T_i$ to $\sum T_i(2 + R_a)$.

This would have the effect on the ith individual shown in Fig. 2(C). Under municipal borrowing, each individual's consumption optimum would be disturbed. Both private borrowers and lenders would have too much after-tax income, and therefore consumption in the first moment and too little in the second. It follows from our assumption that lenders will attempt to restore their original consumption optima by acquiring additional debt (lending) at R_a and that borrowers will attempt to reduce their private liabilities. The question is, will they revert to their original consumption optima? If so, we can conclude that in this case, municipal

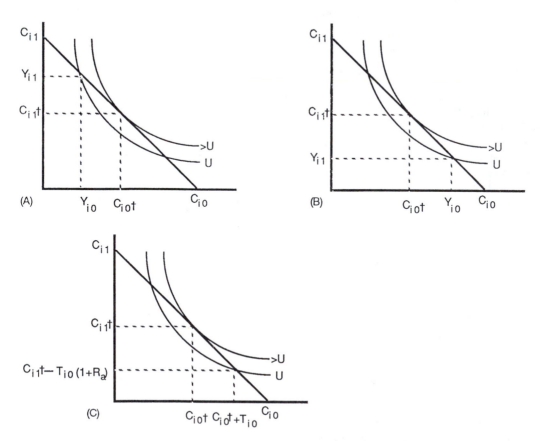

Figure 2 (A) Individual equilibrium where borrower borrows $C_{i0}\dagger - Y_{i0}$ and repays $Y_{i1} - C_{i1}\dagger = (1 + R)(C_{i0}\dagger - Y_{i0})$; (B) Individual equilibrium where lender lends $Y_{i0} - C_{i0}\dagger$ and generates $C_{i1}\dagger - Y_{i1} = (1 + R)(Y_{i0} - C_{i0}\dagger)$; (C) Individual equilibrium, disturbed by municipal debt.

borrowing is identical to private borrowing and that the individuals in our model would be indifferent between municipal property taxes and municipal debt.

In our model either municipal debt will displace private borrowing or it will be purchased with income that would otherwise have been used to pay first-moment property taxes; that is, borrowers replace private borrowing by T_i, and lenders use T_i to purchase municipal debt, thereby accepting municipal debt in lieu of private debt. This implies that attempts to restore private consumption optima will not affect the equilibrium private interest rate $R_p = R_a$, which is to say that in this case, municipal debt is the functional equivalent of private debt.

This conclusion is illustrated in Fig. 3. There, the reduction in private borrowing induced by issuing municipal debt shifts the supply of private debt to the left, from $S(R_a)$ to $S'(R_a)$. Increased private lending shifts the demand for debt to the right, from $D(R_a)$ to $D'(R_a)$. At the initial market clearing interest rate, R_a, the difference between $D'(R_a)$ and $S'(R_a)$ is just equal to ΣT_i, or D_m, the amount of municipal debt issued, although total debt increases to $D_p + D_m$. The new debt equilibrium is at the intersection of $D'(R_a)$ and $S'(R_a) + D_m$.

B. Case 2: Private Equilibrium under a Flat-Rate Income Tax (t)

This case will demonstrate that the equilibrium private interest rate will remain unaffected by municipal borrowing under a flat-rate income tax (t), where interest payments on private debt are tax-deductible for borrowers and taxable as revenue to lenders. To make this point, it is first necessary to show what the equilibrium interest rate on debt would be in the absence of municipal borrowing.

This outcome is identified in Fig. 4, which confirms the simple intuition that the after-tax interest rate will remain R_a, where the after-tax interest rate is equal to $(1 - t)R_p$ and $R_p = R_a/(1 - t)$. In the absence of municipal borrowing, a flat-rate income tax would not affect the quantity of private debt.

Of course, this conclusion follows directly from the assumption that individual behavior is governed by the magnitude of after-tax endowments. This means that individuals would treat an after-tax return of R_a the same as a taxable private return of R_p (where $R_p = R_a/(1 - t)$), since in behavioral terms they are identical. Higher taxes paid by lenders will be just offset by lower taxes paid by borrowers; their after-tax wealth will be unchanged. As in the previous case, borrowers and lenders adjust their consumption patterns by borrowing and lending at rate R_p with an after-tax rate of $R_p(1 - t) = R_a$.

1. Case 2A: The Effect of Municipal Borrowing under a Flat-Rate Income Tax (t)

Again we assume both that the municipality borrows an amount equal to current taxes, and that this has the effect of disturbing the consumption optimum of every property-taxpayer. This in turn leads to behavior intended to restore property tax payers to their consumption optima (i.e., increased lending or reduced private borrowing). The results of these efforts are depicted in Fig. 5, which shows that $R_p = R_a/(1 - t)$ and R_a are unchanged from Fig. 4. Although total debt increases, the increase reflects both a reduction in the supply of private debt and increased demand for debt, since individuals use some of their foregone taxes to buy more debt.

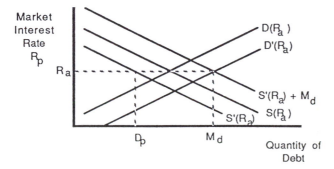

Figure 3   Equilibrium restored.

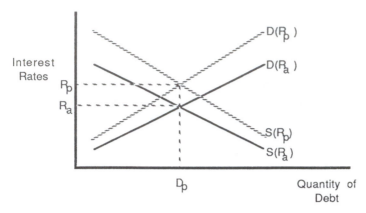

Figure 4   Debt in equilibrium under a flat-rate income tax.

As in Fig. 3, the reduction in private borrowing induced by issuing municipal debt shifts the supply of private debt to the left, from $S(R_a)$ to $S'(R_a)$. Increased private lending shifts the demand for debt to the right, from $D(R_a)$ to $D'(R_a)$. At the initial market clearing interest rate, R_a, the difference between $D'(R_a)$ and $S'(R_a)$ is just equal to ΣT_i, or D_m, the amount of municipal debt issued, although total debt increases to $D_p + D_m$. The new debt equilibrium is again at the intersection of $D'(R_a)$ and $S'(R_a) + D_m$. However, the private rate of interest is grossed up to R_p, as shown in Fig. 4 (Miller, 1977). The reason is, of course, that private debt at R_p taxable at rate t is behaviorally identical to tax-exempt municipal debt at R_a. The key point is that equilibrium consumption levels and choices are not affected by the introduction of municipal borrowing.

C.   Case 3: Private Equilibrium under a Flat-Rate Income Tax (t) when Interest on Private Debt Is Taxable as Revenue but Is not Deductible as Expense

In this section we demonstrate the "contingent" part of the contingent irrelevancy of municipal debt. The general thrust of this section is that under certain exogenously determined circumstances, the municipality can increase the welfare of its citizen taxpayers through its choice of capital structure. A plausible inference that might be drawn from this demonstration is that municipal debt will directly benefit borrowers and indirectly benefit lenders whenever the municipality can borrow at a lower after-tax rate than can private individuals. What we specifically demonstrate, however, is that a municipality can increase utility to the ith individual under a flat-rate income tax (t) by borrowing instead of taxing, when interest on private debt is taxable as revenue but is not deductible as expense.

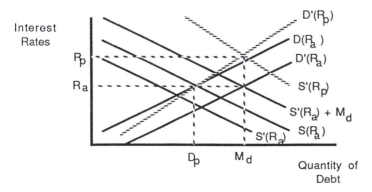

Figure 5   Equilibrium restored under a flat-rate income tax.

Once again we begin our analysis by identifying the debt equilibrium that obtains in this case in the absence of municipal borrowing. As shown in Fig. 6, in where interest on private debt is taxable as revenue but is not deductible as expense, the equilibrium quantity of debt falls from D_p to D_p', and there is also a discrepancy between the after-tax cost to borrowers (R_p) and the after-tax price paid to lenders (R_a). To the left of the kink, the ith individual's budget line (consumption set) has a slope of $(1 + [1 - t]R_p)$; to the right its slope is $-(1 + R_p)$.

1.   Case 3A: The Effect of Municipal Borrowing Under a Flat-Rate Income Tax (t) when Interest on Private Debt Is Taxable as Revenue but Is not Deductible as Expense

For the third time we assume both that the municipality borrows an amount equal to current taxes (at rate R_a) and that this has the effect of disturbing the consumption optimum of all property-taxpayers, which leads them to make an effort to restore to their consumption optima. As a first approximation, the response of lenders in the instant case would be identical to that shown in Fig. 2(C). As long as $-(1 + [1 - t]R_p) = -(1 + R_a)$, lenders in our model remain indifferent between private and municipal debt. Since municipal borrowing in the current moment increases their after-tax income endowment in the present and reduces it in the future, they must acquire additional debt to restore themselves to their previous equilibria.

Municipal borrowing confronts borrowers with a distinctly different situation from that shown in Fig. 2C, when interest on private debt is taxable as revenue but is not deductible as expense. In this instance, borrowers could use their initial-moment property-tax relief (T) to acquire municipal debt (D_m), but they would be much better off if they reduced their nondeductible private debt instead. By so doing they can achieve a higher level of two-moment utility than in Fig. 7(A). The effect of municipal debt on the relevant portion of borrowers' consumption sets is depicted in Fig. 8, which shows that the ith borrower could use his or her deferred initial-moment property-taxes to acquire municipal debt and thereby move along a budget line having a slope of $-(1 + R_a)$ from $C_{i0}\dagger,C_{i1}\dagger$ to $C_{i0} + T_{i0},C_{i1}\dagger + T_{i0}(1 + R_a)$. By reducing private debt, however, the borrower could then move back up a budget line having a slope of $-(1 + R_p)$ from $C_{i0} + T_{i0},C_{i1}\dagger + T_{i0}(1 + R_a)$ to $C_{i0}*,C_{i1}*$. Note that $C_{i0}* \geq C_{i0}\dagger$ and that $C_{i1}* > C_{i1}\dagger$. This means that in this situation, municipal borrowing unambiguously increases the welfare of borrowers.

Thus, in the instant case, the maximum possible future gain to the ith borrower (G_{i1}) would be equal to

$$
\begin{aligned}
G_{i1} &= T_i(1+R_p) - T_i(1+R_a) \\
&= T_i(R_p - R_a) \\
&= T_i[\ R_a/(1 - t)\ -R_a] \\
&= R_a[t/(1 - t)],
\end{aligned}
$$

which is the true tax savings accruing to municipal debt (i.e., the pretax value of the amount by which R_a is grossed up).

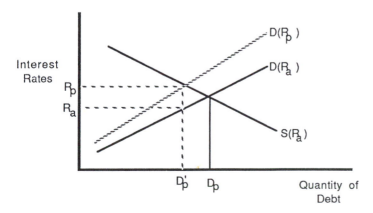

Figure 6   Debt in equilibrium where interest is taxable but not deductible.

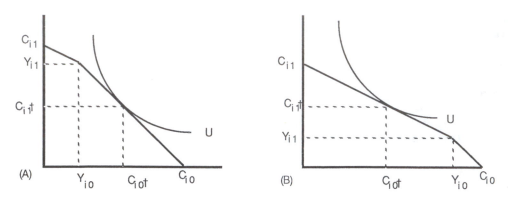

Figure 7 (A) Individual equilibrium where borrower borrows $C_{i0}\dagger - Y_{i0}$ and repays $Y_{i1} - C_{i1}\dagger$; (B) Individual equilibrium where lender lends $Y_{i0} - C_{i0}\dagger$ and generates $C_{i1}\dagger - Y_{i1}$.

It should be obvious that municipal debt would be absorbed by lenders at R_a if and only if borrowers ignored these possible gains. If borrowers reduce private debt to enjoy the gain permitted by municipal borrowing, they must reduce their private debts by the full amount of their deferred property taxes, otherwise there would be a discrepancy between the lenders' demand for debt and the supply of debt at R_a. But this outcome is not consistent with the assumption that the two-moment isoutility schedules of the individuals in our model are convex to the origin. Convexity implies that borrowers will consume some of the wealth gain in the initial moment (as depicted in Fig. 8). If borrowers increase initial-moment consumption, interest rates must rise to absorb D_m since private borrowing is reduced by an amount that is less than T_{i0}.

Thus it also follows that when interest on private debt is taxable as revenue but is not deductible as expense, municipal borrowing should lead to an increase in R_a (and R_p). In that case, *some* of the welfare gain from municipal borrowing will be transferred to lenders in the form of higher interest rates on private and municipal debt. It is not clear how much. The actual distribution of these gains will depend upon the elasticities of supply and demand for debt, but it is possible that every property-tax payer in the borrowing community could benefit from borrowing to reduce current municipal taxes.

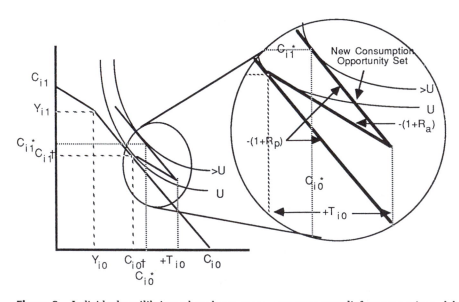

Figure 8 Individual equilibrium where borrower uses property-tax relief to repay private debt.

III. IS OUR MODEL REASONABLE?

Our conclusions follow directly and immediately from our assumptions. Municipal capital structure cannot matter unless the municipality's tax policy somehow influences the consumption behavior of its citizens. Here we must ask whether or not our assumptions are reasonable.

The individuals in our model live in a single-period world. It could be argued that so too do we—that our lives are entirely bound by the present and the future. But we argue here only that this simplifying assumption is widely used and accepted in corporate finance and ought not in this case to bias our conclusions. The assumptions that debt, taxes, consumption, and endowments are certain are also widely used. They are defensible in terms of their utility, if not necessarily their validity.* The assumptions made about utility maximizing, individual utility functions, and the ability of individuals to borrow and lend at the risk-free rate are standard, as are our behavioral assumptions. Only the borrowing/lending assumption appears clearly contrary to fact. However, evidence that municipalities can borrow on better terms than individuals would merely serve to reinforce our inferences about the potential benefits of municipal debt.

Our assumptions about buying and selling real property, tax shifting, and the value of municipal and residential services are all equally arbitrary. They reflect a desire to keep our partial-equilibrium analysis simple and straightforward. Nevertheless, these assumptions can be justified on behavioral grounds. The law of one price, together with the presumption that unusual conditions (e.g., efficiency or inefficiency on the part of a municipality) will be capitalized in ground rents, implies that the net benefit accruing to the citizenry as the result of the delivery of municipal services or from property transactions will be zero at the margin (Bish and Nourse, 1975:79–108). From a behavioral standpoint, only marginal values matter. Moreover, according to Jack Treynor (1982:26) competition prevents landowners and employers operating within a municipality from shifting any part of the tax burden imposed upon them forward onto export customers or backward onto import suppliers. Tax capitalization also means that property owners cannot shift the burden of future taxes onto their successors.

Finally, we have implicitly assumed away the outside world. But why would the rest of the world matter? Presumably the rest of the world was in equilibrium when the municipality issued debt; hence, its individual members were already at their consumption optima. The decision of a municipality to issue debt rather than collect taxes has changed nothing as far as those individuals are concerned—not their income, not their consumption preferences, not their opportunity sets. If nothing has changed for them, their behavior will be unchanged—and they can safely be ignored.

The point is that our assumptions are reasonable; at least they are consistent with those commonly found in models of corporate finance. Ultimately what matters is how well such theories work. Some of them work quite well. If our conclusions are flawed, it is unlikely that the flaw derives from the content of our assumptions. If they are wrong, the probable cause is that our logic misses something significant. James Buchanan (1969:61–69) has, for example, implicitly acknowledged that the logic we have outlined here is correct—as far as it goes—but he insists that it does not go far enough. As Buchanan explains, public-spending decisions are made by public officials. He argues that from *their* standpoint, it may be more costly to finance public spending with taxes than with debt, in which case borrowing would lead to higher than optimal levels of municipal spending and services. Hence, the municipality's tax policy would directly and adversely affect the consumption behavior of its citizens.

The issue that Buchanan very presciently identified is now called the agency problem. Buchanan's logic suggests that since our model ignores the preferences, tastes, and costs that constrain the choices made by municipal officials, it is potentially seriously flawed. However, Buchanan does not show that pay-as-you-go financing serves as a check on public officials, let alone that it serves to bring the interests of municipal officials into line with those of the citizenry. He merely asserts that it does. Elsewhere, however (Choate and Thompson, 1990), we have shown that the agency problem Buchanan (1969:98–102) uses to illustrate his argument about the difference between the costs faced by public officials and the citizenry is either not a problem or is easily soluble.

Scholars tend to be attracted to hard cases. In the agency literature this means situations that are

---

*In an extremely interesting essay, Breton (1977) argues that uncertainty is relevant to the choice of municipal capital structure, but as far as his argument bears on tax-debt policy, it appears to be a variation of the bankruptcy argument in corporate finance. Insofar as the direct costs of bankruptcy are concerned, the evidence is that these are generally too small to influence capital structure (Warner, 1977).

characterized by a high degree of conflict between principal and agent. But intellectual interest ought not to be permitted to obscure reality. Many, perhaps most, potential agency problems have obvious, easily implemented solutions. Lacking any evidence to the contrary, we are unwilling to assume that a potential problem is the same as a real one. After all, agency problems are found in corporate finance as well as in municipal finance, since the interests of corporate managers are also not necessarily identical to those of owners. (See, e.g., Williamson, 1988.) Yet the possibility that the interests of managers and owners may differ is not only irrelevant to normative theories of the firm, it does not appear to undermine the value of positive theories that ignore those differences. Indeed, debt is more often seen as a solution to the agency problem in corporate finance than it is a cause.

IV. DISCUSSION

A good normative model is simply a good positive model run backwards. Our purpose in writing this chapter is as much normative as it is positive. We would like our colleagues in the field of municipal finance to consider the possibility that the emphasis given to capital structure (i.e., short-run budget balancing) is largely misplaced. It seems to us that the critical question about public spending is not the source of financing but what we buy. Since capital budgeting theory is the key to wise investing and efficient operations, it ought to be central to the teaching and the practice of public financial management, and an analysis of benefits and costs should be part of every major decision to change operations, and not merely a issue that arrives in the context of acquiring buildings, building roads and dams, or analyzing make/buy options. That is to say that municipal finance ought to be taught like corporate finance—and practiced that way too.

This is obviously not an unprecedented proposition. Indeed, there are several excellent textbooks that accept it as a given. (See, e.g., Wippern, 1980; Palm and Qayum, 1985.) Some students of public financial management go even further, suggesting that municipal finance should be practically identical to corporate finance (e.g., Buchanan, 1971; see however, Miller, 1981). While we believe that a standard benefit-cost model ought to be a satisfactory guide to most municipal spending decisions, we would acknowledge that the analogy between municipal finance and corporate finance is imperfect—or at best incomplete.

According to Baesel et al. (1981), the modern theory of corporate finance rests on three legs: Fisher separation, the Modigliani-Miller theorem, and the unanimity principle. The unanimity principle says that stockholders implicitly agree to the goal of wealth maximization by their decision to invest in a firm. They explain, "Thus the managers do not have to consult the owners on every decision because all owners agree that the goal is the maximization of their wealth. If a project increases shareholder wealth, all will be in favor of it."

Since the time of Pareto and Lindahl, most students of public finance have argued that unanimity should play a normative role in evaluating government spending, although many are satisfied with potential unanimity; that is, the Kaldor-Hicks applied welfare criterion under which the winners *could* compensate the losers and still be better off. Nevertheless, under the standard canons of cost-benefit analysis, public officials must still consult the preferences of the citizenry on every decision.

Beginning with the pioneering work of Charles Tiebout (1956), a few students of municipal finance have insisted that the analogy between the unanimity principle in corporate finance and municipal finance is far closer in reality than it might appear at first, or even second, glance. In Tiebout models the role assigned wealth maximization in corporate finance is played by maximization of the value of a municipality's private property. (See Breton, 1977; Sonstelie and Portney, 1978; and Treynor, 1982.) It is in fact fairly easy to demonstrate that in the short run, property-value maximization on the part of a municipality is identical to wealth maximization on the part of the firm (Sonstelie and Portney, 1978:272). It is even possible to show that under specified conditions a residential community financed entirely by property taxes would unanimously support public officials who pursued the goal of property-value maximization (276). Hence, it follows that if all the necessary conditions obtain and pursuit of property-value maximization is incentive-compatible, public officials would not have to consult the citizenry on every decision because all citizens would implicitly agree that the municipality's goal is the maximization of their wealth.[*] Nevertheless, while some of the work inspired by Tiebout's insight is highly suggestive, it by no means conclusive.

---

[*]In this vein Treynor (1982:26) asserts that municipal expenditures will benefit a city economically "if and only if they increase the value of the city's private property." He goes on to say that if a municipality's financial goal is maximizing the aggregate value of taxable property, the interest rate on the municipality's bonds will rarely if ever be the proper discount rate for computing the gain or loss from municipal projects" (p. 28). He concludes that "the proper discount rate is the implicit rate used in the valuation of real property" (p. 26). "This rather interesting hypothesis appears to be highly consistent with the information about the systematic risk/return characteristics of municipal debt. (See, e.g., Cohen, 1988.)

We have a hunch that the analogy between the unanimity principle in corporate finance and municipal finance can be strengthened by focusing on governance mechanisms in both sectors. (See, e.g., Williamson, 1988.) That, however, is the topic of a future paper, one that has neither been written nor even thought through. In the meantime, we believe we have demonstrated that the first two legs of the stool are solid—solid enough to support the thesis that municipal finance is more like corporate finance than it is like personal finance.

REFERENCES

Baesel, J. B., Methé, D. T., and Shulman, D. (1981). *J. Finan. Ed.*, *10*: 23–32.

Barro, R. J. (1974). *J. Polit. Econ.*, *82*(6): 1095–1118.

Bish, R. L. and Nourse, H. O. (1975). *Urban Economics and Policy Analysis*, McGraw-Hill, New York.

Bordner, H. W. (1982). *Gov. Acc. J.*, *31*(1): 10–15.

Breton, A. (1977). *Pub. Finance/Fínancés Publiques*, *32*(1): 16–28.

Buchanan, J. M. (1969). *Cost and Choice: An Inquiry into Economic Theory*, The University of Chicago Press, Chicago.

Buchanan, J. M. (1971). *Pub. Choice*, *11*: 1–14.

Choate, G. M. and Thompson, F. (1990). *J. Econ. Behav. Org.*, *14*(3): 393–403.

Choate, G. M. and Thompson, F. (1988). *Pub. Choice*, *58*(1): 3–20.

Cohen, N. R. (1988). *Municipal Default Patterns: An Historical Study*, Enhance Reinsurance Company.

Keown, A. J. and Martin, J. D. (1978). *Finan. Mgt.*, *7*(2): 21–27.

Mikesell, J. L. (1991). *Fiscal Administration*, Brooks/Cole, Pacific Grove, Calif.

Miller, M. H. (1977). *J. Finance*, *32*(2): 261–275.

Miller, G. J. (1981). *Cities by Contract: The Politics of Municipal Incorporation*, MIT Press, Cambridge, Mass.

Modigliani, F. and Miller, M. (1958). *Amer. Econ. Rev.*, *48*(2): 261–296.

Palm, T. and Qayum, A. (1985). *Private and Public Investment Analysis*, South-Western, Cincinnati.

Sonstelie, J. C. and Portney, P. R. (1978). *J. Urban Econ.*, *5*: 263–277.

Tiebout, C. M. (1956). *J. Polit. Econ.*, *64*(5): 416–424.

Treynor, J. L. (1982). *Finan. Anal. J.*, *38*(3): 25–33.

Warner, J. B. (1977). *J. Finance*, *32*(2): 337–348.

Williamson, O. E. (1988). *J. Finance*, *43*(3): 567–591.

Wippern, R. F. (1980). *Cases in Modern Financial Management: Private and Public Sector Perspectives*, Richard D. Irwin, Homewood, Ill.

7

Public Authorities and Government Debt: Practices and Issues

Jerry Mitchell
Baruch College, City University of New York, New York, New York

Public authorities are a major issuer of government debt in the United States. They are the mechanism that governments have devised to build and finance projects the private sector is unwilling or unable to pursue and that the traditional agencies of government seem less capable of implementing. As the issuers of government debt, authorities receive better than average credit ratings—not only because they generate revenues that ensure the repayment of bonds, but also because they make decisions separated from arbitrary political judgments and the uncertainty of investment decisions made by private firms. As independent entities, they are favored by elected officials as a way to remove budget items and unpopular decisions from the dynamics of normal political processes. Taken together, federal, state, and local authorities control significant elements of the nation's natural environment, physical infrastructure, and public economy.

The purpose of this chapter is to examine public authorities as the major agents of government debt financing in the United States. Specifically, this chapter examines the basic purposes and functions of public authorities, the types of projects and services funded "off-budget," the primary influences on authority operations, the key features of the debt-financing process, the various measures of authority performance, and the major financial and political issues that confront authorities. This inquiry is derived from various sources of information, including the collection of secondary documents, in-person interviews with authority officials and municipal bond experts, and a review of recent survey data.

I. THE NATURE OF PUBLIC AUTHORITIES

A. Characteristics

A public authority is a corporate entity that is chartered by one or more governments (national, state, or local); that is governed by an appointed board; and that is responsible for various public service functions. Generally, authorities are characterized by an ability to raise money from private money markets, the right to sue and be sued, the power of eminent domain, the discretion to establish rates and charges, an exemption from property taxation, and the freedom to establish their own personnel and budget systems. Ideally, public authorities operate in the public interest, but in the manner of a self-supporting business, free from political compromise, public pressure, and bureaucratic red tape.

This depiction applies to almost every organization with the name "public authority." It encompasses organizations involved with various public functions, including the following:

- *Alaska Municipal Bond Bank Authority*, which provides loans to businesses for construction and development projects
- *Connecticut Resources Recovery Authority*, which oversees waste-to-energy facilities, solid waste transfer stations, and landfills

- *Delaware Health Facilities Authority*, which supplies financing for the construction and operation of hospitals, clinics, and other health care institutions in the state of Delaware
- *Florida Keys Aqueduct Authority*, which obtains, distributes, and supplies portable water to businesses and residents in the Florida Keys
- *Illinois Sports Facilities Authority*, which manages the new baseball stadium for the Chicago White Sox
- *Jacksonville Transportation Authority*, which maintains a mass transit system and constructs roads and bridges in Duval County, Florida
- *Kansas Development Authority*, which provides low-cost loans to farmers for the purchase of land and equipment
- *Maine State Housing Authority*, which provides assistance for the development and acquisition of low- and middle-income housing
- *New Jersey Turnpike Authority*, which maintains the Interstate 95 toll road from New York City to Trenton
- *Oklahoma Educational Television Authority*, which operates media facilities for educational television
- *Port Authority of New York and New Jersey*, which controls airport and bus facilities, a transit system, bridges and tunnels, marine terminals, industrial development parks, and skyscrapers in metropolitan New York
- *Rhode Island Higher Education Assistance Authority*, which guarantees loans to students in eligible colleges and universities and administers other programs of postsecondary student financial assistance
- *South Carolina Public Service Authority*, which supplies hydroelectric and nuclear power to cooperatives, businesses, and residents in the southeast
- *Tennessee Valley Authority*, which provides hydroelectric power in the Tennessee River Valley
- *Utah Transit Authority*, which manages mass transportation systems for Utah communities, including Salt Lake City and Provo
- *Virginia Agricultural Development Authority*, which furnishes loans, financed with tax-exempt bonds, and technical assistance to farmers
- *Whatcom Transportation Authority*, which operates a bus service for Whatcom County, Washington.

Besides such organizations there are other agencies that are public authorities structurally, but that have "corporation," "commission," or "agency" as titles, such as New York's Empire State Development Corporation, the Ann Arbor Housing Development Corporation, and the New York Mortgage Finance Agency. Many federal agencies, such as Amtrak and the U.S. Postal Service, are also public authorities. However, government-sponsored enterprises (GSEs), such as the Federal Home Loan Mortgage Corporation (Freddie Mac) and the Student Loan Marketing Association (Sallie Mae), are not public authorities; they are privately operated enterprises that work for the federal government. Perhaps most important, public authorities should not be viewed the same as special districts or school districts (even though the Census Bureau lumps authorities together with districts when its counts government organizations in the United States). Special and school districts are different from authorities because they usually have elected governing boards and the power to levy special taxes.

B. Origins

While the basic structure of authorities is relatively well known, it is less obvious when the public authority concept first originated. Roger Wettenhall (1987), an Australian public enterprise scholar, claims that authorities originated in his country in 1841 when the State Savings Bank of Victoria was established as a statutory corporation. The assumption that Australia was the first nation with a public authority is somewhat in doubt, however, because several special commissions and corporations were established during the early 1800s in the United States that much resembled today's public authorities (Gunn, 1988). For instance, the Erie Canal Commission established in New York in 1816 (which financed, constructed, and managed the state's elaborate canal system) had all the characteristics of any public authority operating today (Miller, 1962). But perhaps even before Australia and the United States, Great Britain was the first to experiment with the use of public enterprises. The British monarchy chartered several corporations in the 1700s, principally to operate ports in Liverpool and London (Thurston, 1937). In short, it is only accurate to say that authorities began to appear when many nations established private and municipal corporations during the late 1700s and early 1800s.

By all accounts, the Port of London Authority, created in 1908, was the first organization to bear the authority name. It was so named because every section in its enabling legislation began with the phrase "Authority is hereby given..." (Cohen, 1946). In the United States, the first agency to use the authority name was the Port of New York Authority (later renamed the Port Authority of New York and New Jersey), formed in 1921.

In the United States, the first spurt in the growth of modern-day public authorities began during the campaign for neutral competence in government in the late nineteenth century, the so-called Progressive Era just before the First World War. Much of the rhetoric surrounding the first uses of the public authority model can be attributed to the campaign during the Progressive Era to reduce the influence of political machines and patronage in the conduct of government activities and to enhance the efficiency and effectiveness of government activities. Out of these varied concerns came those bureaucratic organizations that we associate with the "ideal" public authority: financial self-sufficiency, independent decision making, self-management, and neutral competence (Doig and Mitchell, 1992).

The potential benefits of public authorities were truly realized in the early 1930s by pragmatic politicians seeking to efficiently provide public goods without resorting to direct taxation. Reviewing with favor its design and its successes in these early years, Franklin Roosevelt concluded that "this type of disinterested and capable service" ought to be "a model for government agencies throughout the land." FDR, as governor of New York, noted at the dedication of the George Washington Bridge in 1931 that authorities "are chartering the course toward the more able and honorable administration of affairs of government—a course they have proved can be safely steered through political waters with intelligence and integrity at the helm."

Based on his experience with authorities as the chief executive in New York and given his need to carry out massive public works projects, President Roosevelt used authorities extensively to accomplish many aims of the New Deal. During the 1930s the Tennessee Valley Authority was established, and the federal government urged the forty-eight states to authorize public authorities to construct local infrastructure and to meet other human needs. It was not long before local housing authorities and various public utilities were established around the nation. In the decades after World War II, many authorities were utilized by government for expanding the nation's postwar economy. Authorities were given control over transit systems, hospitals, convention centers, airports, recreation facilities, highways, hospitals, schools, and a host of other government projects. Clearly, the leader in the development of new public authorities at the time was Robert Moses in New York, who effectively employed authorities to build much of the infrastructure in his state, including the United Nations, Lincoln Center, and several of the major bridges and tunnels in New York City (Caro, 1974).

Since Moses, authorities have been slowing expanding, albeit in an ad hoc manner, into other policy areas and they have been enlarging their roles as the engines of economic development for state and local governments. There are now over 6,000 (and perhaps as many as 10,000) state and local authorities in the United States (Mitchell, 1991; Axelrod, 1989). There are also at least forty-seven national-level authorities (Axelrod, 1989). Pennsylvania leads all states, with over 2,000 of these entities currently in operation. Among other states, Georgia has over 700 authorities, Texas has close to 400, and New York has nearly 300 (Mitchell, 1992). Although the United States is nowhere comparable to Australia, where over two-thirds of governments are public enterprises (Curnow and Wettenhall, 1990), there is little indication that their numbers will dramatically decrease in the future. In fact, it is common for practitioners and scholars alike to call for the creation and development of new public authorities in the nation.

C. Rationales

Several reasons have been, and continue to be, given to justify the establishment of public authorities. These include:

1. To provide a service that does not coincide with that of any existing general local government. For example, to provide transportation services that cross several county and city jurisdictions.
2. To fund the construction of a needed service with bonds and to repay the bonds with user fees (such as the construction of a highway, convention center, or bridge).
3. To avoid debt or tax ceilings and referenda requirements in the provision of public services.
4. To provide a needed service that the private sector is reluctant to undertake.
5. To make the delivery of a public service more efficient by avoiding cumbersome government contracting procedures and legislative appropriations processes.

6. To remove a public function from the control of politicians or to keep it away from the disputes of competing advocacy groups. For example, an authority could be created to site a hazardous waste facility to avoid close public scrutiny.
7. To attract a skilled, professional workforce to the public sector by eliminating civil service rules and by providing high salaries and other private sector "perks."
8. To assist in the development of businesses or industries. For example, the primary function of industrial development and economic development authorities is to finance facilities for private business uses.

D. Legal Context

Whatever their purpose, it is important to realize that authorities are legally unique entities. First, they must follow enabling statutes that describe their mission, financial power, and overarching governance structure. Second, authorities normally adhere to federal or state laws on contracting, conflicts of interest, and collective bargaining (Douglas, 1990). Third, authorities are subject to federal and state government standards and mandates in such areas as affirmative action, handicapped accessibility, and health and safety regulation. Fourth, a few authorities work within a distinctive set of rules, such as those applied to the Port Authority of New York and New Jersey because of its bistate authorization, and to the Buffalo and Port Erie Public Bridge Authority because of its operation under the auspices of both the New York and Canadian governments. Finally, authorities may legally act as private firms; for instance, most are exempt from civil service requirements when hiring, terminating, and promoting employees.

E. Governance

Authorities are governed by a board whose job is to appoint top management, hold public hearings, authorize the sale of bonds, approve rate increases, and safeguard the public interest. The typical governing board is composed of five members, including citizens appointed for fixed terms by one or more elected officials and ex officio members who serve by virtue of their position in government. While the citizen members tend to be from professional and business fields, there are normally no specific backgrounds or qualifications required for appointment to a governing board (Smith, 1969). From the perspective of appointing officials, the selection of board members may be based on statutory prescription, party or group affiliation, personal loyalty, general expertise in a relevant area, or by district or regional representation. Consequently, there is wide variety in the structure and characteristics of authority boards across the nation. Consider the following examples:

*   *The Delaware Solid Waste Authority* is governed by a board composed of seven members, all of whom are appointed by the governor with the consent of the senate. The governor designates the chair. There must be one member from each of the three counties served by the authority and from the city of Wilmington. Authority members registered in either major political party shall not exceed the other major political party by more than one. The members serve 3-year terms. The members are reimbursed for actual and necessary expenses incurred during their official duties.
*   *The Massachusetts Port Authority* is governed by a board composed of seven members, all whom are appointed by the governor with the advice and consent of the legislature. No more than four members of the board can be of the same political party and the board must include persons with extensive experience in engineering, finance, and commerce, and a bona fide representative of a national or international labor organization. The governor designates one of the members as the chairman. The members serve a 7-year term of office. They receive no compensation, but they are reimbursed for necessary expenses.
*   *The New York Metropolitan Transportation Authority* is governed by a board composed of a chairman and sixteen other members appointed by the governor with the advice and consent of the senate. New York City residency is required for three of the five members appointed by the governor; four members are appointed on recommendation of the major of New York City; and seven members are appointed on recommendation of county executives of the counties in which they must reside, as follows: Nassau, Suffolk, Westchester, Dutchess, Orange, Putnam, and Rockland. Members from the latter four counties cast one collective vote. The term of office for the members is 6 years. The chairman receives a salary of $150,000, the first vice chairman is paid $60,000, and other board members receive $150 per day of service, not to exceed $15,000 annually.

- *The New York Thruway Authority* is overseen by a board composed by three members appointed by the governor with consent of the senate. The governor designates the chairman, who is also the chief executive officer. The members serve 9-year terms. The chairman receives a salary of $25,000 and the other members receive a salary of $17,000.
- *The North Carolina State Ports Authority* is governed by a eleven-member board. Seven members, including the chairman, are appointed by the governor and four members are appointed by the general assembly. Terms for board members appointed by the governor are 6 years, while terms for members appointed by the general assembly are 4 years. The members receive no salary, but are reimbursed for expenses.
- *The Port Authority of New York and New Jersey* is governed by a board of commissioners composed of twelve members, six from New York State and six from New Jersey; appointed by the governors of the respective states with the consent of each state's senate, for overlapping terms of 6 years each. The chairman is elected by the commissioners. The members receive no salary, but are reimbursed for expenses.

F. Administration

Unlike the variation in goverance structures, the management of an authority is relatively straightforward. Authority management is the responsibility of an executive director who is usually appointed by an authority's governing board. The executive director, somewhat like a city manager in municipal government or a chief executive officer in a private corporation, is supposed to carry out board decisions and direct the delivery of services. The executive director and his or her professional staff is expected to be ideologically neutral and to undertake assignments without concern for partisan politics or the views of the community (Horn, 1976). In managing authorities, the executive director is supposed to rely greatly on the technical opinions of engineers, economists, accountants, lawyers, and other experts.

The majority of executive directors have graduate degrees in business and public administration. Their average tenure is 8 years (Mitchell, 1991). They are mostly men who have risen to their position from within their own agency. According to a recent survey of the nation's executives, the primary tasks of an executive director are to work with his or her governing board and to manage authority finances (Mitchell, 1991).

II. AUTHORITY DEBT

The typical public authority issues bonds to finance its operations. Bonds are essentially loans that an authority receives to build a facility or finance a project. Bonds issued by an authority are typically repaid (with interest) to investors by the revenues generated from the project undertaken. Airport authorities may pay back bonds with, for example, fees for landing, concessions, airline gates, and fueling. The interest paid to the holders of authority bonds is exempt from federal income taxes, and therefore authorities can raise capital at a lower cost than the federal government or private firms. Generally, the bonds issued by authorities do not affect the debt ceiling of states or localities because such bonds are not included in the calculation of total debt for a state or locality.

There are two general categories of bonds offered by authorities: (1) short-term bonds, issued for periods not beyond 3 years to provide temporary funding, and (2) long-term bonds, issued for extended periods of time (30 years, e.g.) to provide permanent financing for major capital improvements, construction, and acquisition of capital facilities. The maturity date for these bonds may be term or serial. A term bond matures in lump sums in 1 or 2 years; a serial bond matures over several years, spreading repayments, for example, over the life of a facility.

Authorities use both types of bonds to finance several categories of public policy. Authority bonds finance economic development, education, environmental protection, health care, housing, ports, public facilities, public transportation, and utilities. What follows is a brief description of these areas and an analysis of authority activity with each of them.

A. Economic Development

Bonds issued by authorities for economic development involve the provision of loans, low-cost leases, and other incentives to encourage the development of industry and business. The fundamental objectives are to create new jobs, add economic value to the local or state economy, attract new businesses, and increase tax receipts. The use of authorities to finance economic development began in the 1970s and early 1980s because of federal tax provisions allowing states and cities to issue tax-exempt bonds for commercial development. The extensiveness of such economic development has been noted in a legislative study in New York that found that $770 million in tax-exempt bonds were issued by economic development and industrial development authorities in that state in 1990 alone (New York State Legislature, 1992). While the monetary magnitude is not as great in other states, the trend is similar around around the nation.

A specific example of an authority that issues bonds mostly for economic development in a small state is the Kansas Development Authority (KDC). Using its tax-exempt status, one of its major economic development efforts is a farmer loan program that provides subsidies to banks, which in turn, allows the banks to make low-interest loans to farmers who had not previously owned a significant amount of farmland or who needed to purchase farm implements. The KDC, while not a large authority, provided loans totaling $3.2 million in 1990, with interest rates for the loans averaging 2% to 3% below conventional agricultural lending rates in Kansas.

At least twenty-three states have such independent authorities to finance economic development. The more visible authorities function at the state level; the majority operate in counties and cities. Georgia and New York together have over 600 local economic development organizations. Although they are still popular with state and local officials, the establishment of new economic development authorities and the activity within existing ones has slowed to some extent since the tax-exempt status of industrial development bonds was limited by the Tax Reform Act of 1986 (Lemov, 1989).

B. Education

Bonds issued by authorities for secondary and postsecondary educational purposes are used either to construct, maintain, and operate school facilities, or to provide loans and assistance to postsecondary students. There are twenty-five state-level education authorities in the United States, almost equally divided between those that construct facilities and those that supply financial assistance to undergraduate and graduate college students.

The New York Dormitory Authority represents an authority that issues bonds to finance school construction. Among the largest issuers of tax-exempt bonds in the nation, with a total of $4.11 billion in securities issued in 1990 alone, the Dormitory Authority is the primary developer of school-related facilities in New York. In comparison, the Arkansas Student Loan Authority does not finance capital projects, but rather it issues tax-exempt bonds, and then makes low-interest loans directly to students and purchases qualified students loans from Arkansas lending institutions. As of 1991, this authority had approximately $82 million in bonds outstanding.

C. Environmental Protection

Bonds may be issued by authorities to finance a variety of environmental protection and resource recovery activities. For example, they may finance the construction and operation of sanitary storm sewers and sewage treatment and disposal facilities; support the colleciton, transportation, and disposal of solid wastes, hazardous wastes, and other refuse; and fund irrigation, drainage, flood, and pollution control operations. Within this category we can also include a few authorities that use bonds to conserve, promote, and develop natural resources such as soil, water, forests, minerals, and wildlife. Environmental protection authorities are generally ranked among the safest investments because the demand for their services is not as elastic as it is for authorities that operate bridges, hospitals, toll roads, and the like (Standard and Poor's 1989).

The Delaware Solid Waste Authority typifies the authority that operates facilities designed to protect the environment by disposing of society's wastes. It maintains sanitary landfills, operates recycling facilities, and processes garbage throughout the state of Delaware. In 1990, it disposed of over 5.9 million tons of solid waste, financed in part by approximately $71 million in short- and long-term securities.

This type of authority has become increasingly important in the past two decades (Standard and Poor's, 1989). There has been a particularly rapid growth in the number of authorities that finance public and private pollution control facilities and operations. North Carolina, for example, now has a pollution control financing authority in almost every one of its counties. Overall, there are well over 800 environmental protection authorities in the United States (excluding special districts), existing mostly in California, North Carolina, New Jersey, Pennsylvania, and Texas.

D. Health Care

Many public authorities have been established to issue bonds to fund health care systems. Some of these authorities actually operate hospitals, nursing homes, clinics, or homes for the aged. For example, New York City's Health and Hospitals Corporation manages several public hospitals and clinics in metropolitan New York. Another class of health care authorities exists to finance and construct facilities. In the 1980s, for example, the Idaho Health Facilities Financing Authority provided $300 million in financing for the construction of hospitals, clinics, laboratories, and other facilities in Idaho. For this latter type, the assumption is that public, private, and nonprofit health care institutions cannot financially meet health care demands because they are unable to accumulate excess funds from operating revenues, borrow low-interest capital, or obtain tax-supported subsidies.

As the nation's elderly population has grown, there has been a corresponding increase in the number of health authorities, especially in Florida, Georgia, Indiana, and Pennsylvania. The thirty-two states with such authorities reported an outstanding bond debt of well over $30 billion in 1989 (Standard and Poor's 1989). In Vermont, there has been some discussion of creating a state-level authority to provide comprehensive health care to all state residents. Nonetheless, the continuing debate in the U.S. Congress over the appropriateness of tax-exempt health care financing has caused credit ratings to be downgraded for some health-related bonds, making capital more expensive to obtain.

E. Housing

Many authorities have been created to issue bonds for public housing and private redevelopment projects. Most of these authorities are state-level entities that issue low-interest mortgages to qualified individuals or that provide loans to housing developers. While some local units do issue such debt, most of the local public housing authorities that operate low-income housing projects no longer incur debt, but rather receive their funding from grants provided by the U.S. Department of Housing and Urban Development.

There are over fifty housing authorities that issue tax-exempt bonds. Characteristic is the Colorado Housing and Finance Authority, which began operations in 1974 to provide low- and moderate-income housing to the state's residents. Since its inception, it has issued more $2.2 billion in bonds and has provided financing for more than 37,000 families.

F. Ports

Bonds have long been used by authorities to construct, maintain, and operate anything to do with rivers, lakes, oceans, and other waterways, including canals, harbors, docks, wharves, and terminals. These authorities usually have the word *port* in their titles. They include some of the oldest public authorities in the nation. Modeled after the successful Port of New York Authority, many were created in the 1920s and 1930s as a public response to problems arising from railroad control of commercial port (Sherman, 1985).

There are 108 port authorities in the nation that specialize in the delivery of marine services. Port authorities typically own several facilities, including shipyards, marinas, grain terminals, and docks. Increasingly, port authorities have taken on functions indirectly related to waterways; for example, many port authorities now tout their importance to economic development. This shift into other policy areas has even led port authorities to adopt completely new functions and change their names; for example, the Savannah Ports Authority in Georgia became the Savannah Economic Development Authority in 1989.

A illustrative example of the successful port authority is the Port of Corpus Christi Authority in Texas. From 1987 to 1988 its total assets increased from $25.5 million to over $33.2 million. At the same time, its operating revenues grew from $19.7 million to $24.6 million—a profit after expenses of $1 million. In recent years, the Port of Corpus Christi Authority has not received any federal or state grants, although it has purchased state-owned facilities that now produce additional revenues for the port. To document these successes, the authority produces glossy reports and illustrated publications (very similar to those provided by large private corporations) that detail the authority's extensive economic and social activities.

G. Public Facilities

Many authorities are created for the sole purpose of issuing bonds to pay for new public facilities. Public authorities construct, purchase, lease, maintain, and operate governmental buildings, parking lots, and garages, and build, finance, and operate recreational, cultural, and scientific facilities and activities, including golf courses, playfields, playgrounds, public beaches, swimming pools, tennis courts, parks, auditoriums, stadiums, auto camps, recreation piers, marinas, botanical gardens, galleries, museums, zoos, convention centers, and exhibition halls. The political rationale is to finance capital improvements without increasing taxes. For many facilities, the preferred financing mechanism has been the lease-backed bond that is repaid from the rental payments of a private operator.

There are thirty-four states with authorities that finance and manage public-use facilities. California, New York, and Pennsylvania have the most such authorities. The more prominent of such authorities are ones that build and maintain sports complexes. The Chicago White Sox's new baseball stadium, for example, is the responsibility of the Illinois Sports Facilities Authority. In 1989, the Sports Authority issued $150 million in tax-exempt bonds to finance the construction of the stadium, to eventually be repaid with game tickets and television revenues.

H. Public Transportation

Authorities issue bonds to construct, maintain, and operate highways, streets, and related structures; toll roads, bridges, and tunnels; airports and heliports; and public mass transit systems, such as ferries, buses, trains, and subways. (Transit systems established to transport elementary and secondary school pupils are not included because they are operated by school districts.) Except for airport authorities, many of these authorities emerged in the 1950s, when increased automobile traffic created a demand for new roads and weakened the ability of private businesses to operate mass transportation systems (Doig, 1966).

There are thirty-six states that use public authorities to finance or operate various aspects of transportation. The Institute of Public Administration (1986) found that 56 out of 130 major airport operators were public authorities. Public authorities control large mass transit systems in New York, Philadelphia, Chicago, Atlanta, Boston, Seattle, and several other urban centers. Public authorities also maintain many of the well-known thoroughfares in the country, including the New Jersey Turnpike, the Illinois Toll Road, the Kansas Turnpike, and the Orlando-Orange County Expressway. In most instances, these authorities finance their capital improvements with long-term bonds and repay them with fares, tolls, or fees.

I. Utilities

Authorities issue bonds to support and operate facilities that generate electricity, gas, and water, and also to finance and develop alternative fuels and energy sources, such as nuclear and solar power. Most utility authorities are modeled after the New York Power Authority and the Tennessee Valley Authority, both established in the 1930s. The assumption, although not empirically confirmed, is that power authorities are able to provide larger savings to consumers than are private companies and municipalities (Walsh, 1978).

There are eighteen states with utility authorities; New Jersey and Pennsylvania have the most. Power supply authorities are often significant revenue producers. For example, in 1989, the New York State Power Authority had $1.4 billion in revenues, the Municipal Electric Authority of Georgia had $546 million, and the Lower Colorado River Authority had $306 million. The revenue stream for these utilities is derived from rates charged to residential, commercial, and industrial end users.

III. INFLUENCES ON PUBLIC AUTHORITIES

Public authorities work within a complex environment. At one level, authorities are impacted by physical and technological factors that may mandate their existence or determine the way they deliver certain services. For example, the need to dispose of unwelcome hazardous wastes has led several states to create public authorities for this purpose and to require existing waste disposal authorities to move into the hazardous waste area. Authorities are also greatly influenced by the financial, political, and social spheres of human activity. These influences often determine both the strategic and operational actions of authorities. What follows is a brief review of these influences.

A. Financial Influences

Authorities are strongly influenced by those parties that work in the municipal bond market; that is, the loosely organized system for issuing and selling the securities of public authorities and other governmental units. Several participants interact with authorities in the issuance of debt, including investors, underwriters, financial advisors, accountants, bond counsels, consultants, and credit rating agencies.

Investors in authority bonds may be either private households or large institutions, such as banks and insurance companies. Small households invest in authority bonds mainly to receive uninterrupted payments of interest. In comparison, institutional investors are drawn to authority bonds by their potential to be resold in a secondary market (Feldstein and Fabozzi, 1987). Since the mid-1980s, the number of small investors in authority bonds has been increasing, while at the same time, institutional investors have decreased their holdings of such securities. Generally speaking, investors seek security and high yields from authority bonds. They tend to favor increases in user charges, for example, to pay interest and to maintain cash reserves in case of emergencies (Standard and Poor's, 1989).

Underwriters buy authority securities for resale. An underwriter may be a brokerage house, an investment bank, or a commercial bank. Underwriters make money by selling bonds at a higher price than they bid for them (Walsh, 1978). Underwriters purchase bonds through either a negotiated sale or competitive bidding. The leading underwriters in the nation are the brokerage firms of Goldman, Sachs; Merrill Lynch; Sherson Lehman Hutton; and Smith Barney-Harris Upham. Like individual investors, underwriters seek to purchase bonds with potentially high yields.

Financial advisors help authorities to evaluate market conditions and to negotiate bond contracts with underwriters. The financial advisor determines, for example, how broad a market can be attracted to a sale, when the sale might take place to minimize interest costs, or what might be done to negotiate a private placement. Fundamentally, financial advisors indicate to authorities how they should present their issues during negotiations with underwriters.

Accountants inform potential bond buyers of the issuer's financial condition, as determined by the structure of the security. If the revenue stream underlying the security must be forecast, the accountant may also verify various assumptions and calculations to confirm the stream's contribution to the issuer's ability to repay principal and interest.

Bond counsels lead the effect to inform the structuring of the security in terms of applicable law for the underwriters and authorities. The counsel renders a legal opinion on the bond issue about its tax-exempt status and writes the contract between the issuer and the bondholders. Basically, a bond counsel assures investors that an authority will not default on an obligation because of legal defects in the procedures used to authorize or issue the bonds.

Consultants play in an increasingly important role in authorities as advisors on financial, managerial, and organizational issues. A case study of the Massachusetts Port Authority, for example, discovered that consultants may be used to define policy issues, develop the range of policy issues to consider, recommend courses of action, and prepare justifications for a course of action already taken (Nelkin, 1974).

Credit rating agencies classsify the creditworthiness of authority bonds. The three major rating agencies are Standard and Poor's Corporation, Moody's Investors Service, and Fitch Investors Service. These firms determine the likelihood that the issuer will repay the principal and interest as scheduled. The credit rating process involves four stages. First, the authority submits information relating to its financial, economic, and organizational condition, including several years of audited financial statements, budget documents, feasibility studies, financial reports, and annual updates of relevant statistics (e.g., port authorities must provide data on imports and exports by tonnage, revenues by bulk or passenger, and average dockage or container cranes fees). Second, the credit rating agency compares the issuer's information to the information in its own database, which consists of revenue, expenditure, and debt statistics on all previous issues. Third, a rating committee meets to compare the issuer they are rating with others they rated in the past. Finally, the agency assigns a rating symbol (A, Aaa, B, etc.) indicating the credit quality of an authority issue.

B. Political Influences

These influences include governors, state legislators, courts, local officials, service users, authority peers, interest groups, and federal agencies. Since public authorities are public agencies created by statute and operating for the public interest, they are subject to a wide variety of such influences, even though they are not directly accountable to the political system.

Governors frequently appoint the members to the boards of authorities, thus giving them an opportunity to try to use an authority for their own political purposes. For instance, during Governor Nelson Rockefeller's term of office in New York it was argued that he used authorities to benefit his supporters with authority contracts and various uses of tax-exempt bonds (McClelland and Magdovitz, 1981). In a few cases, governors also have veto power over authority projects, such as in the case of the Port Authority of New York and New Jersey. More indirectly, gubernatorial support may be needed for controversial projects and for the expansion of authority activities into new policy areas (Heiman, 1990). It is hard to imagine, for instance, that the Metropolitan Transportation Authority in New York could raise tolls without the governor's acquiescence.

State legislators have influence over authorities because of their statutory power. Legislatures establish such agencies, and therefore, they can also abolish them (Sayre and Kaufman, 1960). In addition, they may refuse to enact laws giving an authority the powers it needs to embark on a project, or threaten to amend or repeal the statutes under which an authority functions (Sayre and Kaufman, 1960). In particular, state legislatures may play a role in authorities if they are required to provide operating subsidies.

Courts at the federal and state levels must often rule on authority actions and projects. The courts can issue injunctions preventing authorities from using their power of eminent domain or for developing land (Heiman, 1990). Through litigation, courts may also influence governance structures (Muniak, 1990), change personnel practices (Fountain, 1990), and settle disputes between unions and authorities (Douglas, 1990).

Local officials include mayors, county executives, city council members, county legislators, and local bodies, such as planning, zoning, and finance boards (Kraft, 1989). In some instances, these officials actually sit on a governing board. In other cases, they may appoint members to a board, approve the selection of executive directors, or authorize the development of projects. Like governors and legislators, they may provide the political support needed to adopt and implement projects.

The *users* of services can influence authority operations by increasing or decreasing the demand for services. If fees are raised on an authority bridges, for example, the users can stop driving over the bridge. Thus, authority managers must continually evaluate consumer behavior when making decisions regarding the delivery of services (Bosworth, 1961).

The *peers* of authority managers, in both the public and private sectors, exert influence through the power of innovation. Managers may look to their counterparts to discover better methods of delivering services and ways of managing employees. Multiorganizational toll collection systems are one example of the successful transference of knowledge among transportation authorities in the 1980s (Chisholm, 1989).

Interest groups include advocacy groups, civic groups, unions, and other organized collections of individuals. Advocacy groups typically represent users and are interested in financial and safety issues (Heiman, 1990). Civic groups (such as a chamber of commerce) generally line up behind authorities because they like the allegedly nonpolitical, businesslike management of authorities (Sayre and Kaufman, 1960). Unions primarily focus on human resources policies and procedures, particularly with reference to job security and safety (Douglas, 1990).

Federal agencies may influence actions through both legal and financial means. For example, environmental protection authorities are required to work within national guidelines regarding pollution control; transit authorities must implement federal handicapped accessibility standards in order to receive federal mass transportation funds; and housing authorities must adhere to an elaborate set of rules established by the U.S. Department of Housing and Urban Development.

IV.   DEBT FINANCING ACTIVITIES

In issuing bonds, a public authority primarily seeks to satisfy and appease the various actors in its environment. This means that an authority will try to obtain low interest rates and financing costs, to minimize politically imposed restrictions on its activities, and to keep its bonds easy to market (Walsh, 1978). In turn, an authority must find the optimum time to issue its bonds, it must determine the appropriate size of its bond issues, it must package its debt in a way that appeals to investors, and it must account for its revenues, expenditures, and other activities. What follows is a brief review of these important debt-financing activities.

A.   Economic Forecasting

A major activity of authorities is to predict the optimum time to sell bonds. To this end, economists and consultants are employed to evaluate economic conditions and to engage in long-range planning. The objective is to predict the peak of the business cycle to discover the sale date at which interest costs will be lowest.

B. Sizing the Bond Issue

The determination of the bond size is another important debt-financing activity. The size of the bond issue is important because if the bond issue is too small, additional financing must be secured at additional expense; if the bond issue is too large, the borrower will incur unnecessarily high interest costs and may encounter legal problems (Gitajin, 1984). The basic bond size equation is: Total bond size = Net project cost + Net deposit in capitalized interest account + Net deposit in reserve funds + Total issuance expenses.

C. Attracting Bond Buyers

Authorities try to make their bonds attractive to a wide variety of investors. This has become especially important as more individuals and households buy municipal bonds and as banks and insurance companies have slowly been reducing their investments in the municipal bond market. To attract these new bond buyers, several new forms of securities have emerged and various efforts have been undertaken to protect the security of bonds.

Two new forms of securities are unit trusts and zero-coupon bonds. Unit trusts are fixed diversified portfolios of long-term bonds that appeal to individual investors, especially people retired or nearing retirement in the top tax bracket. Zero-coupon bonds are debt instruments with "locked-in yields" sold at significant discounts from their face values with no annual interest payments. Both give investors greater flexibility in the choice of securities to purchase.

To attract new investors, many authorities "guarantee" payment to bondholders in case of default. Along with the guarantee, the authority receives a better credit rating that acts to lower its borrowing costs. These bond guarantees come in several different forms, including: (1) strictly defined insurance policies covering the principal and interest on long-term, fixed-rate issues, (2) letters of credit issued by banks that ensure the repayment of bonds, and (3) a combination of an insurance policy and a bank letter of credit. In 1991, a record $51.6 billion in all municipal issues were guaranteed in some form, up from $33.8 million in 1990 (*New York Times*, Apr. 27, 1992).

D. Accounting

Record keeping is a major debt-financing activity for public authorities. Since the Government Accounting Standards Board took over as the standard setter for government accounting in 1984, the financial reporting procedures for authorities has become standardized and comprehensive. Under the accrual-based accounting system now used by many authorities, transactions must also be recorded when they occur, regardless of when cash is received or disbursed. Furthermore, according to generally accepted accounting principles, the financial statements of authorities must be independently audited, on an annual basis, either by a certified accounting firm or by qualified state or local agency.

The audits of an authority are usually summarized in a report produced each year and available to the public. This annual report usually contains the following information:

- Statutory authorization
- Operating revenues, such as toll revenues
- Operating expenses, such as salaries
- Nonoperating expenses, such as interest income
- Changes in assets and liabilities
- Investments, such as for plants and equipment
- Total debt outstanding
- Status of pension plans
- Lease obligations
- Pending litigation
- Major programmatic accomplishments

V. AUTHORITY PERFORMANCE

While most authorities are required to submit information that details their financial and programmatic activites, this does not mean that it is easy to judge their performance. In fact, it is quite difficult. What exactly does "good" performance mean? What criteria should be used to measure the outcomes of authorities? Does the measurement of performance vary by different types of authorities (e.g., ports vs. housing vs. utilities)? Should authority performance be judged relative to the performance of public or private organizations? Although it is not possible to fully answer these questions in this chapter, it important to briefly consider how authority performance may be addressed.

A. Effectiveness

A first way to examine authority performance is to determine whether or not particular goals have been accomplished. To date, the effectiveness of authorities has been primarily demonstrated by pointing to the projects they have completed. Authorities perform well, in other words, because they have built new baseball stadiums and parks, financed the education of college students, and provided electricity to thousands of citizens.

Consider, for example, the way in which the New York City School Construction Authority specified its performance in 1991. It completed three additions and three minischools to provide spaces for 1,484 students, one modernization, and five athletic fields. It completed 674 improvement projects, including roof and window replacement and security lighting installation. It accelerated the design and construction of six school-based health clinics. It also committed $615 million in capital funds to projects including construction starts for seven new schools, one major modernization, two additions/modernizations, and two athletic fields. Of these commitments, $123 million was earmarked for 425 improvement projects.

It is not only that effectiveness can be used as a standard to measure good performance. Authorities can also be condemned for not accomplishing their goals. For instance, New York's School Construction Authority has been criticized for major delays in the various projects it has completed in New York City (Brooklyn Borough President's Office, 1991).

The problem with such effectiveness measures is that it is difficult to know whether a public agency or private firm could have accomplished the same results as a public authority. For instance, there is no reason to think that a public authority is any more capable of building a sports stadium than are the owners of any sports franchise. The only difference is who benefits and who assumes the financial risks if the project is not completed.

B. Economic Impact Analysis

Another method of assessing the performance of authorities is to assess their larger economic effects. For example, the economic impact of a port authority has been recently explored in a study of the Canaveral Port Authority in Florida. A relatively new port authority, established in 1953, this authority incurred over $20 million in debt and generated over $6.7 million in revenues in 1988. In examining the economic output of the port in 1988, Braun (1990) found that each direct job produced by the port was actually multiplied into 1.38 total jobs, that each $1 of output produced by the port itself required an additional $.55 in supporting production from other parts of the region's economy, and that each $1 of wages paid by the port generated an additional $.57 in wages in the region.

The Port Authority of New York and New Jersey has also reported similar data. The Port Authority summarized its regional impact on New York and New Jersey in 1991 as follows (Marsella, 1992):

- Total monetary impact: $17.7 billion
- Imports: $13.7 billion
- Exports: $ 2.2 billion
- Trade-related services: $ 1.8 billion
- Wages and services: $ 4.7 billion
- Business income: $ 2.1 billion
- Income and sales tax: $ .3 billion
- Jobs: 180,800

To illustrate the broader social benefits of their activities does not truly indicate whether the same benefits could be provided similarly or more equitably by traditional government agencies or private firms. Without a baseline, it is hard to know whether authorities really do provide services better than some other sector.

It can also be argued that the economic benefits of authorities are not really distributed that equitably.

There is a notion that authorities tend to benefit wealthy businesses. It is claimed, for instance, that authorities often construct facilities before private firms have even committed to using them, thereby weakening the position of the authority and local officials in lease negotiations (Walsh, 1978). In using authorities to build stadiums for sports teams, for example, the notion is that wealthy baseball teams obtain the use of a facility at a cost much lower than what they would have had to pay if they owned and operated it themselves (Sullivan, 1987). Clearly, almost every authority decision will make money for someone (Henriques, 1986). It is yet to be determined empirically how benefits are distributed.

VI. ISSUES IN DEBT FINANCE

The measurement of authority performance is not the only problem with authorities. Several other troubles bubble underneath the smooth veneer. First, some authorities have defaulted or nearly defaulted on their bonds. Second, the debt-financing capacity of many authorities has come into question as they have become increasingly dependent on intergovernmental subsidies. Third, authorities have been generally criticized for being "out of control" in their debt-financing activities. In response to these problems, various reforms have been proposed, from changing authority boards to eliminating authority functions.

A. Defaults

At one time it was thought that authorities were almost immune to financial difficulties as they easily funded themselves through revenue bonds repaid by inelastic user fees. In fact, the self-sufficiency of authorities has long been a primary reason for creating new authorities and for supporting the ongoing operation of existing ones (Walsh, 1978; Axelrod, 1989). The basic problem is that many authorities issue bonds to be backed by revenues that now seem less certain and more elastic. Consider a few examples. It is not clear if bonds issued for school loans will be paid back by students unable to obtain jobs, if bonds issued for the construction of a hazardous waste disposal facility will be paid off if there is a failure to site the facility, if parking facilities will be affected by increased competition from private firms, or if increases in a toll will actually cause revenues to drop because of a decrease in demand.

When an authority cannot repay its bonds, the result is financial collapse. In the 1980s, there were a total of 78 bond defaults by authorities, while during the same period there were no defaults of general-purpose governments (Hackbart, 1991). Many of these financial failures were suffered by large, well-endowed authorities, including most notably the Washington Public Power Supply System (WPPSS). In case of the WPPSS default, the problem was that the agency issued bonds for nuclear power projects whose costs were rising so fast that the authority was unable to generate the revenues needed to repay the bonds (Leigland and Lamb, 1986).

There are two concerns here. First, the failure of a few authorities to meet their debt obligations lessens investor confidence in the entire public authority debt-financing system. As this happens, investments could start to slow or crediting ratings might drop systemwide. If the public were to join those banks and insurance companies that have already deserted the municipal bond market since the mid-1980s, the financial survival of many authorities could be in question.

A second concern is that the U.S. Congress or state legislatures may be forced into "bailing out" authorities before they default. While the bonds now issued by authorities are not of the "moral obligation" variety that assumed legislative financial support, there is still pressure on government officials to prevent the financial collapse of authorities. This is because the services provided by authorities are essential to the economy of many states and communities. But providing subsidies to authorities may further weaken the position of authorities by making them to subject to "budgetary politics," like any other government agency. In other words, an authority might have to make fiscal commitments that would not be efficient from the bond market's perspective. It also not clear whether fiscally strapped governments can support the amount of debt being incurred by authorities.

B. Intergovernmental Subsidies

A related issue for many authorities is their growing dependence on funds other than revenue bonds and user fees. More and more authorities now receive funds from a combination of bonds, government grants or loans, user fees, interest on investments, special assessments, mortgage taxes, and donations (Institute of Public

Administration, 1986). The dependence on various sources of income is particularly signficant for authorities that deliver a ongoing service rather than provide financing for solitary projects. Most state and local transportation authorities are highly dependent, for example, on urban mass transportation grants from the federal government. This was made obvious in 1990 when the Niagara Frontier Transportation Authority in Buffalo, New York, almost had to shut down its operations when its expected subsidy from the federal government was not forthcoming.

The operational problem of becoming too dependent on either grants or legislative appropriations is perhaps best exemplified by the nation's housing authorities. Housing authorities were first created in the 1930s and 1940s to carry out the housing policies of the New Deal (Walsh, 1978). In an arrangement similar to that of any other public authority, the basic idea was for a housing authority to issue federally insured revenue bonds to construct housing, and then to repay the bonds and maintain the facilities with tenant rents (Meeham, 1979). This plan changed dramatically in the 1960s when housing authorities began to receive large amounts of intergovermental aid as a way of keeping tenant rents low, a major goal of the War on Poverty (Meeham, 1979). As housing authorities were yoked to federal subsidies, they also became subject to nationwide regulations. Of the many regulations imposed on housing authorities, the most onerous was the rule adopted in the 1970s that required the use of income criteria to determine the amount of rent charged to tenants. This meant, for example, that an authority could not increase rents to account for rising utility costs. In turn, housing authorities lost the revenue-generating capacity that would have allowed them to enter the tax-exempt bond market. As a result, housing authority management was effectively transformed into grant administration for the U.S. Department of Housing and Urban Development.

The various problems that plague housing authorities can be attributed to their "dependency" on federal funds. Without the capacity to issue bonds for new construction, many authority housing projects have become "dilapidated" and "unsatisfactory." The less than businesslike focus of housing authority administration is also a factor that explains, according to several U.S. General Accounting Office reports, the relatively high number of authority executives that have either been criticized for mismanagement or actually convicted of taking compensation for ineligible expenses or engaging in other forms of corruption.

The fear for other types of authorities is that they will also fall into the same trap as housing authorities. A downward financial spiral is possible when authorities become more dependent on subsidies. As an authority relies more on subsidies, it must implement regulations and pay attention to political demands, which reduces its ability to receive a good credit rating, which in turn reduces its capacity to issue new bonds. Housing authorities are the perfect example.

Trying to avoid subsidies, however, may invite authorities to become overburdened with debt. One strategy for an authority confronting a drop in revenues is to diversify its functions and to cross-subsidize them with more debt. The Port Authority of New York and New Jersey has led the way in this strategy. From ports, the Port Authority moved into the construction of bridges, then it operated airports, and now it is in the teliport business. A similar strategy has been undertaken by the New Jersey Turnpike Authority; it has extended the maturity of its bonds through adding new highway lanes (Gillespie and Rockland, 1989) and by purchasing roads from the State of New Jersey (New York Times, May 3, 1991). In another approach to diversification, authorities have began to deliver new services that respond to political pressures or social problems. The Garden State Parkway Authority, for instance, operates a performing arts center. The danger with these strategies is that the economies of scale may become too large to manage, eventually ending in a systemwide collapse.

C.   Out of Control

Diversification is a only one good example of how authorities can act without constraint. Recent survey data indicate that most state and local authorities do not have to seek approval from a parent government for expending surplus funds, setting fees and prices, issuing new bonds, and selecting new capital projects. Similarly, studies have found that many federal-level authorities operate without limits on administrative or capital expenses, Office of Management and Budget apportionments of funds, or line-item reviews. By having so much discretion, the concern is that authorities incur unnecessary debt, spend money unwisely, and engage in questionable activities.

There is evidence that seems to indicate authorities are not controlling their debt issuance. The debt of authorities has been increasing at a much faster rate than for state and local governments. In Illinois, for example, the state's per capita authority bond debt nearly doubled in a decade, from $5.103 billion in 1981 to $9.929 billion in 1990. Similarly, in New York, the debt of state authorities has risen three times faster than direct obligations of the state (Rubenstein, 1992). The outstanding debt of one authority in New York, the Energy Research and Development Authority, rose almost tenfold from 1982 to 1990, from $327 million to $3.7 billion.

Authorities also appear more likely to spend money unwisely. Consider a few examples

- The Port Authority of New York and New Jersy built a luggage tunnel at John F. Kennedy International Airport for $21 million in 1990 even though the airlines said they would not use it. This tunnel was constructed at time when the agency was proposing to increase fares at its bridges (*New York Newsday*, Apr. 16, 1992).
- The Tennessee Valley Authority has developed, by one account, one of the "worst-planned and worst-executed" nuclear power programs in the United States (*Washington Post National*, Apr. 16, 1992). Of 17 plants built since the mid-1970s, eight were canceled after $4 billion had been spent, one closed after a fire, and four others had their operations suspended for safety reasons.
- The Delaware River Port Authority's board chairman benefited as the owner or principal in several construction companies that received $3 million in authority construction contracts between 1954 and 1973 (Henriques, 1986).
- The West New York Municipal Utilities Authority dumped 21 million pounds of pollutants into the Hudson River because it needed to show that it had purchased an efficient treatment process (*New York Times*, Feb. 17, 1991).
- The Louisiana Public Facilities Authority issued $41 million in tax-exempt bonds in 1984 and then retired them in 1987, but for a housing project that was never developed. The bonds, in effect, were low-interest loans to the housing developers (*New York Times*, Jan. 18, 1991).
- The secretary-treasurer of the Kentucky Infrastructure Authority and his father made over $7,000 by buying bonds they knew could be resold to the authority at higher prices. They were indicted by a grand jury in October 1990. (*Wall Street Journal*, Dec. 27, 1990).
- A study of the New York School Construction Authority in 1991 found that in 2 years, it had incurred $105 million in cost overruns; $137 million in new unapproved projects; $216 million in deleted projects; and $332 million ins delayed projects (Brooklyn Borough President's Office, 1991).

Despite such anecdotes, it is still not that easy to know exactly whether or not authorities are out of control. Are these only isolated incidences of misjudgment or is there a overall continuing pattern of mismanagement? Are most authorities out of control or is it only few bad apples? Just because most authorities have dramatically increased their debt does not mean that all authorities try to capitalize on their debt-financing capabilities. And even the fact that some authority boards make unwise financial decisions does not necessarily mean that all authorities are likely to make poor judgments. Yet there is the feeling that authorities are "running wild."

It may also be that authorities are not so much out of control as they are driven by a logic beyond their control. For example, in describing the growth of authorities in New Jersey, Annemarie Hauck Walsh (1978; 339) outlined the consequences of the New Jersey Highway Authority as follows.

> In highway development, a new road generates new growth along its route. This growth in turn generates increased traffic on the road. The growth and the traffic provide the basis for additional lanes or, by similar steps, new tubes for a tunnel, second decks on a bridge. Quantitative traffic studies show that more lanes generate more traffic, which in turn generates more plans. Thus, the four-lane scenic road that Alfred Driscoll proposed (and the Highway Authority built) to allow families to take Sunday drives to the long sweep of New Jersey's ocean shore and beaches has grown into a ten-lane superhighway, spawning population explosions and industrial growth in the shore counties and damaging the resource the road was planned to show off. The concomitant erosion and pollution surprised communities unequipped to handle the water supply needs and wastes of new growth. In some former beachfront towns, high tides now lap the sea wall (built at state and federal expense), and in others, multistory condominiums have their supports planted against the sea wall. County sewer authorities have been established to cope belatedly with some of the wastes; a county "economic development authority" has been created to cope with others—by issuing industrial development bonds for pollution control equipment on private plants. Needless to say, the planners of this scenic road foresaw none of these consequences.

In sum, three questions are unanswered. Are authority managers and board members unable to control authorities? Are authorities effectively biased in particular directions by authority employees or external influences? Are authorities driven by an inherent logic beyond any internal or external controls?

VII. REFORMING AND DISOWNING AUTHORITIES

The dramatic escapades of authorities have provided the rationale for better controlling authorities, for improving the professionalism of authority employees, and for arguing against the creation of new public enterprises—and even the elimination of existing authorities.

A. Federal and State Controls

Some of the possible controls on federal-level authorities that have been proposed include the following:

* Place oversight for authorities in a cabinet-level department to assure that an authority's decisions are consistent with the policies of the administration.
* Require authorities to produce businesslike budgets which, after review by the Office of Management and Budget, should be submitted to Congress as part of the U.S. budget.
* Substitute advisory boards for governing boards to make clear the lines of authority running from the president to executive directors.
* Require the Department of the Treasury to approve the timing and terms of borrowing by authorities and make it consistent with government fiscal and economic policies.

For state and local authorities, the following controls have been proposed or implemented in various jurisdictions:

* Enact statutory limits on the proliferation of authorities.
* Require that the membership of governing boards include the end users of services.
* Require that board members be elected.
* Create regional authorities to oversee several subsidiary authorities, such as is the case with the Illinois Regional Transportation Authority and New York's Metropolitan Transportation Authority.
* Enact a code of ethics for authority management.
* Enact special regulations for authorities with regard to contracting and personnel decisions.
* Create a state-level public authorities control board, such as the one that currently operates in New York State.
* Place a cap on the bond issues offered by authorities.
* Establish investment guidelines that authorities must follow.
* Increase the external audits of authorities by state and local government agencies.

Another response to problems with authorities has been to channel some of their funds to the disadvantaged in society. An example of where the benefits of a public authority have been successfully targeted for the less advantaged was the recent use of excess funds from New York's Battery Park City Authority to finance low-income housing (Eimicke, 1992). In this instance, the Battery Park City Authority issued bonds to finance an upscale commercial and residential complex in the Wall Street area of Manhattan. The profits generated from this development were then used to finance the construction of low-income housing in less marketable areas of the city. While this plan has had its problems, the idea is noteworthy for the effort to distribute public authority benefits more directly and equitably.

B. The Education Alternative

In addition to specific controls, there is much discussion about improving the professionalism of authority employees, especially the executive director and his or her staff. Instead of creating devices and processes that restrain actions and compel accountability, the idea is to further develop the distinctive competence of authority managers (Doig, 1983; Mitchell, 1991; Walsh, 1978). Through education, existing administrative activities could be changed for the better, and college students, the next generation of managers, might be made aware of how to use the power of authorities in a responsible manner. In short, the aim is to allow for the experiment with autonomous government businesses to continue under the direction of a more skilled and ethical cadre of management generalists. Of necessity, the concern is to identify the areas of knowledge and the forms of education useful for authority management.

Port authorities have in fact already started in this direction. A majority of port authorities has management training programs for current and future employees. In addition, many port authority directors have master's degrees in engineering, business, or public administration, even though no educational background is usually required. To further the exchange of professional views, port authorities are also members of the American Association of Port Authorities. By various measures, a professional, businesslike orientation has been critical to the success of port authorities (Boschken, 1982). In turn, this has helped port authorities to consistently obtain good credit ratings in the tax-exempt municipal bond market (Standard and Poor's, 1989) and to integrate the latest technologies and methods of management into port operations (Boschken, 1982).

C. Elimination

The most dramatic response to the problems plaguing authorities has been to advocate turning their functions over to a traditional government agency or to a private sector firm. Instead of better controlling authorities or redistributing their benefits, the idea is that citizens would be better off if authority services and projects were provided by a private firm or traditional government agency (notwithstanding the lack of incontrovertible evidence as to whether the private, nonprofit, public, or quasi-public sectors deliver services more efficiently or effectively).

The argument for turning public authorities over to the private sector is a prescription applied generally to government since the 1980s. In this case, public authorities are lumped together with other agencies of government as social problems. The notion is that government, however organized, thwarts public choice, is less efficient, and a drain on taxpayers; government is the problem, not the solution. It is for these reasons that it has been argued, for example, that transit systems (Ramsey, 1987; Walters, 1987), utilities (Hanke and Walters, 1987), and airports (Roth, 1987) be transferred to private agencies.

Authorities are obviously not too enamored with the idea of transferring their services to private firms. In a letter to the editor of the *Wall Street Journal* (Sept. 19, 1991), Richard C. Leone, the then board chairman of the Port Authority of New York and New Jersey, responded to the proposal to privatize the Port Authority's airports in the following way:

> A major airport is too important to the life of its region to be placed entirely in the hands of a private operator pursuing private gain. Airports generate billions of dollars in direct and indirect income for local businesses, and thousands of jobs for airport and airline employees. Only a responsible public agency can afford substantial capital improvements, and shape policies that meet the diverse needs of customers, airlines, and the entire surrounding region—not just the short-term profit goals of shareholders. Running an airport is a task best left to government, not to a leverage buyout wizard.

It is not clear how far the privatization of public authories will go. Likewise, it is not that obvious whether it is really possible to return functions to a government agency responsible directly to an elected official.

The argument for transferring authority services to a traditional government agency is more specifically geared to the idea that authorities are prone to financial collapse, out of control, and fundamentally unfair. Perhaps the most focused effort to date in this regard has been Massachusetts Governor Andrew Weld's efforts to consolidate the various economic development authorities in the state into a single state gubernatorial agency and to transfer the functions of the huge Massachusetts Transportation Authority to the state's Department of Transportation (*Boston Globe*, Jan. 18, 1992; Aug. 9, 1992). Here the basic argument is that the governor could better coordinate economic development activities and curb the amount of debt incurred by the existing authorities. The governor's plan may not be achieved because of opposition from the authorities and their legislative supporters, but it is interesting nevertheless because it could be a harbinger of what might be proposed in other states.

VIII. CONCLUSION

This chapter has briefly reviewed the complex world of public authorities. The major activities and issues confronting authorities have been reviewed without taking a position on whether authorities are generally "good" or "bad." The problem in making this overall value judgment is that there are so many authorities, a multitude of opinions about what authorities should do, and no standard way to measure their performance.

Further information by which to judge authorities can be found in many different places. Various government agencies cover the activities of authorities, including the U.S. Census Bureau and the Advisory Commission on Intergovernmental Relations. The extent to which authorities are involved with bond issues and public activities can be found by contacting various professional associations, including, for example, the American Planning Association, American Public Power Association, Council of State Governments, Government Finance Officers Association, National Association of Bond Lawyers, National Association of Counties, and the National Council of State Housing Agencies. Last, several books and articles provide good descriptions of authorities; perhaps the most comprehensive is Annemarie Hauck Walsh's *The Public's Business: The Politics and Practices of Government Corporations* (1978).

Overall, it is important to recognize the increasingly important role that authorities play in the nation's future. The discussion about how to control authorities or to make better use of them should be considered with an eye to their potential contributions to the nation and the world. Authorities represent an idea about governance that is still unsettled and unformulated but that is for many reasons appealing to a wide variety of people. It remains to be seen how far the concept can progress.

PRIMARY SOURCES

Alaska Municipal Bond Bank Authority (1991). *Annual Report.*
American Association of Port Authorities (1988). *Mini-Directory of Port Authorities.*
Authorities Association of New Jersey (1990). *Directory of Members.*
Association of Local Housing Finance Agencies (ALFHA). (1989). *Housing Fin. Rep.*, 6.
Canaveral Port Authority (1986). *The Canaveral Harbor Port District.*
City of New York (1992). *The Mayor's Management Report.*
Colby, M. (1990). *City and State*, 11, 25.
Colorado Housing and Finance Authority (1990). *Annual Report.*
Connecticut Resources Recovery Authority (1991). *Annual Report.*
Delaware Health Facilities Authority (1991). *Annual Report.*
Delaware Solid Waste Authority (1988). *Annual Report.*
Florida Keys Aqueduct Authority (1991). *Annual Report.*
Georgia Department of Community Affairs (1986). *Directory of Economic Development Authorities in Georgia.*
Governmental Services, Inc. (1988). *Maine Turnpike Authority: A Comprehensive Review and Analysis of Proposed Improvement Projects*, Augusta, Maine.
Idaho Health Facilities Authority (1988). *Annual Report.*
Illinois Tollway Authority (1987). *A Concise History.*
Illinois Sports Facility Authority (1991). "Developer and Owner of the 'New' Comiskey Park," unpublished brochure.
Jacksonville Transportation Authority (1991). *Annual Report.*
Kansas Development Authority (1991). *Annual Report.*
Maine State Housing Authority (1991). *Annual Report.*
Massachusetts Port Authority Enabling Act, Chapter 465 of the Acts of 1956 as amended through December 1981.
Municipal Electric Authority of Georgia (1988). *Annual Report.*
National Association of State Development Agencies (1989). *Directory of Incentives for Business Investment and Development in the United States: A State-By-State Guide.*
National Council of Health Facilities Finance Authorities (1990). *Directory of Members.*
New Hampshire Housing Finance Agency (1989). *Annual Report.*
New Jersey Health Care Facilities Financing Authority (1987). *Annual Report.*
New Jersey Turnpike Authority (1991). *Annual Report.*
New York State Commission on Government Integrity (1990). *Underground Government: Preliminary Report on Authorities and Other Public Corporations.*
North Carolina State Education Assistance Authority (1990). *Annual Report.*
Oklahoma Educational Television Authority (1991). *Annual Report.*
Pennsylvania Department of Community Affairs (1989). *Directory of Municipal Authorities in Pennsylvania.*
Port of Corpus Christi Authority (1988). *Annual Report.*
Port Authority of New York and New Jersey (1989). *Annual Report.*
Rhode Island Higher Education Assistance Authority (1991). *Annual Report.*
South Carolina Public Service Authority (1991). *Annual Report.*
Tennessee Valley Authority (1991). *Annual Report.*
Utah Transit Authority (1991). *Annual Report.*

United States General Accounting Office (1989). *Chicago Housing Authority Taking Steps to Address Longstanding Problems*, U.S. Government Printing Office, Washington, D.C.
United States Census Bureau (1987). *Government Organization.*
United States General Accounting Office (1989). *HUD Oversight of the Annapolis Housing Authority*, U.S. Government Printing Office, Washington, D.C.
Virginia Agricultural Development Authority (1991). *Annual Report.*
Whatcom Transportation Authority (1991). *Annual Report.*

REFERENCES

Axelrod, D. (1989). *A Budget Quartet: Critical Policy and Management Issues*, St. Martin's, New York.
Boschken, H. L. (1982). *Pub. Admin. Rev.*, 220-226.
Boston Globe (1992). "Weld Panel to Study Agencies," Jan. 18, p. 19.
Boston Globe (1992). "Weld See Intent on Ending Turnpike Authority," Aug. 9, p. 1, 11.
Bosworth, J. C. (1961). *How the Huron-Clinton Metropolitan Authority Responds to Its Public*, Institute of Public Administration, University of Michigan, Ann Arbor.
Braun, B. M. (1990). *Policy Stud. J.*, *18*: 1032-1044.
Brooklyn Borough President's Office (1991). *School Construction: A $750 Million Abuse of Authority*, Brooklyn, N.Y.
Caro, R. (1974). *The Power Broker: Robert Moses and the Fall of New York*, Vintage Books, New York.
Chisholm, D. (1989). *Coordination with Hierarchy: Informal Structures in Multiorganizational Systems*, University of California Press, Berkeley.
Cohen, J. H. (1946). *They Builded Better Than They Knew*, Julian Messner, New York.
Curnow, R. and Wettenhall, R. (1990). *Public in World Perspective* (O. P. Dwivedi and K. M. Henderson, eds.), Iowa State University Press, Ames, pp. 90-114.
Doig, J. W. (1983). *Pub. Admin. Rev.*, 292-304.
Doig, J. W. (1966). *Metropolitan Transportation Policies and the New York Region*, Columbia University Press, New York.
Doig, J. W. and Mitchell, J. (1992). *Public Authorities and Public Policy: The Business of Government* (J. Mitchell, ed.), Greenwood Press, Westport, Conn.
Douglas, J. M. (1990). *Policy Stud. J.*, *18*: 1015-1031.
Eimicke, W. B. (1992). *Public Authorities and Public Policy: The Business of Government* (J. Mitchell, ed.), Greenwood Press, New York, pp. 119-127.
Feldstein, S. G. and Fabozzi, F. J. (1987). *The Dow Jones-Irwin Guide to Municipal Bonds*, Dow Jones-Irwin, New York.
Fountain, J. (1990). *Remedial Law: When Courts Become Administrators* (R. Wood, ed.), University of Massachusetts Press, Amherst, pp. 127-149.
Gillespie, A. K. and Rockland, M. A. (1989). *Looking for American on the New Jersey Turnpike*, Rutgers University Press, New Brunswick, New Jersey.
Gitajin, A. (1984). *Creating and Financing Public Enterprises*, Government Finance Officers Association, Washington, D.C.
Gunn, L. R. (1988). *The Decline of Authority: Public Economic Policy and Political Development in New York State, 1800-1860*, Cornell University Press, Ithaca, New York.
Hackburt, M. (1991). "State Debt Management: The State Special Authority Issue," paper presented at the Annual Meeting of the American Society for Public Administration, Washington, D.C.
Hanke, S. H. and Walters, S. J. K. (1987). *Prospects for Privatization* (S. H. Hanke, ed.), Academy of Political Science, Montpelier, Vt., pp. 104-113.
Heiman, M. (1990). *Policy Stud. J.*, *18*: 974-985.
Henriques, D. (1986). *The Machinery of Greed: Public Authority Abuse and What to Do About It*, Lexington Books, Lexington, Mass.
Hildreth, W. (1987). *Pub. Admin. Q. 11* (3): 314-341.
Horn, K. H. (1976). *Transit J.*, *2*: 15-32.
Institute of Public Administration (1986). *Special Districts and Public Authorities in Public Works Provision*, New York: IPA.
Kraft, J. L. (1989). *News. Auth. Assoc. N.J.*: 1-2, 23.
Leigland, J. and Lamb, R. (1986). *WPP$$: Who Is to Blame for the WPPSS Disaster?* Ballinger, Cambridge, Mass.
Leigland, J. (1990). *West. Polit. Q.*, *43*: 362-380.
Lemov, P. (1989). *Governing*, 32-40.
Marsella, F. J. (1992). *Via Internat.*, 8-9.
Meehan, E. J. (1979). *The Quality of Federal Policymaking: Programmed Failure in Public Housing*, University of Missouri Press, Columbia.
McClelland, P. D. and Magdovitz, A. L. (1981). *Crisis in the Making: The Political Economy of New York State Since 1945*, Cambridge University Press, New York.

Miller, N. (1962). *The Enterprise of a Free People: Aspects of Economic Development of New York During the Canal Period, 1792-1832*, Cornell University Press, Ithaca, New York.

Mitchell, J. (1992). *Public Authorities and Public Policy: The Business of Government* (J. Mitchell, ed.) Greenwood Press, New York, pp. 1-16.

Mitchell, J. (1991). *Pub. Admin. Rev., 51*: 429-437.

Muniak, D. C. (1990). *Policy Stud. J., 18*: 943-960.

Nelkin, D. (1974). *Jetport: The Boston Airport Controversy*, Transaction Books, New Brunswick, N.J.

New York Newsday (1992). "Tube to Oblivion," April 16, p. 3.

New York State Commission on Government Integrity (1990). *Underground Government: Preliminary Report on Authorities and Other Public Corporations*, Albany.

New York State Legislature (1992). *A Kingdom All Their Own: New York State's Industrial Development Agencies: A Report by Franz S. Leichter, 28th S.D., Manhattan*, Albany.

New York Times (1991). "New Jersey Official Quits After Being Charged in Dumping," Feb. 17, p. 49.

New York Times (1991). "State Bond Issuer Challenges I.R.S." Jan. 18, p. D12.

New York Times (1991). "New Florio Move: Selling a Stretch of I-95," May 3, pp. B1, B2.

New York Times (1992). "A Boom in Insured Municipals," April 27, p. D7.

Plous, F. K. Jr. (1990). *City and State*, 16.

Ramsey, J. B. (1987). *Prospects for Privatization* (S. H. Hanke, ed.) Academy of Political Science, Montpelier, Vt., pp. 93-103.

Roth, G. (1987). *Prospects for Privatization* (S. H. Hanke, ed.) Academy of Political Science, Montpelier, Vt., pp. 74-82.

Rubenstein, E. S. (1992). *City J.*, 17-28.

Sayre, W. S. and Kaufman, H. (1960). *Governing New York City: Politics in the Metropolis*, Russell Sage Foundation, New York.

Smith, R. G. (1969). *Public Authorities in Urban Areas*, National Association of Counties, Washington, D.C.

Standard and Poor's Corporation (1989). *S&P's Municipal Finance Criteria*, New York.

Sherman (1985). *Public Port Agencies in the United States and Canada*, American Association of Port Authorities, Alexandra, Va.

Sullivan, N. A. (1987). *The Dodgers Move West*, Oxford, New York.

Thurston, J. (1937). *Government Proprietary Corporations in the English-Speaking Countries*, Harvard University Press, Cambridge, Mass.

Wall Street Journal (1991). "Airport Is Too Important Privatize," letter to the Editor, Sept. 19, p. 23.

Wall Street Journal (1990). "When Bond-Buyers Call, It Pays to Stall," Dec. 27, 1990, p. C7.

Walsh, A. H. (1978). *The Public's Business: The Politics and Practices of Government Corporations*, MIT Press, Cambridge, Mass.

Walters, A. A. (1987). *Prospects for Privatization* (S. H. Hanke, ed.), Academy of Political Science, Montpelier, Vt., pp. 83-92.

Washington Post National (1992). "A New Deal for a Leaner TVA," April 16, p. 31.

Wettenhall, R. (1987). *Public Enterprise and National Development*, Royal Australian Institute of Public Administration, Canberra.

8

Risk Assessment in Government Capital Budgeting

Gerald J. Miller
Rutgers University at Newark, Newark, New Jersey

I. INTRODUCTION

Government allocation decisions have a significant influence on the nation's productivity—its economic efficiency—and particularly on government productivity. Specific allocation decisions, those in budget and regulatory policies, have a profound effect on societal and economic affairs as well. Therefore, understanding allocation decision making can provide insight about just how and with what consequences allocation decisions are made to enhance productivity as well as mollify contending social forces.

One allocation tool, cost-benefit analysis, has grown in popularity, at least among policy analysts in the three most recent presidential administrations, as *the* tool of choice in determining allocations. Therefore, this tool takes on greater significance, and we should wonder how much we understand its foreseen and unforeseen consequences.

Allocation refers to government action to define the country's needs and set priorities for fulfilling them. It is through allocation policy, substantially, that public expenditure policy and regulatory policy are made. Both spending and regulation decisions determine in concrete terms what it is that government agencies and staff members do and how they do it.

Allocation technology is not value-free. In allocation, ideological positions compete for the critical premise or assumption. Allocation policy is quite often framed in terms of equity versus efficiency, with policies and programs that give "to each according to his needs and from each according to her abilities" set against those that suggest projects that result in "at least one person better off and no one worse off."

As a result, determining what technology to employ in making allocation choices has great allure and great controversy. One controversial method of organizing information is *cost-benefit analysis*. In this chapter, we look at the rationale and method of cost-benefit analysis. Then, we critique the use of cost-benefit analysis in achieving productivity. We define productivity as economic efficiency and seek to determine whether or not productivity can be achieved with the methods provided by cost-benefit analysis.

II. RATIONALE AND METHOD OF COST-BENEFIT ANALYSIS

One of the reasons a government exists is to act as the agency of last resort. Government usually gets asked to do those things everyone else is either unwilling or unable to do. Formally, therefore, one of the major concerns of government policy makers has to do with compensating for what markets fail to provide or what markets leave as a consequence of what they do provide. For the purpose of description here, we call government action to remedy market failures, the provision of public goods. This chapter describes the way

---

Adapted from *Public Productivity Handbook*, Marcel Dekker, Inc. (1993).

governments make choices in coping with market failure. First, we reintroduce the fiscal allocation role of government and briefly explain how governments fulfill it. Second, we explain how market failure occurs. Third, we discuss the decision-making process that is used to determine the proper amounts of public goods that should be produced by governments. Finally, we discuss the relatively new concept of "nonmarket failures" and the contributions of economic reasoning to the financial management of government agencies.

A.   Fiscal Functions of Government

Regardless of the forces government fiscal policies are meant to loosen or harness in the name of "doing those things no one else will do," there are certain goods that few will produce—often leaving it to government to provide some things everyone needs. For instance, national defense, the classic case, is a commodity that is too expensive, too complicated, and in general, too hazardous to society to leave for each citizen to provide for herself.

The last reason—hazardous—may be the most important reason for not having an "every-man-for-himself" situation; that is, if everyone had the responsibility to look out for herself, we would have lost the very reason for having a nation in the first place, the acknowledgment that we are one and want to act together to protect and further our collective interest.

In any case, we find government as the provider of last resort when "market failure" occurs. Market failure strikes when the normal processes of the giant auction we call the economy does not work efficiently, specifically when rationing is either not feasible or not desirable (Stiglitz, 1988; Musgrave and Musgrave, 1980).

Rationing is not feasible when no one can be excluded from use of a product or service. Fire services to a complex of abutting apartments may not be feasible since containing a fire in one gives benefits to all. Since no one is excluded, all except the one who pays become free riders. No price system for rationing makes sense.

Rationing may also be undesirable, even though feasible. For instance, an uncrowded bridge could be paid for with a toll device forcing drivers to pay as they entered. Because the bridge is uncrowded, the toll may actually decrease traffic.

In both cases, rationing through normal market mechanisms does not work as it would otherwise. Other methods must be used to decide allocation: how much each apartment dweller should pay for fire protection and how big a bridge to build.

Government's allocation functions relate to the provision of public goods. Generally, the problem is to decide how much and what type of public goods to provide. Decision makers need some sort of mechanism for deciding these questions, and luckily, they have not just one but three mechanisms: the Pareto criterion, the Kaldor criterion, and the mechanism in place that allows us to invoke these criteria.

1.   Pareto Criterion

Named after the nineteenth-century economist, the criterion guides selection of a policy by favoring those in which at least one person is better off and no person is worse off as a result of the policy (Pareto, 1906).

What policies have such an unambiguous goodness attached to them? Education might, but some suffer lost earnings from going to school that they will never recoup. What about water and air quality? There are sunk costs in pollution that we could say one would suffer loss in remedying.

2.   Kaldor Criterion

A second method of dealing with welfare is slightly less demanding. Should we not accept a policy if those in the community benefiting from the policy compensate those who lose by the policy, especially if the winners or beneficiaries still have some gain left over (Kaldor, 1939)?

Consider this example. If the strict private goods only requirement were not relaxed (libertarianism), we would never get such goods as pristine ocean beaches. One finds it extremely difficult to slice up pieces of the ocean in order to allocate maintenance responsibilities to protect the beach. Moreover, nature's ways in forcing erosion and so on would make such coercion folly. Will one person maintain the beaches? Not by the table of benefits, especially when those benefits are held down by the inability to divide the resource or exclude others from its use.

But should the beaches be maintained? If costs equal the expense of maintaining the beaches and benefits equal the sum of everyone's perception of betterment, common sense would tell us yes. For example, in the following illustration, what would the Pareto criterion tell us if the cost were shared equally by all individuals?

Individual	Benefit	Cost	Condition
A	$3,000	$2,000	Better off
B	3,500	2,000	Better off
C	2,000	2,000	No worse off
D	3,000	2,000	Better off
E	2,500	2,000	Better off
Total	$14,000	$10,000	

The Pareto criterion—at least one is better off and no one is worse off as a result of a public program—supports a program, in which costs are shared equally, of $10,000. As the table above shows, that program would make no one worse off—even C—and at least one person—and in this case A, B, and E—would be better off. A $10,000 program passes muster.

The $10,000 program, however, provides greater benefits to some than to others. See the table below. The surpluses range from $1,500 for B to $500 for E.

Individual	Benefit	Cost	Surplus
A	$3,000	$2,000	$1,000
B	3,500	2,000	1,500
C	2,000	2,000	0
D	3,000	2,000	1,000
E	2,500	2,000	500
Total	$14,000	$9,000	

We might say that the $10,000 version of beach cleanup is less equitable than it is efficient. Defining productivity as a balance between equity and efficiency, we want to find the program that would achieve both. The Kaldor criterion is meant to suggest a way to find that program.

Recall the Kaldor criterion provides for winners compensating losers in a given situation. Without assuming any losers, however, we can still create a Kaldor-like result, as the situation below suggests.

Individual	Benefit	Cost	Surplus
A	$3,000	$2,999	$1
B	3,500	3,500	0
C	2,000	2,000	0
D	3,000	3,000	0
E	2,500	2,500	0
Total	$14,000	$13,999	$1

To ensure that the winners bore their fair share of the costs and still stood to reap some gain, the maximum project would have to be $13,999. We can compute this amount by distributing the costs in the same way as the original surpluses so that one person gains $1 of surplus while all others have benefits that equal their costs.

This distribution of costs and benefits underlies the progressive tax structure and redistribution of income programs that guided the construction and maintenance of the American version of the welfare state for some 50 or more years. More to the point of this chapter, however, the Kaldor criterion underlies the measurement of productivity and, especially, cost-benefit analysis. Cost-benefit analysis, like the Kaldor criterion, argues that as long as the benefits exceed the costs of a project, the project should go forward.

3. Voting

The problem with cost-benefit analysis and with the Kaldor criterion is the determination of benefit. In a country that values individualism and decentralized decision making, we assume that each person can value a policy alone. The sum of those values becomes the public welfare. However, that makes it difficult to calculate individual benefits. Instead, the political system, and specifically the voting system, takes care of that.

But what vote should be required—unanimity, majority rule, three-fourths, two-thirds, plurality? The answer lies in the analysis of voting by legislative bodies. Following Buchanan and Tullock (1962), the analysis falls on the interaction of two variables: (1) the loss of value that occurs when we do not include in any decision each individual's calculation of his or her own benefit that would result from the implementation of a given project, and (2) the cost of making an effort to ascertain each individual's preference.

As an alternative to the price system as a method of determining what and how much of a public good to produce, voting applies in finding the expected cost to the individual and to the group or public, which the individual alone can calculate, or implementing a public project. How much effort to exert in finding these individual preferences, or specifically, in determining when we can feel sure we have solicited the opinions of enough people and when enough people desire a project to warrant its implementation, constitutes the basis of voting analysis.

Voting analysis demands that we know individuals' preferences toward a project. Obviously, 100% voting participation resulting in a consensus decision on the project would guide decision makers in making a valid decision. The first variable in voting analysis, therefore, is the probability of violating the Pareto criterion as we depart from unanimous consent. Such a problem occurs in sampling as well as in using majority rule over consensus.

Nevertheless, gaining unanimity has drawbacks, not the least of which is the cost entailed in cajoling participation and informing voting. The counterbalance to total participation and consensus is the cost that both would entail. The more closely we near total participation and consensus in voting, the higher the cost of the voting process. The lower the cost of the voting process, the less likely we will have valid facsimiles of the voters' preferences; that is, majority votes of whatever number of voters may not be valid expressions of the total population's preferences even though such an election may cost less than any method we could use to secure unanimity.

Obviously, the appropriate system of voting involves trading off the cost of exclusion against the cost of the election, a calculation easier than it looks. We seldom have single issues in which individuals have two choices and perfect information about them both. Rather, we have a continuous stream of issues about which individuals have varying levels of intensity of preferences.

It can be shown through studies of public opinion that our knowledge of and attention paid to issues faced by members of Congress is relatively low; over the 10,000 or so measures members see in every session, we as voters probably know something—anything at all—about less than 1% (100) and have intense preferences about even fewer, say 0.1% (10). We probably have full and complete knowledge of even less, say 0.01% (1).

Also, the intensity of preferences among voters tends to form a regular pattern. Very few voters feel intensely about an issue either way. The vast majority—the middle—have no feeling about an issue at all and probably do not find the issue itself salient.

Such arrays of preferences yield themselves to vote trading or logrolling as well as coalition building. In cases in which we have public provision of private goods, we have all the conditions for bargaining: costly participation, isolated issue salience, and unclear estimates of who benefits through policies and by how much.

4. Overspending

In cases in which we have public provision of private goods, we have conditions for overspending, say Buchanan and Tullock (1962), or underspending, says Downs (1960).

Consider an example Buchanan and Tullock offer as support for the idea that logrolling tends to create more expenditure than would ordinarily be the case if economic efficiency controlled. Consider the case of 100 farmers in a locality, each of which is served by a separate access road that requires maintenance. Maintenance of a specific road must be passed by a majority of voters and, if passed, is financed out of general tax revenues levied equally on all farmers. If each road's maintenance is voted on separately and no logrolling takes place, no road improvements would pass under general tax financing. Each road improvement benefits only one person, but the cost is borne by several.

Suppose vote-trading agreements can take place. In order to have his road repaired, each farmer must agree to support the road repairs of 50 other farmers in order to get the 51 votes required for his own. The benefit to this farmer is the benefit of having his own road repaired. The cost to him of the agreement is his share of the repairs to be done on the 50 other roads he agrees to support. In the general case, each of the farmers will attempt to secure an agreement with 50 other farmers and the agreements will probably be overlapping since all 100 farmers want to get their own roads repaired. In the end each farmer will have secured an agreement to have his road repaired. In determining the level of road repairs on each road, the benefit to the farmer whose road is being repaired is weighed against the costs of 50 farmers of repairing it. The costs incurred by the other 49 farmers not included in that particular agreement are neglected. Overall, the cost to all farmers will exceed the benefits from the chosen level of repairs in each road. The logrolling process will have resulted in overexpenditure.

5. Underspending

Anthony Downs (1960) demonstrates the opposite case, the case for spending less than would be necessary. If we consider the same example above but substitute higher education for road repair, we might find that the calculation of benefits each farmer made would result in undervaluing the public expenditure. Arguments, except for the agricultural experiment station, the cooperative extension service, and the college of agriculture at the state land grant university, would probably tend toward belittling most benefits and accentuating higher education's costs. In the end, higher education might be underfunded, given some notion of adequate or efficient funding, and the entire government budget made smaller than economic efficiency might otherwise dictate.

6. Summary

Allocation may be approached through cost-benefit analysis or through logrolling. Cost-benefit analysis is that allocation principle in which a project is selected if the costs and benefits are weighed and the result makes the society better off. The problem with cost-benefit lies in the implementation of the sharing of benefits in such a way that those who bear most of the costs get enough of the benefits to offset their losses.

Logrolling—using the political process to allocate—examines a project in the context of all projects on the agenda for study at one time. The supporters of a project ultimately get their way only because they trade favors with supporters of other projects, resulting in a sharing of costs and benefits so that both sets of supporters as a whole are better off. The problems with logrolling tend to be those related to overspending, a condition supporters of logrolling think is a function of viewing the needs of the individual as greater than the needs of society; that is, those who favor cost-benefit analysis, and who believe logrolling results in overspending, tend to be those who favor the right of the individual to reach her goals in competition with others without government's help. Those who favor logrolling rather than cost-benefit analysis see the needs of society as paramount, at least those needs that in the end make society's benefits greater than society's costs.

III.   ALLOCATION, ORGANIZATION, ANALYSIS—MICRO AND MACRO: AN INTRODUCTION

Cost-benefit structures* drive project-by-project or budget-by-budget decisions. At the micro or project level, an analyst delves into the preferences for that project versus its cost. At the macro or budget level, decision makers must cope with combining into some meaningful whole projects that have overcome micro-level constraints. The systematic aggregation of micro decisions is not truly a macro decision. In reality, budgets are constructed from both micro views and from some systematic macro view—often called an ideology or even a political platform—that details how the entire basket of public goods should be chosen. This section describes both levels of analysis and describes practical ways the two levels may complement each other.

---

*We follow Schmid's organization (1990) here, and the distinction is made for simplicity's sake only.

A.   Micro Cost-Benefit Analysis

To begin a cost-benefit analysis, one has at least one project that can be studied. In this case, the concept is straightforward: determine benefits and costs, then find the ratio of dollar-quantified benefits at their current value to dollar-quantified costs at their current value (B/C). If that ratio is greater than 1, the analysis suggests that the project should be considered for inclusion in the jurisdiction's budget.

The concept as just outlined includes two major ideas that influence the analysis: the notion of measuring benefits and costs and the idea of measuring them at their current value. Measuring benefits and costs involves estimating, forecasting, and costing them, all difficult to do in the public goods sector. The second, calculating benefits and costs at their current value, requires knowledge of preferences about the time value of money.

1.   Uncertainty and the Measurement of Costs and Benefits

Measuring costs and benefits involves carefully considering both the obvious and not so obvious elements that a project will entail, forecasting changes that will occur and affect these elements over time, and including—costing—the elements properly; that is, in both accounting and economic terms. This section describes the hazards of estimating, forecasting, and costing.

a.   Estimating   The first element of measurement is estimation. Estimation deals with the type of cost or benefit to be counted; costs and benefits that are real or pecuniary types, tangible or intangible; as well as direct or indirect benefits. First, real costs and benefits are those that have a real or absolute consequence for society as a whole; that is, on balance the cost or benefit to society was not one in which the cost to one group of individuals was offset by the benefit to another group of individuals. The cost or benefit was not merely redistributed—as a pecuniary cost or benefit would describe—but an absolute change in the well-being of society as a whole.

Second, tangible and intangible costs and benefits describe the difference between those that can be priced or that society can agree relatively easily on a price and those that cannot. A tangible cost-benefit to many is a project such as a dam, with its measurable construction costs and irrigation, flood control, and recreation benefits. An intangible cost might be the endangered species that is destroyed as a result of the dam's displacement and destruction of the species' habitat.

The last type of cost and benefit that must be confronted in estimating the numbers that feed the cost-benefit analysis is the direct-indirect contrast. Direct costs are those immediately apparent from the project. The dam example, both tangible costs and tangible benefits illustrate this idea. The indirect or secondary costs from the dam's construction might include poorer or better drainage in streams and marshes that fed the undammed stream, greater air and noise pollution as a result of recreational equipment used on reservoirs created by the dam, and even climate changes that result from large bodies of water replacing water flows.

In each case, the analysis would not be complete without considering the pecuniary, intangible, and indirect costs and benefits of a project. Most analyses suggest this to be difficult and controversial.

b.   Forecasting   The policy problems and consequences of forecasting are often not based on political differences. Since no forecaster can know the future and instead must monitor various data sets, judgments must be made about what to consider important enough to follow closely, what is novel, and what is a trend. One's assumptions, built not only through political views but also through organizational and professional effort, guide one to search to all three questions (Pierce, 1971: 53). Thus forecasting has great interpretive potential. Likewise one can influence the course of events. If one's view is substantially influential, the guidance this forecast provides can influence the course of events (Pierce, 1971: 41). As Klay (1985) has pointed out, however, what one wants to see can happen. Views do become self-fulfilling prophecies.

Many different classification schemes exist to understand forecasting as a rational exercise. Quantitative methods are those depending on empirical data and in which theories play a central role. Qualitative methods also may come into play. Forecasters may have only a fuzzy understanding of their theories' production under various conditions. Finally, forecasters may combine both forms, implicitly reflecting organization biases; a forecaster may even reason backward from a desirable conjectured state of affairs to the data and assumptions necessary to support the conjecture. (See Dunn, 1981: 195.)

c.   Quantitative Methods   Quantitative methods are those forecasting methods involving data and mathematical analysis. These quantitative methods fall into two basic categories: time-series analytical methods and causal models.

1. Time Series Analysis. A time series is a sequence of observations of phenomena of interest. Usually these observations are spaced at specific and constant intervals. For example, the expenditures of a state government would form a time series when these expenditures, or a specific class of expenditures (the variable), were measured over a period of years. Analysis of a time series involves describing the source of the sequence of realizations, the factor generating the time series. The simplest method of forecasting time series assumes that present trends may be extrapolated. The basic methods used for extrapolation are least squares and other forms of regression analysis.

2. Least Squares and Regression. Simple regression requires that a relationship between two variables exist and that enough history describing this relationship be accessible to determine quantitatively the degree to which movement in one variable may be predicted by movement in the other. Yet, decision makers doubt that what lies ahead will repeat the past. Many discredit regression techniques that try to find linearity where none exists.

3. Causal Models. A model consists of explicitly stated relationships among variables that portray an abstraction of some phenomenon such as taxes and economic growth. Most models build on history, but in addition, elaborate theoretical relationships, such as that involving the curvilinear relationship among productivity, tax rates, and revenue yields illustrated earlier.

Forecasting models range from relatively simple judgmental models to highly complex econometric models.

4. Judgmental Models. A judgmental model is a method of economic analysis that is relatively unstructured and informal. The forecaster generally does not use mathematical equations to represent the economy, but relies instead on any information that seems useful—information about future investment intentions and upcoming political events, judgments, and hunches of people familiar with economic events, and other considerations not explicitly a part of the national income accounts framework.

5. Econometric and Mathematical Models. An econometric model, at the other extreme, is a system of analysis in which the economic system of a country is represented by a complex system of statistically estimated mathematical equations. The number of equations that are needed to adequately represent the economy depends on the number of actors that are to be considered. The larger the number of equations, the greater the number of subtle economic variations that can be accounted for by the model.

6. Policy Analysis with Models. The same model can be used for policy analysis as well as for forecasting. To investigate any specific set of possible government actions, the policy makers simply insert the change into the model and solve to find out what the impact of the action is likely to be. In periods of inflation, the figure for taxes might be raised and expenditures lowered. In periods of depression, the opposite actions might be taken.

An econometric model allows the government to predict the effects of a policy action before enacting it. The quality of the model depends on the accuracy with which it can predict these values. The distinguishing feature of econometric models is, in summary, an attempt to depict the economy by a set of statistically estimated mathematical equations. Particular emphasis is placed on having as many variables as possible explained within the system of equations, on the use of hard economic data, and on the simultaneous solutions of the model without the introduction of other considerations.

d. Qualitative Approaches Qualitative forecasting methods are those in which subjective estimation predominates. Such methods have greatest utility in murky or confusing areas of activity—those areas in which our knowledge of the relevant variables and the patterns of interaction among these variables may not be well developed. Often qualitative methods' loudest partisans are those who reject a priori reasoning or positive theory.

The most basic qualitative forecasting technique is the judgmental forecast. Using judgment, individuals create a relatively unstructured and informal process. Those people with information relevant to the phenomena being considered essentially pool that knowledge and make educated guesses about the future. Hunches and intuition play a large role in the outcome of a judgmental forecasting process.

The Delphi technique is a well-known form of judgmental forecasting (Brown and Helmer, 1962). To employ this method, one empanels a group of experts. These experts respond to a sequence of interrogations in which their responses are communicated to each other. Specifically, their responses to one questionnaire are used to produce a subsequent questionnaire. Any set of information available to some experts and not others is passed on to the others through this sharing process. This information, the method envisions, sharpens judgment among experts and focuses attention and forecasts.

Brainstorming is another information-gathering technology, one useful in aiding judgment and forecasting future events (Osborn, 1953). This method follows a very disciplined format. Criticism of any source of information or of the information provided is banned. In fact, farfetched ideas are encouraged as an aid to eliciting a large number of practical ideas. The quantity of data is emphasized. The first step in the process—the generating phase—rests primarily on creativity. The second phase is a winnowing out phase in which individuals evaluate ideas generated earlier. The third phase builds on the best ideas surviving the second phase by focusing attention on synthesizing these best ideas. Finally, the evaluation phase forces the elimination of all but the best idea or forecast.

Finally, many organizations employ the nominal group technique (Delbecq et al., 1975) to forecast future events. A nominal group is a group composed of the pooled outputs of randomly chosen individuals who have worked alone.

e. Problems in Forecasting   Forecasting in government is hardly ever the prerogative of only one group. Intergroup effort, in fact, describes what takes place when both legislative and executive bodies cooperate, of course (Kamlet et al., 1987), but such effort is also required among different offices within the executive branch (Pierce, 1971).

Common to all whose task is forecasting is ambiguity. Seldom is there a clear definition of cause-effect relationships. Even more seldom is there agreement about what one wants to happen. Thus forecasting is often a judgmental process, p0- especially influenced by forecasters' social construction of reality.

To understand the judgmental process, and thus revenue forecasting, it is necessary to understand the elements that interact to construct cause-effect relationships and desired outcomes. The interaction among actors in forecasting, as in all other organizational and judgmental exercises, assumes that all want stability; all participants interact and confine behavior in ways to trade stable expectations about behavior.

Explaining reality construction solely as an economy of social interactions is incomplete. March and Olsen (1989: 62) suggest that the market centers on bias:

> Although there seems to be ample evidence that when performance fails to meet aspirations, institutions search for new solutions, changes often seem to be driven less by problems than by solutions. . . . When causality and technology are ambiguous, the motivation to have particular solutions adopted is likely to be as powerful as the motivation to have particular problems solved, and changes can be more easily induced by a focus on solutions than by a focus on problems. Solutions and opportunities stimulate awareness of previously unsalient or unnoticed problems or preferences.

All parties to making judgments have a solution in mind. Judgment in a collective choice situation is a matter of convincing other parties of the connection between a preferred solution and the problem at hand.

The argument about one's preferred solution may be easier to make when the party realizes the importance of sequential attention. Parties to the making of judgment have limited time and limited willingness to devote more than a fair share of that time to a given judgment call. Any party realizing the limited time problem can choose to focus attention, or not, on a given solution.

One's ploy may well be to focus on the aspect of the problem that a given solution seems most capable of resolving, or one's time may best be spent in characterizing a problem as one in which a favorite solution has always been chosen by the group to use. In fact, Brunsson (1989) has argued that it is possible to sustain a coalition among members who have what appear to be strictly inconsistent objectives because of sequential attention:

> By adroitly applying technology and expertise, [executives] can manage the assumptions and judgments which must be made to combine . . . forecasts in some reasonable way and predict . . . change.

The recognition of biases, and the understanding that differences may be useful, underscores much research in judgment making (Wright and Ayton, 1987); that is, differences create a healthy skepticism about others' views and assumptions, bringing them out in the open (Golembiewski and Miller, 1981). Research by Klay (1985; 1983) and Ascher (1978) suggest that airing such differences may reduce overreliance on outdated core assumptions, or "assumption drag," in forecasts, improving their accuracy.

f. Costing   Finally, cost-benefit analysts must cope with the assignment of some quantitative value to the stream of costs and benefits. This has proved especially difficult in the public goods sector, since markets have not "priced" these goods due to market failures in either rivalry or divisibility. Three specific costing problems bedevil analysts: estimating shadow prices, final prices, and opportunity costs.

First, the cost of a project or the benefit of it may often be estimated by analogy. Some equivalent market may exist for a project, somewhere; that equivalent is employed as the basis for costing out the elements of the project for analysis. The problems of finding such a shadow or of using the most nearly correct one still create problems.

Second, the lack of a shadow price leads to additional problems; that is, most public goods tend to be oriented toward outcomes rather than mere outputs. Outcomes are extremely hard to envision, much less estimate in dollar-denominated consequences. For example, street sweeping and cleaning are often touted as popular programs, even though they have no meaningful outputs (pounds of garbage collected, raves from residents) but definite outcomes. Clean streets has a meaning all its own and is an end in itself. Such an end in itself is hard to measure for cost-benefit analysis.

Third, a project without a shadow price always carries an opportunity cost that might be measurable and meaningful for analysis. The opportunity cost of any project is the cost and benefit of another project foregone to proceed with the present one. The true cost of any project, therefore, is the cost (and benefit) of the most obvious substitute. Clean streets may carry the cost of an opportunity, such as a rat amelioration program, foregone. The illustration also suggests the problem of lack of adequate quantifiability in opportunities foregone, the biggest problem is calculating costs.

g. *Summary.* Problems abound in estimating, forecasting, or costing project elements for analysis. Estimating costs and benefits accurately requires knowledge that far exceeds that available to an analyst. Forecasting demands an objectivity and a knowledge of theoretical relationships far beyond that normally expected of economics and social observers. Costing public programs has special difficulties in that few analogous, meaningful, or quantifiable projects exist on which to base estimates.

2. *Valuation over Time and by Different Selection Criteria*

The selection of projects through cost-benefit analysis is commonly derived from an investment theory utilizing comparisons between a stream of costs and a stream of benefits *measured at their current value.* Generally, these comparison are made on the basis of one or the other of two calculations, net present value (NPV) or internal rate of return (IRR).

Net present value measures future streams of costs and benefits by "netting" or subtracting current value costs from current value benefits. A variation of this measure is the more popularly known ratio of current value benefits over current value costs. The differences are nil. The criterion for selection in the former is a positive number; the criterion for the ratio is a number greater than unity (1).

A second method of selecting a project is to determine its rate of return (IRR). This calculation suggests that projects whose current value benefits exceed their current value costs by a given rate or percentage are better than those that do not.

The difference between NPV/CB ratio and IRR is in the former's discrimination in favor of large numbers; that is, IRR corrects for extremely large differences in scope among projects. It is more appropriately applied at the macro level where projects compete against other projects than at the micro level where a project's benefits compete against its costs.

a. *Discounting* Nevertheless, the calculation of NPV and the CB ratio depend on establishment of current value costs and benefits. Current value costs and benefits are also known as discounted elements.

Discounting is based on a preference for the time value of money. For example, if given the choice between $100 now and $100 a year from now, most people would prefer to have the $100 now.[*] If forced to wait, we would want the year-from-now choice to be equal in value to the $100 today alternative. The amount that would make the $100 a year from now equivalent in value to the $100 today alternative is our preference for the time value of money. Some of us prefer more under some circumstances than others. To illustrate: the delay in getting the $100, such as when we lend money to a college student daughter to buy an automobile in return for the promise to repay it, we would want to have compensation for the delay. What would the time preference be?

The calculation of time value may shed light on finding preferences. Consider that if you put $100 in a bank at 5% interest, you would have $105 in a year, if interest is compounded annually. The future value of that $100 (the amount it would be worth in 1 year) is $105, or

---

[*]To those like Henny Youngman, this is "nem di gelt" or take the money: "Don't believe all the baloney people tell you about what they'll do for you tomorrow. Take the money" (Youngman, 1990).

Future value of $100 $= \$100 * (1 + 0.05)$
                                    $= \$105$

A sum of $100 at the present time is equivalent to $105 next year at a 5% interest rate. A person's choosing not to put money in the bank tells us that the $100 sum we have today is equivalent to an amount next year of at least $105 and maybe much more. If the person feels that having $100 today or $105 1 year from now are equivalent, then the 5% interest rate represents the time value of money—of waiting 1 year for the money. The 5% interest rate measures the willingness to trade $100 today (present value) for $105 1 year from now (future value).

If we know the interest rate that reflects the trade-off to the citizens of a community between $100 in benefits today versus some greater level of benefits in later years, we can convert the value of the future benefits into their present day's worth. Two examples illustrate the need to know the present value of future benefits. In the first case, many governments often buy fleets of automobiles for their police forces and for many other departments. The government's decision makers face the quandary: Should we buy or should we lease the automobiles? Present valuing the terms of the lease is the only true way to compare, on financial terms, the buy-versus-lease alternatives.

In a second case, governments often sell bonds in the marketplace to finance capital improvements such as roads and bridges. These bonds will be redeemed with principal payments the government will make annually over a period of years. The bond financings are more often than not competitively bid. Investment banks ordinarily bid on bonds by offering an interest rate for each annual principal payment. If a bond financing covered a redemption period of 10 years, an investment bank would often bid on each of ten annual payments or maturities. The government decision maker who evaluates the competing bids must calculate the present value of each principal payment on which the bank submitted a bid because, presumably, the interest rates the banks bid were different, leading to different total amounts of interest the government would pay.

Essentially, we calculate the present value in the opposite way we calculate interest earnings or future value; that is, if the formula for the future value of a sum of money is

Future value = Present value * (one + interest rate)

the formula for finding present value is solved by algebra (dividing both sides of the equals sign by the term "one + interest rate") to get the formula

Present value = Future value / (one + interest rate)

In other words, if we know any two terms—future value, interest rate, or present value—we can find the third. And if we know the future benefits of a project with any certainty at all, as well as the interest rate, we can find the present value of the project.

We should note one fact about terminology related to the time value of money. The rate used to calculate future value is best thought of as an interest rate; most of us are familiar enough with that process through savings accounts and like investments. However, the rate used in present value calculations is known as the *discount rate* because the value of a benefit we receive at some future time is smaller today by comparison because we deduct an amount to compensate us for the delay. In other terms, we deduct from the future value by a factor that relates time and the discount rate.

Projects often begin to have benefits much later than 1 year after they have been built. The construction of a project, for example, may take 3 years. The benefits, while forecast to be a certain amount, may have to be adjusted because of the delay. The adjustment would be done in the same way as three separate 1-year present value calculations; that is, if the present value of a forecasted benefit of $1,000 (at 5%) for 1 year were

Present value $= \$1,000 / (1 + 0.05)$
                                    $= \$952.38$

then the present value for the second year would be

$\$952.38 / (1 + 0.05)$ $= \$907.03$

and the present value for the third year would be

$907.03 / (1 = 0.05)$ $= \$863.84$

The formula may be simplified by

$$\text{Present value (of \$}x\text{ over 3 years at 5\%)} = \frac{\text{Future value}}{(1 + 0.05)^3}$$

Thus, by cubing the discount factor $(1 + 0.05)$, we calculate precisely as we did by the long method formerly.

b. *Annual Costs and Benefits*   Many projects have costs and benefits continually over a period of years. In other words, these projects have a benefit (or cost) stream. To find the total value of the stream from this succession of periods, we add terms to the basic formula for present value that we looked at earlier. If a project had annual benefits for n years, we would use the following formula:

$$\text{Present value} = \text{annual value} * \frac{[(1 + \text{ discount rate})^n - 1]}{\text{discount rate } (1 + \text{ discount rate})^n}$$

Consider the following example. If a city were offered $1,000 for a piece of property valued at $1,500 today that it was leasing to a business for 5 more years at $300 a year with the option of purchase at the end of the 5-year period for $500, which would you advise the city leaders to choose? Using an interest rate of 5%, let's consider the two alternatives.

1. The lease (alternative 1):	
Annual benefit	$=\$300$
One time benefit	$=\$500$
PV annual benefit 300*	$\dfrac{[(1.05)^5 - 1]}{0.05\,(1.05)^5}$
	$=\$1,064$
PV one-time benefit = 500/	$=\$500/(1.05)^5$
	$=\$392$
Total benefits	$=\$1,064 + \$392$
	$=\$1,456$
2. The sale (alternative 2)	
The sale, theoretically, at least, would take	
place today; therefore its present value is	
$1,500	
3. A comparison of the two alternatives:	
Lease/purchase	$=\$1,456$
Sale	$=\$1,500$

We would probably advise the city to sell the property. Of course, the difference is small because, above all, we are dealing with rather small sums. Yet, if the differences were small even with bigger numbers, other considerations would be called into play to decide the question, such as the disposition of the property—given other city policies—if sold, the realiability of payments by the present lessor, and other plans the city might have for adjoining property.

The city's main advantage in knowing the present value of the lease is the ability to compare directly the value of a sale and the value of the lease. These types of calculations make comparisons meaningful, since the cash flow from the lease—[(5 * $300) + $500] = $2,000—might have led decision makers to believe that the lease's value was more than it actually was.

B. Macro Cost-Benefit Analysis or Portfolio Construction

On a project-level evaluation of benefits and costs, the net present value idea has some merit. Certainly, one hesitates to spend taxpayers' money on projects whose worth cannot be shown readily. However, selection problems occur when the comparison is between projects of unequal size or projects of unequal economic or useful lives, as well as when an entire budget of projects is being selected. We find two strategies normally used to overcome these selection problems: a scheduling stategy and a strategy to construct portfolios.

1.   *Cost Benefit Analysis Without Constraint*

First, capital projects are also often submitted with no expenditure ceiling specified. Consequently, more projects are submitted than can be funded. Prioritization is necessary to achieve the required cutbacks.

Prioritization is frequently achieved by scheduling. Scheduling helps alleviate waste by ensuring the construction of facilities required initially; that is, before primary construction. For example, sewers will be scheduled for construction prior to building a street so that it will not be necessary to cut new pavement during sewer construction.

A danger of prioritization by scheduling is that projects are rarely completely eliminated. More often they are postponed and placed further down the schedule. As projects stay on the schedule for several years there can be a maturation effect; they may become bona fide projects with funding, even though they logically do not have a high priority.

Prioritization requires review to ensure the project relates to the overall goals and policies of the jurisdiction. "Projects must be weighed in light of their contribution to programs which, in themselves, are not of equal rank. We emphasize that the project contribution-to-the-program approach, rather than the departmental or functional approach, should dominate thinking" (Schmid) at this level.

2.   *Marginal Rate of Return Analysis*

A second approach to cost-benefit analysis, one that overcomes the scheduling problem, employs marginal analysis in selecting productive projects. This method has greatest utility when projects are quite different in scale or useful life.

Marginal analysis requires three steps. First, a range of discount rates is evaluated to determine the likely field of opportunity costs for projects such as those being evaluated. Second, the analyst determines the IRR for the entire set of projects and discards those that fall below the opportunity costs of capital. Third, the preferred choice is selected by finding that project that has the highest IRR for the employment of capital.

a.   Finding the Range of Discount Rates and Opportunity Costs   Determining opportunity costs of projects provides the information one needs to discount future costs properly; that is, to be systematic in judging the value of public projects, the projects must be compared not only to the population of candidate *public* projects, but also to all investment opportunities, public and private. In this way, the economic efficiency of all institutions is preserved.

An opportunity's cost is the cost of a project foregone; that is, if one chooses one project over another, the true value of the choice is the value foregone to gain it. Consider the example of desserts. If we forego one that weighs in at 1,000 calories for one that has 100 calories, we value the one we chose at its 10:1 savings rate. The one we chose is ten times the value of the one we did not choose.

In this same sense, public projects compete with private sector projects. If we decide to spend money on public capital projects, we forego the economic benefits of leaving the money in the private sector, where, presumably, it generates economic growth.

Since we cannot grasp the long-term costs and benefits of collective goods very well, the opportunity cost gets fixed as a discount rate by which we judge what costs and benefits we do know. We measure costs and benefits and discount this stream by the opportunity cost of capital.

Many consider the market to have done this costing for us, at least in constructing a range of opportunity costs for portfolio purposes. The difference between the tax-free yield on municipal bonds and the taxable yield on these bonds or on corporate bonds of equal risk of default might serve as the floor in our range. The yield on federal long-term yields might be our range's ceiling.

Why these? If the opportunity cost of capital is value foregone, the small difference in the former represents such a comparison. The tax exemption represent the subsidy or cost of pushing investment dollars from private to public sector. These bonds would not be sold, or the projects they finance built, we assume, if they had to be offered at market rates.

The top of the range is that market rate that attracts capital. The federal goverment's long-term taxable bond rate is such a rate.

b.   Determining the Internal Rate of Return of the Projects   Instead of determining a cost-benefit ratio, many analysts follow the private sector practice of solving for the rate of return on investment, or the IRR. Having discovered this internal rate, analysts discard those projects whose rates are less than the opportunity cost of capital—the floor of rates.

Consider the example of a project with an initial outlay of $20,000, annual costs of $10,000, and annual benefits of $13,000, all of which are paid or received at the end of the fiscal year. The projected life of the project is 10 years, and there is no residual benefit at the end of the project. This project's costs and benefits are represented with the following cash flows:

Year	Costs	Benefits
1	−30,000	+13,000
2	−10,000	+13,000
3	−10,000	+13,000
4	−10,000	+13,000
5	−10,000	+13,000
6	−10,000	+13,000
7	−10,000	+13,000
8	−10,000	+13,000
9	−10,000	+13,000
10	−10,000	+13,000

To find the IRR, we determine that discount rate at which the net current value (discounted costs and benefits) are zero. In the table below, we show four possible discount rates and the net current values for the cash flows above.

	Discount rate (%)			
	5	10	15	20
Project A	4,118	253	−2,334	−4,088

Given the numbers that appear in the table, the discount rate of 10.41% brings the discounted benefits and costs into equality; that is, the net costs and benefits are almost zero.

The IRR of a given set of cash flows (outflow in payments for construction and such, inflow in benefits received) is that discount rate at which the current value of the inflow equals the current value of the outflow. Finding the IRR is a matter of eliminating all those discount rates at which the two flows are not equal.

Take, for illustration, three project with unique cash flows.

Project	Capital costs	Annual costs	Annual benefits
A	20,000	10,000	14,000
B	30,000	10,000	15,000
C	50,000	17,000	25,000

With computers, it is possible to program to find the rate, since hunting for it is time-consuming and tedious.

	Discount rate in (%)			
Project	5	10	15	20
A	11,839	6,396	2,684	103
B	10,037	3,450	(993)	(4,038)
C	14,155	3,702	(3,328)	(8,127)

Just as large numbers may be less practical as projects even though benefit-cost ratios make them look better, projects that have large IRR also may not be practical. This may be so in limited budget situations particularly. For example, a budget with a limit of $15,000 simply cannot afford any of the projects, no matter what their IRR. Not only does the IRR calculation limit the population of possible projects to those that exceed the minimum rate or the opportunity cost of capital, but, obviously, it also limits projects to those that a government can afford.

c. *Selecting Projects by Their Marginal Rates of Return* The actual method of choosing a portfolio of projects that have internal rates higher than the minimum is by determining marginal rates of return among those that have not been weeded out already. This method operates on the principle that each additional dollar invested in a project should have at least the same, if not a higher, rate of return than the last. We would first employ the minimum acceptable rate criterion to projects to weed out those projects that alone could not produce a rate of return great enough to justify taxation to finance it. Then we would ask which combination of projects yields the highest marginal rate of return.

Taking the projects just described, and establishing a 7% minimum acceptable rate,[*] arriving at net current values and benefit-cost ratios comes first. The net current values and ratios are displayed below.

	Capital required	Current value (at 7%)	B-C ratio	IRR
A	20,000	9,403	1.11	20.2%
B	30,000	7,081	1.07	13.7%
C	50,000	9,460	1.06	12.4%

Then, the process requires finding the differences between any and all projects. The marginal analysis method requires comparison between successively larger projects—between one project and another with larger capital requirements—and not the other way around (Gohagan, 1980: 209-211).

In our example, our process requires moving from project A to project B (and on to project C) or from project A to project C. We ask whether it is justifiable to spend additional capital to mount a larger project. The marginal additions are portrayed below.

Marginal increase	Initial capital	Annual costs	Annual benefits	Marginal Internal Rate of Return (%)
From A to B	10,000	-0-	1,000	0%
From A to C	30,000	7,000	11,000	7.06%

The analysis suggests two facts. The first is that there is no additional benefit to be gained by investing in project B rather than project A. However, because we set the rate of return floor at 7%, the move from A to C would be justifiable, since the 30,000 extra dollars, invested in what we presume to be a popular project, would return at least that minimum. As a result of our analysis, the marginal IRR calculation would suggest project C to be the most productive use of the public's money.

3. Portfolio Construction

A third approach to cost-benefit analysis deals with the most productive combination of projects by using investment portfolio approaches to choice. Finding this combination is the subject of capital budget deliberations. How does one build a portfolio?

Constructing a portfolio requires three steps. First, we set the minimum rate of return for capital. Second, we determine the marginal internal rate of return for each project or combination of projects over each other project or combination. Finally, we choose that combination that exceeds our minimum rate by the greatest margin.

a. *Setting the Minimum Rate* In our last example, we set the minimum rate at 7%. We will be using the same data; however, let's make the hurdle a higher one, since we will be dealing with large net current values as the following table reveals:

---

[*]This is a fairly low rate. As of this writing, municipal bond rates are in a range averaging 7.5%.

	Capital	Annual benefits	Annual costs	Net Present Equivalent 10%	B/C 10%
A	$20,000	$14,000	$10,000	$6,396	1.08
B	30,000	15,000	10,000	3,450	1.04
C	50,000	25,000	17,000	3,702	1.02
A+B	50,000	29,000	20,000	9,847	1.06
A+C	70,000	39,000	27,000	10,098	1.04
B+C	80,000	50,000	27,000	7,152	1.03

b. Determining Marginal Rates for All Combinations   As with the last group of projects, we will determine marginal rates, but with the portfolio approach, we will also combine projects and calculate IRR and MIRR for those combinations as well. For an illustration of this with our project data, see the table below. In it we report only the largest capital projects. The marginal rate of return is the rate of return on the extra capital invested in projects with higher capital requirements. In the A+C versus A+B example, the A+C required $20,000 more capital than A+B; therefore, the marginal rate is the rate of return on that extra $20,000.

	Marginal B/C	Marginal IRR (%)
A+C over A+B	1.00	10.41%
A+C over C	1.08	20.24%
B+C over A+C	0.68	0.00%

c. Choosing the Best Combination   The criterion for choice is based first on total current value, then marginal benefit-cost ratios, and finally the MIRR. In setting up the last comparison, we took only the portfolio with the highest total current value, A+C with $10,098. Then we compared it to those projects just smaller in capital requirements to determine whether the expenditure of the extra money was justified. The extra $20,000 resulted in at least equal costs and benefits when compared to the combination of A+B and a positive benefit-cost ratio when compared to project C. Each of the MIRR measures—that compared to A+B and that compared to C—were greater than the 10% hurdle we set up. We conclude that the extra $20,000 was a justifiable expenditure on these measures.

If A+C is a justifiable project, what about the next one, B+C, which requires larger amounts of capital? Is the extra $10,000 expenditure justifiable when we select B+C and A+C? According to the chart, it is not. The extra $10,000 represents substantially greater costs than benefits (a marginal benefit-cost ratio of 0.68). Also, the extra capital brings no return at all.

We conclude with the choice of a simple portfolio of projects A and C. The total current value of benefits and costs was a positive $10,098. The marginal gain over the next lowest capital cost alternative was above the minimum rate of return we established, as well.

IV. THE RESEARCH

To test the assumption that the marginal MIRR method will provide the best guide to projects to select, conducted a research project involving seasoned state government executives. We asked them to compute the rates of return, but then asked them to select the best portfolio, using their experience as a guide. The research can suggest some of the important steps actually used in considering which projects are apparently in the best interest of a public authority to fund.

A. Methods

That is, thirty state government analysts, acting as research subjects, were given a cost-benefit analysis to conduct as they saw fit. They were divided into five groups for analysis and discussion in order to ensure that whatever special expertise in urban problems that existed was spread evenly across the groups. The choice concerned the best use of $250,000 in state funds for an economically and socially destitute but politically sensitive (hometown of the governor) area of the state. The groups were given 1 month to decide their portfolios. The five project choices are briefly described below; fuller descriptions are included in the Appendix.

1. A transportation project. A wooden trestle bridge, having an estimated economic life of 25 years, would cost $80,000 for initial construction and would need annual maintenance costing $4,000. The wooden bridge would have to be rebuilt after 25 years, which would require a 1-month closure to traffic. The wooden bridge would be built in an area subject to flooding, one in which the "100-year flood" probabilities indicate some likelihood of a flood that would destroy the bridge up to three times during a 50-year period. There would be intangible, tourism-related benefits to such a structure.
2. A transportation project. A steel replacement bridge, constructed on the same site as, but instead of, the wooden bridge, would have a 50-year economic life. The initial cost would be $160,000, with annual maintenance of $2,000. The bridge would be invulnerable to the 100-year flood.
3. A jobs training program. The journeyman training program would recruit 100 trainees per year for 6 years, 50% from the hard-core unemployed and 50% from nonunion construction workers (who now make $8,000 per year). The trainees would enter a 4-year training program. Once in, students would be paid $7,000 and upon successful completion, would be hired at $14,000. A trainee dropout rate of 10% per year could reasonably be anticipated; graduated journeymen would face an average 10% unemployment rate. Administrative costs for the program would be $100,000 per year.
4. A jobs training program. The clerical training program would also recruit 100 trainees per year over a 6-year period. The trainees would enter a 1-year program and be placed in jobs that paid $7,000 upon successful completion but receive nothing while training. Ninety percent of the trainees would come from the hard-core unemployed. Administrative costs for the program would be $100,000 per year.
5. An urban renewal project. The redevelopment project covers a 100-block area of an urban area and involves land purchases, resident relocation, redevelopment and improvements, public facilities, and administrative costs. The total of tangible costs equals $4.6 million. The total of tangible benefits equals $3.7 million. However, planners and proponents suggest large intangible benefits.

The respondents were asked to use the IRR method to establish relative worthiness and the marginal rate of return method to help identify components of the best mix. They were also asked specifically to include the managerial implications of the portfolio and change recommendations in that light, especially considering fraud and abuse and difficulty in evaluating project success substantively.

B. Findings

Four major sets of findings emerged from the research. First, the cost-benefit analysis could be swayed by both the assumptions built into the projects as well as assumptions projected by the analysts on to the study. For example, many questioned the low dropout rate in the training programs, and this assumption was crucial to the benefit stream. Also, the subjects divided equally over the forecast unemployment rate, with those otherwise favoring the project forecasting a lower unemployment rate than graduate trainees would face in future job markets.

Second, intangibles tended to play a large part in the analysis of social infrastructure programs such as the urban renewal project. Arguments made to include intangibles pointed toward all manner of benefits from redevelopment—from better health of residents to pride in community. Hardheaded numbers analysts deprecated these measures and discarded this project from their portfolios.

Third, all subjects pointed out the fraud potential of the projects and added this factor into their analysis. Urban renewal was the consensus choice of the project most prone to abuse. Training programs were thought to be abused but able to be quarantined from such a problem of good management, an intangible cost.

Fourth, subjects suggested that a short-term bias pervaded analysis. This short-term bias affected judgments about training programs particularly, since their benefits and social consequences may not be apparent for a generation. The short-term bias was also manifested in the consumption-orientedness of the analytical approach. Conservation or patrimony benefits often are difficult to envision much less measure due to their intergenerational quality.

Finally, undergirding all of the findings were the ever-present political considerations. In other words, what would "sell" politically, subjects always wondered. Despite its advantage in IRR terms, "Would a wooden bridge be politically as well as physically vulnerable?" one subject asked. "Could the bridge be explained in the face of conventional opposition, must less justified in the battle for funding by interest groups representing other proposals?"

Some pointed out that the cost-benefit analysis imputed values and demands to individuals without actually verifying them. The value of a bridge, for instance, was the individual's opportunity cost of traveling the next best route. However, no one ever asked an individual whether that was the route she would take or whether he would take that trip at all if there were no bridge. Some mentioned that the analysis would skirt politics when the political process was the only true gauge of what real individuals wanted or were willing to tax themselves to finance.

Politics, in the form of equity, also became an issue. One subject argued, "Cost-benefit analysis is not particularly sensitive to the way in which income is distributed in society." The subject noticed that cost-benefit analysis tended to infer the same amount of value to rich and poor individuals. Also apparent to this subject was the method's conservatism; when used with the five alternatives here, the method tended to minimize the need for government intervention on behalf of the poor.

C. Conclusions

Despite the large number of caveats made to an otherwise quantitative analysis, subjects generally agreed that there are "serious public policy implications in undertaking a project that is not rational with respect to tangible costs that exceed benefits, particularly in times of fiscal austerity." The number of biases that emerge in analyzing the costs and benefits of a range of projects—fraud potential, short-term returns, consumption overwhelming conservation, tangible items to measure—suggested the extreme conservatism of the method to the subjects. Yet, the last comment on fiscal austerity is revealing. It suggests that the political environment for tax policy, the willingness of individuals to pay taxes, and the civic-mindedness of taxpayers serve to condition analysts to the need to be conservative or otherwise in the assumptions and use of bias in analysis. Presumably, times other than fiscal austerity might prompt different analytical procedures.

D. Summary

This research has tested the idea that the IRR method of cost-benefit analysis would guide seasoned state executives in their choice of an optimal, even if hypothetical, portfolio. The findings suggest that a large number of other considerations, both managerial and political, guide judgment in addition to quantitative techniques. However, the surprising finding was the large role that the IRR calculation actually played—that it is not sound, "not rational" to select a project in which tangible costs exceed benefits. Moreover, surprisingly, subjects were loath to project their own political leanings or their social philosophies on the analysis, content instead to act conservatively, in the hope, we would infer, that the political process would take over where they left off in creating an equitable, as well as efficient, portfolio.

V.   ECONOMIC REASONING IN GOVERNMENT FINANCIAL MANAGEMENT

We now place cost-benefit analysis within the even larger body of literature characterizing economic reasoning in government. This review forms a critique and is meant both to support the research findings of the previous section, and to suggest the larger sources and consequences of the approach for choice.

Economics, or more specifically, rational choice theory, exerts a strong influence on thinking about government financial management through cost-benefit analysis. Thus, government productivity is often closely associated with the idea of economic efficiency, which cost-benefit analysis was introduced to maximize.

A.   The Maximizing Behavior of Government Actors and Agencies

The fundamental principle of economic reasoning states that "bureaucratic officials, like all other agents in society, are motivated by their own self interests at least part of the time" (Downs, 1957:2).

In parallel fashion, political actors seek advantage for both themselves and their constituents and tend to maximize gain and minimize loss. Both bureaucratic and political actors reach their targets through a maze of rules—communication and coordination rules for bureaucratic officials and voting rules for political actors. The world within which behavior bends around rules is an unpredictable one, and gaining greater certainty about the acquisition of advantage may offset in part the size of the advantage itself. The actors, therefore, constantly calculate what is literally a risk-return relationship, given their preferences for different kinds of advantages to begin with.

B. Economic Decision Making

Economic decision making tends to be deductive and because of that has an elegance given to mathematicslike precision in detailing "proof" as well as an otherworldliness in which few argue its practicality.

The idea of looking at the world in terms of "decision" instead of some other concept, say sovereignty (another abstraction but one loaded with ideology) or resource problems (topical, practical ways of dealing with phenomena), is tribute to economists following a "scientific" approach to studying the world.

Decisions cut across all of mankind's activities; they occur every minute of every day and cover everything from the mundane to the spiritual and especially the sensible. Dimensions of decisions seem to cover all bases—psychological, political, remunerative—making the decision a truly fundamental element of life.

Having based microeconomics or the theory of the firm on the idea that firm owners maximized, economics could assert something called "optimal decisions." These decisions were based on the thinking of a group of philosophers called "logical positivists."

Logical positivism started in early twentieth century Vienna and became known through the work of A. J. Ayer (1936). Positivists hold that there are only two kinds of statements that have meaning

1. Those which are true merely because of the definitions employed (all bachelors are unmarried).
2. Those that could be shown to be true or shown to be false by some possible sense-experience, such as a scientific experiment (water changes from a liquid to a gaseous state as greater heat is applied). If it cannot be verified by scientific means (empirically verifiable), the statement loses meaning. Thus the statement "There is a God" or "Jane loves Dick" has no meaning.

Logical positivists, not to take it too far, argue that there can be no meaning attributable to that "known" independently of experience. In fact, Ayer himself said (1936: 721)

[T]he admission that there were some facts about the world that could be known independently of experience would be incompatible with one fundamental contention that a sentence says nothing unless it is empirically verifiable.

Ayer and his fellows ran into mathematics—not verifiable independently but the truths that are certain and necessary.

Others had tried to square the two. John Stuart Mill, for instance, had argued that mathematics cannot be proved universally true until we have seen all of the cases. Natural sciences and mathematics, he said, were very similar; their truths are probably so, but we have no guarantee—there may be an exception.

So what happens when an exception is found to a mathematical statement? Suppose, for instance, that we accept as probably true the statement that 2 times 5 equals 10 and, when we count 5 pairs of objects, we find 10 objects. Then, one time we count and do not find 10 objects. In such a case, we would say

1. We were wrong to suppose there were 5 pairs to begin with.
2. An object was taken away when we were not looking.
3. The counting was wrong.

We would explain the phenomena so that it fit the facts, but 2×5 would still $= 10$.

In effect, there is logic and mathematics on the one hand and there is observation and experience on the other. Or as Kant would have it, a synthetic proposition depends on what we see; its validity is determined by the facts of experience, and an analytic proposition is valid solely because of the definitions of the symbols it contains.

Consider a brief example (Ayer, 1936). A statement such as "There are ants that have established a system of slavery" awaits experience for confirmation or falsification. However, a statement such as "either some ants are parasitic or none are" depends solely on "either," "or," and "none" and acquires truth independently of experience. The truth of the matter is we know nothing about parasitic ants after reading the last statement, but we could, through observation, know something about slavery among ants from the first statement. Analytical statements have no factual content. No experience will ever refute them.

There is no lack of use here, in any case. Because, as Lincoln reasoned through the problem of what to do with rebellious Southerners after the War between the States: (1) All Southerners are rebels; (2) All Southerners are Americans, therefore (3) All rebels are Americans.

These statements are tautologies, obvious truths, internally so. The tautological form holds through all analytical propositions: if P implies Q, and P is true, Q is also true.

Still, analytical propositions do not increase knowledge; they are a priori knowledge. In even more direct terms, as Herbert Simon (1976) would say, they are values.

Simon based his thinking on roughly the same analytic-synthetic distinction. Decision making in administrative contexts stems from a set of premises, value premises, and factual premises. Roughly, people having defined the situation in a certain way (provided for themselves the value premise) readily choose the one best way to act (ascertain the facts and choose the optimal way). But Simon went on to show that the latter may not be so.

Thus individuals in administrative contexts have less than full knowledge of or capacity (time, resources) to gather the facts. Rather than optimize, people satisfice or choose the first satisfactory alternative, given their value premise.

Economics steps in via cost-benefit analysis, using logical positivism, in two ways. First, economists argue that given the value premise, and ignoring the individual who is about to make a choice, one can judge from the external situation behavior optimally adapted to the situation. Cost-benefit analysis can provide a standard of optimality against which competing alternatives may be judged.

Second, economicsts also argue the need for aids to calculation that will help individuals suffering with bounded rationality to cope with complex situations. Thus, cost-benefit analysis can uncover masked or hidden facts or even suggest ways to limit one's boundaries to insight.

Cost-benefit analysis is a class of analytical methods that evaluate the economic or the choice—aspects of given decisions. Others are *utility theory*, which examines the relative worth of various alternatives measured subjectively and generally incorporating probability and the decision makers' attitudes toward risk; *cost-effectiveness analysis*, a measure of the relative efficiency of various technologies in achieving an already decided maximum result; and *cost-benefit analysis*, a measure of the relative efficiency of projects economically—"if the intended effects are worth the cost."

The cost-benefit analysis approach has its limits in government decision making, as the research reported here suggested. That is, cost-benefit analysis is often used to justify ex post facto a position already taken; the most significant factor in cost-benefit analysis is often its sponsor. Cost-benefit analysis tends to neglect the distributional consequences of a choice. The method systematically undervalues projects that improve the distribution of wealth and systematically overvalues projects that exacerbate economic inequality. In the Kaldor-Hicks terminology, cost-benefit analysis would recommend a course of action that could potentially allow the winners to compensate the losers so that no one is worse off, but the method does not guarantee that the winners *will* compensate the losers.

Over and above the operational problems with cost-benefit analysis, and by extension, economic reasoning in government, there are intangibles of fundamental importance that cost-benefit analysis cannot conceive. There is, for example, a moral significance in the duties and rights of individuals and of government in relation to the individual that is not comprehended in the measurement of consequences alone. Related to this idea, certain rights such as due process cannot be conceived simply because they are processes valued for themselves rather than outcomes.

Cost-benefit analysis has been blamed for damaging the political system. Some argue that politics is superior to analysis because of the wider scope of ideas and concepts the people practicing politics can fathom. Others argue that analysis enfranchises unelected policy analysts and disenfranchises those who do not understand, who do not believe, or who cannot use analysis to make their arguments to government. Such a situation creates a loss of confidence in government institutions.

To return to cost-benefit analysis's basis in economics, others argue that that basis, insofar as it describes or prescribes government action, is flawed; that is, cost-benefit analysis assumes that there can be no market failure. There are always opportunity costs and shadow prices with which public sector goods can be valued. Research on markets suggests that markets are not perfectly competitive, that that lack of competition leads inevitably to failure, and that public goods are produced to remedy that failure. Without a way to value public goods, therefore, cost-benefit analysis fails to inform the decision-making process.

Another economic idea—that any alternative must be judged in terms of other alternatives—lends support to analysis. These proponents of cost-benefit analysis argue that there is no alternative to cost-benefit analysis, none as explicit or systematic. In fact, cost-benefit analysis's formalized, explicit nature allows the public to hold its public officials accountable to a larger extent than under "normal politics and management." Systematic analysis is less likely to overlook an important fact or consideration that, when placed in an adversarial process such as politics, may lead to the determination of the public interest far sooner than mere impressionistic surmise.

The controversy over the use, misuse, or lack of use of analysis often pits those who believe in government against those who see the market as the predominantly positive force in society. Typically, what cost-benefit analysis overlooks is that most pro-government action proponents find government most useful in providing equity. Pro-market proponents argue that government intervenes for spurious reasons and, in doing so, creates more problems than it solves, certainly leading to less rather than more economic efficiency.

VI. SUMMARY

We have defined productivity in terms of both equity and efficiency in this chapter. We have also shown that the Kaldor criterion for allocating government services fulfills that criterion in theory. In demonstrating the Kaldor criterion, we have demonstrated cost-benefit analysis and have elaborated most of its important technical facets. In doing so, we demonstrated that cost-benefit analysis—and productivity—rely on comparisons made among programs at the suborganization, then organization, then interorganization levels and that the real outcome of these comparisons is the construction of portfolios of investments. The technology that might be used to improve these comparisons, and thus improve productivity, we argued, could be borrowed from portfolio construction models in business investment practice, since they too are based on cost-benefit analytic principles.

We further argued the heuristic if not the absolute determinative value of this technology. Moreover, we demonstrated through a small piece of research that cost-benefit analysis is a crucial learning tool in understanding policy problems. Nevertheless, the research revealed the limited nature of this technology in that real decision makers in a simulated decision-making situation used other different criteria in making final choices. These other different criteria, often more heavily weighted than cost-benefit analysis, included managerial feasibility and a project's tendency toward encouraging fraud and abuse.

In the end, we classed cost-benefit analysis with other methods of thinking that are basically deductive in nature. These methods ignore intuition, feeling, and other means of informing decisions. While practical in a limited way, the analytical methods underlying cost-benefit analysis are often self-defeating. Especially inappropriate to government productivity, the methods defy reality, an administrative reality that must reconcile plural views, each of which describes more than monetized utility, in allocation policy choices.

REFERENCES

Ascher, W. (1978). *Forecasting: An Appraisal for Policy-Makers and Planners*, Johns Hopkins University Press, Baltimore.

Ayer, A. J. (1936). *Language, Truth and Logic*, Knopf, New York.

Brown, B. and Helmer, O. (1962). *Improving the Reliability of Estimates Obtained from a Consensus of Experts*, Rand Corporation, Santa Monica, Calif.

Brunsson, N. (1989). *The Organization of Hypocrisy*, Wiley, Chichester, England.

Buchanan, J. M. and Tullock, G. (1962). *The Calculus of Consent*, University of Michigan Press, Ann Arbor.

Delbecq, A. L., Van de Ven, A. H., and Gustafson, D. H. (1975). *Group Techniques for Program Planning: A Guide for Nominal Group and Delphi Processes*, Scott, Foresman, Glenview, Ill.

Downs, A. (1957). *An Economic Theory of Democracy.* Harper and Row, New York.

Downs, A. (1960). *World Polit., 12* (4): 541-563.

Dunn, W. N. (1981). *Public Policy Analysis*, Prentice-Hall, Englewood Cliffs, N.J.

Gohagan, J. K. (1980). *Quantitative Analysis for Public Policy*, McGraw-Hill, New York.

Golembiewski, R. T. and Miller, G. J. (1981). *Handbook of Political Behavior*, vol. 2 (S. Long, ed.), Plenum Press, New York, pp. 1-71.

Kaldor, N. (1939). *Economic Journal* (September): 549–552.

Kamlet, M. S., Mowery, D. C., and Su, T. (1987). *J Policy Anal. Mgt., 6* (3): 365-384.

Klay, W. E. (1983). *Handbook of Public Budgeting and Financial Management* (J. Rabin and T. D. Lynch, eds.), Marcel Dekker, New York.

Klay, W. E. (1985). *Internat. J. Pub. Admin., 7* (3): 241-265.

March, J. G. and Olsen, J. P. (1989). *Rediscovering Institutions: The Organizational Bias of Politics*, Basic Books, New York.

Musgrave, R. A. and Musgrave, P. B. (1980). *Public Finance in Theory and Practice*, 3d ed., McGraw-Hill, New York.

Osborn, A. (1953). *Applied Imagination: Principle and Procedures of Creative Thinking*, Scribners, New York.

Pareto, V. (1906). *Mannuala Economica Politica*, trans. Ann S. Schweier, Ann S. Schweier and Alfred N. Page (eds.). A. M. Kelly, New York.

Pierce, L. D. (1971). *The Politics of Fiscal Policy Formation*, Goodyear, Pacific Palisades, Calif.

Schmid, A. A. (1990). *Benefit-Cost Analysis: A Political Economy Approach*, Westview, Boulder, Colo.

Simon, H. A. (1976). *Administrative Behavior*, 3d ed., Free Press, New York.

Stiglitz, J. E. (1988). *Economics of the Public Sector*, 2d ed., Norton, New York.

Wright, G. and Ayton, P. (1987). *Judgmental Forecasting*, Wiley, Chichester, England.

Youngman, H. (1990). "'Nem di Gelt (Take the Money)" *New York Times* (July 31): A19.

9

Capital Investment Strategy

Gerald J. Miller
Rutgers University at Newark, Newark, New Jersey

Capital investment among municipalities, often viewed as hit or miss and largely unplanned, may also be viewed as strategic; that is, a rational effort to achieve some future goal underscores and ties together many seemingly unrelated decisions to pave roads, build parks, or buy machinery.

The factors supporting a strategic view are compelling. Capital investment drives all other financial management decisions in a public organization. Capital investments drive the operating budget because these investments prompt the hiring of employees and the scheduling of maintenance and other routine expenditures (Crecine, 1969). Capital investments drive productivity in that purchases of equipment and facilities become the primary source for improvements in efficiency and effectiveness (Swiss, 1991). Capital investments determine the direction community development or redevelopment will take, and they set the balance among forces in maintaining the economic base. Investments also create a community's competitive position among rival residential and industrial locations, affecting future growth in governmental revenues (Schneider, 1989; Pagano and Moore, 1985). Indeed, the controversies engendered by capital investment decisions go far in shaping what communities will be (Adams, 1988).

I. SIGNIFICANCE OF THIS STUDY

This study seeks to fill a void. Capital investment and budgeting suffer from neglect, researchers now realize, despite nearly five decades of concern nationwide with the physical structure—the built environment—of communities. As one researcher put it (Adams, 1988:6),

> For all the concern about the infrastructure problem that is now being expressed by policy makers and policy analysts, little that has been written moves beyond surveying the deteriorating conditions of public facilities and calling for more public investment. We have little information about how public officials go about making investment decisions, and even less about how their decisions affect their communities.

The lack of knowledge exists in all aspects of capital investment and budgetary decision making, leading us in this chapter to try to outline what we know as well as pose questions suitable to finding answers to those things we do not know.

II. CAPITAL INVESTMENT AS STRATEGY

A systematic guide to capital investment eludes researchers and official decision makers alike because there seem to be at least three contradictory explanations for the decisions that should or could be made. The first characterizes investment as the measured, *planned* response to the goals of the organization and community. The second reveals capital decisions as the community's *reaction* to what private markets demand or to what rival locations threaten. The third suggests that capital investments are *opportunistic*; that is, necessarily, nearly random and unrelated to a given purpose. Thus, while we seek to outline what we know and what we do not know about capital investment, we face the three opposed views of choice from the very start.

In all three, however, there are strategic elements, and we may overcome contradiction by viewing capital investments as *strategic* decisions that top managers and elected decision makers must make. Ordinarily, we would use strategy in defining the organization's method of coping with the future through various devices—frameworks, techniques, and plans—to bend the course of future events to their advantage, to eliminate competitive threats to organization survival, or to exploit opportunities for increasing organization wealth and security.

Instead of speaking in terms of an *organization*, however, we often refer to the focus of strategy as the *public interest*, whether the interest is that of the citizenry in a locality, a state, or the nation as a whole. Planning the future, eliminating competitive threats, or exploiting opportunities for the public interest—the community—emerges as strategy and as the focus of capital investments.

Let us illustrate the strategic nature of planned, reactive, and opportunistic capital investments. First, planning incorporates community interests in such a way that a strategic vision of the future comprehends all points of view. This strategic vision becomes the future, almost as if a self-fulfilling prophecy, in the form of infrastructure projects and programs that are put in place to anticipate and guide change, yet those spearheading the consensual forces and those whose analyses inform it sway the process in their own interests.

The second, reactive explanation for investment is a strategy of responding to rival communities and deterring their triumph at one's own expense. Such strategies for investment involve creating a mix of community enhancements that turn one's own disadvantages to advantages. For instance, communities without industry create outstanding school systems to entice families to live in what then becomes an even more attractive bedroom community. Such communities also become irresistible to service industries at such time as the community decides to diversify using its highly educated residential population as a labor force attraction.

The final method is that related to opportunism, each investment exploit of which is only coincidentally related to any other. Individual interests, by implication, get wedded to each other and are rationalized in retrospect.

Each of these types of capital investment strategies has an internal logic of its own, and these logics [1] may be called linear, nonlinear, and opportunistic logics, respectively.

A. Linear Logic

If those who have reviewed large bodies of research could erect a monumental image of strategic management, they would create optimization. Strategy, as such, follows a "linear" logic in which plans precede action. This variation appears to dominate thinking in strategy since the major review of work in not-for-profit organizations (Wortman, 1979), and a set of pictures of its use in organizations outside business (Bryson and Roering, 1988) echoes linear logic by firmly placing what they find studied and practiced in synopticism rather than in competition or a forceful search for advantage (MacMillan, 1978; 1983; Freeman, 1984; Zalid, 1970).

B. Nonlinear Logic

Ironically, just as many tout optimization, the private sector gives heed to strategy's ancient meaning. Popular business organization writers often define strategic effort as instilling organization loyalty and parrying threat (Neuhauser, 1988). This tribal warrior concept conforms to what is meant by the Greek verb *stratego*, "to plan the destruction of one's enemies through effective use of resources" (O'Toole, 1985; Evered, 1983). The reference has also been reversed. Even Clausewitz (1956:121) argues that "it would be better, instead of comparing [War] with any Art, to liken it to business competition, which is also a conflict of human interests and activities."

The military operation connotation comes from Luttwak (1987; Summers, 1987), one of the modern teachers on strategy in war who conceptualizes the logic of strategy as paradox. He contrasts the logic of strategy with linear logic. Linear logic, military style, follows the Latin dictum *si vis pacem, para pacem* or "if you want peace, prepare for peace." In actuality, war follows a paradoxical logic: *si vis pacem, para bellum* or "if you want peace, prepare for war."

According to Luttwak (p. 4), "In war deterrence is all. . . . To be ready to attack is evidence of peaceful intent, but to prepare defenses is aggressive or at least provocative."

Strategy in war is the reversal of opposites. Luttwak continues

[On the battlefield] a bad road can be good precisely because it is bad and may therefore be less strongly held or even left unguarded by the enemy . . . a paradoxical preference for inconvenient times and directions, preparations visibly and deliberately left incomplete, approaches seemingly too dangerous for combat at night and in bad weather, is a common aspect of tactical ingenuity.

If private-sector strategists resemble ancient and modern military ones, they see strategy as nonlinear in its logic and use deception and paradox (e.g., Quinn and Cameron, 1988).

C. Opportunism

Beyond apparently linear logic in the public sector and the nonlinear logic of the private sector, one other exists in Wildavsky's "strategy" for budgeters (1988). His budgetary person is more opportunistic, following neither linear nor nonlinear logic. As if constructing a redoubt, the budgeter builds confidence, finds allies, and shows results. Events occur as if they were assaults on the budgetary base; electoral defeat of mentors in Congress, economic catastrophe for programs or revenues, and changes of allies with issues force ever more ingenious defenses. These same types of events—electoral selection (e.g., natural selection), economic change, or issue mutation—provide opportunities that can be exploited (Wildavsky, 1988:100–119).

This form of strategy resembles the emergent strategy that many have found most appropriate for or characteristic of public sector managers; that is, "the function of emergent strategies would seem to be most compatible with the adhocracy configuration, in which many people—operating personnel, experts and advisors of all kinds, managers at all levels—are potentially involved in the establishment of precedents and, so, the strategies" (Mintzberg and McHugh, 1985:162). To Ring and Perry (1985:282), the point is imperative

> Given previous arguments regarding policy ambiguity, open and intense influence processes and coalition instability, public organizations can be characterized as low on deliberate strategy and high on emergent and unrealized strategy. If this characterization is correct, any manager who is unable, for instance, to relinquish intended strategies in order to pursue emergent strategies is likely to fail.

Something more complex than linear and nonlinear logics—opportunism, perhaps—must be used in describing public-sector strategy.

D. Complex Serial Combinations of "Logics"

Despite reviews and popular writing, research indicates additional, far more complex combinations of concepts in the actual, observed use of strategy. Consider the work by Alfred Chandler (1962). In a survey of American business history, from the canals, to the railroads, on into the industrial revolution, and to modern day developments, he posed the theory that the structure of modern organization emerges from the strategy the business pursues as it defines and capitalizes on opportunities. The pattern of industry development was (1) accumulation of resources, (2) rationalization of the use of those resources, (3) expansion into markets to accumulate more, and (4) "re-rationalization" of the use of these resources and on and on ad infinitum. Thus, strategy—often horizontal mergers to accumulate, vertical mergers to rationalize, for example—led to structure; in this case, he hypothesized structural decentralization followed by centralization.

In the next three major sections, we focus attention on capital investment strategies that follow the three logics. In the first, we concentrate on the capital programming approach, one incorporating cost-benefit analysis and following the linear logic. The second section takes up nonlinear strategies in which competition, and to some extent, deterrence take hold. In the third section, we illustrate cases of investments that follow an opportunistic logic. Finally, we reflect on situations in which the three logics may exist in some serial fashion.

III. THE PLANNING OR LINEAR APPROACH TO STRATEGIC CAPITAL PROJECT CHOICES

Decisions involving what capital investments to make, when to make them, and how much to spend on them create great conflict. For reducing conflict, reformers—planners—plot and follow what amounts to a linear strategy. Recall that a linear strategy is one in which plans precede action. In this section, we examine the linear strategy implied in capital programming and the other procedures involved in reformed capital budgeting,[2] with detailed attention given linear strategy's primary tool, the process of cost-benefit analysis.

The programming approach, in following a linear logic, is based on optimization of resources; therefore, we end the section with a discussion of this logic and its assumptions.

A. Background

Beginning with the Burnham plan of the City of Chicago, modern city planning has connected the city plan with the capital budget through capital improvements programming (CIP; Schultz, 1989; Scott, 1969). The *city plan* is a guide to the physical development of a jurisdiction. It is long-range, covering a period longer than a year, and the plan is comprehensive. The entire geographical area comes within the plan's purview, and the plan includes transportation, housing, land use, utility systems, and recreation elements, attempting to interrelate them in a meaningful way. A *capital project* or capital improvement project, is any major nonrecurring expenditure or any expenditure for physical facilities. A CIP is a schedule of capital improvement projects for several years, showing estimated costs and sources of financing. The most commonly used period for a CIP is the period used for comprehensive land-use planning, with plans of varying generality from 5 to 20 years. A *capital budget* is a list of projects in the CIP, along with costs and financing sources. *Capital budgeting* refers to the whole process of analyses and decisions involved in moving from capital projects to a CIP to a capital budget. Often the first year of capital budget is included in the capital improvements section of the annual operating budget for the upcoming fiscal year.

According to an authoritative survey (Beal and Hollander, 1979), the plan and capital improvements relate in three ways. First, the plan may act as a growth management tool and the CIP may be the yoke for development. For example, development permits may await the completion of infrastructure projects.

Second, the planning function may be made to relate internally to finance by organization means. Urban planning and financial planning are often organized as a single department.

Third, subdivision regulation forces allocation of costs of public facilities between homeowner and government. Developers are required to install some facilities before the city government accepts responsibility for the development through an extension of services.

1. Justification

The need for capital budgeting rests on the accepted fact that public funds are limited. Almost without question, available financial resources fall short of the amount needed to fund what decision makers believe is necessary to cope with all future events. Priority setting being a necessity, the capital program and budget offer an approach that is valued for its perceived rationality.

That is, capital budgeting isolates, for analysis and priority setting, the costly and nonrecurring expenditures from which the community receives long-lived benefits. More specifically, capital budgeting provides a systematic way to prevent unplanned project needs, avoid project duplication, coordinate projects, provide time for technical project design, allow orderly project acquisition, establish priorities, and formulate long-range financial plans. For example (Vogt, 1977), a new park might require land purchase, site development, and new facility construction over several years before the park is open to the public. The benefits of the new park could last for decades or centuries. To pay for the park in one year could be too costly, but the intergenerational benefits might suggest that the park could be paid for over many years. Therefore, the park is a prime capital project which, through the CIP and later the capital budget, receives the study needed to manage the project systematically, efficiently, and equitably.

Thus, according to Vogt (1977), the CIP exists for reasons that suit managers. First, because of size and durability, capital projects have a permanent impact on the community, suggesting the need for careful planning. A multiyear capital program provides time for such long-term planning. Second, the nature and permanence of capital projects usually require special expertise at each stage of management, again necessitating a multiyear planning process. Third, it is much easier to reverse an operating decision once made than to eliminate a capital project once finished. Mistakes are more costly and long-lasting; a multiyear programming period allows details to be worked out and decisions reviewed several times before actually constructing the project. Fourth, because capital expenditures are generally easier to postpone than operating costs, a mechanism to restore this imbalance is needed. A capital program provides the high profile that enables managers to assert the equally important capital investment expenditure. Fifth, capital costs tend not to be constant from year to year. A capital programming approach helps to level the peaks and valleys of capital expenditures.

2. *Planning the Capital Program*

The capital program emerges from the overall plan and planning policies of the community. Ideally, capital projects fulfill long-term operating objectives, and exist as part of an overall plan for service delivery, economic growth, community betterment, or even redistribution of wealth.[3] Within already accepted and well-developed policy directives, general plans, and centralized coordination, capital projects implement land-use plans and policies and comply with projected population densities and commercial or industrial uses.

B. Project Selection and Scheduling with Cost-Benefit Analysis

For a discussion of the rationales, criterions, and methods of cost-benefit analysis used by governments, see Chapter 8, pp. 166–177.

C. Allocation, Organization, Analysis—Micro and Macro

Micro and macro cost-benefit analyses are explored in Chapter 8. At the micro, or project, level, various measurement methods are examined including estimating, forecasting, and costing (see Chapter 8, pp. 166–171). Valuation over time and different selection criteria are also reviewed. At the macro level, cost-benefit analysis without constraint, marginal rate of return analysis, and portfolio construction are explored (see Chapter 8, pp. 171–177).

1. *Conclusions Regarding Cost-Benefit Analysis*

The discussions in Chapter 8 argue that the IRR method of cost-benefit analysis alone would not guide seasoned analysts in their choice of an optimal portfolio. A large number of other considerations, both managerial and political, guide judgement over and above quantitative techniques. However, surprisingly, analysts would probably find that the IRR calculation actually plays a large role—that it is not sound, "not rational," to select a project in which tangible costs exceed benefits. It would not be surprising, moreover, to find that analysts are loath to project their own political leanings or their social philosophies on the analysis, that they are content instead to act conservatively, in hopes that the political process would take over where they left off in creating an equitable, as well as efficient, portfolio.

2. *Conclusions Regarding Other Facts of Linear Strategies*

To follow a linear logic for investment, advocates have urged the use of applied microeconomics (Wetzler and Petersen, 1985). They argue (1985, p. 8) strategy's inherent potency in helping one choose between capital markets and internal sources of financing. More broadly, decision makers actually have two concerns related to financing: whether to borrow money to pay for the project or pay for it out of operating revenues and, if borrowing is involved, what financing technique to use.

To borrow or not for a capital investment has often been answered in equity terms. The payback of borrowed funds spreads the burden across all generations who use the facility, implying a sort of user fee for the facility in the form of taxes that are then earmarked for debt repayment.

As for the use of operating funds, the burden is borne by those in the generation paying taxes until the facility is paid for. If the tax system is proportional or even progressive, this might be somewhat equitable; however, many view local tax systems as regressive.[4] This suggests that pay-as-constructed methods penalize one generation and poorer economic groups.

The use of operating revenues has important frugality arguments—no interest payments—as well as others in which financial management is crucial. For example (Smith, 1990), pay-as-constructed financing from operating revenues is appropriate when high interest rates are not offset by high inflation rates. High inflation—which might make real interest rates negative—and elastic revenues affected by high inflation would offset high interest rates, and make borrowing appropriate. In addition, windfalls in the form of intergovernmental assistance or one-time events may permit operating revenue financing. Finally, in stable growth areas in which capital expenditures are fairly consistent, budgeting can incorporate these investments.

3. *Conclusions about Putting Linear Strategies to Use in Everyday Management*

The linear model of strategy tends to blend applied microeconomics with planning and management for finance officers, yet it fails to deal with two everyday phenomena in public financial management: mandated dependence and conservatism with regard to financing tools.

The ability to act in strategic ways assumes the independence to do so. Mandated programs and spending tend to create problems for a government strategic actor. Less discretion inhibits strategy building. In a survey of financial managers and teachers (Miller, et al., 1987), we asked them the degree to which a major indirect mandate—federal government borrowing—inhibited action by the organizations to which they belonged.

To summarize these findings, we understand financial managers to be buffeted by those who advocate advanced management techniques based on a linear logic, yet conditions outside their control tend to inhibit strategic action. Moreover, understanding strategy's tools, at least in the area of economic develop and infrastructure rehabilitation, has its own limits; financial managers are not yet ready to chance the necessity to defend themselves against charges of profligacy.

4. General Conclusions Regarding Linear Logic in Capital Investment Strategy

For a review of cost-benefit analysis in relation to other linear strategies in government decision making, see Chapter 8, pp. 166–177.

IV. NONLINEAR MODELS OF CAPITAL INVESTMENT STRATEGY

While optimization has substantial support among those who argue that capital investment should follow certain lines of thinking, other models that reflect what is actually done also exist. One of these other models is a nonlinear, as opposed to a linear, model. The nonlinear model is based on the notion of competition, a phenomena spanning zero-sum games (we win to the same degree that our competitor loses) and nonzero-sum games (we win but our competitor does not necessarily lose; Rapoport, 1960:130–139). A nonlinear strategy also employs tactics that involve principles of surprise (paradox) or deterrence (making the hinted-at the obvious), all used in ways that reverse the way we normally view strategy (Luttwak, 1987), whether that strategy involves war making or capital investment.

Nonlinear strategies differ in several regards from linear strategies, as the table below reveals. First, they differ in origin. Nonlinear strategies tend to emerge as multiple competing centers vie for advantage. Linear strategies develop from a simpler, usually centralized structure. Second, they adapt in different ways. Nonlinear strategies tend to adjust in reaction to various conditions as they develop competitively. In economics, such a strategy would be called "price taking." Linear strategies permit much more initiative—are proactive—in setting conditions, as would exist under monopolistic (price-making), rather than competitive conditions. Third, each operates under unique circumstances. A nonlinear strategy is one in which the environment has a great deal of uncertainty but in which there is at least a known payoff for every risk. The environment for linear strategies is much more certain, with little risk ever having to be considered in decisions.

Linear strategies	Nonlinear strategies
1. Forthright goal setting	1. Gaming strategies that employ paradox and surprise
2. Centrism	2. Polycentrism
3. Price makers (monopoly)	3. Price takers (pure competition)
4. Stable, information-rich environments	4. Unstable, risky environments

A nonlinear strategy can underlie capital investment in one major sense; a competitive market exists among communities in seeking taxpayers (Porter, 1985; 1980)—that it, communities in a metropolitan area (or states in a region), offering various residential and industrial locations, may compete to optimize their own residents' housing values, through zoning, schools, or other programs, or to reduce the costs of doing business in the trade or industrial locations they offer. Capital investments in such a competitive market seek to realize a rate of return large enough to entice high-income residents to move in or stay rather than to leave. Investment decisions also encourage preferred businesses and industries to reduce their costs by relocating to the community or remaining, if already there. Localities compete, and *defeating or outrunning* other communities and organizations may be the best way to optimize home values, encourage trade, reduce manufacturing costs, and satisfy all concerns while developing a sturdy tax base.

Three lines of research support thinking about nonlinear strategies: that by Tiebout (1956), Peterson (1981), and Schneider (1989).

A.   Tiebout and "Voting with Your Feet"

The Tiebout idea of markets for local goods includes derivatives of the buyers and sellers of the "real" market. Buyers are community residents, as well as businesses and industries, who locate there. They pay for this location choice through taxes.

The location choice is a summary decision. Based upon preferences and costs, the location, according to Tiebout, is a rational purchase made by *mobile* buyers or buyers who could take advantage of a better opportunity if they could find it.

The local governments, public authorities, and decision makers are the public-goods sellers confronting buyers. Their decisions provide the bundle that buyers find attractive and on which buyers' location decisions are based. Localities' decisions are aimed at providing an attractive bundle at a fair price to a market on which they have focused.

Sellers get feedback as buyers provide it when they enter a market when appropriate and exit otherwise. Sellers may decide that certain public goods are not their forte, and buyers may decide that a particular bundle is not to their liking on the basis of cost or substance. In such cases, sellers then exit.

For example, a mass transit program may be proposed for a community. Some public officials, acting as sellers, may find that mass transit appeals to a group not important to their strategy for the future. Residents, acting as buyers, may feel that a bundle of services including mass transit is not useful to them or is too costly, or both. Sellers exit the competitive mass transit market, and buyers exit the community that provides it.

B.   Peterson and Strategic Budgeting

Such niches, and product selection by the community—based as it is on bundle selection by sellers and buyers—leads naturally to strategic budgeting; that is, community decision makers decide to spend tax revenues in ways that further develop their competitiveness in the niche they have selected.

The foremost proponent of this route to budgeting, Peterson (1981), proposes three categories of expenditures—development, redistribution, and allocation—the levels of which are manipulated to entice or discourage various buyer groups. Development expenditures support growth and include streets, utilities, and other infrastructure items. Redistributive expenditures are usually social welfare, health, or hospital expenditures that transfer tax revenues from high-income groups to provide a safety net for low-income groups. Allocational expenditures are those related to general administration and are housekeeping expenditures.

Strategy dictates that communities encourage the most attractive groups of buyers or residents. In some cases, the community may find affluent buyers the most attractive; in others, a heterogeneous mixture of groups is attractive. In the former case, these buyers may want indirect or group benefits, thus more budget for developmental and less for redistributive expenditures, holding allocational spending constant, emerges as a valid strategy of an affluent (or a wanting-to-become-affluent) community. For a heterogenous community, some balance between developmental and redistributive expenditures must be found, keeping in mind the tendency for redistributive expenditures to drive out developmental ones as well as the affluent taxpayers who are paying for redistributive expenditures.

Competition, of course, exists in providing the most attractive balance of expenditures at the least cost to taxpayers. For example, upscale communities compete for high-income residents whose consumption patterns attract upscale retailers. These retail businesses bear the tax burden that permits greater developmental expenditures (and reduces the relative burden on residents' properties), in turn making the locality more attractive to upscale residents.

C.   Schneider and the Competitive City

The competition among cities has permitted greater scrutiny of actors, constraints, and strategies in an effort to determine how nonlinear strategies emerge.

1.   Actors and Interests

Residents want to ensure the flow of dollars into the community's coffers without increasing their own tax bills. Strategies to achieve this trick include shifting the burden of taxes to the business sector or to taxpayers outside the community, increasing intergovernmental aid, or reducing expenditures.

Firms wants to reduce their costs and increase profits. Reducing costs may include reducing taxes.

Increasing profits may be brought about by increasing the income of a firm's clients or markets—by assuming the burden of their taxes—making them larger buyers of the firm's goods and services. The differences among industries is great. National and international industries face much greater competition, making price important. Regional firms may be less interested in lowering costs and more interested in creating quality markets. The former, therefore, may be interested in lower taxes; the latter may tend to support higher taxes, of which they are willing to accept the burden as long as these taxes support developmental expenditures to entice affluent buyers to locate in a particular community. These businesses may be able to shift the burden of taxes through price increases to the parts of their markets outside the jurisdiction, with such methods as mail-order businesses.

Bureaucrats may want larger budgets or even more simply, more utility, defined as greater flexibility or slack that larger budgets and other factors influence. Slack may be created, in fact, by adding the number of workers as well as or instead of salaries that a larger budget would imply. However, departments with large capital (developmental) expenditures may collide with departments with larger redistributive expenditures. The former departments' strategies would seem to jibe with strategies for winning the intercommunity competition for more affluent buyer markets, but who wins the bureaucratic wars is not as clear.

In fact, bureaucrats' choices depend for their realization on the strategic positions they hold in the collective choice process. Clearly, planners set the basic assumptions about development, influencing future decisions about appropriate projects and groups to be rewarded. Public works chiefs decide what sequence and even what priority projects will have in a multiyear framework. These same chiefs implement plans, forcing substitutions and change orders that have a significant effect on outcomes as well. Finance officers have a say in what the government can afford and in how and when existing plans may be financed. City managers, having citywide welfare in mind, use the power of triage to close down facilities to optimize those the locality can afford. The officials often act in less than consensual fashion, and their strategic positions allow them to construct vetoes over others' choices.

Politicians want reelection (Downs, 1957; 1967), and to that extent, satisfying enough voters to win reelection is their chief aim. Attracting a majority is a matter of keeping services to some level that permits keeping taxes low. Thus Schneider argues (1989:35), "politicians benefit from improving their community's tax base, since this allows more demands to be satisfied within a given tax rate."

Schneider's research supports Peterson's strategic budgeting of developmental expenditures, in the main. Residents wanting low tax bills, firms wanting higher income markets, bureaucrats wanting greater slack and having the position to attain it, and politicians wanting the support of residents for reelection may be viewed as determining a competitive strategy that *win* over other affluent communities and impoverishes communities with strategies promoting redistribution.

2. *Constraints*

The constraints that tend to affect politicians and bureaucrats are those related to partisanship; that is, partisanship (Key, 1949) or strong political party organization sometimes increases the size of government as those who vote demand government-provided services, increasing the size of budgets, work forces, or both. Nonpartisanship may have the opposite effect.

Others, however, see the size of government influenced less by party organizations than the decision rules that bureau officials follow in determining service delivery (Lineberry, 1977). As argued above, for example, a city manager's position in the choice process and the decision rule of triage can determine what is eliminated or kept in the city budget, promoting the size of the budget.

With these constraints, therefore, what strategy tends to follow? Schneider's reading of the evidence (1989:37–38) leads to the following:

> Democrats are less likely to oppose bureaucratic demands for services and hence Democratic control of local governments would lead to larger local governments. . . . Furthermore, in reformed cities, bureaucrats are supposedly more responsive to the demands of the middle class for less spending and lower taxes.

Highly Democratic communities seem likely to follow a strategy aimed at higher taxes than would reformed cities, yet reformed cities without large middle classes demanding lower taxes may follow the same strategy. Apparently, only reformed cities in which the middle and upper classes set tax relief as the top priority would follow a strategy of developmental spending policies in the interest of being competitive in the market for affluent residents and high-tax-paying businesses (Peltzman, 1980).

The federalist governmental structure in the United States and the capitalist economic system may also explain capital investments made by local governments. Likewise, local decision makers optimize residents' housing values by reducing expenditures to hold down taxes. This may be done by constructing infrastructure with money from intergovernmental transfers or from capital markets.

So far, then, economic determinism and resident or consumer sovereignty prompts capital investment strategies. Far more needs to be known about a locality, its decision makers, and the decision rules they follow when elected or appointed to office and delegated the authority to invest. Far more needs to be known about flexible local finance structures that are responsive to the very different, sometimes contradictory imperatives dictated by corporate, consumers', and residents' concerns.

V. AMBIGUITY AND OPPORTUNISTIC LOGIC IN CAPITAL INVESTMENT STRATEGIES

There are other views on capital investment that deny its strategic elements and argue its deterministic nature. Some point out that the larger national economy may determine capital investment decisions far more than local initiative (Peterson, 1981). Industrial location decisions, for instance, may result from national and regional market considerations rather than local amenities; the fiscal impact of these "foreign" decisions then force local capital investments.

How? At the most fundamental level, these national decisions push governments to pursue development policies to accommodate these national movements and to control their consequences. First of all, a national firm's industrial location decisions prompt local land development succeeded by local land improvements, including transportation amenities, water systems, and waste treatment facilities. Development and improvements then prompt changes in land-use patterns that have implications for a considerable number of capital items that governments take the responsibility to provide, such as items to support fire services, police services, schools, and parks. Thus, any local discretion at these stages usually revolves around making land available, zoning those parcels appropriately, and handling the consequences.

The consequences of these development decisions require capital investment for education and training, child care, and health care. To some extent in a few of these areas and to a greater extent in others, these investments, originally a private-sector responsibility, have become a public one (Castells, 1977; Harvey, 1973; 1982). If these services are not provided, a different, far more dire set of consequences develops.

All of the local initiatives that might take place to force national firms' decisions in one way or another tend to be constrained by capital markets to whom local officials turn as fiscal stress grows. For example, should a local community have small but inelastic revenues as most do, and face the choice to zone to keep a piece of land vacant for possible future business development rather than immediate housing development, the resulting revenue loss can determine the outcome. That loss of revenue may be the difference in the ability to afford another needed asset. The same problem exists for communities that want to entice development with amenities. Which amenities do which firms want or need; can communities afford to simply guess? Will the firms locate for the amenities communities can provide even if they do not know for sure which firms are even looking?

Therefore, the decision to locate an industry in a particular place, and the government's decision to invest in a particular asset, might be more randomly related than consciously so (Pagano and Moore, 1985). It is this randomness, as well as the decisions that follow, that create a pervasive ambiguity when we refer to capital investment. Thus, capital investment might be thought of as opportunistic, taking advantage of situations as they appear at the time, rather than strictly linear or even nonlinear.

What is ambiguity and how do opportunistic strategies relate? In a web of organizations, a decision is an outcome of the convergence of several relatively independent "streams," each produced by one of the organizations in the web (Cohen and March, 1986:81). A decision is a product of *contextual rationality* or the tendency of people, problems, solutions, and choices to be joined by relatively arbitrary accidents of timing rather than by their relevance to each other.

The accidents of timing emerge, and what we think of what happened is an "interpretation." There is no such thing as a right interpretation; one's interpretation of an event that was created through the random interaction of variables is usually a matter of opportunism in rationalizing that event in an appropriate and favorable way after the fact (Daft and Weick, 1984; Cohen et al., 1972; 1974). Opportunistic strategies make fact out of accident and plausibility out of happenstance, and they permit at least primitive organizing to emerge.

Interpretations are borne out of metaphors that are carried around in leaders' heads to rationalize their methods of making choices as well as the choices themselves; what leaders use in hindsight to portray events springs from a metaphorical view of the world they hold. For instance, Cohen and March's study of university governance (1986) produced seven such metaphors that they found used by university presidents on their organizations and their work. These metaphors are adapted to government and organizations and portrayed in Table 1.

Each metaphor carries with it a reasonably independent method of management and resource allocation decision making. For example, the first five in Table 1 tend to be linear, strategic metaphors, whether a lone autocrat or a democratic process forces a decision. The competitive market metaphor underlies nonlinear strategy.

The anarchy metaphor is different still. It provides that the leader be the catalyst who brings together independent streams of only partially interested parties in choice situations that make use of superior information. The university president (Cohen and March, 1974:39) "gains . . . influence by understanding the operation of the system and by inventing viable solutions that accomplish . . . objectives rather than by choosing among conflicting alternatives." Subtle adjustments in the form of managing unobtrusively, giving more time, exchanging status for substance, facilitating opposition participation, overloading the system, and providing many opportunities in which problems, participants, solutions, and choice situations come together, work to the catalyst's interest in making choices (Cohen and March, 1974:209–211).

Organizations, according to Cohen and March (1986), vary in the metaphorical requirements they have.

Table 1   Metaphors of Strategy

1. *Plebiscitary autocracy metaphor.* An autocrat makes all decisions on behalf of the organization until such time as a plebiscite is called to ratify the autocrat's performance. The autocrat serves at the overwhelming approval of the electorate or abdicates. Decisions to be made are technically complicated relative to the amount of time and knowledge available to organization members, and the variance of objectives among participants is so small that small amounts of time and interaction may make up for it.
2. *Collective bargaining metaphor.* Assuming fundamentally conflicting interests within the organization, citizens, managers, politicians, and other interested parties resolve conflicts by resorting to bargaining, often through representatives, using formal "contracts" and social pressure for enforcement.
3. *Democratic metaphor.* The organization can be viewed as a community with an electorate of organization members and clients. Major decisions are made by resorting to voting, and votes are swayed by promises of one sort or another.
4. *Consensus metaphor.* To achieve agreement, organization members resort to some procedure, including discourse and assembly which have typically relied on those with high interest and large amounts of time for involvement and participation. Unanimity is possible because of the relative lack of both interest and time among organization members.
5. *Independent judiciary metaphor.* Authority is bestowed by some relatively arbitrary process— birth, cooptation, revelation—on a group of current leaders. This method assumes that "there are substantial conflicts between the immediate self-interests of current constituencies and the long run interests of future constituencies." (p. 84). It is possible to train a judge to recognize the long-run interests and to convince constituencies to accept judgments made in this way.
6. *Competitive market metaphor.* Government organizations provide a bundle of goods and services in a free market. All needing these goods and services select among alternative providers and choose those that come closest to serving perceived needs.
7. *Anarchy metaphor.* The organization's members make autonomous decisions. Resources are allocated by whatever process emerges but without explicit accommodation and with explicit reference to some superordinate goal. Decisions produced in the organization are a consequence produced by the system but intended by no one and decisively controlled by no one. The statistical properties of a large number of these autonomous decisions are such that they will reliably produce jointly satisfactory states.

Source: Cohen and March, 1986: 81–84.

Variance in most regards is a matter of the amount of attention the organization members can give a choice situation as well as the flow of problems and solutions involved. The patterns underlying the apt application of a metaphor might be a matter of how independent, exogenous, and rapid the flow of the streams of problems, solutions, participants, and choice opportunities might be.

The application to investment strategy's unique problems follows these premises. Capital investments represent simultaneous flows of information through various choice structures. Picture an ecology of games (Long, 1958) as an appropriate way to suggest the various interpretations involved. One's problem is another's solution. Many solutions—indicated by the number and type of participants on a given day—swamp the number of problems. Moreover, the number of choice opportunities—times in which a formal decision should be rendered—may vary from time to time. As Long (1958:58) illustrates

> [A] particular highway grid may be the result of a bureaucratic department of public works game in which are combined, though separate, a professional highway engineer game with its purposes and critical elite onlookers; a departmental bureaucracy; a set of contending politicians seeking to use the highways for political capital, patronage, and the like; a banking game concerned with bonds, taxes and the effects of the highways on real estate; newspapermen interested in headlines, scoops, and the effect of highways on the papers' circulation; contractors eager to make money by building roads; ecclesiastics concerned with the effect of highways on their parishes and on the fortunes of the contractors who support their churchly ambitions; labor leaders interested in union contracts and their status as community influentials with a right to be consulted; and civic leaders who must justify the contributions of their bureaus of municipal research or chambers of commerce to the social activity.

Each agenda and each choice opportunity are related by chance, making the outcome predictable only through random association.

March and Olsen's model (1989) illustrates two points that need to be kept in mind in discussing opportunistic investment strategy. The first is the contextual nature of decisions and, especially, the role of timing in decision results; that is, a decision is not made in the abstract but in the context of actual people interpreting events on a given day and determining an outcome with the information they have at the time and the metaphor they use to define the problem and to structure the problem-solving process.

The second idea relates to the role of institutions (Kaufman, 1960; Selznick, 1957). Permanent procedures and organizations make the randomness associated with contextual decision making a little easier to understand. Institutions provide stability where none may exist otherwise. Institutions also epitomize enduring values and attachments that members recall as they make decisions. With these values and the procedures that go with them, institutions act as homogenizing influences, helping gain conformity in an otherwise fragmented system of attachments and work.

A. Applying Contextual Rationality and Anchoring Institutions to Capital Investment

Understanding the role of institutions in capital investment may seem difficult in the face of ambiguity. In fact, a few institutions have become issues themselves[5] because they had too much control over ambiguity.[6] The purpose of this section,[7] then, is to shed light on the institutions that thrive on ambiguity, how these institutions operate, and, most important of all, how and what opportunistic strategies public organizations use to budget and finance capital projects.

We turn next to a brief overview of the argument our observations lead us to make followed by

1. An explanation of the form of institutionalization that takes place to permit opportunistic strategies to emerge
2. A description of process of mobilizing bias that underlies opportunistic strategies
3. A classification of capital investment strategies that provide opportunities to mobilize bias, construct reality, and rationalize ambiguous events

1. Institutionalization
Financing strategies emerge from a set of people who form a team; this semipermanent institutional form has the responsibility for formulating and implementing the major parts of the investment strategy. Formulation tends to involve some form of bargaining among team members, with bargaining positions developed over long periods of network—team members and their multiple contacts—development through direct and

indirect contact (Miller, 1985; Hildreth, 1986; 1987; Sbragia, 1983). Strategy implementation may best be described as the mobilization of bias through the classification of information. Classification emerges out of the efforts of those directly involved in the sales and the larger network of market participants of which they are a part.

Such a description of reality suggests something far different than a principal-agent model of strategy formulation suggested by both linear and nonlinear forms of capital investment strategy (Eisenhardt, 1989). We argue here that investment team members have different goals, and the outcome of their effort is more likely to be a least common denominator of these different goals than a rational pursuit of the issuer's end.

The basic assumption made in this argument is that each organization represented on the team pursues a goal suited to that organization's survival and success. In this research, we use an interorganizational network model that behaves as a political economy. Under some conditions, which we outline, the network members' stability or experience with each other becomes a major factor in the network's success. That experience, in turn, depends on the various bargains struck within the network. These bargains, in turn, reflect the larger pattern of interaction among network members and the outside world.

This approach also provides an alternative view to linear and nonlinear strategies, showing that capital investment is much more of a bargain struck among peer organizations. In fact, the amalgamation of positions after the bargain is hard to reconcile with prior positions, along strictly means-end terms; rather, the appropriate framework might go beyond such simple views to incorporate this network bargaining.

a. Principal and Agent Models.   The myth of agency in conventional strategy formulation lies in the believed relationship between capital budgeting and debt financing; that belief forms the ideal for practice in communities,[8] and it has led reformers to point their efforts in the wrong direction.

The foremost proponents of the myth and of conventional public-sector financing strategy, Wetzler and Peterson (1985), portray it as a rational process, as shown in Table 2; that is, strategy requires principals formulating strategy (managers) to choose among projects of different rates of return and levels of risk in order to exploit targeted capital markets that will through time convert resource and tax-base contributions to a higher-performing portfolio of assets. This is very much what we described as the linear logic underlying some forms of capital investment strategy in earlier parts of this chapter.

The strategy may be formed by employing agents (financial advisors, legal counsel, accountants, and other consultants). These agents provide the analyses of what measures will connect the project to a capital market that can finance it in return for the promise to repay implicit in a stream of revenue directly, indirectly, or not at all connected to the project itself.

b. Network Models.   On the other hand, the strategies that emerge in financing capital improvements may actually result from substantial interaction among many parties, all of which have relatively insular views about the specific strategic and tactical moves to be made to ensure success in financing. In fact, it is the insularity, the individual positions parties bring to the bond-sale team, that makes bargaining rather than mere computation possible.

Table 2   The Conventional (Linear) Strategic Choice Process for Capital Projects

Step	Description
1. Examine the environment	Examine locality's competitive position (e.g., industrial location)
2. Assess the current situation	Determine current condition of public goods or enterprises (e.g., infrastructure)
3. Set goals	Determine public goods or enterprises to be developed
4. Identify the alternatives	Identify debt instruments and investment vehicles, interest-rate cycles, markets, and tax policies in effect or pending
5. Analyze alternatives via return on investment	Determine the savings or earnings per dollar committed by considering the capital project's lifetime costs and benefits as well as the costs of financing by the various means surveyed
6. Select optimal alternative	Choose the time and method of financing

Source: Wetzler and Petersen, 1985.

That bargaining may be the only accountability mechanism available, and it is one the agency myth overlooks; that is, the agency myth forces the reformer to blame public managers and to promote efforts to rein them in. The network approach can argue the benefits of bargaining in forcing team members to stabilize their relationships in order to achieve efficiency, and under certain circumstances, the public interest.

In the description of actual roles and behaviors in strategy formulation and implementation, we have discussed the market-making efforts that go into creating a bond sale, then shown how information is pooled, classified, and interpreted by this team through bargaining. The bargaining involves not only those directly involved in market making—the team—but also an even larger network of important decision makers that includes credit-rating agencies, competing issuers of debt, and ultimately, bond buyers, all of whom we have described and related to one another in Miller (1992).

Strategy implementation, which we describe in the next section, involves determining the opportunistic strategies actually used in capital investment.

A.   Opportunistic Strategies for Capital Investments

There are an infinite number of variations[9] among financing strategies from which communities may choose when funding capital improvements, and most cities can find one that fits their own unique legal, economic, financial, and political constraints. How then do they choose?

Despite the fact that mangers do not have values that permit innovation, outright devotion to innovation occurs and rather comprehensive innovations take place every year.[10] The answer, we argue, lies in the idea advanced earlier that managers themselves do not decide what reality is; if they did, their values would tend to limit their innovativeness. Instead, managers participate with others in constructing a reality that many managers find particularly useful. This reality is constructed specifically to cope with an uncertain environment outside the organization; the innovations constructed create stability, in line with managers' values, perhaps, while still promoting innovation.[11]

This section offers proof of innovation in its description of the ways in which state and local government financial managers reacted to uncertainty in their capital financing activities over the last 15 years.[16] The period had a breathtaking volatility when viewed from its end. Merely reciting the financial condition of New York City at the beginning and the end of the period—near default in 1975, embarking on major service increases and capital improvements with large surpluses in 1985, entering a period of fiscal stress in 1990—perhaps portrays the bust to boom to bust character of many, if not all, state and local governments during this period. The rest cover all bases: boom to bust (Phoenix), still busted (Detroit), and bust to boom (Dallas).

As a matter of surprise to no one now, the period witnessed some of the greatest instability among prices, interest rates, and markets in this century. For example, prices increased at rates in the double digits for the first time since World War II. Interest rates on long, municipal bonds took a leap into double digits for the first time since *The Bond Buyer* began keeping records. As both cause and effect, the distinction among credit market participants, especially the issuer and the intermediary, became obscure (Peterson, 1981). Since the rate instability period, the market has had instability, especially in 1987 and 1989, yet the 1980s witnessed one of the longest periods of stability in the century.

The reaction may be described in terms of coping strategies (Hickson et al., 1971:217), prevention, absorption, and information.

Preventative strategies reduce the probability of shocks occurring so that resources flowing to the organization do not vary widely.

Absorption strategies adjust to events by making a given financial system operate within new and changing confines. Offsetting the effects of variations in resources, particularly the ravages of inflation and interest rate increases, shock absorbers exist to hedge against change, to adjust to the variations in interest rates, and to level consumer demand.

Information strategies deal with uncertainty in capital investment by forcing a reinterpretation of reality by the strategizing organization or by the larger world. This often entails reinterpreting the agenda of issues that frame the need for investment (Kingdon, 1984). Agenda setting in the strategy formulation process encompasses the simple act of identifying a problem, thereby setting in motion the apparatus for solving it. The apparatus involves various institutional arrangements that act to aggregate resources.

The next section catalogs each coping strategy, briefly noting and explaining it.

B. Coping by Prevention

Prevention efforts have attempted to forestall uncertainty. Generally, managers aim these efforts at reducing the probability of shocks occurring so that resources flowing to the organization do not vary widely. State and local financial managers have followed four basic strategies to prevent excessive variability: diversifying,[12] merging,[13] leveraging,[14] and securitizing.[15] The prevention of uncertainty through design of systems that increase the potential pool of resources and the willingness to use the resources has marked state and local government finance. Diversification and merger have gained new life. New techniques, such as leveraging and securitizing, have future value, yet present needs require a great deal of absorption of uncertainty.

C. Coping by Absorption

Action during a period of uncertainty often occurs as absorption activities. Absorbing uncertainty means adjusting to it by making a given financial system operate within new and changing confines. Offsetting the effects of variations in resources, particularly the ravages of inflation and interest rate increases, uncertainty absorption tactics, and strategies used by state and local government financial managers come in several forms. At least four groups of shock absorbers exist: hedging techniques to "insure" against inflation,[16] new inflation and interest rate-sensitive debt products,[17] new advance refunding routines for adjusting existing debt to the variations in interest rates,[18] and leveling demand efforts by which issuers find new bondholders.[19] The uncertainty absorption activities of state and local government financial managers have led to the use of hedging programs to deal with interest rate risk exposure; new financial instruments that move with the changes in interest rates but also allow bondholders the opportunity to sell the security if necessary; advance refunding programs to convert relatively high-interest-rate debt service to lower rates as interest rates fall; and programs that entice an ever-larger group of investors into the market to maintain demand.

D. Coping by Information

Not only does the network political economy play a major part in the social construction of reality through the imagery of prevention and absorption activities, but the activities that serve to reinterpret the agenda of work or the roles of those involved—coping by information activities—also help construct a reality on which network members can agree.

Coping by information with the ambiguity of project finance has emerged as a reinterpretation of the agenda of issues (Kingdon, 1984). Agenda setting in the policy-making process encompasses the simple act of identifying a problem, thereby setting in motion the apparatus for solving it. The apparatus involves various institutional arrangements that act to aggregate resources.

The last full national issue-attention cycle neared its waning moments at the beginning of the period between 1975 and 1990 that I have chosen for study; that is, the civil rights/urban disorders cycle of the late 1960s had exhausted itself to be replaced by the fiscal crisis, then by the infrastructure crisis, and now by a defensive effort to fend off mandates passed down by higher levels of government intent on balancing their budgets but still ensuring certain political debts are paid—a mandate crisis.

The fiscal crisis actually combined two issues, city financial emergencies and tax limitation. The financial emergency side began with New York City's 1975 crisis. The tax limitation movement was ignited by the passage of an expenditure "cap" law in 1976, ultimately spreading with California's proposition 13 in 1978.

In a sort of policy dialectic, the fiscal crisis gave way to a new issue-attention cycle of the 1980s, infrastructure problems and their repair and replacement. Fiscal crisis solutions tended to lead ultimately to proposals for higher taxes. Tax limitation and antigovernment solutions barred the rise in taxes. In the standoff or vacuum, the opportunity arose for resetting the agenda.

With the opportunity for agenda setting came the opportunity for someone or group not on either side to synthesize the proposals. Infrastructure provided the obvious candidate for synthesis, and public financial managers and investment bankers became the obvious issue entrepreneurs. The direct consequence of the fiscal problem was the declining facilities cities faced. At the heart of the tax limitation/antigovernment movement was the question of redistribution of wealth.

The infrastructure movement could solve both sides' greatest fear: that economic problems were not getting solved. Economic problems of cities might not get solved through infrastructure replacement, but the multiplier effect of government spending on infrastructure would have an ameliorative effect (and those standing for election might have something to distribute). Economic problems of individuals might not be solved by infrastructure, but the new emphasis might produce productivity improvements and spark economic expansion (and to the middle class blunt the redistribution of wealth carried on through social programs).

Likewise, infrastructure joined heretofore sparring institutions. Infrastructure repair could join federal departments: Transportation for roads, bridges, and mass transit; Housing and Urban Development for general-purpose development and public administration professionalism; and Environmental Protection for sewer and water systems. These departments, with infrastructure dominating the agenda, might appear to be doing what they intended—something "new," "innovative," or "pioneering"—even if it involved the most standard, traditional, and mundane of activities and dealt with mere "upgrading of existing services." The infrastructure issue would also get the departments out of the "social engineering" morass and make managers responsive to the rising Frost Belt coalition of public officials.

The trick of getting infrastructure off and running in the face of tax-limitation movements and federal budget contraction turned out to be financing. Who would pay for such a massive group of construction projects? Direct taxation or pay-as-you-go as well as direct federal aid having been eliminated, the only alternative left was long-term debt. Seeing such a demand, investment bankers and financial managers literally reshaped public capital financing as well as short-term cash management.

The entire "rebuilding America's cities" movement, as well as the "good schools" movement, represent agenda setting of a high order, but are something that the mandate crisis could stall in its tracks. Swamped with mandates that higher levels of government will not finance and representing responsibility they refuse to assume, local government will have little discretion or money left. The mandate crisis is agenda setting of an even higher order, a power play by those who see the last best chance of decreasing the size of government in turning up the heat on state and local governments. The taxing power of these governments is so weak relative to federal government that project finance will wither. The ambiguity that results is not one that is internal to the network political economy. The ambiguity is one involving localities, private-sector forces, taxpayers, and policy makers fearful of defeat. The ambiguity spells stalemate, and the result is reality construction by cross-veto.

1. Conclusions and Summary

This section of the chapter has discussed the reaction to ambiguity finance officers had in the period from 1975 to 1990. The reaction has taken the form of administrative notions known as "coping." In that period, finance officers coped in direct ways, through prevention and absorption.

The nagging question remains, however: Did financial managers cope or did they depend on their network of investment bankers, attorneys, auditors, and other advisors who aided the effort? Coping suggests a more knowledgeable and sophisticated profession than existed before 1975. Coping also suggests a deep understanding of the capital financing process, the political process that underlies it, and the credit markets that support it, subjects about which most research suggests finance advisors are somewhat less than completely knowledgeable.

If not coping but the more likely case of dependence, the question focuses attention on those central to coping outside government, the financial advisors, who may be leading government financial managers into what amounts to greater ambiguity, to a casinolike world in which puts and floaters, hedges and straddles, and arbitrage and speculation contribute to the creation of debt for the sake of creating debt.

The evidence in this section of the chapter lends credence to the explanation advanced earlier that managers themselves do not decide what reality is; if they did their values would tend to limit their innovativeness. Instead, managers participate with others in constructing a reality that many managers find particularly useful. This reality is constructed opportunistically to cope with an uncertain environment outside the organization; the innovations constructed create stability, in line with managers' values, perhaps, while still promoting innovation.

E. Capital Investment in Communities Revisited

This chapter has surveyed three major approaches used in structuring, formulating, and implementing strategies that pertain to capital asset production in communities. The conventional approach to this form of strategy resembles classic rational decision making in its singleminded insistence of clear priorities and its employment of cost-benefit analysis.

However, we outlined two other counterapproaches. The first, a nonlinear or competitive approach, describes what economists have either portrayed or projected onto suburban communities that vie among themselves for better-quality tax bases.

The second, an opportunistic approach to strategy, pertained to communities that face more uncertain environments. Such communities also have decision makers and interested parties who are randomly related, have unclear goals, and who interact to make choices irregularly. Such a high degree of ambiguity creates vacuums of one sort or another and opens the way for opportunism by all involved.

NOTES

1.   "Think of a logic as simply a line of argument that is shaped around several basic ideas or principles" (Gilbert et al., 1988, p. 5).
2.   Many textbook accounts will parallel the discussion here; however, this section rests on the fine presentations in Vogt (1977; 1975), as well as those in Wacht (1987) and Gordon and Pinches (1984). See also Moak and Killian (1964), Steiss (1975), and the references in Bozeman (1984).
3.   The overall plan, as well as the capital budget represents communitywide interests; that is, capital programming is a complicated process whose outcomes have far-reaching impacts, not only for the departments involved, but for the community as a whole. The process produces considerable involvement from various actors trying to influence capital programming. Following Vogt (1977) and Moak and Hillhouse (1975), the actors should include department heads, central budget staff and chief administrative officer, the governing body, and the taxpayers as a whole. Estimating capital requirements generally begins with a call from the central budget staff for estimates and by distributing forms. The estimates may be developed under various instructions. The central authority may or may not place a ceiling on the department requests. A ceiling forces the department to realistically set priorities for projects and makes the budget staff's work easier. On the other hand, such an approach tends to stifle imagination and innovation through the initial negative approach of an estimated ceiling. The establishment of a ceiling inhibits the department in transmitting overall capital needs which may heighten awareness at central levels within the organization. A key element of strong capital programming and the one element most often missing is a strong central budget authority. In this context a strong central budget authority not only monitors and reviews the budget, but also coordinates the overall planning process. This requires strongly centralized planning and well-articulated organizational policies. Utilizing planning tools, such as cost-benefit analysis, a strong central budget authority can balance one type of project against another to achieve the overall plans, goals, and priorities of the community. With a strong central coordinating body and centralized planning, it is impossible to evaluate objectively the need for a new water treatment plant versus the need for a new arterial thoroughfare or a new park. Each of these projects is so different that without central planning they cannot be compared to each other. A central budget authority promotes a *trickle-down* effect rather than a *percolate-up* type budget. The trickle-down budget relies on major policy and program decisions made at a centralized level with department heads asked to submit specific budget proposals in support of these policy decisions. A percolate-up budget, on the other hand, utilizes recommendations formulated by the operating agencies and forwarded to a centralized budget staff. The budget staff has to pick and choose among the various alternatives that lack a central theme. The central executive must act as adjudicator between the various department heads and the central budget authority. He or she makes sure the budget as submitted reflects his or her own understanding of policy directives and objectively judges the adequacy of the various proposals and their contribution to the overall mission of the organization. The chief executive must ensure that the proper decisions are made among competing priorities and that the programs submitted are properly integrated into the overall function of the organization. Objectivity is necessary to formulate good, sound recommendations but is often impaired by anticipated political responses. The desire for a good "batting average," unfortunately, may outweigh the staff's special responsibility to bring objectivity to the process.

The role of the governing body is to set policy. The legislators must judge the capital budget and its consistency with their policies. At this level, objectivity often breaks down due to the politically expedient or pet project that one or more legislators may be supporting, not necessarily because of its overall importance, but because of a localized importance, especially if ward policies are involved. The legislative body should hold public hearings to obtain citizen input on the various proposals (Moak and Hillhouse, 1975:112).

However, according to authorities on the matter [the legislative body should not be brought into the capital programming process prior to completion of the executive budget. Compromises in this direction tend to invite persistent legislative attempts to influence decisions all along the way with a resultant weakening of the executive's responsibility for budget formulation. Since they have the final decision, legislators should wait for the legislative review stage, at which point their voices will be heard.]

The legislature's function is to establish the upper level of capital outlays consistent with overall fiscal policy. The legislature resolves conflicts that might exist between an expert's view and those of laypersons. Legislators also assess opposing viewpoints of citizens and citizen groups and furnish political leadership on major investments and capital decisions. The citizens and taxpayers at large are also actors in this process. They view the capital budget as an important investment of their tax dollar and personally want some of the benefits of such investment. They will push for one particular project or another, which may or may not have a priority in the context of the overall plan but which is nevertheless important to the individual citizen of group. Pressure is frequently exerted by these individuals or groups.

4. Economists traditionally view local sales tax-based or property tax-based revenue systems as regressive. Both tend to penalize those who spend the largest proportion of their incomes on consumption (either house or retail goods). Generally, this group is the poorest economic group. For more discussion on this, as well as views to the contrary, see Stiglitz (1988).

5. By some calculations, public authorities, for example, issue and manage between one-fifth and one-fourth of all long-term municipal securities. Given present forecasts, the 1990 total would suggest a market of some $25 billion. They are attacked (Walsh, 1978) for having too much responsibility and too little accountability, which in this case may mean too little ambiguity.

6. For work on the Washington Public Power Supply System see Leigland and Lamb (1986); for work on sidestepping the normal political accountability mechanisms with public authorities in order to build public facilities, see Bennett and DiLorenzo (1983), Henriques (1982), and Walsh (1978).

7. This section is based on a paper delivered at the annual meeting of the American Political Science Association, Washington, D.C., Sept. 2, 1988. I thank Robert T. Golembiewski and W. Bartley Hildreth for their comments.

8. See the recent action by the State of California regarding this ideal linkage, which they legislated into practice (Walters, 1990).

9. While we talk about financing strategies primarily as borrowing strategies, that is not the broadest picture one could paint. One strategy involves an all-borrowing policy utilizing current revenues to finance debt incurred as the result of bonds issued to fund capital improvements. An all-borrowing approach is appropriate when inflationary increases exceed the interest that is paid on long-term debt. A capital reserve strategy uses funds saved in an investment account with the investment earnings applied to the project cost. This strategy is useful when inflation is not particularly high or when the project can be deferred for a period of time.

   Several strategies are combinations of other strategies, including a partial pay-as-you-go plan whereby a portion of the project is paid utilizing current revenue or capital reserves and the balance is funded by bonds. Another combination might be referred to as a pay-as-you-spend plan. Particular phases of the project, such as engineering, land acquisition, and construction are financed from current capital resources. Engineering could be financed for the first year, land acquisition the second and third years, and construction the fourth or fifth year. Such an approach allows flexibility as resources can be accumulated for the anticipated larger construction phase over the 4-year engineering and land acquisition phase, or alternatively, debt can be issued the fourth year to fund the construction cost.

10. In fact, two programs have done a great deal to show the substantial regularity and depth of these innovations; that at Rutgers University (Center for Public Productivity, Department of Public Administration) and LOGIN, Norris Institute, as well as that at Harvard University's John F. Kennedy School of Government.

11. This section is based in part on Miller (1985).

   The period roughly dates from the publication of one U.S. Advisory Commission on Intergovernmental Relations study of note (Patton and Hempel, 1975), and covers about 15 years, from 1975 to 1990.

12. Diversification in state and local governments has applied primarily to revenue sources. The search for alternative revenues to the property tax at the local government level and to the income tax at the state level has become one of the clearest trends of the last decade. States have diversified to a lesser extent than simply raising taxes. Nevertheless, so-called sin taxes have gained intense scrutiny and debate among state-level financial managers. Cigarette taxes, especially, have risen in the face of federal tax cutbacks.

13. *Merger.* Two major types of horizontal mergers and a form of vertical merger have entered the scene to provide much preventive potential for financial managers.

   Horizontal mergers. Annexation, the first type of horizontal merger, reports the U.S. Bureau of Census, has fallen, but still remains the merger technique of choice in the South and West (U.S. Bureau of the Census, 1980). Horizontal mergers with the private sector have gained a great deal more notice as well as notoriety. "Privatization" of public functions has a substantial following and applies to almost any activity in which former public functions are shared with private sector or profit-oriented groups. There are at least seven major forms of horizontal merger through privatization.

1. *Equity "kickers"* (*Wall Street Journal*, 1982). In several instances, the government has demanded an equity position in the project as well as the yield from the security financing the project. This has been especially true in short-lived industrial development bond financings in which cities have acted as issuers. However, the equity position has also become a negotiating object when cities have formed partnerships with private parties in using federal funds for redevelopment purposes. The city of Chicago, for example, demanded an equity position in a downtown hotel

development project, in the form of a share of future earnings attributable to the improvements funded by city participation. Other cities exhibiting Chicago's behavior include the following:

a. Louisville, Kentucky, which will receive 50% of the cash flow (after the developer gets a 15% return on his equity) and 50% of the future appreciation in a hotel project in return for aiding a development company with financing for a $50 million project.

b. San Diego, California, which, in a $200 million project downtown, including retail space, office space, and a hotel, the city and the developer agreed that the developer would lend the city $4 million, interest-free, for 4 years to assemble a parcel of blighted acreage. The developer then would buy the land for $1 million. In return, the developer will pay the city 10% of rental income in excess of the base rent for 50 years along with 31% of the parking revenue.

c. New Haven, Connecticut, which transformed an old brass mill into a research facility. The city created a nonprofit corporation as developer and sold the project's tax breaks to investors through limited partnerships to raise project equity. Construction financing was as a no-interest loan from federal community development block grant money. Permanent financing came from construction unions' pension funds. To meet pension law requirements, the city persuaded the state of Connecticut to guarantee the first mortgage. An urban development action grant helped underwrite a second mortgage.

2. *Tax increment financing.* Unlike revenue streams caused by increased sales or rental of facilities, tax increment financing creates a stream of revenue from the increased value of property and from the resulting taxes on that property after development financed by tax increment securities. The method relies first on a calculation of old and new property values. The issuing entity must establish a base year and value property in that base or pre-development year. The entity must also decide the allocation of base-year valuation and tax among those other entities relying on the property tax, such as school boards. Next, the entity estimates the value of the property during and after construction and redevelopment and through the immediate future. With these estimates, the entity creates a revenue stream from the incremental difference in postdevelopment tax revenues. The stream relies on the difference between redevelopment-era property valuation and base-year valuation, multiplied by tax rates and subtracted from base-year allocations due other taxing entities. The financing method has its opponents. Much opposition arises from competing taxing jurisdictions. These jurisdictions, in effect, face a static tax base for the term of the repayment period. Defenders argue that tax increment financing reduces the likelihood of further tax-base erosion. Moreover, they add, redevelopment adds jobs and activity that may work to increase the value of property in other areas in which houses of workers and businesses servicing these workers exist and that form the property tax base on which all jurisdictions' tax bases rely.

3. *Private—public partnerships.* With tax-exempt leverage lease financing, private partnerships assure production of capital goods. Using such a financing plan, a taxable third party builds and owns a facility. The third party, acting as lessor, leases the facility to an operator, including in the lease the cost of maintenance, repair, and insurance. The jurisdiction in turn enters into a service contract with a lessee/operator. The service contract secures the builder's loan; the loan comes from tax-exempt revenue bonds, but the builder contributes 20 to 40% of the purchase price. Revenues from the facility's customers to the city would the service contract.

4. *On-behalf-of issuers.* Assuming congenial state and local law, issuers can create nonprofit corporations that act as issuers "on behalf of" the original issuer, usually a state, county, school board, or city. The authority for the creation of an on-behalf-of issuer rests in federal law. Generally, the government entity forms the corporation for the purpose of leasing real property or equipment from the corporation. The corporation issues bonds or other securities. The lease payment stream from the government to the corporation acts as the underlying security.

5. *Sale and leaseback.* Using an on-behalf-of issuer, a jurisdiction can remove certain assets, but also liabilities, from its books. A city with a facility wholly owned might decide to create a "municipal assistance corporation" (MAC), an on-behalf-of issuer that might buy the facility and lease the facility back over a period equal to the facility's "useful life." The MAC then would sell securities based on the lease payments the city pledged.

6. *Annuities and pension plans* (Yacik, 1985). Jurisdictions now shift their pension liability to the private sector through tax-exempt borrowings. For example, Essex County, New Jersey, sold general obligation bonds to purchase an annuity contract from Metropolitan Life Insurance Company, which, after Metropolitan invests the bond proceeds, will be obligated to pay out $10 million more in pension benefits. Thus the county issued bonds totaling $48 million, and will pay over the life of the bonds principal and interest of $94.9 million. Metropolitan will fully fund the pension system with $105.8 million.

7. *Tax-exempt leasing* (Vogt and Cole, 1983). A tax-exempt lease resembles the on-behalf-of issuing corporation technique. In a tax-exempt lease/purchase agreement, the government entity, as lessee, signs an agreement with a bank, investment bank, or leasing company, as lessor. The lessor raises funds through a lender or investor to pay for the objects covered by the lease. In return, the lender receives a security interest in the equipment of all rights and title under the agreement, and a stream of lease rental payments (principal and interest) of which the interest is tax-exempt. Due to the size of the transaction, more than one lender may participate. Certificates of participation can be issued, allowing lenders to share in a proportionate amount of the stream of the rental payments.

Vertical mergers. While intergovernmental sharing of responsibility, especially that involving federal aid, continues to diminish, state aid to local governments in all forms actually may have increased. Most important are new structures such as the following:

1. *Equipment loan funds* (*The Bond Buyer*, 1983). Several states and counties have issued bonds to fund equipment loan pools for hospitals or other nonprofits or departments within governments. These programs loan funds on an intermediate-term basis, but the value lies in spreading the financing costs of the bonds over a number of equipment users. Credit-enhancement techniques allow merger of smaller or weaker credits to stronger ones.
2. *Bond banks* (Forbes and Petersen, 1983). The larger, unlimited object version of equipment loan funds is the bond bank. Public financing authorities, which pool capital financing for government entities into single large bond issues, came into being around 1970 in the state of Vermont. By pooling obligations, the issue attracts more interest, spreads underwriting costs, and lowers rates. Evidence exists, however, to show at least superficially that the cost of the bond bank is more than made up by reduced interest costs and earnings from bond proceeds investment.
3. *Other forms of state assistance* (Forbes and Petersen, 1983). States also provide assistance to communities in marketing bonds. California's Health Facilities Construction Loan Insurance Program insures local revenue and general obligation bonds that finance health facilities' construction and comply with state health plans. In addition, the Michigan Qualified School Bond Fund operates a revolving loan fund to provide emergency assistance to school districts in meeting debt service. The state of Texas commits royalties from state oil extraction sales to secure local school board bonds. The royalties suffice to back up the creditworthiness of large bond issues from all areas of the state, yielding an AAA rating. Minnesota's Bond Guarantee Fund insures any local general obligation bond issue. State law allows the state to levy a special property tax on a locality, if default occurs.

14. *Leveraging.* With newer revenue sources based on an income stream, similar to an annuity, a government can leverage these streams, or borrow based on them by using them as pledges of collateral. Such approaches amount to simple revenue bonds; however, newer methods, in which various revenue streams act together as "leverage," provide the potential for new and more reliable sources of capital financing funds.

    Cross-source leveraging (Bayless, 1985). One of the best examples of leveraging various revenue streams occurred in New Jersey recently. Through the New Jersey Turnpike Authority, the state's transportation trust fund will gain $12 million a year to restore transportation infrastructure. The state's three toll roads earmark a portion of revenues for the trust, a combined total of $25 million yearly over a 20-year period to service and repay the bond issues financing repair work. Those contributions will be highly leveraged; every dollar contributed by the toll roads could be used to raise another $5, then matched 9 times over by the federal government. The legislature appropriates funds and combines them with the annual contributions from the state's toll roads and a portion of the gasoline tax. This revenue stream guarantees the necessary work provides for debt service on bonds.

15. *Securitization.* Traditionally, communities have financed limited-benefit capital improvements through pledges of receivables. For example, paving a residential street often has depended upon the willingness of the residents to pledge monthly repayments for the work. If the pledges emerged, the local government issued bonds with that revenue stream securing it. Private sector borrowers call this procedure "securitization of assets." Involving an illiquid loan or lease agreement, the securitization process transforms the asset into a liquid security. Virtually any asset with a payment stream and a long-term payment history is an eventual candidate for securitization. State and local government lease agreements—that is, any fee-based service—produce such streams and histories. As a result, their capitalization might rest on securitization of the payment stream. Likewise, capital improvements capable of "exclusion" or unit-benefit analysis, might submit to securitization. Capital goods usually defined as "public goods," such as streets, sidewalks, and even fire stations and police precinct houses (where fire calls and police calls may be defined as exclusive services) could become candidates. The reverse could work financially. Regulatory fees for pollution control, whereby the entity pays regularly based on its emission level, could act as securitization for the capital facilities that might ameliorate the problem. In addition, cities might benefit by private corporations' greater liquidity. A vendor using receivables-backed securities might offer better than the usual trade terms. Liquidity would not be affected because the receivables would be sold. Cities would get better terms because repayment forms a receivable of a given length susceptible to securitization. A city's cash flow could improve, providing it with the foundation for cash management and investment.

    According to some sources (Shapiro, 1985; Sloane, 1985), bankers have begun to look at securitizing other kinds of assets. Beyond assets with a payment stream and a payment history, which can be tracked over a sufficient period of time, "The next generation is an asset that doesn't have a predictable cash flow associated with it. And it might not have any cash flow associated with it except when it's sold." An example would be commodity-backed agreements in which one could pledge or sell a group of assets to back securities (e.g., natural resources, site improvement incentives, zoning abatements, and more abstract forms of assets such as the esthetics of the community or the quality of the school system as they affect business location).

16. *Hedging to absorb uncertainty.* Hedging involves the use of futures or options contracts or both to anticipate movements in interest rates. Futures contracts are agreements to deliver or receive cash or securities at a specified time or place. Options give investors the right but not the obligation to buy or sell something, such as a futures contract or a security, at a specified time or place.

    Hedging strategies. Hedging strategies have developed as futures and options markets have offered new products. Basic hedging involves the purchase of a futures contract, or an option on a physical or futures contract, to guard or lock in an interest rate.

17. *Absorbing uncertainty with new, rate-sensitive debt products.* The fastest growing, and the most often used method of

absorbing uncertainty today has emerged as "creative capital finance" activities. The nature and type of these "creative" techniques has changed as quickly as the volatile trends affecting both borrowers/issuers and lenders/securities holders. These techniques span all dimensions that exist to describe capital financing: short- and long-term, interest-sensitive and insensitive, borrower-tilted and lender-tilted, general and specific use-oriented, and relatively more tax weighted versus less. Six techniques have attained widespread use over the past 15 years: stage financing, commercial paper, floating rate bonds, put option bonds, guarantees, and stepped coupons.

Stage financing. To respond to an expected population growth and service demand life cycle of a growth area, stage financing creates a fixed amount of debt-service capacity that a governmental unit can maintain over a period of time. For example, a unit may decide to set its tax stream at a fixed mill levy for debt-service purposes. In many cases this will be an average rate, seemingly high in the initial stages of growth, but low in the later ones. This millage devoted to debt service permits the unit a borrowing capacity great enough in the early stages to anticipate growth and service demand. The millage devoted to debt service in the later stages is not so great that undue burdens are placed on a stagnant or even declining revenue base.

Tax-exempt commercial paper (Klapper, 1980). Tax-exempt commercial paper, an unsecured, tax-exempt loan with a shorter than 1-year maturity, offers another opportunity to limit exposure in a period of volatility. Interest rates on commercial paper follow the short-term debt market and generally fall below taxable Treasury bill rates. A commercial paper program requires refinancing of existing issues upon maturity. Because paper is unsecured, a letter of credit from a bank normally backs the program.

Floating-rate bonds. Floating or variable-rate financing has emerged because chaotic conditions in the municipal bond market reduced reliance on traditional, long-term, fixed-rate issues. Investors who witnessed bond interest rates fluctuating between 5 1/2% and 14 1/4% over the 5-year period from Sept. 1977 to Jan. 1982 had little demand for a bond bearing a fixed rate for 20 to 30 years, yet the majority of city issuers prefer to finance for as long a term as possible. The interest rate on variable-rate bonds for each interest payment period is not fixed at the time of issuance but instead will "float" or adjust as market conditions change. As such, the rate is tied to an index or a market indicator reasonably sensitive to market conditions. Pricing strategy is by far the most important factor in structuring and marketing variable-rate securities. The strategy relies heavily on some index thought to mirror trends in competing investments of similar risk and maturity. The index provides a time series that can be compared to the interest rates of existing short- and long-term tax-exempt and taxable securities over a relatively long period of time. The interest rate indices run the gamut from London Interbank Offered Rates (LIBOR) to federal securities interest rates to indices set by banks for their own customers. The variable rate has obvious attraction. The issuer borrows in the short-term market at a rate generally 2% to 4% lower than the traditional long-term market rate.

"Put" option bonds. A bond carrying a put option allows the bondholder to sell the bond back to the issuer on a given number of days' notice. Superficially, the "put" evens the sides, giving the bondholder a method of seeking the advantage the issuer always has had with a "call" feature. The put option allows the holder of any bond to demand that the bond be purchased by a remarketing agent on a given day by presenting the bond to the remarketing agent on that day or upon notice specified on the bond. The bondholder receives the principal amount (par value) plus accrued interest, if any, to the date of purchase. The remarketing agent finds a new buyer for the bond sold back by the old buyer exercising the put. If the remarketing agent cannot remarket a bond, a trustee draws on a "liquidity facility," a letter of credit or other liquid financial guarantee of payment usually provided by a bank to pay the principal and accrued interest. Generally, put options carry with them the need for further guarantees of payment, generally a letter of credit. The put feature allows issuers to sell long-term bonds with yields close to those on short-term issues, because the notice period required before the bond is put, in effect, acts as the bond's maturity. Issuers can save as much as 3% on the interest rate they must pay. The put feature first appeared on issues in 1980 and has gained popularity as interest rates have become volatile.

Third-party financial guarantees (Forbes and Petersen, 1983). Default by the Washington Public Power Supply System in 1983 has created a desire by borrowers and lenders to "guarantee" the payment of principal and interest on bonds. Essentially, borrowers buy an insurance policy to guarantee payment to bondholders in case of default. Along with the guarantee comes the insurer's AAA credit rating that acts to lower the borrower's cost. Bond guarantees come in several different forms. First, there are strictly defined insurance policies covering the principal and interest on long-term fixed-rate issues, such as general obligation and revenue bond issues. Second, surety bonds are used when the guarantor has no license for municipal bond credit insurance or, for other legal reasons such as state regulations, cannot issue insurance outright. Practically, surety bonds differ very little from insurance. Third, banks issue letters and lines of credit. Letters of credit generally fit new types of financings carrying put features. Fourth, layered guarantees provide a mix of security features that no bank can provide alone. Industrial development bonds (IDBs) issued by a tax-exempt entity on behalf of a private company may be small and the issue relatively unknown outside its locality. The anonymity and accompanying fear of default on the part of bond buyers may be alleviated somewhat by a letter of credit. The size of the issue may be less of a problem if issues are combined. A first layer of security provided by a multitude of unknown issuers, companies, and banks can get added security by another layer of security (e.g., a large regional bank's letter of credit). A third layer of security may be needed, however, if the regional bank has no credit rating that the individual investor can rely upon. Therefore, a rated bank, of which there are only a handful in the United States, may provide another letter of credit, relying on the financial well-being of the regional bank. With the third letter of credit, the issue receives a AAA rating, and the letter of credit issuers share the risk of default. Finally, a variety of interest rate swaps, segmented market penetrations, interest rate caps and floors, and secondary market deals have appeared.

Stepped coupons (Forbes and Petersen, 1983). A stepped coupon bond uses maturities in which the coupons are "stepped" upward to increase yields over the life of the issue. All of the bonds may yield 7% in 1 year, for example, and 10% the next. The security looks like both a short-term and a long-term issue; moreover the investor has some protection from interest rate volatility. The rate-sensitive debt instruments and financing techniques discussed here were developed in direct response to the volatile interest rates encountered throughout the last 10 years. When rates fall and stabilize, however, governments take advantage of the condition by locking in the lower rates through an advance refunding.

18. *Absorbing uncertainty through advance refunding.* The concept of refinancing an existing indebtedness is a long-established practice utilized not only by state and local governments but also by corporations and individuals to reduce interest costs. New, relatively lower interest rate debt replaces debt issued at relatively higher interest rates. Advanced refunding programs most frequently are used to reduce debt service costs, with the most common refunding process involving issuing the refunding bonds at an interest rate that is lower than the rate of the refunded bonds. However, an advanced refunding may also be employed to restructure debt payments or to update overly restrictive bond indenture covenants. Therefore, refunding has several characteristics: (1) it is a "clean" swap of the outstanding bonds with the refunding bonds; (2) outstanding bonds would immediately cease to have any pledge of revenues; (3) the yearly debt service reduction may, if desired, begin immediately; and (4) the holders of the outstanding bonds would have, as security for the outstanding bonds, a portfolio of qualifying securities.

     Arbitrage and escrowed municipal bonds. A new and potentially more useful advanced refunding technique developed in the early 1980s has increased the savings and uncertainty absorption potential available to state and local governments. The method employs the floating rate and put option debt features we have already discussed, but it also includes investment in municipal bonds. The new technique requires two innovations. First, the refunding bonds are sold at floating rates with put features. The bond proceeds then are invested in fixed-rate, tax-exempt municipal bonds, which in the late 1970s had reached unusually high levels. While a variable-rate refunding bond reduces debt service, an escrow of fixed-rate municipal securities multiplies these savings. Assume that a refunded bond at, for example, 8.5% is matched against a refunding bond with a variable rate averaging 6.5%. Future debt service is reduced by the difference. Next, since the old refunded bond may not be able to be called until a first call option point, for instance, 5 years from now, the refunding bond proceeds can be invested. An investment in municipal bonds at about 8.5% could yield substantial savings. The 2% savings on debt service would be added to the 2% earnings on the municipal bond investment. Therefore, escrowed municipal bonds and variable-rate refunding bonds with a put option accrue considerable savings in a volatile market. Moreover, no restrictions exist to prevent an issuer from borrowing at a tax-exempt floating rate and investing the proceeds at a tax-exempt fixed rate. The use of rate-sensitive instruments in both general obligation and advance refunding situations provided governments a way to absorb the uncertainty, even shock, of interest rate increases to unusually high levels. However, giving debt instruments rate sensitivity also made them more competitive and helped attract new bond buyers. Increasing the demand for debt instruments, moreover, had unique potential to absorb uncertainty by leveling or stabilizing demand.

19. *Leveling demand through new bond buyers.* One major source of variation that state and local governments had to absorb in the last decade lay in changes in demand due to changes in the types of bondholders. In fact, as banks and insurance companies stopped buying bonds due to tax law changes and their own low profits, individuals and households started. Significant new forms of securities have emerged to take advantage of these new buyers, such as unit trusts, zero-coupon bonds, bonds with warrants, and book-entry procedures for accounting for bond interest and principal payments as well as ownership.

Unit trusts. Fixed, diversified portfolios of long-term municipal bonds have entered the market to appeal to individual investors and households. One marketer describes their appeal as aimed to "income oriented people in their mid-50's or older. They wall into the 40 or 50 percent top income tax brackets. They want a tax-free stream of income, and a packaged product appeals to them" (Vartan, 1985). Unit trusts come in several forms. For instance, they may carry insurance. They may allow a double (or even triple) tax exemption because the trusts hold same-state securities and sell to investors in that state.

Mutual funds. Both closed-end funds, operating like unit trusts, and open-end funds now exist to pass on tax-exempt income to individual investors. The basic difference between mutual funds and unit trusts is the funds' management, or its ability to buy and sell bonds for the portfolio to continually achieve higher returns, rather than merely buying a portfolio one time and holding it to maturity. Several different types of funds have emerged to expand the municipal market. Closed-end funds have a finite size; open-end funds may expand as demand changes. Some of both are oriented to short-term municipals, others to longer term municipals oriented toward safety, yield, or both.

Zero-coupon bonds. Zero-coupon bonds are debt instruments sold at significant discounts from their face values with no annual interest payments. Over the life of the bond, the increased value is the original discount offering price compounded semiannually at the original yield. The zeroes are aimed at individual investors facing volatility in the economy. Specifically, the investor can lock in the yield desired with a zero-coupon bond, ultimately benefiting if prevailing interest rates fall. The investor, nevertheless, gambles. If prevailing interest rates rise above the zero's yield, the zero-coupon bond falls in price.

Bonds with warrants. A bond with a warrant attached allows the purchase of additional bonds. The entitlement to purchase additional bonds carries what amounts to a "reverse call" option on the security. If prices on bonds rise (when interest rates fall), the reverse call would have a high value, and this potential entices bondbuyers.

Book entry of bond certificates. Like the Federal Reserve System's electronic book-entry system for U.S. Treasury and other federal agency securities, the law now allows municipals issuers to alleviate the paperwork involved in offering genuine engraved bond certificates to bondholders. The paperless system registers all long-term securities, as federal law now mandates, and utilizes electronic transfer of funds (Petersen and Buckley, 1983). Such a book-entry system, offered by many bank trust departments, establishes the ownership and records the trades in new issues. An audit trail for tax purposes, as well as a record of interest coupon and principal payment, now exists. The initial test and evidence of bond buyer enthusiasm for book entry (and the lack of resistance to having anything other than the genuine article in hand) came with the state of Utah's successful sale of a $10 million general obligation issue in July 1984. The state of Massachusetts sold $140 million a month later using a similar book-entry system.

REFERENCES

Academy of State and Local Government. Becker, S. (1984). *Intergovern. Perspect., 10* (2): 20.
Adams, C. T. (1988). *The Politics of Capital Investment: The Case of Philadelphia*, Temple University Press, Philadelphia.
Aronson, J. R. and Schwartz, E. (1987). *Management Policies in Local Government Finance* (J. R. Aronson and E. Schwartz, eds.), International City Management Association, Washington, D.C., pp. 400–421.
Bayless, P. (1985). *Institut. Invest., 19* (January): pp. 253–254.
Beal, F. and Hollander, E. (1979). *The Practice of Local Government Planning* (F. S. So, et al., eds.), International City Management Association, Washington, D.C., pp. 153–182.
Bennett, J. T. and DiLorenzo, T. (1983). *Underground Government: The Off-Budget Public Sector*, Cato Institute, Washington, D.C.
The Bond Buyer (1983). (August 1): p. 11.
Bozeman, J. L. (1984). *Pub. Budgeting and Finance, 4*(3): 18–30.
Bryson, J. M. and Roering, W. D. (1988). *Pub. Admin. Rev., 48*: 995–1004.
Castells, M. (1977). *The Urban Question: A Marxist Approach*, MIT Press, Cambridge, Mass.
Chandler, A. D. (1962). *Strategy and Structure: Chapters in the History of the American Industrial Enterprise.* MIT Press, Cambridge, Mass.
Clausewitz, C. B. (1956). *On War*, Vol. 1 (trans. J. J. Graham), Barnes and Noble, New York.
Cohen, M. D. and March, J. G. (1986). *Leadership and Ambiguity: The American College President*, 2d ed., Harvard Business School Press, Cambridge, Mass.
Cohen, M. D., March, J. G., and Olsen, J. P. (1972). *Admin. Sci. Q., 17*(1): 1–25.
Crecine, J. P. (1969). *Government Problem Solving*, Rand McNally, Chicago.
Daft, R. L. and Weick, K. L. (1984). *Acad. of Manag. Rev., 9*: 284–295.
Downs, A. (1967). *Inside Bureaucracy*, Little Brown, Boston.
Downs, A. (1957). *An Economic Theory of Democracy*, Harper & Bros., New York.
Dunn, W. N. (1981). *Public Policy Analysis*, Prentice-Hall, Englewood Cliffs, N.J.
Eisenhardt, K. M. (1989). *Acad. Mgt. Rev., 14*(1): 57–74.
Evered, R. (1983). So what is strategy? *Long Range Planning, 16*(3): 57–72.
Forbes, R. W. and Petersen, J. E. (1983). *Creative Capital Financing for State and Local Governments.* (J. E. Petersen and W. C. Hough, eds.), Municipal Finance Officers Association, Chicago.
Freeman, R. E. (1984). *Strategic Management: A Stakeholder Approach*, Pittman, Boston.
Gilbert, D. R. Jr., et al. (1988). *A Logic for Strategy*, Ballinger, Cambridge, Mass.
Gordon, L. A. and Pinches, G. E. (1984). *Improving Capital Budgeting: A Decision Support System Approach*, Addison-Wesley, Reading, Mass.
Harvey, D. (1973). *Social Justice and the City*, Johns Hopkins University Press, Baltimore.
Harvey, D. (1982). *The Limits to Capital*, University of Chicago Press, Chicago.
Henriques, D. (1982). *The Machinery of Greed: The Abuse of Public Authorities and What to Do about It*, Princeton University Press, Princeton, N.J.
Hickson, D. J., Hinings, D. R., Lee, C. A., Schneck, R. E., and Pennings, J. M. (1971). *Admin. Sci. Q., 16*: 216–229.
Hildreth, W. B. (1986). "Strategies of Municipal Debt Issuers," paper presented at the National Conference of the American Society for Public Administration, Anaheim, Calif.
Hildreth, W. B. (1987). *Pub. Admin. Q., 11*(3): 314–341.
Jones, (1981).
Kaldor, N. (1939). *Econ. J.,* (September): 549–552.

Kaufman, H. (1960). *The Forest Ranger: A Study in Administrative Behavior*. Johns Hopkins University Press, Baltimore.

Key, V. O. (1940). *Am. Pol. Sci. Rev.*, *34*(6): 1137–1144.

Kingdon, J. W. (1984). *Agendas, Alternatives and Public Policies*, Little Brown, Boston.

Klapper, B. (1980). *Standard and Poor's Perspective*, (September 17): 1.

Klay, W. E. (1985). *Internat. J. Pub. Admin.*, *7*(3): 241–265.

Leigland, J. and Lamb, R. (1986). *WPP$$: Who Is to blame for the WPPSS Disaster*, Ballinger, Cambridge, Mass.

Lineberry, R. (1977). *Equality and Urban Services*, Sage, Beverly Hills, CA.

Long, N. (1958). *Am. Pol. Sci. Rev.*, *64*: 251–261.

Luttwak, E. N. (1987). *Strategy: The Logic of War and Peace*, Belknap Press, Harvard University Press, Cambridge, Mass.

MacMillan, I. (1978). *Strategy Formulation: Political Concepts*, West Publishing, St. Paul, Minn.

MacMillan, I. (1983). *Advances in Strat. Mgt.*, *1*: 61–82.

March, J. G. and Olsen, J. P. (1989). *Rediscovering Institutions: The Organizational Bias of Politics*, Basic Books, New York.

Miller, G. J. (1985). *Internat. J. Pub. Admin.*, *7*(4): 451–495.

Miller, G. J. (1992). Capital investment and budgeting. In J. Rabin (ed.) *Handbook of Public Budgeting*. Marcel Dekker, New York: 419–502.

Miller, G. J., Rabin, J., and Hildreth, W. B. (1987). *Pub. Product. Rev.*, *43*: 81–96.

Mintzberg, H. and McHugh, A. (1985). *Admin. Sci. Q.*, *30*: 160–197.

Moak, L. L. and Hillhouse, A. M. (1975). *Concepts and Practices in Local Government Finance*, Municipal Finance Officers Association, Chicago.

Moak, L. L. and Killian, K. W. (1964). *A Manual of Suggested Practice for the Preparation and Adoption of Capital Programs and Capital Budgets by Local Governments*, Municipal Finance Officers Association, Chicago.

Neuhauser, P. E. (1988). *Tribal Warfare in Organizations: Turning Tribal Conflict Into Negotiated Peace*, Ballinger, Cambridge, Mass.

O'Toole, (1985).

Pagano, M. A. and Moore, R. T. (1985). *Cities and Fiscal Choices: A New Model of Urban Public Investment*, Duke University Press, Durham, N.C.

Pareto, V. (1906). *Mannuala Economica Politica*, trans. (Ann S. Schweier and Alfred N. Page, eds.), A. M. Kelly, New York.

Patton, J. N. and Hempel, G. H. (1975). *Understanding the Market for State and Local Debt*, U.S. Advisory Commission on Intergovernmental Relations, Washington, D.C.

Peltzman, S. (1980). *J. Law and Econ.*, *23*: 209–287.

Petersen, J. E. and Buckley, M. P. (1983). *A Guide to Registered Municipal Securities*, Munic. Finance Officers Assoc., Washington, D.C.

Peterson, P. E. (1981). *City Limits*, University of Chicago Press, Chicago.

Pierce, L. D. (1971). *The Politics of Fiscal Policy Formation*, Goodyear, Pacific Palisades, Calif.

Porter, M. E. (1980). *Competitive Strategy: Techniques for Analyzing Industries and Competitors*, Free Press, New York.

Porter, M. E. (1985). *Competitive Advantage: Creating and Sustaining Superior Performance*, Free Press, New York.

Quinn, R. E. and Cameron, K. S. (1988). *Paradox and Transformation: Toward a Theory of Change in Organization and Management*, Ballinger Publishing Company, Cambridge, Mass.

Ramsey, (1897).

Rapoport, A. (1960). *Fights, Games and Debates*, University of Michigan Press, Ann Arbor.

Ring, P. S. and Perry, J. L. (1985). *Acad. of Manag. Rev.*, *10*(2): 276–286.

Sbragia, A. M. (1983). *The Municipal Money Chase: The Politics of Local Government Finance* (A. M. Sbragia, ed.),

Scott, M. (1969). *American City Planning since 1890*, University of California Press, Berkeley.

Schneider, M. (1989). *The Competitive City: The Political Economy of Suburbia*, University of Pittsburgh Press, Pittsburgh.

Selznick, P. (1957). *Leadership in Administration*, Row, Peterson, Evanston, Il.

Schultz, S. K. (1989). *Constructing Urban Culture: American Cities and City Planning 1800–1920*, Temple University Press, Philadelphia.

Shapiro, H. D. (1985). *Institut. Invest.*, *19*(May): 197–202.

Sloane, L. (1985). *New York Times*, (July 20): 32.

Smith, B. (1990). *Gov. Finance Rev.*, *6*(3): 22–24, 48.

Steiss, A. W. (1975). *Local Government Finance*, Lexington Books, Lexington, Mass.

Stiglitz, J. E. (1988). *Economics of the Public Sector*, 2d ed., Norton, New York.

Summers, H. G. Jr. (1987). "When Is a Bad Road Good? A review of *Strategy: The Logic of War and Peace by Edward N. Luttwak*," *New York Times Book Review*, Aug. 30: 22.

Swiss, James E. (1991). *Public Management Systems: Monitoring and Managing Government Performance*, Prentice-Hall, Englewood Cliffs, N.J.

Tiebout, C. M. (1956). *J. of Pol. Econ.*, *64*: 416–424.

U.S. Bureau of the Census (1980). *Number of Inhabitants*, PC80-1-A, Chapter A, Superintendent of Documents, U.S. Government Printing Office, Washington, D.C.

U.S. Bureau of the Census (1989).

U.S. General Accounting Office (1983).

Vartan V. G. (1985). Tax-exempt trusts flourish, *New York Times* (August 22): 31.

Vogt, A. J. (1975). *Pop. Gov.*, *41*: 12–13.

Vogt, A. J. (1977). *Capital Improvements Programming: A Handbook for Local Officials*, Institute of Government, University of North Carolina, Chapel Hill.

Vogt, A. J. and Cole, L. A. (1983). *A Guide to Municipal Leasing*. Municipal Finance Officers Association, Washington, D.C.

Wacht, R. F. (1987). *A New Approach to Capital Budgeting for City and County Governments*, 2d Ed., research monograph no. 87, Business Publishing Division, College of Business Administration, Georgia State University, Atlanta.

Wall Street Journal (1982). Cities getting part of profits for giving aid to developers. (September 29): 27.

Walsh, A. H. (1978). *The Public's Business: The Politics and Practices of Government Corporations*, MIT Press, Cambridge, Mass.

Walters, D. (1990). *MuniWeek*, Oct. 8: 29.

Wetzler, J. W. and Petersen, J. E. (1985). *Gov. Finance Rev.*, April: 7–10.

Wildavsky, A. (1988). *The New Politics of the Budgetary Process*. Scott, Forsman and Company, Glenview, Ill.

Wortman, M. (1979). *Strategic Management: A New View of Business Policy and Planning* (Dan E. Schendel and Charles W. Hofer, eds.), Little Brown, Boston.

Yacik, G. (1985). *The Bond Buyer* (May 28): 10.

Zald, M. N. (1970). *Organizational Change: The Political Economy of the YMCA*, University of Chicago Press, Chicago.

10

Strategic Planning and Capital Budgeting: A Primer

Arie Halachmi
Tennessee State University, Nashville, Tennessee, and Netherlands Interuniversity Institute of Government (NIG), University of Twente, Enschende, The Netherlands

Gerasimos A. Gianakis
Kent State University, Kent, Ohio

I. INTRODUCTION

Capital expenditures—that is, capital outlays for public improvements—are important in determining the direction and the degree of community development. Now more than ever decision makers find themselves facing conflicting demands for the use of scarce financial resources. Thus, they have to decide whether to extend infrastructure to a rapidly developing area, to rehabilitate infrastructure in older established neighborhoods, or to upgrade information technologies to be more efficient and effective in the delivery of its services (Robinson, 1991). Decisions about capital expenditures are made while putting together the capital budget. The capital budget itself is the current slice of a multiyear program of improvements, yet even though each capital expenditure involves sizable sums of public funds, all too often such expenditures are discussed as unrelated, individual items rather than integrated components of the total community structure (Levitan and Byrne, 1983:585).

Capital budgeting has to do with the key changes or improvements of a community's infrastructure, buildings, equipment, or the capacity to provide services. Such projects are financed through individual bond issues or other forms of borrowing. However, for lack of in-house expertise or the will or the ability to secure outside help, decisions about the financing of such projects are made sometimes without adequate consideration of their impact on present and future financial sources or the proper physical development of the community. The undesired consequences of poor capital budgeting decisions may affect not only future capital projects but the regular daily operations of government agencies. Public capital investment decisions ultimately influence private decisions to invest human, fiscal, and physical capital within a jurisdiction. The totality of these decisions determines economic growth and thus the revenue base for underwriting the operational budget of the jurisdiction.

The above is a common characteristic of budgeting practices at the state and local levels of government. However, it should be noted that capital budgeting is not treated as strategic planning in the fullest sense of the word at the federal level either. The U.S. General Accounting Office noted in 1981 that "the Federal Government has never had a Capital Budget in the sense of financing capital or investment-type programs separately from current expenditures (General Accounting Office, 1981:46). Capital budgeting at the national level is also a part of the economic stabilization function of the resource allocation process. For these reasons this chapter concentrates mainly on the typical state and local government capital investment process, with particular emphasis on the latter.

In the process of the research for this chapter we met with individuals involved in developing and consolidating the budget at the state and local level. They all suggested that the observation by Levitan and Byrne (1983:585) about the disjointed nature of the budgeting process is as true today as it was 10 years ago. It was also pointed out to us that with the growing dependency on contracting out and the creation of special "functional" districts (e.g., for transportation, health, or economic development) the situation is moving from bad to worse. Coordination and consolidation of budgetary decisions is almost impossible under these new trends because of the multiple players, each with the legal authority to mobilize and to use financial resources, even though each of these independent budgetary decisions affects the same (or segments of the same) population. Is this situation inevitable? Can governments approach such important matters in a more sensible and a more responsible way? The answer to the first question is no and the answer to the second is maybe. Making a coherent and consistent whole out of these independent and disjointed decisions may be feasible only if all the decision makers are willing to make the necessary effort to commit resources and some of their time to strategic analysis and planning.

The purpose of this chapter is to illustrate how strategic planning may be conducive to more responsible and sensible capital budgeting. Our discussion will help the reader see why and when the political context of budgeting decisions may constrain the effectiveness of strategic planning. The chapter starts with a brief discussion of some key terms followed by a presentation of a simple model of strategic planning. It goes on to discuss some important aspects of capital budgeting with cross-references to concepts and elements of strategic planning and management and special attention to possible implications for local governments. The chapter concludes with a look at some cases and a brief assessment of the possible relationship between an effort to integrate strategic planing and capital budgeting and the experience with the introduction of the planning programming budgeting system (PPBS).

II. OVERCOMING THE "STRATEGIC" TERMINOLOGY BARRIER

What is a strategy? What is strategic analysis or strategic planning? What is strategic management? These terms are related but are not synonymous. However, some managers use one of these terms to mean any one of the other terms. For example, when managers say "our strategy is" or "our strategic plan calls for" or "on the basis of a strategic analysis" they may mean to say the same thing or they may mean to imply different things. When it comes to academic writing the situation is not much better. According to Bloom (1986:258) "a problem with strategic planning literature is the lack of uniformity in terminology. What is described in one set of terms in one article may be described differently in another." Without a clear understanding of the context and the nature of the discussion a listener may be easily confused. The inconsistent use of these terms is in stark contrast to the precise use of the terminology of capital budgeting. Thus, the purpose of the following discussion is to clarify some of the concepts behind each of the terms because often they are used interchangeably.

A strategy is "a pattern of actions and resource allocations designed to achieve the goals of the organization" (Bateman and Zethaml, 1993:142). Quinn (1992:5) suggests that

> a strategy is the pattern or plan that integrates an organization's major goals, policies and action sequences into a cohesive whole. A well strategy helps to marshall and allocate an organization's resources into unique and viable posture based on its relative internal competencies and shortcomings, anticipated changes in the environment and contingent moves by intelligent opponents.

According to Mintzberg (1992) a strategy is a plan, a pattern, a ploy, a position, or a perspective. To Nutt and Backoff (1992:59) a strategy provides a focus ("which helps to coordinate activity toward an agreed upon direction"); it provides consistency (as it "indicates what is wanted, which concentrates effort and satisfies peoples need for order and predictability in their affairs"); and it provides a purpose (since it "not only directs effort but gives meaning to both organizational members and outsiders").

Strategic analysis involves the collection and analysis of data in an effort to generate the necessary intelligence for assessing the organization's options in terms of its strengths and weaknesses, the opportunities it may exploit, and the threats it needs to avoid. Strategic analysis involves a study of the past, present situations, emerging trends, and alternative scenarios of the future. The purpose of strategic analysis is to establish the parameters for strategic choices.

Bryson defines strategic planning as "a disciplined effort to produce fundamental decisions and actions shaping the nature and direction of an organization's (or other entity's) activity within legal bounds" (Bryson, 1993:12). Rider (1993:27) suggests that "the strategic plan forms a basis for broad regulations governing activity centers. These regulations may take the form of performance standards which allows the private sector greater discretion when making investment decisions." For our purposes here it is important to note that the difference between strategic and tactical planning seems to correspond in part to the difference between capital and operational budgeting, namely, an emphasis on long- versus short-range considerations and frames of reference (Quinn, 1992:6). Strategic planning, like capital budgeting, is involved with (relatively speaking) long-range considerations of benefits and costs. Tactical planning uses a narrower framework that characterizes in many cases the second half of the annual budgeting process. As pointed out by Levitan and Byrne (1983:585), "municipal budgets ordinarily are restricted to one year by law, whereas the effects of expenditures for new improvements on the finances of a municipality will extend greatly over a number of years and the projects themselves will have a long term effect on the physical development of the community."

The capital improvement program (CIP), as will be explained below must evolve through a process that resembles strategic analysis and the strategic planning process. Robinson (1991:66) defines CIP as a multiyear plan that forecasts spending for all anticipated capital projects. As such it addresses both repair and replacement of existing infrastructure as well as the development of new facilities to accommodate future growth. She claims that an effective CIP consists of both an administrative process to identify the location, scale, and timing of needed capital projects and a fiscal plan to provide for the funding of those projects linking a jurisdiction's planning and budgeting functions (Robinson, 1991:66). According to Levitan and Byrne (1983:587) "the program [i.e., the CIP] is to be so constructed that, implicitly, it will consider the growth and the development of the community in toto as well as anticipate the financial repercussions involved." Though using the vernacular of another professional group Levitan and Byrne seem to follow many of the basic tenets of strategic planning.

McCaffery (1989) suggests that the technical tools of strategic planning are found in the environmental scanning process of strategic management, in which various organizational, economic, and political factors are considered, but they are only part of a process that seeks to provide coalignment of internal and external variables of the agency and its environment. According to Nutt and Backoff (1992:3), "strategic management is applied by leaders to align an organization's direction with the organization's aim. This alignment takes place when needed changes in clients or customers, services, procedures, policies and the like are devised and put into practice." The CIP, in comparison, is "a process of sound municipal administration which links the 'physical' and/or capital needs of a municipality with its ability to pay for these needs" (Levitan and Byrne, 1983:587).

Strategic management, in the broadest sense, involves the launching, monitoring, and involvement in the strategic analysis effort, the development of the strategic plan, and the implementation and revision of the plan as time goes on. According to Halachmi (1992:551), strategic management is an effort to capitalize on the strengths of the organization by taking advantage of favorable conditions inside or outside the organization. It involves minimization of cost by making operations consistent and predictable and by avoiding challenges to structure and organizational culture. According to Hatten and Hatten (1987:1) "strategic management is the process by which organizations *formulates objectives* and is managed to achieve them" (emphasis added). Bozeman (1983:3) uses a narrower perspective and suggests that strategic management "involves the development of contingent managerial strategies that can effectively respond to changeable policies and priorities." As will be shown below, CIP may seem at first sight as if it is inconsistent with Bozeman's view of strategic management, although it is in line with the other views we quoted above. This impression is misleading, however. As noted by Levitan and Byrne (1983:587) the CIP "process must be able to absorb political upheavals, organizational changes, and the evolving priorities of the community." In other words, the CIP also involves the preparations for dealing with different contingencies.

As can be seen from the above there are different interpretations of the term *strategy*. At this time there is no one definition of strategy that is acceptable to all, and the chances for some consensus in the near future are slim. For our purposes, it is important to note two points of controversy: one about the relationship between strategy and organizational goals or mission and the other about the origin, or the way strategies evolve. Although beyond the scope of this chapter, it should be noted that the controversy about each of the two points is not independent from the position some writers take about the other.

As pointed out in an earlier paper (Halachmi, 1986) there are two views of the relationships between strategy and the organizational mission (Eadie, 1983:448). The first looks at strategy as a plan of action that is being derived from a predetermined mission statement or organizational goals (Kovach and Mandell, 1990). The strategy is the mean, the blueprint for action, by which managers hope to take advantage of emerging opportunities and for avoiding threats to the organization or to its ability to carry out its mission. Bozeman's (1983) definition of strategic management, as listed above, reflects this approach. A second approach assumes that the scanning of the environment for opportunities and threats to the organization, independently of any existing mission statement, comes first. The selection of a mission statement and objectives results from the effort to take advantage of organizational strength and to minimize the significance of possible weaknesses.

According to this second perspective, which is reflected in the above definition of strategic management by Hatten and Hatten (1987:1), following the strategic analysis the organization may find itself pursuing new objectives. The same approach is conveyed by Preble's (1983) comparison of goal setting in the public and private sectors. According to Preble (1982:140)

> a specific step in most strategic planning systems is that of goals setting. Goal setting as part of planning in the private sector is carried out by a few planners and top executives within the firm. Decisions concerning goals in the public sector are largely a political process involving various branches of government, public interest group, political parties and constituents.

For those following the notion that goals exist before the strategic planing process begins, the definition of the desired results stays untouched and the search is on for a promising plan of action—a strategy—for reaching them. In the second case, where the strategic planning process is assumed to start with a clean slate, the capabilities and limitations of the organization are defined in the context of likely scenarios about the future. These scenarios are derived from the use of alternative assumptions about the ways the existing environment and the organization are likely to evolve or change in the future. Ultimately the effort is to find the best way of capitalizing on any likely development by anticipating it and being ready for it. According to Quinn (1988:3), the strategic decisions that result from strategic analysis

- Intimately shape the true goals of the enterprise
- Help delineate broad limits of operations
- Delineate both the resources of the enterprise that will be accessible for its tasks and the principle pattern in which these resources will be allocated
- Determine the effectiveness of the enterprise—whether its major thrusts are in the right directions given its resources potential—rather than whether individual tasks are performed efficiently

As we see it, this broader vision of strategic planning (i.e., a vision that assumes that mission statements and the definitions of objectives and goals are products of strategic analysis) is consistent with the garbage can model (Cohen et al., 1972) of decision making. The selection of a strategy according to this vision is the matching of problems with promising courses of actions to resolve them. As will be pointed out later on, such a perspective is very relevant to the capital budgeting process in general and to the development of the CIP in particular. The reason is that capital budgeting is an articulation in monetary terms of an effort to deal with a concrete problem (or to take advantage of a specific situation) that cannot be handled within the regular (i.e, the operational) budget.

The second controversy involves a question about the way a strategy evolves: is the organizational strategy the deliberate and identifiable single result of a rational planning process? Mintzberg (1992:14) contends that the traditional approach incorrectly assumed so. He claims that strategy evolves as a pattern in a stream of decisions or actions. That pattern is a product both of whatever aspects of an organization's intended (planned) strategy are actually realized and of its emergent (unplanned) strategy. Looked upon in this way the emergent strategies may be more appropriate than the organization's intended strategy since they represent a more concrete reaction to concrete situations. A strategy in the sense of "a plan," Mintzberg (1992:14) claims, can go unrealized while patterns may appear without preconceptions: "For a strategy to be truly deliberate—that is, for a pattern to have been intended exactly as realized—would seem to be a tall order" (Mintzberg, 1992:14).

Some students of management may be aware of the view that organizational strategy evolves over time and outside the structured and institutionalized strategic planning process that can be depicted by a clear flowchart. Mintzberg's claim tarnishes the luster of strategic planning as the desired proactive management style. In fact, it replaces it by the less recommended reactive approach that implies that the strategy can be described and defined only in retrospect.

For the general case of strategic management the significance of this possible switch from proactive to a reactive management posture should not be blown out of proportion; after all, it was always recognized that all plans are blueprints for changes. Planners and managers know that the planning process can never generate the insights they can get from involvement in the implementation of the plan. Since it is unwise to ignore such insights or the opportunity to modify the plan in response to any unforseen developments within the organization or in the environment, all plans are subject to change. Yet, for our purposes it should be noted that in the case of capital budgeting the implications of changes in the plan may be different from the ones in the general case.

Capital budgets, as will be shown below, represent choices and priorities not only within but among discrete categories of services or problems. An item in the capital budget reflects not only a choice between a library and a school but among these two and the building of an airport, replacement of a existing bridge, or the development of a new landfill. Modification of the plan, as a result of insight gained during the implementation and in response to unforeseen circumstances, changes the stream of benefits and costs over the lifetime of a given project, and may be enough to change its attractiveness or priority relative to those of the other projects that were not funded. Since such a prospect may reopen the initial decision for questions, there is a risk that administrators will continue to implement the original plan without the necessary modifications to avoid the risk of such questions about the wisdom of the initial decision. The overconstruction of power stations in the late 1970s by the Tennessee Valley Authority or the completion of the Tallico Dam in Tennessee by the Army Corps of Engineers following lengthy and fierce court battles about the endangered snail darter are cases in point. In either case, the sunk cost was as political as it was economic. The reluctance to modify the plan resulted in both cases in a negative return on the investment.

Capital budgeting, when done right, can be an important instrument of strategic management because it, too, is capable of providing a focus, consistency, and a purpose. These three are the qualities of strategy as defined by Nutt and Backoff (1992:59). Strategic management is a process. It involves an assessment of organizational capabilities and shortcomings in relation to evolving trends in the environment for the purpose of capitalizing on the former and exploiting the latter. Depending on the position one takes concerning the nature of strategy, strategic management involves the development or the implementation of the strategy. When the organization is capable of taking advantage of environmental conditions and using existing capacity to improve on past performance, strategic management means exploiting an organizational strength. When the organization must roll back its operations because it lacks the capacity to deal with adverse environmental conditions it has a weakness. In this case strategic management means averting a threat or a risk to the organization or to its mission.

The strategic manager uses a variety of administrative means to collect data that may indicate an evolving environmental trend, an organizational strength, or a weakness. The manager needs to identify principles of action that will allow the organization to take advantage of opportunities and to maintain control over the organizational response to changing environmental conditions. When the manager has little control over the selection of the proper response to changing environmental conditions, the organization has a greater weakness (or is facing a greater threat) than the organization whose administrator can be choosy.

To retain control over the organizational response to emerging environmental trends, either for taking advantage of a strength or to avoid a threat because of a weakness, the manager has to maximize the number of operational options open to him. For the same reason, the manager has to minimize, if not avoid, commitments that may restrict the choice of an organizational response to changing environmental conditions. In order to get the various components of the organization to work in tandem, the strategic managers must have effective means for communicating to all involved where the organization is heading and how it intends to go there. Annual and multiyear operational budgets may offer the manager an effective tool for planning and retaining control over the organization's capacity to respond to changing conditions. However, as pointed out by Halachmi and Boydston (1991), the regular budget is not a good tool for strategic management. It is hypothesized here that the capital budget may prove to be a better means for this purpose for at least two reasons. First, it is better because the information it contains (e.g., about building, major purchasing, or upgrading and renovations) is more tangible and meaningful to most employees than the aggregate numbers concerning various categories of operational expenses. Second, once it is adopted, it should not change too often or in a radical ways.

Hill and Jones (1992) suggest that strategy implementation requires achieving a fit among the organization strategy, structure, and controls. While annual and multiyear budgets for operations are expected to facilitate and to provide such a fit, capital budgeting has to do with the decision about how to achieve and retain said fit over time. For that reason, while annual and multiyear budgets can accommodate emergent strategies, they may be resistant to these forces of change. The implication is that capital budgeting favors and is favored by those who look at budgeting as a proactive rational planning process that attempts to reduce ambiguity about the purpose and direction of organizational efforts.

III.   A SIMPLE MODEL OF STRATEGIC PLANNING

The purpose of strategic planning is to produce both a strategy and a tentative blueprint for carrying it out. An ideal process of strategic planning entails several iterations. It involves investigation (i.e., a deliberate effort to formulate a strategy following the recognition of the need for it), and data collection (about past performance, present activities and strategies, present missions or goals, etc.; emerging/projected trends; and expectations of internal and external stakeholders), through analysis of the data (which may include comparisons with benchmarks and other information about the performance of related entities), selection of the most promising strategy and a tentative sequence of activities to carry it out, and last but not least, an ongoing evaluation to ascertain the validity of the strategy and the strategic plan as a whole.

As the planning effort moves forward, deliberate efforts should be made to examine and scrutinize the implications and the adequacy of earlier assumptions. With the progress of the planning process, better knowledge and insights are gained about the expectations of internal and external stakeholders, legal matters, emerging trends, impending problems or future needs, and the implications of alternative courses of action. The learning benefits from the planning process should be used to improve the plan as soon as they become available. The following discussion describes and explains the seven steps of Halachmi's simple model of strategic planning (Halachmi, 1992).

A.   Developing the Meta Plan

The first step in the planning process involves a general investigation of the internal and external environments of the agency. The purpose of the investigation is to establish the boundaries of the relevant environments and the existence of a genuine need for developing a strategic plan. Defining or redefining the relevant boundaries may in turn change the prospect that there is a need to start a strategic planning process. For example, determining that the boundaries of the relevant environment coincide with the city limits or the county limits may lead to a different decision about the need for strategic planning than a determination that the boundaries coincide with the state line or a region that includes parts of several states.

In preparation for the strategic planning process public administrators must determine that (1) there is a need for one, and (2) the likely benefits (in political or economic terms) outweigh the cost. Only following that determination should managers move on to make the second set of decisions about the planning process. This second set of decisions will influence the nature and value of the strategic analysis, which establishes the key parameters for the planning process. Some of the decisions that make up this set include the following:

- What issues, considerations, organizations, constraints, groups, or individuals should be included in the strategic analysis and what should be left out?
- What is an adequate time frame for making and using projections in the plan?
- What is within the domain of the agency (i.e., what is legitimately within its authority, technical/technological capacity, or sphere of influence), and what should be considered to be outside of it and left for other levels of government or other public or private entities?
- What forces exist in the agency's immediate (i.e., operating) environment and what forces shape this environment by influencing the general environment?

Dror (1968) stresses the need to establish a clear framework for action that is commensurate with the authority and resources of the agency. He uses the term cutoff points or horizon to delineate time, territory, and spheres of social activity beyond which the effect of a policy, or in our case a strategy or a capital budget, can be ignored. One way of arriving at the cutoff horizon is by "stakeholder analysis" (Freeman, 1984).

A preliminary stakeholder analysis consists of several steps. First, it involves the identification of groups and individuals within and outside the organization with a stake in the status quo. Second, it calls for the verification of the reasons or forces that may bring these individuals and groups to form or join a coalition to support the status quo. Next, the analysis requires the identification of issues that are important in the present and those that will become important within 5 to 10 years. Then, the potential influence and interest of each stakeholder in issues of importance, either in the present or in the future, must be estimated. Those coalitions, groups, or individuals that do not seem to have a direct or a long-term stake in what the agency is doing or in issues that are important to the agency may be excluded from the analysis. The same goes for issues that are not salient on the agenda of any important stakeholder.

A cutoff horizon can reduce the strategic planning effort to a manageable task. However, this benefit is not without the risk of ignoring some important issues, groups, or individuals. Some of the risk results from the fact that groups and individuals may relate to a given issue in more than one capacity (Freeman, 1984). It is not easy to estimate whether a group or an individual is consistent in its reactions to a given issue as its capacity or involvement changes. For example, employees of local courts may have various reactions toward a new tax for paying the bonds that allow the city to improve its waterfront or parks to attract corporate offices that are looking to relocate. Some of these employees may react as taxpayers. They will not support a strategic plan or a specific capital project because they fail to see the indirect connection between the plan and the strength of the tax base that influences their job security and standard of living. They may perceive the whole thing in their capacity as taxpayers rather than as city employees or parents and resent an increase in their property tax when their earning are not likely to change. A second subgroup may support the idea but would prefer to see an increase in the sales tax or in user fees as the method for financing the improvement. A third group, which consists mainly of young parents, may support the idea provided that it is done after the city fixes the woes of its school system. In other words, as employees of the city courts are asked to take a position about the pending projects some may vote one way on a given proposition during the general election and differently when it comes to the position their union or the PTA should take about it. A discussion of the reason for this inconsistent behavior is beyond the scope of this chapter. However, for our purposes the implication is clear; in order to secure the approval of a plan, the strategic managers must understand what makes up and what it takes to put together the winning coalition at that given time.

During the meta stage the organization should make every effort to reduce the possible consequences of overlooking the interest of any significant stakeholder. One way of doing it is to request one of the professionals (preferably an outsider) to challenge the assumptions and considerations that were used to frame the boundary of the analysis. Such examinations should be woven into the planning effort itself as part of the planned iterations. The strategic plan may also include set intervals for reevaluation of the said assumptions during the implementation stage. Such examinations may coincide with the development or review of the proposed operational and capital budgets for subsequent years.

The purpose of the investigation is to establish the backdrop and the framework for the strategic planning process. Even though it is usually limited in scope it should give the individual(s) in charge of designing the planning process some insight into the issues that should be dealt with during the planning effort. In other words, the meta planning phase is the time when the organization sorts the wheat from the chaff by determining what constitutes a strategic issue and what does not. The importance of the investigation for strategic issue diagnosis is that it delimit and constrain subsequent information collection, evaluation, and choice (Dutton et al., 1989).

Bryson (1988) suggests that "identifying strategic issues is the heart of the strategic planning process." He points out that the purpose of this step is to identify the fundamental policy choices facing the organization (Bryson, 1988:139). The model that is presented in this chapter uses a different approach to avoid some of the difficulties that were identified by Bryson. The effort to identify strategic issues is an attempt to define the forces that will shape a given environment and influence the freedom of action of a whole government or one of its subunits. The model assumes that only after a force field analysis has been completed may the agency be in a position to identify "fundamental policy choices." Using this approach, which allows for redefinition of the force field or any of its elements, the model creates an analytical framework conducive to an orderly development of the strategic planning process.

Our model makes two important assumptions. First, it assumes that the effort to determine what forces are going to affect the agency is going to be less trying for the participants if the agency is divorced from the effort to select a course of action for dealing with such forces. Second, the model assumes that participants in the planning process are more likely to cooperate if the basic blueprint, which contains a tentative and preliminary inventory of critical issues, is produced by the coordinator of the planning process instead of by any one of them. Knowing that the inventory can and is likely to be revised as the planning process progresses and not having to defend any position before the beginning of the process can induce cooperation. In other words, by developing a working paper before the beginning of the planning process, the coordinator of the process can allow the participants to question and research the issues without attacking or putting anybody on the defense.

The investigation is part of the meta planning phase because its results should influence the scope, timetable and organization of the planning process. To use an analogy, the investigation during the meta phase of the planning process corresponds to the work of a grand jury. The products of the investigation establish the case for subsequent action. It provides the justification and framework for a more comprehensive effort of data collection and analysis.

The meta planning effort serves two purposes. First, it develops a preferred model for the proposed planning process. This model is a logical presentation of the different steps or analytical efforts and the sequence of activities that would lead to the development of the strategic plan. Its purpose is to help would-be participants to understand and anticipate the various stages of the process. The model should help participants see how each step of the process will lead to the next, and how and why each step forward requires a review of implications for earlier work. The second purpose of the meta phase is to estimate the necessary time and resources for completion of each step, control and coordination mechanisms for facilitating the process (e.g., a PERT network), and the apparatus for evaluating the quality of the strategic plan and the process for its development. In essence, the purpose of the meta phase is to provide the individual in charge of strategic planning with the necessary information to carry out the planning process and to evaluate it.

B.   Taking Stock

The second step of the strategic planning process involves a comprehensive and in-depth collection of data. With advances in information technology most of the effort may involve retrieval of information from sources inside and outside the organization. The convenience and the efficiency of such an approach should always be evaluated in each case. The reason for such an assessment is the likelihood of errors, noise, or built-in bias because the data in question were originally collected for other uses.

The purpose of the data collection is to take a snapshot of the relevant "reality"—the proper context for assessing the existing situation and alternative courses of action. To facilitate this step the leader of the planning effort should consult with prospective participants in the planning process or users of the strategic plan to define the set of questions that should guide the collection of data. The questions may be grouped into distinct categories, such as the following:

- What are the legal requirements, mandates, or constraints that must be observed by the government entity for which the plan is developed? What authority does it have? What is the scope of its discretion in exercising this authority? What other bureaus can influence or be influenced by what the agency is doing? What is the relationship between all of these and the evolving economic, political, and social trends?
- What is the relationship between past and present performance and the interest of various stakeholders? What is the common interest of coalitions, groups, or individual stakeholders in each policy arena? How strong is the interest of each member of such coalitions in what the agency is doing (or in how it does it)? What is the likelihood that any of them may change their stated position and join another coalition? What may cause such a change?
- What are the indicators of a popular desire to see a change in the formal definition of the agency's mission? What indicates a wish for a change in the agency's formal structure or administrative practices as established by the enabling legislation? What forces are seeking to affect interpretation of the law, informal practices, and the use of discretion?
- Using professional standards, what can be said about subcomponents of the involved government entity or elements of the program(s) under its jurisdiction? What are the horizontal and vertical interdependencies among subunits? What is the functional nature of these interdependencies (Wintrobe and Breton, 1986), and which ones are critical? Do top administrators, rank and file employees, preliminary service recipients, and other stakeholders recognize and agree on the existence of interdependencies?
- What is the reputation of the agency among legislators, the media, central staff units that regulate and determine the allocation of such resources as budgets or personnel, or groups other than the primary stakeholders?
- What are the expectations and preferences of top officials about such issues as: substantive results, use of resources, organizational structure, administrative practices, relationships with various stakeholders, new initiatives?
- What are the possible implications of changes in office and information technology given the political, social, and economic trends?
- When it comes to the services the agency provides to different publics, what are (and what should be) the relationships among such variables as capacity, quality, queuing, equality (equity), automation, staffing levels, client group awareness, multisite operation, use of vendors, user fees?

C. Strategic Analysis

The third step of the analysis involves a critical review of the answers to all the questions about the involved government entity and its operations, structure, the way it relates to the external environment in the present, and the way it should relate to it in the future. One of the important products of the third step of the strategic planning process is a list of alleged strengths and weaknesses. A strength is a virtue; for example, well-trained personnel or an experience the government entity may have that is useful for dealing with existing problems or projected conditions within or outside its organizational boundaries. A strength indicates a capacity to operate without the presence or the prospect of interference. A weakness is a deficiency. It indicates a potential threat to organizational capacity or the value of the goods or services it provides unless there is a change, inside or outside the agency. Low morale, burnout, poor image, inadequate facilities, lack of experience, or insufficient resources are common reasons for weakness among public agencies.

The disclosed strengths or weaknesses of a government entity provide clues about the desired direction for developing alternatives for action. A strength suggests where the organization may capitalize and take advantage of an opportunity. A weakness reveals the constraints on action and areas in which change is necessary to avoid deterioration. The exact definitions of what constitutes a strength or a weakness must be developed during this stage and requires direct input from top administrators as well as the rank and file. The reason is that what may constitute a weakness for one subunit may be a source of strength for another. For example, one chief of police may consider a public image of a trigger-happy police force as a helping factor because it contributes to deterrence. The head of another government agency may consider the police image as an obstacle to effective action by its own people because it reduces the trust and ability to communicate openly with minority groups about other critical issues.

D. Alternative Generation

The fourth step of the strategic planning process is identification (or generation) and comparative analysis of alternative courses of action. Using the strengths and weaknesses that were identified in the previous phase of the planning process as guidelines, the organization seeks ideas about what can be done, what should not be done, and the main arguments for and against each of these. In order to identify as many ideas and alternatives as possible, the meta plan for the strategic planning process may call for the simultaneous use of several independent efforts. Some of the techniques for generating ideas through mobilization of insights and different kinds of knowledge include the use of expert systems (Ashmore, 1989), focus groups (Morgan, 1988; Stewart and Shamdasani, 1990), brainstorming sessions (Moore, 1987), a Delphi or simulations, consultants, advisory groups, or electronic bulletin boards (BBS).

There are at least five reasons for the simultaneous use of several of these techniques. The first reason is to assure that no viable option is ignored. Yet it is important to remember that some of the above techniques are better than others when it comes to helping individuals with various levels of formal education or outside stakeholders to articulate insights, observations, or their expectations about the agency, its management, or programs. Second, the effort to establish an inventory of options can facilitate the collection of information and opinions so that the virtues and implications of each option are not over- or underestimated. Use of different techniques reduces the odds that an important issue that should be considered by the planners will be overlooked. The third reason is that simultaneous use of different techniques can speed up the process and prevent a stalemate. The fourth reason is that by use of alternative techniques and by involving different groups the organization increases the odds for overcoming cognitive deficiencies (Stubart, 1989; Haley and Stumpf, 1989). Such deficiencies can mar the initial identification of strategic factors and the development of the meta plan. The fifth reason is that the use of multiple techniques will allow the organization to involve more individuals. Broader participation increases the odds that important stakeholders will feel empowered and develop a sense of ownership in the strategic plan. Empowerment and a feeling of ownership may lead to commitment and greater effort by those involved to assure a successful implementation of the strategic plan. Reflecting on the experience in one hospital system Shultz (1991:10) offers the following observations:

> In an effort to more thoughtfully and fairly make choices among projects, the system adopted a progressive approach that involved employees and physicians in establishing capital expenditure priorities. The system wide six-month-long planning process required a real understanding of market needs as well as understanding of how best to respond to those needs and the financial implications of capital investment alternatives.

To the extent that this observation is accurate it suggests that participation is not only desired but feasible.

The various alternatives for interpreting the enabling legislation (the mission), the options for organizing the agency (the grand strategy), and possible administrative practices (functional strategies) should than be ranked on the basis of two considerations: first, the extent to which they take advantage of agency strengths and avoid its weakness; and second, the extent that they are in line with the preferences of important stakeholders. Ignoring either consideration may defeat the whole purpose of developing the strategic plan.

E. Strategic Choices

In the fifth step of the planning process the organization chooses one of the options for implementation. This includes commitments to achieve specific annual objectives, to follow particular functional strategies and policies, to institutionalize the strategy, and to establish control (Pearce and Robinson, 1985). In selecting an option for implementation the organization determines the following:

- What is the agency out to achieve?
- What will be done to achieve it?
- Who is responsible for each element of the program?
- What is the timetable for carrying out the plan?
- What resources are going to be used in the process?
- Where are these resources going to be obtained?
- How and when will the organization get the necessary resources?
- What will be done if there is a problem with any of the above?

F. Organization Leadership and Support

The implementation of any plan requires preparation. The purpose of this sixth step of the strategic planning process is to tie the necessary preparation to the planning process itself. Lack of resources or any other constraints on making the necessary preparations should be taken into consideration and influence the development of the plan.

Sometimes the preparation for implementing a strategic plan may call for special training (Gainer, 1989), purchasing of new services or equipment, modification of facilities, or rewriting of manuals. Some of the preparations may require a lead time. The gap between selection of a strategic plan and the beginning of the implementation process provides a fertile ground for rumors and other activities that may jeopardize the success of the plan. Therefore, even before preparing to implement the plan, the organization must embark on a campaign to educate all employees and other stakeholders about it and how the organization is going to prepare for it.

Managers should treat the implementation as an introduction of a planned change. They must be ready to provide leadership and to be willing to get involved in mobilizing support. According to Holden (1985), if strategic planning is to be a productive management function, support for it must exceed the resistance against it. It follows that in the absence of strategic leadership, the creation of an overall sense of purpose and direction that guides integrated strategy formulation and implementation (Shrivastava and Nachman, 1989; Westley and Mintzberg, 1989), or a sufficient level of support within the organization is unlikely, and the wisdom of engaging in strategic planning should be questioned.

G. Review and Evaluation

During the seventh step, the organization establishes milestones and a framework for monitoring and evaluating the implementation process. Establishing this framework in advance of implementation prevents the temptation to rationalize (or excuse) deviations from the plan. It helps the manager to identify such deviations and to scrutinize assumptions that were used for developing the plan.

The evaluation framework defines the quantitative and qualitative measures of input, process, and output of each subsystem of the agency. Classifying an administrative subunit as a revenue, cost, or responsibility center (Anthony and Young, 1988) allows the manager to compare expected and actual performance (i.e., the stream of benefits present and expected to be incurred and anticipated costs). Also, this stage allows the organization to trace the relative contribution(s) of each subunit to the benefits or the cost side with reference to its use (or generation) of resources.

IV. CAPITAL BUDGETING

This section describes the purpose, structure, and theory of the capital budget process. Selected research is examined in an effort to establish the potential of the capital budgeting process as a vehicle for implementing a strategic management capacity on the local government level. Finally, several case studies related to integrating capital budgeting and planning are reviewed.

A. The Capital Budgeting Decision-Making Process

Mikesell (1991) suggests that capital expenditures secure assets that are expected to last for several years; specifically, the items acquired continue to produce benefits beyond the accounting period in which they were purchased. According to Lyden and Lindenberg (1983:174), public sector capital projects have at least three distinct features that make them different from activities normally included in operating budgets. First, project construction and financing is multiyear in nature. Second, once facilities and equipment are constructed, purchased, or leased, they have a relatively long life. Third, the end products of such projects may be thought of in relatively simplistic terms as a form of capital good, which, when combined with operating expenses such as labor or materials, helps produce actual service. The treatment of capital budgeting by both Mikesell and Lyden and Lindenberg highlights the fact that the most significant characteristic of capital budgeting is the duration of the projects it will underwrite. This relative long duration has direct implications for the immediate and future impact on the community, and the kind of analysis that must be carried out before a project is approved for funding, as well as for selecting the proper mix of the financial instruments (e.g., short- and long-term borrowing, revenues produced by it, grants, and donations) that will pay for it. The operating budget is different. It is made up of line items that are classified as personnel, operating, and capital outlays. The last category includes capital items that have a relatively short design life, are expected to be replaced periodically, and have a moderate price tag relative to the resources of the jurisdiction ($1000 to $10,000 for a medium-sized city); a personal computer might fit this category. These capital expenditures are part of an individual department's overall operating budget, but limits are often placed on spending in this category and the department's operating capital expenditures may compete for funding directly with the capital requests of other departments.

A separate capital budget is prepared for capital expenditures that meet the following criteria:

1. The item has a relatively long useful life, usually a minimum of 10 to 15 years. This criterion may not be applicable to projects that make extensive use of the rapidly changing information technology.
2. The cost of the item is high, given the resources available to the jurisdiction.
3. The expenditure is nonrecurring.
4. The item constitutes a fixed asset.
5. The item is related to other government functions that the government entity must provide by law (Robinson, 1991:68).

In the case of a local authority an example of this level of capital expenditure is the construction of a civic center, jail, bridge, or wastewater treatment plant. Expenditures on these items are considered separately from the operating expenditures of any one department, although they are part of the annual budget and although any department may submit annual budget requests that call for capital expenditures. This category encompasses most of what is defined as the physical infrastructure of the local authority.

Funds for these large capital expenditures are often appropriated separately for the following stages of the project: land acquisition (if necessary), design, construction, and (less frequently) the inspection of the final product. The actual capital budget usually extends for only 1 year, but the projects may take several years to complete. It is now common practice for the jurisdiction to prepare a 5- or 6-year CIP document (Doss, 1987); the annual capital budget appropriation constitutes the first year of this program. The CIP thus consists of a series of the above stages for the range of selected projects scheduled over a 5- or 6-year period.

CIP projects are also segregated by funding source. Funding sources include: transfers from the general fund; general obligation bond issues; restricted revenue sources, such as the gasoline tax for road projects; revenue bond issues backed by user fees, enterprise fund charges, development impact fees, special assessments, or by special bondable revenues such as guaranteed intergovernmental transfers; and grants. Different stages of projects may be located in different funding areas, or a project might be eligible for funding from several sources. Projects identified in the "out years"—years 2 to 6—of the CIP may be transferred between funds on the basis of projected cash flow constraints.

Funding sources can generally be divided into "pay-as-you-go" sources, such as general fund transfers—often from reserves set aside for the project over several years—grants, and borrowed funds, which are repaid over the life of the capital asset. The former approach serves to ensure that there is a widely perceived need for the acquisition of the asset—although the availability of grant funds in a specific area can distort perceptions of local needs—while the latter entails interest payments and administrative costs in addition to the cost of the asset. However, the borrowing option better serves the "benefits principal" of allocating the burden of funding public services; that is, those who benefit from the asset over its life span pay its cost by providing the funds to retire the debt that financed its acquisition. This is the "intergenerational equity" criterion.

Additional reasons for employing a separate budget for the acquisition of costly capital assets include the following:

1. Capital asset acquisitions have significant financial and service ramifications; separate considerations help decision makers to focus their attention in order to avoid mistakes, and allow for the application of special analytical techniques, such as present value calculations and cost-benefit analysis.
2. Separate accounting of capital revenues and expenditures serves to smooth out operating outlays; costly, nonrecurring capital expenditures would make operating budget outlays "lumpy" and erratic over time.
3. Capital budgets help to stabilize property tax rates; for general obligation bond rates may be increased to cover debt service only rather than to cover the entire cost of a capital asset, and this enhances the political feasibility of large projects.

The separation of operating and capital budgets may contribute to better scrutiny of each individual budget proposal by managers, the staff of the central budget office, and legislative bodies. However, as noted by Lyden and Lindenberg (1983), this separation is not without its pitfalls. As they see it "the conceptual separation of capital and operation budgets has contributed to the separate design, negotiation, implementation, and monitoring of capital and operating activities that are vitally interrelated." Thus they caution that "treating operating and capital budgeting decisions separately may result in failure to consider the implications that one set of decisions has on the other" (Lyden and Lindenberg, 1983:174).

The capital budget serves as a tool for managing financial resources; Robinson (1991:67) characterizes it as the "linchpin of financial management for local governments." For Robinson, the CIP links planning and budgeting, and through the former, relates the latter to the jurisdiction's comprehensive land-use plan. She suggests that "[i]f a community has developed a strategic plan, it will likely be implemented through the capital improvement plan" (Robinson, 1991:67). However, this assumes several things: first, that participants in the capital project selection process begin by enunciating community goals and objectives; second, that they are fully cognizant of existing goals and objectives; and third, that they consider these goals and objectives before selecting new projects for the CIP. The existence of a planning mechanism—even in a process with an extended planning horizon and a history of encouraging the use of analytical techniques— does not guarantee that such planning will occur. In the development of the operating budget, planning and budgeting are often antithetical processes (Schick, 1966), and the capital budgeting process can be subject to the same political pressures and compromises.

Steiss (1985) contends that the CIP development process *must* begin with the identification of guiding goals and objectives. However, these are often familiar community goals reflecting abstract values and exhorting decision makers to "do good." The CIP process often involves sophisticated financial analyses and can be quite technical in nature; yet traditionally it has been very open to community participation. This openness is part of the political nature of goal setting in the public sector (Preble, 1983). This complex process is used not only to define goals but to forge the broad political consensus that is often required in order to secure financing. For example, general obligation issues require a referendum. For the same reason goals are likely to be defined loosely, following some sort of stakeholder analysis, to preempt potential political conflict during the public hearing. The articulation of conflicting interests and opinions at early stages of the planning process may undermine the broad-based support that is needed to secure the approval of the plan. Yet, because of their ambiguity general goals can not serve as guides to strategic or operational decision making.

The CIP should be based on data regarding impending changes in the environment, such as general and local demographic trends, forecasts of the demand for service by local or neighborhood, and estimates of economic factors that may influence service levels and funding options (Steiss, 1989). In the past there was a tendency to consider the CIP as the exclusive domain of the public works department. As noted by Matson (1976:42), it was assumed that since capital improvements were largely in the nature of construction projects, the planning was of an engineering nature. Today, the reality is different. Take, for example, the introduction of new information technology. Although such a project may involve some construction, the bulk of the cost and most of the difficult decisions about it are likely to deal with its purchasing and smooth introduction—matters that are foreign to most public works managers. Nevertheless, capital projects are always taken to address an existing or imminent public need. The involved process of identifying community needs generates the justification for capital investment in light of the existing goals and objectives. Although less comprehensive in scope, this phase of the CIP development corresponds to strategic analysis, the third step of Halachmi's (1992) simple model of strategic planning that we described earlier. This similarity is important because it suggests that at least in theory the two analytical efforts may be fused to form one unified process.

In the private sector—from which much of the terminology and many of the methods used in public sector capital budgeting are derived—this process can be reduced to a simple calculation. The reason is that the firm is usually seeking to maximize only a single criterion—profits—whether they are expressed as current return on investment (ROI), return on equity (ROE), rate of growth, or market share. When it comes to capital budgeting, even in the private sector decisions are not easy. According to Gale and Branch (1987:21) "a virtually undisputed principal of capital budgeting and value-oriented measurement is this: invest (when and if you can) to beat the cost of capital (or the required rate of return)." However they are quick to add that "although the principle of value oriented measurement is conceptually unassailable, applying it is not an easy matter." To start with, in the public sector performance must satisfy multiple and many times inconsistent criteria. As observed by Preble (1983:140)

the goal setting process is likely to be more complex in the public sector and often results in the setting of broader goals and performance measures than would be achieved in the private sector. These goals are also a lot more difficult to measure as they are not tied to any single criterion like the private sector.

The public sector has developed a variety of consensus-building and collaborative problem-solving techniques, as well as methodologies for comparing alternatives to aid in these processes (Robinson, 1991). Also, some organizational structures are more likely to encourage the development of CIP. For example, Doss (1987) found that council-manager cities were more likely involved in the full range of capital budgeting, including preparation of a CIP and the use of more sophisticated analytical techniques than mayoral cities. One possible implication of this finding is that the capital budgeting process is perceived as a more technical endeavor in council-manager forms. If that is the case the comprehensiveness of the process would be less likely to be compromised by political conflicts.

Rehabilitation of an existing facility, the replacement of an existing facility, the construction of a facility manifesting a new approach to meeting community needs, or the continued maintenance and repair of an existing facility are some of the alternative ways for dealing with a pressing issue. Several factors may influence the relative attractiveness of each of these options in developing the CIP. One of the more important factors is the availability of alternative funding sources for each option that may determine the ease or the difficulty of securing the necessary funds and the cost of using them. The process should also include an assessment of all the possible risks that could result from the selection of each option (e.g., for meeting the need and underwriting the involved costs). In addressing this issue the analysis should provide conservative estimates of the following:

- What percentage of the need will be met by pursuing each of the relevant options (coupled with the alternative methods of funding in each case)?
- How long would it be before the same need will have to be addressed again?
- What negative externalities may result from selecting a given option and a particular method of underwriting it?
- What factors could significantly affect projected results such as usage rate or expected income from user fees (when applicable)?
- What are the best- and worst-case scenarios for the involved cost estimates?
- What methods and what assumptions have been used to verify the soundness of the financial plan? What is (are) the experience or credentials of the individual(s) that evaluated the financial plan?

- Overall, what are the minimum benefits and the maximum costs of the project to address the stated need?
- Why can't the stated need (or parts of it) be met through marginal changes to ongoing or other future projects?
- Can a marginal expansion of the proposed project (i.e., a preferred option for meeting a need coupled with a preferred method of underwriting it) alleviate the urgency of dealing with some other need?
- What are the likely consequences of deferring the decision or for addressing only parts of the need during the present cycle of the CIP?

The answers to these questions are important for educated decisions about each element of the CIP. The reason for this is that together they provide elected officials with some basis for assessing political and economic implications of each choice for the community at large as well as for their own constituents. With the answer to such questions at hand politicians are better ready to deal with the issue of accountability; that is, to defend and explain their vote on the CIP. To further help elected officials reach a decision on the CIP most jurisdictions employ some sort of ranking system to arrive at a final list of capital undertakings. The following criteria are typical of those used to select and evaluate capital projects (Hatry et al., 1984:7–16):

1. Fiscal impacts, including capital, operating, and maintenance costs, revenue effects, energy requirements, and legal liability
2. Health and safety effects on both the citizenry and government employees
3. Community economic effects on the tax base, employment, incomes of people and businesses, and neighborhoods
4. Environmental, aesthetic, and social effects on the quality of life in the community
5. Disruptions and inconvenience created during the work on the project
6. Distributional effects across age and income groups, neighborhoods, business and individuals, people with and without automobiles, and people with and without handicaps
7. Feasibility in terms of public support, interest group opposition, special federal or state permitting procedures, consistency with comprehensive plans, and legal questions
8. Implications of deferring the project to a later year
9. Amount of uncertainty and risk with regard to cost and other estimates, technology, and the like
10. Effects on relationships with other governments or quasi-governmental agencies that serve the area
11. Effects on the cost or impacts of other capital projects

The criteria considered in the selection process demonstrate the dynamic interplay that occurs between the enunciated goals and objectives of the community, the political feasibility of the project, and financial considerations, including private sector and environmental outcomes. Financial considerations, of course, may affect perceptions of the political feasibility of the project, as well as its relationship to the overall goals of the jurisdiction. For instance, Kamensky (1984) suggests that a movement to user fees as a funding source for capital projects may result in a decrease in demand for those projects. However, the criteria recommended above clearly encompass areas that must be considered in a strategic planning approach to capital investing in the public sector.

The final scheduling of the various stages of the selected projects over the course of the 6-year CIP may also be influenced by financial criteria, namely projected cash flows within each funding source. Too many projects with the same funding source scheduled for a single year will create revenue gaps and necessitate the postponement of selected project stages. Shortfalls in projected revenues, or changes in state or federal legislation can have the same effects, or can cause projects to be shifted to other sources. However, many CIPs do not identify actual funds in a realistic manner until a project slides into the annual capital budget; they often simply focus on projected expenditures and costs. Although this practice weakens the financial planning dimensions of the process, it permits more political demands to be met in the out years of the CIP. Since the capital budget is the only part of the CIP with legal standing (in most jurisdictions), these demands do not have to be revisited until they are scheduled to become part of the annual capital appropriation. These facts point to the need to constantly monitor and update the CIP.

This brief overview has described a capital budgeting process that manifests some potential as a comprehensive service and financial planning process. However, the fact that the structures necessary to support such a process are found in the CIP development process does not assure that the process will function in that way. For example, it is often difficult to collect the data necessary to consider the impact that capital projects will have on the operating budget during the capital budgeting process—that is, the costs of the personnel, materials, and maintenance necessary to operate a facility once it has been constructed. For a project initially assigned to the out years it is difficult to get the capital programming participants to even focus on this issue, despite the fact that it is an important determinant of the overall cost of the project.

Pagano (1984) cites the lack of attention given to the maintenance issue as one of the prime causes of the widely recognized "infrastructure crises." For him, the capital budgeting process is incomplete if it does not somehow explicitly make funds available for this purpose. To address this issue the decisions about design and construction of a capital facility must be effectively linked to the costs of operating it. The capital budgeting process must be woven into the strategic management process to assure its integration with the operating budget process. When such integration is achieved the capital programming process becomes an integral and important element of the strategic planning framework. Such integration is also essential for the overall strategic management of any government entity as will be explained below.

1. A Note on Cost-Benefit Analysis

The capital budgeting process has historically been more hospitable to the application of analytical techniques than the operating budget process has been. The capital budgeting process is more likely to be viewed as a technical activity, and technical experts have been able to exert more influence in that process. The longer planning horizon, comparatively large costs, relatively complicated financing options, and the required project management expertise associated with capital projects have all contributed to this perception.

The fact that it is more amenable to the application of structured analyses may make the capital budgeting process appear to be more conducive to strategic planning. However, the application of analytical techniques is itself never a value-neutral endeavor, and capital budgeting is rarely reduced to a purely analytical process. Although it is more hospitable to the influence of structured analyses, these techniques can only inform the political processes that produce the capital budget. The technical aspects of capital budgeting may limit access and participation, but the process is inevitably political, if only on an organizational level.

The analytical technique most closely associated with capital budgeting is cost-benefit analysis. A comprehensive explication of the cost-benefit analysis process is beyond the scope of this chapter, but components of the technique are reviewed here in order to illuminate the above issues. Briefly, cost-benefit analysis seeks to identify the costs associated with and the benefits to be derived from a capital investment over the life of the project or facility. These costs and benefits are expressed in monetary terms, and the present values of these streams of future costs and benefits are calculated. The costs and benefits are compared in order to determine whether a single project is worthwhile, which of several projects will maximize net benefits, or what particular mix of projects is optimal. The cost-benefit model consists of the following elements: the specification of the objectives of the investment process; the identification of the alternatives available in light of the objectives; the determination of the costs and benefits of each alternative; the construction of a formal model that depicts the relationships between the components of each alternative and their effects in order to facilitate the identification of relevant costs and benefits; and the development of a criterion for selecting the best alternative(s).

The process of selecting the objectives of the investment effort would tie cost-benefit analysis to a strategic planning capacity. However, this process occurs outside the formal cost-benefit model, and the technique does not free the political process from this responsibility. Cost-benefit analysis thus cannot transform the strategic planning process into a purely rational, analytically based procedure. The alternatives to be considered are also usually limited to those that are politically rather than simply economically feasible. At best, the results of analyses of the options associated with alternative investment objectives can be fed back to the political process in order to better inform decision makers.

The cost-benefit model is built on the time value of money, and the selection of an appropriate discount rate is a crucial component of the analytical process. Identical benefits will have different present values if they are realized at different periods in the future; the farther into the future a given benefit occurs, the less its present value. Discount rates may represent private interest rates, or the cost of borrowing money, or they may reflect estimated inflation rates. Social discount rates adjust private interest rates to account for the general public's shortsightedness in regard to saving and investing, as well as in delaying present gratification in favor of future consumption. Generally, the lower the discount rate employed in the cost-benefit model the easier it is to justify investment. However, the cost-benefit model offers little guidance in the selection of an appropriate rate, and the rate utilized will reflect the values and assumptions of the analysts.

The cost-benefit model employs three distinct criteria to determine the optimal investment scenario: the cost-benefit ratio; the net present value, or benefits minus costs criterion; and the internal rate of return. The cost-benefit ratio is particularly sensitive to the definition of costs and benefits; negative effects associated with each alternative must consistently be either added to the cost side or subtracted from the benefit stream. The net present value criterion is biased in favor of large projects; a small project with a favorable cost-benefit ratio may yield less net present value than a large project manifesting a much less favorable ratio. In the internal rate of return method, the discount rate that sets the present value of the benefit stream equal to the present value of the stream of costs is identified; if this discount rate exceeds the cost of borrowing funds, the project is justified. Like the other criteria, it assumes that the situation existing at the time that the analysis is undertaken will define the relevant variables over the life of the project. Some cost-benefit solutions may be sensitive to changes associated with future contingencies, thus the process of selecting the appropriate criterion is rife with value judgments and assumptions.

The cost-benefit models reflect the level of knowledge regarding cause-and-effect relationships among the salient variables. The uncertainty associated with future contingencies is coupled with uncertainties regarding cause-and-effect relationships. Although analytical techniques exist that are designed to test the sensitivity of model solutions to changes in the assumptions on which the models are based, these uncertainties cannot be eliminated. Thus, there is always a certain amount of risk associated with adopting cost-benefit model solutions as guides to capital investments.

Another area of uncertainty is the assignment of prices to costs and benefits. Public goods are provided by governments because these are not amenable to pricing through private markets. These prices must be estimated, and the estimated prices are usually a function of the values of the estimator. This is particularly true of benefits associated with public goods, especially those benefits that are "intangible." The uncertainty and thus the risk, associated with estimated benefits biases the cost-benefit model in favor of those projects in which costs and benefits are more easily quantifiable; in these cases, the model yields a less uncertain solution. Another value judgment to be made is whether or not the costs borne by those who are not in the sponsoring jurisdiction are actually costs that should be assigned to the project under consideration.

The assignment of a dollar value to the costs and benefits of a project actually serves as an estimate of the utility that the benefits hold for those who will receive them. According to the standard cost-benefit model, a project is justified when the total benefits exceed the total costs, and the benefits are great enough that those who receive them can theoretically compensate those who bear the costs or losses associated with the project. However, the benefits may have less utility for the groups that benefited than the losses had for those who bore the costs—regardless of the dollar value assigned to each. Dollar value does not measure the relative utility that something has for a particular group. Neither does the cost-benefit model typically consider the distributional effects of alternative projects; weighting schemes are useful here, but these can be arbitrary and they inevitably reflect the values of the analysts. The increased use of revenue bonds to finance capital facilities raises additional questions of equity associated with user fees.

The above value judgments are initially made at the departmental level, where the projects are initially developed and grouped. The perspective employed at this level may be suboptimal for the organization and the community as a whole, particularly in regard to the allocative and distributional effects of the project. The availability of intergovernmental grants for particular types of capital facilities may also distort local priorities. Finally, the cost-benefit model assumes that if a project yields net benefits it should be funded. However, government organizations must operate within a total budget constraint regardless of the number of projects that appear to be attractive according to this criterion. The jurisdiction must make trade-offs among projects, and the cost-benefit model offers no guidance in this area.

The cost-benefit model serves to highlight issues on which decision makers should focus. It also provides an arena for a dialogue between technical analysts and decision makers, as well as a common filter for the wide variety of capital projects that surface at the local government level. But the technique will not allow decision makers to simply "calculate" their capital investment portfolio, nor can it serve as a vehicle for calculating a strategic plan for the jurisdiction.

B. Capital Budgeting Theory and Concepts

The next two sections examine some of the limited research literature that focuses on capital budgeting with special emphasis on the case of local authorities. There is no universally accepted theory of either private sector investment planning or public sector capital programming; however, unlike the latter, the former has benefited from an extensive range of normative studies of corporate financial management conducted during the past 60 years (Bozeman, 1984). The techniques and processes employed in public sector capital budgeting are derived from these private sector studies. In short, public sector capital budgeting is not fully developed as a field of research; many studies have focused on related substantive issues, such as the "infrastructure crisis." Particular attention is paid here to those factors related to the issue of integrating strategic management and capital budgeting through the strategic plan—specifically, the degree to which capital budgeting can be coordinated with the formal planning process. The following section focuses directly on the strategic management issue.

Since the turn of the century, reform in local government budgeting has been associated with the application of analytical techniques to provide the information necessary to enhance efficiency, and with the idea that the latent role of formal planning—which is inherent in budgeting—must be made more manifest. Performance budgeting focused on work planning and technological efficiency, the planning programming budgeting system (PPBS) aspired to allocative efficiency on the basis of centralized policy planning, and zero-based budgeting (ZBB) highlighted agency-level planning to achieve planned service levels. The reforms met with variable success at the various levels of government, but by 1990 Rubin was able to write that: "Increasingly, planning is merging with budgeting" (1990:182).

It is no small irony then that capital budgeting evolved in the late 1920s "in recognition that planning must be accompanied by realistic appraisal of a community's ability and willingness to pay for what has been planned" (Bozeman, 1984:191). At the same time that operating budget reformers were seeking to make the substantive meaning of the annual budget numbers more explicit and enhance efficiency and responsiveness by wedding it to a formal planning process, capital budget reformers were attempting to give weight to what were often the lofty goals of city planners by tying them to the realities of the budget constraint. Responsibility for developing the capital budget began to move from the planning department to the finance department. The operating budget and capital budget reformers were often, of course, the same people, but by 1984 J. Lisle Bozeman could write that: "The coordination of planning and budgeting is far more apparent in capital budgets than in operating budgets" (1984:195).

The coordination of planning and budgeting in the capital budgeting process may be facilitated by the idea that the decisions to be made are more technical than political in nature. Private sector capital investment decisions are viewed in this way, and the public sector process has borrowed many of the analytical techniques—such as present value analysis and cost-benefit algorithms—employed by private sector organizations. However, the outcome measures demanded by these analytical models are much less precise in the public sector, where ambiguous and often contradictory goals can be pursued simultaneously. In the absence of the common bottom line that exists in the private sector—that is, profits and dollar rate of return on investments—the use of formal decision criteria and project ranking schemes merely moves the political battle from the alternative projects to the content and substance of the formal criteria. Rubin (1993) suggests that the capital budgeting process may involve more intense political competition than the operating budget process because the former entails costly long-term commitments with extensive distributional ramifications.

The integration of planning and budgeting is facilitated by the use of output, or outcome-oriented budget formats (O'Toole and Stipak, 1991; Schick, 1966). This in turn makes the prospect of integrating capital budgeting with the strategic planning process an evolutionary rather than a revolutionary development.

Capital budgets focus on tangible outputs, although the ultimate outcomes or results of these investments may be difficult to specify in terms of formal goals and objectives. The strategic planning process, and even more the strategic management process, can be greatly assisted by the use of such multiyear budget documents as the CIP. However, the CIP is itself more of a plan than a formal budget, particularly when projections are limited to expenditures and actual future revenues are not committed or identified. Indeed, Doss (1987) found that 12% of the respondents to his survey of municipal governments reported having a CIP without having a separate capital budget. This disjointed isolation of planning and budgeting would be less likely to exist when the CIP is synchronized on a regular basis with the operational budgeting process. Coordination is clearly easier when individual budget items are tied to specific revenue sources—such as capital projects often are—particularly when they are financed through borrowing or restricted user fees.

However, in the same way that these elements can enhance the coordination of planning and budgeting, they can also provide for a misleading appearance of real integration. Indeed, some of the same factors outlined above may militate against effective integration of planning and budgeting. For example, once they are adopted, budgets can be rigid and difficult to change. Consequently, multiyear budgeting can be dysfunctional by constraining the adaptability of long-range planning (Halachmi and Boydston, 1991). Earmarked revenues may limit the capacity of the capital budgeting process to respond to real community needs and to mount a comprehensive planning effort. Pagano (1984) points out that the availability of revenue in particular areas rather than a real need may drive the planning process. An unexpected revenue is even more likely to trigger a call for new project(s). Following the logic of the garbage can model of decision making (Cohen et al., 1972), in which solutions are floating around looking for problems, assertive entrepreneurs with monies to lend, development plans, extra service capacity, goods to sell, or a simple desire for growth and profit may influence the evolvement of a need for a private idea to an item on the public's agenda. Subjecting such "ideas" to the rigorous scrutiny of the strategic planning process may slow down the rush to commit idle resources (which includes the residual borrowing capacity) to new ventures that generate more private fortunes than public goods. The promulgation of long-range community goals and objectives through output-oriented budget formats and a demonstrated commitment to them through the planning of "concrete" facilities may serve to exacerbate political conflicts.

In any case, Pagano and Moore (1985) suggest that capital budgeting resource allocation decisions may be inexorably incremental in nature, particularly in those areas that must compete with the operating budget process for general fund resources. This would clearly militate against formal integration with a strategic management process. These authors contend that this incremental nature makes the capital budgeting process responsive to salient political issues—such as the infrastructure crisis—but it also makes a strategic approach vulnerable to the vagaries of changes in political leadership. The fact that the vast majority of CIP processes commit funds for only 1 year is also testimony to the incremental nature of the capital budgeting process. In this vein, McClain (1981) finds that budgeting is often the only formal management tool employed in many local governments. He concludes that asking any budget process to serve as a formal planning process and a financial decision-making process is asking too much. McClain suggests that although it is possible to coordinate planning and budgeting, they should be separate processes. This position is contrary to the position we take. As we see it there are clear advantages to fusing the CIP effort with strategic planning, when possible, in the same way that there are clear advantages for using the operational budget as a tool of strategic management when possible.

The infrastructure issue serves to highlight some of the planning shortcomings associated with capital budgeting. Petersen (1978) identified five measures of the physical condition of a jurisdiction's capital infrastructure

1. Direct observation
2. Reported maintenance and replacement cycles
3. Amount of capital investment needed to improve capital stock to "adequate" standards
4. Monetary losses attributable to the condition of the public stock
5. Data on annual capital and maintenance expenditures

However, none of these provides clear criteria for investment decision making. Kamensky (1984) suggests that the "crisis" of infrastructure condition can be alleviated and much of the apparent need for increased investment can be met by simply relaxing existing standards, which are ultimately determined through the political process. In this regard, the reporting of depreciation—largely ignored in the public sector—would give some objective indication of the need for reinvestment. Thomassen (1990) recommends that jurisdictions use depreciation to distinguish between gross and net investment; depreciation could be charged in operating budgets and debt could be restricted to net capital formation.

The separation of operating and capital budgets constitutes an additional issue. Pagano and Moore (1985:5–6) contend that local governments do not generally develop comprehensive capital budgets

> If capital budgets are records of the fixed assets of cities, then they should include records of activities that clearly support or maintain that fixed investment. Capital budgets should have operating budget components that pertain directly to the maintenance expenditures of facilities . . . that either extend the useful design life of a facility, or allow the predicted useful life of the facility to be reached.

In Pagano's view (1984), much of what is called the infrastructure crisis is rooted in inadequate maintenance of capital facilities. Because maintenance costs are relegated to the operating budget—where they are vulnerable to cuts in order to meet immediate service needs—the full costs of capital facilities are not reported in the capital budget. Most maintenance costs associated with a capital facility occur after it has been operational for some years, and neglect in this area points to a limited planning horizon, as well as to a fragmented approach to financial planning. The capital programming participants focus on the provision of capital investments, and these issues are also evidence of the limited utility of techniques such as cost-benefit analysis to support maintenance expenditures in the face of political demands for additional capital facilities that may entail fewer economic benefits for the community as a whole.

A survey conducted by Botner (1991) indicated that capital budgeting has been enjoying increasing attention in recent years, and the infrastructure crisis has focused attention on the capital programming process. But it emerges here once again as a process that must be effectively managed rather than as a straightforward application of a set of analytical techniques borrowed from the private sector. Management of the CIP is in itself an additional salient issue affecting integration with the planning process. The design and construction of capital facilities can be subject to innumerable delays, partly because the management process is shared by the substantive service agency requesting the project, the jurisdiction's planning, public works, engineering, budget, and finance departments, as well as the private sector firms contracted to do the work. Each of these agencies often seeks to optimize different criteria; identifying someone to take "ownership" of the project is sometimes problematic. These delays can compromise the long-range planning process. Miller (1991) has characterized capital disbursements as the "wild card" of the cash management function, because these are difficult to project, time, and control for the purposes of cash budgeting. Integration of capital budgeting with the strategic planning process means among other things that progress according to schedule is something the strategic managers must worry about.

From an organizational point of view, whatever helps the government entity to stay on schedule is a source of strength, while the causes of a delay are the sources of weakness. Being cognizant of the involved strengths and weaknesses is important for a realistic assessment of the organization's capacity or ability to exploit an opportunity or avoid a threat. Thus, for example, an organization that experiences delays because of bickering over ownership by subunits is not likely to be able to use a defender's strategy (Nutt and Backoff, 1992) to protect its turf when a rival agency tries to move in or attempts to change the enabling legislation. The competing alliances of subunits with outside stakeholders may cripple lobbying efforts to block "unfriendly" initiatives by elected officials who find it easy to resist fragmented demand for change but succumb when faced with a cohesive request to take action.

Despite the issues, problems, and constraints outlined above, capital facilities must be planned for, their costs forecasted, and sources of revenue identified and committed. In short, decisions involving strategic ramifications are made by local governments; Steiss (1989) explicitly recognizes the development of the CIP as a strategic planning process in local government. Mercer (1991) contends, however, that strategic planning is not effective unless it is tied to operational planning; the most effective way of accomplishing this is to integrate the CIP and the operating budget development process. Among the issues we must now consider is first, whether capital budgeting theory and structures have been sufficiently developed for that process to serve as a vehicle for strategic planning, and second, if CIP can be tied to the operational budget process as part of a strategic management effort in general, and in the case of local governments, where in-house capacity is limited and hard to come by in particular.

Considering this last question in the context of earlier research reports suggests a possible paradox. Greenwood (1987:296), for example, suggests that "local authorities with greater range of responsibilities and a more complex environmental context operate best with a complex, highly differentiated set of departments, each department aligned to its segment of the environment, and a complex network of interdepartmental integration devices." He contrasts this with the case of smaller organizations that "operate better with less differentiation, use simpler integrative devices and greater centralization" (Greenwood, 1987:296). The implication of this observation is that those government entities that are in a better position to develop the capacity for using an integrated strategic planning and capital budgeting process are less likely to benefit from it. This implication is contrary to our empirical observations, which suggest precisely the opposite, namely, that local authorities in a more turbulent environment stand to benefit more from a centralized effort to realign operations and resources in anticipation of emerging trends, strengths, and possible threats. A move toward the integration of the two efforts, the one for creating (and thus reviewing and revising) the strategic plan with the one for developing the CIP, is also consistent with the current call to reengineer the work process by linking parallel activities, capturing information once and organizing around outcomes, not tasks (Hammer, 1990). In comparison, in the case of smaller local authorities such reengineering of strategic planning and capital budgeting is not as critical because of the magnitude of the involved resources. For smaller jurisdictions a weakly coordinated effort of strategic management or a less-than-optimal management of financial resources is not a sign of excellence but it does not rule out a change of course midway or the prospect of quick recovery after a bad decision.

V. THE PROSPECTS FOR STRATEGIC CAPITAL BUDGETING AND PLANNING

When strategic management is done right one of the likely results is a seamless integration of the strategic planning process with the organization's management of its various resources. This in turn ensures that all resource allocation decisions serve to optimize the pursuit of strategic goals (Koteen, 1989). In the private sector, the boundary line between strategic management and capital investment planning tends to blur (Clark et al., 1989). This is because all of the resource allocation decisions of the firm are directed to maximize the bottom line. The process of planning for long-term survival, through retention or expansion of market share, return on investment and on equity, dovetails into the process of managing the firm's resources. The manager who makes the programmatic decisions is also the one to make the decisions about the allocation of resources. The bottom-line profit orientation of the private firm functions as a centripetal force in the organization, which serves to integrate the organization's component systems.

Unfortunately, "public management is most like business management at the operating level and less like it at the strategic level" (Bozeman and Straussman, 1990:34). Government entities separate programmatic decisions from financial ones. The decisions about what a government entity or one of its subunits is going to do and how it is going to do it may be separated from the decisions about how and where to get necessary resources. These last decisions are the domain of the budget office and are viewed as part of a broader decision(s) on fiscal policy. Unlike their counterparts in the private sector most public managers do not get involved in crafting the plan for mobilizing the necessary resources beyond the development of a proposed budget. Usually program directors do not get engrossed in studying the relative merit and cost of using a user fee, taxing the general public or parts of it, borrowing in the marketplace, or soliciting grants and funding from other private or public sources. Public administrators who are not exposed to this aspect of public management may not develop a realistic perspective and an accurate understanding of the context and the conditions under which their organization operates.

Because of the political context of all government operations, strategic planning may be attractive to public administrators. Not only has strategic planning promised to make the planning process systematic and rational but it can be touted as a method for "transcending" the political process (Swanstrom, 1987). However, the attempt to couple resource allocation decisions with strategic planning increases the risk of complicating the last one significantly through the introduction of another source of potential conflicts. Nevertheless, the potential effectiveness of capital budgeting as an instrument of strategic management can make the benefit of the effort to integrate it with strategic planning exceed the cost.

For local authorities the attempt to integrate strategic planning and capital budgeting may be an acid test for the extent (or the possibility of developing) an organizationwide strategic management capacity. It was pointed out in an earlier paper (Halachmi and Boydston, 1991) that the regular budget holds little promise of providing the public administrator with an effective tool for monitoring and influencing the implementation of the strategic plan. However, as will be pointed out below, capital budgets may be different. If the capital budgeting process cannot be effectively integrated—the component that Steiss (1989) *equated* with strategic planning on the local level—the prospects for systemwide strategic management would appear to be dim.

Before dealing with the question of whether or not strategic budgeting should be integrated with the strategic planning and management process we must answer two other questions. First, can the logic and the analytical methods of capital budgeting undermine the integrity of the strategic planning process? Second, given the intricate nature and the complexity of capital budgeting and strategic planning as discrete processes, can a process that merges the two in real time be feasible?

The answer to the first question is no. The logic and methods of the two are likely to be consistent, and if anything, the relationship between the logic and the methods of strategic planning and capital budgeting or the development of the CIP can be described as complementary or synergetic. The answer to the second question is not as simple or obvious. In theory there is no reason why the two can not be combined. However, under real conditions the answer might be different. The reason is that maintaining the necessary organizational capacity and finding the right individuals (e.g., those with the talent, skills, and experience) may prove to be a very tall order for most government entities. Going back to the initial question about the integration of strategic planning with capital budgeting, it seems that the issue is not "whether it should be integrated" but "whether it could be integrated." The difference between the two questions is that the first inquires about the normative value of such integration (i.e., its desirability), and the second probes the practical aspect (i.e., if it is a feasible proposition). Obviously, the answer to the second question is likely to be agency-specific and may change with time.

The importance of the capital budget as a tool for strategic management is that when done right, it forces top managers to consider both short- and long-term implications of past and pending commitments of organizational resources (which includes the ability to borrow). The short-term implications and previous commitments mortgaged a future that is now the "present" for the organization. This present situation affects the organization's future and thus it influences its capacity and its cost for mobilizing the necessary resources for carrying out the strategic plan. The long-term implications and pending commitment of resources have to do with the creation of constraints and limiting the freedom of choices of programmatic decisions in the future. Evaluating any addition to the CIP in these terms can be very different from its evaluation by the use of a simple benefit-cost analysis. In other words, integration of capital budgeting with the strategic planning process may provide the necessary context and a better perspective for assessing each item of the CIP on its own and against the overall planning and priorities of a given government entity.

For the rank and file, the CIP establishes a clear and a mutual frame of reference through the sharing of common information about the direction in which the organization is going—information that is driven from knowing that some major improvements are about to take place. Another result of this shared knowledge is that even without any action by top officials it may lead to spontaneous coordination and channeling efforts by various members in different parts of the organization in the same general direction.

Unlike the operational budget that may change overnight or from one fiscal year to the next, capital budgets convey a more permanent sense of priorities and direction. Although the funding of capital budgets is done through annual appropriations, many times its approval amounts to the passing of a multiyear budget. According to Axelrod (1988:277), governments use multiyear budgeting to change the direction of budget priorities, to help stabilize the priorities of programs and projects, to control expenditures, to discourage piecemeal decisions, and to lighten the budgetary workload. In addition to its possible contributions as a form of a multiyear budget, capital budgets can help program managers develop a better understanding of the opportunities and the constrains on future action. With the addition of a new office building or the introduction of a new information technology system to the CIP, a practicing manager could tell that the odds of seeing an affirmative action on a request to build another building or to purchase another system shortly after are low. From a strategic management point of view the important thing is that all managers at all levels and across the board are likely to get a similar message about the future of any such requests. At the same time it may encourage individual managers to search independently of each other for ways to exploit the new opportunities that result from such an improvement. Any success in this regard amounts to an improvement on the rate of return on the involved investment. Knowing that by the end of a given period the organization is going to have a new capacity in any respect may encourage managers to look for opportunities to take advantage of it, possibly by initiating new or different programs or work processes. Here, too, the logic of the garbage can model of decision making illustrates how possible solutions can start floating around in search of problems. These initiatives by managers may prevent inertia from settling in. This, in turn, can diminish the risk of overlooking an emerging threat, a likely event when inertia does settle in.

Strategic management is designed to cut across departmental lines and functional areas in pursuit of the strategic plan. The development of a capital budget follows the same approach with results that are very different from the ones usually obtained from the regular budgeting process. It is only a slight exaggeration to suggest that it is only during the annual budget cycle that the individual departments of a local government, for example, are forced to acknowledge that they are indeed part of the same agency. The needs of central staff units such as finance, personnel, electronic data processing, and purchasing are not likely to be factored into the workplans of the individual operating departments. Managers develop workplans for their respective units without worrying about the budgetary implications for other line and staff units. Resolving such problems is assumed to be the domain of the budget department or the top manager. It is not uncommon for staff and line units to organize their individual operations on the basis of a narrow, provincial view of the public's needs; this serves as an enormous centrifugal force in the local government organization.

The fusing of the strategic planning and the capital budgeting process may weaken some of the centrifugal forces and thus is conducive to strategic management. However, carrying out such a unified planning (and thus an analytical) process may be beyond the ability of many small and midsize government entities. The use of too much outside help in developing the strategic plan may undermine the effort of organizations to empower their own employees or clients. The organization may lose other important advantages that result from broad and direct participation in the strategic planning process, as discussed above. At the same time the use of outside expertise that does not follow the tenets of action research and training (Halachmi, 1980) may increase the odds of overlooking or missing important clues about future developments within or outside most government entities.

VI. CASES IN THE INTEGRATION OF CAPITAL BUDGETING AND STRATEGIC MANAGEMENT

The following section consists of two parts. The first part addresses an earlier attempt to introduce an integrated system of management and financial control. The second recounts the more recent experiences of several jurisdictions.

A. The Comeback of PPBS?

After reading the earlier parts of this chapter the reader must wonder why we go to the trouble of describing both strategic planning and capital budgeting to make the case for their integration into a unified one. After all, a similar logic was used almost 30 years ago to make the case for the use of PPBS by government entities. Bozeman (1984:24) has noted that "the characteristics of PPBS are closely related to the characteristics of capital budgeting." In the case of PPBS there was not much argument at the beginning against the logic behind the concept. However, acceptance and successful implementation of PPBS proved to be illusive. Some of the more salient reasons for the demise of PPBS as the management system of choice are very similar to the ones that are likely to interfere with the integration of strategic management and capital budgeting. In the case of PPBS these factors included the tendency to consolidate power and decision making at the top, giving lower levels of management a sense of disempowerment, making extraordinary demands on the time and other resources of managers at lower levels, and contributing to the absence of the necessary expertise and training for complying with the requirements of PPBS even when there was a will to do so. With this in mind it is easy to see that the question we asked earlier about the feasibility of the integration is a very real one.

The question we need to answer at this junction is what has changed since the attempt to introduce PPBS that is most likely to successfully integrate strategic management and capital budgeting. For one thing we know some of the mistakes involved in the introduction of PPBS, and hopefully we will not repeat them. For example, our discussion of either strategic planning or capital budgeting highlights the importance of empowering lower levels and encouraging participation throughout the organization. We also have a better educated workforce now, and it can participate in a meaningful way in carrying out the integrated process It can adjust more easily to the time and skill demands of the integrated system since its demands are not likely to exceed the demands that result from having strategic management and capital budgeting as two separate processes. In particular, changes in information technology and the expected requirements of service accomplishment efforts (SEAs) reporting are going to allow the collection and analysis of most of the necessary data as by-products of other operations. Computer networks and databanks will allow even small local authorities to give the integrated process a chance. The reason is that the development of a generic template would make it relatively inexpensive to import the integrated system and secure expert advice without having to pay hefty travel expenses. In addition, it should be noted that once the system is up and running the use of expert system software that demonstrates the implications of alternative contingencies for debt management and other important decisions would allow small authorities to use the integrated process.

PPBS was popular at a time of relative resource abundance; indeed, one of the driving factors behind the system at the federal level was the redistribution of this fiscal bounty. We are now in a time of relative resource scarcity, and local governments are finding that they must become increasingly self-reliant in terms of fiscal resources. Productivity enhancements must extend beyond technological fixes at the individual program level to encompass entire decision-making systems and central staff functions.

Last but not least, although conceptually the integration of strategic management and capital budget resembles the logic of PPBS, the implementation requirements of the two are different. In the case of PPBS, agencies had to choose between all or nothing. Because PPBS involved a multiyear system of planning and reviews, it did not allow for gradual introduction. The merging of strategic planning and capital budgeting is more conducive to gradual action. As a matter of fact, we suspect that there are more local authorities with a capital budgeting system in place than local authorities with basic experience with strategic planning. Augmenting the capital budget process by gradually broadening the scope of the analysis may not be something as threatening as PPBS was to line managers.

B. Case Studies

The research literature does not contain a single case study describing an attempt by a local government to integrate its capital budgeting process with a strategic management capacity. This section reviews case studies of issues and processes that would necessarily precede or be logically related to such an effort; these include the development of mission statements, goals, and objectives, the enunciation of a strategic plan for the community, and the identification of the capital improvement component of such a plan. The efforts of selected cities are reviewed first, and the effects of the Growth Management Act of the state of Florida are reviewed as a special case.

1. Selected Municipalities

The focus on the local government level excludes the many long-range policy planning efforts that have occurred at the state level in recent years; these usually covered a range of policy areas and were typically the product of special commissions known as "Future," "Tomorrow," or "2000" (Chi, 1991). However, several local governments have invested in similar efforts. Wheeland (1993) described the strategic planning process employed in Rock Hill, North Carolina, entitled "Empowering the Vision" (ETV). The process was designed and initiated by the city manager, and it included community organizations, city institutions, and private citizens; it was chartered to provide substantive responses to the economic and demographic changes the city had experienced. According to Wheeland, "ETV has altered Rock Hill's policy-making process by institutionalizing strategic planning as a collaborative problem-solving process involving a large number of citizens who are aware of the city's plan and who want to discuss proposals in light of the plan" (p. 71). However, the details of the implementation stage are not addressed, and the specific linkages with organizational decision-making processes are not identified. The ETV process comes to resemble more of a reinvigorated town hall than an institutionalized strategic planning capacity; indeed, the few capital improvement projects specifically identified seemed to have been implemented more to assuage the feelings of the minority community, which felt that it had been excluded from the process, rather than to address any substantive issues identified in the planning process.

Mercer (1991) reported on Savannah, Georgia's "Target 2000" program. The program's goal was "to help the Savannah community decide what kind of place Savannah will be at the end of this century and what programs and actions must be taken so that the community can become what it wants to be" (p. 177). Substantive areas for action included economic development, education, housing, recreation, transportation, facilities, human services, and land use planning. The effort was initiated by the city manager, but the process was multijurisdictional and involved task forces comprising community leaders. These task forces were assisted by a technical advisory committee staffed by executives from community organizations and local governments, as well as by a consultant. The consultant was also responsible for preparing a "blueprint for action," which would summarize the recommendations of the task forces, and for compiling the multiyear capital projects plan, which would list, schedule, and identify financing for each of the projects proposed by the task forces. The process for deciding among the projects is less clear. The report would also serve as a guide for the development of the comprehensive land use and growth management plan. The Savannah approach recognized the institutional elements necessary to bring the 2000 plan to life, but the required decision-making processes were not identified; this would seem to be a serious weakness, particularly in light of the multijurisdictional nature of the plan.

The shortcomings of the "community vision" approach were summarized by Hall and Weschler (1991) in their review of Phoenix, Arizona's "Futures Forum." This program was very similar to Rock Hill's ETV process and Savannah's Target 2000. However, Hall and Weschler found that it was difficult for the citizen groups to carry over the enthusiasm associated with "creating vision" to the realities of taking action. At the implementation stages the participants often "lost the vision mode" and reverted to a more "incrementalist" decision-making process. It would seem that the strategic planning process should be housed in or at least integrated with the implementing institutions and process in order to facilitate the ultimate implementation of the resulting vision. Since the plans tend to center on physical development, the capital budgeting process would appear to be an indispensable component. However, the political consensus required for the design of an acceptable plan calls for community organizations that are more ad hoc and informal in nature.

The above examples focus on efforts to involve the community in the development of a citywide strategic plan in response to perceived threats to the future development of the municipalities. Another approach to strategic planning is to focus on the capacity of the local government organization to deliver services and to identify and adapt to change in the environment. This is a less grandiose level for strategic planning, but an assessment of internal strengths and weaknesses and the development of an environmental scanning capacity would seem to be prerequisites for effective and responsive strategic planning and management.

Mercer (1991) also describes the development of a mission structure by the city of Charlotte, North

Carolina, which often serves as a first step in internal organizational assessment for strategic planning and management. One of the authors of this chapter was closely involved in a similar project in the city of St. Petersburg, Florida. A four-person task force made up of city employees spent 18 months meeting with the management staffs of all of the city's 106 programs, and a mission statement, as well as goals, objectives, and outcome measures (or workload measures if outcomes were not measurable) were negotiated for each program. However, the city manager was reluctant to identify goals for the programs in his office; when he was persuaded to do so, he focused on internal managerial responsibilities rather than on overarching community goals. Thus, the programmatic structure of the city was mapped without reference to community goals or internal organizational goals. Additionally, a mission structure was not negotiated for the CIP, partly because it was more procedural than programmatic in nature and several department participated in the process, and partly because the only community goals available to guide the process were the ambiguous "do good" goals typically enunciated by elected legislative bodies. This points to the strength of the centrifugal forces at work in the typical municipal government organization—forces that are mirrored by the community and with which the CIP and budgeting processes must contend.

The city of St. Petersburg also recently sought to develop a 3-year strategic plan for meeting service demands, downsizing the organization, and increasing productivity. The forces outlined above also influenced this process. It was designed as a bottom-up process in which the individual departments assumed primary responsibility for their own strategic responses; guiding principles were few, despite the conflicting components of the planning mandate. Predictably, the plans represented incremental approaches to change, and any difficult decisions were usually assigned to the out years of the plan. Additionally, capital programming decisions were not made an integral component of the planning process. The individual operating departments had never assumed full responsibility for the identification of capital program projects, and the fact that they were assuming responsibility for the development of strategic plans did not result in the integration of strategic planning and capital programming; indeed, such an integration in this scenario would further fragment the capital budgeting process. Thus, even when the strategic planning process is oriented to the internal workings of the local government organization—that is, the process occurs under a unified chain of command—the integration of strategic planning and capital budgeting in a strategic management framework remains problematical.

Bryson and Roering (1988) analyzed the efforts of eight public agencies in the Twin Cities area of Minnesota to initiate a strategic planning effort. The authors identified the elements necessary for a the successful initiation of such a project, as did Wheeland (1993) and Hall and Weschler (1991), above. Bryson and Roering also point out the fragile, fragmented nature of initial efforts, and the fact that (p. 1000) "the efforts at the initiation of strategic planning were almost always out of sequence with the units' normal planning and budgeting processes, so that it was difficult for most to integrate strategic planning efforts with normal planning and budgeting processes." The authors concluded that private sector models of the strategic planning process may not transfer well to the public sector, and that governmental units may not be able to institutionalize all elements of the strategic planning process. Among those amendable to formal institutionalization are the development of a mission structure and policy objectives, and the periodic identification of strategic issues. This implies an internal organizational focus for the strategic planning process rather than a purely environmental orientation.

The above review of the literature on capital budgeting indicated that some believe that the capital programming process is a strategic planning process, and integration with the fiscal plan of the jurisdiction would create a nascent strategic management capacity. Dayton, Ohio's capital programming process features a strong role for the finance director, who participates by maintaining an inventory of capital facilities and infrastructure and by closely monitoring the condition of these investments, as well as through his financial expertise (Riordan et al., 1987). In this way, the finance director operationalizes a public sector counterpart of the accounting concept of depreciation. However, this does not make the capital programming plan a strategic plan. Dayton's plan is geared to the repair and maintenance of existing facilities, and projects included in the replacement schedule take priority over new projects. The city's comprehensive plan would seem to drive the capital programming process; the capital budget policies specifically preclude the funding of projects that conflict with that plan. Comprehensive plans are often conservative, typically incremental, and usually difficult to amend. In this scenario, capital projects may have strategic implications, but the capital programming process does not constitute a strategic planning capacity.

Bernhard and Lachman (1984) described Milwaukee's effort to integrate comprehensive planning and multiyear budgeting for allocating its community development block grant (CDBG) funds among projects.

The comprehensive planning process had yielded a strategy that emphasized the preservation of the city's economic base and residential neighborhoods. The plan was operationalized through a CDBG funding allocation guide that described the geographic areas in which the grant funds would be spent, as well as the approved program categories and the percentage of the CDBG funds to be allocated to each program category. The guide also set 3-year program goals and budget targets, which were reviewed annually. However, the guide did not list specific projects, but rather target spending levels with the broad categories; the three major categories were social services, planning and management, and physical development. Thus, city departments and community groups still competed for funding on an annual basis, and the 3-year budget horizon functioned as a CIP. The "strategy" lay in the general emphasis on restoration and physical development, and the process was never fully integrated with the capital budgeting process; the guide simply provided another selection criterion for capital programs in what remained an incremental process.

Milwaukee was also featured in a study on strategic fiscal planning by McCann and Daun (1989). This approach focused on the concept of the long-term "fiscal-service" balance of the city, and it addressed such questions as: what the continuation of current service and fiscal policies will mean for the future financial condition of the city, and what fiscal or budgeting changes are necessary to maintain current services in the future. The effort sought to identify future threats to the city's financial condition in light of current spending levels and available resources. This approach highlights the role of the finance director and the salience of organizational resources in the strategic planning framework. The city developed a computerized fiscal impact model that allowed it to ask "what if" questions related to fiscal issues such as labor negotiations and capital investing, and to test alternative strategies. Strategic fiscal planning is not simply multiyear budgeting; however, the link between the strategic planning effort and formal budgeting that would institutionalize the process had not yet been established. The authors speculated that "this could be accomplished through executive budget guidelines" (p. 11).

The city of Sunnyvale (California) instituted a performance audit and budgets system (PABS) in order to clearly define the overall objectives of the city, and to integrate long-range planning and evaluation with its resources allocation process. The city's planning and management system (PAMS) integrated policy making and service delivery through evaluation information and performance-monitoring data. PAMS was viewed as the policy-developing process and PABS as the policy-implementing component; in this way, policy making guides the resource allocation process through goal setting, although planning and budgeting remain separate and distinct activities. Rather than pointing to substantive strategies that have been pursued in an integrative manner as examples of the benefits of this approach, the authors outline benefits in the area of organizational development and capacity building—that is: awareness of service delivery systems, missions, and goals; allocation of resources on the basis of performance data; clearly defined service levels and greater awareness of responsibilities by managers; and greater ownership of organizational goals and policies. However, the organization–development benefits of the implementation of a strategic planning/management capacity constituted a common theme in these case studies.

2. The Florida Growth Management Act

The above studies examined communitywide strategic planning efforts, the development of organizationwide mission structures, the strategic role of the finance department and resource availability, and attempts to implement strategic management systems. This section focuses on an approach related to Chapman's (1988) work regarding the strategic relationship between budgetary and development decisions. The substance of the Florida Growth Management Act of 1985 is outlined, and its implications for the formal integration of strategic planning and capital investment on the local government level are examined.

Over the last 20 years the population of Florida has doubled. Until recently, development and growth were emphasized at the expense of sound planning; the supporting infrastructure was provided through deficit financing based on the idea that growth would eventually pay for itself, or else service levels were simply allowed to deteriorate. After various attempts to implement state and local comprehensive planning—partly in response to perceived crises in the availability of potable water, the impact of growth on the natural environment, and the capacity of the transportation infrastructure—the comprehensive intergovernmental Omnibus Growth Management Act was passed by the state legislature in 1985. The purposes of the act were to: require local governments to prepare multiyear capital improvement plans that included feasible financing sources; to encourage growth in areas that have been previously developed and to mandate that the required infrastructure support be in place prior to project completion; and to provide for the coordination of plans among jurisdictions.

Several of the elements required by this comprehensive approach were already in place. The state produced a state plan that provided policy guidance to local governments in the areas of potable water, land use, and transportation. Local governments were required to adopt comprehensive plans that addressed the areas of solid waste, drainage, potable water, recreation, housing, roads, and the natural environment. Regional planning areas had been previously established, and the intergovernmental coordination element required local governments to indicate steps they had taken to ensure that their plans were consistent with those of neighboring jurisdictions, the regional planning area, and the state plan and policies. Thus, the issues of vertical and horizontal consistency in comprehensive planning were also addressed. Two components introduced in the 1985 act gave Florida the most comprehensive and stringent growth management policy in the nation: the capital improvements element of the comprehensive plan, and the concurrency requirement.

All capital improvements related to any of the elements of the comprehensive plan were required to be listed in the capital improvements element (CIE) of the plan; these could also be listed in the jurisdiction's traditional CIP along with nonqualifying capital improvements, such as a new city hall. The CIE would list qualifying capital improvements for 5 future years. Most significantly, the jurisdictions were required to identify a feasible funding source for each project. This was designed to demonstrate the fiscal feasibility of the comprehensive plan and to establish a "truth in planning" standard. Additionally, local governments were required to identify desired levels of service (LOS) for each of the comprehensive planning elements, and the CIE would map how those standards would be achieved.

The concurrency requirement mandated that the infrastructure necessary to support new development must be in place before the issuance of the necessary development permit, or the permit could be issued on the condition that it be in place before a certificate of occupancy is issued. Any development that adversely impacted current LOS measurements triggered the concurrency requirement; downtowns were excluded, because the act was designed to drive new development into areas that were already developed in an effort to curtail urban sprawl.

The act virtually mandates the development of a strategic planning capacity by local governments. One observer commented (Koenig, 1988:33)

> To pull it off, communities must undergo a critical self assessment, asking themselves the fundamental questions: What are we? What do we want to be in the future? And how are we going to become that? Few communities have ever gone through such analysis.

The act also mandates strategic fiscal planning and management—directly over a broad range of service delivery areas and indirectly over the jurisdiction as a whole—in an effort to force communities to "pay as you grow." The CIE coordinates and integrates land use decisions, fiscal resource allocation decisions, and capital investment decisions to meet LOS standards; it also requires communities to describe how they will manage the concurrency process.

This mandated top-down implementation of strategic planning and management means that local governments lose some flexibility in their capital project planning process. The requirement that actual funding sources be identified is the first step to committing these resources to the project; this, coupled with the likelihood that development decisions will be made on the basis of identified future projects, means that jurisdictions must avoid the tendency to fill the out years of the plan with "wish lists" or "dog projects." They maintain some discretion in establishing LOS standards, but the act grants citizens the standing to sue if the standards are unrealistic or if they are ignored. Local governments can encourage current development and guide location decisions through the LOS standards, and then gradually raise the standards to control growth. Finally, the act virtually mandates the imposition and collection of a broad range of impact fees, and thus enables a new revenue source to fund pay as you go development.

VII. CONCLUSIONS

A strategic management effort in the local government sector does not just differ from private sector approaches because it must address the range of political demands in the community. It is also operationalized through a variety of "miniorganizations" that comprise the "holding company" that is the municipal organization. Wetzler and Petersen (1985) have suggested that the history of PPBS and ZBB point to an evolutionary trend to strategic management. However, this view ignores the failures and partial implementations associated with these budgeting innovations; they have most obviously failed as tools for centralizing budgetary control or providing for the reprogramming of departmental budgets. Klay (1991:289) concludes that "[s]trategic management does not provide a solution to the macrobudgeting problem of establishing fiscal control."

The conflict inherent in the budget process is mitigated by the idea that what is lost this year may be won the next. The capital budget benefits from the fact that fewer departments participate, as well as the ease with which questionable projects can be relegated to the out years of the CIP. According to Swanstrom (1987), the strategic planning process actually serves to limit participation and lessen political conflict. In this view, strategic planning—which was developed in the private sector—is biased toward business interests, and these interests usually initiate and control the process. This perspective also points to the weakness of overall community goals as a unifying focus for the strategic management framework.

Thus, some researchers have concluded that the strategic management effort should be confined to the level of the individual service department (Halachmi, 1986; Klay, 1991). The local government would operationalize a variety of strategic plans in functional areas; these long-range plans would also serve to rationalize the budget process (Klay, 1991). Wechsler and Backoff (1987) point out that different public agencies respond to different action environments, and a single strategic approach would not be appropriate in any case. However, if a capital budget is an integral part of a strategic plan, a comprehensive approach to capital budgeting that is separate from the political pressures of the operating budget process may be difficult to achieve in this scenario. Capital expenditure requests will be part of individual strategic plans in decentralized strategic management systems that will compete with others in the resource allocation process.

Chapman (1988) points out that local government efforts to optimize service levels and levels of physical development are intertwined; he concludes that the responsibilities of land use planners and finance personnel must be more effectively coordinated. This points to a strategic management process that is located in a limited number of staff-level departments. Rather than eliminating an organizationwide approach to strategic management and allowing each department to focus on a functional area, as above, this approach would limit the strategic management function to a few functional areas that have strategic importance for the local government organization and the community as a whole. These strategic functions would seem to include the capital budgeting process and would make the process more amenable to a comprehensive approach. This approach could be combined with the departmental-level approach, but the locus of the capital budgeting function would become problematical.

In any case, the implementation of a strategic management capacity would require a substantial organizational change effort. The sixth element of Halachmi's strategic planning model—organizational leadership and support—may be the most crucial. A fourth alternative is to focus the strategic management process on this change effort; this is, to focus the process on the internal workings of the organization as a preliminary to expanding the focus to the community and the political environment—or as a strategic management effort in itself. The internal structures and process that limit the utility and potential of strategic management can be made the targets of a strategic management process (isolationism, provincialism, the use of narrow decision criteria, weaknesses of formal measurement systems, lack of analytical data in the budget process, the building of specialized constituencies, etc.).

Many of these same issues affect the capital budgeting process, which was separated from the operating process partly in an effort to avoid them. An additional internal strategic focus that relates directly to the viability of the capital programming process is the securing of stable revenue sources and increasing the overall productivity of the local government organization. Wetzler and Petersen (1985) have identified the finance department as an area for strategic planning in this regard, and the capital programming process would be an integral part of this effort. "Simply because governments provide public services that generate *political* dividends, rather than monetary profits, this must not obscure their importance as representatives of very large financial enterprises" (Wetzler and Petersen, 1985:7).

One of the areas that such an effort could address is the forecasting function, which plays an integral part in the capital budgeting process as well as in establishing the extended CIP. A recent survey conducted by Frank and McCollough (1992) indicates that local government capacities in this are not well developed. An additional area of need is accurate and realistic measures of agency performance and service level indicators; this is an issue currently being addressed by the Governmental Accounting Standards Board (GASB). Poister and Streib (1990) have established that the use of analytical techniques for decision making is becoming more widespread among local governments despite the general failures of the budgeting systems that introduced many of them.

A brief strength = weakness = opportunity = threat (SWOT) analysis of the typical capital budgeting process is presented below. This serves as a concise summary of the issues outlined in this section, and the framework is somewhat apropos. The overall objective is to integrate the capital budgeting process with a comprehensive strategic management approach to decision making in a local government. The capital improvement plan should buttress the strategic management framework, and the strategic approach should augment the efficiency and responsiveness of the capital budgeting process.

Strengths
1. The CIP is often the only formal long-range planning process institutionalized in a local government.
2. The CIP provides a forum for a comprehensive approach to meeting the needs for capital investment.
3. Much of the CIP does not compete directly with the operating budget process.
4. There is less immediate pressure to balance revenues and expenditures in the capital budget.
5. The capital budgeting process has a history of allowing for the application of analytical techniques to rationalize the resources allocation plan.
6. The limited number of departments participating reduces political competition.
7. Capital facilities provide a concrete interface between the organization and the community.

Weaknesses
1. The level of sophistication in forecasting tools appears to be weak, as well as the incentive to forecast close to the true revenue constraint.
2. Capital project management and scheduling can be erratic and haphazard for planning purposes.
3. The analytical techniques available to enhance the rationality of the resource allocation process—such as cost-benefit analysis—may be biased toward easily quantifiable projects.
4. The existence of earmarked revenues, enterprise funds, and restrictions on user fees serves to limit the comprehensiveness of the capital budgeting process.
5. It is difficult to measure the need for capital investment.
6. Once they have been formally adopted, budgets can be rigid and make it difficult to adapt to changing circumstances.
7. It is difficult to enunciate missions at the organizational level that can serve as guides to action.

Opportunities
1. The so-called infrastructure crisis has served to highlight the need for an integrated, analytical, and comprehensive approach to local government capital investment.
2. There is strong public and professional consensus to reexamine how government services are organized and delivered.
3. The GASB may mandate the reporting of the service-level measurements that would assist and highlight capital planning efforts.

Threats
1. Political discontinuity can further politicize the capital budgeting process if it is tied to a strategic management plan.
2. The maintenance requirements of existing facilities have not been effectively integrated with the capital budgeting process, and this could undermine the comprehensiveness of a strategic approach to resource management.
3. The existence of strong centrifugal forces in local government organizations could undermine a comprehensive approach to capital programming if it is tied to a centralized strategic management capacity.

VIII. CONCLUDING REMARKS

In 1990 the government of New South Wales (Australia) made a commitment "to producing long term strategic plans for capital expenditure and to making them available to industry and community. These plans will be borne out of agencies' corporate and overall strategic plans and will reflect a 'total assets management' approach to capital expenditure planning" (*Guidelines for Capital Expenditure Strategic Plans*, 1990:1). It is too early to determine whether or not the promised has been fulfilled; however, as we pointed out in several places in this chapter the idea of merging the two efforts is rather attractive. With the recent call for reengineering, the idea of fusing the two planning processes into one is even more intriguing; yet the real question is whether such a venture is feasible and desirable in the long run.

On the one hand, advances in information technology (e.g., the use of expert software, groupware, and networking) provide governments with unprecedented management capabilities. However, these advances, which improve the planning capacity of government agencies, can augment and complicate the politics of putting together the strategic plan or the CIP.

Until the late 1970s, once elected officials made up their minds about the proper definition of desired goals or funding priorities, the rest of the "planning" was left to the professionals. In recent years, however, and partly because of the developments in information technology, growing involvement of the public in all stages of planning and implementation is creating a new reality. Information technology provides interest groups with the ability to monitor the development and implementation of strategic plans and CIP online. Consequently, planners are being directed and redirected to modify plans because at each step of the process a new compromise is made to facilitate the move to the next phase of the planning or the implementation. The risk of this mode of planning, we assert, is that the cumulative affect of the compromises that are being forged during the implementation process erodes the rationale of the initial strategic plan or the CIP. If this assertion is valid, keeping strategic planning (where planners are more susceptible to consider the political ramifications of alternative options) and capital budgeting (where planners pay close attention to economic consequences) apart is consistent with the American preference for systems that provide checks and balances. In other words, keeping the two efforts relatively independent of each other may improve the final results. The reason is that such separation may prevent costly mistakes by subjecting every decision to prolonged scrutiny. By keeping the two efforts apart a government entity could differentiate between a planning process that has strategic implications for a jurisdiction, such as the CIP, and a planning process that is conscientiously strategic. Having said this we must also emphasize that each government entity must consider its own situation at any given time. Some small communities may benefit from a consolidated process, as may some large ones under some circumstances. The recent move toward SEA reporting, for example, may create such circumstances for some government entities but not for others.

REFERENCES

Anthony, R. N. and Young D. W. (1988). *Management Control in Nonprofit Organizations*, 4th. ed., Irwin, Homewood, Ill.
Ashmore, G. M. (1989). *J. Bus. Strat.*, *10*(5): 46–50.
Axelrod, D. (1988). *Budgeting for Modern Government*, St. Martin's Press, New York.
Bateman, T. S. and Zeithaml, C. P. (1993). *Management: Function and Strategy*, 2nd ed., Irwin, Homewood, Ill., p. 142.
Bernhard, A. S. and Lachman, M. L. (1984). *Gov. Finance* (Sept.): 3–7.
Bloom, C. (1986). *J. Plan. Lit.*, *1*(2): 253–259.
Botner, S. B. (1991). *Pub. Budgeting Finan. Mgt.*, *3*(2): 443–456.
Bozeman, B. (1983). *State Gov.*, *56*(1): 2–7.
Bozeman, B. and Straussman, J. D. (1990). *Public Management Strategies*, Jossey-Bass, San Francisco.
Bozeman, J. L. (1984). *Pub. Budgeting and Finance*, *4*(3): 18–28.
Bryson, J. M. and Roering, W. D. (1988). *Pub. Admin. Rev.*, *48*(6): 995–1004.
Bryson, J. M. (1988). *Strategic Planning for Public and Nonprofit Organizations*, Jossey-Bass, San Francisco.
Bryson, J. M. (1993). *Strategic Planning for Public Service and Non-Profit Organizations* (J. M. Bryson, ed.), Pergamon Press, Oxford, U.K., pp. 11–19.
Chapman, J. I. (1988). *Pub. Admin. Rev.*, *48*(4): 800–806.
Chi, K. S. (1991). *J. State Gov.*, *64*(1): 3–11.
Clark, J. J., Hindelang, T. J. and Pritchard, R. E. (1989). *Capital Budgeting: Planning and Control of Capital Expenditures*, 3rd ed., Prentice-Hall, Englewood Cliffs, N.J.
Cohen, M. D., March, J., and Olsen, J. P. (1972). *Admin. Sci. Qu.*, *17*: 1–25.
Doss, C. B. Jr. (1987). *Pub. Budgeting and Finance*, *7*(3): 57–69.
Dror, Y. (1968). *Public Policy Reexamined*, Chandler, San Francisco.
Dutton, J. A., Walton, E. J., and Abrahamson, E. (1989). *J. Mgt. Stud.*, *26*(4): 379–397.
Eadie, D. C. (1983). *Pub. Admin. Rev.*, *43*(5): 447–452.
Frank, H. A. and McCollough, J. (1992). *Internat. J. of Pub. Admin*, 15(9): 1669–1695.
Freeman, R. E. (1984). *Strategic Management: A Stokeholder Approach*, Pittman, Boston.
Gainer, L. (1989). *Training Dev. J.*, *43*(9): S5–S30.
Gale, B. T. and Branch, B. (1987). *Sloan Mgt. Rev.*, *29*(1): 21–31.
General Accounting Office (1981). *A Glossary of Terms Used in the Federal Budget Process*, 3rd ed., U.S. General Accounting Office, Washington, D.C., PAD-81-27.
Greenwood, R. (1987). *Pub. Admin.*, *65*(3): 295–312.
Guidelines for Capital Expenditure Strategic Plans (1990). NSW Premier Departement, New South Wales Government, Sydney.
Halachmi, A. (1980). *Computers Environ. Urb. Syst.*, *5*(1–2): 35–42.
Halachmi, A. (1986). *Pub. Produc. Rev.*, *6*(4): 35–50.
Halachmi, A. (1992). *Public Productivity Handbook* (Marc Holzer, ed.), Marcel Dekker, New York, pp. 551–564.

Halachmi, A. and Boydston, R. B. (1991). *Pub. Budgeting Finan. Mgt.*, *3*(2): 293–316.
Haley, U. C. V. and Stumpf, S. A. (1989). *J. Mgt. Stud.*, *26*(5): 477–498.
Hall, J. S. and Weschler, L. S. (1991). *Nat. Civ. Rev.*, *80*(2): 135–157.
Hammer, M. (1990). *Harvard Bus. Rev.*, *68*(4): 104–112.
Hatten, K. J. and Hatten, M. L. (1987). *Strategic Management*, Prentice-Hall, Englewood Cliffs, N.J.
Hatry, H. (1984). *Guide to Managing Urban Capital*, vol. 5, (H. Hatry and G. E. Petersen, eds.), the Urban Institute, Washington, D.C., pp. 7–16.
Hill, C. W. L. and Jones, G. R. (1992). *Strategic Management*, Houghton Mifflin, Boston.
Kamensky, J. M. (1984). *Pub. Budgeting and Finance*, *4*(3): 3–16.
Klay, W. E. (1991). *Public Budgeting Finan. Mgt.*, *3*(2): 273–392.
Koenig, J. (1988). *Florida Trend* (yearbook): 31–34.
Koteen, J. (1989). *Strategic Management in Public and Nonprofit Organizations*, Praeger, New York.
Kovach, C. and Mandell, M. P. (1990). *State Local Gov. Rev.*, *22*(1): 27–36.
Levitan, D. and Byrne, M. J. (1983). *Handbook on Public Budgeting and Financial Management* (J. Rabin and T. D. Lynch, eds.), Marcel Dekker, New York.
Lyden, F. J. and Lindenberg, M. (1983). *Public Budget in Theory and Practice*, Longman, New York.
Matson, M. C. (1976). *Gov. Finance*, (Aug. 5): 42–58.
McCaffery, J. L. (1989). *Managing Public Programs* (R. E. Cleary and N. Henry, eds.), Jossey-Bass, San Francisco, pp. 193–210.
McCann, J. A. and Daun, M. J. (1989). *Gov. Finance Rev.* (June): 7–11.
McLain, L. F. Jr. (1981). *Gov. Finance* (June): 35–40.
Mercer, J. L. (1991). *Strategic Planning for Public Managers*. Quorum, New York.
Mikesell, J. L. (1991). *Fiscal Administration*, 3rd ed., Brooks/Cole, Pacific Grove, Calif.
Miller, G. (1991). *Local Government Finance*, GFOA, Chicago, pp. 241–62.
Mintzberg, H. (1992). "Five Ps for Strategy" reprinted with deletions from a 1987 paper in *The Strategy Process* (H. Mintzberg and J. B. Quinn, eds.), Prentice Hall, Englewood Cliffs, N.J., pp. 12–19.
Moore, C. M. (1987) *Group Techniques for Idea Building*, Sage, San Francisco.
Morgan, D. L. (1988). *Focus Groups as Qualitative Research*, Sage, San Francisco.
Nutt, P. C. and Backoff, R. W. (1992). *Strategic Management of Public and Third Sector Organizations*, Jossey-Bass, San Francisco.
O'Toole, D. E. and Stipak, B. (1991). *Pub. Budgeting Finan. Mgt.*, *3*(2): 317–332.
Pagano, M. A. (1984). *Pub. Budgeting and Finance*, *4*(3): 31–40.
Pagano, M. A. and Moore, R. J. T. (1985). *Cities and Fiscal Choices: A New Model of Urban Public Investment*, Duke University, Durham, N.C.
Pearce, J. A. and Robinson, R. B. (1988). *Strategic Management*, Irwin, Homewood, Ill.
Petersen, G. E. (1978). *The Fiscal Outlook for Cities* (R. Bahl, ed.), Syracuse University Press, Syracuse, N.Y., pp. 49–74.
Preble, J. F. (1982). *Amer. Rev. Pub. Admin.*, *16*(2): 139–150.
Quinn, J. B. (1992). *The Strategy Process: Concepts and Context* (H. Mintzberg and J. B. Quinn, eds.), Prentice Hall, Englewood Cliffs, N.J., pp. 4–12 (first published in 1980).
Quinn, R. E. (1988). *Beyond Rational Management*, Jossey-Bass, San Francisco.
Rider, R. W. (1993). *Strategic Planning for Public Service and Non-Profit Organizations* (J. M. Bryson, ed.), Pergamon Press, Oxford, U.K., pp. 23–31.
Riordan, T., Oria, M. E., and Tuss, J. P. (1987). *Gov. Finance Rev.* (April): 7–13.
Robinson, S. G. (1991). *Local Government Finance* (J. E. Petersen and D. R. Strachota, eds.), GFOA, Chicago, pp. 65–84.
Rubin, I. S. (1993). *The Politics of Public Budgeting*, 2nd ed., Chatham House, Chatham, N.J.
Rubin, I. S. (1990). *Pub. Admin. Rev.*, *50*(2): 179–189.
Schick, A. (1966). *Public. Admin. Rev.*, *26*(Dec.): 243–258.
Schick, A. (1990). *Pub. Admin. Rev.*, *50*(1): 26–34.
Shrivastava, P. and Nachman, S. A. (1989). *Strat. Mgt. J.*, *10*: 51–61.
Shultz, M. L. (1991). *Trustee*, *44*(10): 10–11.
Steiss, A. W. (1985). *Strategic Management and Organizational Decision Making*, Brooks/Cole, Pacific Grove, Calif.
Stewart, D. W. and Shamdasani, P. M. (1990). *Focus Groups: Theory and Practice*, Sage, San Francisco.
Stubart, C. I. (1989). *J. Mgt. Stud.*, *26*(4): 325–328.
Swanstrom, T. (1987). *J. Urban Affairs*, *9*(2): 139–157.
Thomassen, H. (1990). *Pub. Budgeting and Finance*, *10*(4): 72–86.
Wechsler, B. and Backoff, R. W. (1987). *Amer. Plan. Assoc. J.* (Winter): 34–43.
Westley, F. and Mintzberg, H. (1989). *Strat. Mgt. J.*, *10*: 17–32.
Wetzler, J. W. and Petersen, J. E. (1985). *Gov. Finance Rev.* (April): 7–10.
Wheeland, C. M. (1993). *Pub. Admin. Rev.*, *53*(1): 65–72.
Wintrobe, R. and Berton, A. (1986). *Amer. Econ. Rev.*, *76*(3): 530–538.

11

State Capital Budgeting: The Case of New Jersey Under Thomas Kean

William H. Eldridge
Kean College, Union, New Jersey

Despite its vital importance, capital budgeting is one of those areas that has eluded routine discussions of American government and politics. The subject of the construction of roads, bridges, sewer plants, prisons, and buildings is not one that has proven to be of interest, either to the general public or to the media. The area is rather complicated, full of detail, and not a subject readily discussed in the tabloids or on an "eyewitness news" broadcast.

In addition, a great many superficial analyses of capital budgeting have referred merely to "pork barrel" projects. Such analyses have been based on the premise that capital projects have become nothing more than objects that are traded back and forth among lawmakers. The premise was "you vote for my project and I will vote for your project."

While there was probably some truth to the notion that capital projects could be abused (what concept has not), it fails to reflect the fact that many dams, roads, and other projects were needed to create energy, transport goods, house prisoners and train soldiers. In addition, it did not reflect broader capital needs that were required to span election districts, state boundaries, or city lines. After all, what would America be like if the federal government had not constructed the interstate highway system under President Eisenhower.

A third issue is the rather strange collection of requirements that have been designed to ensure that a variety of groups can either issue debt or prevent its issuance. For example, the number of state-level purpose governments with debt outstanding rose from 224 to 354 from 1977 to 1987, a gain of nearly 60%. These purpose governments consist of authorities, commissions, corporations, boards, administrations, associations, banks, centers, companies, cooperatives, councils, districts, funds, hospitals, ports, systems, and turnpikes.

On the other hand, state governments either by constitution or statute have limited their authority to incur state general obligation borrowing. These include voter approval for borrowing, extraordinary legislative majority approval required for borrowing, flexible debt limits tied to collection of revenue or property values to include voter approval for borrowing, dollar limits on debts tied to voter approval by referendum, and other restrictions.

Furthermore, the level of state long-term debt outstanding has risen from about $87 billion from 1976 to 1977 to about $264 billion from 1987 to 1988, an increase of over 203%. The growth in state debt reflected the need to finance many public purpose activities and aging capital stock within the restraints of increasingly restrictive operating budgets. Long-term debt became a preferred alternative to "pay-as-you-go financing" to deal with capital projects.

These increases in long-term debt have led to the increasing reluctance of voters to approve large capital projects. Recently, these have even included rejection of major programs in New York and California designed to protect the environment (1990 referenda).

These same elements were present in New Jersey during the early 1970s. They led the governor and the legislature to give special attention to the capital needs of the state as well as to its capital budgeting process.

After the voters had rejected a series of proposed bond issues, including those to improve higher education, the state's chief executive and legislators decided to take a detailed look at the reasons for the voters' unwillingness to approve expenditures for long-term capital projects.

A special commission, the McNaughton Commission, composed of members of both political parties, and the executive and legislative branches, as well as representatives from business and labor were appointed to study the problem. What they needed to determine were the reasons voters kept rejecting valuable capital projects.

After consulting with voters and opinion leaders throughout the state, they discovered that the average citizen did not believe that capital projects had been adequately reviewed before they had been placed on the ballot for voter approval. Clearly, citizens had little confidence that their elected officials were giving these proposals careful consideration.

Apparently, voters had also reached the conclusion or been taught that capital projects were merely pork barrel activities placed on the ballot in order to satisfy some political objective. The commission also found that the citizens did not have a detailed knowledge of the specific provisions of the bond issues on which they were being asked to vote.

In addition, the investigating commission discovered that voters were generally suspicious of substantial governmental spending. This was particularly true with respect to the millions of dollars needed to finance the large capital projects that appeared on the ballot. All of these factors combined to result in regular defeats by voters of bond issues that governmental officials believed were critical to the state's well-being. In fact, eight of the sixteen bond issues appearing on the ballot from 1967 to 1976 were rejected by the electorate.

After the investigating commission had done its review, it recommended that a permanent commission be established, its purpose being to review all capital projects independently from the governor and legislature. The special commission believed that this would help restore the confidence of the public in the capital budgeting process. After conducting public hearings, the legislature passed and the governor signed legislation creating the permanent New Jersey Commission on Capital Budgeting and Planning.

The legislation creating the commission defined a capital project as any undertaking that is to be financed or funded by the issuance of bonds, notes, or other evidence of indebtedness of the state or any public authority thereof; or any undertaking that is to be financed or funded or is requested to be financed or funded by an appropriation in the annual budget, where the expenditure therefore is, by statute, or under standards as they may be prescribed from time to time by the Department of Treasury, a capital expenditure.

The legislation created a permanent commission consisting of twelve members selected as follows: the state treasurer, and three other members of the executive branch designated by the governor to serve at his or her pleasure; two members of different parties from the General Assembly to be designated by the speaker; two members of different parties from the Senate to be designated by its president; and four members of the public at large of different parties for 6-year terms to be appointed by the governor with the advice and consent of the Senate in a staggered manner. The chairman was to be designated by the governor from among the public members.

The commission was authorized to employ an executive director and to be staffed by the Division of Budget and Accounting of the Department of Treasury. The division was also authorized to create a bureau of capital planning for this purpose. The commission was also allowed to employ clerical and other assistance and to incur expenses as deemed necessary to perform its functions. The ability to obtain a budget is particularly important for any government agency and this provision recognized the importance of the commission as outlined in the enabling legislation.

The commission was mandated to prepare a state capital improvement plan containing its proposals for state spending for capital projects that shall be consistent with the goals and provisions of the state development and redevelopment plan adopted by the State Planning Commission. Copies of the plan were to be submitted to the governor and the legislature no later than December 1 of each year.

The act required that the plan provide a detailed list of all capital projects that the commission recommended be undertaken or continued by any state agency in the next 3 fiscal years, together with information as to the effect of such capital projects on future operating expenses of the state, and with recommendations as to the priority of such capital projects and the means of funding them.

The provisions of the act required that the plan provide forecasts from the commission as to the requirement for capital projects of state agencies for the 4 fiscal years following the 3 years previously mentioned and for any additional periods required for adequate presentation of particular projects. This provision was clearly designed to permit the commission and other state agencies to develop meaningful forecasts of the state's future capital needs.

The act also required a schedule for the next fiscal year of recommended appropriations of bond funds from issues of bonds previously authorized. In light of the drafters' previous concern about the voters' lack of confidence in bond issues, this provision helped ensure a specific review of how the bonds were being spent, as well as an examination of how they will be spent in the future.

The law required a review of capital projects that have recently been implemented or completed or are in the process of being implemented or completed. This provision helped ensure that there was a review of the actual projects as well as the expenditures associated with the projects.

The enabling legislation also required that the plan contain recommendations as to the maintenance of the physical properties and equipment of state agencies. This provision was particularly important when enacted, and remains important now.

Throughout the nation, the country's infrastructure has been collapsing regularly because of the lack of maintenance. Almost daily, one sees television or newspaper reports of collapsing bridges or highways. There has been very little of this with respect to the facilities of the state of New Jersey.

The act further requires that the state agencies provide, by August 15, a detailed list of capital projects that the state agency seeks to undertake or continue in the next 3 fiscal years, together with information as to the effect of such capital projects on future operating expenses, forecasts as to requirements for future capital projects, requests for appropriations of bond funds from issues of bonds previously authorized, a report on capital projects being implemented or completed, a report as to the maintenance of its physical properties and capital equipment, and any other information it may request.

This section of the enabling legislation helped give teeth to the commission's activities by requiring agencies to give the commission all the information it needed to perform its functions.

The act also mandated a review by the commission of any bill introduced in either house of the legislature that makes provision for an appropriation for a capital project or for the issuance of bonds, notes, or other evidences of indebtedness of either the state or a state agency containing a pledge of the state. The commission was mandated to study the necessity, desirability, and relative priority of such appropriation or indebtedness and to prepare and forward its recommendation on the bill to the house in which it was introduced.

This provision gave the commission a very substantial degree of power because it prevented the legislature from introducing and passing bills relating to capital projects without a recommendation with respect to the desirability of the expenditure from the commission.

The enabling legislation went on to permit the commission to conduct public hearings to further its purposes and to request the appearance of officials and to solicit the testimony of interested groups and the general public. The ability to conduct these hearings became of vital importance to the commission's activities in future years.

I.   THE POLITICAL ENVIRONMENT

After the legislation was enacted, the commission's members were appointed. Because the executive and legislative branches were controlled by the Democratic party, eight of the original twelve members were Democrats. This could have raised substantial questions about the commission's impartiality. However, this problem was resolved when the commission named a Republican who had an outstanding career in business as executive director. This appointment helped give the commission significant credibility with political, business, and labor leaders, as well as with the state's opinion leaders.

The newly appointed executive director further added to the credibility of the commission when he announced that he was willing to accept a salary reduction because of a state budget crisis. This offer achieved wide circulation throughout the media, and gave both the executive director and the commission an impressive beginning.

Because the governor and legislature had only recently passed the legislation as well as having only recently witnessed various bond issues being defeated by the voters, they had a strong interest in having the commission succeed. The scope of the enabling legislation indicates this, and they also gave the commission full support.

In terms of capital projects it should be recognized that legislators have certain interests in mind. Most capital projects are supported by legislators because they believe there is an actual need for them. This is particularly true of large-scale statewide projects. Many legislators discover a personal interest and believe it is important for the state to accomplish this objective.

One legislator may become interested in the problems of the homeless and offer a bond issue to help this group. Another legislator may decide that what the state needs is a new baseball stadium in order to attract major league sports. A third may become concerned about the state's bridges and regularly offer bond issues to ensure that they are maintained in top condition. A fourth may have an abiding interest in the state's highway system, and a fifth may believe it is important to maintain and increase the state's parks and recreational areas.

In addition, the various agencies of the state government all have a variety of real and imagined capital needs. The human services areas have very large facilities that are similar in scope to small-sized cities. In these facilities they house or care for a variety of people with special problems or needs.

For example, there are enormous hospitals that care only for the mentally ill. Scattered around the state are facilities to care for the elderly. Still other facilities care for the mentally retarded or children with extraordinary physical difficulties or health problems. One can imagine the enormous capital needs of a department with facilities having the mission of taking care of people with these special problems.

Another department with tremendous capital needs is the state department of transportation. This department has the responsibility of building new highways throughout the state. Much of its funding comes through the federal government. However, these federal funds are available only if the state has a percentage of matching funds available. This puts enormous pressure on the state to have sufficient capital funds in the pipeline.

The department of transportation also has the responsibility for repairing the state's roads. If roads are maintained well, the costs of keeping them in top condition are relatively minor. On the other hand, if the roads are allowed to deteriorate for more than 7 years, the cost of maintaining the roads goes up dramatically. This means that the department requires a steady influx of capital funds.

Another department that has very substantial and regular capital needs is the Department of Higher Education. This department supervises approximately 30 universities, as well as state and county colleges. These centers of higher education contain hundreds of buildings that need constant maintenance and repair. If the state wishes to construct new or newer facilities, initial and future costs are even higher.

The Department of Correction's mission is to house the thousands of prisoners in the state. Because of the rapid increase in the number of prisoners committed for drug-related offenses, the need for prison space has grown significantly. Again, if one adds the future costs associated with repair and maintenance, the need for capital funds increases substantially.

The Department of Environmental Protection maintains huge amounts of open spaces and parklands. The costs of maintaining them are quite significant. In addition, the increasing urbanization of the state of New Jersey has spurred calls for additional capital funds to acquire new property in order to protect wetlands and other vital natural resources of the state.

In brief, many people who have done capital budgeting have found that there are a great many valuable purposes for capital funds. Some of these purposes are suggested by legislators and some of them are derived from the agencies. In periods of limited funds, some mechanism will develop to resolve the interests that compete for available monies. The real issue may be how rational the process is that makes the allocation decision.

Traditionally, many decisions were made through a variety of trade-offs either among legislators or between legislators and the executive branch. This is the traditional definition of *logrolling* in the sense that legislators take turns voting for each other's capital projects or the executive branch members and the legislators take turns supporting each other's projects. The executive branch can engage in the same process; each of the major department heads can take turns supporting each other's capital projects.

This appears to be the practice in most states and to have been the experience in New Jersey before the establishment of the Capital Budgeting and Planning Commission. While this process has the advantages of relative simplicity, a certain sense of fairness, and a balancing of political interests, it does not have the advantages of a more formal allocation system to include rational, systematic priority-setting mechanisms, evaluation of long-term financing costs, and consideration of future operating expenses.

One of the commission's first tasks was to move toward a more formalized system and to convince the executive and legislative branch members to move away from the old logrolling method and toward a more rational approach. Another objective of the commission was to inform the state's political leaders and voting public that a new, formalized, rational mechanism for evaluating capital projects was now in place. Similarly, the commission staff had to develop methods of communicating this to the various agencies, governmental branches, media, opinion leaders, and public.

The commission and its staff also needed to develop methods for collecting information, presenting and evaluating that information, and establishing criteria for making decisions about approving various capital requests. The commission and its staff also needed to develop means of communicating its decisions to the various stakeholders in a timely fashion. This was particularly important with respect to bond issues that needed to be approved by the legislature, printed on ballots, and approved by the public.

In addition, the commission and its staff needed to develop more specific criteria for evaluating capital projects and to deal with issues involving long-term versus shorter-term funding. Other questions involved the speed of the implementation of capital projects resulting from voter approval of substantial bond issues, as well the evaluation of additional operating costs resulting from new capital projects. Similarly, savings resulting from the rehabilitations of capital facilities needed to be factored into the equation. The next section considers how the commission and its staff resolved these political and financial considerations.

II. DEFINING THE ROLE OF THE CAPITAL BUDGETING AND PLANNING COMMISSION

The first step was to make the commission's advisory role essential to the governor's and legislature's constitutional roles related to the approval of all capital expenditures. To that objective, the commission immediately concentrated on working with the legislature and the chief executive of the state government to develop a workable capital program. The commission and its staff focused first on the most critical capital needs.

The commission first retained a full-time staff of individuals with strong backgrounds in finance as well as in the areas of capital planning and budgeting. The commission then developed three primary objectives in preparing the capital plan. They are: (1) to develop and maintain on an ongoing basis short- and long-range capital spending plans for the state; (2) to analyze and report on the impact of capital spending plans on future operating budgets; and (3) to present the plans for short- and long-range capital investments. The commission recommends to the governor and the legislature items for inclusion in the annual budget. The commission also suggests the means by which capital projects should be funded and comments on capital projects recently completed or presently under construction, as well as making recommendations on the maintenance of state facilities.

While the commission was created to develop a systematic and concentrated focus on the investment of New Jersey's limited capital resources, it began its work slowly by concentrating first on those departments that were capital-intensive. As the commission matured, it gradually expanded its role to encompass all the responsibilities outlined in the enabling legislation. This included its responsibilities of oversight with respect not only to the executive and administrative departments of the state, but also to public authorities and other instrumentalities of the state government (P.L., 1975, c.208, Sec. 1d).

The commission developed specific criteria for recommending the expenditure of funds for capital projects. These are

1. The need must be critical and well defined.
2. Careful planning must proceed each capital project.
3. Maximum utilization must be made of available federal matching aid.
4. Expenditures must be cost-effective, with a minimal impact or future operating budgets, and with priority given to projects that would help reduce annual maintenance expenses.

The commission modifies these criteria slightly in developing bond issue recommendations to ensure the prompt and effective use of bond funds.

In addition to monitoring capital spending and making annual capital appropriations recommendations, the commission and its staff regularly consider capital needs of the state that would be funded by future bond referenda. The commission evaluates these needs, which may be presented to the voters each November, and forwards these recommendations to the governor and the legislative branch as soon as they are determined.

It is useful to take a more detailed examination of each of these criteria and how the commission applied them; first, "the needs must be critical and well defined." This has been–and remains–a difficult objective to attain. A major task of the commission's staff was to force the departments to examine and reexamine their capital projects to ensure that only the most important projects were being presented.

Given the limited resources available for capital projects and the large number of valuable projects that could be financed, it was essential for the staff to ask the departments to return to their subordinates and to sort out projects that could be deleted or delayed. This required the commission's staff and the departments to be rigorous in their demand for the agencies to set priorities more effectively than they had done in the past.

While this was a difficult process, the commission's staff developed a constructive relationship with the professionals in the departments and the various agencies. This ultimately led to a more careful analysis of capital projects and a more thoughtful consideration of capital needs.

This was particularly important with respect to proposed bond issues. Only a few bond proposals can appear on the ballot in any 1 year. This is true for a number of reasons. First, bond proposals are particularly well scrutinized by the media and opinion leaders. If the needs appear less than critical, they are likely to be rejected.

Second, at some point a ceiling is reached in terms of the dollar amount that the voters will approve in any one election. In New Jersey, the rule of thumb seemed to be about $150 million. If the amount became higher than that level, the voters seemed to rebel against one or more of the bond proposals.

Third, because of the general unwillingness of the electorate to approve governmental expenditures, it takes some resources and a considerable amount of effort to convince citizens that a bond issue should be approved. It is much easier to gain voter approval if there are only one or two bond proposals. It is important that the needs underlying the bond issue be critical if it is to gain the support and approval of the voters.

The second major criterion was that careful planning precede each capital project. This was not something that had been required of the departments or agencies prior to the establishment of the commission, and was certainly not required of the various members of the legislature.

The commission staff required that there be plans for each major project rather than merely one plan for a group of capital projects. The staff asked that the plans demonstrate why the project was important, how it would impact on future operating expenses, when the project would begin, what the period of construction would be, and when the ending date would be, what the methods of financing would be. Part of the commission's concern was to encourage the agencies to develop a more general outlook with respect to their projects; that is, if the projects are not only useful with respect to that agency, but also of significance to the state as a whole.

A great deal of effort was devoted to analyzing the time frame for completion of the projects. One of the purposes was to prevent the costs of the projects from rising because of delays and resultant inflation. Another purpose was to ensure that needed projects were finished quickly in order to benefit the state. A third purpose was to bolster the image of government competence and to reduce the impression of governmental inaction and inefficiency.

Part of the planning process related to the exact sources of financing for the project. This was particularly important for those departments that derive a significant percentage of their financing from the federal government. Considerable effort was devoted to attracting these funds. This was the genesis of the transportation trust fund. By dedicating a significant stream of state revenues, the Department of Transportation was able to secure a large amount of federal funds in order to build and repair major highways throughout the state. The construction of these major arteries helped spur the rapid economic growth in New Jersey during the 1980s.

The third basic criterion was to obtain maximum utilization of federal matching funds. This objective has been referenced previously, but its importance cannot be overstated. This is particularly true in New Jersey, which has traditionally ranked close to the bottom of states in terms of attracting federal funds. Because of the large number of sites in the state that require cleanup of hazardous waste, New Jersey is highly dependent on contributions from other levels of government.

No state can be expected to bear the enormous cost of cleaning up these sites by itself, and New Jersey is no exception. Therefore, it became imperative for the state to develop cleanup programs in a manner that would attract the maximum amount of federal monies. It was particularly important to do so quickly before federal funding was exhausted by requests from other states.

To a lesser extent, other departments were also able to attract federal funds if the capital projects were structured correctly. This became an important goal for the commission, its staff, and the people who handled capital budgeting for the departments and their subunits.

The fourth objective was that expenditures must be cost-effective with a minimal impact on future operating budgets, and with priority given to projects that would help reduce annual maintenance expenses. Given the public image of capital projects as mere pork barrel, it was particularly important that the commission demonstrate that it was especially concerned about controlling costs. Because the state has limited resources available for capital projects and restrictive annual operating budgets, it was necessary for the commission to demonstrate that it was concerned with restraining costs.

Its focus on keeping costs under control helped the commission gain and retain credibility with the public, opinion makers, and leaders in state government. In addition, it helped give the commission and its staff a strong sense of focus.

For the first time in state governmental history, departments were being asked to give special attention to the relationship between capital project and operating budgets. Those capital projects that actually reduced maintenance costs and annual operating costs were given first priority. Other projects were ranked, partially based on how they would affect the annual budget.

Departments and agencies began to develop capital budgets that incorporated these objectives. As a result, they contained fewer projects that would add to annual operating costs and more projects that would reduce these costs or at least not increase them.

This criterion has been particularly helpful with respect to bond issues presented to the public. New Jersey has not been plagued with scandals involving capital projects or multibillion debt proposals, as has been the case in some other states. The voters could feel confident that only the most critical and cost-effective proposals were being presented to them for approval. This helped reduce some of the skepticism of the public with respect to capital projects.

A fifth criterion of the commission was to favor capital projects that ensured prompt and efficient use of bond funds. This objective was partially related to the perception that bond funds were being proposed, being passed by the voters, and then not being spent. While this perception probably reflected a limited understanding of the complexity of capital project planning and implementation as well as the length of time necessary to issue bonds, appropriate funds, and spend the monies, it was still an issue that needed to be addressed.

Members of the commission staff often found that members of the public believed erroneously that approved bond issues were simply piles of money that were sitting around in the state treasury and could be used for whatever purposes the governor and the legislature wanted. They also did not understand that it was often cheaper for the state to borrow money at tax-exempt rates than to use current operating funds. As a result the commission and its staff made a concerted effort to ensure that capital projects were given additional priority if they ensured that bond funds were used for the purpose approved.

III.   EVALUATING NEW JERSEY'S CAPITAL BUDGETING EXPERIENCE

One way to begin evaluating the capital planning process in New Jersey is to assess how the public has reacted to the commission's efforts in terms of bond referenda proposed for the voters' approval. Generally, the public appears to have considerably more confidence in the process than previously. Much of the old pork barrel image seems to have disappeared. Instead, there is a greater understanding of the value of improving the state's infrastructure, specifically in the change in the passing rate of bond issues. In the years prior to the establishment of the Capital Budgeting and Planning Commission the voters approved only eight of sixteen bond issues (a passing rate of 50%).

In contrast, the voters have endorsed 33 of 35 bond issues placed before them in the 13 years after the commission's creation. This turnaround demonstrates that the public seems to have greater confidence in the process utilized for evaluating capital programs before they are presented to the electorate. It also seems to show that the public values the independent review performed by the commission before it recommends any bond issues.

One of the commission's tasks is to increase its contact with the public in order to make the electorate more aware of both the commission's role and the process of capital budgeting and planning. The commission believes that "the people of New Jersey should be aware of the intense review process that bond proposals receive, and of the monitoring of these funds once the bond proposal is authorized." A brochure outlining the duties and responsibilities of the commission has been prepared and circulated among various groups. Staff members regularly participate in seminars and panel discussions both inside and outside the state.

Articles describing the commission's functions and activities have appeared in various newspapers and other publications. Budget directors from other states have inquired about the process, the plans requested from the various agencies, and the methods of evaluating proposed capital projects. At the federal level there has been extensive discussion regarding creation of a federal capital budget that would place federal capital projects outside the normal default-ridden operating budget.

New Jersey is, at the very least, in a position in which it can obtain monies to finance those capital projects necessary to maintain one infrastructure that undergirds the state's economy. Some states have allowed the infrastructure to deteriorate so badly that their economy has been harmed.

More than one director of state budgets has told this author that the state's declining infrastructure has hurt its ability to attract business to the state. At the same time, the state's poor economy has prevented the state from convincing voters that money is needed for infrastructure repairs. In short, it is the worst of all possibilities. It is not one that has been seen in New Jersey.

New Jersey's financial position with its triple-A bond rating places it in the top tier of the nation's states. As of December 31, 1989, New Jersey had an authorized debt of $7.06 billion. Of this total, $2.9 billion is outstanding and $2 billion has been retired. An amount of $2.2 billion remains to be issued. The annual debt service of New Jersey is about 3% of the total budget, which is relatively conservative when compared to other states.

One of the issues that the commission and its staff has had to confront during its entire existence is that of debt financing as opposed to pay-as-you-go financing put on the annual budget. Although one could argue that debt financing is particularly appropriate for capital projects because of their long life, the commission and its staff has constantly suggested that capital projects be financed from the operating budgets as much as possible for several reasons.

First, annual financing of capital projects reflects the constant need for such projects. This is particularly true in the case of maintenance activities, which are needed continually.

A second major argument in favor of pay-as-you-go financing is that it limits the need for financing through general obligation bond issues. This by itself has enormous advantages for the state in terms of both capital and operating budgets.

First, the bond-reviewing organizations prefer that states issue as little long-term debt as possible. When the amount of bond debt is low, the bond rating tends to be high. This saves the state and its taxpayers a considerable amount in lower interest payments. Given the length of these bonds, the savings to the citizens can be very substantial.

Second, as was noted above, it is extremely difficult to sort out all the possible capital projects and select those that should be placed on the ballot. If more can be financed by operating budgets, less needs to go through this process. This allows greater consideration of the more critical capital needs of the state, and their placement on the ballot. As was discussed previously, it is not easy to gain voter approval of bond proposals for a variety of reasons. It takes a considerable amount of effort to persuade the state's opinion leaders and electorate to favor large capital expenditures. If the number of proposals on the ballot are limited, those that remain have a better chance of gaining acceptance.

The commission and its staff have worked diligently to maintain a high degree of confidence in the capital budgeting process. By urging more pay-as-you-go financing, they help reduce the chances that less-than-critical capital needs will be presented to voters, and the odds that this confidence will be maintained are increased.

Another reason for advocating pay-as-you-go financing is that it helps shelter capital projects from the vagaries of the annual budget process. When funds are built into the annual budget it makes it difficult to take them out in future years when budgets are tight. This is particularly true of maintenance projects designed to reduce operating expenses. While one can argue that certain programs can be deleted in periods of budgetary crisis, its difficult to argue against projects that actually reduce operating costs.

Another method of evaluating the capital budgeting process is to look at how the commission pared budget requests from the various departments and agencies down to the most critical needs. While each year's results were somewhat different, the general trend was that the commission tended to recommend to the executive and legislative branches about 50% to 65% of the amount of current operating funds requested by the departments for capital projects. The commission recommended a much higher percentage (70% to 80%) of funds derived from previously approved bond funds requested by the various state departments. This indicated a careful screening of projects to ensure that they complied with the voters' wishes when the bonds were approved.

It is useful to look at some of the specific capital projects and how they were financed. For this purpose, the commission's capital improvement program for June 1990 is referenced. For example, the Department of Environmental Protection regularly needs funds for the reconstruction of various recreational lake dams, park road systems, and maintenance facilities.

The department submitted these projects to the commission along with many others. The incremental annual costs were estimated at $0. The estimated total capital costs for these projects is $23 million. Of this amount $4 million had already been made available from previous appropriations. The Capital Budgeting Commission recommended approval of $5 million for the current year. The estimated cost of these projects for the next 2 years is $14 million, and there is no additional estimated cost for the remaining 4 years in the 7-year capital improvement program.

The Department of Environmental Protection also requested that its existing program for sewage plant construction be continued. The total estimated cost consists of $522.6 million. This amount would be derived from $79.6 million in general funds, $359.6 million from federal funds, and $83.4 million from other funds.

Looking at the total plan one can see that $182 million was made available in previous years, $104 million was recommended by the commission for the current fiscal year, $134 million was the estimated cost for the next year, $88 million was estimated for the following year, and $14 million was the estimated cost for the final 4 years of the capital improvement program.

The Department of State requested approval of a study related to the expansion for the state museum in Trenton. The department estimated that the study could find ways of reducing operating costs by approximately $3 million per year. The commission recommended that $273,000 be approved to continue the study of the museum's renovation and expansion.

The Department of Transportation requested funds for its road building program. The estimated cost was approximately $5.1 billion. Of this amount $2.9 billion was to be derived from the state's general fund and $2.2 billion would be from federal funds.

In previous years, $768 million had been made available. Of this amount, $331 million had come from state funds and $437 million had come from federal funds. The commission recommended that another $331 million be made available for the next year, which when combined with federal funds of $566 million, made a total of $897 million available.

The remainder of the department's 7-year plan asked for $365 million in the next year, which would also allow the state to acquire $327 million in matching federal funds, for a total of $692 million. In the following years the department's plan requested another $365 million which, in combination with federal funds of $206 million, gives a total of $571 million. In the subsequent 4 years the department's plan would provide for $1.5 billion and federal matching grants of $734 million, for a total of $2.2 billion.

This illustrates the value of effective long-term planning with an objective to maximizing the value of state and federal funding. In addition, the completion and repair of state roads had a positive effect on the state's economy, which generated additional revenues for the state government.

It is useful to look at the Department of Corrections to observe how the state's capital needs often grow based on particular pieces of legislation. The overwhelming issue that the department faces is prison overcrowding. This has resulted predominantly from the effects of the revision of the state's narcotic statutes in 1987 (the Comprehensive Drug Reform Act of 1987), the 2c criminal code (enacted in 1979), and the Parole Act of 1979 (reenacted in 1980).

The department observed that the state prison population has almost tripled (from 3,750 to 11,100) since enactment of 2c while the youth complex population had doubled (from 2,050 to 3,932). In addition to the inmates housed in facilities directly operated by the Department, approximately 2,900 state inmates were backed up in county facilities awaiting admission and another 600 state inmates were housed in county facilities under the County Assistance and County Contract Programs. Along with this increase in population, there was also an increase in time served as result of 2c's mandatory minimum term provisions. From 1979–1988, approximately 13,500 (almost 38%) of the 36,000 inmates sentenced to state prison under 2c received mandatory minimum terms. Approximately 53% of current state prison inmates are serving mandatory terms.

Under the Parole Act of 1979, releases have fluctuated widely. In 1980, releases increased substantially, dropped again in 1981 and 1982, increased dramatically in 1983, dropped in 1984, and increased to 4,800 in 1985. A slight increase was experienced in 1986, and 1987 represented the first year of over 5,000 releases. Another substantial increase was experienced in 1988, when over 6,000 inmates were released. During fiscal 1989, release volume increased to 6,200, and is expected to continue to increase.

As noted above, another significant problem is the backup of state-sentenced offenders in county jails, despite a significant increase in the number of offenders admitted to the state prison complex over the last several years, as a result of massive capital construction projects. Almost 2,900 inmates are backed up in county correctional facilities. The housing of state-sentenced offenders in county facilities only further exacerbates the county population problems which also have increased under the new criminal code.

The imposition of long parole ineligibility terms that are not reduced by good time, work, and minimum custody credits has a serious impact on the usages of maximum and medium bed spaces. The increase in the length of stay under these sentences results in offenders who have a greater propensity to act out and become management control problems, and are also more likely to attempt escape. Because of this combination of factors, these offenders pose a higher security risk and must be housed in a medium or maximum security facility for longer periods of time than offenders receiving similar sentences under the 2A criminal code without mandatory minimum or parole ineligibility terms.

The population trends resulting from the legislation in combination with the impact of the speedy trial program are awesome. The governor's task force on prison overcrowding has projected the state's inmate population to increase substantially through 1990 under current sentencing and parole release practices.

The interacting effects of the current statutes, particularly as they relate to the imposition of long minimum terms (without parole eligibility) have necessitated the review of several of the recommendations of the correctional master plan, most notably those that have to do with the "nonconstruction" alternative. Under New Jersey's code of criminal justice, the need to provide safe, humane, and secure facilities for violent and repetitive offenders who are receiving long minimum parole ineligibility terms is paramount. To this end, the department has shifted this philosophical position of nonconstruction to one of "new construction and expansion" of existing facilities, specifically in relation to medium and maximum custody bed spaces. The experience of the new code thus far, coupled with the projection of its impact, made by the governor's task force on prison overcrowding, requires the department to look for permanent bed space solutions that will provide custody and care for long-term offenders who are being committed under the code.

The Department of Corrections has taken significant steps to address policy and facility planning issues raised by the New Jersey code of criminal justice and the new parole act. The capital construction program for the state correctional system has included major capital improvements necessary for both the replacement of substandard beds and the addition of medium security beds to meet the expected increase in the number of state offenders. The department has added approximately 6,500 new beds. Renovation of the New Jersey state prison and construction of the Southern State I and II River Front correctional facilities form the core of the department's efforts. In addition to this original initiative, the department received a supplemental appropriation from the legislature in fiscal year 1985 and funding from the Correctional Bond Act for additional bed space construction. By the end of 1991 it is anticipated that the department will have added approximately 9,600 new beds.

The department is pursuing other modified local correctional alternatives. Bond funds approved in the Public Purpose Construction Bond Act of 1980, the Correctional Facilities Construction Bond Act of 1982, and the Correctional Facilities Bond Act of 1967 have been appropriated for the construction of new jails and renovations of present facilities on the county level in return for the allocation of bed spaces for state offenders. The department has completed agreements with Gloucester, Passaic, Middlesex, Atlantic, Morris, Ocean, Mercer, Monmouth, Bergen, Camden, Cumberland, Union, Hudson, Somerset, and Salem Counties through the department's county assistance program. It is anticipated that 999 medium security beds will be allocated for state offenders in return for construction and renovation costs obtained through this source.

This new bed space program was planned with the assumption that the existing bed spaces totaling approximately 7,100 would continue to be available for inmate housing. Therefore, the second initiative in the department's capital construction program was the development of a plan for the maintenance of the existing physical plant to ensure the availability of these bed spaces and to minimize further deterioration. This initiative also includes the necessary improvements that must be made at all facilities to meet various new codes with regard to fire safety and environmental concerns.

The third area of emphasis is the need for improvement and expansion of support areas at various facilities. With the rapid increase in the inmate population within the department it was not feasible to include the improvement or expansion of such areas as infirmaries, kitchens, recreation, and day space areas within the facilities. In fiscal year 1989 the department received appropriations to begin design work on various "support area" projects. Design work has been initiated on those projects, therefore, this year's capital budget submission includes several requests for funding to implement construction. The fiscal year 1991 submission also includes a number of new projects for which funding for design work only is being requested, with construction funds to be identified in subsequent fiscal year requests.

In summary, the department's capital construction program can be categorized into the following areas:

1. Addition of new bed spaces
2. Maintenance and improvement of existing facilities
3. Improvement and expansion of support areas

Continued implementation of this program will not only ensure the availability of required bed spaces but will also serve to protect the investment the state has made in prior capital construction programs.

The Department of Corrections' capital program illustrates a number of key points. A careful review of the department's plan demonstrates how it built it around the changes in its environment and the tremendous increase in its capital needs. It also reflects how a change in a few pieces of legislation can have an enormous and sometimes unexpected impact on the state's infrastructure.

One issue for the state continues to be how it passed legislation and the impact of such laws on the operating and capital budgets. Each piece of legislation is supposed to be accompanied by fiscal notes that analyze the impact on the state's budget. However, the examples cited by the department demonstrate how inadequate these notes can be. The legislature may have decided in response to public concern that it was necessary to impose harsher penalties with respect to drug-related crimes, but it did not adequately consider the costs of constructing prisons to house these criminals. In this instance, the department has responded well to situations to a large degree beyond its control.

One department with a wide degree of responsibilities in fields of increasing importance is the Department of Environmental Protection. It is useful to look at aspects of its plan, which was submitted to the Commission on Capital Budgeting and Planning in accordance with its criterion.

The Department of Environmental Protection is responsible for the conservation and restoration of New Jersey's natural resources. Consequently, the department's capital improvement program reflects a wide spectrum of projects that includes programs for wastewater treatment, flood control, hazardous waste cleanup, shore protection, open space acquisition, resource recovery, water supply, and parkland development.

The Bureau of Trust Fund Management prepares the department's capital budget and long-range plan in addition to coordinating its bond fund administration and financial analysis. Its primary purpose is to act as an effective coordinator for the programs. The Bureau of Capital Improvements is professionally staffed with an engineering group to coordinate the implementation of projects for state facilities through the Department of Treasury's Division of Building and Construction.

The Division of Water Resources is responsible for assistance to local communities for sewage facility construction and water systems rehabilitation. As part of the environmental trust program, a $150 million wastewater treatment fund and a $40 million wastewater treatment fund were created in fiscal year 1986 to provide low-interest loans and loan guarantees to local governmental units for the construction of wastewater treatment plants.

In 1987, water quality amendments to the Clean Water Act created the state revolving fund, which utilizes federal funding to continue to provide the state's share of the wastewater treatment financing program through fiscal year 1990; $540 million worth of loans were made to local governments to upgrade their wastewater treatment facilities.

The Division of Water Resources is also responsible for statewide water supply planning. Once planning is completed, constructing and operating state water supply facilities becomes the responsibility of the New Jersey Water Supply Authority. The Water Supply Authority operates and maintains the D & R Canal, the Spruce Run–Round Valley Reservoirs, and the Manasquan Reservoir. The Wanaque Reservoir is operated by the North Jersey District Water Supply Authority.

In addition to statewide water supply planning, the division also has several loan programs in place to provide low-interest loans to local governments. These include the Water Rehabilitation Program, which provides loans to municipalities to upgrade their water supply facilities, the Contaminated Wellfield Program, and the Water Supply Replacement Trust, which provides loans to municipalities to add additional waterline connections as a result of private wells being contaminated either by nitrates or toxic substances.

The development of acceptable alternatives to landfill disposal of municipal solid waste is being undertaken through the development of resource recovery facilities. The 1985 Resource Recovery and Solid Waste Disposal Facility Fund of $85 million and the 1980 Natural Resources Fund's allocations of $33 million are being used to provide zero-interest loans to local governmental units for the construction of resource recovery facilities or solid waste disposal facilities. A $48 million loan was awarded to Essex County, and the department has been negotiating with other counties that have received appropriations in anticipation of loan closing taking place by the end of 1991.

The department is recognized nationwide as the leader in hazardous waste cleanup. The Division of Hazardous Site Mitigation is continuing its aggressive hazardous waste cleanup program, utilizing in excess of $2.2 billion that is committed to that effort. This cleanup program is funded with monies provided by the state's spill fund, the $100 million 1981 Hazardous Discharge Bond Funds, the $200 million 1986 Hazardous Discharge Bond Fund, a yearly capital appropriation of $40 to $50 million for a 6-year period, the balance of a fiscal year 1986 state capital appropriation of $150 million, and federal Superfund monies allocated to New Jersey's national priority list sites. In addition, the department has private commitments in excess of $1 billion for the cleanup of hazardous waste by responsible parties.

The Division of Parks and Forestry manages the state's parks, forests, marinas, natural areas, and historic sites to help meet the recreational needs of New Jersey's citizens. The division provides and maintains state facilities for camping, swimming, historic interpretation, boating, and winter activities.

Recognizing the need for adequate maintenance of the existing facilities, the division has undertaken a program of renovation and rehabilitation. The division has incorporated in its design requirements for future recreational facilities standards that will assure construction of facilities having reduced maintenance costs.

The Green Acres Administration is responsible for the acquisition of lands for state parks, forest preserves, reservoirs, and wildlife areas. Unlike the Green Trust and earlier bond acts, the Green Acres Administration provides, through loans and grants, major assistance programs for the acquisition and development of local parklands.

Protecting the state's wildlife resources along with regulating hunting, fishing, and shell fishing, is the responsibility of the Division of Fish, Game and Wildlife. The division has undertaken a major maintenance and improvement program to maintain and upgrade existing facilities and to increase fisherman access to lakes and rivers.

The Division of Coastal Resources is responsible for the implementation of the Shore Protection Program. Funds have been made available by the 1977 Beaches and Harbor Fund, the 1983 Shore Protection Fund, and a $12 million capital appropriation in fiscal year 1988. The program includes major construction and beach restoration projects. The division is also responsible for the state's inland waterways—maintaining, marking, and dredging the channels.

The Mosquito Control Commission ensures that efficient and environmentally safe techniques are used in the control of mosquitoes. The commission's equipment loan program is available to the counties for approved projects, and provides more effective mosquito control by coordinating county needs on a statewide basis. In addition, annual capital appropriations provide funding for grants to counties.

The Palisades Interstate Park Commission's capital program includes upgrading of existing recreational support facilities and renovations and improvements to the Palisades Parkway. This interstate commission operates and manages land in both New Jersey and New York.

This plan is another example of the value of the Capital Budgeting Commission. Prior to its inception, it was unlikely that executive departments would have done such an exemplary and comprehensive job on their capital plan. The process established by the commission staff facilitated a more thoughtful examination of each of the subunit's capital needs.

Another department worth examining in detail is the Department of Treasury. It has responsibility for the construction of various governmental facilities throughout the state of New Jersey. Its capital improvement plan reads as follows:

"The Department of the Treasury, through its General Services Administration (GSA) and Office of Management and Budget (OMB) is responsible for a number of functions that directly affect the construction, operation and maintenance of capital facilities throughout the state. Specifically, the Department is responsible for:

1. Providing the necessary project planning and supporting facilities in the capital complex.
2. Providing for the administration of construction projects.
3. Providing the necessary assistance for improving maintenance at state facilities.
4. Administering certain statewide capital programs in the areas of asbestos removal and fire and life safety code compliance.
5. Integrating facilities development functions within GSA and provide a more precise multi-year definition of the state's office space requirements.

The GSA's Division of Building and Construction (DBC) is responsible for providing necessary professional-level planning, architectural/engineering design, and construction management/inspection functions to state departments and agencies. Through effective management and supervision of these functions, the division ensures that the approved capital development plans are completed in full compliance with program needs, within budget, within appropriate time constraints, and to a high level of quality. This includes compliance with prevailing design and construction codes and regulations. In summary, the division provides all necessary services for the development, and in support, of the capital development plans for the affected state departments and agencies.

Also, the division is responsible for the maintenance and day-to-day operations of the Trenton Capitol Complex and the Richard J. Hughes Complex. The Capitol Complex, which houses most of the state's administrative offices, is comprised of 34 government buildings. These buildings include the State House, the State House Annex, the Labor and Industry Building, the Health and Agriculture and Education buildings, the State Library, a museum, and a planetarium. The support of the various departmental operations and the ensuring of the safety and well-being of thousands of state employees require an extensive maintenance operation. For example, over 400 state and private sector custodial workers, craftsmen, and engineers service over 4.1 million square feet of building space. This staff ensures the proper operation and maintenance of power plants and various electrical, plumbing, heating, ventilating, and air conditioning systems.

The construction of four additional office buildings for the Departments of Environmental Protection (DEP), Transportation, and other state departments is complete. The construction of these facilities is being financed through the State Building Authority (P.L. 1981, c. 120). The authority is authorized not to have more than $250 million in bonds and notes outstanding. Specific projects proposed for financing by the authority must be approved by the New Jersey Commission on Capital Budgeting and Planning, the legislature, and the governor. The DEP general office and commerce buildings are maintained and operated by the Division of Building and Construction.

In addition to the above, the Division of Building and Construction is responsible for the coordination of the Statewide Maintenance Improvement Program.

The program's goals are to promote the effectiveness of maintenance operations in state facilities and to provide the administrative support for maintenance at the department and agency levels. In summary, the program's tasks are

1. To identify equipment and systems necessary to the operation of each facility
2. To establish a preventive maintenance program, including schedules, procedures, and tasks
3. To establish a work order system
4. To provide a computerized management information and control system
5. To determine organizational and staffing needs with recommendations for training of personnel
6. To promote the effectiveness of maintenance management and operations to ensure that the state's investment in buildings and facilities is adequately preserved.

The program has been implemented at Trenton State College, the University of Medicine and Dentistry of New Jersey, the Yardville and Bordentown correctional institutions, the Ancora and Hunterdon mental health facilities, and at the Capitol Complex and the Richard J. Hughes Complex.

During fiscal 1986–1990 the program was expanded to sixty-six additional institutions within the Departments of Human Services, Higher Education, Corrections, and Transportation. A major enhancement to the program was the utilization of microcomputers instead of a mainframe. This provided greater flexibilities and efficiencies in operations at the facility level with significant reductions in costs.

The eventual goal is to incorporate the program at all major state institutions. Once this goal is accomplished, the increase in the efficiency and effectiveness in maintenance operations will have a significant impact in preserving the state's capital investment in buildings and equipment.

For fiscal 1991, the GSA's capital request totaled about $48 million for equipment and structural modifications, replacement and repairs, and planning studies. Among the projects proposed were emergency fire safety compliance, deferred maintenance, state-owned and -leased office space refurbishments, un-planned asbestos studies and removal, space/interior planning studies, and capital city redevelopment infrastructure improvements.

Also, GSA's Office of Leasing Operations (OLO) has the responsibility of providing office space for the various state departments and agencies through lease, purchase, and other arrangements. The lack of adequate, centrally located office space has resulted in the dispersal of government offices throughout the

Trenton area. Such dispersal tends to be costly, produces inefficiencies, and causes inconveniences to the public.

Specifically, the facilities planning unit in OLO has three components. First, strategic planning gathers space requirements data from program agencies, develops conceptual solutions, and performs economic analyses of alternatives. The second component focuses on the technical review, evaluation, and modification of architectural and engineering specifications of proposals and plans for leased facilities; major reallocation of existing space; and/or new building construction. Lastly, space planning and interior design centers on the development and programming of specific projects utilizing a computer-aided space design system to create state-of-the-art office layouts which emphasize efficient space utilization and productive working environments."

One of the commission's objectives is to track the expenditures from approved bond issues and to ensure that projects are in conformance with the purpose of the bonds approved by the electorate. As noted previously, the commission was established in 1976. A review of the bond issues illustrates the wide range of purposes and capital projects that have been approved by New Jersey's voters. The total authorization is $7.060 billion. Of this amount $4.904 billion has been issued, and a total of $1.999 billion has been retired, leaving an outstanding amount of $2.905 billion. Of the total amount authorized by voters, the legislature has appropriated $4.919 billion, leaving a balance of $1.503 billion to be appropriated (as of December 31, 1969). The list of bond funds follows:

Highway improvement and grade crossing elimination bonds (1930).
The proceeds of this $58,000,000 bond issue were used for road and bridge construction, construction of roads at state institutions, and right-of-way acquisitions.
Water development bonds (1958).
This act authorized $45,850,000 to research and develop water supplies for potable, industrial, irrigation, and other purposes.
State institution construction bonds (1960).
An amount of $40,000,000 was authorized to renovate and improve or construct facilities at various state institutions established for mental health, charitable, public health, training, or correctional purposes.
State recreation and conservation land acquisition bonds (1961).
This act authorized $60,000,000 to provide funds to the state, and for grants to local governments for the acquisition of land for recreation and conservation purposes.
New Jersey institutions construction bonds (1964).
A $50,000,000 bond issue was authorized for construction of, or renovations and improvements to, state facilities for mental health, charitable, hospital, training, and correctional purposes.
State higher education construction bonds (1964).
This act authorized $40,100,000 for construction, reconstruction, and equipment of facilities and for the purchase of land, if necessary, for Rutgers University, New Jersey Institute of Technology, and the state colleges.
State housing assistance bonds (1968).
An amount of $12,500,000 was authorized through this act of provide funds to spur construction and rehabilitation of housing to be occupied by families of low and moderate income.
Public building construction bonds (1968).
This act authorizes $337,500,000 for the construction or reconstruction and rehabilitation of various institutions and the equipment necessary for the operation of the facilities. Among the types of institutional facilities included in the act are mental health and mental retardation, correctional, higher education, including state and county college, vocational education, and facilities to establish a public broadcasting system within the state of New Jersey.
State transportation bonds (1968).
This act authorized $640,000,000 to improve the public transportation system of the state. Of this amount, not more than $200,000,000 was to be used for mass transportation facilities, with the remainder to be used for the improvement of highways.
Water conservation bonds (1969).
This act authorized $271,000,000 for planning, developing, constructing, and maintaining facilities to provide adequate supplies of water for potable, industrial, commercial, irrigational, and recreational purposes.
Higher education construction bonds (1971).

Facilities of state institutions for higher education and county colleges are being constructed, rehabilitated, or equipped using funds authorized by this act totaling $155,000,000.

State recreation and conservation land acquisition bonds (1971).

An amount of $80 million was authorized for the acquisition of land by the state and by municipalities through state grants for recreation and conservation purposes.

State facilities for handicapped bonds (1973).

This act authorized $25,000,000 for the expansion and renovation of the Marie H. Katzenbach School for the Deaf and to establish regional schools throughout the state to educate severely handicapped children.

State recreation and conservation land acquisition and development bonds (1974).

As with the Recreation and Conservation Land Acquisition Acts of 1961 and 1971, this act provides funds for the acquisition of land by the state and municipalities through state grants for recreation and conservation purposes. In addition, this act also provides funds for state and local development of acquired lands to expand and enhance their utilization for recreation and conservation purposes. A total of $200,000,000 was authorized.

Clean waters bonds (1976).

This act authorized $120,000,000 for the conservation and development of water resources through construction of water supply and wastewater treatment facilities.

Institutions construction bonds (1976).

An amount of $60,000,000 was authorized to provide safe and humane facilities at institutions for the mentally ill, mentally retarded, and incarcerated through the construction of new facilities or the rehabilitation and improvement of existing facilities.

State mortgage assistance bonds (1976).

This act authorized $25,000,000 to spur construction, rehabilitation, and maintenance of housing for senior citizens and families of low and moderate income and to provide funds for second mortgage assistance.

Medical education facilities bonds (1977).

This act provided for the issuance of general obligation bonds of the state to refinance revenue bonds issued in 1974 by the New Jersey Health Care Facilities Financing Authority. The refinancing would reduce interest costs for the construction of the teaching hospital at the University of Medicine and Dentistry of New Jersey and would also provide substantial savings ($25 million) that can be made available for other needed purposes.

Natural resources bonds (1980).

This act authorized $145,000,000 for development, acquisition, and construction at resource recovery facilities, sewage treatment facilities, water supply facilities, dam restoration projects, and harbor cleanup.

Water supply bonds (1981).

This act authorized $350,000,000 for state or local projects to rehabilitate, repair, or consolidate antiquated, damaged, or inadequately operating water supply facilities and to plan, design, acquire, and construct various state water supply facilities, all as recommended by the New Jersey Statewide Water Supply Plan.

Hazardous discharge bonds (1981).

This act authorized $100,000,000 for the identification and cleanup and removal of hazardous discharges.

Farmland preservation bonds (1981).

This act authorized $50,000,000 for the purchase of development easements on farmland and to provide state matching funds for soil and water conservation projects.

Community development bonds (1982).

This act authorized $85,000,000 to capitalize the New Jersey Local Development Financing Fund and to provide support for revitalization, development, and creation of urban industrial parks.

Correctional facilities construction bonds (1982).

This act authorized $170,000,000 for correction facilities, their planning, erection, acquisition, improvement, development, and equipment. The funds will be used to alleviate present and anticipated problems of overcrowding in state and county prisons.

Bridge rehabilitation and improvement bonds (1983).

This act authorized $135,000,000 to rehabilitate and improve bridges in the state's rail and road system.

Shore protection bonds (1983).

This act authorized $50,000,000 for the researching, planning, acquiring, developing, construction, and maintaining of shore protection projects.

New Jersey Green Acres bonds (1983).

This act authorized $135,000,000 to enable the state and local governments to continue acquisition and development of land for recreation and conservation purposes.

Science and Technology Bond Act (1984).

This act authorized $90,000,000 to develop advanced technology centers at New Jersey's research universities in high-growth, job-intensive fields, and undergraduate science and engineering facilities and programs at New Jersey's public and private universities and colleges and 2-year community colleges.

New Jersey human services construction bond act (1984).

An amount of $60,000,000 was authorized for the rehabilitation and improvement of aging human service facilities for the mentally ill and mentally retarded, as well as veterans' homes, making them safer and providing a more homelike environment.

Wastewater treatment bond fund (1985).

This act authorized $190,000,000 for the purpose of providing local government units with loans, grants, and other forms of financial aid for the construction of wastewater treatment systems.

Resource recovery and solid waste disposal facility fund bond (1985).

This act authorized $85,000,000 for the purpose of making state loans to local government units for the construction of resource recovery facilities and environmentally sound sanitary landfill facilities.

Pinelands infrastructure trust bond (1985).

This act authorized $30,000,000 for the purpose of providing grants and loans to local units in the Pinelands area for infrastructure projects necessary to accommodate development in regional growth areas.

Hazardous discharge (1986).

An amount of $200,000,000 was authorized for identification, cleanup, and removal of hazardous discharges.

Correctional Facilities Bond Act (1987).

An amount of $198,000,000 was authorized for the construction of prison facilities.

Green Acres Cultural Centers and Historic Preservation Bond Act (1987).

An amount of $100,000,000 was authorized for the purpose of financing the construction and development of cultural centers and the restoration, repair, or rehabilitation of historic structures.

Jobs, Education and Competitiveness Bond Act (1988).

An act that authorizes $350,000,000 for the construction and improvement of higher education facilities; and the construction and establishment of advanced technology centers sponsored by the New Jersey Commission on Science and Technology; $308,000,000 is dedicated for higher education facilities, and $42,000,000 toward advanced technology centers.

Open Space Preservation Bond Act (1989).

This act authorized bonds for $300,000,000 for acquiring and developing lands for recreation and conservation purposes, purchasing farmland soil and water conservation projects, and funding development potential transfer banks.

Public Purpose Buildings and Community Based Facilities Construction Bond Act (1989).

This act authorized $125,000,000 for human services institutions and community facilities, and state correctional facilities. Of the total, $90,000,000 is for state and community-based human services facilities for the developmentally disabled and the mentally ill, and $35,000,000 is for construction of additional state correctional facilities.

Stormwater Management and Combined Sewer Overflow Abatement Bond Act (1989).

This act authorized $50,000,000 for the purpose of providing grants and low-interest loans to local government units for the costs of projects to manage stormwater and abate combined sewer overflows into the state's waters and other improper connections of stormwater and sewer systems.

New Jersey Bridge Rehabilitation and Improvement and Railroad Right of Way Preservation Bond Act (1989).

This act authorized $115,000,000 to finance the rehabilitation and improvement of state, county, and municipal bridges and the preservation and acquisition of railroad rights-of-way.

IV. FUTURE OF CAPITAL BUDGETING

The ability of all levels of government to finance their capital needs will have a significant impact on their economies. The infrastructure of a nation or state provides the foundation on which its commerce rests. Those states that are able to keep their infrastructure in good shape will be in the best position to compete in a changing economy.

As a result, the processes relating to the approval or capital projects will assume even greater importance in the future. The experience of New Jersey's Commission on Capital Budgeting and Planning has been widely regarded as a model for the nation. It has been extremely effective in educating the public with respect to capital projects, evaluating the plans of the various departments, and establishing priorities for bond proposals and other capital projects. While these processes and procedures have been useful for the state, reduced governmental resources and increased demands will require even more thoughtful planning in the future.

Maintaining the state's infrastructure is one of government's primary activities. Indeed, one could argue that it is government's most important function. In the future, it would be useful to think of capital budgeting in more strategic terms. While New Jersey has managed to avoid many of the crises that have plagued other states, a longer-term perspective would be helpful.

A useful first step could be to develop longer-term capital budgeting plans that can gain executive and legislative support. Traditionally, this has been difficult to achieve for a number of reasons. Often members of the executive branch who prepare the budget do not want to limit their flexibility by being bound by long-term plans.

While longer-term commitments will somewhat limit the flexibility of the budget process, the disadvantage is minor in the area of capital projects. In comparison with the operating budget, capital expenditures are relatively small. In addition, while one can reasonably debate the wisdom of operating expenses, sewer plants, bridges, and roads must be built and buildings must be maintained, regardless of which political philosophy prevails. Therefore, capital projects and infrastructure repair may be the one area that needs to be sheltered from the vagaries of the sometimes political budget process.

The Transportation Trust Fund can serve as an example of the advantages of long-term commitments to necessary capital projects. The fund allowed the state to accomplish several objectives. First, it ensured that state funds were available to obtain matching federal funds. This could be accomplished in a number of areas that would allow New Jersey, traditionally ranked near the bottom in acquiring federal funds, to gain a better return on the dollars it sends to Washington.

Second, it permitted a steady flow of funds into the department, which allowed better overall planning and the completion of a number of unfinished roads. It also facilitated bidding procedures and the other processes necessary for completing, building, and repairing roads. This helped the economy of New Jersey because of the expenditure of construction funds and the multiplier effects that such expenditures generate. It also stimulated commercial and residential construction along the completed roads and highways.

Many corporate executives place great emphasis on the status of the state's infrastructure when making decisions regarding the location of their company. Mundane items such as sewer plants, roads, and reservoirs became important to businesses' fortunes for several reasons. If the infrastructure is in place, it helps their businesses succeed. If it is not in place, the businesses will have to pay for it.

Longer-term commitments would stimulate economic growth, promote savings, and help acquire federal assistance. For New Jersey, this would be particularly important in the area of hazardous waste cleanup and highway construction and repair. The most urbanized state in the nation would particularly benefit from such a strategy.

Another issue that ought to be addressed is that of annual pay-as-you-go financing versus long-term general obligation bond financing. Generally speaking, steady annual financing has several advantages. It reflects more accurately the regular capital needs of the various departments of the state. In addition, annual expenses do not need to be approved by the voters, as do general obligation bonds. On the other hand, annual capital expenditures do not have the political "sex appeal" of other programs, and may be the first ones eliminated in periods of budget cutbacks. Once bond issues have been approved, the monies must be used for the capital projects intended, and the funds will be spent for those purposes.

Ideally, one could build a combination of annual and bond financing that would combine the advantages of each and ensure a regular flow of capital funds into the departments. One of the weaknesses of the American system of government is the failure to reach some concensus as to its proper roles. It would be useful for the various levels of government to think more strategically. One place to begin is in the area that is most important to the citizens; effective and efficient capital budgeting benefits all citizens, regardless of economic standing or position.

12

State and Local Debt Policy and Management

James R. Ramsey
Western Kentucky University, Bowling Green, Kentucky

Merl Hackbart
University of Kentucky, Lexington, Kentucky

During the 1980s, a transformation took place in the fiscal federalism of the United States. A stated policy of the federal government during this period of time was to shift more program responsibilities to state and local government, but funding for such programs often did not accompany this shift (Ramsey and Hackbart, 1993). For example, revenue-sharing monies were cut for local governments in 1987. Also, the Environmental Protection Agency (EPA) grants to local governments for sewer projects were eliminated and replaced with state-administered loan programs. These are just examples of areas in which state and local governments were required to replace federal funds for state and local programs.

The 1980s were also a decade of uneven economic growth. In the early 1980s, a severe recession impacted the country. The period of 1983 to 1990 was generally one of sustained economic growth nationally, however, economic growth was uneven among regions of the country and the concept of a "rolling recession" became prominent. Some believed that while the national economy was immune from recessions, regions would experience periods of slow growth or no growth. Clearly this belief was proved to be unfounded with the national recession that began in the summer of 1990. That recession further increased fiscal pressures on state and local government.

Court orders and other federal mandates have also required state and local governments to spend new and additional resources on various programs. For example, many states have been under court orders to spend funds for the improvement of their prison systems. In recent years, federal mandates have created a fiscal crisis in health care as states have faced uncontrolled costs for health care-related programs such as Medicaid.

For all the reasons cited above, state and local governments have experienced fiscal pressures that have caused budgetary strains. Further, unlike the federal government, state and local governments are almost always required to balance their budgets on an annual basis. This requires state and local governments to manage revenues and expenditures to produce a balanced budget.

A distinguishing characteristic of state and local finance is that most state and local governments prepare both operating and capital budgets. Operating budgets for state and local governments generally consist of current expenditures such as salaries, utilities, travel, and other items that are consumed during one accounting period. Capital budgets, on the other hand, address the financing of assets with a multiyear life, such as construction projects. At one time, state and local governments financed much of their capital budgets with current revenue sources, such as taxes, federal funds, and earnings on investments. However, during periods of tight budgets, state and local governments have found it increasingly difficult to spend current revenue for capital items. As a result, state and local governments have been active participants in the bond market to borrow funds to pay for capital projects (*Bond Buyer Yearbook*).

While state and local governments have been participants in the credit markets for many years, greater focus and attention has been given to the municipal credit markets in recent years due to (1) increased volume of state and local borrowing, (2) changes in federal tax laws that have constrained the ability of state and local governments to borrow, and (3) pressures to finance more functions of government by borrowing. For example, the technology explosion of recent years has required state and local governments to expend large sums of money on computer and information systems. Since these hardware and software systems have a multiyear life, many state and local governments have financed the acquisition of computing hardware and software in the credit market. This policy raises an interesting issue since computer hardware and software become technologically obsolete in a short period of time. As will be discussed later, the credit markets are normally thought to be appropriate only for those assets with a multiyear useful life. Another example of the increased use of the credit markets is borrowing for economic development. Interstate competition for new and expanded industrial opportunities has led many state and local governments to raise funds in the capital market to provide incentives and inducements for plant and industry location (Hackbart and Ramsey, 1993).

In light of these trends, the focus of this chapter is to discuss the municipal credit markets. It will begin with a discussion of two critical issues: the appropriateness of borrowing to finance capital projects, and the issue of how much borrowing is appropriate. It will be shown that borrowing can be an important source of funding for state and local governments if a sound debt management program is developed by a municipal government. Given the appropriateness of borrowing to finance certain types of projects, a discussion will then follow on the characteristics of the tax-exempt marketplace. The most important and distinguished characteristic of the market for state and local debt is that the interest paid by state and local governments on their bonds is exempt from federal income taxes, and in most instances state income taxes. Therefore, an investor facing several investment alternatives must factor into his investment decision-making process the fact that the interest he receives on a municipal security is free from federal income tax.

After this discussion, an overview of the security provisions of municipal bonds will be provided. This will be followed by a discussion of the general characteristics of state and local bonds. A discussion will then follow on the mechanics and process for issuing state and local debt. The players in the structuring and marketing of a bond issue will be described, as will the detailed process by which a bond issue is sold and funds are made available for spending purposes.

Included in this discussion will be the concept of the rating agencies and the rating process. The chapter then concludes with a discussion of several special topics, including a discussion of refunding, and the distinction between current and advance refundings and economic and legal refundings. This topic has proven to be very important in recent years, given the historically low levels of interest rates. Another special topic to be discussed is that of federal tax reform and its impact on state and local borrowers. The most significant federal legislation to impact both supply and demand for municipal debt has been the Tax Reform Act of 1986 (TRA86). This legislation was extremely complicated, and dramatically impacted municipal borrowers. Several statutory and regulatory changes have been made since 1986 to reduce the onerous burden on state and local government of many of these provisions. Any comprehensive analysis of the market for state and local debt would be incomplete without at least a cursory overview of the topic of tax reform and its impact on municipal borrowers.

I. RATIONALE FOR STATE AND LOCAL BORROWING

A question often raised by the press, legislators, and the public in general is whether or not borrowing by state and local government is appropriate. It is often stated that borrowing mortgages the future of our children and grandchildren and borrowing represents a financial weakness that should be avoided. Therefore, it is desirable to focus briefly on the rationale for borrowing by state and local government.

We often identify three economic functions of government. These are the allocation function, the redistribution function, and the stabilization function. The allocation function relates to the fact that while our economy is said to be a private market economy, we know that there are times where the private marketplace will not produce certain goods and services because it is impossible for private business to do so and earn a profit. Without going into a complete explanation of the various situations in which the private marketplace breaks down and fails, it is reasonable to believe that one function of government is to provide those goods and services that we as taxpayers demand, but that the private sector will not provide. For example, we normally believe that national defense is a good that the private sector would not provide. It is also normally believed that education is a good that if left strictly to the private sector would be provided, but at a cost and level that would not encourage education for large numbers of people. These are examples of the allocation function of government.

A second function of government is the distribution function. Even if markets were perfectly efficient and provided us with all the goods and services that we demand, the distribution of these goods and services might be socially undesirable. Therefore, government has the role of redistributing income. This redistribution function of government has been long accepted in the United States and is reflected in both our revenue policies (e.g., our progressive income tax) and our expenditures (e.g., programs for low-income individuals such as Aid to Families with Dependent Children, Medicaid, and food stamps). Again, a theoretical discussion of the distribution function of government is beyond our scope at this time, however, intuitively we recognize that this function of government does exist.

The final function of government is the stabilization function. After periods of economic growth followed by recessions, depressions, and no growth, the Congress of the United States finally formulated in 1946 the government's responsibility to provide an economic environment that assures economic growth, price stability, and full employment. Again, a detailed discussion of the stabilization function of government is beyond our scope, as is a detailed discussion of the tools that governments may use to achieve these stabilization goals (i.e., monetary and fiscal policy).

Now, given these three functions of government, an appropriate question to be raised in a federalistic government such as we have in the United States is "What is the appropriate level of government to perform each of these functions?" That is, should the federal government perform one function, state government another function, and our local governments the third function, or is there some mix of federal, state, and local government that is best suited to performing these three functions? Wallace Oates argues that the distribution and stabilization functions are best performed by the federal government. He indicates that the allocation function should be split among federal, state, and local governments and that the appropriate level of government to perform this function is that level most closely tied to the beneficiaries of the program being provided. For example, since everyone throughout the United States benefits from national defense, Oates would argue that national defense should be provided by the federal government. On the other hand, since police and fire protection primarily benefits the residences of a specific community then these functions are best provided locally (Oats, 1972).

We are aware that the federal government has extensively used debt financing over time. This is most often justified as one means of achieving the stabilization function of government. For example, if the national economy is experiencing slow or no growth then appropriate fiscal policy to stimulate the economy is to increase government spending and to reduce taxation; a combination that will lead to federal deficits. Therefore, federal borrowing is most often rationalized as appropriate for achieving the stabilization function of the federal government. On the other hand, since the only function that state and local governments perform (at least from a theoretical perspective) is the allocation function, it is argued that the state and local government rationale for borrowing is to help achieve the allocation function.

The conventional wisdom of state and local finance is that current expenditures (salaries, operating expenses, utilities, travel, etc.) should be paid for from current or recurring revenue sources (taxes collected, grants received, investment income, etc.). At the same time, the conventional wisdom of state and local finance suggests that capital expenditures may be appropriately financed by borrowing. This conventional wisdom is based on the benefit principle of taxation that states that one who benefits from the consumption of a public good should pay for that good. Since capital goods have a multiyear asset life, future taxpayers will benefit from the consumption of these capital goods. One way to ensure that future taxpayers pay their fair share of the capital goods they consume is to require that a portion of their taxes be used to amortize the debt needed to finance the capital project (Oats, 1972).

For example, consider the construction of a highway. The normal life of a road might be 20 years; so individuals over a 20-year span will benefit from driving on the highway. Highway projects are extremely expensive and it is often difficult for state governments to raise the current revenues necessary to finance a road on a pay-as-you-go basis. Therefore, states often finance major highway projects with the proceeds of bond issues. In this case it would be appropriate according to the conventional wisdom to finance the capital projects with 20-year bond issue since the project has an expected asset life of a 20 years. With this policy, future users and beneficiaries of the highway will be required to pay a portion of the cost of the highway through the utilization of their future taxes to amortize debt over the life of the bonds.

It should be noted that not all observers of state and local finance subscribe to the notion of this conventional wisdom. In fact, some have challenged the conventional wisdom, indicating that under certain circumstances it is impossible to shift costs forward to future users. A discussion of the challenge to the conventional wisdom is again beyond the scope and purpose of this discussion (Oats, 1972). We will accept the conventional wisdom and say that borrowing by state and local governments may be an appropriate means of financing capital projects.

Given the conventional wisdom of state and local finance, a second critical issue then becomes how much debt is affordable. Just as there is a limit to how much debt an individual can incur with a given level of income, it should be expected that there exists a debt ceiling or limit for state and local governments. Two levels of discussion have evolved as to the appropriate level of debt for state and local government. The first examines the issue of debt affordability. Most of this literature has attempted to identify income and wealth variables that define a historical level of debt utilized by a municipal government. This research hypothesizes that if a state or local government has maintained a relationship between its debt service payments and these income and wealth variables over time without creating undue budgetary strains, then growth in these income and wealth variables can be used to predict service levels that may be incurred in the future without placing undue fiscal constraints on the state and local government's budget (Hackbart and Ramsey, 1990).

A second and more practical level of analysis has developed with the rating agencies as state and local governments have attempted to convince the rating agencies that their levels of debt are affordable and will not create undue budgetary constraints that jeopardize the repayment of bonds outstanding. Many states, for example, have identified rules of thumb to determine an appropriate level of debt outstanding. These practical debt policies are similar conceptually to the more theoretical approaches that were mentioned above. However, these more practical approaches are generally based on a public policy perception of an appropriate ceiling and the development in most cases of nonstatistically derived rules of thumb (Ramsey et al., 1988). While neither the theoretical approach nor the practical approach is absolute, both focus public policy attention on the critical issue that there exists some undetermined point at which debt service begins to "crowd out" operating programs from the budget. These periods of crowding out are most likely to occur in a recessionary period, in which revenues do not grow at historical rates and/or during periods of extreme expenditure pressure resulting from mandated programs such as Medicaid.

Therefore, we will conclude this section by indicating that state and local borrowing may be appropriate for financing the acquisition of many types of capital expenditures. At the same time, it is recognized that there is a limit to the amount of debt that can be incurred, so that even in a true capital budgeting process in which a variety of projects are deemed to be economic viable, not all such projects may be budgetarily affordable.

II. THE TAX EXEMPTION ON STATE AND LOCAL BORROWING

The most important characteristic of bonds sold by state and local governments is the exemption of the interest paid to the purchaser of the bonds from federal income taxation. This federal tax exemption has a long history and is based on statutory and not constitutional law.[*]

The tax exemption on state and local bonds has important implications for municipal issuers. It allows state and local governments to borrow funds at interest rates lower than those available to individuals, corporations, and even the federal government. A full discussion of the tax exemption of municipal bonds is beyond the scope of this presentation. However, the exemption represents a subsidy from the federal government to state and local governments.

Table 1 illustrates the value of the tax exemption. This table is constructed from the perspective of an individual investor. As shown in the table, an individual investor may be faced with three alternative investment choices: (1) the purchase of a municipal bond at a 10% rate of interest, (2) the purchase of a corporate bond at a 13% rate of interest, and (3) the purchase of a stock yielding a dividend of 6%. Column 1 shows that for an investment of $30,000, the investor's before-tax interest income will be $3,000. Since this

---

[*]A recent Supreme Court case has reiterated that the tax exemption on muncipal bonds is statutorily determined by Congress and is not a constitutional right of the state. This issue was addressed in the case of *Baker* v. *South Carolina*. It is further noted that this case originally raised the issue of the federal requirement that bonds sold by state and local government be registered. The U.S. Supreme Court ruled that the federal government could require such registration of state and local bonds and the opinion then went further to address this tax exemption. It also should be noted that certain types of bonds sold by state and local governments may be deemed to be taxable (depending upon the nature of the project the proceeds are used to finance) and that the interest on certain state and local bonds may be subject to the federal alternative minimum tax.

Table 1   The Value of the Tax Exemption: A Comparison of Investment Alternatives

	10% Tax Exempt Bond ($)	13% Taxable Bond ($)	Stock Paying 6% Dividend ($)
Cash investment	30,000	35,502	76,923
Pretax return	3,000	4,615	4,615
Tax in 35% bracket	0	1,615	1,615
Net after-tax return	3,000	3,000	3,000

interest income is exempt from federal income taxes, the investor's after-tax return is the same as her pretax return. For the corporate bond, the investor's pretax income is $4,615; assuming the investor is in a 35% tax bracket, the investor will pay $1,615 taxes to the federal government and will net $3,000 after taxes. The table is constructed to show that an investor would be required to invest 5,502 additional dollars in a corporate bond to receive the same after-tax dollars from her investment that she received on a tax-exempt bond. The final column illustrates the same point for the investment in a common stock. For an investment of $76,923 the investor will receive a pretax return of $4,615, and again assuming a 35% tax bracket the investor's after tax-return will be $3,000 or the same amount received on a much lower investment in tax-exempt bonds.

As a result of the tax exemption on municipal bonds, investors (individuals, banks, insurance companies, etc.) utilize municipal bonds as a means of sheltering income from taxes (i.e., a legal tax loophole). The greater the tax bracket an individual or business is in, the greater the value of the tax exemption. It is interesting to note that the discussion of increased taxes on high-income individuals in 1993 caused a significant increase in the demand for tax-exempt securities. This point illustrates the importance of the tax exemption to investors; the possibility of a tax increase can cause investors to reshuffle their investment purchases. The implication of this ability by state and local governments to borrow on a tax-exempt basis is that investors are willing to lend money to state and local governments at a lower interest rate than they are willing to lend money to corporations and/or the federal government.

This federal subsidy to state and local governments has been the focus of changes in federal tax policy. Over time, various tax reform and tax legislation efforts have attempted to restrict the types of projects that may be financed with tax-exempt bonds. Again without a detailed discussion, it can be noted that federal legislation has defined two broad categories of municipal bonds: (1) governmental bonds and (2) private activity bonds. Governmental bonds are defined by the federal government to be those bonds sold by state and local governments to finance pubic purpose projects (e.g., schools, prisons, and highways). These projects have been defined by the federal government to have a broad-based public purpose with the benefits accruing to society at large. On the other hand, private activity bonds are defined as securities sold to finance projects that directly benefit an individual or a private entity. An example of a private activity bond is a single-family mortgage revenue bond or a student loan bond. While society generally agrees that affordable housing and greater access to higher education are both worthwhile social goals, the direct beneficiaries of both these types of bond programs are individuals. As a result, recent tax law changes may make the interest paid on these types of bonds subject to taxation. Finally, it should be noted that certain types of projects cannot be financed with tax-exempt bonds. Direct lending programs to business and industry as a means of promoting economic development are no longer eligible projects for financing with tax-exempt bonds.

The tax exempt status of municipal securities gives rise to a very important issue for the municipal credit markets—the concept of arbitrage. Arbitrage can be most easily defined as borrowing funds at one interest rate and reinvesting the proceeds of the borrowing at a higher interest rate. Bank profitability is a function of arbitrage; banks borrow funds from depositors and pay the depositor an interest rate such as 3% on a 90-day certificate of deposit. Banks then invest this money in a loan to one of the bank's customers at a higher interest rate, say 6%. The spread between 3% and 6% represents revenue, and hence profitability to the bank.

In like matter, municipal bond issuers have the ability to borrow in the tax-exempt market and reinvest their proceeds at a higher interest rate in the taxable securities market. For example, in the 1993 credit market environment, a municipal issuer could borrow funds on a 20-year basis at an interest rate of approximately 5% and then reinvest these funds in a 20-year government security at an interest rate of approximately 6%. As a general rule, a municipal issuer would have no reason to invest funds for such a long period of time. Rather, the issuer would generally expend the proceeds of the tax-exempt bond for such purposes as the construction of a project or facility or perhaps the acquisition of equipment. However, as will be noted in a later discussion, it is common for municipal issuers to borrow as part of their bond issue funds to establish a debt service reserve. The debt service reserve will then be held throughout the life of the bonds. Historically, issuers have created debt service reserves to enhance the security provisions of their issue but to also earn arbitrage income. Further, it has sometimes been the case that the spread relationship between tax-exempt interest rates and taxable interest rates have allowed municipal issuers to borrow in the tax-exempt market on a long-term basis and to earn an arbitrage in the short-term taxable market. Finally, some issuers have borrowed in the municipal market without a defined purpose for the proceeds of the finance. As a result, these issuers have used the proceeds for arbitrage. Recently the federal government has effectively limited the arbitrage opportunities for state and local issuers. As a general rule, if a municipal issuer borrows funds on a tax-exempt basis and earns an arbitrage, the issuer is required to pay back to the federal government the interest rate differential between the tax-exempt and taxable market.

III. STRUCTURING A TAX-EXEMPT BOND: AN OVERVIEW

Thus far we have discussed the theory of tax-exempt financing in the context of the capital budgeting process and the significance of the tax exemption. We will now turn our attention to the actual structuring and mechanics of a bond issue. We will begin with an overview of concepts important to the structuring of a tax-exempt bond issue. At the completion of this discussion, a detailed discussion of the mechanics of a bond issue will be presented.

A. Security and Credit Provision of a Tax-Exempt Bond

As with any loan there are two parties involved with a bond issue, the borrower and the lender. Before a lender will make a commitment to loan funds, the lender will do a credit analysis to determine the probability or likelihood of being repaid the principal amount of the loan as well as the interest on the loan. A more complete discussion of the rating agencies and detailed credit considerations will be presented later. At this time, however, it is worthwhile to discuss the general types of credit that secure tax-exempt bonds. These are: (1) general obligation pledges, (2) revenue bond pledges, (3) moral obligation pledges, and (4) industrial revenue bond pledges. Each of these will be discussed below.

A general obligation security pledge is a pledge of the full faith and credit of the borrower; that is, a city or state that issues a general obligation bond is borrowing money and is pledging or promising the lender that it will do anything and everything required to repay the loan, including increasing taxes if necessary. A general obligation pledge also includes a commitment of all of the financial assets and resources of the issuer to the loan repayment. A general obligation security is the strongest pledge a borrower can make to a lender, and therefore presents the lowest credit risk. Because of the nature of a general obligation pledge, many cities and/or states require voter approval prior to issuing general obligation debt (Hackbart et al., 1990). In other cities and states, general obligation debt is not legally permitted at all.

A revenue bond is secured by the cash flow of the project financed with the proceeds of the bond issue. For example, if bonds are sold to finance a toll road, the only source of repayment of principal and interest to the bond holder is the revenues generated from the tolls. In many cases, the project itself is also pledged as collateral on revenue bond issues. In the example previously given, if the toll road did not generate sufficient cash flow to make the principal and interest payment on the bonds, the bondholder could theoretically take possession of the toll road as the collateral for the bonds. For revenue bonds, detailed credit analyses are required to determine the financial viability of the project. Often individual investors do not have the time or expertise to perform such analysis, and as a result will rely upon the credit rating assigned by one or more of the major rating agencies. Again, the rating process will be discussed in more detail later. However, it is very important to recognize the risk involved with revenue bonds and to realize that the nature of the project as well as the political support for it are important credit considerations.

A moral obligation bond is one in which the credit or security pledged to the bondholder is the revenues generated from the project, but in addition there is an implied or moral obligation on behalf of the issuer that if revenues from the project are not sufficient to meet principal and interest cash flow requirements for the bonds, the issuer will use other revenue sources and assets to make payment to the bondholder. With moral obligation credits, the issuer is not obligated or required to fill in the gap with any shortfalls in revenues, but the issuer has a moral obligation to ensure that the bonds do not default. There are varying degrees of moral obligations that are utilized by state and local government, and some are viewed in the credit market as stronger than other types. As a general statement, moral obligation bonds are not viewed as being as creditworthy as general obligation bonds, but they are stronger credit than revenue bonds.

In an effort to attract business and industry over the years, many state and local governments have issued tax-exempt bonds on behalf of private users such as private companies. Such bonds have provided lower financing costs to private companies than could be obtained by the companies in other credit markets. Such financings are referred to as "conduit financings" since the issuer (i.e., the city or state) is merely providing its name and ability to borrow funds in a tax-exempt market to a private company. The private company has full and total responsibility for repayment of the loan. Industrial revenue bonds or private activity bonds have a long history of use in the United States and their use was greatly expanded throughout the early 1980s (*Bond Buyer Yearbook*). As a result, the federal government attempted to limit the uses of such financings through the enactment of TRA86. The key point, however, is that industrial revenue bonds are almost always a pledge of security of the company for which the bonds were issued and are not a credit obligation of the issuer of the city or state. A city or state has neither a legal nor moral obligation to make the repayment of principal and interest. Politicians have often raised the issue of whether or not a default of an industrial revenue bond would impact the credit of the city or state. As a general rule, this would not be the case since the credit markets generally understand the risk associated with industrial revenue bonds and lenders would not seek recourse from the issuer itself in the case of a default.

B. Maturity Structure of Bonds

Bonds, like any other type of loan, may be structured for long or short periods of time. The theory of debt finance discussed earlier indicated that the maturity of the bond issue should be tied directly to the life of the asset being financed with the bonds. As a result, we normally think of tax-exempt bonds being issued for time periods of between 15 and 30 years. However, there are circumstances in which prudent debt management would suggest the issuance of shorter-term bonds, and a discussion of these circumstances will be provided.

Long-term bond issues may generally be structured as (1) serial bonds, (2) term bonds, (3) zero coupon bonds, or (4) a combination of these. Serial bonds are bonds that are structured so that a portion of the principal outstanding on the bonds is repaid annually. It is a conventional practice that interest on tax-exempt bonds be paid semiannually. Therefore, with a serial bond the bondholder is receiving interest on an ongoing basis and a portion of the principal is paid annually. Figure 1 is the cover page from an official statement for a Murray State University bond issue, an example of a serial bond structure. As can be seen, the total amount of the loan is $4,625,000; in the first year $90,000 in principal is repaid. In the final maturity or year of the bond issue $390,000 in principal is paid. Most of us are familiar with serial loans since we structure our home mortgages as serial loans.

Term bonds, on the other hand, are bonds that repay interest on a semiannual basis, but the principal is repaid at one time. Term bonds are sometimes referred to as bullet maturities or balloon loans.

Zero coupon bonds, on the other hand, are bond issues that do not pay principal or interest until a final maturity date. Many of us are familiar with the series EE savings bonds sold by the federal government. The investor may invest $25 today and receive $50 at some date in the future. There is no repayment of interest or payment of principal from the date the investment is made until the final maturity of the loan. This is an example of a zero coupon bond.

Finally, some bond issue will be structured to include features of serial, term, and zero coupon loans; that is, there are some investors who have a preference for serial bonds, other investors who have a preference for term bonds, and still others with a preference for zero coupon bonds. Therefore, some issuers, particularly on larger bond issues, will find the overall lowest interest rate can be obtained by including all three types of bond structures into one issue.

We can also classify long-term bonds as either fixed-rate or variable-rate bonds. Again, a proper analogy would be the homeowner who finances his home purchase by borrowing. Some homeowners prefer a fixed-rate mortgage, a loan for which the interest rate is fixed over the entire life of the mortgage. In other cases, the homeowner may prefer an adjustable rate mortgage, in which the interest rate on the mortgage is reset on a periodic basis, such as annually or quarterly. In like manner, a city or state that sells long-term bonds must determine whether to borrow on a fixed-rate or a variable/adjustable rate basis.

Official Statement Dated March 10, 1992

NEW ISSUE   Moody's Rating: Aaa
                                                        Standard & Poor's Rating: AAA
"BANK QUALIFIED"   (See "Ratings" herein)

In the opinion of Bond Counsel, Rubin Hays & Foley, interest on the Series H Bonds is exempt from Federal and Kentucky income taxation under existing statutes, court decisions, regulations and published rulings, and under existing laws the principal of the Series H Bonds is exempt from ad valorem taxation by the Commonwealth of Kentucky and any political subdivision thereof, assuming compliance by the University with certain tax covenants. For a more complete statement with reference to the foregoing see "Tax Exemption" and "Special Tax Exemption Considerations" herein.

$4,625,000
MURRAY STATE UNIVERSITY
Consolidated Educational Buildings Revenue Bonds
Series H

Dated: March 1, 1992   Due: May 1, as shown below

The Series H Bonds bear interest payable on each Interest Payment Date (May 1 and November 1 of each year), commencing November 1, 1992. Principal shall be payable at the principal office of Citizens Fidelity Bank and Trust Company, Louisville, Kentucky (the "Registrar and Paying Agent"), and interest shall be payable by check or draft mailed by the Paying Agent no later than the due date thereof to the registered owners thereof of record as of the close of business on the 15th day of the month preceding each interest payment date (April 15 and October 15). The Series H Bonds shall be issued only as fully registered bonds in the denominations of $5,000, or integral multiples thereof, and shall mature on May 1, in accordance with the following schedule:

Payment of the principal of and interest on the Bonds when due will be insured by a municipal bond insurance policy to be issued by AMBAC Indemnity Corporation simultaneously with the delivery of the bonds.

AMBAC.

SCHEDULE OF MATURITIES

Due May 1	Amount	Rate	Price or Yield	Due May 1	Amount	Rate	Price or Yield
1993	$ 90,000	3.50%	100%	2003	$220,000	5.75%	100%
1994	140,000	4.00	100	2004	235,000	5.90	100
1995	150,000	4.50	100	2005	250,000	6.00	100
1996	155,000	4.75	100	2006	265,000	6.00	6.10
1997	160,000	5.00	100	2007	285,000	6.00	6.20
1998	170,000	5.10	100	2008	305,000	6.10	6.25
1999	180,000	5.20	100	2009	325,000	6.20	6.30
2000	185,000	5.30	100	2010	345,000	6.20	6.35
2001	200,000	5.45	100	2011	365,000	6.20	6.40
2002	210,000	5.60	100	2012	390,000	6.20	6.40

(Plus Accrued Interest from March 1, 1992)

The Series H Bonds are subject to redemption prior to maturity as described herein.

The Series H Bonds maturing 2006 through 2012 will be issued at an original issue discount as more fully described under "Original Issue Discount" herein.

The proceeds of the Series H Bonds will be used for the replacement of the Underground Steam Lines and to renovate the old Fine Arts Building, as more fully described under "Description of the Series H Project" herein.

The Series H Bonds constitute special obligations of Murray State University and do not constitute a debt, liability or obligation of the Commonwealth of Kentucky nor a pledge of the full faith and credit of the Commonwealth. Principal of and interest on the Series H Bonds are payable solely from the revenues of the Consolidated Educational Buildings Project, on a parity as to security and source of payment with the outstanding Series B, C, D, E, F Refunding and G Bonds.

The Series H Bonds are issued subject to the approval of legality by Rubin Hays & Foley, Louisville, Kentucky, Bond Counsel.

Figure 1 An example of a serial bond structure—cover page from an official statement for a Murray State University bond issue.

Rates for variable/adjustable rate bonds will always be lower than for fixed-rate bonds when sold. In the mid-1980s, when fixed interest rates were high and the spread between fixed rates and variable rates was wide, many cities and states found it advantageous to borrow on a variable-rate basis as a means of reducing debt service cost and therefore saving money. On the other hand, a variable bond issue imposes interest rate risks on the issuer. As long as interest rates stay the same or go down, the issuer will be better off in the long run with the issuance of variable-rate debt. However, an increase in interest rates can mitigate such savings. The decision to borrow on a fixed- or variable-rate basis is a policy decision that must be addressed in structuring a bond issue.

It should also be noted that variable-rate bonds are more complicated and involve more costs of issuance than fixed-rate bonds. Again, many issuers of variable-rate bonds often believe that the potential cost savings from lower interest rates make up for any increased administrative burden and any higher initial front-end costs.

As suggested earlier, it would not be financially prudent to finance an asset with a 2- or 3-year life with a 20-year bond. Conversely, it is often prudent to use short-term bonds with a 1- or 2-year maturity structure. We generally identify three major purposes for short-term borrowing. First, an issuer may have expenditure needs today but revenues and taxes will not be collected until some point in the future. Therefore, it may be prudent to borrow funds today to meet these expenditure requirements and then to repay the loan with the anticipated revenues that will be received in the future. Such short-term loans issued in the anticipation of future revenue or tax collections are called revenue anticipation notes or tax anticipation notes. Often the maturity of such notes will be 1 year or less since revenues and taxes are due in the immediate future.

In like manner, cities and states may find that they are to receive a grant to provide the financing for a project. However, a condition of the grant may be that the project is finalized and inspected prior to the disbursement of any of the grant funds. In such a case, the issuance of grant anticipation notes may be appropriate. As the name implies, grant anticipation notes are short-term bonds or notes sold in anticipation of future funding from grant funds. Grant anticipation notes will be of a short-term nature, generally 1 to 3 years. Once the grant is received, then the short-term loan will be repaid.

Finally, some cities and states have utilized short-term borrowings known as bond anticipation notes. Bond anticipation notes are short-term borrowings in anticipation of the issuance of long-term bonds at some point in the future. For example, suppose a city or state is undertaking a capital construction project and the complete scope or size of the project is unknown. The city or state may issue bond anticipation notes to borrow the money to be spent on the construction, then later issue bonds to provide for the permanent financing. Bond anticipation notes have also been used during periods of high interest rates when issuers did not want to lock in permanent financing; they therefore borrowed for a short-term period and did their permanent financing at some point in the future. As can be surmised, the future direction of interest rates is unknown and the issuance of bond anticipation notes involves an interest rate risk.

C.   Financing Team

Prior to the structuring and marketing of a bond issue, the members of the financing team must be assembled. Each member of the financing team has a role to play and it is important to identify the specific role each member plays.

The most important member of the financing team is the issuer. It is the issuer who is incurring a liability that must be repaid in the future. It is the issuer's debt! Often other members of the financing team will provide advice on the appropriate structure and marketing of an issue. While the issuer need not have a detailed knowledge of the credit markets, the issuer should understand the structure of their transaction since they are responsible for the repayment of the loan over its life. Issuers may ask questions of other team members and must attempt to understand the terms and provisions of the loan that they are receiving.

Issuers are oftentimes boards or commissions of a state or city. These boards and commissions are frequently composed of public officials and lay members appointed to the board by a governor or mayor. Issuers should have professional staffs to assist them in anlayzing advice received from other financing team members.

A required second member of the financing team is the bond counsel. In Fig. 1 a summary of the bond counsel's opinion on the tax-exempt status of the bonds is provided at the top of the official statement. This opinion is:

In the opinion of Bond Counsel, Rubin Hays & Foley, interest on the Series H Bonds is exempt from Federal and Kentucky income taxation under existing statutes, court decisions, regulations and published ruling, and under existing laws the principal of the Series H Bonds is exempt from ad valorem taxation by the Commonwealth of Kentucky and any political subdivision thereof, assuming compliance by the University with certain tax covenants. For a more complete statement with reference to the foregoing see 'Tax Exemption' and 'Special Tax Exemption Considerations' herein.

This opinion is critical since the lenders, or the buyers of the bonds, will rely upon this legal opinion to assure them that the interest income they will receive on the bonds is exempt from federal income taxes. Earlier we talked about the importance of this tax exemption and its impact on investment decisions that are made by investors. An investor whose financial goals mandate investing in a tax-exempt security does not want to run the risk that at some future date she will be required to pay taxes on the interest that she received. Therefore, lenders and potential bond buyers depend heavily on the opinion of bond counsels to provide them with assurances that interest on purchased bonds is exempt from federal and many cases state income taxes. Bond law is a specialized area of the law with training that requires expertise in those sections of the U.S. Internal Revenue Service code that deal with the tax exemption on the municipal security. Therefore, it is unlikely that a general counsel for an issuer or a city attorney has the background and expertise to provide a recognized and accepted legal opinion. Most bond investors will look to legal tax opinions rendered by recognized bond council firms. A publication called the *Municipal Bond Dealers Directory* or the *Red Book* provides a listing of law firms throughout the United States that have provided legal opinions on municipal securities on prior transactions (Bond Buyer). Therefore, it is normally desirable for the issuer to employ a legal firm that is recognized in the *Red Book*.

It should finally be noted that bond counsels may be selected as a member of the financing team in several different ways. Bid procedures may be developed that solicit prices from recognized bond counsels and contracts may then be awarded to the lowest bidder. At one time it was generally believed that bond attorneys' services could not be acquired on a price bid. However, over time the bidding of legal services has become a more standard practice and today many issuers select their legal counsel on a price bid basis. In addition, it should be noted that the bond counsel is employed by the issuer and therefore must be compensated by the issuer. A more complete discussion of compensation will be provided in a later section dealing with the sizing of the bond issue.

Most issuers of tax-exempt bonds will utilize the services of an investment banker as a member of the financing team to assist them in the structure and marketing of the issue. Investment banking firms may be national firms such as Merrill Lynch or Goldman Sachs, or firms that concentrate their business activities in regional areas. To fully understand the role of the investor banker, it is necessary to first discuss the three methods for selling and marketing tax-exempt bonds.

An issuer may elect to sell their bonds via a competitive sale, negotiated sale, or a private placement. In a competitive sale, the bonds are sold on the basis of a price (interest rate) bid and the bidder that offers to purchase the bonds at the lowest interest rate is the winning bidder. Sealed bids are normally taken at a designated time and an award is made to the low-interest-rate bidder. In a competitive transaction, the investment banker plays the role of financial advisor to the issuer, offering advice with regard to numerous structural issues, such as whether to sell long-term bonds on a fixed-rate or variable-rate basis, or whether serial bonds are more attractive than term bonds. The investment banker will also assist the issuer in marketing its bonds (e.g., obtaining a rating, advertising the bond issue, and preparing the official statement). It should again be noted that the final decisions are the issuer's; however, the advice offered by the financial advisor can be very important in making prudent financial decisions. At the same time, an issuer must remember that financial advisors are paid consultants and in some cases their advice will reflect the investment banking firm's biases. That is why it is critical for an issuer to understand the advice it receives so that it makes the best financial decision possible.

A second type of sale is a negotiated sale process. In a negotiated sale an issuer again will select an investment banking firm, and the firm will perform the same services provided in a competitive sell. However, now instead of the issuer's advertising for sealed interest rate bids the issuer will negotiate the terms and conditions and interest rate with the investment banker. The investment banker wears a "dual hat" during a negotiated process: both the role of a financial advisor and the purchaser of the bond. It should be noted that the investment banking firm has little desire to purchase the bonds to hold in its portfolio as an investment. Its incentive is to purchase the bonds in the primary market and then to resale the bonds to banks, insurance companies, individuals, mutual funds, and the like, in the secondary bond market. The investment bank's profits are derived from the difference between the price that it pays, the price or interest rate negotiated in the primary market, and the price for the interest rate paid in the secondary market. To determine a fair price or interest rate in the primary market an issuer should examine the interest rate on other similar transactions being marketed at the same time as the issuer's bond issue and should compare the proposed interest rate on the negotiated sale with various bond indices that are published. In this way, the issuer can ensure that the interest rate negotiated is a market interest rate.

A decade ago approximately 60% of all municipal issues were sold on a negotiated basis; now approximately 75% of all issues are sold on a negotiated basis (*Bond Buyer Yearbook*). While it is generally believed that an issuer will receive a better interest rate with a competitive sale than with a negotiated sale, this may not always be the case. Again as a general rule, negotiated issues are warranted for larger transactions, refunding transactions, complicated structures, and transactions in which an issuer does not have an established or "seasoned" name in the credit market. In each of these cases, the investment banking firm buying the bonds in the primary market can do significant premarketing and advertising work in the secondary market to encourage participation in the transaction by banks, insurance companies, individuals, mutual funds, and the like. Without such premarketing and advertising, bidders will often have a reluctance to bid on bonds in the primary market, and no bids or perhaps only one bid would be received. As a result, the competitive transaction can in some cases cause higher interest rates. For smaller, straightforward established issuers, this is probably not the case.

As with a competitive sale, the investment banker is employed and paid a fee by the issuer for negotiated issues. It is interesting to note that an issuer may select the investment banking firm with which it will negotiate the final terms and conditions of a transaction in the negotiated market through a competitive bid process; that is, most often issuers will develop requests for proposals (RFP) that ask investment banking firms for information on the type of financing structure that they propose, the firm's experience with particular types of transactions and suggested fees. Issuers will then evaluate this information and develop a scoring system to select the investment banking firm with which the sale is ultimately negotiated.

Finally, it should be noted that in a minority of cases, municipal governments will market their bonds through a process known as the private placement. With a private placement, the issuer negotiates the sale of their bonds directly with the ultimate buyer of the bonds, such as a bank or insurance company. In the case of a private placement, the services of the investment banker may not be necessary since the terms and conditions are tailored to meet the demand of the ultimate buyer. In other cases an investment banking firm may be employed in a private placement to represent the issuer in the negotiation with the ultimate buyer.

A commerical bank is also usually employed as the final member of the financing team on a tax-exempt bond issue. The bank may wear one or more of the following "hats": (1) trustee, (2) registrar, and (3) paying agent. The bank, in its trustee function, is employed to hold the proceeds of the tax-exempt bond issue until the proceeds are spent for construction and/or acquisition. These funds must be held somewhere, and normally a commerical bank is employed to hold these funds in a trust account specifically for the purposes for which the bonds were sold.

In addition, banks provide the registrar function services. Prior to January 1, 1984, most tax-exempt bonds were issued as coupon bonds or bearer bonds. This means that the issuer provided to the bondholder a document with coupon payments attached to the bond issue. As interest became due on the bonds, the holder or bearer of the bonds would clip the coupon and take it to a local bank for payment, in the same fashion that a check would be taken to a bank for payment. The holder or bearer of the bonds was forced to clip the coupon to receive the interest due on his or her bonds on a semiannual basis. If a coupon bond was lost by one individual and found by a second individual, the second individual could clip the coupon and redeem it for cash, hence the term bearer-bonds; coupons were payable on presentation by the bearer of the coupon.

While the interest on municipal bonds is exempt from federal, and in most cases state income taxation, municipal bonds may trade in the marketplace as stocks trade day to day; that is, Mr. Smith may buy a tax-exempt bond from Merrill Lynch for $5,000, and if interest rates decline, Mr. Smith may later sell that bond back to Merrill Lynch or some other individual for more than $5,000. Again, as in a stock transaction, Mr. Smith would have earned a capital gain on the sale of the municipal bond. This capital gain is subject to federal income taxation. The U.S. Department of the Treasury and the Internal Revenue Service believed that capital gains on tax-exempt bonds were often unreported since there were no records of the holders of the bonds. As a result, in 1983 legislation was enacted by Congress requiring that all bonds sold after January

1, 1984 be registered.* Hence, an issuer must keep a written record of the holders of his or her securities. If Mr. Smith sells his securities, the issuer must erase Mr. Smith's name and add the name and address of the individual who purchased the security from Mr. Smith. This information must then be reported on an ongoing basis to the Internal Revenue Service so that it can track capital gains earnings and ensure that such earnings are reported as taxable income. As a practical matter, most state and local issuers do not have the time or the staff to keep track of all of the holders of their outstanding bonds. Therefore, this function is generally contracted to a bank to perform. This is the registrar function of the bank.

Finally, banks also perform the role of paying agent on bonds. Since bonds today are not coupon bonds, the issuer is required to mail to the holder of the bonds on a semiannual basis, principal and interest due. Again, the issuer generally contracts with a bank to perform this paying-agent function. The bank will print the check and mail the check to the bondholder.

An issuer could have three banks perform these three functions. However, most often the same bank will serve as trustee, registrar, and paying agent. Further, most issuers will select the bank to perform these functions based upon a competitive selection process. Most banks have experience as trustee, registrar, and paying agent, so often a price bid may be developed and the trustee, registrar, and paying agent selected based upon the lowest price bid.

In summary, the issuer working with the bond counsel, the investment banker, and the bank forms the team that is necessary to structure and market a tax-exempt bond issue. In the case of the bond counsel, the investment bank, and the bank, a fee is paid for services. It is important that the issuer have a strong working relationship with each of the members of the financing team so that the issuer and financing team members may attempt to get the lowest interest rate possible.

D. Structuring the Issue

The following section details the process for actually structuring a bond issue. The steps involved are: (1) sizing the issue, (2) determining other structural considerations, (3) making rating and credit market considerations, (4) advertising the sale, (5) making the actual sale, and (6) closing and investing the bond proceeds. Each of these will be briefly discussed below.

When an issuer elects to sell bonds to finance a capital project, the architects and engineers for the project will generally provide the issuer a cost estimate for the project. Let us assume that we have a $4,000,000 project that needs to be financed. If we sell bonds to finance it, the first consideration that needs to be reviewed is how much actually needs to be borrowed to provide the $4,000,000 needed to meet the construction cost of the project. Most often, tax-exempt issuers will find that they must borrow an amount greater than the construction amount of the project to cover the associated costs of the bond issue. Again, the best analogy would be the individual home owner who purchases a home but must pay an appraisal fee, a title search fee, legal fees, and so forth upon closing the transaction. To analyze the sizing of a tax-exempt bond issue, we should first address a chart of accounts that might typically be established for such an issue. Figure 2 provides a typical chart of accounts for a tax-exempt issue.

The construction fund is established as a depository for the bond proceeds until they are expended. If our proceeds are being used to pay for the construction of a building, the actual construction time may be 1 year or longer. The construction fund is established as a separate account to maintain the construction funds until fully expended. It should also be noted that the construction fund may be invested to earn interest income until the proceeds are used. This raises the first policy issue that must be addressed in sizing a bond issue; that is, whether we fully fund or net fund the construction fund.

A fully funded construction fund is one in which $4,000,000 is borrowed for a $4,000,000 project. Obviously, investment income will be earned over the life of the construction fund, so the construction fund will ultimately have an amount in excess of $4,000,000. In this case, this investment income may be used for potential cost overruns or other purposes related to the project.

Alternatively, an issuer could elect to borrow less than $4,000,000 and use the investment income earned on the construction fund to bring funds available up to the required construction amount; that is, depending on interest rates and the length of the construction project, an issuer may need to borrow only $3,500,000 to finance a $4,000,000 project. Borrowing less than the amount of the project and relying on investment income

*In the *Baker v. South Carolina* case, the treasurer of the state of South Carolina challenged the federal government's ability to require the issuance of such registered securities. (See footnote on p. 258)

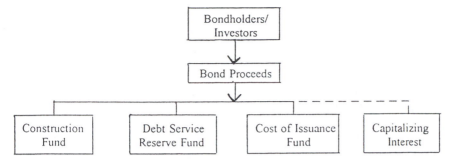

Figure 2 A typical chart of accounts for a tax-exempt issue.

to complete the project is known as net funding the project. The advantage of net funding construction projects is that less money is borrowed and hence the annual debt service requirements on the bond issue are less than with a fully funded bond issue. Again, this is a policy decision to be made by the issuer when sizing the issue and structuring the bonds.

A debt service reserve is often established on bond issues as a source of security to the bondholder. The typical debt service reserve is established in an amount equal to the maximum annual principal and interest payment on the bond issue. This amount is held in a separate account, in escrow, to be used only in the event that the project does not generate sufficient cash flow to make the debt service payments. Debt service reserves are often necessary on revenue bonds and used less on general obligation-type issues.

Prior to TRA86, the debt service on an issue could be invested at an unlimited interest rate (i.e., an issuer could arbitrage on the reserve). The TRA86 indicated that if in fact an issuer establishes a debt service reserve and earns arbitrage on the reserve, the difference between the borrowing costs of the bond issue and the earnings on the debt service reserve must be rebated or paid to the federal government. For example, suppose that our $4,000,000 project will have a maximum annual debt service of $400,000 a year. This amount of funds is generally borrowed as a part of the bond issue and then deposited in an escrow account with the trustee bank. If the interest rate on the bonds was 6% but market conditions allow the issuer to earn 7%, then the 1% differential in borrowing cost and investment earnings must be rebated to the federal government. While debt service reserves are a security provision on a bond issue, prior to 1986, issuers had financial incentives to establish debt service reserves. Today, issuers generally utilize debt reserves for security provisions only and often do not utilize reserves unless necessary for credit enhancement.

Issuers may also elect to capitalize or borrow interest to make debt service payments on issues in the early years of the issue; this is most often utilized on revenue bond issues. For example, an issuer may borrow money today for a toll road project. The issuer is required to make principal and interest payments during the construction phase of the project—prior to its completion and hence the collection of tolls. Since the project is not generating revenues to meet the debt service requirement, the issuer capitalizes interest or borrows the interest due until the project is completed.

A final account that will need to be established for most municipal bond issues is the cost of issuance account. As already noted, the structuring of a municipal bond involves the employment of the services of specialized attorneys and consultants. These businesses will need to be paid for their services. These firms could be paid from the operating budget of the city or state. However, as a general rule, most cities and states do not plan for or incorporate these costs associated with the issuance of bonds into their operating budgets. Further, from a conceptual perspective, these costs are appropriate for amortization over the life of the bond. As a result, most municipal issuers will estimate the fees required as part of a bond issue and these fees are then borrowed as part of the financing. These estimated costs are then deposited into a separate cost of issuance account normally held with the trustee bank. After the successful sale and closing of the bond issue, the issuer will authorize the trustee to make payments to the various members of the financing team from the cost of issuance account. Normally the cost of the issuance account is a short-term account that can be closed once all of the various costs of issuance are paid.

There are a number of other structural issues that must be addressed in the preparation in the sale of a bond issue. One of the most important of these structural issues is the "call" provisions for the transactions. The call provisions of the issue will impact the marketability of the bonds and the issuer's future ability to refund or refinance the bonds. To illustrate, let's suppose that a municipal issuer sells 20-year bonds at a fixed interest rate of 8%. The issuer would like to retain the option of refinancing these bonds at some point in the future should interest rates decline. This again is analogous to home owners with long-term fixed-rate mortgages who want to take advantage of a falling interest rate environment to refinance their houses and save on their monthly mortgage payments. In like manner, cities and states wish to maintain their option to refinance bonds at some point in the future. On the other hand, the purchaser of the bonds has made an investment decision based upon today's interest rate structure. This investor would like to avoid having her investment refinanced at some point in the future and being required to then reinvest her funds at a lower interest rate.

As a general rule, municipal issuers will offer some type of call protection to the municipal investor; that is, an issuer will convenant to the investor that the bonds the investor has purchased will not be recalled for a certain period of time, say 10 years. Hence, an investor in a 20-year fixed-rate bond of 8% is assured that for at least 10 years will continue to hold his 8% bond. After 10 years, standard practice is for the issuer to have the ability to call or purchase the bonds back from the investor so that the issuer may take advantage of the lower interest rate environment. The more call protection the issuer is willing to provide to the investor the more marketable the bonds will be (i.e., the lower the interest rate). On the other hand, the more call protection given to the investor, the more difficult it is for the issuer to refund its bonds at some point in the future.

There are other structural issues that must be addressed by the issuer. A full discussion of each of these is beyond the scope of this presentation. However, it should again be noted that the issuer working in concert with its bond counsel or investment banker should analyze each of these structural issues and determine what is in the best interest of the issuer.

E. The Rating Process

An integral part of marketing of a municipal bond issue is the decision of whether or not to have the issue rated by one or more of the major rating agencies. There are currently three major rating firms for municipal bonds in the United States: Moody's Investors Service, Standard and Poor's, and Fitch, Inc. Each of these rating agencies will analyze a municipal issuer and its credit and issue a letter rating that may be used by the issuer in the marketing of its bonds. It is important to note that the issuer pays a fee to the rating agency to obtain this rating. Further, the issuer must provide detailed information to the rating agencies that may be analyzed and reviewed in determining the rating that will be assigned. Further, once an insurer has provided information to a rating agency, it cannot decide not to use an unfavorable rating. Ratings are a disclosure item in the official statement of an issuer, and the issuer is obligated to inform potential buyers and investors of the rating that is assigned.

Not every municipal bond issue will find it necessary to have a rating assigned by one or more of the major rating agencies. A small local issuer may borrow a relatively small amount of funds and will find that it can successfully market its bond issue to local banks and investors who are familiar with the issuer and its credit. In these cases, therefore, it is unnecessary to pay the expense associated with a rating.

Ratings are most often sought by issuers who frequently borrow in the capital markets or who issue large bond issues that require a broad array of investors. For example, a state that is preparing to borrow $30,000,000 may find it necessary to attract potential buyers from outside the state's geographical boundaries. Many large institutional buyers of tax-exempt bonds are located in New York, Chicago, San Francisco, Boston, Hartford, and the like. These institutional buyers often provide a critical market for a state's bond issue. Some of these institutional buyers will have their own credit departments that perform credit analysis on issuers to ascertain whether or not a particular municipal bond meets its investment criteria. Other institutional buyers rely upon ratings as a guide to credit quality. More specifically, many institutional buyers formulate investment policies that dictate the amount or percentage of a particular issuer's credit that they are willing to hold in their portfolio. For example, a bank may restrict itself to no more than 5% of a particular credit in its portfolio. Such a policy ensures credit diversification, and such diversification is an accepted portfolio management strategy for diversifying risks. Therefore, larger issuers and issuers that are somewhat frequent borrowers will generally elect to obtain at least one rating to assist in the marketing and sale of their securities. Large issuers that frequently access the credit markets may in fact determine that it is in their best interest to obtain multiple ratings (i.e., separate ratings) from Moody's, Standard and Poor's, and Fitch. This might be particularly important for a state that borrows several times during the year and is dependent upon a large and diverse market to provide an outlet for its bonds. These issuers need to work closely on an ongoing basis with the rating agencies to provide them with current and up-to-date information so that the rating agencies have the best available information upon which to base their rating decision.

There does not exist a standard formula utilized by one or all of the rating agencies in determining credit quality and that therefore may be used to predict an issuer's rating. Numerous research efforts have been conducted to try to model the variables that are analyzed by the rating agencies in determining their rating assignment (Wilson, 1986; Horton, 1969; Osteryoung and Blevins, 1978). It is beyond our scope to discuss this research in detail; however, it is valuable for us to identify the broad areas of focus that the rating agencies review in assigning issuers a specific rating. A review of the credit reports of the rating agencies and other literature provided by the rating agencies suggests that there are four broad areas that the rating agencies focus upon in the assignment of a rating (Standard and Poor's Corporation, 1989). These are: (1) the economic conditions of the issuer, (2) the financial strength of the issuer, (3) the demographics of the issuer, and (4) the management strengths of the issuer. Each of these will be briefly discussed below.

It is logical to believe that the rating agencies will look at the economic conditions of an issuer as a primary measure of the issuer's ability to pay. For example, for a state or local government, economic variables such as employment/unemployment and personal income are primary measures of the revenue potential of the issuer. One would believe that the greater the employment growth in an area, the more people are working and earning income, and thus the greater the tax base for the community. Therefore, rating agencies will be interested in time series data that show the employment/unemployment patterns for an area.

In like manner, personal income is a measure of a state or local government's ability to pay, in much the same way as gross domestic product is a measure of economic well-being for the federal government. It might well be that an area has experienced strong employment growth but that the majority of the jobs are in lower-paying service industries. Therefore, an examination of employment/unemployment variables alone may sometimes be misleading and personal income growth may give a better measure of overall economic well-being. There are numerous other economic variables that will also be of interest to rating agencies.

The key point, however, is that these economic variables are a proxy or measure of the ability to repay principal and interest on debt. Throughout this chapter, we have often used analogies of an individual home owner in our discussion of the tax-exempt market. We know that a bank evaluating a loan to a potential home owner will be interested in that individual's employment record and income level, and the same holds true for state and local borrowers.

A second area of interest to the rating agencies is the financial reports and statements of the borrower. Historical data is generally required so that the rating agencies may discern trends and patterns of financial strengths or weaknesses. Most often, the rating agencies will review an issuer's budget. The budget document itself is a projection of revenues and expenditures for a future time period. The rating agencies will access the reasonableness of these revenue and expenditure plans. For example, rating agencies will be cautious if they believe that revenues have been unrealistically estimated. The expenditure plan of an issuer is important since the allocation of dollars by a governmental body is a reflection of the policies and priorities of that issuer. In addition to the budget, the rating agencies will be interested in reviewing an issuer's balance sheet and income and expense statements. A historical review of these financial statements allows the rating agencies to determine changes in the fund balance of the issuer and its overall financial strength. The income and expense statement is a document that summarizes revenues collected and expenses incurred over a period of time. The rating agencies use this information to compare projected revenues with actual revenues and projected expenditures with actual expenditures. Also, it is important to review the difference between revenues and expenditures. If revenues exceed expenditures, the fund balance of the issuer will increase, providing a greater cushion or "rainy day fund" for the issuer. This cushion or rainy day fund may need to be a source of revenues for the payment of future debt service in a recessionary or financially tough period. If expenditures exceed revenues, then the issuer has run a deficit and this deficit will draw down or deplete existing cushions and rainy day funds of the issuer. The rating agencies will also be interested in the accounting procedures used to develop these financial statements.

A complete discussion of accounting and auditing principles is again beyond our scope of presentation here. However, the rating agencies, as well as institutional buyers of municipal bonds, will strongly prefer that the financial statements of the issuer be prepared in accordance with generally accepted accounting principles (GAAP). Generally accepted accounting principles ensure uniformity in recording and reporting financial transactions and allow the rating agencies to make "apples-to-apples" comparisons among issuers, as well as for a particular issuer over time.

The third area of review by the rating agencies is the demographic characteristics of the issuer. For example, a growing population generally indicates a greater population base for the support and payment of future debt service liabilities. On the other hand, a declining population base might indicate that there will be fewer people available to work and make tax payments to support the repayment of debt over the life of the capital project. In addition, other detailed demographic information may also be valuable from a credit perspective. An aging population would indicate a declining workforce and increased demands for governmental services. The same might be true of a very young population, which indicates a need for more schools, playgrounds, parks, and similar expenditures. Migration patterns are also an important credit consideration and are reviewed as part of the demographic analysis by the rating agencies.

Finally, the rating agencies analyze the management strengths and weaknesses of the issuer. The management of an organization is critical to the financial operation of that organization both in the private and public sectors. The public sector is sometimes regarded as having political appointees with minimal professional capabilities and this is an important consideration in the assignment of a rating. Rating agencies' personnel will often attempt to visit an issuer to have the opportunity to meet with its financial management team and determine its professionalism. In other cases, rating agencies will encourage issuers to visit them in their offices in New York, in part for the same reason.

Rating agencies collect information that we have discussed above and analyze it in detail. Often credit analysts working for the rating agencies will ask specific questions of an issuer about a project being financed with the proceeds of tax-exempt bonds or other questions about the issuer. Once these questions have been answered and the analysis of the rating agencies is complete, a rating will be assigned to the issuer. As seen in Fig. 1, the rating is prominently displayed at the top of the cover page of the official statement. Further, a section of the official statement will discuss the rating in greater detail. Figure 3 shows a listing of ratings assigned by Standard and Poor's Corporation and the definitions ascribed to each rating level.

It should also be noted that a recent trend in the municipal bond market has been for issuers to purchase municipal bond insurance in an effort to enhance their ratings; that is, an issuer who is rated A may wish to improve its rating to AAA. It can do so only by buying an insurance policy from a municipal bond insurer. As with any insurance, the issuer must pay a premium to the insurance company to buy this policy. An issuer should examine the cost of an insurance policy with the present value of the projected savings in debt service cost due to the higher rating and lower interest rate; that is, a AAA-rated bond issue should sell at a lower interest cost than an A-rated issue. If a municipal bond insurance policy has a present value savings of $700,000 to the issuer from reduced interest payments and the cost of the policy is $500,000, then the purchase of municipal insurance is economically viable. Most issuers will evaluate the cost benefits of municipal bond insurance on issues prior to their marketing.

Once the issue has been structured, the rating has been obtained, and the issue has been marketed, the actual sale of the bonds takes place. As previously noted, the two frequent sales methods are the competitive sale and the negotiated sale. Again, with the competitive sale the issuer advertises a sale date and takes sealed interest rate bids at that time. The award of the sale may be based on either the lowest net interest cost basis or the lowest true interest cost basis. The calculation of these interest costs is beyond the scope of this presentation and computer programs are readily available to make these calculations. It is sufficient to note at this time that the concept of the net interest cost and true interest cost provides alternative calculations for incorporating the cost of issuance and the future debt interest payments of the issuer into a common cost measure for all bidders on the bonds.

Alternatively, the bonds may be sold to a negotiated sale that, as previously described, would involve the issuer negotiating the interest rate with an investment banking firm. An advantage of a negotiated sale is that the issuer has greater flexibility in setting the actual sale date; that is, with a competitive sale a specific date for the sale of the bonds is chosen and then advertised to the potential bond bidders. If market conditions change and the chosen date is not appropriate for the sale, the issuer must cancel the sale, select a new date for issuing the bonds, and readvertise. On the other hand, with a negotiated sale the issuer has great flexibility in selling the bonds on a day that they believe will offer the lowest interest cost.

Once the interest rate is established on the bonds, the issuer must plan for the closing of the bond issue. Again, the closing on a bond issue is analogous to a home mortgage. The closing represents the point at which the transaction is finalized and the issuer exchanges the bonds for commitments to repay for funds. Between the time of the sale and the closing, the bonds must be printed and other provisions made for the closing. The period between the sale and the closing is often around 3 weeks. During this period of time the bond counsel will ensure that all of the proper closing documentation is finalized. The issuer will work with the bond trustee to arrange for the transfer of bonds and money. On the date of the closing when the actual exchange of bonds

DESCRIPTION OF MUNICIPAL BOND RATINGS

Municipal Bond Ratings

Standard & Poor's. A Standard & Poor's municipal obligation rating is a current assessment of the creditworthiness of an obligor with respect to a specific obligation. This assessment may take into consideration obligors such as guarantors, insurers or lessees.

The debt rating is not a recommendation to purchase, sell or hold a security, inasmuch as it does not comment as to market price or suitability for a particular investor.

The ratings are based on current information furnished by the issuer or obtained by Standard & Poor's from other sources it considers reliable. Standard & Poor's does not perform an audit in connection with any rating and may, on occasion, rely on unaudited financial information. The ratings may be changed, suspended or withdrawn as a result of changes in, or unavailability of, such information, or for other circumstances.

The ratings are based, in varying degrees, on the following considerations:

I. Likelihood of default- capacity and willingness of the obligor as to the timely payment of interest and repayment of principal in accordance with the terms of the obligation;

II. Nature of and provisions of the obligation;

III. Protection afforded by, and relative position of, the obligation in the event of bankruptcy, reorganization or other arrangement under the laws of bankruptcy and other laws affecting creditors' rights.

AAA Debt rated "AAA" has the highest rating assigned by Standard & Poor's. Capacity to pay interest and repay principal is extremely strong.

AA Debt rated "AA" has a very strong capacity to pay interest and repay principal and differs from the highest rated issues only in small degree.

A Debt rated "A" has a strong capacity to pay interest and repay principal although it is somewhat more susceptible to the adverse effects of changes in circumstances and economic conditions than debt in higher rated categories.

BBB Debt rated "BBB" is regarded as having an adequate capacity to pay interest and repay principal. Whereas it normally exhibits adequate protection parameters, adverse economic conditions or changing circumstances are more likely to lead to a weakened capacity to pay interest and repay principal for debt in this category than in higher rated categories.

Plus (+) or Minus (-): The ratings from "AA" to "B" may be modified by the addition of a plus or minus sign to show relative standing within the major rating categories.

Provisional Ratings: The letter "p" indicates that the rating is provisional. A provisional rating assumes the successful completion of the project being financed by the debt being rated and indicates that payment of debt service requirements is largely or entirely dependent upon the successful and timely completion of the project. This rating, however, while addressing credit quality subsequent to completion of the project, makes no comment on the likelihood of, or the risk of default upon failure of, such completion. The investor should exercise his own judgment with respect to such likelihood and risk.

Moody's Investors Service. A brief description of the applicable Moody's Investors Service rating symbols and their meanings follows:

Aaa Bonds which are rated Aaa are judged to be of the best quality. They carry the smallest degree of investment risk and are generally referred to as "gilt edge." Interest payments are protected

(*continues on page 727*)

Figure 3 A list of ratings assigned by Standard and Poor's Corporation and Moody's Investors Service and the definitions ascribed to each level.

and money takes place, the funds received by the issuer must be deposited into the appropriate accounts and funds previously described. Provisions should also be made for the investment of these monies until utilized for construction, payment of cost of issuance, and the like.

IV. REFUNDINGS

Much as individual home owners will refinance their existing mortgages when interest rates drop significantly, state and local governments find it advantageous to refinance or refund outstanding debt. Normally, a state

by a large or by an exceptionally stable margin and principal is secure. While the various protective elements are likely to change, such changes as can be visualized are most unlikely to impair the fundamentally strong position of such issues.

Aa Bonds which are rated Aa are judged to be of high quality by all standards. Together with the Aaa group they comprise what are generally known as high grade bonds. They are rated lower than the best bonds because margins of protection may not be as large as in Aaa securities or fluctuation of protective elements may be of greater amplitude or there may be other elements present which make the long-term risks appear somewhat larger than in Aaa securities.

A   Bonds which are rated A possess many favorable investment attributes and are to be considered as upper medium grade obligations. Factors giving security to principal and interest are considered adequate, but elements may be present which suggest a susceptibility to impairment some time in the future.

Baa Bonds which are rated Baa are considered as medium grade obligations; i.e., they are neither highly protected nor poorly secured. Interest payments and principal security appear adequate for the present but certain protective elements may be lacking or may be characteristically unreliable over any great length of time. Such bonds lack outstanding investment characteristics and in fact have speculative characteristics as well.

Bonds in the Aa, A, Baa, Ba and B groups which Moody's believes possess the strongest investment attributes are designated by the symbols Aa1, A1, Baa1, Ba1 and B1.

Moody's Short Term Loan Ratings- There are four rating categories for short-term obligations, all of which define an investment grade situation. These are designated Moody's Investment Grade as MIG 1 through MIG 4. In the case of variable rate demand obligations (VRDOs), two ratings are assigned; one representing an evaluation of the degree of risk associated with scheduled principal and interest payments, and the other representing an evaluation of the degree of risk associated with the demand feature. The short-term rating assigned to the demand feature of VRDOs is designated as VMIG. When no rating is applied to the long or short-term aspect of a VRDO, it will be designated NR. Issues or the features associated with MIG or VMIG ratings are identified by date of issue, date of maturity or maturities or rating expiration date and description to distinguish each rating from other ratings. Each rating designation is unique with no implication as to any other similar issue of the same obligor. MIG ratings terminate at the retirement of the obligation while VMIG rating expiration will be a function of each issuer's specific structural or credit features.

MIG1/VMIG1 This designation denotes best quality. There is present strong protection by established cash flows, superior liquidity support or demonstrated broad-based access to the market for refinancing.

MIG2/VMIG2 This designation denotes high quality. Margins of protection are ample although not so large as in the preceding group.

MIG3/VMIG3 This designation denotes favorable quality. All security elements are accounted for but there is lacking the undeniable strength of the preceding grades. Liquidity and cash flow protection may be narrow and market access for refinancing is likely to be less well established.

MIG4/VMIG4 This designation denotes adequate quality. Protection commonly regarded as required of an investment security is present and, although not distinctly or predominantly speculative, there is specific risk.

Source: Standard and Poor's Debt Ratings Criteria, (New York), 1986.

Figure 3 (*Continued*)

or local government will refinance outstanding debt to reduce annual debt service payments (i.e., to save money). A second type of refunding which is not economically motivated but is an attempt to modernize and update covenants made by the bondholder in prior years is called a legal defeasement.

Economic refundings are undertaken with the primary objective of saving money. Economic refundings may be either current refundings or advance refundings. As was noted in the prior discussion dealing with the structuring of state and local debt, issuers of state and local bonds will often provide call protection to the buyers of their bonds. It has been somewhat of a standard practice that bond buyers are given 10 years of call protection. This means that the buyer of the bonds cannot have her bonds recalled or purchased by the issuer for a 10-year period. It has been standard practice that call provisions after the tenth year often provide that the bondholder be paid a premium (a price greater than the par value of the bond) for several years leading up to the final maturity on the bond. As was noted earlier, call protection is an important marketing consideration for issuers since many investors purchase state and local bonds with the intent to hold them until their final maturity. If in fact his bonds were called prior to maturity, the investor would be required to take the proceeds from his called bonds and try to find other investments to replace those that were called.

Refundings that are undertaken after the call date on a bond issue are referred to as current refundings. For example, suppose the city of XYZ sells a 20-year bond with 10-year call protection to the purchaser. If, in year 11, XYZ sells new bonds at a lower interest rate than the original bonds and takes the proceeds from the new or refunding bond issue to pay off the old or refunded issue, this transaction constitutes a current refunding. Current refundings are simple, straightforward, and purely economically motivated. To use the home owner analogy that we referred to earlier, a current refunding is analogous to an individual with a 10% mortgage refinancing that mortgage at 7% to save on her monthly mortgage payments. In the case of the home owner, the new loan is not used to purchase a new home but rather to pay off the principal on the existing higher-interest-rate loan. This is how a current refunding works.

An advance refunding is also undertaken to reduce debt service cost; however, advance refundings are more complicated to structure. An advance refunding exists when the issuer sells refunding bonds prior to the call date on the existing bond issue. We have already said that the call provision provides protection to the bondholder of the outstanding bonds, therefore, in the case of an advance refunding the issuer cannot take the proceeds from the refunding bonds and immediately pay off the outstanding bonds that carry the higher interest cost. Rather, the issuer must take the proceeds of the refunding bonds and establish an escrow of investments that will be used to make the debt service payment on the outstanding bonds until the call date, at which time the escrow will be used to call or pay off the outstanding bonds. For example, suppose XYZ sold a 20-year bond issue at a 10% interest rate and with 10 years of call protection. Five years after the original bonds were sold at a 10% interest rate, interest rates have fallen to 7%. City XYZ may elect to do an advance refunding; that is, the city may realize that interest rates are lower now than when the original bond issue was sold and may believe that if it waits until the call date (5 years later) to attempt a refunding, interest rates may no longer be at this reduced level. Therefore, the issuer makes a policy decision to take advantage of the lower interest rates today rather then assume the interest risk that exists until it can do a current refunding. In this case, XYZ would sell advance refunding bonds. The issuer would take the proceeds of the advance refunding bonds, and structure an escrow of investments or securities so that the escrow will make the debt service payments on the outstanding bonds in years 6, 7, 8, 9, and 10. The escrow would also be used in year 10 to pay the principal outstanding on the refunded bonds. The issuer will then pay debt service on the newer lower-interest-rate bonds beginning in year 5. So even though the issuer has not been able to pay off the outstanding bonds prior to the call date, the issuer has established an escrow of investments that will make the debt service payments on the old bonds. Needless to say, structuring of the escrow is critically important so that the escrow of investments will yield a perfectly matched cash flow to the debt service requirements on the outstanding bonds. Advance refunding bond issues are more complicated for this reason than new money bond issues or current refundings. As a result, advance refunding involves more costs of issuance.

It should be noted that the Internal Revenue Service has promulgated regulations dealing with the structuring of escrows on advance refundings. As a general rule, an issuer must structure the escrow of investments so that the investment yield on the escrow does not exceed the interest rate on the new refunding bonds sold. In the example cited above, the yield on the escrow would be limited to 7%.

V. TAX REFORM AND ITS IMPACT

The most significant and comprehensive attempt to redefine the utilization of tax-exempt bonds occurred with the passage of TRA86. The TRA86 was enacted after several years of debate and discussion focused on reducing the federal deficit. The TRA86, in its final form, was over 2000 pages in length; approximately 200 pages of the tax bill focused on tax-exempt bonds. A full discussion of TRA86 as it applies to the municipal bond market is beyond the scope of this presentation as it is very detailed and legalistic in its focus. Furthermore, TRA86 was confusing and dependent upon the promulgation of administrative regulations for the implementation of specific features of the act. As a result, the Arbitrage Rebate Regulations of 1989 and the Arbitrage Rebate Regulations of 1991 are important components of the implementation of the TRA86. Also, in 1989 Congress clarified and undid some provisions of TRA86 with the passage of the Revenue Reconciliation Act of 1989. As has already been discussed, one of the most significant features of TRA86 and subsequent regulations was the impact on the ability of state and local issuers to earn arbitrage. As previously noted, TRA86 effectively attempted to limit the ability of municipal issuers to earn legal arbitrage. There are, however, exceptions that apply to small issuers (those issuers that do not sell more than $5 million in bonds in a calendar year) and for issuers who are able to complete their construction projects in a specified time period. Still, as a general rule, if an issuer earns an interest rate on the proceeds of a tax-exempt bond issue that exceeds the borrowing cost on the issue, these funds must be rebated to the Internal Revenue Service. This requirement has forced issuers to do such things as keep records and file reports, which were not previously mandated.

The TRA86 also defined categories of bonds that we previously discussed: governmental bonds and private activity bonds. As previously noted, private activity bonds are now subject to the federal alternative minimum tax. This is significant in that the federal government does in fact tax the interest received on certain types of municipal securities. The TRA86 also placed a limit on the number of advanced refundings that an issuer could undertake. This impacts the planning and behavior of municipal issuers. Finally, TRA86 determined that certain types of activities, such as wholesaling and retailing, could not be financed with the proceeds of tax-exempt bonds; that is, industrial revenue bonds, long an industrial development tool of state and local government, could now only be used to support manufacturing and very limited other types of economic activities.

VI. SUMMARY AND CONCLUSIONS

Debt financing and debt policy emerged as key state and local government financial management issues in the 1990s. The increased public attention and scrutiny accorded these issues to a large degree resulted from the "coming together" of a series of related issues and circumstances of the 1980s. Among these factors were the uneven performance of the U.S. economy, which included wide swings in the rate of economic growth and differential rates of economic growth among regions; the massive federal debts and deficits; court decisions requiring increased funding for corrections and education; and emerging public priorities that left state and local governments financially strapped. Such financial stress emerged at the very time that state and local governments were attempting to finance the restructuring and expansion of their public infrastructure systems to ensure they were positioned to facilitate economic growth in the next decade and beyond.

These various interrelated financial trends encouraged and in some cases forced state and local governments to increase their use of municipal debt financing of their capital investments and infrastructure. This change brought with it new financial management challenges. State and local governments had to develop overall debt use and management policies, acquire staffs with the financial knowledge required to work with the financial community in the debt-financing process, and become active managers of debt policy and debt-marketing and -financing processes.

This chapter has focused on reviewing the emerging financial management environment, the debt management and policy issues, and the numerous processes and procedures involved in the use of debt financing as an integral component of the capital budgeting process. It also highlighted some of the critical changes in federal tax policy that have impacted the ability of state and local governments to use this financing option. Certainly, state and local debt policy and management are major issues for the 1990s and beyond. An understanding of the major issues in this area of financial management will benefit policy makers and state and local government financial managers as they continue to evolve optimal policies, procedures, and practices in this important state and local government area.

REFERENCES

Bond Buyer Yearbook, American Banker, New York, various years.
Bond Buyer, *Municipal Bond Dealers Directory*, various issues.

Hackbart, M., Leigland, J., Riherd, R., and Reid, M. (1990). *Debt and Duty: Accountability and Efficiency in State Debt Management*, Council of State Governments, Lexington, KY.

Hackbart, M. and Ramsey, J. (1990). *Municipal Fin. J.*, *11* (1).

Hackbart, M. and Ramsey, J. (1993). *The Handbook of Municipal Bonds and Public Finance* (R. Lamb, J. Leigland, and S. Rappaport, eds.), New York Institute of Finance, New York.

Horton, J. (1969). *Finan. Anal. J.*, March/April.

Oats, W. E. (1972). *Fiscal Federalism*, Harcourt, Brace and Jovanovich, New York.

Osteryoung, J. S. and Blevins, D. R. (1978). *Growth and Change*, July.

Ramsey, J., Gritz, T., and Hackbart, M. (1988). *Internat. J. Pub. Admin.*, *11* (2).

Ramsey, J. and Hackbart, M. (1993). *Handbook of Comparative Public Budgeting and Financial Management* (T. D. Lynch and L. L. Martin, eds.), Marcel Dekker, New York.

Standard and Poor's Corporation (1989). *S & P's Municipal Finance Criteria*, New York.

Wilson, S. (1986). *Gov. Finance Rev.*, *2* (3).

13

Developing Formal Debt Policies

Richard Larkin
Standard & Poor's Corporation, New York, New York

James C. Joseph
Government Finance Officers Association, Chicago, Illinois

As the demand for public-sector investment in infrastructure continues to grow, the issuance of debt has become an increasingly important component of state and local government capital programs. In the absence of policies and procedures to monitor capital financing practices, this greater dependence on borrowed funds can have a significant negative impact on a government's credit quality. While the issuance of debt is frequently an appropriate method of financing capital projects at the state and local level, it also entails careful monitoring of such issuances to ensure that an erosion of the government's credit quality does not result.

An approach being utilized by many governments to address potential credit concerns is the development, adoption, and implementation of formal debt policies. Such policies are designed to provide guidance to all participants in the capital improvement process as project requests are evaluated and funding decisions are made. By clearly spelling out the policy objectives of the government and delineating the acceptable parameters of debt issuance and management, formal debt policies can make an effective contribution to the capital funding process.

Debt policies typically address the following:

- The level of indebtedness the government can reasonably expect to incur without jeopardizing its credit standing
- The purposes for which various types of obligations will be sold
- The appropriate uses and amounts of short-term debt
- The structure of each type of issue

The degree of detail contained in debt policies can vary considerably. Some governments have concluded that their management objectives are well served by the adoption and implementation of debt policies that offer only broad direction to administrative personnel. Others have chosen to use such policies to address borrowing practices in considerable detail. Either approach can be effective, as long as the government has a clear idea of its policy goals. Care must be taken, however, not to expect debt policies, however detailed, to anticipate every future contingency in the capital program. Sufficient flexibility must be maintained to enable governmental staff to respond to unforeseen circumstances or new opportunities, where appropriate. Some considerations used to formulate debt policy are:

- How long is the capital planning period?
- Have all nondebt sources of funds been considered?

Adapted from *Government Finance Review*, Aug. 1991: 11-14 by permission of the Governmnet Finance Officers Association.

- How are borrowing plans reviewed internally?
- What level of debt is manageable in order to maintain or improve the government's credit quality?
- How much "pay-as-you-go" financing should be included in the capital plan?
- How much short-term borrowing will be undertaken, including both operating and capital borrowings?
- How much debt will be issued in the form of variable-rate securities?
- How does the redemption schedule for each proposed issue affect the overall debt service requirements of the government?
- What types of affordability guidelines will be established to help monitor and preserve credit quality?
- What provisions have been made to periodically review the capital plan and borrowing practices?
- What is the overlapping debt burden on the taxpayer?
- How will the formal debt policies be integrated into the capital planning and funding process?

When formal debt policies are adopted and integrated into the capital planning process, public officials are able to evaluate accurately the impact of each funding decision on the government's debt position and credit quality. In this way, debt policies can contribute to more efficient financial management by enabling officials to identify and address potential credit concerns before they are raised by underwriters, the rating agencies, or potential investors.

The fact that a government has gone to the effort to develop formal debt policies and incorporate these into its comprehensive capital improvement program demonstrates a strong commitment to the control of borrowing practices. This recognition of the importance of sound debt management is a very positive factor in the municipal market's assessment of credit quality.

I. COMPONENTS OF A DEBT POLICY

While a first-time home buyer may have an idea of what kind of house he or she would like, the decision to buy or not to buy is usually based on cost and the resultant monthly mortgage payment. In much the same way, a government's debt policy should begin with a review of affordability. Planning departments and elected officials are charged with identifying and prioritizing the capital and infrastructure needs of their governmental entities. What may be desired for the optimal efficiency of government or the achievement of some ideal quality of life, however, may be unattainable due to limited resources. Affordability, therefore, should be the first item addressed in any forecast of debt needs and planned issuance.

In addition to the constraints of how much debt a government can afford to carry, there are other practical limitations. Very large issuers, such as the states of New York and California, need to be sensitive to the timing of their debt offerings. The sheer magnitude of any one sale by these issuers can have a significant effect on the municipal securities market. As a result, these issuers are careful not to flood the market when other issuers have planned sales, particularly issuers from the same state.

Many investors and institutional buyers have geographic limitations on their holdings of securities; a flood of paper from one state or region may force some potential buyers to pass on a current offering because their portfolios are already full. This was one of the reasons for the creation of debt advisory commissions in California and Oregon. These groups coordinate the timing of state and local debt offerings to assure relatively unclogged access to the markets.

This consideration also should be kept in mind when an issuer is contemplating debt in various modes such as revenue bonds, certificates of participation, and tax anticipation notes. While these vehicles may create additional market capacity for buyers who favor different security pledge types, the name–concentration factor still could have a detrimental effect on market access if there is too much supply. The use of different security pledges does not create a blank check for unlimited market access. For this reason and others, debt policies should incorporate plans for all debt issuance, not merely general obligation debt.

A government's borrowing history, future needs, and affordability will all have a bearing on the amounts issued, sizing, and timing of bond sales. A small community, such as Washington Township in Morris County, New Jersey, may be faced with an extraordinary need for debt to build a town complex, resulting in an increase in per capita debt in that town of as much as $500. Since the town is an infrequent borrower, even a relatively small issue of $10 million may create a challenge for smooth market access.

One option in this case would be the sale of two or more small issues over the period of time necessary to construct the facility. Several smaller school districts, such as Alief and Katy independent school districts in the Houston area, have been successful in managing large capital programs through this method. The advantage is that the increased debt costs are phased in to avoid taxpayer shock. In addition, the gradual funding of the capital plan helps establish market knowledge and acceptance of the issuer's credit. This approach is effective when the government has prepared a multiyear capital plan that investors can rely on.

II. TEN CONSIDERATIONS FOR DEBT POLICY

Most of the items that should be included in a comprehensive debt policy statement are described below. These include sample debt measurements for policy goals or targets, suggested benchmarks for measuring affordability, and examples of current planning documents from issuers that incorporate some or all of these concepts.

A. How Much to Borrow

Good debt planning starts with a good capital improvement plan (CIP), one that reviews the status of current infrastructure, identifies replacement and renovation needs, and proposes new capital projects. In the process of developing the CIP, funding priorities are developed that permit the ranking of proposed projects, ranging from those that are essential to health and welfare to those items that are considered niceties, or wish list items. This is the first step toward determining what may be affordable, given the underlying economic base or the anticipation of shifting economic fortunes during a recession.

B. Affordability Targets

A debt policy with targets or ceilings on each type of obligation provides evidence of intention to keep debt manageable. There are various measurements that can be used for these targets. The first set of targets measures debt levels compared to economic indicators. When using these, the debt measurements should include "overlapping" debt, or debt issued by other coterminous governments. For a city, these ratios should include the common share of county, school district, or other special district debt that places a burden on the common tax or economic base. Common examples of these debt ratios are

- Per capita debt
- Debt as a percent of taxable market value of property
- Debt as a percent of total income

These benchmark ratios used by ratings agencies in measuring debt load are rough guides and may be adjusted because of unusual circumstances. Figure 1 provides examples of how these ratios are used in the assessment of credit quality to determine the relative burden of a government's debt obligations.

Other affordability guidelines are frequently used to measure the cost of debt relative to budget resources. One of the key measures used in a credit analysis is annual debt service as a percent of operating revenue, or expenditures, in the general and debt service funds. These benchmarks also will vary by type of government and according to unusual factors. In general, the more specialized governments in terms of services, such as school districts, show higher thresholds for debt service targets. Examples of these benchmark ratios are shown in Figure 2.

Measurement	Low	Medium	Above Avg	High
Per capita debt	< $500	$500-$800	$800-$1200	> $1200
% of market value	< 2%	2-5%	5-8%	> 8%
% of income	< 4%	4-7%	7-10%	> 10%

Figure 1   Use of ratios to assess credit quality.

Type of Government	Low	Medium	High
States	0-2%	2-6%	> 6%
Counties	0-7%	7-12%	> 12%
Cities	0-8%	8-15%	> 15%
School districts, etc.	0-10%	10-20%	> 20%

Figure 2   Debt service as a percent of budgeted expenditures guides.

C. Review of Plans

Most governments provide for annual review of the capital improvement plan and adjustment of debt issuance, as necessary. Ideally, these annual adjustments will be minor. One of the goals of the capital improvement process is to offer market credit analysts a reasonably accurate picture of the government's long-term funding schedule. However, not even the best planning process can anticipate every economic, financial, or political change that may require an adjustment in the government's spending plans. As a result, governments, both large and small, should provide for a regular review of their long-term borrowing plans.

D. Planning Period

The purpose of multiyear planning is to make better short-term decisions in light of other priorities that may arise in later years as well as to examine the longer-range implications and effects of debt issuance in the second, third, and fourth years, when the payments become budget items. A 5-year capital improvement plan includes new planned debt, retirement of previously issued debt, and pro forma debt levels if the plan is carried out. A useful addition is a multiyear forecast of annual debt service requirements; this will clearly delineate the consequences of the proposed levels of debt issuance. Rapidly increasing debt service costs are major contributors to the large budget gaps now being addressed in New York City and the state of California.

E. Debt Included in the Plan

All debt, regardless of the source of revenue pledged for repayment, represents some sort of cost to taxpayers or ratepayers; there is no such thing as a free lunch. A plan or forecast that shows a leveling off of general obligation (GO) debt, at a time when there is an acceleration of water revenue debt that formerly was financed with GOs, would be misleading without a description of the plans for revenue bond issuance. And while lease-secured and certificate of participation obligations may not be debt under strict legal definitions, they still require future appropriations, and are a fixed charge. These lease payments and other nonbond obligations are added as de facto debt by most security analysts when calculating an issuer's debt ratios.

F. Nondebt Capital Funding Sources

One of the fundamental principles of capital finance is that it is always better to use someone else's money—especially if one is not required to pay it back or if one can pay it back at an artificially low interest rate. Good debt management policies will recognize the value of external sources of capital other than debt and incorporate these into the CIP. As the CIP is reviewed and amended each year, public officials need to identify all alternative sources of funding and examine the availability of these sources for each project being considered. While it is more difficult these days to find sources that do not require repayment, there are low-interest loan programs and matching fund programs that are still available to assist with the cost of capital projects. Including, in detail, these other sources of funding in the capital planning documents will help identify opportunities to keep debt as low as possible, as well as point out areas of potentially soft funding that might require additional debt if the anticipated funding source does not materialize.

G. The Role of Pay-as-You-Go Financing

Pay-as-you-go financing can be viewed as the equivalent of the down payment in the home-buyer analogy. It acts to keep debt manageable, indicates to investors governmental support for a debt-funded project, and provides some budgetary flexibility in future years, if temporary revenue gaps occur. Baltimore and Pittsburgh have adopted formal pay-as-you-go targets in their debt policies. In the early 1980s, Pennsylvania appropri-ated substantial funds for economic development loans, reversing previous policies which funded these loans 100% from borrowed proceeds. When recent budget gaps led them to revert to bonding for these projects, the credit markets did not perceive this as bonding for operating expenses. Changes in laws for tax-exempt borrowing make pay-as-you-go financing more attractive, since there are no penalties for the use of taxpayer money on projects that might be deemed "private use" by the federal government. Given the current fiscal constraints of local governments, debt policies which establish a target of 3 to 5% of annual spending as a pay-as-you-go capital contribution would be beneficial.

H.   Length of Debt Maturities

A common guideline for debt maturity on traditional brick and mortar projects is for approximately 50% of the principal amount to be retired over 10 years. The useful life of the facility may justify a longer amortization, but financial considerations warrant a different review. Longer debt, or debt with retirement back-ended to the later maturities, tends to keep the debt burden longer, at a time when additional debt may have to be stacked on for big-ticket items, such as a replacement of water mains or new schools. A more rapid debt redemption schedule creates additional borrowing capacity—as debt is paid off, new debt becomes more affordable. For example, although the state of Maryland is a high-debt state, its debt maturities tend not to exceed 15 years. Therefore, despite a significant increase in debt for new schools in the 1970s, Maryland has been successful in maintaining steady debt ratios. This was helpful when the state unexpectedly needed to borrow to fund losses in state-insured savings and loan institutions in the mid-1980s.

Good debt policies should contain self-established limitations on the use of traditional short-term debt instruments such as tax and revenue anticipation notes, commercial paper, and variable rate demand bonds. Short-term borrowing is attractive from an interest rate perspective, but puts a government at refinancing risk if there are temporary budget problems or if there are disruptions in the capital markets because of external events. In normal circumstances, they are a valuable financing tool, but care must be taken to ensure that they are carefully scrutinized and used prudently. An issuer without outstanding short-term obligations, especially those that require refinancing, is stronger than an issuer that must rely on the annual or seasonal good will of lenders for operating or capital cash. A government's debt policies can recognize the inherent risk in short-term securities and set reasonable limits to their use.

I.   Monitoring the Plan

Debt policies are only as good as their implementation and follow-through. The guidelines established by the governing body should not be immutable; changing circumstances require flexibility and revision. Targets can pursue the objective of funding needed capital improvements in the most efficient manner possible while recognizing that anticipation of every future contingency is unrealistic. When adjustments are necessary, the reasons for such policy changes need to be well documented if the government wishes to demonstrate to the credit markets and its citizens that its commitment to sound debt management principles is unchanged.

J.   Overlapping Debt

Superior debt policy planning documents incorporate the needs and plans of coterminous units. In Washington Township, New Jersey, town leaders failed to take overlapping debt into account and underestimated the concern of residents over the high tax and debt burden in 1990 when a proposal was made to bond for a municipal building. It did not matter that the town itself was virtually debt free—the elementary and high school districts had recently completed large projects in the 1980s to meet growth demands, and new township facilities were viewed as unaffordable, despite general agreement that they were needed. As a result, the referendum for the complex failed in the election.

Government officials' decisions concerning the taxpayer's burden for capital funding are only one piece of a larger picture; the individual taxpayer must bear the burden of all overlapping jurisdictions, both for operating and capital purposes. Government cooperation in the management of that burden helps each unit to meet its policy objectives. The metropolitan governments in the Minneapolis/St. Paul area are generally recognized as leaders in cooperative debt planning and management, due to their success in coordination and planning of debt by the member governments. An article in the April 1989 issue of *Government Finance Review* describes the development of their comprehensive debt management program.

III. CONCLUSION

The planning, development, and implementation of formal debt policies can be an important component of a government's overall capital program. A decision to borrow money binds a government to a stream of debt service payments that can last 20 years or more. In the absence of sound debt issuance and management policies, it is very difficult for public officials to accurately evaluate the long-term consequences of these funding decisions. The consistent application of carefully developed debt management policies can benefit governments in a number of areas. Foremost among these benefits are enhanced credit quality and improved access to the tax-exempt and taxable credit markets. By demonstrating a strong degree of management control of this important element of financial management, governments send a clear message to credit analysts, underwriters, and investors that the borrowing program is aware of the market's concerns and will be administered in a responsible manner.

The concepts described in this chapter offer governmental officials the basic tools necessary to prepare effective debt management policies. Every public-sector manager should consider how these concepts can be applied in their jurisdictions to improve debt issuance and management practices. Over time, the administrative effort to develop, administer, and implement such policies will pay significant dividends.

14

Understanding and Forecasting Condition or Ability to Repay Debt: Report of the Capital Debt Affordability Committee on Recommended Debt Authorizations for Fiscal Year 1993

Capital Debt Affordability Committee, State of Maryland
Annapolis, Maryland

I. INTRODUCTION

A. Background

The creation of the Capital Debt Affordability Committee was an outgrowth of two events: the dramatic increase in outstanding debt during the mid-1970s and the release of the Department of Fiscal Services' 2-year study on the state's debt picture, titled *An Analysis and Evaluation of the State of Maryland's Long-Term Debt: 1958–1988*.

In response to this study and the rising level of state debt, the 1978 session of the General Assembly enacted the current State Finance and Procurement Article, Section 8-104, et seq., which created the committee as a unit of the executive department. The members currently are the treasurer (chair), the comptroller, the secretaries of the Departments of Budget and Fiscal Planning and Transportation, and one person appointed by the governor. The committee is required to review the size and condition of the state debt on a continuing basis and to submit to the governor, by September 10 of each year, an estimate of the total amount of new general obligation debt that prudently may be authorized for the next fiscal year. Although the committee's estimates are advisory only, the governor is required to give due consideration to the committee's findings in determining the total authorizations of new state debt and in preparing a preliminary allocation for the next fiscal year. The committee is required to consider

- The amount of general obligation debt that will be outstanding and authorized but unissued during the next fiscal year
- The capital program and the capital improvement and school construction needs during the next fiscal years
- Projected debt service requirements for the next 10 years
- Criteria established or used by recognized bond rating agencies in judging the quality of state bond issues
- Other factors relevant to the ability of the state to meet its projected debt service requirements for the next 5 years or relevant to the marketability of state bonds
- The effect of new authorizations on each of the factors enumerated above

In addition to these tasks, the committee has generally reviewed, and made recommendations concerning, other types of public debt issued by state or state-created authorities or agencies.

Adapted with permission of Hon. Lucille Maurer, Treasurer, State of Maryland.

In keeping with a narrow interpretation of its statutory charge, the committee's efforts through 1986 focused mainly on bringing the state's general obligation debt in line with certain parameters. In 1987, however, the committee began to adopt a more comprehensive view of state debt that included all tax-supported debt in addition to general obligation debt.

The main basis for adopting this broader view was that the rating agencies and investment community take a more comprehensive view of Maryland's debt when analyzing the state's obligations. Many discussions with rating analysts over the last several years in conjunction with the reviews associated with the savings and loan program and concerning stadia and infrastructure financing all indicated that rating analysts were interested in *all* tax-supported debt. Summaries of rating agency reports indicate the measure of debt used is "net tax-supported debt"—the sum of general obligation debt, consolidated and county transportation debt (net of sinking funds), capital lease commitments, and bond anticipation notes.

A second reason for adopting a more comprehensive view of debt was that other forms of long-term commitments were becoming more common. Lease, particularly lease purchase, obligations were at least more visible, if not more widely used. The bonds issued by the Maryland Stadium Authority for the Baltimore stadia are supported by lease arrangements; the state has consolidated a significant amount of equipment lease obligations; and the Motor Vehicle Administration was using the capital lease method for expanding or relocating its service center network. Although these leases do not represent debt in the constitutional sense, any default on these leases would be viewed by the market in the same light as a default on state bonds.

This broader and more comprehensive view was ultimately codified and included in the committee's statutory charge by Chapter 241, *Laws of Maryland, 1985.*

The 1989 General Assembly further expanded the committee's charge as part of legislation relating to higher education debt (Chapter 93, *Laws of Maryland, 1989*). As enacted, the statute directs the committee to review on a continuing basis the size and condition of any debt of the University of Maryland system, Morgan State University, and St. Mary's College of Maryland; take any debt issued for academic facilities into account as part of the committee's affordability analysis with respect to the estimate of new authorizations of general obligation debt; and finally, to submit to the governor and the General Assembly an estimate of the amount of new bonds for academic facilities that prudently may be authorized in the aggregate for the next fiscal year by the University of Maryland system, Morgan State University, and St. Mary's College of Maryland.

B. 1990 Recommendations and Subsequent Events

The following lists the recommendations of the 1990 Capital Debt Affordability Committee and subsequent events related to those recommendations.

- The committee recommended that new authorizations of general obligation debt should be limited to $330 million.

    The 1991 General Assembly, at its regular session, authorized $330 million of new general obligation debt, of which $329 million was signed into law. No additional new general obligation debt was authorized at the June 1991, special session.
- The committee recommended that new authorizations for academic facilities at the three university systems should be limited to an aggregate of $43 million.

    The 1991 General Assembly authorized new academic facility bonds to be issued by the University of Maryland System in the amount of $42.700 million for approved projects totaling $42.759 million. No academic bonds or projects were authorized for the other two university systems.
- The committee recommended that the state should proceed with a "one-time" general obligation bond authorization to finance an office space program in Baltimore (in addition to the $330 million).

    Legislation was proposed (HB 311) to authorize $88 million for a lease conversion program; it received unfavorable committee reports.
- The committee recommended that capital leases for real property be counted against the limit for new general obligation bond authorizations unless that capital lease was a component of a program explicitly outside the annual limit.

    No new authorizations to be financed with capital leases for real property were enacted. During the interim, however, the Senate Budget and Taxation Committee and the House Appropriations Committee reviewed a proposal to exercise the option to purchase for $22 million part of the St. Paul Plaza Building currently leased by the attorney general's office. The letter to the Board of Public Works stated the committee's agreement with the CDAC recommendation to count individual capital leases against the limit.

- The committee recommended that the authorization for the county transportation bonds be repealed. Legislation was not introduced to repeal this provision.
- In addition to authorizing specific academic projects for the University of Maryland system, Chapter 610 also increased the maximum allowable net amount of debt outstanding (for both academic and auxiliary facilities) for the University of Maryland system from $370 million to $442.7 million. The maximums for Morgan State University and St. Mary's College of Maryland remain unchanged at $28 million and $15 million, respectively. Furthermore, Chapter 610 eliminated finance costs during construction and for the first year, debt service reserves, and administrative expenses as eligible for funding with bond proceeds.
- Legislation was introduced (HB 1307) prohibiting Maryland Environmental Services (MES) from issuing revenue bonds to finance projects for the benefit of state units. In lieu of enacting such legislation, certain projects that originally were included in the proposed capital budget to be funded with revenue bonds were added to the consolidated capital bond loan to be funded with general obligation bonds. Language contained in the joint chairman's report expressed the intent of the committees that MES not use revenue bonds to fund water and wastewater facilities improvements at state facilities, with the exception of Eastern Correctional Institute (ECI).

II. TAX-SUPPORTED DEBT: TRENDS AND OUTLOOK

The state of Maryland has issued in recent years five types of tax-supported debt: (1) general obligation debt, which pledges the full faith and credit of the state; (2) bonds and notes issued by the Department of Transportation and backed by the operating revenues and pledged taxes of the department; (3) bond anticipation notes (BANs) issued in support of the savings and loan program; (4) capital leases; and (5) debt incurred by the Maryland Stadium Authority.

A. General Obligation Bonds

1. Structure

General obligation bonds are authorized and issued to provide funds for general construction of, and capital improvements to, state-owned facilities, including institutions of higher education; grants to local educational authorities for construction of, and capital improvements to, public schools; and financial assistance in the form of both repayable loans and grants to local governments and the private sector for special capital projects where a state interest or need has been demonstrated. Financial assistance to local governments and the private sector is provided primarily for capital projects related to water quality improvements, jails and detention facilities, community colleges, economic development, community mental health facilities, historic preservation, private higher education, and other community projects.

Prior to 1971, the counties and Baltimore City were responsible for financing public school construction. Also prior to 1971, the state had a program which provided, on a formula basis, for a sharing of capital expenses for local schools. In addition, the state lent its credit for this purpose by selling state general obligation bonds under the general public school construction loan program (GPSCL), the proceeds of which were used to fund the construction of local public schools. The debt service on GPSCL bonds was recovered from the subdivisions. By 1971, however, it appeared that many of the subdivisions had not provided for sufficient construction, and a deficiency in school facilities was evident. To assist the local units in correcting this deficiency, the state assumed the direct responsibility for future school construction under the state public school construction and capital improvement loan program (SPSCL) and undertook to reimburse local governments for the costs of debt service on certain prior bonds issued for school construction.

2. Trends in Outstanding General Obligation Debt

Both Fig. 1 and the following table direct the substantial growth between 1966 and 1978 in the state's general obligation debt. During the 1971–1978 period, the growth in general obligation debt accelerated principally as a result of the large authorizations for public school construction made during the 1971–1975 sessions of the General Assembly. Since fiscal 1978, general obligation debt has remained relatively level.

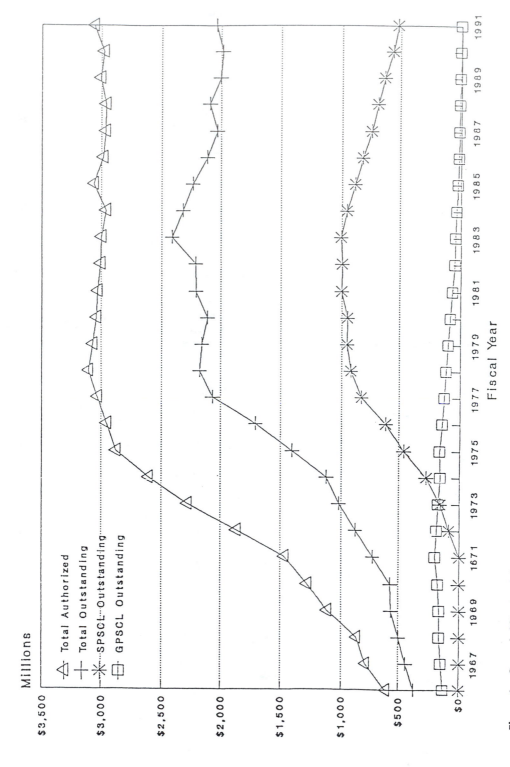

Figure 1   General obligation debt outstanding at June 30.

Fiscal period	Average annual general obligation debt		Average annual SPSCL debt	
	Authorized	Issued	Authorized	Issued
1966–1970	$180,905	$80,104	$ -0-	$ -0-
1971–1978	316,540	270,747	152,250	122,374
1979–1987	211,509	181,006	42,033	57,172
1988–1991	301,661	248,970	52,000	50,012

Note: All figures in thousands.

As depicted in Fig. 2, adjusted general obligation debt service grew annually from a level of $24 million in fiscal 1966 to $408 million in fiscal 1986 and then declined slightly to $393 million in fiscal 1991. Adjusted general obligation debt service represents the burden on the general fund and state property tax for debt service. Adjusted debt service is the total principal and interest payments on general obligation bonds with two adjustments, both of which are related to the funding of local public schools. First, general obligation debt service is reduced by the amount of debt service on "repayable" loans that is recovered by the state from the local subdivisions on the GPSCL loans. (Typically, this repayment is made in advance of the payment due date of the related debt service.) Second, general obligation debt service is increased by the amount of nonstate local school debt service that was assumed by the state in 1971 with the advent of the new school construction program.

Also depicted in Fig. 2 is the dramatically increasing reliance on general funds to support general obligation debt service from 1971 to 1986. After 1986, the general fund requirement fell and was expected to fall through fiscal 1993. While state property taxes are constitutionally pledged to the payment of debt service, it has been state policy for many years to maintain a stable property tax rate and rely on general funds, appropriated either to the annuity bond fund or to the Aid to Education program of the State Department of Education, to provide the majority of funding for general obligation debt service. In fiscal 1966, property tax revenues provided the funding for 89% of the general obligation debt service; in fiscal 1991, property taxes provided only 44%.

The growth in debt service (Fig. 2) reflects both the increase in debt outstanding through 1978 (Fig. 1) and dramatic increases in interest rates in the early 1980s. Figure 3 depicts the average interest rates paid on state general obligation debt (derived by dividing interest paid in a fiscal year by the average debt outstanding during that year) and the average rates of interest incurred on new issues during each fiscal year. The average interest rate paid on outstanding debt ranges from a low of 2.74% in fiscal 1966 to a high of 7.26% in fiscal 1987. The average of interest rates on all new issues during a year ranged from a low of 3.25% in 1966 to a high of 10.27% in 1982; most recently, it was 6.7% in fiscal 1991.

3. Capital Program Structure

The state's annual capital program presently includes projects funded from state general funds, state general obligation bonds, certain special and federal funds appropriated in the state's annual operating budget, and bonds and other financing obligations issued by various state agencies, including the Department of Transportation and the various higher education systems.

The general obligation bond-financed portion of the capital program consists of the Maryland consolidated capital bond loan (MCCB) and other initiatives. The MCCB is a consolidation of projects formerly authorized by the general construction loans and by various administration-sponsored bond bills. The general construction-type projects are typically state-owned; the other projects are typically capital grants or loans associated with statutory programs for nonstate-owned facilities such as local elementary and secondary schools, local jails, community health facilities, and local water treatment plants.

The general obligation bond-financed portion of the capital program has traditionally been supplemented by general fund capital appropriations customarily added to the operating budget. The use of operating funds to finance capital projects can reduce debt issuance as well as expand capital programs beyond the level that can be financed prudently with general obligation bonds. The use of operating budget resources, moreover, is sometimes necessary to avoid unnecessary expenses associated with compliance with restrictive federal statutes. For example, the federal Tax Reform Act of 1986 imposes certain constraints that either limit the

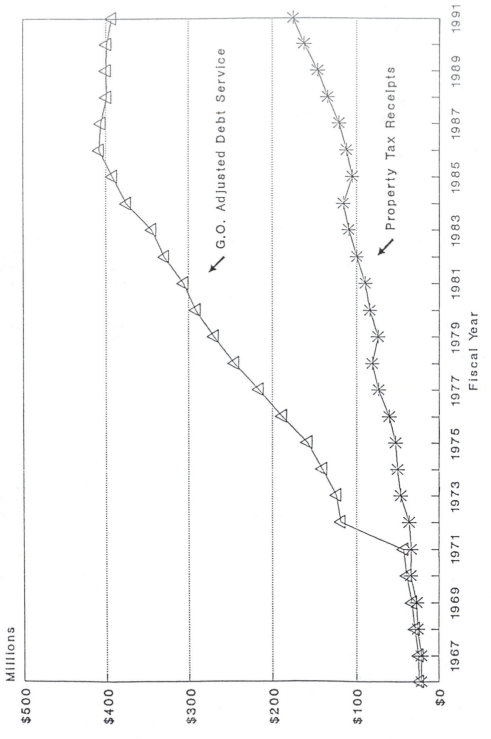

Figure 2 General obligation debt service adjusted for assumed debt and repayables.

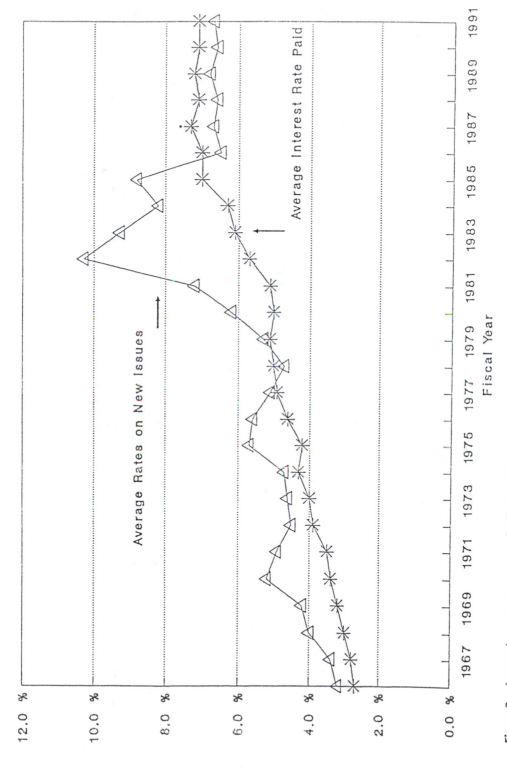

Figure 3 Average interest rates on general obligation debt.

degree of tax exemption or create arbitrage problems for bonds issued to establish mortgage insurance reserves, subsidize industrial development, or serve as capitalization fund for the state revolving fund.

Although the state's policy may be to provide additional capital funding in the operating budget, the financial reality is that in certain years the operating budget does not have the flexibility to fund a significant PAYGO appropriation. For example, for fiscal year (FY) 1990, the PAYGO appropriation was $212 million; for FY 1992, the PAYGO appropriation is $30.6 million, virtually all of which is associated with programs for which issuance of tax-exempt bonds is difficult.

4. Estimated General Construction Requests: FY 1993–1997

Agency requests for state-owned projects over the next 5 years total approximately $1.5 billion or an average of $305 million per year. These requests include construction, renovation, and expansion of health and correctional facilities; public office buildings; district courts; facilities at institutions for higher education; and state parks. In addition, there are small but needed programs for handicapped accessibility and asbestos abatement, which will total $4 to $5 million each year.

Agency *requests* for state-owned construction projects are as follows:

Agency	FY 93	FY 94	FY 95	FY 96	FY 97	Total
Comm. College of Baltimore	$12.2	$12.3	$12.8	$ 0.9	$ 0.0	$ 38.2
Education	4.4	0.0	14.1			18.5
Environment (asbestos)	3.0	3.0	3.0	3.0	3.0	15.0
Health & Mental Hygiene	17.9	13.4	17.1	15.3	10.4	74.1
Housing & Comm. Develop.	4.7	4.7	11.9	3.0	0.4	24.7
Judiciary	19.0	15.8	9.3	4.1	6.1	54.3
Juvenile Services	3.8	5.5	11.6	1.7	9.6	32.2
Military Department	5.4	0.2	10.5			16.1
Morgan State University	26.9	20.5	17.7	27.0	28.3	120.4
Natural Resources	11.5	15.0	11.2	7.2	11.3	56.2
Md. Environmental Serv.	12.6	2.3	2.2	1.0	0.9	19.0
Off. for Handicapped Indiv.	1.2	1.0	1.0	1.0	1.0	5.2
Public Broadcasting	0.9	0.4	1.0	0.4	1.6	4.3
Public Safety & Cor. Serv.	82.3	97.3	102.0	67.0	19.5	368.1
Board of Public Works	18.2	7.3	17.5	82.9	39.1	165.0
St. Mary's College			0.3	3.5	0.3	4.1
Univ. of Md. System	112.4	88.9	103.9	88.9	90.2	484.3
Athletic facilities	3.0	5.0	7.0			15.0
Computer research	7.0					7.0
Veterans Commission	0.9		1.3			2.2
Veterans Home Comm.	0.9					0.9
Total	$348.2	$292.6	$355.4	$306.9	$221.7	$1,524.8

Note: All figures in millions.

5. Estimated Administration-Sponsored Program Requests: FY 1993–1997

There are many different administration-sponsored bond programs through which state agencies provide financial assistance to nonstate entities. This is accomplished primarily through capital loans and grants to local governments, private organizations, nonprofit institutions, and individuals for economic, environmental, and social purposes. These include grants for sewer and water facilities, economic development, housing, and various community facilities. The SPSCL program, which previously funded 100% of allowable construction costs for approved school projects, now funds between 50% and 75% of eligible construction costs, depending on a variety of factors.

Prior to the 1990 session of the General Assembly, funding for most programs providing capital grants, loans, and other financial assistance to nonstate entities was authorized in separate general obligation bond enabling acts. In 1990, the funding for many of these programs was consolidated into the MCCB. State funding for private higher education facilities and local jails, however, continues to be provided through separate and individual project-specific enabling acts.

There has been an increase in the amount authorized for administration-sponsored bond programs in recent years. Future funding is primarily expected to increase most rapidly in environmental programs. As the trend toward deinstitutionalization continues, significant increases are probable for community-based health, juvenile, and social service programs. The local jail requests of $106 million during the next 5 years reflect the need to comply with legislation enacted in 1986 that requires local jails to house prisoners with sentences of 12 months or less.

Requests for administration-sponsored bond bills are expected to total almost $1.5 billion in the next 5 years, or an average of $308 million per year. Many programs of the Department of Housing and Community Development and the Department of Economic and Employment Development, previously funded with general obligation bonds, may no longer easily be funded by tax-exempt bonds because of the new provisions of the Tax Reform Act of 1986; consequently, these programs and the funds to be set aside to purchase the Peabody Conservatory art collection are expected to be financed with operating budget funds. Expected *requests* for nonstate-owned administration-sponsored programs are as follows:

	FY 93	FY 94	FY 95	FY 96	FY 97	Total
Aging						
Elderly citizen centers	$ 1.3	$ 1.3	$ 1.3	$ 1.3	$ 1.3	$ 6.5
Environment						
Hazardous substance control	8.7	13.8	16.3	8.9	10.6	58.3
Water supply	5.0	5.0	6.0	7.0	8.0	31.0
Water quality	24.9	28.7	29.7	44.6	46.2	174.1
Health & Mental Hygiene						
Community mental health facil.	9.0	9.0	9.0	9.0	9.0	45.0
Adult day care	1.0	1.0	1.0	1.0	1.0	5.0
Housing & Comm. Develop.						
Md. Historical Trust	0.7	0.7	0.7	0.7	0.7	3.5
	6.0	6.0	6.0	6.0	6.0	30.0
Human Resources						
Homeless facilities	1.0	1.0	1.0	1.0	1.0	5.0
Juvenile Services						
Juvenile residential facil.	1.2	1.2	1.2	1.2	1.2	6.0
Natural Resources						
Comprehensive flood mgt.	3.0	3.0	3.0	3.0	3.0	15.0
MES-recycling grants	1.0	1.0				2.0
Solid waste facilities	2.0					2.0
Local schools						
Public school construction	218.5	191.7	114.6	160.2	162.4	847.4
Miscellaneous						
U. Md. Medical System	10.0	10.0	10.0	10.0	10.0	50.0
Public community colleges	16.0	15.0	15.0	15.0	15.0	76.0
Private higher education	6.0	5.5	5.5	5.5	5.5	28.0
Local jails	20.9	35.8	16.8	18.8	13.5	105.8
Christopher Columbus Center	17.3					17.3
Md. Bioprocessing Fac.	15.0					15.0
Baltimore Zoo	5.0	2.5	2.5	2.5	2.5	15.0
Total	$373.5	$332.2	$239.6	$295.7	$296.9	$1537.9

Note: All figures in millions.

6. Other Initiatives

In addition to administration-sponsored bond programs, many other bond bills are introduced to fund programs established by statute or projects initiated by members of the General Assembly. These bills principally provide grants to subdivisions and private nonprofit sponsors for a multitude of local projects.

While it is not possible to predict accurately future demand, a decrease is not anticipated. Requests for other initiatives over the next 5 years are expected to total $500 million and average $100 million annually.

7. Summary of Capital Program FY 1993–1997

The total capital requests are estimated at $3.5 billion for the next 5 years. Based on an analysis of programs traditionally funded by general obligation debt, the Department of Budget and Fiscal Planning anticipates that the FY 1993–1997 general obligation bond-financed capital program will total approximately $2.4 billion. The total capital program will depend upon the level of general funds available for capital funding. The level of general funds available to supplement the bond-funded program will largely be dependent on the state's financial conditions.

	FY 1993–1997 requests	FY 1993–1997 anticipated capital program
State-owned construction projects	$1,525	$1,035
Administration-sponsored programs	1,538	1,310
Other bond bills	500	75
Total	$3,563	$2,420

Note: All figures in millions.

B. Transportation Bonds

Consolidated transportation bonds and county transportation bonds are limited obligations issued by the Department of Transportation, the principal of which must be paid within 15 years from the date of issue. The consolidated transportation bonds are issued for highway and other transportation projects. The gross outstanding aggregate principal amount of consolidated transportation bonds is presently limited by statute to $950 million. The county transportation bonds are bonds issued on behalf of the counties and Baltimore City for local transportation projects; the debt service on the county bonds is recovered from the local units by the state through deduction from amounts otherwise due them from state-collected shared highway user revenues.

Debt service on consolidated transportation bonds is payable from the department's shares of the motor vehicle fuel tax, the motor vehicle titling tax, all mandatory motor vehicle registration fees, and a portion of the corporate income tax, plus all departmental operating revenues and receipts. The holders of such bonds are not entitled to look to other sources for payment. The department has covenanted with the holders of outstanding consolidated transportation bonds not to issue additional bonds unless the excess of revenues (credited to the transportation trust fund) over expenses (of departmental operations) in the preceding fiscal year, which is available for debt service, is equal to at least twice the maximum amount of debt service for any future fiscal year (including debt service on the additional bonds to be issued) and total proceeds from taxes pledged to debt service for the past fiscal year equal at least twice such maximum debt service.

Debt service on county transportation bonds is secured by revenues distributed by law to the subdivisions from transportation trust fund sources. These sources include shares of the corporate income tax, titling tax, motor fuel taxes, and vehicle registration fees.

Both consolidated and county transportation bonds issued before June 1, 1989 utilized sinking funds with respect to the payment of debt service. In the case of consolidated bonds, at the time of issue, debt service due on that issue in the current calendar year and in the following calendar year was placed in the sinking fund. Thereafter, on each January 1, an amount equal to the debt service due for the following calendar year was placed in the fund. For county bonds, the practice was identical, with the exception that debt service was reserved on a fiscal year basis. In measuring debt outstanding, most credit analysts reduce gross debt outstanding by the amounts in sinking funds and by the amounts of defeased bonds, if any.

As a result of state legislation enacted in 1989, advance funding of future debt service requirements is no longer mandatory with respect to consolidated and county bonds issued after June 1, 1989. As a matter of policy, however, the department is continuing the practice of advance funding of future debt service on county bonds.

Figure 4 depicts outstanding consolidated and county transportation bonds (after being reduced by the amounts in the two sinking funds) for the historical period FY 1979 through 1991 and the department's current

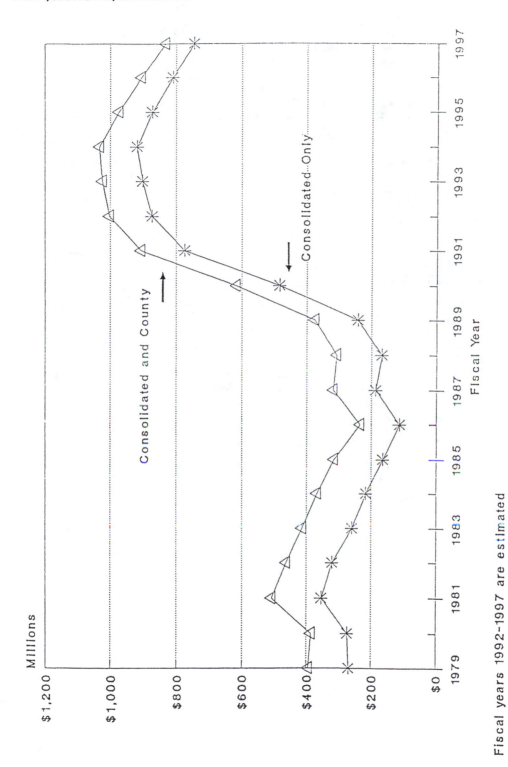

Millions

Fiscal years 1992-1997 are estimated

Figure 4   Transportation debt outstanding (net of sinking funds).

projections for FY 1992 through 1997. During the 10 years from fiscal 1979 to fiscal 1988, departmental revenues were of a magnitude such that new consolidated bond issues of only $245 million, excluding short-term notes, were needed to augment operating revenues to fund the transportation capital program. This modest level of issuance reflected, among other factors, the impact on customary transportation revenues of several gas tax increases (from 9 cents per gallon in fiscal 1982 to 13.5 cents in fiscal 1984, and to the current level of 18.5 cents per gallon effective June 1, 1987) and of permanent allocations to the transportation trust fund of a portion of corporate income tax receipts and the balance of the titling tax. In the most recent years, the level of new issuances accelerated to $100 million in 1989, $260 million in 1990, and $310 million in 1991.

The slowdown in department revenue, however, limited the amount of bonds the department could issue; in fact, the full issue of $120 million, associated with the increase in Motor Vehicle Administration fees, was its only sale of consolidated transportation bonds projected for FY 1992. Annual sales in 1993 and 1994 were expected to be limited to the $50–55 million range. Thereafter, no new sales of consolidated transportation bonds were anticipated under the current revenue structure.

Issuances of county transportation bonds are expected to average $10 million per year over the 6-year period 1992–1997.

C. Bond Anticipation Notes

In response to the savings and loan crisis in May 1985, the General Assembly authorized $100 million in general obligation bonds that could be used, among other purposes, to facilitate mergers or to make capital investments in state-chartered savings and loan associations when such investment would ensure that the association would receive federal insurance. Chapter 452, Laws of 1990, canceled the authorization.

Three-year BANs were issued to associations in connection with pending insurance applications. In exchange for the BANs, the state received net worth certificates representing an equity share in the participating associations. The divided rate on the net worth certificates was in all cases 1½% higher than the interest rate on the BANs. The following table summarizes activity with the BANs that were issued in exchange for net worth certificates.

Fiscal year	Outstanding (beginning of fiscal year)	Issues	Redemptions	Outstanding (end of fiscal year)
1986	$ —	$26,410	$11,250	$15,160
1987	15,160	746	—	15,906
1988	15,906	—	7,758	8,148
1989	8,148	—	7,402	746
1990	746	—	746	—
1991	—	—	—	—

Note: All figures in thousands.

Two additional BANs were issued in connection with the savings and loan program. One for $46.7 million, subsequently canceled, was issued to the Maryland deposit insurance fund in connection with the purchase of deposits; one for $15 million, subsequently redeemed, was issued as security for a short-term bank loan to facilitate a distribution to depositors.

Since the bond authorization has been canceled and since all insured deposits have been paid, there will be no additional BANs issued under this program.

D. Lease and Conditional Purchase Financings

A development in the state's capital funding programs over the past several years is the use of capital lease financings in which the state earns an equity interest in the leased property and gains title to such property at the end of the leasing period. Such capital leases are considered debt of the state by financial analysts and under generally accepted accounting principles.

For financial statements to reflect generally accepted accounting principles, leases that are in essence a vehicle for financing assets must be "capitalized" (i.e., reflected on the balance sheet). To the extent that meaningful financial reporting requires this, rating agencies and credit evaluators will incorporate leases of this nature into their overall calculation of the state's debt burden.

Under generally accepted accounting principles, if a lease financing meets *any one* of the following four criteria at its inception, the lease shall be classified as a capital lease by the lessee:

- The lease transfers ownership of the property to the lessee (user) by the end of the lease term.
- The lease allows the lessee (user) to purchase the property at a bargain price.
- The term of the lease is 75% or more of the estimated useful economic life of the property.
- The present value of the lease payments is 90% or more of the fair value of the property.

If state leases meet *any* of these four criteria, the state's audited financial statements will reflect the capitalization of those leases, and the state will be judged by knowledgeable reviewers as having incurred debt. The additional state liability and debt service resulting from financing leases currently is not large relative to the state's general obligation debt liability and debt service and is not anticipated to grow materially in the near future.

Capital leases are used for the acquisition of both real property and equipment. Under current practice, capital leases for equipment, primarily data processing and telecommunications equipment, are generally for periods less than 5 years. Real property capital leases, on the other hand, have tended to be longer term—in the range of 20 to 30 years—and have been used to acquire a wide variety of facilities, such as regional motor vehicle service centers, a highway support center, an upgraded environmental facility for a state prison, and multiservice centers.

The following table summarizes tax-supported capital lease financings for FY 1984 through 1990 and estimated amounts for fiscal 1991.

Tax-Supported Capital Leases

Fiscal year	Present value of minimum lease payments (in thousands)
1984	$ —
1985	—
1986	—
1987	12,743
1988	47,579
1989	48,702
1990	46,779
1991	64,614

The future use of capital leases for acquiring real property is not well defined. On the one hand, there are no approved programs to develop state facilities under a capital lease, either by private investors or local governments. On the other hand, there continue to be proposals put forth under which the state would acquire real property through a capital lease arrangement. Since the committee's last report, the Maryland Stadium Authority and the State Highway Administration developed but did not finalize a proposal to finance a headquarters facility for the administration at Camden Yards. Also, a proposal by the Maryland Environmental Service to finance a number of sewage treatment and solid waste disposal facilities for state facilities through certificates of participation secured by leases between the service and the using agency was limited by the 1991 General Assembly to a single facility supporting the ECI. Furthermore, it is possible that there may be capital leases associated with the comprehensive office space acquisition program described in Sec. V.

For the purposes of this report, it is assumed that $10 million in real property projects, excluding components of the comprehensive office space acquisition program, will be financed by capital leases. It is further assumed that these projects are not projects for which general obligation bonds are authorized; hence, there will be no offset in the amount of general obligation bonds issued or outstanding.

It is also believed that future capital leases for equipment will be reasonably constant over time, averaging about $15 million a year, except in FY 1992, during which an additional $10 million capital lease will finance two new helicopters. The one major deviation from this scenario is a possible $50-60 million capital lease through which the Department of Transportation will acquire light-rail cars to be used on the central light-rail line.

E. Maryland Stadium Authority

The Maryland Stadium Authority was created in 1986 for the purpose of proposing a site for one or more new professional sports facilities in Maryland and financing and directing the acquisition and construction of such facilities. The authority is authorized to issue revenue bonds, subject to prior approval of the Board of Public Works. The 1987 General Assembly placed an aggregate limit of $235 million on the issuance of such bonds, of which $200 million may be issued as tax-exempt securities prior to January 1, 1991, under a transitional provision of the Tax Reform Act of 1986.

In May 1989, the authority issued $60.8 million in taxable lease revenue notes for the acquisition and preparation of the property site of new sports facilities. The authority also entered into a lease arrangement with the state whereby the state will lease the facilities from the authority. The authority's note and subsequent bond issues are secured by the lease with the state, and the state's rental payments to the authority approximate the debt service on the authority's notes and bonds. The state will sublease the facilities back to the authority and the authority's rental payments to the state approximate the authority's net income. At the conclusion of the lease term, title to the facilities will transfer to the state.

In October 1989, the authority issued $137.5 million of tax- exempt lease revenue bonds to finance the construction of a baseball stadium; a portion of the proceeds was used to defease $43.4 million of the first issue due in December of 1989 and December of 1990.

Funds for the lease of the baseball stadium will be provided by: (1) two to four annual sports lotteries; (2) an annual payment of $1 million from Baltimore City; (3) interest earnings on the facilities fund and on any debt service reserve fund; and (4) net operating revenues of the authority.

For the purposes of this report, it was assumed that the Stadium Authority would issue $81.8 million in additional debt to construct a football stadium, an amount that fully utilized the maximum debt outstanding allowed. It was also assumed that the debt would be issued in fiscal 1993, consistent with the current National Football League expansion schedule, and would be a taxable issue since the special tax-exempt provision provided by the transition rule for the Tax Reform Act of 1986 expired.

III. AFFORDABILITY ANALYSIS

The objective of an affordability analysis is to draw a proper balance between two basic considerations: the state's capital needs and its ability and/or willingness to repay the debt issued to finance those capital needs.

A. The Concept of Affordability

The ultimate test of affordability is the willingness and ability of the state to pay the resulting debt burden when due. Apart from revenue sources which are dedicated by law, the allocation of future resources between debt repayment and other program needs is a matter of judgment. The whole issue of affordability is, therefore, a judgmental one, dependent upon complex considerations such as perceived needs, the relationship between debt authorization and debt issuance, available and potential funding mechanisms, overall budgetary priorities, and revenues.

The committee believes that the crux of the concept of affordability is not merely whether or not the state can pay the debt service; rather, affordability implies the ability to manage debt over time to achieve certain goals. Maryland has a long tradition of effectively managing its finances and debt. The challenge of debt management is to provide sufficient funds to meet growing capital needs within the framework of the state's debt capacity, thereby maintaining the triple-A credit rating.

B. History of Affordability Criteria

Based upon an analysis of available material (including the responses to a questionnaire sent to a number of experts on Maryland's finances in 1979 and subsequently updated in 1984), the following affordability criteria were developed and employed in the 1979 and subsequent reports:

- That outstanding debt be reduced toward a target level of 3.2% of state personal income as rapidly as practical
- That adjusted debt service be reduced toward a target level of 8% of state general fund and property tax revenues as rapidly as practical
- That new authorizations be kept in the range of redemptions of existing debt over the near term.

These criteria were adopted by the committee solely for the analysis of general obligation debt. The committee had considered its major task to be primarily the analysis of general obligation debt in keeping with the tenor of the statute establishing the committee.

Criteria 1 and 2 represented traditional measures and criterion 3 reflected a discretionary policy position that the state should "get out of debt." Given the committee's view that the first two criteria were goals to be achieved over time, the final criterion became controlling over the short term.

In 1987, while retaining the first and second criteria for evaluating the expanded definition of debt and debt service, the committee concluded that the third criterion was no longer an applicable guideline. The basis for its conclusion was threefold. First, there were legislative and executive commitments to provide an increase in the level of bonded debt to finance needed transportation projects and the new stadia. Second, the high ratings of the state's general obligation and transportation bonds indicated that the existing level of debt and the planned increase were acceptable to the rating agencies. Third, adherence to the criterion ties yearly authorizations to events of 15 years before, thereby producing highly variable bond authorizations which are inconsistent with either good debt management or a stable capital program.

In 1988, a detailed survey of credit analysts was undertaken to obtain their views on the committee's comprehensive approach to reviewing debt and to the criteria the committee have been using for 10 years. The survey affirmed the committee's decision to take an expanded view of debt; in addition, criteria 1 and 2 were almost universally approved.

C. 1991 Affordability Recommendation

The committee recommended a $350 million limit for new general obligation debt authorizations in 1992.

In its 1988 report, the committee discussed the elements of the current environment which dictated its program of new authorizations. First, the state clearly needs more capital investment. This need has always existed; as time passes, however, and unmet needs accumulate, the urgency of addressing the backlog intensifies. While the capital program may have kept pace with inflation, it has not kept up with the operating budget. At the same time, the state's clients and population continue to grow, and the state's infrastructure continues to age, while the federal government is retreating as a provider of capital. These circumstances are by no means unique to Maryland, but rather mirror the national phenomenon of a burgeoning backlog of critical capital projects combined with shrinking federal assistance for capital construction, acquisition, rehabilitation, and renovation. Second, the tax-supported debt capacity is, and continues to be to an increasing degree, able to accommodate increased levels of new authorizations. In that report the committee proposed the following program:

General Assembly Proposed Programs

1989	$295
1990	315
1991	330
1992	350
1993	370
1994	395

The 1989 General Assembly was fortunate to enjoy a level of unanticipated general fund revenues, potentially of a nonrecurring nature, such that an unusually significant amount was available for capital projects. Consequently, the General Assembly limited new general obligation debt authorizations to $280 million—rather than to authorize the maximum limit of $295 million recommended by the committee. The following year, the committee's recommendation recycled the $15 million authorization not needed in 1989, thereby maintaining total authorizations of $610 million for the 2 years (1989 and 1990). For the 1991 session, the committee recommended a limit of $330 million and the General Assembly enacted bond bills totaling $330 million.

The committee continues to believe that the underlying reasons for the committee's prior recommendations are still valid. The committee also believes the 5-year program originally recommended in 1988 and reaffirmed in 1989 and 1990 continues to be consistent with prudent debt management.

D.   Comparison of Recommendation and Criteria

To analyze the relationship of the committee's recommendation for general obligation debt to the affordability criteria, each component of tax-supported debt and debt service is projected.

The assumptions for the growth in nongeneral obligation components of tax-supported debt and debt service are as described in Sec. II. The Department of Transportation debt was expected to continue to grow through 1992 and then decline significantly over the next 4 years, as reported in Sec. II.D. The Maryland Stadium Authority's issuance debt was as projected in Sec. II.F. No new BANS would be issued over the forecast period, since the authorization was canceled. It was assumed that approximately $10 million in new capital leases for real property and $15 million in new capital leases equipment would be executed in each year except in 1992 during which an additional $10 million would be executed in connection with the acquisition of two helicopters.

With respect to general obligation debt, it is necessary to project the pattern of issuance of both new and current authorizations. Newly authorized bonds are not immediately issued; in fact, less than half of the bonds authorized in a year are typically issued within the next 2 fiscal years. Consequently, the impact of a limit on any year's debt authorizations translates slowly into issuances and affects the outstanding level of debt with a substantial lag. Appendix B-1 converts, on the basis of historical patterns, the recommended levels of new general obligation bond authorizations into a projected level of annual issuances and assumes that all authorized debt with the exception of $11 million authorized for Program Open Space will be issued. Although some authorizations may ultimately be canceled, such cancellations are expected to be immaterial to the analysis.

Adjusted general obligation debt services is as displayed in Appendix B-4 and assumes a pattern of future interest rates similar to that projected by the WEFA forecasting service.

Based on the committee's projections, outstanding tax- supported debt rises steadily over the near term, reflecting moderate growth in the level of general obligation bonds, and near-term growth in the level of consolidated transportation bonds and in the construction of the football stadium in Camden Yards (Table 1). The growth in debt outstanding for fiscal 1992 and 1993 is slightly greater than the growth in personal income; consequently, the ratio of debt outstanding to personal income rises from 2.91% in 1991 to 2.97% in 1993. After 1993, the growth in personal income is equal to or greater than the growth in debt. As a result, the key ratio begins to drop modestly. Throughout the whole forecast period, the ratio of debt outstanding to personal income is well below the affordability criterion of 3.2%.

With respect to the other affordability criterion, the ratio of debt service to revenues, the pattern is distinctly different. In every year, this ratio, which is a proxy for the burden of the debt on the operating budget, shows marked improvement (Table 2). In 1991, the ratio is 7.2%; in 1997, the ratio is projected to be 6.20%.

The committee's total program is expected to result in a pattern of debt issuances, debt outstanding, and debt service payments that are well within the affordability standards. The state is no longer in the same posture as it was in the early years of the committee when the committee was recommending a policy that would bring debt and debt service within affordability limits over time; rather, the state already meets the accepted affordability standards and the goal is to maintain those standards with a margin for contingencies. The improvement in the state's debt position is even more dramatic in that the same criteria, which through 1986 applied only to general obligation debt, are now applied to a more comprehensive definition of tax-supported debt.

E.   Comparison of Recommendation and Capital Program

The committee's projections of tax-supported debt fully incorporate the most current capital program proposed by the Department of Transportation; a statutory change raising the ceiling on consolidated transportation

Table 1 State-Tax-Supported Debt: Outstanding Components and Relationship to Personal Income

Fiscal year	General obligation a,b	Department of Transportation c			Capital leases	Stadium Authority	Bond anticipation notes	Total Tax-supported debt	
		Consolidated	County	Total					
State tax-supported debt outstanding ($ in thousands)									
1987	2,030,415	186,683	131,086	317,769	12,062	—	15,906	2,376,152	1987
1988	2,090,820	168,047	140,301	308,348	47,580	—	8,148	2,454,896	1988
1989	2,005,360	241,838	133,266	375,104	45,026	60,845	746	2,487,081	1989
1990	1,986,907	482,691	133,727	616,418	43,602	155,000	—	2,801,927	1990
1991	2,038,445	773,671	135,841	909,512	73,263	155,000	—	3,176,220	1991
1992	2,148,360	874,770	127,926	1,002,696	100,540	154,880	—	3,406,476	1992
1993	2,312,030	903,689	120,414	1,024,103	112,585	235,000	—	3,683,718	1993
1994	2,490,940	920,576	111,641	1,032,217	122,671	233,165	—	3,878,993	1994
1995	2,656,722	873,756	100,990	974,746	129,350	231,200	—	3,992,018	1995
1996	2,836,633	811,511	95,551	907,062	133,010	228,152	—	4,104,857	1996
1997	3,020,059	744,663	89,435	834,098	136,352	224,891	—	4,215,400	1997
State-tax-supported debt outstanding as a percent of personal income (affordability criteria standard = 3.2%)									
1987	2.46%	0.23%	0.16%	0.38%	0.01%	—	0.02%	2.87%	1987
1988	2.31%	0.19%	0.15%	0.34%	0.05%	—	0.01%	2.71%	1988
1989	2.04%	0.25%	0.14%	0.38%	0.05%	0.06%	0.00%	2.53%	1989
1990	1.90%	0.46%	0.13%	0.59%	0.04%	0.15%	—	2.68%	1990
1991	1.87%	0.71%	0.12%	0.83%	0.07%	0.14%	—	2.91%	1991
1992	1.85%	0.75%	0.11%	0.86%	0.09%	0.13%	—	2.93%	1992
1993	1.86%	0.73%	0.10%	0.83%	0.09%	0.19%	—	2.97%	1993
1994	1.88%	0.70%	0.08%	0.78%	0.09%	0.18%	—	2.93%	1994
1995	1.88%	0.62%	0.07%	0.69%	0.09%	0.16%	—	2.82%	1995
1996	1.87%	0.54%	0.06%	0.60%	0.09%	0.15%	—	2.71%	1996
1997	1.86%	0.46%	0.06%	0.51%	0.08%	0.14%	—	2.60%	1997

*Reflects presumed new authorizations as follows:

General Assembly session:	For fiscal year:	
1992	1993	$350 million
1993	1994	$370 million
1994	1995	$395 million
1995	1996	$415 million
1996	1997	$435 million
1997	1998	$455 million

b Assumes debt service on minibonds is paid at maturity and no minibond put options are exercised.

c Assumes future issues of consolidated transportation bonds are consistent with recent revenue enhancements and debt service coverage requirements.

Table 2 State-Tax-Supported Debt Service: Components and Relationship to Revenues

State tax-supported debt service ($ in thousands)

Fiscal year	General obligation[a]	Department of Transportation		Total	Capital leases	Stadium Authority	Bond anticipation notes[b]	Total tax-supported debt service
		Consolidated	County[b]					
1987	405,905	19,919		19,919	4,838	—		430,662
1988	398,979	23,685		23,685	5,259	—		427,923
1989	399,441	35,195		35,195	8,423	—		443,059
1990	399,125	48,842		48,842	8,544	11,113		467,624
1991	388,399	64,261		64,261	9,149	11,984		473,793
1992	349,044	80,211		80,211	14,159	12,104		455,518
1993	332,329	89,886		89,886	21,017	17,742		460,974
1994	346,253	97,936		97,936	23,984	21,832		490,005
1995	401,311	111,983		111,983	28,193	21,836		563,323
1996	420,560	122,932		122,932	31,742	22,735		597,969
1997	440,655	125,510		125,510	32,471	22,701		621,337

State tax-supported debt service as a percent of revenues (affordability criteria standard = 8%)

Fiscal year	General obligation[a]	Department of Transportation		Total	Capital leases	Stadium Authority	Bond anticipation notes[b]	Total tax-supported debt service
		Consolidated	County[b]					
1987	8.52%	2.55%		2.55%	0.10%	—		7.77%
1988	7.63%	2.65%		2.65%	0.10%	—		6.99%
1989	7.15%	3.72%		3.72%	0.15%			6.78%
1990	6.80%	5.16%		5.16%	0.15%	100.00%[c]		6.85%
1991	6.60%	7.29%		7.29%	0.16%	100.00%		6.99%
1992	5.35%	8.51%		8.51%	0.22%	100.00%		6.09%
1993	4.92%	9.12%		9.12%	0.31%	100.00%		5.94%
1994	4.79%	9.65%		9.65%	0.31%	100.00%		5.93%
1995	5.19%	10.73%		10.73%	0.36%	100.00%		6.41%
1996	5.08%	11.38%		11.38%	0.38%	100.00%		6.38%
1997	4.96%	11.23%		11.23%	0.37%	100.00%		6.20%

[a] Assumes debt service on minibonds is paid at maturity and no minibond put options are exercised.
[b] Repayments from counties and from savings and loan institutions equal or exceed debt service requirements.
[c] Transfers from the Stadium Facilities Fund to the Stadium Authority are assumed to be just sufficient, when coupled with the authority's own-source revenues, to meet debt service requirements. Assumes proceeds from future bond issues will be used to make certain principal payments.

bonds outstanding, however, will be necessary to execute this program. The committee's projections of tax-supported debt also incorporate issuance of all $235 million available to the Maryland Stadium Authority for the construction of sports stadia. The committee's recommendation of general obligation authorizations does not, however, provide for full funding of the general obligation capital program.

The general obligation capital program funding requirements as presented in Sec. II.A are $2.4 billion for FY 1993 through 1997; for the same period, the committee proposes $1.96 billion, or 81%, in new general obligation bond authorizations. In terms of expected level of requests for capital funding by state agencies and legislative sponsors, the committee's plan would provide bonds sufficient to finance 55% of the total requests. The committee recognizes that the affordable amount does not meet all capital needs and may fall substantially short if new capital demands occur, either as new programs emerge or as the federal government continues to reduce its support for state and local programs.

There are basically only two options for meeting the capital needs normally funded by general obligation bonds while staying within debt-affordability limits. The state can commit a level of funds in the operating budget sufficient to fund unmet general obligation capital needs. Alternatively, the state can shift priorities among the components of tax-supported debt, thereby allowing for a greater level of new general obligation authorizations.

F. Affordability Risk Analysis

1. Background

In its 1989 and 1990 reports, the committee introduced and analyzed the concept of affordability risk—the risk that a particular 5-year general obligation bond authorization plan, if followed over time, leads to a breach of the committee's affordability limits, even though the plan was deemed affordable at the time it was proposed. The concept of affordability risk arose because the committee has been faced with what appears to be substantial unused affordability capacity. Again this year as in the committee's reports for 1989 and 1990, the committee's 5-year general obligation bond plan is expected to result in ratios of outstanding debt to personal income substantially below the 3.2% affordability limit in each year of the forecast period.

2. Components of Risk

There appear to be four basic risk components in making a judgment about the ultimate affordability of a 5-year general obligation program of authorizations.

- Changes in personal income
- Changes in the definition of tax-supported debt
- Changes within the general obligation bond program
- Changes in the bond issuance plans of other, including new, components of tax-supported debt

3. Changes in Personal Income

Over the past decade, there has been substantial change in personal income estimates. These changes result from (1) after-the-fact measurement changes by the federal statisticians, and (2) revised projections by the committee. The former risk is clearly beyond the committee's control. Although the federal estimates of personal income for a year may change by material amounts in the first 2 years after the close of the year, subsequent adjustments can, on the basis of experience, be expected to be small and to increase measured personal income (expand affordable capacity). The committee's projections of the 6-year growth in personal income, on the whole, have been conservative and, therefore, subsequent reports tended to portray an increase in affordable capacity. As a consequence, last year's report indicated that the risk from a downward revision of personal income was "deemed small if the Committee maintains its tradition of conservative long term projections."

The depth of the recession, however, was not reflected in the committee's projections in the 1990 report. The forecasts from WEFA of Maryland personal income are substantially below the levels used in last year's report. Essentially, the new projections reflect a loss of a year's growth in personal income. Last year, 1992 and 1993 personal income were projected to be $123 billion and $131 billion, respectively; it was projected that 1993 and 1994 personal income would be $124 billion and $132 billion, respectively. This downward revision of projected personal income has had a major effect. Table 1 indicates that the ratio of debt outstanding to personal income at June 30, 1993, and June 30, 1996, was projected to be 2.97% and 2.71%, respectively. If last year's estimates of personal income were used, the ratios would be 2.79% and 2.53%, respectively.

The committee continued to believe that the risk associated with reductions in anticipated levels of personal income was not great. The committee was anticipating that personal income would grow by an average 6.85% annually over the next 6 fiscal years. The average growth rate for the 10 years ending with the depressed FY 1991 was 7.9%. Even if the committee's projections were too optimistic, the committee's program would remain affordable. For example, if the growth rate of personal income were only 4.8%, or 2% per year lower than the committee's estimate, the ratio of debt outstanding to personal income would be 3.03% or less throughout the period 1991–1997.

4. Changes in the Definition of Tax-Supported Debt

Changes in the definition of tax-supported debt will typically only occur whenever an outside authoritative group changes definition. To be sure, there may be state reviews of individual transactions that prompt the reclassification of a specific transaction or set of transactions. Such internally initiated reclassifications, however, are apt to be minor. On the other hand, there would be a major impact if, for example, the bond rating agencies would decide to count state housing agency debt as tax-supported debt or if the Governmental Accounting Standards Board would require long-term operating leases to be included on the state's balance sheet. Although changes in standards of outside authoritative groups might have a major impact on measured affordability, such changes are likely to be implemented with ample lead time and would either only affect the out years of the program or provide the committee with time to adjust its program.

5. Changes within the General Obligation Bond Program

Changes within the general obligation bond program may arise because of changes in: (1) the types and costs of facilities and other projects financed by general obligation bonds, or (2) changes in the speed with which authorized bonds are issued.

Changes of the first variety do not of themselves affect affordability but rather may lead to a reallocation of resources. The committee's recommendations are made in terms of a specific dollar amount of bonds and not in terms of a specific set of programmatic facilities, grants, or other capital projects. Changes in construction costs, the availability of PAYGO funding, the need for new prisons or hospitals, federal tax laws, and a host of other variables will certainly influence both the need for general obligation bonds and the committee's view of the appropriate share of the affordability limit that is to be used; such changes affect the amount of real assets that can be acquired within a specific dollar amount of program. Such changes by themselves, however, affect neither the dollar amount of the committee's 5-year plan nor the ratio of debt outstanding associated with that specific plan to personal income. Therefore, without committee or General Assembly action to alter the dollars to be authorized in the committee's 5-year plan, there is no affordability risk resulting from such changes within the general obligation plan.

Changes in the speed with which authorized bonds are issued, however, may affect affordability. Bonds authorized by the General Assembly at any session are not immediately sold. Rather, the bonds are sold over an extended period of time as the projects are developed and cash is required to pay property owners, consultants, contractors, and equipment manufacturers. Any systematic force that would accelerate or retard the speed with which bonds are brought to market will increase or decrease the amount of bonds outstanding and affect the ratio of debt outstanding to personal income. Over the life of the committee, there has been no major systematic force. The proposed federal regulations on the use of bond proceeds for reimbursement, however, might be such a major systematic force. As discussed in Sec. V.C, the proposed regulations, if ultimately adopted, may well lead to an acceleration of the issuance of general obligation bonds. The potential impact is estimated to be an increase in the ratio of debt outstanding to personal income in the .05% to .14% range.

6. Changes in the Bond Issuance Plans of Other Components of State-Tax-Supported Debt

Changes in the bond issuance plans for other components of tax-supported debt probably present the greatest risk to the eventual affordability of a specific 5-year program. These changes can take the form of expansion of existing programs, as was the case with the expanded consolidated transportation debt issuance associated with the 1987 gas tax increase, or a totally new program, such as the Maryland Stadium Authority in 1987.

There are basically four classes of changes.

1. There are changes in existing programs associated with external events. For example, the NFL could delay the designation of the expansion cities and, as a result, the "projected" sale of bonds for the football stadium would be delayed.
2. There are known proposals to expand existing programs or create new programs that the committee may believe to have a high probability of enactment, but the exact timing of the enactment and the amount of new debt were less certain. For example, the 1990 General Assembly created a Convention Center Authority which was studying the need for and options related to expanded convention facilities in Baltimore City. It was highly likely that the 1992 General Assembly will consider a major state-backed revenue bond proposal for new facilities.
3. There are known proposals that the committee may believe to have a low probability of enactment. For example, in both 1990 and 1991, the General Assembly considered a large bond authorization for accelerating land purchases under Program Open Space and directed the Department of Budget and Fiscal Planning and the Department of Natural Resources to study the proposal. The proposal was similar to the original design of Program Open Space which was abandoned when transfer tax receipts were more than adequate to meet the acquisition program's cash needs.
4. There are bond programs that are not known at the time the committee develops its plan and analyzes it for conformity with affordability standards. Two years ago when the committee was considering its plan for 1990–1994, there was no proposal for state assistance for an expanded convention center; now it was quite possible that tax-supported debt related to the convention center would be outstanding by 1994. Clearly, this fourth type of risk is most likely to affect that last 2 years of any 5-year period as opposed to the first 2 years of the period.

7. FY 1993–1997 Risks

In considering the affordability risk associated with the 1993–1997 plan in this year's report, the major risk appeared to be related to potential changes in other components of tax-supported debt. There was also a risk association with the proposed federal reimbursement regulations. On the other hand, the committee's projections of personal income were conservative; personal income was projected to grow at 6.8% per annum in the next 6 years as compared with the 7.8% per annum rate experienced during past 10 years. There was no evidence that the rating agencies or the Governmental Accounting Standards Board contemplated changes in standards that would expand the definition of tax-supported debt.

The major elements of affordability risk from changes in the issuance plans of other components of tax-supported debt are an expanded transportation capital program, a convention center bond program, and a one-time general obligation program to replace leased state office space in Baltimore with state-owned space. Other known programs—Program Open Space and the Maryland Stadium Authority—do not appear at this time to increase affordability risk. In the judgment of the Department of Budget and Fiscal Planning, sufficient justification does not exist for a major bond-funded component of Program Open Space; moreover, the General Assembly has reviewed this proposal in its most recent two sessions and declined to enact the program. With respect to the Maryland Stadium Authority, there was the possibility that the NFL would postpone its expansion plans again or not include Baltimore in such plans. A bond issue for the football stadium was included in the base analysis; it was believed that the conservative approach was to retain the football stadium bonds in the base case since the "risk" was of an action that would improve the chances that the affordability limits were not breached. The Department of Transportation proposed a $52 million issue of certificates of participation as part of a foreign tax-favored (cross-border) lease arrangement for the acquisition of light-rail cars. The Swedish tax climate, at this time, did not appear favorable for the transaction.

The Department of Transportation was currently experiencing revenue attainment problems that were seriously limiting its capital program. The department was expected to spend almost $900 million on capital projects in fiscal 1992; spending on capital projects was projected by the department to decline by more than two-thirds by fiscal 1997. It was unlikely that capital spending on the state's vital transportation network would be allowed to decline to that level. In order to maintain an adequate capital program, the department estimated that it would need to issue a minimum of $870 million consolidated transportation bonds in addition to the $225 million currently anticipated. For purposes of this affordability risk analysis, it was assumed that $65 million in additional bonds would be issued in fiscal 1993, $135 million in fiscal 1994, $245 million in fiscal 1995, $205 million in fiscal 1996, and $220 million in 1997.

The Convention Center Authority, established in 1990, has developed a financing plan and begun design work for an expanded convention center in Baltimore which would enable Baltimore City to compete for larger conventions. In accordance with the action by the 1991 General Assembly, the financing plan will be presented to the 1992 General Assembly. For the purposes of the affordability risk analysis, it is assumed that the ultimate cost of the convention facilities would be $125 million and that the revenue bonds to finance the facility would be backed by a lease arrangement similar to that backing the revenue bonds of the Maryland Stadium Authority. To be conservative, the analysis assumed that a $10 million initial issue of bonds for planning would occur in fiscal 1992 and that the remaining bonds would be issued in fiscal 1993.

As discussed in Sec. V of this Chapter, the committee recommended that the state undertake a bond-financed program to acquire state-owned space in Baltimore for headquarters operations and similar activities which was currently in leased space. For purposes of this affordability risk analysis, it was assumed that the total program cost will be $100 million. It was further assumed that $50 million in bonds would be issued in fiscal 1992 and $25 million in each of FY 1993 and 1994.

The effect of the three potential bond programs on the ratio of bonds outstanding to personal income is as follows:

Ratio of Debt Outstanding to Personal Income

Fiscal year	Base plan	Plan including potential programs
1992	2.93%	2.94%
1993	2.97%	3.16%
1994	2.92%	3.23%
1995	2.82%	3.29%
1996	2.71%	3.27%
1997	2.60%	3.24%

In the committee's base plan, which does not incorporate any of the potentially expanded or new programs, the ratio is significantly below the 3.2% limit for each year. If the three potential bond programs are added, there is no unused capacity; in fact, the ratio exceeds the 3.2% affordability limit in most years. The ratio in excess of the 3.2% affordability limit in the last years of the plan, moreover, suggests that there may be even additional risk in the out years of the plan as new, but not yet identified, needs and programs might materialize and require capacity.

If federal reimbursement regulations would adopted in a form similar to those proposed, there was even more danger that the outstanding debt would exceed the 3.2% affordability limits during the 1993–97 period. If the impact of the regulations were at the lower end of the range suggested in Sec. V, the ratio of outstanding debt to personal income would exceed 3.3% in 1995; if the impact were closer to the high end of the range, the ratio for the same year would be 3.4%.

8. Conclusion

The analysis suggests that, although the committee's current projection of general obligation bond authorizations is currently affordable, the apparent unused capacity may easily be absorbed by a combination of the response to the proposed federal reimbursement regulations and new and expanded components of tax-supported debt such as discussed above. The committee realizes that the potential scenario discussed above is a projection based on certain assumptions. These assumptions may not materialize: the assumed programs could be authorized at higher or lower levels; the assumed timing of the issues could be more protracted; all of the assumed programs may not be adopted while other programs, not assumed for this analysis, may be adopted. The assumptions underlying the potential scenario are not unreasonable; the additional debt associated with the assumptions represents a distinct possibility. The committee, therefore, deems it prudent to limit its affordability recommendation to the same 5-year plan of new authorizations for general obligation bonds that is consistent with the past 2 years' reports.

IV. HIGHER EDUCATION DEBT

A. Background

Chapter 93, *Laws of Maryland, 1989*, altered the revenue bonding framework and authority of the University of Maryland system, Morgan State University, and St. Mary's College of Maryland, and also assigned certain duties relevant to those alterations to the Capital Debt Affordability Committee.

The statute provides a new framework for the issuance of higher education debt. In particular, the statute distinguishes between auxiliary facilities (which generate fees or income arising from the use of the facility) and academic facilities (which are used primarily for instruction of students and any facilities which are not auxiliary). It also authorizes institutions to issue bonds to finance either auxiliary or academic facilities (maximum terms of 33 and 20 years, respectively) with the stipulation that any academic facilities so financed are first expressly approved by an act of the General Assembly as to both project and amount.

Furthermore, the statute specifies fund sources that can be pledged as security as opposed to those that can be used for debt service payments. Specifically available to be pledged as security are auxiliary fees (defined as fees and rents arising from the use of the auxiliary facility) and academic fees (defined as tuition and student fees). The systems specifically cannot pledge: a state appropriation; contracts, grants, or gifts; or any other source not expressly authorized by the General Assembly. Debt service on bonds for either or both auxiliary or academic facilities is payable solely from auxiliary fees, academic fees, a state appropriation expressly authorized for that purpose, or revenues from contracts, gifts, or grants.

The statute and subsequent annual amendments to the statute establish the maximum allowable amount of outstanding debt for the University of Maryland system at $442.7 million, Morgan State University at $28 million, and St. Mary's College of Maryland at $15 million. Debt for both academic and auxiliary facilities, including capital leases for real property, are subject to the maximum.

For 1989, Chapter 93 authorized three facilities (total project cost of $51.0 million) to be financed with bonds in an amount of $58.7 million. For 1990, Chapter 121 authorized three facilities (total project cost of $41.6 million) to be financed with bonds in an amount of $45.8 million. For 1991, Chapter 610 authorized three facilities to be financed with bonds in an amount of $42.7 million.

In addition to defining higher education bond authority and authorizing certain projects, Chapter 93 directs the Capital Debt Affordability Committee to

"review on a continuing basis the size and condition of any debt of" the University of Maryland system, Morgan State University, and St. Mary's College of Maryland

"In preparing an estimate with respect to the authorization of any new State debt" (i.e., general obligation debt) to "take into account as part of the affordability analysis any debt for academic facilities to be issued by a system"

"submit to the Governor and the General Assembly the Committee's estimate of the amount of new bonds for academic facilities that prudently may be authorized in the aggregate for the next fiscal year" (by the University of Maryland system, Morgan State University, and St. Mary's College of Maryland)

The charges pose two basic questions for the committee. How is higher education debt to be "taken into account" in the committee's affordability analysis? How is the committee to determine a "prudent" amount of new academic debt that may be authorized?

B. Incorporating Higher Education Academic Debt into the Affordability Analysis

The new language in the statute expanding the committee's charge states: "In preparing an estimate with respect to the authorization of any new State debt [i.e., general obligation debt], the Committee shall take into account as part of the affordability analysis any debt for academic facilities to be issued by a system." This language is somewhat ambiguous as to what constitutes "to take into account." Neither the statute nor the committee narrative in the report of the chairmen on the 1991 capital budget specifically directs the committee to include higher education debt as a component of state-tax-supported debt for purposes of the capacity criteria or affordability analysis or the committee's recommendation relating to new authorization of general obligation debt.

Second, during their February 1989 presentation to the joint fiscal committees, both attending rating agencies were quite explicit in describing their approach to debt measurement that debt issued by institutions of higher education was not considered by them to be state-tax-supported debt. The debt of the three systems, either currently outstanding or related to future issuances, will not, under current rating agency policy, be counted by the rating agencies in determining the rating of the state's general obligation bonds.

Third, both the statutory structure of higher education debt and the current budgetary policies related to higher education debt underscore the separation of higher education debt and tax-supported debt. The statute provides that higher education debt may not be secured by a pledge of the issuer's general fund appropriation. The statute further provides that no general funds may be used to pay debt service unless specifically authorized in the budget. Not only has no budget included such authorization, but also the secretary of budget and fiscal planning has stated in a letter to the committee that there is no commitment on the part of the administration to provide general fund support for higher education debt service.

There appears to be no basis, therefore, for including higher education debt as a component of state-tax-supported debt. At the same time, however, the committee must in some way "take into account" higher education academic debt. The committee believes that through careful analysis, discussions, and deliberations of higher education debt levels, capacity, and needs it is meeting legislative intent. It should be noted that outstanding higher education debt, including both academic and auxiliary debt as projected was less than 0.4% projected personal income in FY 1992 and a maximum of 0.42% during the forecast period.

C. Recommending a Prudent Level of New Higher Education Academic Debt to Be Authorized

The committee's charge is to submit an "estimate of the amount of new bonds for academic facilities that prudently may be authorized in the aggregate for the next fiscal year by the University of Maryland System, Morgan State University, and St. Mary's College of Maryland." This charge, therefore, requires the committee to distinguish between burdens imposed by academic debt as opposed to those imposed by auxiliary debt in arriving at a recommendation for academic debt alone. From a credit analyst's point of view, the aggregate level of a system's debt is critical, while the type of debt (academic versus auxiliary) has less relevance to the credit analysis.

One approach to determining a prudent amount of new academic debt to be authorized is to start with the aggregate level of debt that each system anticipates issuing. If it is estimated that level of debt is prudent over time, then it is reasonable for the committee to accept that aggregate total and to also accept the breakdown (between academic and auxiliary) proposed by a system.

This approach does not address the issue of the maximum level of debt outstanding allowed by statute for each system. While the committee believes that "caps" on amounts of debt outstanding are outside the statutory charge of this committee, the analysis of system debt capacity may prove useful to the governor and General Assembly in setting limits for debt outstanding.

The guidelines initially adopted by the committee to judge debt manageability are those contained in the rating methodology used by one of the major rating agencies. Standard and Poor's uses five factors to rate a public institution's debt (over a time frame of several years): (1) the rating of the state, (2) the state's general financial support for higher education as a whole, (3) the state's financial support for the particular institution, (4) the institution's demand and financial factors, and (5) the security pledge.

The first, second, and fifth factors are the same for all three systems. All systems benefit from the state's AAA/Aaa rating; all are part of public higher education in Maryland; and all can offer the same types of security.

The third factor is only relevant to Morgan State University and St. Mary's College of Maryland since the University of Maryland system, as now constituted, receives approximately 94% of the state's general funds appropriated to the three systems.

The fourth factor, the institution's demand and financial factors, encompasses a host of data dealing with the student body, financial performance, and components of debt. The specific guideline related to debt burden is twofold. First, the most accurate measure of debt burden is judged to be debt service as a percent of the sum of unrestricted current fund expenditures plus mandatory transfers. Second, if that ratio exceeds 10%, the institution is considered highly leveraged. It should be noted that although the threshold ratio for excessive debt is deemed to be 10%, the average ratio in 1988 for public institutions was 1.9%. Surprisingly, for private institutions, that average ratio was 3.7% and for private institutions with a AAA bond rating, it was 8.5%.

Table 3 displays various components of debt for each of the three higher education systems. In analyzing

Table 3　Education Debt: Total Auxiliary and Academic ($ in thousands)

	Projected issuances		Debt outstanding	Debt service	Unrestricted current fund expenditures plus mandatory transfers	Ratio of debt service to UCF expenditures plus mandatory transfers
	Auxiliary	Academic				
University of Maryland system						
1992	30,000	40,000	391,614	33,216	1,196,575	2.78%
1993	30,000	40,000	449,643	41,590	1,244,940	3.34%
1994	30,000	40,000	505,292	46,782	1,320,806	3.54%
1995	30,000	40,000	558,360	52,388	1,401,409	3.74%
1996	30,000	40,000	608,726	59,100	1,488,006	3.97%
1997	30,000	40,000	656,252	64,749	1,582,856	4.09%
Morgan State University	None anticipated					
1992			26,599	459	46,400	0.99%
1993			26,400	352	50,350	0.70%
1994			26,187	1,246	52,740	2.36%
1995			26,187	1,823	56,135	3.25%
1996			26,187	1,603	59,808	2.68%
1997			26,187	1,603	63,794	2.51%
St. Mary's College of Maryland						
1992	0	None	4,134	391	17,200	2.27%
1993	2,500	antici-	6,389	390	18,050	2.16%
1994	0	pated	6,123	574	19,049	3.01%
1995	0		5,790	628	20,091	3.13%
1996	0		5,491	579	21,209	2.73%
1997	0		5,175	582	22,431	2.59%

the data, it is important to recognize that there are two levels of higher education debt measurement. One consists of the sum of the components that count toward the statutory ceiling, and the other measure consists of the sum of the components that count for the purpose of credit analysis. It is presumed for purposes of this analysis that the relevant measure is the one that encompasses all components of debt—one that mirrors the measure used by credit analysts.

Only one of the three systems anticipated issuing new academic debt. The University of Maryland system's academic debt projection included the projects specifically authorized during the 1991 session, the bonds for which would be issued during fiscal 1992, and approximately $40 million a year thereafter; the university's auxiliary debt projection included $30 million to be issued in fiscal 1992 and each year thereafter. Morgan State University issued $26.2 million in auxiliary bonds in May 1990 for a project to rehabilitate existing dormitories and add approximately 600 new dormitory beds. Morgan had no plans to issue additional debt. St. Mary's College of Maryland anticipated issuing $2.5 million in auxiliary debt during fiscal 1993 for the renovation of a gymnasium.

As can be seen from the final column of each panel in the table, each system was well within the criteria suggested by Standard and Poor's for measuring debt burden. The debt burden ratios were, in fact, more favorable for the University of Maryland system than displayed last year. The primary reason for the improved ratios for the university was greater capacity. The last 2 years' report did not fully reflect the major increase in resources committed to higher education in the fiscal 1989 and 1990 budgets. For example, last year it was projected that the University of Maryland's 1992 unrestricted current fund expenditures plus mandatory transfers would be $1.1 billion; the current estimate is $1.2 billion. The debt burden ratios for Morgan and St. Mary's were somewhat worse than last year. Again capacity is the key factor. Last year Morgan projected capacity to grow over 9% per year; the current estimate is 6.5% per year. In the case of St. Mary's, the reduced capacity mainly reflects reductions in the 1991 and 1992 budgets.

Since each of the system's debt issuance plans would result in a debt burden level well below the 10% "highly leveraged" threshold established by Standard and Poor's, there appears to be no basis for the committee's recommendation to differ from the systems' plans at this time. The committee recommends a limit of $40 million of new bonds for academic facilities that prudently may be authorized in the aggregate for the next fiscal year. This amount represents financing of academic facilities by the University of Maryland system.

V. OTHER ISSUES

A. State Ownership of Office Space

1. Background

In its last two reports, the committee has addressed the issue of converting rented office space to state-owned space.

The members of the committee have long been aware of the economics implicit in the rent/purchase decision. Rental space is very flexible and can be procured quickly and abandoned when service demands change or program demands diminish, but the flexibility comes at a price. Not only does the state receive no equity for its rental payments, but the rental payments generally reflect the landlord's higher cost of capital, shorter desired capital recovery period, and requirement to pay local real estate taxes. All evidence—the analyses of individual projects brought to the Board of Public Works, the Department of Budget and Fiscal Planning's analysis in connection with the Annapolis office complex plan adopted by the General Assembly 1990, and the same department's 1990 analysis for the committee of a program to convert leased headquarters and support space in Baltimore to state-owned space—supports the committee's judgment that it is generally more economical to utilize owned space than rental space wherever the demand for the activities using the space are long-lasting. Permanency of demand is particularly present for headquarters and support activities for major state departments.

The committee also recognized that the significant economic advantages to office building ownership are not always persuasive in a capital budget process—especially one that is constrained by a limit on new general obligation bond authorizations.

In the last report, the committee recommended that the state proceed with a "one-time" general obligation bond authorization to finance a program to convert the use of leased space to the use of owned space for headquarters and support activities in the Baltimore area. The committee further recommended that this authorization be considered in addition to the normal affordability limit.

2. 1991 Update
The Department of Budget and Fiscal Planning provided the committee with an updated analysis of the cost of acquiring state-owned space for agencies currently in leased space. Rather than tie the analysis to specific candidate buildings, the department segregated the demand for space into the demand for class A space and class B space. The department then determined the expected cost of the requisite space by applying an average cost for each class of space. The expected cost of class A and class B space was estimated by the Department of General Services at $175 per square foot and $75 per square foot, respectively.

The total anticipated cost associated with the department's updated lease conversion analysis is $97 million. The total anticipated cost for 152 thousand square feet of class A space, for the office of the attorney general and the Department of Economic and Employment Development, is $30 million. The total anticipated cost for 661 thousand square feet of class B space is $57 million. To these two amounts the department added the $10 million lease buyout cost for the recently leased Towson District Court.

3. Committee Recommendation
The committee strongly supports the concept of a lease conversion program for headquarters and support space in the Baltimore area.

The committee believes that a well-conceived program to replace rental space with state-owned space for headquarters and support activities has the potential to improve the state's true fiscal position. Although operating payments are only a footnote disclosure in the state's financial statements, the rental payments represent a true long-term liability to the state and a claim on future state tax dollars. To be sure, the future liability for rental payments is not as fixed in amount as debt service; but realistically, the rental payments for today's headquarters activities are likely to increase over the long run. Debt service on bonds issued to buy office space can be viewed as a substitute for rental payments. To the extent that there is an economic advantage to buy rather than rent, as there usually is, *the increase in debt service* (related to the additional bonds issued for the conversion of rental space to owned space) *actually improves the state's fiscal position.*

The committee again recommends that the state proceed with a one-time general obligation bond authorization to finance an office space program in Baltimore. Because the compelling and competing needs for schools, prisons, and other facilities will always take precedent over a program to convert office space, this authorization would be considered in addition to the $350 million recommended (in Sec. III of this report).

B. County Transportation Bonds

1. Background
In each year of the committee's 6-year projection period (1992–1997), county transportation debt represents over $100 million of state-tax-supported debt. Although the county transportation debt is used exclusively to make loans to counties and is secured by taxes imposed and collected by the state but payable to the counties, the debt is issued by the Department of Transportation and is state debt. As state debt, the county transportation debt uses up valuable state capacity that could be used for needed state projects.

The issue before the committee was whether programs such as the county transportation bonds still made sense in light of their impact on the state's debt capacity.

2. History of State Extensions of Credit to Local Governments
In the late 1940s and early 1950s, the state initiated programs to provide financial assistance to local governments by issuing state bonds. The proceeds of these bonds were to be loaned to local governments, and the repayment of the bonds was secured by a lien on the "local share" of state-collected taxes. The programs reflected the state's desire to accelerate the construction of vital schools and roads and the knowledge that many local governments would be unable to borrow in the public markets or could borrow but at higher costs than the borrowing costs typically incurred by the state.

Over time, the state bond programs for loans to local governments for schools and transportation grew substantially. The school program grew until 1971, at which time over $205 million was outstanding; however, the program declined dramatically after the state's assumption of a major share of the cost of local school construction. The last loan authorization for the school program was enacted in 1981; as of June 30, 1991, only a small amount of such bonds remained outstanding, and there were no bonds authorized but unissued. The transportation program, on the other hand, continues to function. In November 1990, the Department of Transportation issued $16.6 million in county transportation bonds for six counties; as of June 30, 1991, the outstanding balance of these bonds, net of sinking fund amounts, was $135.8 million. The department expects to continue to issue bonds under this program over the committee's planning period at the rate of approximately $10 million per year.

In addition to the issuance of bonds for local transportation and school projects, the state also issued state bonds, the proceeds of which were loaned to local governments for other types of projects. In 1989, the state sold bonds to make a $2.5 million loan to Ocean City and Worcester County for the local share of the costs of the beach erosion project at Ocean City; more recently the local share has been financed with local government debt. Over the years, the state has loaned proceeds of general obligation bonds to local governments for water and sewer projects. As of June 30, 1991, the outstanding balance on loans for such projects was approximately $17 million. It is not expected that general obligation bonds will continue to be a major source of loans for local water and sewer projects, since the newly created Maryland Water Quality Financing Administration has begun to issue revenue bonds for that purpose.

3. County Transportation Bonds

The county transportation bond program clearly has a benefit to local governments. Many of the counties are able to borrow at more favorable interest rates than if they issued bonds directly, since the county transportation bonds are obligations of the Department of Transportation. The bonds are typically rated double A; only nine of the counties presently have a double A rating from a recognized bond rating agency. There are savings to the counties, since the fixed portion of the issuance costs are spread over a larger amount of bonds. There are also similar savings in the paying agent function and in monitoring the market for potential opportunities to refund or to redeem early. There are advantages to some counties in avoiding either legal or customary debt limits or procedures; the bonds, however, are county debt in the bond rating agency analyses and are included in the county's audited financial statements.

Although there are financial advantages to the counties to participate in the county transportation bond program, the absence of the program is unlikely to leave its participants without access to the bond market. As displayed in Figure 5, in the most recent 5 years, 35% of the bonds were issued on behalf of Prince George's County, an experienced issuer in the tax-exempt market. Almost 75% of the bonds issued in the last 12 years were issued on behalf of two of the state's most populous and financially sophisticated jurisdictions. All but three of Maryland's counties have a single A or better rating. Of the remaining three, one is investment grade and the other two are not rated. In the absence of the program, all or any of the counties could issue bonds through the state's infrastructure program and retain some of the advantages of the county transportation bond program. Alternatively, legislation would be enacted, establishing within the Department of Transportation, a bond bank program similar to the Water Quality Financing Administration's program.

There are, of course, options to assure that the counties do not experience any loss; for example, state provision of bond insurance or an interest subsidy. These options, however, would require an expenditure of state tax revenues.

The committee recommends that the General Assembly consider eliminating the state's liability for future issues of county transportation bonds while providing an alternative that embodies the key aspects of the program. It is the committee's judgment that the counties can adequately access the national securities markets without the aid of the county transportation bond program, and that the interest subsidy afforded the counties under the program is insufficient to justify the use of valuable state bonding capacity.

C. Proposed Federal Reimbursement Regulations

1. Background

The state traditionally issues general obligation bonds to fund the estimated near-term cash requirements associated with the entire capital program that has been authorized by bond bills. Although care is taken to estimate the cash needs associated with each bond authorization, especially the authorizations for local projects, the typical outcome is that more bonds are issued for some loan accounts (bond bills) and too few

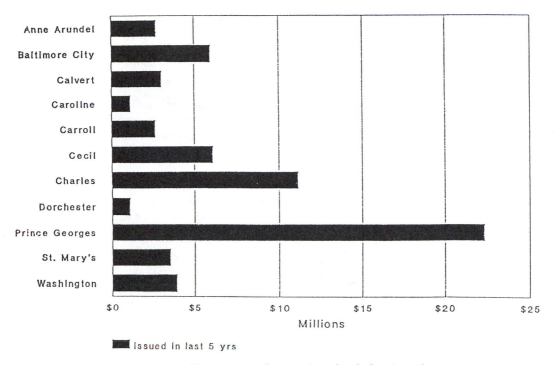

Figure 5   County transportation bond program (total amount issued in the last 5 years).

bonds are issued for other loan accounts. This mismatch causes few problems because the state has enough cash in the aggregate loan fund account to advance money to the projects in loan accounts for which some bonds have been sold but which presently do not have enough money. These advances create "red balances" in the loan account to which the funds are advanced. The red balances are liquidated by issuing the appropriate amount of bonds in the next bond sale. Since the enactment of the Tax Reform Act of 1986, almost 63% of the proceeds from eleven regular general obligation bond issues have been used to reimburse. In only two issues were less than half the proceeds used to reimburse.

The federal government has become very concerned about the level and use of tax-exempt bonds. The federal Department of the Treasury is concerned that state and local governments are issuing "too much" tax-exempt debt and/or are issuing tax-exempt debt "too early." In the Treasury's view, too great or too early issuances increase the amount of tax-exempt debt outstanding and, presumably, decrease federal income tax revenues. A particular concern is that state and local governments, in looking for ways to augment revenues, identify projects for which they paid cash, issue debt for such projects, assert they "spent" the bond proceeds on the projects (thereby freeing the proceeds from the arbitrage rebate restrictions), and then invest the proceeds at taxable interest rates. This supposed abusive gambit is called the "pyramid bond" (akin to the Egyptian government now issuing bonds to reimburse itself for the construction costs of the pyramids).

To date, Maryland has not had a problem with early or excessive issuances. The state's policy of advancing cash and subsequently reimbursing the red balances results in the state issuing fewer bonds earlier than would be required if all loan accounts had to have adequate cash prior to construction.

2.   The Proposed Reimbursement Regulations

On April 15, 1991, the Internal Revenue Service issued proposed regulations relating to the "proceeds of Bonds Used for Reimbursement." The regulations were originally scheduled to be effective for bonds issued after September 6, 1991, but the effective date has been postponed.

The proposed regulations outline a very detailed procedure which must be followed if any of the proceeds of the tax-exempt bonds are to be recognized as "spent" when used to reimburse a prior expenditure. The procedure spells out very specific rules on how the intent to reimburse is to be declared, the time frame for the declaration of intent, the time frame for reimbursement, the type of expenditure that may be reimbursed, and antiabuse provisions.

The regulations as originally proposed appear to impose an unreasonable level of recordkeeping and monitoring on a government with a varied capital program carried out by different units and entailing an enormous number of projects, some of which must be flexibly defined. The proposed regulations also provide penalties for failing to reimburse once a declaration of intent has been made.

If not materially amended, the proposed regulations will make it exceedingly difficult to continue its current practice of advancing funds for some capital projects and reimbursing the advance when bonds are sold. The proposed regulations, as currently structured, may effectively require the state to issue its debt earlier and in greater amounts. Estimating the amount of additional debt outstanding is not clear-cut.

3. Estimated Range of Impact

Clearly, the impact of the regulations on debt outstanding and the affordability criteria will depend upon what policies and procedures the state will adopt and the state's success in carrying out such policies and procedures.

There is a wide spectrum of policies that the state could employ to deal with the reimbursement regulations. Through the use of bond anticipation notes, it may be possible for the state to retain its current procedures for the issuance of the general obligation bonds; however, a bond anticipation program is essentially a short-term borrowing program that would require legislation. Traditionally, short-term borrowing has not been viewed favorably in Maryland government. Alternatively, all general obligation bonds could be structured to be reimbursement bonds. This alternative would require a change in legislation, a substantial increase in the amount of cash advanced, and a monitoring system to assure that reimbursement occurred within the allowed time frames. A conservative alternative is to issue bonds prior to any expenditure. This alternative does not require legislation and obviates the need to implement a complex monitoring and accounting program in tight fiscal times.

The analysis assumes that the state will only use bond proceeds on hand to pay expenditures for all general obligation bond-financed capital projects and grants. Such a policy will minimize the possibility that a "reimbursement problem" arises. One approach to estimating the impact is to see what the impact of such a policy would have been had it been in place during recent years *and* the state had been very accurate in estimating needs. Another approach to estimating the impact is to accelerate the issuance schedules assumed in the preliminary affordability analysis tables. These two approaches can be used to establish a range of impacts.

If the state had been able to anticipate precisely all of its reimbursement needs and sold sufficient bonds in each preceding sale so that the red balances would not have occurred, there would have been approximately $50 million in additional debt outstanding on June 30, 1991. Over the period since 1987, the largest amount of additional bonds that would have had to be outstanding at any time was approximately $95 million in early 1990. Over the same period, the average amount of additional debt outstanding at fiscal year end would have been approximately $49 million or about 56% of the first sale of the subsequent fiscal year. Applying this percentage to the issuances included in the committee's affordability analysis, the impact on outstanding debt in dollars (millions) and as a percentage of personal income would be

1992	1993	1994	1995	1996	1997
$57.8	$63.5	$67.2	$67.9	$66.2	$58.1
.05%	.05%	.05%	.05%	.05%	.05%

It is very unlikely, however, that the state would be able to anticipate precisely the actual cash needs—even for a period as short as 6 months. It is more likely, in fact, that cash estimating would be extremely conservative in order to be certain that no ready-to-proceed project would have to be held up because of inadequate cash. A fairly conservative set of assumptions concerning the possible impact of the reimbursement regulations on the state's general obligation issuance schedule is (1) currently authorized but unissued bonds are sold one half year earlier than assumed in the affordability analysis tables (see Appendix B-1); (2) an additional 15% of each year's new authorizations are sold in the year following authorization; and (3) an additional 5% of each year's new authorizations are sold in the second year following authorization. Applying these assumptions to the committee's affordability analysis, the impact on outstanding debt in dollars (millions) and as a percentage of personal income would be

1992	1993	1994	1995	1996	1997
$126.5	$143.0	$185.5	$198.5	$198.0	$201.8
.11%	.12%	.14%	.14%	.13%	.12%

4. Conclusion

The above analysis suggests that an approach whereby payment of project expenditures be limited to bond proceeds on hand would increase the outstanding debt to personal income affordability measure by something more than .05% but less than .12–.14%. Although this may not appear to be a major impact, it is. The county transportation bond program absorbs .06% to .11% of the same measure in the committee's forecast period. Capital leases absorb .08% over the period.

Given the size of the possible impact and the fact that the additional bonds do not provide additional capital projects, it may be worthwhile to explore seriously other options such as more frequent sales, the use of bond anticipation notes, more control over issuers who will be considered as part of the state, and the eligibility of certain types of already completed capital projects for state bond funding.

APPENDIX A–1

Maryland Personal Income and Population: Historical Data and
Projections

Calendar year	Personal income (millions)	Change (%)	Population (thousands)	Change (%)
1981	50,847	37.8	4,257	1.1
1982	54,411	7.0	4,273	0.4
1983	58,647	7.8	4,301	0.7
1984	64,544	10.1	4,349	1.1
1985	70,154	8.7	4,393	1.0
1986	75,685	7.9	4,461	1.5
1987	82,683	9.2	4,536	1.7
1988	90,633	9.6	4,622	1.9
1989	98,159	8.3	4,694	1.6
1990	104,543	6.5	4,781	1.9
1991	109,000	4.3	4,830	1.0
1992	116,100	6.5	4,882	1.1
1993	124,100	6.9	4,935	1.1
1994	132,400	6.7	4,987	1.1
1995	141,400	6.8	5,035	1.0
1996	151,400	7.1	5,085	1.0
1997	162,100	7.1	5,136	1.0

Note: Personal income: 1980–1990—Official Statement State and Local Facilities Loan of 1991, third series (U.S. Department of Commerce, Bureau of Economic Analysis), 1991–1997—BRE (WEFA—regional forecast, first quarter 1991); population: 1980–1990—Official Statement State and Local Facilities Loan of 1991, third series (U.S. Department of Commerce, Bureau of Census), 1991–1996—projected using percentage changes in the current forecast of the Maryland Office of Planning.

APPENDIX A–2

Maryland State Revenue Projections ($ in millions)

Fiscal year	General fund revenue	Property taxes	Total	Transportation revenues	Stadium-related revenues	Total revenues
1981	2,703.4	88.8	2,792.2	486.7		3,278.9
1982	2,925.0	99.5	3,024.5	497.9		3,522.4
1983	3,096.5	109.2	3,205.7	531.9		3,737.6
1984	3,416.8	116.1	3,532.9	660.5		4,193.4
1985	3,809.2	104.8	3,914.0	689.8		4,603.8
1986	4,164.1	112.2	4,276.3	730.7		5,007.0
1987	4,642.0	121.2	4,763.2	780.5		5,543.7
1988	5,093.2	134.9	5,228.1	892.5		6,120.6
1989	5,442.3	147.0	5,589.3	945.3		6,534.6
1990	5,705.2	162.5	5,867.7	946.1	11.1	6,824.9
1991	5,710.0	175.0	5,885.0	882.0	12.0	6,779.0
1992	6,338.6	187.7	6,526.3	942.0	12.1	7,480.4
1993	6,555.4	203.4	6,758.8	986.0	17.7	7,762.5
1994	7,009.3	217.7	7,227.0	1,015.0	21.8	8,263.8
1995	7,487.6	238.3	7,725.9	1,044.0	21.8	8,791.7
1996	8,013.9	260.7	8,274.6	1,080.0	22.7	9,377.3
1997	8,596.6	286.0	8,882.6	1,118.0	22.7	10,023.3

Note: General fund: 1981–1990—supplemental financial data of the comptroller, 1991–1997—Bureau of Revenue estimates; property tax revenues: 1981–1990—supplemental financial data of the comptroller, 1991—1992—Commission on State Debt, 1993—fiscal 1993 CPS for public debt, 1994–1997, Bureau of Revenue estimates; transportation revenues: Department of Transportation, office of asst. sec., finance; stadium revenues: transfers from the Stadium Facilities Fund to the Stadium Authority are assumed to be just sufficient, when coupled with the authority's own-source revenues, to meet debt service requirements.

APPENDIX B–1

Projected General Obligation Debt—Authorized but Unissued ($ in millions)

General Assembly session	Proposed authorizations[b]	Estimated issuances during fiscal year[a]										Total issues
		1992	1993	1994	1995	1996	1997	1998	1999	2000	2001	
1992	350	0	88	88	70	70	18	18	0	0	0	350
1993	370		0	93	93	74	74	19	19	0	0	370
1994	395			0	99	99	79	79	20	20	0	395
1995	415				0	104	104	83	83	21	21	415
1996	435					0	109	109	87	87	22	413
1997	455						0	114	114	91	91	410
1998	475							0	119	119	95	333
1999	495								0	124	124	248
2000	510									0	128	128
2001	540										0	0
Total		0	88	180	261	347	383	421	441	461	480	3,060
Current authorizations[b]	1,013	310	253	180	119	59	37	30	27	0	0	1,013
Total issuances		310	340	360	380	405	420	450	467	461	480	4,073

[a]Percentage issuance assumptions by fiscal years:

Fiscal year following year of authorization	1st	2nd	3rd	4th	5th	6th
Percentage of original authorization issued:	25%	25%	20%	20%	5%	5%

[b]Net of $10 million—the remaining bonds authorized by the Outdoor Recreation Loan of 1969 which are unissued at June 30, 1991. This amount will be canceled.

APPENDIX B–2

Projected General Obligation Debt Authorized but Unissued ($ in thousands)

Fiscal year	Authorized but unissued debt at beginning of year	New debt issues		New debt authoriza-tions	Projected cancel-lations	Authorized but unissued debt at end of year
		Bond issues[a]	Capital leases			
1992	1,022,766	310,000	0	350,000	1,000[b]	1,061,766
1993	1,061,766	340,000	0	370,000	1,000	1,090,766
1994	1,090,766	360,000	0	395,000	1,000	1,124,766
1995	1,124,766	380,000	0	415,000	1,000	1,158,766
1996	1,158,766	405,000	0	435,000	1,000	1,187,766
1997	1,187,766	420,000	0	455,000	1,000	1,221,766
1998	1,221,766	450,000	0	475,000	1,000	1,245,766
1999	1,245,766	467,266	0	495,000	1,000	1,272,500
2000	1,272,500	461,000	0	510,000	1,000	1,320,500
2001	1,320,500	479,750	0	540,000	1,000	1,379,750

[a]As projected in Appendix B-1.
[b]Projected cancellations are $1 million per year for outdoor recreation.

APPENDIX B–3

Projected General Obligation Debt Outstanding ($ in thousands)

Fiscal year	Outstanding at beginning of year	New issues[a]	Redemptions[b]	Increased debt resulting from accreted interest on capital appreciation bonds	Outstanding at end of year
1992	2,038,445	310,000	200,085		2,148,360
1993	2,148,360	340,000	176,330		2,312,030
1994	2,312,030	360,000	181,090		2,490,940
1995	2,490,940	380,000	214,218		2,656,722
1996	2,656,722	405,000	225,089		2,836,633
1997	2,836,633	420,000	236,574		3,020,059
1998	3,020,059	450,000	248,018		3,222,041
1999	3,222,041	467,266	232,726		3,456,581
2000	3,456,581	461,000	262,827		3,654,754
2001	3,654,754	479,750	280,578		3,853,926

[a]As projected in Appendix B-1.
[b]Assumes debt service on minibonds is paid at maturity and no minibond put options are exercised.

APPENDIX B–4

Projected General Obligation Debt Service ($ in thousands)

Fiscal year	Gross debt service			Adjustment		Adjusted general obligation debt service
	Bonds currently outstanding[a]	New issues	Total	Debt service on "repayable" bonds[b]	Nonstate debt service assumed[c]	
1992	339,326	6,253	345,579	(1,353)	4,818	349,044
1993	302,640	27,906	330,546	(1,358)	3,141	332,329
1994	294,455	50,306	344,761	(654)	2,146	346,253
1995	303,964	96,538	400,502	(653)	1,462	401,311
1996	279,425	140,427	419,852	(652)	1,360	420,560
1997	254,011	186,944	440,955	(647)	347	440,655
1998	229,219	235,742	464,961	(642)	64	464,383
1999	177,579	287,626	465,205	(209)	0	464,996
2000	177,795	340,450	518,245	0	0	518,245
2001	152,149	392,964	545,113	0	0	545,113

[a] Assumes debt service on minibonds is paid at maturity and no minibond put options are exercised.
[b] Represents debt service which is repaid to the state by local subdivisions prior to the debt service payment due date.
[c] Represents debt service assumed by the state on bonds issued by local subdivisions for public schools.

APPENDIX C–1

Historical Data—General Obligation Debt ($ in thousands)

Fiscal year	Authorized[a]	Canceled	Issued	Redeemed	Outstanding	Authorized but unissued	Gross total	Adjustment[b] Repayable	Adjustment[b] Assumed	Net	Adjusted debt service
1965	157,250	818	69,290	27,062	329,651	252,377	35,070	(13,608)	0	(13,608)	21,462
1966	57,047	396	73,795	28,887	374,559	235,233	38,519	(14,661)	0	(14,661)	23,858
1967	207,122	2,680	95,785	28,176	442,168	343,890	39,690	(15,311)	0	(15,311)	24,379
1968	113,754	4,414	86,235	31,549	496,854	366,994	45,498	(16,628)	0	(16,628)	28,870
1969	322,388	34,857	99,505	34,178	562,181	555,021	50,986	(18,561)	0	(18,561)	32,425
1970	204,214	1,589	45,200	39,166	568,215	712,446	58,277	(19,672)		(19,672)	38,605
1971	268,203	40,358	194,720	42,103	720,832	745,571	64,854	(22,047)	0	(22,047)	42,807
1972	470,786	17,065	204,040	48,696	876,176	995,251	80,138	(7,309)	46,608	39,299	119,437
1973	463,565	9,152	193,505	51,017	1,018,664	1,256,159	88,836	(9,912)	45,766	35,854	124,690
1974	412,827	16,058	162,150	59,823	1,120,991	1,490,778	105,394	(9,405)	45,684	36,279	141,673
1975	375,956	35,267	353,615	72,452	1,402,154	1,477,852	125,787	(11,581)	44,674	33,094	158,881
1976	180,181	20,465	391,605	83,416	1,710,343	1,245,963	155,462	(11,072)	44,186	33,114	188,576
1977	169,908	653	448,200	92,633	2,065,910	967,018	184,751	(11,963)	43,425	31,462	216,213
1978	190,896	4,577	218,145	111,095	2,172,960	935,192	216,797	(14,066)	42,459	28,393	245,190
1979	155,887	61,422	115,350	134,235	2,154,075	914,307	244,653	(14,503)	39,599	25,096	269,749
1980	205,510	72,819	117,310	162,255	2,109,130	929,688	269,054	(15,052)	37,425	22,373	291,427
1981	182,418	16,335	271,065	176,140	2,204,055	824,706	286,003	(15,946)	35,841	19,895	305,898
1982	184,998	22,391	188,180	184,575	2,207,660	799,133	311,372	(16,253)	33,947	17,694	329,066
1983	190,250	8,851	392,230	190,000	2,409,890	588,301	330,491	(14,062)	28,328	14,266	344,757
1984	203,150	24,467	116,700	212,275	2,314,315	650,284	361,279	(12,750)	27,209	14,459	375,738
1985	331,387	11,187	138,990	222,010	2,231,295	831,495	380,089	(11,809)	24,146	12,337	392,426
1986	219,034	49,892	124,585	245,805	2,110,075	876,052	396,768	(9,204)	20,227	11,023	407,791
1987	230,950	7,575	164,645	244,305	2,030,415	934,782	394,568	(5,104)	16,441	11,337	405,905
1988	254,228	13,601	304,860	244,455	2,090,820	870,549	389,993	(4,649)	13,635	8,986	398,979
1989	294,997	3,545	160,000	245,460	2,005,360	1,002,000	393,388	(4,240)	10,293	6,053	399,441
1990	328,219	103,063	234,227	252,680	1,986,907	992,930	395,068	(4,260)	8,317	4,057	399,125
1991	329,200	2,570	296,795	245,256	2,038,446	1,022,766	388,399	(1,349)	6,352	5,003	393,402

[a] Authorizations for a fiscal year represent those authorizations effective for that fiscal year; therefore, authorizations for FY 1988 exclude $15 million for the Salisbury Multi-Service Center which authorization is effective 7/1/88.

[b] Adjustment to debt service: "repayable" represents debt service on loans the repayment of which is received by the state, from nonstate entities, concurrently with, or prior to, debt service payment dates. "Assumed" debt represents payments made by the state for debt service on nonstate debt.

APPENDIX C-2

Historical Data—School Debt ($ In thousands)

Fiscal year	State public school construction and capital improvement loans						General public school construction loans						Supplemental public school construction loans					
	Authorized[a]	Issued	Redeemed	Outstanding	Authorized but unissued	Debt service	Authorized/(Cancelled)	Issued	Redeemed	Outstanding	Authorized but unissued	Debt service	Authorized	Issued	Redeemed	Outstanding	Authorized but unissued	Debt service
1965	0	0	0	0	0	0	50,000	20,910	10,511	122,597	74,975	13,608	0	0	0	0	0	0
1966	0	0	0	0	0	0	0	26,570	10,926	138,241	48,405	14,661	0	0	0	0	0	0
1967	0	0	0	0	0	0	50,000	28,380	10,922	155,699	70,025	15,311	0	0	0	0	0	0
1968	0	0	0	0	0	0	0	28,110	11,755	172,054	41,915	16,628	0	0	0	0	0	0
1969	0	0	0	0	0	0	0	11,405	12,796	170,663	30,510	18,561	0	0	0	0	0	0
1970	0	0	0	0	0	0	50,000	24,380	14,042	181,001	56,130	19,672	0	0	0	0	0	0
1971	150,000	0	0	0	150,000	0	0	40,105	15,453	205,653	16,025	22,047	0	0	0	0	0	0
1972	300,000	90,340	0	90,340	359,660	1,986	0	4,580	16,406	193,827	11,445	24,080	0	0	0	0	0	0
1973	220,000	73,000	0	163,340	506,660	5,218	0	3,770	16,561	181,036	7,675	23,903	25,000	0	0	0	25,000	0
1974	212,000	114,400	0	277,740	604,260	9,154	0	0	18,125	162,911	7,675	25,064	0	0	0	0	25,000	0
1975	160,000	186,000	5,170	458,260	578,260	20,623	0	5,830	18,651	150,090	1,845	25,100	0	20,000	0	20,000	5,000	0
1976	50,000	162,700	9,685	611,585	465,560	34,242	0	0	18,241	131,849	1,845	24,222	0	0	0	20,000	5,000	1,113
1977	69,000	230,900	16,590	825,895	303,660	52,119	0	0	18,384	113,465	1,845	23,713	0	0	0	20,000	5,000	1,113
1978	57,000	121,650	27,240	920,305	239,010	70,941	0	1,695	17,465	97,695	150	22,172	0	5,000	1,060	23,940	0	2,289
1979	62,000	70,750	37,285	953,770	230,260	85,335	0	0	16,890	80,805	150	20,981	0	0	1,125	22,815	0	2,409
1980	45,000	48,210	52,195	949,785	227,050	99,952	0	0	16,085	64,720	150	19,551	0	0	1,190	21,625	0	2,412
1981	45,000	111,200	61,860	999,125	160,850	111,679	(150)	0	14,875	49,845	0	17,707	2,000	0	1,540	20,085	2,000	2,688
1982	32,000	65,500	69,120	995,505	127,350	124,968	0	0	13,040	36,805	0	15,291	2,000	0	1,630	18,455	4,000	2,694
1983	22,000	86,350	75,410	1,006,445	63,000	134,258	0	0	10,605	26,200	0	12,337	900	4,000	1,725	20,730	900	2,810
1984	36,000	36,500	87,025	955,920	62,500	146,099	0	0	8,515	17,685	0	9,765	0	900	1,825	19,805	0	2,985
1985	34,600	24,000	94,685	885,235	73,100	153,339	0	0	7,765	9,920	0	8,623	0	0	1,935	17,870	0	3,187
1986	44,300	38,000	103,545	819,690	79,400	149,417	0	0	5,375	4,545	0	5,845	0	0	2,215	15,655	0	3,359
1987	57,400	34,040	111,190	742,540	102,760	163,947	0	0	1,465	3,080	0	1,691	0	0	2,395	13,260	0	3,413
1988	53,000	55,750	109,295	688,995	100,010	157,696	0	0	1,085	1,995	0	1,235	0	0	2,535	10,725	0	3,414
1989	44,000	52,000	110,090	630,905	91,010	155,959	0	0	725	1,270	0	817	0	0	2,695	8,030	0	3,424
1990	53,000	35,300	106,395	559,810	109,710	148,422	0	0	775	495	0	824	0	0	2,870	5,160	0	3,437
1991	60,000	57,000	94,910	521,900	112,710	133,620	0	0	155	340	0	175	0	0	780	4,380	0	1,174

[a]FY 1987 authorizations include 13,500,000 for systemic renovations.

APPENDIX C-3

Historical Data—Department of Transportation Debt: Consolidated Transportation Bonds ($ in thousands)

Fiscal year	Gross debt outstanding (beginning of year)	Issued	Defeased	Redeemed	Gross debt outstanding (end of year)	Sinking fund(s) balance[c]	Net debt outstanding (end of year)	Deposits to refunding sinking fund	Principal redeemed	Interest	Total
1979	354,900			35[b]	354,865	85,727	269,138	30,491	35	19,076	49,602
1980	354,865	45,000			399,865	125,826	274,039	27,924		20,559	48,483
1981	399,865	120,000[a]			519,865	165,346	354,519	22,924		23,943	46,867
1982	519,865	60,000		60,000	519,865	198,770	321,095	20,924		28,945	49,869
1983	519,865	40,000		60,000	499,865	240,601	259,264	20,924	60,000	32,884	113,808
1984	499,865				499,865	283,617	216,248	20,924		29,219	50,143
1985	499,865				499,865	335,241	164,624	20,924		29,219	50,143
1986	499,865		354,865	3,000	142,000	29,299	112,701	10,462	3,000	19,547	33,009
1987	142,000	100,000		7,000	235,000	48,317	186,683		7,000	12,919	19,919
1988	235,000			8,000	227,000	58,953	168,047		8,000	15,685	23,685
1989	227,000	100,000		17,000	310,000	68,162	241,838		17,000	18,195	35,195
1990	310,000	260,000		20,000	550,000	67,309	482,691		20,000	28,842	48,842
1991	550,000	310,000		18,000	842,000	68,329	773,671		18,000	46,261	64,261

Note: On 2/15/78, $354.9 million of refunding bonds were issued that refunded $346.9 million in outstanding state highway construction bonds ($99.4 million) and consolidated transportation bonds ($247.5 million). Therefore, at 6/30/78, $354.9 million was outstanding. These bonds were fully defeased by the end of fiscal 1986.

[a] Includes $60 million consolidated transportation bonds plus a 1-year bond anticipation note for $60 million. The 1-year BAN was reissued the following year.

[b] Specifications for the use of certain federal funds received by the department required retiring debt; therefore, during fiscal 1979, the department purchased on the open market $35,000 of the refunding bonds.

[c] For those bonds issued prior to 7/1/89, sinking fund balances reflect the net effect of: deposits into the fund, one calendar year in advance, of debt service; fund earnings; and payments from the sinking fund, to bondholders. Bonds issued after 7/1/89 do not require such a sinking fund.

[d] Represents payments to the refunding bond sinking fund plus payments of principal and interest to the bondholders. Amounts may differ from budgetary amounts (budgetary amounts represent payment to sinking funds).

Historical Data—Department of Transportation Debt: County Transportation Bonds ($ in thousands)

Fiscal year	Gross debt outstanding beginning of year	Issued	Defeased or refunded	Redeemed	Gross debt outstanding end of year	Sinking fund(s) balance[c]	Net debt outstanding (end of year)	Deposits to refunding sinking fund	Debt service[d]		
									Principal redeemed	Interest	Total
1979	156,595	4,645		655	160,585	35,898	124,687	9,832	655	8,708	19,195
1980	160,585			215	160,370	48,491	111,879	9,882	215	8,822	18,919
1981	160,370	59,270			219,640	67,056	152,584	9,473		11,187	20,660
1982	219,640	5,700		255	225,085	85,295	139,790	9,266	255	13,843	23,364
1983	225,085	34,875		2,625	257,335	104,373	152,962	9,216	2,625	15,681	27,522
1984	257,335	22,270		2,985	276,620	124,619	152,001	8,749	2,985	18,061	29,795
1985	276,620	24,210		4,435	296,395	144,595	151,800	7,214	4,435	19,591	31,240
1986	296,395	8,795		5,720	299,470	177,185	122,285		5,720	12,099	17,819
1987	299,470	40,590[a]	180,405[b]	7,090	152,565	21,479	131,086		7,090	12,336	19,426
1988	152,565	18,255		8,920	161,900	21,599	140,301		8,920	11,766	20,686
1989	161,900	7,285		9,895	159,290	26,024	133,266		9,895	11,931	21,826
1990	159,290	9,950		11,535	157,705	23,978	133,727		11,535	11,695	23,230
1991	157,705	16,550		12,875	161,380	25,539	135,841		12,875	11,619	24,494

Note: On 5/25/78, $155.725 million of refunding bonds were issued that refunded $153,685 million in outstanding county highway construction bonds and county transportation bonds. At 6/30/78, $155.725 million of the refunding bonds were outstanding. These bonds were fully defeased by the end of fiscal 1986. Also outstanding at 6/30/78 was $870 thousand in old county highway construction bonds that were not refunded.

[a] Represents the ninth series issue of $11.415 million plus a refunding series of $29.175 million issued to refund $24.680 million. The $29.175 million will mature from fiscal 1988 through fiscal 1998.

[b] Represents the defeasance of $155.725 million and the refunded $24.680 million.

[c] Sinking fund balances reflect the net effect of: deposits into the fund, one fiscal year in advance, of debt service; fund earnings; and payments, from the sinking fund, to bondholders.

[d] Represents payments to the refunding bond sinking fund plus payments of principal and interest to bondholders. Amounts may differ from budgetary amounts. (Budgetary amounts represent payments to sinking funds.)

15

City Debt Policy: Policy Options Analysis for Debt Service, Capital Program, and Bond Schedule

City of Dallas Department of Budget and Management Services
Dallas, Texas

I. BACKGROUND

A. History of Prior Bond Programs

The city of Dallas has held bond programs every 3 to 4 years. $893,487,000 has been authorized through the 1978, 1979, 1982, and 1985 bond programs. Almost 48% of this amount was authorized in 1985. The 1982 bond program comprised 28% of the total, while the 1978 bond program made up 18%. The comparatively small 1979 bond program accounted for 6% of all authorizations from 1978 to 1985.

Street and traffic control improvements received almost 51% of the total authorization. Park and recreation, cultural and library facilities improvements received 28%; 11% went toward flood protection; and 9% was authorized for public safety and municipal services. The total authorizations for each bond program are shown in Table 1.

B. Current Situation

The 1985 bond program authorized $428.1 million in bond sales to fund construction of capital improvement program projects. The principal and interest (debt service) payments on these bonds were paid primarily from ad valorem taxes. It was initially envisioned these bonds would be sold over a 4½-year period with an average of $106.1 million issued annually. The slowdown in the local economy placed greater pressure on the debt service (DS) tax rate than assumed in 1985. The current practices below have been followed to minimize the impacts.

- The program was lengthened to a 6-year schedule. The last currently planned 1985 bond program sale was anticipated for October 1991.
- Annual bond sale amounts have been reduced to approximate the amount of principal being retired each year. This action maintains total outstanding debt level. Appendix I details total current outstanding debt.
- Operating and maintenance (O & M) impacts are examined prior to issuing bonds. Facilities which will have an operating cost impact (recreation centers, fire stations, libraries) have been deferred to minimize impact on the general fund (GF). New fire station construction has been scheduled to open one station per fiscal year.
- Bonds are issued on 20-year schedules with equal annual principal payments. This "level principal" structure is an aggressive method of retiring debt, quickly reducing outstanding indebtedness.
- Bonds are sold at a discount rather than at par scale. At a discount scale where bonds are sold below face

Adapted with the permission of Jody Puckett, Assistant Director, Budget and Management Services, City of Dallas, Texas.

Table 1 Bond Programs Authorized (000's)

	1978	1979	1982	1985	Total
Total authorized	$163,735	$54,622	$247,070	$428,060	$893,487
Percentage of total auth. (1978–1985)	18.33%	6.11%	27.65%	47.91%	100.00%

value, the underwriter derives a profit by getting 1% of the sale proceeds up front and structuring the bonds at a market interest rate throughout their maturity schedule. At a par scale, bonds trade at the face value and the underwriter derives profit by structuring above-market interest rates in the early years. To discount all 20 years DS cash flows to present value, the discount scale can save approximately $600,000 for a $50 million bond sale at 7.5%.

The city has currently issued 52% of the 1985 bonds authorized. The status of the 1985 bond program is shown in Table 2.

A comparison between Dallas' 1985 bond program and Houston's $595 million 1984 bond program is illustrated in Appendix II.

C. Project Priority Process

As part of the annual budget development process, project schedules are examined and the bond sale schedule is developed to align funding with (1) anticipated construction schedules, (2) availability of O & M funds for new capital facilities, (3) availability of fund cash balances, and (4) compliance with the financial management performance criteria. Bonds are sold only for projects which are ready for construction and will have funding available for O & M when the facility is open. Table 3 outlines the projected bond sale schedule as incorporated in the FY 1988–1989 capital budget:

Of the $222.4 million issued to date, $148.5 million was for street system and flood protection improvements. Compared to other facilities improvement projects, this type of capital improvement does not require significant O & M costs, but enhances and preserves the tax base by providing infrastructure beneficial to economic development.

The 1985 bond program has provided initial or complete funding for a variety of projects identified as important to the vitality of the city. Since that time, critical projects requiring funding have emerged. North Central Expressway will require approximately $43.7 million for right-of-way acquisition, outfall drainage, and the provision of alternate routes during construction. In addition, flood protection improvements for Middle Five Mile Creek will need immediate funding. Final cost estimates for these flood protection

Table 2 Current Status of 1985 Bond Program

Program	Authorized	Issued	Remaining
Arts district land preservation	$28,000	$28,000	–0–
Dallas Zoo improvements	12,000	8,300	3,700
Fair Park	9,375	5,679	3,696
Fire protection facilities	13,527	4,046	9,481
Library services facilities	1,943	50	1,893
Park and rec. fac. & improve.	39,811	21,233	18,578
Police and multiple svc. fac.	19,510	5,547	13,963
Solid waste disposal fac.	2,120	1,100	1,020
Storm drainage & flood protect. fac.	56,049	26,451	29,598
Street system improvements	244,525	122,020	122,505
Trinity Park	1,200	–0–	1,200
Total	$428,060	$222,426	$205,634

Table 3 1985 Bond Program Bond Sale Schedule ($000's)

Previous issued	October 1989	October 1990	October 1991	Remaining issue
$222,426	$67,526	$69,960	$68,148	$205,634

improvements will be determined at a later date. Alternate means of financing could be created in accordance with specific criteria and with prior city council approval (Table 4).

D. Bond Rating History and Current Situation

The city of Dallas has held a continuous AAA bond rating from Moody's since 1973 and from Standard and Poor's since 1978. This highest achievable rating allows the city to sell bonds at a lower interest rate than would otherwise be possible. Many factors are assessed by the rating agencies in their determination of the creditworthiness of proposed debt. They have praised the city's effort to balance the budget in a tough economic environment. They also have expressed some concern with several relevant economic indicators, including population, employment, assessed valuation, and sales tax revenues. In particular, the increasing share of the total tax rate that is devoted to DS is being carefully watched. In FY 1984–1985, DS comprised 24.5% of the total tax rate. In FY 1988–1989 it was 32.0%. Both bond rating agencies have warned that future ratings could be jeopardized by adverse developments in the city's economy, financial position, or debt burden.

The AAA rating is a tangible asset of the city, saving millions of dollars in interest costs over the years. Interest rates on AA bonds could be expected as much as 10 to 47 basis points higher than AAA bonds. The historical interest rate comparison among AAA, AA, and A ratings is included in Appendix III. It was estimated this difference would amount to $1.5 million in additional costs on the general obligation (GO) bond issue of $55.9 million in October 1988 had they been issued as AAs.

Efforts to maintain the AAA rating have led to caution on the size of annual bond sales. Smaller bond sales place limits on the amount of construction funds available. The suggestion has been made by several area economists that the city should issue additional debt in order to take advantage of relatively low construction costs and provide infrastructure improvements to stimulate economic development. The potential for economic development must be weighed against higher tax rates, higher per capita debt burdens, and the prospect of additional costs due to the reduction of the AAA rating if this course of action is to be chosen.

E. Financial Management Performance Criteria

The financial management performance criteria (FMPC) are a measure of management effectiveness and fiscal responsibility of the bond programs and associated bonded indebtedness. Because debt level and structure are important factors in credit ratings, an issuance rate that overburdens the city may lead to rating downgrades. However, low debt burden may be perceived as evidencing underinvestment in the infrastructure and thus an impediment to future economic growth. With so many variables involved in the management of debt, an effective management tool is essential. The FMPC adopted by the city council in March 1978 provides benchmarks to guide managerial decisions in efficient city operations. It also provides a means of communicating the city's performance measures to the city council and bond rating agencies. The criteria pertaining

Table 4 Immediate Needs (1989–1990)

Project	Cost estimate ($000's)
North Central Expressway R-O-W	11,846
North Central Expressway outfall (phases I & II)	31,868
Flood protection—Middle Five Mile Creek	Amounts and sources being reviewed

to the capital program and debt management define acceptable levels of bonded indebtedness and are standards used in determining the financial stability of the city. The FMPC are calculated for each bond issuance, for proposed budget recommendations, and to determine the city's financial status as of the end of the fiscal year. The criteria set limits on net GO debt, overlapping debt, bond maturities, annual GO debt, and per capita debt.

Criteria are noted below.

* Any capital project financed through the issuance of bonds shall be financed for a period not to exceed the expected useful life of the project.

Prudent use of debt dictates that the bond's term matches the useful life of the facilities being financed.

* The net (non-self-supporting) GO debt of Dallas will not exceed 4% of the true market valuation of the taxable property of Dallas.

This evaluates the relative level of outstanding bonded indebtedness to the tax base and sets limitations on net GO debt.

* Total direct plus overlapping debt shall be managed so as not to exceed 8% market valuation of taxable property of Dallas.

This criterion sets limitations on overlapping debt of all local jurisdictions. An overly burdened municipality may be subject to a rating downgrade by financial analysts.

* Average (weighted) GO bond maturities shall be kept at or below 10 years.

This criterion is calculated based on the total outstanding principal payments weighted by the number of years remaining to pay. This is a measure of swiftness of debt retirements.

* Annual GO DS (contribution) shall not exceed 20% of the total locally generated, nonenterprise, operating revenue.

This criterion compares annual DS to annual GF revenue. Annual GF revenues include funds generated by property, sales, alcohol, and franchise taxes; licenses and permits; fines and forfeitures; and service charges. The 20% criterion is a sensitive measuring tool and fluctuates as debt is incurred or decreased and as GF revenues are increased or remain stagnant. Financial analysts consider this ratio to be the true measure of debt capacity. Particular attention has been given to this criterion in recent years as it has exceeded 19% due to increasing debt service costs without an accompanying increase in GF revenues.

This relationship is measured as follows:

DS = Net debt service contribution (debt service revenues net of transfers from enterprise funds)
GF = Locally generated, nonenterprise, operating revenue (total general fund revenue less inter-governmental and interfund revenues)

$$\frac{DS}{GF + DS} \leq 20\%$$

Table 5 provides the city's historical performance and projected values for the 20% criterion for FY 1985–1986 through FY 1990–1991.

The criterion is gradually moving toward the 20% cutoff and exceeds the limit in FY 1990–1991 under the current projected bond sale schedule and GF revenue estimates.

Key to the 1985 bond program 20% criterion was the assumption of continued growth in the tax base.

Table 5 Performance and Project Values of the 20 Percent Criterion (FY 85–86 through 90–91)

FY 85–86	FY 86–87	FY 87–88	FY 88–89	Estimate FY 89–90	Projected FY 90–91	Projected FY 91–92	Projected FY 92–93
17.27%	19.57%	19.40%	19.31%	19.61%	20.58%	21.39%	19.74%

Continued tax base growth translates to increased GF revenues and the capacity to keep annual DS at a reasonable percentage (i.e., 15% to 20%) of overall revenues. Our actual experience reflects a flat tax base in FY 1987–1988 and FY 1988–1989 and a decline was projected for the next year. This produced flat revenues and an associated increase in the criterion. The percentage was projected to exceed 20% in FY 1990–1991. The FY 1981 to FY 1989 historical performance of FMPC pertaining to capital program and debt management is illustrated in Appendix IV.

II. POLICY OPTIONS ANALYSIS

Bond programs are issued as long-term financing for capital improvement projects. Bond financing of infrastructure improvements enables the cost to be spread out over the useful life of the project, normally 20 years. The bond program development process identifies projects by doing a needs assessment based upon a quantitative and/or qualitative set of criteria. Other criteria include projects having a legal mandate, projects that have strong citizen interest, or those of an ongoing nature. The city council reviews the proposed bond program, holds further public hearings and considers the impacts the program will have upon taxes, and the benefit to the quality of life in Dallas, as well as the infrastructure needs of the community. Once a new program is approved by the public, a long-range bond sale schedule is established, reviewed, and approved by the city council. The bond sale schedule is determined by the funding priorities of the program.

The current bond sale schedule allows completion of the 1985 bond program while maintaining a stable outstanding debt level and sustaining adequate cash needs for project construction (Table 6).

Given this schedule, current projected tax rate impact for the 1985 bond program follows in Table 7.

A. Project Priority and Debt Impact Analysis

In order to meet new and 1985 bond program priorities, without deferring current planned sales, the tax rate impact is shown in Table 8.

In addition to projects authorized in the 1985 bond program, new priority projects have arisen. In order to maintain good faith with the voters while accomplishing new priorities, increased debt could be issued. Advantages of this include completion of the 1985 bond program as planned, provide funding in alignment with current construction schedules, provide for urgent needs immediately, and promotion of economic development and job creation in the city. Disadvantages include increased tax rate impacts, increased outstanding debt, impact on GF for O & M impacts, and exceeding the FMPC 20% criterion. Because of the poorer economic conditions that currently exist, the priorities of many projects may be in need of reexamination. It is important to determine the current priorities for projects already funded and to examine priorities of projects which remain authorized but unissued in the 1985 bond program.

These currently unissued projects should also be reviewed to examine the possibility of deauthorizing them from the approved program. This would eliminate the need to sell bonds for these projects in the future, thereby increasing the city's capacity to fund new projects with higher priorities (e.g., North Central Expressway).

The following projects approved in the 1985 bond program are possible candidates for deauthorization as shown in Table 9.

Deauthorization of 1985 bond program projects could create additional capacity for the issuance of alternative debt (certificates of obligation) or a small bond program to fund new higher priority projects.

Table 10 illustrates the tax rate requirements due to the above deauthorizations.

The tax rate reduction due to this is shown in Table 11.

To accomplish the review of changing project priorities, the capital budget review committee should

Table 6 1985 Bond Program: Proposed Remaining Target Amounts ($000's)

FY 89–90	FY 90–91	FY 91–92
$67,526	$69, 960	$68, 148

Table 7 1985 Bond Program Tax Rate Need

	1988–89	1989–90	1990–91	1991–92	1992–93
Tax rate (cents)	17.31	17.17	18.19	20.41	22.14
Tax rate increase	(0.14)	1.02	2.22	1.73	(2.31)
Total tax rate (cents)	17.17	18.19	20.41	22.14	19.83
Additional tax revenue required		$4.9 M	10.9 M	8.7 M	(12.0 M)

Table 8

	FY 89–90	FY 90–91	FY 91–92	FY 92–93
1985 bond—planned schedule ($000's)	67,526	69,960	68,148	–0–
New priorities	–0–	43,714	–0–	–0–
Total bond sale	67,526	113,674	68,148	–0–
Total tax rate (cents)	18.19	20.94	23.19	20.81
Additional tax revenue	$4.9 M	13.5 M	11.3 M	(12.4 M)

Table 9 Possible Candidates for Deauthorization

	Remaining unissued ($ millions)
Multiple Services	
Dallas West Site Acq.	4.085
Dallas N. Service Ctr.	2.6
S. E. Equip. Service Ctr.	2.5
Street System	
Jefferson-Houston	2.0
Denton Drive-Webb Chapel to Lombardy	2.0
Fair Park Link	4.25
Total	17.435

Table 10

	FY 89–90	FY 90–91	FY 91–92	FY 92–93
1985 bond—planned ($000's)	67,526	69,960	68,148	–0–
Deauthorizations	–0–	–0–	(17,435)	–0–
Total sle amount	67,526	69,960	50,713	–0–
Total tax rate (cents)	18.19	20.41	21.97	19.45
Additional tax revenue required ($ million)	4.9 M	10.9 M	7.8 M	(13.1 M)

Table 11

	FY 89–90	FY 90–91	FY 91–92	FY 92–93
1985 bond—planned (cents)	18.19	20.41	22.14	19.83
With Deauthorizations (cents)	18.19	20.41	21.97	19.45
Reduction due to deauthorizations (cents)	–0–	–0–	0.17	0.38

undertake a new task to review priorities of new and unissued projects. This committee would meet on a semiannual basis to review currently approved projects and recommend to the city manager's office a list of projects to be eliminated. This list would be presented to the finance committee and ratified by the city council. Following council ratification, then citizens approve deauthorization.

Due to their urgency, several unfunded projects have been identified as new priorities, such as North Central Expressway project and flood protection for Middle Five Mile Creek. To deauthorize unsold 1985 bond program projects, the substitution of alternative debt issues for planned 1985 bond program issues would allow funding for the new priorities.

This would replace all or a portion of an annual 1985 bond program sale in order to maintain stable outstanding debt. This would lead to further protraction of the 1985 bond program, although it would maintain projected DS costs, tax impacts, and FMPC implications for the first 3 years.

In the following example a portion of the bond sale schedule would be replaced for the first 3 years by alternative debt issuance and then added back to the end of the schedule, thus expanding the 1985 bond program from 6 to 7 years. The tax rate impact for displacing a portion of the 1985 bond program with financing for new priorities such as Central Expressway right-of-way and ($11.8M) Central Expressway outfall ($31.9M) is shown in Table 12.

This schedule's impact would not differ from the current 1985 bond program schedule until FY 1992–1993. It would take an additional year to complete all 1985 bond projects. Projected annual tax increases would be the same as the planned schedule until FY 1992–1993.

Table 13 compares the planned 1985 bond program schedule to a schedule with funds for new priorities.

B. FMPC Sensitivity Analysis

If the present bond program was completed as scheduled, the 20% criterion (see Sec. II) for future years was estimated at (Table 14):
Under the current planned schedule, FY 1990–1991 exceeds the limit.

In order to reduce the FY 1990–1991 criterion to 20%, one of three options must be chosen:

1. Debt service must decrease. Debt service must decrease by approximately $4.2 million in FY 1990–1991 in order to meet the criterion. This represents a total bond sale reduction of approximately $70 million

Table 12 Tax Rate Impact for Displacing a Portion of the 1985 Bond Program

	1989–90	1990–91	1991–92	1992–93
1985 bond program ($000's)	67,526	26,246	68,148	43,714
Deauthorization	0	0	0	(17,435)
New priority sale schedule ($000's)[a]	0	43,714	0	0
Total sale amount ($000's)	67,526	69,960	68,148	26,279
Tax rate impact (cents)	1.02	2.22	1.73	(2.00)
Total tax rate (cents)	18.19	20.41	22.14	20.14
Additional tax revenue required ($ million)	4.9 M	10.9 M	8.7 M	(10.4 M)

[a]Includes North Central Expressway; does not include flood protection for Middle Five Mile Creek.

Table 13 Debt Service Incremental Tax Rate Increase (cents per $100 valuation)

Program option	1989–90	1990–91	1991–92	1992–93	1993–94
1985 bond—planned schedule	1.02	2.22	1.73	(2.31)	(1.54)
Substitution w/new priorities deauthorization	1.02	2.22	1.73	(2.00)	(1.27)
Net impact	–0–	–0–	–0–	0.31	0.27

by FY 1990–1991. In order to stay within the 20% criterion with the assumption of long-range financial forecast (LRFF) revenues, the bond sale schedule must be limited as follows in Table 15.
2. General fund revenues must increase. General fund revenues in FY 1990–1991 must increase by approximately $17.5 million above the LRFF projected level. To balance at 20% for future years, the following GF revenue increases above LRFF levels must be realized (Table 16).
3. A combination of DS decrease and GF revenue increase must occur. The combination of bond sale and GF revenues is a modified approach to stay within the 20% criterion. It will reduce the impact on the bond sale schedule and increase funds to meet O & M needs, but it would impact the tax rate, user fees, and future new priority projects. Table 17 illustrates alternative combinations of these two factors by reducing DS and increasing locally generated revenues which would reduce the FY 1990–1991 criterion to below 20%.

The above analysis examines and balances FY 1990–1991 only. In order to maintain the FMPC criterion below 20% for all years, the following exemplifies one combination of bond sale schedule and GF revenue adjustments needed (Table 18).

With the economy still in a sluggish condition and no anticipated growth in the tax base, the city may need to exceed the 20% limit for a short period of time or increase the limit in order to complete the 1985 bond program as currently scheduled. This may be necessary if the city is to continue investment in its infrastructure improvement with no offsetting GF increases from property taxes. It should be noted that GF increases are not only fueled by property tax increases but increases in other revenue streams; fines, licenses, permits, and service charges should also be explored.

The downside to a criterion exceeding 20% is the possibility of a negative bond rating response. Presently, Standard and Poor's measures the debt burden against the tax base and considers debt burden high when DS exceeds 20% of the combined GF and DS contribution.

As part of any future bond program process, the city should consider a new FMPC to limit the size of a proposed program. The methodology to develop a new criterion will be presented to the finance committee and ratified by council at a later date.

C. Extended Bond Maturity Schedules

Currently, the city issues bonds with 20-year maturities. Lengthening the maturity schedule to 25 or 30 years is an option available to reduce annual requirements in the front of the schedule, but total financing costs over the entire length of the schedule increases. Appendix V details the estimated payment schedules for the currently scheduled October 1989 $67.5 million sale. It shows that while the annual requirements are lower for the 25- and 30-year schedules for the first 15 years compared to the 20-year schedule, total interest costs increase from $54.9 million for the 20-year schedule to $65.5 million and $78.7 million for the 25- and 30-year schedules, respectively. Table 19 compares average annual costs, interest rates, and total interest savings for each maturity schedule.

Table 14

FY 89–90	FY 90–91	FY 91–92	FY 92–93	FY 93–94	FY 94–95
19.61%	20.58%	21.39%	19.74%	18.79%	17.91%

Table 15

	1989–90	1990–91	1991–92	1992–93
Bond sale	67.5 M	–0–	36.0 M	102.1 M
Criterion	19.61%	19.99%	19.99%	18.97%

Table 16

	FY 89–90	FY 90–91	FY 91–92	FY 92–93
GF revenues	–0–	17.5 M	40.5 M	–0–

Table 17

	Option A (FY 90–91)	Option B (FY 90–91)
DS decreases	$1 M	2 M
GF increases	$13.5 M	11.5 M
Criterion	19.96%	19.89%
Equivalent bond Sale reduction	16.8 M	33.7 M

Table 18

	FY 89–90	FY 90–91	FY 91–92	FY 92–93
Bond sale shedule ($000's)	67,526	53,160	38,148	46,800
GF revenue increase needed (above LRFF revenues)	–0–	13.5 M	26.6 M	–0–

Table 19

	20 years	25 years	30 years
Avergage annual cost	6.1 M	5.3 M	4.8 M
Interest rate	7.50%	7.55%	7.60%
Interest savings	22.8 M	12.6 M	–0–

In addition to lower interest rates and cost savings, 20-year maturity schedules more properly align financing with expected project life. Also, due to its more aggressive debt retirement, 20-year schedules are preferred by bond-rating agencies. Extended maturity schedules would also slow the city's debt retirement.

III. RECOMMENDATIONS

The city of Dallas has maintained sound capital improvements through various bond programs. Economic prosperity for the future of Dallas depends on the quality of its public facilities and services. Because of the size of the capital program and commitment to Dallas's tomorrow, the debt burden has increased through continued bond issuance. Therefore, in order to continue the city's infrastructure improvement while maintaining financial health and good bond ratings, examination of policy options has become necessary for the future capital improvement program. Policy alternatives for DS and the capital program must be continually examined to determine their adequacy and timeliness. Based on the above analyses the following alternatives are recommended:

- Deauthorize and defer lowest priority capital projects.
- Use alternate financing or small bond programs to fund new priority projects.
- Use a combination of reduced bond sales and increased GF revenues to stay within the 20% criterion.
- Continue the allocation of resources necessary to maintain the AAA rating.
- Consider a new FMPC to limit size of future bond programs.
- Meet new and 1985 priorities by increasing debt.
- Still under review is the $4.9 million DS gap. Consider reducing through project closeouts and excess interest earnings.

APPENDIX I: EXISTING DEBT STRUCTURE ON REMAINING PAYMENT SCHEDULES: BONDS

FY	$521,199,844 issue, 8-15-85 ($ in million)			$65,000,000 issue, 12-1-85 ($ in millions)			$122,319,000 issue, 5-1-86 ($ in millions)			$4,000,000 issue, series 1983 ($ in millions)		
	Prin.	Int.	Total	Prin.	Int.	Total	Prin.	Int.	Total	Prin.	Int.	Total
88–89	36.2	30.2	66.4	3.3	4.7	7.9	6.1	7.9	14.1	2.0	0.1	2.1
89–90	47.0	27.2	74.2	3.3	4.4	7.6	6.1	7.4	13.5			
90–91	44.7	23.8	68.5	3.3	4.1	7.3	6.1	6.9	13.0			
91–92	47.9	20.3	68.2	3.3	3.8	7.0	6.1	6.3	12.4			
92–93	43.5	16.7	60.2	3.3	3.5	6.7	6.1	5.8	11.9			
93–94	33.9	13.5	47.4	3.3	3.2	6.4	6.1	5.3	11.4			
94–95	15.2	29.7	44.8	3.3	2.8	6.1	6.1	4.7	10.8			
95–96	26.4	11.0	37.4	3.3	2.5	5.8	6.1	4.2	10.3			
96–97	25.7	8.8	34.5	3.3	2.2	5.5	6.1	3.8	9.9			
97–98	24.7	6.6	31.3	3.3	2.0	5.2	6.1	3.4	9.5			
98–99	23.5	4.5	28.0	3.3	1.7	5.0	6.1	3.0	9.1			
99–00	20.7	2.6	23.2	3.3	1.5	4.7	6.1	2.6	8.7			
00–01	18.3	0.8	19.1	3.3	1.2	4.4	6.1	2.2	8.3			
01–02	3.4	11.3	14.7	3.3	1.0	4.2	6.1	1.8	7.9			
02–03	2.9	11.0	13.9	3.3	0.7	4.0	6.1	1.4	7.5			
03–04	1.4	5.8	7.2	3.3	0.5	3.8	6.1	1.1	7.2			
04–05				3.3	0.3	3.6	6.1	0.7	6.8			
05–06				3.3	0.1	3.4	6.1	0.4	6.5			
06–07												
06–08												
08–09												
	415.2	223.8	639.0	58.5	40.2	98.7	110.1	68.8	178.8	2.0	0.1	2.1

$11,628,000 issue, 11-1-86 ($ in millions)			$76,545,000 issue, 11-15-87 ($ in millions)			$55,855,000 issue, 11-1-88 ($ in millions)		
Prin.	Int.	Total	Prin.	Int.	Total	Prin.	Int.	Total
0.6	0.7	1.3	3.8	5.5	9.3	0.0	3.3	3.3
0.6	0.7	1.2	3.8	5.2	8.9	1.9	3.8	5.7
0.6	0.6	1.2	3.8	4.8	8.6	2.8	3.7	6.4
0.6	0.6	1.2	3.8	4.5	8.2	2.8	3.5	6.2
0.6	0.5	1.1	3.8	4.1	7.9	2.9	3.3	6.1
0.6	0.5	1.1	3.8	3.8	7.6	2.9	3.1	5.9
0.6	0.4	1.0	3.8	3.5	7.2	2.9	2.9	5.7
0.6	0.4	1.0	3.8	3.1	6.9	2.9	2.7	5.5
0.6	0.4	0.9	3.8	2.9	6.6	2.9	2.5	5.3
0.6	0.3	0.9	3.8	2.6	6.4	2.9	2.3	5.1
0.6	0.3	0.9	3.8	2.4	6.1	2.9	2.1	4.9
0.6	0.3	0.8	3.8	2.1	5.9	2.9	1.9	4.7
0.6	0.2	0.8	3.8	1.8	5.6	2.9	1.7	4.5
0.6	0.2	0.8	3.8	1.5	5.3	2.9	1.5	4.3
0.6	0.1	0.7	3.8	1.3	5.0	2.9	1.3	4.1
0.6	0.1	0.7	3.8	1.0	4.8	2.9	1.1	3.9
0.6	0.1	0.6	3.8	0.7	4.5	2.9	0.9	3.7
0.6	0.0	0.6	3.8	0.5	4.2	2.9	0.7	3.5
0.6	0.0	0.6	3.8	0.2	4.0	2.9	0.5	3.3
						2.9	0.3	3.1
						2.9	0.1	2.9
11.0	6.4	17.4	71.7	51.4	123.1	55.9	43.1	99.0

Existing Debt Structure Remaining Payment Schedules: Notes

FY	$11,000,000 equip. note issue, 1-1-87 ($ in millions)			$2,720,000 equip. note issue, 5-1-87 ($ in millions)			$6,240,000 equip. note issue, 1-1-88 ($ in millions)			$6,295,000 equip. note issue, 5-24-89 ($ in millions)			Fiscal year totals for bonds and notes ($ in millions)		
	Prin.	Int.	Total	Prin.	Int.	Total	Prin.	Int.	Total	Prin.	Int.	Total	Prin.	Int.	Total
88–89	2.2	0.4	2.6	0.5	0.1	0.7	1.5	0.3	1.8	0.0	0.0	0.0	56.1	53.2	109.4
89–90	2.2	0.3	2.5	0.5	0.1	0.6	1.5	0.2	1.7	0.7	0.5	1.2	67.5	49.8	117.3
90–91	2.2	0.2	2.4	0.5	0.0	0.6	1.5	0.2	1.6	1.4	0.3	1.7	66.7	44.6	111.3
91–92	2.2	0.1	2.3	0.5	0.0	0.6	1.5	0.1	1.5	1.4	0.2	1.6	70.0	39.3	109.3
92–93										1.4	0.1	1.5	61.5	34.0	95.5
93–94										1.4	0.0	1.4	51.9	29.3	81.2
94–95													31.7	44.0	75.7
95–96													42.9	24.0	66.9
96–97													42.3	20.6	62.9
97–98													41.2	17.3	58.5
98–99													40.1	14.0	54.1
99–00													37.2	10.8	48.1
00–01													34.8	7.9	42.7
01–02													20.0	17.2	37.2
02–03													19.5	15.9	35.3
03–04													17.9	9.6	27.5
04–05													16.6	2.7	19.3
05–06													16.6	1.7	18.2
06–07													7.2	0.7	7.9
07–08													2.9	0.3	3.1
08–09													2.9	0.1	2.9
	8.8	0.8	9.6	2.2	0.2	2.4	5.8	0.8	6.6	6.3	1.3	7.5	747.4	436.9	1,184.3

APPENDIX II: COMPARISON WITH HOUSTON

GO Bond Issued Comparison

	Year after voter approval						Total
	Year 1	Year 2	Year 3	Year 4	Year 5	Remainder	
Dallas	90.0 M	–0–	76.5 M	55.9 M	67.5 M	205.6 M	428 M
	21%	21%	39%	52%	68%	100%	
Houston	100.1 M	55.0 M	90.1 M	157.2 M	–0–	192.6 M	595 M
	17%	26%	41%	68%	68%	100%	

Actual GO Expenditure Comparison

	FY 84–85	FY 85–86	FY 86–87	FY 87–88	Total
Dallas	82 M	129 M	127 M	125 M	463 M
Houston	54 M	118 M	116 M	102 M	390 M

APPENDIX III: ANNUAL AVERAGES 1960–1988

Year	Composite	Aaa	Aa	A
1988	7.56	7.35	7.48	7.59
1987	7.59	7.12	7.35	7.73
1986	7.32	6.95	7.16	7.43
1985	9.08	8.60	8.93	9.20
1984	9.94	9.61	9.88	10.15
1983	9.45	8.80	9.20	9.64
1982	11.63	10.88	11.31	11.84
1981	11.09	10.42	10.89	11.31
1980	8.34	7.84	8.06	8.44
1979	6.27	5.89	6.12	6.34
1978	5.87	5.52	5.68	5.99
1977	5.64	5.20	5.39	5.86
1976	6.61	5.65	6.12	7.17
1975	7.05	6.42	6.77	7.37
1974	6.19	5.89	6.04	6.30
1973	5.20	4.95	5.09	5.29
1972	5.30	5.04	5.19	5.38
1971	5.52	5.22	5.36	5.61
1970	6.41	6.12	6.28	6.49
1969	5.73	5.45	5.58	5.82
1968	4.48	4.20	4.31	4.54
1967	4.00	3.74	3.86	4.08
1966	3.90	3.67	3.76	3.95
1965	3.34	3.16	3.25	3.38
1964	3.29	3.09	3.19	3.32
1963	3.28	3.06	3.16	3.30
1962	3.30	3.03	3.17	3.32
1961	3.60	3.27	3.46	3.66
1960	3.69	3.26	3.51	3.77

APPENDIX IV: FINANCIAL MANAGEMENT PERFORMANCE CRITERIA (FY 1982–1989)

	FY 81–82	FY 82–83	FY83–84	FY 84–85	FY 85–86	FY 86–87	FY 87–88	FY 88–89
Any capital project financed through the issuance of bonds shall be financed for a period not to exceed the expected useful life of the project.			------	--Implemented--	------			
The net (non-self-supporting GO debt of Dallas will not exceed 4% of the true market valuation of the taxable property of Dallas.	1.61%	1.06%	1.10%	1.10%	1.19%	1.13%	1.18%	1.91%
Total direct plus overlapping debt shall be managed so as to not exceed 8% market valuation of taxable property of Dallas.	3.11%	2.27%	1.90%	2.30%	2.33%	2.29%	2.29%	2.39%
Interest, operating, and/or maintenance expenses will be capitalized only for enterprise activities.			------	--Implemented--	------			
Average (weighted) GO bond maturities shall be kept at or below 10 years.	7.78 years	7.56 years	8.06 years	7.55 years	7.80 years	7.04 years	6.80 years	6.64 years
Annual GO debt service (contribution) shall not exceed 20% of the total locally generated, nonenterprise, operating revenue.	13.25%	13.48%	15.60%	15.10%	17.27%	19.57%	19.40%	19.31%
Per capita GO debt will be managed to not exceed 10% of the latest authoritative computation of Dallas's per capita annual personal income.	4.64%	4.74%	4.90%	5.20%	4.775	4.54%	4.78%	4.82%

APPENDIX V: PROJECTED PAYMENT SCHEDULE

20-Year Bonds ($67.526 million sale)

Principal	Coupon rate	Interest	FY total
		0.00	
		4,220,375.00	4,220,375.00
3,306,000.00	7.500%	2,532,225.00	
		2,408,250.00	8,246,475.00
3,380,000.00	7.500%	2,408,250.00	
		2,281,500.00	8,069,750.00
3,380,000.00	7.500%	2,281,500.00	
		2,154,750.00	7,816,250.00
3,380,000.00	7.500%	2,154,750.00	
		2,028,000.00	7,562,750.00
3,380,000.00	7.500%	2,028,000.00	
		1,901,250.00	7,309,250.00
3,380,000.00	7.500%	1,901,250.00	
		1,774,500.00	7,055,750.00
3,380,000.00	7.500%	1,774,500.00	
		1,647,750.00	6,802,250.00
3,380,000.00	7.500%	1,647,750.00	
		1,521,000.00	6,548,750.00
3,380,000.00	7.500%	1,521,000.00	
		1,394,250.00	6,295,250.00
3,380,000.00	7.500%	1,394,250.00	
		1,267,500.00	6,041,750.00
3,380,000.00	7.500%	1,267,500.00	
		1,140,750.00	5,788,250.00
3,380,000.00	7.500%	1,140,750.00	
		1,014,000.00	5,534,750.00
3,380,000.00	7.500%	1,014,000.00	
		887,250.00	5,281,250.00
3,380,000.00	7.500%	887,250.00	
		760,500.00	5,027,750.00
3,380,000.00	7.500%	760,500.00	
		633,750.00	4,774,250.00
3,380,000.00	7.500%	633,750.00	
		507,000.00	4,520,750.00
3,380,000.00	7.500%	507,000.00	
		380,250.00	4,267,250.00
3,380,000.00	7.500%	380,250.00	
		253,500.00	4,013,750.00
3,380,000.00	7.500%	253,500.00	
		126,750.00	3,760,250.00
3,380,000.00	7.500%	126,750.00	
		0.00	3,506,750.00
67,526,000.00		54,917,600.00	122,443,600.00

25-Year Bonds ($67.526 million sale)

Principal	Coupon rate	Interest	FY total
		0.00	
		4,248,510.83	4,248,510.83
2,726,000.00	7.550%	2,447,181.50	
		2,446,200.00	7,619,381.50
2,700,000.00	7.550%	2,344,275.00	
		2,344,275.00	7,388,550.00
2,700,000.00	7.550%	2,242,350.00	
		2,242,350.00	7,184,700.00
2,700,000.00	7.550%	2,140,425.00	
		2,140,425.00	6,980,850.00
2,700,000.00	7.550%	2,038,500.00	
		2,038,500.00	6,777,000.00
2,700,000.00	7.550%	1,936,575.00	
		1,936,575.00	6,573,150.00
2,700,000.00	7.550%	1,834,650.00	
		1,834,650.00	6,369,300.00
2,700,000.00	7.550%	1,732,725.00	
		1,732,725.00	6,165,450.00
2,700,000.00	7.550%	1,630,800.00	
		1,630,800.00	5,961,600.00
2,700,000.00	7.550%	1,528,875.00	
		1,528,875.00	5,757,750.00
2,700,000.00	7.550%	1,426,950.00	
		1,426,950.00	5,553,900.00
2,700,000.00	7.550%	1,325,025.00	
		1,325,025.00	5,350,050.00
2,700,000.00	7.550%	1,223,100.00	
		1,223,100.00	5,146,200.00
2,700,000.00	7.550%	1,121,175.00	
		1,121,175.00	4,942,350.00
2,700,000.00	7.550%	1,019,250.00	
		1,019,250.00	4,738,500.00
2,700,000.00	7.550%	917,325.00	
		917,325.00	4,534,650.00
2,700,000.00	7.550%	815,400.00	
		815,400.00	4,330,800.00
2,700,000.00	7.550%	713,475.00	
		713,475.00	4,126,950.00
2,700,000.00	7.550%	611,550.00	
		611,550.00	3,923,100.00
2,700,000.00	7.550%	509,625.00	
		509,625.00	3,719,250.00
2,700,000.00	7.550%	407,700.00	
		407,700.00	3,515,400.00
2,700,000.00	7.550%	305,775.00	
		305,775.00	3,311,550.00
2,700,000.00	7.550%	203,850.00	
		203,850.00	3,107,700.00
2,700,000.00	7.550%	101,925.00	
		101,925.00	2,903,850.00
2,700,000.00	7.550%	101,925.00	
		0.00	2,801,925.00
67,526,000.00		65,506,417.33	133,032,417.33

30-Year Bonds ($67.526 million sale)

Principal	Coupon rate	Interest	FY total
		0.00	
		4,276,646.67	4,276,646.67
2,276,000.00	7.600%	2,480,488.00	
		2,479,500.00	7,235,988.00
2,250,000.00	7.600%	2,394,000.00	
		2,394,000.00	7,038,000.00
2,250,000.00	7.600%	2,308,500.00	
		2,308,500.00	6,867,000.00
2,250,000.00	7.600%	2,223,000.00	
		2,223,000.00	6,696,000.00
2,250,000.00	7.600%	2,137,500.00	
		2,137,500.00	6,525,000.00
2,250,000.00	7.600%	2,052,000.00	
		2,052,000.00	6,354,000.00
2,250,000.00	7.600%	1,966,500.00	
		1,966,500.00	6,183,000.00
2,250,000.00	7.600%	1,881,000.00	
		1,881,000.00	6,012,000.00
2,250,000.00	7.600%	1,795,500.00	
		1,795,500.00	5,841,000.00
2,250,000.00	7.600%	1,710,000.00	
		1,710,000.00	5,670,000.00
2,250,000.00	7.600%	1,624,500.00	
		1,624,500.00	5,499,000.00
2,250,000.00	7.600%	1,539,000.00	
		1,539,000.00	5,328,000.00
2,250,000.00	7.600%	1,453,500.00	
		1,453,500.00	5,157,000.00
2,250,000.00	7.600%	1,368,000.00	
		1,368,000.00	4,986,000.00
2,250,000.00	7.600%	1,282,500.00	
		1,282,500.00	4,815,000.00
2,250,000.00	7.600%	1,197,000.00	
		1,197,000.00	4,644,000.00
2,250,000.00	7.600%	1,111,500.00	
		1,111,500.00	4,473,000.00
2,250,000.00	7.600%	1,026,000.00	
		1,026,000.00	4,302,000.00
2,250,000.00	7.600%	940,500.00	
		940,500.00	4,131,000.00
2,250,000.00	7.600%	855,000.00	
		855,000.00	3,960,000.00
2,250,000.00	7.600%	769,500.00	
		769,500.00	3,789,000.00
2,250,000.00	7.600%	684,000.00	
		684,000.00	3,618,000.00
2,250,000.00	7.600%	598,500.00	
		598,500.00	3,447,000.00
2,250,000.00	7.600%	513,000.00	
		513,000.00	3,276,000.00
2,250,000.00	7.600%	427,500.00	
		427,500.00	3,105,000.00

Principal	Coupon rate	Interest	FY total
2,250,000.00	7.600%	342,000.00	
		342,000.00	2,934,000.00
2,250,000.00	7.600%	256,500.00	
		256,500.00	2,763,000.00
2,250,000.00	7.600%	171,000.00	
		171,000.00	2,592,000.00
2,250,000.00	7.600%	85,500.00	
		85,500.00	2,421,000.00
2,250,000.00	7.600%	85,500.00	
		0.00	2,335,500.00
67,526,000.00		78,748,134.67	146,274,134.67

APPENDIX VI: BOND SCHEDULE, DEBT SERVICE, AND CAPITAL PROGRAM

A. Issues

This appendix examines many important issues in DS and capital program relating to the City of Dallas. They include

- What is the current status of the 1985 and 1989 bond programs?
- What options could be considered for future bond sales?
- What is the DS tax rate impact related to these schedules?
- What impact do these schedules have on the city's FMPC?
- What has been the trend of expenditures in DS over the last 10 years? What is projected?
- What are bond rating factors?
- Can commercial paper be an innovative financing alternative for general purpose capital improvement projects?
- What is our future capital improvement program plan?

B. Background

Historically, the city of Dallas has held bond programs every 3 to 4 years, with the most recent in 1989. Bond programs provide for the construction of assets with a long-term life. General obligation debt programs are approved by the citizens of Dallas and this debt is backed by the "full faith and credit" of the city. The issuance of bonds once they are authorized by the voters is dependent upon economic and financial factors. As bonds are issued, they are rated by bond rating agencies. This rating provides investors with an indication of the relative creditworthiness of the bonds.

The costs of bonds (i.e., principal and interest) are budgeted as DS. The primary source of revenue for the DS is the ad valorem tax. State law establishes that the tax rate for DS be separate from the rate for operations. Specific FPMC have been developed to monitor bonded indebtedness. The 20% criterion is most often cited as the guideline for DS. This criterion specifies that annual contributions to DS cannot exceed 20% of total locally generated, nonenterprise operating revenue.

The bond programs of 1978, 1979, 1982, 1985, and 1989 authorized a total of $954,187,000 in bond sales. Almost 45% of this amount was authorized in 1985. The 1982 bond program represents the next significant percentage with 26% of the total, while the 1978 bond program is 17%. The 1979 and 1989 bond programs each represent approximately 6% of the total authorizations from 1978–1989 (Table 20).

Street and traffic control improvements received 52% of the total authorization. Park and recreation, cultural and library facilities improvements received 27%; 12% was authorized for flood protection; and 9% was authorized for public safety and municipal service projects (Table 21).

1. Outstanding Debt

General obligation bonds are a direct obligation of the city for which its full faith and credit are pledged, and are payable from taxes levied on all taxable property located within the city. Although GO bonds are pledged

Table 20 Bonds Authorized Status (000's)

Year	Amount	Percent
1978	163,735	17.16
1979	54,622	5.72
1982	247,070	25.89
1985	428,060	44.86
1989	60,700	6.37
Total	954,187	100.00

to be paid from property tax revenues, some of the city's outstanding debt is self-supporting from contributions from other sources. The difference between total outstanding debt and self-supporting debt is the net oustanding net, that amount supported by property tax revenues. Table 22 illustrates the trend of GO outstanding debt for the last 10 years.

Figure 1 illustrates the amount of outstanding GO debt per person in Dallas.

2. Debt Service Tax Rate Impact

In 1982–1983, the DS portion of the property tax rate was 11.76¢. The current DS tax rate is 21.72¢. The DS tax rate was 23% of the total tax rate in FY 1982–1983. The DS tax rate for FY 1991–1992 is 34.5% of the total tax rate. The DS tax rate has had an annual average increase of 7.38% over the 10 years from FY 1982–1983 to FY 1991-1992. Table 23 provides a 10-year history of the city's DS tax rate.

3. Bond Program Development

General obligation bonds are issued as long-term financing for capital improvement projects. Bond financing of infrastructure improvements allows the cost to be spread out of the useful life of the project, which is normally 20 years.

The bond program development process identifies projects by doing a needs assessment based upon a quantitative and/or qualitative set of criteria. Other criteria include legal mandates, strong citizen interest, or ongoing projects. The city council reviews the proposed bond program, holds public hearings, and considers the impacts the program will have upon taxes, the benefit to the quality of life in Dallas, as well as the infrastructure needs of the community.

Once a new program is approved by the public, a long-range bond sale schedule is established, reviewed, and approved by the city council. The bond sale schedule is developed, based on several factors which include funding priorities of the program, affordability of DS within the financial management guidelines approved by the city council, and the availability of O & M funds within the operating budget.

Economic factors which affect the city's ability to issue and service new debt include interest rates, assessed property values, and the amount of GO debt currently outstanding. The fact that the city of Dallas has held a Aaa bond rating continuously from Moody's since 1973 and held a AAA bond rating from Standard and Poor's since 1978 has resulted in interest cost savings.

Assessed property value influences the city's ability to service outstanding debt and afford new debt

Table 21

1978–1989 bond programs authorized	Percent
Street and traffic control improvements	52.15
Parks & rec. and cultural improvements	26.59
Flood protection	12.46
Public safety and municipal services	8.80
Total	100.00

Table 22   Outstanding GO Debt: 10-Year
History (millions)

FY	Total	Net
82–83	456.5	386.1
83–84	457.9	456.5
84–85	510.6	521.2
85–86	674.6	606.9
86–87	644.4	656.3
87–88	685.5	664.0
88–89	691.3	631.7
89–90	697.1	635.7
90–91	635.4	569.2
91–92 (budget)	593.0	520.9

issues. As property values rise, the city has more revenue available to meet DS obligations. Conversely, as property values fall, managing new debt costs at an existing DS tax rate is impacted.

4.   Current Practice and 1985 and 1989 Bond Program Status

The slowdown in the local economy in recent years placed greater pressure on the DS tax rate than was assumed in 1985. The following practices have been undertaken to minimize the impact:

- The program was lengthened initially to a 6-year schedule and ultimately to a 9-year schedule. The current schedule anticipates the last 1985 bond sale in the first quarter of FY 1993–1994.
- Bonds are issued in amounts equal to principal amounts retired each year. This action levels the total outstanding debt.
- Impact on O & M costs are examined prior to issuing bonds. Facilities which have an operating cost impact (recreation centers, fire stations, libraries) have been deferred to minimize impact on the GF. New fire station construction has been scheduled to open one station per fiscal year.
- Bonds are issued on 20-year schedules with equal annual principal payments. This "level principal" structure is an aggressive method of retiring debt, quickly reducing outstanding indebtedness.
- Bonds are sold at a "discount" rather than at "par." When bonds are sold below face value or "discount," the underwriter derives a profit by getting 1% of the sale proceeds up front and structuring the bonds at a market interest rate throughout their maturity schedule. At "par," bonds trade at the face value and the underwriter derives profit by structuring above-market interest rates in the early years. For example, discounting all DS cash flows to present value could save approximately $600,000 on a $50 million bond sale at 7.5% over a 20-year period.
- Interest rates and economic conditions are assessed on an ongoing basis for refunding opportunities by city staff and the city's bond counsel.

5.   1985 and 1989 Bond Program Status

The city has currently issued 57.53% of the 1985 bonds authorized. The status of the 1985 bond program is shown in Table 24:

The 1989 bond program authorized $60.7 million in capital improvement projects identified as critical needs. The 1989 bond program provides for Central Expressway right-of-way acquisition, outfall drainage, and flood protection improvements for Middle Five Mile Creek and Rochester Area Levee. With $8.5 million remaining to be sold, the 1989 bond program is 86% issued.

6.   Capital Program Alternatives under Examination

Continuous examination and review of existing bond authorizations are conducted for opportunities to reduce DS requirements of existing bond programs should the property tax base decline. The primary focus of review is to identify opportunities for reprioritization of existing (issued) bond projects and reprogramming of existing unspent bond proceeds. The reviews are conducted in such a way as to ensure that equity within the city is

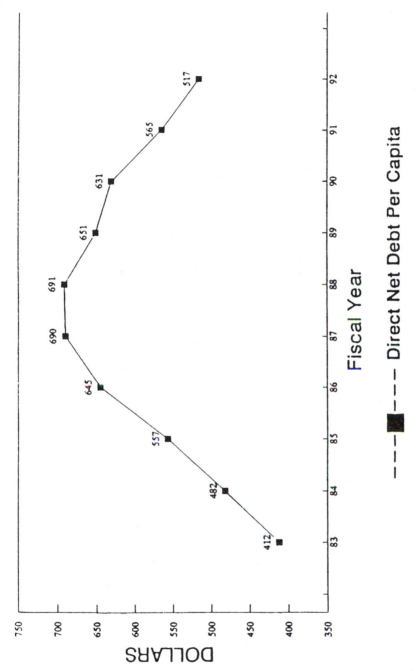

Figure 1 Dallas general obligation debt per capita for fiscal years 1983–1992.

Table 23 Debt Service Tax Rate Trend

FY	Cents
82–83	11.76
83–84	11.83
84–85	12.05
85–86	12.68[a]
86–87	15.96[a]
87–88	17.31[a]
88–89	17.17
89–90	17.17
90–91	20.25
91–92	21.72

[a]Reflects primary impact of loss of federal revenue sharing.

addressed. Identification of these funds continues as an ongoing effort by the responsible construction departments and budget and research.

7. Bond Sale Schedule Development

As part of the annual budget development process, project schedules are examined and the bond sale schedule is developed to align funding with (1) anticipated construction schedules, (2) availability of O & M funds for new capital facilities, (3) availability of fund cash balances, and (4) compliance with the FMPC. Bonds are sold only for projects which are ready for construction and will have O & M funds available when the facility is opened. Table 25 outlines the bond sale status for the 1985 and 1989 bond programs.

Of the $298.5 million issued to date, $221.3 million was for street system and flood protection improvements. Compared to other facilities improvement projects, this type of capital improvement does not require significant O & M costs, but assists in the enhancement and preservation of the tax base by providing infrastructure beneficial to economic development.

8. Current and Alternate Bond Sale Schedules

The current bond sale schedule (option A) with two anticipated issuances was identified during fiscal year 1990–1991 and fiscal year 1991–1992. The current bond sale schedule would issue $90.4 million in bonds

Table 24 Current Status of 1985 Bond Program (000's)

Program	Authorized	Issued	Remaining
Arts District land preservation	$28,000	$28,000	–0–
Dallas Zoo improvements	12,000	8,300	3,700
Fair Park improvements	9,375	5,779	3,596
Fire protection facilities	13,527	4,896	8,631
Library services facilities	1,943	50	1,893
Park and rec. fac. & improvements	39,811	22,539	17,272
Police and multiple Svc. Fac.	19,510	6,505	13,005
Solid waste disposal fac.	2,120	1,100	1,020
Storm drainage flood protect. fac.	56,049	33,571	22,478
Street system improvements	244,525	135,511	109,014
Trinity Park	1,200	–0–	1,200
Total	$428,060	$246,251	$181,809
Percentage	100%	58%	42%

Table 25 1985 & 1989 Bond Sale Status (000's)

	Previous issued	Remaining issue
1985 program	$246,251	$181,809
1989 program	52,200	8,500
Total	$298,451	$190,309

during the first quarter of fiscal year 1992–1993, and the remaining $99.9 million in the first quarter of FY 1993–1994.

In addition, two alternate bond sale schedules are examined. Option B provides for one sale which would allow completion of the 1985 and 1989 bond programs by fiscal year 1992–1993. This schedule would issue the entire amount of $190.3 million in fiscal year 1992–1993. Option C provides for reducing the issue amounts and extending the current bond sale schedule for 2 years to eliminate projected tax rate increases which are reflected in both the option A and option B bond sale schedules.

All three schedules shown below assume a decline in the tax base of 3.9% in FY 1992–1993, and an additional decline of 2.0% in FY 1993–1994, followed by 1.0%, 2.0%, and 3.0% increases in subsequent years. In addition, these bond sale options do not include issuance of certificates of obligation for Fair Park of $9.7 million or Walker consent decree debt of $13.2 million.

The advantages of option A (Table 26) include:

- The 1985 bond program would be issued in 9 years.
- It balances affordability with citizen expectations.
- The required tax increase in FY 1993–1994 is minimal compared to option B.

The disadvantage of option A is

- It requires tax rate increases in FY 1993–1994 and FY 1994–1995.

The advantages of option B (Table 27) include:

- It completes the 1985 bond program.
- It is the most aggressive issuance option.

Its disadvantage is that

- It requires the most significant tax increase of three options.

The advantage of option C (Table 28) is that

- There is no tax rate impact.

Its disadvantages include

- The 1985 bond program is extended beyond 10 years.
- It likely delayed the next bond program.
- It creates significant pent-up demand.

Given the above three schedules, the projected tax rate impact for the 1985 and 1989 bond program is as follows in Tables 29, 30, and 31.

Table 26 Option A: Current Schedule, 1985 and 1989 Bond Programs ($000's)

	FY 92–93	FY 93–94	FY 93–94	FY 94–95	Total
1985 bond programs	$81,885	$99,924	–0–	–0–	$181,809
1989 bond programs	8,500	–0–	–0–	–0–	8,500
	$90,385	$99,924	–0–	–0–	$190,309

Table 27 Option B: One Sale Schedule, 1985 and 1989 Bond Programs ($000s)

	FY 92–93	FY 93–94	FY 93–94	FY 94–95	Total
1985 bond programs	$181,809	–0–	–0–	–0–	$181,809
1989 bond programs	8,500	–0–	–0–	–0–	8,500
	$190,309	–0–	–0–	–0–	$190,309

Table 28 Option C: No Tax Rate Increase Schedule, 1985 and 1989 Bond Programs ($000s)

	FY 92–93	FY 93–94	FY 94–95	FY 95–96	Total
1985 bond programs	$81,885	$30,000	$46,000	$23,924	$181,809
1989 bond programs	8,500	–0–	–0–	–0–	8,500
	$90,385	$30,000	$46,000	$23,924	$190,309

Table 29 Option A: Current Schedule, 1985 and 1989 Bond Programs Tax Rate Need

	FY 92–93	FY 93–94	FY 94–95	FY 95–96
Additional tax revenue required (000's)	–0–	1,239	5,939	–0–
Tax rate (cents)	21.72	21.72	22.02	23.43
Tax rate increase	–0–	.30	1.41	–0–
Total tax rate (cents)	21.72	22.02	23.43	23.43

Table 30 Option B: One Sale Schedule, 1985 and 1989 Bond Programs Tax Rate Need

	FY 92–93	FY 93–94	FY 94–95	FY 95–96
Additional tax revenue required (000's)	–0–	12,481	–0–	–0–
Tax rate (cents)	21.72	21.72	24.72	24.72
Tax rate increase	–0–	3.00	–0–	–0–
Total tax rate (cents)	21.72	24.72	24.72	24.72

Table 31 Option C: No Tax Rate Increase Schedule, 1985 and 1989 Bond Programs Tax Rate Need

	FY 92–93	FY 93–94	FY 94–95	FY 95–96
Additional tax revenue required (000's)	–0–	–0–	–0–	–0–
Tax rate (cents)	21.72	21.72	21.72	21.72
Tax rate ncrease	–0–	–0–	–0–	–0–
Total tax rate (cents)	21.72	21.72	21.72	21.72

Note: Interest rate is based on 6.25% for all new bond issues.

9. Preservation of Bond Authorization

All bond authorizations are expected to be issued within 10 years. Although bonds remaining unissued after 10 years can be nullified at the discretion of the attorney general, there are two measures that can be taken that may preserve the bond authorization should it become necessary to extend issuance of the 1985 bond program beyond 10 years as with option C.

The first measure for extending a bond authorization is by council statement stating that the needed projects remaining unissued after 10 years are deferred, not abandoned. The resolution could be prepared in conjunction with each upcoming bond issuance resolution. A statement was included in the resolution authorized by the city council when $8.5 million in GO debt was issued in April 1991. Second, at the time of issuing the deferred project bonds, certification would be required stating the reasons for the delay. The city has received approval from the attorney general for this process of preserving the authorization.

10. Financial Management Performance Criteria

The FMPC are primarily measures of management effectiveness and the fiscal responsibility of bonded indebtedness. Their purpose is to communicate performance to the city council, the public, and the bond rating agencies.

The FMPC were adopted by the city council in March 1978 as standards to guide managerial decisions and to promote efficient city operations. The criteria pertaining to capital programs and debt management define acceptable levels of bonded indebtedness and are standards used in determining the financial stability of the city. The criteria set limits on net GO debt, overlapping debt, bond maturities, annual GO debt, and per capita debt. One of the most significant indicators of the city's financial management strategy is the 20% criterion. Under this criterion, the city's annual contribution to DS shall not exceed 20% of the total locally generated nonenterprise operating revenue.

Below are the projected FMPC 20% criteria for the current and both alternate bond sale schedules (Table 32). These projections assume GF revenues remain constant based on the FY 1991–1992 budget. Under these assumptions, the city does not exceed the FMPC 20% criterion under any of the three bond sale schedule scenarios.

11. Operating and Maintenance Impact

In addition, the GF will be required to absorb new costs as a result of completing projects in the 1985 bond program. Of the remaining 1985 bonds to be issued, a substantial portion in the amount of $56.8 million has associated O & M costs that will impact the GF budget. The remaining issues have relatively higher O & M costs due to the city's past cost reduction practice of issuing debt for projects that have little or no O & M cost impact. The following tables illustrate the O & M impact associated with all unissued bonds for the next 5 years based on the option A (Table 33) and option B (Table 34) bond sale schedules. Although the O & M

Table 32

Option A: Projected FMPC 20% Criteria—Current Schedule			
FY 92–93	FY 93–94	FY 94–95	FY 95–96
17.62%	18.44%	18.71%	17.31%

Option B: Projected FMPC 20% Criteria—One Sale Schedule			
FY 92–93	FY 93–94	FY 94–95	FY 95–96
18.05%	19.54%	18.66%	17.26%

Option C: Projected FMPC 20% Criteria—No Tax Rate Increase Schedule			
FY 92–93	FY 93–94	FY 94–95	FY 95–96
17.62%	18.13%	17.82%	17.06%

Table 33 Option A: Projected Operating and Maintenance Impact—Current Schedule

	92–93	93–94	94—95	95–96	96–97
Total O & M cost ($000's)	$803	$1,735	$2,678	$2,424	$2,426
Tax rate increase (cents)	0.18	0.21	0.22	–0–	–0–

cost associated with option C bond sale schedule is anticipated to be less than the other two options, it cannot be accurately determined until the specific projects are identified from each bond sale.

C. Debt Service Trend Analysis and Forecast

As a result of conservative debt management practices, the city is now approaching a reversal in its increasing DS expenditure trend. Debt service expenses have, as shown in Table 35, increased 69% in actual dollars and 15% in constant dollars over the 10-year period from FY 1982–1983 to FY 1991–1992.

Projections of DS expenditures, for both the current bond sale schedule and both alternate schedules, indicate a downward trend has begun. This trend is demonstrated in Table 36 and in Figure 2.

1. Refunding Opportunity Analysis

As interest rates have declined, the city's financial advisors along with city staff have monitored the market for refunding opportunities to reduce DS costs. The Tax Reform Act of 1986 specifies that bonds issued before January 1, 1986 may be refunded two times. Due to restrictions imposed by the Tax Reform Act of 1986, "opportunity costs" became a significant factor in analyzing the cost savings associated with an advance refunding. A recommended threshold for accounting for this opportunity cost is a present value savings equal to 5% of the amount of the refunded bonds.

Current refunding consideration includes a portion of the series 1985 refunding bonds, the series 1985A bonds issued in December of 1985, and the 1987 bonds. The refunding of these three series has a present value savings expressed as a percentage of refunding bonds of 5.95%. This is based on current market rates as of January 28, 1992. The refunding of these series, in the amount of $174,450,000, results in an aggregate DS reduction to the city of approximately $23,563,589 and present value savings of approximately $9,482,129.

D. Bond Rating Factors

The purpose of bond ratings is to provide investors with an indicator of the relative creditworthiness of specific debt obligations. The rating serves as an opinion of the issuer's ability and willingness to repay its debt obligations, and it affects overall perceptions in the market and the probable reception of the offering by investors. Maintenance of Dallas' AAA rating is related to the city's willingness to pay debt obligations through a tax increase and/or its willingness to reduce bond sale amounts to lighten debt burden and ensure that the city has the ability to pay its obligation.

Bond ratings are assigned upon request of the issuer each time an issue is brought to market. A higher bond rating will result in a lower interest rate. Ratings are affected by a variety of objective and subjective indicators related to the city's economic, debt, fiscal, and administrative factors. No single factor is viewed as most important, and each area is weighted within the context of its potential impact on the issuer's ability and willingness to repay the debt.

Table 34 Option B: Projected Operating and Maintenance Impact—One Sale Schedule

	92–93	93–94	94–95	95–96	96–97
Total O & M cost ($000's)	$792	$2,661	$2,441	$2,373	$2,374
Tax rate increas (cents)	0.18	0.43	–0–	–0–	–0–

Table 35 Debt Service 10-Year Expenditure History

	Actual dollars	1982 constant dollars	FMPC (20%)
1982–83	70,036	70,036	13.48%
1983–84	69,605	64,499	15.60%
1984–85	73,068	65,239	15.10%
1985–86	77,998	68,419	17.27%
1986–87	96,759	81,999	19.57%
1987–88	102,737	83,526	19.64%
1988–89	109,385	84,795	19.07%
1989–90	119,233	87,671	18.28%
1990–91	119,857	84,406	18.76%
1991–92 (budget)	118,436	80,569	18.79%

1. Economic Factors

The economy is probably the least controllable and often the most difficult factor in credit analysis. It is important for an area to offer economic diversity in its tax and service base. The bond rating agencies during recent ratings have been particularly concerned with the city's unemployment rate and future employment prospects, and the growth (decline) in the tax base. In addition the rating agencies examine building permit numbers and dollar value, the leading taxpayers' assessed value, per capita effective buying income trends in retail sales, and other indicators to measure the sensitivity of a municipal government's financial condition to the performance of the local economy. Job creation and adequate income levels are elements used in measuring the city's ability to repay debt. Demonstrating strength in past economic performance and future outlook should result in favorable debt ratings.

2. Debt Factors

Debt factors include the type of security being pledged to debt repayment, overall debt burden, and debt history. Debt burden is measured against certain aspects of the ability to repay, including the municipality's total budget resources. Debt history trends as well as future projected debt needs are other rating factors. Control of debt position is particularly critical to any kind of rating analysis.

   The relationship between the magnitude of debt to be repaid and the perceived benefit to be derived from the uses of that debt has become very critical. A municipal government desiring a good bond rating should be able to demonstrate both effective planning and public necessity for undertaking the proposed capital projects, as well as proving economic feasibility.

3. Fiscal and Financial Factors

Regardless of economic, spending, and tax realities, the city must balance its budget. Therefore, annual operating performance and year-end position are the ultimate measures of management's control. The balance

Table 36 Five-Year Debt Service Expenditure Projection (000's)

	92–93	93–94	94–95	95–96	96–97
Option A—current schedule	111,120	106,405	108,488	98,773	93,840
Option B—one sale schedule	114,242	114,524	108,175	98,460	93,528
Option C—no tax rate increase schedule	111,120	104,220	102,059	97,047	94,133

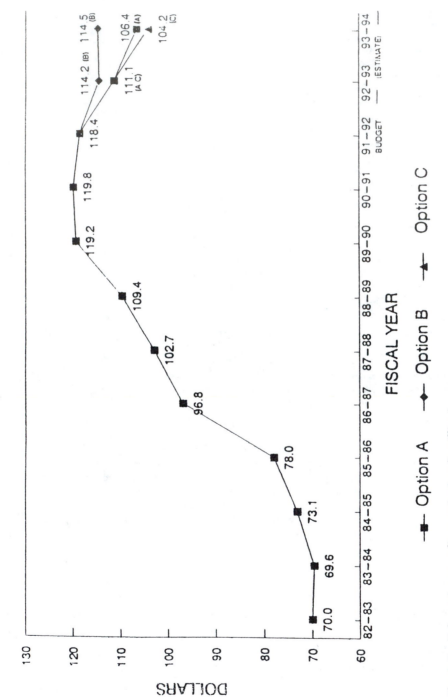

Figure 2   Debt service expenditure projections (in millions).

sheet for the operating account is examined with emphasis on current financial position and fund balances, as well as trend analysis. Rating agencies are also concerned with the reduction of liability exposure through risk management as well as active and prudent investment of cash balances.

The degree of flexibility in providing municipal services is a relevant concern of the rating agencies. Some proportion of budgeted expenditures is likely to be fixed, including debt payment, contractual obligations, and pension liabilities. Prudent funding of expenditures is therefore critical for maintaining good bond ratings.

4. Administrative and Management Factors

A rating is also based on judgment of how well the city's policy makers and management run its operations. Thus, the quality of policy and management decisions is a significant consideration in the rating process. For example, the tax rate, levy limitations, debt limitations, and current unused margin are important policy and management decisions. The city council's willingness to make hard decisions can lead to a high-grade credit. Although the local economic base usually is not under the direct control of the city council and management, the resolve to make a determined response to economic fluctuations becomes an important credit consideration. Management turnover ratio, legal and political restraints evident in the issuing entity's structure, and environment are also evaluated.

Rating agencies are concerned with the city's ability and willingness to pay its obligations. Bonds which are rated Aaa or AAA are judged to be of the best quality, because they carry the smallest degree of investment risk. The city of Dallas has held the longest continuous Aaa rating from Moody's (since 1973) and AAA from Standard and Poor's (since 1978) of cities with an estimated population over 400,000. The ratings agencies continue to praise the city's efforts to take the difficult steps required to balance the budget in a tough economic environment. However, both agencies expressed some concern with several relevant economic indicators, including population, employment, assessed valuation, and sales tax revenues; and various financial indicators, including fund balances and reserve balances. Both rating agencies have warned that future ratings could be jeopardized by adverse developments in the city's economy, financial position, or debt burden.

E. Commercial Paper

Commercial paper is a project funding source that has been successfully used by Dallas Water Utilities. Rather than increasing the revenue bond debt by funding projects that may not have immediate cash requirements, commercial paper is used to support project awards. At a later date when the outstanding commercial paper reaches a sufficient level, revenue bonds are issued to provide for commercial paper retirement. This results in lower DS costs and provides for greater cash flow flexibility.

Commercial paper authorizations are approved quarterly by the city council for Water Utilities construction projects. On January 8, 1992, the city council approved a $15.8 million authorization for the second quarter of FY 1991–1992. The issue brought the total commercial paper outstanding to a projected $61.9 million as of March 31, 1992. The maximum limit of commercial paper outstanding at any one time is $100 million.

Aside from commercial paper being used for interim short-term financing, it is also used to refinance, or roll over, previously issued commercial paper. Only the principal amount of the paper is rolled over. The interest is paid when it is due from Water Utilities' operating funds budgeted for DS.

There are several advantages to using commercial paper rather than revenue bonds alone. First, since commercial paper is not classified as long-term debt, there is no affect on the equity ratio or coverage ratio. Second, commercial paper can be issued on an "as-needed" basis rather than "in bulk," as with bond sales. This decreases the amount of total debt outstanding. Finally, as presented in the Water Utilities Department's commercial paper quarterly progress report, as of December 31, 1991, a $16.3 million present value savings has been realized with commercial paper and refunding bonds, as compared with financing through revenue bonds only. This is due to the lower interest costs of commercial paper. Dallas's commercial paper carries the highest rating given both by Standard & Poor's Corporation and Moody's Investors Service.

There are two disadvantages to commercial paper. First, the secondary market activity is very limited. The limited activity is based on the nature of commercial paper being short-term. Maturities range from 1 to 270 days, with an average maturity of 30 to 60 days. The limited secondary market is not a major disadvantage when the short maturity of commercial paper is considered.

Perhaps the primary disadvantage of commercial paper is that it must be supported by a pledge of revenue bonds. State law prohibits commercial paper from being secured by a pledge of GO bonds. This limits commercial paper to be used only by revenue-generating entities or enterprise funds such as Dallas Water Utilities.

A bill in the last Texas legislative session that would have allowed commercial paper to be guaranteed by the pledge of GO bonds failed in the House of Representatives. According to Texas Municipal League staff, the bill will be reintroduced at the next legislative session. The Government Finance Officers Association of Texas (GFOAT) has prepared legislation and asked the Texas Municipal League to lobby for the removal of the prohibition of pledging ad valorem taxes to support short-term securities such as commercial paper. Allowing commercial paper to be backed by ad valorem taxes would let the city use commercial paper to support general purpose capital improvement projects which currently are supported by GO bonds. This option could be quite helpful in providing immediate interim financing for continued work on high-priority or urgently needed projects. Under this scenario, commercial paper could be issued just before a contract award date without the GO bonds being issued. When the GO bonds were issued at their scheduled date, the bonds could then provide for retirement of the commercial paper.

In order to utilize commercial paper as an interim financing mechanism for GO projects, development of policy guidelines (i.e., ceiling and FMPC) and procedures would be required. For example, the Water Utilities commercial paper policy guidelines limit the amount of commercial paper that may be outstanding, not to exceed $100 million at any time. Once the outstanding commercial paper reaches this limit, it is retired with an issuance of bonds.

F. Future Capital Improvement Program Plan

Historically, bond elections have been held every 3 to 4 years; however, development of new bond programs has been impacted by economic constraints.

1. Election Date Information

State law requires that the ordinance formally calling a bond election must indicate the date of the election, the propositions to be voted on (exact ballot wording), and the polling places to be used. The law further requires the ordinance be passed not less than 15 days or more than 90 days prior to the date of the election. The ordinance can be passed any time within that period. (For example, the ordinance calling the August 3, 1982 election was passed on June 16, 1982; the ordinance calling the November 5, 1985 election was passed on September 4, 1985.)

A sufficient amount of time is necessary for proper election administration. Administration of an election improves when more time is available. As absentee balloting begins 20 days prior to the election, an approximate 45-day lead time between the calling of the election and the election day is recommended. State Election Law, Sec. 41.001 (1987) requires election dates be held on the uniform election dates unless the city council, by resolution or ordinance, finds in a conclusive and incontestable manner, that holding the election on a date other than a uniform election date is in the public interest. Uniform election dates are as follows:

Third Saturday in January
First Saturday in May
Second Saturday in August
First Tuesday after the first Monday in November

Bond elections do not have to be held on uniform election dates. An election could be anticipated during the fall of 1993 or after the complete issuance of the 1985 and 1989 bonds.

2. Development Process and Capital Improvements Planning

The bond program development process generally begins with a council workshop to determine needs for and timing of the next bond program. Given the council's direction, the city manager appoints a staff bond task force to examine which projects from a staff perspective should be considered for inclusion as part of the next bond referendum. These projects are identified by doing a needs assessment based upon a quantitative and/or qualitative set of criteria, such as the relationship between the volume of traffic on certain streets and the need for upgrading. Other criteria include projects having a legal mandate, projects having strong citizen interest, or those of an ongoing nature. During this time, the city council holds a series of advertised public hearings and town hall meetings to gather preliminary citizen input. Workshops are held with the city council regarding projects currently under consideration and public comments. Based upon the input of the city council during the workshops, the city manager attaches priorities to the projects and finalizes the proposals for the council. The proposal also includes an effort to determine future operating expenses, revenues, and savings by project.

The city manager's proposal is then submitted to the city council, which reviews the proposed bond program, holds further public hearings, and considers the various impacts the program will have upon taxes, the benefit and quality of life in Dallas, as well as the infrastructure needs of the community. The city council completes review and approves the final program proposal which will be put to a public vote. At this point, the city council seeks citizen volunteers to serve on the Dallas City Bond Committee. This committee raises funds for the bond program promotion from private sources and promotes the program.

Once a new program is approved by the public, a long-range bond sale schedule is established, reviewed, and approved by the city council. The bond sale schedule is determined by the funding priorities of the program. These schedules are reexamined each year during the capital budget development process to ensure that capital project priorities are being met within the tax levy limit, that the O & M cost of new capital facilities are available, and that the FMPC are being maintained.

3. Candidate Projects

Candidate projects for the new bond program would include Walker consent decree mandates and projects which included only engineering funding in prior bond programs, as well as new infrastructure priorities. Departmental staff recently developed a list of candidate projects for a future bond program. A summarized version of the potential projects is provided in section H.

G. Recommendations

Given the city's revenue requirements to meet DS obligations as well as provide for its infrastructure, the recommendations listed below will be incorporated into the FY 1992–1993 budget process:

- Continue to meet urgent infrastructure needs.
- Provide updated analysis based on revised projections of the tax base.
- Continue to assume current bond sale schedule.
- Modify schedule if needed based on updated analysis.
- Reexamine projects identified in FY 1992–1993 sale to ensure equity of allocation.
- Monitor issuance against availability of GF monies for O & M costs.
- Continue to examine refunding opportunities to minimize tax impact for future fiscal years.
- Proceed with development of future bond program.
- Refer commercial paper alternative to legislative committee for consideration in city's legislative package.

H. Potential Projects for New Bond Program

Economic development
Public/private partnership
Street system improvement program
Neighborhood petition street paving
 (current backlog of 42 petitions for $10,820)
Neighborhood petition alley paving
 (current backlog of 10 petitions for $300)
Reconstruction of streets
Reconstruction of alleys
Reconstruction of curb, gutter, sidewalks
Resurfacing
 (current backlog of over 260 lane miles)
Sidewalk improvements/barrier-free ramps
 (current backlog of 4 projects for $120)

Street modifications and bottleneck removals
 (current backlog of 25 projects)
Advanced acquisition for street right-of-way
Railroad crossing improvements
Barrier-free ramps (ADA new requirements)
Subdivision participation paving
Street and freeway lighting
Participation with other government agencies
 (includes FAUs, pass, county bond program thoroughfares, intersections, and TXDOT interchanges)
County and state participation projects
 (additional supplemental requirements)
Denton Drive and Denton/Hines connection from Webb Chapel to Farmers Branch city limit
Haskell–East Grand to Fitzhugh
Oak Lawn IH 35E to Maple
Red Bird Ln.—Duncanville Rd. to Cockrell Hill
Regal Row—CRI&P RR to IH 35E
Singleton—Hampton to Canada
IH 30 ramps/frontage rds. at Fair Park
IH 30 ramps/frontage rds. for racetrack
IH 30 ramps at Beckley
Parkdale Drive Bridge UPRR
Dickerson St. at Osage Branch
Stemmons/Thornton bypasses (10% row participation)
LBJ Freeway corridor improvements
Highway construction amenities
Sidewalk improvement participation at DART stations
Street paving/intersection IMPS near DART stations
Reconstruction of bus lanes
Fair Park area streets
Dallas City Center improvements, phase II
Landscaping improvements on thoroughfares
Bridge repair and modifications
Houston Street viaduct restoration
Target neighborhood paving program
Major and secondary thoroughfares
Arts District street/Streetscape IMPS
CBD projects
Trolley expansion
Downtown greenspace, including Jubilee Commons
Peak/Bryan phase II/Bryan Burley St.
Old City Park expansion
PIDs
 Uptown
 Downtown
 Residential
State—Thomas TIF
South Port area/Foreign Trade Zone
Traffic signal improvements
Storm drainage improvements
Miscellaneous erosion control projects
 (current backlog of 32 projects)
Major erosion control projects/8 projects
Floodplain mgt. drainage projects
 (road, bridge, channel improvements)/161 projects
Floodplain mgt. drainage projects:

remove over 1100 structures on 60 projects
Storm drainage relief systems over $100,000:
 52 projects/77 flooded structures
Storm drainage relief systems less than $100,000:
 35 projects/55 flooded structures
Street and private property flooding:
 23 projects
Floodplain mgt. studies
Flood alert system expansion
Trinity Floodway System improvements/4 projects
Police and multiple services
Police academy phase I
 (includes pistol range, driving course, and classrooms)
New police headquarters
Mounted patrol headquarters—Pan American Bldg. Fair Park
Major maintenance of city facilities
 (includes roofing, mechanical systems, asbestos/hazardous material/abatement, landscaping amenities)
Northeast offices for street and sanitation
Northwest sanitation office (replacement)
Southeast operations site acquisition/site development
Communications: replace 12 microwave towers
Radio tower—WRR (repaint)
Microwave link in lieu of cable
ADA accessibility (retrofit existing facilities)
Library facilities
Branch renovations/abatement (17 branches)
Replacement furnishings (10 branches)
Central library replacement furnishings/carpet/shelving
Graphics package for library system
Mall kiosks (4)
Fire protection facilities
New headquarters (Dolphin Rd.)
Retrofit existing stations w/diesel exhaust systems
Station replacements (including site acq.)
 Sta. 34—8003 Lake June
 Sta. 35—3822 Walnut Hill
 Sta. 36—3241 N. Hampton
 Sta. 27—8401 Douglas
 Sta. 31—9365 Garland Rd.
 Sta. 25—4607 S. Lancaster Rd.
 Sta. 33—754 W. Illinois
Public health facilities
Health clinic expansion—Los Barrios
New office/clinic, East Dallas
Multipurpose in Pleasant Grove
Expand West Dallas Multipurpose
Cultural affairs
Freedmans Cemetery
Artist Square, phase II, theater/studio
Neighborhood cultural centers
Opera/performing arts feasibility study
Other major improvements
Parking facilities—Dallas City Center Main Street improvements
GIS/DALIS systems
Farmers Market revitalization, phases II, III

Park and recreation improvement projects
Building additions—various sites
Gym floor replacements—various sites
HVAC replacements—various sites
Recreation center construction—3700 block of Dixon
Recreation center construction—Grauwyler Park
Recreation center construction—Randall Park
Recreation center construction—Rhodes Terrace Park
Recreation center construction—Umpress Annex Park
Recreation center construction—George B. Dealey (replacement)
Facility construction—Crawford Maintenance Center (replacement)
Facility construction—Mt. Creek Lake Maintenance Center (replacement)
Building renovations—various sites
Roof replacements—various sites
Courts/slabs new construction and replacement—various sites
Equipment replacement—various sites
Erosion control improvements—various sites
Fair Park master plan implementation
Cotton Bowl renovations
Hall of State renovations
Athletic field improvements—various sites
Handicapped access—various sites
Land acquisition—general parkland
Land acquisition—open space
Lighting improvements—various sites
Master plan implementation—various park sites
Paving/parking lot improvements—various sites
Park road overlays—various sites
Trail paving improvements—various sites
Pool construction—Redbird Park
Pool improvements (handicapped access)—various sites
Pool renovations (miscellaneous)—sites not specified
Site improvement—various sites
Zoo renovations—various facilities
Wilds of Africa additions—various facilities

16

Intergovernmental Cooperation Produces a Comprehensive Debt Management Program in Saint Paul, Minnesota

Gary Norstrem, Greg Blees, and Eugene Schiller
Department of Finance, City of Saint Paul, Saint Paul, Minnesota

During the late 1960s and early 1970s, general obligation debt was being issued by the city of Saint Paul, Minnesota (population 264,782) and its various overlapping governmental units at an extremely rapid pace. As a result, by year end 1976 the total outstanding overlapping general obligation (GO) debt was $286,522,000, or $983.46 per capita. This situation placed Saint Paul among the cities having the highest per capita debt in the nation. As the debt grew, the rating agencies looked more closely at Saint Paul and eventually the city's bond rating dropped from AAA to AA.

These activities were not going unnoticed by city staff or the elected officials. The elected officials, aware of the necessity to maintain and upgrade the infrastructure, were deeply concerned that the financing means to do so be addressed. In March 1975, the city council passed a resolution which pledged communication with other political subdivisions within the city so that mutual capital financing needs could be discussed, priorities established, and the citizens advised of the combined taxing impact of such political subdivisions. Early in 1976, the Budget Office circulated a work program for a city bond consultant and a request for a proposal for a comprehensive study of its debt and bonding policies.

The newly elected mayor, George Latimer, upon taking office in June 1976, requested three actions of city council

- Approval of the $6.0 million in 1976 capital improvement bonds, instead of the previously approved $6.5 million; approval of $1.0 million instead of the requested $1.5 million in Housing Rehabilitation Program bonds; and approval of $660,000 in water revenue bonds
- Approval of the funds necessary to formulate a GO debt policy for the city tax base
- Approval of a unified capital improvement program and budget process for the city of Saint Paul

It was at this time also that the Minnesota Taxpayers Association released a report analyzing Saint Paul's overlapping GO debt, stating that it was excessive and had a stranglehold on the city.

I. JOINT DEBT ADVISORY COMMITTEE

The concerns for the total amount of GO debt pledged against the Saint Paul property tax base—both directly and indirectly—prompted the mayor and council to pursue a debt policy which would continue to maintain

---

Adapted from *Government Finance Review*, April 1989: 17–20 by permission of the Government Finance Officers Association.

and develop the city's infrastructure while, at the same time, reducing the GO tax burden. The council provided funding for a consultant to study all bonding activities contemplated by all governmental subdivisions that issue bonds against the Saint Paul property tax base. And upon the recommendation of the mayor, officials of the major governmental units relying on the city tax base agreed to meet to address bonding needs and the overlapping debt situation.

On April 15, 1977, a joint debt advisory committee was formed, consisting of the

- Mayor, council president, and two council members of Saint Paul
- School board chair, vice chair, and clerk of Independent School District #625
- Board president and two commissioners of the Port Authority of Saint Paul
- Board chairman and two commissioners of the county of Ramsey

A technical advisory staff was appointed to assist the Joint Debt Advisory Committee. Led by Saint Paul's budget director, it included staff from each of the participating governmental entities, along with their fiscal consultants.

It was mutually agreed at the first meeting that elected officials, staff, and the citizens all needed a better understanding of GO debt. The first meeting also resulted in decisions to review joint-use policies, to attempt to determine annual bonding priorities, and to identify opportunities for joint planning, joint funding, and joint legislation.

In the months that followed, the fiscal consultants, the advisory committee technicians, and the committee studied the above issues and developed an estimate of general needs for GO bonding during the 10 years ending 1985. Bonding priorities were identified by each entity and there was discussion relating to priorities within entities, but at no point during the development of the first plan was it necessary to recommend any reductions from what was presented as needs. All were accommodated.

II. REDUCING OVERLAPPING DEBT

The following goals for reducing GO debt by 1985 were adopted by the Saint Paul city council in January 1978:

- The reduction of Saint Paul's GO debt per capita for all local government units from $983 to $900 or less per person
- The reduction of Saint Paul's GO obligation debt as a percentage of market value for all local government units from 8.5% to 6% or less.

The above goals had been formally endorsed by the Joint Debt Advisory Committee in December. As there was some reluctance by other governing bodies to formally adopt these goals, similar resolutions were not brought before them.

During the following 10 years, Saint Paul's city treasurer and budget director closely monitored GO per capita debt and debt as a percentage of market value. Progress on the adopted goals was tracked and reported to the citizens, elected officials, and rating agencies annually, in conjunction with the city's sale of GO debt, but the goals were not updated.

By 1985, the results were more pleasing than had been expected. Overlapping GO debt outstanding had declined from $286,522,000 in 1976 to $223,908,000 in 1985, as shown in Fig. 1, and the per capita debt, at $836.07, was substantially lower than the $900 target figure. General obligation debt as a percentage of market value, expected to drop from 9.4% to 6% during the 10 years, had actually dropped to 3.5% by year end 1985. A good share of this decline was brought about by substantial reductions in school district debt.

Sparked by this success and the need for new long-term overlapping debt goals, the mayor in May 1986 invited the same governing bodies to reconvene and develop a new GO bonding policy for financing the communities' capital needs under the direction of Saint Paul's new director of finance and management services. Of special concern at this time was the significant reduction in federal grants available for financing capital improvements and economic development. The mayor also invited the chairs of the local delegations of the state legislative delegation, who are responsible for gaining approval of the respective capital improvement bonding authorization at the state legislature. This is an alternative to referendum in Minnesota. The reconvened Joint Debt Advisory Committee consisted of fewer members from each local government entity than did the original committee.

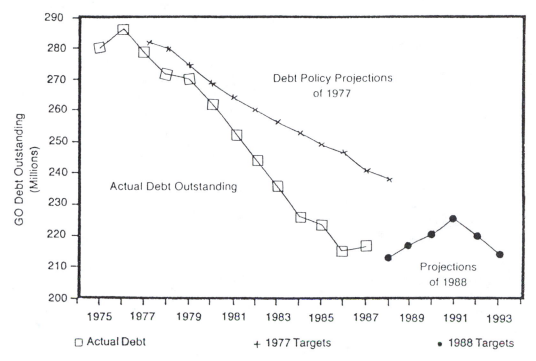

Figure 1   Saint Paul overlapping GO debt (city, port authority, school, county).

III. A NEW DEBT REDUCTION PLAN

Preliminary discussions of the committee determined that a 10-year plan, such as the original, entailed too long a time frame for realistic assumptions and projections. A 5-year plan, updated annually, was viewed as more realistic due to the variety of rapidly changing federal, state, and local funding mechanisms and mandated changes that drastically impact local government financing programs. The committee first developed and set forth a mission statement and specific goals and objectives (see Fig. 2), which were considered necessary to successfully implement an effective 5-year debt strategy.

Each government unit was then requested to develop a plan for its individual capital needs for the next 5 years. This was difficult for the county, which traditionally had issued very few GO bonds but now faced substantial needs for facilities for expanded county services and road repair as well as a decision whether to remodel or build a new county administrative building which also housed the court system. Staff representatives from the various units of government worked together in the development of these plans and, with considerable effort, molded all the component plans into a master plan for the committee's review.

The committee, evaluating the data on existing and projected GO bonding, grouped the GO bond issues into the following major categories for each unit of government:

- Property tax-financed debt
- General obligation debt financed with dedicated revenue sources
- Tax increment-financed GO debt

This classification highlighted the important distinction between GO bond issues, which are financed by citywide property taxes, and those issues that have revenue sources other than a citywide tax levy.

The committee also reviewed an inventory of capital projects to be considered for financing during the 5 years of the plan. Projects were sorted by the following broad categories: new facilities, facility expansion, facility replacement, facility rehabilitation, consolidation/joint use, energy retrofitting, handicap accessibility, streets/sewers, and private development inducement.

During this data-gathering process, committee members met with representatives of the two major rating

Mission Statement

To develop and update on an annual basis a five-year general
obligation debt policy for the St. Paul tax base which
recognizes the long-range capital program needs of the City
of St. Paul, Independent School District #625, St. Paul Port
Authority, Ramsey County government; and the tax payers'
ability to pay.

Goals/Objectives

*To establish reasonable debt level targets which recognize
 projected inflation and planned capital needs for each unit
 of government.
*To seek opportunities to finance capital projects with
 revenues other than general obligation bonding.
*To seek opportunities to finance debt service for general
 obligation bonds with revenues other than property taxes.
*To structure debt retirement to relate more closely to those
 who benefit.
*To produce a debt policy which will maintain and improve
 our credit ratings.
*To coordinate the scheduling of bond sales.
*To jointly support bonding programs for legislative approval
 for the city, port authority, county and school district.
*To consider opportunities such as refinancing, restructuring
 or redefeasance of existing general obligation debt which
 would reduce existing debt service.

Originally adapted: September 3, 1986
Reviewed and revised: January 28, 1988

Figure 2   Joint Debt Advisory Committee.

agencies—Standard & Poor's and Moody's Investors Service—in an attempt to improve bond ratings. The
feedback from both agencies was that they were impressed with the joint cooperation and communication
exhibited by the city of Saint Paul, the county of Ramsey, the Port Authority, and the Saint Paul School
District.

The fiscal consultant prepared a new debt study, and presented it to the committee. This 1986 report,
Debt Comparison of the City of Saint Paul with Comparable Cities, compared credit data used by Moody's
Investors Service in the ranking of Saint Paul and 20 similar cities and documented the change from 1977
to 1986 in a number of key debt measures and ratios. The report found Saint Paul ranking far below the
20-city average in total overlapping GO debt in 1986, whereas in 1977 it was more than 50% above the
average. The report stated, "The city's most marked improvement is a 40.5 percent reduction of overlapping
debt compared to an average 40.0 percent increase for the 20 cities analyzed." This positive achievement
was viewed as testimony to the fact that a commitment by elected officials to a joint debt/GO planned bonding
policy can produce desirable results.

It should be noted that this report found that the GO direct and overlapping debt ratio as a percent of
full market value averaged 3.3% for the 20 cities analyzed, and was 4.1% for Saint Paul. This finding became
the basis for the major goal statement of the Joint Debt Advisory Committee recommendations.

After reviewing existing debt schedules as well as the consultant's report and rating considerations with
representatives from the rating agencies, the committee examined the projected bonding proposals identified
by each unit of government. These proposals were considered against the trend of reduced federal financing
for local improvements and tax base development, and against the projected impact on property tax levies

for Saint Paul taxpayers. From this multifaceted review, the Joint Debt Advisory Committee's findings and recommendations were set forth on January 1987. The recommendations are displayed in Fig. 3.

The findings and recommendations were packaged with a substantial amount of relevant information and documentation and forwarded by Mayor Latimer to the legislative body of each unit of government with a request that they be formally endorsed. Within 60 days, formal resolutions were adopted by all units: the city of Saint Paul, Ramsey County, the Port Authority of Saint Paul and Independent School District #625. These resolutions are meaningful in Minnesota because capital improvement bonding authority is granted by the legislature. It has been helpful for the state policy makers to have assurance that officials of all the governmental entities were working together in the best interest of Saint Paul citizens.

Figure 1, which shows the GO debt reduction progress made between 1975 and 1987, also illustrates the projected targets for each year through 1993.

IV. STATUS REPORT

The process works well today and is helpful to all units of government. The "Five-Year Debt Management Strategy," as this program now is referred to, was updated in late 1987 with projections for 1989 through

---

RECOMMENDATIONS
January 20, 1987

1. The elected officials representing the citizens of Saint Paul adopt as their major debt goal:

   By 1992, the maximum amount of overlapping general obligation debt for the Saint Paul tax base should not exceed 3.5 percent of the estimated market value of taxable properties.

2. In order to meet the 1992 debt goal, the following targets for general obligation debt as a percent of estimated market value should be strived for by each unit of government:

City of Saint Paul	2.5% of city tax base
Port Authority	0.1% of city tax base
Independent School District	0.25% of city tax base
Ramsey County	1.0% of county tax base

3. The Ramsey County legislative delegation should support the following requests for general obligation bonding authority:

   City of Saint Paul:
   CIB and Urban Renewal Bonding:

1988	$12,100,000
1989	$12,900,000
1990	$13,700,000
1991	$14,500,000
1992	$15,400,000

   Saint Paul School District:
   Construction and Remodeling Bonding:

1987	$15,000,000 to $17,000,000

Ramsey County:
General Purpose Bonding

1987	$8,500,000
1988	$8,500,000
1989	$8,500,000
1990	$8,500,000
1991	$8,500,000
1992	$8,500,000

Cityhall and Courthouse Infrastructure Repair Bonding:

1987	$20,000,000

Building Space Needs:

1988	$30,000,000*

Port Authority:
No GO Bonding Authority Is Being Requested

*Preliminary figure used by the Joint Debt Advisory Committee prior to actual determination of need by Ramsey County Board of Commissioners.

4. The Joint Debt Advisory Committee should reconvene each November to review and update the five-year strategy for controlling overlapping general obligation debt for the Saint Paul tax base.

5. Beginning in February of 1988 an annual *Status Report Of Overlapping General Obligation Debt* should be prepared by the mayor's office in order to measure progress towards the Joint Debt Advisory Committee's 1992 goal. The status report should be distributed to the Saint Paul City Council, the Port Authority, the Ramsey County Board of Commissioners, the Saint Paul School Board and the Ramsey County legislative delegation.

Figure 3   1986 Joint Debt Advisory Committee representing the Saint Paul tax base.

CreditComment

St. Paul's innovative debt management

This week's $14.5 million sale of St. Paul, Minn.'s general obligation bonds is the first issue under an innovative five-year debt management strategy that is drawing national attention *(see analysis, page 26)*. Four governments overlapping the St. Paul tax base are being brought together in one of the rare occasions that neighboring municipalities coordinate a policy to finance the area's capital needs. The plan addresses the concern that increasing debt can adversely affect capital planning as well as municipal bond ratings, particularly where overlapping governmental units compete for resources.

St. Paul's strategy could become a model for other municipalities. Given declines in federal grants and revenue sharing, which many localities had used to finance capital needs, tax-supported debt is likely to assume a larger role in municipal capital financing. This can become a problem, especially for fast growing suburban areas and older cities that are replacing infrastructure. In many cases, increasing debt is compounded because an area's counties, cities, school districts, and other special districts issue debt independently and do not coordinate their plans with underlying or overlapping jurisdictions. (All participants have G.O. bond ratings of 'AA +' except for the school district which is not rated.) The result can be unexpectedly rapid increases in an area's overall debt, which overburdens taxpayers and could affect credit quality.

Coordinated bonding policy

To prevent this in St. Paul, Mayor George Latimer convened a meeting in 1986 of representatives of St. Paul, Ramsey County, St. Paul Independent School District 625, and the Port Authority of St. Paul to develop a coordinated G.O. bonding policy. The plan was written by a joint debt advisory committee, and was adopted as public policy during 1987 by each respective governing body.

A schedule of participants' bond sales for 1988–1992 was developed and will be updated annually. The goal is to maintain overlapping G.O. net debt at not more than 3.5% of taxable properties' market value and $860 on a per capita basis. The advisory committee based the plan on conservative projections for tax base and population growth. Total debt issuance reflects only the highest priorities of the four units' capital plans, after taking into account dedicated revenue streams to finance G.O.

St. Paul area's plan to share debt

	New G.O. debt (mil. $)		—Total G.O. debt— (mil. $)			
	1988–1992	1988	1989	1990	1991	1992
St. Paul	80.6	155.0	160.1	165.9	171.8	176.3
Ramsey Cnty.*	33.1	43.0	43.8	44.4	45.6	46.7
Indep. Sch. Dist. 625	0.0	46.0	38.3	30.4	23.0	15.2
Port Authority	0.0	9.1	7.7	6.3	4.9	3.5
Total	113.7	253.0	249.9	247.0	245.3	241.7

*53% overlapping share of debt.

debt service as well as intergovernmental mandates and financial assistance. Each unit has been assigned a target percentage of the tax base as its maximum net G.O. debt *(see table)*.

The St. Paul plan offers a refreshing glimpse of intergovernmental cooperation on debt management. It points the way for communities across the country to tackle debt burden concerns. S&P views this cooperation favorably and recognizes the credit quality enhancement produced by strong planning and management.

Paul J. Flynn (212) 208-1781
Arthur J. Grisi (212) 208-1754
Jay Abrams (212) 208-1366

Figure 4   Standard & Poor's debt rating of Saint Paul (1988).

1993. At that time there was a slight change in the wording of the mission statement, but no change in the goals or objectives.

Saint Paul's debt rating has been upgraded by Standard & Poor's from AA to AA+ and this joint debt management program was highlighted in Standard & Poor's *Creditweek* magazine on February 22, 1988, as shown in Fig. 4.

The process of cooperatively developing and monitoring a debt management strategy has led to reinforcing a positive working climate and intergovernmental perspective among elected officials and staff. This, in turn, has led to successful joint ventures on other issues. For example, an agreement was reached between the city and the county on financing a $48 million rehabilitation of the 60-year-old joint city hall and courthouse building. As part of this action, the county will manage the building and assume all of the debt in exchange for the city granting clear title to five other buildings to the county.

Another outcome was a joint lobbying effort during the 1988 legislative session resulting in a new special capital improvement tax levy authority for Ramsey County which may be used to support either GO debt or pay-as-you-go financing for capital projects. The Minnesota legislature was impressed by these joint efforts and made the capital improvement legislation applicable to all counties in Minnesota.

Most recently, the city and the county have begun discussions on consolidation of their health department services.

17

The Pay-As-You-Go Concept in Municipal Financing

Bernard Smith

Department of Finance, City of Halifax, Halifax, Nova Scotia, Canada

The pay-as-you-go method of funding means simply that capital works are paid for from the government's current revenue base and that the municipality does not take the more usual approach of issuing bonds and then repaying those borrowings over time. The advantage is that paying interest on bonds is avoided. The reader who is based in a jurisdiction which enjoys tax-exempt status for municipal borrowing clearly does not have the potential to avoid paying bond interest at rates (presently around $11\frac{1}{2}\%$ in the Canadian market) which approach those in that marketplace. But, given time, even those jurisdictions may need the pay-as-you-go concept.

I. COST IMPLICATIONS

The following example (Fig. 1) illustrates the cost implications of a program of continual financing. Analyzing a hypothetical case, the figure shows the financial impact of a program of capital works where $20 million per year is financed in each year at an assumed 11% interest cost and with a 10-year term with equal annual payments of principal in each year for each bond issue. The reader will note that only for years 1 through 7 is the amount being paid annually for debt service less than the $20 million annual cost of the capital program. From year 7 out, the actual level of payments required to service the bonds exceeds the level of the pay-as-you-go program. At year 20, an equilibrium point is reached for the debt-financed option where $43 million are paid out each year to fund this $20 million capital program. An even more sobering statistic is that, at this point of equilibrium, $379 million remains to be paid in order to discharge the existing obligations over the future years.

What has been achieved by financing this $20 million annual program each year? For the first 7 years, payments were less than $20 million per year. Starting at less than $1 million in year 1, they rose to $20 million over the 7-year term. In fact, the payments averaged about $12 million per year over this 7-year period and, as a result, $57 million (7 years at an average of $8 million per year) in payments were deferred until after year 7. However, in order to defer those $57 million in payments until years 8 through 14, an eventual payment of $43 million per annum is incurred and an ongoing obligation of $379 million. Surely food for thought.

Offsetting these costs should be the rate of inflaton over the period. The higher the rate of inflation, then the less the case to be made for pay-as-you-go capital funding. In order to put this into perspective, one should examine the same graph net of inflation. The case then becomes less dramatic but still valid.

Figure 2, showing the same hypothetical situation taking into account the impact of inflation, assumes that interest costs are again at $11\frac{1}{2}\%$ and inflation is at $4\frac{1}{2}\%$. This gives a real interest cost of 7%, which

Adapted from *Government Finance Review*, June 1990: 22–24, 48 by permission of Government Finance Officers Association.

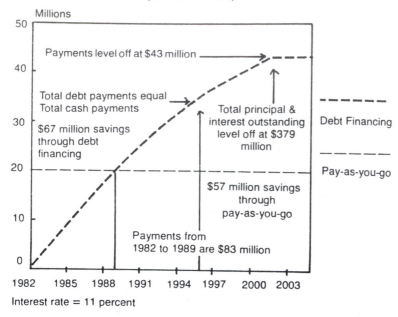

Figure 1   Capital program financing analysis—hypothetical case.

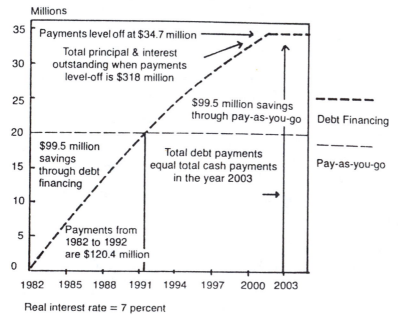

Figure 2   Capital program financing analysis—hypothetical case.

is the net real interest cost figure shown in Fig. 2. Note that the number of years over which real outflow of funds is below the $20 million level is extended from 7 to 11 years. The time required to reach the equilibrium point of $34.7 million in real dollars is lower but still very significant. The real cost encountered by the $20 million borrowing plan are still significant.

Figure 3 illustrates a case which is probably closer to reality in which the impact of an assumed 4% inflation rate is taken into the equation together with an assumed 11% interest cost. The equilibrium point is never reached as a result of the inflationary impact, but the costs of the ongoing debt load is even more dramatic at $453 million at year 18, which then continues to escalate. A sobering testimony to the merits of a pay-as-you-go capital program.

II. CIRCUMSTANCES FAVORING PAY-AS-YOU-GO

Some of the characteristic situations in which a pay-as-you-go approach may be most appropriate include

- In areas in times of high interest rates unless they are offset by even higher rates of inflation
- In stable or relatively little-growth areas that have an ongoing capital works requirement which is fairly consistent from year to year
- Where a window in capital needs requirements or a previously unavailable (possibly temporary) source of funds permits a move to pay-as-you-go
- Where the fiscal projections for the municipality do not permit the ongoing escalation of borrowing costs.

A.   In Areas or Times of High Interest Rates

Times of high interest rates should be examined in terms of the actual real interest cost. Even if inflation is running at high levels at the time of debt issuance, it can be dangerous to allow the municipality to become locked in to high nominal interest rates for extended terms, since these may have to be repaid in times of low inflation that may follow. For some communities, it may be possible to move to a pay-as-you-go approach in

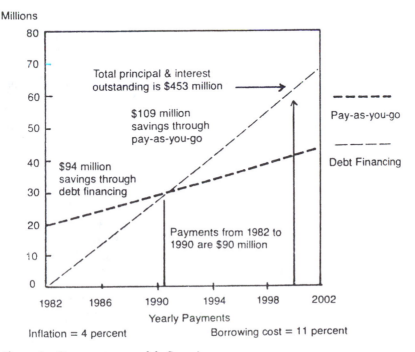

Figure 3   Pay-as-you-go vs. debt financing.

times of high interest rates because the interest charges plus the capital repayment represent such a significant amount.

B. In Areas Which Are Stable, Showing Little Growth

When a municipality reaches a point of stability and is showing little growth, an examination of its capital program reveals that much of the work is of a maintenance nature. A case can be made that since the municipality is only maintaining its existing structure and is not adding to its tax base, the program can most advantageously be financed from current revenues, particularly where the program is at a steady level from year to year.

C. Where There Is a Window in Capital Needs

It is difficult to change from a debt-financed to a pay-as-you-go basis. Depending upon the term of the bonds outstanding for the municipal unit and the ongoing demand these present on current revenues, it takes about 5 to 7 years before an appreciable amount of funds are freed up as a result of reduced debt service costs such that an adequate program of capital works can be put in place paid for on the pay-as-you-go basis.

How does the municipality bridge that gap? In the case of the city of Halifax, a new capital assistance program was put in place from a senior level of government. With $8 million annually in funds earmarked for the pay-as-you-go capital program and a little belt tightening in terms of the capital program to be put in place, the gap is being crossed. Clearly, the objective must be to deal with essential needs over the "bridge" period and with some combination of reducing funds for essential projects only to get to the point of payoff at about 7 years out, where a normal volume of capital works can be handled again.

D. Where the Projections for the Municipality Do Not Support an Ongoing Program of Borrowing

Where the tax base of the municipality is not expanding and where the projections show every likelihood of continuing fiscal difficulty, then it is particularly appropriate to attempt to get the municipality on to a debt-free status.

III. PAY-AS-YOU-GO NOT APPROPRIATE

There are times and situations when it may not be appropriate to embark on a pay-as-you-go approach. Some of the major contraindications are pointed out in the ensuing sections.

A. Where the Capital Works Are Adding to the Tax Base

In these instances, the expanded tax base can be used to support the capital works; the facilities servicing the expanded tax base should not be loaded onto the existing base. Clearly, some of the cost is still going to be paid by the existing base, unless the costs of the capital works are paid over time by some form of area levy to the newly serviced areas. Even if the burden is spread over the existing base plus the new base, there is some case to be made for financing under these circumstances.

B. Where a Major Capital Expenditure Is Contemplated Which Does Not Fit into the Normal Routing Level of Capital Works and Which Would, As A Result, Distort the Whole Tax Structure of the Municipality

The pay-as-you-go concept is intended to fund the normal and routine level of capital spending. The unusual "once in a generation" capital expenditure which overshadows all routine capital works and which would totally distort any particular year or even several years of normal activity probably should be financed by issue of bonds.

C. Where Real Interest Costs Are Negative

During the latter half of the 1970s, real interest costs were negative. It was possible to borrow at moderate interest rates, which were at times lower than the rate of inflation at the time of the bond issue. That was a time when it was right to borrow. Capital structures put in place at that time were being utilized while being paid for in increasingly less valuable dollars. The experience of the investment community over that period and the eventual awakening which took place resulted in the very high real interest rates of the 1980s. No one can predict when the next period of negative interest rates will arrive.

IV. THE CITY OF HALIFAX EXPERIENCE

Debt servicing costs had traditionally run at a level approaching 14% of current revenues in the city of Halifax. Only 8.5% of current revenue was actually being used and put into place as capital works; the balance between the 8.5% and the 14% was interest costs. By paying down the existing debt, it should be possible to provide for a program of capital works at a rate of 8.5% of current revenues. Shown in Fig. 4 is a schedule of what has actually been achieved to date in terms of reducing debt in the city of Halifax. Debt service costs to 1990 have been reduced from 14% of current revenues at the beginning of the decade to below 5% 10 years later; of course, a period of inflation makes these percentages look especially good.

V. RECURRING QUESTIONS

The negative of pay-as-you-go financing plans is that it is extremely difficult to achieve a discipline whereby an elected body will annually tax for and set aside for capital purposes millions of dollars in cash at a time when politically it may be having difficulty justifying the taxation levels required. To bring this about requires a carefully crafted, preagreed policy that will regularly set specified levels of cash transfers into the pay-as-you-go program.

    Underlying the pay-as-you-go versus borrowing debate are several basic questions that must be addressed. When raised by the citizen-taxpayer, they usually are phrased in the following terms:

- "Why should this generation pay for assets which will be used by the next generation?" A response to that concern is that the established practice of claiming to associate repayment periods with the useful life of

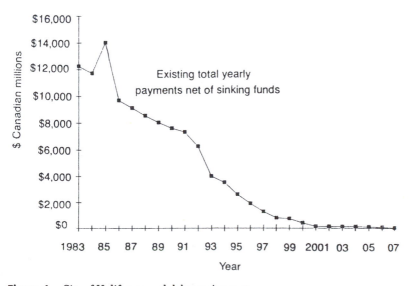

Figure 4   City of Halifax annual debt service costs.

the asset was only partially accurate, at best. There are, in fact, billions of dollars worth of existing assets fully paid for, but still in use. Thus, the effort to spread cost over useful life did not work for those assets—the benefits are still being enjoyed and no one is paying. But heavy, one-shot capital assets are not recommended as candidates for the pay-as-you-go approach; inclusion of that type of asset is generally disruptive to the program. It is the routine, ongoing mass of small-ticket capital items which make up the bulk of most capital programs—these can and should be paid for without resorting to borrowing.

- "Why should I pay for that sewer or sidewalk all in 1 year?" The rejoinder points out that even though all taxpayers may be contributing to one particular set of assets in any given year, that same group has the use of another set of assets that were paid for by another combination of taxpaying residents in the preceding year. A city's residents have the benefit of a whole range of existing municipal infrastructure which is maintained, replaced, and marginally extended on a revolving basis. This infrastructure is generally uniform from year to year, why not pay cash for it and avoid the debt costs?

- "Will going to a pay-as-you-go basis result in the municipal unit gaining less assistance from other levels of government?" It may, and each municipality would have to answer this question within its own environment. In the case of the city of Halifax, a reduction of debt service costs equivalent to 5.5% on revenues as a result of an elimination of interest would require an increase in grants by other levels of government by about 75% in order to make the "borrow to get grants" scenario pay off. This is not likely to come about in the current environment.

VI. THE CHOICE

As logical thinking beings, city officials do not have to put their governments into debt with the consequent incurrence of interest costs before they can bring themselves to the point of setting aside funds for capital works. If municipal government has the self discipline to set aside funds sufficient to maintain its routine capital requirements (calculated for Halifax at 8.5% of revenues), the program will work. If it does not have enough self-discipline to do this, then it is doomed to pay a greater portion of its revenues for its capital facilites (calculated historically in the city of Halifax at 14% of current revenues). In Halifax, this is an interesting choice which is being remade in favor of the 8.5% option each year.

18

State Practices for Financing Capital Projects

United States General Accounting Office
Washington, D.C.

I. INTRODUCTION

We have been examining the concept of capital budgeting as a step in strengthening financial management within the federal government. We have reviewed various aspects of this issue.* Last year, we released an exposure draft (*Budget Issues: Capital Budgeting for the Federal Government*, GAO/AFMD-88-44, July 1988) which proposes restructuring the unified budget into operating and capital components.†

Most states have had experience with capital budgeting and related financing techniques. In our 1986 study of states' capital budgeting practices, 37 of 45 states responding indicated they had some form of a capital budget. Furthermore, 21 states replied they used long-term borrowing to finance capital assets. According to the U.S. Bureau of the Census, the 50 states spent over $34.5 billion in 1986 on capital assets.

The federal government, on the other hand, has limited experience using a capital budget as a decision-making tool during the budget process. Its unified, cash-based budget treats outlays for capital and operating activities the same. This should not be the case. Capital outlays, whether they are for buildings or loans, produce future streams of benefits to the government or the economy. The benefits may be cash flows, facilities to carry out government operations, or other such economic returns. Although the current budget provides a comprehensive report of cash receipts and outlays, it does not distinguish between expenditures for capital investments and current operations.

While our previous work provides an overall framework for capital budgeting at the federal level, a number of issues must still be resolved prior to implementing a capital budget within the unified federal budget. One of those issues concerns developing specific procedures for defining and identifying capital assets. A second issue is how capital acquisitions should be financed. A third issue, which has generated congressional interest, is whether borrowing maturity can or should be linked to the life of the capital asset. We examined how the states budget for and finance capital investments. Their experiences could provide useful information to the Congress, the Office of Management and Budget (OMB), and federal departments and agencies as they evaluate and discuss the concept of implementing a capital budget for the federal government.

Adapted from a work in the public domain.

Budget Issues: Capital Budgeting Practices in the States (GAO/AFMD-86-63FS, July 15, 1986); *Capital Budgeting for the Federal Government* (GAO/T-AFMD-88-3, December 8, 1987); and *Budget Reform for the Federal Government* (GAO/T-AFMD-88-13, June 7, 1988).

†The term *capital budget* is not universally defined. In our capital budget proposal, we define a capital budget as that part of the unified budget which segregates capital revenues and investments from the operating budget's revenues and expenses. Capital revenues and capital investments are excluded from the calculations of the operating budget's surplus or deficit, but the operating budget is charged for depreciation.

A.   Objectives, Scope, and Methodology

The principal objectives of this study were to (1) identify the criteria states use for defining a capital asset and the procedures they use in developing their capital budgets, (2) identify the methods states use to finance capital assets, and (3) determine the extent to which states link borrowing maturities to the useful life of a capital asset.

To achieve our study objectives, we reviewed related books, articles, and other published reports, including prior GAO reports, for information on state budgeting practices for financing capital assets. In addition, we selected nine states for detailed study.

In selecting these states, we used our 1986 report (*Budget Issues: Capital Budgeting Practices in the States*, GAO/AFMD-86-63FS, July 15, 1986) which identified nineteen states that (1) used long-term borrowing for financing capital assets and (2) linked borrowing maturities to asset life. From these nineteen states, we wanted to select states which were responsible for a majority of the capital expenditures. For the nineteen states, we reviewed (1) the amount of the state's total capital outlays, (2) the state's capital outlays as a percentage of total state expenditures, (3) the amount of the state's long-term debt, and (4) the percentage of the state's capital outlays financed by long-term debt. For our current study, we wanted to determine whether and, if so, how the states directly link borrowing maturities to asset life.

As a result of considering the above criteria, we selected a judgmental sample of eight states for study—Florida, Georgia, Illinois, Kentucky, New Jersey, New York, Pennsylvania, and Virginia. These eight states accounted for 73% of the capital expenditures made by the nineteen states in our 1986 survey. In addition, we selected Colorado because it not only uses a capital budget, but it also responded to our 1986 survey that it does not link long-term borrowing maturities to asset life. Colorado also identified long-term borrowing as its largest source of revenue for capital expenditures. In addition, Denver, Colorado, is the home of the National Conference of State Legislatures, where we obtained valuable information for this study.

In each of the nine states, we interviewed various state officials to obtain information regarding their capital budgeting approach and process and to gather data on their respective state's debt. We also used U.S. Bureau of the Census data on capital expenditures if the information we obtained from the individual states was not presented in the format necessary to complete our review.

The results of our review are presented in the following three chapters. Section II describes the criteria states use for defining capital assets and the procedures they use in developing their capital budgets, and it also provides specific details on the nine states in our survey. Section III discusses the states' general methods of financing capital projects. Section IV examines whether there is a linkage between the financing method or borrowing maturity and a capital asset's useful life.

II.   STATE BUDGETING FOR CAPITAL ASSETS

A majority of the fifty states use a capital budget, segregating capital and noncapital expenditures. Furthermore, most states have established (1) criteria for defining capital assets and (2) specific capital budgeting procedures. The nine states we reviewed all use a capital budget and most have defined capital assets and developed capital budgeting procedures.

A.   Defining Capital Assets

Capital assets are often defined as those intended for long-term use or possession. They are relatively permanent in nature, and they are not intended for resale. Usually, they are classified into general groups, such as land, buildings, and equipment. The general classifications represent many types of capital projects which cover various functions such as medical and educational facilities, prisons, parks and recreation, general public buildings, airports, and highways.

In fiscal year 1986, the fifty states reported that they spent about $34.5 billion on capital projects. Table 1 provides the fifty states' capital expenditures by function, according to the U.S. Bureau of the Census. The table also includes the capital expenditures made by the nine states included in our study. Because most states in our study presented their expenditures by departmental or cabinet structure rather than listing them strictly along functional lines, we used the Census Bureau's data on capital expenditures.

According to the National Council of State Legislatures, there are seven states which have no specific written definition for a capital asset. In the nine states we visited, most have developed strict definitions for

Table 1 States' Capital Expenditures (Fiscal Year 1986)

	All states (in billions)	Nine states in GAO review (in billions)
Highways	$20.4	$6.8
Education	5.1	1.2
Natural resources	1.1	0.3
Hospitals	0.8	0.3
Correction	1.6	0.4
Parks and recreation	0.4	0.1
Public buildings	0.4	0.2
Health	0.3	0.2
Police	0.3	0.1
Airports	0.2	0.1
Other	3.9	2.1
Total	$34.5	$11.8

Source: U.S. Bureau of the Census, *State Government Finances in 1986.*

determining what constitutes a capital asset, while others have only general and broad criteria. The criteria each of the nine states uses to define capital assets are discussed below. For purposes of the following discussion, the terms capital asset, capital project, and capital items are used interchangeably, depending on the state's choice of terminology.

Colorado—A capital asset is any nonstructural improvement to land—such as land grading, drainage, roadways, or sewers—which costs more than $100, but less than $5,000; any alteration or repair which costs more than $100, but less than $15,000; and any equipment, furniture, etc. with a useful life over 1 year, which is continuously used, and which costs $100 to $50,000. Projects such as site purchase or development, major repairs or renovations, building construction or equipment purchases which cost more than $50,000 are considered capital construction.

Florida—A fixed capital outlay is real property (land, buildings, appurtenances, fixtures and fixed equipment, structures, etc.), including additions, replacements, major repairs, and renovations to real property which materially extend its useful life or improve or change its functional use. Also, it includes the capital outlay necessary to furnish and operate a new or improved facility.

Georgia—This state's budget office determines what constitutes a capital asset. It bases its decision primarily on an estimated useful life determination of proposed capital projects. The life of the capital asset or project should equal or exceed 5 years. Additionally, the project must be "bondable," that is, market conditions are favorable for selling bonds, and bond ratings will not be adversely affected.

Illinois—This state's budget office also determines, at its discretion, what constitutes a capital asset. It relies on the project's bondability in determining whether it can be classified as capital. For bonding, projects must meet certain criteria, including: the project is of a durable nature; the project is not subject to inherent risk of failure or intended to fulfill temporary needs; expenditure of funds must appreciably increase or enhance the interest of the state; the state must have a direct interest; and project expenses must exceed $25,000.

Kentucky—Capital projects are any construction item, or any combination of capital construction items necessary to make a building or utility installation complete which are estimated to cost $200,000 or more and major items of movable equipment estimated to cost $50,000 or more.

New Jersey—This state defines capital projects as any undertaking proposed to be funded by general obligation bonds, or by an appropriation in the annual capital budget. They include the acquisition of land and the purchase of construction and equipment which exceed $50,000.

New York—Capital projects are any projects which would be financed through debt issuance by the state, funded by an appropriation from the capital projects funds, or funded by an appropriation from the Capital Projects Budget Bill. Capital projects are those involving the acquisition, construction, demolition, or replacement or major repair of a fixed asset.

Pennsylvania—Capital projects include any building, structure, facility, or physical public betterment or improvement; any land; any furnishings, machinery, apparatus, or equipment for any public betterment or improvement; or any undertaking to construct, repair, renovate, improve, equip, furnish, or acquire any of the foregoing, provided that the project is designated in a capital budget as a capital project. The project or equipment must have an estimated useful life in excess of 5 years and an estimated cost in excess of $100,000.

Virginia—Capital items include real property acquisitions; new construction greater than 5,000 square feet or greater than $75,000; improvements to existing facilities greater than $200,000 or resulting in operating costs greater than $15,000; and equipment, if financed through revenue bonds. The detailed descriptions and criteria for property and improvements, plant and improvements, and equipment are provided in state budgeting procedure guidelines.

B. How States Budget for Capital Assets

A prior GAO report* on capital budgeting issues reported that 37 of 45 states responding said they have a distinct capital budget where capital amounts are reported separately. The report also provided the following information about the states that responded:

* Seventeen states maintain separate capital and operating budgets.
* Thirteen states combine capital and operating amounts into an overall budget total.
* Seven states use various other procedures to report capital.

In November 1987, the National Conference of State Legislatures completed a study, *Capital Budgeting and Finance: The Legislative Role*, regarding the legislative role in the capital budgeting and finance process for the states. One of the recommendations the study made to the states was that the "executive branch should be required to submit to the legislature a single capital budget that includes all capital requests for the forthcoming budget period, by priority, across agencies, presented by funding source." The study's authors favor a single and separate capital budget request because they believe that

* Presenting all capital requests, arranged by proposed funding source, in one separate document enhances the examination of alternative financing mechanisms for various projects
* Showing all requests in one place and ranking them allows legislators to better consider the trade-offs among different projects across state agencies

Because capital budgeting practices in the nine states we visited vary from state to state, it would be very difficult to call any one state typical. Some states are more centralized than others, with greater decision making on capital projects within the governor's office. On the other hand, some states are strong legislatively and use legislative committees to establish priorities.

For example, in Florida, Kentucky, and New Jersey, all state agencies are required to prepare a capital facilities plan every year. In Florida and Kentucky, the governor's office reviews and consolidates the plans before submitting them to the legislature. In New Jersey, the state's Office of Management and Budget is charged with coordinating the agencies' plans. The final plan is then presented to the State Capital Planning Commission, which develops and maintains, on an ongoing basis, short- and long-range capital spending plans and makes final recommendations to the governor for inclusion in the annual state budget. In contrast, Colorado has a permanent legislative committee, known as the Capital Development Committee, which is charged with ranking capital construction projects in order of importance for annual recommendation to the Joint Budget Committee.

All nine states we visited maintain distinct capital budgets, but only five combined the capital and operating budgets into one overall budget. For instance, as part of its annual financial report, Kentucky prepares combined general purpose financial statements showing sources of revenue, including proceeds from bond sales, and overall expenditures, including those for capital projects. In addition, the financial report provides more detailed statements for individual funds such as the general fund, special revenue funds, and federal funds. One of these individual funds is the capital projects fund. According to Kentucky's annual financial report, the capital projects fund accounts for financial resources appropriated by the General

---

Budget Issues: Capital Budgeting Practices in the States (GAO/AFMD-86-63FS, July 15, 1986).

Assembly for the acquisition, construction, or renovation of major capital facilities, and for the acquisition of major equipment, other than items financed by proprietary funds, certain trust funds, and university and college funds.

Similarly, Illinois's state budget provides summary statements indicating general uses for all appropriated funds. However, the budget also provides detailed financial data for all the state's departments, agencies, and programs. The capital program is included in the budget report as a separate program. It provides information regarding the sources of capital funds and a description of all current and proposed capital projects.

III. METHODS OF FINANCING CAPITAL ASSETS

States finance capital assets primarily through the use of current revenues and long-term debt. In a 1986 GAO survey (*Budget Issues: Capital Budgeting Practices in the States*, GAO/AFMD-86-63FS, July 15, 1986), 29 of the 37 states who responded that they used a capital budget indicated that one of their primary funding sources for financing capital assets was current revenues (state revenues and intergovernmental funds from the federal government and local governments). Similarly, 21 of the reporting states indicated that long-term borrowings were also a primary source of funds for financing capital assets.

A. Current Revenues

Current revenues consist of state revenues and intergovernmental funds. State revenues are collected primarily from taxes, current charges, and miscellaneous general revenues. Taxes constitute the largest segment of state revenues, with sales and gross receipts taxes, income and license taxes being the major kinds of taxes.

Miscellaneous general revenues comprise the second largest type of state revenues. These revenues include interest earnings, rents, royalties, lottery net income, donations, and fines and forfeitures.

Current charges are the third largest type of state revenue. States receive such revenues from the public for performing specific services benefitting the person charged, such as rents and sales from furnishing commodities or services, and intergovernmental transfers.

In addition, states receive intergovernmental funds. These funds include federal funds and funds from local governments. The federal funds are frequently grants for physical capital investments, such as highways or community and regional development projects. The funds from local governments are for shares in the financial support of state-administered programs, reimbursements for services performed or expenditures made for them by the state, payments on debt service of state debt issued for their benefit, and repayment of advances and contingent loans extended to them.

In some of the nine states we visited, current revenues fund most capital expenditures, with a majority of those revenues provided by the federal government. In Georgia, a state official told us that the state's 1988 projected capital outlays would be about $900 million. Current revenues, including state revenues of $180 million and federal funds of $315 million, would finance 55% of the total capital expenditures. The federal funds were earmarked for Georgia Department of Transportation projects.

In Virginia, the 1987 capital budget program was projected at $343 million. Except for $36 million of long-term debt, the program was financed entirely from current revenues. For the 1987–1988 fiscal year, New York planned capital outlays of $2.2 billion. Approximately 50%, or $1.1 billion, would be derived from current revenues. Of that portion, federal funds would comprise 62%.

In six of the states that we visited, lottery revenue is used to support specific programs. Pennsylvania, for example, primarily uses its net lottery revenues for programs in its Departments of Aging or Public Welfare. However, some states are beginning to use lottery revenues for capital projects. For instance, Colorado's 1988–1989 budget has dedicated lottery proceeds to finance $16.5 million in capital projects.

We also found that state governments use current revenues for lease payments in order to finance capital projects. Leasing is a capital financing mechanism that allows a state to pay for the purchase or use of a facility or equipment in installments rather than all at once. State governments use leasing as an alternative to bond financing or full cash payments.

There are several types of leases. The two more common forms are operating leases and capital leases. An operating lease is a short-term rental agreement where the state leases an asset for only a fraction of the asset's useful life. As the lessee, the state uses the asset in return for regularly scheduled rental payments, which are classified as current expenses. The lessor, normally a manufacturer or vendor, provides the asset in return for the agreed-upon payments. The lessor is usually responsible for maintenance, insurance, and taxes. These responsibilities enable the lessor to claim the tax benefits of ownership.

A capital lease, also known as a lease-purchase agreement, is one where the ownership of the asset normally transfers from the lessor to the lessee at the end of a lease term. This agreement establishes periodic payments divided into both principal and interest, and a date when title to the asset may transfer, if the lessee meets all contractual requirements. A capital lease may involve a single item or multiple items.

States reported they use leasing instead of borrowing for several reasons

- A state is unable to enter the bond market with a new issue because it has reached its legal debt limit.
- A state is unable or unwilling to enter the bond market because of high interest rates.
- The need for voter approval on bond issues makes leasing more attractive.
- The useful life of an asset or changing technology makes issuance of long-term bonds an inappropriate financing mechanism. Lease agreements are typically 4, 6, or 8 years, whereas long-term bonds are normally for 10 years or more.

Some of the nine states we visited use leases extensively. Florida leased nearly $400 million worth of equipment in 1986. Kentucky leases $35 million to $40 million a year in small equipment. Similarly, Colorado's state agencies had issued about $26 million in lease-purchase agreements through 1985. New York planned to issue about $426 million of lease-purchase debt to finance about 20% of its 1987–1988 capital program.

B. Debt Financing

States use a combination of short-term and long-term debt to finance capital expenditures. Short-term debt consists of interest-bearing debt payable within 1 year from the date of issue, such as bond anticipation notes, bank loans, and tax anticipation notes and warrants. States use short-term debt mostly in anticipation of tax receipts; it is seldom used to finance the start of capital projects.

Long-term debt, however, is the most frequently used debt-financing tool for capital assets. In 1988* we reported that the use of long-term debt by the 50 states increased, in aggregate current dollars, from about $19 billion in 1961 to over $212 billion in 1985. During the 1981–1985 period, state debt grew at an annual rate of 12%.

There are two major forms of long-term debt—full faith debt and nonguaranteed debt.

1. Full Faith Debt

When a state issues full faith debt, it promises to repay the debt using, if necessary, its taxing powers to obtain the needed funds. Full faith debt is generally issued in the form of general obligation bonds. A distinction does exist between general obligation bonds payable from unlimited taxing powers, and those where the power to tax for debt repayment is subject to some kind of limitation. In either case, the bondholders rely on the state government to take whatever action is necessary to ensure repayment. For this reason, general obligation bonds generally have lower interest rates than nonguaranteed debt.

The states we visited finance varying portions of their capital projects with general obligation bonds. In New York, new general obligation debt totaling $365 million was planned to finance about 17% of the 1987–1988 capital plan. Georgia was planning on issuing $405 million of general obligation bonds to finance 45% of its $900 million capital program.

Another category of full faith debt is zero coupon bonds. These bonds are offered at a discounted rate and are payable at maturity at their full par value. Of the nine states in our review, Illinois was the only state that was using this financing method. The state is calling the bonds "general obligation college savings bonds," and they are issued in denominations which have maturity values in $5,000 multiples. Illinois's first zero coupon bond issue in 1988 was for about $93 million. Officials indicated that they sold out immediately and probably could have sold about three times the state's initial issue.

a.   Debt Limitations   Most states have constitutional or statutory debt limitations to prevent state and local

---

Budget Issues: Overview of State and Federal Debt (GAO/AFMD-88-11BR, January 27, 1988).

government fiscal mismanagement and to protect the interests of bondholders. One common form of debt limit restriction is placing a limit on the dollar amount of the debt the state may incur. This amount is either given as an absolute value or as a flexible limit, such as a percentage of the state's revenue receipts or a percentage of the assessed value of the state's property tax. For example, Pennsylvania's constitution establishes a debt limit at 1.75 times the average of the state's annual tax revenues for the previous 5 years. In Georgia, the constitution restricts borrowing to 10% of the previous year's net revenue. At the other extreme, Colorado's constitution prohibits the state from issuing any full faith and credit debt.

A second type of debt limit restriction requires that debt be issued only for certain public purposes. Generally, those purposes must be related to capital projects. In Florida, for example, the state constitution states that state bonds pledging the full faith and credit of the state may be issued only to finance or refinance the cost of state fixed capital outlay projects.

A third type of debt limit restriction is one that requires voter approval in order to exceed certain dollar limits for debt or to simply issue any debt. In Kentucky, there are no constitutionally imposed limits on debt, but all debt financing must have prior approval by the state's General Assembly, which sets the limits on the volume of bonds issued. In Florida, full faith and credit bond issuance is generally subject to voter approval.

2. Nonguaranteed Debt

Nonguaranteed debt is payable solely from a specific pledged source, as opposed to general obligation bonds, where the full faith and credit and taxing power of the issuing state are pledged for the repayment of the debt. Nonguaranteed debt is financed primarily through revenue bonds. They are secured by user fee repayments (revenue generated from the project itself) or earmarked revenues. In case of default, the issuing state does not have a legal liability to pay the debt from general tax revenues. Its liability only extends to the specific revenue pledged to repay the debt. In fiscal year 1986, state nonguaranteed debt represented over 73% of all long-term debt for the 50 states.

The principal advantages of revenue bonds over general obligation bonds are that they normally do not require voter approval, and the generally are not subject to constitutional or statutory debt limitations. Other advantages are that capital projects are usually paid for by user fees, and bond issuers can adjust their rate structure to keep up with inflation and pay operating costs. The major disadvantage is that revenue bonds are issued for a long time period in order to provide a safe margin for covering costs and debt charges. This extended maturity increases the bond interest rate.

There are three broad categories of revenue bonds. Government enterprise bonds, the traditional category of revenue bonds, are used to borrow funds for constructing or improving facilities, such as utilities, airports, and bridges. In such instances, utility payments, landing fees, and bridge tolls provide revenues to fund the debt service.

Public bonds for private purposes are issued to support activities such as housing, economic development, construction, industrial pollution control, student loans, or other activities. The private beneficiaries of the bonds' proceeds repay the debt through lease payments or other kinds of periodic payments which cover debt service over the life of the bonds.

A third category of revenue bonds, government lessee bonds, differs from the previous two types in that repayment is usually from taxes, not revenue-producing activities. In these cases, one state entity with borrowing authority issues bonds and uses the debt proceeds to acquire facilities for another state entity. The two entities enter a lease agreement which requires the entity using the facility to make lease payments to the entity that issued the bond. The lease payments are usually funded by tax revenues and are used to liquidate the debt.

Revenue bonds are issued by a state or public authority. For example, Florida's state government had $605 million in revenue bonds outstanding at the end of fiscal year 1987. These bonds financed roads, bridges, and other capital projects and will be paid from revenue sources other than state taxes. In Kentucky, which has not issued any general obligation bonds since 1965, revenue bonds are used to finance capital projects. These bonds are secured by revenue from the projects financed, not the full faith and credit of the state or state taxes.

In addition, revenue bonds may also be issued by a political subdivision of a state, referred to as a "public authority." A public authority is a public bond-issuing entity generally established by statute to finance public facilities that have not or cannot be financed by an existing state agency or that can be better financed by an authority. Authorities usually do not have taxing power, but accomplish their financing with revenue bonds.

There are several different types of public authorities. Some authorities are established to finance public projects that can be repaid with user fees. Others are set up as building corporations to issue debt for constructing state offices and other facilities and repay the debt from leases to the state. A third type of authority provides an interest subsidy (tax-exempt status) to a private activity defined as being in the public interest (e.g., health facilities authorities).

The actions of a public authority can affect a state's credit, regardless of whether the authority's issues are backed by the state. Furthermore, public authorities are viewed by some as a means of "backdoor financing" because they are normally beyond the control of voters and legislators.

In the nine states we visited, we found that such authorities are used to finance specific projects. For instance, New Jersey has 13 public authorities, which had outstanding debt of almost $15 billion at the end of 1986. On August 31, 1987, five Illinois state authorities had outstanding debt totaling over $700 million. Colorado also makes extensive use of public authorities, and their cumulative indebtedness as of 1985 was nearly $3 billion. New York has 29 major authorities which had $24.1 billion in outstanding revenue and nonrecourse bonds at the end of 1986.

Another type of nonguaranteed debt is "moral obligation bonds." Typically, these bonds are issued by state agencies under legislation that implies that the state will secure the debt if default is threatened. Usually, the issuing agency must establish a debt service fund from bond sale proceeds. The agency will then use income from its normal sources to meet debt service costs as they become due. However, if this income is not sufficient to meet costs, money is advanced from the debt service reserve fund to make payments. The state, in turn, may then make appropriations to restore the debt service fund.

Moral obligation bonds are not enforceable against the legislature, and the legislature has the legal right to elect to forego such payments. On the other hand, it is assumed that, because the state legislature authorized such debt under these terms, it incurred a "moral obligation" to meet the revenue shortfalls needed for debt service. New York's public authorities, for example, had $15.4 billion in moral obligation bonds outstanding at the end of September 1986.

As stated above, state debt limits do not apply to nonguaranteed debt, because state debt limits either are silent on the issue, and such debt is generally not considered a legal obligation of the state, or specifically exclude this type of debt from constitutional limitations. As a result, nonguaranteed debt is occasionally used to circumvent or avoid a state's debt limit requirements. Indeed, officials in several of the states we visited indicated that they relied heavily on nonguaranteed debt, partly because it was easier to issue since they did not have to follow the states' legislative limitations regarding debt.

IV. LINKAGE BETWEEN BORROWING MATURITY AND ASSET LIFE

The nine states we visted generally do not directly link the financing method and borrowing maturity to a capital asset or its useful life. It is sometimes held that linking debt maturity to estimated asset life assures that those who benefit from the asset will be the ones who help pay for it (through their annual taxes used for debt service). However, the states we visited link the type and maturity of the financing more directly to factors other than asset life, such as prevailing market conditions, the states' desire to achieve the best economic results, the need to maintain a high-quality bond rating, legislative limitations on the type and amount of debt, and other considerations.

In our review, Kentucky was the only state that attempts to match an asset's useful life to the financial life of its debt. In that state, useful life is determined according to capitalization and depreciation procedures. User agencies advise the financing agency and the budget office of the useful life based on their maintenance and obsolescence experience. However, there are no written state guidelines for determining useful life.

Two of the nine states—Pennsylvania and New York—statutorily require that the life of the project be longer than the project's financing. Although their laws require that the bond life be shorter than the project life, market conditions and the need to keep interest rates as low as possible actually determine the life of bonds issued for capital projects in these two states. Virginia state officials said that financing terms are designed to provide the best economic result for the state and are not tied directly to the individual asset. However, these officials added that financing is not undertaken where the life of the asset would not at least match or exceed the term of the financing.

Generally, we found that the nine states we visited do not link borrowing maturity to a specific asset's life. In Pennsylvania, for example, there is no attempt to associate a specific type of financing with specific assets. Debt issues are usually influenced by general bond market conditions, and they are tied to state programs rather than to specific capital assets. In Georgia, general obligation bonds are the only long-term financing used. According to a Georgia budget official, many factors influence the decision to finance certain assets with debt. These factors include overall fund availability, amount of other commitments or agency requests, market factors, the useful life of the assets, the specific nature of the assets being financed, the size of the bond package, and the legislative attitude about bonds.

Although the nine states generally are not linking borrowing maturity to asset life, some states are using a form of financing known as certificates of participation, where specific assets or a pool of assets are used to secure the debt. The certificates are usually issued for a relatively short period of time, normally 5 years. More importantly, they are not a full faith and credit obligation of the state because the capital assets financed are security for the certificates.

New Jersey is one state that uses certificates of participation, primarily to finance equipment purchases. The state is consolidating all outstanding equipment lease purchase agreements under certificate of participation arrangements. In 1987, for example, New Jersey issued certificates of participation which would give the certificate holders a proportionate share of lease payments that would be made for certain items of equipment, such as computers and helicopters. The certificates' security is the equipment itself, which is specified in detail in the offering prospectus.

Florida also uses certificates of participation, but its process varies somewhat from New Jersey's. Florida's certificates are being used to create a financing pool which can be drawn down as needed for equipment acquisition. However, the certificates' security remains the equipment itself or more directly the "program rental" that will be paid by state agencies for the equipment's use. The equipment that can be acquired under Florida's program is described as "computers, copiers and office equipment, office automation/word processing equipment, typesetting equipment, tractors, telecommunications or telephone system equipment."

New York is also using certificates of participation. However, it imposes a statewide limit of $160 million. The governor recommends that agencies use certificates of participation for funding the installment or lease purchases of real and personal property.

19

Stability and Turnover in Self-Serving Debt Networks

Gerald J. Miller
Rutgers University at Newark, Newark, New Jersey

Characterizing the 1990s, large U.S. budget deficits, compounding large amounts of debt held by corporations, state and local governments, and households, have strained the financial system's supply of capital. In matching investors to borrowers, financial intermediaries, as ever, have played a creative role under strained conditions in finding new investors and inducing existing ones to infuse even more capital.

Debt management—broadly conceived as activities involving intermediaries, lenders, and borrowers—has gained far more importance under these conditions. This research argues that, as debt management's importance has increased, governments' dependence on debt intermediaries has grown. Often, public managers, who nominally head debt management networks in issuing and selling debt to investors, only reluctantly question decisions intermediaries make, and they fail to force accountability through methods these networks provide. Cases of default and waste illustrate this dependency.

I. WASHINGTON PUBLIC POWER SUPPLY SYSTEM DEFAULT

In the detailed analyses of the default of the Washington Public Power Supply System (WPPSS; Leigland and Lamb, 1986; Myhra, 1984; Jones, 1984), two causes bear out facets of an extreme lack of foresight or cooperation. First, Leigland and Lamb (1986) describe the absence of any sense of responsibility on the part of the individuals involved—from WPPSS, bankers, bond counsel, and various subcontractors—stemming from a network significantly lacking cross-checks or the incentives to challenge assumptions made by the others. For example, they point out (1986: 207) that WPPSS executives left policy planning (assessing demand for the power plants) to the board, public utility districts, and the regional planning system. Top managers left project management to private contractors and particularly architect-engineers. The Nuclear Regulatory Commission was left to lead quality assurance.

However, the board left much of its work for others, too. Planning fell to the Bonneville Power Administration and regional utility groups. Effective management of the organization without substantial oversight was left to top management. Leigland and Lamb observed that the board occupied itself almost exclusively with details, such as individual change order approvals, without looking at the broader implications involved.

The intermediaries easily evaded responsibility as well. Leigland and Lamb (1986: 208) found that during the financing of the WPPSS projects, bond salesmen and analysts attached disclaimers to published reports on the WPPSS bonds to avoid responsibility for statements that were sometimes little more than good promotional copy. Underwriters and financial advisers concentrated on selling bonds at increasing interest rates leaving WPPSS the responsibility of understanding and solving the underlying problems that were undermining its creditworthiness. Bond fund managers and institutional investors carefully reviewed legal opinions to reassure themselves that all responsibility for WPPSS debts would rest squarely with the project participants.

In addition, the bond rating agencies could claim, as a reason for ignorance of problems besetting the system and impending default, as did one (Blumstein, 1983: 24F), "I react to information that's given to us."

The lack of responsibility ultimately led to the "tar baby syndrome," or what Jones (1984) called vector politics. As the system's problems began to attract public attention on a broader national scale, "everyone involved with WPPSS quickly became afraid of being associated with, and even more, responsible for, those problems—of being stuck to the tar baby" (Leigland and Lamb, 1986: 209). The tar baby appeared even stickier when it became known that some congressional bailout effort was underfoot. To Jones (1984: 72), "numerous participants in the [process] all pulled hard to represent their separate interests and the resulting absence of compromise left no alternative to default.... Default was the result of vector politics."

The technical causes also point out the exploding consequences of decisions the system managers made. Myhra (1984) argues the exploding effect of the capitalized interest financing plan. The strategy involved issuing bonds that would pay for interest on earlier issues of bonds. This plan, often thought also to be a proximate cause of the New York City fiscal crisis (Morris, 1980: 128–139), led to inverted pyramiding in which larger and larger bond issues had to sell to pay for old interest, new construction, and new interest. As the issues grew larger, the creditworthiness of each one became more questionable since no new revenue-generating capacity had come onstream through power plants.

II.   THE PENNSYLVANIA NEGOTIATED BOND DEAL WASTE CONTROVERSY

The second instance of looming debt management problems began with a study of Pennsylvania local governments' unique bond sales practices (Forbes and Petersen, 1979). Today, Pennsylvania law directly and indirectly gives preference to *negotiated general obligation* municipal bond sales to underwriters rather than *competitively bidded* sales.

What is the difference between a general obligation bond sale and any other? What is the difference in a competitive sale and a negotiated one? Think of the distinctions as two dimensions describing how to classify all municipal bonds: the first, the type of security, the second, the method of sale to investors.

The type of bond depends on the strength of the contract backing repayment. General obligation debt is that guaranteed to be repaid with interest based on the "full faith and credit" promise of the debt issuer. This promise implies that the issuer will use all revenues necessary to repay debt before using those same revenues for such things as salaries, supplies, other operating expenses, and other nonguaranteed debt.

Nonguaranteed debt, as the name implies, relies on a pledge rather than a full faith and credit promise. The pledge relates to a stream of revenue that is expected to produce sufficient funds to cover debt *and* operating expenses. Typical of nonguaranteed debt are revenue bonds such as those representing obligations of water and sewer enterprises organized and run by municipalities. The independent public enterprise's use of nonguaranteed debt—for example, the New Jersey Turnpike Authority's pledge of highway toll revenue to repay bonds—is even more typical of this type of debt.

A sale of a bond issue may be competitive or negotiated for either guaranteed or nonguaranteed debt. See Table 1 for the advantages and disadvantages of each.

In the Pennsylvania case, Forbes and Peterson tried to determine whether or not most governments paid excessive interest costs for the money they borrowed.

Following methods common at the time, the Forbes and Peterson work showed that such might be the case. They found local government's bond interest rates were somewhat higher than those paid in other states in the region. However, they also found that (p. 24) :

> General Obligation negotiated issues in Pennsylvania carry Net Interest Costs that are 29 basis points higher than competitively-sold issues within the Region (excluding New York).
> GO negotiated issues in Pennsylvania sell at NICs that are 25 basis points higher than competitively sold GO bonds in Pennsylvania in the same size range.

Their analysis of underwriter spreads—compensation in the bond issue for work done by bankers to sell the securities to investors—revealed larger amounts than was common among local governments in New York. Variation in state-specific laws, policies, and procedures suggest little statistical effect on interests costs or underwriter spreads.

Table 1 A Comparison of Competitive and Negotiated Bond Sale Characteristics

Competitive sale

Definition: Competitive underwriting is the method of bond sale in which the issuer sells its bonds to the underwriter offering the lowest bid meeting the terms of the sale. In a competitive underwriting, the issuer, typically with a financial advisor or investment banker, conducts all the origination tasks necessary for the bond offering. These tasks include structing the maturity schedule, preparing the official statement, verifying legal documents, obtaining a rating, securing credit enhancement, and timing the sale. The issuer then advertises the sale of the bonds in advance of the specified sale date through a notice of sale (NOS). The NOS contains relevant information on the proposed issue and the criteria by which the bonds will be awarded. At the specified date, time, and venue, the issuer opens all bids and awards the right to purchase the bonds to the underwriter with the best bid based on the criteria specified in the NOS.

Advantages:

1. *Competitive environment.* The issuer's ultimate goal in a financing is to protect the public's interest by obtaining the lowest possible interest cost. Consequently, the most compelling argument in favor of a competitive sale is that the competition among underwriters provides the incentive for keeping the effective interest cost as low as possible. Under the competitive bid process, market forces determine the price.

2. *Historically lower spreads.* While the gross underwriting spreads (management fee, expenses, underwriting fee, and takedown) between competitive and negotiated bond sales have been narrowing over the past decade, competitive underwriting is still generally viewed as the best means of reducing underwriting costs. While one may argue that equating spreads is an *apples versus oranges* comparison and that any advantage in spread should be weighed against other costs of the financing, data since 1982 indicate that competitive issues hold an edge in terms of lower underwriter fees paid on general obligation and revenue bond issues.

3. *Open process.* The other positive feature of competitive sale is that the issuer generally avoids allegations of unfairness or impropriety in the selection of the underwriter because the bonds are sold through a public auction.

Disadvantages:

1. *Risk premium.* Underwriters bidding on a competitive sale have no guarantee of being awarded bonds. Thus, underwriters cannot be expected to conduct the same level of presale marketing (canvassing prospective investors before the sale) as in a negotiated sale. To compensate for uncertainty about market demand, underwriters may include a hedge or a risk premium in their bids, which can show up either in the spread or the reoffering scale. The amount of the risk premium, however, should also be weighed against the total cost of the financing.

2. *Limited timing and structural flexibility.* An issuer's ability to make last-minute changes is limited by the competitive sale process. With regard to timing, competitive bidding entails a 15-day lag between the time documents are completed and the actual sale date, due to legal notice requirements. Hence, the issuer's ability to speed up the sale process, if necessary, is restricted. While a NOS can be structured to allow for postponement of a competitive sale and subsequent reoffering with a minimum of 2 days prior notice, the competitive sale process remains less flexible than its negotiated counterpart.

Table 1 (*continued*)

In addition, the competitive sale restricts the issuer's ability to adjust major structural features, such as final maturity and call provisions, to match the demand realized in the actual sale process. Again, while a properly structured NOS can increase the flexibility of competitive sale by allowing for changes in the size of the issue (within certain parameters), principal maturity amounts, and the composition of serial versus term bonds, a negotiated sale still holds the advantage if flexibility in structuring is of paramount consideration.

3. *Minimum issuer control over underwriter selection and bond distribution.* In competitive underwriting, the bonds are sold to the underwriter submitting the best bid, based on the NOS criteria. The issuer exerts little influence over which underwriting firms actually purchase the bonds and how these bonds are ultimately distributed. For example, the issuer's ability to ensure that regional firms are included in the underwriting syndicate of a large issuer, or that a portion of the bonds are sold to certain types of investors (e.g., retail or regional investors) is limited. In competitive sale, market forces determine the distribution of the bonds. This lack of control, however, should only be disadvantageous to the extent that the issuer is interested in influencing the composition of the underwriting team or the distribution of the bonds.

Negotiated sale

Definition: In a negotiated sale, the terms of purchase are subject to negotiation between the issuer and the underwriter. Whereas the issuer accepts or rejects the underwriter bids in a competitive sale, the issuer can and is expected to negotiate with the underwriter over the price of the bonds and the spread in a negotiated sale.

In a negotiated sale, underwriter selection is one of the first steps taken by the issuer. Because the issuer selects an underwriter without fully knowing the terms under which that underwriter is willing to purchase the bonds, the issuer's selection is based on other criteria, which generally include the underwriter's expertise, financial resources, compatibility, and experience. Once the underwriter is selected, both the underwriter and the issuer participate in the origination and the pricing of the issue. A financial advisor or other investment banking firm will often represent the issuer's interest in a negotiated sale.

Advantages:

1. *Assistance in originating the issue.* While the underwriter's primary role in a negotiated sale is as the purchaser of the issue, the underwriter can also assist the issuer in performing origination tasks such as preparing the official statement, making presentations to rating agencies, and obtaining credit enhancement—in essence, "one-stop shopping." Some issuers, however, prefer to engage a financial advisor or another investment banking firm for assistance in a negotiated sale. In a competitive sale, the issuer performing the origination tasks or pays for these services separately.

2. *Effective presale marketing.* Because the underwriter in a negotiated offering is assured the right to purchase the bonds, the underwriter can conduct more effective presale marketing than in a competitive sale. By developing information about market demand for the bonds, the underwriter can reduce inventory risk, presumably leading to a lower risk premium in the pricing. Presale marketing is especially important for issuers who have not developed a reputation among investors or whose securities are not widely held among investors.

3. *Timing and structural flexibility.* Another advantage of negotiated underwriting is flexibility—the ability to sell the bonds at any time and to change the structure of the issue in response to changing conditions. Although the issuer may announce a negotiated sale date, this date is considered a target and can be changed if deemed necessary (because of a large supply of similar securities or unfavorable interest rate movements, for example). Similarly, negotiated underwriting allows the issuer the flexibility to adjust the structure of the issue up until the time of sale to meet either the issuer's or the investor's needs.

4. *Influence over underwriter selection and bond distribution.* In a negotiated sale, the issuer exercises more influence over underwriter selection and bond distribution. The choice of the underwriter in a negotiated sale is based on a variety of criteria that may target certain types of underwriting firms and establish distribution goals. Issuers trying to reach certain market sectors may be able to negotiate with the underwriter to allocate the bonds accordingly. Again, this type of control should only be relevant to issuers wishing to include certain firms in the underwriting syndicate or wanting to make sure that certain types of customers receive a portion of the bonds.

Disadvantages:

1. *Lack of competition in the pricing.* In a negotiated sale, the bond pricing is less subject to the rigors of competition, as the underwriter obtains the exclusive right to purchase the bonds in advance of the pricing. Unless the issuer is vigilant during the pricing, the interest rates may be structured to protect the profit margin of the underwriter, not to keep the issuer's borrowing costs as low as possible. Although some underwriters may exercise restraint in the pricing to protect their reputation and promote future business, issuers should take the responsibility to obtain market information on comparable transactions at the time of pricing.

Source: California Debt Advisory Commission (1992). Used with permission.

Later research modified somewhat the bold assertion of this research. Bland (1985) succeeded in showing that Forbes and Peterson overstated their case, as his research suggested that experience may well inform the negotiation governments pursue with underwriters. In some cases, experience leads to substantial interest costs savings when compared to that paid by less experienced negotiating governments. The differences in costs associated with experience hold up against costs for competitively bid bond sales by local governments in New Jersey and Ohio as well.

Specifically, Bland's analysis suggests that as a negotiated sale issuer's experience increases, interests rates decline; that is, "when all other determinants of NIC are held constant, a negotiating issuer with the experience of four previous sales will obtain an interest rate that is 24 basis points lower than an issuer with no previous experience in the past decade" (p. 236). The difference holds up when experienced negotiators are compared to competitively bid issues.

> the sales of negotiating issuers with experience . . . imply that they are able to negotiate interest rates that are statistically comparable to what the most sought after competitive issues receive. The implication is that with some market experience, the management team of an issuer is capable of matching wits with the representatives of the underwriting syndicate and is able to negotiate an interest rate comparable to that which could be obtained if the issue were to receive seven or more competitive bids.

Finally, Bland found that negotiating issuers with no experience incur much the same interest costs as do those that receive three or fewer bids. Penalties, in other words, reward inexperience in making a market for a debt issue—making the issue attractive to a larger number of bidders—as much as it does inexperience in dealing with one underwriter through negotiation.

In summary, WPPSS led to a spiral ultimately ending in default. The Pennsylvania market potentially combines both, if as Forbes and Peterson claim, the insularity of these negotiated deals could lead to the partitioning of responsibility, as in WPPSS, so that no one party has the incentive to question others' assumptions.

III. THE GENERAL PROBLEM

The problem common to these instances of scandal, default, and waste is one of information poverty and undue deference to those who seem to help make up for it. Such situations are somewhat like the cobweb economists use to explain market instability and sellers' imperfect knowledge (Heilbroner and Thurow, 1984: 126–127); that is, markets in constant flux never provide enough certainty—information that lends itself to a patterned image—to compensate for a decision maker's lack of insight. The decision maker constantly decides matters either in terms of the reality of the past, often compounding past error, or through deference to those more likely to be privy to the secrets or nuances of a complex process or system.

To illustrate, permanent networks, which were to compensate for the inexperience of WPPSS managers, failed to remedy many of the gaps in knowledge and obstacles to taking responsibility. Leigland and Lamb (1986: 207–8) imply that some team at the helm taking overall responsibility might have compensated for the diffusion of responsibility and guilt. Conceivably, if these intermediaries had some enduring interest in stabilizing relations, then foresight, as well as institutional memory, might have developed.

The Pennsylvania controversy suggests that permanent networks within the municipal bond market for guaranteed debt create excessive interest costs, when compared to competitively bid issues. However, when handling debt issues that are sold less as commodities and more as craftwork, such as nonguaranteed and off-budget enterprise debt, teams relying on negotiated issues seem to learn as time passes, decreasing costs.

The conflict appears rather starkly if a little too simply at this point. The WPPSS and Pennsylvania cases involve use of stable routines and stable sets of advisors. In both cases, permanent networks that are useful for their ability to "learn" from the past or for their special access to information, become insular, self-serving sources of advice for governments. Is the problem this simple?

A. The Management Literature

The evidence from the literature, especially that on interorganizational networks, suggests conflicting tendencies toward insularity on the one hand or learning on the other. By a network, I mean the "totality of all the units connected by a certain relationship" (Jay, 1964: 138; Aldrich, 1979; Tichy et al., 1979). A network is constructed by discovering all the ties that bind a given population of organizations (Aldrich and Whetten, 1981). Stability evolves through the work of linking-pin organizations that have extensive and overlapping ties to different parts of a network. The links may be thought of functionally as communications channels between organizations, resource conduits among network members, and even models to be imitated by other organizations in the population. Thus, an accounting firm might channel information about a reporting standard from rating agencies to bond issuers; the firm might direct clients to financial advisors the firm's members respect as a result of previous bond sales; or the firm itself, through one or more of its many services, might serve as a model for a municipal finance office.

All organizations within a network are linked directly or indirectly, and stability depends on the strength of these links. Aldrich and Whetten (1981: 391) hypothesize

> The ultimate predictor of network stability is the probability of a link failing, given that another has failed. This, in turn, is a function of the probability of any one link failing and two network characteristics: the duplication of linkages and the multiplicity of linkages between any two organizations.

The stability of a network implies both the permanence of its membership and the redundancy of its members' ties with others inside and outside that network.

Such redundancy hypotheses find confirmation in the literature on public management. Landau (1969) argued that redundancy tends to ensure performance. Golembiewski (1964) has argued that duplication works, in symbiotic interrelationships, to prevent the exercise of vetoes by powerful subunits.

B. The Behavioral Literature

The small group literature provides further evidence which might apply to debt management networks. Compensating qualities can substitute for the lack of cohesion in financing teams, a problem some point to as compounding and others as remedying the insularity that grows as the same members continually work with each other (Shaw and Shaw, 1962; Sukurai, 1975; Murnighan and Conlon, 1991).

One of these compensating qualities is heterogeneity. Hoffman (1966) has shown that group members with heterogeneous backgrounds tend to work together more effectively, up to a point, because of the greater diversity of information they bring. Since group membership permanence tends to lead to a homogenizing of views (Sherif, 1935; Festinger, 1950), diversity might counter that tendency.

Diversity implies turnover, however. Trow (1960) suggests that turnover leads to short-run decline in performance as the group undergoes reorganization. Katz (1982), on the other hand, found that among 50 R&D teams he studied, long-time membership on a team reduced the team's performance. While performance increased in the first 2 years, it fell thereafter. After 5 years, performance declined to below that which existed when the team members began their work together.

A second quality compensating for either too much or too little cohesion in financing teams is equality of status or even more likely, settled status. Research shows that groups are more productive when members can avoid status struggle, either because positions of members (who's the leader) are relatively stable or because the method of cost sharing or surplus sharing are settled (Moulin, 1989).

Finally, the research indicates that either stability or turnover might result in a greater willingness to take risks and greater adaptability. Richly joined networks provide for greater opportunity for trial and error and for the spread of innovation (Aldrich, 1979: 282; Terreberry, 1968), yet Price (1977) argues that turnover provides the chance for infusing new knowledge and technology through the replacement of old network members who were more comfortable following familiar patterns and methods.

Thus, neither turnover nor stability inevitably leads to higher performance, greater innovation, or, in other words, smart adaptation to changing circumstances (Hom et al., 1995: 531–582).

C. The Knowledge from Actual Practice

Assume a simplistic situation, momentarily, a small municipal financing network consisting of a financial advisor, an accounting firm, and a law firm (Lemov, 1990). The three are richly joined in the following ways:

1. The law firm acts as corporation counsel to the other two organizations.
2. The accounting firm audits the transactions of the other two organizations; moreover, auditors have been recruited and have joined the financial advising firm from time to time as principals.

3. The three organizations are active in the new-issue market for municipal securities with all other possible participants, and they serve together on a team for a bond sale for an issuer.

An issuer becomes the beneficiary of knowledge about changes made by Congress in tax laws relating to municipal debt, about specific needs for information by rating agencies, and new debt structures that may be designed to appeal to specific segments of the market. The richly joined network ultimately results in the issuer's ability to adjust to complex and changing environments.

Now consider a more complex example. Assume that among a population of law firms that act as bond counsel, the firms tend as a matter of principle to differ in their approach to interpreting the law as it regards various creative capital financing structures, some firms being indulgent, others strict. Assume, furthermore, that in a population of accounting firms asked to forecast the revenue stream that would generate principal and interest payments for various creative capital financing structures, some firms would tend to be liberal, others tight. Finally, assume that among a population of financial advisors, the same sort of variation would exist among opinions about the applicability and marketability of debt structures.

Random selection of a combination of these firms by an issuer—through competitive bidding, for example—would yield a team advising the issuer to take a particular course of action, one in which the knowledge each advisor had, as well as the expectation each had of the other's interpretation and its effect on the market for the issue, would play a part. The result would produce a bargain in which a security configured in a unique way was rated and sold.

Now assume a second random selection of firms by an issuer and a second sale. What knowledge does the second team have about the configuration of the first security? What keeps the second team from relying on an incorrect interpretation of what the first team did? What keeps the second sale from "missing the market?"

D. The Experience with Debt Sales

The process of issuing debt involves four steps. Initiation of a sale rests on the choice of the market. Which investors will/should buy the securities? Tax laws, the economic cycle, and the habitual purchasing practices of individuals and institutions combine in various ways. They create choices based on the probability that legislators, interest rates, and consumers will behave in reasonably predictable ways.

The second step in the process involves structuring a debt issue to confront two problems: the predilections of the market chosen and the capacity of the issuer. The market choices put a premium on accuracy, but the ability of the issuer to manage the debt provided in the structure sets limits.

The structure directly connects the market with disclosure of the issue and the issuer, the third step. What facts will be disclosed, and more important, what interpretation will be presented for these facts in the major document for disclosing information, the offering statement (OS), and the presentations to ratings agencies?

The final step is the sale, at which time all parties decide the price of the issue. The sale confirms the assumptions made by the team about the structure of the issue and the level of demand for the quantity provided. In viewing the sale another way, it becomes a confirming piece of information about where the sale fell on the cobweb. If the guess about supply and demand resulted in a spiral inward, I can say the team "learned."

Consider what factors might encourage "learning." I would expect that the number of links among members of the team leads to stability, and stability, in turn, leads either to insularity or to learning and adaptation. An expectations approach helps to understand richly linked organizations in the bond team context; that is, each member of the bond team must be guided in each other's assigned task by expectations of the behavior of others. The financial advisor cannot select a market unless the advisor can expect to have counsel's positive legal interpretation of the structure that would most logically follow the selection of that market. Likewise, the advisor cannot select a market without the expectation that the CPA will interpret the various issuer capacities in such a way as to support the structure the market suggests. No decision made by any member of the team, in the end, can be made in a vacuum, without the knowledge of what the other members are likely to do. Otherwise, the decisions made by the members form an endless iteration—a loop—in which market choice forces structure but is confounded by disclosure leading to a new market and a new structure and interpretations wedded to the previous structure.

One solution to the problem of expectations is to live with the short-term chaos that lies in individuals getting organized, as the small group literature suggests. Another solution might exist in a richly linked network of organizations. Rich links lead to knowledge of likely behavior under varying circumstances. Assumptions at extremely general levels are shared or at least made widely known through large numbers of activities in which the linked organizations jointly participate. Rich links also provide multiple avenues for testing expectations under widely varying conditions. For example, the legal interpretations a bond counsel is likely to submit may be expected based on the legal interpretations the bond counsel has traditionally issued in the capacity of the corporate counsel, as the earlier illustration depicted.

If rich links lead to shared expectations of behavior, these links contribute either to insularity or to learning. Consider the argument for specific types of teams in municipal finance. The negotiated rather than the competitive sale invites the sort of stability and exploitation of existing rich links among potential members of a team. Negotiated sales require the issuer to choose precisely those members who have apparently learned the market as well as each other in terms of the market. A negotiated sale provides an opportunity to choose the market (especially when the sale is privately placed), opening the way or creating the need for innovation (craft work rather than routine technology) in the type of issue structure chosen. The negotiated sale also provides incredible overlap and duplication in the work involved.

Such rich links and the opportunities provided by the negotiated sale invite learning. Stigler (1961) indicated that buyers and sellers accumulate information from their experience in the marketplace that allows them to obtain more favorable conditions in each successive transaction. More specifically, Bland (1985) found that issuers using multiple negotiated sales received more favorable terms through each successive sale *up to a certain point*. He concluded (p. 236): "Local governments with previous bond market experience are capable of assembling a management team that can negotiate an interest rate comparable to what the most sought after competitive issues obtain."

Nevertheless, the evidence indicating that either competitive or negotiated sales are preferable is inconclusive. In a wide-ranging review of studies comparing both methods of sale in the tax-exempt and corporate markets, Leonard (1994a: 3) concluded that "many good arguments . . . favor the proposition that municipalities opt for negotiated sales of bonds more often than they should," but that "competitive bidding has not always been the lowest cost method of sale" (1994b: 36). He went on to say that perhaps the decision rules followed by issuers have led to proportions of each sale that are appropriate.

E.   Rich Links and Relative Wealth

Within networks, status, especially that created by wealth, makes possible economies of influence. We would expect that wealth differences encourage or preclude influence, as the case may be. Wealth creates advantage, and lack of wealth results in dependence on sources of information. Such a dependency would reduce creativity, making links among network members and the larger environment poorer rather than richer.

F.   Rich Links and Incentives

Dreams of changing one's status as well as the appearance of opportunity creates an incentive system that serves to encourage creativity. The poor seek opportunities that help their unique positions, making their information or their energy to gain information valuable to the network. The rich take advantage of opportunities to increase wealth even if it advantages everyone in the network, but they foresee developing opportunities. They influence the image of events people, and they coopt important skills, broadening their own view and encouraging status changes.

G.   A Recap

A network's stability or instability interacts with the wealth and number of links among its members and the incentives offered by the network to its members. The literature conflicts. One direction the literature takes suggests that the greater the stability, the greater the opportunities for learning, and the greater the amount of learning, the greater the chance for innovation and adaptation. From the literature that takes another direction, I infer that the greater the stability, the more likely it is that network members try to impose their view of the world; this view may or may not be tenable, making risk greater and error more likely.

If an efficient market is one that allocates scarce capital among competing uses, and assigns appropriate prices (interest payments to the issuer and bond prices and yields to the investor) to structures at particular levels of repayment capacity, under what conditions does network stability or instability lead to market efficiency? The answer lies in the test of a network stability model against a network instability model.

IV. THE PROPOSITIONS

Does stability among bond sale team members or the market as a whole have any bearing on the tendency for events to explode out of control? What effect does wealth and the incentive to increase that wealth have on this tendency? We explore these factors in an experiment involving relatively knowledgeable and ambitious research subjects. There are three basic propositions in this research.

Proposition 1: The more stable the group, the faster the learning; that is, the more often individuals work together, the sooner they derive a common view of events, as well as mechanisms for processing and acting on novel events. The common view enables them to see the patterned uncertainties on which they may act profitably.

Proposition 2: The greater the initial equality of resources among members of the group, the greater the learning; that is, the fewer the differences in status among members, the sooner these differences are settled, the sooner the group is organized, and the sooner the group can process and act on information to the common benefit of the group's members.

Proposition 3: The greater the willingness of the group to match individual contributions with individual rewards (to provide payoffs proportional to contributions), the greater the learning. Matching risk with reward provides incentives to learn; that is, to get organized to process information.

V. THE EXPERIMENT

My research design aimed at isolating the factors gathered from the literature that coexisted with learning in the face of randomness. Basically, I employed a repeated measures design. I recruited graduate master's of public administration students to participate in a game ostensibly related to the stability of budgets and the prediction of environmental resource change over time (based on Pfeiffer, 1974). For a more detailed description of the experiment, see Table 2, the Appendix, and Miller (1993).

VI. FINDINGS

The research leans toward confirming that stable groups breed insularity and not learning. In short, the more unstable the membership of a group, the faster the learning. The first and most basic observation of this finding is portrayed in Fig. 1.

Unstable teams' error rates, although initially higher than those of stable teams, declined sharply, as measured

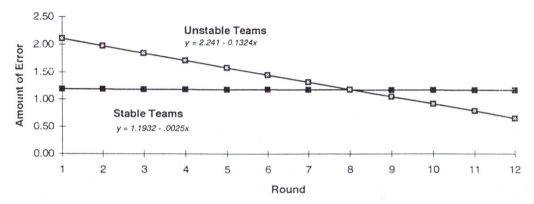

Figure 1 Error rates among stable and unstable teams.

by the statistic and the equation. Those rates among stable teams failed to decline at all. Among stable teams, the slope of the line failed to gain significance; that is, the inference that the slope equals zero is substantially greater than chance.

A. Stability and Wealth

To measure the differences that equal wealth among participants may have had on the ability to learn, I removed those groups from the stable side that started out with unequal resources; there were no such groups among unstable groups. While this left only two stable groups (compared to eight unstable groups) and threatened any inference I draw, the direction is toward even less learning. (See Fig. 2.)

As Fig. 2 suggests, the error rates of the two stable teams actually increased instead of decreased. The lack of statistical significance, however, fails to allow me to say that the slope of the line is not zero. The slope of the line describing Fig. 2's stable groups' error rates and those stable groups in Fig. 1 is significantly/not significantly different, in fact.

B. Stable Groups and Incentives

Finally, I removed the groups with reward structures that did not give incentives to take risks from those that did. That left only one stable group, threatening inferences again. However, as Fig. 3 portrays, the stable team's error rate declined a bit, but not to the same degree as unstable groups with rewards proportional to risks taken.

The Fig. 3 results, however, should not be generalized without question to all stable groups in the situations such as those we describe, WPPSS or Pennsylvania local governments. The difference in the slope of the error rates of the Fig. 3 stable group and those in the larger samples is not significant statistically.

VII. DISCUSSION

The small groups here, and their results, give some insight into the mechanics of stable and unstable teams. Unstable teams learn faster in an uncertain problem-solving situation than do stable groups. Why? Consider four groups of explanations.

The management literature suggests that stronger links among network members led to stability, a trait that might yield learning and adaptability. The inference from this research project suggests otherwise; in fact, the opposite. Very little learning occurred in the stable groups I observed. The generalization that network members feather their own nests when there is little uncertainty might hold; it finds confirmation in many cases such as those described at the beginning of this chapter.

The behavioral literature suggests that diversity leads to instability and a short-run performance decline, and yet also long-term effectiveness. I found confirmation for this idea in this research. The generalization, especially to the Pennsylvania local government case, is that *competitively bidded sales (and advice) might be just as effective as negotiated sales* in all but the most uncertain situations.

The literature on practice suggests that richly joined network members (stable teams) may find it easier than less richly joined members to form an image of an uncertain situation such as a constantly changing market. The question was left open as to whether or not the image was tenable. The real question, however, may be whether stable teams can change their quickly formed image rapidly if wrong. The evidence from this research suggests otherwise. In fact, unstable teams may well adapt more quickly. The necessity to adapt is clear in the cobweb illustrated earlier; adaptability prevents an exploding cobweb, a situation in which the reality of the past is the only reality and one that compounds error.

From debt issuance experience, I read that mutually predictable expectations among team members reduce the time required to negotiate a common view of the world; in short, to understand market reality. My research suggests that this may be the case, as evident in the lower initial errors made by stable teams. However, the lower error rates existed only in the short term as error rates of stable teams quickly rivaled and then surpassed those of unstable teams. I generalize that the diversity inherent in an unstable team may provide opportunities for devil's advocates to question comfortable views and to offer a healthy skepticism overall.

Finally, the role played by the initial wealth of group members and the group's incentive system became only marginally clearer. Because my findings did not achieve statistical significance, careful generalization

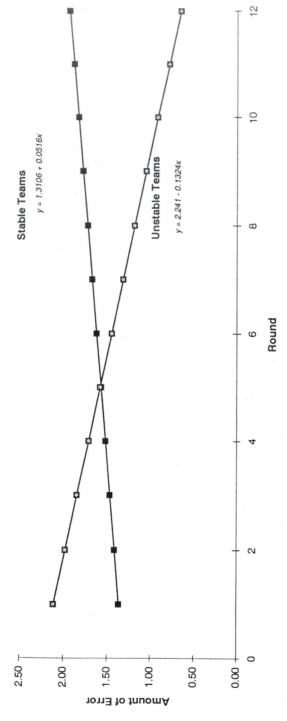

Figure 2   Error rates among stable and unstable teams that began with equal resources among members.

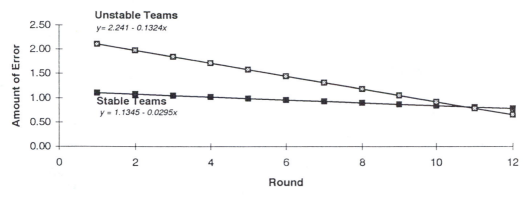

Figure 3   Error rates among stable and unstable teams that provided payoff incentives proportional to members' contributions.

is essential. I conclude that rewards and incentives do play a role. Rewards may decrease dependence and advantage while increasing the potential for learning. Incentives that are proportionate to risk do seem to encourage reduction of error. Further research will shed light on the interaction among these variables.

In summary, what disciplining strategy does this research suggest for the WPPSS default and the Pennsylvania interest cost controversy? First, my research sides with competition among members in a debt management network. Clearly, that seems the case for the vast majority of state and local government bond sales.

Second, my research suggests the need for extremely clear priority schedules on the part of government financial managers. Clear priorities can aid in applying discipline to network members, especially if it is clear that market competition, budget slack, or interest cost savings is of paramount interest.

Finally, work among members of a debt management network may not require rich links as described here; however, redundancy and mutual expectations must exist. Decentralizing debt management networks (creatively following Golembiewski, 1964; Eccles and Crane, 1988) to the government department level could easily promote redundancy of the most creative type; that is, some departments' needs may favor leasing over bond financing, and some may require negotiated rather than competitive bidding. Yet, all must have ways of inducing competition. Others will require some financing technique tailored more closely to the project or financial needs unique to them.

Multiple, sometimes overlapping teams—from inside the government organization as well as from outside—serve these different needs. Counsel, audit, and financial advising functions inside government could act as redundant functions with those from outside government.

High-level integration would enforce mutual expectations. Priorities—marketing, budgetary slack, or cost savings—might differ across departments, but high-level comparisons of these decentralized units would focus attention on those units that are failing and promote emulation of those units that are succeeding. Decentralization actually reduces barriers to communication—counsels could talk to counsels across financing projects about tax legislation, for example—enforcing the disciplinary strategy being pursued.

Suggesting that diversity has short-term costs but even greater long-term benefits, this work on debt

Table 2   Diagrammatic View of Research Design (stable versus unstable team)

	Wave 1						Wave 2							
Team	1	2	3	4	5	6	1	2	3	4	5	6	7	8
Membership	S	S	S	C	C	C	S	S	S	C	C	C	C	C
Initial distribution	E	U	U	E	E	E	E	U	U	E	E	E	E	E
Payoff distribution							E	R	P	P	P	P	P	P

Note: S = stable; C = changing; E = equal; U = unequal; R = random; P = proportional.

management networks has attempted to resolve the conflict between the certainty of routine financial advising and insularity that often comes along with that same certainty. At all costs, this research sheds light on and even promotes competition, clear priorities, and redundancies in such a system. While further research on both empirical and practical fronts will sharpen the conclusions here, what has emerged so far accords with long-standing management thinking that should influence financial management as well.

APPENDIX

The explanation to the students began with the following directions:

> This exercise presents you with two tasks—to be thorough and to win. In the exercise, you will bid for a series of payoffs. You will not know the precise value of any one payoff, but you will know the range of possibilities. Along with other members of your group, you must risk your personal assets in order to compile the bid.

In a first wave, students were organized into six teams of four students each. Each group was given resources (in the form of stones) representing $10. The amounts given each individual in the group varied even though each group's total was the same; in some groups, members got equal amounts and in others unequal amounts.

Each group had to bid for each of a series of ten payoffs, the exact amount of which they did not know. All groups were, however, given information about the range of payoffs over the ten rounds plus the amount of the largest and smallest payoff. Each group's bid required a contribution from each group member.

The groups, as organized, varied not only in equal/unequal resources given each group member at the start of the bidding; the groups also differed in the stability of members. Three of the groups remained intact through the ten rounds. The other three groups had unstable membership. Members, by design, went from one group to one of the other two after each round; none of these groups ever had the same members for two consecutive rounds.

To vary incentives, a second wave of graduate MPA students underwent a similar auction exercise. The same basic conditions applied although there were eight rather than six groups. In addition to variations in initial resources for each group member, the reward structure varied as well; that is, some groups' rules provided that should they win, their winnings had to be divided in one of three specified ways—equally, proportionally to contribution, or randomly—no matter what the method of contribution specified.

Group members were asked to record the amounts of their personal contributions and the group's bids and winnings.

The two waves appear in diagrammatic form in Table 2.

The learning was suggested by the difference between the payoff and each group's bid and between the payoff and each group's bid in the subsequent round. Statistics were computed to distinguish groups: ordinary least squares and its inferential referents.

REFERENCES

Aldrich, H. E. (1979). *Organizations and Environments*, Prentice-Hall, Englewood Cliffs, N.J.
Aldrich, H. E. and Whetten, D. A. (1981). *Handbook of Organizational Design, vol. 1* (P. C. Nystrom and W. H. Starbuck, eds.), Oxford University Press, New York.
Bland, R. L. (1985). *Pub. Admin. Rev.*, 45: 233–237.
Blumstein, M. (1983). "The Lessons of a Bond Failure." *New York Times* (Aug. 14): Business (Section 3), pp. 1, 24.
California Debt Advisory Commission (1992). *Competitive versus Negotiated Sale of Debt*, issue brief no. 1, Sacramento.
Eccles, R. G. and Crane, D. B. (1988). *Doing Deals: Investment Banks at Work*, Harvard Business School Press, Cambridge, Mass.
The Economist (1991a). "The World Bond Bazaar" (Sept. 21), p. 95.
The Economist (1991b). "Broken Bonds" (Sept. 21), pp. 18–19.
Farrell, C. (1991). "Did Salomon's Scheming Raise Interest Rates?" *Business Week* (Sept. 2): 69.
Festinger, L. (1950). *Psych. Rev.*, 57: 271–292.
Forbes, R. W. and Petersen, J. E. (1979). *Local Government General Obligation Bond Sales in Pennsylvania: The Cost Implications of Negotiation vs. Competitive Bidding*, Government Finance Research Center, Municipal Finance Officers Association, Washington, D.C.
Golembiewski, R. T. (1964). *The Acct. Rev.*, 39: 333–341.
Heilbroner, R. L. and Thurow, L. C. (1984). *Understanding Microeconomics*, 6th ed., Prentice-Hall, Englewood Cliffs, N.J.

Hoffman, R. L. (1966). *Advances in Experimental Social Psychology, vol. 2* (L. Berkowitz, ed.), Academic Press, New York, pp. 99–132.

Hom, P. W., Griffeth, R. W., and Carson, P. P. (1995). *Handbook of Public Personnel Administration* (J. Rabin, T. Vocino, W. B. Hildreth, and G. J. Miller, eds.), Marcel Dekker, New York, pp. 531–582.

Jay, E. J. (1964). *Man, 64:* 137–139.

Jones, L. R. (1984). *Pub. Budgeting and Finance* (winter): 60–77.

Katz, R. (1982). *Admin. Sci. Q., 27:* 81–104.

Kleinbaum, D. G. and Kupper, L. L. (1978). *Applied Regression Analysis and Other Multivariable Methods*, Duxbury Press, North Scituate, Mass.

Landau, M. (1969). *Pub. Admin. Rev., 29:* 346–358.

Leigland, J. and Lamb, R. (1986). *WPP$$: Who Is to Blame for the WPPSS Disaster*, Ballinger, Cambridge, Mass.

Lemov, P. (1990). *Governing* (June): 52–58.

Leonard, P. (1994a). *Review of Studies of Competitive and Negotiated Financing of Municipal and Corporate Bonds*, Public Securities Association, New York.

Leonard, P. (1994b). *Municipal Fin. J., 15* (2): 12–36.

McNamee, M., Woolley, S., and Weiss, G. (1991). *Bus. Week* (Oct. 14): 102–103.

Morris, C. R. (1980). *The Cost of Good Intentions*, McGraw-Hill, New York.

Miller, G. J. (1991). *Government Financial Management Theory*, Marcel Dekker, New York.

Miller, G. J. (1992). *Investment Banks, Bidding Syndicates, Network Stability, and Government Productivity*, paper prepared for the British Conference on Public Administration, London, Aug. 1992.

Miller, G. J. (1993). *Pub. Admin. Rev., 53:* 50–58.

Moulin, H. (1989). *Axioms of Cooperative Decision Making*, Cambridge University Press, Cambridge, U.K.

Mundell, R. A. (1975). *The Phenomenon of Worldwide Inflation* (D. Meiselman and A. B. Laffer, eds.), American Enterprise Institute, Washington, D.C., quoted in Wanninski, J. (1978). *The Way the World Works*, Touchstone/Simon & Schuster, New York, Chap. 6.

Murnighan, J. K. and Conlon, D. E. (1991). *Admin. Sci. Q., 36:* 165–186.

Myhra, D. (1984). *Whoops!/WPPSS*, McFarland, Jefferson, N.C.

Pfeiffer, J. W. (1974). *A Handbook of Structured Experiences for Human Relations Training*, vol. 2, rev. (J. W. Pfeiffer and J. E. Jones, eds.), University Associates, La Jolla, Calif., pp. 58–61.

Price, J. L. (1977). *The Study of Turnover*, Iowa State University Press, Ames.

Sukurai, M. M. (1975). *Sociometry, 38:* 234–242.

Sharp, E. (1986). *Amer. Polit. Sci. Rev., 80:* 1271–1288.

Shaw, M. E. and Shaw, L. M. (1962). *J. Social Psych., 57:* 453–458.

Sherif, M. (1935). *Archives Psych., 27* (187).

Stigler, G. J. (1961). *J. Polit. Econ.,* (July/Aug.): 706–738.

Terreberry, S. (1968). *Admin. Sci. Q., 12:* 590–613.

Tichy, N. M., Tushman, M. L., and Fombrun, C. (1979). *Acad. Mgt. Rev., 4:* 507–519.

Trow, D. B. (1960). *Human Relat., 13:* 259–269.

Weiss, G., Spiro, L. N., and Foust, D. (1991). *Bus. Week* (Sept. 2): 66–70.

20

Choosing an Underwriter for a Negotiated Bond Sale

Tom McLoughlin
Government Finance Officers Association, Washington, D.C.

The increased use of the negotiated sale as a means of issuing bonds has been a striking characteristic of the municipal securities market during the past 20 years. In a negotiated sale, the securities are offered to an underwriter or underwriting syndicate which is selected in advance of the sale date by the issuer. The terms are subject to negotiation between the issuer and the purchaser. As Figs. 1 and 2 illustrate, both the volume and the percentage of bonds that have been sold in this manner have risen dramatically since 1973.

The proliferation of limited-obligation bonds to finance public improvements has contributed to the pronounced trend toward negotiated sales. Unlike general obligation bonds, which are secured by a full faith and credit pledge of the issuer, limited obligation securities depend exclusively upon the stream of revenue provided from an enterprise or from an annual budget appropriation. The issuer's obligation to pay debt service is subject to the sufficiency of the pledged revenue stream. As a result, these obligations are usually not subject to public referendum. The absence of a referendum is an important consideration for state and local government issuers because of the prevalent sentiment against higher taxes.

To compensate for the weaker security features or unusual payment structure of limited-obligation security instruments, the issuer and its underwriter must identify potential purchasers earlier in the issuance process in order to convince them to make a substantial investment. The underwriter's sales representatives are not likely to spend a considerable amount of time assessing the unique features of a limited-obligation bond unless they have a reasonable assurance that the issuer will provide them with an inventory of bonds to sell. In a competitive sale, the issuer cannot make such an assurance. By adopting the negotiated sale as the method of choice, the issuer can encourage a more concerted marketing effort from the underwriter's sales force.

State and local governments also turn to the negotiated sale with greater frequency when the municipal securities market becomes more volatile. Even the most sophisticated managers of competitive bidding accounts can suffer substantial financial loss when interest rates fluctuate abruptly. In volatile markets, such as those in 1981–1982 and again in 1986 prior to the enactment of the Tax Reform Act, issuers cannot be assured of receiving aggressive bids for their securities in a competitive environment. By negotiating the sale of bonds directly with a managing underwriter selected in advance, market conditions can be monitored more closely to the issuer's advantage.

Although there are certain instances when a negotiated sale is a useful alternative to the receipt of competitive bids, the finance officer's responsibility to safeguard the public trust also becomes more acute when negotiation is chosen as the preferred method of sale. The inherent protection afforded by open competition is absent. The issuer must take an active role in determining the underwriter's compensation, participate in the development of a comprehensive marketing plan, and monitor market conditions to assure that the true interest

Adapted from *Government Finance Review*, June 1990: 28-30 by permission of Government Finance Officers Association.

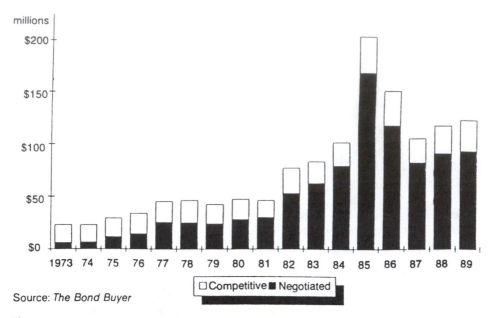

Figure 1   Increase in the dollar volume of negotiated sales.

cost is an accurate reflection of the existing yield curve for similar securities. The willingness and ability of the finance officer to meet this responsibility is crucial to the success of a negotiated sale.

I. THE REQUEST FOR PROPOSALS

Many issuers have chosen to issue a request for proposals (RFP) as a means of selecting an underwriter or underwriting syndicate. The RFP enables the finance officer to choose an experienced underwriter from a

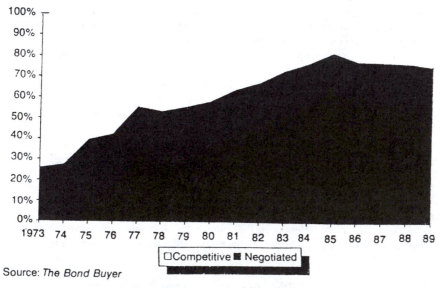

Figure 2   Percentage of long-term municipal bonds financed through negotiation.

very large group of capable firms. Each RFP will differ due to the unique circumstances surrounding the issuance of the securities. At a minimum, however, the RFP should describe the purpose for which the bonds will be issued, the source or sources of revenues expected to be pledged to bond security, the anticipated size and term (or life) of the issue, and a description of the criteria that will be used to select the underwriter(s).

Any limitations on the structure of the proposed issue, such as the maximum amount of debt service that the issuer can afford to pay in any given year, also should be described in detail. All too often, a state or local government issuer will receive a well-crafted proposal from an experienced firm which will be rejected because of a misunderstanding about the political or budgetary constraints faced by the issuer.

Once the project is described in sufficient detail to generate interest among members of the underwriting community, the RFP should request information about the firm's experience in underwriting similarly secured bond issues. For example, the underwriting firm may be able to provide the services of an investment banker well versed in the structuring and marketing of lease revenue bonds or certificates of participation. If the proposed financing has such special features, the ability of the underwriter to demonstrate the availability of an acknowledged expert is indispensable.

Some types of issues, such as variable-rate demand obligations, require the services of an underwriter with a strong institutional sales force. For other types of issues, the ability of the underwriter to sell bonds to the growing number of individual investors is desirable. This latter type of marketing ability is especially important for issuers in states with a relatively high income tax rate. In these states, individual investors are likely to accept a lower rate of interest than institutional investors because of the unique advantages that tax exemption provides for their personal investment strategy.

The ability of the managing underwriter to maintain a secondary market for the issuer's bond issue also should be assessed. Although the secondary market for municipal securities is less organized than the one for corporate equities, some firms do specialize in the purchase and resale of certain types of securities. Some regional investment banks specialize in trades involving bonds issued by a particular state or one of its political subdivisions. The ability of the managing underwriter to "make a market" in the issuer's bonds after the sale is consummated is an important consideration because the liquidity of the investment will affect the rate of interest demanded by the investor.

In summary, the RFP for underwriting services needs to be specific enough to allow for a fair comparison of multiple proposals, but general enough to permit creative responses to the issuer's financing needs.

II. COMPENSATION

In the vast majority of cases, the underwriting spread is the largest component of total issuance costs. According to the preliminary results of a survey completed by the Financial Markets Research Center of the State University of New York at Albany, the underwriting spread ranged from 48% to 88% of the total cost of financing a long-term debt issue. The actual percentage varied depending upon the amount of bonds being sold.

In a negotiated sale, the underwriter is compensated for its services by the initial discount that it receives on the purchase of the bond issue. The amount of the discount, or "gross underwriting spread," will vary depending upon market conditions and a number of other factors. At a minimum, however, the discount should be based upon a reasonable interpretation of the amount of effort required to structure the bond issue and to sell the securities at a favorable rate of interest.

The underwriting spread is often quoted on the basis of "dollars per bond" with each bond representing $1,000. Although most long-term bond issues are now sold in $5,000 denominations, the use of a $1,000 face amount in determining the underwriter's compensation is a vestige of an earlier era in public finance when most municipal bonds were sold in the smaller $1,000 denomination. Thus, an underwriting spread of $12 per bond would equal 1.2% of the principal amount of the bonds. On a $20 million issue, the discount would be equal to $240,000.

The spread comprises four components, each of which is priced separately. The *management fee* compensates the investment bankers on the public finance staff of the underwriter for their work in the development and implementation of the financing. The amount of the management fee will vary considerably because it is largely dependent upon the amount of time and effort involved in structuring the bond issue. Complicated and time-consuming bond financings will demand a higher management fee than the fee accorded more conventional issues.

The issuer also is expected to reimburse the underwriter for out-of-pocket expenses. In effect, the *expense* component of the spread represents the cost of operating the syndicate. The largest expense associated with the underwriter's participation usually is the fee charged by underwriter's counsel. If the issuer chooses a managing underwriter who does not maintain a public finance office in the local area, the cost of travel also can constitute a significant expense for which the issuer will be liable. In its RFP, the issuer also should state whether the underwriter should include the cost of printing the official statement as an itemized expense. As the concern for adequate disclosure grows, publication costs also are likely to increase.

The *underwriting fee*, also called the *"risk"* component of the spread, sometimes is included in proposals from interested firms. The fee is designed to compensate the underwriter for taking the risk of purchasing the entire bond issue before it has received offsetting orders from investors for all of the bonds. In effect, the fee is supposed to offer some protection to the underwriter in case of an abrupt increase in the rates of interest demanded by investors before the firm has had a chance to sell all of the bonds. However, the actual risk experienced by the underwriting syndicate in a negotiated sale is less than the risk inherent in a competitive issue. In a negotiated sale, the underwriter will have received a substantial number of firm orders at the proposed yield prior to making a commitment to the issuer to purchase the bond issue. If a very large portion of the issue was placed with investors prior to purchase, the underwriter may agree to waive the underwriting fee. The willingness of the underwriter to waive the fee in case of a strong reception from the market for the issuer's bonds should be determined early in the issuance process.

The *takedown* is generally the largest component of the underwriter's spread. It represents the discount at which syndicate members buy or "take down" bonds from the overall underwriting account. The takedown also is used to determine the salespersons' compensation for marketing the bonds. The amount of the takedown varies with the degree of difficulty involved in selling the bonds on behalf of the issuer. In general, longer maturities require a higher takedown fee than shorter maturities.

Although the issuer will pay the entire takedown fee regardless of which underwriter actually sells the bonds, it is worthwhile to note that there are two distinct parts of the takedown. In order to encourage other municipal bond dealers who are not members of the syndicate to sell bonds on behalf of the issuer, some syndicates offer other firms a "concession." The concession represents a discount on the par value of the bonds. By purchasing bonds at the concession, and subsequently selling them to an investor at par, other dealers are able to make a small profit. The remainder of the takedown, often termed the "additional takedown," is retained by the underwriting syndicate for its own profit. However, if the bonds are sold directly to an investor by a member of the underwriting syndicate, then that firm is entitled to the entire takedown.

The request for proposals for underwriting services resembles other RFPs to the extent that it should request information about the fee that will be charged by the interested bidder for its services. The underwriter should be able to provide a firm indication of the size of the gross spread necessary to sell an issue such as the one described in the RFP. Two components of the spread, the management fee and underwriting fee, can be provided with certainty. The other two components, takedown and the expenses, must be estimated in light of current market conditions (though usually underwriters are prepared to offer a cap on expenses).

Upon receipt of the proposals, the finance officer will be tempted to examine the proposed fees immediately and select the firm with the lowest spread. Resisting this temptation is advisable for two reasons. First, the proposals will contain other equally valuable information by which to judge the merits and abilities of the underwriters. For instance, each proposal must be examined to determine which firm has made the most appropriate staff assignments. Ideally, the assigned bankers should have some prior experience in arranging similar types of financing. The marketing plan also should be reviewed to ascertain whether the interested firm will be able to identify those investors who can provide the most favorable interest rates. The issuer also should not rely solely upon the estimate of the spread for a second reason. On occasion, some firms may offer to underwrite a bond issue for an exceptionally low spread. Most often, this will result in a takedown which is not large enough to generate much interest among the underwriter's sales force to work hard on behalf of the issuer. In effect, their sales commission is not large enough to warrant much effort trying to identify investors willing to purchase the bonds at the most favorable interest cost to the issuer. The issuer's desire to reduce the initial discount should be balanced against the goal of obtaining the best rate of interest over the life of the issue. For the largest and most active bond issuers, whose presence in the market demands attention from underwriters and investors alike, this balance is more easily struck than for smaller issuers.

Perhaps the most valuable tool in choosing an underwriter is the telephone. Finance officers are encouraged to contact other units of government with similar characteristics and financing needs. The performance of the underwriter on behalf of a neighboring government is the best indication of its future ability to work on behalf of another community. For a negotiated sale to result in the lowest overall cost of financing, the finance officer must be prepared to spend a considerable amount of time reviewing the underwriter's past performance, independently gauging current market conditions, and assessing the likely market for the bond issue prior to pricing the securities.

21
Municipal Bond Issue Structuring

Amy V. Puelz
Edwin L. Cox School of Business, Southern Methodist University, Dallas, Texas

I. INTRODUCTION

A serial municipal bond issue is typically a long-term commitment by a locality or state with a portion of the debt maturing each year until the final maturity date. This chapter focuses on the serial bond issue structuring process. In structuring a bond issue, an issuer has a number of decisions such as the type and size of coupon payment to attach to the bonds, whether insurance or another form of a guarantee should be purchased, if and when a call provision should be attached to the bonds, how the sale of the bonds should be handled, and who should be responsible for the sale. These decisions, along with a myriad of other financial and regulatory considerations, must be addressed in the bond-structuring process. This chapter addresses these decisions from the perspective of the issuer of tax-exempt debt and how cost-effective debt issues must be structured so as to meet the requirements of their investing markets while capitalizing on their unique tax status.

The remainder of this section discusses why the issuance of cost-effective bonds is so critical in the new municipal bond market. Section II presents the participants in the process followed by an enumeration of the decision that must be made. The remainder of the chapter discusses each decision in detail and how each affects the cost of issuing debt.

Traditionally, issuers of tax-exempt debt have not been required to structure bond issues with the precision required by today's market conditions. Prior to the mid-1980s issuers of municipal bonds supplied a market characterized by a relatively stable demand from banks and property and casualty insurance companies that purchased the debt for legal and profit-sheltering reasons. In addition, there were opportunities for the bond issuer to earn risk-free arbitrage profits by investing the proceeds from low-cost bond issues in higher-yielding taxable securities. During the mid-1980s and early 1990s declining demand for municipal bonds by banks and insurance companies caused by changes in tax laws, defaults and near defaults of exempt issuers, taxpayer revolts, and federal government regulatory changes, helped to shape the new tax-exempt marketplace. In order to compete with the taxable sector for the funds in these new markets, municipal financiers must be innovative and produce a more marketable product that matches the public's needs. While many ideas from the taxable sector can be applied to the problem, the tax-exempt market requires special examination on a number of topics. The individual needs of tax-exempt issuers such as states and local governments and the consideration of the political, regulatory, and legal environments in which they must operate necessitate a specialized approach to the structuring of tax-exempt debt.

Momentum promoting change in municipal finance was initiated through the federal government's Tax Reform Act of 1986 (TRA 86). The sections of this legislation directed at issuers of tax-exempt debt virtually eliminated arbitrage opportunities, limited the number and type of issuers of private activity bonds, and reduced the tax incentive afforded the largest markets for municipal bonds—banks and property and casualty insurance companies.

The virtual elimination of arbitrage profits (which are profits earned when relatively inexpensive tax-exempt dollars are invested at higher taxable rates) was one of the major impacts of the TRA 86. The practice of reinvesting low-cost exempt funds in higher taxable investments was common practice prior to TRA 86 because potential earnings were high. The spread between taxable and tax-exempt rates represented the risk-free return for the issuer of the tax-exempt debt.[*]

Opportunities for arbitrage profits before the TRA 86 were abundant. For example, an issuer must in many cases hold a bond reserve fund equal to 10% of the bond proceeds. This reserve fund was held for the duration of the bond issue and used to retire debt in the final year of the serial maturity. Before TRA 86, reserve funds could be invested at substantially higher taxable yields with few or no restrictions. Arbitrage profits were also commonly generated in the issuance of bonds to fund construction of some form. Construction projects typically do not require proceeds to be paid out when the funds are received, but over the time period of the construction. Therefore the unused portion of the construction fund could be invested at higher yields until the funds were actually spent. In some cases, governments found it cost-effective to issue debt in advance of spending in order to enter the market at a more attractive time or to bundle several projects together and structure a larger bond issue (Bland, 1984; Hildreth, 1993). Again, arbitrage profits could be generated on these funds until the proceeds were actually used to fund projects.

In the past these practices were tolerated by the federal government since arbitrage profits were only captured for short periods of time by issuers with legitimate public needs. However, because of tremendous monetary incentives to exploit tax-exempt benefits, abuses such as issuing an amount greater than that required for the proposed project, issuing the bonds well in advance of the time when the funds were actually required, and issuing bonds for the sole purpose of generating arbitrage profits were present in the market. An example of a municipality overissuing for a proposed project was seen in a planned bond issue by Caldwell, Texas. The community attempted to issue $2.4 billion in 30-year bonds to build two power plants capable of generating power for a city 28 times the size of Caldwell. Another example of abuse is seen in the Guam Economic Development Authority's generation of 300 million in tax-exempt dollars costing 6-3/4% to build multifamily housing with no apparent plans of actually constructing such units in the near future. With the proceeds invested at that time in 9% government securities, arbitrage profits earned from the issue had the potential to climb as high as $25 million over a 3-year period. Even issuers such as the state of California's treasury admitted to issuing $1 billion additional 1-year bonds in order to realize approximately $10 million in arbitrage profits (Weberman and Schifrin, 1986).

The abuse of arbitrage opportunities lowered federal government tax revenues and resulted in the placement of strict earning limitations on tax-exempt dollars, the reduction of the number of issues eligible for tax-exempt status, and the virtually elimination of arbitrage profits in any form. Under the amended TRA 86, all but a very few small issuers must carefully account for all earnings on tax-exempt funds and refund any earnings in excess of the cost of the funds to the federal government.

As arbitrage profit opportunities were being removed, new regulations were also being put into place that distinguished between projects being funded for the public good and those serving private interests. The former are referred to as governmental bonds and the latter as private activity bonds. Private activity bonds used to finance private interests may now be subject to some form of federal income tax. Those that do retain tax-exempt status are subject to federally imposed ceilings on total dollars issued.

The federal government's incentive to make such a distinction can be attributed in part to the increase in the volume of tax-exempt issues and a dramatic increase in the number and type of projects financed with tax-exempt dollars. The total volume issued in long-term municipal bonds grew from $29.3 billion in 1975 to $204.3 billion in 1985. Even after the rush to market in 1985 the volume remained relatively high at $117.0 billion in 1988 (Bland and Chen, 1990). From 1982 to 1990 the ratio of total state and local debt as a percentage of personal income increased from 16% to 19% (Bahl and Duncombe, 1993). Among the many reasons for the increased volume of new bond issues were (1) local governments felt the pinch of federal government budget cuts, causing revenue sources to be reduced or eliminated, (2) budget cuts had caused a reduction in intragovernment transfers, and (3) state and city governments had to meet employee demands for improved benefit packages and increased wages in order to retain competent personnel (Inzer and Reinhart, 1984). Also, a deteriorating infrastructure necessitated increased expenditures for repairs and replacement; cities and states faced a formidable task in repairing and rebuilding roads, bridges, transit systems, and water and sewer lines.

As with arbitrage restrictions, new regulations affecting the issuance and tax status of private activity

[*]The required yield on tax-exempt bonds is typically close to 23% lower than the required yield on taxable bonds.

bonds were set forth in the TRA 86 because of perceived abuses associated with the issuance of tax-exempt funds for the benefit of private enterprises. An example of the use of tax-exempt dollars to fund projects for private interest is seen in K Mart's leasing stores built with the use of tax-exempt dollars generated through the issuance of industrial revenue bonds (Kaufman, 1981).

Most private activity bonds are now classified as alternative minimum tax (AMT) bonds. An AMT bond is subject to the federal alternative minimum tax and hence taxable to the investor if he or she is subject to a minimum tax liability.[*] Because of this potential tax liability, the required yield on AMT bonds has been as much as 70 basis points higher than tax-exempt bonds (Brown, 1988). If an issuer is issuing AMT bonds then the required yield will be higher than for tax-exempt bonds but lower that comparable taxable bonds (Puelz and Puelz, 1991).

Another major change has been a shift in the market for the municipal bonds. Commercial banks have in the past been the largest holder of tax-exempt debt. Banks held as much as 50.5% of tax-exempt debt in 1972. Reduction of the tax-sheltering potential from municipal bonds combined with battered profits caused by volatile interest rates and increased competition have caused commercial banks to reduce their holdings of tax-exempt debt. Bank holdings of municipal bonds dropped by a total $136 billion, an amount equal to 59% of their holdings, between 1986 and 1990 (Petersen, 1991).

Property and casualty insurers have historically been the second largest market for municipals. Their demand for municipals is directly influenced by insurance underwriting profits and losses. As profitability increases, their demand for the tax-exempt instruments also increases. As profitability decreases, demand decreases. Like banks, insurers have experienced decreased profitability over the past 10 years. In the short run this trend appears to be continuing, however, due to changes in the insurance underwriting cycle the same inference is difficult to make over the long run. Presently, property and casualty insurers are required to limit the amount of underwriting loss deductions based on the amount of interest received on tax-exempt securities. This has served to further reduce their incentive to hold municipals during periods when underwriting losses are predicted.

During the mid-1980s, as demand for municipals bonds by banks and insurance companies dropped, a new, more demanding market for tax-exempt debt was emerging in individual investors. In the 1980s the number of households in high marginal tax brackets grew and tax reform eliminated many individual tax shelters such as individual retirement accounts (IRAs). Both these events caused individual households to become a larger potential market for tax-exempt debt even though individual marginal tax rates were reduced during the same period. To date, individual household investors have become the largest market for municipal bonds. By 1990 individuals were estimated to hold 62% of all tax-exempt bonds: $349 billion in individual bond holdings and $184 billion in shares of tax-exempt mutual funds (Peterson, 1991). Required rates of return by individuals are directly tied to marginal tax rates. With the reduction of the top marginal tax rate in the 1980s, households with less need to shelter income required higher returns from municipal bonds in order for them to be a financially viable alternative.

If local governments are to continue to tap this new pool of funds, issues must be structured to meet the needs of the new market of affluent individual investors who are more demanding in terms of investment liquidity and credit disclosure practices than banks and insurers have been in the past. Formerly, local governments had relatively little incentive to offer liquidity to investors. Banks, who historically held 50% of the market, were willing to hold large amounts of long-term illiquid debt primarily because large banks had access to other forms of liquidity not available to the general market.[†] Individuals, on the other hand, do not have the same opportunity to balance illiquid assets. Requiring premiums on illiquid investments is especially prevalent during periods of volatile interest rates, which has been characteristic of the recent past.

This new market of individual investors also has less access to information regarding the creditworthiness of investments than banks and insurers. Individual investors therefore require that more credit information be supplied by the issuer or a premium will be charged for the additional risk assured. Improved disclosure practices include information concerning the issuer's financial status, the soundness of the proposed project,

---

[*]Several authors have written about the characteristics of AMT bonds and the minimum tax (Brown, 1988; Petersen 1987 and 1988; Aalberts and Utley, 1988; Poterba, 1989; and Puelz, 1993).

[†]Through the use of liability management, banks can sell interest sensitive liabilities and concentrate the municipal portion in longer-term, higher-yielding bonds (Kidwell et al., 1983).

and projected revenue flows. Most institutional investors, including those operating tax-exempt mutual funds, require the issuer to adhere to tighter disclosure requirements than in the past (Hildreth, 1993).

At the same time that issuers of tax-exempt debt were feeling the effects of tax reform and higher debt costs, events occurred that increased the perceived risk of holding municipal bonds. The greater the perceived risk of any investment the higher the required yield on that investment, therefore, the cost of issuing tax-exempt debt was increased further. Events serving to reduce the public's confidence in the municipal bond market included defaults and near defaults of large issuers, taxpayer revolts, and legal questions regarding the constitutionality of tax-exempt status afforded local governments.

The near default of New York City is argued by some to have caused an immediate and long-term increase in the perceived risk in general obligation issues (Hoffland, 1974). The default of the Washington Public Power Supply System in 1983, despite high ratings by both major rating agencies, put into question the ability of these agencies to evaluate tax-exempt debt instruments, especially on debt from smaller issues (Zonana and Hertzbreg, 1981). Taxpayer revolts such as proposition 13 in California further reduced the public's confidence in the tax-exempt sector. Since 1978 seventeen states have enacted laws similar to proposition 13 limiting state government spending and/or authority to raise funds (Joyce and Mullins, 1991). Limiting a government's authority to tax casts doubt on its ability to raise funds for debt servicing through taxes. The near default of New York City on its general obligation debt and the limitation movement have caused investors to realize that the probability of default is present even if the bonds are backed by a large tax base.

The legality of the tax-exemption afforded local governments has also been put in question. The federal tax exemption for bonds issued by other units of government was established in 1819 in *McCulloch versus Maryland*. In 1895 the federal taxation of municipal bonds was ruled unconstitutional even though interest on those bonds was not exempted in the new tax code established a year prior. Numerous attempts have been made to eliminate this tax-exempt status, beginning in 1922 when a constitutional amendment was proposed and rejected. Since that time, a half dozen unsuccessful attempts have been made to change the exemption status (Winders, 1981). The 1988 Supreme Court decision on *South Carolina versus Baker* set forth that tax exemption is not a constitutional right but a congressional decision. This creates a new, imposing risk for issuers, the risk relative to the future tax-exempt status of the interest income.

In summary, the TRA 86 and subsequent amendments reducing the demand by banks and insurers and reducing the top marginal tax rate of high-income individuals has caused shift in the yield curve, resulting in higher debt costs to insurers. Increased perceived risk associated with municipal bonds has further increased the cost of issuing debt. The effects of higher costs are compounded by the increased monetary needs of state and local governments for funds and the loss of all arbitrage profit opportunities. Faced with a competitive market and a continuing need to raise funds through the issuance of debt, tax-exempt issuers are forced to find methods to tap new money sources and raise necessary funds in a cost-effective fashion. The individual needs of tax-exempt issuers such as states and local governments and the consideration of the political, regulatory, and legal environments in which they must operate necessitate a specialized approach to the structuring of tax-exempt debt.

II. THE MUNICIPAL BOND STRUCTURING PROCESS

In this section the participants in the process of the isssuance of debt are identified and their responsibility summarized. Then the decisions to be made during the issuance process are set forth. The remainder of the chapter addresses each of these structuring decisions and how it impacts the overall effectiveness of raising funds in the debt market.

A.   Participants in the Issuance of Debt

The participants in the issuance of debt and their relationship to each other is presented in Fig. 1 and examined in detail by Hildreth (1993).

Figure 1 illustrates the primary relationships between the participating parties. Lines between participants indicate the direction of interaction during the structuring and issuance process. Not all parties are participants in the process on all types of issues, and the basic relationships may change from issue to issue.

The issuer works with a financial advisor to address the financial aspects of the bond issue such as the proceeds required from the issue, and the financial options available to the issuer. It has been estimated that

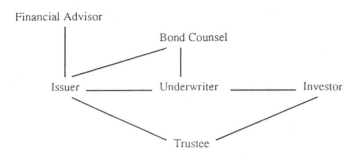

Figure 1 Participants in the bond structuring and issuance process.

80% of all issuers use the services of financial advisors (Mysak, 1990). Moak (1982) outlines the eleven areas in which the financial advisor assists the issuer. These areas include making presentations to rating agencies, calculating the timing of bond sales, and determining the costs for different financing alternatives. In a negotiated issue an underwriter may perform some of the functions of the financial advisor.[*] Some have questioned the soundness of the decision to use an underwriter as a financial advisor when it is the underwriter who will eventually be responsible for sale of the bonds (Mysak, 1990). The question arises whether there is a conflict of interest and whether the underwriter can give impartial advice to the issuer.

The bond counsel addresses the legal considerations of the issue. One of the most important function performed by the bond counsel is to ensure that the requirements set forth by the federal government for tax-exempt status are met. If the requirements are not met the interest income from the issue may be taxable to the investor. The bond counsel is instrumental in providing the investor with the confidence that all regulatory constraints have been adhered to and the interest income will be tax-exempt.

The underwriter's functions vary, depending on the type of bidding. In a negotiated issue the underwriter will act in some aspects as a financial advisor, assisting the issuer in all phases of the structuring process. In a competitive issue the underwriter bids on the chance to sell all or a portion of the new bonds. In a competitive issue the issuer typically determines the maturity schedule before the underwriters bid on the option to sell the bonds. In both cases, negotiated and competitive, the underwriter is charged with reselling the bonds in the market. The spread between the price paid by the underwriter for the new bonds and the price received by the underwriter when the bonds are resold to the investing public is the underwriter's fee.

The trustee, typically a bank, acts as an intermediary between the issuer and the investor after the bonds have been sold. The trustee transfers interest payments from the issuer to the investor who is the final and arguably the most important participant in the process.

B. Structuring Steps

This section lays out the major steps that must be taken in the process of raising funds through the issuance of tax-exempt debt. These steps are not necessarily presented in the order in which they would be performed, but all represent critical components of the structuring process.

1. *What type of bond should be issued.* The issuer must determine if general obligation, or revenue, should be issued. It must also determine if the bonds will be categorized as governmental or private activity bonds.
2. *How the bonds are to be sold.* The decision involves the selection of the underwriter who will be responsible for selling the bonds to the investing public. In some cases large issuers bypass the underwriter entirely and market the bonds directly to the investing public.
3. *What type and size of coupons should be attached.* This decision is critical to the overall cost to the issuer. Innovations in the municipal bond market have created a number of ways by which issuers can transfer interest income to investors, making this decision more complex than it has been in the recent past.

---

[*]The difference between a negotiated and a competitive bid issue is addressed in Section IV.

4. *How to estimate required proceeds.* This estimate may be the maximum proceeds that can be issued based on debt ceilings and/or minimum requirements necessary to fund the proposed project.
5. *How to estimate revenue flows.* Revenue flows may result from the available tax base in the case of a general obligation issue or from revenues generated from a pledged revenue flow in the case of a revenue issue. The issuer must ensure that pledged revenues are sufficient to cover debt-servicing requirements for the life of the bond issue. An important component in this step is the forecasting of future revenue flows.
6. *Whether or not to include call provisions.* Currently a large proportion of municipal bonds are callable before maturity. The inclusion of call provisions is an important factor in determining the total cost and underlying risk of the issue.
7. *Whether or not to include credit enhancements.* Credit enhancements such as private bond insurance and bank guarantees reduce the perceived risk and therefore reduce the required return on the bonds. The issuer must evaluate the cost of the credit enhancement relative to the reduced cost of the funds.
8. *Whether to employ tools to aid in the structuring process.* A number of tools are available to assist in the bond-structuring process. The decision to employ a structuring tool must be made based on an analysis of the cost incurred and benefits derived as a result of using the tool.

III. TYPES OF TAX-EXEMPT BONDS

One of the first decisions to be made by the issuer is whether the debt will be financed from general tax revenues or from pledged revenue flows. The issuer must also determine whether the new bonds will be classified as governmental purpose bonds or private activity bonds.

A. General Obligation vs. Revenue

One of the first decisions an issuer must make is whether the bonds are to be revenue or general obligation. In a revenue issue, debt servicing is funded from pledged project revenues or a specified tax. An example of a project being funded by project revenues would be the use of a season ticket surcharge to fund the construction of a football practice field. An example of a project being funded by a specific tax would be using a portion of cigarette tax revenues to fund a hospital renovation. A general obligation issue financing is backed by the full taxing power of the issuer. General obligation issues normally require public approval through a pubic referendum.

In the past general obligation issues were perceived by the general investing public to be substantially less risky and therefore lower yields were tolerated. The low-risk characteristic of general obligations was diminished somewhat by the New York City financial crisis causing a near default of their general obligation debt. This was compounded by taxpayer revolts limiting local government authority in matters of taxation. These events have increased the perceived risk associated with the general obligation debt of even the largest municipal issuers as doubt was cast on the issuer's ability to raise funds to service debt through taxation.

The volume of new revenue issues has increased relative to general obligation issues. From 1982 to 1989 revenue bonds as a percentage of the total debt burden of the United States increased from 51.1% to 71.3% (Bahl and Duncombe, 1993). This shift toward revenue issues has been attributed to several factors. First, most revenue bonds do not require a voter referendum, which can be a very time-consuming and risky process. By avoiding the time lag associated with a referendum, the issuer has more flexibility to enter the market during periods when costs are relatively low. Second, revenue issues are typically funded by those who benefit from the project rather than the entire taxable public. This approach may be appealing to constituents not willing to pay for programs or projects from which they do not directly benefit. Third, projects being funded are becoming more technical in nature and require the formation of special authorities that do not have the ability to tax and must therefore rely on revenue bonds (Fisher, 1980).

B. Governmental Use vs. Private Activity

Following the TRA 86, tax-exempt bonds were classified as governmental use and private activity bonds. Bonds are categorized as governmental use bonds if the proceeds are used for traditional governmental purposes such as schools, sewers, and roads. If the proceeds are used to finance a project to be used by a private enterprise, the bonds are categorized as private activity bonds. The distinction between the two is important for several reasons. First, private activity bonds are subject to annual volume caps. Second, most private activity bonds are subject to the minimum tax, making their required yield higher than governmental use bonds. These bonds are referred to as AMT bonds. The required yield on these bonds falls between then required yield on governmental use bonds and taxable bonds of comparable risk (Puelz and Puelz, 1991). The bond counsel serves an important function in determining under which category the bonds must be issued.

IV. UNDERWRITERS

The issuer's decision as to the selection of an underwriter affects how the resulting bonds will be structured and eventually sold in the market. The underwriter bids for the right to purchase the new issue bonds from the issuer and resale the bonds to the investing public. The difference between the price at which the new bonds are bought from the issuer and the price at which the bonds are resold to the investing public is the fee charged for the underwriter's services. This fee is referred to as the gross underwriter spread. Two common methods by which underwriters bid for the right to resale municipal bonds are negotiated and competitive.

In a negotiated bid issue, the underwriter is selected and a contractual agreement is entered into before the issue is structured and marketed. The underwriter works closely with the issuer in all stages of the issue development process, acting in many regards as a financial advisor. Conversely, a competitive issue involves a public auction in which bids are requested by the issuer. The bidders typically are given information concerning the maturity structure and possible coupon rate restrictions. The bidders then assign coupon rates to the various maturities and bid for the right to sell the issue at those rates. The issuer selects the underwriter submitting the schedule of coupons that result in the lowest interest cost.

In the past the competitive method has been more popular, but this appears to be changing (Braswell et al., 1983). About 79% of the volume of long-term municipal debt in the first quarter of 1987 was sold through negotiation as compared with 23% in 1973. This implies that the majority of issuers prefer to work directly with the underwriter throughout the structuring and marketing of the bonds as in a negotiated issue rather than in the final stages as in a competitive issue (Fabozzi and West, 1981; Dyl and Joehnk, 1976; Ederington, 1976).

Whether the cost of issuing debt is lower for a competitive or a negotiated bid issue is long-standing controversy in municipal finance. The gross underwriting spread in a negotiated issue, in which the underwriter is under contract to structure the issue, assign coupon rates, and sell the resulting bonds, is generally substantially higher than in a competitive issue.[*] In some cases the higher cost associated with negotiated underwriting may be offset by the reduced interest cost on the bonds. Research comparing the two methods of bidding suggests the method that will result in the lowest overall debt cost is a function of: (1) the number of bids expected from a competitive bid solicitation, (2) the market volatility, (3) the importance of timing the placement of the bonds in the market, (4) the frequency with which the issuer issues debt, (5) the experience of the issuer, and (6) the complexity of the issue to be structured.

Both Kessel (1971) and Cook (1982) find that a competitive bid issue is most cost-effective if a sufficient number of bids are received. This means for small issuers who typically do not attract a large number of bids the advantage of competitive bidding is minimal if any. Therefore, when it is predicted that there will be relatively few underwriter bids, there may be an incentive to choose negotiated underwriting.

Studies comparing negotiated and competitive underwritten issues in the taxable sector find that competitive sales with a sufficient number of bids result in lower interest costs in normal (stable) market conditions (Dyl and Joehnk, 1976; Ederington, 1976; Maese, 1985). However, in unstable conditions such as those seen in the 1970s and 1980s, a negotiated issue tends to be more cost-effective. One reason for this is that the underwriter under a negotiated contract is able to utilize superior information about the issue and the issuer and therefore structure a more efficient issue that meets the current market demands as well as the needs of the issuer (Fabozzi and West, 1981). Another reason is that with a negotiated bid issue the placement of the bonds in the volatile market can be timed to minimize cost. In a competitive bid issue there is little timing flexibility as bidding announcements are made for a set date and underwriters bid based on market conditions at that time (Hildreth, 1993). During periods of unstable market conditions, timing the sale of the bonds can be a significant factor in the overall cost of the debt.

---

[*]During the first half of 1992 the average gross underwriting spread was $8.68 per $1000 of par value on competitive issue and $9.74 per $1000 of par value for negotiated issues (King, 1992).

Negotiation is likely to be more cost-effective when complex issues are being structured for several reasons. First, by working directly with the underwriter the issuer can better analyze all alternative financing strategies. Second, as tax-exempt issues become more complicated, the ability to accurately analyze and rank bids in the short time available in the competitive bidding process is greatly reduced.

In support of the proposition that negotiation is more cost-effective for complex issues, Miller points out that "when handling debt issues that are sold less as commodities and more as craft work . . . teams relying on negotiated issues seem to learn as time passes thus reducing costs" (Miller, 1993). Miller's statement suggests not only that negotiated bidding may be appropriate for complex issues but that inexperienced issuers might realize lower costs by soliciting competitive bids. Bland (1985) comes to the same conclusion and suggests that only experienced issuers can achieve comparable interest rates through negotiated or competitive bidding. Inexperienced and infrequent issuers comprise the majority of the tax-exempt debt issuers in the market. There are an estimated 80,000 municipalities empowered to issue tax-exempt debt, and 30,000 of those issue bonds only once in 5 years (Mysak, 1990).

The increasing number of negotiated bond issues relative to competitive bond issues is most likely explained by the increased complexity of bond issue structures.[*] Financing innovations in the new municipal market such as variable rate and zero coupon bonds, put options and interest rate swaps make the structuring process more complicated and therefore the negotiated bidding process possibly more cost-effective in the long run.

V. INTEREST COST MEASURES

In structuring a bond issue the issuer must have measures to evaluate the interest cost associated with raising funds in the debt market. Debt interest cost measures are essential in facilitating the selection between various financing alternatives or between competing bids. In this section three methods of computing interest costs are presented: net interest cost (NIC), true interest costs (TIC), and present value of interest cost (PIC). The NIC technique, although the standard approach in the past, does not account for the time value of money. TIC is a variation of the internal rate of return (IRR) of the issue, which is a standard measure used in financial mathematics. PIC is a method that discounts future interest cost cash flows back to the present based on projected future interest rates.

A.   Net Interest Cost

The first measure of interest cost, NIC, is relatively simplistic and highly inaccurate. The NIC measures the value of a dollar received today as being equal to the value of a dollar received in the future.[†] Net interest cost is defined as

$$NIC = \frac{\sum_{t=1}^{n} (t \cdot A_t \cdot c_t) + D}{\sum_{t=1}^{n} (t \cdot A_t)}$$

where

n   =   number of maturities
A_t =   principal amount due in year t
c_t =   annual coupon rate assigned to maturity t
D   =   gross underwriter spread

Using NIC as a method to evaluate interest costs ignores the timing of payments. Serial issues that are front-loaded (high coupons on early maturities) and issues that are back-loaded (high coupons on later maturities) having the same NIC should not be considered equally attractive alternatives from the issuer's perspective. For example, consider a 2-year $20,000 proceed serial issue with $10,000 maturing each year. Assume that the underwriter's spread is zero. A front-loaded issue might have coupon rates assigned as

---

[*]Others might attribute the predominance of negotiated bid issues in the market to political favoritism (McCorry, 1987).
[†]See Hopewell and Kaufman (1974a and 1974b) for a more detailed description of NIC.

$c_1 = 0.20$ and $c_2 = 0.15$

The NIC would be calculated as[*]

$$NIC = \frac{1 \cdot 10{,}000 \cdot 0.20 + 2 \cdot 10{,}000 \cdot 0.15}{1 \cdot 10{,}000 + 2 \cdot 10{,}000} \approx 0.167$$

A back-loaded issue might have a coupon assignment of

$c_1 = 0.10$ and $c_2 = 0.20$

The NIC for this issue would be calculated as

$$NIC = \frac{1 \cdot 10{,}000 \cdot 0.10 + 2 \cdot 10{,}000 \cdot 0.20}{1 \cdot 10{,}000 + 2 \cdot 10{,}000} \approx 0.167$$

The NIC calculations are identical for the two issues. The back-loaded issue would, however, be preferred to the front-loaded issue. This is because although both issues pay $5000 in interest costs over 2 years, with the back-loaded issue, $1000 less is paid during the first year. Assuming the first-year savings of $1000 on the back-loaded issue could be invested at 10%, the issuer would save $100 over the front-loaded issue. In actual practice the savings would be much greater.

One of the best examples of misuse of NIC is seen in a 1973 $25 million issue by the state of Minnesota. The bids for the competitively issued bonds were ranked and chosen using NIC criteria. It is estimated that the total present value of extra cost to the state for not using a time value of money approach to rank the bids was $1.25 million, or 5% of the par value of the issue (Bierwag, 1976). In 1972 and 1973 it is estimated that one-half of the winning bids awarded on an NIC basis were not cost-effective (Hopewell and Kaufman, 1974a and 1974b).

NIC was originally preferred because (1) other methods that took into account the time value of money were too time-consuming and costly, and (2) municipal finance officers were often part-time employees with little or no financial background and therefore unable to understand or apply more complicated measures. The availability of computer software and even calculators that compute IRR quickly and efficiently makes this first argument antiquated. The widespread use of IRR and its presence in most business schools' curricula invalidates the second argument.

If NIC is to be employed, then structures closer to the optimal least-cost structure can result if constraints are placed on coupon rate assignments. For example, a constraint requiring that coupons be nondescending in maturity order results in a structure close to the optimal least-cost bid for the purpose of ranking financing alternatives or competitive bids (Kaufman, 1983).

B. True Interest Costs

A preferred technique for measuring interest costs takes into account the time value of money. Several such techniques have been applied to tax-exempt finance. The most popular measure is TIC. TIC is similar to the IRR of the issue. TIC is the interest rate that discounts the dollar principal and interest cash flows back to the price or proceeds of the issue. An equation defining TIC assuming semi-annual coupon payments and compounding is

$$P = D + \left(\sum_{t=1}^{n} \frac{A_t}{(1 + TIC/2)^{2t}} + \sum_{i=1}^{2t} \frac{c_t/2 \cdot A_t}{(1 + TIC/2)^i} \right)$$

where

P   =   proceeds of the issue

Deriving TIC for alternative bond issue structures, the issuer more accurately calculates the overall interest cost by accounting for the time value of money. Consider again the front-loaded example above that is a 2-year $20,000 proceed serial issue with $10,000 maturing each year and has the coupon rates

$c_1 = 0.20$ and $c_2 = 0.15$

---

[*]All coupons are assumed to be set at par value.

The TIC calculated for the issue is 16.75%. The back-loaded issue with the same maturity schedule and the coupons

$c_1 = 0.10$ and $c_2 = 0.20$

has a TIC equal to 16.50%. Clearly the back-loaded issue with the lower TIC is more cost-effective.

C. Present Value of Interest

Another approach to determining the interest cost of an issue is the PIC. This technique is proposed as a theoretically superior measure of interest cost. PIC incorporates expectations of future interest rates in determining the interest cost of the issue.[*]

PIC is calculated as follows:

$$PIC = \sum_{t=1}^{n} \frac{I_t}{\prod_{j=1}^{t} (1 + r_j)} + D$$

where

I_t = the total interest cost period t
r_j = the expected one-period borrowing rate during period j

Although PIC is theoretically superior to other measures, there is a question of its practicality, as its calculation involves the estimation of forward rates expected to prevail in the future. If forward rates are not estimated with accuracy, then the PIC measure is prone to error. One method of calculating forward rates involves using current interest rates for different maturities. The calculation is

$$r_j = \frac{(1 + R_j)^j}{(1 + R_{j-1})^{j-1}} - 1$$

where

r_j = the one-period borrowing rate expected to prevail in period i
R_j = the current "i"-period borrowing rate
R_{j-1} = the current "i–1"-period borrowing rate

In order to calculate the PIC of an issue, the forward rates for the duration of the issue must be derived. Consider again the $20,000 proceed serial issue with $10,000 maturing each year. The forward rates for the four 6-month periods of the issue would be calculated from the current 6-month, 1-year, 18-month and 2-year borrowing rates

$R_1 = 7.0\%$, $R_2 = 7.5\%$, $R_3 = 8.0\%$ and $R_4 = 8.5\%$

where

R_1 = the current 6-month borrowing rate
R_2 = the current 1-year borrowing rate
R_3 = the current 18-month borrowing rate
R_4 = the current 2-year borrowing rate

The expected 6-month borrowing rates would be calculated as

$r_1 = 7.0\%$, $r_2 = 8.0\%$, $r_3 = 9.0\%$, and $r_4 = 10.0\%$

The PIC of the front-loaded issue with the coupons

$c_1 = 0.20$ and $c_2 = 0.15$

---

[*]See Osterman et al. (1979) for a more detailed discussion of PIC.

is calculated $4287. This represents the expected present value of the $5000 in interest costs over the 2 years. The back-loaded issue with the coupons

$$c_1 = 0.10 \text{ and } c_2 = 0.20$$

has a PIC equal to $4216. In this case, as with the TIC approach, the back-loaded issue with the lower PIC is preferred.

VI. REQUIRED RATE OF RETURN

In the previous section three measures to evaluate the interest cost of a bond issue are presented. Underlying each of these interest cost measures is the estimated required rate of return on each of the bond maturities. The required rate of return of an investment is the interest rate that investors require on the investment in order to assume the risks associated with it. For any investment, the required rate of return is a factor of the term of the investment and the risk associated with payment of interest and principle. Cook (1982) presents a summary of the explanatory variables in the determination of the required rate of return for municipal bonds. They include

1. Bond issue characteristic such as call provisions and coupon types
2. Issuer characteristics such as bond rating and issue purpose
3. Marketing factors such as whether the issue is negotiated or competitive, the number of bids received on a competitive issue, and whether or not the bonds are bank eligible
4. Regional market conditions such as municipal bond supply and demand
5. Other factors such as bond issue size, national market conditions, and marginal tax rates

Typically, the longer the term of the investment the greater the required rate of return. Although there have been periods in which long-term rates were lower than short-term rates (referred to as a downward sloping yield curve), an upward sloping curve is the norm. In addition to the term of the investment, the greater the risk associated with the payment of principal and interest, the higher the required rate of return on the investment.

A. Taxable vs. Tax-Exempt Rates

If two bonds are identical in every aspect except tax status, the required rate of return on the taxable bond will exceed the required rate of return on the tax-exempt bond.[*] The relationship between the tax-exempt expected return or yield and the taxable expected return or yield is

$$R_e = R_t\,(1-T)$$

where

R_e = yield on the tax-exempt bond
R_t = yield on the taxable bond
T = the applicable tax rate

This simplistic relationship, however, is not observed in the market. Some argue that this does not mean that there is not a relationship between taxable rates and tax-exempt rates but rather the two bonds compared are not identical with regard to risk. Trzcinka (1982) suggests that rather than attempting to compare two bonds with identical risk, a more appropriate relationship would include a risk premia τ to account for the differential in risk. The relationship is then defined as

$$R_e = \tau + R_t(1 - T)$$

If τ is positive, the tax-exempt bond is more risky than the taxable bond. If the return on a risk-free government security R_f is used as the taxable yield the relationship becomes

$$R_e = \tau + R_f(1 - T)$$

---

[*]The ratio of tax-exempt to taxable bonds post-TRA 86 has been relatively stable at 75% (Petersen, 1991).

In this case the risk premia τ is equal to the total risk of the tax-exempt bond.

In academic literature there are three theories that address the issue of the yield spreads between taxable and tax-exempt bonds. These three theories as outlined by Mitchell and McDade (1991) deal with tax arbitrage, capital structure, and market segmentation. Fama (1977) suggests the spread is explained by the tax-arbitrage practices of commercial banks. However, because of the declining market in commercial banks it would be expected that their influence on yield spreads is minimal. Miller (1977) explains the spread as a function of the capital structure decisions by nonfinancial corporations. The third theory, formulated by Kidwell and Koch (1983) and others, suggests that market segmentation is a significant factor in explaining the observed spread.

A somewhat consistent observation seen in comparing taxable and tax-exempt yields is that the tax-exempt yield curve typically has a steeper slope than the taxable yield curve. This relationship can be explained from the analysis of the ratio model developed by Liebowitz (1983). What the steeper yield curve for municipals means is that as the term increases, tax-exempt yields approach taxable yields. Even during periods in which the taxable yield curve is inverted or downward sloping, the municipal curve is consistently upward sloping.[*]

B. Cyclical Economic Effects

The inability to directly relate taxable yields to tax-exempt yields has led some to conclude that the major determinant of municipal bond yields is not the movement of taxable yields but rather cyclical economic factors affecting supply, demand, and volatility. Support for the relationship between economic cycles and tax-exempt rates is found when one observes 4 years in the recent past when corporate tax rates were decreased: 1965, 1970, 1971, and 1979. Rather than a corresponding increase in the ratio of tax-exempt yields to taxable yields, the ratio actually decreased and continued to decrease for several months following the corporate tax rate reduction.[†] These decreasing ratios in the wake of tax reductions is explained by the inflationary economy reducing profit margins for banks and property and casualty insurers. Reduced profit margins reduce the need for tax shelters found in municipals.

Research has shown that the primary influence on taxable yields is inflationary expectations (Yohe and Karnosky, 1969). Since municipals are affected by the same inflationary cycles, it would appear that taxable yields should serve as a proxy for tax-exempt yields even if a cyclical theory of bond yield determination is assumed.

In the past the cyclical pattern of municipal yields was explained by the stop-and-go bond demands of insurers and banks (Kochan, 1983). Kimbal in 1977 shows that marginal tax rates on interest income is inversely related to demand by banks and property and casualty insurers for tax shelters. However, as the municipal sector is becoming increasingly dependent on the individual investor and competing more directly with the taxable sector for funds, one would expect the cycles that affect taxable yields to exert a similar influence on tax-exempt yields.

Municipal yields do tend to move with taxable yields; however, they tend to increase more with market retreats than taxable yields. This is an indication of the perceived superior bond liquidity and safety associated with the taxable sector.

Yawitz, Maloney, and Ederington's 1985 model of tax-exempt yields uses the risk-free rate as a proxy for tax-exempt yields. The relationship is

$$R_e = \frac{(1 - P_m)(1 - \alpha_T)}{P_m} + \frac{(1 - T)R_f}{P_m}$$

where

R_e = the rate of return on tax-exempt bonds
R_f = the risk-free rate of return
P_m = the probability of payment
α_T = capital gains or losses that are included in taxable income
T = marginal break-even tax rate for P_m

---

[*]Inversion implies short-term rates are higher than long-term rates. Inversion of the taxable yield curve normally occurs during periods of high inflation (e.g., Oct. 1981, Jan. 1981, and June 1980; Laufenberg, 1983).
[†]This implies that municipal yields increase as tax rates increase.

This model implies a linear relationship between municipal and risk-free returns, but the slope and intercept are nonlinear functions of the tax rate and the probability of payment. Several relationships were found in empirical tests of the model that support its validity. First, the probability of payment P_m was directly related to the bond's rating, as would be expected. Second, estimated break-even tax rates increased with increasing maturity. This is consistent with the segmentation hypothesis in municipal finance (Hendershott and Kidwell, 1978).

VII. COUPONS

A bond coupon payment is typically a semiannual interest payment made from the issuer to the investor through the bond trustee. A par bond is one for which the annual coupon payment rate is the same as the annual required rate return on the bond. A par bond will sell at a price equal to the face value of the bond. A bond will sell at a discount (premium) relative to its face value if the coupon rate is lower (higher) than its required rate of return. In making the decision regarding coupons an issuer must not only select the coupon size but must also determine if fixed coupons or variable coupons are more cost-effective.

A. Coupon Size

The size of the coupon payment attached to a bond is always made relative to the required rate of return on the bond. If coupon payments are at a rate greater than the required rate of return, then the bonds sell at a premium. The investor is receiving the return on the investment earlier in the term of the bond and receives a final payment at maturity that is less than the price he or she originally paid for the bond. On the other hand, if coupon payments are at a rate less than the required rate of return, then the bond will sell at a discount. The investor is receiving coupons that are below the required rate of return and receives a final payment at maturity that is greater than the price he or she originally paid for the bond.

The relationship between the price, annual coupons, and required rate of return is given as

$$P_0 = \sum_{t=1}^{n} \frac{C_t}{(1 + R)^t} + \frac{A_n}{(1 + R)^n}$$

where

P_0 = the price of the bond
A_n = the principal payment at maturity
C_t = the coupon payment at year t
R = the annual required rate of return on the bond (yield to maturity)
n = the number of years in the term of the bond

In order for a bond to be marketable to the investing public at its minimum required rate of return, the coupon attached to it must lie within some acceptable range from par value. If the coupon lies outside this acceptable range, the cost to the issuer will increase (Wiengartner, 1972; Buse, 1976). Hopewell and Kaufman (1974a and 1974b) analyzed the costs to the issuer of relatively high (above par) and relatively low (below par) coupons. They found that limiting the range of coupon rates to a small interval around the required rate of return reduced the magnitude of these costs.

There are situations, however, in which an issuer or underwriter may desire that coupons be set above or below par values. For example, if the bond issue is to be competitively bid and if the NIC is to be used to evaluate the bids, underwriters have an incentive to set higher coupons on short maturities than they would if a time value of money approach is used to evaluate the bids. If coupons on short maturities are relatively high, the issuer is paying more for the generated funds on a time value of money basis, increasing the price at which the underwriter can resale the bonds to investors. In this situation the issuer can minimize or eliminate the problem of inefficient coupons several ways. One method would be to set upper limits on coupons with short maturities or to require that coupons increase with maturity. Another and preferred alternative is to evaluate bids using a time value of money approach such as TIC or present value of money approach (PIC).*

---

*See Section V for a detailed description of interest cost valuations. Hopewell and Kaufman (1974a and 1974b) provide a detailed description of the misuse of NIC in evaluating bids in municipal finance.

Original issue discount or zero coupon bonds are bonds that have coupons set at a rate below the required rate of return or at zero. In this case the bonds sell at a discount from par. An issuer might consider this type of financing if the investor's reinvestment risk associated with par coupons is high. Reinvestment risk is the risk that the investor will receive coupon payments from the bond and be forced to reinvest the money at a lower rate of return than the original investment. If no coupons or relatively low coupon payments are received and the bond interest is received in the form of a final payment at maturity, the reinvestment risk is eliminated or reduced. In this situation, the issuer would require a lower rate of return on the bonds since no payments are received until maturity. On the other hand, because no payments are made until maturity, the creditworthiness of the issuer is more of a critical factor than if interest income is received on a regular basis.

One of the drawbacks with discount or zero coupon bonds is that the par value of the bonds that will be repaid at maturity is significantly higher than the proceeds received from the sale of the issue. Legally this might be a concern in the calculation of the debt limitations, or politically it might be unwise. Capital appreciation or compound-interest bonds are similar to zero or original issue discount bonds in that the issuer eliminates or reduces the reinvestment risk for the investor. However, capital appreciation bonds are sold at par because interest payments are held by the issuer and compounded at a specified rate and paid to the issuer at maturity. The major benefit with capital appreciation bonds is that the bonds are sold at par and not at a discount from par (Petersen, 1991).

Another innovation seen in the setting of coupons is the use of stepped coupons. In the stepped coupon bonds offered by Lee County, Florida, in 1982, all bond maturities in the issue paid the same coupon with the coupon rate increased from time to time during the term of the issue. The advantage of stepped coupons is that the issuer is able to lower interest cost in the early years of the issue and reduce the total level of debt at a faster rate than with conventional fixed-rate coupons (McCorry, 1982). The cost to the issuer will be a higher overall required rate of return, as the investor will be receiving the return on his or her investment later than if level coupons were employed.

B.   Fixed vs. Variable

Variable-rate coupons first appeared in the municipal sector in the mid-1960s. Variable-rate coupons reduce the price risk for the investor because the coupons are adjusted periodically and remain relatively close to par. Reduced price risk results in a lower required rate of return and a lower total interest cost to the issuer. However, the issuer is also assuming additional interest rate risk, as debt-servicing requirements are tied to market rates and can vary significantly from period to period. These risks to the issuer can be limited by placing caps on the percentage of change in the variable-rate coupons from year to year and/or over the life of the issue.

Variable-rate securities are most attractive to the issuer when long-term interest rates are high relative to short-term rates. In the mid-1980s when long-term interest rates were very high, 20% of the dollar volume of bond sales were variable (Petersen, 1991). This is explained by the fact that issuers were more than willing to attach variable-rate coupons in the hope that interest rates would fall and the cost of the debt would decrease. As the yield curve flattened and long-term rates dropped in 1990, the volume of bond sales that contained variable-rate coupon dropped to 7% (Petersen, 1991). In an environment of relatively low long-term rates, issuers are more likely to lock in fixed-rate coupons. The issuer must realize that offering variable-rate coupons in an financial climate in which long-term rates are high and expected to decline will result in higher required yields on the bonds sold. Offsetting a portion of the cost of higher yields is the typically lower underwriting charge for variable rate issues.[*]

Aside from required rate of return, the issuer and underwriter should consider the effect on risk of default when variable rates are offered. If the revenue stream that is to be used to service the debt does not vary with interest rates, then the inclusion of variable-rate coupons will more than likely increase the risk of default on the issue. If the revenue stream used to service debt varies directly with the level of interest rates, the inclusion of variable-rate coupons will decrease the risk of default on the issue. The relationship between revenue flows used to finance the debt and market interest rates must be considered when determining whether variable or fixed-rate coupons should be attached to the bonds.

---

[*]Underwriting charges on variable-rate issues vary from 0.5% to 0.8%, as opposed to 0.8% to 1.5% for fixed-rate bonds issues (Petersen, 1991).

Bond structures developed with variable-rate coupons should be analyzed with regard to total debt-servicing requirements under various scenarios of rate fluctuations. These figures can then be compared to the debt-servicing requirements on the fixed-rate issues. Rate expectations might be estimated, as suggested in Section V, through forward rates and various scenarios compared. In this type of "what if" analysis, the best, worst, and expected case scenarios from the issuer's perspective if variable rates are attached would all be identified and the interest cost for each alternative estimated. For example, the best case scenario might correspond to an annual decrease of 20 basis points, the worst case scenario might correspond to an annual increase of 20 basis points, and the expected case scenario might correspond to constant rate expectations. Tables 1, 2, and 3 present the present value of debt service for a 7-year serial maturity bond issue sold at par with coupons of 5.5% paid semiannually. There is assumed to be no maximum or minimum level for changes in variable-rate coupons that are adjusted annually. The discount rate used is 5.5%. With constant rate expectations the present value of debt servicing is $5,470,446. In Table 2, where rates are expected to increase by 20 basis points annually, the present value of total debt service is $85,834 higher than when rates are expected to remain constant. In Table 3, where rates are expected to decrease by 20 basis points annually, the present value of interest costs is $85,834 lower than if rates are expected to remain constant, and $171,668 lower than if rates are expected to increase by 20 basis points annually.

The effect of rate changes on present value total debt service when variable-rate coupons are present is more pronounced as the duration of the issue increases. This means that as the retirement of principal is delayed, the effect of changing rates is magnified. The impact of fluctuating rates can be reduced by placing a upper and/or lower limit on the amount that coupon rates can change per year and/or over the life on the bonds.

Put options may also be attached to variable-rate coupon bonds. Put options give the investor the right to sell the bonds back to the issuer. This option makes the bonds more attractive to the investor and therefore reduces the required rate of return. From the issuer's standpoint the put option increases the risk it bears, as the investor retains the right to sell the bonds if rates drop significantly. If rates increase significantly the investor also has the option to sell the bonds and reinvest the proceeds at a fixed rate, locking in the higher return. From the issuer's perspective, if the put option is exercised and coupons reflect the current market interest rates, the issuer should be able to raise additional funds at the same rate it was paying on those funds when the put was exercised. If the investor pays a premium upon exercising the put option then some or all of the issuance costs associated with refinancing the debt if the put is exercised can be captured.

C. Interest Rate Swaps

Interest rate swaps are a technique used in corporate financing and have started to come into use in municipal financing. A swap involves an issuer's trading the payments for its bond issue with the payments from another bond issue. Typically a issuer would trade a variable-rate payment schedule for a fixed-rate schedule or visa

Table 1 Constant Rate Expectation

Year	Maturity amount	Interest rate (%)	Price	Present value debt service
1	$600,000	5.50	$600,000	$856,962
2	$625,000	5.50	$625,000	$804,697
3	$650,000	5.50	$650,000	$754,365
4	$700,000	5.50	$700,000	$726,149
5	$750,000	5.50	$750,000	$696,692
6	$780,000	5.50	$780,000	$651,807
7	$1,350,000	5.50	$1,350,000	$979,774
	$5,455,000		$5,455,000	$5,470,446

Note: Variable rate coupon = 5.5%

Table 2 Increasing Rate Expectation

Year	Maturity amount	Interest rate (%)	Price	Present value debt service
1	$600,000	5.50	$600,000	$856,962
2	$625,000	5.70	$625,000	$813,539
3	$650,000	5.90	$650,000	$768,969
4	$700,000	6.10	$700,000	$743,723
5	$750,000	6.30	$750,000	$714,560
6	$780,000	6.50	$780,000	$667,464
7	$1,350,000	6.70	$1,350,000	$991,062
	$5,455,000		$5,455,000	$5,556,280

Note: Variable rate coupon = 5.5%

Table 3 Decreasing Rate Expectation

Year	Maturity amount	Interest rate (%)	Price	Present value debt service
1	$600,000	5.50	$600,000	$856,962
2	$625,000	5.30	$625,000	$795,854
3	$650,000	5.10	$650,000	$739,760
4	$700,000	4.90	$700,000	$708,575
5	$750,000	4.70	$750,000	$678,824
6	$780,000	4.50	$780,000	$636,150
7	$1,350,000	4.30	$1,350,000	$968,487
	$5,455,000		$5,455,000	$5,384,612

Note: Variable rate coupon = 5.5%

versa. One reason for interest rate swaps is to more accurately match payments to revenue flows. Another reason is that an issuer may be able to raise funds in a particular market more cost-effectively through variable-rate (fixed-rate) bonds, but it desires fixed-rate (variable-rate) interest payments. Because interest rate swaps are relatively new in the municipal market, transaction costs are high. With increased use and standardization in the future, interest rate swaps may become as standard in the municipal market as they are in the corporate market.

VIII.   ESTIMATING REQUIRED PROCEEDS

The proceeds of the issue are the dollar amount received by the issuer from the sale of the bonds. From the proceeds of the bond sale the issuer must deduct all costs of issuance such as the gross underwriter fees, rating fees, and insurance premiums. There are potential upper and lower bounds on the proceeds generated from an issue. Maximum proceeds requirements are imposed by such government regulations as debt ceilings. Depending on the type of issue and the issuer's current total debt outstanding, debt ceilings may or may not be a concern. Minimum proceed requirements are the funds required to meet the current financial need of the municipality.

To illustrate the calculation of minimum proceeds assume that proceeds are to be used to fund the construction of a municipal facility. The construction account is the account that will hold the funds from which construction costs will be paid as they come due. The minimum proceeds requirement is based on the total dollar cost and the timing of cash outflows for the project for which the generated funds are to be used.

Before the TRA 86, municipalities had an incentive to issue bonds to cover all project construction costs, bond reserve fund costs, and issuance costs.[*] The interest earned on the bond reserve and construction accounts contained arbitrage profits that could be used to retire debt and pay interest costs.[†] Post-TRA 86 this is no longer true, as current tax laws all but eliminate arbitrage profits. Regulations restrict an issuer's earnings rate to the interest cost on the debt issue. This interest cost is reflected in the true interest cost of the bond issue (TIC). Any earnings on the funds in excess of the cost of the funds must be refunded to the government.[‡] An issuer faced with an increasing cost of capital would have an incentive to issue fewer bonds and fund construction from the interest earnings on the bond reserve and construction accounts.

The calculation of minimum proceeds assumes that the issuer has an increasing cost of capital and it finds it in its best interest to use interest earnings to fund construction. Further, it is assumed that TIC reflects the issuer's interest cost for the funds and therefore the maximum return on idle funds. The minimum proceeds requirement P_l for an issue would be estimated as

$$C = P_l + \sum_{t=1}^{m} TIC(P_l - B_t - S) - q(P_l - S_b) - S$$

where

C	=	the estimated total cost of the proposed construction project
m	=	the time to complete the proposed construction project
TIC	=	the true interest cost
B_t	=	the cumulative cash outflow for construction through time t
TIC $(P_l - B_t - S)$	=	the interest earned on the construction fund during time period t
$q(P_l - S_b)$	=	the amount to be placed in a required bond reserve fund
S	=	underwriter spread and issuance costs (including insurance premiums)
S_b	=	amount of S not to be included in the calculation of the bond reserve fund
q	=	proportion bond reserve fund requirement

In determining the required proceeds the issuer must estimate the timing of expected cash outflows for the construction of the project. This is because during the period of time in which proceeds are being used to finance the project the interest earnings on idle funds would be used to offset project construction costs. When the cash outflows for project financing are finished, the interest earnings on the proceeds can be used to offset debt-servicing costs.

In order to be in compliance with arbitrage restrictions, any amount earned in excess of this maximum earning rate of TIC must be refunded to the federal government. Because the TIC of the issue is typically not known with certainty until the bonds are issued, an estimate must be derived. If the estimate of TIC is too high (low) the proceeds generated from the issue will be below (above) that required for the project.

For example, consider a bond issue described by

C	=	$5,000,000–the estimated total cost of the proposed project
m	=	3–the time to complete the proposed project
TIC*	=	6.0%–the initial target total interest cost
B_1	=	1,000,000–the cumulative project financing cash outflow year 1
B_2	=	3,000,000–the cumulative project financing cash outflow year 2
B_3	=	5,000,000–the cumulative project financing cash outflow year 3
S	=	$50,000–borrowed underwriter spread and issuance costs
S_b	=	0
q	=	10%–bond reserve fund requirement

In this example the minimum required proceeds are calculated as $5,184,300. This calculation assumes that the final maturity is at the end of year 3 and that the bond reserve fund is used to retire debt during the third and final year. If the TIC is 5.5% rather than 6.0% the minimum required proceeds are $5,214,400.

---

[*]The amount held in the bond reserve fund is typically 10%.

[†]This is true only during periods of positive carry, where interest earned on taxable securities is greater than that paid on tax-free securities. Although there have been periods in which a negative carry existed, when taxable rates were less than tax-free rates for some maturities (most recently in the second half of 1986), it is rare.

[‡]Some small issuers are exempt from these arbitrage restrictions.

In an insured issue the determination of the minimum proceeds becomes more complicated when the insurance premium to be paid out of borrowed funds is a percentage of the total debt service. Like TIC, total debt service is not known until the bond issue is actually structured. Therefore, an estimate of the premium is determined. If the estimate is too low (high) the proceeds generated will be higher (lower) than those required to finance the proposed project.

Another factor that can further complicate the determination of required proceeds is allowing underwriters in a competitive issuance to bid on portions of the bond issue. Inzer and Reinhart (1984) suggest that this approach will result in lower interest costs for the issuer because the underwriters bid only on those maturities that they can market in a cost-effective fashion to their clientele rather than having to bid on the whole package of bonds. If the issuer decides to employ this approach there is a risk that some of the maturities that are deemed unattractive by the market will not be purchased and the proceeds will be lower than anticipated.

IX. DEBT SERVICING

Debt servicing of a bond issue is defined as semiannual payment of coupon interest and maturing principal to the investors through a trustee. The funds required for debt-servicing needs must be available from tax revenues in the case of a general obligation bond issue or from a pledged revenue source in the case of a special purpose revenue bond issue. Revenue flows must be forecast into the future for the duration of the bond issue to ensure that the funds will be available when required. When future revenue flows are uncertain the issue must be structured so as to minimize the probability that the debt-servicing needs will exceed the revenues available, and the bond issuer will be in default.

A. Forecasting Revenue Flows

Because the types of revenue flows used to fund the debt servicing on bonds varies from issue to issue and issuer to issuer, the best forecasting technique for estimating future cash flows also varies. In predicting future revenue flows, patterns, trends, and/or causal relationships must be identified. In this section three techniques for forecasting revenues are presented: exponential smoothing, time series analysis, and causal models. The interested reader can refer to any number of statistical or forecasting reference books for a more detailed description of forecasting (e.g., Sobol and Starr, 1993).

1. Exponential Smoothing

Exponential smoothing is a simple forecasting technique that generates the next period forecast from historical revenue figures. The technique smoothes the historical data based on a selected smoothing constant that minimizes the forecast error. One-parameter exponential smoothing is appropriate for data for which there is no perceivable long-term growth or decay in revenues over time, and two-parameter smoothing is appropriate when there is growth or decay in the trend over time.

The one-parameter forecast of revenue flows in year t, F_t, is derived as

$$F_t = (1-\alpha) \cdot F_{t-1} + \alpha(A_{t-1})$$

where

F_{t-1} = the revenue forecast for the previous year (t−1)
A_{t-1} = the actual revenue for the previous period (t−1)
α = the smoothing constant

The smoothing constant is the weight that is placed on the last period's actual revenues and one minus the smoothing constant is the weight that is placed on the last period's forecast. In this manner, historical revenue flows are smoothed and the next period forecast is generated. Table 4 illustrates the use of one-parameter exponential smoothing.

The average difference between actual revenues A_t and forecast revenues F_t is a measure of the accuracy of the forecast. The lower this average difference the better the forecast. By adjusting the smoothing constant the issuer can select the best forecasting model using one-parameter smoothing.

Table 4 Revenue Forecast: One-Parameter
Exponential Smoothing ($\alpha = 0.2$)

Time	Actual revenue ($000)	Forecast revenue ($000)	Difference between A_t and F_t ($000)
t	A_t	F_t	
1	76	76.0	0.0
2	93	76.0	17.0
3	60	79.4	19.4
4	78	75.5	2.5
5	86	76.0	10.0
6	75	78.0	3.0
7	60	77.4	17.4
8	85	73.9	11.1
9	65	76.1	11.1
10	66	73.9	7.9
11	79	72.3	6.7
12	80	73.7	6.3
13	55	74.9	19.9
14	70	70.9	0.9
15	60	70.8	10.8
16	80	68.6	11.4
17	78	70.9	7.1
18	77	72.3	4.7
19	67	73.2	6.2
20	68	72.0	4.0
		Average difference between A_t and F_t ($000)	8.875

Figure 2 illustrates the one-parameter exponential smoothing example in Table 4 with the actual revenue flow series (A_t) and the forecast revenue series (F_t) plotted when one-parameter exponential smoothing is used to forecast. The forecast is a smoothed average of the previous period's revenue flows. The greater the variation in revenues the smaller the optimal smoothing constant in the one-parameter model.

Two-parameter exponential smoothing is appropriate when there is a trend in the revenue time series. In two-parameter exponential smoothing there are two smoothing constants, α and β. As in the one-parameter model, α is used to smooth actual revenue flows. The second smoothing constant, β is used to smooth the trend or change from period to period. The forecast trend for time period t in two-parameter exponential smoothing T_t is derived as

$$T_t = T_{t-1} + \beta(F_t - F_{t-1})$$

where

F_t and F_{t-1} = the one-parameter revenue forecast for the years t and t–1, respectively
β = the trend smoothing constant

The two-parameter forecast for period t, FIT_t, is derived as

$$FIT_t = F_t + T_t$$

Table 5 illustrates the use of two-parameter exponential smoothing, given historical revenue figures.

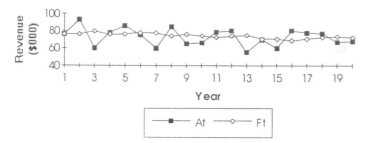

Figure 2   Revenue forecast—one-parameter exponential smoothing.

As with one-parameter exponential smoothing, the average difference between the actual revenues A_t and forecast revenues FIT_t is a measure of the accuracy of the forecast. By adjusting the smoothing constants α and β the issuer can select the best forecasting model using two-parameter smoothing. Figure 3 illustrates the two-parameter example in Table 5 with the actual revenue flow series (A_t) and the forecast series (FIT_t) plotted. The increasing trend and smoothing in the historical revenue flows is easily observed.

2.   Times Series Analysis

Like exponential smoothing, in time series analysis the revenue flows are forecast based on historical data. In time series analysis, four components are isolated and their effects of revenue flows captured. The four components are seasonal, trend, cyclical, and irregular.

Table 5   Revenue Forecast: Two- Parameter Exponential Smoothing ($\alpha=0.2$ and $\beta=0.4$)

Year	Actual revenue ($000) A_t	Forecast revenue ($000) F_t	Trend ($000) T_t	Forecast ($000) FIT_t	Difference between A_t and FIT_t ($000)
1	76	76.0	0.00	76.0	0.0
2	93	76.0	0.00	76.0	17.0
3	108	79.4	1.36	80.9	27.2
4	128	85.1	3.65	88.8	39.2
5	196	93.7	7.08	100.8	95.2
6	175	114.2	15.26	129.4	45.6
7	141	126.3	20.13	146.5	5.5
8	236	129.3	21.30	150.6	85.4
9	256	150.6	29.84	180.5	75.5
10	190	171.7	38.27	210.0	20.0
11	227	175.3	39.74	215.1	11.9
12	299	185.7	43.87	229.6	69.4
13	403	208.3	52.94	261.3	141.7
14	282	247.3	68.51	315.8	33.9
15	288	254.2	71.29	325.5	37.5
16	387	261.0	73.99	335.0	52.0
17	484	286.2	84.07	370.3	113.7
18	384	325.7	99.90	425.6	41.6
19	330	337.4	104.56	442.0	112.0
20	497	335.9	103.97	439.9	57.1
				Average difference between A_t and FIT_t	54.08

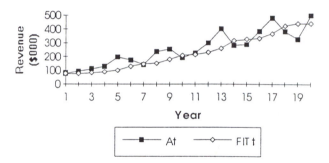

Figure 3   Revenue Forecast—two-parameter exponential smoothing.

The seasonal component of a revenue time series is the predictable fluctuations within a set period of time. Typically seasonal patterns would be seen in quarterly or monthly revenue flow data. Figure 4 illustrates a quarterly revenue flow time series in which seasonal patterns are apparent. Actual revenues flows and seasonally adjusted revenue flows are both plotted. Revenue flows are seasonally adjusted using a seasonal index derived from the data. In this example, revenue flows increase slightly in quarters 2 and 3. In quarter 4 there is a significant increase in revenues followed by a drop in revenues during quarter 1. Issuers would need to account for this seasonal trend in revenue flows, given that coupon payments are made semiannually.

The trend in a revenue time series is the long-term growth or decay of revenues. In Fig. 4 the increasing linear trend in quarterly revenue flows is apparent from the seasonally adjusted data. Trends may be linear or nonlinear in nature. The magnitude and direction of the revenue trend is critical in bond-issue structuring. If revenues are increasing over time, the issue should be structured so as to minimize the debt-servicing requirements in the initial years of the offering. In such a situation the issuer might consider offering zero coupon or original issue discount bonds.[*] On the other hand, if revenue flows are expected to decrease over the duration of the issue, the issue should be structured so as to minimize the debt-servicing needs in the later years of the issue. This could be accomplished by offering premium bonds or by reducing maturity amounts in the later years of the issue.

The trend component is quantified using simple linear regression. The regression equation using ordinary least squares is

$$\hat{y} = a + b \cdot t$$

---

[*]See Section V for a discussion of these types of coupons.

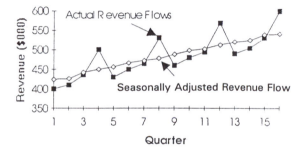

Figure 4   Quarterly revenue.

Table 6 Model Parameter Estimates

Contant (a)	416.3
Coefficient (b)	7.9
R^2	0.99

where

$\hat{y}$ = the revenue forecast
a = estimated model constant
b = estimated model coefficient
t = quarter

The regression model derived from the data presented in Fig. 4 is summarized in Table 6. Briefly, the regression equation for this model is

$$\hat{y} = 416.3 + 7.9 \cdot t$$

The coefficient (b) reveals that the expected increase in revenues per quarter is $7.9 thousand.

The R^2 is the proportion of variation in revenues that is explained by time. In other words, 99% of the uncertainty associated with revenues is explained by time. Therefore, the issuer is fairly certain that revenue flows will increase by $7.9 thousand per quarter. There is of course still uncertainty with a forecast based on regression models. Discussion of how the issuer handles uncertainty in revenue flow forecasts follows in the next section.

The cyclical component is typically fluctuations that are not predictable with any level of accuracy. Cyclical patterns are movements that are influenced by the local, national, and/or global economy. The final component is the irregular component. Like the cyclical component, forecasting based on random occurrences that may happen in the future is difficult if not impossible. An example of an unpredictable event that might affect revenue flows would be a large liability claim filed against the issuer. However, issuers may have information on events that will effect future revenue flows. This information should be incorporated into the revenue flow forecast. An example of a predictable factor that would affect revenue flows would be the anticipated relocation of a large employer to another locality, significantly reducing the issuer's tax base.

3. Causal Models

In a causal model the issuer identifies those factors that are expected to influence revenue flows. These factors might include population or economic performance measures. A predictive model incorporating these factors would be used to develop a forecasting framework for revenue flows. As in simple linear regression, a causal model would be derived from historical revenue flow data. Those factors predicted to influence revenue flows would be estimated and used to forecast revenues.

B.   Handling Uncertainty in Revenue Flows

As with any forecast there will always be a level of uncertainty. Uncertainty will not be eliminated in forecasting and issuers must be prepared to deal with it. The common measure of uncertainty in statistical analysis is standard deviation or variance. In statistical regression analysis several tests can be performed to determine the accuracy of model measures and forecasts. The measures of uncertainty associated with this model are presented in all statistical packages and can be used to develop confidence intervals for estimates from the model. A confidence interval is a range over which the issuer has some level of confidence that the estimated parameter will fall.

To illustrate the effect of uncertainty the time series presented in Fig. 4 and Table 6 is used. By using standard statistical analysis the confidence intervals for the change in revenues per period is derived. In this example, the 95% confidence interval for the change in revenues per period is estimated as 7.62 to 8.28. The means the issuer is 95% confident that revenues will increase between 7.62 and 8.28 thousand per quarter. This information could be used in a "what if" analysis in determining the risk associated with various financing alternatives.

When the regression model is used to forecast revenues the issuer should consider the accuracy of the prediction. This is accomplished by generating a confidence interval for the prediction. For a given year the forecast is generated by substituting the year for t and solving for y. For example, the forecast for quarter 17 is

$$\hat{y} = 416.3 + 7.9 \cdot 17 = 550.6$$

This forecast is subject to error because the model is just estimated from sample data, and time period is not a perfect predictor of revenues. A confidence interval for a prediction is the range over which the issuer has a level of confidence that the revenues will fall.

I.   Debt Coverage Ratio

The issue must be set up in such a manner so as to facilitate the issuer's ability to service debt. If debt-servicing requirements exceed revenues and there is no other means to service the debt, the issuer will be in default. To protect against default the expected debt-servicing requirement for any one period should not exceed the projected revenue flows for that period. Preferably the revenues should provide some cushion amount over the required debt-servicing needs. This cushion is referred to as the debt coverage ratio (DCR). The DCR is calculated as the ratio of pledged revenue to debt service. The higher the DCR the lower the risk that sufficient revenues will not be available to service the debt.

Table 7 presents a sample bond issue, with the debt-servicing requirements and the revenues available to service the debt outlined for each year in the 7-year maturity issue.

In this example the DCR varies from 3.38 to 1.37, with the greatest protection against default afforded the issuer in the early years of the issue when the DCR is high. The issuer would probably be better off with more protection in the form of higher DCR in the later years of the issue, as the further out in the future revenue flows are estimated the greater the uncertainty.

X.   CALL PROVISIONS

Call provisions permit the issuer to retire all or a portion of the outstanding debt before its maturity date at par or at a stated premium above par. In the municipal sector call provisions are common; 98% of municipals are callable. The average first call to final maturity ratio is .42 for revenue issues.[*] Call options allow the issuer to refinance the bond issue to either reduce borrowing costs or eliminate undesirable bond covenants. The presence of a call provision will increase the required rate of return demanded by the investor and therefore the cost to the issuer. It should be determined how varying the amount of callable funds, the deferment period, or the call order will affect the price of the issue. These figures then would be compared to the projected savings from the call provision.

The primary determinant of the premium required when a call provision is included is the level of interest rates at the time of the issue (Van Horne, 1978). If rates are relatively high and expected to drop, the market will require a larger premium for a call provision than if rates are relatively low. This is because of the increased probability that the market price will exceed the call price on the call date when rates are relatively

---

[*]For example, on a 10-year serial issue the first date the bonds would be callable would be 4 years after the issue date (Kidwell, 1976).

Table 7   Debt Coverage Ratio Calculation

Year	Maturity amount	Coupon rate	Price	Debt service	Pledged revenue	DCR
1	$735,000	5.1500%	$735,353.91	$1,050,222.50	$3,546,000	3.38
2	$775,000	5.1500%	$772,821.23	$1,052,370.00	$2,980,508	2.83
3	$810,000	5.5000%	$806,689.88	$1,047,457.50	$2,417,453	2.31
4	$855,000	5.6500%	$848,979.13	$1,047,907.50	$2,248,177	2.15
5	$905,000	5.8500%	$895,374.78	$1,049,600.00	$2,226,435	2.12
6	$1,515,000	6.0500%	$1,496,317.28	$1,606,657.50	$2,201,068	1.37

high. When this happens the bond will be called and the investors will have to place the proceeds in relatively lower-yielding securities.

Yawitz and Marshall (1981) estimate the increase in required yields on bonds when call provision are included. In their analysis they found the MOOD index to be a statistically significant proxy for call premiums. The MOOD index is a consumer sentiment index developed by Fair (1971).

The required premium is lower on discount bonds than on par bonds because discounted coupon bonds will have a lower market value than current coupon bonds and therefore will have less probability of being called (Friedlander, 1983). Variable-rate coupon bonds typically would not be callable because the interest rate adjusts with the prevailing rates. However, if a lower limit is placed on the level in which coupons can fall, the issuer may consider a call provision in the event that rates are expected to drop below the lower limit on the variable-rate coupon.

There are numerous procedures to calculate the required premium of callable bonds. One of the most common used by practitioners and academics is the Black-Scholes option pricing model (1972). The derivation and application of the model is discussed in most finance or portfolio textbooks (e.g., Levy and Sarnat, 1984). One of the difficulties is deriving call price from the Black-Scholes model is the estimation of price volatility. Elton and Gruber (1972) develop a technique based on the Markovian analysis. As with the Black-Scholes model, one of the major problems with employing the model to estimate call premiums is in the estimation of the probability distribution of future price movement.

The economic value of a call provision to the issuer is the dollar savings expected if interest rates fall. Spivey (1989) empirically tested the relationship between the value of the call provision and the premium required on callable bonds. The conclusion was that they are equal. In other words, the additional cost to the issuer of including the call provisions in the issue are exactly offset by the expected savings due to the ability to refinance.

XI. CREDIT ENHANCEMENTS

A number of defaults and near defaults over the past 20 years have served to erode the public's confidence in the safety of municipal debt, even when it is backed by the full taxing power of the issuing government. The near default of the general obligation issues of New York City is argued by some to have caused an immediate and long-term shift in the perceived risk on general obligation issues (Hoffland, 1974), while others studies indicate that the effect of the near default was temporary, if present at all (Kidwell and Trzcinka, 1982). Whether the market correctly perceived the risk in the municipal bond market before the New York City crisis is arguable. The event does serve to point out that a general obligation issue is only as secure as the security inherent in the tax base of the issuer. General obligation bonds, such as the ones nearly defaulted in New York City, are secured by the full taxing power of the state or municipality, but state and local governments regardless of the size of their tax base do not have unlimited funds with which to service debt. As Michael Satz, senior vice president and chief executive officer of AMBAC, a municipal insurer, said, the industry could no longer assume "that simply because the issuer was a government it was fail safe" (Hawthorn, 1986).

This diminishing confidence in the creditworthiness of municipal bonds has resulted in the market requiring higher yields to compensate for higher perceived risks. In addition, investors are requiring more information regarding the issuer's financial status and ability to service debt. Disclosure practices in the past have been insufficient; issuers must improve disclosure or incur the increased costs associated with increased perceived risk on the part of the investors.

One reaction by the issuers of municipal debt to the market's increased perceived risk is seen in the increased use of insurance and guarantees. By purchasing insurance or guarantees the issuer protects the investor against the probability of the issuer's not being able to meet debt-servicing requirements and being in default. The use of municipal bond insurance has gained in popularity, especially among smaller insurers, in order to reduce costs (Roche, 1985). In the decision as to whether to purchase insurance or guarantees the issuer must weigh the costs of insurance against the savings resulting from the reduction in perceived risks. Several studies have addressed this issue (Joehnk and Minge, 1976; Horton, 1970; Feldstein, 1983).

A. Rating

Two commercial rating agencies provide rating services. Moody's and Standard and Poor's. A high rating received by an issuer, AAA or Aaa, signals to the market that the rating agency has evaluated that issuer and the bonds to be issued as a very low-risk investment, hence the issuer with a high rating will be able to sell the bonds at a lower required rate of return.

In 1983 the highly rated revenue bonds of the Washington Public Power Supply System (WPPSS) defaulted, although both commercial rating agencies gave WPPSS their highest rating. The inaccurate rating of WPPSS resulted in a market demand for better information regarding the creditworthiness of their tax-exempt investment. The market sentiment was that commerical rating agencies were paid large fees for ratings services and oftentimes, especially on smaller issues, lacked adequate information to make accurate judgments (Zonana and Hertzbreg, 1981). With approximately 80,000 municipalities authorized to issue tax-exempt debt, analysts making recommendations in the new municipal market must have some expertise in the type of project being funded and the underlying creditworthiness of the issuing government. Municipal analysts are starting to pay less attention to a bond's rating and more to the bond's financial characteristics in developing recommendations. The result is that revenue and general obligation bonds are being more carefully scrutinized than in the past.

Ingram et al. (1983) looked at the effect of rating changes on municipal bond yields. In the corporate market, rating changes have relatively little impact on yields, as information contained in rating changes has already been incorporated in the price. In the municipal market, however, rating changes do impact bond yields. Ingram et al. suggest this is true in the municipal market because of time lags in the release of financial disclosure information, and because of the high cost associated with gathering information. Hsueh and Kidwell (1988) address the value of obtaining ratings from both rating agencies. The hypothesis is that if one rating signals the creditworthiness of the issuer, then two ratings should provide a stronger signal. They find that two ratings do provide information to the market and reduce borrowing costs to the issuer from 5.2 basis points to 21 basis points, depending on whether or not the ratings are identical.

B.   Insurance

Municipal bond insurance has been available since 1971. Savings resulting from the purchase of insurance are measured in terms of the reduced debt-servicing costs due to reduced risk of default and increased marketability. Kidwell et al. (1987) estimate the average net interest saving for insurance as 22.4 basis points. However, the benefit varies, depending on the underlying creditworthiness of the issuer. The benefit received from insurance varies from 3.8 basis points for Aa-rated bonds to 59 basis points for Baa-rated bonds. This means that an issuer with a high rating without insurance would receive lower cost savings from insurance than an issuer who has a lower credit rating without insurance.

Insured bonds automatically receive the highest credit rating from both commercial rating agencies. Insured AAA-rated issues do not, however, have required rates as low as uninsured AAA rated general obligations. Uninsured general obligations issues that receive the AAA rating based on their own creditworthiness are deemed by the public to be less risky than a bond that receives a AAA rating because of its underlying insurance. The differential in yields between the two issues has ranged from 25 to 65 basis points (Feldstein, 1983). Insured AAA rated bonds tend to sell at yields closer to A- or AA-rated uninsured bonds. When estimating the savings resulting from the purchase of insurance the issuer should be careful not to assume insured required rates would equal uninsured AAA required rates.

Another benefit for small issuers is improved marketability. Small issuers unknown in outside markets are better able to sell bonds over a larger market area if they have purchased insurance. The insurance performs an informational function for the investors in outside markets as to the creditworthiness of smaller issues (Kessel, 1971; Rubinfeld, 1973). Quantifying this cost may be difficult, but small issuers could compare rates received on uninsured and insured tax-exempt bonds from issuers of similar size and/or in similar markets. Hsueh and Liu (1990) argue that insurance does not provide a signaling benefit to issuers but that the net benefit is caused by some other factor such as market imperfections. Puelz (1992) suggests Hsueh and Liu's conclusions are based on an incorrect definition of signaling.

The Joehnk and Minge (1976) model of the savings resulting from the purchase of insurance is[*]

---

[*]The notation is changed slightly from Joehnk and Minge. G_m* is replaced by G_t and S_t is replaced by T_t.

$$T_t = C_t^{\,n} - C_t^{\,w} + G_t$$

where

Tt   = savings in period t
$C_t^{\,n}$ = cash outflow at time t on an uninsured bond
$C_t^{\,w}$ = cash outflow at time t on a insured bond
Gt   = the portion of the borrowed bond fee that is amortized at principal payment time t*

The savings T_t must then be discounted back to present value terms. The applicable discount rate is the expected IRR on the tax-exempt issue. The present value of savings resulting from insurance is defined as

$$\sum_{t=1}^{n} \frac{T_t}{(1+.5 \cdot i)^{2t}} - M_{t\,0} + U_{t0}$$

where

n   = the number of years to maturity
M_{t0} = the miscellaneous costs of obtaining insurance at the time 0 (i.e., rating fees)
U_{t0} = savings due to the increased marketability of the issue at time 0
i   = the applicable discount rate

If the saving resulting from the purchase of insurance is greater than zero then it should be purchased.

Table 8 illustrates the evaluation of the insurance purchase decision. In this example all costs of insurance are borrowed. The present value of debt service is higher by $1,253 when insurance is purchased.

The issuer must be cautious in evaluating insurance savings when there is a call provision on the issue. When a bond is called before maturity the savings resulting from lower debt servicing after the call date are eliminated. The issuer should evaluate the savings to the first call date and every year thereafter, including the maturity date. Expected total savings would then be weighted as to the probability that the market price will exceed the call price and the bond will be called during that year.

Puelz (1991) simulated the cost savings associated with insurance that are forfeited when call provisions are present. The simulation results presented in Figure 5 illustrate the effect of the call premium on forfeited cost savings. This example assumes interest rates are stationary. This does not mean rates are constant, but that the expected net change in rates over time is zero. Forfeited cost savings are presented relative to the standard deviation of rate changes. The larger the standard deviation of rate changes the more variable the rates. The more variable the rates, the greater the probability of a call and the greater the forfeited cost savings. The simulation results also illustrate the effect of the call premium on forfeited cost savings. The higher the call premium the lower the probability that the issuer will find it cost-effective to call the bonds and the lower the forfeited cost savings

Figure 6 illustrates the forfeited cost savings given different interest rate climates: stationary, increasing (+.2% per year), and decreasing (-.2% per year). As illustrated before, in all cases the more variable interest rates the greater the forfeited cost savings. If rates decrease, the magnitude of forfeited cost savings increases significantly. This is because as rates drop the issuer is more likely to find it profitable to call the bonds and refinance at lower interest rates. However, even when rates are expected to increase there is still a low expected forfeited cost saving. If the bonds are called and refinanced, then a portion of the cost savings may be recovered if the new issue bonds are insured (Boyle, 1992).

C. Bank Guarantees

A bank guarantee, like bond insurance, is a guarantee that the bank will make interest and principal payments to the investor if the issuer defaults. Unlike bond insurance the term of a bank guarantee is typically 5 to 10 years rather than the entire term of the bond issue. The bank and the issuer have the option to renew the agreement. If the agreement is not renewed there may be special provisions to protect the investor, such as substitute guarantees or mandatory redemption (Petersen, 1991).

As with bond insurance the underlying creditworthiness of the bank is an important consideration in

---

*This is assuming that the insurance premium is paid at time zero from borrowed funds rather than from general funds already available. Joehnk develops another model if the latter is true. The borrowed premium scenario is the more appropriate model as the rate earned on the general funds is probably greater than the rate paid for the tax-free funds.

Table 8 Evaluation of Insurance Purchase Decision

	With insurance			Without insurance			Present value uninsured debt service minus insured debt service
Year	Maturity amount	Coupon rate	Present value debt service	Maturity amount	Coupon rate	Present value debt service	
1	$620,000	4.75%	$611,726	$615,000	4.80%	$607,087	($4,639)
2	$650,000	5.05%	$636,779	$645,000	5.10%	$632,479	($4,300)
3	$685,000	5.30%	$669,335	$680,000	5.40%	$666,287	($3,048)
4	$720,000	5.65%	$707,496	$715,000	5.70%	$703,834	($3,662)
5	$755,000	5.70%	$740,681	$750,000	6.00%	$745,337	$4,656
6	$800,000	5.90%	$790,235	$795,000	6.10%	$793,175	$2,940
7	$1,405,000	6.15%	$1,405,290	$1,400,000	6.30%	$1,412,091	$6,801
	Total		$5,561,542			$5,560,289	($1,253)

Note: Discount rate = 6.146%.

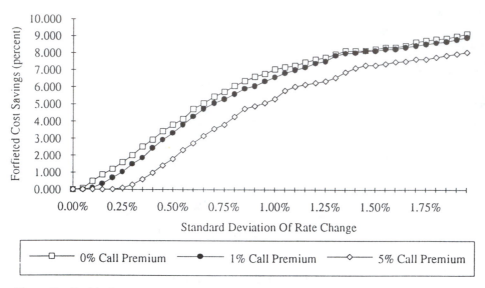

Figure 5 Forfeited cost savings given stationary rate expectations.*

Figure 6 Forfeited cost savings given level debt servicing.*

*Reprinted with permission from *Municipal Finance Journal*, Winter 1991, *12*(4), Panel Publishers, New York (see Puelz, 1991).

evaluating the cost-effectiveness of the bank guarantee. In addition, long-term bonds secured with short-term bank guarantees will not be as secure as the same bonds secured with conventional insurance would be.

XII. TOOLS FOR STRUCTURING

Numerous mathematical programming models have been developed to aid in the structuring process. An issuer should consider the dollar cost and benefit derived from using one or several decision aids. The costs of employing a decision aid are the time, equipment, and expertise required to set the decision aid in place and to operate it. The dollar benefit derived is in terms of cost savings due to the development of more cost-effective issue structures.

Many of these models utilize linear programming techniques to assign coupon rates to the serial maturities. Most of the earlier models use NIC to measure the interest cost of the issue (Cohen and Hammer, 1965 and 1966; Wiengartner, 1972; Nauss and Keeler, 1981). More recent models utilize TIC as the criterion (Nauss, 1986; Bierwag, 1976; Puelz and Lee, 1989 and 1992). All of these models (with the exception of Cohen and Hammer's work in 1966 and Puelz and Lee's in 1989 and 1992) were developed for use in competitive bidding. These models assist the underwriter in submitting bids to the issuer by determining the optimal coupon rates to assign to predetermined maturity schedules. Many of these models are evaluated on their computation speed because of the time constraints associated with submitting bids.

In a negotiated issue the underwriter works closely with the issuer throughout the structuring process and is not under the same time constraints as in a competitively bid issue. Cohen and Hammer (1966) designed a linear programming model to assign coupon and maturities amounts simultaneously. Their objective was to create an issue in which the debt servicing was level throughout the bond's life. Their model utilized NIC, which was the standard of the time. Puelz and Lee (1992) developed a model to derive the optimal maturity and coupon schedule that minimizes the TIC. Both of these models address only the decision as to optimal coupon and maturity schedules.

Puelz and Lee (1989) developed a decision support system (DSS) to aid in the entire process of bond structuring. A DSS is a supportive decision-making tool to be used in unstructured decision-making environments. If a DSS is properly designed and implemented, it should improve the effectiveness of the decision making. Effectiveness involves the identification of what should be done and the utilization of the appropriate selection criteria. The dynamic environment of municipal finance and the complexity of the decision make the use of a DSS in municipal bond structuring a valuable aid. The DSS developed in their research is divided into ten modules. The first group of modules includes: required rates of return, call provision, marketability, proceeds, projected revenue flows, and total interest costs. These modules are utilized to generate input into the priority structure module, which in turn generates input for the goal programming (GP) module. Output from the GP module is the least cost-maturity and coupon schedule for the bond issue. This bond structure is then used as input into the variable rate and the insurance modules where those decisions are evaluated.

REFERENCES

Aalberts, R. L. and Utley, J. C. (1988). *J. Taxa. Invest.*, 6: 267-285.
Bahl, R. and Duncombe, W. (1993). *Pub. Admin. Rev.*, 53 (1): 31-40.
Bierwag, G. O. (1976). *Mgt. Sci.*, 22 (11): 1175-1185.
Black, F. and Scholes, M. (1972). *J. Finance*, 27 (2): 399-418.
Bland, R. L. (1984). *Pub. Budgeting and Finance*, 4 (1): 53-59.
Bland, R. L. (1985). *Pub. Admin. Rev.*, 45: 233-237.
Bland, R. L. and Chen, L. (1990). *Pub. Admin. Rev.*, 51 (1): 42–48.
Boyle, N. (1992). *Bond Buyer*, 299 (28843): 1.
Braswell, R. C., Nosari, E. J., and Sumners, D. L. (1983). *J. Money, Cred. Bank.*, 15 (1): 102-106.
Brown, D. (1988). *Municipal Fin. J.*, 9: 42-48.
Buse, A. (1976). *J. Finance*, 25 (4): 809-818.
Cohen, K. J. and Hammer, F. S. (1965). *Mgt. Sci.*, 12 (1): 68-82.
Cohen, K. J. and Hammer, F. S. (1966). *Mgt. Sci.*, 13 (3): 161-166.
Cook, T. Q. (1982). *Econ. Rev. Fed. Res. Bank Richmond* (May-June): 14-39.
Dyl, E. A. and Joehnk, M. D. (1976). *Bell J. Econ.*, 7 (2): 680-689.
Ederington, L. H. (1976). *J. Finance*, 31 (1): 17-28.
Elton, E. J. and Gruber, M. J. (1972). *J. Finance*, 27 (4): 891-902.

Fabozzi, I. J. and West, R. R. (1981). *J. Finan. Quant. Anal.*, *16* (3): 323–340.

Fair, R. C. (1971). *A Short-run Forecasting Model of the United States Economy*, Heath, Lexington, Mass.

Fama, E. (1977). *A Pricing Model for the Municipal Bond Market*, unpublished manuscript, University of Chicago.

Feldstein, M. (1983). *The Municipal Bond Handbook, vol. I* (F. F. Fabozzi, S. G. Feldstein, I. M. Pollack, and F. G. Zarb, eds.), Dow Jones-Irwin, Homewood, Ill., pp. 404-411.

Fischer, P. J. (1980). *J. Money, Cred. Bank.*, *12* (1): 71-83.

Friedlander, G. (1983). *The Municipal Bond Handbook, vol. I* (F. F. Fabozzi, S. G. Feldstein, I. M. Pollack, and F. G. Zarb, eds., Dow Jones-Irwin, Homewood, Ill., pp. 340-353.

Hawthorn, F. (1986). *Inst. Investor, 20* (2): 223-226.

Hendershott, P. and Kidwell, D. (1978). *J. Money, Cred. Bank.*, *10* (3): 337-347.

Hildreth, W. B. (1993). *Pub. Admin. Rev.*, *53* (1): 41-49.

Hoffland, D. L. (1974). *Finan. Anal. J.*, *30* (2): 65-70.

Hoffland, D. L. (1977). *Finan. Anal. J.*, *33* (2): 36-39.

Hopewell, M. H. and Kaufman, G. G. (1974a). *J. Finance, 29* (1): 155-164.

Hopewell, M. H. and Kaufman, G. G. (1974b). *Nat. Tax J., 27* (4): 531-541.

Horton, J. J. (1970). *J. Bank Research, 1, 4*: 29-40.

Hsueh, L. P. and Liu, Y. A. (1990). *J. Risk Insur., 57* (4): 691-700.

Hsueh, L. P. and Kidwell, D. S. (1988). *Finan. Mgt.*: 46-53.

Ingram, R. W., Brooks, L. D., and Copeland, R. M. (1983). *J. Finance, 38* (3): 997-1003.

Inzer, R. B. and Reinhart, W. J. (1984). *Gov. Finance, 13* (6): 25-29.

Joehnk, F. J. and Minge, D. (1976). *Rev. Bus. Econ. Res., 12* (1): 1-18.

Joyce, P. G. and Mullins, D. R. (1991). *Pub. Admin. Rev., 51* (3): 240-253.

Kaufman, G. C. (1981). *Efficiency in the Municipal Bond Market* (G. C. Kaufman, ed.), JAI Press Inc., Greenwich, Conn., pp. xi-xvi.

Kaufman, G. C. (1983). *The Municipal Bond Handbook, vol. I* (F. F. Fabozzi, S. G. Feldstein, I. M. Pollack, and F. G. Zarb, eds.), Dow Jones-Irwin, Homewood, Ill., pp. 252-274.

Kessel, R. (1971). *J. Polit. Econ., 79* (4): 706-737.

Kidwell, D. S. (1976). *Nebr. J. Econ. Bus., 15* (4): 63-70.

Kidwell, D. S. and Trzcinka, C. A. (1982). *J. Finance, 37* (5): 1239-1246.

Kidwell, D. S., Fabozzi, F. J., and Moore, C. M. (1983). *The Municipal Bond Handbook, vol. I* (F. F. Fabozzi, S. G. Feldstein, I. M. Pollack, and F. G. Zarb, eds.), Dow Jones-Irwin, Homewood, Ill., pp. 94-110.

Kidwell, D. S. and Koch, T. W. (1983). *J. Money, Cred. Bank., 15* (1): 40-55.

Kidwell, D. S., Sorensen, E. H., and Wachowicz, J. M. (1987). *J. Finan. Quant. Anal., 22* (3): 299-313.

King, S. R. (1992). *Bond Buyer, 300* (28956): 1.

Kochan, J. L. (1983). *The Municipal Bond Handbook, vol. I* (F. F. Fabozzi, S. G. Feldstein, I. M. Pollack, and F. G. Zarb, eds.), Dow Jones-Irwin, Homewood, Ill., pp. 326-339.

Laufenberg, D. (1983). *The Municipal Bond Handbook, vol. I* (F. F. Fabozzi, S. G. Feldstein, I. M. Pollack, and F. G. Zarb, eds.), Dow Jones-Irwin, Homewood, Ill., pp. 275-283.

Leibowitz, M. L. (1983). *The Municipal Bond Handbook, vol I*, (F. F. Fabozzi, S. G. Feldstein, I. M. Pollack, and F. G. Zarb, eds.), Dow Jones-Irwin, Homewood, Ill., pp. 297-325.

Levy, H. and Sarnat, M. (1984). *Portfolio and Investment Selection: Theory and Practice*, Prentice/Hall, Englewood Cliffs, N.J.

Maese, J. E. (1985). *Financ. Mgt., 14* (1): 26-32.

McCorry, J. (1987). *Bond Buyer, 4* (16): 1.

McCorry, J. (1982). *Bond Buyer* (April 14).

Miller, M. H. (1977). *J. Finance, 32*: 261-275.

Miller, G. J. (1993). *Pub. Admin. Rev., 53* (1): 50-58.

Mitchell, K. and McDade, M. D. (1992). *J. Money, Cred. Bank., 24* (4): 529-552.

Moak, L. (1982). *Municipal Bonds: Planning Sale and Administration*, Government Finance Officers Association, Chicago.

Mysak, J. (1990). *Bond Buyer, 293* (28496): 30.

Nauss, R. M. (1986). *Mgt. Sci., 32* (7): 870-877.

Nauss, R. M. and Keeler, B. R. (1981). *J. Bank Res., 11* (4): 174-181.

Petersen, J. E. (1987). *Nat. Tax J., 40*: 393-402.

Petersen, J. E. (1988). *Pub. Budgeting and Finance, 8*: 22-34.

Petersen, J. E. (1991). *Nat. Tax J., 44* (4): 11-28.

Porteba, J. M. (1989). *Reg. Sci. Urban Econ., 19* 537-562.

Puelz, A. v. and Lee, S. M. (1989). *Municipal Fin. J., 10* (2): 153-171.

Puelz, A. v. (1991). *Municipal Fin. J., 12*: 23-33.

Puelz, A. v. and Puelz, R. (1991). *The Effect of Alternative Minimum Tax Bonds on Optimal Bond Portfolio Choice*, proceedings of the 1991 Annual Meeting of the Decision Sciences Institute, Miami Beach, Fl., pp. 138-140.

Puelz, A. v. and Lee, S. M. (1992). *Mgt. Sci., 38* (8): 1186-1200.

Puelz, A. v. (1993). *Finan. Serv. Rev. 3*(1): 59–73.

Puelz, R. (1992). *J. Risk Insur. 59*: 499–503.

Roche, P. B. (1985). "Use of Municipal Bond Insurance Gaining Among Small Insurers." *Wall St. J.*, Jan. 13: 15.

Rubinfeld, D. (1973). *Nat. Tax J. 26* (1): 17-27.

Sobol, M. G. and Starr, M. K. (1993). *Introduction to Statistics for Executives*, McGraw Hill, New York.

Spivey, M. F. (1989). *J. Finan. Res., 12*: 203-216.

Trzcinka, C. (1982). *J. Finan., 37* (4): 907-923.

Van Horne, J. C. (1978). *Financial Market Rates and Flows*, Prentice-Hall, Englewood Cliffs, N.J.

Weberman, B. and Schifrin, M. (1986). *Forbes*, Feb. 10: 50.

Weingartner, H. M. (1972). *Mgt. Sci., 19* (4): 369-378.

Winders, J. J. (1981). *Efficiency in the Municipal Bond Market* (G. C. Kaufman, ed.), JAI Press, Greenwich, Conn., pp. 257-260.

Yawitz, J. B., Maloney, K. J. and Edenington, L. H. (1985). *J Finan.*, *40*(4): 1127–1139.

Yohe, W. P. and Karnosky, D. S. (1969). *Fed. Res. Bank St. Louis Rev., 51*.

Zonana, V. S. and Hertzbreg, D. (1981). "Moody's Dominance in Municipal Markets Is Slowly Being Eroded." *Wall St. J.*, Nov. 1.

22

The Objectives of Municipal Disclosure: Epitomizing the Issuer's Credit Quality

Thomas A. Dorsey
AMBAC Indemnity Corporation, New York, New York

I. THE NEED FOR DISCLOSURE

An important factor affecting the need for disclosure today is the growing shift in the ownership of municipal fixed-income securities. Over the last decade, particularly after the Tax Reform Act of 1986, the ownership of municipal debt has shifted dramatically to the retail market and the individual investor. (See Figure 1.)

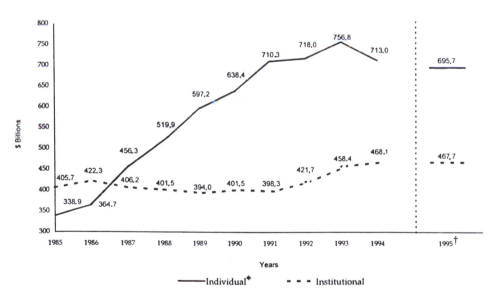

Figure 1 Holders of municipal debt: (*) "Individual" includes mutual fund investments, (†) figures are preliminary and unadjusted for first quarter. (*Source: The Bond Buyer*, June 16, 1995.)

The opinions expressed in this paper are solely those of the author and do not reflect the views of the ownership or management of AMBAC Inc. or AMBAC Indemnity Corp.

As investors these bondholders are less sophisticated than the institutional investors that dominated earlier markets. Accordingly, their needs for clear and accurate disclosure are greater.

The problem is whether or not individual purchasers of bonds are fully capable of assessing the implications of the data presented in an offering statement (OS). Assuming that investment in tax-exempt municipal bonds correlates with higher income and education levels (a fairly supportable assumption), the average individual investor should find the basic demographic and economic information useful and should appreciate its general implications.

The problem of risk assessment will arise in the attempt to relate the basic data to the *security* and *structural* conditions involved in the transaction. Here the private individual will be affected by his or her knowledge of state municipal finance law and practices that govern the repayment of debt. These provisions interact with the disclosed economic data to make the interpretation of risk more difficult. In order to understand these consequences of disclosure and address some basic issues concerning the use of data we need to examine standard disclosure data.

II. CREDIT IMPLICATIONS IN THE USE OF EMPIRICAL DATA

Disclosure today presents a "snapshot" of the issuer. The credit picture is fixed in time and is limited to descriptive data applying solely to the municipality, without reference to any contrasting norms. Nevertheless, this information is very useful and represents a substantial improvement over the disclosure of a decade ago. The level of disclosure also effectively deals with a principle well documented by decision-making theories; namely, that it is impossible to have perfect knowledge. Thus, the "market" must suboptimize to produce an OS that is comprehensive to the individual investor but also produced with "due diligence." The result is disclosure which inherently imposes choices on the manner in which the issuer presents relevant information. These choices revolve around the following factors.

A. Congruent Data

First, the data provided may not be presented in a comprehensive format; that is, the various data elements do not have a common basis for conformity. This can arise from several causes. Some data may be substantially out of date. They may be badly lagged from the current year. Various data sets will not be compatible either temporally or geographically (e.g., county-level data versus municipal data), requiring the reader to make "knowledgeable" adjustments.

Finally, key data elements that allow the inference of other conclusions may not be available or may be omitted. The result may be that the composite picture normally presented is lacking in some troublesome aspect. *To the knowledgeable analyst the absence of information is more significant than its presence, and lacunae in disclosure are treated with strong suspicion.* As a result, comprehensiveness and completeness are essential to successful disclosure. We will discuss some cases below.

B. Consistency

Second, *data may be presented in a manner consistent with industry practice* but arrayed in a manner that frustrates its interpretation in a useful manner. Issuers must focus on the use of data to confirm and elaborate on factors relating to the security (e.g., taxes) pledged to the repayment of debt. Breaking away from standard disclosure to provide certain data items can enhance the argument for creditworthiness. However, some data cannot be reconciled by the preparer of the OS to achieve unambiguous interpretation. In these cases the narrative discussion and the total presentation must deal with any deficiencies. We will discuss some cases below.

C. Comparisons

Third, data are rarely, if ever, presented with comparative examples *even though this is the very basis for most credit analysts' evaluation of creditworthiness.* Industry analysts are trained to compare all credits of a like type to all other credits they have evaluated to test for narrow degrees of credit or rating distinctions. *It is this comparative approach that provides the additional depth in evaluating creditworthiness in the municipal market. As a result the presentation of selected comparative data may be viewed by market participants as helping in risk evaluation. However, the choice of comparison will inevitably be criticized by knowledgeable market participants.*

D. Erroneousness

Fourth, in rare cases the disclosure is erroneous or deliberately misleading (usually by omission). In these cases the purchaser, and even the professional analyst, has little recourse to other means of assessing risk. Customarily the market relies on the opinion of bond counsel and underwriters' counsel to aver that the disclosure is material in all respects. However, the degree of responsibility and the effect of reliance on other experts is still not fully defined in the law. (See discussion below.) In short, there is no real protection from deliberate attempts to disguise negative information.

The following discussion is intended to provide municipal officials, providers of municipal data, and others associated with bringing municipal debt transactions to market with some insight into how substantive disclosure is used and evaluated. In order to focus the discussion we will use the suggested disclosure guidelines prepared by the National Federation of Municipal Analysts (NFMA) for general obligation bonds, which is reproduced in the appendix.

Wherever possible, concrete examples rendered anonymous by removing identifying elements are presented to assist the reader. For brevity's sake only certain sections of the NFMA outline can be examined in detail. In particular, we have omitted any discussion of debt description, project and capital program, and financial practices.

Since disclosure is an art and not a science, this chapter offers no conclusions about the exact way to proceed; rather, we raise some points about industry guidelines and try to suggest techniques that will enhance the story the issuer is trying to tell and about which its officials should be aware.

III. CONCEPTS OF MATERIALITY IN DISCLOSING EMPIRICAL DATA

The legal environment in which the disclosure of empirical data describing municipal credit conditions occurs is not well developed or particularly clear. Case law in this area deals with the broad application of disclosure rules, and the specifics of data accuracy are rarely considered. Thus, determinations about the correct treatment of data must be inferred from the available law.

The basic point of departure is the Securities Exchange Act of 1933 and rules attendant thereto. Under the 1933 act the standard is "full and fair disclosure" as presented in a registration statement. Joint and several liabilities are imposed on the issuer, the underwriters, and all experts providing information or analysis for "material misstatements in, or omissions from, the registration statement" (15 USC 77k). A defense to liability is provided if the parties had reasonable grounds, after reasonable investigation, to believe that the facts presented are true and accurate. Section 11 of the act provides that "the standard of reasonableness [is that] required of a prudent man in the management of his own property."

Since the 1933 act does not govern tax-exempt financings, these standards are not applied to municipal transactions. Moreover, the treatment of the "due diligence" standard present in rule 176 (17 C.F.R., 230.176) is also applied as a flexible test that depends on the circumstances of the financing and the issuer. Case law governing registered securities has required independent verification of information without reliance on the issuer or issuer's counsel. Moreover the Security and Exchange Commission (SEC) has indicated that it is the duty of the underwriter to evaluate the correctness of the disclosure statement.

Section 12(2) of the 1933 act exempts the majority of municipal bond transactions from the effect of the act, including, by inference, the test of negligence as a standard of liability. This conclusion has been stated in the American Bar Association's *Report on Disclosure Roles of Counsel in State and Local Government Offerings* (1987) as follows:

> Since issuers incurring absolute liabilities under Section 11 must be shown under Section 12(2) to have been negligent, and since municipal securities are expressly exempt from both Sections, taking the entire framework of regulation into account anything more onerous than a scienter standard would appear to be an inappropriate level of culpability for state and local governments under the antifraud provisions (p. 40).

The standard of "scienter" is effectively expressed as "knowledge" in that the party must know or have reason to believe that the information is incorrect or misleading. This standard can apply to cases in which there is some unresolved doubt in the mind of the expert that he or she would ordinarily check in the reasonable conduct of their own affairs. Thus due diligence is a matter of judgment "that . . . is best left a general and flexible standard . . . determined in most cases by the particular circumstances of the public offering of either municipal or corporate securities" (*Disclosure Roles*, p. 76).

The adoption of the standards as guidelines by the municipal securities industry has been amplified in recent years by the efforts of the Government Finance Officers Association (GFOA) to promulgate disclosure guidelines. That work has been followed by that of the NFMA in preparing the *Disclosure Handbook for Municipal Securities* (1990). Both of these developments are significant steps in the industry's efforts to provide complete standards for disclosure without turning to regulation.

In this context it should also be noted that the Securities Act amendments of 1975, which established the Municipal Securities Rulemaking Board (the MSRB), specifically prohibited the MSRB from requiring the issuance of disclosure documents. Even though the MSRB is the regulatory body for the industry, the rationale for this action is founded in the large number of issuers, the wide discrepancies in the size of offerings, and the variety of bond security types. Thus, while the MSRB does require the underwriter to provide final OS's to its customers, the form and nature of the disclosure is still governed by the guidelines suggested by the GFOA and the NFMA.

Specific tests of the accuracy of data disclosure are essentially nonexistent in the case law of municipal bond transactions. Generally the quality of specific data elements is not at issue. Rather, comprehensiveness or inferential value of the facts becomes the focus of any controversy. One excerpt from an SEC-reported opinion illustrates this premise.

> there is an underwriter obligation to ensure that sales literature is founded upon an adequate investigation so that [it] accurately [reflects] all material facts which a prudent investor should know.
> the Commission indicated that the underwriter should have conducted an investigation of the financial condition of the owner-developer involved in the particular offering and of the property to be developed. The investigation of the property would have disclosed the distance of the property from schools and shopping areas and its location on an airport approach [Walston and Company, SEC Rel 34-8164 (Sept. 22, 1967) 1966-67 Transfer Binder, FED SEC L Rep (CCH) p77, 474].

IV.   AN EXAMINATION OF THE NFMA GUIDELINES

A.   Description of Issuer

1.   *The Entity*

A concise, well-written *history and background* of the issuer, which places it in a socioeconomic context in its state and region, is a powerful tool of disclosure that is frequently omitted. Carefully crafted, this introduction can serve as the context for presenting all the additional data in the OS. It can deal with preexisting negative perceptions or it can provide the first impression for a reviewer unfamiliar with the issuer. A detailed *map* with good graphics can be an essential component of this description.

Poor background, or failure to describe unique characteristics of the issuing entity, can be damaging or can fatally prejudice the reviewer's opinion, as seen in the following example:

> A key reviewer of the OS knew that the city of Squeedonk was unique because it was situated on Native American tribal lands leased to the residents on a 99-year (perpetual) lease approaching its renewal date. Similar treaty arrangements were familiar to the reviewer and were not deemed to be a problem; the failure to disclose the matter (while not material) was viewed negatively.

2.   *Management and Administration*

The background, selection, and experience of *management* is a critical element for understanding credit quality. Reviewers' confidence with municipal officials (and professional mangers) is frequently critical to a positive outcome, particularly when fiscal stress is evident. Disclosure of this information is common for tax-exempt enterprise issuance (hospitals, housing agencies, utilities) but much more infrequent for tax-backed general obligation issuance. The reasons for this are unclear. It would appear that disclosure of background is closely correlated with the existence of professional credentials by municipal managers. This seems one-sided since years of hands-on experience can be much more valuable than several semesters of academic training.

The occurrence of a *default*, nonappropriation for lease debt, or bankruptcy is a mandatory element of disclosure. Indeed, any suggestion of fiscal malfeasance, no matter how well resolved, has to be addressed by disclosure. Institutional memory in the tax-exempt municipal market is very long and cynicism runs deep. Conversely, it is neither desirable nor constructive to raise spurious matters to a level of materiality, and issuers should discuss such matters carefully with bond counsel or their fiscal advisors. For example

> Several years ago the city of Malurb was subject to a probe by a state commission of investigation on certain fiscal practices. No sanctions resulted from this activity. When Malurb's next debt issue was being prepared, a municipal official in a public information session answered a vague question about the commission's probe by saying 'the FBI investigation never resulted in any indictments.' None of the participating reviewers were aware that the FBI had also investigated allegations of graft in Malurb. The proposed issue was withdrawn from the market for some time, but eventually sold.

The form and *organization of government* and the allocation of functions (municipal services) are rarely described, despite the fact that these matters differ significantly from state to state. In New York, for example, each type of municipality (city, county, town, village, etc.) and class of municipality within each type, can have different service obligations. By contrast, in Florida, *municipality* is a generic term, regardless of the local designation (city, town, village), and all municipalities can perform the same functions. Counties, however, perform a separate set of functions. This information is important in assessing the scope of obligations, particularly where mandated service obligations are causing fiscal stress with the withdrawal of federal and state aid.

The *budget process* and the *physical assets* of the issuer should be succinctly described with emphasis on *timing*, as it affects the security pledged to the bonds, and the relation between the purposes of the current financing to other capital projects and assets. Reviewers are primarily interested in evidence of essentiality of purpose, scope and cost of the project, and consistency within the capital plan. *Municipal labor force* information should be presented to address cost factors, adequacy of service delivery, contract status, personnel relations, and adequacy of pension funding. The delight with which private individuals voluntarily inform reviewers that labor unrest may impair the issuer's functions or budget is surprising.

3. Economic Factors

Land use and *demographic data* have been fairly standard disclosure items for years. Often they are not well integrated and certain elements have been emphasized to serve special characteristics of the issuer. For example, disclosure dealing with development district financings often overdisclose land use patterns and underdisclose demographic breakdowns. There are two reasons for this: (1) the data disclosed are legitimately what are available and (2) detailed disclosure of cohort distribution or wealth indicators could give an undesirable impression.

In particular circumstances care should be given to explaining apparent inconsistencies. For example, *enrollment data for school districts* is always disclosed, usually on an aggregate basis by year. On the other hand, breakdowns by age groups are rarely provided, so it is difficult to ascertain if a "bulge" exists in the annual flow of students through the system. In a recent issue of the Outback Central School District the data showed a long-term *decline* of 10% in the aging municipal population of the town coterminous with the school district. School enrollment, however, showed a modest but persistent increase of 2% per year. What was the cause? An inquiry to the financial advisor produced the explanation "They are having more babies." Who? If the population is declining (and aging) fertility rates should not be rising, particularly if the base population is not being replaced. Clearly something was unresolved, either in the statistics or their interpretation.

Employment characteristics are important data usually well disclosed but often inconsistently or without regard to context. The following example is fairly typical of standard GO disclosure and provides an adequate response to the need for employment data. However, the time periods do not compare (July to December) between labor force and unemployment data. This is a minor point that could easily be adjusted. Also, the county and state data have little direct relationship since the county is so small. Finally, the data do not explain why the county and state positions have *reversed* in the 6 months from December to July.

A more complex limitation of employment data is the inability to relate the place of work with the place of residence. This is particularly difficult in the case of a semirural residential population center without any major employers in its boundaries. Unemployment is nominal, but commutation to the nearest urban area is

Table 1 Labor Force Statistics

	Outback County July 1990	State of Noname July 1990
Civilian labor force	6,172	8,527,900
Total employed	5,846	7,990,300
Total unemployed	326	537,600
Percentage unemployed	5.3%	6.3%

Unemployment rates	December 1989	December 1988
Outback County	6.5%	8.1%
State of Noname	5.8%	6.2%
United States of America	5.1%	5.0%

Source: State Employment Commission.

a trip of an hour or more. Where do these people work? The answer cannot be deduced from the data. As a result it is difficult to assess the long-term economic vitality of the issuer. However, a narrative discussion describing the local employment environment can add to understanding.

Retail sales data (and related tax collections) are most useful when the bonds are secured by a sales tax pledge. As an indicator of economic health these data are only generally helpful. It is increasingly common for suburban municipalities to contain major sales tax generators (e.g., a regional mall) that are strongly affected by externalities. Supporting information is needed to paint a full picture.

Building permit data can be even more difficult to evaluate. The basic problem is the lack of distribution by the number of permits in each value class. Fifty commercial permits for $50 million can involve one $49.5 million building and 49 minor improvements. Disaggregation of the data into useful profiles is essential for analysis. The data should explain what is being built, not how much is being added (Table 2).

V. TERMS OF DEBT

A. Nature of Security

The elements of this portion of the disclosure do not involve the presentation of empirical data. Nevertheless, this narrative is critical to the interpretation of the data on pledged revenue. This is particularly true when

Table 2 Building Permits

	1984		1985	
	Permits	Valuation	Permits	Valuation
New construction				
Residential	1,321	$65,429,443	702	$61,052,315
Commerical	222	99,505,000	65	75,531,224
Industrial	17	3,924,504	28	8,238,257
Other	217	36,235,023	295	31,200,646
Total new construction	$1778	$205,093,970	1,090	$176,022,442
Total repairs, alternations/additions	3,845	$191,618,347	3,584	$178,112,185
Grand total	5,623	$396,712,317	4,674	$354,134,627
New residential units	2,127		1,937	

Source: Department of Safety and Permits, building inspection annual reports.

less familiar forms of tax revenues or intergovernmental transfers are employed. One example will have to suffice. Often facts needed to interpret distribution formulas become important in understanding creditworthiness (a point not clearly identified in these guidelines).

A good example is Florida's authorization to localities to pledge the 1/2 cent optional sales tax proceeds to the repayment of bonds. These taxes are distributed on the basis of the revenues generated in the county and apportioned on the basis of the population of incorporated and unincorporated areas in the county. A "floor" of 40% is established for counties. In a recent county financing, the county share of the revenue (62%) adequately covered debt service. However, it was not disclosed that in the prior year an unincorporated portion of the county had considered incorporating. Is this material? As a historical event it may only be interesting to a bondholder, but to other reviewers it becomes a strong signal to apply the worst case test of a 40% distribution to evaluate the resulting debt service coverage. Otherwise, disclosure of sales tax proceeds or retail sales data may be ineffective in measuring risk.

B. Debt Description

Traditionally, debt is well documented but the measurers of its burden are always calculated based on other data. Thus, good population and good tax base values are essential to good measures of debt per capita and debt to full value. More important, however, debt figures vary widely by state and locality with no clear norms for analysis. A number of important variables affect these figures, including: (1) age and status of existing infrastructure, (2) age and growth rate of the issuing municipality, (3) mandated services provided to its residents, and (4) infrastructure and zoning effects on future ratables.

The traditional measures are evaluated in a vacuum and are useful only in the context of the individual analyst's cognitive map of similar cases. Comparative data would enhance the analysis. However, access to debt per capita means or medians for Texas cities, or cities of 100,000 or less, only provides limited understanding. Disaggregation and comparison by (1) rate of growth, (2) proximity to urban centers, or (3) whether or not future capital obligations are needed could be more informative.

VI. FINANCIAL DATA

A. Property Tax Policy, Structure, and Collections

Information relating to taxable valuation, major taxpayers, and tax rates are also well-organized disclosure items. Items that are suggested by the NFMA guidelines but frequently omitted, are data on exemptions and the total tax impact on a "typical" residential unit. Occasionally taxpayer information is not well developed, often because it is difficult to sort out from the total assessment roll.

The problem with property tax data is not its availability but rather its interpretation. While the data can be presented in well-structured formats the differences in treatment from state to state can substantially cloud interpretation of the data. Differences between uniform and classified valuation systems, equalization processes, optional and mandated exemptions, tax rate allocations, and other legal and administrative procedures make analysis quite complex. The narrative discussion setting forth local tax administrative procedures thus becomes a key element of disclosure.

B. Reports, Financial Practices, and Operations

Fiscal reports and policies are often not covered in a separate discussion, and many key questions can be resolved by good presentation of fiscal procedures. The process for interfund transfers and the conditions under which they are allowed is a good example of an item recommended in the NFMA outline. Nothing is less comprehensible than a series of intrafund transfers that balance but that cannot be separated into their components or rationalized to one another. Experienced analysts often have to resort to calling the issuer's accountant or financial officer to provide the underlying explanation for the sources of the transferred funds.

Categorization of revenues and expenditures into broad types often may not help resolve questions raised in other parts of the disclosure. For example, revenues broken down into (1) taxes and special assessments, (2) licenses and permits, (3) intergovernmental, (4) charges for services, (5) fines and forfeits, (6) interest income, and (7) miscellaneous, may disguise certain facts. If "intergovernmental" is 25% of revenues, how much is state and how much is federal? Declining federal aid or state aid rollbacks can have implications here but the magnitude cannot be measured. Similar questions can be raised about other categories, not the least of which is "miscellaneous."

Expenditure categories raise similar questions. Listings such as "public safety," "health and welfare," and "culture and recreation" do not answer questions about police costs or discretionary versus mandatory expenditures. If libraries are closed because of fiscal stress how much in savings results? If the mayor just proposed hiring 5000 policemen what is the estimated budgetary impact on the police department's budget? The concerned reviewer has to call the financial advisor or the appropriate municipal fiscal officer to find out. The individual bondholder may simply be left relying on published rating reports.

The growing utilization of audited financial statements, the widespread use of recognized auditing firms, and the professional education courses offered by such firms has vastly improved this aspect of disclosure. Current limitations in this regard have more to do with state and local standards for financial reporting by municipalities than with the services of the accounting profession.

VII.   IMPENDING CHANGES: RULE 15c2-12 AND "CONTINUING DISCLOSURE"

Since 1988, increasing SEC and MSRB involvement in disclosure is placing additional emphasis on the need for clear, prompt provision of pertinent fiscal information. Rule 15c2-12 requires underwriting firms to provide "nearly final" official statements before bidding commences. Final OSs must be made available within 2 days of sale to any person requesting such information. The effect of this rule will be to increase the attention and resources applied to preparing official statements, emphasizing the need for very current information. It will encourage well-prepared discussions of economic, financial, and structural conditions and other relevant risk factors.

The "continuing disclosure" requirement—applying essentially to secondary market transactions—requires a focused update (limited to 3 pages) of pertinent disclosure information. This approach to disclosure is currently in a voluntary pilot phase. The implications, however, are significant for larger frequent issuers whose bonds are traded extensively. Here the burden will be placed on bond trustees and issuers to maintain market liquidity by establishing a current and relevant disclosure data base relating to their debt that can be digested and made available to purchasers in the municipal markets.

The central question present here is "How much disclosure is appropriate?" Limiting submission size helps control data flows, but may exclude useful information. In particular, financial statements, which are the heart of continuing disclosure, require substantial space (paper or electronic) to be stored. Sandardizing information will facilitate management but will cut against the special needs of particular issuers or "nonstandardized" bond types. Issuers that seek to "epitomize" their presentation of data may, in fact, set themselves a higher (or unreasonable) standard that they may have to maintain in the future. Conversely, allowing adequate flexibility to disclose specialized data is probably essential to adequately serving the retail market. The effort involved to reach a happy medium is high but ultimately worth the time it should receive.

VIII.   STRATEGIES FOR EPITOMIZING THE ISSUER

Epitome is defined alternatively as (1) a brief presentation, and (2) a typical or ideal example. One objective of disclosure in an OS should be to briefly describe the ideal quality of the issuing entity with the purpose of persuading investors to want to act as the municipality's creditors. Well-structured disclosure can serve that purpose.

The profile of the issuer should attempt to focus on the most current data that describe its creditworthiness. Population figures, if estimated, should be attributed to the source. Employment data should be cited to a central common source such as the Bureau of Labor Statistics. If state or regional data are more current or show a recent favorable trend, they should be presented as *complementary information*. Reviewers should not be put off by two separate data sources unless they are inherently contradictory.

Explanatory linkages should be established *across data sets* whenever possible. If the largest employer is the largest taxpayer and is expanding its physical plant these data should be brought together as evidence of economic growth. Without supporting explanations the large concentration of employment and tax liability (and an unexplained blip in building permit values) may be viewed as additional risk.

A good picture is also realistic, and the subject should not be "airbrushed." For example, many municipalities are experiencing fiscal stress today. Those conditions should be clearly described in addition to the strategy planned to resolve related financial difficulties. A reasonable fiscal plan usually involves incurring debt. Very few debt issuers are precluded from the market because of tight finances. Market access is more directly affected by the inability to describe a course of solution.

Disclosure does not need to be limited to the snapshot strategy, particularly when the financing requires broader understanding by the investor. Presentation of data that place the issuer in context in its labor market, its regional economy, and its standard metropolitan area (SMA) rounds out the reviewer's sense of the credit. Economic activity relevant to the evaluation of the pledged security can be related to the overall economy, often resulting in greater comfort with the creditor.

Although not frequently used, comparative data on a like class of issuers can substantially enhance understanding of the creditworthiness of the issuer. Some frequent issuers include these types of data in rating agency presentations because they know the rating officers will have to compare the proposed rating with the ratings of similar issuers in order to maintain consistency. Similar comparative data can place issuers in "good company" on a regional or national level. This depends, however, on the availability of a data base with sufficiently accurate and current information to support such a presentation. Unfortunately this type of data base, focused on *credit quality data*, is not readily available from a national source.

Finally, there is a clear need for greater narrative discussion accompanying complex local government financings secured by intergovernmental revenue transfers or new forms of taxes. As local issuers are increasingly forced back on their own resources, state legislatures are authorizing more complex transactions. Recent examples include tax allocation bonds, excise tax allocations, mortgage transfer tax bonds, and a host of other "non-ad valorem" financings. Here careful discussion of the operation of the tax and the allocation of the revenue stream is required to provide complete understanding. Discussion of contingencies that can affect the security on the occurrence of some future event (e.g., a decennial census) is essential.

This approach is necessary so that basic data can be interpreted in the context of the security and structure of the financing. It would be unreasonable to expect the average investor to understand the connection between the standard disclosure and the operations of the revenue program without the narrative linkage.

The evident conclusion is that as municipal debt financings become more complex, disclosure must also become more complex. Thus we have two effects operating in this area today. First, various actors are seeking to clarify and improve basic disclosure. Second, the form and structure of local government financing is becoming more complex, requiring greater explanation. These two forces will demand better data, broader data sources, and greater understanding of local government finances if private investors continue to become major participants in the tax-exempt municipal market.

APPENDIX

Tax-Supported Debt

State and local governments must accept increasing responsibility for municipal services because of changing federal policies. The importance of accurate historical and current information on the tax base, tax structure, financial management, and policies are crucial to assessing the entity's ability and willingness to meet its obligations.

General Obligation Bonds

I. Description of issuer
    A. The entity
        1. History
        2. Location and size (map where necessary)
        3. Principal officers
            a) Professional history
            b) Manner of selection; terms of officers
            c) Name, address, and telephone number for issuer's chief financial officer or contact person
        4. Default record, if any
    B. Administration and management
        1. Form of government and organization

      2. Services provided
      3. Nature, condition, and capacity of existing facilities
      4. Budgetary (operating and capital) process
      5. Labor force
         a) Breakdown by category and trend of work force
         b) Contract history, terms of agreements, and status
         c) Pension funding status
  C. Economic factors
      1. Land area and description
         a) Land use breakdown and trends
         b) Annexation trend and practices
      2. Population characteristics
         a) Current estimate and growth trend
         b) Composition by age and by income group
         c) School enrollment trend, if applicable
         d) Per capita (and median family) income levels, current estimates—trend and comparison with state
      3. Employment characteristics
         a) Labor force, employment, and unemployment—5-year trend
         b) Employment by sector—5-year trend
         c) Unemployment rates—5-year trend
         d) Largest employers—5-year trend
      4. Retail sales volume and tax collections, as applicable—5-year trend
      5. Building permit classifications and value, as applicable—5-year trend
II. Terms of debt
  A. Nature of security
      1. Debt limitation rules and calculation of remaining legal capacity
      2.. Legal features
         a) Discussion of pending proceedings that could materially affect entity's ability to perform its obligations (or could trigger an extraordinary call), e.g., legislation, litigation and/or any official act
           (1) Description of threatened proceedings
           (2) Opinion as to possible outcome and potential cost, if determinable
         b) Taxation
         c) Validation or procedure that could have been used to validate
         d) Litigation
         e) Events of default and remedies
      3. Redemption provisions for all possible circumstances
      4. State role in debt oversight, approval, and debt service (or debt service assistance) payments from state sources
  B. Debt description
      1. Issuance structure
         a) Authorization process (and margin, if voter-approved)
         b) Amount unissued
      2. Amount
         a) Description of all direct tax-supported debt, including short-term debt, leases, contractual obligations, and applicable sinking funds
         b) Detail of overlapping debt, with valuation and debt percent applicable to issuing entity
         c) Short-term borrowing history (5 years) with recent cash flow statement
      3. Debt service
         a) Principal and interest schedule for outstanding and proposed debt
         b) Annual lease and contract payments, etc.
III. Capital improvements
  A. Bond proceeds/the project
      1. Application of proceeds and total cost

    2. Construction schedule, if applicable
    3. Nature, capacity, and use of facility, if applicable
  B. Capital program
    1. Description and anticipated sources of funding
    2. Infrastructure evaluation policy
    3. Future borrowing requirements, including proposed bond elections

IV. Financial data
  A. Property tax policy, structure, and collections
    1. Assessed and full values, with discussion of reassessment policies, revaluations, or tax base changes—5 years
    2. Tax rate composition
      a) Rate limitation rules
      b) Breakdown and trend of rates—5 years
    3. Exemption and abatement policies
    4. Tax payment schedule and penalties
    5. Tax levies and collections, including penalties—5 years
    6. Estimated total property tax bill (on typical residential unit)
    7. Ten largest taxpayers and their respective valuations
  B. Reports and financial practices
    1. Listing of available financial/budgetary reports
    2. Annual audit and key comparisons with prior year
    3. Interfund transfers—identification and governing policies
    4. Basis of accounting and budgeting
    5. Fund balance composition, breakdown, and application
  C. Operations
    1. Major funds' revenues and expenditures by individual fund—5 years
    2. Major funds' breakdown of revenues and expenditures by individual funds; breakdown also by source or function
    3. Balance sheets for major funds with undesignated balances—5 years
    4. Management summary of operations, including comparison of budgeted with actual
    5. Pension fund statistics
      a) Funding plan and contribution structure
      b) Assets, liabilities, and funding ratios—5 years
      c) Amortization schedule for unfunded liabilities
      d) Summary of actuary's report on the system's soundness, including disclosure of key assumptions regarding investment rate, inflation, etc.

V. Secondary market disclosure
  A. Annual audits and routine financial and debt-related information should be made available on a timely basis
  B. Supplemental information and updates (generally contained in annual financial or audit reports)
    1. Property tax system (base, rates, and collections)
    2. Economic base (population, unemployment, building permits, etc.)
    3. Debt program (direct and overlapping debt, payout, future borrowing plans)
    4. Changes in key management personnel or investor contact
    5. Any other changed information that could have been a significant aspect of disclosure at the time of the sale, including litigation and legislation

23

Municipal Securities Disclosure: Amendments to U.S. Securities and Exchange Commission Rule 15c2-12

United States Securities and Exchange Commission
Washington, D.C.

On November 10, 1994, the SEC adopted amendments to SEC Rules 15c2-12, on municipal securities disclosure. The board is reprinting the adopting release of the SEC rule 15c2-12 amendments. The amendments to SEC rule 15c2-12 prohibit a dealer ("participating underwriter") from purchasing or selling municipal securities unless the participating underwriter has reasonably determined that an issuer of municipal securities or an obligated person has undertaken in a written agreement or contract for the benefit of holders of such securities to provide certain annual financial information and event notices to various information repositories; and prohibit a dealer from recommending the purchase or sale of a municipal security unless it has procedures in place that provide reasonable assurance that it will receive promptly any event notices with respect to that security.

Dealers should note the various effective and compliance dates of the amendments to SEC rule 15c2-12 stated in the release.

I. SUPPLEMENTARY INFORMATION: INTRODUCTION AND SUMMARY

The commission has long been concerned with disclosure in both the primary and secondary markets for municipal securities.[1] As part of the Securities Acts Amendments of 1975, Congress established a limited regulatory scheme for the municipal securities market. This limited regulatory scheme included mandatory registration of municipal securities brokers and dealers, and the creation of the Municipal Securities Rulemaking Board (MSRB). In 1989, acting in response to consistently slow dissemination of information in connection with primary offerings of municipal securities, the commission, pursuant to its authority under Exchange Act section 15(c)(2),[2] adopted rule 15c2-12[3] and an accompanying interpretation concerning the due diligence obligations of underwriters of municipal securities.[4] In 1993, the commission's Division of Market Regulation conducted a comprehensive review of many aspects of the municipal securities market, including secondary market disclosure.[5] Findings in the September 1993 *Staff Report on the Municipal Securities Market (Staff Report)* regarding the growing participation of individual investors, who may not be sophisticated in financial matters, as well as the proliferation of complex derivative municipal securities, underscored the need for improved disclosure practices in both the primary and secondary municipal securities markets.[6] Information about the issuer and other obligated persons is as critical to the secondary market,[7] where little information about municipal issuers and obligated persons is regularly disseminated, as it is in primary offerings, where, as a general matter, good disclosure practices exist. As one industry group

Adapted from *MSRB Reports, 14*(5): 25-50 (in the public domain).

testified, today "secondary market information is difficult to come by even for professional municipal analysts, to say nothing of retail investors."[8]

Notwithstanding voluntary industry initiatives to improve disclosure, particularly primary market disclosure, the *Staff Report* recommended that the commission use its interpretive authority to provide guidance regarding the disclosure obligations of municiple securities participants under the antifraud provisions of the federal securities laws, and that the commission amend rule 15c2-12 to prohibit municipal securities dealers from recommending outstanding municipal securities unless the issuer has committed to make available ongoing information regarding its financial condition. In order to assist issuers, brokers, dealers, and municipal securities dealers in meeting their obligations under the antifraud provisions, in March 1994, the commission published the *Statement of the Commission Regarding Disclosure Obligations of Municipal Securities Issuers and Others* ("interpretive release"),[9] which outlined its views with respect to the disclosure obligations of market participants under the antifraud provisions of the federal securities laws in connection with both primary and secondary market disclosure.

Concurrent with the publication of the interpretive release, the commission published Securities Exchange Act Release no. 33742 ("proposing release"),[10] which requested comment on amendments to rule 15c2-12 ("proposed amendments") designed to enhance the quality, timing, and dissemination of disclosure in the municipal securities market by placing certain requirements on brokers, dealers, and municipal securities dealers. In proposing the amendments, the commission intended to further deter fraud by preventing the underwriting and recommendation of transactions in municipal securities about which little or no current information exists. Brokers, dealers, and municipal securities dealers serve as the link between the issuers whose securities they sell and the investors to whom they recommend securities. Investors, especially individual investors, place their reliance on these securities professionals for their recommendations of municipal securities.

The amendments to rule 15c2-12 ensure that brokers, dealers, and municipal securities dealers will review the secondary market disclosure practices of issuers and other obligated persons at the time of an offering of municipal securities.[11] This scrutiny at the time of initial issuance of municipal securities will result in the dissemination of important information by issuers and other obligated persons throughout the term of the municipal securities. As a result of the amendments, brokers, dealers, and municipal securities dealers will be better able to satisfy their obligation under the federal securities laws to have a reasonable basis on which to recommend municipal securities, as well as their obligations under the rules of the MSRB.

The availability of secondary market disclosure to all municipal securities market participants will enable investors to better protect themselves from misrepresentation or other fraudulent activities by brokers, dealers, and municipal securities dealers. A lack of consistent secondary market disclosure impairs investors' ability to acquire information necessary to make intelligent, informed investment decisions, and thus, to protect themselves from fraud.

In the proposing release, comment was requested on each aspect of the proposed amendments, as well as on standards for recognition of nationally recognized municipal securities information repositories (NRMSIRs). In response to the request for comments, the commission received over 390 comment letters representing over 475 groups and individuals. The commenters represented all types of participants in the municipal securities market, including issuers, underwriters, investors, counsel, analysts, financial advisers, banks, insurance providers, disclosure services, and the MSRB.[12] The comment letters presented a variety of thoughtful views on the issues raised by the proposing release.[13] The commission has determined to adopt amendments to rule 15c2-12, with certain modifications that are designed to address concerns expressed by commenters.[14] In addition, the suggestions of a group of industry participants that cooperated to assist the commission in its efforts to improve disclosure in the municipal securities market have been valuable.[15]

Commenters across a broad range of market participants supported the goal of improved secondary market disclosure for the municipal securities market, but emphasized that flexibility is necessary, given the diversity that exists in the municipal securities market.[16] As adopted, the amendments to rule 15c2-12 will further that goal by prohibiting underwritings unless there are commitments to provide ongoing disclosure, while, at the same time, providing issuers with significant flexibility to determine the appropriate nature of that disclosure. The amendments retain the requirement that a participating underwriter ascertain that an issuer or obligated person has undertaken to provide secondary market disclosure, including notices of material events, to information repositories, but rely on the parties to the transaction to establish who will provide secondary market disclosure, and what information is material to an understanding of the security being offered.

The amendments build upon and reinforce current market practices that have provided, as a general matter, good quality disclosure in official statements, and extend those practices to the secondary market. As is currently the practice, under the amendments, the participants in an underwriting would continue to determine which persons are material to an understanding of the offering. Information concerning those persons would be included in the final official statement. Financial information and operating data that is material to an offering at the outset generally remains material throughout the life of the securities. Under the amendments, that information would be provided on an annual basis. Put simply, the amendments reflect the belief that purchasers in the secondary market need the same level of financial information and operating data in making investment decisions as purchasers in the underwritten offering.

The proposed amendments would have prohibited a broker, dealer, or municipal dealer from recommending the purchase or sale of a municipal security, unless it had reviewed the annual and event information provided pursuant to the undertaking. Commenters anticipated that such a prohibition would have a considerable negative impact on secondary market liquidity. Furthermore, brokers, dealers, and municipal securities dealers considered the proposed recommendation prohibition to be problematic from a compliance perspective. The commission has modified this provision to require instead that brokers, dealers, and municipal securities dealers recommending municipal securities in the secondary market have procedures to obtain material event notices. Because under existing law brokers, dealers, and municipal securities dealers are required to use information disseminated into the marketplace in forming a reasonable basis for recommending securities to investors, the rule does not impose mechanical review requirements on a trade-by-trade basis.

The amendments contain an exemption to minimize the effect on small issuers. Offerings in which neither the issuer nor any obligor is obligated with respect to more than $10 million in municipal securities outstanding following an offering will be exempt from the amendments, on the condition that there is a limited undertaking to provide upon request, or annually to a state information depository, at least the financial information or operating data they customarily prepare, and that is publicly available. In addition, the undertaking must meet the amendment's requirement regarding notices of material events.

II.   DESCRIPTION OF AMENDMENTS TO RULE 15c2-12

A.   Amendments with Respect to the Underwriting of Municipal Securities

Under the amendments to rule 15c2-12, a broker, dealer, or municipal securities dealer ("participating underwriter")[17] will be prohibited, subject to certain exemptions, from purchasing or selling municipal securities in connection with a primary offering of municipal securities with an aggregate principal amount of $1,000,000 or more ("offering"),[18] unless the participating underwriter has made certain determinations.[19] Specifically, the participating underwriter must reasonably determine that an issuer of municipal securities or an obligated person, either individually or in combination with other issuers of such municipal securities or other obligated persons,[20] has undertaken in a written agreement or contract for the benefit of holders of such securities, to provide, either directly or indirectly through an indenture trustee or a designated agent, certain annual financial information and event notices to various information repositories.[21]

The "reasonable determination" required by the amendments to rule 15c2-12 must be made by the participating underwriter prior to its purchasing or selling municipal securities in connection with an offering. A participating underwriter would, therefore, need to receive assurances from the issuer or obligated persons that such undertakings would be made before agreeing to act as an underwriter. A dealer could look to provisions in the underwriting agreement or bond purchase agreement that describe the undertakings for the benefit of bondholders made elsewhere, such as in a trust indenture, bond resolution, or separate written agreement.[22] In a competitively bid offering, such assurances also might be found in a notice of sale. Of course, representations concerning commitments to provide secondary market disclosure, like any other key representations by an issuer, are subject to specific verification, such that a participating underwriter has a reasonable basis to believe that such representations are true and accurate. Thus, investigation of an issuer's or obligated person's undertakings to provide secondary market disclosure would be an element of the participating underwriter's professional review of offering documents.[23]

Because the amendments prohibit participating underwriters from purchasing or selling securities in the absence of undertakings in a written agreement or contract, such agreement or contract would have to be in place at the time the issuer delivers the securities to the participating underwriter.[24] As discussed below, in conditioning the closing of an offering on the existence of an agreement or contract, this provision of the amendments permits flexibility as to where undertakings for continuing disclosure are memorialized.[25]

The amendments to the definition of final official statement will affect the obligations of participating underwriters under rule 15c2-12. Rule 15c2-12(b)(1) requires that a participating underwriter, prior to bidding for, purchasing, offering, or selling municipal securities, obtain and review a DFOS.[26] The commission expects that participating underwriters will review the DFOS with a view to ascertaining that it contains information satisfying the definition of final official statement in rule 15c2-12.[27] The commission further expects that the quality of disclosure in the DFOS will improve in a manner that is commensurate with the changes in final official statement disclosure.[28]

Rule 15c2-12(b)(2) requires, for all except competitively bid offerings, from the time a participating underwriter has reached an understanding with an issuer of municipal securities that it will act as a participating underwriter, until the final official statement is available, that the participating underwriter send, to any potential customer, no later than the next business day, a copy of the most recent POS, if any. The commission expects that the participating underwriters' obligations with respect to dissemination of the POS will not change.

1. Determining the Required Scope of the Undertaking to Provide Secondary Market Disclosure

Under the amendments as adopted, the financial information and operational data to be provided on an annual basis pursuant to the undertaking will mirror the financial information and operating data contained in the final official statement with respect to both the issuers and obligated persons that will be the subject of the ongoing disclosure, and the type of information provided. The amendments govern the core financial and operational data to be provided. It does not address the textual disclosure typically provided in annual reports, leaving the scope of that disclosure to market practice.[29] To clarify the intended quantitative focus of the rule, as adopted, the rule uses the term *"financial information and operating date"*.

a. The Starting Point—Definition of Final Official Statement

1. Information Concerning Persons Material to an Evaluation of the Offering. The proposed amendments would have revised the definition of final official statement to require that financial and operating information, including audited annual financial statements, regarding the issuer and any significant obligor be included in order to provide a fair presentation of the issuer's and significant obligor's financial condition, results of operations, and cash flow.

Commenters objected to various aspects of the proposed definition, including the general requirement that financial and operating information be presented in the final official statement.[30] Commenters also objected that the use of the term *the issuer*, in specifying whose financial information should be included in the final official statement, failed to take into account a variety of situations in which the governmental issuer does not have any repayment obligations on the municipal securities (as with conduit issuers), as well as other situations (such as revenue bonds) in which the payments will be derived from entities, enterprises, funds and accounts that do not prepare separate financial statements. Some commenters took the position that in certain instances, inclusion of the financial statements of the general municipal issuer of which the enterprise is a part may be misleading.[31]

In view of these comments, the definition of final official statement has been revised to require that financial information and operating data be provided for those persons, entities, enterprises, funds, and accounts that are material to an evaluation of the offering.[32] Thus, the definition eliminates the reference to "the" issuer. In addition, the definition no longer requires that the official statement provide information about specific "significant obligors." It leaves to the parties (including the issuer and participating underwriters) the determination of whose financial information is material to the offering (including, without limitation, the credit supporting the securities being offered).

The definition does not set its own form and content requirements on the financial information and operating data to be included; in particular, the proposed requirement for audited financial statements has not been adopted. Instead, it provides the flexibility that many commenters asserted is necessary in determining the content and scope of the disclosed financial information and operating data, given the diversity among types of issuers, types of issues, and sources of repayment.[33]

The fact that the amendments rely on the final official statement to set the standard for ongoing disclosure should not serve as an incentive for issuers to reduce existing disclosure practices in the preparation of the final official statement. Market discipline and regulatory requirements should ensure that those practices continue at current or improved levels. While issuers remain primarily responsible for the content and accuracy of their disclosures,[34] as noted, participating underwriters must review the DFOS in a manner consistent with their obligations.

As the commission recognized in the interpretive release,[35] the extensive voluntary guidelines issued by the Government Finance Officers' Association, and the industry—specific guidelines published by industry groups such as the National Federation of Municipal Analysts, are followed widely in the preparation of official statements.[36] The commission anticipates that such sound practices will continue and develop beyond that mandated by the amendments. Although those guidelines are not mandatory, the commission encourages market participants to continue to refer to those voluntary guidelines and the commission's interpretive release[37] in preparing disclosure documents. In addition, as noted in the interpretive release,[37] final official statements are subject to the prohibition against false or misleading statements of material facts, including the omission of material facts necessary to make the statements made, in light of the circumstances in which they are made, not misleading.

2. *Use of Cross-References to Publicly Available Information.* The proposing release requested comment on the appropriateness of satisfying disclosure needs through a reference to other externally prepared and located documents. In response, a number of commenters stated that the concept of incorporation of information should be explicitly included in the rule,[38] and that the ability to incorporate information should not be conditioned on a minimum dollar amount of securities in the hands of the public—commonly known as "public float."[39] Some commenters also suggested that any limitation of this practice to "seasoned issuers" should include all investment-grade issuers.[40] Some commenters further noted that the final official statement should not have to set forth information that has been filed with the commission in accordance with its periodic reporting requirements.[41] The commenters suggested one significant prerequisite for permitting cross-referencing—the availability of the information in some public repository.[42]

The definition of final official statement has been revised to make explicit[43] that a final official statement may include financial information and operating data either by setting forth the information in the document or set of documents composing the final official statement, or by including a specific reference to documents already prepared and previously made publicly available.[44] For purposes of the amendments, documents will be considered to be publicly available if they have been submitted to each NRMSIR and to the appropriate state information depository or, if the information concerns a reporting company, filed with the commission. If the document is a final official statement, it must be available from the MSRB.

If cross-referencing is used, for purposes of determining the appropriate scope of the ongoing information undertaking, the final official statement will be deemed to include all information and documents that have been cross-referenced.[45] The amendment does not place limitations on the type of issuer that may use cross-referencing. This approach is consistent with the goal of making the repositories the principal source of information concerning municipal securities. Once received by a repository, the referenced information should be readily available regardless of the nature of the issuer.

As commenters noted, permitting cross-referencing to other externally prepared and available information should result in official statements that are clear and concise, yet provide information material to the offering.[46] Moreover, the use of cross-referencing also should ease some expressed apprehension about the ability of some issuers to obtain information about parties not within their control, to the extent that information about these parties is made available to the repositories or, if a reporting company, filed with the commission.[47]

3. *Description of Information Undertakings.* The definition of final official statement also has been changed from the proposed amendments to include a requirement that the undertakings provided pursuant to the rule be described in the final official statement.[48] As the commission recognized in the interpretive release[49] and a number of commenters echoed,[50] it is important for investors and the market to know the scope of any ongoing disclosure. By including a description of the undertaking in the final official statement, market participants will know the identity of the entities about which information will be provided, and the type of information to be provided. By reviewing the final official statement, investors in the secondary market will be able to ascertain the scope of that undertaking and whether it has been satisfied.

Critical to any evaluation of a covenant is the likelihood that the issuer or obligated person will abide by the undertaking. The definition of final official statement thus has been modified to require disclosure of all instances in the previous 5 years in which any person providing an undertaking failed to comply in all material respects with any previous informational undertakings called for by the amendments.[51] This information is important to the market, and should, therefore, be disclosed in the final official statement. The requirement should provide an additional incentive for issuers and obligated persons to comply with their undertakings to provide secondary market disclosure, and will ensure that participating underwriters and others are able to assess the reliability of disclosure representations.[52]

The amendments do not prohibit participating underwriters from underwriting an offering of municipal securities if an issuer or obligated person has failed to comply with previous undertakings to provide secondary market disclosure. However, if a failure to comply with such previous undertakings has not been remedied as of the start of the offering, or if the party has a history of persistent and material breaches, it is doubtful whether a participating underwriter could form a reasonable basis for relying on the accuracy of the issuer's or obligated person's ongoing disclosure representations.

b.   Entities About Which Information Must Be Provided to the Secondary Market.   It is critical that current financial information and operating data is provided to the secondary market about the persons that would be important to investors in evaluating the security. The proposed amendments would have required the participating underwriter to determine that the issuer had committed to provide, at least annually, current financial information concerning the issuer of the municipal securities and any significant obligor.[53] The identity of persons about which information should be provided to the secondary market was the subject of a substantial number of comment letters.[54] As with the proposed definition of final official statement, a large number of commenters expressed particular concern about the provision of information on a continuing basis for conduit issuers who have no ongoing liability for repayment of municipal securities.[55] There also were a significant number of comments received critiquing the concept of significant obligor.[56]

Under the amendments as revised, the identity of the persons for which information must be provided on an annual basis is determined by the information included in the final official statement. If the final official statement includes financial information or operating data on a person, information about that person must continue to be provided to the secondary market if the person is committed by contract or other arrangement to support payment of the obligations on the municipal securities.[57] Thus, the obligation to provide ongoing information relates to those persons for which financial information or operating data is included in the final official statement *and* that have a contractual or other connection to repayment of the municipal obligations.

1.   The Obligated Person Concept.   The proposed amendments defined a significant obligor as "any person who, directly or indirectly, is the source of 20 percent or more of the cash flow servicing the obligations on the municipal security." The proposed definition generated a significant amount of comment, including concerns that it could be interpreted to include significant taxpayers and customers,[58] credit enhancers (including banks that are letter of credit providers and insurers providing bond insurance),[59] providers of guaranteed investment contracts,[60] as well as state and federal governments that provide revenue sharing, grant, state and local aid, and other cofinancing arrangements.[61] Commenters raised technical concerns as to the appropriate percentage of repayment obligation necessary to trigger inclusion in the definition of significant obligor,[62] and when the percentages were to be measured.[63] Some commenters also expressed concern that, in the bond pool context, the definition of significant obligor may not have permitted sufficient flexibility in determining which obligors in a pool would be the subject of the requirement to provide information on an ongoing basis.[64]

Commenters suggested a number of modifications to the significant obligor concept. First, a number of commenters indicated that the definition of significant obligor should include a requirement that a contractual relationship exist between the obligor and the repayment of the obligation before a continuing information obligation is imposed.[65] Second, commenters recommended modifying the definition to include different percentages of cash flow, ranging from a low of no threshold to a high of 50% of cash flow.[66] Third, some commenters suggested replacing the entire definition of significant obligor with the concept of materiality, in which the issuer and the other offering participants would determine, on a continuing basis, whose information would be provided.[67]

As suggested by a number of commenters, the amendments eliminate the reference to significant obligor.[68] Instead, the amendments include a definition of "obligated person," which means a person (including an issuer of separate securities) that is committed by contract or other arrangement structured to support payment of all or part of the obligations on the municipal securities.[69] By including a nexus to the financing through a commitment that is structured to support the payment obligations, the amendments address concerns raised by many commenters that the term *source of cash flow* in the definition of significant obligor was overbroad and could encompass persons with no relationship to the financing.[70] The requirement for a contractual or other arrangement will assist participating underwriters in identifying the persons for which information should be provided pursuant to an undertaking.

Some commenters recommended that the commitment with respect to payment of the obligation on the securities consist of a contractual obligation to and enforceable by bondholders.[71] Instead, the definition includes a broader notion of a contract or arrangement that is structured to "support payment," without specifying that it run to bondholders. The definition is intended to include contracts or arrangements where payments are made either to bondholders, to issuers to be used to pay obligations on municipal securities, or through conduit structures.[72] Similarly, the reference to "obligations on municipal securities is intended to be broad enough to cover debt obligations, lease payments, and any other repayment obligation on or resulting from the municipal securities.

As was the case with the proposed significant obligor concept, the term *obligated persons* includes, but is broader than, the concept of issuers of separate securities under rule 131 pursuant to the Securities Act of 1933 (Securities Act)[73] and Exchange Act rule 3b-5.[74] Also, in response to comments raised that the terms *issuer* or *significant obligor* do not sufficiently address financings in which the source of repayment is not a separate person or entity, but a dedicated revenue stream from a specified project, segregated tax revenues or other enterprise, fund or account,[75] the definition includes persons which are obligated generally, such as with full recourse to the person, or, in a more limited manner, such as through an enterprise, fund or account of such person, including a dedicated revenue stream. As noted above, the obligation to provide information must cover all such enterprises, funds or accounts, whether or not there is a separate entity. In such a case, the information undertaking could be provided by the governmental unit or financing authority of which the enterprise, fund, or account is a part.[76] For example, a participating underwriter could accept an information undertaking from a state issuing bonds secured solely by funds collected under a special tax, to report financial information relating to the special tax; for issues supported both by contracts of assistance of separate authorities or funds in addition to the issuer's own revenues, undertakings from the separate authorities, as well as the issuer could be provided. Accordingly, although the definition of significant obligor has been eliminated, that modification does not reflect a change in the commission's assessment of the importance of ongoing information concerning the ultimate sources of payment on the securities.

Unlike the significant obligor concept in the proposed amendments, there is no need to include a specified percentage of payment in the definition of obligated person, because the issuer and other participants will determine at the time of preparation of the final official statement which obligated persons are material to an offering.[77] In making that materiality determination, the parties to a financing will evaluate the facts of the offering.[78]

Determining the obligated persons in pooled financings requires more flexibility, because the composition of the pool may vary over time. Rather than identifying the specific persons for which information will be provided on a continuing basis, under the amendments, bond pools must describe in their official statements, and the undertaking, the objective criteria (presumably including percentage of payment support) they will apply consistently, both in the final official statement and on a continuing basis, in determining whether information concerning an obligated person will be provided.[79] The amendments permit, but do not require this approach for nonpooled issuers. The objective criteria approach ensures that financial information and operating data will be provided about those persons that, at the time of disclosure, meet the objective standards described in the undertakings. Obligated persons could commit to the issuer, at the time of initial participation in a pooled financing, through an undertaking to provide information when and if they satisfy that criteria. Obligated persons that no longer meet the objective criteria will no longer need to provide ongoing information. In order to ensure that the selection method is incorporated into the undertaking, the amendments require that participating underwriters reasonably determine that the undertakings identify those persons for which the information will be provided, either by name or by the objective criteria to be used to select such persons.[80]

Commenters were divided on whether providers of bond insurance, letters of credit, and other liquidity facilities, should be excluded from the definition of significant obligor.[81] The concept of "obligated person" encompasses these entities because they are committed, at least conditionally, to support payment of principal and interest obligations. Moreover, these persons normally are material to an understanding of the security, and, therefore, official statements should contain financial information concerning such persons either directly or by reference to publicly available materials. A number of commenters stated, however, that it would be inappropriate to put the onus on the issuer to provide information on such providers on an annual basis, particularly where that information is otherwise available to investors either upon request or in public reports that have been submitted to appropriate regulatory authorities.[82]

Commenters indicated a willingness by providers of bond insurance, letters of credit, and other liquidity facilities to deposit publicly available reports in a repository, or otherwise note where such reports may be easily obtained.[83] The issuer or other obligated person providing the undertaking may then refer to such reports in their annual financial information and indicate the location where any such current annual reports can be obtained. Based upon such representations, providers of bond insurance, letters of credit, and liquidity facilities have been excepted from the definition of obligated person to eliminate the need to separately obtain and disseminate annual information about such providers.

The commission encourages industry participants to work together to adopt appropriate disclosure practices, both with respect to information concerning the provider contained in primary offering materials and on an ongoing basis in the annual financial information. The commission will monitor developments in this area regarding the nature and quality of information made available about credit enhancers and liquidity providers, and the manner in which information is made available to determine whether further steps are necessary to assure access to this important body of information.

2. *Who Must Undertake.* A related question to whose information must be given is who must provide the information undertaking; the person providing the undertaking may not necessarily be the person about which the information relates. The proposed amendments would have required that the continuing information undertaking be provided by the issuer. A significant number of commenters raised concerns about which of potentially several persons that could be considered an issuer of municipal securities[84] would be expected to provide the undertaking and who would make that determination.[85] This was a particular concern in light of the potential liability of the issuer providing the undertaking for the provision and the content of information regarding other issuers and significant obligors—persons not necessarily under their control. Commenters made a number of suggestions to address these perceived ambiguities, including requiring that each issuer of a municipal security and each significant obligor undertake to provide the information only with respect to itself.[86]

In response to these concerns, and consistent with the general approach to affording underwriting participants significant flexibility, the undertaking provision has been revised to provide that the undertaking may be made by any issuer of the municipal securities being offered, or by any obligated person for which information is provided in the final official statement. An issuer of a municipal security may provide the undertaking, regardless of whether it is obligated on the municipal security. In addition, obligated persons may provide the undertaking regardless of whether they are deemed an issuer of municipal securities. These obligated persons may be the main, if not the only, credit source for repayment of the obligations on the municipal securities. This approach should allow the governmental issuer to shift to the obligated person the responsibility to provide information on a continuing basis.

Thus, a participating underwriter need only reasonably determine that an issuer of municipal securities or an obligated person for which financial information or operating data is presented in the final official statement has agreed to provide the information called for by the rule; it will not be necessary to obtain an undertaking from all possible issuers and obligated persons. Moreover, to respond to the expressed concern that separate undertakings should be permitted, the amendments have been revised to recognize that undertakings may be provided in combination with other issuers and other obligated persons. In all cases, however, the undertakings, either individually or collectively, must constitute a commitment to provide information with respect to all the persons about which information must be provided on an annual basis.

The amendments have been revised to clarify that dissemination responsibilities may be delegated to designated agents or to indenture trustees. As commenters pointed out, there are circumstances in which third parties may be effective in assisting issuers and obligated persons in disseminating the information.[87] Moreover, indenture trustees have expressed concerns about being considered "designated agents" in performing any dissemination role, based on the scope of, and standards affecting, their responsibilities as indenture trustees.[88] The language has been revised in response to clarify that, in addition to designated agents, issuers or obligated persons may contractually empower indenture trustees to disseminate information that an issuer or obligated person has agreed to provide. The parties may authorize an indenture trustee to provide certain information through specific instruction or on its own initiative upon becoming aware of particular facts.

c. Scope of Financial Information and Operating Data to be Provided on an Annual Basis

1. Definition of Annual Financial Information. The amendments provide a definition of the term *annual financial information,*[89] a concept that was used, without definition, in the proposed amendments. The definition of annual financial information specifies both the timing of the information—that is, once a year—and, by referring to the final official statement, the type of financial information and operating data that is to be provided to the repositories. If financial information or operating data concerning an obligated person (or category of obligated persons in the case of financings using the objective criteria approach) is included in the final official statement, then annual financial information would consist of the same type of financial information or operating data. For example, if anticipated cash flow information is provided in the final official statement for a revenue bond financing, cash flow data reflecting actual operations must continue to be provided on an annual basis. Only the annual financial information called for by the undertakings need be sent to the repositories; other types of financial information and reports that may be prepared by the issuer or obligated persons are not subject to the rule's dissemination provisions.

Many commenters addressed the issue of whether the rule should specify form and content of the information that should be provided on an annual basis, as well as for event-specific information.[90] Some commenters argued that the rule should include specified formats for information to be provided, including financial statements and certain industry reporting formats,[91] while other commenters contended that no form or content should be specified and that the parties should be permitted to make determinations based on materiality alone.[92] As discussed below, the flexibility afforded by the concept of annual financial information addresses these concerns by providing a minimum standard for ongoing disclosure, but allowing the parties to define that standard with respect to each offering of municipal securities.

2. Financial Information. The proposal to mandate audited financial statements produced considerable comment. As with the proposed definition of final official statement, commenters expressed concern with the availability of audited financial statements on an annual basis, as well as the relevance of financial statements for certain types of financings.

Some commenters indicated that some municipalities were not required by law to have independently audited financial statements, and any such requirement would impose a significant new expense.[93] A number of commenters also expressed doubt as to whether audited financial information could be delivered on an annual basis, because audits may not be completed for a number of years following the close of the fiscal year.[94] Commenters noted that in some cases, financial statements for certain types of entities were audited every year, and in other cases every 2 to 3 years.[95] Therefore, some of these commenters argued that the requirement for annual audited financial statements would have an adverse impact on an issuer's ability to access the public securities markets or increase its costs of financing.[96]

A number of commenters also raised concerns regarding the availability of full financial statements for certain issuers, whether or not audited.[97] As examples, commenters noted that some issuing entities do not have their own financial statements and may be included in the financial statements of a larger issuer or entity.[98] Commenters from two states indicated that governmental units of the states may be encompassed in the state's comprehensive annual financial report and that there may be only supplemental schedules that described the governmental units.[99]

Some commenters raised the point that financial statements of a general governmental unit may not necessarily be relevant in certain project and structured financings.[100] As an example, one commenter noted that in some asset-backed financings, information about the governmental issuer may be relevant only with respect to its experience in managing programs of loan pools.[101]

Commenters proposed a number of alternatives to the requirement to provide annual audited financial statements. Among the alternatives was a suggestion that financial statements be required in the form customarily prepared by the issuer promptly upon becoming available and that audited financial statements be provided to the extent available.[102] Other suggestions included limiting the requirement to those entities required by state or federal law to have audited financial statements.[103]

In view of the comments received, the amendments do not adopt the proposal to mandate audited financial statements on an annual basis with respect to each issuer and significant obligor. Instead, the amendments continue to require annual financial information, which may be unaudited, and may, where appropriate and consistent with the presentation in the final official statement, be other than full financial statements. While it is anticipated that full financial statements will be provided for entities with ongoing revenues and operating expenses, it is possible that in the case of dedicated revenue streams and certain types of structured financings, other types of special purpose financial statements, project operating statements, or reports may be used to reflect the financial position of the credit source for the financing. However, if audited financial statements are prepared, then when and if available, such audited financial statements will be subject to the undertaking and must be submitted to the repositories.[104] Thus, as suggested by a number of commenters, the undertaking must include audited financial statements only in those cases where they otherwise are prepared.

The amendments adopt the proposed requirement that the undertaking specify the accounting principles pursuant to which the financial information provided as part of the annual financial information will be prepared.[105] As discussed in the proposing release, it is important that financial information be prepared on a consistent basis to enable market participants to evaluate results and perform year-to-year comparisons.[106] The undertaking also must specify whether audited financial statements will be provided as part of the annual financial information.[107]

The amendments do not establish a standardized format for presentation of financial information, or any specification of the content of the information, other than by reference to the final official statement. The annual financial information may be presented through any disclosure document or set of documents, whatever their form or principal purpose, that include the necessary information. The amendments, as adopted, contemplate that sequential final official statements prepared by frequent issuers may meet the standards of the rule. As in the case of final official statements, annual financial information submitted to a repository also may reference other information already submitted to repositories or the MSRB, or filed with the commission.[108]

3.   *Operating Data.*   The proposed amendments[109] would have required that the undertaking call for pertinent operating information, and that the parties specify the pertinent operating information to be provided on an annual basis. The basic concern of commenters regarding this provision, in addition to issues of specification of form and content discussed above, was that the use of the term *pertinent* did not provide sufficient guidance as to who would determine what was pertinent and what independent obligations participating underwriters would have with respect to such evaluation.[110]

The amendments have been modified to respond to these comments. The phrase pertinent has been deleted from the reference to operating information and the word *data* is used to emphasize the intended quantitative nature of the information. Operating data is included as a subset of annual financial information, and the operating data to be provided annually also is determined by reference to the type of operating data presented in the final official statement. Thus, the parties will determine at the outset, presumably with the assistance of applicable industry guidelines, what operating data will be provided both initially and on an ongoing basis. For example, in a conduit health care financing, under current industry practice, an official statement typically provides information relating to the obligated party—the hospital—in an appendix. In addition to a discussion describing the hospital, its administration and management, economic base and service area, and capital plan, operating statistics such as bed utilization, admissions and type, patient days, and payor utilization often is provided. Under the amendments, in this type of transaction, parties at the outset of a transaction will determine which operating data will be included in the hospital appendix; such information, in turn, will be the type of "operating data" to be provided annually.

Some commenters expressed concern that the proposed amendments were not sufficiently flexible to permit parties to address changing conditions because the undertaking would have to describe the financial and pertinent operating information to be provided in the future.[111] Nonetheless, the requirement that the undertaking specify in reasonable detail the type of data that will be provided on an ongoing basis, including the identity of the persons (or category of persons) about which the information will relate has been retained. As is the case with financial information, the intent of the amendments is to give investors and market participants the ability to evaluate the security through comparisons of the quantitative operating data provided. Contrary to the suggestion of some commenters, the undertaking would be meaningless if issuers and obligated persons could unilaterally determine that certain types of information were no longer necessary or meaningful to investors.

Because the amendments require that the undertaking specify only the general type of information to be supplied, there should be sufficient flexibility to accommodate subsequent developments that may require adjustments in the financial information and operating data that should be provided annually. Of course, nothing in the undertaking will prevent a party from providing additional information, particularly where such disclosure may be necessary to avoid liability under the antifraud provisions of the federal securities laws. Similarly, the amendments make specific provision for adjusting the persons about which information is provided. As required in the case of pooled financings, parties may identify the persons covered by reference to objective selection criteria that will be applied on a consistent basis between the offering statements and with regard to annual financial information. Moreover, the party providing the undertaking need not continue to provide information concerning persons that are no longer obligated persons with respect to the municipal securities.

A new provision has been added to the amendments which permits the written agreement or contract to have a termination provision with respect to any obligated person that is no longer directly or indirectly liable for repayment of any of the obligations on the municipal securities.[112] Once an obligated person no longer has any liability for repayment of the municipal securities, whether through termination or expiration of its commitment to support payment, or as a result of a defeasance of the municipal securities with no remaining liability, then the obligation to provide annual financial information and notices of events may terminate.

2. Notice of Material Events

Commenters generally agreed that issuers and obligors should be subject to an undertaking to provide event information to the market.[113] Brokers, dealers, and municipal securities dealers supported these provisions of the proposed amendments, because the use of a list provides guidance as to what events should be covered.[114] Other commenters, however, felt that the list should be deleted from the rule and that the concept of materiality should be relied upon to determine what events should be the subject of notices.[115] Some commenters believed that the list of eleven events should be expanded to include a provision that would cover any other event that might reasonably be expected to have a material adverse effect on the holders of the bonds.[116]

The list of eleven events has been retained in the amendments.[117] As indicated in the proposing release, the list of eleven events was proposed in response to requests for guidance to issuers and other participants in the municipal securities markets as to those events that normally would reflect on the credit supporting the municipal securities, as well as on the terms of the securities that they issue, and thus normally would be considered material. Under the amendments, only the occurrence of one of the specified events will, if material, create an obligation to send a notice to the repository.

The determination of whether other events also should be the subject of notification pursuant to the information undertaking is left to the parties. For example, some commenters requested that the list of events be expanded to address circumstances when the notified events have been cured or rectified, as well as other favorable developments.[118] The parties would be free to add such matters to the undertaking. Issuers also may wish to send information regarding material developments to the repositories, to ensure equal access to that information by all investors and participants in the market, regardless of whether the particular development is subject to the undertaking.[119]

Some commenters were concerned that permitting issuers and obligors to send any notices or information they wished would flood the repositories. Given the fact that event notices generally are short, it appears that the repositories would be able to handle the flow of notices. The commission will, however, monitor developments in this area.

Some commenters expressed concern that the event described as "matters affecting collateral" was too broad.[120] In response to such observations, that reference has been revised to reflect more clearly the types of events relating to collateral that could affect the creditworthiness of the security being offered. For instance, the item was not intended to require disclosure in the event of a drop in revenues or receipts securing payment. Rather, as more clearly indicated in the revised amendments, it is intended to encompass the release, substitution, or sale of property securing repayment of the securities being offered.[121]

Commenters also questioned whether the event relating to adverse tax opinions or events affecting the tax-exempt status of the security would include events not specific to an issuer, such as tax law changes which may affect a multitude of issuances and which are broadly reported.[122] They argued that there is no need for each issuer to make that disclosure, which may overwhelm the repositories. The amendments do not include a uniform requirement for notification of events having widespread impact that are widely reported. Frequently, individual issuer disclosure may not affect the total "mix" of information available to investors, for example where Congress amends tax rates or alternative minimum tax rules that could affect an investor's yield. On the other hand, it may not be clear, absent individual disclosure, which classes of outstanding securities are affected by the general events, for example, where the tax law change affects a particular type of municipal security or financing structure.

It is possible that an "event" affecting the tax-exempt status of the security may include the commencement of litigation and other legal proceedings, including an audit by the Internal Revenue Service, when an issuer determines, based on the status of the proceedings and their likely impact on holders of the municipal securities, among other things, that such events may be material to investors.

Commenters expressed concern that the party providing the undertaking may not have knowledge of the occurrence of events affecting other parties that might be called for by the provisions of the rule.[123] This concern should be addressed by the revised approach of enabling the parties to the transaction to determine who will provide the undertakings. For example, in the conduit context, the covenant could be provided by the person that is committed by contract or other arrangement to support payment of debt service, rather than the conduit issuer.

The timing for providing the notification has not been changed from the proposed amendments, which required that the notice be provided on a "timely" basis. The amendments do not establish a specific time frame as timely, because of the wide variety of events and issuer circumstances. In general, this determination must take into consideration the time needed to discover the occurrence of the event, assess its materiality, and prepare and disseminate the notice.

A new paragraph has been added to the amendments[124] that would require a participating underwriter to reasonably determine that the undertaking includes an agreement to notify the appropriate repository if the annual financial information is not provided in the stated time frame. Given the expressed concerns of some commenters regarding the difficulty that they would face in determining whether an issuer or other person was in compliance with any of its undertakings,[125] this provision will help inform market participants if annual financial information for such persons has not been made available in the agreed-upon time frame.

3. Location of Undertaking in a Written Agreement or Contract

The proposed amendments called for the undertaking to be contained in a written agreement or contract for the benefit of holders of municipal securities. Commenters provided a variety of views as to where the undertakings should be memorialized, who should be parties to such undertakings, and the need for flexibility to modify undertakings in the future. Commenters suggested, for instance, that the undertakings could be included in the trust indenture, bond resolution, ordinance, or other legislation, a separate written agreement, or the underwriting agreement or bond purchase agreement.

As discussed in the proposing release, many offerings of municipal securities are issued pursuant to a trust indenture setting out the covenants of the issuer for the benefit of the holders of the municipal securities. If there is no trust indenture as part of an offering, as is the case with general obligation and certain other types of bonds, there may be a bond resolution, ordinance, or other legislation. Most commenters addressing this issue considered the trust indenture, bond resolution, ordinance, or other legislation to be appropriate for undertakings to provide secondary market disclosure, because they would create a direct obligation by issuers to bondholders.[126] Commenters also suggested the use of a separate written agreement between the issuer and the trustee as an appropriate method of memorializing undertakings.[127]

Several commenters suggested that the inclusion of the undertakings in an underwriting agreement or bond purchase agreement would be sufficient for purposes of rule 15c2-12,[128] although another commenter suggested that a promise running to the benefit of the underwriter, whether in a bond purchase agreement or in a separate agreement, would be enforceable by existing and future bondholders only on the basis of a third party beneficiary theory, the availability of which may vary from state to state.[129]

Because commenters were supportive of leaving the determination of the location of the undertaking to the parties, the relevant language of the proposed amendments, requiring a participating underwriter to look to "undertakings in a written agreement or contract for the benefit of holders of such securities" has been adopted as proposed. Therefore, undertakings may be included in a trust indenture, bond resolution or other legislation, or a separate written agreement. Undertakings also may be included in the bond form itself. This general requirement will create a direct obligation to bondholders, yet will be flexible to address variations in state law, as well as the wide variety of types and structures of offerings in the municipal securities market.

The commission also recognizes that an issuer's ability to contract may be limited under state law. To the extent that issuers are restricted by statute from entering into long-term contractual arrangements, the undertaking may include a qualifier to its obligation, such as that it is subject to appropriation.[130]

Commenters generally took the view that, while a statement in the final official statement describing any undertakings to provide secondary market disclosure would be an important addition to undertakings in a written agreement or contract, in order to make clear that the undertaking is an obligation of the issuer or obligated person that is enforceable on behalf of bondholders, the undertaking should be in writing signed by the issuer or obligated person.[131] Statements regarding an issuer's or obligated person's provision of secondary market disclosure made exclusively in an official statement would not satisfy the terms of rule 15c2-12(b)(5) because they would not create a contract enforceable on behalf of bondholders.

Commenters addressing the inclusion of undertakings in various documents were concerned that the failure to provide continuing disclosure pursuant to the undertakings could be deemed a potential event of default on the securities.[132] Although a failure to comply with the undertaking would be a breach of contract, the rule does not specify the consequences of an issuer's breach of its undertakings to provide secondary market disclosure. As called for by the joint response, as well as other commenters, remedies for breach of any undertaking under applicable state law are a subject for negotiation between the parties to the offering. To avoid uncertainties of enforcement, the parties to a transaction are encouraged to enumerate the consequences in the undertaking, including the available remedies, for breach of the information undertaking.

B. Recommendation of Transactions in Municipal Securities

The proposed amendments would have prohibited any broker, dealer, or municipal securities dealer from recommending the purchase or sale of a municipal security unless it had specifically reviewed the information the issuer of such municipal security had undertaken to provide.[133] The purpose of this provision of the proposed amendments was to assist dealers in satisfying their obligation to have a reasonable basis to recommend municipal securities by requiring them to consider the most current information before making a recommendation.

In view of the importance of secondary market liquidity in municipal issues, the commission requested comment on whether the proposed amendments would have a substantial or long-lasting effect on market liquidity. This request for comment was based on concerns raised about whether municipal securities dealers would be willing to effect secondary market transactions in a broad range of municipal securities if review was required on a recommendation by recommendation basis.

Many commenters strongly criticized this provision of the proposed amendments. The majority of commenters responded that requiring the review of information prior to making a recommendation on the purchase or sale of a municipal security would create substantial compliance burdens for dealers.[134] Commenters also noted that the specific requirement to review information either would impel dealers to hire larger research and analysis staffs,[135] or, more likely, would cause dealers to restrict the issuers whose municipal securities they would trade to a smaller number of large and frequent issuers.[136] Commenters predicted that, as a result, liquidity for all but the largest and most frequent issuers would be reduced.[137]

Commenters proposed alternatives to the recommendation prohibition, including basing the type of review of a municipal security, and disclosure about such review, on whether the investor was an institutional or retail investor,[138] or on the type of municipal security recommended.[139] Other commenters suggested the continued reliance on the reasonable basis standard inherent in the MSRB's suitability rule, G-19, and the antifraud provisions, as discussed by the commission in the 1988 and 1989 releases proposing and adopting rule 15c2-12, as well as the interpretive release.[140]

As adopted, this provision has been modified in a number of respects to respond to concerns expressed by commenters. In particular, the amendments replace the proposed review standard with a requirement that dealers have procedures in place that provide reasonable assurance that they will receive promptly any notices of material events regarding the securities that they recommend. The events are any of the eleven events disclosed as described in rule 15c2-12(b)(5)(i)(C), or the notice of failure to provide annual financial information in accordance with an undertaking as described in rule 15c2-12(b)(5)(i)(D) with respect to that security. Many dealers currently subscribe to electronic reporting systems that give notice of significant events made public by municipal issuers. To comply with the rule's requirement, these dealers should make certain that these systems receive, directly or indirectly, material event notices for issues the dealer recommends. In addition, dealers should develop procedures to ensure that notices of such events will be available to the staff responsible for making recommendations.

In the commission's view, the recommendation provision, as modified, should substantially reduce the concerns of commenters with respect to compliance burdens and effects on liquidity. It also will help ensure that dealers will consider the material event notices that issuers produce, thus enabling them to have an adequate basis on which to recommend[141] municipal securities.

Moreover, even though the amendments do not require that dealers directly review an issuer's ongoing disclosure before making each recommendation, the commission agrees with those commenters that said that additional information made available by issuers will be taken into account by dealers making recommendations regarding that security, under the MSRB's fair dealing and suitability rules, and the antifraud provisions.[142] In addition to the commission's past interpretations of the responsibilities of dealers to have a reasonable basis for their recommendations, the MSRB repeatedly has emphasized that secondary market disclosure information publicized by issuers must be taken into account by dealers to meet the investor protection standards imposed by its investor protection rules. Specifically, MSRB rule G-17 requires dealers to disclose material facts of a transaction to the customer, MSRB rule G-19 requires dealers to ensure that any transaction recommended to the customer is suitable for that customer, and MSRB rule G-30 requires dealers to ensure that the prices set for customer transactions are fair and reasonable. In its comment letter, the MSRB noted that "[I]f a dealer is not aware of major financial and other material developments affecting an issuer's securities, it is difficult or impossible for the dealer to comply with these requirements."[143]

For example, if a dealer reviews an electronic reporting system for material events relating to a security, and finds that an issuer has submitted a notice that it has failed to provide annual financial information on or before the date specified in the written agreement or contract,[144] that fact would be a significant factor to be taken into account when the dealer formulates the basis for a recommendation of such securities. While the dealer would not be prohibited per se from recommending such municipal securities, notice that the issuer has failed to provide annual financial information would be the type of material information required to be disclosed to the customer pursuant to MSRB rule G-17.[145] Such a notice also would trigger a further inquiry by the dealer to assure itself that it is cognizant of the condition of the issuer or obligated persons, despite the absence of promised information. This also would be true if a dealer attempts to obtain an issuer's annual financial information, finds that it has not been submitted to any repository, and the dealer had no record of the issuer submitting a notice to this effect. In such cases, further research may be necessary or advisable prior to making a recommendation in the issuer's securities.

C. Information Repositories

1. Background

Under rule 15c2-12, as adopted in 1989, NRMSIRs essentially serve the function of disseminators of official statements on behalf of participating underwriters.[146] The option of participating underwriters to transfer their final official statement delivery obligations to NRMSIRs has encouraged the development of NRMSIRs.[147] The three existing NRMSIRs are private vendors that gather and disseminate final official statements pursuant to rule 15c2-12. In addition, although not required under existing provisions of the rule, they provide other current information about municipal issuers to the primary and secondary municipal securities markets.[148]

As a result of the amendments, NRMSIRs will play an expanded role in the collection and dissemination of secondary market information. In addition to the collection and dissemination of final official statements, they will collect and disseminate annual financial information, as well as notices of material events. The commission is sensitive to the need of NRMSIRs for flexibility, especially with respect to the timing requirements for the dissemination of notices of material events. The commission will monitor developments in the municipal securities market as participants adapt to the changes in rule 15c2-12, and fully expects that the current and potential NRMSIRs are capable of adjusting to their expanded role. The commission is of the view that NRMSIRs, as private information vendors, will have sufficient economic incentives to serve their expanded functions resulting from the amendments to rule 15c2-12, even in the absence of the more specific review requirement of the recommendation prohibition of the proposed amendments.[149]

2. Definition of Nationally Recognized Municipal Securities Information Repository

The commission requested comment on whether the term *NRMSIR* should be defined in rule 15c2-12, and whether specific standards should be established for NRMSIRs. If standards were to be established in the rule, the commission requested comment on whether proposed standards set forth in the release were adequate.[150] The majority of state-based information gatherers and disseminators, and other NRMSIRs that addressed the issue of defining the term NRMSIR supported maintaining the guidelines already established by the commission in the 1989 release.[151] After reviewing the comment letters, the commission has determined that the guidance established in the 1989 release for NRMSIRs should be modified only as necessary to reflect the amendments to rule 15c2-12. In determining whether a particular entity is an NRMSIR the commission will now consider, among other things, whether the repository

1　Is national in scope
2　Maintains[152] current, accurate[153] information about municipal offerings in the form of official statements, and annual financial information, notices of material events, and notices of a failure to provide annual financial information undertaken to be provided in accordance with rule 15c2-12
3　Has effective retrieval and dissemination systems
4　Places no limits on the persons from which it will accept official statements, and annual financial information, notices of material events, and notices of a failure to provide annual financial information undertaken to be provided in accordance with rule 15c2-12
5　Provides access to the documents deposited with it to anyone willing and able to pay the applicable fees
6　Charges reasonable fees

While NRMSIRs may charge reasonable fees[154] for the dissemination of information, they may not charge issuers for accepting information provided by issuers in accordance with rule 15c2-12.[155] In response to concerns raised by commenters, the commission also notes that giving preferential treatment to certain brokers, dealers, and municipal securities dealers by giving them market information before it is made available to all customers would be wholly inconsistent with recognition as a NRMSIR.[156]

Comment also was requested on the ability and willingness of both potential NRMSIRs, and those presently operating under no-action letters, to meet the dissemination standards discussed in the proposing release. NRMSIRs responded that they can meet these standards.[157] In order to implement these standards, the commission has determined that existing NRMSIRs should reapply for recognition from the commission under the revised criteria to continue to function as NRMSIRs.

3.　State Information Depositories

The commission also requested comment on whether a state-based depository could serve as an effective means to disseminate information to the market for a nationally traded security, thus enabling the appropriate parties to fulfill their disclosure obligations using a state-based depository. Commenters expressed divergent views on this issue.[158] No state responded directly in response to the commission's request for comment on whether states are willing to make the necessary financial commitment to create a state-based system. The comptroller of the state of New York pointed out, however, that his office already collects financial data from local governments, and that there "is an appropriate and important function which the states may perform in the secondary market disclosure process."[159] A number of third party state-based information collectors also stated that they were in the process of creating state-based repositories.[160] Other such third party state-based information collectors pointed out that they already had working depositories in place.[161]

Based on these comments, and in light of existing disclosure mechanisms and recent legislation in several states designed to enhance secondary market disclosure,[162] it appears that states can play a beneficial role in enhancing disclosure in the municipal securities market.[163] State-based depositories will be in a special relationship with filers of disclosure information to provide for convenient and efficient dissemination. The commission therefore encourages states to develop state-based depositories.

To encourage the development of state-based depositories, the commission has amended rule 15c2-12 to require that participating underwriters reasonably determine that the information undertaken to be provided, in addition to being submitted to the NRMSIRs, or, in some cases, to the MSRB, will be submitted to a state information depository (SID), if an appropriate SID has been established in that state. Further, as discussed below,[164] an exemption conditioned on making annual financial information available upon request or to a SID, and providing notices of material events to each NRMSIR or the MSRB, and to a SID, has been adopted. An appropriate SID would be a depository operated or designated[165] by the state that receives information from all issuers within the state, and makes this information available promptly to the public on a contemporaneous basis.[166] The commission staff is prepared to provide guidance in particular instances regarding a SID's qualification for purposes of the rule.

4.　Information Delivery Requirements

The proposing release asked to whom the required information should be delivered. It also requested comment on the feasibility of requiring NRMSIRs to inform the MSRB when they receive disclosure information from issuers, and whether such information also should be required to be placed with the MSRB, in addition to or in lieu of an NRMSIR. The NRMSIRs did not address the issue of requiring them to inform the MSRB whenever they received disclosure information from an issuer, although one commenter argued that designating the MSRB as a repository only would add an unnecessary layer to the dissemination process.[167] Other commenters suggested designating a single central repository.[168] Similarly, some commenters suggested imposing a requirement that disclosure information be delivered to all NRMSIRs,[169] while others suggested that NRMSIRs be required to share the information received with other NRMSIRs,[170] and a third group preferred the establishment of a central index.[171] State-based information gatherers and disseminators had diverging views on this issue.[172]

Based on these comments, the commission has determined to require that annual financial information undertaken to be provided be deposited with each NRMSIR and the appropriate SID in the issuer's state. Any audited financial statements submitted in accordance with the undertakings also must be delivered to each NRMSIR and to the SID in the issuer's state, if such a depository has been established. The requirement to have annual financial information and audited financial statements delivered to all NRMSIRs and the appropriate SID is a modification of the proposed amendments. This modification will ensure that all NRMSIRs receive disclosure information directly. It also permits the commission to adopt the amendments without a delay for the creation of a central index or a system of information sharing among NRMSIRs.[173] The requirement to send information to all NRMSIRs rather than a single NRMSIR of the issuer's or obligated person's choice, should not impose significant burdens or costs, other than duplication and mailing costs. Furthermore, this requirement to deliver disclosure to the NRMSIRs and the appropriate SID also allays the anticompetitive concerns raised by the creation of a single NRMSIR.

In contrast to annual financial information, under the amendments, notices of material events, as well as notices of a failure by an issuer or other obligated person to provide annual financial information must be delivered to each NRMSIR or the MSRB, and the appropriate SID. The commission is of the view that permitting issuers and obligated persons to file such notices either with each NRMSIR or with the MSRB (as well as the appropriate SID) will facilitate prompt and wide disclosure. The amendments reflect the preference of some commenters for filing such notices in one central place, such as the MSRB, rather than having to file with multiple NRMSIRs. The commission expects that if notices are filed with the MSRB, the MSRB will make these notices available to all NRMSIRs on a prompt and contemporaneous basis.

5. Timing of Dissemination

Due to the time sensitive nature of notices of material event and failures to provide annual financial statements, it is important that such notices are disseminated quickly. These market requirements will dictate that disseminators have a system in place by which information vendors can make such notices available to broker-dealers and investors quickly and contemporaneously.

NRMSIRs and other information vendors have indicated in their comment letters that under certain circumstances a 15-minute turnaround[174] time for notices of material events, and a 24-hour turnaround period for annual financial information may be feasible, and, in some instances, already is in place.[175] Nonetheless, because the ultimate scope of the information undertakings was not known to the existing and potential NRMSIRs at the time they submitted their comments, the commission intends to discuss with the NRMSIRs during the recognition process appropriate and practicable turnaround standards for information redissemination. Because SIDs are alternative sources of information for every type of disclosure, the commission does not intend to impose strict turnaround times for SIDs. Instead, SIDs should provide the commission and users with a clear statement of turnaround times that they will meet consistently.

6. Technological Considerations

The commission also received many suggestions from information gatherers and vendors on streamlining the filing of disclosure information. These suggestions included requiring electronic filing of disclosure information, providing filings on computer disks, and providing information on NRMSIRs as images of original source documents rather than exclusively as coded text.[176] Rather than dictate standards, the commission encourages municipal securities market participants to coordinate their requirements and preferences on an industrywide basis.

D. Exemptions

The proposed amendments contained two new exemptions, which are being adopted with certain modifications. A third new exemption from the annual financial information requirement, for short-term securities, also is being adopted. In addition, rule 15c2-12's limitation to primary offerings of municipal securities with an aggregate principal amount of $1,000,000 or more, and its existing exemptions, also apply to the amendments.[177]

1. Small Issuer Exemption

The proposed amendments would have exempted from the provisions of the undertaking and recommendation prohibitions of the rule municipal securities issued in offerings by issuers that had (1) less than $10,000,000 in principal amount of securities outstanding, including the offered securities and (2) issued less than $3,000,000 in aggregate amount of municipal securities in the most recent 48 months preceding the offering.

A number of commenters discussed the appropriateness of the proposed dollar exemption, with comments ranging from a call for increased thresholds to no thresholds at all.[178] Some commenters believed that the thresholds should be increased, because many small municipalities would exceed these thresholds if they delay their financings in order to issue a greater amount of bonds at one time. The commenters argued that these are small, infrequent issuers with limited trading in the secondary market and the cost of compliance would outweigh the benefits received from improved secondary market disclosure.[179]

Other commenters took exception to the proposed thresholds because they were too high. These commenters argued that the exemption as proposed would exclude from coverage of the rule the types of issuers who have historically had deficient disclosure practices and disproportionate numbers of defaults.[180] A number of commenters also argued that the $3 million/48-month component of the threshold was too complex.[181]

As adopted,[182] the exemption retains the aggregate $10,000,000 limitation, but eliminates the $3,000,000 threshold. Instead, in addition to falling under the $10,000,000 in outstanding securities threshold, the exemption is conditioned upon an issuer or obligated person providing a limited disclosure undertaking. Under this undertaking, financial information and operating data concerning each obligor for which financial information or operating data is presented in the final official statement, must be provided upon request to any person, or be provided at least annually to the appropriate SID. The undertaking would specify the type of financial information and operating data that will be made available annually, which must include financial information and operating data that is customarily prepared by the obligated person and is publicly available. The final official statement must describe where and how the financial information and operating data can be obtained.

Financial information and operating data of governmental issuers generally are subject to freedom of information laws, and thus would be publicly available for purposes of this condition of the exemption. Conduit borrowers generally provide annual financial information to trustees, credit enhancers, or the financing agency that issued the municipal securities, and thus would have no difficulty complying with this standard if that information is made publicly available. To the extent that an obligated person does not currently publicly disclose that information, they are free to specify the type of information they are undertaking to provide on an ongoing basis, but they must agree to provide some information. That information need not be the same type of information presented in the official statement. Nor would these exempt persons have to release their audited financial statements, unless they otherwise customarily prepare and make their audited financial statements publicly available. Moreover, the limited disclosure undertaking need only cover those obligors for which financial information or operating data is provided in the official statement.

In addition to providing financial information and operating data annually, notices of material events must be sent to each NRMSIR or to the MSRB, and the appropriate SID. This public information condition has been adopted in response to comments highlighting the need for information regarding small issuers accessing the public debt market.[183]

The threshold of $10,000,000 has been retained, notwithstanding comments that it was too high or too low. According to statistics provided by one commenter,[184] in 1993, 71% of the approximately 52,000 municipal issuers had under $10,000,000 in outstanding municipal securities. Accordingly, the amendments as proposed already provided significant exemptive relief for small issuers. Indeed, the fact that a majority of issuers fall below that threshold supports conditioning the exemption on a commitment to provide a limited amount of secondary market information from exempt issuers. Even with that condition, a significant percentage of offerings would remain totally exempt from the amendments as adopted, because over 20% of the total issuances in 1993 were under $1,000,000.[185] As these statistics demonstrate, the exemption should exclude a large percentage of small infrequent issuers.

Commenters also questioned how the aggregate thresholds were measured, including whose securities would be included and whether the exemption applied only to outstanding securities that were sold in offerings subject to the rule.[186] Many commenters indicated that the thresholds should be separately applied to each issuer of municipal securities and each underlying obligor.[187] Thus, in the case of conduit issuers that have no liability on the municipal securities, commenters argued that the thresholds should be determined by reference to the persons who are the beneficiaries of the financing.[188] Some commenters argued that those issuers that had different types of financings that relied on separate revenue streams for repayment, such as dedicated tax revenues, should not be foreclosed from relying on the small issuer exemption for each financing.[189]

To address the first of these concerns, the amendments have been revised to clarify that the availability of the exemption turns on the amount of outstanding municipal securities for which an issuer or obligated person also is an obligated person. An issuer of municipal securities would need to satisfy the threshold only if it were an obligated person with respect to the security being offered. Under this approach, if a financing agency that is offering obligations that have some recourse to the agency, only those outstanding securities of the agency that likewise are recourse would count toward the threshold. If the financing agency does not issue recourse securities, the exemption will be unavailable only if a conduit borrower obligated on the municipal securities being offered is an obligated person with respect to more than $10,000,000 in outstanding municipal securities. If any one obligated person in an offering exceeds the threshold, then the entire offering, including all obligated persons, will be subject to the rule. Subsequent nonrecourse offerings by the financing agency would not be affected, but would be subject to a similar test.

With respect to the second concern, however, the amendments require that an obligated person aggregate all its outstanding obligations, even if some are payable from separate dedicated revenue sources. For example, a city or county that issues securities for a number of different purposes could not qualify as a small and infrequent issuer merely because its outstanding securities are payable from separate revenue streams. Thus, while a governmental issuer's outstanding obligations need not be aggregated with that of nongovernmental obligated persons, a governmental issuer could not avoid aggregation of its securities by restricting repayment to separate revenue streams.[190]

Commenters also discussed a related issue of what securities would be included in the calculation. Commenters contended that only publicly offered securities should be included in the calculation. Other commenters questioned how short-term obligations such as bond anticipation notes, refunded bonds, and installment/lease purchase agreements would be treated. Several commenters suggested that the threshold should be measured only against publicly offered, long-term bonds.[191]

The amendments have been clarified in this respect to exclude from the threshold calculation securities that were offered in transactions exempt from rule 15c2-12 because they were otherwise exempt as private placements and short-term financings. In addition, to the extent that an issuer or obligated person is no longer liable for repayment on bonds, as with certain defeased bonds, then such bonds would not be included in the calculation of the threshold for such issuer or obligated person.

A number of commenters indicated that an exemption should be available based on the number of holders of the municipal securities.[192] However, in accordance with concerns voiced by other commenters regarding the difficulty in ascertaining the number of holders due to the fact that most municipal securities are held in street name through a very limited number of depositories,[193] the amendments do not adopt any exemption based on the number of holders of the municipal securities.

A variety of other comments were raised relating to exemptions, and a number of alternative exemptions were proposed, including exemptions based on the type of issuer or the existence of an investment-grade rating.[194] Commenters also believed that an exemption should be available for securities covered by bond insurance or other credit enhancement, such as bank letters of credit.[195] Except as described above, the exemptions have not been revised to adopt these suggestions. Commenters, including some bond insurance providers,[196] expressed the view that the existence of credit enhancement does not necessarily eliminate the need for information regarding the underlying credit.

A number of commenters also argued that new exemptions should be added that would mirror exemptions under the Securities Act.[197] Some commenters argued that exemptions should be included for nonprofit entities that would have their own exemption from registration under the Securities Act.[198] The commission is not including any exclusion in the amendments for any such issuers. Issuers accessing the tax-exempt public securities markets have obligations to promote the integrity and efficiency of those markets. As the commission noted in the interpretive release, the high level of defaults in sectors such as health care, lifecare, retirement homes, and multifamily housing, relative to other market sectors,[199] and the past problems with the sufficiency of information in many of these sectors, weighs heavily against adopting such exclusions.

2. Exemption from the Annual Financial Information Requirement for Short-term Securities

A new exemption has been added to exempt from the requirement for an undertaking calling for annual financial information, offerings of securities with an 18-month or shorter maturity.[200] The new exemption is in response to comments suggesting that the rule not require annual financial information in situations where the securities would mature shortly after, or possibly even before, the annual financial information would be due.[201] The provisions of the amended rule relating to notices of material events, however, would apply to these offerings absent some other rule 15c2-12 exemption.

3. Exemptions from the Recommendation Prohibition

The proposed amendments also included a new exemption,[202] which would have permitted the recommendation in the secondary market of securities that were not subject to the underwriting prohibition, either because they were sold in a primary offering[203] of municipal securities with an aggregate principal amount of less than $1,000,000, or came within the existing exemptions for limited placements, short-term securities, and securities with demand features,[204] or within the new exemption for small, infrequent issuers.[205] This exemption has been adopted as proposed,[206] with the exception that securities sold in an exempt offering that is subject to the limited undertaking condition,[207] are not exempt from the application of the recommendation prohibition. Pursuant to this element of the small issuer exemption, dealers must have in place procedures to receive notices of material events.[208]

4. Transactional Exemption

The existing rule 15c2-12 transactional exemption[209] permits the commission to exempt any participating underwriter from any requirement of the rule. Because rule 15c2-12, as amended, places requirements on brokers, dealers, and municipal securities dealers in the secondary market, the transactional exemption has been amended to clarify that the commission has exemptive authority with respect to both participating underwriters, in connection with offerings, and with respect to brokers, dealers, and municipal securities dealers recommending transactions in the secondary market.[210]

E. Transitional Provision

The rule as amended contains a transitional provision for the amendments to rule 15c2-12.[211] The underwriting prohibition applies to a participating underwriter that has contractually committed to act as an underwriter in an offering on or after the effective date of the rule, July 3, 1995; provided that issuers need not undertake to provide annual financial information for fiscal years ending prior to January 1, 1996. The recommendation prohibition will become effective on January 1, 1996. The commission is of the view that this delay of 6 months beyond the effective date of the amendment relating to the underwriting of municipal securities is sufficient to permit participants in the municipal securities market to design procedures for compliance with the provisions of rule 15c2-12. Brokers, dealers, and municipal securities dealers must, therefore, have procedures in place to comply with the recommendation prohibition on or before January 1, 1996. Finally, the limited undertaking condition to the small issuer exemption need not be satisfied for offerings commencing prior to January 1, 1996.

III. EFFECTS ON COMPETITION AND REGULATORY FLEXIBILITY ACT CONSIDERATIONS

Section 23(a)(2) of the Exchange Act[212] requires the commission, in adopting rules under the act, to consider the anticompetitive effects of those rules, if any, and to balance that impact against the regulatory benefits gained in terms of furthering the purposes of the Exchange Act. The commission has considered the amendments to rule 15c2-12 in light of the standard cited in section 23(a)(2) and believes the adoption of the amendments will not impose any burden on competition not necessary or appropriate in furtherance of the Exchange Act.

In addition, the commission has prepared a final regulatory flexibility analysis (FRFA), pursuant to the requirements of the Regulatory Flexibility Act[213] regarding the proposed amendments to rule 15c2-12. The commission requested comment on the extent to which current practice deviates from the requirements of the proposed amendments, and the extent to which additional costs may be imposed on small issuers, brokers, dealers, and municipal securities dealers if the amendments are adopted as proposed. The FRFA indicates that the amendments to the rule could impose some additional costs on small broker-dealers and municipal issuers. Nonetheless, the commission is of the view that many of the substantive requirements of the amendments already are observed, absent access to the continuing information provided by the amendments, by issuers, brokers, dealers, and municipal securities dealers as a matter of business practice, or to fulfill their existing obligations under the antifraud provisions of the federal securities laws. To the extent that the proposed amendments would have imposed additional costs on small issuers, brokers, dealers, and municipal securities dealers, in response to commenters' concerns, the commission has modified the amendments as described.

NOTES

1. Both the Securities Act and the Exchange Act were enacted with broad exemptions for municipal securities from all of their provisions except the antifraud provisions of the Securities Act section 17(a) and Exchange Act section 10(b). Municipal securities received special exemptions not only based on considerations of federal-state comity, but also due to the lack of perceived abuses, at the time of enactment, in the municipal securities market as compared with the corporate market. Furthermore, until recently, the typical purchasers of municipal securities were institutional investors with financial expertise.
2. Section 15(c)(2) of the Exchange Act prohibits municipal securities dealers from effecting any transaction in, or inducing or attempting to induce the purchase or sale of, any municipal security by means of a "fraudulent, deceptive, or manipulative act or practice," and authorizes the commission, by rules and regulations, to define and prescribe means reasonably designed to prevent such acts and practices. Exchange Act section 15(c)(2), 15 U.S.C. 78o(c)(2). Rule 15c2-12 also was adopted pursuant to the commission's authority under Exchange Act section 2, 3, 10, 15, 15B, and 23; 15 U.S.C. 78b, 78c, 78j, 78o, 78o-4, 78q, and 78w.
3. 17 CFR 240.15c2-12. Rule 15c2-12 was proposed for adoption in 1988, and adopted in 1989. See Securities Exchange Act release no. 26100 (Sept. 22, 1988), 53 FR 37778 (1988 release); Securities Exchange Act release no. 26985 (June 28, 1989), 54 FR 28799 (1989 release). Rule 15c2-12 requires an underwriter of municipal securities (1) to obtain and review an issuer's official statement that, except for certain information, is "deemed final" by an issuer prior to making a purchase, offer, or sale of municipal securities; (2) in negotiated sales, to provide the issuer's most recent preliminary official statement (if one exists) to potential customers; (3) to deliver to customers, upon request, copies of the final official statement for a specified period of time; and (4) to contract to receive, within a specified time, sufficient copies of the issuer's final official statement to comply with the rule's delivery requirement, and the requirements of the rules of the MSRB.
4. The 1989 release also stated that issuers are primarily responsible for the content of their disclosure documents, and may be held primarily liable under the federal securities laws for misleading disclosure. See 1989 release at note 84.
5. Since September 1993, other initiatives related to the municipal securities market have been taken. On April 7, 1994, the commission approved changes to MSRB rule G-19 concerning suitability of recommendations, and rule G-8 concerning recordkeeping. Securities Exchange Act release no. 33869 (April 7, 1994), 59 FR 17632. These changes are designed to ensure that dealers, before making recommendations to customers, take appropriate steps to determine that the transaction is suitable. Concurrently, the commission approved MSRB rule G-37 relating to the linkage between political contributions and the municipal securities business. Securities Exchange Act release no. 33868 (April 7, 1994), 59 FR 17621. The rule seeks to end "pay to play" abuses in the municipal securities market by prohibiting dealers from conducting certain types of business with an issuer within 2 years after any contribution by the dealer or certain affiliated persons of the issuer who could influence the awarding of municipal securities business. On June 20, 1994, the MSRB filed with the commission a proposal to amend MSRB rule G-14 concerning reports of sales or purchases, and procedures for reporting interdealer transactions. Securities Exchange Act release no. 34458 (July 28, 1994), 59 FR 39803. The proposed rule change is a first step to increase transparency in the municipal securities market by collecting and disseminating information on interdealer transactions. On December 19, 1993, the commission issued a release proposing for public comment amendments to the rule regulating money market funds, rule 2a-7 under the Investment Company Act of 1940. Investment Company Act release no. 19959 (Dec. 28, 1993), 58 FR 68585.
6. By 1993, individual investors, including those holding through mutual funds and money market funds, held approximately 76% of municipal debt outstanding, as compared with 44% in 1983. The Bond Buyer, "Holders of Municipal Debt," (July 1, 1994) at 5.
7. The municipal securities market is not the only market for debt securities that suffers from information inefficiencies. For that reason, the commission also is exploring means to increase the amount of information concerning issuers of corporate debt securities. See Securities Exchange Act release no. 34139 (June 7, 1994), 59 FR 29453.
8. Statement of Gerald McBride, chairman, Municipal Securities Division, Public Securities Association, before the House Committee on Energy and Commerce, Telecommunications and Finance Subcommittee (Oct. 7, 1993) at 5.

9. Securities Act release no. 7049 (March 9, 1994), 59 FR 12748.
10. Securities Exchange Act release no. 33742 (March 9, 1994), 59 FR 12759. Also on March 9, the commission published Securities Exchange Act release no. 33743, which proposed the adoption of rule 15c2-13. Proposed rule 15c2-13 would have required broker, dealers, and municipal securities dealers to disclose markup information in riskless principal transactions in municipal securities; and to disclose when a particular municipal security is not rated by a nationally recognized statistical rating organization (NRSRO). Due to the recent development of proposals by the MSRB and market participants to make pricing information available to investors, the commission has determined to defer the riskless principal markup proposal for 6 months. In addition, the portion of proposed rule 15c2-13 that would require disclosure if a municipal security is not rated by an NRSRO has been deferred, and will be withdrawn if the MSRB acts to adopt similar amendments to its confirmation rule, rule G-15. See Securities Exchange Act release no. 34962 (Nov. 10, 1994).
11. Participating underwriters generally maintain a market in an issue of municipal securities in the period following an offering. Failure by a participating underwriter to receive assurances with respect to undertakings to provide secondary market disclosure will increase the difficulty of its formulation of a reasonable basis on which to recommend a municipal security during this period of secondary market trading.
12. Among others, the commission received 232 letters representing the views of 242 issuers and issuer associations; 52 letters representing the views of 57 brokers, dealers, and municipal securities dealers; and 8 letters representing the views of 8 investors and investor associations.
13. The commission has given consideration to the views of some commenters who questioned the commission's authority to adopt the amendments to rule 15c2-12. See, e.g., letter of ABA Business Law Section; letter of Hawkins Delafield & Wood, letter of NABL. The commission believes that it has ample authority to adopt the amendments.
14. The comment letters and a summary of the comment letters prepared by commission staff are contained in public file no. S7-5-94. See also public file no. S7-4-94.
15. See *Joint Response to the Securities Exchange Commission on Releases Concerning Municipal Securities Market Disclosure*, prepared by American Bankers Association's Corporate Trust Committee, American Public Power Association, Association of Local Housing Finance Agencies, Council of Infrastructure Financing Authorities, Government Finance Officers Association, National Association of Counties, National Association of State Auditors, Comptrollers and Treasurers, National Council of State Housing Agencies, National Federation of Municipal Analysts, Public Securities Association (Joint Response).
16. See, e.g., joint response; letter of Chapman and Cutler; letter of Florida Division of Bond Finance of the State Board of Administration; letter of J. P. Morgan Securities, Inc.; letter of National Association of Bond Lawyers (NABL); letter of Orrick, Herrington & Sutcliffe (Orrick Herrington); letter of Public Securities Association (PSA).
17. See rule 15c2-12(a).
18. The amendments also include an exemption for small and infrequent issuers. See Section II.D.1., infra.
19. Rule 15c2-12(b)(5)(i).
20. These concepts are discussed in Section II.A.1.b., infra.
21. Information repositories are discussed in Section II.C., infra.
22. See letter of Merrill Lynch, Pierce, Fenner & Smith (Merrill Lynch).
23. As noted in the 1988 release, the obligations of managing underwriters and underwriters participating in an offering differ. An underwriter participating in an offering need not duplicate the efforts of the managing underwriter, but must satisfy itself that the managing underwriter reviewed the accuracy of the information in the official statement in a professional manner and therefore had a reasonable basis for its recommendation. Underwriters participating in offerings, however, have a duty to notify the managing underwriter of any factors that suggest inaccuracies in disclosure, or signal the need for additional investigation. See 1988 release at n. 87.
24. See letter of Kutak Rock; letter of Section of Urban, State and Local Government Law, American Bar Association (ABA Urban Law Section); letter of Colorado Municipal Bond Supervisory Board.
25. In contrast to the requirement in rule 15c2-12(b)(5) that participating underwriters reasonably determine that issuers or obligated persons have undertaken to provide secondary market disclosure prior to the time they "purchase or sell" municipal securities, rule 15c2-12(b)(1) requires participating underwriters to obtain and review an official statement deemed final by the issuer (DFOS) prior to the time they "bid for, purchase, offer, or sell" securities. Thus, under rule 15c2-12(b)(1), in a competitive underwriting, a participating underwriter must obtain and review the DFOS prior to placing a bid on an issue of municipal securities. Because the term *offer* encompasses the distribution of a preliminary official statement, as well as oral solicitations of indications of interest, in a negotiated underwriting, a participating underwriter is required to obtain and review the DFOS prior to the time it distributes the preliminary official statement to potential investors. If no offers are made, the participating underwriter is required to obtain and review the DFOS by the earlier of the time it agrees (whether in principle or by signing the bond purchase agreement) to purchase the bonds, or the first sale of bonds. See Mudge Rose Guthrie Alexander & Ferdon (April 4, 1990): interpretive release at Section III.C.6.
26. Information regarding the offering price, interest rate, selling compensation, aggregate principal amount, principal amount per maturity, delivery dates, any other terms or provisions required by an issuer of such securities to be specified in a competitive bid, ratings, other terms of the securities depending on such matters, and the identity of

the underwriters, may be omitted from the official statement reviewed by the participating underwriter for purposes of rule 15c2-12(b)(1).

27. Whether information is in fact known or not reasonably ascertainable at the time the participating underwriter must obtain and review the DFOS pursuant to the rule is best determined in the context of each offering by the issuer, the participating underwriter, and their respective counsel. See Public Securities Association (May 29, 1992).

28. As a practical matter, the DFOS and the preliminary official statement (POS) are often the same document. See Mudge Rose Guthrie Alexander & Ferdon (April 4, 1990).

29. See Association of Local Housing Finance Agencies, *Guidelines for Information Disclosure to the Secondary Market* (1992); Government Finance Officers Association, *Disclosure Guidelines for State and Local Government Securities* (Jan. 1991); Healthcare Financial Management Association, Principles and Practices Board, *Statement Number 18—Public Disclosure of Financial and Operating Information by Healthcare Providers* (May 1994); National Council of State Housing Agencies, *Quarterly Reporting Format for State Housing Finance Agency Single Family Housing Bonds* (1989) and *Multi-family Disclosure Format* (1991); National Federation of Municipal Analysts, *Disclosure Handbook for Municipal Securities 1992 Update* (Nov. 1992).

30. See, e.g., letter of Indiana Bond Bank; letter of Kutak Rock; letter of NABL; letter of Texas Public Finance Authority; letter of Goldman Sachs & Co. (Goldman Sachs).

31. See, e.g., letter of Department of Community Trade and Economic Development, state of Washington; letter of American Public Power Association (APPA); letter of Municipal Treasurer's Association; letter of Orrick Herrington.

32. See rule 15c2-12(f)(3).

33. See, e.g., letter of Association of Local Housing Financing Agencies (ALHFA); letter of treasurer, state of Connecticut Office of the Treasurer (Treasurer of the state of Connecticut); letter of Council of Development Finance Agencies (CDFA); joint response; letter of Securities Industry Association (SIA); letter of Morgan Stanley & Co., Inc. (Morgan Stanley).

34. See 1989 release.

35. Interpretive release at Section III.B. The interpretive release is cited in the preliminary note to rule 15c2-12 as a source of guidance as to the disclosure obligations of issuers of municipal securities, as well as the role of brokers, dealers, and municipal securities dealers.

36. See note 31, supra.

37. See interpretive release at Section III.A.

38. See joint response.

39. See letter of ABA Urban Law Section; letter of Bose McKinney & Evans; joint response; letter of Mudge Rose Guthrie Alexander & Ferdon (Mudge Rose); letter of Domitory Authority of the State of New York (New York Dormitory Authority).

40. See letter of Mudge Rose; letter of New York Dormitory Authority.

41. See letter of ABA Urban Law Section; letter of Kutak Rock; letter of Texas Public Finance Authority.

42. See, e.g., letter of Bose McKinney & Evans; joint response. One commenter also stated that if cross-referencing was permitted, there should be a delay between the distribution of the official statement and the offering. The delay would enable potential purchasers and others to obtain any materials that were referenced in the official statement and make an informed investment decision. See letter of Prudential Investment Corp.

43. See 1989 release (discussing the definition of "final official statement" in rule 15c2-12 as originally adopted, and stating that the definition recognizes that the issuer's final official statement may be composed of one or more documents).

44. Rule 15c2-12(f)(3). To avoid confusion with the technical aspects of incorporation by reference for registrants under the commission's registration rules, the amended rule does not use that term. At least two states, New York and Texas, have prepared a standard disclosure document for state information.

45. Participating underwriters and other market participants must keep in mind their obligations under the rule with respect to the DFOS and final official statement, and under the antifraud provisions of the federal securities laws. To the extent that cross-references are used, the DFOS should be disseminated in sufficient time for review by participating underwriters, and the POS should be made available in time to enable prospective purchasers to make informed investment decisions based upon the referenced materials. See interpretive release at Section III.C.6.

46. See, e.g., letter of New York Dormitory Authority; letter of the treasurer of the state of Connecticut.

47. See, e.g., letter of Fieldman, Rolapp & Associates; letter of state of Florida, Office of Auditor General; letter of San Francisco International Airport; letter of Texas Water Development Board; letter of State of Washington, Office of the Treasurer.

48. Rule 15c2-12(f)(3).

49. See interpretive release at Section III.C.4.

50. See, e.g., letter of Chemical Securities, Inc. (Chemical Securities); letter of Ferris Baker Watts; letter of National Federation of Municipal Analysts (NFMA).

51. See rule 15c2-12(f)(3).

52. See letter of PSA.

53. Paragraph (b)(5)(i)(A) of the proposed amendments.

54. See, e.g., letter of Fidelity Management and Research Company; letter of First Albany Corporation; letter of Maine Municipal Bond Bank; letter of NAB; letter of National Council of Health Facilities Finance Authorities (NCHFFA); letter of Realvest Capital Corporation; letter of South Carolina Economic Developers Association, Inc.

55. See, e.g., letter of ABA Urban Law Section; letter of Gilmore & Bell, P.C. (Gilmore & Bell); letter of New York Housing Finance Agency, state of New York Mortgage Agency, New York State Medical Care Facilities Finance Agency (New York State Housing Finance Agency); letter of Orrick Herrington.

56. See, e.g., letter of Section of Business Law, American Bar Association (ABA Business Law Section); letter of treasurer of the state of California (treasurer of the state of California); letter of Goldman Sachs; letter of IDS Financial Corporation; joint response; letter of Kutak Rock; letter of Morgan Stanley; letter of National Association of State Treasurers (NAST).

57. Providers of bond insurance, letters of credit, and liquidity facilities have been excepted from the definition of obligated person to eliminate the need to separately obtain and disseminate annual information about such providers. See Section II.A.1.b.(1). infra.

58. See, e.g., letter of American Municipal Power—Ohio, Inc. (AMP—Ohio); letter of Gilmore & Bell; letter of treasurer of the state of California.

59. See, e.g., letter of Financial Guaranty Insurance Company (FGIC); letter of Goldman Sachs; letter of Hawkins Delafield & Wood; letter of Thacher Proffitt & Wood.

60. See, e.g., letter of Kutak Rock.

61. See, e.g., letter of ABA Urban Law Section; letter of Kutak Rock; letter of state of Washington, Office of the Treasurer.

62. See, e.g., letter of APPA; letter of George K. Baum & Co.; letter of CDFA; letter of Eaton Vance Management; letter of NCHFFA.

63. See, e.g., letter of ABA Business Law Section; letter of Electricities, Inc.; letter of Hawkins Delafield & Wood; letter of Kutak Rock; letter of Mudge Rose; letter of San Francisco International Airport.

64. See, e.g., letter of ABA Urban Law Section; letter of A. G. Edwards & Sons, Inc.; letter of Council of Infrastructure Financing Authorities (CIFA); letter of Hawkins Delafield & Wood; letter of Program Administration Services, Inc.

65. See, e.g., letter of ABA Business Law Section; letter of APPA; letter of city of Everett, Washington; letter of Goldman Sachs; letter of Hawkins Delafield & Wood; letter of Merrill Lynch; letter of Morgan Stanley; letter of Mudge Rose; letter of Orrick Herrington. Certain of these commenters noted that by including a contractual or similar relationship between the entity making payments and the financing, customers and taxpayers, having no connection to or responsibility in connection with the financing would not inadvertently be swept within the scope of the definition.

66. See, e.g., letter of APPA; letter of George K. Baum & Co.; letter of city of Everett, Washington; letter of IDS Financial Corporation; letter of Standish, Ayer & Wood, Inc.

67. See, e.g., letter of ABA Business Law Section; letter of ALHFA; letter of PSA.

68. See, e.g., letter of FGIC; joint response; letter of NABL; letter of PSA.

69. See rule 15c2-12(f)(10).

70. See, e.g., letter of Bose McKinney & Evans; letter of Mudge Rose; letter of New York Dormitory Authority; letter of Orrick Herrington.

71. See, e.g., letter of Bose McKinney & Evans; letter of Goldman Sachs; letter of Indiana Bond Bank; letter of Hawkins Delafield & Wood.

72. For example, if all or a portion of a project financed by bonds is used by a party that has committed, by contract or other arrangement (written or oral) to pay for such use, and such payments support payment of debt service on the bonds (as structured at the time of issuance), continuing information on the party would be appropriate. Accordingly, parties that support debt service through payments under a lease, loan, installment sale agreement, or other contract relating to use of a project are included in the definition, regardless of whether the financing is a conduit arrangement (such as a nonrecourse loan to a manufacturer to finance acquisition of a new facility or to a hospital to acquire equipment) or system or project financing (such as a lease to a particular carrier of a terminal in an airport system or sale of the output of a facility pursuant to a take-or-pay [or take-and-pay] contract). Major customers purchasing power from a municipal light department that, in turn, is under a take-or-pay contract with a joint action public power agency would not be included in the definition, although the municipal light department would likely be included in the definition. Similarly, major taxpayers in a municipal general obligation issue would not be included in the definition; however, an undertaking covering a developer that is the sole landowner in a development district assessment financing in which the future collection of assessments to service the borrowing is dependent upon the developer as part of the structure of the financing may be appropriate.

73. 17 CFR 239.131.

74. 17 CFR 240.3b-5.

75. See, e.g., letter of Fidelity Management and Research Company; letter of Mudge Rose; letter of NABL; letter of Texas Public Finance Authority.

76. See rule 15c2-12(b)(5)(i).

77. Under the revised amendments, the concerns of some commenters that the definition of significant obligor failed to take into account short-term arrangements (i.e., the arrangements with persons providing cash flow were shorter than the term of the securities) is also alleviated in two ways. First, the issuer determines at the outset if an obligated person is material to the offering. Second, assuming an obligated person is included in the final official statement,

the undertaking to continue to provide information on such obligated person may be terminated once it no longer has liability for any obligation on or relating to repayment of the municipal securities. See rule 15c2-12(b)(5)(iii); letter of APPA; letter of Hawkins Delafield & Wood.

78.   Guidelines and practices that have developed in other contexts may be useful in analyzing both the materiality of an obligated person to the municipal financing and the appropriate level of disclosure relating to such obligated person. For example, in connection with securitization of nonrecourse commercial mortgage loans, the 10% and 20% property assets concentration tests described in staff accounting bulletins 71 and 71A are applied. These percentages are applied by analogy in other asset-backed financings.

79.   Although the amendments do not specify the scope of the objective criteria, the criteria description should be clear as to when and how they are applied.

80.   See rule 15c2-12(b)(5)(ii).

81.   See, e.g., letter of ABA Urban Law Section; letter of Blackwell Industrial Authority, Blackwell, Oklahoma; letter of Davis Polk & Wardwell; letter of IDS Financial Corporation; letter of Kutak Rock; letter of Oregon Economic Development Department; letter of Realvest Capital Corporation; letter of Thacher Proffitt & Wood. Some commenters also were concerned as to whether the definition would encompass providers of guaranteed investment contracts and other investments. See, e.g., letter of ABA Urban Law Section; letter of Kutak Rock, on behalf of AMBAC Indemnity Corporation, Capital Markets Assurance Corporation, Capital Reinsurance Company, Enhance Reinsurance Company, Financial Guaranty Insurance Company, Financial Security Assurance, Inc., and Municipal Bond Investors Assurance Corporation (Kutak Rock on behalf of Financial Guaranty Insurers). A functional approach determines whether providers of investments should provide ongoing information. For example, if the proceeds of an offering are invested in guaranteed investment contracts (GICs), and the income from the GICs is the predominant source of revenue to repay the obligations on the securities, information about the provider may be material to the offering, including on an ongoing basis. If, however, other sources of revenue are committed to support payment of the obligations, the relative importance of the provider of the GIC to investors may be diminished.

82.   See, e.g., letter of ABA Urban Law Section; letter of Smith, Gambrell & Russell; letter of Texas Water Development Board. Some commenters noted difficulty in obtaining information from credit enhancers. See letter of Association of Bay Area Governments; letter of New York State Housing Finance Agency; letter of state of Washington, Office of the Treasurer.

83.   See, e.g., memorandum of Aug. 10, 1994 meeting with Davis, Polk and Wardwell and various banks; letter of Kutak Rock on behalf of Financial Guaranty Insurers. One commenter recommended that bond insurers and banks providing letters of credit, who are not subject to periodic reporting requirements of the federal securities laws, send publicly available reports to the repositories. See letter of ABA Urban Law Section.

84.   The term *issuer of municipal securities*, as defined in rule 15c2-12, includes issuers of separate securities as well.

85.   See, e.g., letter of ALHFA; letter of Hawkins Delafield & Wood; letter of Kutak Rock; letter of National State Auditors Association; letter of the treasurer of the state of North Carolina.

86.   See, e.g., letter of ABA Urban Law Section; letter of ALHFA; letter of Kutak Rock; letter of NABL.

87.   See, e.g., letter of Bond Investors Association; letter of PSA; letter of Texas Public Finance Authority.

88.   See, e.g., letter of Bank One Corporation; letter of Reliance Trust Company; letter of State Street Bank and Trust Company.

89.   Rule 15c2-12(f)(9).

90.   See, e.g., letter of Dean Witter Reynolds, Inc. (Dean Witter); letter of National League of Cities; letter of NFMA; joint response; letter of PSA; letter of Tillinghast, Collins & Graham; letter of the treasurer of the state of Connecticut.

91.   See, e.g., letter of Dain Bosworth, Inc.; letter of First Albany Corporation; letter of MSRB; letter of NFMA; letter of Standish, Ayer & Wood, Inc.

92.   See, e.g., letter of CDFA; letter of Chapman and Cutler; letter of CIFA; joint response; letter of H. M. Quackenbush; letter of NABL.

93.   See, e.g., letter of Texas Water Development Board; letter of state of Washington, Office of the Treasurer.

94.   See, e.g., letter of city of Barling; letter of Dain Bosworth, Inc.; letter of Friday, Eldridge & Clark.

95.   See, e.g., letter of AMP—Ohio; letter of state of Indiana, State Board of Accounts; letter of state of Montana, Department of Natural Resources and Conservation; letter of Washington Finance Officers Association.

96.   See, e.g., letter of AMP—Ohio; letter of Washington Finance Officers Association.

97.   See, e.g., letter of ABA Business Law Section; letter of Florida Division of Bond Finance; letter of Gust & Rosenfeld; letter of Office of the State Auditor, Texas (Texas Office of the State Auditor).

98.   See, e.g., letter of treasurer of the state of North Carolina; letter of Texas Office of the State Auditor.

99.   See, e.g., letter of the treasurer of the state of North Carolina; letter of Texas Office of the State Auditor.

100. See, e.g., letter of ABA Urban Law Section; letter of APPA; letter of Goldman Sachs; letter of Gust & Rosenfeld; letter of the Hospital & Higher Education Facilities Authority of Philadelphia; letter of Morgan Stanley; letter of NABL; letter of New York State Housing Finance Agency.

101. See letter of ABA Urban Law Section.

102. See, e.g., letter of ABA Business Law Section; letter of Association of Bay Area Governments; letter of North East Independent School District; letter of PSA; letter of Washington Finance Officers Association.

103. See, e.g., letter of the treasurer of the state of North Carolina; letter of Washington Finance Officers Association.

104. See rule 15c2-12(b)(5)(i)(B).
105. See rule 15c2-12(b)(5)(ii)(B).
106. See proposing release. A number of commenters reponded for comment on specification of the use of generally accepted accounting principles (GAAP) and generally accepted auditing standards (GAAS). See, e.g., letter of comptroller of the state of California; letter of Government Accounting Standards Board (GASB); letter of NAST; letter of National State Auditors Association; letter of Prudential Investment Corp. The amendments as adopted do not mandate the use of either GAAP or GAAS.
107. See rule 15c2-12(b)(5)(ii)(B).
108. Of course, any required information must be the subject of an undertaking, and if the information cross-referenced has not been submitted to a repository or the MSRB, or filed with the commission, the undertaking will not have been complied with.
109. Paragraph (b)(5)(i)(A) of the proposed amendments.
110. See, e.g., letter of APPA; letter of Fidelity Management and Research Company; letter of Hawkins Delafield & Wood.
111. See, e.g., letter of Chapman and Cutler; joint response; letter of Kutak Rock.
112. See rule 15c2-12(b)(5)(iii).
113. See paragraph (b)(5)(i)(B) of the proposed amendments. See also, letter of A. G. Edwards; letter of Chemical Securities; letter of J. J. Kenny Co., Inc. (J. J. Kenny Co.); letter of MSRB.
114. See, e.g., letter of Chemical Securities; letter of Goldman Sachs; letter of George K. Baum; letter of PSA.
115. See, e.g., letter of CDFA; letter of Gust & Rosenfeld; joint response; letter of Municipal Treasurers Association; letter of Rauscher Pierce Refsnes, Inc.; letter of Standish Ayer & Wood, Inc.
116. See, e.g., letter of Chemical Securities; letter of Edward D. Jones & Co.; letter of Finance Authority of Maine; letter of Ferris Baker Watts; letter of Norwest Investment Services, Inc.; letter of Prudential Investment Corp.
117. The introduction to the list also has been clarified to indicate that the events relate specifically to the securities being offered. See rule 15c2-12(b)(5)(i)(C).
118. See, e.g., letter of NAST; letter of the treasurer of state of California.
119. Several commenters have expressed concern that statements by various elected officials made in a political context relating to an issuer must now be included in information provided to a repository. The amendments contain no such requirement. Moreover, these concerns appear to be based upon a misunderstanding of the reminder to issuers in the interpretive release that investors may rely on a variety of formal and informal sources for continuing information on municipal issuers, including public statements and press releases concerning an entity's fiscal affairs made by municipal officials, particularly in the absence of a more standardized mechanism for disseminating information about the municipal issuer to the market as a whole. The caution contained in the interpretive release that the antifraud provisions may apply to releases of information to the public reasonably expected to reach investors and the trading market does not mean, as some commenters inferred, that such statements are per se material; nor do the amendments require that such statements, even where material, be provided to the repositories.
120. See, e.g., letter of ABA Business Law Section; letter of ABA Urban Law Section; letter of NABL; letter of NCHFFA; letter of New York State Housing Finance Agency; letter of Orrick Herrington.
121. See rule 15c2-12(b)(5)(i)(C)(10).
122. See, e.g., letter of ABA Urban Law Section; letter of Kutak Rock; letter of Orrick Herrington.
123. See, e.g., letter of First Southwest Company; letter of New York Dormitory Authority; letter of the treasurer of the state of North Carolina; letter of city of Pullman, Washington.
124. See rule 15c2-12(b)(5)(i)(D).
125. See, e.g., letter of Gust & Rosenfeld.
126. See, e.g., letter of Merrill Lynch. Certain commenters considered that undertakings in a trust indenture could prove inflexible, as well as difficult to modify if they became inappropriate to the future. Letter of ABA Business Law Ssection. Other commenters considered that the issue of flexibility could be addressed through careful drafting. Letter of Morgan Stanley; letter of Rauscher, Pierce, Refsnes, Inc.
127. See letter of Chapman and Cutler (suggesting that an agreement could be made between an issuer and a trustee or between the issuer and an NRMSIR); letter of Rauscher, Pierce, Refsnes, Inc. These commenters noted that such agreements provide flexibility for the future modification of the type, timing, or presentation of secondary market disclosure, as well as remedies in the event of a breach of the agreement.
128. See, e.g., letter of Mudge Rose.
129. See letter of Morgan Stanley. Morgan Stanley also suggested that an underwriting agreement was an unsatisfactory vehicle for undertakings to provide secondary market disclosure because an underwriter of a specific bond issue should not be the recipient of a long-term contract of this type. See letter of Morgan Stanley. Other commenters agreed that undertakings should be for the benefit of holders of municipal securities, and that there should be no requirement that undertakings be made for the benefit of participating underwriters. See, e.g., letter of Merrill Lynch (noting that "the holders of the securities have the greatest interest in enforcing the covenant to provide information and are in the best position to evaluate whether affirmative efforts to enforce the covenant should be undertaken").
130. Some commenters were concerned that in some jurisdictions, an issuer's ability to agree to provide information beyond a 1-year period might be restricted by state law. To address such concerns, inclusion of a condition

subsequent in the covenant, such as subject to appropriation, might be appropriate. It is anticipated, however, that should funds that would enable the issuer to provide the agreed-upon information not be appropriated, disclosure of such fact would be made by notice to the repositories pursuant to rule 15c2-12(b)(5)(i)(D).

131. See, e.g., letter of Chemical Securities; letter of Dain Bosworth, Inc.; letter of Dillon, Read & Co., Inc.
132. Commenters argued that an issuer's failure to comply with undertakings to provide secondary market disclosure should not result in an event of default. See, e.g., letter of ABA Urban Law Section; letter of state of Washington, Office of the Treasurer; letter of Colorado Municipal Bond Supervision Advisory Board.
133. See paragraph (c) of the proposed amendments.
134. See letter of PSA [noting that paragraph (c) would require dealers to create records showing that they had reviewed municipal securities].
135. See, e.g., letter of Chapman and Cutler (brokers with fewer analysts will be at a competitive disadvantage); letter of Morgan Stanley [noting that in order to comply with paragraph (c) as proposed, reliance on third-party service providers for information analysis would be required].
136. See, e.g., joint response; letter of PSA; letter of Gabriel, Hueglin & Cashman.
137. See, e.g., joint response; letter of PSA.
138. Letter of Investment Company Institute (ICI). See also letter of MSRB; letter of NABL. NABL suggested disclosure by dealers as to whether a party has committed to provide secondary market disclosure, and if not, the consequences of investing in the securities.
139. See, e.g., letter of Edward D. Jones & Co. (suggesting application of the proposed amendments only to nonrated or special assessment bonds); letter of NABL (suggesting exemptions from the amendments to rule 15c2-12 for issuers that obtain and maintain an investment grade rating, and for general obligation bonds and revenue bonds issued to finance essential government purposes).
140. See, e.g., letter of PSA; letter of A. G. Edwards & Sons, Inc. (reviewing issuer's disclosure is not the only way to form the basis for a recommendation).
141. As noted in the proposing release, most situations in which a dealer brings a municipal security to the attention of a customer involve an implicit recommendation of the security to the customer.
142. See, e.g., letter of MSRB (emphasizing that, in the board's view, dealers would be responsible for continuing disclosure information available in NRMSIRs even without the specific "review" requirement); letter of Paine Webber.
143. Letter of MSRB (noting the requirements of the MSRB's rules in commenting that the proposed amendment's requirement to review periodic information is not a practical option for dealers).
144. See rule 15c2-12(b)(5)(i)(D).
145. See MSRB manual (CCH) ¶ 3581.30 (interpreting MSRB rule G-17 to require that a dealer disclose, at or prior to a sale, all material facts concerning the transaction, including a complete description of the security). See also 1988 release at note 50 and accompanying text.
146. Under rule 15c2-12(b)(4), underwriters must deliver final official statements to potential customers for a 90-day period after the close of the underwriting period. The underwriters' 90-day delivery obligation is shortened to 25 days if the final official statement can be obtained from an NRMSIR.
147. Since the commission adopted rule 15c2-12, the Division of Market Regulation issued three no-action letters recognizing national information vendors as NRMSIRs, based on the standards set out in the July 1989 release. See letters from Richard G. Ketchum, director, Division of Market Regulation to Joseph V. Riccobono, executive vice-president, American Banker-Bond Buyer (Jan. 4, 1990); J. Kevin Kenny, president, chief executive officer, J. J. Kenny Co. (Jan. 4, 1990); and Michael R. Bloomberg, president, Bloomberg, L.P. (Jan. 11, 1990). Recently, the commission has received inquiries from additional information vendors desiring to be recognized as NRMSIRs.
148. NRMSIRs are not the only source of information in the municipal market. The MSRB has developed its Municipal Securities Information Library (MSIL) system, which presently collects information and disseminates it to market participants and information vendors. The Official Statement and Advance Refunding Document-Paper Submission System ("OS/ARD") of the MSIL collects and makes available on magnetic tape and on paper official statements and advance refunding notices. Securities Exchange Act release no. 29298 (June 13, 1991), 56 FR 28194. As a part of the MSIL system, the MSRB commenced operation of its continuing disclosure information (CDI) pilot system in Jan. 1993. The CDI system is a central repository for voluntarily submitted official continuing disclosure documents relating to outstanding municipal securities issues. Securities Exchange Act release no. 30556 (April 6, 1992) 57 FR 12534. Neither the MSIL OS/ARD system nor the CDI system is an NRMSIR; the commission has previously indicated that it would consider the competitive implications of an MSRB request for NRMSIR status. See Securities Exchange Act release no. 28081 (June 1, 1990), 55 FR 23333, 23337 n.26.
149. See, e.g., letter of PSA (noting that the suggestion made by some market participants that municipal securities dealers will not utilize information they have long sought is implausible), letter of Ferris Baker Watts (information will be used if it is available).
150. The commission suggested that NRMSIRs (1) maintain current, accurate information about municipal securities, including final official statements, the issuer's annual final information, and issuer's notices of material events; (2) have effective systems for the timely collection, indexing, storage, and retrieval of these documents; and (3) be capable of national dissemination of final official statements, annual financial information, and notices of material

events through electronic dissemination systems, in response to telephone inquiries, and hard copy delivery via facsimile, by mail, and by messenger service. The commission also stressed the importance of timely public availability upon receipt of information by a NRMSIR.

151. See, e.g., letter of Bloomberg L.P.; letter of Cypress Capital Corp. (a dealer chosen by the Louisiana Municipal Association to assist it in developing a repository to collect and disseminate information on Louisiana issuers of municipal securities). In discussing NRMSIRs in the 1989 release, the commission noted that in determining whether a particular entity is an NRMSIR, it would look, among other things, at whether the repository: (1) is national in scope; (2) maintains current, accurate information about municipal offerings in the form of official statements; (3) has effective retrieval and dissemination systems; (4) places no limit on the issuers from which it will accept official statements or related information; (5) provides access to the documents deposited with it to anyone willing and able to pay the applicable fees; and (6) charges reasonable fees. See 1989 release at note 65.

152. In the past, the Division of Market Regulation has required that each NRMSIR maintain copies of all disclosure documents. In view of recent requests from information collectors and disseminators, the Division of Market Regulation will review, on a case by case basis, NRMSIR proposals to satisfy the requirement to maintain copies of disclosure documents through a contract with another entity (including the MSRB) that will maintain copies. See letters from Laurence M. Landau, vice president, Dow Jones Telerate, to Elizabeth MacGregor, Division of Market Regulation, SEC, (July 18, 1994) and to Guatam S. Gujral, Division of Market Reagulation, SEC (Aug. 4, 1994). See also letter of Storch & Brenner (on behalf of R. R. Donnelly Financial). This flexible approach, requested by industry participants, may allow NRMSIRs to reduce the cost at which they can collect and disseminate disclosure information to broker-dealers and investors.

153. It should be noted that NRMSIRs are not being required to verify the accuracy of the information provided them. NRMSIRs are required to accurately convey the information provided to them.

154. See 1989 release.

155. See, e.g., letter of Maine Municipal Bond Bank; letter of National Association of Independent Public Financial Advisors (NRMSIR users, not issuers, should pay the NRMSIR costs).

156. See, e.g., letter of Colonial Management Associates, Inc.

157. Letter of Bloomberg L.P.; letter of J. J. Kenny Co.; letter of the *Bond Buyer*.

158. With one notable exception, national information vendors generally did not see a need for state-based repositories and argued that state-based repositories would indeed add to the complexity of collecting and disseminating information. See, e.g., letter of J. J. Kenny Co. Some state-based information gatherers and disseminators, however, argued that they already had created mechanisms for the collection and dissemination of information, and their systems are working well. The National Association of State Auditors, Comptrollers and Treasurers (NASACT) pointed out that issuers and other obligors will probably file with state-based repositories, with whom they are accustomed to working and with whom they typically must file in any event for regulatory purposes unrelated to secondary market disclosure. NASACT argued that while the state repositories do not wish to compete with NRMSIRs, state-based repositories can serve an important role in enhancing the accessibility of disclosure information for repackaging by the NRMSIRs. See letter of NASACT.

159. See letter of the Office of the State Comptroller, state of New York.

160. See, e.g., letter of Cypress Capital Corporation (Louisiana Municipal Security Disclosure Board "intends to be in a position to comply with the standards developed by the Commission for NRMSIRs").

161. See letter of Municipal Advisory Council of Texas; letter of Ohio Municipal Advisory Council.

162. South Carolina recently enacted legislation requiring issuers to agree in a bond indenture to file an annual independent audit within a specified number of days of the issuer's receipt thereof and certain event information with a central repository. South Carolina Senate Bill 1182, (effective Sept. 1, 1994) to be codified in S.C. Code Ann. Chapter 1, Title 11, Section 11-1-85 (1976). Similarly, Tennessee recently adopted legislation authorizing the adoption of rules to facilitate secondary market disclosure by any public entity, including the form and content of that disclosure. Tenn. Code Ann. Sec. 9-21-151 (a) and (b)(2).

163. See, e.g., letter of the Office of the State Comptroller, state of New York.

164. See Section II.D.1. infra.

165. There is no requirement that SIDs be instrumentalities of a state. A number of private organizations already function as state-based repositories, at times at no cost to the taxpayer. The commission defers to each state's determination whether to have a private or public entity be its SID.

166. As with NRMSIRs, for a SID to give preferential treatment to a NRMSIR by giving it market information before it is made available to other NRMSIRs would be wholly inconsistent with functioning as a SID.

167. Letter of Bloomberg L.P.

168. See, e.g., Artemis Capital Group, Ltd. (proposing that the commission designate the MSRB's MSIL system as the single central repository); letter of Chapman and Cutler (there should be one central source of information).

169. See, e.g., letter of J. J. Kenny Co.; letter of National Association of Independent Public Financial Advisers.

170. See, e.g., letter of MSRB; letter of Richard A. Ciccarone.

171. Letter of Storch & Brenner (on behalf of R. R. Donnelly Financial); letter of the *Bond Buyer*.

172. The Ohio Municipal Advisory Council stated that it is feasible to require repositories to inform the MSRB as to which issuers have released information to it. Under Cypress Capital Corporation's proposal, the indexing party

would receive descriptions of all materials received by the Louisiana Repository. But see, letter of NASACT (requirement that a repository be required to notify a central index each time an item of information is received by the repository is unduly burdensome and unnecessary).

173. Some commenters expressed an interest in creating a central index and an information-sharing system. Letter of Storch & Brenner (on behalf of R. R. Donnelly Financial); letter of Dow Jones Telerate, Inc. The commission is prepared to review such mechanisms for centralized collection and dissemination if requested to do so.

174. The commission considers "turnaround time" or "turnaround period" to mean the time between which an NRMSIR initially receives information, and the time when such information is made available to the public. NRMSIRs will be required to make available the full text of notices of material events, and post the receipt and availability of other documents within the designated turnaround time period.

175. The *Bond Buyer* stated that it broadcasts, through its Munifacts News product, material events and time criticial announcements within 15 minutes of their receipt to municipal market participants throughout the country. It stated that it also posts documents within 24 hours of a document's receipt to the *Bond Buyer's* On-line Index which is updated throughout the day. Letter of the *Bond Buyer*. Similarly, Dow Jones Telerate stated that electronic dissemination will allow the turnaround time of 24 hours for an official statement and 15 minutes for secondary disclosure documents on material events to be feasible. Letter of Dow Jones Telerate. Material information is electronically disseminated on a "real time" basis by Bloomberg L.P. Letter of Bloomberg L.P.

176. J. J. Kenny Co. requested that documents be required to be filed as images of original source documents rather than exclusively as coded text. Dow Jones Telerate requested that official statements be filed along with one electronic disk copy of the original word processing\desktop publishing file with the label marked as to which software and version was used. For secondary market disclosure documents, Telerate advises using the NFMA proposed worksheets. The *Bond Buyer* stated that "collection would be most efficient if documents were in ASCII and a common word processing or publishing format."

177. Former paragraph (c) of rule 15c2-12 was proposed to be, and has been redesignated as paragraph (d)(1). This paragraph exempts primary offerings of municipal securities in authorized denominations of $100,000 or more, if such securities: (1) are sold to no more than 35 investors, each of whom the underwriter reasonably believes is capable of evaluating the investment and who is not purchasing with a view to distribution; (2) have a maturity of 9 months or less or; (3) at the option of the holder may be tendered to an issuer at least as frequently as every 9 months.

178. See, e.g., letter of ALHFA; letter of CDFA; letter of NFMA; letter of National Association of Independent Public Finance Advisors; letter of Prudential Investment Corp.; letter of PSA; letter of Washington State Auditor.

179. See, e.g., letter of NAST; letter of SIA.

180. See, e.g., letter of Chemical Securities; letter of Eaton Vance Management; letter of Edward D. Jones & Co.; letter of Morgan Stanley; letter of National Association of Independent Public Finance Advisors; letter of Norwest Investment Services.

181. See, e.g., letter of APPA; letter of the Bank of New York; joint response.

182. See rule 15c2-12(d)(2).

183. See joint response. A number of other commenters expressed concern about the lack of information on issuers in market segments in which the higher proportion of defaults have occurred. See note 182, supra and accompanying text. The effective date for this information undertaking condition on the small issuer exemption will be delayed until Jan. 1, 1996. See Section II.E., infra.

184. See letter of the *Bond Buyer*.

185. See letter of the *Bond Buyer*. The requirements of rule 15c2-12, as amended, may not be avoided by breaking up an offering into several offerings of less than $1,000,000, where the offerings are of the same class of securities and are for the same purpose.

186. See, e.g., letter of ABA Urban Law Section; letter of CIFA; letter of Colorado Municipal Bond Supervision Advisory Board.

187. See, e.g., letter of ALHFA; letter of CDFA; letter of Hawkins Delafield & Wood.

188. See, e.g., letter of Alaska Municipal Bond Bank; letter of Bose, McKinney & Evans; letter of CDFA; letter of Oregon Economic Development Department.

189. See, e.g., letter of ABA Business Law Section; letter of Chapman and Cutler; letter of NABL.

190. Significant indicia of whether an issuer in a revenue-type financing is in fact a part of a larger municipality would be whether the issuer's accounts are reflected in the municipality's financial statements and whether the municipality's officials or personnel manage the separate financing programs.

191. See, e.g., letter of ABA Business Law Section; letter of Day Berry & Howard; joint response; letter of Kutak Rock; letter of the Treasurer of the state of North Carolina.

192. See, e.g., letter of ABA Business Law Section; letter of Kutak Rock; letter of Mudge Rose; letter of National League of Cities.

193. See, e.g., letter of Bank One Corporation; letter of Reliance Trust Company.

194. See, e.g., letter of ICI; letter of McDonald & Company Securities; letter of NABL; letter of National League of Cities; letter of NFMA; letter of New York Dormitory Authority; letter of Putnam Investment Management; letter of state of Utah, Office of the State Treasurer; letter of state of Washington, Office of the State Treasurer.

195. See, e.g., letter of Delaware County Industrial Development Authority; letter of Financial Security Assurance; letter of McNair & Sanford; letter of Smith, Gambrell & Russell.

196. As some commenters indicated, the existence of credit enhancement or other programmatic enhancement features does not eliminate the need for information on underlying obligated persons, particularly where there is a long-term guarantee, because of the potential impact of a default on the pricing of the securities. See letter of Kutak Rock on behalf of Financial Guaranty Insurers; letter of FGIC; letter of Prudential Investment Corp. See also Securities and Exchange Commission, *Report by the Securities and Exchange Commission on the Financial Guaranty Market: The Use of the Exemption in Section 3(a)(2) of the Securities Act for Securities Guaranteed by Banks and the Use of Insurance Policies to Guarantee Debt Securities* (Aug. 28, 1987).

197. See, e.g., letter of ABA Business Law Section; letter of Goldman Sachs; letter of Morgan Stanley; letter of Mudge Rose; letter of Thacher Proffitt & Wood.

198. See, e.g., letter of Morgan Stanley; letter of Mudge Rose; letter of New York Dormitory Authority.

199. Interpretive release at Section III.D. See also letter of the *Bond Buyer*.

200. Rule 15c2-12(d)(3).

201. See, e.g., letter of ABA Urban Law Section; letter of Chemical Securities; letter of Day, Berry & Howard; letter of Kutak Rock; letter of Maryland Department of Economic and Employment Development.

202. See paragraph (d)(3) of the proposed amendments.

203. The exemption has been modified to clarify that the recommendation prohibition will not apply to primary or secondary market trading where municipal securities are exempt at the time of their original issuance. Several commenters noted that the inclusion of the term *a primary offering of* created confusion, based on the stated purpose of the exemption in the proposing release. See, e.g., letter of Kutak Rock; letter of ABA Urban Law Section; letter of Colorado Municipal Bond Supervision Advisory Board; letter of Day, Berry & Howard. The exemption has been modified to delete that term, thus giving the exemption its intended meaning.

204. See paragraph (d)(1) of the proposed amendments.

205. See paragraph (d)(2) of the proposed amendments.

206. Rule 15c2-12(d)(4).

207. See rule 15c2-12(d)(2).

208. See rule 15c2-12(b)(5)(i)(C).

209. Former paragraph (d) of rule 15c2-12.

210. The transactional exemption also has been redesignated as paragraph (e) of rule 15c2-12.

211. See rule 15c2-12(g).

212. 15 U.S.C. 78w(a)(2).

213. 5 U.S.C. 604.

24

Municipal Bond Ratings and Municipal Debt Management

Anthony L. Loviscek
W. Paul Stillman School of Business, Seton Hall University, South Orange, New Jersey

Frederick D. Crowley
Indiana University/Purdue University–Fort Wayne, Fort Wayne, Indiana

I. INTRODUCTION

What are municipal bond ratings? What is their relationship with municipal bonds? What is their purpose in local government finance? How are they determined? What variables influence the ratings? What are their policy implications for debt management? These questions serve as the foundation for this chapter. While the discussion of the first four questions provides an overview of municipal bond ratings, their purpose, and the bond rating process, the heart of the chapter lies with the discussion of the last two questions. In fact, the overriding purpose of the chapter is to forge a new direction in the thinking about active bond rating management. Integral to this purpose, and any substantive analysis of the municipal bond market, is an in-depth discussion of the variables thought to influence municipal bond ratings. This deceptively simple yet unresolved issue continues to create considerable controversy among government officials, investors, bond analysts, and researchers.

The chapter is divided into six major sections. The first section, the introduction, provides background material. Subsections are devoted to municipal bonds, municipal notes, bond ratings, their implication for debt management, and the bond ratings process. The second section examines the issue of bond rating determinants. The subsections include summaries of major studies to date on municipal bond ratings, patterns in the studies, and a critique of them. The third section deals with new directions in bond rating determinants. In the subsections, arguments are presented on what variables should be the focus of municipal finance officials. The fourth section is concerned with a new analytical method for active management of bond ratings, with a subsection on its application. In light of the results, the fifth section offers suggestions for debt management strategies. The sixth section provides a summary and conclusion.

A. Municipal Bonds: Types and Features

At local government levels, few issues are less contested than the need to maintain and upgrade area roads, bridges, sewers, schools, rail systems, and airports. These capital-intensive projects—often referred to as investments in "social overhead capital" or "infrastructure"—require large outlays and yield long-term benefits. Given the nature of their cost-benefit structure, rather than attempting to pay the cost of the projects in a single lump sum, the payment is spread over the projected life of the projects by governments issuing long-term bonds, or debt. In the nomenclature of finance, the bonds are called "municipals" or "munis," and are long-term debt instruments supported by a local government's revenue-raising ability.

Any bond, whether issued from public or private sources, is a legal contract that promises to pay the

buyer, or investor, a stated rate of interest and to repay the principal at the date of maturity.* Municipal bonds
are no exception. They represent debt from a broad category of issuers, such as cities, counties, parishes,
towns, boroughs, villages, and special districts (such as a toll bridge authority). As with all other bonds in
general, their maturities are at least 10 years, and usually up to 30 years.†

As of 1993, there were over 1 million municipal bonds, which make up the vast majority of a U.S.
municipal finance market valued at over $1 trillion. The bonds fall into three broad categories: general
obligation bonds, which are usually referred to as "GO" bonds; limited obligation bonds, the most significant
category being revenue bonds; and industrial development bonds.

Since their inception in the early 1800s by New York City, tax-supported GO bonds have been regarded
as one of the safest long-term investments in the United States. They finance projects that provide the greatest
and most diverse social benefits, and from which no individual profits directly. Examples of such projects
include roads and bridges. The bonds are often called "full faith and credit bonds" because the pledge to make
timely interest and principal payments is strong. That strength comes from the local government's taxing power,
which can be thought of as a lien upon all property owned by the government and the residents within its
jurisdiction.‡ The bonds have been major workhorses for capital fund-raising, and will likely continue to be so
well into the twenty-first century. They currently constitute about 35% of the total volume of municipal issues.

Compared to GO bonds, revenue bonds finance projects somewhat more narrow in their scope of benefits.
These projects fall under the general category of municipal-owned businesses, including parking garages,
airports, hospitals, and stadiums. At a minimum, revenues from the projects must cover operating expenses
and debt payments. During the 1970s and 1980s, revenue bonds became particularly popular for several
reasons: reliance on user fees rather than the unpopular property tax, which creates a lien on people's homes;
the limited capacity of local governments to issue more GO debt; and market innovations that have continued
to favor revenue bond issues.§

Because revenue bonds are not backed generally by taxes, concern over the default risk of the bonds
can be greater than for GO bonds. This observation means that bonds secured from limited revenues should
be evaluated on the basis of revenues over and above that needed for operating expenses. To illustrate, an
airport may be obligated to charge fees sufficient to pay operating expenses after providing 125% coverage
of debt payments.

Industrial development bonds have become integral components in active economic development
strategies designed to finance selected industrial and commercial projects. The goal is to expand local
employment opportunities and, therefore, the tax base. Examples of projects include hotels, shipping ports,
and technology-driven ("high-tech") research centers (e.g., for computer software). Because of the risk of
default for an individual project, the bonds typically represent "pools," or a number of projects. This way, if
one project should fail, revenues from other projects can be used to maintain debt payments.

How safe are these bonds? Alternatively, what is the likelihood that a local government will be able to

---

*A promise to pay interest and principal, however, need not make the bonds marketable. From the issuing authority's view,
"marketable" means selling them at a price (or offering an interest rate) that the authority deems reasonable. From the investor's
viewpoint, marketable denotes the ability to easily price the bonds or, alternatively, convert the bonds into cash. To illustrate, no
investor would buy the risky bonds of a bankrupt corporation that promised to pay interest equal to that earned on safe U.S.
Treasury bonds. In other words, not all promises are created equal. To compensate for the risk that a promise may be broken,
investors demand higher interest rates, or yields. The greater the risk of a broken promise, the higher the yield investors will
demand.
†As of 1993, several corporations have begun successfully issuing 100-year bonds. One expects municipalities and municipal
bond buyers, sooner or later, to embrace longer maturity schedules for municipal bonds. Another feature of bonds, including
municipals, is "callability." If the bonds are issued with a call feature, it allows the issuer—in this case a municipality—to buy
back the bonds if market interest rates fall below the level being paid on the bonds. While this is viewed favorably by
municipalities, it is viewed negatively by investors. As a result and as compensation for the callability risk, investors demand
that callable bonds have slightly higher average rates of return than noncallable bonds.
‡It should be pointed out that a pledge of full faith and credit takes various forms. Unlimited tax-backed bonds represent the
strongest pledge. Limited tax-backed bonds carry legal limits on tax rates that can be levied to support the bonds. Despite the tax
limit, they may be rated as high as unlimited tax-backed bonds if there is sufficient margin within the tax limit to raise the tax
levy easily. There are also "double-barreled" bonds. They are secured by revenues from the project, and are supported by taxes
only if there is a revenue shortfall.
§The increasing popularity of revenue bonds reduced the dominance of GO bonds during the 1970s and most of the 1980s. Between
1987 and 1992, however, GO bond issuance jumped from about 29% of new municipal bonds issued to 35%.

make timely payments of interest and principal? How do local governments and investors monitor this likelihood? These questions are ultimately concerned with the risk that a bond issue will fall into bankruptcy; that is, a local government will default on its payment obligations. Because information on such risk is generally lacking, and because assembling such information can be a formidable task for prospective investors, the market for any municipal bond issue is narrow.[*] To help overcome these information problems or, alternatively, to broaden the market for their bonds, local governments will often have the bonds rated for quality. In this context, "quality" means the safety from the risk of default.[†]

Of the three groups, industrial development bonds are the most controversial and the most risky. While GO bonds are supported by government taxing powers, and revenue bonds by fees charged from the project, industrial development bonds are supported by the creditworthiness of the beneficiary enterprise, not by the government's ability to make timely payments of interest and principal. Support for this point can also be found in current tax law. The 1986 Tax Reform Act eliminated the tax-exempt status of industrial development bonds while maintaining that status for the other municipal bonds.[‡]

Regardless of the type of bond issued, local government officials have a tremendous incentive to issue only the highest-quality bonds. The higher the quality of a bond, the higher its rating will be. This higher rating reflects a lower default risk, making it easier to attract risk-averse investors. The more attractive investors find the bonds, the easier it is for a community to raise the needed capital at a reasonable price, or rate of interest. Yet the potential benefits do not end here. The lower the interest rate, the lower the borrowing costs, which reduces the burden for local governments to raise the needed revenue to make timely interest and principal payments. A lower burden coupled with greater benefits to a community from the projects implies a well-managed government, translating to political support for the incumbent government.

B. Municipal Notes and Commercial Paper: Types and Features

In conjunction with the municipal bond market are the municipal note and commercial paper markets. While the bond market is centered on long-term issues, the note and commercial paper markets represent short-term securities. Municipal notes represent temporary borrowing by local governments to either address mismatching in the timing between the receipt of revenues and the disbursements for operations or to temporarily finance capital projects. They have the same legal features as bonds with the exception that their maturity schedules are much shorter. They are usually issued for a period of 12 months, although some are issued for periods as short as 3 months and others may be up to several years.

As suggested by their definition, it is reasonable to divide municipal notes into two major categories: cash flow notes and bond anticipation notes. Cash flow notes are often referred to as "tax anticipation" notes and are used to even out cash flows. For example, a local government may receive the majority of its annual property tax revenue in December; however, to cover ongoing payments for wages and salaries for the period from July through November, it may issue tax anticipation notes. In another instance, because of a legal mandate to annually balance a budget, tax anticipation notes would be used to cover an operating deficit.

Bond anticipation notes are used for interim financing of capital projects. Three reasons support their existence. First, there is the opportunity to lower borrowing costs. The more funds readily available for a capital project, the more favorable borrowing terms can be. In short, the notes were designed to provide the funds with the sale of bonds used to retire the notes.

---

[*]The information costs could be lessened and the market for municipal bonds could be broadened if there were a larger number and wider variety of investors of the bonds. As part of trading the bonds, the investors would naturally pressure the municipal bond market for timely and accurate information about the financial condition of municipalities. The result would be reliable information at a low cost. However, because of their long-term characteristics and their tax-free interest features, municipal bonds generally appeal only to a selected group of investors. Traditionally, these investors are high-income individuals, banks, and insurance companies. Because this selected group often holds the bonds to maturity, the outcome is not only a narrow market but one in which the bonds are infrequently traded. As a result, not much is generally known about the quality of municipal securities.

[†]Because this view of quality is concerned only with default risk, it is narrow. It does not consider any other kind of investment risk, such as inflation, rising interest rates, or adverse changes in tax laws.

[‡]Local governments claim that they need the no-tax incentive to attract investors. Closer inspection, however, suggests that the reasons are more political than economic. As such, the tax-exempt feature works as an inconspicuous subsidy to local governments. If it were a line item in the federal budget, it might be jeopardized by political vagaries. In fact, Metcalf (1993) offers theoretical and empirical support for the view that federal tax rates affect the desired debt levels of state and local governments. He concludes that there is little economic justification for the tax-exempt status of the bonds.

Second, there is the possibility of efficiency gains. Over a wide variety of projects, municipalities have the choice of either issuing many different bonds or issuing many different notes to be retired by a single bond issue. In practice, the latter approach offers the opportunity of lower finance costs. Third, and often most important, is the potential to reduce long-term interest costs. Notes can be issued in anticipation of changing market conditions. For example, if a drop in long-term interest rates is forthcoming, it behooves municipalities to issue notes now, before the drop in long-term rates, and bonds later, after the drop in long-term rates.

Similar in design and purpose to municipal notes is commercial paper, a short-term, continuously offered, unsecured debt instrument. Its maturity is generally up to 270 days; however, because it is continuously offered, the commercial paper program may be years in duration. As a result, unlike municipal notes, commercial paper is closely linked to the issuing government's long-term debt position. In addition, and further differentiating it from municipal notes, it is generally supported by the issuing government's liquidity position, such as the issuer's liquid assets, a bank line of credit, or a combination of the two.

A caveat is in order. Whether with municipal notes or commercial paper, short-term borrowing is designed to complement long-term borrowing. If short-term structural imbalances exist over the long term in the municipality's financing arrangements, then short-term debt, especially commercial paper, may impinge negatively on the credit quality, or safety, of a government's bonds. If sustained, the result will be higher default risk, which ultimately means a lower bond rating.

C. Municipal Bond, Note, and Commercial Paper Ratings: Definition, Description, and Purpose

A municipal debt rating is a qualitative indicator of the creditworthiness of a local government with respect to specific payment obligations on its debt. A rating is provided for a fee by financial services, such as Moody's Investor Services and the Standard & Poor's Corporation, the two most widely known rating agencies. Ratings are based on three primary considerations: likelihood of bankruptcy or default, the purpose behind the debt, and any protection (e.g., insurance, legal restrictions, and reorganization agreements) for the prospective buyer or investor. Of these three criteria, the overwhelming concern is with the likelihood of default.

Table 1 provides an overview of the ratings and an interpretation of each classification, from the highest grade, such as "Aaa/AAA" or "blue chip," to the lowest grade, "C/D" or default.* Bonds rated from Aaa/AAA to Baa/BBB are known as "investment-grade." Bonds rated below Baa/BBB are "noninvestment grade," and are often referred to as "speculative" or "junk."†

Short-term debt ratings are similar, but on the whole, the range of ratings is not as wide. It runs from a high on notes of "MIG 1/SP-1" to a low of "MIG 4/B-C," and from a high on commercial paper of "P-1/A-1+" to a low of "P-3/A-3" (where MIG stands for Moody's investment grade and SP stands for Standard & Poor's).

Given that bonds make up over 90% of the dollar volume of municipal securities, most of the remaining discussion will be with them and their associated ratings. Moreover, as will be seen, all substantive work on ratings has been concerned with bonds, and usually GO bonds. More discussion on the complementary relationship between bonds and notes will take place under the discussion of the policy implications that underlie municipal bond rating determinants.

While a bond rating or any debt rating is qualitative, it has quantitative implications. The rating is inversely related to the interest rate, or coupon rate, offered on the series of bonds that are rated. Thus, the higher (lower) the bond rating, the lower (higher) the interest cost the issuer must pay to compensate bond buyers for the perceived default risk of the bonds.

The fundamental purpose behind the ratings is to provide prospective investors with a summary measure

---

*Table 1 gives the major classifications. Between each pair of classifications, there are degrees of Aa (AA), A (A), Baa (BBB), etc. For example, Moody's may assign any of the following Aa categories: "Aa1," "Aa2," or "Aa3." Similarly, Standard & Poor's may use "AA+," "AA," or "AA-." For brevity as well as clarity, this study will refer only to the major classifications, which is the standard used in discussion of bond ratings.

†The name *junk bond* originated in the 1980s. It has been more closely associated with corporate finance than municipal finance. Companies engaged in the purchase of other companies often financed the transactions with low-grade bonds, thus the terms *leveraged buyout* with *junk bonds* became part of the nomenclature of financial markets. Nonetheless, mounting fiscal pressures and tax base erosion for U.S. cities, resulting in part from the exodus of population and industry from city districts, may be the harbingers for many new junk bonds in the municipal sector during the 1990s and the twenty-first century.

Table 1   Overview of Debt Ratings

Bond ratings by		
Moody's	Standard & Poor's	Description
Aaa	AAA	Highest grade of bond. Capacity to pay interest and principal in a timely manner is generally believed to be extremely strong.
Aa	AA	Bonds in this category are considered to have a very strong ability to repay principal and interest in a timely manner. They differ in a small degree from bonds in the first category.
A	A	Bonds with this rating have a strong capacity to repay principal and interest, yet are somewhat more susceptible to fluctuations in economic conditions.
Baa	BBB	These bonds are normally considered to have adequate capacity to repay interest and principal. Adverse economic conditions are more likely to lead to a weakened condition and capacity to make payments than bonds in higher categories.
Ba	BB	Bonds rated in this category are lower medium-grade issues with speculative characteristics about them.
B	B	These are low-grade bonds. Default is a possibility.
C	D	These are the lowest-rated bonds. They are in default with very poor prospects of making up payments in arrears and ever repaying principal.

Municipal notes		Municipal commercial paper		
Moody's	Standard & Poor's	Moody's	Standard & Poor's	Description
MIG-1	SP-1	P-1	A-1+	Exceptionally high degree of safety to make timely interest and principal payments
MIG-2	SP-2	P-1	A-1	High degree of safety to make timely interest and principal payments
MIG-3	SP-3	P-2	A-2	Acceptable to strong degree of safety to make timely interest and principal payments
MIG-4	B-C	P-3	A-3	Satisfactory safety to make timely interest and principal payments but may be more vulnerable to adverse conditions than higher rated instruments

of confidence that a municipality will make timely payment of interest and principal. Given the enormous variety of credit characteristics among municipal bonds, as discussed below, ratings represent a convenient method of distinguishing among bonds that appear equally safe. It should be noted, however, that a rating is not a recommendation to investors to buy, hold, or sell a local government's bonds. It only represents, clearly more than any other factor, the likelihood that the bonds will fall into bankruptcy.

How valuable is a rating? This is a crucial question for two reasons. First, bond ratings are an elective;

that is, there is not a legal mandate for an issuing local government to have its bonds rated. The need to have bonds rated lies with the potential market for the bonds. For example, a local bank or insurance company may agree to underwrite the entire municipal bond issue at a satisfactory market rate of interest. In such instances, bond ratings are unnecessary.

On the other hand, if an issue is especially large, the local financial community may be unable to accommodate the municipality's request for financing a capital project. As a result, a bond rating—especially a high one—carries two potential benefits. It affords investors unfamiliar with the community an opportunity to readily assess the default risk of the issue, and at the same time, it expands the potential market for the municipality's bonds. As a result, investor decision making is facilitated, and with access to more investors, the community is much more likely to raise the necessary funds without having to resort to intense competition with other investments (e.g., U.S. government bonds, corporate bonds, and stocks); that is, without having to offer a significantly higher rate of interest as an incentive to attract investors. In short, bond ratings aid both buyers and sellers of bonds.

Second, should a community feel that a bond rating would give it access to more potential investors, it should also be aware that an efficient municipal bond market renders rating information superfluous.[*] This is indeed possible, especially when viewed in light of the time-consuming and laborious bond rating process (discussed below). The municipal market, however, unlike its federal government and corporate counterparts, is not as well known. In addition, municipal bonds are traded infrequently. Consequently, municipal financial information is incorporated into municipal securities more slowly than information for other securities markets. The implication is that a substantive reason exists to have a simple, information-enhancement mechanism, such as ratings. Without them, the municipal bond market would have much more difficulty incorporating new and relevant information into the price, and therefore the rate of return, of a bond issue.[†] As a result, it is reasonable to conclude that a rating serves as a valuable predictor of the credit quality of a municipal bond issue.

In theory, the ratings range is wide. Unlike some corporate bond issues, however, municipal bonds have low default risk because few local governments have ever defaulted.[‡] Moreover, even if a local government should fail to make timely interest and principal payments, it does not, unlike a private enterprise, cease as a going concern. This is because it still must provide basic services, from police and fire protection to water treatment. As a result, the vast majority of municipal ratings are in the investment-grade categories, or Baa/BBB and higher.

The low default risk need not translate into many Aaa/AAA ratings, however, nor does it mean that debt is never rated as noninvestment grade. To illustrate, Table 2 displays bond ratings on GO debt, as of July 1993, for some of the nation's major metropolitan areas. The table shows that Moody's awarded the Aaa, or blue-chip, rating to the debt of only two cities, Los Angeles and San Diego. On the other hand, Moody's gave its lowest investment grade rating (Baa) to the debt of three cities: New Orleans, New York, and St. Louis. It gave noninvestment grade, or junk ratings, to the bonds of Detroit (Ba) and Philadelphia (Ba).

By comparison, Standard & Poor's judged only the GO bonds of Dallas to be worthy of an AAA rating.

---

[*]In the finance literature, an "efficient" municipal bond market has come to mean one in which all new and relevant information about a local government is rapidly incorporated into the price of its bonds. This outcome, so the argument goes, stems from the behavior of investors who stand ready to immediately tap any profitable opportunity. Given that the rating process may take up to several months, especially for new governments with new bond issues, it is conceivable that the bond market assimilates the informational content of a bond rating well before the rating is published.

[†]When viewing the "thinness" of the municipal bond market—the specialized investors and the infrequency with which the bonds are traded—and the lack of easily available information about the past, current, and future financial condition of local governments, it is not surprising that bond ratings may be viewed as valuable predictors of creditworthiness.

[‡]The major exception in the twentieth century occurred during the depths of the Great Depression between 1929 and 1933. Over 4,700 municipalities defaulted on almost $3 billion of debt. However, most of these problems were corrected by 1940, an enviable record compared to private financial and nonfinancial corporations for that period. Since World War II, the most famous case of municipal bond default was New York City in 1975. Rating agencies responded predictably and strongly. During the year, Moody's lowered the New York's general obligation rating from A—investment grade—to Caa—highly speculative or junk. Standard & Poor's suspended the city's rating until March 1981, when it reinstated an investment grade rating of BBB. Curiously, the city's debt was downgraded in the late 1960s, but then upgraded in the early 1970s after considerable pressure was placed on rating agencies. However, the default by New York City was not the largest dollar default in history. That notoriety goes to the Washington Public Power Supply System. In 1983, it defaulted on $2.25 billion of municipal bonds. In bond circles, the issue has come to be known derisively as "Whoops." As of 1993, investors into the Whoops issue had recovered only $0.34 on the dollar.

Table 2   Bond Ratings for Selected Municipalities
(July 1993)

Municipality	Rating Agency	
	Moody's	Standard & Poor's
Atlanta, Ga.	Aa	AA
Baltimore, Md.	A	A
Chicago, Ill.	A	A
Cincinnati, Ohio	Aa	AA
Cleveland, Ohio	A	A
Columbus, Ohio	Aa	AA
Dallas, Tex.	Aa	AAA
Detroit, Mich.	Ba	BBB
Houston, Tex.	Aa	AA
Los Angeles, Calif.	Aaa	AA
Milwaukee, Wis.	Aa	AA
Nashville, Tenn.	Aa	AA
New Orleans, La.	Baa	A
New York City, N.Y.	Baa	A
Philadelphia, Pa.	Ba	B
Phoenix, Az.	Aa	AA
Saint Louis, Mo.	Baa	BBB
Saint Paul, Minn.	Aa	AA
San Antonio, Tex.	Aa	AA
San Diego, Calif.	Aaa	AA
San Francisco, Calif.	A	AA
Seattle, Wash.	Aa	AA

The bonds of Detroit and St. Louis were rated BBB, while those of Philadelphia were rated B, noninvestment grade. Note as well that the two agencies do not necessarily agree on the likelihood of default risk. This has occurred for the bonds of eight cities—Dallas, Detroit, Los Angeles, New Orleans, New York, Philadelphia, San Diego, and San Francisco—more than one-third of the sample. In all cases, they differ by one rating. In five of the cases, Standard & Poor's had the higher rating. Although not shown in the table, a similar pattern exists at the county level. Of the hundreds of counties whose GO debt was rated by both agencies, only about 10% received an Aaa/AAA rating.* This is further evidence of the exacting requirements necessary to achieve a blue-chip rating. As indicated in Table 1, local governments should note well the phrase "capacity to pay interest and principal in a timely manner is generally believed to be extremely strong."

Although most municipal debt is rated as investment grade, the penalty for not having the highest bond rating, or receiving a bond rating decrease, can be severe. Noting that higher bond ratings carry lower interest rates, it is easy to see that the difference in interest costs between ratings can translate into millions of dollars of additional revenue that must be raised to cover interest and principal payments. To illustrate, during the 1980s and early 1990s, Moody's rated the GO debt (which is supported by the local government's taxing authority) of San Diego as Aaa. As a result, the city's bonds were easily sold to investors, had low interest costs, and carried a small tax burden for the city.

On the other hand, for the same period, Moody's judged the default risk of New York City's general obligation debt to be Baa, owing in part to ongoing financial concerns that stemmed from its bankruptcy in 1975. This meant that New York had to pay about one-half a percentage point higher in interest than its western counterpart. Thus, New York City's bonds were more difficult to sell, had higher interest costs, and

---

*Additional information on bond ratings is found in Moody's *Municipal and Government Handbook* (1992) and Standard and Poor's *Municipal Ratings Handbook* (1993). These issues are annual. Standard & Poor's also publishes a weekly supplement called *Creditweek: Municipal*. It contains current information on financial and economic developments of state and local governments.

carried a higher tax burden. More precisely, in interest costs alone, New York City had to raise about $70 million more per year in taxes than if its debt had been rated as Aaa.*

The role and importance of municipal bond ratings is likely to increase into the twenty-first century for at least four reasons. First, it is unlikely that the municipal bond market—in itself a complex market because of the long-term and tax-free interest characteristics of the bonds—and municipal financing in general will become simpler, rendering ratings obsolete. As well, it is unlikely that the municipal market will be as efficient as the U.S. Treasury or corporate bond markets, in which the issues are much more frequently traded and in which much more is known about the issuers.

Second, and related to the first point, beyond guidelines set by the Government Accounting Standards Board, there is neither a set of uniform reporting procedures for municipal revenues, costs, and debt, nor a set of specific guidelines for determining the creation of the numbers. As a result, the need remains for an independent assessor to facilitate the demand for and supply of municipal bonds. For the foreseeable future, that need will be filled by bond rating agencies.

Third, the ongoing realignment of U.S. government responsibilities, with the federal government parceling out more duties for local governments, pressures municipalities into new and higher expenditure and revenue obligations. As evidence, during the 1980s and into the early 1990s, long-term local government debt levels jumped from approximately $300 billion to $600 billion, more than double the nation's inflation and income growth rates. Because not all of this debt has been easily sold, local governments have increasingly relied on bond ratings, and will likely continue to do so, to broaden the market for their bonds.

Fourth, an aging infrastructure and expanding populations eventually will require renovations and increases in social overhead capital. Local governments will have to respond by issuing more long-term debt. As regards the third point, the result is increased reliance on bond ratings. This point further suggests that the ability of local governments to finance renovation and expansion of their infrastructure by bonds and to minimize the corresponding interest costs will depend in part on the way rating agencies perceive the creditworthiness of local governments.

D.   Municipal Bond Ratings, Debt Management, and Good Government

What are the implications of bond ratings for debt management of local governments? Although specific recommendations on answers to this question will come later, there is the need at a basic level to point out the link between the ratings and debt management. Because the ratings reflect the interest cost of borrowing, and because borrowing costs on GO debt are supported by taxes, a local government needs to properly time the issuance of its bonds. For example, if its GO debt has an AA rating but the rating agency gives it a negative outlook, it behooves the government to issue the bonds as soon as possible, ahead of any potential or predictable downgrade in its rating. Issuing the bonds after a downgrade narrows the market for the bonds, which pushes up interest costs and eventually the taxes needed to make timely debt payments. However, if an upgrade appears imminent, it would be prudent to postpone the issue until after the rating determination, thus holding down interest costs and taxes. The government may even inquire with the rating agency as to what is needed for a higher rating, or to maintain the current rating, such as the acquisition of more property or the attraction of new industry. Yet underlying the question of the timing of the bond issue is the following question: What variables influence bond ratings? In other words, which variables should municipal officials monitor to increase the likelihood that the bond issue is properly timed? This important question is treated in depth in a later section.

The relationship between debt management and bond ratings has implications for the ongoing debate between "good" versus "bad" government, or "efficient" versus "inefficient" government. Abnormal increases in local government debt may be viewed as a signal of government inefficiency: unnecessary projects, sloppy tax revenue generation, and inferior debt management practices. If prolonged, the consequence may be a lower bond rating, pushing up interest costs. Overall, the result is a general decline in social welfare. While always cause for concern, two points are in order. First, government, or public,

---

*The half percentage point, or .005, multiplied by the city's approximately $14 billion in debt equals $70 million. Although this is an oversimplification, it does show the consequences of having less than a blue-chip rating. It should be kept in mind that this difference is not constant. Between 1981 and 1985, for example, the difference was almost an entire percentage point, which would have roughly doubled the interest payments.

investments in infrastructure are designed to complement, not conflict, with private sector activity. Such investment from the private sector, when it does occur, is less than optimal because the incentive to provide it is relatively small, owing to the characteristics of the project (e.g., private cost of building, maintaining, and charging tolls on a major highway is prohibitive). Second, because such projects yield a long-term stream of benefits, it is imminently sensible to practice the matching principle of accounting: finance the project over the life of the benefits. Combined, these two points argue that increased debt may be a sign of efficiency rather than inefficiency.

Bond ratings can play a unique and substantive role in the debate. A positive external effect of bond ratings—essentially a check against bad debt management—is that the greater the perceived inefficiency of a project, the more likely the added debt burden will be viewed unfavorably. The result may be a downgraded bond rating. This is because inefficient projects drain the revenue-raising capacity of a government. As a result, eventually a government's ability to make timely debt payments is called into question, putting downward pressure on the rating.

A direct and immediate effect of a downgraded rating is a more narrow market for the local government's bonds. There are, however, significant indirect effects. The more unfavorable the rating, the more likely that the taxes that ultimately support the bonds, or fees that the government must charge for the services, will be increased. The higher this increase, the greater the likelihood of a voter protest, which serves as a check on inefficient project and debt management. In addition, because a bond rating is designed to reflect the long-term features of the bond issue, an unfavorable rating is one sign of potential long-term financial difficulties.

Unfortunately, in recent times long-term financial pressures have become increasingly problematic for governments at all levels to correct. For local governments, higher revenue has traditionally come from higher property taxes. As is well known, however, the property tax has been increasingly unpopular with voters, owing to its sometimes low correlation with income, the vagaries of property tax assessment procedures, and its conspicuousness. In addition, and further limiting government power to raise taxes, bond-financed projects may be subject to a voter referendum.[*]

Because bond ratings reflect a long-term financial commitment, only strong and substantive change in a community's debt payment ability (e.g., change in the long-term growth of the tax base) will lead an agency to change a bond rating. The incentive for rating agencies to do otherwise is virtually nonexistent. The more often they change a rating, the more they invite criticism that they are unsure of the government's debt repayment abilities.

The behavior of rating agencies carries an important implication for debt management: a lower bond rating is not likely to be reversed in the near future. Thus, the community's revenue-raising ability likely comes under additional pressure. The obvious lesson is that municipal officials need to be circumspect of proper debt management as it applies to bond ratings. The failure to do so, as pointed out in the case of New York City, whose rating was suspended by Standard & Poor's between 1975 and 1981, results in greater financial burden on a community, exacerbating the problem of providing infrastructure renovation and expansion at a tolerable cost.[†]

To sum up and conclude, a bond rating may serve as a check against fiscal mismanagement, increasing the likelihood of government support for the correct mix of public and private goods and services. Upgrades may be interpreted as one sign of improved government management, while downgrades may be viewed as a

---

[*] As evidence of the unpopularity of the property tax, in 1978 California's Proposition 13 limited total public debt to 1% cash value of the property tax base and severely limited increases in property tax rates. In 1981, voters in Massachusetts passed legislation that limited debt throughout the state to 2.5% of property value. The ramification of these debt and tax ceilings has been mounting budgetary difficulties, as witnessed in 1991 by the bankruptcy of Bridgeport, Connecticut and the fiscal duress faced by Philadelphia. In 1991, the result for GO bonds—not unexpectedly—was more downgrades than upgrades. In 1992, Standard & Poor's gave more upgrades than downgrades, but the dollar volume of downgrades was greater. As expressed here, a voter referendum is cast in a somewhat negative light. On the positive side, a referendum is one gauge of community support for a project. Moreover, Standard & Poor's says that the degree of community support may affect the rating it gives a bond issue.

[†] This is not to say that the municipal market is without vexing institutional problems. Because of the municipal bond market's complexities and information problems, there have been assertions that the market suffers from undue political influence (e.g., local officials having close ties with investment bankers), disclosure difficulties (e.g., standard information on the "ability to pay" for municipals is nonexistent), and poor pricing (e.g., securities are infrequently traded and usually little information is known about the quality of the issue).

move in the opposite direction.* More specific information on bond ratings in this regard is provided in a later section.

E.   Municipal Bond Rating Process

The bond rating process is, in a word, complex. This is supported by the wide range of projects financed by rated bonds with diverse characteristics. For example, GO bonds have a large variety of credit characteristics. There are both unlimited and limited tax GO bonds. Some governments are well below their imposed taxing limits. Other communities, however, are critically close to their limits. Some communities require a referendum to issue GO bonds, while other communities issue bonds without any backing by property tax revenue. Moreover, some bonds are fully supported by property tax revenue; however, the revenue largely originates from one source, such as a local industry (which may or may not be in sound financial condition.) How do investors choose from among all these diverse GO bond characteristics? Bond ratings provide a convenient means of standardizing all of these attributes. This provides investors with a criterion to select from a large pool of bonds that appear on the surface to have equally safe features.

The same kind of discussion applies to revenue bonds. Some of the projects financed by bonds that agencies rate are water and sewer facilities, gas lines, airports, parking garages, ports, toll facilities, transportation equipment, hospitals, and marinas. Nonetheless, there are projects financed by bonds that agencies in general will not rate, owing to the unpredictability and volatility of the credit conditions that affect the projects. These include recreational and sports facilities that are supported only by the revenue generated by the enterprise, and housing projects in which the sponsoring agency has little or no operating experience.

Even more complex, and indeed risky, are industrial development bonds. As mentioned, these bonds are used to finance aggressive economic development strategies designed to attract growth industries such as high-tech companies to expand the employment base. Here is where the controversies—financial, economic, and legal—begin. What are growth industries? What variables attract them? What are their chances for success? How long will they locate in the area? These questions, and others, lead to bond issues that vary widely in structure and volume. Nonetheless, there is a common feature across development strategies. Planned revenues to be generated from the projects are pledged as payment for debt obligations. Because of the underlying risk associated with an individual project, rating agencies generally rate only "pools" of these bonds across several different projects. Even these bond pools are deemed risky; rating agencies are slow to rate them above an A and are inclined to give them noninvestment grade, or junk, ratings.

Regardless of the type of bond to be issued, rating agencies require preparation of detailed financial statements, an oral presentation that outlines the debt and the reasons for it, research by bond rating analysts, analysis of the issue's quality by the rating agency, discussion of the analysis by the rating agency's rating committee, and determination of the rating. In addition, there is the possibility for the issuing government to appeal the decision before it is made public.

The rating process for a new bond issue is depicted as series of steps, listed below in the order in which they occur.

1.   The government requests a rating.
2.   The government completes the rating agency's application form and sends it to the rating agency.
3.   The rating agency assigns a rating team to review the material and complete any additional research into the bonds and the issuing government.
4.   The rating research team reports to the rating committee.
5.   The rating agency meets with the issuing government.
6.   The rating agency prepares a rating profile for the issuing government's bonds.
7.   The rating committee discusses and votes on both the quality of the issue and the issuing government's ability to make timely debt payments.

---

*There are limits to the interpretation of this statement, however. As will be seen, bond rating decreases may occur for reasons apart from government inefficiency. For instance, population and industry have been moving south and west since the colonial era. As a result, some communities have experienced bond rating downgrades not because they have necessarily become inefficient but because their economic bases, on which taxes depend, have shrunk. Regardless of efficiency considerations, all else being equal, a shrinking tax base makes it more difficult to meet debt obligations. The implication is that the key lies in the change in the rating, not the rating itself. In the end, one should be cautious in claiming that, for example, one community's AA-rated debt reflects greater efficiency than similar A-rated debt of another community.

8. The rating agency notifies an authorized representative of the issuing community of the rating.
9. There is public disclosure of the rating.

The minimum information rating agencies reportedly need to rate GO and revenue bonds can be summarized and divided into the following categories:

1. Annual financial reports for at least the last 3 years and audited by independent certified auditors (e.g., accountants or state/local auditors)
2. Current budget statement
3. Current capital renovation and expansion program
4. Official statements of financing
5. Description of the specific program requiring financing
6. Planning document, including zoning provisions
7. Statement of cash flow, especially if short-term borrowing is foreseen
8. Description of current short-term and long-term debts, including maturity dates of each issue
9. Legal documentation on debt issuance and service, plus information on borrowing and tax levy capacities
10. Statement on source(s) and allocation of projected revenues to cover the interest and principal payments

To be safe, the local government should prepare its financial statement according to guidelines set by the Government Accounting Standards Board. As mentioned, however, these guidelines provide for considerable latitude. Thus, a detailed description of the accounting procedures used in the compilation of the data is necessary. Any deviations from these guidelines must be reported to the rating agency, and any accounting change that affects financial statements needs to be explained in detail.

At a minimum, municipalities need to report evidence of their past, present, and future ability to meet their debt obligations in a timely manner. They must assemble key balance sheet data for a 3-year period, with 10-year trends on annual debt service (generally as a percentage of total expenditures) and tax revenue coverage, if the issue is one of general obligation. As part of this reporting, property assessment, a major indicator of revenue enhancement potential, should be provided for at least the next 5 years and broken down into its basic components: residential, industrial, utility, and commercial. The issuing government must also describe any borrowing to cover operating expenses and deficits, and whether any debt service has been met by loans from other governments. In addition, qualitative information affecting either the issue or issuer should be provided. This includes evidence of community support, legislation affecting the issue, and whether or not any consultants used in estimating the feasibility of the project were connected to the issuer as a bondholder, underwriter, employee, or financial advisor.

Ratings are monitored, and remain in effect as long as the agencies are apprised of current developments on an ongoing basis. For GO bonds, these include annual financial reports, budgets, changes in taxpayer and employment bases, and changes in state and federal aid. For revenue bonds, these include progress reports, engineering updates, and revenue generation.

Regardless of the type of bond issued, a rating reflects the long-term financial and economic features of a municipality, necessitating a steady flow of information from municipality to rating agency. If a local government fails to supply the information on a timely basis, the result is a withdrawal of the rating. A long-term rating may also be withdrawn if critical information is not provided on the issuance of short-term debt that has no rating. This information should encompass current cash flows and lines of credit.

Because rating agencies are private organizations with a professed goal of profit maximization, they charge fees for their services. The approximate range is from $2,500 to $75,000, depending on the size and complexity of the issue. As a guide, the fees are based on the size, frequency, and complexity of the debt issuance, in addition to the time and expense associated with the rating process.

II. DETERMINANTS OF MUNICIPAL BOND RATINGS

What are the variables that influence municipal bond ratings? One way of answering this question is to check published sources of Moody's and Standard & Poor's. Following Cluff and Farnham (1984, pp. 90–91), we find that Moody's reportedly examines four categories: debt analysis, financial analysis, government analysis, and economic analysis. The agency asserts that it analyzes thirty variables. Examples across the four categories include debt burden, debt history, assessed property value, tax rates, tax structure, revenue trends, expenditure trends, form of government, locational advantages, family income, age of housing, and industrial shifts.

Standard & Poor's also declares that four areas are critical; however, compared to Moody's the categories and components are somewhat different. The categories are as follows: economic base, financial factors, debt factors, and administrative factors. The total number of components or variables is twenty-seven. Examples across the categories include income levels and rate of income growth, employment mix and labor force growth, population, age and composition of the housing stock, revenue structure, debt burden, debt issuance history, debt payout schedules, form of government, and impressions of professionalism.

As implied in the discussion, it would be fair to say that Moody's relies more on financial analysis (e.g., debt and revenue variables) than its counterpart, while Standard & Poor's relies more on economic base characteristics (e.g., income and population variables). While knowledge of these variables may help narrow the range of choice among hundreds of possible variables, the list leads to important unresolved questions. For example, precisely what is meant by "debt burden?" Should tax rates be high or low? What is meant by "revenue structure?" Which form of government is viewed in the best light? In addition, does Moody's truly rely on all thirty variables? If it does, are the variables weighted equally? If they are not, what weight should be placed on each variable? The same questions apply to the twenty-seven variables reportedly used by Standard & Poor's. Although rating agencies have offered their services for over 50 years, satisfactory answers to these questions continue to be elusive.

Leading into the studies, we can ask these same questions more specifically. Do financial accounting variables, such as per capita debt, debt to assessed property value, and cash flow, strongly influence the ratings? Do demographic variables, such as population growth, affect the ratings? Do economic variables, as represented by income and employment figures, matter? If there are affirmative answers to these inquiries, to what degree does each of the variables matter? However appealing and simple answers to such questions appear, widespread disagreement exists among municipal officials, underwriters, investment analysts, and researchers on the answers. This has serious implications. Without consensus, little can be concluded or recommended beyond the discussion thus far, about possible improvements in municipal bond financing and debt management.

Why has consensus proved elusive? There are several reasons. First, the rating process is qualitative; it does not reportedly rely on a simple formula or on criteria that are easily understood. Second, rating agencies reportedly examine a wide variety of criteria: balance sheet information, business cycle data, and legal restrictions. It has proved difficult to pinpoint, on average, which criteria are the most important.

Third, the information in the second point can be grouped into four categories: debt burden, budget management, revenue generation, and socioeconomic environment. However, there seems to be significant differences between the two major rating agencies in their respective approaches toward these four categories. As will be seen, Moody's appears to emphasize financial and budgetary aspects, while Standard & Poor's reportedly leans toward the economic environment.* Fourth, there is no published information that indicates precisely what lies behind a rating.

The fourth point deserves further discussion. Rating agencies have never publicly revealed either what variables are, on average, the prime determinants of bond ratings, or the weight to assign each variable. Presumably there are several reasons for this. First, given the number and diversity of municipalities (e.g., cities, counties, boroughs, parishes, villages), and their varying characteristics, the agencies hesitate to claim that a "common thread" may connect the communities. In other words, they wish to avoid the accusation of comparing municipal "apples" to municipal "oranges." Second, and as an extension of the first point, rating agencies do not operate from government mandate, subpoena powers, or voter referendum. The nature of the business—a financial service offering recommendations on the quality of securities—is such that "reputation is everything." In other words, confidence in rating agencies rests with the belief that the ratings are systematically the result of a sound, objective, and thorough examination of the quality of the bonds, which

---

*For further information, and to compare the criteria used by Moody's and Standard & Poor's, see Moody's *Municipal and Government Manual* (1992) and *Standard & Poor's Municipal Finance Criteria* (1993). Differences in rating criteria appear to extend to bond insurance as well, the oldest potential rating enhancement method for supporting payment of interest and principal. Traditionally, Moody's does not appear to view bond insurance as significant support, choosing instead to rate the bonds on the merits of the project and the payment ability of the issuer. Standard & Poor's, however, reportedly sees bond insurance in a positive light. It has claimed to give AAA ratings to bonds issued by primary insurance corporations, such as the Municipal Bond Insurance Association or the American Municipal Bond Assurance Corporation.

includes the ability of the issuing government to make timely debt payments. Understandably, rating agencies wish to protect their reputation, and therefore are very selective in their release of information, especially if they perceive it may be controversial. In short, they wish to avoid two accusations: either using the wrong information or using the right information incorrectly.

In light of the discussion, what have researchers concluded in their studies of municipal bond ratings? Has there been any move toward consensus? What has been learned from the studies? Where are the pitfalls in the studies? How can the studies be improved? Addressing these issues is a major purpose of this chapter, and considerable time and attention are given to them in the next section. The implications of these issues are critical to policy analysts and practitioners. As mentioned previously, for efficient debt management, they need to know which variables are the most likely to change bond ratings and, in turn, how they might effect desired changes in these variables. If even modest movements in this direction are not possible, then any attempt at substantive improvement in government efficiency, which encompasses the proper mix of public and private goods and services, is frustrated.

A. Studies on Municipal Bond Ratings at a Glance

Although the municipal rating services offered by Moody's and Standard & Poor's were begun in 1918 and 1940, respectively, studies that have attempted to discern municipal bond rating determinants did not begin until the late 1960s. This is largely because until then bond ratings and their determinants were not a public issue. Of the three kinds of bonds, the studies have been overwhelmingly concerned with replicating GO bond ratings, and primarily those of Moody's, owing to the availability of data. Although hundreds of articles have been written on municipal bond ratings, the focus in this study is on research that has relied on statistical modeling. These studies tend to offer more systematic and objective evidence of the variables that influence the ratings compared to purely descriptive studies. As will be seen, as of the 1990s, there have been about twenty published studies based on a variety of models and many variables.

The construction of models on municipal bond ratings was stimulated when Moody's downgraded New York City's debt in 1965 from A to Baa, followed by a similar move by Standard & Poor's in 1966. In a contentious report delivered before a congressional subcommittee, Goodman (1968) seriously questioned the methods the rating agencies used to assign ratings. The implication was that they used unreasonable if not arbitrary criteria. This prompted several polemical studies that either supported Goodman's testimony or tried to show why municipalities and investors should have confidence in the agencies (e.g., Reilly, 1968; Harries, 1968; and Riehle, 1968). The Twentieth Century Task Force (1974) studied these concerns by discussing the fairness of rating agencies, their ability to measure risk, and their responsiveness to changes in market conditions. Despite the questions raised about the criteria, researchers have studied the bond rating issue under the assumption that rating agencies reasonably judge the credit risk of municipal debt.

The variables used in the studies are dominated by financial accounting criteria, including various measures of debt, revenue, expenditure, and cash flow. Other categories of variables are geography, population, race, and income.[*] Two statistical techniques have been used across the studies. One is discriminant analysis, a method that assigns a municipality's rating to one of two or more groups [i.e., the method discriminates between (among) two (or more) groups based on a set of variables]. The other is regression analysis, a method in which independent variables (e.g., financial accounting measures) are used to help explain various bond ratings.[†] Despite the difference in names, in theory the two methods have many similarities.

To date, the emphasis has been on the ability of the variables to replicate GO bond ratings. Unfortunately, despite the systematic attempts, the results have been very mixed. Some studies report that the models replicated 80% or more of the ratings. Others report results that are far less sanguine, usually not much better than chance. Close inspection of the studies shows that many different variables have been used, with over

---

[*] A distinction between financial accounting variables and income variables is in order. A financial accounting variable is one that attempts to measure managerial performance based on generally accepted recording principles (e.g., debits and credits). An economic variable, although it, too, reflects performance, is one that measures the behavioral aspects of an enterprise based on optimal resource allocation.

[†] As will be explained, two regression models, known as "linear probability" and "probit," have been used. They are special cases of the classic textbook regression model. Discussions of each kind of model can be found in any of a number of textbooks that deal with model building and applications in business and the social sciences. One such textbook is Maddala (1988).

60% being classified as financial accounting. The dominant tool has been discriminant analysis, which has been used in about 75% of the studies. As mentioned previously, the studies have not reached consensus, as will be seen by the number and types of variables concluded to be primary determinants across the studies. These include debt as a percentage of income, short-term debt as a percentage of general revenue, working capital as a percentage of total debt, housing characteristics, a community's dependence on tourism, and the percentage of the population that is black.

Beyond the differences in specification across the models, at this stage it should be pointed out that the application of discriminant analysis in virtually every study that employed it may be flawed. Evidence and explanations for why this may be so, such as violations of basic assumptions or an incorrect application of discriminant analysis, are in forthcoming sections. Suffice it is to say that the results from the discriminant models are questionable, and in some studies highly so.

B.   Overview of the Major Studies

For two reasons, it behooves the current study to provide a summary of each of the major studies. First, the summary provides practitioners, bond rating analysts, and researchers with a perspective on the evolution of bond rating studies. In doing so, it points out possible problems and pitfalls in the studies, facilitating perusal of the literature, comparison of the studies, and an assessment of a difficult literature. Second, it provides a foundation for the comments, questions, and criticisms that the current study raises about research to date and its attempt to address them.

At the outset, to keep the focus on bond ratings, it should be noted that the overview examines studies whose primary concern has been to isolate the variables that determine municipal bond ratings. As such, it deals with the methods used and the results obtained in major studies to date on bond ratings of U.S. metropolitan areas. As mentioned earlier, the discussion is restricted to studies that involve the application of statistical modeling. These studies have the greatest likelihood of revealing the determinants of municipal bond ratings, and therefore hold the greatest promise for new insights into municipal financial management.

Because the studies under examination have dealt with GO bond ratings, little will be said about revenue bonds, school bonds, sewer bonds, and the like. Nothing will be said about state bond ratings. Also, although there will be some discussion of the relationship between bond ratings and interest costs, no attempt will be made to evaluate the research on this relationship. This is because its primary purpose has not involved the issue of bond rating determinants.

One of the very first studies was done by Tyler (1968). He used a debt-wealth index to indicate a community's ability to pay its debts. He specified the index to be a function of thirty variables comprising debt, revenue, income, and employment measures that he claimed his company used in assessing default risk. He used the specification to grade municipal debt on a scale of 00 to 100, where 00–14, 15–29, 30–44, and 45–59 indicate, in order of increasing default risk, four investment grades (equivalent to Aaa, Aa, A, and Baa). Bonds rated 60–100 were considered to be noninvestment grade. Although he did not subject his method to statistical tests, his approach is significant in that every major subsequent study used a subset of the types of variables he felt influenced municipal bond ratings.

Carleton and Lerner (1969) provided the study that strongly influenced all major subsequent studies on municipal bond ratings. As a result of the issues surrounding New York City's downgrading in the late 1960s, they attempted to replicate five classes of Moody's bond ratings, from Aaa to Ba, for 491 communities nationwide for 1967. Beginning with six variables, they pared the variable selection to four and applied discriminant analysis to debt as a percentage of assessed property value, average tax collection rate, the logarithm of population size, and a dummy variable for school districts. The first two variables are financial accounting variables and are thought to measure managerial performance of municipalities—an appealing way of trying to explain municipal bond ratings.

To support their results and to adjust for classification biases, they applied their model to another sample—usually referred to as a "holdout sample"—which included 200 communities.[*] They found that all four variables were significant discriminators; however, replicative accuracy was only 53% for the original

---

[*]The statistical literature has shown that the classification accuracy of discriminant analysis is biased upward without a holdout sample. A holdout sample is formed by splitting the original sample into two groups, the holdout usually being the smaller of the two. The discriminant function is estimated for the larger group. The estimated function is then used to classify the holdout group, which results in a more conservative classification accuracy. For further information, see Eisenbeis (1977, pp. 893–894).

sample (491), and only 50% for the other sample—not better than chance. However, rather than concluding that rating agencies may be remiss in their duties, they suggested that a different specification and a different application of discriminant analysis were needed.

Horton (1969 and 1970) used Carleton and Lerner's data base in an attempt to improve upon their results. Instead of using discriminant analysis, as Carleton and Lerner did, he used regression analysis. He also used a somewhat different set of variables. Like Carleton and Lerner, he used debt as a percentage of assessed property valuation and population; however, he relied on geographic location rather than tax collections and school districts.[*] His objective was rather different, as well. He attempted to classify Moody's ratings into either investment grade (Baa and higher) or noninvestment grade (Ba and lower).

He used a sample of 150 communities nationwide, 75 of which had investment grade ratings. To adjust for possible classification bias, following Carleton and Lerner, he also applied his model to a holdout sample of 50 communities, 25 of which had investment grade ratings. His results implied that the population, debt burden, and geographic location variables exerted the strongest influence on the ratings. Of the original sample, 83% were classified correctly; of the second sample, 80%. Overall, he concluded that his study was superior to that of Carleton and Lerner.

Like Horton, Bahl (1971) employed regression analysis to help determine which variables accounted for the difference in credit risks across communities. Compared to Horton's two-classification approach, however, he examined each of the top four bond ratings. In other words, he tried to explain why one municipality's GO bonds were rated Aaa while another municipality's bonds were rated Baa. (Horton was concerned only with whether or not a municipality's bonds were rated Baa or higher.)

Another unique aspect of his work was a comparison of Moody's ratings with Standard & Poor's. He examined GO debt rated by both agencies for 473 communities nationwide between 1969 and 1971. He tried to explain the differences in bond ratings across communities and across rating agencies by using debt as a percentage of personal income, debt as a percentage of property value, per capita debt, and population.

In both groups, he found that only per capita debt influenced bond ratings. Unlike Horton, he did not test the model for classification accuracy. He speculated that the model could be improved by using economic base variables, such as income and employment, and other financial accounting variables, such as revenue–expenditure imbalance and a community's dependence on a single revenue source. However, he did not support his discussion by testing these variables.

In contrast to previous studies, Hempel (1973) did not examine bond ratings per se; however, his study is well within the scope of studies on bond ratings. He examined two sets of communities, those that defaulted on their debt and those that did not. He applied both discriminant analysis and regression analysis to financial accounting and population variables for 45 Michigan cities—28 of which had defaulted on their debt payments—for 1930 through 1937. Beginning with 23 variables, and in spirit with the study by Carleton and Lerner, he concluded that the essential variables were as follows: debt as a percentage of assessed property value, percentage of taxes uncollected, per capita notes outstanding, population growth, debt as a percentage of taxes levied, and a tax levy per $1000 of assessed property value. The model correctly classified 76% of the cities. As did previous researchers, he adjusted his model for classification bias by using the equivalent of a holdout sample. The classification accuracy, however, dropped to 56%, but was still somewhat higher than what Carleton and Lerner achieved.

Rubinfeld (1973) expanded the efforts of, in particular, Horton, Bahl, and Hempel. Using regression analysis, he derived a rating index based on Moody's four highest ratings for New England communities for 1970. Unlike previous studies, the issue he addressed was to determine the variables that led to an Aaa rating. The Aaa rating was a function of eight variables. Four dealt with financial accounting data: overlapping debt, net debt to assessed property value, total assessed property value, and the percentage of taxes uncollected. One variable measured income, two variables controlled for communities with debt rated below Aaa, and one variable controlled for geographic location; specifically, whether or not a community was in Massachusetts.

The results showed that overlapping debt, median family income, the dummy variables for ratings below Aaa, and geographic location had the strongest association with a Aaa rating. The model correctly classified

---

[*]He controlled for geographic location by using a 0–1 variable, sometimes referred to as a dummy or dichotomous variable because it can assume only one of two values. As an example, if a community is located in, say, the Northeast, the community is assigned a "1." If it is located in any other region (e.g., Midwest or South), it would be assigned a "0." In effect, the test is to see if there is a significant difference or pattern in bond ratings between communities given a 1 versus those given a 0.

67% of the bond ratings. He also applied discriminant analysis to the same variables and found the classification accuracy, at 68%, to be noticeably higher than that achieved by Carleton and Lerner at 53%. Although he did not use a holdout sample to adjust for possible classification bias, he concluded that his approach was satisfactory.

In line with Bahl's objective, Morton (1975) compared the investment-grade bond ratings of Moody's with those of Standard & Poor's for 1972. He selected eleven variables. They represented a combination of those used in previous studies, such as per capita debt, ratio of debt to true property value, interest payments as a percentage of expenditures, population, geographic region, and per capita income. Two unique variables included in the model were a community's dependence on tourism and the percentage of the population that was black.

In Morton's national sample of 223 cities, Moody's rated the bonds of 170 cities; Standard & Poor's rated 112. Following previous research, he also adjusted his model for classification bias by examining 24 additional ratings of Moody's and 19 ratings of Standard & Poor's. For the entire sample, his method correctly classified 58% of Moody's ratings and 66% of Standard & Poor's. For the additional ratings, the classification accuracy was 46% for Moody's and 63% for Standard & Poor's.

Overall classification accuracies were only marginally higher than what Carleton and Lerner achieved. In general, Morton concluded that Moody's relied more on financial accounting information, such as the ratio of debt to assessed property value, whereas Standard & Poor's relied more on socioeconomic data, such as per capita income. He also found that the two agencies agreed on 70% of the ratings. Of the 41 cases that differed, Standard & Poor's rating was higher 39 times.

Michel (1977) tried to replicate Moody's investment grade bond ratings (i.e., Aaa to Baa) from 1962 through 1971 for the fifty largest U.S. cities. Following previous research, especially that of Carleton and Lerner, he applied discriminant analysis to twelve financial accounting variables, such as per capita debt, per capita revenue, uncollected taxes as a percentage of debt service, and debt as a percentage of assessed property value. Dividing the period under study in half and forming two sets of samples consisting of 115 cases each enabled him to perform four sets of analyses.

He concluded that the most significant discriminators were per capita debt, per capita revenue, and uncollected taxes as a percentage of debt service. The classification accuracies ranged from 35.7% to 59.6%, with 58.2% for a holdout group. These results were no more accurate than what Carleton and Lerner achieved.

Unlike any previous studies, however, his results, along with those found in previous research, led him to criticize investors and researchers. He concluded (p. 587) that the variables "typically used to assess risk do not accurately reflect the underlying risk associated with municipal issues," and this is largely because these variables "are not reflective of economic reality." There are two significant points to this quote. First, it assumes that Moody's used an approach that was easily approximated by discriminant analysis applied to financial accounting variables. Second, and curiously, Michel's remarks seem either to have been unnoticed or disregarded. With one exception, as will be seen, every subsequent study was strongly influenced by the variable selection used by Carleton and Lerner.

Aronson and Marsden (1980) attempted to reproduce the bond ratings for twenty-four of the twenty-five cities that Moody's highlighted in a 1977 study . Their sample was for communities rated from Aaa to Baa. In addition to attempting to replicate ratings across these categories, they sought to do the same to a two-rating classification, Aaa–Aa and A1–A–Baa, where A1 is between A and Aa. They applied discriminant analysis to seven financial accounting variables—which included per capita debt, average tax rate, and net debt as a percentage of true property value—and two socioeconomic variables, which included the percentage of the population that was black.

Their findings differed from previous studies in two ways. First, they found that the black population variable was the most powerful discriminator. Second, the classification accuracy across the five categories was 83.3% and across two categories was 95.8%, both big jumps over the accuracies achieved by Carleton and Lerner, as they noted. Both percentages were far and away the highest to date. They also found that a specification with the black population variable, debt as a percentage of true property value, and surplus revenue as a percentage of total revenue correctly classified 81% of the ratings across two categories. However, they did not use a holdout sample in any of their applications.

Stock and Robertson (1982) criticized previous studies, such as Carleton and Lerner, Horton, and Michel, for failing to consider different types of GO bonds. They examined whether or not classification accuracy would increase over that of previous studies by applying discriminant analysis separately to 152 city bonds, 75 of which comprised a holdout sample, and 392 school bonds, 193 of which comprised a holdout sample.

They confined their study to bonds issued in Oklahoma and rated in the late 1970s by the Municipal Rating Committee of Oklahoma, not by Moody's or Standard & Poor's. They examined the four highest ratings. Eight of their ten variables dealt with financial accounting information, including net debt per capita, logarithm of net debt, net debt as a percentage of assessed property value, and a sinking fund levy. The remaining variables were the logarithm of population and average per capita income.

For both types of bonds, they concluded that the debt—particularly the logarithm of net debt—and population variables had significant discriminatory power. They found tax variables to be more influential with the ratings of school bonds than with the ratings of city bonds. The classification accuracy of the holdout sample for city bonds was 71%; for school bonds, 87%. For a holdout sample, the accuracies were clearly the highest found to date.

Raman (1981) departed from previous studies by trying to replicate changes in either direction from Moody's A rating (1975–1979) nationwide for thirty cities with populations of 50,000 or more. He applied multiple discriminant analysis to twelve variables. Similar in spirit to the variables used by Carleton and Lerner, Horton, and Michel, he used ten financial accounting variables, such as per capita debt, per capita revenue, and the ratio of debt to general revenue. The two remaining variables dealt with population and geographic region. He examined upgraded and downgraded ratings, with several stages used to test the stability of the results.

His results showed that per capita revenue, the ratio of short-term debt to general revenue, and a dummy variable for geographic region were generally the strongest predictors. He found that classification accuracies ranged from 80% to 100%, significantly higher than in most previous studies. Classification accuracy was verified with a holdout method used for small samples. This procedure is called Lachenbruch's U Method.[*]

Raman (1982) used the same techniques in an attempt to replicate Moody's ratings for twelve cities. Each city had a population over 300,000 and had either an unchanged A rating or was downgraded from an A rating between 1971 and 1980. He used five financial accounting variables, three of which dealt either with cash flow from operations or net working capital as a percentage of GO debt; therefore, they were different from the variables used in his other study.[†] He concluded that short-term debt as a percentage of revenue, working capital as a percentage of debt, and cash flow were the primary predictors. The classification accuracy was 83%, high compared to previous studies.

Copeland and Ingram (1982) examined the timeliness and reliability of financial accounting data in predicting changes in Moody's ratings. They applied discriminant analysis to a subset of twenty-eight financial accounting variables thought to influence bond ratings. The variables were calculated for each of 168 cities nationwide for the period from 1975 to 1977. By rating change, 35 cities experienced downgrades in their debt, 77 received upgrades, and 56 had no change. Two models were constructed. One model was used to test the data 1 year prior to the rating change. Another model was used to test the data 1 year after the rating change. Copeland and Ingram employed eight variables in the prior-year model and seven variables in the postyear model. These variables included short-term debt turnover, total per capita revenue, per capita revenue from own sources, reliance on the property tax, revenue from own sources as a percentage of total revenue, "vital" expenditures as a percentage of total expenditures, and revenue diversification.

They found that short-term debt turnover, property tax reliance, and revenue from own sources as a percentage of total revenue to be the main predictors. The classification accuracy of the prior-year model for the entire sample was 79%. For the postyear model, it was 83%. However, when adjusting for possible classification bias, they found that each accuracy declined to 55% and 70%, respectively. As a result, they (p. 287) felt that financial accounting data can accurately reflect past changes in bond ratings but may not be sufficiently reliable "to instill faith in their usefulness as predictors of risk change."

Farnham and Cluff (1982) questioned the results obtained in previous studies in three ways. First, some samples either were too small (e.g., the twenty-four in Aronson and Marsden's study) or were confined to a single region (e.g., Rubinfeld's study). Thus, general inferences drawn from these studies are suspect. Second, classification accuracy has varied according to the number of rating categories used (e.g., Carleton and Lerner used five, Raman used three, and Horton used two). Third, they criticized the variables used in previous studies.

---

[*] For a description of this approach, see Eisenbeis (1977, pp. 893–894).
[†] Caution needs to be used when reading Raman's paper. It is not clear whether cash flow is divided by GO debt, because he (p. 47) defined two variables to be the same.

In an attempt to overcome these weaknesses, they used a sample of 680 cities nationwide that had Moody's ratings of Baa and higher for 1977. They applied discriminant analysis to 35 variables that Moody's cited as bond rating determinants. They separated the variables into four groups: "debt" (e.g., debt as a percentage of assessed property valuation), "financial" (e.g., total general revenue, percentage change in total revenue, and assessed property valuation), "economic base" (e.g., population, percentage of population that is nonwhite, and occupied housing units) and "administrative" (e.g., percentage of current taxes collected). Following previous research, of the 680 cities, they used 205 to control for classification bias.

Given the variables used, their findings departed somewhat from those in prior research. They found that only one financial accounting variable—assessed property valuation—was among the ten most significant variables. They also found that the logarithm of population and the percentage of houses built before 1940 were very significant. Classification accuracies ranged from 62% to 68%, higher than in some previous studies (e.g., Carleton and Lerner, 1969; 50%) but lower than in others (e.g., Stock and Robertson, 1981; 87%).

They also split their sample into four population categories to examine the effect of city size. When using all 35 variables, they found that the overall classification accuracy improved to over 70%. They obtained similar results to these when controlling for geographic location. Overall, they concluded that Moody's employed considerable information to arrive at ratings, suggesting that future studies need to incorporate a larger set of variables than had been normally used in studies to date.

Cluff and Farnham (1984) examined Moody's ratings of 976 cities and Standard & Poor's ratings of 271 cities for 1977. Their objective was to compare the rating criteria between the two agencies, as both Bahl and Morton did. Unlike either author, however, they employed a special form of regression analysis designed to more accurately measure the importance of variables than discriminant analysis and ordinary regression methods.[*] They employed 23 of the 35 variables used in their previous study. The difference was in the number of financial accounting variables. Only four of the variables—compared to fifteen in their earlier study—were specified: per capita debt, total general revenue, percentage change in total revenue, and assessed property valuation. The remaining variables were either socioeconomic (e.g., population density, percentage of the population that was nonwhite, and percentage of total housing that was owner-occupied) or locational in nature (e.g., cities located in the Northeast).

They found that housing variables, such as the percentage of owner-occupied houses and the percentage of one-unit structures, were the primary influences on the ratings of both agencies. The financial accounting variables, such as per capita debt and assessed property valuation, were found to significantly influence Moody's ratings but not Standard and Poor's. Overall, the results supported Morton's findings.

Departing from previous work in scope and purpose, Loviscek and Crowley (1988) examined changes in bond ratings assigned by Moody's to examine whether or not a community received a bond rating increase. Their purpose, however, was not to analyze classification accuracy but to test the extent to which bond rating upgrades could be explained by economic base and population variables. In contrast to previous studies, they did not employ any financial accounting variables. Their argument was that financial accounting information was too controversial to be used reliably. They supported their argument by citing the conclusions reached by Michel and by Copeland and Ingram, both of whom questioned the reliability and usefulness of financial accounting information as a predictor of bond ratings.

The model used was simple. Three of the four variables were unique in the sense that no previous study had employed them. The variables measured the diversification of the industrial base, an income variable designed to measure the ability of an area to attract economic activity, and a variable to control for whether or not a community was located in an energy-surplus area.[†] The fourth variable measured population growth.

They examined changes in bond ratings for 117 counties between 1971 and 1980, a period of high and rising energy prices. Using regression analysis, they found that all four variables helped explain bond rating upgrades, and concluded that future studies on bond ratings needed to give greater weight to economic base variables and less weight to financial accounting variables.

Loviscek and Crowley (1990) used a similar theme to address the following question: What is in a Aaa

---

[*]The regression technique is known as "probit analysis" and was created specifically to handle some of the problems of applying ordinary regression analysis to data sets similar in nature to those used in bond rating studies.

[†]An energy-surplus area was defined as one that exports more coal, oil, and natural gas than it imports. Following the logic used in previous studies, if a community was located in an energy-surplus area, say Texas, it was assigned a 1; otherwise, it was assigned a 0.

rating? However, rather than using population growth and energy-surplus variables, they used debt as a percentage of assessed property value and a dummy variable for Aa ratings. Using a number of techniques, they concluded that industrial base diversification, income, and debt to assessed property value were the primary influences on Moody's determination of a Aaa rating. They also reported, using a holdout technique, classification accuracies that exceeded 80%, one of the highest achieved to date.

C. Patterns in the Studies: A Critical Analysis

Of the published studies, Bahl (1971), Morton (1975), and Cluff and Farnham (1984) examined the ratings of Moody's and Standard & Poor's. Thus, there have been twenty attempts to model the behavior of rating agencies. Overwhelmingly, replicating Moody's ratings has been the dominant concern, having been attempted twenty times to three times for Standard & Poor's ratings.[*]

Three conspicuous patterns emerge from the studies. First, beginning with Carleton and Lerner's study, financial accounting variables, particularly debt burden and revenue variables, dominated the variable specifications used in the studies. Second, discriminant analysis was the preferred model, having been used in thirteen of the twenty attempts. Third, a major concern was with the replicative accuracy of a model. With the exception of Horton, who used regression analysis and examined two categories, investment-grade or noninvestment-grade, the models used up through Michel's study had low replicative accuracy. The later studies, from Aronson and Marsden through Loviscek and Crowley, had noticeably higher classification accuracies. We now turn to a critical examination of each of these three patterns.

1. First Pattern: Variables

A total of 122 different variables was specified among the models, of which 73, or 60%, can be classified as financial accounting.[†] Revenue variables were used 15 times; per capita debt, 14 times; and debt as a percentage of assessed property value, 14 times. Population, income, and geography variables comprised 27, or 22%, of the variables. Population measures were used 15 times; variables accounting for geographic region, 10 times; income measures, 8 times; and racial mix composition, 6 times. The findings suggest that rating agencies relied on debt burden, revenue, and population variables, with consideration given to geographic location and racial mix composition.

Perusal of the results across all the studies suggests that there was a marked tendency for researchers to use a variety of debt, revenue, and "other" variables, many of which were found to be significant. As a result, a closer inspection of these categories is in order. Considerable variation, for example, exists among the revenue variables found to be significant. These include general revenue, percentage change in general revenue, surplus revenue as a percentage of general revenue, tax levies, sinking fund levies, general revenue as percentage of income, per capita revenue, tax collection rate, and the degree of reliance on the property tax.

Substantial variation is also present in the debt variables found to be significant. In addition to per capita debt and debt as a percentage of assessed property value, there is the logarithm of total debt, total debt as a percentage of general revenue, total debt as a percentage of income, short-term debt as a percentage of total debt, short-term debt as a percentage of general revenue, and working capital as percentage of total debt.

The same statement can be made, and more strongly, for significant "other" variables. A sample of them includes assessed property value, housing characteristics, vital expenditures as a percentage of total expenditures, the educational level of the population, municipal payroll, the logarithm of the number of municipal employees, a community's dependence on tourism, a dummy variable for school districts, and a dummy variable for Aa bond ratings.

Although some pairs of the significant variables could be strongly related, the variety of variables makes

---

[*]Readers should be aware of some inconsistencies and omissions in the studies. For example, Rubinfeld did not define a variable (AGROWS) among his nine-variable model. Raman (1982, p. 47) defined two of his cash flow variables to be the same. Farnham and Cluff erred in reporting their discriminant results. They reported the generation of results from a nonlinear, or quadratic, routine; however, in reality, they used a linear routine. All possible versions of the *Statistical Package for the Social Sciences* (1975 and 1983) that they reportedly used produce only linear results.

[†]This is not to imply that there are no similarities in the 122 variables. Some of them, such as the ratio of debt to assessed property value and the ratio of debt to true property value, are strongly related.

inferences drawn from the results across all studies risky. Moreover, the most significant variables in many of the studies came from the "other" categories: per capita notes outstanding (Hempel), overlapping debt (Rubinfeld), logarithm of net debt (Stock and Robertson), short-term debt to general revenue (Raman), short-term debt turnover (Copeland and Ingram), a community's dependence on tourism (Morton), percentage of the population that is black (Aronson and Marsden), housing characteristics (Farnham and Cluff), and income potential (Loviscek and Crowley). In the end, it is difficult to arrive at a consensus from the disparate results.

Even where similarity exists, questions can be raised. For instance, although geographic region and racial mix composition variables were found to be significant in a number of studies, they beg several questions. Why is a particular region viewed (un)favorably? Is it due to the region's industrial base, market growth, or natural resource base? If so, this effect should be incorporated in economic base and income variables. In fact, as Cluff and Farnham have reported, Standard & Poor's typically relies on economic base information more than financial accounting information, as seen in the following statement: "The economic base is the most critical element in determining an issuer's rating" (*Municipal Finance Criteria*, 1993, p. 20). Regardless, none of the researchers who controlled for geographic region offered an explanation.

Why does racial and ethnic composition matter? An explanation cannot be found in the studies. Because bonds and not people are rated, accusations that rating agencies are racially and ethnically biased are misplaced and would be damaging to the reputations of the agencies as independent assessors of bond quality. Is it because too many of these individuals have low incomes? Conceivably, their social needs could cause government expenditures to increase but contribute little to tax revenue, thus limiting a local government's ability to meet its debt payments. This effect, however, should be observed in income, government expenditure, or tax variables.

2. *Second Pattern: Applications of Discriminant Analysis*

Having been used in thirteen of the twenty studies, we find discriminant analysis to have been the dominant tool. Although not reported so far in the summary of the studies, there are different methods of applying discriminant analysis. Expectedly, some are to be preferred over others, depending on the characteristics of the data. To keep the discussion simple, which fits the purpose at hand, there are two types of discriminant analysis, linear and nonlinear. The nonlinear version is quadratic discriminant analysis. It can be applied in either a stepwise—one variable at a time—or continuous fashion. Of the twelve studies that used discriminant analysis, nine used the linear approach, with eight of them employing stepwise estimation (which is critically discussed in the next section.) The other three applications were reportedly quadratic.

To achieve an optimal solution under the linear method in municipal bond rating studies, at a minimum, two criteria must be met. First, the variance, or dispersion, of the variables of one group (e.g., bonds rated Aaa) must equal the variance of the variables of the other group (e.g., bonds rated Aa and below). (In the case of several groups, the variances across all of them must be equal.) Second, the variables taken together must be, in a statistical sense, normally distributed.

In practice, the two assumptions are easily violated, with a strong possibility of biased results. Municipal bond rating studies are no exception. How sensitive have researchers been to possible violations in these assumptions? This issue is now examined.

When the variance assumption is violated, linear discriminant analysis is no longer applicable. The nonlinear, or quadratic, rule now applies. Understandably, researchers prefer to avoid the quadratic approach. As shown by Eisenbeis and Avery (1972), it is much more difficult to apply and the results are much more difficult to interpret. Nonetheless, the evidence suggests that this rule should be used as the sample size decreases, as the number of independent variables increases, and as the difference in variances across the groups of ratings increases (Dillon, 1979).

Only Raman (1981), Stock and Robertson, Copeland and Ingram, and Farnham and Cluff tested for the equality of the variances. Judging from the variables used, it appears that Hempel, Aronson and Marsden, and Raman (1982) should have tested for this equality as well. Each used small samples and twenty-three, nine, and five variables, respectively. Moreover, following Pinches and Mingo (1975), we conclude that the variables used by Carleton and Lerner, Rubinfeld, and Morton mandated the quadratic rule, a line of reasoning cited by Stock and Robertson.[*]

---

[*] In each study, a dummy, or (1,0), variable was used. Unlike a continuous variable, such as per capita debt, this variable usually creates problems for the linear rule. At a minimum, the sample needs to be split by the dummy variable.

Concerns can be raised about the studies in which the equality of variances was tested. Raman found that the variances were not equal but used the linear discriminant rule, claiming that it may be robust to violations in the assumption of equal variances. Eisenbeis and Avery (1972, pp. 8, 16, 37–52) and Dillon (1979, p. 373) offer substantive reasons to seriously question Raman's position. Studies by Farnham and Cluff (1982, p. 436), and Stock and Robertson (1981, p. 156), and Copeland and Ingram (1982, p. 281) reportedly tested the assumption but provided little evidence of their test.

The last point leads to a facet of these three studies that is potentially more disturbing. The authors claimed that the variances were unequal, and therefore reportedly employed quadratic discriminant analysis. Conceptually, this is correct; however, the evidence suggests they used a linear rule. First, they did not report coefficients for the squared and interaction terms that are integral to the quadratic rule. Second, Stock and Robertson (1981, pp. 156, 158, 159) and Copeland and Ingram (1982, pp. 281–283) reported the coefficients occur only if the linear rule is used.[*] Moreover, the statistical routines that Farnham and Cluff used are set up only for linear methods. The upshot, of course, is the disconcerting thought that the results generated and conclusions drawn in each of these studies, as reported, may well be invalid.

The second assumption, which concerns the normal distribution of the data, has significant implications for significance tests and classification accuracies. The greater the violation of this assumption, the more wary researchers should be about their results and conclusions. Unfortunately, if the data are found to be badly skewed, short of deleting the problem variable—an approach that should be avoided—the only viable recourse is getting more data, which still may not correct the problem. Even taking a transformation of a nonnormally distributed variable may produce normality for one variable but does not assure normality for all variables taken together.

None of the authors reportedly tested for normality of the variables. Some, such as Carleton and Lerner (1969), Raman (1981), and Farnham and Cluff (1982), used logarithmic transformations but did not report any tests of normality for any of their samples or subsamples. Consequently, and once again, there is reason to doubt the validity of the results found and conclusions drawn in studies that have applied discriminant analysis. At this stage, one can only hope for one of two things: either the variables were at least close to a normal distribution or discriminant analysis is insensitive to violations in the normality assumption.

3. Third Pattern: Replicative Accuracy, the Success of Later Studies, and Stepwise Estimation

The studies by Aronson and Marsden (1980) through Cluff and Farnham (1984) either had higher replicative accuracy or were able to isolate the determinants of ratings more clearly than the authors of earlier studies. Of the earlier studies, only Horton had considerable success. On the surface, the pattern suggests considerable progress toward isolating the determinants of ratings. However, as implied in the previous sections, questions can be raised about the degree to which bond rating determinants have been isolated. For example, 80 variables were specified in the studies by Aronson and Marsden (9), Stock and Robertson (10), Raman [(1980) 12], Raman [(1981) 5], Copeland and Ingram (9), and Farnham and Cluff (35). Unfortunately, none of the variables is common to all the studies. Per capita debt appeared four times. Debt as a percentage of property value was used in three studies. Population, total property value, income, nonwhite population, and housing ownership each were used in two studies. This would not be a significant problem if, as mentioned previously, there was not substantial variation in the variables concluded to be significant.

As an additional concern about the variables used across the studies, note the tempered conclusions of Aronson and Marsden (1980) as well as of Raman (1982). Aronson and Marsden (p. 103) downplayed the influence of their strongest discriminator, the percentage of the population that is black: the variable "may well be a proxy for a large set of measures." They concluded (p. 104) that "a larger sample and perhaps a greater number of variables is needed."[†] Their view supports the questions raised earlier about the efficacy of racial mix composition variables. Raman's model (p. 46), by his own admission, is questionable: "given the small sample size, the number of explanatory variables had to be kept to a minimum." As evidence,

---

[*]At a very technical level, as can be found in each of the articles, the authors reported the percentage of total discriminating power accounted for by each variable by considering the size of the standardized discriminant coefficient relative to the proportional variance accounted for by each discriminant function. This method is valid only when the variances are equal; that is, for the linear rule (Eisenbeis, 1977, pp. 884–885).

[†]Their statements should not be underemphasized. Parry (1985) showed that Aronson and Marsden's results are very likely biased. For example, through statistical validation techniques, he concluded that their high classification accuracies were significantly overstated.

although he examined changes in bond ratings in both of his studies, he used seven fewer variables in his 1982 study compared to his 1981 study. When coupled with the other questions raised about Raman's studies, one is led to doubt the validity of his conclusions.

Lovell (1983) has shown that stepwise estimation is part of "data mining," or the search for significant results without regard for theory or accurate general inferences. The result of data mining is significant bias in the results. Thus, inferences about the population of bond ratings, if not ruled out, are very limited. Adding to the problem is the fact that a number of stepwise estimation methods are available.[*] Seven of the studies involved stepwise estimation. These include those by Carleton and Lerner (1969), Morton (1975), Michel (1977), Aronson and Marsden (1980), and Raman (1981 and 1982). Of these, the work of Aronson and Marsden is especially open to criticism, because they used three different stepwise routines.

4. Summary

In summary, although the results suggest that measures of debt burden, revenue, population, geographic location, and racial mix composition influenced bond ratings, major concerns can be raised about the findings. Over 100 variables—60% of which were financial accounting—were used across the specifications, leading to wide variation in the variables found to influence ratings. In the applications of discriminant analysis, researchers often overlooked the need to check carefully for violations in the assumptions that underlie discriminant analysis. In addition, the broad use of stepwise estimation calls into question the generality of the results. In the end, it is difficult to conclude that researchers have satisfactorily addressed the issue of rating determinants.

III. NEW DIRECTIONS

The purpose of this section is to offer new directions in municipal bond rating studies, directions that, we hope in the end, will move municipal officials, underwriters, and researchers toward consensus among the many possible municipal bond rating determinants. To take an eclectic stance with respect to the literature, we follow the recommendations of Michel (1977) and Loviscek and Crowley (1990). Combined, their essential arguments may be expressed threefold. First, rather than relying exclusively on financial accounting information, we propose that economic data be the primary reference. Second, industrial base diversification, a variable that has only begun to be explored systematically for its impact on municipal finance costs, should be examined as part of the replacement set for financial accounting information. Third, in the interest of a parsimonious set of variables, we argue for a smaller and more easily managed set. Several views motivate the suggestions.

First, recall that Michel (1977) concluded that the financial accounting statistics used to date, undoubtedly the primary information source in bond rating studies, fail to reflect accurately the underlying risk associated with municipal issues and fail to reflect economic reality. This is an obvious call for more accurate measurement of "ability to pay." The candidate we propose is income data, such as wages, salaries, dividends, interest, and rent. The data also have the advantage of being "tighter"; that is, much less subject to manipulation and misinterpretation than financial accounting information.

Second, unquestionably the relationship between the rate of return from municipal bonds and default risk is positive, indicating that buyers of bonds wish to avoid risk and will certainly not take on greater risk without greater return. Yet offering investors greater returns carries a serious trade-off for local governments: higher interest costs and ultimately higher taxes. How can the risk and, in turn, interest costs be reduced? Although one obvious approach is simply not to issue more debt, an alternative recommendation, which relies on active management of the local economy, is to promote a diversified industrial base. An economy that has a diversified industrial or economic base depends on a variety of industries for its economic well-being. As Loviscek and Crowley (1990) have strongly argued, it allows the risk of untimely interest and principal payments to be spread over a number of sources, rather than just one or a few. In short, we embrace the well-known phrase "Don't put all your eggs in one basket."

Third, unlike much of the literature, we propose a small number of variables. As justification, we cite

---

[*]The stepwise method can be either forward or backward. In the forward case, variables are entered one at a time until a threshold is reached. In the backward case, all variables are initially included. Then they are deleted one by one until a threshold is reached. The threshold can be any of many statistical criteria.

the large body of evidence from the social sciences suggesting that a relatively simple model may effectively capture most of the expert judgments in such situations as that of bond rating determination. For example, in judicial proceedings, it is argued that judges overestimate the weight they place on minor details and underestimate the importance they give to a few primary variables. In addition, the subjects—perhaps even bond raters—are largely unaware of their actions. As further support, Kaplan and Urwitz (1979) cited this body of studies to construct a model on bond ratings.[*]

A. Income Variables: Measures of Ability to Pay

Previous studies have, both explicitly and implicitly, argued that tax variables are the primary determinants of bond ratings. Undoubtedly, variables such as per capita revenue and assessed property value can strongly influence the flow of tax revenue used to make timely debt payments. Nonetheless, such variables do not measure the *ability* to tax. A municipality's personal income, the sum of its earnings from wages, salaries, rents, interest, profits, dividends, royalties, and transfer payments is well grounded in economic theory and evidence as the primary engine of tax revenue generation. Even an implicit tax variable, assessed property valuation, ultimately rests on the income of the property owners. Moreover, it needs to be emphasized that it is not what investors view to be the correct variables but what rating agencies perceive as the proper variables. As a result, we propose that personal income variables replace tax variables as indicators of a community's ability to make timely interest and principal payments. All else being equal, the higher its personal income level, the greater the maturity of the municipality and the more confident investors will be in its ability to raise the revenue necessary to make timely debt payments. The result, all else being equal, is a higher bond rating.

By themselves, income levels may not be completely satisfactory. While they indicate economic maturity and a strong current ability to pay debts in a timely manner, they may not accurately indicate *future* payment ability. As an additional variable, income *growth* of a community may be as important because the key lies in the municipality's long-term future ability to make timely payments. The more robust the income growth and the more predictable that growth is for the long term, the more likely a municipality will receive and maintain a high bond rating.

As another critical adjustment, ability to pay should be measured in relative terms, not in absolute terms. By their sheer size, large communities have higher personal income levels than small ones. As a result, there is a size bias in the data. A reasonable alternative is personal income per person or per taxpayer. For yet greater accuracy, and where possible, the income should be adjusted for both inflation and cost of living.[†]

B. Industrial Base Diversification: Measures of Risk Reduction

The timely flow of tax revenue is influenced not only by income but by the base upon which the income is driven. That base represents a community's employers—its industrial base. In what follows we argue that industrial or economic base diversification promotes stability of revenue and therefore reduces the default risk of a municipality's bonds.

The assertion comes from the argument that a diversified industrial base reduces cyclical movements in economic activity—the "ups" and "downs" in the economy.[‡] These movements, or swings in income, create uncertainty, which translates into risk, because the debt payments must be paid whether the economy is in a "boom" or "bust" period. Unfortunately, the busts—when debt payment ability is most in doubt—are difficult to predict. Thus, municipalities must stand ready to shield themselves as much as possible from the risk of economic downturns. One way of doing so is to promote a diversified industrial base. A diversified base ensures that the revenue used to meet debt obligations comes from a variety of sources. The result is a more predictable flow of revenue and a lower default risk.

Traditionally, the variability in economic activity is inversely related to the degree of diversity in the

---

[*]Unlike the studies reviewed, Kaplan and Urwitz examined corporate bond ratings. Since Moody's and Standard & Poor's each use the same rating scheme for both municipal and corporate bonds, and since a similar controversy about municipal bond ratings exists for corporate bond ratings, Kaplan and Urwitz's argument applies.

[†]Another variation is called "income potential." Recognized by regional and urban analysts, it is a measure of the ability of an area to attract additional economic growth. As mentioned, Loviscek and Crowley (1988) used a measure of it in their study.

[‡]For a rigorous analysis of diversification, see Conroy (1974) and Brewer (1985).

employment base. All else being equal and put simply, the more a community depends on a single industry for its employment and revenue generation, the more prone it is to wide swings in economic activity. The result is greater uncertainty about its debt payment abilities, which significantly reduces the likelihood of receiving a high bond rating.

As an illustration of the implications of diversification for municipal finance, energy-surplus states, such as Louisiana, Oklahoma, and Texas, enjoyed above-average growth rates during the 1970s. This was a period of a dramatic increase in energy prices—a fivefold increase that brought a surge in economic growth. However, the surge was short-lived. The sharp decline in energy prices during the 1980s brought a rash of economic problems that severely affected, among other industries, real estate and banking, leading to a surge in bankruptcies. One financial consequence of this swing in economic and financial activity was lower bond ratings for many communities.[*] In short, communities that depend on one or a few industries for their economic well-being are vulnerable to any shock that negatively affects these industries.[†] The key to reducing the impact of these shocks and, therefore, promoting a stable flow of revenue, is a diversified industrial base.

How is industrial base diversification measured? Fortunately, there are several measures available. In all cases, one begins with area employment data. The simplest measure is to employ a "naive" one. Following the research of Evans and Archer (1968) on asset diversification, we can link the naive approach to the total number of employers in the community. The hypothesis is that the larger its employment base, the more likely a municipality's economic base will be diversified. As an analogy, the larger a shopping mall is, the more likely a consumer will find a wide variety of stores. From this measure, one can move to more sophisticated measures, which rely on a comparison of the municipality's employment per industry to the nation's employment per industry. As discussed by Mathur (1970), Kort (1981), and Brewer (1985), the measures are the "coefficient of specialization," "national average," and "entropy."

C. Financial Accounting Variables

In terms of new directions in bond rating research, the emphasis so far has been exclusively on economic base variables: income and diversification. Is there a role for financial accounting variables? We argue that the answer is "yes," although the role is significantly reduced compared to studies to date. Four considerations motivate this position. First, of the seventy-plus financial accounting variables used to date, the one used most frequently and found to be a significant predictor of municipal bond ratings is total debt outstanding to assessed property value. Second, this variable is not easily approximated from either income or diversification variables. Third, as judged from its manuals and the publication of local government data, Moody's seems to emphasize this variable. Fourth, while personal income is arguably the best measure of a taxpayer's "ability to pay" taxes on residential property, it falls short when commercial and industrial properties are considered. These are critical components of property tax revenue.

With respect to financial analysis, bond rating agencies seem to view debt as a percentage of assessed property value as a measure of municipal "leverage." In corporate financial analysis, municipal leverage is analogous to debt as a percentage of the firm's equity or market value. Put simply, the ratio of debt to assessed value is a measure of financial risk; specifically, debt burden capacity. All else being equal, the more debt the municipality has issued, the more leveraged its financial structure, and the greater the financial risk that the municipality may not be timely with its interest and principal payments. Thus, to round out the specification, we propose that total debt outstanding to assessed property value be the third and final variable.

As a summary, three points have been argued. First, as a measure of the ability to pay debts in a timely manner, income variables are more accurate measures than financial accounting variables. Second, by promoting a diversified industrial base, a community may systematically reduce the default risk of its debt. Third, studies on municipal bond ratings should rely on a smaller set of variables than typically recommended in the literature. To conclude, it is recommended that three variables be used: real per capita income, industrial base diversification based on area employment, and debt to assessed property value. In the next section, a test of these three variables is conducted, along with application of a technique designed to reveal

---

[*]As evidence, both New Orleans and Houston lost at least one bond rating between 1982 and 1987. Moreover, prior to 1982, Houston's GO debt was rated by Moody's as Aaa.

[†]Other illustrations include Flint, Michigan, and its dependence on automobile production; Gary, Indiana, and its reliance on steel production; and Charleston, West Virginia, and its link to the coal industry.

how a community may enhance its efficiency by using these three variables. The result is a higher bond rating, which manifests itself in lower interest costs on debt.

IV. A NEW APPROACH

Rather than relying on either discriminant analysis or regression techniques, we propose a new approach. It is based on a branch of economics known as "welfare economics." Not to be confused with income support programs, the idea of welfare economics is grounded in resource use, specifically efficiency. In the broadest sense, efficiency may be viewed as a guide to resource use, whether it be for labor, capital, raw materials, or time. In short, resources should be used to produce the maximum amount of output with a given level of inputs. Conversely, the goal is to use a minimum amount of inputs for a given level of output. In welfare economics, this has come to mean the point at which society cannot make some individuals "better off" without making others "worse off." Reaching this point means that resources are allocated as well as possible; they cannot be reallocated overall to increase society's welfare.[*]

One obvious difficulty with this concept of absolute efficiency in welfare economics is applicability. What is meant by better off? How is it measured? What is input? What is output? Fortunately, despite the obstacles of measuring this concept on an *absolute* basis, there is a relatively new technique available that measures it on a *relative* basis. It is known as "data envelopment analysis," which is an application of mathematical programming applied to questions concerned with optimal resource use.[†]

Broadly speaking, data envelopment analysis (DEA) was designed to help evaluate the efficiency of one unit compared to all other units. Unlike conventional mathematical programming applications (e.g., linear programming) that strive to minimize a cost function or maximize a revenue function from varying inputs, DEA measures how efficiently several inputs contribute to one or more output goals of an organization. For example, DEA can be used to measure the relative efficiency of individual businesses by examining the input mix of labor, machinery, rent, land, and so forth—inputs that contribute to output, such as sales and profit. In particular, DEA is well suited to evaluate relative efficiency of units whose outputs are difficult to assess, such as schools, hospitals, and governments. As of this writing, however, there has been no work on the application of DEA to municipal finance issues, including bond ratings and interest costs.

How does DEA measure relative efficiency? To place the discussion within the context of municipalities, it constructs a hypothetical (or composite) municipal government from all other governments in a given data base and compares it to each of the governments under study. The operating efficiency of a municipality is determined by comparing its output to those of the hypothetical composite, or benchmark, government. The composite government uses optimal weighted inputs determined from the municipal governments in the data base. This is done by constraining the composite municipality's output to be greater than or equal to the output of the municipality under evaluation. The municipality under evaluation is said to be *inefficient* if the benchmark government requires fewer inputs to generate the same levels of output. As a guide, any unit—a municipality in this case—that is found to be inefficient (relative to the benchmark unit) is assigned a value less than 1. Any unit determined to be relatively efficient is given a 1.

Any units that are assigned values less than 1 are candidates for improvement. The DEA actually shows what areas are the targets for reducing inefficiency. In other words, within the context of this study, DEA might suggest that a local economy's industrial base diversification is too low, or that its debt as a percentage of assessed property value is too high. Relative to the composite local government, DEA indicates to what extent the variables need to be altered to achieve efficiency. This is accomplished by examining what DEA refers to as "slack" variables. As the name implies, a slack variable indicates an inappropriate amount of input. For example, a metropolitan area's industrial base may be underdiversified or its debt may be too high relative to its assessed property value.

As with any tool, DEA is not without its limitations. One, of course, is that it makes relative comparisons. It does not have an absolute criterion against which the performance of a unit can be measured. A unit may

---

[*]The idea of not being able to make some individuals "better off" without making others "worse off" has been termed "Pareto optimality," after the Italian economist, Vilfredo Pareto, who developed the concept.

[†]Data envelopment analysis is an application of linear programming, a method used to achieve optimal solutions subject to a series of constraints. For applications of data envelopment analysis outside the municipal finance area, see Charnes et al. (1981), Banker and Morey (1986), Ludwin and Guthrie (1989), and Diamond and Medewitz (1990).

be relatively inefficient when compared to one group; however, it may be classified as efficient when compared to a second group. For this reason, it is critical that the units under study have comparable input resources and share similar output goals.

A second limitation of DEA is that it cannot distinguish between the worth of any pair of inputs. To illustrate, assume that DEA is applied to assessing the relative efficiency of how different counties employ their inputs to achieve a minimum interest rate cost. If the researcher were to include as an input, say, the number of parks in the county, and only one of the counties had parks, then DEA would most likely identify that having parks can reduce debt. It is highly doubtful that either rating agencies or financial markets would agree with this assessment.

A third limitation of DEA is that it is sensitive to the value of the inputs. For example, a school system may be measuring the performance of its students on a test relative to students in other school systems who took the same test. If the number of school days missed is considered an important input, it should be stated in positive terms rather than in negative terms; that is, one should express the input as the number of class days attended rather than the number of class days missed. This means that a variable such as debt as a percentage of assessed property value needs to be expressed as its inverse—assessed property value as a percentage of debt.

A.   An Application of Data Envelopment Analysis

To illustrate the application of DEA and to discuss its policy implications more fully, we turn to economic base and financial accounting data for ten U.S. counties. The counties are of varying population size and are part of major metropolitan statistical areas, as follows: Bexar (San Antonio, Texas), Cook (Chicago, Illinois), Dade (Miami, Florida), Fulton (Atlanta, Georgia), Lane (Eugene, Oregon), Los Angeles (Los Angeles, California), Lucas (Toledo, Ohio), Ramsey (Minneapolis, Minnesota), Wayne (Detroit, Michigan), and Westmoreland (Pittsburgh, Pennsylvania).

The issue at hand is to determine if the counties are making (relative) efficient use of their resources to effect a favorable bond rating and ultimately a minimum interest cost on municipal debt. This interest cost serves as the output measure and is expressed as a percentage. In keeping with the recommendations discussed in the previous section, we choose not only a small number of input variables but one financial accounting variable and two economic base variables, as follows:

1.   Total debt as a percentage of assessed property value
2.   Diversification, as measured by the "coefficient of specialization"
3.   Inflation-adjusted (1987=100) per capita income

Of the three variables, the coefficient of specialization requires further discussion. The measure relies on local area employment. It can be thought of as a two-step comparison. First, it compares the employment in a specific industry against total area employment. Second, the local area result is contrasted with national employment in that industry relative to total nationwide employment.[*] Of several diversification measures available, Loviscek and Crowley (1990) showed that this measure strongly influences municipal bond ratings. The coefficient is defined as follows:

$$CS = \frac{\Sigma \left| \dfrac{e_i}{e_c} - \dfrac{E_{i_n}}{E_N} \right|}{2}$$

where

e_i =   employment in industry "i" in county "c"
e_c =   employment in county "c"
E_{in} =   employment in industry "i" in the nation
E_N =   employment in the nation

The coefficient has a range of approximately 0 to approximately 1. A zero indicates that the county's employment base is comparably diversified to the nation's. As a county's value for the coefficient approaches

---

[*]Additional discussion of the coefficient of specialization may be found in Mathur (1970).

1, its employment base is said to depend increasingly on a limited number of industries. This less diversified employment base may easily lead to unstable income for the county. The result is a questionable ability of the county to raise the revenue necessary to make timely payment of interest and principal, which translates to a lower bond rating.

The data for the one output and three input variables—indeed, reliable data sources across a number of variables—are found primarily in three sources. The employment data for the diversification variable can be found in *County Business Patterns*. The income data are readily accessible from the *Survey of Current Business*. Debt as a percentage of assessed property value is more problematic; however, the data may be obtained from various government publications, such as *Compendium of Government Finances*. Information on municipal bonds, bond ratings, and interest costs, as well as assessed property value, may be obtained from *Moody's Municipal and Government Manual* (1992).* As of this writing, the latest common period available across the four variables was 1990.

The coefficient of specialization was calculated by stratifying employment into one of ten categories: agriculture, mining, construction, manufacturing, transportation, wholesale trade, retail trade, finance, services, and "unclassified." The interest cost was estimated by taking an average of the interest rates associated with the county's debt rating.

The data are presented in Table 3. The counties are listed alphabetically, followed by each county's bond rating as assessed by Moody's. The four variables are listed at the top of the table. Before applying DEA to the data, further discussion of the data is in order. The highest figure for debt to assessed property value—the most financially leveraged of the counties—goes to Pittsburgh's Westmoreland County, while the lowest is for Detroit's Wayne County. Concerning diversification, Toledo's Lucas County is clearly the most diversified across the ten industrial employment categories, registering a coefficient of 0.0833. At 0.225, Atlanta's Fulton County has the greatest concentration in a few industries. On the other hand, Fulton County has a per capita income of $20,425, clearly the highest of the group, while San Antonio's Bexar County has the lowest per capita income at $13,340. As can be attested to by the bond ratings, Minneapolis' Ramsey County enjoys a debt rating of Aaa and the lowest interest cost, 6.61%. This is contrasted with Westmoreland County, which has a Baa rating and the highest interest cost, 7.58%.

With respect to the output and input variables, DEA attempts to answer the following question: Given a county's debt to assessed property value, economic base diversification, and real per capita income, how may it minimize its interest costs relative to a composite municipality? To answer the question from the information provided, data envelopment analysis constructs a composite municipality from all possible municipalities under investigation. In this case, the criteria for constructing this composite, or benchmark, come from the three input variables. All municipalities under study are compared to a benchmark to determine if they are managing their resources efficiently.

*Owing to the detailed financial data provided, the *Manual* can be awkward to use, especially for bond ratings. As a suggested alternative, see *Moody's Bond Record* (1992), a monthly publication.

Table 3   Observations for Data Envelopment Analysis

County	Debt to assessed value	Coefficient of specialization	Per capita income	Interest cost
Bexar (Aa)	0.0522	0.1073	13340	6.94
Cook (A)	0.0461	0.1404	18454	7.39
Dade (A)	0.0854	0.1490	16874	7.33
Fulton (Aa)	0.0417	0.2252	20425	6.86
Lane (Aa)	0.0500	0.1889	13973	6.91
Los Angeles (Aaa)	0.0438	0.1885	18790	6.67
Lucas (A)	0.0394	0.0833	16247	7.27
Ramsey (Aaa)	0.0393	0.1108	18466	6.61
Wayne (Baa)	0.0226	0.1347	16137	7.52
Westmoreland (Baa)	0.0925	0.1088	14695	7.58

As stated previously, DEA is "input dependent"; that is, it works under the assumption that the selected inputs are appropriate. The technique strives to minimize the amount of input necessary to achieve the output. Outputs are assumed to be a "good"—more is preferred to less—and need to be expressed accordingly. Inputs need to be similarly expressed. To reflect these characteristics, some of the data in Table 3 have to be modified. For one, interest expense, the output variable, was redefined as 100% minus interest cost. For the input variables, debt to assessed property value was redefined as its inverse, assessed property value as a percentage of total debt. Similarly, recalling that the smaller the coefficient of specialization, the more diversified an economy's industrial base, we need to use its inverse. No change was needed for per capita income. The changes in definition enable the employment of the output and inputs in a manner consistent with the DEA technique. The transformed values of the observations are presented in Table 4.

The results from the DEA technique are presented in Table 5. Along the left-hand column, "Wt" in front of each county stands for "weight" (which will become clear by illustration in a moment). Counties that are relatively efficient have the value 1.000. Any county with this score does not need to alter the composition of its inputs; in this case assessed value as a percentage of debt, diversification, and per capita income. Therefore, an efficient county will always have a weight of 1.000. As seen from Table 5, seven of the counties—Bexar, Dade, Fulton, Lane, Los Angeles, Ramsey, and Westmoreland—registered this value. As a result, none of them needs to alter its input mix.

Three counties, Chicago's Cook, Toledo's Lucas, and Detroit's Wayne, were found to be relatively inefficient. Of the three, at 0.821 Lucas County is the most inefficient; at 0.977 Wayne County is the least inefficient. The value of 0.821 means that a composite county could in theory be constructed from the other counties that would provide the same cost of interest but require only 82.1% or less of the inputs used in Lucas County. Similarly, a composite county could be constructed for Cook County that would use 91.7% or less of Cook County's inputs.

Reading down the column for Cook, we see that such a county could be constructed by using 14.5% of Dade's inputs ("WtDade"), 31.3% of Lane's inputs ("WtLane"), and 50.3% of Los Angeles' input (WtLos Angeles). Also, a composite county for Wayne County could be constructed by using 62.8% of Lane's inputs (WtLane) and 37.2% of Los Angeles' inputs (WtLos Angeles).[*] Finally, and in some ways most interestingly, the results for Lucas County suggest that it would do well to use Bexar County (WtBexar, 100%) as a role model, because Bexar could achieve the same interest cost with only 82.1% of Lucas's inputs.

The policy implications for the results are found in the slack variables. Slack 1 represents the "idle capacity" associated with assessed property value as a percentage of debt. Slack 2 is the idle capacity associated with diversification. Slack 3 represents the idle capacity associated with per capita income. Of

---

[*]The numbers were determined by means of the optimization routine that DEA employs. As suggested by the different results for Cook and Wayne counties, owing to the unique features of each county, the input mix for achieving efficiency will vary across counties.

Table 4   Transformed Observations for Data Envelopment Analysis

County	Assessed value to debt	Coefficient of specialization	Per capita income	Interest cost
Bexar	19.1431	9.3195	13340	93.06
Cook	21.6818	7.1250	18454	92.61
Dade	11.7068	6.7126	16874	92.67
Fulton	24.0000	4.4405	20425	93.14
Lane	20.0000	8.4104	13973	93.09
Los Angeles	22.8267	5.3050	18790	93.33
Lucas	25.3968	12.0021	16247	92.73
Ramsey	25.4545	9.0253	18466	93.39
Wayne	44.3312	7.4239	16137	92.48
Westmoreland	10.8108	9.1904	14695	92.42

Table 5 Results from Data Envelopment Analysis

	Bexar	Cook	Dace	Fulton	Lane	Los Angeles	Lucas	Ramsey	Wayne	West-moreland
Efficiency	1.000	0.917	1.000	1.000	1.000	1.000	0.821	1.000	0.977	1.000
WtBexar	1.000	0.000	0.000	0.000	0.000	0.000	1.000	0.000	0.000	0.000
WtCook	0.000	0.000	0.000	0.000	0.000	0.000	0.000	0.000	0.000	0.000
WtDade	0.000	0.145	1.000	0.000	0.000	0.000	0.000	0.000	0.000	0.000
WtFulton	0.000	0.000	0.000	1.000	0.000	0.000	0.000	0.000	0.000	0.000
WtLane	0.000	0.313	0.000	0.000	1.000	0.000	0.000	0.000	0.628	0.000
WtLos Angeles	0.000	0.503	0.000	0.000	0.000	1.000	0.000	0.000	0.372	0.000
WtLucas	0.000	0.000	0.000	0.000	0.000	0.000	0.000	0.000	0.000	0.000
WtRamsey	0.000	0.000	0.000	0.000	0.000	0.000	0.000	1.000	0.000	0.000
WtWayne	0.000	0.000	0.000	0.000	0.000	0.000	0.000	0.000	0.000	0.000
WtWest-moreland	0.000	0.000	0.000	0.000	0.000	0.000	0.000	0.000	0.000	1.000
Slack 1	0.000	0.000	0.000	0.000	0.000	0.000	1.710	0.000	22.262	0.000
Slack 2	0.000	0.000	0.000	0.000	0.000	0.000	0.535	0.000	0.000	0.000
Slack 3	0.000	0.000	0.000	0.000	0.000	0.000	0.000	0.000	0.000	0.000

the three variables, slack occurs in diversification and assessed value of the inefficient counties; however, there is no slack in per capita income.

Wayne County has a slack value of 22.262 for the assessed value variable. Within the context of municipal financing, the interpretation of this value is subject to some debate, as will be pointed out. Nonetheless, one reasonable interpretation is that Wayne County has much more collateral backing its bonds than would normally be expected. This suggests that Wayne County may be able to raise additional debt without significantly altering its cost of funds.

At 1.710, Lucas County also has slack in its assessed value measure; however, the more interesting observation is concerned with the slack in its level of diversification. A value of 0.535 may be a sign of overdiversification. If correct, this suggests that the county can afford to become less diversified in its employment base without endangering its bond rating of A; that is, without causing investors to question its ability to make timely debt payments.

As mentioned, the interpretations offered for the slack variables for Wayne and Lucas Counties are open to further discussion. If one holds the premise that the rating agencies are not always correct in their assessment of municipal bond quality, it might be argued that Lucas County should have a lower cost of debt given the slack it has in the diversification of its employment base and in its assessed value as a percentage of debt; that is, its employment base is considerably more diverse—in fact, the most diversified of the group—but does not seem to enjoy the benefits of a lower interest cost on the debt. Similarly, Wayne County does not benefit from a lower cost of debt, even though it has significant collateral reserve, or "community equity," relative to its debt. Indirectly, therefore, one may argue that DEA may also be a test of the efficacy of bond rating agencies. This suggests there may be more room for substantive give and take between municipalities and rating agencies than commonly thought.

There could be other interpretations, depending upon the output and inputs specified. The above slack observations are unique—they apply only to the list of variables used. A different set of variables may well lead to different conclusions, even with the inclusion of the same three variables. The result may be a new set of policy recommendations. Subjectivity aside, the application of DEA to the issue of municipal financing suggests that it holds considerable promise as a valuable tool to policy makers when assessing the relative financial performance of municipal governments that share comparable input and outputs.

V. DEBT MANAGEMENT STRATEGY

While undoubtedly an understanding of municipal bond ratings, the rating process, and bond rating determinants is necessary for effective debt management, it is not sufficient. Equally important is an understanding of four areas: the term structure of interest, bond duration, yield to maturity, and municipal bond clientele characteristics. Together with bond ratings, these four areas constitute the foundation for effective debt management strategies.

A. The Term Structure of Interest

Interest rates are the result of an interaction of opportunity costs of borrowing and inflationary expectations (e.g., issuing long-term securities as opposed to short-term securities when expected inflation is low).[*] While the determination of appropriate opportunity costs and inflationary expectations is beyond the scope of this discussion, the fundamental relationship can be used to draw inferences from financial markets. This can be done by examining the "term structure of interest," the relationship between interest rates and maturity schedules of debt instruments.

The term structure of interest contributes to an understanding of interest rate determination. Because it may be used as an integral component in municipal debt management, a short discussion of the term structure is in order.[†] It may be viewed at any time, with the reference points being interest rates on U.S. Treasury securities of varying maturities. Figure 1 illustrates the term structure of interest for October 1993. The interest return (expressed as "yield to maturity") is read from the vertical axis; the maturity schedules from the horizontal axis. The upward-sloping feature of the curve is referred to as a "classic" curve—one frequently observed from U.S. data. The yield to maturity gradually increases as the length of maturity increases. What determines the shape of this curve as well as that of other curves? Three hypotheses, to which we now turn, have been put forth as explanations. They are known as "liquidity premium," "segmentation," and "expectations."

---

[*]The relationship is formally known as the Fisher effect, named after the economist Irving Fisher.
[†]Most texts on money and financial markets provide a more thorough discussion of the term structure than that found here. One recommendation is Kohn (1993).

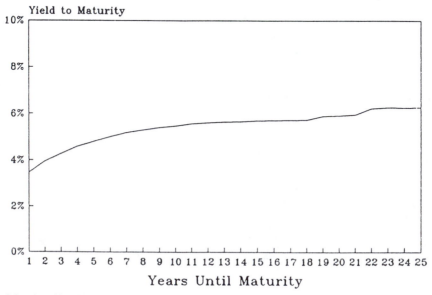

As of October 27, 1993

Figure 1 Term structure of interest.

1. Liquidity Premium

The liquidity premium hypothesis argues that short-term interest rates should be lower than long-term interest rates. It argues that an investor who lends money for a long period is giving up more opportunity than an investor who lends money for a short period. There is also greater uncertainty about inflation risk associated with long-term investments than with short-term investments. Finally, long-term bonds have greater duration values than short-term bonds.[*] Advocates of the liquidity premium hypothesis believe the term structure of interest curve is best described as shown in Fig. 2.

2. Segmentation Hypothesis

The segmentation hypothesis argues that investors and borrowers have different horizon requirements for their funds. Supply of and demand for funds for any given maturity schedule determine the interest rate for the bond. For example, insurance companies, given their long-term outlook, tend to be concerned with long-run matching of their inflows and outflows. On the other hand, commercial banks are concerned with intermediate-term maturity schedules, and cash budget managers are concerned with short-term maturity schedules. Different maturity schedules for securities attract respective clientele.

Advocates of the segmentation hypothesis argue that it is not unusual for temporary "anomalies" to exist in the classic curve. These anomalies can lead to, for example, a higher return on an intermediate-term bond than on a long-term bond. However, the anomalies, so the proponents argue, are not sufficient to cause clientele who prefer long-term bonds to shift to intermediate-term bonds. This type of anomaly is depicted in Fig. 3.

3. Expectations Hypothesis

The expectations hypothesis argues that investors seek maximum expected return regardless of the maturity schedule of the bond. It also assumes that borrowers, such as municipal governments, are indifferent to the maturity of the bond they issue. As a result of investors actively seeking out high yields, bond yields fluctuate. The result of these activities is that on average an investor should be indifferent between, for example, a single 5-year bond versus five successive 1-year bonds. Specifically, it states

---

[*]Duration can be described as the relative responsiveness of bond prices with respect to interest rates. All else being equal, the bond with the greater duration value will experience a greater percentage change in its value for a given percentage change in interest rates. Duration is discussed in more detail in the next section.

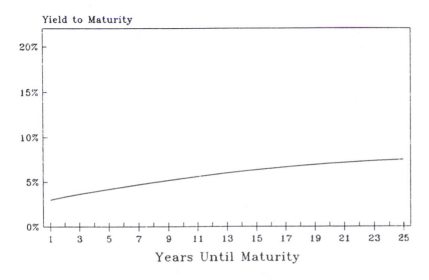

Figure 2   Term structure of interest (classic yield curve).

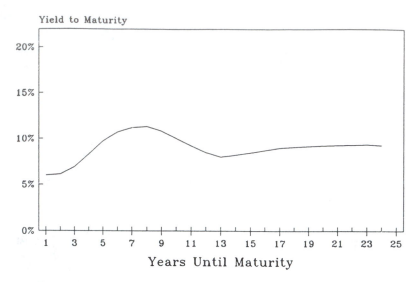

Figure 3   Term structure of interest (anomaly in interest rates).

Single 5-year bond = five 1-year bonds

$$V_5 = \$1000(1 + {_0}i_5)^5 = \$1000(1 + {_0}i_1)(1 + {_1}i_2)(1 + {_2}i_3)(1 + {_3}i_4)(1 + {_4}i_5) \qquad (1)$$

For example, assume that the single 5-year rate of interest is 8.01% (${_0}i_5$). It will have a value of $1,470.00 at period 5. The five single-period interest rates could be as follows:

Period 0 to end of year 1—6.11% (${_0}i_1$).
Period 1 to end of year 2—6.32% (${_1}i_2$).
Period 2 to end of year 3—8.13% (${_2}i_3$).
Period 3 to end of year 4—9.13% (${_3}i_4$).
Period 4 to end of year 5—10.227% (${_4}i_5$).

As the economy expands, the quantity of money demanded in the economy increases. Provided the quantity of money supplied lags this demand, the "pent-up" demand for liquidity will lead to an increase in short-term interest rates. The result may be an inverted yield curve. This is illustrated in Fig. 4. If the term structure of interest has an inverted yield curve, the expectations hypothesis would argue that market forces would interact to reduce interest rates, especially short-term interest rates. This is illustrated in Fig. 5. Put simply, supply and demand factors endogenous to the economy and investor clientele will contribute to declining short-term interest rates.

4. Inflationary Expectations

As stated previously, interest rates are related to opportunity costs plus inflationary expectations. With differing inflationary expectations, everything else held constant, the term structure of interest could very well retain its classic shape. The only difference would be in the level of expected inflation, which acts to shift the term structure, as illustrated in Fig. 6.

Despite the varied shapes of the term structure of interest, the differing hypotheses, and the inflation premia, general observations are possible. First, inflationary expectations contribute to higher interest rates, with short-term rates tending to rise faster than long-term rates as the economy expands. Second, anomalies do appear in the term structure. Third, long-term bonds have a greater responsiveness to changes in price with respect to interest rates than do short-term bonds. This is the concept of duration, to which we now turn.

B.   Duration

Duration is a measure of the relative responsiveness (or "elasticity") of a bond's price with respect to interest rates. A bond's duration is important for at least three reasons. First, in the event that the segmentation

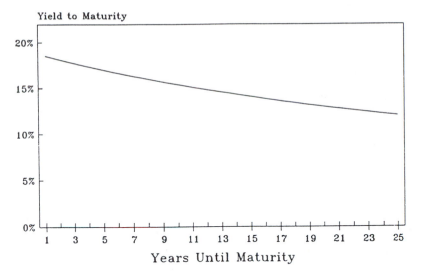

Figure 4 Term structure of interest (inverted yield curve).

hypothesis is correct, bonds of a given duration will attract specific investor interest. Second, if the liquidity hypothesis is correct, bonds of higher duration, such as GO bonds, are perceived to be riskier and less liquid than those of lesser duration, such as tax anticipation notes. Third, the implications of duration for investors in the municipal market—indeed, any bond market—are broad. These include bond portfolio management, interest futures, bond swaps, and attempts to protect a bond portfolio from price volatility induced by fluctuating interest rates. Duration is defined as follows:

$$D = \sum [t(C_t)/(1+i)^t]/P \tag{2}$$

where

t   = time period
C_t = cash flow in period t
i   = market discount rate
P   = price or present value of the bond

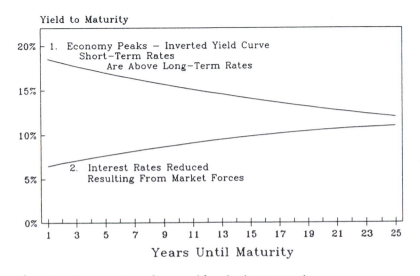

Figure 5 Term structure of interest (changing interest rates).

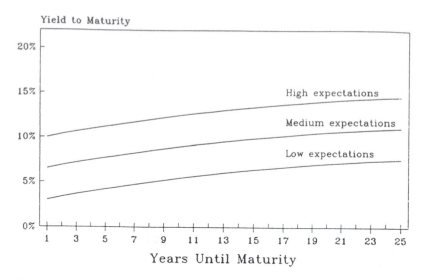

Figure 6   Term structure of interest (inflationary expectations).

The calculation of a bond that has 5 years before it matures, has a coupon rate of 8%, and has a yield to maturity of 10% is demonstrated in Table 6.

Duration may also be defined in terms of elasticity, as follows:

$$D = [(\Delta P/P)/(\Delta i/(1+i^*))] \tag{3}$$

where

P   = price or present value of the bond
ΔP = change in the price
Δi = change in market interest rates (discount rate)
i* = current market interest rate

Rearranging the equation and solving for the change in a bond's price (ΔP) gives the following expression:

$$\Delta P = -D[(\Delta i)/(1+i^*)]P \tag{4}$$

Duration values are influenced by both maturity lengths and market rates of interest. The relationship is direct, implying that as the years to maturity increase, the duration of the bond increases. This is demonstrated in Fig. 7. However, interest rates play a role as well. As market rates of interest increase, duration decreases. This is shown in Fig. 8.

Table 6   Duration Calculation

t	C	$C_t/(1+i^*)^t$	$t(C_t/(1+i^*)^t)$
1	80	72.737	72.73
2	80	66.116	132.24
3	80	60.105	180.33
4	80	54.641	218.56
5	1080	670.595	3352.98
Sum		924.194	3956.84

D = 3956.84/924.194
D = 4.2814

1. Changes in Bond Values

During the life of a bond, any bondholder, whether an individual investor or a bond portfolio manager, is faced with possible changes in a bond's value. Two factors govern this change: interest rates and the term to maturity. For a given bond, what should happen to its price if interest rates are expected to rise, for example, from 10% to 11%? Using the data in Table 6, with 5 years to maturity, we see that the current price of the bond is $924.19. With the increase in interest to 11%, present value theory indicates that the bond will decrease in value. From Eq. (4), the change in price can be expected to be -$35.64. The calculated present value of the bond in Table 6 would be $889.12, resulting in a very small prediction error of $0.58. However, had the bond's duration value been greater, there would have been a larger decrease in price. This implies that the size of the error is directly related to a bond's duration. Given the data in Table 6, with the exception that interest rates are now 11%, we should expect the duration of the bond to decrease. The recalculated duration for this bond is 4.2658. As expected, its duration decreased as interest rates increased.

C. Estimated Yield to Maturity

Bond prices are determined by taking the present value of future flows at a market rate of interest. From information about the maturity, interest payments, and purchase price of a bond, it is possible to determine the estimated yield to maturity, as follows:

$$\text{Yield to maturity} \approx \frac{\text{interest} + [\text{maturity} - \text{cost}]/n}{.6(\text{cost}) + .4(\text{maturity})} \tag{5}$$

where

interest	=	annual dollar amount of interest the bond pays
maturity	=	maturity value of the bond
cost	=	current price of the bond
n	=	number of years until maturity

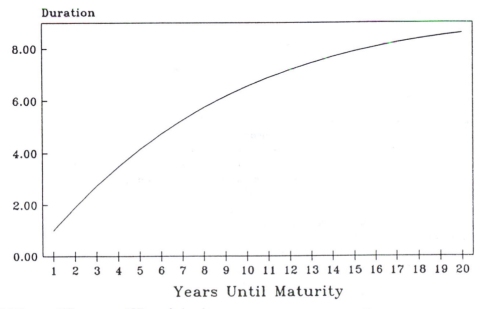

$1,000 par; 10% coupon; 12% market rate

Figure 7 Bond duration (for different maturity schedules).

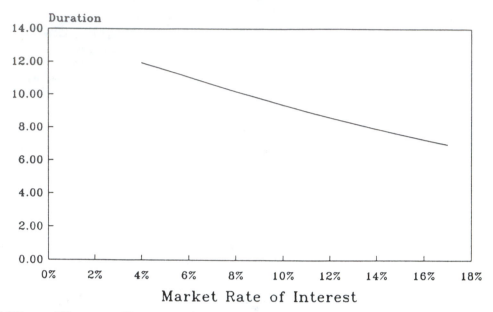

$1,000 par; 10% coupon; 20 yrs maturity

Figure 8   Bond duration (for different market interest rates).

The information in Table 6 was based on a bond that has a market value of $924.18, has 5 years to maturity, and pays $80 in interest per year. The true yield to maturity for this bond is 10%. If this were not known, Equ. (5) could be used to approximate the yield, as follows:

$$\text{Yield to maturity} \approx \frac{80 + (1000-924.18)/5}{.6(924.18) + .4(1000)}$$

Yield to maturity ≈ 9.96996%

The estimated yield to maturity formula is easy to use and produces acceptably accurate approximations for yield.

D. Municipal Bond Clientele Characteristics

The segmentation hypothesis argues that certain types of securities attract particular groups of investors. This is especially true of municipal bonds. Interest income on these bonds is exempt from federal taxation. This feature has especially contributed to attracting commercial banks and individuals with high marginal tax rates. These two groups constitute "clienteles" for municipal bonds. Together they hold approximately 73% of the outstanding municipal debt. Commercial banks also benefit from investing in municipal bonds through an interest deductibility feature that permits them to create an arbitrage situation—one of riskless profit.[*]

Individuals should be indifferent between normal taxable interest and tax-exempt interest if the net after-tax returns are equal, as follows:

$$R_{norm}(1 - T_{norm}) = R_{mun}(1 - T_{mun}) \tag{6}$$

_____

[*]Local governments also have an arbitrage opportunity. Metcalf (1990) has shown that the tax-exempt status of the bonds may lead governments to issue bonds at the tax-exempt interest rate (say, 6%), invest the proceeds at a higher taxable rate (say, 8%), and collect the difference (2%). This practice, however, is illegal.

where

R_{norm} = return on taxable investments (assume 10%)
T_{norm} = tax rate on normal taxable investments (assume 30%)
R_{mun} = return on municipal investments (assume 8%)
T_{mun} = tax rate on municipal investments (assume 0%)

Solving for R_{norm}, it can be shown that the tax-exempt status of municipal bonds effectively equates the tax-free return to a significantly higher taxable return, as follows:

$$R_{norm} = R_{mun}(1 - T_{mun})/(1 - T_{norm})$$
$$R_{norm} = 0.08(1 - 0)/(1 - .3)$$
$$R_{norm} = 0.1143$$

Therefore, the investor has a choice of earning a 10% fully taxable return or an 8% tax-exempt return. The net benefit of the tax-exempt return could only be replicated if the investor could obtain a taxable return of 11.43%. Because of the higher wealth accumulated with an investment in the municipal bond, the investor becomes a client of that market.

Commercial banks are in a similar but more favorable situation. Prior to 1983, 100% of the interest expense incurred from its own loans taken out for the purposes of investing in municipal bonds was fully tax-deductible. Effective in 1983, only 80% of the interest expense on debt purchased after December 31, 1982 was tax-deductible. In accordance with the Tax Reform Act of 1986, none of the interest expense was tax-deductible on municipals purchased after August 7, 1986, with one exception. If a municipality issues debt for qualified public purposes, such as for schools or sewers, and the issue is less than $10,000,000 per year, then the deductibility of 80% still applies for the investing bank.

Table 7 illustrates the after-tax characteristics of a bank's investment in municipal bonds. Situation A depicts the interest expense as being fully tax-deductible. Situation B represents 80% of the interest expense as being tax-deductible. Situation C assumes that 80% of the interest expense is tax-deductible, but only for specific assets. The net effect of the loss of interest expense deductibility is to decrease the attractiveness of the municipal bond to the bank. In the above illustration, this results from an effective T_{mun} of 5%.

E. Debt Management: Bond Ratings and the Four Areas

At the outset of this section, it was mentioned that active debt management required an understanding of bond ratings and four additional areas: the term structure of interest, duration, yield to maturity, and clientele characteristics. In general, the management of municipal debt should include an effort to time the issuance of new debt to correlate to low long-term interest rates. For example, if a community's economic base shows increasingly favorable characteristics, it behooves the community to postpone issuance of new debt until a more favorable bond rating is secured.

While higher bond ratings can clearly reduce the interest cost of debt, further interest cost reductions are possible. An examination of current interest rate movements, both short-term and long-term, can help ease the costs. For example, with a classic yield curve, if short-term rates have been dropping, then long-term rates likely will as well. It behooves a municipal government to issue short-term debt, such as tax anticipation notes and commercial paper, and postpone bond issuance until after long-term rates have fallen. When linked to the likelihood of a higher bond rating, the reduction in interest costs may indeed be significant.

As another illustration, an inverted yield curve is often observed near expansion peaks prior to interest rate reductions. It pays the municipality, therefore, to postpone debt issuance until after interest rates have fallen. On the other hand, signs of higher inflationary expectations will cause the classic yield curve to shift upward, signaling a jump in short-term and long-term interest rates. As a result, municipalities should issue long-term debt at the first signs of such signals, especially if a more favorable bond rating is not expected.

Municipal governments, however, need to note that the market for their issues may be "thin," owing to duration issues and clientele effects. The length of time for which a bond is issued influences its duration, a significant input to an investor trying to estimate the stability of a bond's value relative to changes in interest rates. This attracts investors with special preferences. The duration of the bonds in the portfolio and that of alternative bonds on the market can influence a decision to hold a bond. This could adversely affect the marketability of a municipal issue if its duration characteristics are inconsistent with investors' desires. While the yield to maturity may be attractive and easy to compute for an investor, the yield may be outweighed by potential losses in principal if an interest rate increase takes place and an investor is holding a high duration

Table 7 Comparison of After-Tax Returns on Taxable and Tax-Exempt Investments for Commercial Banks

Situation A—100% tax deductible	Taxable investment	Municipal investment
Maturity value	100,000	100,000
Coupon rate	8%	6%
Yearly interest income	8,000	6,000
Applicable federal tax rate	30%	—
Federal tax	2,400	0
After-tax interest income	5,600	6,000

Situation B—Deduction of interest on loans used to raise funds to invest in municipal bonds is 80% tax deductible

Assume
- Total interest expenses are $2,000,000.
- Average amount of municipal securities held 1986 that qualify for exclusion.
- Average amount of assets for the year is $40,000,000.

Calculation of nondeductible interest expense
- Proportion of municipals to total is 1,000,000/40,000,000 = 2.5%.
- Nondeductible interest expense = (0.2)(0.025)(2,000,000) = 10,000.

Situation C—After-tax interest earned allowing for partial deductibility of interest expense on the municipal bond in situation A

	Taxable investment	Municipal investment
Maturity value	100,000	100,000
Coupon rate	8%	6%
Yearly interest income	8,000	6,000
Applicable federal tax rate	30%	—
Average interest expense (5%)	5,000	5,000
Lost interest deduction (20%)	0	1,000
Increased tax liability (30%)	0	300
Federal tax	2,400	0
After-tax interest income	5,600	5,700

bond. Risk-averse investors wish to avoid such situations, and municipalities need to be sensitive to these concerns if they wish to hold interest costs to a minimum. As a result, municipalities that expect bond rating upgrades, which reduce the risk of principal losses, may be well advised to advertise this possibility as a means to allay risk-averse investors.

The section on data envelopment analysis pointed out the possibilities for a municipality to learn how to more effectively manage its economic and financial base. Doing so increases efficiency. If sustained, the result is a more favorable bond rating and reduction in the cost of debt. Given that a strong clientele exists for municipal debt instruments, a more favorable bond rating coupled with the tax environment provides a tangible incentive to high-income individuals to invest in municipal bonds. To a lesser extent, the same is true for commercial banks, especially if the bonds finance public-purpose projects and amount to less than $10,000,000 per year in borrowing. With this information, along with monitoring interest rates and inflationary expectations, a municipality should find itself in a more favorable position to take advantage of timely situations and serve more effectively the needs of its constituency.

VI. SUMMARY

This study has provided an overview of municipal bond ratings, qualitative indicators of the creditworthiness of municipal bonds. The areas covered have included a description of the ratings, the importance of the ratings to local governments and investors, the determinants of the ratings, and the role of ratings in debt management. It has been argued that the ratings play unique and substantive roles in municipal finance, providing local governments with opportunities to improve financial management. These opportunities include broadening the market for a bond issue, issuing bonds at the correct time, and managing variables that influence the ratings.

Two areas received special attention: determinants of the ratings and debt management. To predict changes in municipal bond ratings, and ultimately the interest cost of debt, it was argued that municipal finance officials, investors, and researchers would be well advised to focus on three variables: total debt as a percentage of assessed property value, industrial base diversification, and per capita income. As support for this argument, the variables were used in an application of data envelopment analysis to show how local governments might improve their efficiency. If efficiency gains are sustained, the result should be a higher bond rating.

Knowledge of bond ratings, the bond rating process, and bond rating determinants, while necessary for effective debt management, is not sufficient. Also required is an understanding of the term structure of interest, duration, yield to maturity, and municipal bond clientele characteristics. These four areas are critical to the prediction of interest rates and investor preference for bonds of varying maturities. Together with bond ratings, the four areas serve as the foundation for effective debt management, which places municipal governments in a more favorable position to take advantage of changing market conditions. The result is the opportunity to provide higher-quality service at a lower cost.

REFERENCES

Aronson, J. R. and Marsden, J. R. (1980). *Pub. Finance Q.*, 8: 97–106.

Bahl, R. W. (1971). *Proceed. Nat.l Tax Assoc.* (Sept.): 600–622.

Banker, R. D. and Morey, R. C. (1986). *Mgt. Sci.*, 32: 1613–1627.

Brewer, H. L. (1985). *J. Reg. Sci.*, 25: 463–470.

Carleton, W. T. and Lerner, E. M. (1969). *J. Money, Cred. Bank.*, 1: 750–764.

Charnes, A., Cooper, W. W., and Rhodes, E. (1981). *Mgt. Sci.*, 27: 668–697.

Cluff, G. S. and Farnham, P. G. (1984). *Q. Rev. Econ. Bus.*, 24: 72–94.

Conroy, M. E. (1974). *J. Reg. Sci.*, 14: 31–46.

Copeland, R. M. and Ingram, R. W. (1982). *J. Acct. Res.*, 10: 275–289.

Diamond, A. M. Jr. and Medewitz, J. N. (1990). *J. Econ. Ed.*, 21: 337–354.

Dillon, W. R. (1979). *J. Marketing Res.*, 16: 370–381.

Eisenbeis, R. A. (1977). *J. Finance*, 32: 875–900.

Eisenbeis, R. A. and Avery, R. B. (1972). *Discriminant Analysis and Classification Procedures*, Lexington Books, Lexington, Mass.

Evans, J. L. and Archer, S. H. (1968). *J. Finance*, 23: 761–769.

Farnham, P. G. and Cluff, G. S. (1982). *Pub. Finance Q.*, 10: 427–455.

Goodman, R. (1968). *Finan. Anal. J.*, 24: 59–65.

Harries, B. (1968). *Finan. Anal. J.*, 24: 68–71.

Hempel, G. H. (1973). *J. Finance*, 28: 523–530.

Horton, J. J. (1969). *Finan. Anal. J.*, 25: 72–75.

Horton, J. J. (1970). *J. Bank Res.*, 1: 29–40.

Kaplan, R. S. and Urwitz, G. (1979). *J. Bus.*, 52: 231–261.

Kohn, M. (1993). *Money, Banking, and Financial Markets, second edition*, Dryden Press, New York.

Kort, J. (1981). *Land Econ.*, 57: 596–608.

Lovell, M. C. (1983). *Rev. Econ. Stat.*, 65: 1–12.

Loviscek, A. L. and Crowley, F. D. (1988). *Urban Stud.*, 25: 124–132.

Loviscek, A. L. and Crowley, F. D. (1990). *Finan. Rev.*, 25: 25–53.

Ludwin, W. and Guthrie, T. L. (1989). *Pub. Produc. Rev.*, 12: 361–372.

Maddala, G. S. (1988). *Introduction to Econometrics*, Macmillan, New York.

Mathur, V. K. (1970). *J. Reg. Sci.*, 15: 81–91.

Metcalf, G. E. (1990). *Rev. Econ. Stat.*, 72: 390–396.

Metcalf, G. E. (1993). *J. Pub. Econ.*, 51: 269–285.

Michel, A. J. (1977). *J. Finan. Quant. Anal.*, 12: 587–598.

Moody's Investor Services (1991). *Moody's Bond Record*, New York.

Moody's Investor Services (1992). *Moody's Municipal and Government Manual*, New York.

Morton, T. G. (1975). *Rev. Bus. Econ. Res.*, winter: 74–81.

Parry, R. W. (1983). *Pub. Finance Q.*, 11: 79–93.

Pinches, G. E. and Mingo, K. A. (1975). *J. Finance*, *30*: 201–206.
Raman, K. K. (1981). *Acct. Rev.*, *56*: 910–926.
Raman, K. K. (1982). *J. Acc. Aud. Finance*, *6*: 44–50.
Reilly, R. (1968). *Finan. Anal. J.*, *24*: 65–66.
Riehle, R. (1968). *Finan. Anal. J.*, *24*: 71–73.
Rubinfeld, D. L. (1973). *Natl. Tax J.*, *26*: 17–27.
Standard & Poor's Corporation (1993). *Creditweek: Municipal*, New York.
Standard & Poor's Corporation (1993). *Municipal Ratings Handbook*, New York.
Standard & Poor's Corporation (1993). *Municipal Finance Criteria*, New York.
Statistical Package for the Social Sciences: User's Guide McGraw-Hill, New York. 1975 and 1983.
Stock, D. and Robertson, T. (1981). *J. Bank Res.*, *12*: 153–160.
Twentieth Century Fund Task Force (1974). *The Rating Game*, Twentieth Century Fund, New York.
Tyler, W. H. (1968). *Instit. Investor*, May: 26–28, 77–79.
U.S. Department of Commerce, Bureau of the Census (1989). *Compendium of Government Finances*.
U.S. Department of Commerce, Bureau of the Census (1993). *County Business Patterns*.
U.S. Department of Commerce, Bureau of Economic Analysis (1993). *Survey of Current Business*.

25

Formal Regulatory Handle Needed for NRSRO Designation: Part I

Richard Y. Roberts
United States Securities and Exchange Commission, Washington, D.C.

I. INTRODUCTION

As some of you may be aware, during a commission meeting dealing with the adoption of amendments to rule 2a-7 under the Investment Company Act, I expressed concern with the commission's increased reliance on the judgment of so-called nationally recognized statistical rating organizations (NRSROs). I initially became concerned with the NRSRO designation process, and the absence of standards therefore, during the commission's rule-making proceedings leading to the adoption of the Multijurisdictional Disclosure and Modifications to the Current Registration and Reporting System for Canadian Issuers (MJDS).[1]

The MJDS rules hinge more favorable regulatory treatment on the issuance of a high rating by an NRSRO; and as a result, the two Canadian rating agencies, the Canadian Bond Rating Service (CBRS) and the Dominion Bond Rating Service Limited (DBRS), were prompted to seek designation by the commission as NRSROs. Thus the commission's increasing dependence on the judgment of NRSROs has resulted in the designation of a rating agency as an NRSRO being not only of domestic interest, but of international interest as well.

To illustrate further, in addition to CBRS and DBRS, the commission has received numerous inquiries from domestic and international rating agencies, as well as inquiries from foreign governments, regarding the criteria and process used to designate rating agencies as NRSROs. It is obvious that commission NRSRO designation has become a sensitive and controversial issue of global significance, particularly in the absence of published standards for such designation. Today it is my intention to discuss some of the alternatives available that could provide for more appropriate treatment of rating agencies under our federal securities laws.

II. HISTORICAL DEVELOPMENT OF THE TERM NATIONALLY RECOGNIZED STATISTICAL RATING ORGANIZATION

The term *nationally recognized statistical rating organization* originally was adopted by the commission solely for purposes of distinguishing different grades of debt securities under its net capital rule, Exchange Act rule 15c3-1.[2] Rule 15c3-1 requires broker–dealers, when computing net capital, to deduct from net worth certain percentages of the market value ("haircuts") of their proprietary securities positions. A primary purpose of the haircuts is to provide a margin of safety against losses incurred by broker-dealers as a result of market

---

The views expressed herein are those of Commissioner Roberts and do not necessarily represent those of the commission, other commissioners, or the staff. Adapted with the permission of Richard Y. Roberts.

fluctuations in the prices of their proprietary positions. Various provisions of rule 15c3-1 set forth: (1) the haircuts for commercial paper that has been rated in one of the three highest categories by at least two NRSROs; (2) the haircuts for nonconvertible debt securities that are rated in one of the four highest rating categories by at least two NRSROs; and (3) the haircuts for cumulative, nonconvertible preferred stock rated in one of the four highest rating categories by at least two NRSROs.[3]

In 1973, the commission first considered the use of ratings of "nationally recognized statistical rating services" for regulatory purposes in certain revisions to its capital rules. Specifically, the commission decided to recognize the use of the ratings of nationally recognized statistical rating services as a basis for determining the haircuts for commercial paper and nonconvertible debt securities under rule 15c3-1. This initial determination to rely on ratings was based on the general recognition that ratings are primarily criteria of investment quality, measuring credit risk but ignoring interest risk, purchasing power risk, and the price risk inherent in convertibles selling above face value. Essentially, ratings were considered yardsticks of the relative safety of interest and principal payments.

In considering whether the commission, by using ratings in rule 15c3-1, would be indirectly taking a position on the investment worth of particular securities, it was noted that various securities exchanges, including the New York Stock Exchange, used rating agencies to determine haircuts for purposes of their net capital rules. After some study, a determination was made that the proposed use of ratings in prescribing haircuts for commercial paper and debt securities was solely to avoid setting haircuts that would be harsher than necessary for many securities and would not result in the commission taking a position as to the investment worth of particular securities.

Two somewhat related purposes were sought to be accomplished by using the ratings of nationally recognized rating agencies. First, ratings provided a means of distinguishing between commercial paper that generally is underwritten and issued by those dealing in the commercial paper market and illiquid, short-term promissory notes of companies for which there generally is no secondary trading market, the latter having no value for net capital purposes. Second, by recognizing securities that are highly rated by rating agencies, as opposed to those with no rating or with low ratings, the commission is able to recognize that group of securities which are considered creditworthy by broker-dealers and institutional investors as well as by the rating agencies themselves.

III.   THE EXPANDED USE OF THE TERM NRSRO

A.   Internationally

The globalization and securitization of the international financial markets have expanded the role of credit ratings in countries other than the United States. Credit ratings currently are incorporated into regulatory schemes in, among other countries, Australia, Canada, France, Japan, the United Kingdom, Mexico, and Switzerland, and in the Eurobond market. Nevertheless, credit ratings have not yet obtained the degree of importance in the domestic markets of other countries as they have in the United States.

B.   Domestically

[T]he regulatory use of credit ratings in the [United States] is both longer-established and more far-reaching than in other countries. . . . This emphasis on credit ratings reflects both the importance of the [United States] corporate bond and [commercial paper] markets and the regulatory response to dislocation of the securities markets in the early 1930s, and again in the 1970s.[4]

In the federal securities laws and rules and regulations thereunder, the use of certain debt ratings by NRSROs as the basis for awarding benefits that otherwise are not available to securities that are unrated or rated in a lower rating category has expanded well beyond the original intended use of the concept in the net capital rule. For example, Congress, in certain mortgage-related legislation,[5] and the commission, in its regulations promulgated pursuant to the Securities Act,[6] the Exchange Act,[7] and the Investment Company Act,[8] have chosen to use the ratings of NRSROs to distinguish "investment grade" debt securities from those which are "noninvestment grade." Moreover, the board of governors of the Federal Reserve System in its regulation T also uses the term NRSRO.[9] In each of these instances, NRSRO is defined as it is used in the net capital rule. The commission, however, never has issued a definition of the term NRSRO.

When ratings originally were used in the net capital rule, it was determined that it was appropriate to limit recognition to only those rating agencies which were recognized nationally. At that time, it was decided that it was appropriate to recognize only Standard & Poor's Corporation, Moody's Investor Service, and Fitch Investors Service. This decision was based, in part, on findings that, when considered together, these three agencies rated most of the commercial paper and corporate debt issued in the United States, although frequently an issue was rated by only one of the three rating services. Nevertheless, the possibility that other rating agencies subsequently would be added to the list was not ruled out if they were to gain national recognition by receiving broad acceptance from the investment community, broker-dealers, and issuers.

Currently, any rating agency that wishes to be designated as an NRSRO for purposes of our securities laws must send a letter to the staff of the commission's Division of Market Regulation (the division) requesting that its application for recognition be approved. If the organization's structure and debt rating process, among other things, satisfies criteria the division finds generally necessary for recognition of the entity as an NRSRO, the division will prepare a letter stating that it will not recommend an enforcement action to the commission if broker–dealers consider the particular rating agency an NRSRO for purposes of the net capital rule. By memorandum, the division advises the commission of its intention to send the no-action letter to the rating agency unless the commission objects to this action. If the commission does not object, the division will send the rating agency a no-action letter designating the agency as an NRSRO for purposes of various paragraphs of the net capital rule.

As discussed above, the term NRSRO has been used, in addition to its use in the net capital rule, in various other provisions of the commission's rules and regulations, as well as in legislation and in regulation T. Moreover, because in each of these instances NRSRO is defined as it is used in rule 15c3-1, the effect of the division's no-action letter is to designate the rating agency as an NRSRO under other provisions of the commission's rules and regulations that use the term NRSRO, in addition to the agency's designation for purposes of the net capital rule.

Since the designation of the first three NRSROs, the division has been contacted by other agencies seeking such designation. These agencies have sought the designation because the proliferation in the use of the term, especially its use in rule 2a-7 and in the MJDS, has turned such status into a competitive advantage. Using the no-action letter process described above, the division has recognized four additional NRSROs (i.e., Duff & Phelps, MCM, IBCA, and Thompson BankWatch).

While the division's no-action process has worked well in the short-term, given the fact that NRSRO designation has risen to the level of an international trade issue, a more formal process appears to be necessary for the long term. I believe that uniformity and comparability of ratings will be available only if each rating agency designated as an NRSRO is required to meet the same minimum published standards. Nevertheless, I recognize that one must balance such concerns with recognition that all rating agencies add value to the market by developing their own qualitative approach to credit analysis.

IV. RECOMMENDATIONS FOR THE REGULATORY TREATMENT OF RATING AGENCIES

There are several alternatives for addressing the question of what is the appropriate regulatory treatment of rating agencies for purposes of the federal securities laws.

A. Alternative 1: Revision of the Current System so that the Division No Longer Relies on the Ratings of NRSROs for Purposes of the Net Capital Rule or Designates Rating Agencies as NRSROs

I am inclined to believe that doing away with the concept of NRSRO in the commission's rules and regulations is not a realistic solution to dealing with the question of rating agencies. As discussed above, the practice of using ratings for regulatory purposes has become well established and is growing. When the division first proposed using ratings, it carefully evaluated the appropriateness of their use in the net capital rule and determined that ratings of nationally recognized rating agencies could be of value. Since that time, the use of ratings has been deemed valuable for purposes of other commission rules and regulations, as well as the rules of other regulatory bodies in the United States and abroad. Therefore, at this time, I would not recommend discontinuing the use of the term NRSRO.

B. Alternative 2: Continuation of the Current System of Designating Rating Agencies as NRSROs

With the expanded use of the term NRSRO in other commission rules and regulations, obtaining designation as an NRSRO has become of increased importance to rating agencies and also has resulted in increased scrutiny of rating agencies and their ratings. When the commission first used the term NRSRO in the net capital rule, it designated three rating agencies as NRSROs (i.e., Fitch, Moody's, and S&P). In the next 7 years, it added two more to the list (i.e., Duff & Phelps and MCM; the latter, of course, is no longer an NRSRO). Since October 1990, the commission has designated two additional rating agencies as NRSROs (i.e., BankWatch and IBCA); and the division currently has, as I mentioned earlier, active requests pending for the recognition of a number of additional foreign and domestic rating agencies. Nevertheless, rating agencies remain the only participants in the securities markets to be largely unregulated, despite the fact that their importance and influence is growing and is heavily documented.

Now just because some securities activity is not regulated by the commission does not necessarily mean that I am interested in regulating that activity. However, the combination of the commission's increasing reliance on NRSROs in our rules and regulations and of the growing number of rating agencies seeking NRSRO designation, particularly internationally, does lead me to believe that the commission should have minimum published standards for NRSRO designation. I am unaware how the commission could promulgate standards for NRSRO designation and for eligibility for continued designation without bringing NRSROs under direct commission oversight.

Currently all rating agencies designated as NRSROs are registered as investment advisers pursuant to the Investment Advisers Act (Advisers Act). Because of this registration as investment advisers, the commission receives the information the agencies are required to file as part of their registration under the Advisers Act. Additionally, the agencies are subject to inspection as part of the Division of Investment Management's examination program for investment advisers. However, if challenged, I am not entirely certain that the commission could require rating agencies to register under the Advisers Act.

The only other means of authority that the commission has over the rating agencies is through the no-action letters designating the agencies as NRSROs. Each rating agency designated as an NRSRO is directed to bring to the division's notice any material change in the facts of the no-action letter. If the division determines that the facts so warrant, it can then withdraw the letter.

In reality, however, despite the importance of rating agencies and ratings to the securities markets, the commission receives little information about the rating agencies and their operations. Often the division receives only informal information about the rating agencies, usually through business publications or from competing rating agencies. For example, the division learned about McGraw-Hill Inc.'s, S&P's parent company, acquisition of J. J. Kenny Co., a brokers' broker, from a *Wall Street Journal* article.[10]

As discussed above, although the NRSROs and their ratings have significant impact on the commission's rules and on the securities markets, I do not believe that the division has any meaningful authority over these organizations and their rating practices. Due to the continued growth in the use of ratings in the commission's rules and the important role of rating agencies in the securities markets, it appears to me that the commission should pursue a course of action that will bring NRSROs within the direct regulatory oversight of the commission.

C. Alternative 3: Propose Amendments to Rule 15c3-1 that Would Define the Term NRSRO, Require the Registration of NRSROs, and Set Forth Certain Minimum Standards to Govern the Operations of NRSROs

Although, as discussed above, the term NRSRO originally was used in the net capital rule, the rule does not define the term. Therefore, I would urge the division to consider recommending to the commission amendments to rule 15c3-1 that would define the term NRSRO. Based on its work in the area, the division has developed sufficient knowledge of the ratings industry to allow it to formulate a definition of this term. Additionally, these potential amendments to the net capital rule should require that NRSROs register with the commission in their capacity as NRSROs and that they establish and maintain certain minimum criteria in order to be considered NRSROs and in order to continue their NRSRO eligibility.

I believe that the promulgation of such amendments is necessary to ensure that the use of ratings in the commission's rules and regulations continues: (1) to enhance the financial safety and soundness of regulated entities, (2) to promote investor protection, and (3) to serve as a proxy of market liquidity and efficiency.

Obviously at this juncture I am discussing only a proposal. Any such proposal would of course be published and subject to the comment process. Further, even if any such proposal was eventually finalized, no rating agency would be forced to seek NRSRO designation. That action is voluntary. A rating agency must elect to "opt in" for regulatory treatment.

V. CONCLUSION

In conclusion, at least as a more formal solution to the need that I believe exists for direct commission oversight of NRSROs, I urge that the division consider recommending to the commission that it propose amendments to the net capital rule. These amendments should: (1) define the term NRSRO, (2) require the registration of these entities with the commission, and (3) set forth certain minimum standards or criteria that rating agencies must meet in order to obtain and maintain this designation.

NOTES

1. *See* release nos. 33-6902; 34-29354; 39-2267; IC-18210; 56 Fed. Reg. 30,036 (July 1, 1991).
2. See *Adoption of Amendments to Rule 15c3-1* and *Adoption of an Alternative Net Capital Requirement for Certain Brokers and Dealers*, Exchange Act release no. 11497 (June 26, 1975).
3. Paragraphs (c)(2)(vi)(E), (F) and (H) of rule 15c3-1.
4. J. Harris, "Inside Information for Outsiders." *Fin. Times*, July 22, 1991, p. 11.
5. The Secondary Mortgage Market Enhancement Act of 1984, Pub. L. no. 98-440.
6. See, e.g., regulation S-K; form S-3; forms F-2 and F-3.
7. See, e.g., rule 10b-6; rule 15c3-1; form 17-H.
8. See, e.g., rule 2a-7; rule 10F-3.
9. 12 C.F.R. part 220.2.
10. See "McGraw-Hill Plans to Buy J. J. Kenny." *Wall St. J.*, Dec. 13, 1989, p. A4.

26

Formal Regulatory Handle Needed for NRSRO Designation: Part II

Richard Y. Roberts
United States Securities and Exchange Commission, Washington, D.C.

I. INTRODUCTION

As some of you may be aware, during a commission meeting dealing with the adoption of amendments to rule 2a-7 under the Investment Company Act, I expressed concern with the commission's increased reliance on the judgment of so-called nationally recognized statistical rating organizations (NRSROs). I initially became concerned with the NRSRO designation process, and the absence of formal standards therefore, during the commission's rulemaking proceedings leading to the Multijurisdictional Disclosure and Modifications to the Current Registration and Reporting System for Canadian Issuers (MJDS).

The MJDS rules hinge more favorable regulatory treatment on the issuance of a high rating by an NRSRO; and the MJDS could well become the model for other such international accords. The result of all this is that the commission's increasing dependence on the judgment of NRSROs has resulted in the designation of a rating agency as an NRSRO by the commission being not only of domestic interest, but of international interest as well.

II. GROWTH OF THE ROLE OF NRSROs IN THE REGULATORY ARENA

The term *nationally recognized statistical rating organization* originally was adopted by the commission solely for purposes of distinguishing different grades of debt securities under its net capital rule, Exchange Act rule 15c3-1. However, the use of certain debt ratings by NRSROs, as the basis for awarding benefits that otherwise are not available to securities that are unrated or rated in a lower rating category, has expanded well beyond the original intended use of the concept in the net capital rule. The MJDS rules are one example. There are other examples which crop up in commission regulations promulgated pursuant to the Securities Act, the Exchange Act, and the Investment Company Act. The amendments adopted to rule 2a-7 are the latest example. I have suggested extending the concept myself by recommending that the commission propose a rule that would impose on broker–dealers a written suitability requirement when they sell unrated or low-rated municipal bonds to retail investors.

Since I have brought up the subject of municipal securities, that area serves as a good example of the prominent role played by rating agencies in our capital formation system. The importance of ratings to municipal securities market participants cannot be overemphasized. These ratings are relied upon by

The views expressed herein are those of Commissioner Roberts and do not necessarily represent those of the Commission, other Commissioners or the staff. Adapted with the permission of Richard Y. Roberts.

investors, municipalities, and underwriters. They have enormous impact on the investment decisions of both individual and institutional investors as well as the access to capital by municipal issuers.

Investors use ratings as part of their analysis in making an investment decision, including whether or not the entity is permitted to add a particular security to its investment portfolio or is required to divest itself of securities that it already holds; underwriters look at ratings in deciding whether to underwrite a particular issue; and brokers use ratings as part of their research reports for investors when making recommendations on particular securities. Moreover, the particular rating an issuer receives is an important factor in providing access to the market and in determining the interest rate that the municipality has to pay. In fact, ratings "enjoy universal use in the municipal bond market. They assist in the marketing of the many, and otherwise highly diverse, types of securities by compressing them into a few, relatively homogenous groupings."*

While the term NRSRO has expanded beyond the original intended use of the concept in the net capital rule, it is always defined as it is used in the net capital rule. Oddly enough, however, the commission has never actually issued a definition of the term NRSRO. It is time that the commission did so.

A couple of days ago in another presentation and in an attempt to provide standardization for NRSRO designation, I urged the commission's Division of Market Regulation (the division) to strongly consider recommending to the commission that it propose amendments to the net capital rule that would, among other things, define the term NRSRO. However, there are a couple of alternatives available for addressing the question of what is the appropriate regulatory treatment of rating agencies for purposes of the federal securities laws, other than proposing amendments to rule 15c3-1. I wish to briefly go through them with you.

A. Other Alternative 1: Revision of the Current System so that the Division No Longer Relies on the Ratings of NRSROs for Purposes of the Net Capital Rule or Designates Rating Agencies as NRSROs

I am inclined to believe that doing away with the concept of NRSRO in the commission's rules and regulations is not a realistic solution to dealing with the question of rating agencies. The practice of using ratings for regulatory purposes has become well established and is growing. When the division first proposed using ratings, it carefully evaluated the appropriateness of their use in the net capital rule and determined that ratings of nationally recognized rating agencies could be of value. Since that time, the use of ratings has been deemed valuable for purposes of other commission rules and regulations, as well as the rules of other regulatory bodies in the United States and abroad. Therefore, at this time, I would not recommend discontinuing the use of the term NRSRO.

B. Other Alternative 2: Continuation of the Current System of Designating Rating Agencies as NRSROs

With the expanded use of the term NRSRO in commission rules and regulations, obtaining designation as an NRSRO has become of increased importance to rating agencies and also has resulted in increased scrutiny of rating agencies and their ratings. When the commission first used the term NRSRO in the net capital rule, it designated three rating agencies as NRSROs (i.e., Fitch, Moody's, and S&P). In the next 7 years, it added two more to the list (i.e., Duff & Phelps and MCM; the latter, of course, is no longer an NRSRO). Since October 1990, the commission has designated two additional rating agencies as NRSROs (i.e., BankWatch and IBCA); and the division currently has active requests pending for the recognition of a number of additional foreign and domestic rating agencies. Nevertheless, rating agencies remain the only participants in the securities markets to be largely unregulated, despite the fact that their importance and influence is heavily documented.

Now just because some securities activity is not regulated by the commission does not necessarily mean that I am interested in regulating that activity. However, the combination of the commission's increasing reliance on NRSROs in our rules and regulations and of the growing number of rating agencies seeking NRSRO designation, particularly internationally, does lead me to believe that the commission should have minimum published standards for NRSRO designation. I am unaware how the commission could promulgate standards for NRSRO designation and for eligibility for continued designation without bringing NRSROs under direct commission oversight.

---

*See *Commission Staff Report, Transactions in Securities of the City of New York*, Aug. 1977: 5-5.

Currently, all rating agencies designated as NRSROs are registered as investment advisers pursuant to the Investment Advisers Act (Advisers Act). Because of this registration as investment advisers, the commission receives the information the agencies are required to file as part of their registration under the Advisers Act. Additionally, the agencies are subject to inspection as part of the Division of Investment Management's examination program for investment advisers. However, if challenged, I am not entirely certain that the commission could require rating agencies to register under the Advisers Act.

The only other means of authority that the commission has over the rating agencies is through no-action letters designating the agencies as NRSROs, which is a process that I will expand upon to some degree in a few minutes. Each rating agency designated as an NRSRO is directed to bring to the division's notice any material change in the facts of the no-action letter. If the division determines that the facts so warrant, it can then withdraw the letter.

In reality, however, despite the importance of rating agencies and ratings to the securities markets, the commission receives little information about the rating agencies and their operations. Often, the division receives only informal information about the rating agencies, usually through business publications or from competing rating agencies. For example, the division learned about McGraw-Hill Inc.'s S&P's parent company, acquisition of J. J. Kenny Co., a brokers' broker, from a *Wall Street Journal* article.*

As I have already discussed, although the NRSROs and their ratings have significant impact on the commission's rules and on the securities markets, I do not believe that the division has any meaningful authority over these organizations and their rating practices. Due to this continued growth in the use of ratings in the commission's rules and the important role of rating agencies in the securities markets, it appears to me that the commission should pursue a course of action that would bring NRSROs within the direct regulatory oversight of the commission. Thus, in my judgment the division should strongly consider recommending to the commission amendments to rule 15c3-1 that would, among other things, define the term NRSRO. Today it is my intention to flesh out to some extent what I believe should be provided in those amendments.

III. PROPOSED AMENDMENTS TO RULE 15c3-1

Any proposed package of amendments to the net capital rule should of course first define the term NRSRO. It is my opinion that the division has developed sufficient knowledge of the ratings industry to allow it to formulate a definition of this term. Such proposed amendments should also provide specific criteria which must be met by a rating agency in order to satisfy the definition of NRSRO and thereby achieve NRSRO designation. Further, the proposed amendments should require that NRSROs register with the commission in their capacity as NRSROs in order to ensure continued satisfaction of the NRSRO criteria.

Currently, as I mentioned earlier, any rating agency that wishes to be designated as an NRSRO for purposes of our securities laws must work through the division's no-action letter process. If the rating agency is successful in its quest, the division will ultimately send the rating agency a no-action letter designating the agency an NRSRO for purposes of the net capital rule. Through this no-action process, the division has formulated certain minimum standards that a rating agency must meet to be designated as an NRSRO. It appears to me that these standards should be used as the criteria upon which a formal NRSRO designation process should be bottomed.

The first and single most important criterion appears to be that the entity be recognized in the United States by the preeminent users of rating services as an issuer of credible and reliable ratings. It is the integrity and responsiveness of the rating agencies that determines their reputation for credibility. The reputation of a rating agency is the sum: (1) of its rating methodology, which must be seen as credible, thorough, and comprehensive; (2) of its analysts and management personnel, who must be seen to be unbiased and immune from outside pressures; and (3) of its ratings, which must be viewed as timely and useful to issuers and investor alike. If the agencies do not develop these attributes, the value of their ratings will decline and so will the use of these ratings.

Rating agencies themselves recognize that their reputation for integrity and reliability is their most valuable asset. Officials for S&P have noted that

---

*See "McGraw-Hill Plans to Buy J. J. Kenny." *Wall St. J.*, Dec. 13, 1989, p. A4

ratings are of value only as long as they are credible. Credibility arises primarily from the objectivity which results from the rater being independent of the issuer's business. The investor is willing to accept the rater's judgment only where such credibility exists. When enough investors are willing to accept the judgment of a particular rater, that rater gains recognition as a rating agency.*

The other specific criteria that the division has determined are important to ensuring that a rating agency has a minimum level of operational capability and that its ratings are reliable are: (1) the availability of sufficient financial resources (to permit the agency to operate independent of economic pressures); (2) adequate staffing (so that the entity is capable of thoroughly and competently evaluating an issuer's credit); (3) the agency's reputation for integrity in the marketplace (this goes to the question of whether the agency has national recognition as a credible and reliable source of ratings); (4) systematic rating procedures (which are necessary to ensure credible and accurate ratings); and (5) the agency's establishment and compliance with internal procedures designed to prevent misuse of nonpublic information.

The division also has determined that it is important for the NRSROs to disseminate their ratings publicly. This is because the ratings of the organizations are used in the net capital rule, among other of the commission's rules, and should be readily available for use and comparison. Nevertheless, not all of the rating agencies disseminate their ratings to newspapers or wire services, and copyright law may prevent such media sources from publishing the ratings without the express approval of the rating agencies. In any event, the division believes that it is necessary to require the public dissemination of ratings by the NRSROs. Of course, most public disseminations of ratings (i.e., except for press releases) are ordinarily accompanied by disclosures of consideration received in order to avoid violating section 17(b) of the Securities Act.

The division's efforts to develop minimum criteria and standards for NRSROs has been complicated by both the different uses of the term in regulations and the differences in the uses of ratings in markets worldwide. However, if, as I expect, ratings of NRSROs will continue to be employed as an integral and growing part of the commission's regulatory program, they should meet certain published minimum standards of uniformity or comparability. Otherwise, users of ratings, including investors, issuers, and broker-dealers, will be confused or uncertain as to whether or not a particular rating agency's rating qualifies a security for certain regulatory treatment. Additionally, without uniform standards, it will become more difficult for the commission's and the self-regulatory organization's examiners to monitor compliance with the commission's rules that use ratings.

Thus, while I believe that uniform standards are necessary, I am of the opinion that uniformity and comparability of ratings will be available only if each rating agency designated as an NRSRO is required to meet the same formal minimum standards.

IV.   CLARIFY AUTHORITY OF COMMISSION TO PROPOSE AMENDMENTS

The adoption of amendments to the net capital rule is necessary to make sure that the use of ratings in the commission's rules and regulations continues: (1) to enhance the financial safety and soundness of regulated entities, (2) to promote investor protection, and (3) to serve as a proxy of market liquidity and efficiency.

The difficulty with this approach, however, is that there remain lingering questions concerning the extent of the authority of the commission to promulgate rules to require the registration of NRSROs or to regulate the ratings activities of these agencies. Without legislative authority to require such registration and to regulate these entities, it is possible that the commission's authority to promulgate rules governing NRSROs may be challenged. Therefore, although in my view the commission should propose for comment amendments to rule 15c3-1 that would define the term NRSRO, require the registration of these entities with the commission, and establish certain minimum standards or criteria that must be maintained by these entities, clarification of commission authority to do so may be in order. Consequently, the commission should also consider seeking from the Congress legislation that would define the term NRSRO for purposes of section 3 of the Exchange Act and that would clarify the commission's authority with respect to NRSROs.

By defining the term NRSRO in the Exchange Act, Congress would provide certainty to a term that, although it appears in many instances throughout the federal securities laws, is nowhere defined. Additionally, there do appear to be sound and persuasive reasons for bringing the NRSROs squarely under the regulatory

---

*"Standard & Poor's Updates Its Guide to Rating Criteria." *Bond Buyer*, Dec. 23, 1983, p. 12.

oversight of the commission. As discussed previously, rating agencies, despite the great degree of influence that they exert in the financial markets, are not formally regulated. By obtaining the legislative authority to regulate the NRSROs, the commission's regulatory authority to promulgate rules that would provide for both registration of the NRSROs and regulatory oversight over their actions would be clarified.

V. CONCLUSION

In conclusion, it is my judgment that, in addition to proposing amendments to the net capital rule that would define the term NRSRO, require the registration of NRSROs, and set forth certain minimum standards to govern the operations of NRSROs, the commission should also consider recommending to Congress that it pass legislation that would define the term NRSRO for purposes of section 3 of the Exchange Act and that would clarify the commission's oversight authority with respect to NRSROs.

27

Information Needed for Rating Municipal Bonds and Notes

Tax-Supported Bond Anticipation Notes

Primary Documents

Official statement or prospectus

Notice of sale (if public sale)

Legal opinion

Law(s) under which the notes are to be issued (this requirement is waived if the law has been previously submitted and has not been subsequently amended)

Note resolution or ordinance

Bond resolution or ordinance

Annual reports or audits for the last three years

Current operating budget

Engineer's report, if available

Bond purchase commitment letter, if sale of the bonds has been pre-arranged (i.e.,

to an agency of the United States Government)

Support Documents
(for information not contained in any of the aforementioned documents)

Maturity schedule for all bond anticipation notes, including final statutory maturity date for this and outstanding notes

Basis for interest rate computation

Complete debt statement of issuer, including debt-incurring capacity

Interest rate limitations on bonds and notes

List of last five bond issues of the type that will fund the notes, including amount, sale date, number of bids received (if public sale), and net interest cost for each

Enterprise-Supported Revenue Bonds

Primary Documents

Official statement or prospectus

Notice of sale (if public sale)

Legal opinion

Trust indenture, bond resolution, or ordinance and any other legal documents (i.e., lease or escrow agreements, supplemental resolution or indenture) if applicable

Annual reports or audits for the last three years; include interim financial results for recently concluded but unaudited period, or year-to-date results and comparable period in prior year

Most recent operating budget

Capital budget or planning document

Engineering report on feasibility and construction, if available

Financial feasibility study including projections, if available

Rate study, if available

Support Documents
(for information not contained in any of the aforementioned documents)

Description of enterprise, including system capacity and trend of usage, particularly customers and consumption (output) by year for past five years; percent of service purchased by each major user

Description of rate setting process; record of revisions for past five years

Public employees: number employed and trend; status of contracts, unions, and pension funds

Economic data for service area

Debt (outstanding and new): segregate by security; actual principal maturities and interest requirements for each year, pro-forma debt service schedule for new debt including interest rate assumptions

Investment policy: formal document or brief description of practices

Major customers based on usage and revenues

Statement describing any outstanding environmental or permitting issues

Enterprise-Supported Revenue Bond Anticipation Notes

Primary Documents

Official statement or prospectus

Notice of sale (if public sale)

Legal opinion

Law(s) under which the notes are to be issued (this requirement is waived if the law has been previously submitted and has not been subsequently amended)

Note resolution or ordinance

Bond resolution or ordinance, trust indenture, and any other legal documents relevant to the bonds and notes

Annual reports or audits for the last three years

Current operating budget

Engineer's report on feasibility and construction, if available

Bond purchase commitment letter, if sale of the bonds has been pre-arranged (i.e., to an agency of the United States Government)

Support Documents
(for information not contained in any of the aforementioned documents)

Maturity schedule for all bond anticipation notes, including final statutory maturity date for this and outstanding notes

Basis for interest rate computation

Complete debt statement of issuer, including debt-incurring capacity

Interest rate limitations on bonds and notes

List of last five bond issues of type that will fund notes, including amount, sale date, number of bids received (if public sale), and net interest cost

Enterprise system description

Major customers based on usage and revenues

Statement describing any outstanding environmental or permitting issues

Lease Rental Bonds and Certificates of Participation Secured by an Underlying Lease

Primary Documents
(as applicable)

Official statement or prospectus

Notice of sale (if public sale)

Legal opinion of qualified bond counsel for overall transaction and specifically opining on validity and binding obligation for both trust and lease agreements (if private sector lessor is involved, Moody's also requires an opinion covering insolvency issues relating to the lessor)

Trust agreement, indenture of trust, master trust, mortgage trust

Lease agreement, lease purchase agreement, facility lease, master lease

Assignment agreement

Agency agreement

Site lease

Authorizing resolution of governing body

Description of lessee functions, services, and management

Project description

Certificate of essential use

Construction or acquisition schedule

Asset appraisal (applicable when utilizing existing asset to secure lease)

Useful life of any equipment financed

Annual reports or audits of lessee for the last three years

Most recent operating budget of lessee

Capital budget or planning document of lessee

Copy of local charter or document which describes governmental structure of lessee

For school districts: 10-year enrollment trend and projection; school plant description, including facilities and capacity

Lease Rental Bonds and Certificates of Participation
Secured by an Underlying Lease *continued*

Notes: If there is private sector involvement, please refer to the following Moody's *Municipal Credit Reports*: "Private Sector Involvement in Municipal Leasing: Analytical Rating Approach," dated May 6, 1991, and "Bank-Related Involvement in Municipal Leasing: Analytical Rating Approach," dated December 6, 1991.

In the case of secondary market securitization, please contact a member of the lease specialty group.

Support Documents
(applies to lessee for information not contained in any of the above documents)

Assessed valuation for the last five years

Equalization ratios for the last five years

List of 10 largest taxpayers, their assessed valuation, and description

Current population and latest census estimates

Tax rates and levies for the last five years, including collection of current year's levy and total tax collections; tax rates of overlapping jurisdictions

Tax assessment and/or collection procedures, including due dates and penalty rates

Tax and/or levy limitations

Debt or interest rate limits

Statement of direct debt and debt of overlapping debt issuers, including allocable share

Annual principal and interest payments of outstanding debt, with bonds segregated by security and projects defined

Future plans for debt issuance

Number and dollar amount of building permits over the last five years

Number of governmental employees, whether unionized, and contract status

Statement regarding status of employee pension funds; latest actuarial study, if available

Local and area unemployment rate

List of 10 leading employers, number of employees, and type of business

Area of the issuer (in square miles) and percentage of land that is developed

Investment policy: formal document or brief description of practices

Enterprise system description, if relevant, including: system capacity and trend of usage, particularly annual customers and consumption (output) for past five years; percent of service purchased by each major user; description of rate setting process; record of rate revisions for past five years

Tax and/or Revenue Anticipation Notes (Operating Loans)

Primary Documents

Official statement or prospectus

Notice of sale (if public sale)

Legal opinion

Note resolution or ordinance and other pertinent legal documents

Cash flow statements: include at least one full fiscal year actual; current fiscal year through note maturity (see accompanying form for general format and level of detail) *Note:* The cash flows are on a cash basis

and should not include or show negative receipts or disbursements or negative balances

Annual reports or audits for the last three years

Current operating budget and next year's budget (proposed or adopted, as available)

Law(s) under which the notes are being issued (this requirement is waived if the law has been previously submitted and has not been amended subsequently)

Tax and/or Revenue Anticipation Notes (Operating Loans) *continued*

Support Documents
(for information not contained in any of the aforementioned documents)

Assumptions used in preparing cash flows

Tax rates and levies for the last five years; current and total collections; tax rates of overlapping jurisdictions

Tax assessment and collection procedures, including due dates and penalty rates

Maturity schedule for all tax and/or revenue anticipation notes outstanding, including final statutory maturity dates

Tax and levy limitations

List of operating loan borrowings over the last five fiscal years, including type and amount issued in fiscal year, and amount outstanding at year end, and interest rates on the notes

Explanation of segregation procedure, if any, of funds for the payment of the notes

Status of employee contracts and pension plans

Investment policy: formal document or brief description of practices

Note: For information requirements on pooled tax and revenue note transactions, please contact a regional ratings manager.

Sample Cash Flow Summary Table

CASH FLOW SUMMARY (millions of dollars) [1]

Name of Issuer: _____

Period Covered: [2] _____

Month									
Balance									
RECEIPTS	XXXXXXX	XXXXXXX	XXXXXXX	XXXXXXX	XXXXXXX	XXXXXXX	XXXXXXX	XXXXXXX	XXXXXXXX
Property taxes									
State aid									
Sales taxes									
Federal aid									
Other									
Loans from other funds									
Note proceeds									
*									
TOTAL RECEIPTS									
DISBURSEMENTS	XXXXXXX	XXXXXXX	XXXXXXX	XXXXXXX	XXXXXXX	XXXXXXX	XXXXXXX	XXXX	
Salaries & benefits									
Services & supplies									
Capital outlays									
Note principal repayments									
Note interest repayments [3]									
**									
TOTAL DISBURSEMENTS									
Balance									
REPAY FUND***	XXXXXXX	XXXXXXX	XXXXXXX	XXXXXXX	XXXXXXX	XXXXXXX	XXXXXXX	XX	
Balance									
Receipts									
Disbursements									
Balance									

*Other major categories; e.g. Business taxes, utility taxes, fines, use of money and property; transfers in, reimbursement/repayments from other funds, etc.
**Other major categories, e.g., repayment of other loans, transfers out, etc.
***Applicable if resolution or statutes requires segregation of funds for note repayment

1 Includes General, _____
2 Actual Data through _____
3 Assumed rate of _____%
  Actual rate of _____%

Grant Anticipation Notes

Primary Documents

Official statement or prospectus

Notice of sale (if public sale)

Legal opinion

Note resolution or ordinance and other pertinent legal documents

Cash flow statements: include all relevant funds during construction period until notes are due

Annual reports or audits for the last three years

Current operating budget and next year's budget (proposed or adopted, if applicable)

Law(s) under which the notes are being issued (this requirement is waived if the law has been previously submitted and has not been amended subsequently)

Copies of executed grant agreements/ contracts

Engineer's report for the grant project, if available

Support Documents
(for information not contained in any of the aforementioned documents)

Assumptions used in preparing cash flows

Investment policy: formal document or brief description of practices

Enterprise system description, if relevant, including: system capacity and trend of usage, particularly annual customers and consumption (output) for past five years; percent of service purchased by each major user; description of rate setting process; record of rate revisions for past five years

Hospital Revenue Bonds

Primary Documents

Official statement or prospectus

Notice of sale (if public sale)

Legal opinion

Relevant legal documents including, but not limited to, the master trust indenture (if applicable), trust indenture and loan agreement

Annual audited financial statements for the past five years and unaudited year-to-date interim statements (with figures for prior year's comparable period)

Historical inpatient and outpatient utilization for the past five years and year-to-date interim figures (with figures for prior year's comparable period)

Financial feasibility study, if available, or management's own utilization and financial projections

Management letters (a.k.a. accountant's letter of recommendation) for past five years

Sources/uses of funds for proposed debt

Support Documents
(for information not contained in any of the aforementioned documents)

Description of hospital and its services

Description of corporate organizational structure

Physician staff information (i.e., number of total staff; number of active staff; number of active staff that are board certified; number of admissions attributed to, and age of, the 10 leading admitting physicians; deletions and additions to active staff for past five years; average age of active staff)

List of competitors and relevant utilization information; include market share analysis, if available

Number of full-time equivalent employees for past five years

Medicare case mix index

Percent of gross patient revenues for past five years by payor type

Schedule of annual principal and interest payments for new and outstanding debt

Mortgage-Backed Housing Bonds

Primary Documents

Official statement or prospectus

Notice of sale (if public sale)

Legal opinion; other opinions as applicable

Trust indenture, bond resolution or ordinance, and any other legal documents (e.g., supplemental resolution or indenture, investment agreement(s), origination and servicing agreement) if applicable

Annual reports or audits for the last three years; include interim financial results for recently concluded but unaudited period, or year-to-date results and comparable period in prior year

Cash flow projections including all assumptions

Support Documents

(for information not contained in any of the aforementioned documents)

For All Programs

Description of issuer's administrative activities

List of program investments; description of investment policies

Reserve Fund levels and history of any previous draws below requirements

For Single Family Programs

Mortgage interest rate(s); types of loans (fixed rate, GEM, GPM, etc.); term(s) of loans

Number and dollar amount of loans in portfolio (original and current)

Dates first and last loans originated

Uncommitted lendable funds: dollar amount (if any)

Insurance coverage: percentage breakdown by private mortgage insurance, VA, FHA, uninsured

Percentage breakdown of private mortgage insurance loans by insurer

Pool coverage: insurer; amount of coverage; which loans are covered

Description of self-insurance funds; claim experience

Loan characteristics: percentages of new construction loans; condominiums loans; planned developments financed

Delinquencies: 30, 60, 90 days, and in foreclosure (percent of total)

Real estate owned properties: number and dollar amount

Claims on pool policy: number and dollar amount

Description of any rejected insurance claims (primary or pool); number and dollar amount of any uninsured foreclosure losses.

For FHA-Insured Multi-Family Programs

List of projects; number of units in each project; project locations

Number and dollar amount of loans outstanding

Dates of initial and final FHA endorsement for each loan

Description of any present or past loan delinquencies

Status of any FHA insurance claims

General comment on physical condition of projects

For All Other Multi-Family Programs

List of projects; number of units in each project; project locations

Dates construction completed for each project

Occupancy levels for each project; description of any past occupancy problems

HUD contract rent for each unit (if applicable)

Project cash flow experience

General comment on current physical condition of buildings; whether renovations, rehabilitation or major maintenance have been performed or planned

Frequency of on-site inspections

Number and dollar amount of mortgage loans outstanding; description of any delinquencies, defaults or other problems meeting mortgage payments

Casualty and other insurance coverage

Higher Education/University Revenue Bonds

Primary Documents

Official statement or prospectus

Notice of sale (if public sale)

Legal opinion

Trust indenture

Resolution or bond ordinance

Annual reports or audits for the last three years; include interim financial results for recently concluded but unaudited period, or year-to-date results and comparable period in prior year

Most recent operating budget

Capital budget or planning document

Debt statement of all parity and separately secured issues; actual principal maturities and interest requirements for each year

Enrollment: five-year trend of actual and five-year trend of projected enrollment

Application pool information and 10-year trend analysis

Tuition and room and board trends for the last five years

Support Documents
(for information not contained in any of the aforementioned documents)

Latest endowment fund balances (restricted and unrestricted)

Investment policy: formal document or brief description of practices

Financial aid: percent of students receiving; types of aid; dollar amount

Five-year trends of gifts, grants, and bequests

Employees: number employed and trend, status of contracts, union representation, pension funds

Catalogue of courses offered

Student Loan Revenue Bonds

Primary Documents

Official statement

Notice of sale (if public sale)

Legal opinions, including bond counsel opinion and perfected security opinion

Trust indenture, bond resolution, and any other legal documents (e.g., supplemental resolution, investment agreement(s), swap agreement, origination and servicing agreements, custodial and depository agreements), if applicable

Secondary market annual reports or audits for the last three years, including interim financial results for recently concluded but unaudited period

Cash flow projections including all assumptions under various stressful scenarios

Support Documents
(for information not contained in any of the aforementioned documents)

Description of issuer's administrative activities and controls

Student loan portfolio information (including, but not limited to, school type, loan type, repayment status, delinquencies, historical defaults, default projections)

Loan servicing statistics, including rejection rates

Guarantor portfolio and reimbursement information, including three years past "trigger" rates, reserve levels, annual guarantee volume, recovery rates, and any outstanding sanctions or fines with the Department of Education, as well as information on portfolio characteristics

Letter-of-Credit-Backed Issues

Primary Documents

Official statement or prospectus

Notice of sale (if public sale)

Legal opinion

Trust indenture

Resolution or bond ordinance

Letter of credit and reimbursement agreement

Loan or lease agreement

Bank counsel enforceability opinion (foreign and domestic)

Preference (bankruptcy) opinion

Bond purchase agreement

Support Documents

(as applicable, for information not contained in any of the aforementioned documents)

Remarketing agreement

Tender agent agreement

Pledge and security agreement

Guaranty agreement

Mortgage and/or collateral documents

Standby bond purchase agreement

Interest rate swap agreement

Guaranteed investment contract

Refunded Bonds

Primary Documents

Escrow agreement or letter of instructions (in draft form if the refunding closing has not occurred, otherwise an executed copy)

Primary legal instruments for both the refunded and refunding bonds (i.e., trust indenture, resolution, bond ordinance)

Official statements for both the refunded and refunding bonds

A verification report attesting to the sufficiency of funds in the escrow, which must be prepared by either a certified public accountant or some other person or entity acceptable to Moody's

Escrow agent's attestation of the securities purchased and held in the escrow account

Defeasance opinion (if available)

Preference opinion (if applicable)

Section 362(a) opinion (if applicable)

Notes: In order to facilitate the rating process, Moody's recommends that we receive the refunded documents in draft form prior to the refunded closing date. Early receipt enables us to work with the issuer and other parties to ensure that the provisions of the escrow meet our criteria, thereby eliminating the need to supplement the documents after the closing date.

28

The Role of Economic Factors in Moody's Credit Analysis

Edward Krauss and Alfred Medioli
Moody's Investors Service, New York, New York

In determining long-term credit quality and an issuer's ability to repay its debt, economic factors usually play a major role. Although the economy is probably the least controllable of the four main credit factors, it is critical to Moody's analysis of general obligation credit quality because the economic base is ultimately what generates the resources to repay municipal debt.

While an issuer's tax base is what provides the resources, the capacity to pay is also measured, in part, by an area economy's stability in periods of economic slowdown and uncertainty, as well as by growth trends exhibited in more normal times. In our evaluation, Moody's analyzes economic data received at regular intervals from the federal, state, and local governments to assess current conditions and to aid in predicting future performance.

Q. What weight does Moody's give to economic factors in determining a credit rating?
A. When the evaluation of a municipal issue is first undertaken, no single area of analysis is considered by Moody's to be most important. As analysis of an issue proceeds, however, one factor may become more important because it represents a particular vulnerability of strength for the credit. Of the four broad areas of analysis Moody's examines, the economy is most often the area that results in rating distinctions among municipalities. Such distinctions recognize that communities with more diversified, broader economies and favorable socioeconomic indices are generally equipped to ride out periods of slow growth and recession better than places with narrow and limited economic bases. Therefore, even though good management, low debt levels, and strong financial operations are present for a number of municipalities, those with healthy and diverse economic bases may receive moderately higher debt ratings.

Q. What sort of information does Moody's consider when analyzing an issuer's economy and economic performance?
A. Because the capacity to repay debt is determined to a great extent by a community's economic resources, Moody's economic analysis focuses on the relative size and value of the tax base, economic performance, population trends, employment rates, and various other indicators. In addition to examining these overall measures of the economic base, Moody's is also concerned with the characteristics of the resident population itself. Furthermore, a number of measures are examined to determine an area's economic direction. Since Moody's examines a broad array of statistical data, no single measure predominates our judgment.

Q. Can you discuss some of the specific measures Moody's considers when evaluating a community's economic resources?
A. When assessing an issuer's ability to support debt and pay for services, a municipal credit analyst must evaluate the extent of a community's overall wealth. Although no single aggregate measure fully quantifies a community's wealth, the assessed and full values of all taxable property are useful proxies. Moody's

Adopted from *Municipal Issues* (Oct. 1991): 7-9 by permission of Moody's Investors Service.

analyzes data for a period of years to determine significant trends in overall growth as well as the composition of that growth. By looking at various supporting data, Moody's can determine whether a community is experiencing increased values through price appreciation or through new and additional development; whether the tax base is keeping pace with inflation; and if current and historical tax collection rates are stable or improving. Since tax data is compiled on a local or state level, and methods used for calculation generally differ, it is not very useful to compare this data between states in a given geographic region or nationally.

The percent and direction of an area's population change is a good measure of economic vitality. A diverse economic base—one that is not vulnerable to a single employer or type of industry—will tend to grow steadily as population growth keeps pace with general economic growth. An economy that is completely dependent on a cyclical industry may surge or stagnate in terms of population, or even demonstrate declines. Consequently, steady population growth is usually viewed as a favorable credit factor. Stagnation or decline in population may raise concerns, while sudden dramatic growth may be viewed with caution, in that it does not necessarily indicate a true trend. The density of an area and local zoning regulations are also important in terms of assessing whether there is room for growth.

Current and historical labor force and employment data indicate economic performance over long- and near-term periods and provide us with a measure of stability or cyclicality. Unemployment rates are perhaps the most current measure of an area's economic health. Equally important are unemployment trends, which may demonstrate a municipality's ability to withstand changes in national or regional economic fortunes. These measures are most useful when compared with similar information for neighboring communities, the state, and the nation.

Q. What measures are used to evaluate the character of the resident population?
A. Moody's relies on a variety of socioeconomic data, much of which is provided by the U.S. Census Bureau. Two of the most useful statistics for determining an area's economic well-being are per capita earned income and median family income. The various measures of income are particularly meaningful when compared to state, regional, and national norms compiled by Moody's, so that relative costs of living and other differences can be accounted for. The rate of income growth relative to other places is also important in that it may reflect an improving, declining, or stable economy.

Q. At what indicators of economic direction does Moody's look?
A. Analysts consider the credit quality and market position of a region's largest employers and the strength of its largest taxpayers. Moody's Public Finance Department analysts consult regularly with analysts in Moody's Corporate Department for information on the performance of a local government's largest corporate employers or taxpayers and/or any overview of a particularly dominant industry.

Especially critical in our evaluation are indicators of economic growth. The economic statistics that Moody's examines will vary, depending upon the forces that drive the area's economy. Moody's analysts look favorably on steady increases in retail sales, building permits, and other indicators that measure aspects of economic activity. Information regarding utility hookups and housing prices are received periodically from municipal issuers and are other important indicators of economic health or potential problems. Information about these various activities becomes even more critical when an entity has its finances or debt supported by any of these sources.

Q. From where and how often does Moody's receive its economic information?
A. Moody's has an extensive economic data base that contains information on over 25,000 communities. This data is received periodically from the U.S. Census Bureau and other governmental agencies and provides demographic, employment, and other economic statistics. Moody's also receives tax base information and various other indicators of economic activity and growth from state and local governments.

Moody's receives the latest Bureau of Labor Statistics (BLS) employment data for all communities on an annual and monthly basis, thereby allowing us to assess historical and current conditions. Other census information is received as it becomes available. Various population, income, and housing information from the 1990 census is now being received, so changes that have occurred locally and across the nation since 1980 can be examined. Tax and other local data is received at least annually and, in many cases, more frequently.

Q. How important is economic diversity?
A. Economic diversity is important in that it can provide long-term resilience to the local economy and protection against a decline in any one sector. Although concentration in one industry or company carries with it inherent vulnerabilities, at the same time, the presence of a major facility can benefit a local tax base and create primary and secondary jobs. The stability of such a company or industry is a prime concern for Moody's analysts. Many places have economies highly dependent on one sector or industry, or even on a single employer, which could leave them vulnerable to an economic downturn and periods of high unemployment during recessions. In this regard, our analysts consider the strength and performance of a municipality or region's largest employers and taxpayers as well as a dominant industry or sector. Recent and historical employment trends both for the community and company are analyzed. Our analysts are also interested in the nature of the product line and the extent of duplicate facilities elsewhere. Moody's Corporate Department analysts are consulted regularly for information on a dominant company or industry.

It is essential that a distinction is made between true diversity—as is generally present in a major metropolitan area—and local diversity within an area that is fundamentally not diverse. To illustrate, Billings, Montana, is locally diverse, in that it has substantial trade, banking, financial services, etc., but all these industries serve the primarily agricultural and mineral-based region of eastern Montana. In this example, local diversity does not provide full protection against declines in oil—as occurred in Billings in the late 1980s. Billings' local diversity did, however, provide some insulation against the negative effects of the regional decline.

Q. What about economic stability, as opposed to great diversity?
A. The value of diversity lies in its ability to provide long-term resilience, and conceptually, stability achieves the same end. Thus, a single employer such as a state university or an important and well-managed power plant can provide long-term stability, even in an area that is not particularly diverse. However, the economic bases served by such a large, stable employer probably would not be as strong as those of a large metropolitan area that enjoys true diversity and that, to some extent, can grow its own economic base.

Q. Does Moody's favor a rapidly growing economy?
A. Not necessarily. With growth comes new challenges and often, the need to take on new debt to build and maintain expanded services. In some instances, rapid growth creates more crises and long-term credit problems than benefits. On the other hand, although stability can have great merits, it can also be an indication of economic stagnation which, in turn, might indicate an eventual decline. Because these characteristics are qualitative, Moody's analysts are careful in interpreting quantitative measures to arrive at conclusions regarding economic growth.

Q. What is the relationship between municipal ratings and the corporate ratings assigned to a municipality's largest taxpayers, employers, etc.?
A. The relationship is an indirect one. While the strength of a municipality's leading companies is sometimes an important credit factor, it cannot be assumed that a given company's strength determines economic stability. For example, a corporation with *Aaa*-rated debt might be so rated because it is quick to dispose of unprofitable operations; therefore, the presence of a factory owned by this corporation in a town is a worthwhile component of the local economy only to the extent that the factory has value to the corporation. For this reason, Moody's Public Finance analysts consult regularly with our corporate analysts to discuss the outlook and overall operating approach of dominant taxpayers and/or employers.

29

The Role of Financial Factors in Moody's Credit Analysis

Paul Devine and Robert W. Stanley
Moody's Investors Service, New York, New York

Financial performance is an integral factor in Moody's credit analysis, often reflecting the degree to which the other primary credit factors—debt, administration and economy—are favorable or unfavorable for a given municipal issuer. Annual operating performance and resultant year-end financial position will reflect the strength of a municipality's management, the area's economic conditions, and debt practices employed. Furthermore, financial operations and performance are critical because, regardless of economic, spending, and taxing realities, a municipal government is expected both to remain solvent in order to meet the service demands of its constituents, and to balance its budget.

Q. What areas does Moody's examine in assessing an issuer's level of financial control?
A. In order to assess an issuer's degree of financial control, our analysts must know the scope of municipal services that need to be provided, and the degree of flexibility and extent of resources the issuer has to provide those services. The municipal entity's mission, budgetary responsibilities, and revenue-raising ability should be clearly delineated.

It is important to note that an established trend of financial control is more important to Moody's than year-end figures alone. Budgetary planning, daily spending control, policies on spending growth, use of surplus, and shortfall contingency plans are all critical to maintaining budget balance and are, therefore, examined in our credit analysis.

Q. What role does an issuer's revenue-raising authority play in the evaluation of its finances?
A. Revenue-raising flexibility is an important component in determining how much financial control an issuer is able to exert. The existence of broad powers to raise tax rates and other fees independently provides a strong means of determining future budget conditions. The Moody's analyst is particularly interested in the way revenue-raising authority is used. Moody's views timely tax and fee increases most favorably because, if revenue reviews are not undertaken as part of the annual budget process and tax rate adjustments are implemented only during a crisis situation, tax rate increases can become traumatic events.

Moody's also likes to see a diverse array of revenue sources so that there is not an overreliance on any one revenue stream. An administration's success in developing and implementing innovative sources of revenue is also looked upon favorably in our credit analysis.

Q. What are some of the key financial indicators examined by Moody's during the course of credit analysis?
A. Some financial indicators examined are general fund balance as percent of revenues; annual percentage

---

Adapted from *Municipal Issues* (Dec. 1991): 5-6 by permission of Moody's Investors Service.

growth in revenues and expenditures; the amounts of and reasons for interfund transfers; primary revenue sources and expenditure items; the composition of assets and liabilities; cash position; and actual financial performance relative to budget.

Q. And what are the important qualitative factors with regard to finances?
A. Qualitative factors include the level of control an issuer has over financial operations; the scope of municipal services to be provided; revenue-raising and spending flexibility; and accuracy and consistency of accounting procedures.

Q. What role does an issuer's local economy play in the analysis of financial performance?
A. Because an issuer's revenue-raising powers are important, the relative strengths and weaknesses of its local economy can have an impact on financial performance. Economic control is measured in terms of how sensitive a municipality or enterprise's financial condition is to the performance of the local economy. Cyclical sensitivity of some revenue sources—personal and business income taxes, sales taxes, and fees and charges to industrial or commercial users—can be an indicator of financial vulnerability. Property taxes are a more predictable and stable source of revenues; therefore, local governments that rely on ad valorem taxation for the bulk of their resources require a thinner cushion of reserves than those governments that rely on more economically-sensitive taxes and user fees.

Q. Will my rating suffer if I resort to one-shot revenues to achieve a balanced budget?
A. One-shot revenues definitely have a legitimate use in municipal budgets if used appropriately. One-shots do not raise analytic concerns if they are used to meet nonrecurring expenses, such as the financing of a capital project, costs associated with a legal judgment, or any other extraordinary item. Moody's generally takes a dim view of one-shot budget fixes, however, when they are not part of an overall plan to restore recurring balances. Financial operations become vulnerable to deterioration if one-shots are used to meet recurring expenditures since such revenue sources are not likely to be available on an annual basis.

Q. Does Moody's recommend any particular course of action to address a budget imbalance?
A. Although such decisions are best made by local representatives, an issuer should keep in mind that strategies can differ for short-term versus long-term objectives. If a temporary imbalance must be surmounted, then deferral of some expenses might be an appropriate response. If an operating imbalance is expected to persist in the absence of corrective action, then the response should achieve ongoing budget balance while also maintaining essential service provision and an adequate physical plant.

Q. How would Moody's view an operating deficit?
A. The reason behind an operating deficit can be more important than the deficit itself. Since Moody's looks for a structural balance between recurring operating revenues and expenditures, a deficit caused by an imbalance in this area poses the risk of further financial deterioration if remedial action is not taken. However, a deficit caused by events not likely to be repeated, or incurred as part of a larger plan that is designed realistically to achieve lasting structural balance, or for which management demonstrates the ability and willingness to take corrective action, poses far less risk of continued financial deterioration.

Q. Does Moody's consider short-term borrowing to have a negative effect on financial position?
A. As is true for one-shot revenues, short-term borrowing can be acceptable, and even favorable, if used prudently. For many local governments, the timing of receipts and disbursements do not coincide, giving rise to a legitimate need for cash flow borrowing. In other instances, short-term borrowing is undertaken to accommodate or "roll-over" an accumulated deficit. The latter activity is not viewed favorably by Moody's as it is merely a way of continuing fundamentally unbalanced operations. In addition, an issuer reliant on such a practice to balance its budget runs the risk of not being able to access the short-term market and meet expenses in a timely manner.

Q. In the evaluation of general fund balance, what does Moody's consider to be of major importance?
A. The availability of adequate financial reserves that can be used to address unforeseen contingencies is

imperative if an issuer is to control its financial position. The presence of such reserves—or fund balance—provides a cushion to protect against unexpected or temporary operating imbalances. Essentially, a solid fund balance can give an issuer some time to take corrective action. The actual level of fund balance should be related to the likelihood of drawing upon such reserves. A credit rating need not suffer from a relatively small balance if a low level of reserves is justified by a long-term trend of annual budget surpluses. Conversely, a larger fund balance may be warranted if budget revenues and expenses are economically sensitive or not easily forecast.

Although general fund operations are often a key focus in the analysis of general obligation debt, Moody's analysts are interested in the financial position of all funds, including special revenue funds and enterprise funds. Because we are concerned about how an issuer deals with expenditures that it must fund from its own resources, we tend to place special emphasis on those funds over which the issuer has discretion, as opposed to those that are state or federal pass-throughs.

Q. Is there a certain level of which fund balance must be maintained in order to receive a good rating?
A. There is no specific size fund balance that is ideal in all circumstances. As a general rule of thumb, Moody's likes to see a general fund balance equal to at least 5% of revenues, but factors such as the magnitude of operations, volatility and predictability of revenue sources and expenditures, and history of achieving budget targets may dictate larger or smaller balances. We also place strong emphasis on the examination of margins available in revenue sources and the degree of expenditure flexibility that can be relied upon to meet contingent needs. Finally, the demonstrated ability of the locality's management to meet budget targets and cope with unplanned events leaves the analyst more comfortable with a smaller fund balance than if such a history is lacking.

Q. Does Moody's consider large fund balances to be indicative of sound finances?
A. Large fund balances often reflect sound financial management, but not always, for two reasons. First, overly large balances can lead to discontent among employees and taxpayers, who may question the need for such reserves when the money could be used for salaries or lower taxes. Second, the fund balance is a measure of financial position, but financial structure is important as well. For example, Moody's looks to see if there is a trend of recurring revenues being sufficient to meet recurring expenditures, what funds the issuer has complete discretion over, whether interfund transfers are made, etc.

Q. What kinds of accounting/financial reporting does Moody's require?
A. Although there is no specific Moody's requirement as to the type of financial statement submitted or the reporting basis used, we generally prefer GAAP (generally accepted accounting principles) reporting. Adherence to GAAP permits the analyst to gather, compare, and evaluate financial information efficiently on a comparative basis. What is most important, however, is how well financial statements allow the analyst to assess whether a borrower's finances and budgeting practices are weak or sound.

30

The Role of Administrative Factors in Moody's Credit Analysis

Michael Johnston

Moody's Investors Service, New York, New York

Although frequently thought of as more subjective and less quantifiable than other rating factors, an evaluation of a municipal entity's administrative factors is critical to Moody's analysis of municipal credit quality. Indeed, in today's slowing economic and tightening fiscal environment, management issues may be more important than ever. Two of the cities highlighted in this edition of *Municipal Issues*—Cambridge, Mass. and South St. Paul, Minn.—are excellent examples of the positive influence good management can have on a municipality's credit standing.

What follows are answers to some of the most frequently asked questions concerning the analysis of administrative and governmental factors.

Q. What does the analysis of administrative factors involve?
A. Included in Moody's analysis of administrative factors are such issues as the legal and structural organization of a given municipal entity, the services that entity is responsible for providing, the amount of flexibility it has in providing those services, its revenue structure, and management's experience and record of accomplishments.

Since providing even the most basic services can be costly, Moody's analysts also focus on the powers and abilities of governmental entities to draw on the economic resources available in the region within which they operate, and any associate legal or statutory constraints. Intergovernmental relationships must also be assessed, particularly when services are provided to a common group of tax or rate payers. In some cases, a given entity may be responsible for providing services in tandem with other levels of government. At one extreme are relatively independent units that provide all local government services that in other places are traditionally provided by multiple layers of government. At the other extreme are governmental arrangements where even such basic services as police and fire are the responsibility of independent special service districts. The Moody's analyst must assess the legal structure of these intergovernmental relationships, as well as the political environment and level of community support for the various services provided.

Q. How does Moody's evaluate the administrative factors?
A. Our evaluation of administrative factors typically focuses on two broad categories: management issues and structural issues. To evaluate the quality of management we concentrate on results: financial trends; the history of budgeted to actual results; the availability and size of contingency reserves; the timeliness of tax,

Adapted from *Municipal Issues* (June 1991): 6-7 by permission of Moody's Investors Service.

revenue, or rate increases; the size and scope of capital plans; the efficiency of revenue collection and cost containment; and management's general recognition of and responsiveness to constraints or problems.

The structural issues evaluated include the municipal entity's legal organization and statutory limitations; its mission and mandates; interrelationships with other entities, particularly the state government; the level of unionization and contract status; and governmental structure. The revenue structure and management's ability to live within its means—particularly given such factors as rate restrictions or economically-sensitive revenue streams—are also evaluated.

A proven ability to achieve budget targets consistently, to implement programs of cost control and revenue enhancement successfully, and to plan for the future—all while functioning within its structural constraints—demonstrates to Moody's the degree of control a municipal entity is willing and able to exert over its financial condition.

Q. Is the level of government a factor in evaluating credit quality?
A. In the regional ratings group's analysis, the answer is generally no. The relationship between the government's service responsibilities and its resources is usually more significant than the level of government itself. In order to understand the relative operating flexibility of any municipal government, a credit analyst must first know the degree and scope of its service responsibilities. The various levels of government generally provide different services. Since a particular service may be more difficult or costly to provide than others, a given municipality may have more difficulty in providing that service.

For example, municipalities and entities required to fund mandated expenditures such as social services or environmental protection improvements, with minimal associate revenue increases, have a pronounced reduction in flexibility. In addition, these costs are subject to unanticipated escalation.

Q. Is there a difference in the way you look at different forms of government?
A. Again, the answer is generally no. All types of government (strong mayor, council-manager, board of directors/general manager, etc.) are capable of providing services efficiently. Any governmental structure must be conducive to the successful performance of the entity's administrative responsibilities and have sufficient oversight and supervision to ensure that its tasks are completed efficiently. It has been Moody's experience that fractional governments without a central or coordinated approach have difficulties as priorities change or new pressures arise. Any government structure that allows decisions to be made and implemented fairly and efficiently is adequate, however.

Q. Why are administrative factors important in determining a credit rating?
A. Since debt repayment is ultimately based on an issuer's ability and willingness to tap its resources to meet its obligations, the powers and abilities of governmental entities to do so is a critical credit factor. Therefore, an evaluation of administrative capabilties is essential. In addition, administrative factors have a direct impact on other key analytic areas such as finances, debt management, and, to some extent, even on the economic viability of the area.

Well-managed budget processes and long-term capital plans that can realistically be achieved are significant, positive credit factors. The reverse is true for poorly maintained financial operations, a lack of checks and balances, and future plans that are based on overly optimistic growth projections.

Q. What weight does Moody's give to administrative factors in determining a credit rating?
A. In general, all the factors involved in Moody's review of relative credit quality are of equal weight. However, an individual municipality may have unique strengths or weaknesses that make one of the rating factors more significant than the others in relation to a particular debt issuance. Administrative factors are often thought of as being more important during periods of fiscal strain and/or economic slowdown. While operations may require more careful monitoring when finances are tight, the municipal entities that manage most effectively during cyclical downturns are frequently those that are managed carefully and with forethought during times of relative growth and plenty.

31

The Role of Debt Position and Debt Management in Moody's Credit Analysis

Steven Bocamazo
Moody's Investors Service, New York, New York

The demand for capital funds is expected to increase over the next several years as governmental entities address an aging infrastructure, enironmental concerns, and a host of social issues. As new debt is added to the burden many municipalities already carry, Moody's hears many questions regarding the analytic process from issuers coming to market with new series of bonds, as well as from those seeking a rating upgrade on existing debt.

It is important to keep in mind that Moody's rates debt issues, not issuers. A debt rating is not a judgment of a municipality as a place to live; rather, it is an assessment of the willingness and ability of a municipality to meet its debt obligations.

Q. What weight does Moody's give to debt factors in determining a credit rating?
A. The nature of the debt security under review is the driving factor that determines how Moody's analysis will proceed. The first question an analyst must ask is "What is the nature of the obligation, and what is the legal security behind it?"

Having answered those questions, the analyst proceeds to examine those areas relevant to the obligation and its security. In general, these are debt position and management, the local economy, the issuer's finances, and the strength of local management. No one of these factors is considered to be most important at the start of our analysis; as analysis proceeds, however, one element may take on more importance than the others because it represents a particular strength or vulnerability for the credit.

Q. What factors does Moody's examine when analyzing an issuer's debt position and debt management?
A. Moody's examines debt levels, the pressure that debt obligations place on the budget, debt structure, expectations about future borrowing, and the capital plan. The debt obligations of overlapping governmental units also are considered. Although this overlapping debt is not within the direct control of the issuer under review, it is included in the credit analysis because it represents additional responsibilities of the same group of taxpayers.

Q. What are some of the measures Moody's uses to evaluate debt levels?
A. The two measures most frequently used by Moody's to assess relative debt levels are debt burden and debt per capita. Debt burden measures the burden that all tax-supported debt places on a particular tax base.

Adapted from *Municipal Issues* (Dec. 1990): 3-4, 8 by permission of Moody's Investors Service.

It is a ratio between the issuer's net debt plus the net debt of overlapping entities, and the estimated full value of taxable property. Net debt is calculated by taking the issuer's gross debt, and netting out short-term operating debt and bonds fully supported by enterprise revenues. Debt per capita is a measurement of a community's debt in relation to its population. In analyzing an issuer's debt levels, Moody's compares both debt burden and debt per capita to medians we have developed for municipalities of similar size.

In recent years, as issuers have increased their reliance on revenue bonds and reduced their reliance on general obligation debt, Moody's has begun exploring other indicators of debt levels in an effort to measure not just tax-supported debt, but all debt taxpayers will pay, including those paid with user charges.

Q. How much debt is too much debt?
A. Although rapidly rising or high debt levels often serve as a warning signal to the analyst, the determination that a given level of debt is too high for a specific issuer will depend on the individual situation and the relative strengths of the key factors mentioned above. Favorable trends in financial operations and the local economy, as well as sound management practices, may serve to mitigate an analyst's concern regarding high debt levels.

It also is worth noting that, just as increased levels of debt are not necessarily cause for concern, neither will a reduction in debt level, in and of itself, necessarily lead to a higher rating.

Q. What does Moody's include in a debt statement when analyzing general obligation bonds?
A. A debt statement is a "snapshot" of a municipality's debt.

It should be noted that only debt principal is shown on the debt statement; interest payments are not included.

Q. Is the debt statement adjusted to reflect how much cash is available in the debt service fund?
A. Moody's generally does not make adjustments to the debt statement for cash in the debt service fund, primarily because debt service monies typically are used to pay interest as well as principal and, as noted, the debt statement shows only principal obligations. In addition, general obligation debt service funds are usually held by the municipality rather than a third party and typically are not segregated from the issuer's other funds; in some instances, they may be used for purposes other than debt repayment.

Q. How does Moody's determine whether a debt issue is self-supporting?
A. A bond issue is considered to be self-supporting when there is evidence that the obligation is paid from a specific source other than the issuer's tax base. Revenue bonds, for example, are always treated as self-supporting, unless the municipality subsidizes the revenue bond's debt service from its general fund; for a revenue bond, the municipality has no legal obligation to use any revenue sources other than the specific enterprise earnings pledged to pay debt service.

In those instances where general obligation bonds are issued on behalf of an enterprise system (e.g., water, sewer, health care, parking facility), the Moody's analyst will review the finances of the system to determine whether its net revenues have been sufficient historically to cover debt service, and whether service charges are sufficient to ensure that future debt can be paid solely from system earnings. If such is the case, then the debt is considered to be self-supporting.

Moody's often is asked by issuers how we treat bonds that are partially paid from enterprise earnings. Our policy is to view the entire bond issue as non-self-supporting, and to include it in our calculation of an issuer's direct net debt.

Q. How does Moody's treat nonbonded debt?
A. Nonbonded debt paid from general revenues, such as most capital leases, certificates of participation (COPs), and lease rental obligations is considered to be part of an issuer's direct debt. From Moody's point of view, the credit quality of a municipal borrower's debt depends on the issuer's ability and willingness to meet all of its obligations, including those involving leases. Therefore, even if lease obligations are not legally defined as debt for a particular municipality, Moody's includes leases on the debt statement and in our calculation of debt burden and debt per capita.

Q. Why aren't sales tax, special assessment, and tax increment bonds considered to be self-supporting?

A. Although a property tax levy may not be necessary to support the debt service requirements for sales tax revenue, special assessment, or tax increment bonds, the revenues that will repay them nevertheless are derived from the issuer's tax base rather than from user charges. Because the issuance of debt backed by taxes other than property taxes has increased in recent years. Moody's currently is exploring new debt measures that will evaluate tax-supported debt in relation to a variety of different measures of a community's capacity for debt repayment. The full value of all property nevertheless will continue to be an important proxy for a community's wealth. When evaluating the overall impact of sales tax, special assessment, and tax increment bonds, we do take into account special assessment collection rates, annual growth in sales tax collections, and the captured tax base growth in tax increment districts.

Q. How are short-term financing instruments handled?

A. In general, Moody's expects short-term financing instruments to be repaid from anticipated operating revenues and taxes. Therefore, we deduct from the debt statement short-term obligations such as revenue anticipation notes (RANs), tax anticipation notes (TANs), and tax and revenue anticipation notes (TRANs). Bond anticipation notes (BANs), however, are not deducted from the total gross debt; since they will be redeemed by the issuance of long-term debt, they represent an anticipated long-term obligation of the issuer. Grant anticipation notes (GANs) are deducted from the gross direct debt only if Moody's can ensure that the expected grant will be received in sufficient time and amount to redeem the note.

Q. What role does debt structure play in Moody's analysis?

A. Debt structure, or the type of debt the issuer has taken on, is very important in assessing credit quality. Perhaps most important, it can reflect the debt management practices of the issuer. A debt structure that shows heavy reliance on such things as short-term debt, balloon maturities, rapidly escalating debt service requirements, or a slow payout of principal may reflect stress in some sector of the municipality, such as a lack of growth in taxable values. On the other hand, a slower payout could reflect an expectation that some future development will have a positive impact on the municipality's ability to support the debt.

A key statistic examined in the evaluation of debt structure is debt payout, which measures the rate of principal retirement within a set period of time. The rate of debt payout sometimes is considered to be a proxy for an issuer's willingness to pay. If debt retirement is rapid, the issuer may be viewed as being very willing to draw upon its resources to repay its obligations. Conversely, if debt retirement is unduly slow, concerns may be raised regarding willingness to repay.

Q. Does Moody's have any "rule of thumb" regarding debt payout for general obligation bonds?

A. As a standard of comparison, Moody's traditionally has looked for the repayment of at least 50% of outstanding general obligation debt within 10 years. This standard derived from the time when most debt issues had a life of 20 years. More recently, however, widespread use of an increasing variety of financing structures has made that standard less uniformly applicable. Although a slower rate of repayment is not necessarily a negative credit factor, one fundamental principle underlying repayment has not changed: a debt payout schedule should be in line with the useful life of the project being financed.

Q. Is voter approval of a debt issue considered by Moody's to be a positive credit factor?

A. Not necessarily, since in many areas of the country voter approval is not required for various types of debt. In those areas where it is required, however, the margin of the authorization can be a credit factor because it may reveal the level of community support for the project and thus some evidence of the taxpayers' willingness to pay the debt service of the obligation. Conversely, in those instances where alternate financing mechanisms are used to circumvent voter approval, questions may be raised regarding public support for the proposed project.

32

The Role of Legal Factors in Moody's Credit Analysis

James H. Burr and Katherine McManus

Moody's Investors Service, New York, New York

Q. What is the role that legal documents play in the analytic process?

A. The legal documents set forth the legal parameters and terms under which the debt is issued. In particular, Moody's looks to the legal documents to determine the actual security behind the bond, identify the issuer's responsibilities in the transaction, identify the bondholder's recourse should there be a payment default, and get comfort as to the issuer's legal right to issue the debt.

Q. How much does Moody's rely upon legal documentation in assigning a rating?

A. The significance of relevant legal documents varies with the complexity and structure of a transaction. For a simple, straightforward general obligation bond, standard documents and an opinion from bond counsel as to the legality of the issue are usually adequate. By contrast, a large financing for a resource recovery plant, with multiple contracts for construction, operation and/or ownership of the plant, will entail substantial evaluation by the analyst of a greater number of legal documents.

Q. What legal opinions does Moody's require in order to rate a transaction?

A. Again, the number and type of legal opinions will vary with the nature of the financing to be rated. At a minimum, Moody's requires an opinion from independent counsel, attesting to the legality of the debt and the pledged security for its holders. If there are other parties to the transaction, and payment of the debt is in any way dependent upon the performance of those parties, Moody's may require a legal opinion from counsel stating that those parties may legally enter into the arrangement and that the parties' obligations under the applicable state or federal law are enforceable. In addition, when the presence of private sector entities in the transaction could interrupt or otherwise affect the payment of debt service should the private sector entity file (or be filed against) under the Federal Bankruptcy Code, Moody's may seek opinions from counsel indicating that the bankruptcy risks have been essentially eliminated.

Q. Does Moody's have any requirements as to the provider of the bond counsel opinion?

A. Moody's requires that the counsel providing any legal opinion be qualified to deliver the opinion, either by demonstrated experience in the field or, under certain circumstances, by demonstrating sufficient legal research to give us comfort that the conclusions reached in the opinion are accurate. Moody's typically requires that the counsel demonstrate its experience by meeting the standards for listing maintained by the *Bond Buyer's Municipal Marketplace* listing of municipal bond attorneys.

Adapted from *Municipal Issues* (April 1992): 11-12 by permission of Moody's Investors Service.

Q. Does Moody's ever refuse to accept a legal opinion?
A. Yes. Moody's will refuse to accept a legal opinion if the provider does not meet the qualifications we feel necessary to render such an opinion, or if the conclusions reached in the opinion are not in accordance with our understanding of the law. In any instance in which the accuracy of a legal opinion is in question, Moody's reserves the right to (1) refer the matter to our own outside counsel for independent verification of the conclusions reached in the opinion in question, and (2) decline to rate the issue to which the legal opinion in question applies unless and until the accuracy of the conclusions stated in the opinion can be verified to our satisfaction.

Q. Does Moody's include in its analysis any assumptions of performance by a fiduciary, such as a bond trustee or registrar and paying agent?
A. Yes. Moody's assumes that a fiduciary will follow the terms set forth in a legally binding contractual obligation, such as a trust indenture, that create the fiduciary responsibility.

Q. Does Moody's give any analytic weight to an issuer's "moral obligation" pledge?
A. The term *moral obligation*, as applied to the commitment of a governmental unit, is a term without a standard definition. Historically, the term was used to describe one element of security in state issuances in which the state would pledge revenues as the primary security and agree to fund and subsequently replenish a debt service reserve as the secondary security. Such an obligation has been traditionally referred to as a "moral obligation." Over time, the term has been used to refer to any commitment signifying an expectation on the part of the purchaser of the bonds that the issuer will stand behind a bond or note issue, even though there is no legal commitment to do so. In contrast, when a municipality commits its general obligation pledge to a debt issue, it has a legal obligation to pay bondholders in full and on time.

Moody's does not give analytic weight to a "moral obligation" in the rating process. While Moody's recognizes that the governmental entity having such an obligation may choose to honor it for a variety of reasons when called upon, we cannot determine with any degree of certainty just when an entity will or will not elect to do so.

Q. How does Moody's define default?
A. A default is a breach of some covenant, promise, or duty imposed by the bond contract, such as failure to pay principal, interest, or both when due. A "technical" default results when specifically defined events of default occur, such as a breach of a trust indenture covenant. In some cases, a breach of covenant may not technically reach the level of a default until a cure period has lapsed. In other cases, the covenant breach is defined as an event of default that can be cured within a specified period of time. If such a technical default occurs and is not cured, the bondholders or trustee may exercise legally available rights and remedies for enforcement of the bond contract.

Q. How does Moody's feel about violations of the terms of the documents, covenant breaches, or technical defaults for the debt that it rates?
A. Moody's takes very seriously an issuer or obligor's promises to take certain actions and to refrain from taking other actions. Although we realize that there may be some circumstances in which the issuer or obligor is not at fault, generally a technical default is viewed negatively. If the covenant breach or default raises questions as to the willingness of the issuer or obligor to meet the debt obligations, there can be negative credit consequences for all debt obligations issued by that obligor.

Q. Does Moody's view the legal protections for holders of contractual obligations not legally defined as debt (e.g., lease rental or installment purchase contract appropriation bonds, or certificates of participation) differently from those applicable to holders of a governmental unit's direct debt obligations?
A. Moody's recognizes that debt limits, legal obstacles and restrictions, and the difficulty of obtaining voter approval for unpopular but necessary projects (such as jails or residential drug treatment facilities) may lead governments to issue obligations not legally defined as debt—or "nondebt debt" financing vehicles. Although we understand the reasoning behind such issuances, it is undeniable that there are additional risks to holders of nondebt debt obligations than there are to holders of a governmental unit's direct bonds or notes.

Depending on state legal restrictions, the risks result from either (1) the governmental unit's ability to legally terminate its obligations for nondebt debt by simply not appropriating the funds to make the payments on the lease or contract ("appropriation risk"), or (2) the governmental unit not being required to make (or, in some states, actually being legally prohibited from making) the payments if it does not have beneficial use or occupancy of the property or equipment financed with these obligations ("abatement risk"). In dealing with abatement risk, Moody's may require reserve funds and rental interruption insurance as additional protections for holders.

In all nondebt debt transactions, Moody's may reflect the risks in a lower rating, the level of which is determined by evaluating appropriation risk or abatement risk as relevant, and by evaluating the perceived essentiality (or lack thereof) of the project being financed.

Q. Would a rating be affected if the debt issue is subject to legal or executive action?
A. The increased use of nondebt debt financings has elicited a number of legal challenges by taxpayers who perceive themselves to have been disregarded by their governmental leaders when a nondebt debt instrument is issued so that voter approval laws may be circumvented. To date, despite several adverse and subsequently reversed decisions at the state supreme court level, no outstanding nondebt debt has been held to be illegal. In one decision made by the highest court of the state of New Mexico, the court found that such obligations did, in fact, constitute legal debt. The holding was prospective only and did not invalidate previously issued obligations.

Q. How closely does Moody's monitor litigation and when would Moody's take a rating action in the event of an adverse judgment?
A. Moody's follows very closely any litigation that contests (1) the legal validity and enforceability of the debt (examples of some problems include voter approval not being required for debt issuance, exceeding debt limits, and failure to follow legal authorization procedures); or (2) the issuer's legal obligation to pay the debt (problems include illegality of take-or-pay contracts or inability to pledge general obligation funds for purposes of debt).

To the extent that the governmental unit is engaged in other litigation, Moody's will focus on the litigation to the extent an adverse judgment either (1) is expected to have a material adverse effect on the government's financial operations, or (2) will have a material negative impact on bondholder security. Typically, Moody's will not take rating action in the event of an adverse judgment at a lower court level, assuming that we are informed that an appeal will be forthcoming. In the event that the judgment is final, Moody's will then explore both the potential consequences of the judgment and any actions that may be taken to minimize the impact of the judgment on the governmental unit before any final rating action is taken.

Q. Is a debt instrument's tax status considered a rating factor by Moody's?
A. No. Moody's rates debt obligations without regard to the issue's tax status.

33

Bid Evaluation for Competitive Bond Sales: NIC vs. TIC

Tom McLoughlin
Government Finance Officers Association, Washington, D.C.

Municipal bond market participants have been embroiled in a perpetual debate about the most cost-effective method of issuing securities. Proponents of the competitive sale process cite the inherent protections afforded by open competition as sufficient justification for the receipt of public bids. Others have argued that a negotiated sale is more advantageous because the managing underwriter will devote more resources to presale marketing efforts and will be more capable of changing the structure of the bond issue to satisfy the demands of investors. The controversy is likely to continue without a definitive resolution. In the June 1990 issue of *Government Finance Review*, the merits of preparing a formal request for proposal to choose an underwriter for a negotiated sale were discussed in detail. The selection process in competitive sales warrants equal attention.

In a competitive sale, bonds are awarded at a public auction to the underwriting firm, or group of firms, that provides the issuer with the best bid for its securities. The bidding parameters are established in a document called the *official notice of sale* that issuers use to solicit bids from prospective purchasers. Among other items, the notice of sale will announce the time and place of the sale, the schedule of principal maturities, and the method by which the issuer will determine the winning bid. The winning bid should be the one that provides funds to the state or local government at the lowest effective interest cost. There are two techniques for calculating the effective interest cost of different bids.

I. NET INTEREST COST

Until recently, the most prevalent method of evaluating public bids was through the use of a net interest cost (NIC) calculation. The NIC is the average interest rate on a bond issue calculated on the basis of simple interest. The formula for calculating the NIC of a bond issue is illustrated in Equation 1. To establish the numerator, the sum of all interest payments payable over the life of the bond issue is adjusted by the amount of the premium or discount offered by the bidder. The total number of bond-year dollars is used as the denominator. The total number of bond-year dollars is calculated as the sum of the product of each year's maturity value and the number of years to its maturity. Alternatively, the denominator may be the product of the par value of the issue and the average life.

$$NIC = \frac{\text{total amount of interest payments} +/- \text{ premium or discount}}{\text{number of bond-year dollars}} \qquad [1]$$

The advantage of the NIC method is the ease by which the percentage rate is calculated. The disadvantage of the NIC calculation method is that it gives equal weight to each interest payment regardless of the date on

Adapted from *Government Finance Review* (Oct. 1991):38–39 by permission of the Government Finance Officers Association.

which it was paid. Similarly, the bidder offers to purchase the securities at a discount; the amount of the discount is considered to be similar to any coupon payment and subtracted from the total amount of the numerator. Clearly, while the NIC calculation considers the aggregate amount of interest payable in relationship to the amount borrowed and term of borrowing, it is completely insensitive to the time value of money.

II. TRUE INTEREST COST

The preferred method of ascertaining the effective interest cost of a particular bid is through the calculation of a bond issue's true interest cost (TIC). Unlike the NIC calculation, the TIC technique takes account of the time value of money by treating debt service payments in present-value terms. This method gives greater weight to earlier payments than to later payments of an equal dollar magnitude because the obligation to pay a dollar today is more onerous than the obligation to pay a dollar 10 years from now. Presumably, a borrower could take a much smaller amount of money, invest it today, and let the compounded interest accumulate until the borrower has the needed amount 10 years from now.[1]

The TIC calculation is complicated where there are a variety of coupon rates being used. Although the discount rate is not known, the present value of the stream of payments is readily identifiable as the amount of bond proceeds. The TIC is the annual percentage rate that discounts the aggregate amount of debt service payments to the present value of the bond proceeds on either the dated date of the bond issue or the settlement date. Unlike the NIC calculation, there is no algebraic formula for the TIC calculation. Instead, it must be calculated through a series of iterations on a computer or through a more time consuming process of using compound interest rate tables. Prior to the widespread use of the microcomputer, the complexity of calculating the true interest cost was a discouragement to its use. Now, however, there are numerous software programs on the market to make the TIC calculation very quickly.

III. THE SAME BOND ISSUE BUT DIFFERENT RESULTS

The use of NIC as a means of determining the best bid occasionally can result in the award of the bonds to the wrong bidder. The potential for an error is best illustrated through example. A hypothetical bond issue comprising three maturities is provided in Table 1. For the purposes of this example, the official notice of sale announced that the best bid would be determined on the basis of the lowest NIC without any other constraints. As Table 1 illustrates, Firm A's coupon rate scale has a normal positive slope. Conversely, Firm B has placed the highest coupon rates at the front end of the maturity schedule. In doing so, Firm B has structured a bid with a low NIC but with an undesirable debt service schedule for the issuer. Based upon the results, the issuer may be obliged to choose the winner by random lot based upon the selection criteria included in the official notice of sale.

Investors generally prefer to receive their interest earlier rather than later and will pay a higher price for a security that carries a higher rate of interest. Prospective underwriters therefore have an incentive to

Table 1   General Obligation Bond Issue (par amount: $3,000,000; dated date: Aug 1, 1991; due dates: Aug 1, 1992–1994)

Maturity schedule	Firm A		Firm B	
	Coupon rates	Annual debt service	Coupon rates	Annual debt service
$1,000,000	6.50%	$1,210,000	20.00%	$1,292,000
$1,000,000	7.00%	$1,145,000	4.60%	$1,092,000
$1,000,000	7.50%	$1,075,000	4.60%	$1,023,000
$3,000,000		$3,430,000		$3,430,000
	NIC:	7.16666	NIC:	7.16666
	TIC:	7.15705	TIC:	7.28834

structure their bids with higher interest rate coupons in the early years of a maturity schedule. If NIC is used as the determinant of lowest interest cost, only the aggregate amount of interest matters. The timing of the payments does not. Table 1 demonstrates the inherent danger of awarding a bond issue on the basis of NIC without placing other constraints on the coupon rates. The calculation shows that Firm B has an equal chance of being awarded the bonds despite the fact that its bid requires the issuer to pay $82,000 more in the first year of the debt service schedule. Perhaps even more importantly, the ability to refinance the outstanding obligations is diminished when the winning bid results in a high-to-low coupon rate scale.

To avoid some of the pitfalls inherent in the NIC calculation, many state and local governments have established rules that constrain prospective purchasers from making inefficient bids. For instance, some issuers prohibit coupon rates from varying too widely. Often called the "maximum coupon spread constraint," the prohibition prevents the bidder from submitting excessively high coupons for the first few maturities. Other issuers insist that prospective purchasers submit a bid that has nondescending coupons. This constraint assures the state or local government that the coupon rate on each maturity is equal to or greater than the coupon on all preceding maturities. This type of constraint is often used when the issuer wants to preserve the option of refinancing the debt at a later date.

The inclusion of these types of constraints reduces, but does not eliminate, the possibility that an NIC award will identify the wrong bidder as the winner. The TIC calculation remains preferable for at least two reasons. First, the use of TIC already in effect incorporates many of the constraints in its calculation. As demonstrated in Table 1, bidders who submit very high coupons will be penalized. Second, the TIC calculation is better suited to identifying the best bid whenever the issuer permits a discount bid. The NIC calculation adds the amount of the discount to the total amount of interest payable on the bonds. But, it does not attach any importance to the fact that issuers must pay this discount immediately from bond proceeds. The TIC calculation, on the other hand, incorporates the notion that a discount is equivalent to a coupon payment by the issuer at the time of settlement.[2] For these reasons, state and local governments are encouraged to use the TIC calculation whenever possible to identify the lowest effective interest rate on future bond issues.

NOTES

1. California Debt Issuance Primer (1988). California Debt Advisory Commission, Sacramento, pp. 5–53.
2. Center for Capital Market Research (1977). "Improving Bidding Rules to Reduce Costs in the Competitive Sale of Municipal Bonds," University of Oregon, Eugene, p. 50.

34

The Valuation of Municipal Bond Bids: Four Solutions

Harold Bierman, Jr.
Samuel Curtis Johnson Graduate School of Management, Cornell University, Ithaca, New York

When the captain of U.S.S. New Jersey gives the order "right standard rudder," the helmsman obeys immediately, but the ship continues on its way for hundreds of yards before it changes course significantly. And so it is with the municipal bond bidding process. The theoretical literature criticizing past and current practice is well established, but there is very little change in course. Any issue of *The Weekly Bond Buyer* will contain many notices of sale of notes and bonds that indicate the bid will be chosen by the use of the net interest cost (NIC) or the Canadian interest cost (CIC) method.

This article considers four possible solutions to the optimum bid choice decision facing a municipality with a pending bond issue. We shall see that two of the four methods are in error (one more so than the other) and that the other two methods are correct (but one is easier to apply). The four methods are

1. Net interest cost (NIC)
2. Canadian interest cost (CIC)
3. Present value
4. None of the above

Our ultimate preference is "none of the above." The solution offered is easy to apply and theoretically correct.

I. NET INTEREST COST

A. Computation Method

The computation of the NIC of a bond issue is relatively easy. The steps are

1. Add the total interest payments to be made over the life of the bond (subtract any bond premiums). If 40 bonds with face values of $1,000 are paying .10 per year ($100) interest for 8 years, the total interest to be paid is 100(40)(8) = 32,000. We are assuming a conventional balloon-payment debt.
2. Compute the total "bond years." If 40 bonds are outstanding for 8 years, there are 320 bond years.
3. Divide the number obtained in step 1 by the number obtained in step 2 to obtain the annual interest cost

$$\text{Interest cost} = \frac{32,000}{320} = 100$$

Adapted from *Municipal Finance Journal*, 6 (fall 1985): 263–268 by permission of Panel Publishers, Inc.

4. Divide the number obtained in step 3 by 1,000 to obtain the NIC per dollar of debt:

$$\text{NIC} = \frac{100}{1,000} = .10$$

Note that with a conventional balloon-payment debt with a single maturity date, the NIC is equal to the yield to maturity of the debt if the debt is issued at par.

Continuing the above example, assume that $60 of period-8 interest is now paid at time 1. The shifting of interest back to time 1 will increase the yield-to-maturity cost of the debt to the issuer, but does not change the NIC. The NIC remains at .10 even though the yield to maturity is now larger than .10. Any amount of interest can be shifted in time and be replaced by an equal dollar amount at a different moment in time without changing the NIC.

B. Problems

The fact is that, in general, the NIC does not effectively consider the time value of money. This is a measure that cannot be used to give reliable preference rankings of different bids. This conclusion has been effectively pointed out in the finance literature.* Other authors have pointed out how the bidder can exploit for profit this deficient calculation.

To illustrate the deficiencies of NIC, consider the choice between issuing $32,000 of conventional balloon-payment 2-year bonds paying .08 per year with an NIC of .08, or issuing the following mixture of 1-year and 2-year bonds also with an NIC of .08:

Years to maturity	Interest rate	Annual interest per bond	Number of bonds	Total interest over life	Bond years
1	.50	500	8	$500 \times 8 \times 1 = 4,000$	8
2	.01	10	24	$10 \times 24 \times 2 = \underline{\;\;480}$	48
			32	4,480	56

$$\text{Interest per bond year} = \frac{4,480}{56} = 80$$

$$\text{NIC} = \frac{80}{1,000} = .08$$

The cash flow of the .50 and .01 bond issues are

0	1	2	
+ 32,000	− 4,000		($4,000 is the interest of the .50 bonds.)
	− 8,000	−24,000	(Principal payments.)
	− 240	− 240	(Interest of the .01 bonds.)
+ 32,000	−12,240	−24,240	

The yield to maturity is .082 for the overall bond issue consisting of 8 bonds paying .50 and 24 bonds paying .01. Figure 1 shows graphically the two alternatives.

If the interest-rate cost to the municipality is larger than .08, the 8% debt is to be preferred despite the fact that the NIC of both alternatives is the same. In fact, if the cost of funds to the municipality is greater than .066, the 8% debt is better.

---

*H. Bierman, Jr., "Alternative Debt Bids by State and Local Governments," *Financial Management*, Winter 1982, pp. 51–54; H. Bierman, Jr., "A Comment on Optimizing Municipal Bond Bids," *Journal of Bank Research*, Summer 1983, pp. 173–174; M. H. Hopewell, C. G. Kaufman, and R. R. West, "Lowest Bond Bid Costs Minnesota Extra One Million Dollars," working paper, October 1972; R. R. West, "The 'Net Interest Cost' Method of Issuing Tax Exempt Bonds: Is It Rational?" *Public Finance* (No. 3, 1968), pp. 346–354.

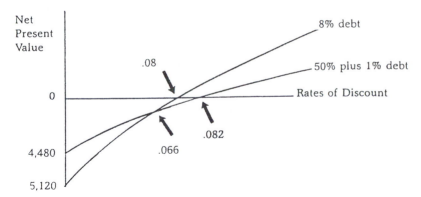

Figure 1   Comparison of two issues using NIC.

The failure of NIC could be illustrated more dramatically by lengthening the time horizon (so that the time value factor would become more important), but it should be obvious that any procedure that omits the time value of money cannot be used effectively to evaluate alternatives when time is important.

II.   CANADIAN INTEREST COST

The CIC method is actually the equivalent of using the yields to maturity (or the internal rates of return) to evaluate bids. In Fig. 1, the alternative with the lower yield is likely to be the better choice (as long as the entity's cost of money is larger than .066). However, if we change the example, the CIC method may also give a faulty decision. Consider the following two financing alternatives:

	0	1	2	CIC
Alternative 1	+1,000	−1,080		.08
Alternative 2	+1,000		−1,210	.10

Alternative 1 has the lower CIC, and thus would be chosen using that criterion. However, Fig. 2 shows that if the municipality's time value factor is larger than .1204, the .10 debt is better than the .08 debt.

The CIC method, since it is an internal-rate-of-return calculation, is not a reliable method of choosing between mutually exclusive alternatives. Since only one bid will be accepted, the bids are mutually exclusive. To place the objection in perspective, the CIC calculation is a tremendous improvement over NIC because it does consider the time value of money and its faults are of less practical significance. If the choices are limited to NIC or CIC, CIC wins the contest. But there is no reason to limit the choice in this fashion.

III.   PRESENT VALUE

Using the present-value method, one computes the net present values of all the debt alternatives and chooses the bid with highest positive (for lowest negative) net present value. Using Fig. 2, the .10 debt would be chosen if the interest rate to be used is larger than .1204. If the interest rate is smaller than .1204, then the .08 debt is more desirable, since it has a higher net present value.

The major problem with using the present-value method is the choice of the interest rates to be used. The calculation is made complex when the term structure of interest rates is not constant, and a different interest rate should be chosen for each time period. The choice between alternative bids will depend heavily on the choice of interest rates, and whatever rate schedule is used will be subject to second-guessing by those observers with an economic interest in the outcome. While theoretically correct, the use of present value does have operating difficulties. But despite these difficulties, it is better than either NIC or CIC since it does allow the explicit inclusion of the municipality's cost of money in choosing the best bid.

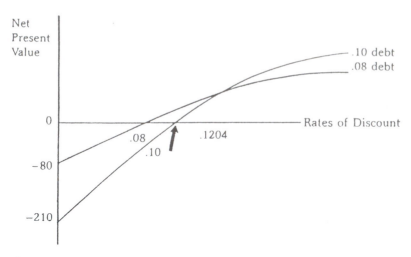

Figure 2   Comparison of two issues using CIC.

IV.   NONE OF THE ABOVE

What is the best valuation method? The winner is "none of the above." Fortunately, it is not necessary to use any of the three methods that have thus far been illustrated to determine the optimum bid. All that is necessary is to turn the bidding process upside down. Instead of asking the investment banking firms to submit a bond contract including the specific principal and interest payments, the issuing governmental body will design the debt security (with the assistance of financial experts), and the investment community will be asked to bid a price for the security. Since the security is exactly defined by the issuing body and is the same for all bidders, the issuing body will only have to decide which bid is the highest. Obviously this is a much less difficult task than evaluating a larger number of contracts that differ in many significant ways. All reasonable persons will be able to agree on which bid offers the most immediate cash.

V.   SHIFT VALUATION TO THE BIDDERS

The complex valuaton problem will be shifted to the firms bidding for the bond contract. Firms that insist on using calculations equivalent to NIC will find themselves bidding the wrong amounts for the proposed contracts and will rapidly disappear (more likely, NIC will never be used). The bidding firms can be expected to have the necessary expertise to arrive at theoretically valid amounts for the given bond issues.

As long as issuing bodies indicate that NIC will be used to evaluate bids, intricate games will be played by bidders to minimize NIC, and maximize the internal rate of return (or net present value) subject to the constraints defined by other contractual provisions imposed by the issuing entity. The use of NIC imposes an unnecessary cost on the taxpayers of the cities, counties, and states of this country, since it tends to ensure that the lowest-economic-cost bond issue will not be chosen.

In the past 30 years, a large segment of the business community has learned to take the time value of money into consideration in a theoretically correct manner. It is past time for the use of NIC to cease and for the tax-exempt-bond-issuing community to take time discounting into consideration in a theoretically correct manner. Fortunately, this step can be accomplished in an effective manner by merely revising the bidding procedure. If this recommendation is not acceptable, then the issuing bodies should learn how to apply the present-value method.

35

Applying the Bierman Technique: Municipal Bond Bid Valuation

Robert W. Zinn*
Pinellas County Government, Clearwater, Florida

In the fall 1985 issue of *Municipal Finance Journal*, Professor Harold Bierman, Jr., analyzed and rejected the three commonly used methods for the valuation of competitively bid bond issues, putting forth instead a fourth technique of his own, the innovative NOTA (for none of the above),[†] or Bierman technique.[‡] In theory, this technique would allow the bond issuer to set the payment schedule and determine its own future cash flows, in effect turning the tables on the bidding process. In the winter 1986 issue, Daniel Anderson responded to Bierman's innovation with an article refuting the new method as being oversimplified, favoring instead the more traditional Canadian interest cost (CIC) and present-value techniques.[§]

This article picks up the debate where it was left off by presenting an example of Bierman's theory being put into practice. In October 1991, Pinellas County (Florida) successfully applied the Bierman technique to an actual bond issue, despite Anderson and the resistance of various underwriters, financial advisors, and bond counsels. This chapter begins with a brief review of the Bierman and Anderson articles as background, then describes the Pinellas County experience with the Bierman technique.

I. EVALUATIONAL SOLUTIONS IDENTIFIED

The Bierman article defined four evaluational techniques and ranked them in order of increasing desirability, as follows:

1. Net interest cost (NIC)
2. Canadian interest cost (CIC)
3. Present value
4. None of the above (NOTA)

The criticisms advanced on the first three methods, which resulted in the Bierman recommendation of NOTA are summarized as follows:

Adapted from *Municipal Finance Journal* 13 (spring 1992): 51-60 by permission of Panel Publishers, Inc.

[†]Bierman, Harold, Jr. "The Valuation of Municipal Bond Bids: Four Solutions," *Municipal Finance Journal*, 6 (fall 1985):263–268.

[‡]In the cited articles, the fourth solution for evaluating competitively bid bond issues has been identified as the NOTA method. Throughout much of this article, that term has also been used for the sake of consistency with these earlier analyses. However, the method is more appropriately called the Bierman technique, in honor of its originator, and that term is also used herein.

[§]Anderson, Daniel "Comments on the Valuation of Municipal Bond Bids (or Theory May Be More Expensive than Practice)," *Municipal Finance Journal*, 7 (fall 1986):45–48.

*Current affiliation: Consultant, Indian Rocks Beach, Florida.

- *NIC.* The NIC technique is the least acceptable method because it ignores the present value of money.
- *CIC.* Although the CIC technique does involve time value of money, the internal-rate-of-return calculation that it uses is unreliable for choosing between mutually exclusive alternatives, since it accepts only one bid.
- *Present-value.* The present-value technique is better than the CIC technique because it involves the issuer's cost of money; however, the choice between alternative bids depends on the selection of assumed interest rates (including those individual rates applicable to each time period). This dependence is its weakness, since the chosen rate schedule will be subject to second-guessing.

To apply the NOTA "theory," the issuer designs the debt security (with expert financial assistance) and then requests the investment community to bid for the security. The best bid is the one that offers the most immediate cash.

II.   THEORY MORE EXPENSIVE (NOTA REJECTED)

The Anderson article rejected the NOTA notion for being an oversimplification, favoring CIC and present-value methodologies. Anderson's responses to earlier criticisms of CIC and present-value techniques are summarized as follows:

- *CIC.* Issuers do not generally have a precise sense of the appropriate discount rates, since they enter the market infrequently and must rely on the bond auction (or the bidding process) for price determination. Furthermore, insensitivities to cash flow differentials between exclusive alternatives are resolved by calling for bids with minima and/or maxima constraints.
- *Present-value.* Bierman's criticism of this type of valuation was recognized as the difficulty of choosing appropriate discount rates. However, it was unclear to Anderson how a given bond issuer might know an appropriate discount rate for a present-value evaluation and consequently reject a CIC evaluation.

Aside from addressing the technical comments, the Anderson article identifies the NOTA notion as having been recommended "because it leaves nothing for underwriters to manipulate." Moreover, the Anderson article continues the defense of CIC and present-value techniques which, unlike NOTA, require underwriter participation in the design process.

Under commonly used NIC, CIC, and present-value techniques, it is recognized that underwriter participation adds value to a competitive bond bid. In particular, the underwriting process tailors bond issues to the needs and buying habits of a wide range of potential bondholders who are clients of the underwriting community. To the extent a bond issue is easily and quickly resold (reoffered), an underwriter (or group) can bid aggressively and minimize its risk of holding for resale.

III.   NOTA THEORY APPLIED

As a Florida municipal issuer, Pinellas County recently accepted the Bierman invitation to "turn the bidding process upside down" by applying the NOTA theory. With this approach, the selected bid will be the one that offers the greatest amount of immediate cash.

A.   Issuer Preparation

Zero coupon (or no-interest) bonds require each annual principal maturity to be discounted to represent the interest components of an established stream of future payments. Consequently, it is the greatest amount of immediate cash made available under an established stream of promised future payments which, in practice, determines the best bid for no coupon (or no-interest) bonds.

Using the established no-coupon bond concept of a stream of promised future payments, the next step is to lower the discount (adjustment to market prices) by including predetermined interest coupon rates. With both predetermined annual maturities and related interest rates set forth by the issuer for a bid response, Bierman's theory is ready to be put into practice.

Pinellas County has entered the competitively bid bond market in only two instances since the Tax Reform Act of 1986. The services of a financial advisor were engaged to assist in structuring principal maturities with predetermined interest coupon scales in the third instance. An independent bond counsel also was employed to ensure legal and tax compliance. Although an issuer may enter the market infrequently, there are a number of rate indexes available for current and up-to-date market yields. Whether a proposed issue has the small $5 million issue benefit, or is bank qualified at the $10 million limit, such national (and local) indexes offer benchmarks from which to key off interest rates acceptable to a local or statewide situation.

B. True Interest Cost Practices

Florida municipal issuers generally award competitively bid bonds according to the true interest cost (TIC) method. TIC is defined as a discounted cash flow analysis, which is used by selecting a discount rate and applying it to a known future series of payments to calculate their present value. Frequently the selected discount rate is the expected rate of inflation or a known cost of borrowing.*

In other words, the TIC method utilizes techniques previously identified with CIC and present-value. When minima and/or maxima constraints are added to initial bid specifications, the TIC methodology is unquestionably improved. The alternate choices (or assumptions) used for interest (or inflation) rates, however, can continue to skew the results. In spite of the availability of software systems for TIC calculations, some Florida issuers continue to publish the less favored NIC rates.

Replacement of established TIC practices with Bierman's untried NOTA theory caused considerable consternation with the underwriting, financial, and bond counsel communities. Nevertheless, the issuer continued to prevail.

C. Proposed Bond Issue

Using inexpensive PC software, the issuer structured $89,320,000 in capital improvement revenue bonds, to be dated October 1, 1991, with principal and interest payable solely by a lien upon and pledge of its infrastructure sales surtaxes.

The infrastructure sales surtax revenue stream was established for a 10-year period by a local referendum held November 7, 1989. This dedicated 1% surtax became effective February 1, 1990, for the state of Florida to collect along with its 7% statewide sales taxes. The first monthly remittance received from the state was in April 1990. Since the bonds are dated October 1, 1991, 102 months of the sales surtax revenue stream (on a cash basis) remains for the security and payment of a proposed 8-year issue.

In the October 8, 1991 preliminary official statement for the bonds (dated October 1), the schedule of issuer predetermined principal and interest payments (with cents rounded) was published, as shown in Table 1.

The interest coupon rates stated in the preliminary official statement were purposely set low to ensure an original issue discount. Otherwise, any premium gained from the sale would be subject to excess proceeds penalties.

D. Coverage and Pricing

The long-standing policy of the issuer is to maximize annual coverages on its financing and use these excess coverage amounts for pay-as-you-go capital improvement projects. This "trading on an equity in revenues" created from released cash flows permits an ongoing capital improvement program with sufficient cash to timely meet both bond and nonbond financed construction payments. Moreover, the trading on the revenue equity concept offers added protection to the bondholders.

With annual debt payments predetermined, maximum debt service coverage is then set, as illustrated in Table 2.

The initial issue pricing used for establishing the $13,995,000 annual maximum debt assumed an aggressively priced A-1 rated issue. The aggressiveness of this scale was based on an expected issue discount ranging from .75% to 1.50% of par. In terms of dollars, this sets a midpoint discount of $1,004,850.

Moody's Investor Service, Inc. statement upgrading to Aa from A-1, however, generated $672,512 in estimated gross interest savings for a calculated present value of $576,592. With a recalculated issue discount ranging from no more than .8545% of par to no less than .0105% of par, a new discount midpoint was

---

*See Government Finance Officers Association, Research Center *BONDCALC II, User's Manual*, April 1987.

Table 1 Stated Maturities, Interest Rates, and Debt Payments Amounts (interest paid semiannually and principal paid annually)

Maturity		Interest		Annual debt
Date	Principal	Rate	Payments	Payment amount[a]
1992	$9,380,000	4.40%	$4,611,453	$13,991,453
1993	9,795,000	4.75%	4,198,732	13,993,732
1994	10,260,000	5.00%	3,733,470	13,993,470
1995	10,770,000	5.20%	3,220,470	13,990,470
1996	11,335,000	5.30%	2,660,430	13,995,430
1997	11,935,000	5.40%	2,059,675	13,994,675
1998	12,580,000	5.45%	1,415,185	13,995,185
1999	13,265,000	5.50%	729,575	13,994,575
	$89,320,000		$22,628,990	$111,948,990

[a]These columns will be replaced in the Official Statement by "Price."
Note: Accrued interest to be added.

determined at $334,950. Consequently, concern over resetting coupon scales with higher interest rates to avoid an original issued premium was allayed.

E. NOTA Bid Call/Award

The official notice of sale (released October 16, 1991) called for sealed bids from the underwriting community to be opened on October 22, 1991 at 11:00 A.M. in Clearwater, Florida. All bids were to be unconditional, presented on the official bid form, and enclosed in a sealed envelope with a good faith check for $900,000. The official notice clearly stated "the bonds will be awarded to the best bidder whose proposal shall result in the greatest amount of proceeds to the Issuer (the highest dollar amount of purchase price)." With TIC abandoned in favor of NOTA, the question was "How will the underwriting community (including its potential bondholder clients) react?"

Six sealed bids were received, which are listed as follows in descending order of proceed amounts:

1. $88,693,477.10
2. $88,298,807.40
3. $88,019,875.30
4. $87,998,064.60
5. $87,991,019.20
6. $87,735,934.55

Table 2 Maximum Debt Service Coverage

Year ended Sept. 30	Sales tax revenue	Annual maximum debt service	Coverage
1992	$31,305,000	$13,995,000	2.24
1993	32,564,000	13,995,000	2.33
1994	33,825,000	13,995,000	2.42
1995	35,270,000	13,995,000	2.52
1996	36,177,000	13,995,000	2.58
1997	37,104,000	13,995,000	2.65
1998	38,060,000	13,995,000	2.72
1999	39,053,000	13,995,000	2.79
2000 (1/2 year)	19,517,000	0	N/A
Total	$302,875,000	$111,960,000	

The greatest amount of proceeds is clear-cut and indisputable, and bid award is made instantly. At last, the TIC mindset was broken with the award of bid 1 at 99.298564% of par!

F. NOTA Analysis

Although award is to bid 1 according to the greatest amount of immediate cash, the issuer requested each bidder's reoffered rates to generate NIC and TIC comparisons, including the breakout of discount amounts, which are shown in Table 3.

A further comparison of each underwriter's reoffered scale compared with the issuer's stated coupon rates is illustrated in Table 4.

In this instance, the order in which NOTA had ranked the bids is consistent with both the NIC and TIC methods. It can be argued that the wide dispersion in TIC rates results from undue restraint on the underwriters. Moreover, concern may exist over some bidders' having superior information, while others do not.

The process, however, had the issuer establishing its payment stream according to its desires rather than as a result of being exposed to any potential underwriter manipulation. All potential bidders received preliminary official statements (with the bidding forms). Since the sealed bids were presented and opened at a specific time, the determination of the best price was solely in the hands of an underwriter or syndicated group of underwriters.

The differences in the various bidders' reoffered annual maturities indicate that an underwriter's client base does vary in its buying needs and habits. Nevertheless, the issuer is limited to accepting only one bid for the entire issue.

The fact that the successful bidder had to reoffer the 1999 maturities (with a 5.5% stated interest coupon rate) at 20 basis points more is a remarketing issue between it and its client base. It does not change the issuer's obligation to pay semiannual interest at 5.5% per annum for this maturity, and at the stated rates for the entire issue.

Perhaps an ideal bidding procedure would be to bid separately each maturity with its stated interest coupon rate (including an underwriter discount) and allow an issuer to award "pieces" of the "whole." Since the underwriting community is unlikely to fully accept this "piecemeal" suggestion, the issuer must continue to consider the "whole" as the crux of the issue.

G. Debt Service Comparison

Maximum annual debt service using the issuer's debt payment amounts (at the stated rates), and the successful bidder's reoffered scales are shown in Table 5.

It should be obvious that annual payment amounts are more level at the issuer's stated coupon scales than what these payments would have been if these scales had been adjusted to the successful bidder's reofferings. More especially, there is a $353,570 gross savings to interest payments over the life of the issue. The present value of these interest savings is $289,730 to equate to the original issue discount of $285,320 of the successful bidder. The difference (although immaterial) between present value interest savings and original issue discount did not translate into a loss to the issuer.

Table 3 NIC and TIC Comparisons

	Methods		Discount amounts		
Bid	NIC	TIC	Total	Underwriter	Original issue
1	5.500776	5.483563	$ 626,523	$341,203	$285,320
2	5.616632	5.593823	1,021,193	446,600	574,593
3	5.699613	5.672175	1,300,125	589,799	710,326
4	5.718103	5.678316	1,321,935	410,851	911,084
5	5.701194	5.680301	1,328,981	669,900	659,081
6	5.768729	5.752299	1,584,065	803,880	780,185

Table 4 Comparison of Underwriters' Reoffered Scales

Maturity	Issuer's stated rate	Bidder					
		1	2	3	4	5	6
1992	4.40%	4.40%	4.50%	4.40%	4.40%	4.50%	4.50%
1993	4.75	4.75	4.90	4.80	4.75	4.80	4.90
1994	5.00	5.10	5.10	5.00	5.10	5.00	5.15
1995	5.20	5.15	5.25	5.30	5.50	5.25	5.35
1996	5.30	5.30	5.40	5.45	5.60	5.45	5.50
1997	5.40	5.40	5.55	5.60	5.60	5.60	5.60
1998	5.45	5.60	5.65	5.70	5.75	5.70	5.70
1999	5.50	5.70	5.75	5.85	5.85	5.80	5.80

With a lower and more level annual debt service, additional released cash from annual revenue flows is made available for pay-as-you-go capital fundings. This improves the "trading on the revenue equity" concept where more revenues are owned by the issuer.

H.   Reoffering Distribution

The distribution of the reoffered $89,320,000 maturity purchases is illustrated in Table 6.

The distribution amounts were obtained 2 weeks after the bidding from a major Florida-based firm, which served as lead manager of a syndicated group with five comanagers. Sales of comanagers were not available and are identified as maturities listed under "other." The lead underwriter, however, did venture an approximation of a fifty-fifty split for "other" as being between mutual funds and institutional investors. Otherwise, there were no mutual fund sales specifically reported.

IV.   SUMMARY AND CONCLUSION

The application of the NOTA method to "real life" practice demonstrates how an issuer can determine its own future principal and interest payment commitments to its advantage. As a competitive bid process, it places the responsibilities squarely on the underwriting community to compete fairly; only underwriters have the disciplines necessary to assess the risk/reward responsibilties and the skills necessary to market an issue. These expert disciplines and skills can be combined to assist the issuer with one readily understood number (the whole). Otherwise, the underwriting community should be willing to accept separately awarded bids for each maturity.

Table 5 Maximum Debt Service and Bidders' Reoffered Scales

Maturity	Debt payment amount	Reoffered scales
1992	$13,991,453	$14,041,728
1993	13,993,732	14,044,007
1994	13,993,470	14,043,745
1995	13,990,470	14,030,485
1996	13,995,430	14,040,830
1997	13,994,675	14,040,075
1998	13,995,185	14,040,585
1999	13,994,575	14,021,105
Total	$111,948,990	$112,302,560

Table 6 Distribution of Reoffered Maturity Purchases

Maturity	Unsold	Insur. Co.	Trust Dept.	Institutions	Retail	Other
1992					$200	$9,180
1993		$9,595	$ 50			150
1994		10,260				
1995		6,485	625		25	3,635
1996		6,925	325			4,085
1997	$8,540		500			2,895
1998			250			12,330
1999			125	$8,610		4,530
Totals	$8,540	$33,265	$1,875	$8,610	$225	$36,805

Note: Dollars in thousands

Since coverage is an important element for ratings, it would benefit underwriters to consider assisting their clients with planning and selling bond issues to permit additionally planned pay-as-you-go fundings (trading on the revenue equity).

Perhaps the most important issue is the public perception of the underwriting community and the issuers involved in bond financings. From the point of view of the taxpayer, the use of NIC, CIC, and TIC can seem to be confusing nonsense. Unfortunately, this perception adds to the general public's distrust of both the underwriters and issuers.

With NOTA, public confidence in municipal financings is easily improved because the phrase "the one with the biggest check wins" is a simple and straightforward description of the way that it works. Certainly there is a constant stream of creative and dynamic financing techniques flowing from the underwriting community to benefit the issuers. Perhaps NOTA can be accepted as an approach that also encourages public trust.

36

Understanding the Underwriting Spread

California Debt Advisory Commission
Sacramento, California

I. INTRODUCTION

One of the issuer's primary goals in any public debt offering is to borrow needed funds at the lowest possible cost. Inevitably, this entails not only obtaining favorable interest rates, but also holding other borrowing costs to a minimum. A major cost component of public debt issuance is the underwriter's compensation, which usually takes the form of the *underwriting spread*. While the amount of the underwriting spread will vary significantly depending on the characteristics of (1) the issuer, (2) the project, and (3) the financing, a general discussion of its components can prove valuable to an issuer evaluating proposed underwriting spreads.

The amount of the underwriting spread poses more of a concern to issuers offering debt through negotiated rather than competitive sale. In a competitive sale, the bonds are awarded to the underwriter offering the lowest qualifying bid (combined interest and spread), regardless of the level of underwriting spread which is imbedded in the bids. For instance, an underwriting firm with a superior distribution network might be able to offer the lowest bid even while setting the underwriting spread at a higher level than its competitors. By contrast, a negotiated sale requires the issuer and the underwriter to agree on the terms and conditions of the bond sale. These negotiations focus on the interest rate pricing and on the other major cost factor in the sale of bonds: the underwriting spread. Because the underwriter has obtained the exclusive right to purchase the bonds, the issuer cannot rely on competition between underwriters to keep the underwriting costs down. Consequently, it is critical that issuers become familiar with the various components which make up the underwriting spread.

II. THE UNDERWRITING SPREAD

The underwriting spread is defined as the difference between the price at which an underwriter purchases bonds from an issuer and the price at which the bonds are resold to investors. Bonds are generally offered in $5,000 increments. Spreads, however, are typically quoted in dollars per $1,000 bond. Thus, if an underwriter purchases a $1,000 bond from the issuer at $990 and reoffers it to investors at the face value, the underwriting spread is $10, or 1%. If the underwriter purchases bonds at par or at a premium, the underwriting spread is earned by reoffering the bonds to investors at a higher premium. Hence, if an underwriter purchases a $1,000 bond from the issuer at the full face value, the bonds could be reoffered at $1,010 to generate a spread of $10, or 1%. The underwriting spread compensates the underwriter for certain services rendered and is the source of underwriting profits.

Small issues generally require only one underwriter to distribute the bonds. Consequently, one under-

---

Adapted from Issue Brief No. 2 (March 1993) by permission of the California Debt Advisory Commission.

writer assumes all the risks of the transaction and receives all the profits from the reoffering of the issue. Large issues, however, often require the purchase and selling power of an underwriting *syndicate*. A syndicate is a group of underwriters convened to collectively purchase and reoffer an issue. Syndicate members share the liability of, and the profits from, the purchase and the resale of the issue. Generally, a syndicate is headed by a *senior manager* (and *co-senior managers*, if any) who usually negotiates with the issuer, signs all contracts on behalf of the syndicate, and allocates the bonds among the syndicate members. A syndicate may also have *co-managers* who assist the issuer in preparing the issue for the sale.

In an underwriting syndicate, the senior managers typically take on the highest share of the underwriting liability. Accordingly, they receive the highest share of the syndicate profits. The senior managers are followed by the co-managers in terms of level of liability and share of the profits. The remaining members of the syndicate typically assume the smallest share of liability and profits. In addition to, or in lieu of, a syndicate, the underwriter may opt to form a *selling group*. A selling group consists of dealers and brokers brought together to help sell bonds. They do not share the underwriting risk and, consequently, do not receive a share of the syndicate profits.

III. THE FOUR COMPONENTS OF THE SPREAD

As indicated earlier, the spread is where the underwriter recoups the costs of providing investment banking services and derives its profits. The four components of the spread are *management fee*, *expenses*, *underwriting fee*, and *takedown*. While it is customary for the underwriting spread to be quoted as a percentage of the issue size, some components of the spread, such as the management fee and certain expense items, can be quoted in fixed terms, irrespective of the issue size.

A. Management Fee

The management fee compensates the underwriter for the investment banking services provided to the issuer, above the amount of compensation earned from other components. In the case of an issue underwritten by a syndicate, the management fee is paid to the senior manager (and co-senior manager, if any) for managing the affairs of the syndicate. Depending on the conditions agreed upon by the syndicate and the issuer, a management fee may also be paid to the co-managers for providing services to the issuer. Some of the services covered by the management fee include

- Development of a financing plan and a maturity schedule best suited to the needs of the issuer. These activities may be conducted in coordination with the financial advisor.
- Origination and marketing tasks such as preparation of bond documents, rating agency presentations, and circulation of disclosure information.
- Assessment of market conditions and advice on the timing of the sale.
- Preparation of reports on the postsale results of the transaction.

The management fee can vary significantly from one transaction to another depending upon the time and effort expended by the underwriter.

B. Expenses

This component of the spread reimburses the underwriter for out-of-pocket costs incurred in the course of the sale. The biggest expense item is usually the underwriter's counsel fee. In addition, travel expenses can be a significant expense item, especially if the underwriter does not have an office located near the issuer or access to necessary professional expertise in the vicinity of the issuer. Other expense items include advertising and printing costs, computer services, bond clearance, communications (phone, FAX, courier, messenger services), Municipal Securities Rulemaking Board fees, and California Debt Advisory Commission fees.

C. Underwriting Fee

Because the underwriter cannot always be certain that all of the issuer's bonds will be readily purchased by investors, the underwriter may charge a fee to cover the possibility that some of the bonds may have to be reoffered at a lower price or taken into the underwriter's inventory. The size of the fee is directly related to the market risk involved. In a strong and stable market, characterized by an abundance of buyers, all the bonds may already be pre-sold. In this instance, the underwriting fee can be waived because the underwriter's risk has been eliminated.

D. Takedown

The takedown is the biggest and perhaps the most confusing component of the spread. Essentially, the takedown is a sales commission paid to the underwriter. In order to obtain the most favorable interest rates, the issuer has to provide the underwriter's sales force sufficient incentive, in the form of the takedown, to work hard at finding investors willing to accept the lowest rates.

In effect, the takedown functions as a discount from the listed reoffering price given to the firm that sells the bond to the investor. The takedown consists of two parts: the *concession* and the *additional takedown*. [Note that the term *additional takedown* does not refer to an amount *in addition to* the takedown. Rather, it refers to a subcomponent of the takedown.] Apportioning the takedown between the concession and the additional takedown is basically a convention that provides an incentive for *nonmember firms* to sell bonds. If a syndicate member sells the bonds directly to investors, that firm receives a discount equal to the sum of the concession and the additional takedown, or the *full takedown*. When a nonmember firm sells the bonds, it takes down the bonds from the syndicate *at the concession*—at a discount equal to the concession—and reoffers them to investors at the listed reoffering price. The remaining portion of the takedown, the additional takedown, stays with the syndicate as profit.

Each maturity in a bond issue carries a separate takedown. Generally, the takedown bears an inverse relationship to credit quality and a direct relationship to the length of principal maturities. For example, a triple-B credit maturing in 10 years typically will have a higher takedown than a triple-A credit of the same maturity because a lower rated bond is more difficult to market. In addition, bonds which mature in the twentieth year will normally have a higher takedown than bonds from the same issue which mature on the first year because short maturities are usually more marketable than long maturities. Because the takedown varies among different maturities within the same bond issue, the *average takedown*—the average of the takedowns for each maturity in the issue—is often used when discussing the total spread.

IV. AN ILLUSTRATION OF UNDERWRITING SPREAD

For a more concrete understanding of the underwriting spread, consider the following illustration of a hypothetical $10 million negotiated serial bond issue. Leaving the interest rate pricing aside for the purposes of this discussion, assume that the underwriter offers to purchase the issue for $9.9 million with a plan to reoffer it to the public at par or face value—leaving a $100,000 underwriting spread.

Table 1 breaks down the underwriting spread of $10 per $1,000 bond. (The spread figures used in this illustration were chosen for ease of calculation only and may not reflect current or historical spreads.) Of this amount, $1.50 per $1,000 bond (a total of $15,000 for the issue) is designated as the management fee, paying for such services as developing the debt service schedule and obtaining a rating. If this issue is being underwritten by a syndicate, the management fee also compensates the senior underwriter for negotiating with the issuer, allocating the bonds, and confirming customer orders. Another $1.50 per $1,000 bond (a total of $15,000) is designated reimbursement for the underwriter's expenses such as bond counsel fee, travel, and printing.

Table 1 also shows that the underwriting fee is 75 cents per $1,000 bond, or $7,500 for the entire issue. Remember, the underwriting fee compensates the underwriter for the possibility that it may not be able to sell all the bonds at the listed reoffering price. The presence of a $7,500 underwriting fee suggests that at least some portion of the bonds remains unsold at the time of the sale. Essentially, this amount serves as the hedge for the syndicate in the event that the remaining bonds cannot be sold at par. However, if the underwriting syndicate manages to sell all the bonds at par, it keeps this amount free and clear. Considered part of the syndicate profits, this amount will be divided among the members of the syndicate based on the proportion of each member's participation (share of the liability) in the underwriting. Say, for example, that this issue is being underwritten by a six-member syndicate consisting of two senior managers with 25% participation each ($2.5 million liability each), two co-managers with 15% participation each ($1.5 million liability each), and two members with 10% participation each ($1 million liability each). The $7,500

Table 1 Hypothetical Underwriting Spread: $10 Million Issue

Components	Amounts per $1,000 bond	Percentage of issue	Total for issue
Management fee	$1.50	0.150%	$15,000
Expenses	1.50	0.150	15,000
Underwriting fee	0.75	0.075	7,500
Average takedown	6.25	0.625	62,500
Concession	(3.75)	(0.375)	(37,500)
Additional takedown	(2.50)	(0.250)	(25,000)
Total spread	$10.00	1.00%	$100,000

underwriting fee will be divided according to their liability, with each of the senior managers receiving $1,875 (25%), each co-manager receiving $1,125 (15%), and each member receiving $750 (10%).

The average takedown for this issue is $6.25 per $1,000 bond or $62,500 for the entire bond issue. Of that amount, $3.75 represents the concession and $2.50 represents the additional takedown. As noted in the previous section, however, the average takedown is a figure used mainly for general discussion purposes. The takedown of the bonds actually varies by maturity. To fully understand the mechanics of the takedown, it is necessary to look at each maturity in the issue.

A. Takedown Distribution

Table 2 shows the ten maturities of the hypothetical $10 million serial bond issue, as well as the takedown for each maturity. As indicated earlier, members of the syndicate take down the bonds at the full takedown—at a discount equal to the sum of the concession and the additional takedown. For instance, the 1995 maturity carries a full takedown of one-fourth of 1% (1/8 concession + 1/8 additional takedown) or $2.50 ($1.25 concession + $1.25 additional takedown) for every $1,000 bond. Hence, if firm A, which is a member of the syndicate, takes down a $1,000 bond from the 1995 maturity, it would pay the syndicate $997.50 ($1,000 – $2.50) for the bond and reoffer the bond to investors at par (the listed reoffering price). A firm that is not a member of the syndicate, however, purchases or takes down the bonds from the syndicate at the reoffering price less the concession. Hence, for the 1995 maturity, nonmember firm B would receive a one-eighth of 1% ($1.25 concession) discount for every $1,000 bond it takes down. This means that firm B would purchase a $1,000 bond from the syndicate at $998.75 ($1,000 – $1.25) and reoffer it to investors at par. The syndicate, in turn, would retain one-eighth of 1% ($1.25 additional takedown) for every $1,000 bond in the 1995 maturity sold by a nonmember firm as part of its profits. This amount will eventually be divided among the syndicate members based on their participation, in the same fashion as the underwriting fee.

Table 2 Hypothetical Takedown by Maturity: $10 Million Issue (per $1,000 bond)

Maturities	Amounts	Coupon rates	Prices/ yields	Conc./add TD (fractions)	Conc./add TD (dollar amounts)
1994	$1,000,000	4.65	100	1/8 + 1/8	$1.25 + $1.25
1995	1,000,000	5.15	100	1/8 + 1/8	1.25 + 1.25
1996	1,000,000	5.30	100	1/8 + 1/8	1.25 + 1.25
1997	1,000,000	5.50	100	1/4 + 1/8	2.50 + 1.25
1998	1,000,000	5.65	100	3/8 + 1/4	3.75 + 2.50
1999	1,000,000	5.80	100	1/2 + 1/4	5.00 + 2.50
2000	1,000,000	5.90	100	1/2 + 1/4	5.00 + 2.50
2001	1,000,000	6.05	100	1/2 + 1/4	5.00 + 2.50
2002	1,000,000	6.15	100	5/8 + 1/2	6.25 + 5.00
2003	1,000,000	6.25	100	5/8 + 1/2	6.25 + 5.00

As an example of the variation of the takedown between maturities in the same issue, compare the total takedown for the 2003 maturity with the total takedown for the 1995 maturity. The $11.25 per $1,000 bond total takedown for the 2003 maturity is significantly higher than the $2.50 per $1,000 bond total takedown for the 1995 maturity. The profit margin for the longer maturity is obviously bigger. Thus, if a syndicate member sells bonds from the 2003 maturity, it would receive a discount from the listed reoffering price (par) equal to $11.25 ($6.25 concession + $5.00 additional takedown) for every $1,000 bond taken down versus $2.50 for every $1,000 bond taken down from the 1995 maturity. A nonmember firm taking down bonds in the 2003 maturity would receive the $6.25 (concession) discount from par for every $1,000 bond versus $1.25 for every $1,000 bond from the 1995 maturity.

V.   NEGOTIATING THE UNDERWRITING SPREAD

The breakdown of underwriting spread shown above is for illustrative purposes only. It is not intended to represent an ideal spread distribution. Actual spreads vary between issues due to differences in credit quality, maturities, debt service payment sources, tax status, and a host of other factors. Two issues of the same size sold at the same time will not necessarily have the same spread. Two issues with the same spread will not necessarily have the same distribution of spread among component parts. The following section offers suggestions for negotiating proposed underwriting spreads.

A.   Setting Spread Parameters in the RFP

One approach used by some issuers to control costs, while retaining the flexibility to adjust the spread to reflect the underwriter's performance in the sale, is to set spread parameters in the request for proposals (RFP). Under this approach, the issuer requires underwriters to indicate an estimate for each component of the spread in their responses to the RFP. Given that the takedown and underwriting fee are closely tied to the interest rate pricing which occurs much later, it is sometimes unrealistic to expect a concrete estimate for these two components. However, the issuer can obtain fairly sound estimates for the management fee and expense components. To hold the underwriters true to these estimates, the issuer specifies in the RFP that the estimates will be considered as bids and the selected underwriter's bids will function as caps for the management fee and expense components. Thus, while the issuer may want to leave final spread negotiations until closer to the sale date, it can set the parameters for at least the management fee and expense components of the spread based on the underwriter responses to the RFP.

B.   Management Fee

When negotiating the management fee, issuers should consider the level and the quality of the services provided by the underwriter. An underwriter that helps the issuer structure a complex offering might merit a higher management fee. However, for a straightforward issue, the management fee is often waived or nominal. If financial advisory tasks such as developing the financing plan, structuring the issue, and obtaining a rating are performed in-house or by a financial advisor, the issuer should also seek a waiver or nominal management fee.

C.   Expenses

It is important that issuers hold underwriters accountable for expense reimbursements. At the outset, the issuer and the underwriter should identify which expenses are eligible for reimbursement. The issuer should require the underwriter to provide a line-item listing of reimbursable expenses, including underwriter's counsel fees. Issuers should not be shy about asking underwriters for explanations of questionable items.

D.   Underwriting Fee

Issuers should not agree to pay any underwriting fee unless, during the pricing process, there is evidence of the risk that the underwriter cannot sell all the bonds at the listed reoffering price. Hence, when negotiating the underwriting fee, issuers should monitor the progress of the bond orders. If the underwriter receives orders for a significant portion of the bonds by the end of the initial order period, the issuer should look for a nominal, if any, underwriting fee. If all of the bonds have been pre-sold to investors during the initial order period, the underwriter faces no inventory risk and should not be paid an underwriting fee. Issuers should also be aware that some managers are willing to commit their capital to a successful sale, even if it means underwriting a portion or all of the issue. Thus, issuers should always explore the possibility of waiving the underwriting fee at the outset of the negotiations for every offering.

E. Takedown

Obtaining orders at market rates while paying the lowest possible takedown is the issuer's challenge. However, a singleminded pursuit for the lowest takedown without regard to the interest rate pricing, would not necessarily serve the issuer's interest. The takedown provides an incentive for the sales force to aggressively market competitively priced bonds. If the takedown is set too low, there is less motivation for the sales force to find investors willing to accept the issuer's rates. Thus, when maturities are *undersubscribed* (not receiving sufficient orders) during the initial order period, the issuer should recognize that it may be able to generate adequate orders for some of the undersubscribed maturities by increasing the takedowns, rather than raising the rates. If the issuer insists on keeping the takedowns at low levels, the only option would be to raise the rates to generate sufficient orders for the undersubscribed maturities. On the other hand, when maturities are *oversubscribed* (receiving more orders than there are bonds available) during the initial order period, the issuer should not be shy about pursuing reductions in the interest rates or the takedowns for those maturities.

37

Tax-Exempt Debt and U.S. Department of Treasury Regulations

George J. Whelan
Commerce Department, City of Philadelphia, Philadelphia, Pennsylvania

Michele M. Patrick
Office of the Managing Director, City of Philadelphia, Philadelphia, Pennsylvania

A considerable amount of fairly comprehensive and technical literature has been written explaining the legal and regulatory requirements of arbitrage rebate as it applies to the issuance of tax-exempt debt.

As defined by the Department of Treasury Regulations, arbitrage is the gain a tax-exempt investor may be able to obtain by borrowing at a tax-exempt rate and investing at a taxable rate.[1] The Tax Reform Act of 1986, and subsequent amendments relating to the issuance of tax-exempt debt and arbitrage regulations, had a dramatic affect on all issuers of tax-exempt debt. The issuers are primarily state and local governments or the instrumentalities of state and local governments. These instrumentalities are most often authorities that are empowered by state and local governments to issue debt for certain public purposes such as health care, education and, to some extent, certain public economic development-type projects.

Perhaps the most difficult aspect of these new requirements (and the explanatory texts) has been the need to calculate arbitrage rebate. *Arbitrage rebate* refers to the requirement to rebate to the federal government investment earnings derived with the proceeds of tax-exempt debt that are in excess of the earnings that would have been earned had the proceeds of the debt been invested at the same interest rate as that paid to the holders of the tax-exempt debt. (In a few restricted instances, such earnings do not have to be rebated; this will be discussed in greater detail later in this chapter.)

For example, if bonds have been sold at an overall interest rate of 7%, and the proceeds were invested to earn at a rate of 8%, the difference in earnings (the "arbitrage") as a result of that 1% "spread" would have to be rebated or paid to the Internal Revenue Service.

As may be expected, due to the complexity of the regulations, the term arbitrage rebate has become encased in a lot of nuances and misunderstandings. Moreover, as alluded to above, there is a great deal of available literature that explains in a comprehensive manner the various complexities and specific regulations.

This is not the thrust of this chapter; on the contrary, this chapter is meant to be an instructive primer for the practitioner and the student. The basic underlying mathematics and central concepts involved in calculating arbitrage rebate will be discussed and demonstrated by means of several representative examples. It is hoped that this approach will enable the reader to gain both a thorough understanding of the central principles surrounding arbitrage financing and arbitrage rebate, and the "knack" of how to do the calculations.

At this juncture, we must caution, however, that when undertaking arbitrage calculations, it is imperative to work with the appropriate legal, financial, and accounting advisors to ensure compliance with an extremely complicated series of laws and regulations.

The authors wish to acknowledge the assistance of Frederic L. Ballard, Jr., Esq. of Ballard, Spahr, Andrews and Ingersoll, Washington, D.C., for reviewing certain legal and regulatory sections of the text.

I. A BRIEF HISTORY: ARBITRAGE BEFORE 1969

Before 1969, it appears that the federal government was unconcerned with arbitrage opportunities. State and local governments, because of federal tax exemption on their obligations, were allowed to earn unlimited arbitrage. The tax-exempt status was not intended to serve as an opportunity for local governments to borrow in order to gain arbitrage, but to attract capital and therefore lower their costs of borrowing.

II. ARBITRAGE FINANCING EXAMPLE

The following example, taken from the Internal Revenue Service announcement 89-66, Table 1, has been somewhat adjusted to demonstrate the possible advantage, in arbitrage earnings, to any state or local entity.

City XYZ issues $10 million of general obligation bonds on March 1, 1989, in order to undertake various capital projects. The bonds are issued at par and have a term of 20 years. The yield on the bonds is 7% per year, compounded annually. On the issue date, City XYZ invests $2 million of the bond proceeds in a 1-year certificate of deposit paying 6% interest per year, compounded annually. Another $5 million is invested in a 2-year certificate paying 7.5% interest per year, compounded annually, and the remaining $3 million is invested in a 3-year certificate paying 8% interest per year, compounded annually. Assume that City XYZ receives the interest payment annually. Also assume that the bond proceeds invested in the certificates and all the interest are immediately spent on the project when the principal and interest from these investments are received (Table 1).

Yes, arbitrage has some potential reward, which would reduce the cost of borrowing for construction projects, but it also entails risk. For example, during the closing months of a given year, reinvestment rates for the borrower entity may be less than those paid for the loans; consequently, a loss would be realized in that year.[2]

Although the preceding example is, obviously, quite simplistic in nature, it does illustrate the basic concept of arbitrage. More importantly, this example has been placed here in order for the reader to familiarize himself or herself with the basic terms. The same example will be employed, again, when discussing the "classical" or exact rebate method and the effect of future value calculations.

Eventually, as state and local governments began to more fully utilize opportunities for arbitrage income, the U.S. Treasury Department began to show signs of increasing opposition to the practice.[3] Congress first specifically addressed the arbitrage issue in the Tax Reform Act of 1969. This act amended the IRS code of

Table 1

Date	Receipt	Explanation	Future value as of 3/1/94 at 7% compounded annually
I. Future value of receipts			
3/1/90	$2,735,000.00	Principal and interest from certificates	$ 3,585,027.09
3/1/91	$5,615,000.00	Principal and interest from certificates	$ 6,878,616.45
3/1/92	$3,240,000.00	Principal and interest from certificates	$ 3,709,476.00
Future value of receipts			$14,173,119.54
II. Future value of payments			
3/1/89	$10,000,000.00	Purchase certificates	$14,025,517.31
Future value of payments			$14,025,517.31
III. Rebatable Arbitrage as of 3/1/94			
Future value of receipts		$14,173,119.54	
Less future value of payments		− $14,025,517.31	
Arbitrage earnings:		$147,602.23	

Source: IRS announcement 89-66, Table 1 ("Federal Income Tax Principles of Municipal Bonds"), "Compilation of Rebatable Arbitrage."

1954 and established that the penalty for issuing an "arbitrage bond" would be the loss of the tax-exempt status of the interest on the bonds, retroactive to the date of issuance.[4]

Although the penalty for an arbitrage bond has remained unchanged since the 1969 act, the definition of arbitrage bond has gone through several permutations. Originally, in 1969, it was an issue that did not comply with rules that required that the yield on the investments with bond proceeds not be materially higher than the yield on the bonds. Of course, as always with arbitrage regulations, there were various exceptions.[5]

New arbitrage regulations were adopted in 1979 as "yield restriction regulations." In general, these very comprehensive and detailed regulations permitted arbitrage profits that were incidental to the borrowing plans of a government, as long as it appeared that the only motive for borrowing the funds was to finance a particular project. Thus, under the yield restriction regulations, arbitrage bonds are those for which the amount, timing, or life of the bond issue is unusual, in order to arbitrage profits.[6]

It must be noted that since the crux of this chapter is a discussion of arbitrage *rebate* regulations and calculations, further discourse on the 1979 yield regulations is unnecessary. They have been noted in order to provide the reader with a more complete historical framework for arbitrage rebate.

At the beginning of the Reagan years, a bond issuer was permitted to earn arbitrage proceeds for up to 3 years, but only on the portion of the bond proceeds that were used to pay for legitimate capital costs. A "temporary period" for a bona fide debt service fund, within which unlimited arbitrage earnings were allowed under the 1979 regulations, was established at 13 months and remains so under the June 1993 arbitrage regulations, pursuant to the Tax Reform Act of 1986. A reasonably required reserve fund, pursuant to the 1993 final regulations, put further limits on arbitrage earnings (e.g., 125% of average annual debt service).[7.] As time went on, at the administrative level, Treasury regulations were often amended to combat innovative arbitrage techniques that were undertaken by state and local governments.[8] Clearly, as reflected in the 1993 regulations, that regulatory activity is continuing.

III. HISTORY OF REBATE REQUIREMENTS

The original 1969 arbitrage rule carried no rebate requirements. It primarily dealt with yield restrictions, temporary periods, and reserve funds. In 1980, Congress passed legislation that required that the issuers of bonds to finance home mortgages rebate any arbitrage profits to homeowners. As an alternative, issuers were allowed to pay the rebate to the federal government (Internal Revenue Service). Finally, in 1985 Congress extended the rebate requirement to industrial development bonds; this time, however, paying the rebate to the federal government was the only option. Officially, the 1985 regulations were passed because the federal government did not want state and local entities to issue bonds solely for the purpose of obtaining arbitrage income.[9]

IV. 1986 FEDERAL TAX REFORM ACT

The Federal Tax Reform Act of 1986 [additional sections 148 and 149 (d) to the IRS code by section 1301 (100 Stat 2602)] imposed significant new requirements for all issuers of tax-exempt debt. The crux of the new legislation is that investment earnings derived with the proceeds of tax-exempt debt, that are in excess of the earnings that would have been realized had the proceeds of the debt been invested at the same interest as that paid to the holders of tax-exempt debt, must be rebated to the federal government. Moreover, a specified formula must be utilized in order to determine the required rebate. All tax-exempt bonds are now subject to this rebate requirement.

As officially stated, the purpose of the Tax Reform Act of 1986 is "To eliminate significant arbitrage incentives to issue more bonds, to issue bonds earlier, and to leave bonds outstanding longer than necessary to carry out the governmental purposes of the tax exempt issue" (*Federal Register*, May 15, 1989). In effect, the rebate requirement forces state and local governments to pay to the Internal Revenue Service all the arbitrage earnings that they had previously been permitted to accrue under the yield restriction rules. Consequently, the new rebate requirement eliminates any arbitrage benefits. If a state or local government does not adhere to the rebate requirements, it forfeits the tax-exempt status of the interest on the bonds, retroactive to the date of issue.[10]

Perhaps more importantly, the central requirement of the rebate regulations requires that the amount of the rebate, which must be paid to the federal government, be computed using the "future value" method. A full discussion of this method, including examples and the mandated computation dates, will follow a brief discussion of the exceptions to the 1986 Tax Reform Act.

V. EXCEPTIONS TO THE 1986 REBATE REQUIREMENT

The 1986 version of the rebate requirement allowed five exceptions.[11]

1. A bond issue, the gross proceeds of which are to be expended for the purpose of the issue within 6 months of the issue date. This is known as the "safe harbor rule." (Originally this was the only exception based on expenditure of proceeds.)
2. Issues from "small governmental units." A small governmental unit is an issuer whose total financing in a calendar year is not expected to exceed $5 million. Industrial development bonds cannot qualify for this exception, but do not count toward the $5 million limit.
3. Issues that are invested in tax-exempt obligations.
4. Issues whose proceeds are invested in "demand deposit SLGs." These securities are only offered to state and local governments by the Department of the Treasury.
5. Debt service funds; however, there are certain exceptions, such as limiting the size of earnings to $100,000 in certain cases.

It is necessary to again caution the reader that when discussing arbitrage, there are numerous regulations and often an exception to every rule. Thus, this section on exceptions to the rebate requirement is not meant to be all-inclusive.

Furthermore, since 1986 there have been a number of changes to the tax law that have somewhat altered these ancillary points without changing the fundamental rebate and future value requirements. For example, as discussed later in this chapter, a 2-year exception was added to the statute in 1989 and an 18-month exception was added in 1993.

VI. FUTURE VALUE REBATE REQUIREMENTS

As previously noted, the crux of the 1986 Tax Reform Act, as amended, is the use of the "future value" method to determine the amount of arbitrage rebate that is due the federal government. Basically, under a "rebatable arbitrage" scheme, the purchase price of investments, called "payments," are "future valued." In other words, they are computed as of a computation date and by using an interest rate equal to the rate on the issue. Under normal circumstances, computation dates occur at the end of every 5 bond years. A fuller discussion of computation dates will follow. The receipts from investments are also future valued. The difference between the aggregate future value of all payments, and the aggregate future value of all receipts, is the *rebatable arbitrage* that is due the federal government.[12]

The term *payment* and *receipt* are somewhat misleading. It may help to think of the payment as the proceeds of the bond issue being invested at the time of issuance. That investment is the payment. As the investments are liquidated and used to pay the cost of construction, they can be thought of as receipts that are expended. The regulations specifically exclude receipts that are automatically reinvested (not spent) from future value calculations.

Concerning computation dates, Treasury regulations require that an issuer compute rebatable arbitrage 5 years after the issuance of the respective bond issue. At that time, the issuer must pay at least 90% of the required arbitrage within 60 days. The issuer must then recalculate and redetermine its rebatable arbitrage on successive computation dates (falling after 5-year periods) and pay the required amount within 60 days. When the issue is finally retired, the remaining balance must also be paid within 60 days.[13]

By again employing the example we used earlier—keeping the same terms, but this time future valuing the payments and receipts—to calculate future value and the rebatable arbitrage, we can see how the 1986 Tax Reform Act greatly affected issuers of tax-exempt debt. As previously noted:

The City of XYZ has issued $10 million of general obligation bonds on March 1, 1989, in order to undertake various capital projects. The bonds are issued on par and have a term of 20 years. The yield on the bonds is 7% per year, compounded annually. On the issue date, City XYZ invests $2 million of bond proceeds in 1-year certificate of deposit paying 6% interest per year, compounded annually. Another $5 million is invested in a

Table 2

Date	Receipt	Explanation	Future value as of 3/1/94 at 7% compounded annually
I. Future value of receipts			
3/1/90	$2,735,000.00	Principal and interest from certificates	$3,585,027.09
3/1/91	$5,615,000.00	Principal and interest from certificates	$6,878,616.45
3/1/92	$3,240,000.00	Principal and interest from certificates	$3,709,476.00
Future value of receipts			$14,173,119.54
II. Future value of payments			
3/1/89	$10,000,000.00	Purchase certificates	$14,025,517.31
Future value of payments			$14,025,517.31
III. Rebatable arbitrage as of 3/1/94			
Future value of receipts			$14,173,119.54
Less future value of payments			−$14,025,517.31
Excess of future value of receipts over payments			$147,602.23
Less computation date credit			$1,000.00[a]
REBATABLE ARBITRAGE AS OF 3/1/94			$146,602.23

[a]Pursuant to the June 1993 Final Arbitrage Regulations, there is a $1,000 per annum credit allowed. Again, this is another example of the gradually evolving legal and regulatory aspects of arbitrage rebate.
Source: IRS announcement 89-66, Table 1 ("Federal Income Tax Principles of Municipal Bonds"), "Computation of Rebatable Arbitrage."

2-year certificate paying 7.5% interest per year compounded annually and the remaining $3 million is invested in a 3-year certificate paying 8% interest per year, compounded annually. Assume that City XYZ receives the interest payment annually. Also assume that the bond proceeds invested in the certificates and all the interest are immediately spent on the project when the principal and the interest from these investments are received.

VII. MATHEMATICS OF FUTURE VALUE

As previously noted, the rebate calculations we have been discussing require the amount of the rebate to be computed using the future value method. Future value calculations were employed in the previous example.

Mathematically, future value is derived from the more familiar concept known as present value; present value calculations are often undertaken by students of economics and finance. Most simply, present value is the current value of an amount to be paid or received in the future. Present value is calculated using the following accepted formula:

This formula is taken from the *Federal Register*, vol. 54, no. 92, but it can also be found in practically all economics textbooks.

$$PV = \frac{FV}{(1 + i)^n}$$

where

PV = present value of amount to be paid
i   = discount rate, divided by number of compounding intervals in a year
n   = number of compounding intervals during the period beginning on the date as of which the present value is computed and ending on the date the amount is to be received or paid

Future value is, of course, the reciprocal of present value. Utilizing the above equation, in order to isolate FV (future value), it is necessary to multiply each side of the equation by $(1 + i)^n$. Thus, the following equation emerges:

$$FV = PV(1 + i)^n$$

where

FV = future value of what is to be received or paid
PV = present value of what is to be received or paid
i   = interest rate equal to the yield on the bond issue
n   = the number of compounding periods

This is the equation to be used when undertaking future value calculations for the rebate requirement, as required by the Treasury Department.

VIII. CALCULATING FUTURE VALUE INTEREST FACTOR

A final helpful formula in future value calculations is the equation used to determine the "future value interest factor," FVIV.

Let us again examine our future value formula:

$$FV = PV(1 + i)^n$$

If we divide both sides of the equation by the present value PV, we arrive at the following equation:

$$\frac{FV}{PV} = (1 + i)^n$$

where

FV/PV = can be called the FVIF.
   i   = interest rate factor, or bond yield, as defined in the regulations. In other words, it is the overall rate of interest being paid to the bondholders.
   n   = number of compounding periods. This part of the equation allows one to calculate the future value from different times, e.g., 23 months from the end of the first 5-year computation date.

The FVIF equation is an integral part of arbitrage calculations. As we have discussed, the Treasury regulations require that arbitrage earnings not exceed the rate at which the bondholders are earning interest. Another way to state this would be: The arbitrage earnings are not to exceed the rate of interest to the issuer. Thus, by multiplying the stream of payments (investments) and receipts (expenditures) with the future value interest factor, the future value of each of the payments and receipts is determined.

The following example (Fig. 1) demonstrates the importance of the FVIF, as well as how rebatable arbitrage is determined in a "real world" scenario. Note the varied frequency of the requisitions, which is more reflective of an active construction schedule. Each of these requisition dates needs to be future valued from the various times.

The example shows a revenue bond issue for which the rebate liability is calculated at the end of the June 30 fiscal year. Note that the original proceeds plus accrued interest are invested at the date of issuance. All the requisitions (architects, land acquisition, construction, etc.) are listed in sequence.

The number of months until the end of the first 5-year computation date (August 1, 1994) are provided. One of the little quirks in the original May 15, 1989 regulations is that the first bond year can be less than 12 months, depending on the date of issuance (e.g., August 19, 1989 to August 1, 1990).

The central task is to calculate the future value of this stream of payments and receipts. The FVIFs take the monthly bond yield (0.575%) as the "i" in the FVIF formula and the number of months as the "nth" power. In Fig. 1, the last column is the product of those calculations. The yield, or interest rate paid to the bondholders, in this example is 6.9%, or .575 per month. For our purposes, it is sufficient to note here that the regulations prescribe technical methods for calculating the bond yield for an entire issue. As a point of information, these technical methods also involve present value concepts. The total of payments is subtracted from the total amount of receipts. In this example, the payments exceed the receipts so there is no liability. Any rebate is not due until the full 5-year computation period is complete. However, for accounting statement purposes, a community may need to show the accruing liability at the end of each fiscal year within the computation period. In other words, the following example is somewhat informal in that it is an estimate at the end of 1 year rather than the required formal 5-year calculation.

Thus, it is hoped that this illustration will simply give the reader a start on "getting the knack" of how to do arbitrage rebate calculations. We hasten to add that various commercial spreadsheet software packages are very helpful in preparing such calculations.

Clearly, the yield on the investments is less than the yield on the bonds by approximately $1,115,000. Consequently, there is no arbitrage rebate accruing at the end of the first year of the 5-year computation period.

Several additional explanatory comments regarding this example are also in order. This example shows the investment of gross proceeds ($15,000,000 plus accrued interest of $25,000) with the same-day withdrawal of the costs of issuance (e.g., bond insurance and issuance costs). It is more likely, however, that in an actual transaction the *net* proceeds—those proceeds available after paying the costs of issuance—would be the amount invested and future valued as the "payment," while subsequent withdrawals to pay various

Revenue Bonds		Bond Yield Limit	
Date Issued		annual	6.9000000%
08/19/1989		semiannual	3.4500000%
Computation date - August 1, 1994		monthly	0.5750000%
(August 19, 1989 - August 1, 1990)		biweekly	0.2653846%
(First bond year)		daily (360)	0.0191667%

Transaction Date		Calc. Date	Years	Months	Calculation Amount	Monthly FV Factor	Amount
08/19/89	proceeds	08/19/89	4.9	58.8	$15,000,000	1.4009235149	($21,013,852.72)
08/19/89	accrued interest	08/19/89	4.9	58.8	25,000	1.4009235149	(35,023.09)
08/19/89	interest account	08/19/89	4.9	58.8	25,000	1.4009235149	35,023.09
08/19/89	bond insurance	08/19/89	4.9	58.8	100,000	1.4009235149	140,092.35
08/19/89	insurance costs	08/19/89	4.9	58.8	45,000	1.4009235149	63,041.56
08/19/89	underwriters' fee	08/19/89	4.9	58.8	125,000	1.4009235149	175,115.44
10/27/89	requisition	10/27/89		56.5	300,000	1.3828348996	414,850.47
11/17/89	requisition	11/17/89		55.8	100,000	1.3775593034	137,755.93
12/01/89	requisition	12/01/89		55.4	125,000	1.3738788658	171,734.80
12/01/89	requisition	12/01/89		55.4	10,000	1.3738788658	13,738.78
01/26/90	requisition	01/26/90		53.6	15,000	1.3595125132	20,392.69
02/02/90	requisition	02/02/90		53.4	17,000	1.357954445	23,085.23
02/23/90	requisition	02/23/90		52.7	2,300	1.3527737692	3,111.38
02/23/90	requisition	02/23/90		52.7	995,000	1.3527737692	1,346,009.90
02/23/90	requisition	02/23/90		52.7	12,000	1.3527737692	16,233.29
02/23/90	requisition	02/23/90		52.7	3,050	1.3527737692	4,126.86
03/16/90	requisition	03/16/90		51.9	1,203	1.3468404212	1,620.25
03/30/90	requisition	03/30/90		51.5	1,025	1.3432415668	1,376.82
03/30/90	requisition	03/30/90		51.5	2,550	1.3432415668	3,425.27
04/06/90	requisition	04/06/90		51.3	1,240	1.341702146	1,663.71
04/20/90	requisition	04/20/90		50.8	45,000	1.3381170215	60,215.27
05/11/90	requisition	05/11/90		50.1	20,000	1.3327572886	26,655.15
05/11/90	requisition	05/11/90		50.1	195,000	1.3327572886	259,887.67
05/11/90	requisition	05/11/90		50.1	120,000	1.3327572886	159,930.87
05/11/90	requisition	05/11/90		50.1	95,000	1.3327572886	126,611.94
05/18/90	requisition	05/18/90		49.9	1,500	1.330975486	1,996.46
06/30/90	RECEIPT (balance)	06/30/90		48.5	12,666,132	1.3203345836	16,726,172.79

Total amount of payments	$21,048,875.81
Total amount of receipts	(19,933,867.08)

Excess payments over receipts if positive number	$1,115,008.78
Estimated rebate amount if a negative number	

Figure 1   Arbitrage rebate calculations at the end of the June 30 fiscal year.

requisitions would be the "receipts." The authors chose to illustrate the calculation in this way so as to reflect the treatment of all the elements of the transaction in the most conservative manner possible.

Finally, we need to note that this example relies on the assumption that the investment of all the proceeds is undertaken on August 19, 1989, and that all investment income is automatically reinvested. It is also assumed that there is no period of idle funds before the requisitions. These assumptions involve the maximizations of investment returns, whereas in actual practice there may be some periods during which noninterest-bearing accounts are involved in closing the transaction, or paying requisitions. The authors want to note these assumptions in order to more completely illustrate the adaptability of this exhibit.

IX. ADDITIONAL ARBITRAGE PAYMENT REGULATIONS

As indicated, a number and variety of regulations govern arbitrage payment procedures.[14] Perhaps most importantly, the federal government allows a credit on each arbitrage computation date; originally, the credit amount could not exceed $1,000. The amount was raised to $3,000 in 1991, but it was reduced to the original $1,000 by the 1993 regulations. In order for a computation date to be eligible for the credit, it must be at least 1 year since the previous computation date, or at least 1 year since the bond's date of issue—if it is the first computation date.

An issuer is allowed to pay a rebate installment before the mandated computation date. Such payment will count toward the installment due at the next computation date, at the future valued amount.

An issuer may treat a series of issues as a single issue, as long as the issues are redeemed during a 6-month period and as long as no bond in any of the issues has a maturity longer than 270 days.

The regulations do allow an issuer who discovers that through an innocent error he or she has underpaid the required amount to pay a "correction amount" without losing the tax-exempt status of the bond issue. The correction amount is the full amount that should have been paid on the respective computation date, plus interest at the current rate for time deposit SLGs. Under such a scenario, payment must occur within 60 days of the date the error is discovered and must be accompanied by a full explanation. If the IRS does not respond within 90 days, and is not investigating the issue, the mistake will be treated as "honest" and the tax exemption shall be maintained. If the correction amount is less than $50,000, payment does not have to be made for 180 days after the discovery of the mistake, and no explanation is necessary.

If an issue does not qualify under the "innocent error procedures," it can still maintain its tax-exempt status. In this case, the IRS must first determine that the mistake was not a result of willful neglect; then the issuer must pay the correction amount plus a penalty. The penalty is 50% of the unpaid rebate.

In the fall of 1992, the IRS did issue procedures for recovering overpayment.

X. THE SAFE HARBOR TWO-YEAR PENALTY APPROACH

Treasury officials were very thorough when formulating the 1986 Tax Reform Act. They tried their best to devise methods and formulas under a variety of conceivable scenarios to have as much arbitrage earnings as possible rebated to the federal government.

The Government Finance Officers Association and other organizations became very active in convincing Congress to pass legislative relief. The passage of the Revenue Reconciliation Act of 1989 provided an alternative to the rebate requirement, a choice that has been dubbed the "penalty approach."

At the time of bond issuance, an issuer can opt to come under the provisions of the newer legislation rather than the original 1986 rebate legislation. Once the decision has been made, the issuer cannot change his or her mind. Under this alternative, both the "construction test" and the "expenditure test" must be satisfied.

The construction test requires that at least 75% of the net proceeds of a given bond issue be used to pay the construction expenditures on property owned by a state or local government. Construction includes new construction, rehabilitation, or reconstruction.

Under the expenditure test, the proceeds of a bond issue must be expended within 2 years, and furthermore, the rate of expenditure must meet specified targets during that 2-year period.

Specifically, 10% must be expended within 6 months; 45% within 1 year; 75% within 18 months; and 100%—less retainage—within 2 years. The 100% limit at the end of 2 years is considered satisfied if an amount not exceeding 5% of the net proceeds is held as a responsible retainage and expended by the end of 3 years from the original date of the issue.

Failure to meet these targets—in essence, meeting the construction test but not the expenditure test—means that the issuer can opt to pay a penalty to the federal government of 1.5% on the amount of net proceeds of the issue that, as of the close of each 6-month period, is not spent as required. The issuer could also choose, instead of paying the 1.5% penalty, to calculate and pay its rebatable arbitrage for the bond issue. The decision as to whether to opt for the 1.5% penalty instead of the conventional arbitrage rebate must be made at the time of the bond issuance.

Moreover, if less than 75% of the net proceeds are to be used to finance construction (see construction test above), the issuer can still qualify this lesser portion of the bond issue for the penalty approach. Under this scenario, the issuer can also opt to pay the 1.5% penalty instead of calculating its rebatable arbitrage on the lesser portion.

The 1993 regulations [vol. 58, no. 116, sec. (1.148-7) sec. K] extend the 1.5% penalty on shortfalls to include each semiannual period after the end of the fourth period. In other words, the issuer can continue to pay a penalty indefinitely on any shortfall that exists after 2 full years. This penalty is equal to 1.5% multiplied by the unexpended proceeds that remain at the end of each semiannual period.

XI.   THE PENALTY APPROACH

City ABC is undertaking a $30,000,000.00 bond issue to build a new municipal services building. A full 100% of the bond issue, excluding allowable issuing costs, will be used to fund construction. Thus, the project meets the construction tests. Furthermore, city officials believe that project expenditures can meet the requirements of the expenditure test. Consequently, the city government chooses the penalty approach and issues the bonds on January 2, 1990.

Project total cost: $30,000,000.00

$30,000,000.00
  −750,000.00   Cost of issuance (legal, printing, other fees)
$29,250,000.00

The following amounts must be spent:

$2,925,000 or 10% by June 2, 1990 (6 months)
$13,162,500 or 45% by January 2, 1991 (1 year)
$21,937,500 or 75% by June 2, 1991 (18 months)
$27,787,500 or 95% by January 2, 1992 (2 years—allowing for 5% retainage)

But now, let us assume only $20,000,000 is spent by June 2, 1991. Under such circumstances, a penalty of 1.5% on the amount underexpended (in this example $1,937,500), or $29,062.50, would have to be paid to the IRS. Likewise, the penalty would have to be paid should the subsequent 2 year target also not being met.

For the sake of simplicity, this example does not reflect the effect of investment income being added to the principal amounts that are being spent.

When comparing the two methods, a great benefit of the 2-year penalty approach is its simplicity. If a governmental entity reasonably expects to meet the target dates, then it may be wise to elect to use this approach and avoid all the meticulous calculations and detailed record keeping that are obviously required by the traditional future value approach. Moreover, as long as there is only a small shortfall in meeting the expenditure requirements, the penalty will usually be smaller than the rebatable arbitrage amount.[15]

Perhaps more importantly, should the bond issuer earn arbitrage in excess of the yield on the bonds during any period, these earnings can help defray the cost of the project; with the penalty approach, arbitrage is not subject to rebate.

Now, some issuers may not be able to choose this penalty approach because the 2-year target would be too difficult to meet or because their bonds were issued too early. The central question is whether the project is one that can get underway quickly and be completed in a relatively short amount of time. If there is considerable doubt regarding this, the bond issuer should be forewarned that the penalties that can accrue can be substantial. Thus, sound judgment and realistic construction plans are vital prerequisites.

Regarding the penalty approach, a brief cautionary note is in order. Specifically, with overall bond yields of only 5% to 6% being paid to the investor and short-term money market yields of only 3% to 4%, there has generally been little opportunity to realize arbitrage. Issuers who opted for the penalty approach in this environment, and then experienced construction delays, were subject to substantial penalty payments. Obviously, even with its inherent simplicity, the penalty approach was not advantageous in such situations.

It should also be noted that available construction proceeds that qualify for this safe harbor 2-year penalty approach may continue to qualify for it, despite a refunding of the issue.[16] Refundings and rebatable arbitrage will be discussed in the next section.

XII.   REFUNDINGS

The May 15, 1989 temporary rebate regulations greatly altered the requirements for refundings, an important tool for the issuers of tax-exempt debt. To qualify as a refunding issue, an issuer's proceeds must be used to pay the debt service on an outstanding issue. Furthermore, under Treasury Department regulations, if any portion of an issue (issue X) is used to fund either the principal or interest of an outstanding issue, then that issue (issue X) is a refunding issue. Conversely, a new bond issue is one used for any purpose except to fund the debt service on an outstanding issue.

Refundings of a bond issue usually take place when prevailing interest rates are reduced. Thus, by retiring or refunding the one bond issue with another with lower interest rates, the issuer can save a considerable amount in amortization costs.

Virtually all of the new rules, however, were not concerned with arbitrage rebate regulations, but with stopping former practices that the Treasury considered abusive.[17]

Concerning rebatable arbitrage, refundings are now subject to two fundamental rules:[18]

1.   After the proceeds of a refunding issue have been used to pay for a prior issue, any remaining proceeds from the prior issue are transferred to the refunding issue. These proceeds are now subject to arbitrage rebate based on the yield of the refunding issue.
2.   The funds that result from the sale of a refunding bond face no investment restrictions for 30 days after the sale of the bond issue. After that, the applicable yield restriction is the yield on the refunding issue plus an additional de minimis flat .001%, which is subject to rebate.

     Thus, in the case of an advanced refunding—where proceeds are escrowed until call dates, for example—there is no arbitrage to calculate because of the yield restrictions.

XIII.   POOLED CASH OR COMINGLING FUNDS

On May 18, 1992, and subsequently June 18, 1993, the Treasury Department issued additional regulations concerning arbitrage rebate, which solidified, amplified, and clarified a number of earlier items and regulations that had been originally promulgated in the May 1989 regulations. One finance practice, in particular—the treatment of "comingled" funds—received special treatment. This was especially helpful to many issuers of tax-exempt debt, since comingled funds, or pooled cash, is not a rare practice. Yet before the advent of these regulations, there was no guidance with regard to determining the rebatable arbitrage for comingled funds.

Under comingled funds or pooled cash, there exists a physical comingling of cash of all the funds of a governmental entity, except those that must remain separate for legal reasons, regardless of their source. This would include current revenue, tax receipts, bond proceeds, and grants from other governmental bodies. The pooled cash can then be used on an as-needed basis with payrolls, operating disbursements, construction expenditures, and the like being disbursed from the comingled cash. However, a separate accounting of each fund is usually maintained. If any member fund experiences a temporary cash deficiency, an interfund advance can be made from the consolidated cash account; consequently, the temporary use of tax revenues or other operating revenues for capital purposes or the temporary use of capital funds for operating purposes may result. Idle funds in the consolidated cash account may be invested.

To further illustrate, let us assume that on a monthly basis a state or local government entity sweeps the interest earnings from a consolidated cash account, and then credits this interest to the various operating accounts. The entity would then have to allocate the investment earnings on a "reasonable basis" to the proceeds of the different bond issues, which have been invested in the consolidated cash account. Such a reasonable basis could be, for example, the average daily amount of an issue's proceeds that were invested during the month.

MONTH	AVERAGE DAILY G.O. BALANCE	G.O. ISSUE RATE YIC (CANADAN)	CON CASH MTD AVG YLD THIS PERIOD	EARNINGS PER G.O. ISSUE RATE	EARNINGS PER CON CASH MTD AVG YLD	CON CASH MINUS G.O. EARNINGS	COMPOUND EARNINGS PER CON CASH MTD AVG YIELD	TOTAL AMOUNT	CUMULATIVE TOTAL REBATABLE AMOUNT
AUG 87	97,193,257.50	7.80450•%	7.144%	653,191.67	597,911.32	(55,280.35)	(340.07)	($55,620.42)	($55,620.42)
SEPT 87	95,199,482.70	7.80450•%	7.453%	619,153.95	591,268.12	(27,885.83)	(518.64)	($28,404.48)	($84,024.90)
OCT 87	90,177,817.22	7.80450•%	7.499%	666,044.09	582,320.75	(23,723.34)	(673.34)	($24,396.68)	($108,421.57)
NOV 87	85,539,984.35	7.80450•%	7.471%	556,330.96	532,557.69	(23,773.27)	(823.02)	($24,596.30)	($133,017.87)
DEC 87	77,213,570.02	7.80450•%	7.767%	518,917.28	516,423.66	(2,493.62)	(877.10)	($3,370.72)	($135,388.59)
JAN 88	73,096,438.52	7.80450•%	7.281%	491,247.91	458,296.40	(32,951.52)	(1,027.47)	($33,978.99)	($170,367.58)
FEB 88	73,014,739.35	7.80450•%	7.153%	459,040.86	420,721.07	(38,319.79)	(1,243.95)	($39,563.74)	($209,931.32)
MAR 88	73,012,226.87	7.80450•%	6.994%	490,681.96	439,724.25	(50,957.72)	(1,520.55)	($52,478.26)	($262,409.58)
APR 88	72,975,795.89	7.80450•%	7.051%	474,616.58	428,793.61	(45,822.96)	(1,811.12)	($47,634.08)	($310,043.67)
MAY 88	72,975,795.89	7.80450•%	7.154%	490,437.13	449,559.28	(40,877.85)	(2,092.08)	($42,969.92)	($353,013.59)
JUNE 88	72,595,607.43	7.80450•%	7.297%	472,143.92	441,441.79	(30,702.13)	(2,333.31)	($33,035.45)	($386,049.03)
TOTAL						(372,768.38)	(13,260.66)	($386,049.03)	
JULY 88	70,648,691.27	7.80450•%	7.664%	474,797.72	466,249.96	(8,547.75)	(2,604.16)	($11,151.92)	($397,200.95)
AUG 88	68,738,839.47	7.80450•%	8.150%	461,962.47	482,412.99	20,450.52	(2,644.06)	$17,806.47	($379,394.48)
SEPT 88	64,565,423.92	7.80450•%	8.540%	419,917.59	459,490.60	39,573.01	(2,499.01)	$37,074.00	($343,320.48)
OCT 88	60,037,603.73	7.80450•%	8.279%	403,435.42	428,016.42	24,530.99	(2,265.57)	$22,265.43	($320,055.06)
NOV 88	55,859,119.89	7.80450•%	8.513%	363,293.94	396,272.91	32,979.97	(2,104.44)	$30,875.53	($289,179.53)
DEC 88	51,781,561.33	7.80450•%	8.829%	348,000.45	393,682.42	45,681.96	(1,851.25)	$43,830.71	($245,348.82)
JAN 89	48,323,841.56	7.80450•%	8.942%	324,762.56	372,096.26	47,333.71	(1,524.73)	$45,808.98	($199,539.84)
FEB 89	43,788,176.65	7.80450•%	9.545%	265,801.67	325,078.56	59,276.89	(1,152.86)	$58,124.03	($141,415.81)
MAR 89	39,830,692.47	7.80450•%	9.755%	267,683.97	335,269.32	67,585.36	(621.46)	$66,963.90	($74,451.91)
APR 89	36,247,913.83	7.80450•%	9.652%	235,747.49	291,554.05	55,806.56	(154.97)	$55,651.59	($18,800.32)
MAY 89	35,021,730.16	7.80450•%	9.806%	235,365.25	295,725.60	60,360.35	350.94	$60,711.29	$41,910.97
JUNE 89	34,063,361.55	7.80450•%	9.400%	221,339.70	266,829.67	45,289.96	705.84	$45,995.81	$87,906.77
TOTAL						117,533.16	(29,626.38)	$87,906.77	
JULY 89	31,807,567.99	7.80450•%	8.701%	213,784.20	238,319.09	24,554.89	842.62	$25,397.51	$113,304.29
AUG 89	27,796,610.68	7.80450•%	8.746%	186,808.38	209,344.00	22,535.62	1,023.05	$23,558.67	$136,862.96
SEPT 89	23,622,234.34	7.80450•%	9.184%	154,933.94	182,319.50	27,385.56	1,298.95	$28,684.51	$165,547.47
OCT 89	19,950,893.91	7.80450•%	8.756%	134,080.88	150,427.52	16,346.64	1,371.46	$17,718.10	$183,265.57
NOV 89	17,635,937.48	7.80450•%	8.441%	114,699.92	124,054.26	9,354.35	1,400.08	$10,754.43	$194,020.00
DEC 89	14,150,011.73	7.80450•%	8.652%	95,095.79	105,422.30	10,326.51	1,522.45	$11,848.96	$205,868.97
JAN 90	10,887,553.50	7.80450•%	8.092%	73,170.29	75,865.68	2,695.39	1,453.30	$4,148.69	$2,100,017.65
FEB 90	6,351,072.02	7.80450•%	8.155%	38,552.09	40,283.44	1,731.33	1,486.98	$3,218.33	$213,235.98
MAR 90	3,049,817.54	7.80450•%	8.257%	20,496.44	21,684.80	1,188.36	1,524.60	$2,712.96	$215,948.94
APR 90	70,517.58	7.80450•%	8.212%	458.63	482.58	23.95	1,527.24	$1,551.19	$217,500.13
MAY 90		7.80450•%	8.186%	0.00	0.00	0.00	1,533.17	$1,533.17	$219,033.30
JUNE 90		7.80450•%	8.205%	0.00	0.00	0.00	1,547.56	$1,547.56	$220,580.86
TOTAL						233,675.78	(13,094.92)	$220,580.86	

Figure 2 FIFO example of arbitrage rebate calculations at the end of the June 30 fiscal year.

In our discussion of arbitrage up to this point, the scenario has been described as selling bonds, placing the proceeds in a separate segregated account and then drawing against the account as needed.

It is beyond the scope of this chapter to explain the intricacies of pooled or comingled cash, except in the introductory terms we have provided. With regard to arbitrage calculation in pooled cash situations, accounting concepts such as LIFO (last in, first out) and FIFO (first in, first out) become acceptable approaches. [See sec. 1.148-6 (d)(6), vol. 58, no. 116, *Federal Register*, June 18, 1993.]

To illustrate, suppose there are two bond sales within a 2- or 3-year period for general capital improvements within a community. The proceeds of the bonds are comingled in a capital fund and then, in turn, the capital funds are comingled with grant funds and operating funds. Now, the regulations require a consistently applied ratable allocation method. Thus, let us assume that a bond issuer has decided to use an alternative such as average daily balance on a FIFO basis. This would allow calculations for the first bond sale to be done first, while the second issue could be second in line, and so forth. A simplified example is provided.

With respect to our Fig. 2, the reader is reminded of the various nuances and explanations noted in connection with Fig. 1; they apply here as well.

XIV. CONCLUSION

The 2-year penalty approach, refunding, and comingled cash are just three—albeit three of the most important and most common—of the numerous tax-exempt debt issuing situations that are governed by Treasury regulations.

As the debt-issuing scenarios and the calculations become more complex (e.g., variable rate debt), so do the arbitrage regulations. Virtually every debt-financing type is controlled by different regulations.

The future value or exact method is applicable in many situations, as prescribed by the law and various regulations. However, as we have noted, the penalty approach, refunding, and so forth enable an issuer to avoid such tedious calculations.

In this chapter we have attempted to explain the history and mechanics of arbitrage rebate and the calculations required for both the future value method and the penalty approach. We hope that the reader has thus acquired the knack of how to properly undertake arbitrage rebate and penalty calculations.

However, there must be two final words of caution. First, arbitrage regulations are continually changing and any practitioner must be sure to keep abreast of the latest developments. Finally, we must urge yet again that anyone planning to undertake arbitrage rebate calculations for a state or local government convene with the necessary accounting, legal, and finance experts.

Without a doubt, in the 1990s arbitrage rebate has assumed a central role in the issuance of tax-exempt debt and will continue to be a major topic of concern for finance officers, accountants, tax lawyers, and students of these disciplines.

NOTES

1. Gross, K., ed. (1989). *Federal Income Tax Principles of Bond Law*, Aztech Financial Printers, New York, p. 15;
   Moak, L. L. (1982). *Municipal Bonds Planning, Sale, and Administration*, Municipal Finance Officers Association,
   p. 174.
2. Moak, pp. 128–130.
3. Moak, p. 174.
4. Gross, p. 15.
5. Gross, p. 16.
6. Gross, pp. 16–17.
7. June 18, 1993 Final Arbitrage Regulations [vol. 58, no. 116 (sec 1.148-2) (f)(2)(ii)].
8. Gross, p. 16.
9. Ballard, F. L. Jr. (1992). *ABCs of Arbitrage*, American Bar Association Press, p. 2.
10. Gross, p. 41.
11. Ballard, pp. 8–9; Gross, pp. 64–66.
12. Ballard, p. 9.
13. Ballard, p. 8.
14. Ballard, pp. 12–13.
15. Ballard, p. 17.
16. Ballard, p. 19.
17. Gross, p. 74.
18. Ballard, pp. 69–70.

38

The Anatomy of a Municipal Bond Default

W. Bartley Hildreth
Hugo Wall School of Urban and Public Affairs, and F. Frank Barton School of Business, Wichita State University, Wichita, Kansas

Governmental jurisdictions borrow money to help finance the provision of public goods. Debt creation, however, imposes an explicit burden of debt repayment. When the debt repayment conditions fail to be honored, the result is default. In municipal finance, there are defaults and then there are so-called technical defaults. In conventional terms, a default conveys a condition of finality, yet defaults are subject to potential resolution through what is generally termed a "workout." A technical default is a viable candidate for a workout given its nature; that is, normally no loss of principal or interest. This chapter reviews the concept of default, and then examines the structure of a technical default and its workout.

I. THE CONCEPT OF DEFAULT

The intended strategy of personal and organizational finance is to avoid default, but not at all costs. At a theoretical and practical point, the benefits of default outweigh the costs. United States laws permit individuals, as well as corporate and municipal organizations, to seek court protection under default situations, thus, default is always a possibility. Investors must exercise caution in making such loans and stay vigilant throughout the duration of the loan. All too frequently, investors rely solely upon bond ratings to provide an assessment as to the probability of nonpayment of a debt.

Default is often viewed as a single distinct occasion involving nonpayment of a financial obligation. Default involves failure to repay the principal amount borrowed and/or the scheduled interest payments by the agreed-upon schedule. A delay in payment by only a few days still meets the definition of a default even though the delay imposes a negligible economic impact on the bondholders. Continued nonpayment of principal or interest imposes a much more significant burden, thus, as a concept, default has both short-term and long-term dimensions.

Default is also defined by obligations, duties, and responsibilities that are more procedural than economic. In fact, default is typically defined as an omission or failure to keep a promise or perform an obligation. Specific covenants binding the debtor to particular practices and policies are combined into a document termed an indenture. These covenants include pledges to transfer and retain a specified stock of funds in certain restricted accounts; to maintain levels of property and casualty insurance; to revise rates to levels sufficient to cover all expenses and coverage requirements; and numerous other features designed to protect the assets covering the bondholders' claims. Violation of any single covenant results in an "event of default." According to Spiotto (1993: 13.42), "An 'Event of Default' is the agreed upon occurrence that allows the bondholders or their representative (indenture trustee) to take appropriate action, including the institution of the remedies set forth in the indenture." The trustee's remedies include a range of legal actions to force the debtor to take the steps contained in the indenture; to assert the trustee's control over the project to protect bondholders' interests; and/or to accelerate as due and payable all outstanding bonds. Such obligations seek "to prevent default" rather than merely to enforce the payment of delinquencies (Smith, 1979: 245–246).

After an issuer pledges to follow specific procedural terms and conditions, any failure to follow such covenants alerts the bondholders to the possibility of repayment problems. Actually, the indenture serves to anticipate repayment problems before the bondholders incur real economic loss.

Municipal financial analysts assert that a technical default is less significant than a default, because of the distinctions between the violation of procedural covenants and the nonpayment of principal and interest. (See Advisory Commission on Intergovernmental Relations [ACIR], 1985; Feldstein, 1983.) While not necessarily differing on the apparent economic difference between the two, the law is more precise and less tied to economic calculations. Spiotto, perhaps the most prominent municipal default legal expert, clarifies that a "default ripens into an Event of Default after notice has been given to the issuer for the commencement of the grace period and, after a lapse of time, the default remains uncured" (Spiotto, 1993: 13.41).

Despite the appearance that defaults are distinct and final, Spiotto (1986) isolates three default phases. The first phase involves gathering information on the reasons for the default and the correction of any defected security for the debt. For example, if a revenue source appears defective, corrective action might preserve the probability of repayment. As a case in point, the precipitating factor in the largest municipal default in history—the Washington Public Power Supply System (WPPSS)—was a state court invalidation of power sales agreements between the WPPSS and several public utilities. These agreements—termed "take or pay" for their economic value—offered the security upon which WPPSS borrowed money to build nuclear power facilities. With the removal of these financial supports, the WPPSS financing plan collapsed (U.S. Securities and Exchange Commission, 1988). Actions that impair the security of bonds increase the probability of long-term debt default. In contrast, actions to correct the defective security could improve the chances of an end to the default. A defective feature at this stage of the financial history of a project may not lend itself to easy correction, however.

The second phase of a default is the workout, in which the bondholders and the issuer attempt to resolve their differences (Spiotto, 1993). In general finance, a workout occurs "when the parties agree that their financial interests are best served by restructuring the borrower's debt and reorganizing its operations" (General Accounting Office, 1984: 39). This chapter addresses a successful debt default workout.

Failure in the second phase leads to what is generally considered the nature of a default. In the third phase of a default, bondholders assert their rights to obtain payment, including calling the bonds due and payable immediately (acceleration of payments) and using the full force of litigation to uphold their interests.

As demonstrated, the concept of default is not clear and distinct. In fact, the book traditionally used by Moody's Investors Service in the schooling of municipal credit analysts contends that default is of "little significance except within the context of a specific situation" (Smith, 1979: 244). In fact, it calls default "a bogeyman irrationally beclouding municipal credit" (Smith, 1979: 244).

This chapter examines a default according to the situational analysis suggested by Moody's Investors Service (Smith, 1979: 244). Unlike the WPPSS default, in which a workout was unsuccessful (Jones, 1984), this chapter examines the successful uses of the workout to resolve a municipal default. The default under study here was labeled technical, since all principal and interest payments were made on time, albeit from sources unanticipated in the original financing. Using the legal reasoning of Spiotto (1993), however, the case met the definitions of default. This study identifies the structure, or anatomy, of the default and its workout. The issue is important because the willingness of public officials to resolve financial dilemmas such as a default is critical to governing in resource-scarce environments.

II. THE STRUCTURE OF DEFAULT

A default has both general and particular features. In general, debt financing requires the involvement of a large group of participants, not just the borrower and a lender. Defaults themselves are not merely local events; they invoke state and federal interests as well as the functioning of an efficient capital market. A particular default arises out of a milieu involving elements that are both unique and general. According to Spiotto's (1993) default workout phases, success relates to the ability of the key participants to resolve their differences. One way to examine the participants' behavior is within the theoretical perspective of an interorganizational network model. This section introduces each of these points; the case study later illustrates them using situation analysis.

A wide array of parties are involved in debt creation and management. (See Hildreth, 1993.) The participants include the issuer or borrower, the investors with funds to loan for a price, investment bankers to buy the issuer's bonds and sell them to the investors, a bond counsel willing to issue an opinion on the legality of the debt instruments, a trustee to monitor the issuer on behalf of the bondholders, credit raters to assess the probability of default, and state and federal government oversight agencies. The ability of such participants to work together daily in a complex market is demonstrated by the large number of issuers and the sheer dollar volume of the municipal market at any given time.

Defaults in the municipal securities market have implications beyond the local community. The interests of the bondholders, the state, and the federal government are especially tested by a municipal bond default. The bondholders are numerous and often scattered (in an economically random process) around the country. This makes bondholders the constituents of many public officials. Plus, a municipal security issuer is either a state government or a state-created political entity (e.g., a municipal corporation, county, or statutory agency), thus justifying state monitoring. (See ACIR, 1985; Hildreth, 1987b.)

The federal government also has a financial interest in the municipal market. This arises out of the loss of U.S. income taxes (via a tax expenditure) with the issuance of each and every municipal security. The power of Congress to completely eliminate the tax-exempt securities market is constitutionally clear (*South Carolina* v. *Baker*, 1988). As the search intensifies for more U.S. income tax receipts to aid in the federal deficit reduction effort, the tax expenditures associated with tax-exempt market are an enticing target (Carter and Hildreth, 1992). Such a search may focus on defaults as clues for the need to impose tighter federal supervision, thereby creating an opportunity for the federal government to reduce its tax expenditures.

Disclosure is central to federal securities law and the functioning of efficient capital markets. In a theme reminiscent of its 1976 report on New York City's debt problems, the 1988 report of the U.S. Securities and Exchange Commission (SEC) on the circumstances surrounding the WPPSS default of $2.25 billion of municipal revenue bonds noted systematic disclosure problems in the municipal securities industry as well as deficient disclosures to WPPSS investors (U.S. Securities and Exchange Commission, 1976 and 1988). The 1988 report raised questions as to whether or not the official disclosure documents for the bonds adequately revealed significant facts relating to the projects. Without adequate disclosure, investors are unable to make an intelligent decision regarding the probability of repayment. Thus, federal regulators placed municipal debtors on notice regarding the adequacy of their disclosures.

Debt defaults are the culmination of legal, economic, political, managerial, and financial problems. (See generally Hillhouse, 1936; Hemple, 1971; ACIR, 1973 and 1985.) While court invalidation of the power sales agreements hurried the WPPSS default, the original energy demand estimates were unrealistic, the political pressures to keep low power rates were high and growing, the project schedules were too hard to maintain, and the escalating project costs were compounded by a high interest rate environment. (See Jones, 1984; Myhra, 1984.) In another celebrated default, the city of Cleveland, Ohio, defaulted on the repayment of short-term notes (not bonds). While the Cleveland default was precipitated by a political debate between the mayor and the banks holding the notes, the city was experiencing significant underlying managerial and financial problems. (See Swanstron, 1985; Hildreth, 1987b.) Thus, an anatomical study of a default and its workout requires a review of the legal background, the economic dilemmas, the financial reorganization, and the nature of the interactions among key participants.

A theoretical framework for studying a default workout relates to the network of financing participants. The nature of the debt-financing relationships has implications for the success of an issuer's financing goals (Hildreth, 1989 and 1993). Using an interorganizational network model that behaves as a political economy, Miller and Hildreth (1988) posit that each debt-financing team member pursues a self-interest goal of survival and success, yet the network's ability to coalesce around a common solution depends upon the network's stability. While the theory was advanced based upon successive debt financings, it offers a framework for reviewing the behavior of key network links during a debt default workout.

In summary, studying the anatomy of a default opens up many lines of municipal finance concerns. A case study is employed to illustrate the richness of studying the default phenomena.

III. A MIDWEST CITY'S DEFAULT EXPERIENCE

A critical infrastructure for municipalities is solid waste disposal, unless the public sector leaves the arena to the private market for solution. Those communities involving themselves in solid waste services have to consider disposal methods, but face landfill site and capacity constraints. One alternative is to burn solid waste to generate energy (either steam or electricity) for sale to business, industry, and other customers. There are about 140 resource recovery projects in operation now (Kiser, 1992), but only 16 are refuse-derived fuel (RDF) facilities that process and produce fuel on-site. At the forefront of this movement was a midwestern city's recycle energy system (RES).[1] The RES was designed to dispose of 1,000 tons of garbage and trash per day by shredding, removing ferrous materials for sale, and burning the residue to produce steam for sale as a source of energy. It was one of the first (and last) strictly public refuse recovery projects financed solely by revenues generated by the project itself, including fees for dumping garbage into the RES as well as the fees generated from selling the output steam.

A long-term solid waste disposal problem faced the city as it entered the 1970s. Adding fuel to the local dilemma was the private utility company's decision in 1971 to abandon a steam system servicing downtown. The city decided to build a modern resource recovery plant using leading-edge technology to dispose of municipal solid waste and generate the steam required for the loop. The capital financing that eventually emerged was a state and local partnership with tax-exempt securities issued by a state financial intermediary (or conduit), to build what was to be a city-owned and -operated facility.

Frequently in public power projects (Jones, 1984; Feldstein, 1983) technological, economic, and operational risks abound. In this case, the technology was unproven; the economics were uncertain; and the managerial ability to deal with the complex system was questionable. On Standard & Poor's (1984) risk assessment scale, this resource recovery facility scored high. The eventual result was a waste-to-energy project that entered into technical default on its state agency-issued municipal securities.

To assist in a review of the case study, the structure of the RES default is presented in several sections. The first two roughly follow a legal and financial perspective, respectively. Then, a two-step workout sequence is captured by reviewing competing economic premises. The stability of the financing team enhanced the possibility of success; thus, a review of the interorganizational network economy is provided. Finally, to the city that owned the RES but did not issue the bonds in technical default, a major concern was to avoid jeopardizing the city's financial standing, including its general credit quality, while also seeking a solution to a valuable investment for dealing with the community's solid waste disposal needs. This chapter offers an analysis of the city's market disclosure practices related to the RES. This serves as a measure of the city's attempt to keep investors in its own bonds aware of RES facts, and the distinction between the RES default and the city's general credit.

A. Structure of the Financing

A state statutory authority—the state Water Development Authority (WDA)—issued $46 million of municipal bonds in December, 1976 to build the RES. A series of legal agreements secured the bonds with the interrelationships sketched in Fig. 1. The financing was made pursuant to a trust indenture between the WDA and a bank trustee named by WDA to serve in the bondholders' interest. Under a cooperative agreement by and between the WDA, the city, and the county, proceeds from the sale of the bonds were loaned by the WDA to the city to construct and operate the RES. The RES was to generate revenues from both the input and output sides of the system, by requiring the city and other haulers to dump solid wastes into the RES (and pay a tip fee) and by charging users of the steam produced by the facility (many under long-term contracts).

An adequate supply of refuse was essential to the facility's financing. Both the city and county agreed to enact ordinances requiring all solid waste collected in their respective jurisdictions to be disposed of at the RES after payment of the required tip fee. The city enacted the required "flow control" ordinance. It was challenged by several private landfill operators and private solid waste haulers as being in violation of federal antitrust laws and the "takings" clause of the Fourteenth Amendment, as well as other laws. In spite of two appeals to the U.S. Supreme Court, the validity of the city's ordinance was upheld in 1985. The county resisted enacting a similar flow control ordinance.

Contractual arrangements divided steam customers into three classes: uninterruptible, interruptible, and surplus. Uninterruptible customers, located on an old steam loop in the central business district, had no alternative heating sources. Interruptible customers included a downtown-based state university and a large nonprofit hospital, each a large user with existing natural gas alternatives. The surplus or third class comprised a single customer, a large international manufacturing firm headquartered in the city. A series of contracts specified that the three classes of customers agreed to pay rates at a level sufficient to cover the operation and maintenance expenses and to provide 1.5 times the coverage of the annual debt service. These customer's contracts included take or pay provisions whereby they agreed to pay for the contracted level of steam even if the steam was not used.

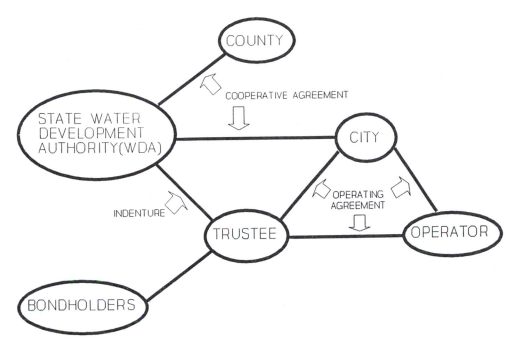

Figure 1   Structure for debt financing.

All RES revenues, including tip fees and steam user fees, were earmarked for operational expenses and to make payments on the loan. Loan payments from RES revenues were to be used by the WDA to make principal and interest payments on the bonds. The city did not extend its full faith and credit guarantee to the WDA bonds; the WDA bonds were state agency-issued project revenue bonds secured by the revenue capacity of the RES. As stated on the cover of the official statement (OS) of the WDA bonds, the bonds "will not constitute a debt or a pledge of the faith and credit of the [WDA], the State or any political subdivision thereof . . . [but] are payable solely from, and secured by a pledge of, revenues derived from the project."

A local engineering firm served as consulting engineers on the project, their first in waste-to-energy systems. To facilitate the bond sale, a nationally recognized engineering firm was paid by the city (on its behalf and on behalf of the bond underwriters) to assess the technical and engineering feasibility and to determine the project's economic feasibility. Despite assurances from this feasibility consultant (in a report reprinted in the OS) that the project was "sound from a technical engineering standpoint," the RES failed to meet its objectives and had to be redesigned later.

Originally scheduled to begin operation in 1979, the RES was not fully completed until January 1983. Major design and mechanical problems requiring extensive modification caused this delay. This increased the costs. The original estimated cost of $56 million was secured by $46 million from the WDA bonds and $5 million each from the city and the county (separately issued general obligation securities). By its completion, however, the RES cost almost $100 million. To make up the difference, the city contributed the proceeds of $8 million of general obligation bonds, the WDA added $16 million from its coffers, and a congressionally mandated U.S. Environmental Protection Agency (EPA) grant (a reallocation of an unused city grant) added $19.7 million.

As a result of these design problems, the RES did not produce the revenues required to make all loan payments. This resulted in a continuing series of events of default under the cooperative agreement, triggering corresponding events of default under the indenture. All payments of principal and interest due the bondholders under the indenture were made, however. The debt service reserve fund provided the funds for 1980 debt payments. The aforementioned city and WDA contributions made up the difference in 1981 and 1982; the EPA grant was used for 1983 payments and set aside for 1984 payments. This left no clear special source of funds from which to make payments in 1985.

The RES plunged into technical default in February 1981, when there were insufficient project funds to make the scheduled loan payment, although the funds were made available from other sources, as outlined above. Asserting its remedial powers, the bondholders' trustee assumed management of the RES during the summer of 1981 in order to preserve the interests of the bondholders and to gain the $16 million infusion from the WDA. Subsequently, a long-term operating service agreement was signed by the trustee, the city, and a private firm providing for the waste management firm to redesign and simplify the RES mechanics for a guaranteed price and then to operate the RES for 10 years under a cost plus fee contract. The fee was set low in the initial years, but escalated at a rapid pace. An incentive fee was also included in the package.

The trustee engaged the services of legal counsel, a consulting engineering firm, and a national accounting firm to assist it in the newly expanded responsibilities. The costs to support the trustee, its entourage, and operator received first claim over RES revenues. Thus, the expenses for the trustee to assume active management and monitoring increased the cost structure of the RES. Although modifications to the RES were made and mechanical difficulties were significantly reduced, the system continued to incur operating deficits. In response, the trustee pressed for operating subsidies from the city and higher rates for RES customers.

B. The Structure of the Financial Dilemma

In late 1983, a newly elected mayor assessed the realities of the RES problems. While the RES was an ongoing question in the mayoral campaign, it was not a decisive matter in the voters' rejection of the incumbent in November. Just days before the new mayor took his oath of office a series of fires and explosions rocked the plant, highlighting the problems facing the new administration. Earlier in the transition period, the following elements in the city's financial dilemma were outlined:

1. As stated in the cooperative agreement between the city, county, and WDA, project revenues were to provide 150% coverage of WDA debt service. To achieve 100% coverage of the debt service would have required steam rate increases of approximately 40% for the uninterruptible customers, 103% for the interruptible customers, and 153% for the surplus sales customer. Even those rate levels assumed that a stock of funds remaining from the special EPA grant would be used to pay all debt service obligations during 1984 since the RES would not generate sufficient funds on its own.

2. The trustee proposed to force rate increases on January 1, 1984—the first day of the new mayoral term. While not sufficient to meet debt service coverage requirements, the proposed rate increases were set at approximately 13% for the uninterruptible customers, 51% for the interruptible customers, and 137% for the surplus sales customer. Tipping fees—the fees paid by both the city and private garbage haulers to dump their loads into the RES—were to increase by 10%. This schedule of rate increase also assumed that the remaining federal grant proceeds would cover the year's debt service requirements. The trustee projected that the rate increases were sufficient to get the RES through 1984, given the assumption that all users would continue the current level of services, but at the higher rates—thus assuming no price inelasticity of demand and no substitutional effect. A further assumption in the scenario was that the RES operation would meet its budget estimates, including no fires or unexpected operational problems (both high-risk assumptions, given past history).

3. Regular and periodic rate increases, in addition to the one just outlined, would be necessary to produce net operating income (NOI; operating revenues less operating expenses). A major RES cost was the contract operator's fixed fee: $130,000 in 1983, $550,000 in 1984, $1 million in 1985, and $1.5 million in 1986. The fixed fee levels agreed to in the long-term operating service agreement were purported to give the private operator a return for assuming the business risk of making the RES operationally viable. Combining modest price increases on utilities and other RES expenses, the fixed fee amounts revealed a need for significant increases in operating revenues each year to cover escalating cost factors.

4. A positive NOI by itself was insufficient to ensure the financial viability of the RES. The loan repayments to WDA, the required stocking of both an equipment and replacement fund, as well as a debt service reserve account, all constituted additional expenses *not* included within the NOI calculation. The 1984 debt service on WDA bonds was $4.266 million; stocking the other accounts required more funds.

5. The long-term operating service agreement stated that if the operator budgeted an upcoming year's positive NOI exceeding the projected NOI figure contained in the contract, the operator would receive an incentive fee set at 60% of the difference between the forecasted NOI and the budgeted NOI. The probability of such an incentive payment was remote given the financial problems besetting the RES.

6. The operator's contract required the operator to prepare a budget, formally called an "annual forecast of costs," for submission to the city and the trustee by October 1 of each year. In response, both the city and the trustee had to give the operator written notice of any budget disputes by November 1—a 1-month review period. The contract specified that when the parties could not amicably resolve the dispute by December 1, the monthly payment to the operator "shall, until the dispute is resolved, be prepared, submitted and paid on the basis of the Annual Forecast of Costs as submitted by the Operator." The operator had neither an obligation to submit a budget generating an NOI nor one that necessarily covered debt service. In fact, the operator had no control over the setting of RES rates; the trustee assumed those responsibilities if the city abdicated its role.

7. With the trustee's assumption of management responsibility, the mayor lost effective budgetary control over the RES budget. In this strong mayor-council city, neither the mayor nor his appointed finance director were able to monitor costs and, if necessary, make budget cuts to offset revenue shortfalls or expense overruns. In fact, the city only received monthly variance reports on expected versus actual costs for the preceding month. Since all steam fees were paid directly to a trustee-controlled bank account (a by-product of the trustee's takeover of the RES), the city did not know the cash flow position of project funds until reported later by the operator and the trustee's financial advisor.

8. The operator submitted a monthly invoice to the trustee and the city for payment of costs to be incurred in the *ensuing* calendar month, as estimated in the annual forecast of costs. As a result, scarce project funds were used to pay for utility fees (a large monthly cost item) before the service was actually used, billed, or paid. For example, the operator would submit the November invoice by October 15, with the invoice paid from project funds by November 1. The RES would use the gas in November but the operator would not be billed until December 10, with payment due on January 10. Thus, the operator enjoyed the cash float from November 1 to January 10. This was at a time when interest rates were quite high.

9. The trustee discounted fears that rate changes could affect usage changes. To users, however, RES rates should not exceed the cost of alternative energy. While many steam users lacked boilers or alternative energy sources, the return on a capital investment is justified under certain pricing scenarios. A business could respond instead by moving from the central business district, striking another blow against a struggling downtown.

10. The demand risk of the RES was reduced through take or pay contracts. Major users entered into contracts specifying their agreement to use the allotted share of RES steam or pay in lieu thereof. For example, a major international manufacturing firm headquartered in the the city had a 25-year contract to buy all the excess steam of the RES. As shown by the experiences of both WPPSS and the Massachusetts Municipal Electric Company (Herman and Seidler, 1988), as economics clash with take or pay contracts, litigation ensues. Major RES users had quietly put the city and the trustee on notice that they would legally challenge the validity of the contracts if pressed on the point.

11. The city's taxing power was supporting part of the total cost of the RES, even though the WDA bonds did not involve the city's full faith and credit guarantee. A long-term city cost was debt service on $13,640,000 in unvoted general obligation bonds—$5 million for the original financial commitment and the rest for subsequent capital repair contributions.[2] The city also paid tip fees to dispose of city-collected residential solid wastes—the cost of hauling the ash generated by the RES—and expenses associated with general city "overhead" (supervisory and monitoring time and expense).

12. The city risked becoming the ultimate risk bearer for the WDA bonds. Under the cooperative agreement (between the city, the county, and WDA) the city agreed to pay tip fees to the RES for disposal of the city's residential solid wastes. Assuming the flow control ordinance and steam contracts were all ultimately held invalid and unenforceable, the city would remain its sole user. This put or pay feature was designed to ensure an adequate supply of refuse. Under such a scenario, the city would have an obligation to charge residential collection customers a rate necessary to offset the tipping fee, up to the contractually agreed to limit of fees "comparable with competitive charges for such services." In such a worst case scenario, the city had the equally unacceptable option of offsetting the necessary residential fee increases with diverted general tax receipts. Adding creditability to this view is Moody's (1987:8) point that the tip fee "can broaden the project's claim on general municipal revenues . . . not unlike a municipality-wide special tax or fee."

13. The city's landfill capacity was projected to reach its limit in approximately 5 to 7 years without the RES, or 20 to 30 years with the RES. No other landfill site was programmed, and it would take 3 to 5 years to complete the process of opening a new landfill. In addition, the state government was intensifying

its regulatory powers over landfill activities. All of these factors pointed to the city's need to reassert the RES as part of the city's entire solid waste collection and disposal system (as it was originally cast), and not just a troubled plant.

14. State law provided for state supervision over municipalities that failed specific fiscal tests, with one being default on a debt obligation. The city's failure to make the loan payments to WDA in accordance with the cooperative agreement appeared to meet this fiscal emergency condition. The elected state auditor had the responsibility to issue the determination, but he had not done so, nor did he during the default period. If the state auditor had acted, a state-created board would have been appointed to oversee the city's entire financial agenda, not just the RES. To some, the city's financial reputation was at more risk with a financial emergency declaration than with a long-term default on RES bonds since those bonds were legally project revenue bonds.

15. Slowly, the city's general financial condition was improving after an economic restructuring that saw many of the major manufacturing facilities close their doors in the preceding decade with a concomitant loss in the city's population. A local income tax provided the bulk of the tax revenue and it reflected the anemic economic changes. Significant budget reductions were in force for several years. The city's bond ratings were downgraded in 1980–1981 to a AA– by Standard & Poor's and an A by Moody's Investors Service. The city was a yearly borrower of funds to finance a systematic and aggressive capital improvements program for which a share of the local income tax was dedicated. While the city's finances were in strong shape given its economic environment, it had little room to maneuver. Any attempt to bail out the RES at the expense of general services would be a budget-busting exercise that would be both politically unacceptable and likely to erode the city's general bond ratings.

C.   The Structure of Competing Economic Premises

The city's financial dilemma required it to balance the risk of a default on state-agency bonds for a city-owned project against the risk of opening the city's treasury to a troubled enterprise operation. Politically, the new mayor could have placed all the blame on "prior" city administrations (all from the "other" political party) during the RES saga, and let the RES dissolve into a legal battle. In fact, the outgoing mayor's administration sought to put the mayor-elect in the position of quickly supporting a large bailout subsidy. The Mayor-elect resisted these initiatives. While preserving his option to abandon the RES, the new mayor instituted steps to test the long-term value of the RES to meet the community's solid waste disposal needs. Designing and implementing the default workout dominated the city's fiscal agenda for over a year.

It is useful to view the default workout as following two phases. Phase 1 started with the initiation of the technical default. It was characterized by the bondholders' trustee assuming management control and leadership over the future of the RES. The dominant economic premise during the first phase was revenue maximization for the RES enterprise. To the new mayor the key to resolving the default was to change the economic premise to one more in keeping with the larger issue, the need for a cost-effective solid waste disposal system. In brief, the first phase of the default workout followed the revenue maximization goal; the city abdicated its responsibility for the RES to nonlocal interests. The second phase of the workout sought to reassert local responsibility over the RES and to redefine the issue as a long-term concern over the community's solid waste collection and disposal system.

1.   Revenue Maximization of the RES

During the first phase of the default workout, the RES operated under a revenue maximization concept. This economic premise emerged out of the trustee's assumption of control following the technical default. It was firmly established in late 1981 when the city and the bondholders' trustee entered into a long-term operating service agreement with a private waste management operator to manage the RES plant. This operating service agreement and its implementation relied upon revenue maximization, not cost control.

In pursuit of revenue maximization, the RES sought to maximize the composition of the refuse supply. A basic flow of refuse was required to run the plant at the desired level of capacity. By the original financing agreement, the city had to use the facility for its collected garbage and pay a tip fee to the RES. Pending final resolution of litigation, the city did not enforce the flow control ordinance requiring private waste haulers to use the RES and pay the required tip fee. The RES depended upon this continuous flow of garbage into the RES to generate an uninterrupted flow of steam to the customers. Any break in the garbage flow or any downtime due to mechanical problems resulted in the burning of gas to produce steam—a wasteful and uneconomical energy conversion. The RES reverted to this costly step many times because of mechanical problems.

Faced with these conditions, the RES had an incentive to attract premium-paying waste dumpers. Accepting out-of-state wastes arranged through brokers was one result. The RES accepted New Jersey waste that did not meet New Jersey disposal laws but did meet the state laws governing the RES. A form of such waste was saw oil, or sawdust laced with certain kinds of oil (including flavors and fragrances, ball bearing and grinding oils, synthetic and organic lubricants, and waste oil bottom sludge). There was a twofold advantage in accepting this waste: it generated a premium payment for the right to dump the waste into the RES and the oil-based product had a high burning yield—it generated more energy than regular wastes.

A primary application of the revenue maximization approach was that steam customers were viewed as a captured market; they would have to pay rates at the required levels to ensure an adequate RES revenue base. This logic clashed with the concept that customers should pay a gas equivalent rate. The concept of a gas equivalent rate recognized that the interruptible and surplus energy customers could immediately switch to an alternative energy system, resulting in a severe reduction in RES steam utilization. Offsetting the potential price inelasticity of the demand and substitution effect was a series of take-or-pay contracts between steam customers and the RES upon which the original WDA capital construction funding was premised. The trustee asserted that the contracts were legal and enforceable if challenged, and thus steam users had to pay the steam rates demanded by the trustee. Major customers took the position that the contracts were unenforceable. The parties were quickly adopting intractable positions.

A revenue maximization emphasis permitted cost control to receive weak attention. As the first phase of the RES workout drew closer to failing, the trustee's legal and monitoring costs escalated. The RES account that the trustee controlled paid the trustee's bills first! Furthermore, the trustee hinted that the last remaining EPA grant funds that were tentatively earmarked for 1984 debt service might have to be used instead for legal expenses if the RES failed to get the requested aid from city coffers and higher rate increases.

In summary, the first phase of the workout eroded local control and was premised on revenue maximization. For example, out-of-state wastes were accepted by the trustee's operator, a politically unacceptable position if the city controlled the RES. The various parties were asserting legal arguments, presaging litigation. Cost control within the RES account was of secondary interests. Furthermore, the revenue maximization premise focused on a subsystem—solid waste disposal of some wastes—of a much larger solid waste collection and disposal system.

2. *Cost-Effective Solid Waste System*

As designed by the new mayor, the goal of the second phase of the default workout was to reorient the RES from its myopic revenue maximization focus to a substitute premise of viewing the RES as part of a local solid waste collection and disposal system judged by cost-effective standards; that is to say, the focus was to develop a solid waste collection and disposal system that would accomplish its responsibilities in a safe manner at minimum costs given local needs. Local control would permit city policy makers (the administration and city council working together) to decide who and what should be processed into the plant, the price citizens should pay for solid waste handling and disposal, and the price steam customers should pay for access to a dependable energy system.

During the second phase of the workout, the contending positions of all parties (including steam customers and the trustee), were used by the mayor as a form of leverage. The point was to keep the customers from going to court too soon or the trustee from pushing steam rates higher than market rates. In fact, the major steam customers agreed to a modest (18%) rate increase and advanced their payments in some cases to help ease the RES's severe cash flow problems as the second phase of the workout took shape.

To build a consensus that the local community had to resolve the default, the mayor appointed a nine-member "blue ribbon" commission of major corporate chief executives, local business leaders, representatives of the major customers, and the chief city and county elected officials. The commission brought financial, legal, and political expertise to the table. A major result of the commission was its focus on the need for a long-term solution. In fact, in its May 1984 report, the commission concluded that the RES was a valuable community investment that provided the only feasible solid waste disposal system available to the area. In the short run, the commission kept the major steam customers aware of the RES and its problems and the damage that a single lawsuit could do to a lasting solution.

In summary, the original workout phase adopted the premise that the RES was a separate entity from the city; it needed a revenue flow to meet all its obligations. On the surface, this was perhaps understandable, given the original financing methods. In fact, this is the premise of revenue-backed municipal securities such as those issued by WDA on behalf of the city's RES. The economics of the facility changed over time, fueled by the imposition of new costs brought on by the initial design failure and subsequent default. Unable to support itself, the RES needed new sources of money or greatly expanded rates on existing customers. In contrast, the second phase of the default workout adopted an operating premise that the RES was a part, albeit a costly and troubled element, of the community's total solid waste collection and disposal system. There were no guarantees that the second phase would work. It depended upon a balancing of competing self-interests to benefit the entire community.

D. The Structure of a Network Economy

A theoretical framework for studying a default workout relates to the network of participants and their incentives to resolve the default. Using an interorganizational network model that behaves as a political economy, Miller and Hildreth (1988) posit that each debt-financing team member pursues his or her own goal of survival and success, yet the network's ability to coalesce around a common solution depends upon the network's stability. While Miller and Hildreth applied the theory to successive debt financings, the theory should apply to the utility of network stability in a default workout.

The stability of the key links in the network is significant in a default workout. In a review of the WPPSS default, Jones (1984) examined the reasons why workout negotiations were unsuccessful. Jones concluded (1984: 72)

> It was not the financial infeasibility of the various resolution plans that resulted in default. Rather, default was the result of vector politics, i.e., the numerous participants in the workout all pulled hard to represent their separate interest and the resulting absence of compromise left no alternative to default. Given the size of the stakes in billions of dollars this outcome is understandable.

The RES case study provides another perspective on the ability of key links in the network economy to work toward a common goal.

The network members in the debt creation process are not immune from involvement in a subsequent debt default. In fact, their own perceived legal liability not only can foster cooperative resolution of the workout, but also can drive the parties to separate legal corners, ready to defend past actions at all costs. As WPPSS litigation demonstrated, issuers, bond counsels, consulting engineers, underwriters, ratepayers, the trustee, and others were all vulnerable to legal questioning in a default scenario. (See U.S. Securities and Exchange Commission, 1988.) This section examines the roles of the city (mayor and council), institutional investors (major bondholders), the trustee, the bond counsel, and the WDA for indications of a successful application of interorganizational network theory.

It is not axiomatic that a mayor and council will agree on how to deal with a troubled municipal enterprise. There were several indications that a cooperative spirit might take hold between the thirteen-member city council and the newly elected mayor. For the first time in over a decade and half, the mayor and a majority of council members were of the same political party. Furthermore, a signal of cooperation was conveyed with the appointment of the council president as the city's public works director (the office responsible for a city-run RES). As a 15-year veteran council member, and one whose private job was as a manager of facilities support services at the headquarters of a major international manufacturing firm, this person not only was well qualified, but council members trusted his political instincts. All of these factors helped the new mayor, because the council was tired of short-term "solutions" that never endured for very long. The council had to be convinced that a financial reorganization would work for the long term and meet the city's competing needs. A confrontational approach was unacceptable, and the council had to be part of the solution. This was quickly put to a test in the first days of the new administration. The trustee pressured for a city council vote on bailing out the RES's 1984 operating deficit with city funds. Following an agreed-upon script, the council expressed strong objections to a city bailout, voting "no" on the ordinance, and called for a long-term solution, not just an operating subsidy that left the debt (and its structures) overhanging the RES. This gave the mayor the city consensus he needed as he confronted other parties to the situation.

Needless to say, bondholders are prone to express strong disapproval at losing their investments, much less any interest foregone on such investment or secondary trading losses. Thus, actions (either real or perceived) taken by network members (or others) that weaken the probability of debt repayment are subject to eventual legal scrutiny by the bondholders. In this case, the trustee was afraid of incurring the bondholders' wrath if the bonds were not repaid and the trustee's actions (or lack thereof) became the subject of legal challenge.

A presumption is that bondholders and the debt issuer are adversaries in a default scenario. In the RES case, a meeting of bondholders was called by the trustee within the first month of the new mayor's term. The purported purpose was to put pressure on the mayor to agree to steam rate increases, or alternatively, to secure bondholders' permission for the trustee to force rate increases—revealing the trustee's legal discomfort over its position. After listening to the mayor explain his pledge to make a good-faith effort to have a long-term solution in place by year's end, the bondholders gave strong support to his workout efforts. The institutional investors at the meeting were supportive of the mayor's early initiatives, especially the so-called blue ribbon commission. In fact, institutional investors instructed the bondholders' trustee to be more cooperative with the mayor's workout agenda. Since institutional investors held over 50% of the outstanding WDA bonds, with the remainder held by about 200 different investors, their influence was significant. Later during a delay in the workout, a private meeting of major institutional investors and bond insurance guarantors (of bonds insured after original issuance) assured the mayor of their continued support and pledge to monitor the trustee's increasingly noncooperative stance.

Bondholders are linked to the bond trustee. The trustee, on behalf of the bondholders, is a signatory to the indenture contract with the debt issuer. This avoids "the impractical requirement that each bondholder read, understand, and accept the complex and long indenture contract" (Sawicki, 1985: 172). Trustees remain in their legal capacity until all bonds mature and are repaid. They are selected to be on the financing team for a variety of reasons, including tradition and local preferences.

The trustee's normal ministerial duty is to process the bondholders' interest and principal payments. As the threat of debtor misconduct increases, the trustee's duties increase according to the indenture. Prior to an event of default, a trustee only has a good-faith responsibility to monitor compliance with the indenture and other factors important to the bondholders' interests. After default, however, trustees generally must meet a prudent person rule, taking care to act as if the assets are personal ones. The indenture specifies the remedies a trustee can take on behalf of the bondholders.

In this case the trustee's role changed over the life of the bond. The trustee had assumed the dominant role in the first phase of the workout by legitimately asserting some of the trustee's remedial powers. According to Sawicki (1985: 191)

> It is in the best interests of the reasonably prudent investor to protect against and try to prevent the termination of the investor's primary source of repayment, i.e., the . . . generating facility, before that source has produced any revenues to meet repayment obligations.

By taking early and decisive steps, investors (or their trustee) preserve their options to attempt a cure for the problems, to aid in rectifying the situation, or to sell the investment so as to redeploy any remaining investment capital (Sawicki, 1985).

The trustee is torn between needing to assert the prudent person rule while also hoping to revert back to the more preferred ministerial role. The first phase of the workout was dominated by the trustee. In the second phase, however, the trustee followed the city's agenda because, in part, of the strong support given the mayor's workout plans by the institutional investors. After spending several years managing the RES, the trustee also likely realized that there were no other viable choices short of total default and litigation. Furthermore, the trustee bank was part of a larger regional bank holding company whose leadership had expressed confidence in the mayor's efforts and offered comfort that the trustee bank would not take any precipitous actions.

Besides a new mayoral administration, perhaps the most critical network member in the case was the bond counsel. The city had utilized the bond counsel services of the same legal firm for over 30 years. This same firm also served as the bond counsel and general legal advisor to the WDA. According to some observers, the bond counsel faced a potential conflict of interest charge over this dual representation. The OS of the WDA on the issuance of the $46 million in bonds named this firm as the WDA's bond counsel, but did not see the need to disclose that the firm also served as the city's bond counsel. An issue was the potential lack of independent review given the original debt security documents to preserve the individual interests of both the city and the WDA. If the default reached a litigation mode, the probability of continuing both arrangements was low, even if handled by different partners of the same law firm. Thus, a major client would leave the firm. Added to the calculus was the fact that the legal firm was one of the most prominent ones in the state; its influence on state policy making was widely recognized. In private, one of the firm's senior partners made it clear that it was in the interest of the state, the city, and his law firm to solve the problem, and that this firm would help in designing a financial reorganization. The law firm was potentially (and actually) of significant help in clarifying the state's interest in a viable local solid waste disposal solution and the risks to the state from a long-term WDA debt default.

While alerting the legal firm to the city's concerns, city officials concluded that network stability in regard to the bond counsel improved the chances for a successful workout. The bond counsel had its reputation on the line, and faced the possibility of legal challenge if bond repayment was interrupted.

The WDA also was a key link in the network. It actually issued the bonds that were in technical default. Its credit reputation was at risk. The bonds were given a CC rating by Standard & Poor's, meaning the highest degree of speculation. As with any conduit financing agency, the WDA's future was tied to its continued market access, thus it was willing to side with whichever party had the strongest agenda (the trustee at first, later the city). With its board appointed by the governor on staggered terms, the WDA was alert to the governor's views on matters affecting the WDA. In the end, the WDA helped fund the final workout with a major financial contribution.

As demonstrated by this brief review of the debt default network links—the city, institutional investors, the trustee, the bond counsel, and the financial conduit agency (the WDA)—the success of the workout was tied to the self-interests of each party in the interorganizational network.

E. The Structure of a Financial Reorganization

A financial reorganization of the RES was required to advance the goals embodied in the planned operating premise of a cost-effective solid waste system. Defeasance of the outstanding WDA bonds emerged as the preferred method. Defeasance is a voluntary financial reorganization to adjust the pattern of debt service payments and to gain release from the original bond indenture. This requires structuring a portfolio of government securities the principal and interest of which are sufficient to meet all future principal and interest payments on the refunded outstanding bonds (Feldstein and Fabozzi, 1987). In a defeasance, bondholders achieve certainty that their interest and principal payments will be paid on time and in full. This relieves the bondholders and their trustee of any concern over the facilities financed by the bonds. A successful defeasance of the outstanding bonds removes the trust indenture, permitting the trustee to revert back to the traditional role of a paying agent of coupons and maturities. The desire to remove the bond indenture confirmed the use of a defeasance, instead of an open-market purchase of outstanding RES bonds, which was unlikely to be successful enough to remove the indenture.

Defeasance of the RES bonds would remove the trust indenture, but not the cooperative agreement. Since the WDA had made several financial loans to the RES, the RES remained responsible for repayment at such time as the plant could support those repayments.

To implement defeasance required a stock of funds, and the mayor sought to tap local, state, and federal sources. Each source needed assurance that its contribution was part of a long-term financial reorganization, not an operating subsidy. Since a state conduit financing agency—the WDA—issued the original bonds, the city could not directly legally defease another issuer's bonds. Thus, the city could not borrow funds to provide the required stock of funds to defease the state agency debt.

The city considered the state government a prime source of funds. In fact, the WDA possessed excess funds from interest earnings on several bond issues, but was unwilling to apply the funds to help out only one city in the state. Although the state's general credit quality was not directly affected by a state conduit financing agency's default, the governor was reminded of how interwoven all debt was that had the state's name on it, even if the WDA securities were not direct legal obligations of the state. On a trip to meet with "Wall Street" analysts about the state's fiscal health, he was told that the WDA default—albeit technical— was a point of concern that affected the state's credit and that would become even more problematic if the principal and interest payments on the RES bonds were abrogated. The governor's position on helping the WDA and the city became more accommodating thereafter, leading to a called meeting with the mayor. Interestingly, the mayor had taken political jabs during the campaign for being too tied to state house concerns (since he was a sitting state legislator) rather than local ones. As a result of the governor's new interest, however, the WDA voted to make the funds available for the RES financial reorganization (backed by an implicit state agreement to replenish the WDA funds).

A strong political relationship between the mayor and the local U.S. congressman helped propel the financial reorganization. This relationship is illustrated by later events when the congressman decided not to run for reelection and supported (politically and financially) the mayor's successful election to Congress. At the time, however, for someone in the city to call on this senior congressman was not new, even to help the RES. With local interests at heart, this congressman had helped the prior mayor (of the opposing political party) secure an earlier EPA grant reallocation (the source for RES debt service). The congressman, working in league with the new mayor, took actions over several months to seed the opportunity for a new grant of congressional funds.

The city received a special EPA grant late in 1984 made available to the city through the cooperation of key members of Congress. The resulting amendment to a continuing appropriations act restricted the city's use of the funds to only "refinance the bond debt" of the RES. Furthermore, the congressionally mandated grant specified that no more than 60% of the refinancing could comprise federal dollars. As a perfunctory condition for the dollars, the city had to allow the RES to serve as a "laboratory facility for municipal waste to energy research." Due to the specified percentage requirement, the federal funds had to be the last dollars into the account. To create the proper paper trail concerning the proper use of the federal funds, the federal dollars had to be the first ones out of the defeasance account. Thus, actual defeasance was delayed to ensure that the federal dollars were the last in but the first out.

In October 1984, the city council approved the mayor's financial reorganization plan. The mayor's plan provided funding for the defeasance with $13 million from the congressionally enacted special EPA allocation, $15 million from the state's WDA, and $6 million from the city. The city also contributed an additional $2 million to cover transition costs. The city's total contribution of $8 million was taken from the city's pay-as-you-go capital budget with the programmed capital projects financed instead by borrowing— merely a matter of fungibility of funds to meet legal requirements. Defeasance would also permit the release of $850,000 held in special RES debt accounts.

Once the city obtained the $13 million EPA check on January 17, 1985, it started implementing the defeasance program. The city relied on a preselected investment banking firm for advice on timing the required open-market purchase of high-yield government securities. Defeasance is usually accomplished by issuing debt, the proceeds of which are invested in a structured portfolio of U.S. government securities specially prepared by the U.S. Treasury. The purpose of this arrangement is to achieve an optimum fit between the U.S. Treasury securities and the debt service schedule of the outstanding (defeased) bonds and to avoid making more interest on the investment than is due on the bonds—an arbitrage issue. In the RES defeasance, no tax-exempt bonds were issued. Thus an open-market purchase was required to purchase a set of outstanding securities that could provide the best possible fit. The constraints involved matching a fixed stock of funds and a fixed debt schedule with an open-market purchase of a portfolio of high-yield government securities. Market drifts made the optimizing decision difficult to achieve for a few weeks.

In late January the city's selected investment banking firm made a bid to sell the required portfolio of government securities at a slightly higher than anticipated, but still acceptable, price of $34.85 million. The bid was accepted pending verification as to accuracy and accomplishment of the defeasance requirements by an independent accounting firm. The delivery of the purchased securities to the WDA occurred about 2 weeks later. Once all the legal documents were finalized, the portfolio of structured securities was transferred to the trustee who then released the RES back to the city for local control and management.

F. The Structure of Disclosure Practices

Disclosure is central to federal securities law and the functioning of efficient capital markets. In its report on the circumstances surrounding the WPPSS default of $2.25 billion of municipal revenue bonds, the SEC (1988) noted systematic disclosure problems in the municipal securities industry as well as deficient disclosures to WPPSS investors. The report raised questions as to whether or not the OS for WPPSS bonds adequately disclosed significant facts relating to the projects, specifically cost estimates, power demand, financing ability, and the validity and enforceability of agreements—the last being the precipitating factor in the default.

From the beginning, this project was linked to evolving disclosure trends. Only after receiving binding construction bids for the project in 1975 did the city consider its financing plans. The city anticipated issuing city revenue bonds, as it was accustomed to for its water and sewer systems.[3] This path was squashed, however, by the storm over New York City's 1975 fiscal crisis, and the near-default of a similar waste-to-energy system in another state.

The city had to put the fixed-fee RES bids it had accepted, but not executed, on hold while it reconfigured the financing. The WDA emerged as a viable conduit for funds, structuring the city's obligations as a loan payment, not a debt under state definitions. There was a scramble for a successful bond underwriting team, and a nationally recognized firm to assess the project's technical and engineering feasibility.

Upon dissemination of the preliminary OS relating to the offering of the WDA bonds, the SEC inquired about the deficiency of certain disclosures. On the first page of the inside introductory statement, the OS stated in its description of the project

> The shredding facility, spreader-stokers and boilers and appurtenant facilities to each (the 'Project Plant') have not previously been assembled in a single operating facility, although facilities similar to the shredding facility and boilers are each in operation at separate locations. The ability of the Project to generate sufficient revenues to meet debt service requirements on the Bonds depends upon its ability to function as designed. The Feasibility Report concludes, 'The Project, as conceived, is sound from a technical engineering standpoint.'

Allegations were made to the SEC that the feasibility report (reprinted in full as an attachment in the OS) failed to make certain disclosures regarding operational difficulties experienced at the installations used to support the technical soundness of the RES. To clear the bonds from any taint that would surely scuttle the bond sale, the WDA and its underwriters mailed a clarifying two-page letter to the potential bond purchasers who had been sent the OS. This letter gave details on the four sites relied upon by the feasibility consultant in assessing the technical engineering viability of the component elements at those sites. Again, the point was made that although the key design components had not been assembled in a single operating facility, they should work together, as conceived. This letter appeared to satisfy the SEC's staff, so the bond sale took place. The SEC's letter, while somewhat boilerplate, ended with the reminder "that the responsibility for providing full and adequate disclosure under the federal securities laws rests with parties to this transaction." The effect was that although the file was closed at this time, it did not preclude the SEC from reopening the matter.

The city was mindful of continuing disclosure responsibilities. To do otherwise would prejudice the capital market for direct city debt. The city's official market disclosure documents included provisions related to the RES. The city issued an "annual informational statement" each year prior to the yearly spring borrowing, at which time a traditional OS was issued referencing and updating (if necessary) the annual informational statement.[4] Few governmental units followed this suggested two-step disclosure practice. (See Municipal Finance Officers Association, 1978.)

Market disclosure documents have become more standardized over the years. The SEC (1988) report on the WPPSS default hints at the need for federal regulation. Market participants have responded with voluntary guidelines for both the primary market (Government Finance Officers Association, 1991) and the secondary market (National Federation of Municipal Analysts, 1990). While suggested guidelines are useful, a disclosure document reflects the circumstances of the issuer. The extent of material needing to be disclosed drives the length of the discussion, and the placement of the material within the document reflects a mixture of model format and strategy.

A study of the city's official disclosure documents can gauge the changing seriousness of the RES default to the city. The extent of disclosure links the city's perspective on the RES to the city's capital market orientation. While a legal rendering of precise content changes has value, this analysis uses the count of words devoted to RES-related matters by location of the discussion in each of the yearly disclosure documents.[5]

It is contended here that the location of the RES discussion reflects strategic decisions. A review of the relevant locations and likely strategic reasoning follows:

RES—A separate section conveyed the significance of the RES situation.
Solid waste—Reflecting the city's postdefault strategy, the entire solid waste collection and disposal system was presented in a separate enterprise-type discussion adjacent to the reviews of other city utilities.
Long-term debt—Since the defaulted RES bonds were not direct city debts for computing the city's debt limitations, but rather a long-term obligation in the form of a loan, discussion in this specialized section along with the other city/WDA loan arrangements alerted readers to the city's contractual obligations to the WDA.
Litigation—Given the potential for claims and litigation to have a material impact on the city's finances, the RES opened the city to actual legal exposures the extent of which required disclosure.

The pattern of the city's market disclosure is shown in Fig. 2 and is measured by the number of words devoted to the RES by the location of the discussion in the disclosure document. Figure 2 reflects the evolving complexity of the issue as well as limited strategic choices. The total number of words devoted to the troubled facility is reflected in the upper curve with its strong upsweep to the peak in 1984 (at 1,808 words), followed by a steady decline for 5 years before increasing again. In 1984, extensive disclosure focused on the blue ribbon commission and its report calling for a restructuring of the RES. The financial reorganization (defeasance) that effectively removed the default was accomplished in the first quarter of 1985, yet the disclosure statement for 1985 reflects additional statements regarding the city's plan to operate the RES with modifications. Disclosure in the 1990s reflects efforts to improve the solid waste system and new calls for repayment of WDA loan advances.

In terms of particular disclosure categories, the RES curve reflects the increasing complexity of the issue. With the loan default in 1981, the disclosure requirements became much more significant. Thus, by establishing a separate section—labeled RES here—interested city investors could clearly identify relevant facts. As the rapidly increasing curve demonstrates, events such as the trustee's assumption of management control, the hiring of a private operator, special funds used to make the scheduled principal and interest payments, and the continued uncertainty of the mechanical operations added up to extended disclosure.

Following removal of the default characterization in 1985, the city revised the disclosure statement. The change reflected the shift in economic focus away from the RES as a separate entity (reflected in the RES curve) to an economic focus on the RES as a subsystem within the larger solid waste collection and disposal system (reflected in the SOLIDWST curve). An uptick starting in 1988 in the SOLIDWST curve reflected a range of developments such as the surplus steam customer converting to an uninterruptible steam customer status (generating extra revenues for the system), the initiation of a curbside recycling program in 1990, and specification of the declining city subsidy ($2.5 million in 1986 to $500,000 in 1992).

Litigation disclosures expended to reflect legal controversies. In the years up through 1985, the litigation disclosure pertained to the federal courts' review of the city's flow control ordinance. The 1985 disclosure statement reported that the U.S. Supreme Court's refusal to rehear the case effectively meant that the city's ordinance was upheld. Subsequent litigation disclosures dealt with explosions that claimed three lives in December 1984 (and an unrelated landfill explosion). Suits were filed against the city (and others) and the city initiated damage claims against the parties who delivered unauthorized hazardous chemicals into the RES. These controversies were discussed in detail in the 1987 document as the litigation ended. This resolution permitted a reduction of words in the 1988 disclosure statement, and a subsequent silent period of 3 years. Renewed disclosure in the 1992 statement reflected a reference to the WDA bringing suit to recover its advanced payments backed solely by project revenues.

Because of the city's frequent use of long-term obligations other than legally defined debt, the disclosure

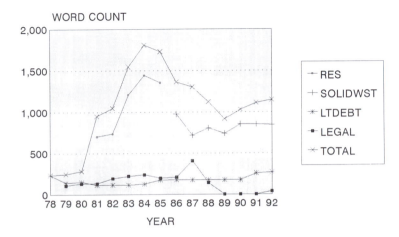

Figure 2   Extent of official disclosure.

document states the legal distinction and the scope of these other obligations, termed loans. The city used the WDA as the conduit financier on each of the loans (which varied from three to six over the years reviewed here for water and sewer utilities as well as for the RES). Thus, the RES bonds issued by the WDA were disclosed within this section of the disclosure document. In the first 3 years, this was a primary location for details concerning the RES bonds. As the RES problems mounted, the LTDEBT section (as those words only pertaining to the RES loan are labeled in Fig. 2) merely contained a reference to alert the reader to turn to the more substantive disclosure section. With defeasance of the RES bonds, the LTDEBT section was expanded to disclose that the WDA had made $31.3 million in advances to the RES. The disclosure indicated the WDA retained no security or property interest over the RES, with reimbursement contingent on the availability of RES revenues when and if available after payments for RES operation and maintenance expenses. Disclosure expanded in 1991 as the WDA sought court action to force the city to repay the advances plus interest.

In summary, the city's disclosure statements over 15 years provide a useful indicator of the city's representation of events surrounding the RES. This helps illustrate the city's strategic decision to shift the emphasis from a narrow view of the RES to a broader focus on solid waste management. Disclosure has market implications, too. In the wake of both the New York City and WPPSS financial crises, a major focus of federal regulators was on the disclosure practices of the respective governmental entities. If the second phase of the RES default workout had failed and recriminations and litigation ensued, investors in city bonds (and other interested parties) would surely have scrutinized the city's past disclosure statements. This environment demands that disclosure not merely provide a static rendering of a community's basic condition, but rather that it serve as a dynamic reflection of events and developments bearing on its ability, and willingness, to pay on an obligation.

IV. CONCLUSIONS

Debt financing carries the risk of default. Bond ratings provide investors with a gauge to measure the probability of an issuer's default. The issuer, wishing to preserve market access, has a strong incentive to avoid debt default. While the incentive may be high for local governments to maximize the use of conduit financing agencies and other forms of innovative revenue debt, there remains a degree of burden if default occurs. Even when default falls under the technical concept—meaning that all principal and interest payments have thus far been paid—the local government incurs pressure to resolve the underlying problems, if only to avoid a long-term default on principal and interest payments. By studying the structure, or anatomy, of a default and its workout, researchers gain a more effective understanding of the implications of debt financing. This is of increasing importance as governments attempt to finance unproven technological facilities to deal with modern service demands.

The financing structure of the RES was instructive, if not all too similar. The RES failed to meet rate, volume, and technical assumptions, similar to the WPPSS. As with the WPPSS, the RES achieved financing based on several risk-sharing arrangements, notably the take-or-pay contracts. The RES used the financing scheme often advanced as a creative means to deal with scarce resources—a conduit debt instrument avoiding the city's legal debt limitation.

The factor that permits the RES case study to be of research interest is the insight it offers into the structure of a default and its workout. Constraints were many and multifaceted. For example, the original intergovernmental risk sharing between the city and the WDA proved to be of significant leverage in gaining state support to resolve the default. The municipal "market" was an ever-present constraint and the city endeavored to deal with market concerns through periodic disclosure statements.

According to Miller and Hildreth (1988), debt-financing participants behave as an interorganizational network economy. Network stability permits network links to coalesce around a joint solution that also meets each member's measure of success. As applied to the case study, the network economy theory offers an explanation for the success of the workout. While most participants were tied to the network because of legal relationships, the continued use of the same city bond counsel facilitated access to critical political, financial, and legal opportunities. The role of institutional investors in guiding their trustees' behavior is a facet of a default network deserving more attention.

A community's strategic response to a troubled bond issue concerns bondholders and the trading market. Disclosure at the time of bond sales and material events constitute the primary points of formal information dissemination. When and how information about municipal securities in general and troubled bonds in particular is circulated to interested parties is a point of sharp discussion at this time (U.S. Securities and Exchange Commission, 1993). This study examined one measure of one community's 15-year effort at disclosure of a project originally shrouded under a default cloud. By doing so, the study revealed a very dynamic response measured by word count and location. Content analysis of disclosure documents has a value in what it can reveal about the borrower's strategic decisions and market orientation.

The details of the case study cannot be generalized except perhaps as they relate to similar refuse disposal facilities, however, the structure of the default offers some insight into the risks of debt financing. The success of the default workout demonstrates how effective financial strategies and strong financial and political skills can enhance the success of municipal financing arrangements.

NOTES

1. In a similar fashion to Hildreth (1983) and Rubin (1982: 145), the name of the city is not disclosed "to preserve the anonymity of informants." Original source documents and meetings with informants enhanced the validity of the case study. I wish to acknowledge the unique contributions of Thomas C. Sawyer to my understanding of this case.
2. After the workout but as part of the financial and operational reorganization, the city issued an additional $2.4 million of unvoted general obligation bonds, primarily to provide additional waste storage capacity.
3. Moody's Investor's Service (1987:8) termed "revenue bonds payable only from . . . plant revenues . . . as a very narrow pledge . . . offer(ing) very little bondholder protection." At that time, Moody's did not have a rating outstanding on any resource recovery systems with that type of "narrow pledge."
4. The city was one of the few jurisdictions in the country to issue an "Annual informational statement" pursuit to the guidelines issued by the then-named Municipal Finance Officers Association (MFOA; 1978). The rationale for a two-step disclosure sequence was stated this way by MFOA (1978: 1).

   Official statements released shortly before the sale of bond issues rapidly become outdated. Investors and dealers in the secondary market need current information on which to base decisions. The information suggested in these Guidelines is intended to assist in the production of documents which will be acceptable for that purpose.

   Evolution of these disclosure guidelines have led to two subsequent publications by the Government Finance Officers Association (1988 and 1991).
5. The timing of the disclosure documents ranged from March to June, with April as the most frequent month. The dates vary, due to financing schedules, strategic delays, and other unknown reasons. The documents increased in size over the 15 years covered by this study, especially by the reprinting of the audited general purpose financial statements. In 1984, for example, the document was 56 pages long and had textual material of about 25,000 words.

REFERENCES

Advisory Commission on Intergovernmental Relations (1973). *City Financial Emergencies: The Intergovernmental Dimension*, U.S. Government Printing Office, Washington, D.C.

Advisory Commission on Intergovernmental Relations (1985). *Bankruptcies, Defaults, and Other Local Government Financial Emergencies*, U.S. Government Printing Office, Washington, D.C.

Carter, R. Y. and Hildreth, W. B. (1992). *Pub. Budgeting Finan. Mgt.*, 4(3):491–527.

Feldstein S. G. (1983). *The Municipal Bond Handbook*, vol. II (S. G. Feldstein, F. J. Fabozzi, and I. M. Pollack, ed.), Dow-Jones-Irwin, Homewood, Ill., pp. 151–162.

Feldstein, S. G. and Fabozzi, F. J. (1987). *The Dow Jones-Irwin Guide to Municipal Bonds*, Dow Jones-Irwin, Homewood, Ill.

General Accounting Office (1984). *Guidelines For Rescuing Large Failing Firms and Municipalities*, U.S. Government Printing Office, Washington, D.C.

Government Finance Officers Association (1988). *Disclosure Guidelines for State and Local Government Securities*, Government Finance Officers Association, Chicago.

Government Finance Officers Association (1991). *Disclosure Guidelines for State and Local Government Securities*, Government Finance Officers Association, Chicago.

Hemphel, G. H. (1971). *The Postwar Quality of State and Local Debt*, National Bureau of Economic Research, New York.

Herman, T. and Seidler, L. (1988). "Credit Markets: Bonds Stage Afternoon Rally Amid Rise in Dollar and Drop in Oil, Gold Prices," *Wall St. J.*, (Sept. 30): 24.

Hildreth, W. B. (1983). *Pub. Produc. Rev.*, 7(3):269–287.

Hildreth, W. B. (1987a). *Pub. Admin. Q.*, *11*(3):314–340.

Hildreth, W. B. (1987b). "State Supervision of Municipal Financial Emergencies," paper presented at National Conference, Urban Affairs Association, Akron, Ohio, April.

Hildreth, W. B. (1989). *Handbook of Strategic Management* (J. Rabin, G. J. Miller, and W. B. Hildreth, eds.), Marcel Dekker, Inc., New York, pp. 279–300.

Hildreth, W. B. (1993). *Pub. Admin. Rev.*, *53*(1):41–49.

Hillhouse, A. M. (1936). *Municipal Bonds*, Prentice-Hall, New York.

Jones, L. R. (1984). *Pub. Budgeting and Finance*, *4*(4):60–77.

Kiser, J. V. L. (1992). *Waste Age* (Nov.):26–36.

Miller, G. J. and Hildreth, W. B. (1988). "The Municipal Debt Financing as a Network Political Economy: Network Stability and Market Efficiency," paper presented at Annual Meeting, American Political Science Association, September.

Moody's Investors Service (1987). "Resource Recovery: Rating the Debt," *Moody's Mun. Issues*, *4*(3).

Municipal Finance Officers Association (1978). *Guidelines for Use by State and Local Governments in the Preparation of Yearly Information Statements and Other Current Information*, Municipal Finance Officers Association, Chicago.

Myhra, D. (1984). *Whoops! WPPSS: Washington Public Power Supply System Nuclear Plants*, McFarland & Company, Jefferson, N.C.

National Federation of Municipal Analysts (1990). *Disclosure Handbook for Municipal Securities*, National Federation of Municipal Analysts, Pittsburgh.

Rubin, I. S. (1982). *Running in the Red: The Political Dynamics of Urban Fiscal Stress*, State University of New York Press, Albany.

Sawicki, T. J. (1985). *Emory Law J.*, *34*:157–199.

Smith, W. S. (1979). *The Appraisal of Municipal Credit Risk*, Moody's Investors Service, New York.

South Carolina v. *Baker* (1988). U.S. Supreme Court, April 20.

Spiotto, J. E. (1993) *State and Local Government Debt Financing*, vol. 2 (M. David Gelfand, ed.), Callaghan & Company, Wilmette, Ill., pp. 13:01–13:56.

Standard & Poor's (1984). "Credit Comment: Resource Recovery Ratings Approach," *CREDITWEEK* (June 4):1–8.

Swanstrom, T. (1985). *The Crisis of Growth Politics: Cleveland, Kucinich and the Challenge of Urban Populism*, Temple University Press, Philadelphia.

United States Securities and Exchange Commission (1977). *Staff Report on the Transactions in Securities of the City of New York*, Securities and Exchange Commission, Washington, D.C.

United States Securities and Exchange Commission (1988). *Staff Report on the Investigation in the Matters of Transactions in Washington Public Power Supply System Securities*, Securities and Exchange Commission, Washington, D.C., September.

United States Securities and Exchange Commission (1993). *Staff Report on the Municipal Securities Market*, Securities and Exchange Commission, Washington, D.C.

39

Current and Capital Budgets

A. Premchand
International Monetary Fund, Washington, D.C.

I. INTRODUCTION

The most important distinction in the budget structure is between current and capital transactions. The idea of separating the budget into two sections, in which the current budget—covering current expenditure—is to be financed, in principle, by taxation, and the capital budget—covering the acquisition of newly produced assets in the economy—is to be financed by borrowing, gained acceptance in the late 1930s. Since then this issue has become controversial, gaining over the years both strong supporters and opponents. Since the introduction of this distinction, several variants have been introduced such as recurring and nonrecurring, ordinary and extraordinary, revenue and capital, current and capital, current and investment, above and below the line, and development budgets. Implementation of development plans led to a frequent association of investment components with the capital budget, and there is a view that such a separate identification facilitates the formulation of plans and fiscal policy. The variations illustrate the great diversity of budget structures and the existence of many types of double budgets, and they make formidable the task of providing a common definition that captures the nuances of these structures. The approaches of national accounts systems or recent experiences do not ease the situation. Some of the industrial countries that had dual budget systems abandoned them during recent years in favor of additional analytical abilities gained in the use of national accounts. At the same time, the need for having a capital budget, as an appropriate check on the spending proclivities of government, is believed necessary in the United States; many developing countries find the use of the dual budget system advantageous and beneficial, and it is not viewed as a mere legacy of the colonial system. The current discussion provides two polar positions regarding the dual budget system—as an anachronism and as an imperative of the current situation. Depending on one's background or the specific situation, a case could be made for giving up the practice or, alternatively, for strengthening and streamlining the system. This underlines the need for a detailed discussion of the nature of the current and capital budgets, the initial influences, the economic, financial, and managerial considerations for it, and the measurement issues.

The meaning of the capital budget varies in the countries where it is in use. Broadly, it reflects, on the revenue side, proceeds from the sale of government property, or taxes that are presumed to be paid from private capital as distinct from income such as death duties and capital levies, and, where practical, in the real sense of the capital budget, depreciation allowances and proceeds from borrowing. The capital expenditure budget has two approaches—a capital expenditure budget comprising outlays on the acquisition of newly produced assets that are a part of a nation's gross investment for the period, and a finance budget comprising depreciation allowances and acquisition of previously produced assets that do not affect the volume of production but that involved a periodic valuation of government assets. The assets may be both real or

Adapted from *Government Budgeting and Expenditure Controls: Theory and Practice* (1983): 292–303 by permission of the International Monetary Fund.

financial, the latter reflecting government lending operations and other financial assets acquired. A capital budget may also be used to denote, on the receipts side, the foreign aid received, and on the expenditure side, projects and programs that are covered by foreign aid. In a number of developing countries, capital budgets are used to reflect the plan programs and investments and their scope and operations are coterminus with development plans, even if some of those activities do not result in acquisitions of assets. Notwithstanding this divergence, the principal accepted feature of a capital budget is that it primarily consists of the proceeds of borrowing, which are then used for the acquisition of assets, leaving the net worth of government unaltered.

During the 1930s, borrowing to build assets was considered acceptable. The increase in government liabilities was matched, in the event, by an increase in assets. But the position would change, however, if the proceeds of borrowing were to be used for financing current expenditures as that would reduce net assets. Viewed in terms of net worth, a distinction became necessary between expenditures that led to the creation of assets and those that did not. As capital expenditures meant an equal and balancing increase in assets, budgetary deficits and surpluses became associated with the deficits and surpluses on the current account.

The equation of borrowing with asset-creating expenditures is derived from commercial practices. The most important way for a commercial firm to maximize its profits would be for its receipts, in addition to covering its operational expenditures, to also cover expenses representing the use of capital. The surplus on its current account would reflect its capacity to augment its net worth and is its measure of profitability. Application of this principle to government, however, is fraught with technical and philosophical issues that are difficult to resolve. In technical terms, the application of the commercial approach to government would need the maintenance of depreciation or amortization for all assets. In turn, this would involve an enormous outlay on people and time with benefits that are, at best, doubtful. More practically, it is found that even in countries with separate capital budgets, no depreciation is made in the budget.* Moreover, the assets in government have multiple uses and because their purpose is to serve as public goods that are not marketable, their valuation becomes intractable.† Also, the private sector practice of allocating costs over time cannot be extended to government. In the private world, outlays on the purchase of real assets, for example, plant and equipment, are capitalized in the year in which they are acquired and are written off over the life period of that asset in the form of depreciation allowances. The phasing of these allowances over a period reduces the volatility in reporting costs and the net income of the firm. In government, the real cost cannot be passed on to future generations and when the timing, as well as the magnitudes of capital outlays, is irregular, as is true during a period of planned development, the inclusion of both capital and current outlays at the time they are incurred will complicate the problem of compiling annual costs and benefits.‡ Moreover, capital equipment in government may have multiple uses and it is difficult to allocate costs for its various uses. Philosophically, it is argued that asset creation tends to relegate the role of government from provision of social services to a lower level and that, in any event, asset creation by itself cannot be an adequate justification for government borrowing. Decisions concerning the resources over which the government seeks control are based on wider considerations. While depreciation would provide for the extension and replenishment of fixed assets and liabilities, it appears that the analogy of the private sector should not be overextended. Nothwithstanding these inherent limitations in the analogy of the private sector, the technique gained easy acceptance because it provided a way out of the depression and also facilitated political aggreement.§

II. ECONOMIC CONSIDERATIONS

Several economic considerations favor the dual budget system. Briefly, these are that the structure clearly shows the current and capital outlays, that it provides a clear identification of borrowing and its utilization, and that it delineates information on the actual capital formation. Implicit in the plea for the separation of

---

*It is, however, imputed in the national accounts. But, as discussed later, this is not without conceptual difficulties.

†In addition, there are problems relating to the valuation of art museums, roads, and battleships.

‡In a way, depreciation allowance does not alter the basic cash position of government. It is a contra-entry in the budget shown as an expenditure on the current account and a receipt on the capital account. But the computation of the costs is difficult. The irregularity in the phasing of outlays is an additional complication. In a perfectly stable program, depreciation allowances could be equal to the new capital outlays, provided annual outlays for new capital outlays had been constant for a period of years equal to the average depreciable life of the assets. This procedure is adopted in the computation of the general government sector in the national accounts of the United States, in which the new outlay is equal to the annual depreciation.

§The United States, which adopted the New Deal policies, did not use the technique of capital budgets.

current and capital outlays is the above-mentioned belief that current expenditures should be financed from taxation and that surpluses thereon should be used, together with borrowing, for financing capital outlays. This has contributed to the emergence of the balance on the current account as a key variable in economic policy. As noted earlier, the attitude that loan funds are less acceptable for current expenditures has led to the adoption of a more stringent approach toward their review and inclusion in the budget. Some contend that the use of current balance as an indicator of development or tax effort has become a theology, and that in the process, the larger purposes of the budget have come to be neglected. For example, from the stabilization point of view, it is the size of the overall deficit and the pattern of its financing that are far more important. Similarly, it is suggested that the application of the current account system on the same basis as an operating surplus in a commercial firm might imply that a deficit on the current account was due to extravagance or wasteful expenditure. It may thus introduce biases in the allocation of resources. Further, the existence of two budgets and the appearance of a balance in them might pose a psychological barrier to adequate taxation during periods of inflation. Various considerations discussed earlier suggest that the need for capital budget should be seen not merely as a rationalization of borrowing but, in the wider context of the formulation of fiscal policy, in terms of overall expenditures and the appropriate mix of taxation and borrowing relevant for the purpose. Expenditures should be subjected to broader tests rather than rushing to facile conclusions that expenditures on the current account do not contribute to the development of the national product. It could also be argued that some of these contentions are based on exaggerated fears on the use of the distinction and that, within limits, the dual budget system offers a rule of thumb or a first approximation. It is only when the system goes beyond a certain stage and becomes an obsession that some of the ill effects are generated. The capital budget has the inherent feature of ensuring outlays that are financed by loans yielding a return higher than the cost of raising them. From a managerial point of view, capital budgets so organized force the decision maker to evaluate the prospective returns and recognize implicitly the capital shortage and the need for its apportionment to obtain the highest returns. The capital budget enables a better determination of the responsibility within government and provides an implicit separation of funds, phased over a period, to be spent on a project. The critics of the dual budget system argue that the need for a return, either in the limited financial sense or in the broader context of the social return, is a view that needs to be applied over a wider spectrum of public expenditure and not confined to capital budget only. Also, borrowing-spending can always be more expansionary than taxation-spending, and persistence of high government borrowing may reduce the funds available for private investment and contribute to raising the interest rates.

As for providing information on capital formation in the government sector, those who favor a budget without these distinctions suggest that the required information should more appropriately be compiled on a supplementary basis rather than on a separation of the budget. Indeed, such calculations are made as a part of the periodic reports on national income. But then it could be argued that the existence of a capital budget (properly organized in terms of the national income accounts), while not a prerequisite, will facilitate the quick compilation of national accounts. During the period when national income accounts are still being refined, as is happening in several developing countries, such a separately organized capital budget may prove a valuable asset. In industrial countries, where national income accounts are forecast and published regularly, the need for such a budget may be less keenly felt.

III. MEASUREMENT ISSUES

The matter of the choice between dual budgets and a unitary budget is also influenced by the more practical considerations relating to the criteria to be used to determine items for inclusion in the current and capital budgets. The formulation of the criteria, however, has been a matter of as yet unresolved dispute, which again illustrates the difficulty in evolving economic principles for daily application. As borrowed funds are the primary means of financing the capital budget, it is natural that an important criterion should be the productivity or the revenue-producing capability of the proposed expenditures. Outlays have been classified, for this purpose, into "self-liquidating," covering those projects that provide an adequate revenue feedback for paying interest as well as the repayment of the principal, and "self-financing" projects consisting of those that can only pay interest charges. The application of this principle to government operations is rendered difficult, partly because revenue receipts form a part of the general pool and partly because most expenditures at the central government level are in the form of transfers to other levels of government and assets, if any, may be created there. Also, while assets may be created, they may not necessarily be revenue producing or they may have an uncertain future. The creation of the asset implies an expectation of income or services but their outcome may be at an indeterminate point of time. A rigorous application of this principle may reveal that expenditures that pass this test should be small.

Yet another suggested criterion is that the classification should be done with reference to the life expectancy of the asset and assets with a life span longer than 1 year should be included in the capital budget. A strict application of this would result in the inclusion of too many items of daily use to be within manageable limits. It is for this purpose that a combination of the asset features and life expectancy have been used for defining the criterion for inclusion. The system of national accounts, for example, views this in terms of capital formation measured by expenditures on tangible assets—"on additions of new durable goods to the stock of fixed assets." The emphasis on tangible assets has, however, been criticized because many development activities that might increase future income may not lead to the creation of tangible assets. The approach of the national accounts system follows the traditional Keynesian lines that were mainly concerned with the stock of capital. Empirical findings have demonstrated, however, that capital accumulation per se was not too significant for the rate of growth, and a greater part of growth was to be ascribed to the increase in the use or efficiency of productive resources. Outlays on family planning, research and development, or the training of civil servants have all the innate potentials of contributing to economic growth. Such potentials are not captured in the tangible or durable goods approach of national accounts. Development economists believe to be appropriate an approach that emphasizes investment for purposes of increasing future income, regardless of tangibility. An extension of this approach is the implicit suggestion that a new set of definitions and conventions should be worked out as a part of the national accounting system.

The definition provided by the System of National Accounts (SNA), however, excludes expenditures on military facilities, including barracks, transportation, and equipment, from tangible assets, presumably in the belief that these outlays are not productive, that they have a high rate of obsolescence and an uncertain future.* More problematic is its treatment of outlays on repairs. In terms of SNA approaches, outlays on current repair are those that keep the assets "in proper working order," while capital outlays on repairs are those that "lengthen the expected normal lifetime use of fixed assets or increase the productivity of these goods significantly" and that, in order to be classified as capital, the outlays should be substantial. Net capital formation is derived from gross capital formation by subtracting the comsumption of fixed capital, which is that part of the gross product that is required to replace fixed capital. In computing net capital formation, no consumption of fixed capital is allowed for assets of government, such as dams and roads, as outlays on their repair and maintenance are assumed to maintain the assets in their original condition.

There are several problems in the measurement of capital items in terms of national accounting concepts. Apart from the conceptual difficulty associated with the narrow scope of tangible assets, the 1-year longevity consideration would contribute to discrepancies, if rigidly adhered to, between quarterly and annual accounts. The distinction between repair and maintenance is arbitrary and, in the last analysis, would imply substituting the judgment of the national accounting statistician for that of the budgeteer.† The measurement becomes more difficult in a context of uneven application of the criteria.

The issue is frequently raised whether the capital budget is developmental or whether the development budget is a capital budget. This has arisen because, as pointed out earlier, these terms have sometimes been used interchangeably and also because a major part of development outlays are met from the capital budget. Development outlays are clearly much broader and ideally would include several elements of capital expenditures and expenditures on the development of human beings and related matters. The capital budget is narrower and inclusion of items in that part of the budget is not necessarily in terms of their development character. Moreover, development outlays as a concept is rather amorphous and ambiguous. It is hard, therefore, to draw demarcation lines between these expenditures. Much is dependent on the time element, for what is developmental today might be a capital asset tomorrow.

---

*It could be argued that the indirect benefits of military outlays could contribute to growth and some of them should be included in the capital account. In Sweden, during the early years of experience with capital budget revenue-producing assets (e.g., military housing) were included in the capital budget.
†The "saving" computed from the application of the above criteria is different from the current account surplus or deficit discussed earlier. Saving is a balancing item in the national income accounts.

IV.   PROBLEMS: ALTERNATIVES

The lack of a settled view on what constitutes capital has contributed to the emergence of a variety of practices. Three main problems are experienced. First, a multiplicity of budget categories that extend beyond the current and capital divisions has developed. Second, comprehensive criteria are rarely articulated for the classification of revenues and expenditures. Third, there is a lack of consistency in the application of the criteria. Thus, terminological confusion has arisen, which in turn generates issues in the compilation of accounts and more significantly in policy formulation. Classification limitation prevents the government from having a clear understanding of the magnitude and composition of investment outlays and of their implications for future resources and their utilization. It may even have contributed to distortions in policy making. These issues are serious enough to warrant a new look at the available alternatives. An idea that has gained some support since the early 1970s, following the recommendations of the U.S. President's Commission on Budget Concepts, has been the unified budget. The recommendation had its origin in the conflicting coverages and conclusions of the administrative, cash, and national income budgets then in vogue in the United States. In considering the relevance of this approach to countries with dual budget systems, the main issue is whether the unification of budgets would avoid the conceptual problems referred to above. The need for information on capital formation, it is believed, can be met from the national accounts and the limitations of the tangible asset approach of the national accounts can be compensated for by classifying expenditures into (1) consumption, (2) investment in tangible assets, and (3) expenditure on future benefits not resulting in the acquisition of assets.* Other limitations on the concepts of maintenance and repair could be similarly refined.

It could also be argued that the use of national accounts does not provide the managerial facility associated with capital budgets. Capital budgets meet this requirement and, notwithstanding conceptual limitations, extended practice over the years has contributed to an understanding among practitioners. For many budgeteers, the provision of funds for the budget categories is the language they understand. National accounts, while essential for policy purposes, are not the basis for allocation of funds or for recording accounts. This is not to deny the need for more improvements. The issue then is should efforts be made to improve the system by refining the classification or should it be abandoned in favor of national accounts? Answers to this are dependent on the pragmatic combination of the relative roles of economic policy and managerial considerations and the status of the national income accounts.

---

*For national accounts only category (1) would be relevant.   For those interested in the wider developmental implications, categories (2) and (3) would be useful.

40

Capital Budgeting for the Federal Government: Managing the Deficit by Redefinition

John L. Mikesell

School of Public and Environmental Affairs, Indiana University, Bloomington, Indiana

The Reagan experiment has provided the United States with its first sustained episode of major peacetime deficits. Before 1981, the deficit had never reached 4% of the gross national product in peacetime; since then, it has always been above that level. It is a legacy that tempts solutions by gimmick—"binding" deficits targets, balanced budget amendments, line item veto, and, finally, capital budgeting. While most would, one way or another, change the political dynamic between Congress and the president to induce the parties closer to fiscal responsibility, the capital budget proposal would handle the deficit more directly. It would simply redefine the manner in which federal spending gets counted and, along the way, probably reduce the deficit about which policy makers (and the public) should be concerned. At the same time, capital budgeting promises some greater attention of the condition of the federal government's capital infrastructure.

I. THE PRESENT FEDERAL SYSTEM

The federal government offers a system no accountant could love. Budgets and accounts focus on outflows of cash and devote little attention to government assets and public facilities. Critics argue that, although the approach is simple, direct, and satisfies the basic need for control of agency operations, it produces three major deficiencies that interfere with sound fiscal decision making. First, the attention to current flows of cash may understate the eventual costs of federal spending choices. A program chosen now may have minimal current cash consequences but major long-run costs. The focus on cash-out-the-door may distort decisions to the benefit of projects that would never be selected in their full costs were assessed. Concealing full costs is a powerful tool in finance of pork barrel programs; if Congress must face the full cost of the project, instead of the annual costs brought forward in each annual budget, it may become less accommodating to big projects that yield minimal national return.

Second, the prevailing decision process is deficient because future benefits which can flow from major capital projects are inadequately considered in the process. The present system essentially expenses capital investment in the first year; benefits may flow for many years, but the project in question can appear excessively expensive because full capital cost (or at least the amount that proponents are willing to admit to) is compared with only the initial benefit. Thus, there is discrimination against capital investment relative to current expenditures as groups of small price items drive out large price, but prospectively large benefit, projects.

And third, the current system may invite gimmick transactions to control deficit levels, a problem

---

Adapted from *SPEA Review*, 8 (2) (spring 1987): 27–29 by permission of *SPEA Review*.

possibly heightened by the need to achieve formal deficit targets enacted in the Balanced Budget and Emergency Deficit Control Act of 1985. Thus, the fiscal 1988 budget proposed the sale of Amtrak, the Naval petroleum reserves, and other real property to generate around $4 billion. Such a sale of government assests counts exclusively as revenue. The current system provides no recognition that the transactions would reduce the net worth of the government. Under accounting practices used in the private sector, such sales of assets would not necessarily increase net income, and sales for less than the amounts invested in them would even count as a loss. But that is not the government system: in it, an asset sale produces revenue not distinct from other sustainable revenue flows that diminish neither government capital holdings nor net worth.

In short, the present structure is defective for policy making. It provides (1) major disincentives for public capital investment, (2) misleading fiscal statistics about the condition of the federal government, and (3) avenues for fiscal management by gimmick. A budgeting system that includes a capital budget has been proposed as part of the solution.

It should be noted that the reasons for support of formal capital budgets at the state and local level do not transfer to the federal level. The federal government is so large that no single capital project is likely to influence its tax rates, it does not require extraordinary physical and financial planning to protect its debt rating, and its choice for debt finance presumably should hinge on stabilization objectives rather than on the character of projects being undertaken. Thus, the case of federal capital budgeting is based more on a decision process than is the more pragmatic case for capital budgeting by subnational units.

II. WHAT A CAPITAL BUDGET WOULD CHANGE

The way out of these problems is a restructuring of the financial decision making and reporting system, and a separate capital budget is a requisite part of the reform. Capital budgeting requires two budgets, a capital budget and an operating budget. All capital spending—spending for infrastructure and other high ticket price, long life, nonrecurring items—would be in the capital budget and only capital spending would be in it. The operating budget would contain all other spending plus a charge for depreciation and obsolescence of the capital stock. Accompanying these revisions would be a redirection of attention from any deficit or surplus to the government's net worth.

No longer would sale of assets be considered revenue. No longer would capital expenditure be considered on the same footing with operating expenditure. No longer would capital investments get undertaken without full attention to eventual operation and maintenance costs, because the capital budget process provides more open scrutiny of such projects. No longer would some types of capital projects be favored over others simply because of their agency and congressional sponsors—all projects would compete together on their own merits as additions to the public capital stock. And finally, uniform, governmentwide application of cost-benefit analysis would be possible, allowing public capital development to be considered along the same investment analysis lines employed in the private sector.

So would capital budgeting cause the measured federal deficit to be higher or lower? That is not easy to predict. Some deficit-reducing tools or gimmicks would be gone and some major spending program incentives will be changed. On the whole, the direction of the change is difficult to forecast. But it is possible to conclude that the change will direct attention away from a cash flow figure—the deficit—and toward the change in the net worth of government. To an accountant, this figure is the one worth watching—particularly should anyone make an offer to buy the company.

III. WHY ISN'T EVERYONE CHEERING?

Capital budgeting and accounting systems that do not focus on simple cash flows are not a secret, new technological innovation. Why hasn't a change been made long before this? Is it simply a grand version of governmental inertia and bureaucratic reluctance to change, or is there more substance involved? The latter is probably the case, and the objections are grounded in both logic and practice.

One basic objection deals with the manner for distinguishing between that which is a capital outlay from other outlays. In the private sector, that distinction—and the correctness of a series of such distinctions—is driven by the marketplace through the success or failure of firms. The distinction is guided by the rules of generally accepted accounting principles and an independent accounting profession. The rules are arbi-trary—not statements of fact—but they are, over time, guided by the experience of successful firm survival and unsuccesful firm failure. For governments, the distinction will be made by politicians and there is no market test. Many fear that distinctions will be driven by political convenience, and the capital budget will be bloated by convenient classification. Why would not proponents of spending for agriculture, education, environmental control, defense systems, and so on not argue that these programs are for America's future and, hence, classifiable as investment? And why wouldn't it be more convenient to talk about controlled operating deficits—or even surpluses—all the while capital spending, as redefined, rages out of control?

A second objection deals with the significance of net worth as opposed to the measured deficit. As the Office of Management and Budget argued in the 1984 federal budget

> The true net worth of the Federal Government is based on the strength of the American economy, not on what the Government owns as physical or financial assets. Most Federal physical assets—defense installations, public facilities, public parks, national forests, etc.—are held as public trusts, not as a source of profit. The primary financial asset of the Government is an asset not available to any private business: the ability to tax. Similarly, the primary responsibilities of the Government—to defend the nation and to promote the general welfare—have no counterpart in the private sector.

The federal government's primary revenue production is not derived from the sale of any service. Indeed, the services it provides generally produce no revenue. Nobody is likely to make an offer to buy the government and an equity issue is not contemplated. Thus, net worth in any business accounting sense is probably neither possible to calculate nor is it likely to be used for any decision.

IV. CONCLUSION

A capital budget for the federal government is unlikely to substitute for political will in the fiscal process. Governments need well-defined capital improvement programs, including both asset inventories and capital development planning. Neither is dependent on having a formal capital budget. Adopting a capital budget process by itself is not a solution to either infrastructure or deficit problems. Until full responsibility for the budget returns to the presidency, until members of the Congress regard the federal budget as something other than a supply shop for spending in their own states and districts, and until the public stops viewing the federal government as a check disbursing agent, there is little hope for deficit progress.

41

Federal Deficits and Financing the National Debt

Marcia Lynn Whicker
Rutgers University at Newark, Newark, New Jersey

One of the most controversial aspects of federal budgeting is the annual deficits the United States has accumulated, especially during the past two decades. These deficits have contributed significantly to the growth of the national debt. By FY 1993, projected deficits were $327 billion. Total outstanding federal debt in 1992 reached $4.08 trillion, more than double than the $1.83 trillion of 1985. Federal debt in 1992 was 68.2% of gross domestic product (GDP), the highest percentage ever since World War II and the Korean War. Net interest on the debt was $199.4 billion.[1]

Federal deficits, then, have driven accumulated national debt to unprecedented levels. Why have deficits grown and persisted? Few argue that massive federal deficits are good; rather, controversy surrounds exactly how bad federal deficits are and what to do about them. Policy makers agree that something should be done, but disagree on what solutions should be embraced. Observers agree, however, that federal deficits have been rising, despite all efforts to abate or even just ameliorate their growth. Plausible methods of reducing the deficit all create political pain, and thus are controversial.

I. WHY DEFICITS HAVE GROWN

Federal deficits have mounted despite the efforts of policy makers to curb them. Critics contend that the budget and spending are out of control. So why have deficits mounted and persisted across the past two decades? Several factors are at work, including the following.

1. *Budgets have dual stabilization and allocation functions that may conflict.* Budgets are used to implement both economic policy goals and specific program needs. This dual purpose of budgets undercuts deficit reduction.[2] Sometimes the goal of stabilizing the economy by reducing deficits, interest paid, and debt may contradict allocation goals of increasing federal spending for desirable social and defense goals.

By allocating monies to programs, policy makers express national priorities.[3] Trend analysis may present a distorted picture of national priorities since a unified national budget, including programs funded through trust fund revenues, was only adopted in the late 1960s. Prior to that time, some government programs, including Social Security, were not included in the budget. However, trend analysis is often used anyway to show shifting national priorities when enacting allocation goals.

Beginning in 1960, this type of analysis of budget shares reveals a decline in defense, followed by a revival of relative funding. National defense received 52.2% of total federal outlays in 1960. This amount declined to 22.7% of outlays in 1980 after the disillusionment of Vietnam, and then began to climb during the Reagan years. By the end of President Ronald Reagan's second term in 1988, national defense constituted 27.3% of outlays; approximately 73% of federal outlays were for nondefense programs. With the end of the cold war, defense spending began to decline relative to other functions, and by 1992 was 21.6% of outlays. Social spending experienced the reverse pattern. Since 1960, human resource spending has experienced a dramatic increase in budget share. In 1960, human resource expenditures constituted only 28% of total federal outlays. By 1987, that share had risen to 49%.[4]

Addressing important defense and social priorities by spending may conflict, however, with the macroeconomic policy goals of reducing deficits by lowering spending.[5] Rising deficits have caused mounting national debt. National debt more than doubled during the Reagan administration. In 1980, when Reagan assumed the White House, national debt was slightly under $1 trillion, at $908.5 billion. By 1989, when Reagan retired from office, national debt had increased to $2,867.5 billion, or almost $3 trillion. Critics contend this growth resulted from deficits accumulated when the supply-side goal of cutting taxes and the allocation goal of increasing defense spending both escalated the gap between receipts and outlays.[6] Interest on the federal debt also increased, both in absolute terms and as a share of total federal spending. Between 1960 and 1987, the budget share going to interests payments on national debt accumulated by past deficits had grown from 9% to 17%. In each budget year, continued spending for important allocation goals received higher priority than deficit reduction.

2. *The budget process is decentralized, with no central policy structure for controlling deficits by coordinating stabilization and allocation.* Federal budgets are a major tool for achieving fiscal policy goals as well as achieving the specific goals of individual programs, yet only in the past two decades has Congress adopted the structure to realize the potential for fiscal policy stabilization goals. Prior to 1974, macroeconomists often theorized about the desired level of federal expenditures to provide the appropriate level of fiscal stimulus, given the existing levels of unemployment, inflation, and interest rates.[7] But in the real world of congressional budgeting, the actual appropriations subcommittee decisions that determined federal expenditures were mostly divorced from any meaningful consideration of the state of the economy and fiscal policy needs. Nor was much weight attributed to revenue limitations, since the two finance committees—the House Ways and Means Committee and the Senate Finance Committee—operated independently in setting tax rates and in establishing modifications, exemptions, and exceptions in the tax code. What drove budget decisions was micro-level attention by members of appropriations subcommittees to incremental requests for increases in program expenditures.

The reality of national budget making was a process impacted more by the highly decentralized structure of the U.S. government and of Congress itself, as well as by interest group politics than by stabilization theory. Major budget reforms have created new institutional actors to increase monitoring of stabilization goal achievement as well as allocations, yet the process remains highly decentralized, with no single actor or institution assuming final responsibility for budgets and deficits. Partisanship increased blame shifting. The largely Democratic Congress charged that the mostly Republican presidents have not submitted balanced budgets and that they are merely responding to presidential lead. Republican presidents, in turn, charged that the mostly Democratic Congress was spendthrift and irresponsible.

3. *The budget process is lengthy, providing many points at which interest groups may block cuts.* Shepherding a federal budget through the various stages of budget development is lengthy and often laborious, filled with points at which the budget can be snagged on some political difficulty and delayed, and spending cuts restored by lobbyists representing powerful interest groups. Concerns over federal deficits may take second place to reelection and lobbying pressures placed on members of Congress to restore cuts or increase spending for specific programs.

The budget process has four stages during which lobbying and pressure may occur. If interest groups fail to achieve favorable spending outcomes at one stage, the lengthy process provides other opportunities for lobbying and influence. The stages of the budget process include planning and analysis, budget formulation, implementation, and audit and review. Interest groups have the greatest access to key decision makers, particularly in the formulation stage, and to a lesser extent in the planning stage, although no stage is immune.

In the planning and analysis phase, available resources are assessed, goals are clarified, and alternative approaches to attain goals are analyzed. This stage is conducted in the executive branch by the budget offices of the federal departments and by the Office of Management and Budget (OMB). In the legislative branch, the budget committee staffs, and especially the Congressional Budget Office (CBO), conduct analyses of policy goals and options. The analyses of CBO have been particularly well regarded for their accuracy, but the analyses from the administration frequently build in assumptions that favor the interest groups that are its major constituents. Agencies also are predisposed to produce analyses that support their clientele.

During the policy formulation phase, the budget is developed and approved. Interest groups have the greatest probability of exerting influence here. Budget development revolves around the budget year (BY)—the fiscal year following the current year. Prior to budget development, executive agencies have submitted quarterly financial plans that provide budget reviewers with estimates of 5-year program costs. Executive departments and agencies receive guidelines from OMB in the form of a budget call to aid in the development of budget figures. Once agency figures are prepared, the remainder of this phase involves budget reviews—first within the executive branch by the department budget offices and OMB, and subsequently within Congress. This stage culminates with the final passage of major appropriations bills. Lobbying efforts are particularly intense in Congress, with multiple possible points of intervention.

4. *Redistribution drives federal budgeting, yet the budget does not include direct explicit information on who gets what.* Often thick, voluminous, weighty, and seemingly dry to the unsophisticated reader oblivious to the clash of values and political battles symbolized by the numbers included, budgets represent a national plan for accomplishing goals within the BY.[8] The budget sets forth estimates of resources required and of resources available, in comparison with previous years and estimates for future year resources. Federal budgets contain five types of information. (See Table 1.) Yet none of the information in the budget deals directly with redistributive impacts that drive the budget process. While beneficiaries may be implied by the nature of programs being funded, details on how much wealth and income are being redistributed among income groups is not in the budget. Such details would likely increase resistance to expenditures that are

Table 1   The Federal Budget and Financing Deficits

Information provided in the federal budget:
Estimates of outlays, revenues, and budget authority for the budget year
Presidential budget requests for current and prior years
Five-year projections for revenues, outlays, and budget authority
Economic projections for the economy
Current services estimates
Federal budget legislation:
1921 Budget and Accounting Act
  Created a national executive budget
  Significantly increased the president's role in the budgetary process
  Created the Bureau of the Budget (BOB)
  Created the General Accounting Office (GAO)
1945 Government Corporations Act:
  Extended GAO audit authority to government corporations
1946 Full Employment Act
  Required that budgetary policy be used to support full employment
  Created the Council of Economic Advisors (CEA) to advise the president on economic policy
1950 Federal Anti-Deficiency Act amendments
  Provided sanctions for officials knowingly overspending
  Expanded presidential impoundment authority
1974 Congressional Budget and Impoundment Control Act
  Created a top-down process to integrate fiscal policy making with allocation goals of funding program needs
  Changed executive impoundments into rescissions and deferrals
  Created Senate and House budget committees and the Congressional Budget Office
  Required 5-year forecasting on new programs, and current services, tax expenditure, and credit budgets
1986 Gramm-Rudman-Hollings Act
  Set deficit reduction targets to achieve a balanced budget by 1991
  Established procedures for automatic spending cuts dispersed equally across social and defense spending if deficit targets were not met
1990 Budget Enforcement Act
  Set new 5-year deficit targets for 1991–1995
  Retained the automatic sequestration of military and civilian expenditures when deficit targets are not met, giving the president some new powers
  Set discretionary spending totals in defense, international, and domestic spending
  Made other process reforms

regressive, increasing the wealth of those already relatively well off. Rather, the information in the budget is more mundane, as shown below.

Outlays, revenues, and budget authority: Each federal budget presents estimates of outlays, revenues, and budget authority for the upcoming year. Both outlay and budget authority figures are presented by agency, function, and account. Outlays are actual federal payments or disbursements during the fiscal year. Outlays represent the liquidation of an obligation, usually by check or disbursement of cash. Most frequently outlays occur in the actual year the obligation was incurred, but not always. Outlays may also represent payment of obligations occurred in prior years. Revenues are anticipated receipts and collections. In addition to outlays and revenues, the federal budget contains budget authority estimates. Budget authority is the legal authority to enter into obligations that will result in immediate or future government outlays. The three basic types of budget authority are appropriations, contract authority, and borrowing authority. Appropriations are the most common type of budget authority and represent a legislative authorization that permits government agencies to incur obligations and to make payments out of the U.S. Treasury for specified purposes. An appropriation usually follows enactment of authorizing legislation. Borrowing authority is the authority that permits an agency to spend borrowed monies (debt receipts), while contract authority permits obligations to be incurred in advance of appropriations or in anticipation of receipts.

Presidential success: The budget provides information to assess past presidential success by including data on the most recently completed fiscal year, and a revised estimate of the fiscal year still in progress. Presidential requests for appropriations may be compared with actual appropriations.

Five-year projections: Five-year projections for outlays, budget authority, and revenues have been included in recent federal budgets, permitting trend analysis, and providing Congress, agencies, and the public with an overview of how the current budget fits into long-term policy. While 5-year projections for certain types of budget authorities make government management easier, they also reduce the flexibility of the budget as a fiscal policy tool. Presumably the purpose of 5-year program cost projections was to reduce providing members of Congress with information about future as well as immediate costs, allowing them to avoid enacting programs whose costs increase rapidly. These projections have not significantly reduced deficits, however.

Economic projections: Economic projections for the economy are the basis for budget projections and are also included in recent federal budgets. The economic projections in the budget represent a summary of more detailed projections presented in the *Economic Report of the President*. If these projections are overly optimistic, they may be used to justify higher spending, which in turn may produce higher deficits.

Current services estimates: The 1974 Congressional Budget Act requires the president to include current services estimates in his budget proposal. A current services budget consists of required outlays to maintain the current service level into the budget year, making changes for adjustments in economic and demographic conditions. The current services estimates provide a baseline for comparing the requests in the president's budget. If inflation is high or economic conditions are otherwise unfavorable, the president's requests may be higher than last year's outlays, but still represent a decrease in actual service level. Current services estimates allow Congressmembers to determine whether the president's requests represent a real increase or a real decrease in the services provided. Current services estimates provide useful information for interest groups lobbying for increased funding by enabling them to argue that services for group members are being reduced, despite increases in nominal funds.

5. *Budgeting has been incremental and "bottom-up."* Congressional budgeting, especially before the 1974 Congressional Budget Act, was very decentralized. Major appropriations bills were examined and marked up by subcommittees of the appropriations committees of each house. The bills were approved by the various subcommittees and passed on to the full appropriations committee for approval at different times, sometimes months apart. Before the 1974 reforms, congressional budgeting was a bottom-up rather than a top-down process.[9] Decision making remained very open to political influence, and focused on program issues rather than on economic policy goals.

No strong incentive existed for the full appropriations committees to consider the budget in its entirety.[10] First, the appropriations bills were forwarded sequentially at different times, a procedure that inhibited examining the budget as a single document requiring trade-offs and priority setting. Second, an informal norm of reciprocity existed between members of the various subcommittees. Members of the appropriations committees in each house typically sought assignments to subcommittees that oversaw spending in programs that affected their own constituencies. Members could then take credit for government spending that their own constituents favored and increase their reelection potential. Not anxious to have their own subcommittee legislation overturned or drastically modified by the full committee, members would often give cursory approval to the legislation originating in other subcommittees in exchange for equivalent treatment for their own subcommittee work. While some debate would occur on the floor of each house once appropriations bills were forwarded, the same incentives to logroll that existed in the appropriations committees diminished the ability of Congress to set priorities, to encourage trade-offs between policy areas, and to curb deficits.

Incrementalism dominated budget decision making. Little attention was directed toward the budget base, the amount of funds that were appropriated last year.[11] Most attention was focused on the budget increment, the additional funds requested for the budget year. One result of bottom-up incremental decision making was rising federal expenditures and deficits. An iron triangle based on a common interest in increasing program expenditures often formed between agency officials, the affected interest groups and clientele of the agency, and the appropriations subcommittee that reviewed budget requests by the agency. Each side of the iron triangle exerted pressure to increase program expenditures. Affected interest groups and clientele were direct beneficiaries of greater funding. Agency officials preferred directing large expanding programs to small shrinking programs—employees and clients were happier and life was easier when expenditures were growing. Since members of appropriations committees typically gravitated toward subcommittees that directly affected their constituencies, they also preferred program growth to program decline. Furthermore, subcommittees that reviewed large growing programs were institutionally more prestigious and powerful than those that reviewed smaller shrinking programs. (See Table 2.)

Incrementalism led to role-playing and strategies by various budget actors.[12] Agency officials, knowing that most attention would be focused on the budget increment, were predisposed to ask for additional funds. Sometimes the incremental requests would be padded or exaggerated in anticipation of cuts by OMB and congressional committees. Agencies that were ordered to reduce spending might argue that programs popular in Congress were the only programs that could be cut, expecting Congress to restore the cuts.

Members of Congress also resorted to strategies to cope with the mountains of budget detail.[13] In addition to focusing primarily on the increment, congressional members would use spot-checks of the figures in the budget base, assuming that if the few items that were examined closely were realistic and accurate, the remainder of the figures must also be solid. Since budget bills constitutionally were required to be initiated in the House of Representatives, House appropriations subcommittees could often play a more extreme

Table 2   Characteristics of Bottom-up and Top-down Budgeting

Characteristics	Bottom-up	Top-down
Time frame	Pre-1974	Post-1974
Decision mode	Incrementalism	Constrained trade-offs and priority-setting
Timing of Decisions	Sequential examination of appropriations bills only	Early examination of the budget as a whole
Initial focus	Budget margin, program issues, and line items totals	Budget base, economic policy goals and broad functional
Decision strategies	Log-rolling, functional and geographic specialization and deference, quadriad power, padding, use of political gaming	Forecasting, expert testimony, greater emphasis on analysis and budgetary justification
Primary constituencies	Special interests, subnational constituencies, specific policy groups of Iron Triangle	National constituencies, finance and economic cross-policy groups
Branch strengthened	President and the bureaucracy	Congress

role—inflating the budget of politically popular programs and slashing unpopular programs—knowing that the Senate could modify the excess.

6. *Major budget actors all have incentives for increasing federal spending.* Major budget actors involved in budget formulation and approval all have strong incentives for increasing funding.

Agency budget offices: Agency personnel are typically advocates of increased appropriations.[14] The duties of agency budget offices may vary somewhat, but generally this is where the initial executive budget is developed. The functions may be quite diverse. Agency budget officials, in conjunction with the appropriate operating officials, develop budget estimates for programs and offices, conduct budget reviews, and recommend budget allocations. These officials justify the submitted budget to OMB and to Congress by using financial and personnel exhibits, budget narrative material, and additional support data. Agency budget officials help prepare agency operating personnel for testimony before both OMB and Congress. Apportionments and allotments are prepared by agency budget officials who also maintain overall control of the agency's financial resources and position allocations. Other functions include ongoing reviews during the fiscal year, making recommendations for reprogramming actions and other funding adjustments. Budget officials are also responsible for assuring sound financial management within the agency and for recommending any changes needed in financial management procedures. Budget officers are usually career civil servants who work closely with politically appointed agency or department heads.[15] These officers serve as contacts with both the legislative branch and the public on financial matters of agency concern. Budget work is often repetitive and seasonal. When the budget is being prepared and deadlines are imminent, the budget officer may log long hours on the job, working late at night and on weekends. Timeliness of information is crucial. Budget officials must cope with deadlines and other pressures, including interest groups anxious to retain program funding. As they conduct their analyses, agency officials may interact with clientele, becoming sympathetic with the clientele's view that more funding is needed. Further, as agencies expand, so do career options and the power of agency officials. Working in an expanding agency is more fun than working in one constantly beset by budget cuts. When judgment calls are made, agency officials, within budget constraints, typically advocate spending more.

Department budget offices: Department budget offices service the entire federal department in the executive branch rather than a single agency, yet many of the functions and activities of department budget officers are equivalent to those of agency budget offices. The scope rather than the nature of budget activity distinguishes the two types of offices. Department budget offices also are generally advocates for increased appropriations for the entire department. In order to maximize department resources, however, the office may recommend cuts in particular agencies within its jurisdiction. Under a fiscally conservative administration, or an administration in which the policy area of the department has fallen out of favor, the advocacy role of the department budget office may be more muted and sub-dued.

Office of Management and Budget: Currently, OMB has the powers of budget development and legislative clearance. Its personnel include a staff of several hundred budget examiners who review agency budget requests. Transferred to the executive office of the president in 1939, OMB has been gaining in power and prestige since its creation in 1921, accumulating additional influence and authority through legislation, executive orders, and reorganization acts. In 1933, it gained the power to make, waive, and modify apportionments of appropriations, a power previously wielded by individual department and bureau heads. This power over apportionment was expanded in 1950 with the passage of amendments to the Anti-Deficiency Act. OMB was reorganized from the Old Bureau of the Budget in 1970 and was given an enlarged mandate. Its authority to act in the president's name extends to the entire federal administration, as well as to state and local governments when federal funds are involved, and to federal contractors. As a result of the 1970 reorganization, legislative clearance was centralized and most policy decisions were subsequently made by political appointees. Previously, decisions made by the OMB director on agency budget requests could be appealed over his head to the president by disgruntled agency officials. After 1970, decisions made by the OMB director were presented as presidential decisions, making appeal much more difficult and unlikely. The general thrust of the Nixon administration reforms and reorganization was to heighten the role of political appointees and to make OMB more responsive to the institution of the president. OMB theoretically may advocate spending cuts rather than increases, especially in conservative presidential administrations. Even conservative presidents, however, may want significant increases in defense and military spending. OMB has not been particularly successful at holding down spending in other areas, either.

House Budget Committee: The House Budget Committee conducts hearings on the state of the economy, appropriate levels of fiscal stimulus, the need for new programs, and overall spending priorities. Along with the Senate Budget Committee, the House Budget Committee is also responsible for developing and passing a first and second concurrent budget resolution, which is the framework of the congressional budget. When first established by the 1974 Congressional Budget Act, the House Budget Committee had 23 members whose membership overlapped in specified ways with the memberships of other powerful financial committees. Five members of the House Budget Committee came from the Appropriations Committee, five from the Ways and Means Committee, 11 from other committees, one from the Democratic leadership, and one from the Republican leadership. Two more at-large members were added in 1975, increasing the total membership to 25. Membership on the House Budget Committee is on a rotating basis, a feature that weakens the committee institutionally vis-à-vis permanent standing committees such as Appropriations and Ways and Means. Originally, members could serve only 4 out of 10 years on the House Budget Committee. Across time, the committee membership has been enlarged and the tenure has been made more generous. By the Ninety-seventh Congress, the committee had thirty members. Tenure was lengthened to allow members to serve 6 out of 10 years before rotating off the committee. House Budget Committee chairs may serve 8 out of 10 years. In theory, the macroeconomic fiscal targets for total revenues and spending hold down deficits. In reality, partisan clashes on the committee at times have been divisive. The committee must rely on moral suasion to persuade revenue committees to increase taxes, or authorizing committees to cut spending authority. Thus, the success of the House Budget Committee in holding down spending has been limited.

Senate Budget Committee: The Senate Budget Committee, also established by the 1974 reforms, fulfills a role in the Senate equivalent to the role played by the House Budget Committee in the House of Representatives. Originally the committee had fifteen members, a number that had been increased to twenty-two by the Ninety-seventh Congress. Like other committees, members of the Senate Budget Committee are chosen by the Democratic and Republican caucuses. Unlike the House Budget Committee, however, the Senate Budget Committee is a standing committee with permanent membership, a fact that enhances its power in the Senate to a greater level than the power achieved by the House Budget Committee. Despite the greater relative power of the Senate Budget Committee, it was more willing during the era of Democratic control of the Senate between 1974 and 1980 to accommodate requests by standing authorizing committees than was the House Budget Committee. Generally, the Senate Budget Committee has been more political and accommodating than the House Budget Committee, which is known for its greater attention to technical budget detail. Many of the limits on increased spending confronting the House Budget Committee are also felt by the Senate Budget Committee.

Congressional Budget Office: The 1974 Congressional Budget Act mandated that assist congressional committees and members by specified hierarchy. Foremost, it is required to provide assistance to the two budget committees; secondarily it provides information upon request to the two appropriations committees and the two revenue committees. Next it is required, to the extent that is practicable, to provide information to additional committees on budget, tax, and economic issues. Finally it is charged to provide information to individual members of the House and the Senate. The CBO director is jointly appointed by the speaker of the House and the president pro tempore of the Senate to a 4-year term. The CBO director has the authority to hire experts and consultants as well as to use CBO staff to secure information from the various executive and congressional agencies. The 1974 Congressional Budget Act charges CBO with providing Congress with two kinds of information—budget analysis and policy analysis. Several CBO duties relate to the provision of budget analysis—the computation of budget and tax estimates. One major budget analysis function is scorekeeping—keeping Congress regularly informed of how enacted appropriations legislation compares with the most recent budget resolution. The agency also keeps committees that report spending and tax expenditure legislation, especially the Appropriations, Ways and Means, and Finance Committees, informed about the compatibility of their legislation with the most recent budget resolution. Five-year cost projections for every authorizing bill reported by a House or Senate committee are the responsibility of CBO, as well as preparing and issuing an annual report soon after the beginning of each fiscal year that projects total spending, revenues, and tax expenditures for the next 5 years. The CBO produces an annual report by April 1 on alternative budget courses that Congress might pursue in the upcoming fiscal year with an emphasis on fiscal policy and spending priorities. The agency also produces analyses requested by the budget committees on specific aspects of federal policy. Scorekeeping (data on the amount of money appropriated toward the budget total so far) and other CBO analyses were designed to curb excessive spending and deficits. Analyses by CBO have gained the reputation of being more accurate and less biased than executive branch estimates, in part because CBO serves so many masters. Once its estimates and analyses are released to members, however, political forces become more powerful. Of major budget actors, then, CBO has among the least incentive to increase spending, but it does have some incentive since Congress is its major client, and Congress as an institution is under pressure to spend on constituents. Mostly in CBO, however, the multiplicity of "bosses," some conservative, some liberal, some moderate, provide countervailing pressures, leaving CBO the most neutral of budget actors.

Congressional authorizing committees: Congressional rules require that a program or agency must first be authorized before funds can be appropriated for it. A two-stage decision process results, where program decision making is separated from financial decision making, to prevent the appropriations committees from subsuming the business of substantive committees and to avoid an excessive concentration of legislative powers. The sharpness of this distinction has eroded across time, although precedents in each house govern what should be separated from appropriations statutes into distinct authorizing legislation. Formal procedures for waiving or bypassing the restriction against substantive legislation in appropriations bills exist in each house. Traditionally, when Congress established a new agency it granted that agency a permanent authorization by specifying that the agency continue to operate indefinitely and with "such sums as necessary" to assure that continuation be appropriated. Permanent authorizations have the effect of removing the authorizing committees from the annual budget process except when the authorizing committees proposed new programs or modified existing ones. The use of permanent authorizations has diminished across time, although they still account for over a third of the federal budget. Currently, the use of permanent authorizations is concentrated in the categories of interest on the national debt; mandatory entitlements such as Social Security, veteran's benefits, and welfare; and the basic operations of most cabinet departments. With the diminishing use of permanent authorizations, the authorizations process has become an avenue for substantive committees to express budgetary preferences by authorizing desired funding levels for particular programs. Increasing numbers of agencies must now appear periodically before their authorizing committees in the first step of the two-stage process required for securing funding. By limiting the use of permanent authorizations, substantive committees have gained a role in the budget process. Agencies now subject to annual authorizations include the State Department, the Justice Department, and the intelligence agencies. Congress has begun to use the authorization power to control executive actions by including specific limitations into the authorizing statutes. Typically, substantive committees are advocates of greater spending for the programs over which they have jurisdiction, and the authorized amount often exceeds the appropriated amount. When the authorized amount exceeds the recommended figure in the president's budget, the appropriations committee has been more likely to follow the latter than the former. For most annual authorizations, especially defense, the amount appropriated closely follows the authorized amount. For many domestic grant programs, however, the gap between authorizations and appropriations has been widening in recent years. The two-stage process within Congress that separates authorization from appropriations contributes to budget uncontrollability and increased expenditures.

Congressional appropriations committees: Each house of Congress has an appropriations committee that has the responsibility for appropriating funds for all government programs and agencies. Historically these committees regarded themselves as watchdogs of the Treasury.[16] Until 1974, few guidelines or restraints other than the budget estimates in the president's budget were available to the appropriations committees as they annually conducted their business. Devolution of decision making from the committee level to the subcommittee level occurred within these committees, as it did within other congressional committees. The 1974 Congressional Budget Act presented the possibility of jurisdictional conflict between the older and established appropriations committees within each house, and the newly created budget committees.[17] The first concurrent budget resolution established targets for overall spending levels, as well as subtotals for major functional areas. Appropriations committees after the 1974 act had to try to work within the time frame established by the act, and within the totals established by the budget committees and approved by both houses of Congress. The act changed the role of the appropriations committees from guarders of the federal Treasury to spenders who must be restrained by the reformed process. The legislative reforms prohibited appropriations decisions before the passage of the first concurrent budget resolution. Appropriations committees must allocate their share of the budget among their subcommittees before reporting any appropriations bills to the floor. Before the House committee brings any bills to the floor, it must review all its bills and report to Congress on how these bills compare with the first budget resolution. A scorecard accompanies each appropriations bill showing its impact on the congressional budget. Despite the hope that scorekeeping would keep members better informed of the cumulative impact of their actions and help to lower spending, members of appropriations committees often serve on subcommittees that disperse monies affecting their constituents and therefore have an incentive to increase spending in specific areas to gain or retain constituent support.

Congressional revenue committees: The House Ways and Means Committee and the Senate Finance Committee are the major congressional revenue committees. Originally, the revenue and appropriations functions were combined in one committee in both the House and the Senate. These functions were separated into two different committees in the House in 1865 and in the Senate in 1867. Until the 1974 reforms, a formal fiscal policy did not exist; tax policy was developed by the revenue committees relatively independently of the appropriations process. The House Ways and Means Committee was particularly powerful in the 63 years between 1911 and 1974. During this time, the Democrats on the House Ways and Means Committee controlled committee assignments for Democratic house members. Democrats seeking committee assignments found their institutional fortunes controlled by Ways and Means Committee members. In 1974, the committee assignment function for House Democrats was moved to the Democratic Steering and Policy Committee. The Ways and Means Committee, however, continues to attract power-oriented rather than issue-oriented members. The Senate Finance Committee has been dominated by members from small and Western states. Both committees historically have been defenders of special tax exemptions for many powerful interest groups, including the gas and oil industry. Since the U.S. Constitution specifies that revenue bills should be initiated in the House, the Ways and Means Committee continues to wield great power. Such is its importance that regardless of the overall ratio of Democrats to Republicans, it traditionally has had a disproportionate number of members from the majority party to ensure its control. The Senate Finance Committee has jurisdiction over the nomination of the secretary of the Treasury, the director of the Internal Revenue Service, tax and customs court judges, members of the International Trade Commission, the commissioner of social security, and many undersecretaries and assistant secretaries of the Treasury. Since both are prestigious, both revenue committees have had a membership with greater than average seniority. The revenue committees, and particularly Ways and Means, are now constrained to postpone any action that changes total federal revenues until after the first budget resolution is passed. Also, as a result of the 1974 reforms, both committees must now deal more openly with tax expenditures. Tax expenditures are now defined and estimated. Despite 1974 reforms that attempted to increase collaboration of the revenue committees with their respective budget and appropriation committees through the budget reconciliation process, this coordination remains loose. Revenue committees are under considerable scrutiny when debating tax increases and are not under mandatory instructions from budget committees or anyone else to do so. Thus, resistance to tax increases within the revenue committees as well as within the entire Congress contributes further to budget deficits.

Agency clientele and affected interest groups: Powerful interest groups impact on several aspects of the budget process, but are particularly visible during congressional budgeting. Affected interest groups are vocal proponents of increased spending for programs for which they are beneficiaries. While both high- and low-income groups are affected by budget authority and outlays, high-income groups in particular stand to benefit from tax expenditures that are part of the post-1974 expanded budget process. Traditional tactics used by interest groups include preparing expert testimony for congressional committees, visiting the offices of members of Congress to present the group's point of view, and monitoring congressional progress on key bills to keep group members informed. Mass tactics, less frequently used, include organizing mass mailings and letter-writing campaigns and mass demonstrations.

7. *Much of the federal budget is now "uncontrollable."* Much of the federal budget is "uncontrollable"; that is, not amenable to change because of long-term commitments and entitlements.[18] For uncontrollable expenditures, the decision about what total outlays will be in any given budget year has been removed from the annual budget process, and lies elsewhere, is dependent on economic conditions, or both.

Across time, a growing share of the federal budget has become uncontrollable. This trend has alarmed budget watchers who feel that the rapid growth in uncontrollable spending has contributed to mounting federal deficits and rising national debt. The OMB estimated that in 1970, 63% of the budget was uncontrollable. By 1983, the estimate of the uncontrollable budget share had risen to 76%.[19] Uncontrollable spending is sometimes called backdoor spending to reflect the fact that growth in these types of expenditures often occurs unobtrusively and unintentionally.

Backdoor spending takes several forms. One form is contract authority, which allows government officials to make legally binding financial obligations, not necessarily in the current or budget years, that must be paid at some future date. Contract authority is used extensively in the procurement of large complex defense weapons systems. Borrowing authority is also a form of backdoor spending since it allows government officials to make legally binding obligations that government will liquidate debt at some specified future point. Interest payments on the debt, another uncontrollable category, grow in response to total debt borrowed and market interest rates rather than explicit decisions by budget makers. Earmarked funds are also considered to be a type of backdoor spending, since funds from a particular source may only be spent for a designated purpose. The Highway Trust Fund and Social Security Trust Funds represent examples of earmarked funds.

A fourth and very large category of backdoor spending is entitlement programs that require the payment of benefits to any person, or unit of government, that meets the eligibility requirements specified in the entitlement program authorizing legislation. Major entitlement programs include unemployment compensation, welfare, food stamps, and veterans benefits. In addition to being uncontrollable, entitlement programs tend to be automatic stabilizers, since entitlement expenditures fluctuate countercyclically.[20] When the economy is booming and inflation is a danger, entitlement spending often falls, as more people are incorporated into the mainstream of economic life. When the economy is depressed and recession is a danger, the rising number of needy individuals eligible for benefits causes entitlement expenditures to grow.

By including a reconciliation provision, the 1974 reforms attempted to deal with the growth in uncontrollable expenditures. The idea of the reform was that in reconciliation, the budget committees could direct authorizing committees to tighten eligibility standards or lower benefit levels if projected spending and consequent deficits were too high. Except for the early years of the Reagan administration, however, when benefit levels and eligibility standards for major social programs were altered to reduce total social spending and social spending budget share, the reconciliation process has not been used successfully to this end. Even in those years under Reagan, deficits did not decrease as a result of social spending cutbacks, but rather increased for social spending reductions were more than offset by increases in defense spending and revenue losses from tax cuts.[21]

II. WHAT HAVE POLICY MAKERS DONE ABOUT DEFICITS?

Policy makers have tried several things to address deficits, some substantive, but many cosmetic.

1. *Adopt a statutory national debt limit.* For many years, the United States has had a national debt limit. Once this limit was approached, if it were not changed, no more borrowing to finance current deficits could occur. The debt ceiling, however, has not been effective, since each time it is reached, Congress and the president jointly increase it. Sometimes the increase in debt levels is temporarily held hostage to an ongoing partisan battle within Congress, or between Congress and the president, but not for long.

2. *Move expenditures off budget.* One strategy policy makers have used is to move federal expenditures off budget, so that they are not counted in expenditure totals and do not increase deficits. Expenses attached to various federal credit programs have been moved off budget in this manner, including costs attached to the savings and loans bailout in the early 1990s.

3. *Move trust funds carrying surpluses on budget.* The Social Security Trust Fund and other funds carrying surpluses have been counted in the budget total. Even though their earmarking restricts fund expenditures to purposes specified in the trust funds' authorizing legislation, the addition of these funds to budget totals allows their surpluses to be used to lower operating deficits. Without the inclusion of the trust fund surpluses, operating deficits would be even higher.

At one point, Senator Daniel Patrick Moynihan (D-NY) introduced legislation to lower Social Security taxes to reduce Social Security surpluses. Moynihan's rationale was that this would force the president to submit a balanced budget. This strategy, however, ignored surpluses in other funds, and would have left the Social Security fund with no cushion for future needs. His proposal was not enacted, but trust fund surpluses continue to offset operating deficits.

4. *Give authority for budget reduction recommendations to a nonpartisan commission.* When faced with

a thorny and sensitive political issue, Congress has sometimes delegated the problem to a nonpartisan commission. This strategy worked when controlling the money supply proved difficult and the Federal Reserve Board—nonpartisan in character—was created. In the 1980s when the Social Security fund was in trouble for unfunded liabilities, a nonpartisan commission was established to study the issue and make recommendations. Although its recommendations were to increase tax rates and modify benefit structures—politically unpopular solutions that could be used to partisan advantage if advocated by one party or the other—these recommendations were subsequently adopted and rescued the fund.

When deficits continued to grow during the Reagan administration, Congress tried the nonpartisan commission solution again, but with less success. The National Economic Commission was established in 1987. It studied the deficit for almost 2 years and made a report, but because deficit reduction must necessarily involve raising taxes—which President George Bush pledged not to do in the 1988 presidential campaign—or cutting expenditures from programs with powerful constituencies, the report was largely ignored.[22]

5. *Introduce a structure for "top-down" budgeting.* One of the two major goals of the Congressional Budget and Impoundment Act of 1974 was to reform budget procedures internal to Congress. The act attempted to centralize budgeting, to create a structure capable of viewing the budget as a whole, to encourage priority setting, and to curb deficit spending in order to reduce the high inflation rates of the mid-1970s. The act created three new congressional units, a budget committee in each house and a support agency—the CBO—to help Congress prepare and manage the federal budget. A major function of the budget committees is to construct a congressional budget as an alternative to the executive budget. CBO was charged with helping the budget committees in budget preparation, as well as providing information on tax expenditures and economic conditions.

The architects of the 1974 reforms wanted to change congressional budgeting from a bottom-up, micro-level, incremental process to more of a top-down, macro-level, nonincremental process. They had two options: a rigid structure that required coordination and formal trade-offs between policy areas once total budget, revenue, and deficit figures were set, or a less rigid structure that relied more on moral persuasion and reasoning than on rigid institutional controls. Some conservatives in Congress were anxious to curb mounting deficits and preferred the more rigid structure.

Liberals, fearful that rigid controls would be used to gut social programs, favored the less rigid structure. Liberals also argued that rigid controls may lead to a failure of the internal congressional budget reforms, causing the entire act to be discredited, including the impoundment portions. Such was the tension between the executive and legislative branches at that time that liberals carried the day. The 1974 reforms relied on informal rather than rigid institutional controls to enforce adherence to limits required by previously established budget totals and the trade-offs such commitment requires.

The revised congressional process sets overall nonbinding targets for budget authority, budget outlays, and deficits.[23] Recommended levels of federal revenues, federal debt, and the amount to increase the statutory debt ceiling are established. The act does not require either a balanced budget or a reduction in national debt. Specific targets are developed for budget outlays and budget authority for each of nineteen major functional categories in the budget, such as national defense, international affairs, commerce and housing credit, income security, and health. Initially, congressional debate centered on the first and second concurrent budget resolutions within each house. Across time, the second concurrent resolution was largely abandoned and the reconciliation process—in which budget committees direct the appropriations committees to cut funds, the taxing committees to raise new revenues, or the authorizing committees to change benefit levels and eligibility requirements—was moved up to closely follow the first concurrent resolution.

The 1974 reforms have been modestly successful in some areas, but not in controlling federal deficits. As a result of the 1974 act, congressional budget decision makers have more information than ever before. Previously relying on the executive branch and interest groups for information about programs, Congress now may use data collected by the CBO and budget committee staffs. Further, information is available linking the impact of program level decisions to fiscal policy goals.

Despite this, the economy was not noticeably improved in the late 1970s in the initial years after the reforms, and some attributed the decline in inflation during the first Reagan administration to executive branch initiatives rather than to congressional ones. In 1981 during the Reagan honeymoon period when the presidency was receiving favorable political coverage, the congressional budget was virtually ignored and the executive budget was adopted almost in its entirety. In addition, the reformed congressional budget process has not noticeably dampened rising deficits.

The 1974 reforms created a structure to force discussion on economic policy goals as well as the impact of federal expenditures upon those goals, but it could not and did not force consensus on those goals. Conservatives and many Republicans continue to place a higher priority on curbing inflation, while liberals and some Democrats continue to place a higher priority on reducing unemployment. Similarly, the reforms created a structure to force discussion on the necessity for trade-offs between different policy areas so that an increase in spending in one area would imply a decrease in another. But it could not and did not require consensus on what those trade-offs should be.

Some inside budget observers argue that the 1974 reforms worked reasonably well in the pre-Reagan years between 1974 and 1981 if success is measured by the resulting levels of federal deficits and debt and by process deadlines being met, although interest rates and inflation were high. In the Reagan years after 1982, separated from the earlier period by the watershed Economic Recovery Tax Act of 1981, neither process nor results were satisfactory. This act eliminated $750 billion in revenues over a 5-year period, or $150 billion a year, virtually assuring massive deficits and an uncontrollable budget. Nor were process deadlines met in the Reagan years. Relatively uninhibited by the 1974 budget structure, congressional Democrats competed with congressional Republicans and President Reagan to see who could give away the greatest share of benefits and contracts through tax cuts and spending increases, particularly in defense. After leaving office, David Stockman, Reagan's OMB director at the time, described the early Reagan years as a period where "the greed level, the level of optimism just got out of control."[24]

Because the 1974 top-down reforms did not curb deficits, additional reforms have been proposed, most dealing with modifications of the budget process, rather than specific content of the budget. Executive branch reforms have typically emphasized efficiency, which indirectly would lower budget totals by achieving more with less. Other proposed reforms are to directly reduce federal deficits.

6. *Introduce budget reforms to enhance efficiency.* Several budget reforms have been introduced in the executive budget process oriented toward increasing efficiency and rationality in budget formulation.[25] While these do not directly reduce expenditures, by achieving service delivery and other government outputs with less inputs, one goal of efficiency is to lower deficits. The politics of budget reform are such that reformers usually must oversell the merits of their proposals to overcome inertia and resistance to change. Initially a flurry of excitement occurs and expectations rise. Since the reform was oversold and since much of the resistance to change is quite real, disappointment and disillusionment soon set in. Dramatic changes do not occur and the budget reform is pronounced a failure, yet a residue of increased rationality may remain after the reform has been formally abandoned.

One such reform was the programming, planning, and budgeting system (PPBS), first introduced in the federal government in the Defense Department in the 1960s, which stressed the use of analysis in the early stages of the budget cycle. Program budgeting and the greater use of data associated with programs were advocated. Output measures and 5-year projections beyond the BY were to be employed. Special studies and analyses were to accompany specific major program issues. While eventually abandoned as unwieldy, many of the procedures advocated by PPBS, such as 5-year projections and the increased use of analyses, were incorporated into the 1974 congressional budget reforms.

A second executive reform was management by objective (MBO), urged upon federal departments and agencies by the Nixon administration. It called for the establishment of specific objectives for agencies and required regular high-level periodic reports on progress toward agency objectives. While this reform also died an early death, some agencies incorporated various aspects of it into their operating procedures.

The Carter administration pushed a third executive budget reform—zero base budgeting (ZBB). A bottom-up approach, ZBB required program managers to create decision packages that link budget figures with activities and objectives. These packages were ranked at each successively higher level of authority. High-ranking packages were funded, while lower-ranking packages may not receive funding. This approach was designed to encourage an annual examination of the budget base as well as the budget increment. While portions of the process have been retained, the procedure generated excessive detail and proved cumbersome.

7. *Advocate constitutional amendments to deal with deficits.* In the 1970s, an amendment to the U.S. Constitution mandating a balanced federal budget was endorsed by many state legislatures who passed resolutions requesting the Congress call a constitutional convention to approve the amendment.[26] This movement fell two states short of the necessary number to initiate a constitutional amendment in this fashion. In the 1980s, President Reagan proposed the amendment as a solution to historically large deficits accruing during his first term, but with no greater success in passing it.[27]

Generally, conservatives have favored the balanced budget amendment while liberals have opposed it. Critics argue that it would vitiate the use of the federal budget as a stabilization tool to achieve fiscal policy goals, and would not directly address the sources of pressure for rising federal expenditures. Proponents argue that safeguards could be built into the amendment so that its provisions could be overridden in the event of a fiscal emergency.

Another amendment to the U.S. Constitution, the presidential item veto amendment, would give the president the authority to veto specific line items within appropriations bills. This reform has been urged by recent presidents, but has not been adopted. Current interpretation of presidential veto power requires that the president either sign into law or veto an entire bill, and does not give him the discretionary power to judge specific narrow parts of budget authority. Yet governors in forty-three states have item veto power. Proponents agree that this additional presidential power would help to hold the line on deficits, while critics are skeptical and fearful that presidents would use the power to thwart congressional intent. The presidential item veto joins a long line of budget reforms that, whatever their economic intent, have tapped long-standing partisan and institutional conflict.

8. *Enact the Gramm-Rudman-Hollings deficit reduction legislation.* The focus of budget reform efforts has been on directly lowering deficits. While neither of the proposed constitutional amendments was successfully adopted, the 1985 Gramm-Rudman-Hollings Act was enacted. Despite continual modification of the federal budget process, by mid-1985 signs of continuing difficulty were plentiful.[28]

- In no year since 1977 had all thirteen annual appropriations bills that in total constitute the federal budget been delivered by Congress to the president for approval by the beginning of fiscal year set in the 1974 act, October 1.
- In two fiscal years, 1986 and 1987, none of the thirteen appropriations bills had been sent to the president by the beginning of the fiscal year, so the entire federal government in those years began the new year operating under a continuing resolution.
- The first concurrent budget resolution was usually passed from 1 to 4 months behind the scheduled date of May 15, the second resolution had been abandoned, and often appropriations bills were being passed before, not after, the prerequisite authorization bills.

In short, the budget process was in disarray by the 1980s, a problem Shuman, a budget insider, attributed to the following four factors:

- The 1974 act made the budget process more complex, with sometimes—as in the case of the second concurrent resolution and reconciliation process—unrealistic completion dates.
- President Ronald Reagan had overloaded and overwhelmed the Congress with more controversial budget and tax proposals than members could digest and act on in a 12-month period.
- Some Senate members insisted on attaching "riders"—unrelated amendments and provisions—on highly controversial social issues such as abortion, prayer in the schools, and busing to authorization and appropriation bills, ignoring the rule that such riders be germane to the bill.
- Periodically House Democrats and Senate Republicans would deliberately delay appropriations bills to gain tactical advantage.

Most troubling, however, was the growth in federal deficits, which increased from the range of $40 billion to $80 billion in the post-Congressional Budget Act pre-Reagan years between 1974 and 1981 to the range of $80 billion to $220 billion in the 1980s. The national debt almost doubled in 4 years, from $914 billion in 1981 to $1,827.5 billion in 1985. Confronted with swelling deficits and national debt, conservatives in Congress responded by proposing the Balanced Budget and Emergency Deficit Control Act of 1985, informally called the Gramm-Rudman-Hollings Act (GRH) after its primary sponsors.

Senator Rudman, one of the sponsors of GRH called it at the time of its passage "a bad idea whose time has come."[29] Its two centerpieces were a schedule of deficit targets designed to balance the budget by 1991 by reducing the deficit an additional $36 billion in each of 5 years, and a mechanism for automatic budget cuts that were to be activated if Congress failed to meet those targets. The act allowed for postponing the deficit reduction if a recession occurred and negating it in the event of war. Proponents of GRH argued that only such a drastic measure could withstand the political pressures from special interest groups for increases in spending. Opponents argued that the law represented a meat cleaver approach to financial decision making.

The process of cutting funds was called sequestration. Its activation would cause sufficient amounts to be automatically withheld from appropriations to meet GRH totals. Cuts were to occur equally in defense and social spending, with certain programs exempted in each category. In defense, contracts such as those on large weapons systems to which the government was legally obligated to make payments were exempted, while on the social spending side, Social Security, reflecting in part the growing political power of an enlarging older population, was exempted. These were not the only areas protected from cuts, however, since more than forty-five programs were totally exempted from reduction. Once a decision to sequester was made, little discretion remained since the amounts to be cut and where the cuts were to occur were specified by law.

While ascertaining that sequestration was required seems like a technical issue, in reality it became political. Estimates of budget deficits may vary widely, depending on the assumptions that are made about overall economic growth and therefore federal tax receipts. Optimistic estimates of economic growth will produce higher estimates of tax receipts and lower deficit estimates, while with pessimistic expectations of economic growth, federal tax receipts will be lower and budget deficits will be larger. Controlling the economic projections and estimates of tax receipts means controlling in some instances estimates of deficits and therefore whether or not GRH sequestration is required.

Shortly after its passage, the constitutionality of the implementation of the sequestration process was challenged by Congressman Mike Synar (D-OK) and eleven colleagues. The initial law required the comptroller general, the head of the General Accounting Office (GAO), to activate the sequestration. Congress placed the GAO comptroller in charge of deficit forecasting to reflect its greater trust in GAO estimate accuracy over executive branch accuracy. The OMB estimates, by contrast, have sometimes been less accurate, due to political pressure to make the most optimistic economic assumptions as possible so deficit estimates will be as low as possible. The Supreme Court, however, found that having the GAO comptroller determine if and when GRH provisions would be activated violated the separation of powers principle. The Court argued that the GAO comptroller was an agent of Congress, the legislative branch, not the executive branch, since unlike executive branch officers the GAO comptroller could be removed by Congress through a joint resolution. The court found this infringed on the executive duties to faithfully execute the law and therefore violated the separation of powers.

Anticipating that the triggering mechanism for sequestration may be found unconstitutional, Congress actually provided for a challenge in the law itself and for a quick Supreme Court review, as well as a backup trigger mechanism. After the Supreme Court decision, the backup trigger mechanism became effective. It calls for the CBO and OMB directors to issue a joint report on August 20 to a temporary joint committee of Congress, consisting of members of the House and Senate Budget Committees. The committee reports a joint resolution to Congress on needed sequestration amounts within 5 calendar days. Each house then has 5 working days to vote final approval on the resolution before it is sent to the president. Typically, Congress is in summer recess during this period in late August and early September. In election years, such as 1988, this resolution addressing the deficit is scheduled for consideration in September, only weeks before the election, placing great pressure on Congress to approve overly optimistic projections and to find alternative strategies for dealing with deficits.

Initially, Congress used "smoke and mirrors," including selling federal assets, using accounting maneuvers, and moving some federal outlays off budget. The surplus in the Social Security Trust Fund that grew after reforms in 1983 increased taxes and altered some benefits, was used to offset federal expenditures and lower the deficit, even though Social Security funds are earmarked for that purpose only. Great pressure was exerted in 1988 and 1989 to keep funding of the savings and loans thrift "bailout" off budget as well. Even so, the revised target was supposed to be $100 billion for 1990, but $140 was anticipated. By the Bush administration, some observers felt that the federal deficit had gotten "stuck" at around $150 billion. Despite numerous budget summits between key budget process actors, no easy solution to large federal deficits appeared in sight.

9. *Adopt the Budget Enforcement Act of 1990.* A massive disagreement over the FY 1991 budget provoked yet another process reform to deal with federal deficits. In the fall of 1990, OMB director Richard Darman presented bleak figures to Congress. Because of the decline in the economy and the massive increase in funds needed for the savings and loan bailout[30]

- The FY 1991 deficit was projected to be $168 billion, not the anticipated $100 billion.
- Including the S & L bailout funds for that year raised the deficit to $231 billion.
- Removing the "masking effect" of the Social Security Trust Fund surplus raised the deficit to $280 to $300 billion.
- The FY 1990 budget deficit was also raised from its previous estimate of $100 billion to $161.3 billion.

Congress was deadlocked, and long days were spent hammering out a budget agreement. Public confidence in Congress and government plummeted; President Bush was forced to abandon his 1988 campaign pledge of no new taxes, an abandonment he later retracted in the 1992 presidential campaign when attacked from the right in Republican primaries by challenger Pat Buchanan. Budget stalemate led to threats to close government down over the 3-day Columbus Day weekend. After 2 1/2 months of negotiation, a 5-year budget agreement was adopted, reducing spending by $500 billion over 5 years between 1991 and 1995. This legislation was technically Title XIII of the Omnibus Budget Reconciliation Act of 1990 (OBRA). Title XIII is called the Budget Enforcement Act of 1990. The following are the two main features of the agreement:

- Most of the reductions would not occur in the first 2 years but in the last 3 years. Only 23% would occur in the first 2 years; the remaining 77% in the last 3 years.
- The reductions were not absolute cuts, but rather cuts from the "current services base-line estimates" (last year's budget adjusted for economic growth, inflation, and other factors).

Subject to changes from presidential reestimates, projected moving deficit targets under the 1990 budget agreement were $327 billion for 1991, $317 billion for 1992, $236 billion for 1993, $102 billion for 1994, and $83 billion for 1995. The 1990 Budget Enforcement Act also included various process reforms, and effectively vitiated the earlier targets of GRH. Sequestration, or automatic cuts in spending if deficit targets were not met, still are to be applied as under GRH to military and civilian accounts separately. Discretionary spending ceilings brought about by a special sequestration procedure applied to three broad categories: defense, international, and domestic spending. A pay-as-you-go "minisequester" could also be enacted. Budget actors remained optimistic that the 1990 agreement would be more successful in curbing deficits than its predecessors, but basic pressures driving federal spending and deficits upward were not altered.

III. CONSTRAINTS ON RAISING TAXES TO LOWER DEFICITS

Lowering expenditures is only one of two possible approaches to lowering deficits. The other is to raise revenues by raising taxes. Confronted with a decentralized and politicized budget process and a budget that is largely uncontrollable, why have politicians not raised taxes to lower deficits? The political reality of raising taxes, however, is if anything more difficult than lowering expenditures.

By the 1980s, a pledge of "no new taxes" from politicians was almost a political litmus test for voter approval. Politicians who acknowledged in the heat of a campaign that they would support raising taxes, such as Democratic nominee Walter Mondale did in the 1984 presidential race, went down to resounding defeat. Politicians who railed against new taxes, such as incumbent present Ronald Reagan did, won by large margins. The key question for policy makers, then, has been how to raise adequate tax revenues to fund government in a democracy in the face of widespread resistance, and during the Reagan years under the supply-side economics, drastic cuts in taxes, especially for the rich. Several constraints operate on the ability of policy makers to raise taxes as demands on government grow.

1. *Low taxes relative to other nations create expectations of continued low taxes.* Despite the seemingly onerous burden of U.S. taxes, they remain lower than those of most advanced European countries.[31] In 1984, after the early Reagan tax cuts, taxes in the United States constituted 29% of GNP. While Japan's taxes constituted a lower percentage of GNP (27%) and Australia (31%) and Canada (33%) slightly higher percentages, of European nations besides Switzerland (32%), only Germany and Britain (at about 38%) were below 40%. Austria, Belgium, Denmark, France, Italy, the Netherlands, and Norway all taxed at percentages ranging between 40% and 50%, and Sweden's taxes exceeded 50% of GNP. Yet relatively low U.S. taxes do not give policy makers greater room to maneuver for more revenues to fund government; rather, low taxes have created an expectation that taxes will remain low. These expectations, in turn, fuel resistance to higher tax levies.
2. *Taxes already constitute a large dollar volume.* Because the U.S. economy is large, the volume of taxes and other government funds is large—$844,949,000,000 for all levels of government in FY 1986.[32] Of this, $471,898,000,000 was collected by the federal government, $228,054,000,000 by state governments, and $144,997,000,000 by all forms of local governments. By FY 1988, total receipts for the federal government totaled $909,200,000,000. In political debate, these large numbers seem overwhelming to many citizens struggling to make ends meet, who erroneously conclude that such a huge dollar volume should be adequate if only politicians were not evil and corrupt.

3. *Heavy reliance is placed on highly visible and despised income taxes.* Compared to other nations, the United States relies heavily on individual and corporate income taxes, which constitute 42% of tax revenues for all levels of government combined. This percentage is somewhat higher for the federal government (55%) and lower for state and local government (21%). When rate structures are progressive, income taxes are the "fairest" of taxes, according to the ability to pay principle. Yet citizens do not judge income taxes to be fair. Perhaps because withholding is taken from weekly or monthly paychecks, and the process of calculating annual taxes every year by April 15 is visible and troublesome, citizens hate the income taxes more than other taxes, increasing resistance to tax hikes.

4. *The growing reliance on payroll taxes also increases resistance.* The importance of payroll taxes, mostly in the form of Social Security taxes, has been increasing in recent decades, and currently makes up over a third of revenues at the national level and a fifth at state and local levels.[33] These payroll taxes, like income taxes, are highly visible, increasing resistance, with the additional disadvantage of being regressive.

5. *Tax overlap occurs across levels of government contributing to resentment of "overtaxation."* Both the federal and state governments have separate constitutional authority to tax, and this contributes to tax overlap, especially between the federal and state governments. Considerable tax overlap exists at all three levels of government. While some specialization exists, with the federal government relying most heavily on income taxes, states on the general sales tax, and local governments on property tax, tax policy more closely resembles the "marble cake" model of federalism, rather than the neatly categorized "layer cake" image. States also tax income. Three-fourths of the states have both sales and income taxes. Some localities have a payroll tax in addition to Social Security at the federal level. Multiple governments taxing the same income or asset adds to taxpayer feelings of being overtaxed.

6. *The federal government raises the most taxes, contributing to perceptions that big government is getting bigger.* The federal government remains the "rich Uncle Sam," collecting 63% of all government revenues. The federal government appears to be the most distant and remote to citizens. Because the biggest government collects the most taxes, some citizens perceive that big government is getting bigger. Further, as concern over federal deficits has grown, intergovernmental transfers from the federal government to state and local government have shrunk. Tax revenues have been increasing at the state and local levels, partially to offset recent declines in federal grants, further contributing to perceptions that government taxing is out of control.

7. *Comparative constancy in the U.S. tax structure has increased resistance to new taxes.* The current U.S. tax structure has remained relatively constant since World War II, when the federal government substantially increased individual and corporate taxes, in part to fund the war. Changes since then, including lowering the tax rates, increasing exemptions and personal deductions, and raising payroll taxes, have not altered the basic structure of the system. The relative constancy of the tax structure made the introduction of new taxes already used in other countries, such as the value added tax (VAT), more controversial.

8. *Tax policy has been used as an instrument for stabilization and redistribution, which sometimes undercuts the goal of raising revenues to fund government.* Tax policy, particularly involving tax cuts, has been used in the past for stabilization: to increase personal savings, to stimulate investment, to reward businesses for hiring minority workers, and to reduce unemployment. Capital gains reductions were passed to stimulate investment. Tax cuts such as oil depletion allowances have had redistributive effects, rewarding some producers over others. Other tax cuts have helped one income group over others. Tax incentives have also been used to encourage energy efficiency. Sometimes proponents of these cuts argue that in the long run growth will occur and the tax base will increase, but each one of these cuts reduces the immediate tax base and undercuts the goal of producing adequate revenues to fund government.

9. *Very little progressive redistribution occurs through the tax system, so no one supports taxes because they are substantially relatively better off.* The tax system is only marginally redistributive. Depending on the assumptions made about who bears the burden of indirect taxes, the system as a whole is either proportional or mildly progressive. State and local taxes remain both regressive and less responsive to growth. Low- and middle-income groups, then, do not become better off relatively as a result of tax policy. If they did, resistance to increases in taxes might diminish. The affluent are best off from low nonredistributive taxes, since progressive taxation would hit them harder. Thus, the nonredistributive nature of the overall tax system keeps high-income groups happy with low taxes, and the lack of redistribution does not encourage low- and middle-income groups to lower tax resistance. Higher taxes

to them, in a nonredistributive system, would mean they were no better off relatively, and were worse off absolutely with lower personal disposable incomes.

10. *Citizens get little formal education about taxes and the role of government in the economy.* Despite the fact that concepts dealing with taxes are no more difficult than those dealing with calculus, finite mathematics, elementary chemistry, beginning physics, or biology, all of which are regularly taught in high schools, basic information about taxes and the role of government in the economy are often not taught. When one-fourth of all high school students drop out prior to graduation, and one-half of those graduating go into the labor force rather than immediately to college, wide exposure to tax concepts must be available in high school or even earlier grades if most citizens are to learn them. Yet taxes, the only inevitability confronting all citizens other than death, are not systematically taught. When taxes are covered, it is usually either within a civics course or in the context of a course designed to praise free enterprise and markets as the only organizing principles for economic activities. Government is often in this context excoriated as being bad and inefficient. Thus, a lack of education and biased education further bias citizens against taxes to fund government services.

IV. TAXES HAVE NEVER BEEN POPULAR

Taxes have been controversial and unpopular throughout the nation's history. Previous tax battles often pitted one group or political party against another. How revenues were raised in earlier years set the stage for tax policy debates today.

A. Early Taxes

In the nation's infancy, as now, how to raise revenues for public purposes was a hotly debated matter. While there was considerable consensus about the appropriateness of tariffs, both to provide government revenue and to protect domestic industries, varied opinions existed about other methods for raising government revenue.

Assuming the Federalists' position, Alexander Hamilton argued strongly for full repayment of Revolutionary War debt and for the use of tariffs to protect manufacturing. Manufacturing represented the future of the country in the Hamiltonian vision of it, and tariffs, despite their negative impact on consumers and southern plantations, were necessary to shield budding industries from foreign competition. The nation adhered to many of Hamilton's positions on fiscal affairs. After the 1787 constitutional convention, the federal government established the First Bank of the United States to pay off Revolutionary War debt, and in 1791 also assumed the debts of the states. Public monies in those early days were raised through customs duties and excise taxes on whiskey, carriages, snuff, sugar, and auction sales.[34]

This first tax system has been described as an economic success but a political failure. Anti-Federalist groups, disgruntled with the revenue system, contributed to the realigning election of 1800 and the election of anti-Federalist Thomas Jefferson to the presidency, after two Federalist presidents, George Washington and John Adams. Among them were farmers, consumers, and large land owners hurt by tariffs, excise taxes, and Hamilton's sound money policies.[35]

Extensive changes were made in the U.S. tax system between 1800 and the War of 1812, during the presidencies of Jefferson and James Madison. These presidents abolished excise taxes, used land taxes to encourage western settlement, and lowered tariff rates. Despite this, the strength of the economy produced substantial tariff revenues until the War of 1812 cut off trade, resulting in a reimposition of excise taxes. Tariffs remained the mainstay of federal revenues for the next hundred years, producing rare agreement between the two political parties. Democrats, in principle, often preferred lower tariffs than did Republicans, but in practice often argued for tariffs on different commodities than Republicans, depending on their respective constituencies. Increasingly, as the South grew more dependent on cotton, it grew more resistant to tariffs, so that the major differences over taxes were regional rather than partisan. Further, tariff revenues were unstable and depended on national and international trends in trade, business cycles, and wars, all largely beyond the control of the U.S. government.

B. Civil War Taxes

In the period between 1841 and 1860, preceding the Civil War, government control was divided, alternating between the Whigs and the Democrats. Democrats managed to lower tariffs early in the period, only to see them raised again when Whigs gained control of both houses of Congress. Most of the high tariffs Republicans imposed during this period remained in effect until 1892, when Democrats recaptured control of the national government.

During the Civil War, two major changes introduced into tax policy were a progressive income tax and an inheritance tax. Republicans, the wealthier partisans, supported a broad application of the income tax, but in a position that foreshadowed the modern capital gains exclusion, opposed applying it to income from stocks, bonds, and land sales. The progressive rate structure was abolished immediately after the war in 1867, and the income tax itself was abandoned in 1872.

The growing industrial elite shaped post-Civil War taxes, so that revenues fell as a proportion of GNP and heavier tax burdens were placed on consumption than on production. Excise taxes on liquor and tobacco were adopted for moral purposes, but also had a regressive impact, placing a greater burden on the poor. Neither individual nor corporate incomes were taxed. Protest from farmers and workers built up against high tariffs, hard money, and lack of credit.[36]

C.   Early Income Tax Policy: 1894–1930

Despite broad support for an income tax from populists, Republicans disagreed and were supported by a reversal of the Supreme Court on the issue. Previously judged to be constitutional, the Republican-dominated U.S. Supreme Court of the period reversed a century of precedents to rule that a tax on incomes was a direct tax and therefore was unconstitutional. Republicans remained the majority party, despite a realigning election in 1896 that changed the basic composition of each party rather than throwing out the party in power.

By the early 1900s, Republican progressives, led by Theodore Roosevelt, advocated a progressive income tax. By that time, the United States had become a net exporter and found high tariffs to be an impediment. Eventually, some conservatives also supported the Sixteenth Amendment, which allowed a progressive personal income tax, in an attempt to avert a proposed tax on corporate income. When the United States entered World War I, the income tax was already in place and was increased to fund the war effort. It soon became the major source of federal revenue, surpassing tariff revenues.

After World War I revenues subsided, but not to their original level, despite the urgings of Secretary of the Treasury Andrew Mellon—now recognized as an early advocate of supply-side economics—to reduce taxes on business and individual wealth. After the crash of 1929, President Hoover increased taxes as classical economic theory advocated to reduce a growing federal deficit. In 1930, to increase federal revenues, Congress approved the highly protectionist Smoot–Hawley Tariff, now widely credited with further depressing the economy and lengthening and deepening the depression. Discontent over these policies contributed to the realigning election of 1932 and the return of Democrats to national power.

D.   New Deal Taxes

The depression forced President Roosevelt to deficit-finance government expenditures. A payroll tax was enacted to finance Social Security on a "pay-as-you-go" basis. The tariff became a foreign policy tool largely controlled by the president, rather than a domestic policy tool that had preoccupied Congress, and by the beginning of World War II, it was no longer a significant source of federal revenue.

Despite Franklin Roosevelt's campaign rhetoric about shifting the tax burden from the lower classes to the middle class and the rich, many New Deal taxes were regressive, including the new Social Security payroll tax placed only on the first $3,000 of income and a processing tax used to fund an agricultural adjustment program at the federal level. States also passed highly regressive sales taxes during this period. Further, some experts have argued that New Deal policies actually prolonged the depression, such as the Revenue Act of 1935, which raised taxes and further slowed economic growth with little impact on income distribution.[37] Partially because New Dealers did not fully control the Congress, the Supreme Court, or state governments, the impact of New Deal policies was not as great as they hoped or as their opponents feared. Eventually, U.S. entry into World War II expunged the lingering effects of the depression.

E.   Current Taxes

Today, the federal tax system relies heavily on income taxes, but draws from other sources as well.

1. Individual Income Tax

When the income tax was first enacted, resistance to new taxes was overcome by applying the tax to a very small portion of the population; only the top 5% of the population was affected. Today, about 45% of all federal tax receipts are raised through the individual income tax, more than from any other source. While other western nations have income taxes, none emphasizes it as much in its revenue structure as the United States. Until 1981, the income tax had a progressive rate structure based on the notion that taxpayers have different abilities to pay. Progressivity has been further eroded by tax expenditures—special exemptions and exclusions—created throughout the years, as well as a significant reduction in the number of tax brackets in 1986.

Before the 1986 Tax Reform Act, the rate schedule for the personal income tax included fourteen brackets. The 1986 changes dropped the number of brackets to two, 15% and 28%, but due to changes for high-income taxpayers in personal exemptions during the phaseout, the effective high rate for a time was 33%, creating a third bracket. After the phaseout, the top bracket reverted to 28%. For taxpayers with high incomes yet low tax liabilities due to income exclusions and other tax expenditures, an alternative minimum tax must be calculated.

Taxes on wages and salaries are collected through a withholding system, first introduced in 1943. Tax payments on other sources of income must be paid in quarterly installments during the year in which the income is received. Since withholding minimizes tax cheating, some reformists have tried to apply that collection system to interest and earnings on intangible assets as well as to earned income.

Across time, taxes on earned income have constituted a greater proportion of total taxes collected from the individual income tax, indicating a greater incidence of failure to pay taxes on income derived from assets and sources other than wages and salaries. These proposed changes in collection procedures, however, have met with great political resistance by the institutions, such as banks and investment houses, that would be responsible for implementing the extended withholding system, as well as from taxpayers who have such sources of income.

In 1982, Congress extended withholding at a rate of 10% to interest and dividend payments exceeding $150 a year, with exemptions for lower-income elderly citizens. When a massive campaign against this measure was launched by banks and savings and loan associations, Congress reversed itself the next year, despite evidence that considerable revenues could be collected from taxpayers not complying with tax law. Tax politics have prevented proposals for extending withholding to earnings on intangible assets from succeeding.

The income tax has been criticized for having a deleterious affect on work incentives and savings. Pechman concludes, however, that historical trends in the U.S. labor supply do not support the view that taxes have had a significant impact on the aggregate labor supply, and that the effect of taxes on savings is even more ambiguous.[38]

2. Corporate Income Tax

First enacted in 1909, Congress levied the corporate income tax as an excise on the privilege of doing business to avoid a constitutional challenge. Congress relied on resentment to "robber baron" corporate empires to enact it. The new tax was challenged anyway, but was upheld by the U.S. Supreme Court, which agreed that the privilege of doing business could be measured by corporate profits.

The history of the corporate income tax has been one of declining importance in the overall federal revenue structure. For 17 of 28 years between 1913 and 1941, corporate income tax receipts exceeded those derived from the individual income tax. Between 1941 and 1967, the corporate income tax was the second most important source of federal revenue, behind the individual income tax. Since 1968, it has been superseded by the payroll tax financing Social Security and has fallen in importance dramatically. By 1986, it accounted for only 8% of total federal revenues, compared to 28% 30 years earlier. During that time frame, corporate tax rates have been reduced from 52% to 34% of taxable profits. The corporate income tax has a flat rate schedule, but is still complicated by the myriad of special applications for various types of businesses and business situations.

Critics of the corporate income tax have charged that its burden is actually shifted forward to consumers so that it is a consumption tax in disguise; that dividend payments to stockholders are "doubly taxed," once as retained earnings within the corporation and again as individual stockholder income; that the tax curtails business investment and retards growth; and that it has been applied in a discriminatory fashion across industries.

Supporters counter that the degree of shifting depends on how competitive markets are, and that there is little shifting in competitive markets. Further, corporations are separate legal entities with many privileges, and corporate income should accordingly be taxed separately from, and in addition to, taxing stockholder income. Supporters also argue that alternative methods of raising government revenue would harm economic growth and investment even more than the corporate income tax. Finally, the elimination of the investment tax credit and the adoption of more realistic depreciation allowances in 1987 have helped to reduce some interindustry distortion resulting from the tax.

3. Social Security Tax

The second largest source of federal revenue, payroll taxes, are used in the United States to finance the Social Security system and benefits. Resistance to this tax was initially overcome by earmarking funds for "pensionlike" benefits. Once a substantial portion of the population depended upon Social Security as a major source of retirement income, further increases in rates could be achieved, albeit with difficulty, to keep the system solvent. By 1990, the tax contribution made by individuals was scheduled to be 7.65% of earnings, up to an income ceiling set to $43,800 in 1987. The ceiling makes the tax more regressive than it otherwise would be. Employee contributions are matched by an equal contribution from the employer. Self-employed persons pay both the employee and the employer contributions.

To help reduce the burden of Social Security on low incomes, Congress has implemented limited "refundable" income tax credits for some groups. One way to reduce the system's regressivity is to remove the ceiling. Alternatively, some reformists advocate abolishing the payroll tax and financing Social Security from a progressive income tax.

4. Other Taxes

In addition to the above, the federal government levies a variety of other taxes, including excise taxes on liquor, gasoline, cigarettes, air travel, long-distance phone calls, and customs taxes. Excise taxes, in essence, are selected sales taxes. Taxes on commodities or services deemed morally or socially undesirable are sometimes called sumptuary taxes. In 1978, to promote fuel efficiency, special automobile excise taxes were imposed that varied with the fuel consumption of the vehicle to which they were applied. In 1980, a crude oil windfall profits tax was enacted.

A very small source of revenue is derived from estate and gift taxes. Applied by the federal government, the gross estate tax consists of all property owned by a decedent at the time of death, including stocks, bonds, real estate, mortgages, and personal property. After many allowable deductions, including a marriage deduction for spouses, the unified estate and gift tax rates begin at 18% on the first $10,000 of taxable transfer and rise to 50% for transfers exceeding $2.5 million. Estate and gift taxes are not broad-based mass taxes, and less than 2% of all those who died in 1985 had estates subject to the tax.

5. A Value-Added Tax?

Unlike many western nations which derive 20% to 30% of their national revenues from a VAT, the United States has not adopted such a tax. A VAT is one form of national sales tax. It is placed on the "value added" at each stage of the production process. Proponents argue that it is relatively productive in the countries where it has been used, and by being incorporated into the price as yet another cost, is largely hidden from the public. Being hidden, in turn, prevents public annoyance and resistance. Proponents further argue that it taxes consumption, or what people take out of society, rather than their income, earnings, or savings, or what they put into it. Because everyone must consume, even those engaged in underground and illegal activities, it taxes people who have previously escaped taxation. The VAT is also self-enforcing in that any attempt by a firm to push the VAT backward to suppliers or forward to consumers will be resisted by those groups, leaving the government its rightful revenue.

Opponents argue that the VAT is the equivalent of a national sales tax, and as such, is regressive. It could also raise the prices of U.S. products, making them less competitive in export markets. Furthermore, it places the heaviest burden on complex manufactured products, including high technology, whose components may change hands several times. It taxes least those services that have little turnover but constitute one of the fastest-growing sectors of the economy. Despite large federal deficits, no serious consideration of the VAT in Congress occurred through the first term of the Bush administration.

V.   DO TAXES MAKE GOVERNMENT AND DEFICITS BIGGER?

Controversy surrounds the question of whether or not taxes cause government growth and make government and eventually deficits bigger. Those concerned with deficits fear that deficits have grown as government has grown, since public expectations outstrip the capacity of taxes to pay for them. Plainly, taxes and spending are positively correlated so that both increase or decrease at about the same time, but what is the nature of the relationship? Economists disagree about whether taxes drive spending, or the reverse.[39] Milton Friedman supports the former view, contending that higher taxes do not lead to lower deficits, but rather lead to more spending and bigger government.[40] James Buchanan, Richard Wagner, and others in the public choice school argue that the manner in which the government obtains the revenues, rather than the level of the revenues, is the most important element in determining government spending.[41]

In the Buchanan-Wagner framework, raising revenues from direct taxation acts as a constraint on government spending, so that when high taxes result in high tax rates, government spending is slowed. By contrast, deficit spending and inflationary finance result in higher rates of government spending. With this latter method, citizens pay "indirect" taxes through higher interest when government financing "crowds out" private financing and through inflation. Further, the economic instability caused by the higher interest rates and inflation expands government further as it intervenes to stabilize the economy.

Related to the Buchanan-Wagner view is the argument that voters routinely underestimate their tax burdens and the cost of public services. Taxes are often hidden, either as product taxes or through withholding. This creates a fiscal illusion that also allows governments to become bigger than they otherwise would be.[42]

Disagreeing with both the Friedman and the Buchanan-Wagner theses, Robert Barro argues that higher spending forces up taxes. Nor does Barro believe that deficit spending creates a "fiscal illusion" that allows politicians to spend public funds irresponsibly.[43] Using annual data for the period from 1946 to 1983, Anderson, Wallace, and Warner find some support for this position, concluding that increases in expenditures lead to higher taxes, but not vice versa. More causal observations of the recent U.S. economy would also support this view, since the increased taxes have appeared to follow increased deficits and debt. Since generalizing from this evidence to a larger arena of circumstances may prove difficult, good minds continue to disagree.

VI.   THE OVERLAPPING REVENUE AND STABILIZATION ROLES OF TAXES

Confounding the allocation function of taxes to produce adequate revenues to fund government services is its concurrent role as a fiscal policy tool for stabilization. Tax legislation is passed by the Congress and signed into law by the president, who may place different priorities on these two roles for taxes. Both Congress and the president agree, however, that lowering taxes is politically popular, while raising taxes is political anathema. As these policy makers construct, debate, and approve new tax legislation, several stabilization aspects of taxes must be considered.

A.   The Multiplier Effect

Tax changes do not have a one-time impact, but rather reverberate throughout the economy for several iterations. Thus, tax changes have implications both for total revenues for government services and for stabilization that are far greater than their initial magnitude. Cutting taxes may have an expansionary effect far greater than the size of the initial amount by which taxes are reduced. The initial amount by which disposable income is increased from the tax cut is then respent, minus taxes, in the second round of effects. In the third round, the amount left at the end of the second round is respent, again minus taxes. The multiplier is a number that measures the size of this expansionary impact. A multiplier of 2.5 means that an initial increase in dollars in the economy will have an expansionary effect 2.5 times greater than the initial expenditures.

Similarly, a tax increase has a contractionary effect greater than the initial additional amount removed from disposable income, and that impact may also be measured by the multiplier. The value for the multiplier is determined in large part by the rate of turnover of dollars in the economy. The impact of the multiplier is influenced by both its own value and the size of the tax change.

B.   The Differential Impacts of Tax and Spending Changes

Taxation is a somewhat less precise fiscal policy tool than government spending. While policy makers can calculate spending increases and decreases in absolute dollars, presumably to obtain the desired stabilization effect, they must set tax rates rather than the absolute amount of tax dollars to be withheld from the economy or added to it. The final impact of a tax change, then, depends on several factors: the size of the rate change; the health of the economy, which influences how many taxpayers there are and their levels of income; and taxpayer attitudes toward the economic future.

Spending changes typically have a stronger impact than tax changes of the same magnitude. When spending for government purchases is increased, the entire amount of the increase is immediately pumped into the economy. When government spending is decreased, the entire amount is withheld. When taxes are increased by an identical dollar amount, however, individuals may draw down savings to initially postpone the impact of the tax increase on their disposable income, delaying and possibly reducing the fiscal policy effects of the tax increase. Similarly, when taxes are decreased by an identical dollar amount, whether or not taxpayers immediately spend the entire additional disposable income depends on their attitudes toward the future. Pessimistic taxpayers who are fearful of the economic future may choose to save a portion of the additional tax dollars, while more optimistic taxpayers may spend the entire amount, or larger portions of it. Thus, the fiscal policy effect of a tax cut is less than that of a government spending increase, because taxpayers benefiting from the tax cut may choose to save rather than spend some of their tax-cut income.

Additionally, whether the tax savings results from a one-time windfall reduction or from a permanent reduction in tax rates may affect taxpayer behavior. Many economists assume that permanent reductions have a stronger impact on consumption behavior than one-time windfalls. Temporary tax changes have some impact on spending, but are less powerful than changes expected to be permanent. This occurs because taxpayers will alter their spending habits and behavior if they think a tax cut is permanent, but not if they anticipate that it is temporary.

Even if these measurement problems did not confound prepolicy enactment calculations about the size of stimulation or contraction being introduced, changes in government spending have stronger than equivalent changes in taxes. The difference derives from the stronger first round effects of a change in government spending, where the entire amount is available for second round spending. By contrast, with a tax cut, consumers save some portion, so the entire first round is not available for second round spending.

In addition to purchases for goods and services, transfer payments made to individuals are also part of total government spending. However, these become personal disposable income, some portion of which may be saved. From the viewpoint of fiscal policy makers, the stimulative effect of a change in transfer payments to individuals is equivalent to the impact of a change in tax rates, rather than an increase or decrease in dollars spent for government purchases.

C.   The Automatic Stabilizing Effect of Taxes

Some tax and expenditure adjustments occur automatically, varying with changes in the economy. These stabilizers supplement the impacts of discretionary changes to diminish economic fluctuations induced by business cycles, and include both income taxes and transfer payments, such as unemployment compensation and welfare payments. Automatic stabilizers, then, are countercyclical in impact, and unlike discretionary tax and spending changes, do not require any action by Congress and the president to be activated.

With the federal individual income tax, the automatic stabilizing effect results from the progressive rate structure and the fact that moving up the income scale implies moving into higher marginal tax brackets, while moving down the income scale means moving into lower marginal tax brackets. The reduction in the number of tax brackets in the federal income tax code and the total progressivity of the system with the adoption of the 1986 tax cuts reduced but did not eliminate the automatic stabilizing potential of the federal income tax.

When the economy is in a recession, personal incomes decline. With the decline in personal incomes, tax burdens fall as individuals slip back to lower marginal tax rates on a progressive income tax schedule, and others either have no immediate income or fall below the income level subject to income tax. As individual tax burdens fall, total tax collections decline, leaving a higher portion of disposable income in the hands of consumers, who spend a substantial part of the additional dollars. The additional spending helps to reverse the recession and pump up the economy.

When reverse conditions prevail and the economy is becoming overheated with escalating inflation, personal incomes rise. As personal incomes rise, taxpayers automatically move into higher marginal tax brackets, where a larger portion of their personal income is paid to the government, reducing their personal disposable income. This reduction dampens personal spending somewhat, thereby reducing inflationary pressures. Reductions in federal income tax progressivity in both 1981 and 1986, leaving larger, fewer brackets and a flatter structure, have reduced the automatic stabilizing impact of taxes.

Transfer payments, such as unemployment and welfare, also serve as automatic stabilizers and vacillate countercyclically to the business cycle. With transfer payments, recession conditions typically increase the number of people who become unemployed and eligible for unemployment compensation or for welfare and other transfer payments. As the economy slumps, the stream of transfer payments automatically increases, reflecting the increase in the number of eligible recipients. The increase in total transfer payments results in more disposable income in the hands of people who otherwise would not have it, and again helps to pump up the economy. When inflationary pressures develop later as the business cycle progresses, more individuals will be working, and transfer payments will fall as the unemployment rate falls, reducing government spending.

D. Potential or High-Employment GNP

The effect of a tax change, or alternatively, of a change in government spending, is considered not only in terms of its impact on the current economy, but also in terms of its impact on a full-employment GNP. Analysts calculate whether a proposed change would result in a deficit or a surplus at full- or high-employment GNP. Two types of budget statements are available for this purpose: the official unified budget and the national income accounts budget.[44] The unified budget is the official accounting statement for the federal government, but it was not designed expressly for the purpose of calculating fiscal policy effects on the economy. The national income accounts budget was designed for this purpose, and is used to calculate full-employment budget deficits and surpluses.

Economists contend that to examine actual surpluses and deficits to determine whether or not fiscal policy is expansionary or restrictive is misleading. Rather, the impacts of proposed policy changes should be examined for the full-employment budget. If the proposed change would result in a full-employment budget surplus, it is restrictive; proposed changes that would result in full-employment budget deficits are expansionary. By this reasoning, proposed changes that result in actual deficits but in full-employment budget surpluses are not inflationary, whereas changes that result in both actual and full-employment budget deficits are inflationary. In recent years fiscal policies have been adopted that produce both types of deficits.

The strength of private demand for consumption and investment determines what fiscal policies are preferred. When private demand is weak, greater economic stimulation is needed. Fiscal policy actions including tax cuts that result in a full-employment budget deficit are appropriate. Alternatively, when private demand is strong, anti-inflationary fiscal policy is called for. Actions including tax increases that result in full-employment surpluses should be pursued.

Despite this logic, critics have argued that fiscal policy has not always been appropriately applied. Full-employment surpluses were sharply increased during the years 1959 to 1960, 1969, and 1974. These increases have been blamed for the recessions of 1960 to 1961, 1970 to 1971, and 1974 to 1975. Excess has also occurred in the opposite direction. By 1965, the full-employment surpluses were wiped out by escalating military expenditures for the Vietnam War, and full-employment deficits grew (1.1% of potential GNP in 1966, 2.4% in 1967, and 1.8% in 1968). The Federal Reserve did not employ monetary policies to offset these expansionary full-employment deficits, and decade-long inflation resulted.[45]

E. Fiscal Dividend or Drag

Both of the terms fiscal dividend and fiscal drag have been used to describe an upward creep in full-employment revenues in times of economic growth. Critics of fiscal drag argue that it is merely a concept used to justify lower taxes that are needed to fund government services. Fiscal dividend and drag result from the elastic nature of the federal tax structure—the fact that tax revenues grow faster than the tax base during expansions and shrink faster than the tax base during periods of retrenchment. The elasticity of the tax structure depends in turn on the fact that it is progressive. Both terms—fiscal dividend and fiscal drag—refer to the same fiscal policy effect. The former, fiscal dividend, refers to the additional revenues the federal government will recoup with economic growth, while the latter, fiscal drag, refers to the depressing effect extracting a larger share of the GNP in taxes will have on personal spending and on the economy.

With fiscal dividend or drag, as the economy grows, leading to growth in personal and corporate incomes, taxpayers move into higher tax brackets, automatically raising tax receipts. Inflation raises tax receipts even more since it increases money or nominal incomes, even though real incomes and purchasing power may not be rising, or may be rising more slowly.

For example, Pechman calculates that at FY 1988 income levels and tax rates, assuming an unemployment rate of 6% and an inflation rate of 4%, federal tax receipts would automatically increase by $60 billion a year, or 1.3% of GNP. This would produce a full-employment budget surplus of approximately $60 billion, minus cost-of-living adjustments in transfer payments. Assuming a 6% inflation rate produces a full-employment budget surplus of $80 billion, or 1.5% of GNP.

Some policy advocates have proposed indexing the tax system as a way of reducing fiscal drag as well as reducing the tax burden on individuals during inflationary periods. With indexing, tax brackets are expanded and exemptions and the standard deduction are increased in rough accordance with the increases in the inflation rate. Federal income tax indexing was imposed during 1985 and 1986 and was scheduled to resume in 1990. Indexing is popular with constituents by undercuts revenues available for government services.

F.   The Interface with Monetary Policy

Taxes and spending share their stabilization role with monetary policy, which also has an impact on the total amount of money in the economy at any given time and on consumer spending. Developed by the independent Federal Reserve system, monetary policy may be compatible with tax and spending policy, developed separately by Congress and the president, or may work at cross-purposes with it. Fiscal policy may be expansionary, but its impact may be partially offset by a tight, contractive monetary policy. The reverse is less common but may also occur.

Monetary policy may be used to expand the money supply to provide for easier financing of federal deficits and debt, so that federal borrowing does not use up all available capital. While centralized coordination of fiscal and monetary policy has often been discussed, their relative independence allows one to be a check on the other.

VII.   TAX POLITICS

A.   Public Resistance to Taxes and Strategies for Overcoming It

Taxes, never popular, became even less so during the 1980s. For politicians, making promises to raise taxes to fund government services as Democratic candidate Walter Mondale did in the 1984 presidential race was almost a guarantee of committing political suicide. By 1988, Republican presidential candidate George Bush gained much attention and support with his pledge "Read my lips—no new taxes," to the American people. Bush received 40 out of 50 states' electoral votes, sending a clear signal to members of Congress that proposals to increase taxes were not popular with the public and eroded ballot box power. Presidential and congressional resistance to considering new taxes during the early Bush administration persisted, despite continuing budget deficits and mounting national debt.

Resistance to tax increases and new taxes is not unique to the current era, but rather has existed throughout the nation's history. Given this resistance, timing and environmental conditions have a substantial impact on when tax increases are proposed and how large the increase is. New taxes are most likely to be proposed when the opposition party is weak and not as able to take advantage of taxpayer discontent or when there is a compelling and obvious need for new revenues. Major expansions in the income tax have coincided with wars and depressions.[46]

Another strategy used for making new taxes politically acceptable is to initially place the tax on a limited number of taxpayers and businesses, and with relatively low rates. When the federal income tax was first passed after the adoption of the Sixteenth Amendment, for example, the exemption level for the tax was so high that most people paid nothing. Even with graduated rates, the top rate was only 7% on incomes over $500,000, a bracket that affected few people in 1913.

When the income tax became the major source of funding to pay for World War I, the exemption level was reduced so that moderate-income taxpayers now had to pay, but to instill a sense of fairness and reduce resistance, rates on the wealthy were increased simultaneously. Despite a reduction in both tax rates and progressivity after World War I, the need to find revenues to fund depression-origin programs drove rates back up again. By the end of World War II, the federal income tax had shifted from being an elite tax to being a mass tax, with the result of a substantial increase in tax receipts and tax yield.

Numerous other strategies are used in proposing, passing, and successfully implementing tax increases or new taxes.[47] Among them are the following:

- Earmarking new tax revenues for politically popular causes, a strategy used with Social Security taxes and the highway trust fund
- Distributing benefits from a tax increase in popular and visible ways as broadly as possible
- Making taxes temporary, a strategy used for the income tax surcharged during the Nixon administration to counter inflation induced from spending in Vietnam and on new social programs
- Stressing accountability to the public
- Making tax increases predictable, by stressing the need to the public consistently and persistently before enactment
- Taxing the economically weak, a strategy that has resulted in a drop in the contribution corporate taxes make to total federal revenues and a rise in regressive payroll taxes and taxes on individuals.

B. Tax Politics and Income Classes

Lower-income groups spend more of their disposable income than do upper-income groups, having what economists call a higher marginal propensity to consume (MPC) and a lower marginal propensity to invest (MPI). Accordingly, tax changes concentrated on lower-income groups have been assumed by economists to have a stronger impact than those focused on upper-income groups. Little empirical evidence supports this view, however, and in fact, contrary evidence exists that the impact of a tax change on consumption is largely independent of its distribution among income groups.

Despite this, political debate over how tax reductions should be dispersed is often couched in terms of stabilization benefits to be derived, rather than in terms of the redistributive benefits to income classes, which really drive much of the politics surrounding tax changes. Democrats, for example, have sometimes argued for tax cuts for the lower and lower-middle income groups, primarily Democrat constituencies, on the stabilization grounds that the cut will be more stimulative, since lower-income groups will spend their tax savings, pumping the money into the economy rather than saving it.

Republicans, by contrast, have more commonly argued for tax cuts for the upper-middle and upper-income groups, primarily Republican constituencies, also on stabilization grounds. Republicans contend that extra disposable income for these groups will be more stimulative than extra money for lower-income groups, because upper-income groups are more likely to spend their additional dollars on consumer durables, such as cars and appliances. These types of expenditures are more stimulative to production, according to Republican logic, than equal dollar expenditures made by lower-income groups for nondurables, such as food and rent. Thus, in the politics of tax changes, rhetoric revolves around stabilization issues while motives and decision making in large part revolve around redistributive concerns.

C. Irregular and Sometimes Infrequent Evaluation of Tax Adequacy

In contrast to government spending, which would not occur without overt action by Congress and the president to pass appropriations annually, once approved, tax rates and schedules remain in place until altered. While the reevaluation and approval of budgets is frequent and regular, the reevaluation and approval of taxes is less frequent and irregular. These process differences compound the measurement difficulties mentioned earlier involved in fine-tuning the use of taxes as a component of fiscal policy. Considerable resistance usually occurs to any proposed tax change, and the fact that reevaluation of the tax code is not incorporated into regular legislative routine makes it easier for special interests to prevent revenue enhancements impacting on them personally.

One goal of the 1974 Congressional Budget Act was to include reevaluation of taxes as a component of fiscal policy into the annual budget process, as well as to more closely coordinate revenue committee activities with those of the budget and appropriations committees. This coordination was to occur through the reconciliation process, when after evaluating macroeconomic stabilization needs, existing program commitments, and requests for new funding, the budget committees were to instruct their respective revenue committees about recommended revenue needs. The revenue committees then were to find new funds in whatever fashion they viewed most appropriate. This coordinating process, however, has remained informal, and revenue committees are free to ignore or sidestep budget committee requests.

Further, the initial timing for this consultation with the revenue committees proposed in the act was unrealistic and abandoned. Initially, the reconciliation process was to occur after the second budget resolution at the end of the summer. Congress, however, did not have enough time to address reconciliation in the short period allowed, and the revenue committees did not have enough time to build the complex coalitions that increasing taxes frequently requires. After effectively abandoning the second budget resolution, the reconciliation, in the form of budget committee directives to the finance committees, was moved to late spring or early summer, shortly after the passage of the first resolution. The process, however, remains nonbinding.

D. Tax Politics and the Lengthy Tax Process

Tax policy exists in a public policy arena in which the language is often arcane, abstruse, and dry, but the impacts on both stabilization and redistribution are tremendous, and the passions run high. Since tax policy affects almost every citizen and business directly, any proposed change is highly debated and scrutinized. Many actors provide advice to the Congress on tax policy, including the legislative counsels of the House and Senate that draft tax bills, experts at the GAO and Congressional Research Service who provide analysis, and economists at the CBO who also provide studies and advice. Just as in budgeting, the decentralized lengthy structure provides many points where powerful interest groups may influence outcomes to their liking.

The Treasury Department: The development of tax bills initiated within the executive branch is supervised by the assistant secretary for tax policy within the Treasury Department. (See Table 3.) The assistant secretary for tax policy has three staffs: the offices of tax analysis to estimate the impacts of revenue changes; the office of the tax legislative counsel to provide legal analyses; and the office of the international tax counsel to examine foreign source income and foreign citizens. Work on a new tax bill begins many months, and often more than a year, before it is submitted to Congress. During this time, the assistant secretary for taxation amasses a great amount of information, impact studies, and analyses on the proposed changes, as well as keeping the White House staff informed of the progress and consulting with other government agencies.

The Joint Committee on Taxation: Along with the Joint Economic Committee, the Joint Committee on Taxation is one of two joint congressional committees established to address major and often controversial policy areas. It is involved in shaping new tax legislation, but unlike the House Ways and Means Committee and the Senate Finance Committee, the Joint Committee on Taxation is not a veto point or gate through which legislation must pass and is not directly involved in the legislative process; rather, its role is advisory.

The House Ways and Means Committee: According to Article I, Section 7 of the U.S. Constitution, all revenue bills must originate in the House of Representatives. Hence, tax bills technically begin in the House Ways and Means Committee, although the Senate carries equal weight in the tax legislative process, and often greatly alters House bills. In the late 1980s, about two-thirds of the House Ways and Means Committee members were Democrats and one-third Republicans. Ways and Means is the most powerful committee in the House, and has jurisdiction over revenue, debt, customs, trade, health, welfare, and Social Security legislation.[48] Committee members work through six subcommittees on many issues, but consider general tax legislation as a committee of the whole. After administration-sponsored tax bills are presented to the House Ways and Means Committee, usually by the secretary of the Treasury, testimony is solicited from bankers, businesspersons, lawyers, economists, and affected interest groups. Often missing from the general lineup of experts, however, are witnesses who represent the general public. Although in recent years public interest groups have been testifying on major tax bills with greater regularity, the bulk of nongovernment testimony still comes from special interests. Hearings may run for months, depending upon the amount of interest sparked by the bill. Following hearings, the committee holds markup sessions, open to the public since 1974, in which the committee makes decisions on the bill. Despite the attempts to make the markup sessions more open, secrecy still abounds. With a recorded vote to enter executive session, the committee can hold closed hearings. This practice has been

Table 3 Tax Process Actors

Executive branch actors

    Treasury Department: Analyzes tax bills and makes recommendations to the president concerning tax policy

        Internal Revenue Service: Collects federal taxes

        Office of Tax Analysis: Analyzes tax issues and makes revenue projections

        Office of the Tax Legislative Council: Reviews and approves IRS regulations

        Office of International Tax Council: Provides legal analyses for foreign source income and related issues

    Office of Management and Budget: Includes revenue estimates in its analyses and advises the president on budget-related revenue measures

    President: Must sign all revenue laws; galvanizes public opinion on tax issues

Legislative branch actors

    Joint Committee on Taxation: Advises Congress on tax issues

    House of Representatives: Initiates all revenue measures and approves tax legislation in floor debate

        House Budget Committee: Holds hearings on macro-level revenue needs, passes the first concurrent budget containing revenue targets, and sends nonbinding directives to the House Ways and Means Committee during the reconciliation process

        House Ways and Means Committee: Has jurisdiction over revenue, debt, customs, trade, health, welfare, and Social Security legislation

        House Rules Committee: Must issue a rule regulating amendments and floor debates for all legislation, including tax legislation

    Senate: Must approve all tax legislation

        Senate Budget Committee: Exercises functions parallel to those of the House Budget Committee

        Senate Finance Committee: Exercises jurisdiction over taxation, foreign trade, health, Social Security, and other financial issues

    Conference Committee: Resolves differences between House and Senate versions of tax bills, with members from each chamber voting as a unit

    Congressional Budget Office: Conducts analyses of tax-related issues, issues revenue and deficit forecasts, and issues an economic report on the impact of government taxing and spending on the state of the economy

---

increasingly common in recent years. Further, many decisions are made by party caucuses of committee members, which occur behind closed doors. The decisions made by the House Ways and Means Committee represent a confluence of partisan and nonpartisan interests. In addition to the actual bill, a committee report is generated, prepared by staff of the Joint Taxation Committee, that may approach several hundred pages in length. The report details the Ways and Means Committee's rationale for the bill, estimates its revenue impact, and provides a section-by-section analysis of the proposed changes. Minority reports of members who disagree may also be included. After committee deliberations, both the bill and the committee report are sent to the House.

The House of Representatives: Because the House is so large, it must limit and set ground rules for floor debate through the House Rules Committee to prevent the passage of bills from becoming unwieldy. Under open rules, bills may be amended on the floor, while under closed rules, they may not be amended. Open rules allow for unrelated issues to be attached as riders, and may cause the tax bill to become hostage to the politics surrounding the rider. Tax legislation typically emerges from the Rules Committee with a modified closed rule that allows separate debate and floor votes on only a limited set of amendments approved by the Ways and Means or the Rules Committee. In contrast to the committee hearings, floor debate transpires in a brief day or two. Only rarely are House Ways and Means Committee bills rejected. Rather, a vote will be held to send the bill back to the Ways and Means Committee, which is instructed to report it back out with one or more amendments appended.

The Senate Finance Committee: The counterpart to the House Ways and Means Committee, although somewhat smaller with twenty members, is the Senate Finance Committee. It exercises jurisdiction over taxation, foreign trade, health, Social Security, and other financial issues. The partisan makeup of the committee is proportionate to the strength of the two parties within the Senate. The secretary of the Treasury also appears before this committee, testifying on the House version of the tax bill. The lineup of expert witnesses before the Senate Finance Committee closely parallels, and is almost identical to, the earlier lineup before the House Ways and Means Committee. Various groups exert strong lobbying efforts here as well as before the House committee. The Senate Finance Committee usually makes major changes in the bill before reporting it to the Senate floor, and in 1982, when the House had no major bill, the Senate Finance Committee tacked its own bill onto some minor tax amendments forwarded by the House. The Senate Finance Committee also prepares a frequently lengthy committee report that has the same purpose as that of the House committee.

The Senate Floor: Discussion and action on the Senate floor is much less fettered than on the House floor. Except for debate on budget reconciliation bills, which is limited to 20 hours, the Senate has no limit on debate or amendments. While in most House floor debates the primary intent of many speakers is to establish an official record for their position, speakers addressing the Senate on pending major tax legislation may actually try to persuade and convert colleagues. Floor debate in the Senate is typically longer and more colorful than in the House, but still very technical and directed toward aspects of the bill that directly benefit or penalize specific groups. Usually amendments proposed on the floor are opposed by either the administration or the Senate Finance Committee or both and are rejected, although occasionally floor amendments survive. Bills that fail to win approval are either sent back to the Finance Committee or are abandoned.

The conference committee: In the increasingly unlikely event that the Senate passes a House tax bill unamended, it is forwarded to the president for approval. More likely, the Senate amends the House bill, making necessary a conference committee, consisting of both Democratic and Republican members from each house. Normally, the numbers from each chamber are equal, and include the senior members of the two tax committees. Usually, four or five majority party members and two or three minority party members are appointed from both the House and the Senate. When voting, each chamber votes as a unit, with the majority party controlling the unit vote. While the mission of the conference committee is to resolve the differences between the House and Senate versions of the bill, sometimes the conference committee exceeds that mandate and inserts provisions that were in neither version of the bill. In the interest of achieving a compromise that meets revenue goals, appointed conferees are usually genuinely interested in reaching an agreement, and access to conferees by interest groups may be eliminated or severely limited. The time for conference committee deliberations varies from a day to a week or two, depending on the degree of disagreement between the House and Senate versions of the bill and its size and complexity. Usually, the House and Senate delegations meet separately using a go-between, and may even deputize the delegation chairs to work out compromises and details when impasse points are reached. The conference committee bill is reported to both houses for final vote and then submitted to the president.

Presidential action: The president consults with OMB and White House advisors before deciding whether to sign or veto a major tax bill. Usually administration officials have exerted great energy and effort to have the bill amended and shaped in earlier stages to eliminate provisions that the administration cannot live with, and to include provisions that it must have. Hence, while every detail of a major tax bill is rarely to a president's liking, rarely also do presidents veto such bills. Only four major tax bills were vetoed in the past 35 years. A presidential statement usually accompanies major tax bills, expressing pleasure for approving it, taking umbrance at some of the provisions despite approving it, or explaining a presidential veto of the bill. The newly enacted tax changes may take effect immediately or be phased in gradually. The IRS gears up to administer the bill, which may include developing regulations. The length of time needed to develop administrative regulations and to fully implement the bill depends in part on its statutory specifications and complexity. In recent years, bills have been so complex that subsequent legislation to correct unforeseen errors has routinely been required.

VIII. "TAX EXPENDITURES" EXACERBATE DEFICITS

Tax expenditures lower tax revenues and exacerbate federal deficits. Tension exists between special interests that wish to chip away at the tax base (the items and income covered by taxes), creating special exemptions and exclusions for their clients and group members, and those concerned with revenue adequacy or fairness, who wish to keep the tax base from being eroded. These exemptions from the tax code are called "tax expenditures," and much of what passes for debate over tax reform is actually debate over the type, nature, and extent of tax expenditures that shall be inserted into the tax code. They benefit a large array of special interest groups, including business. Some of the biggest, such as mortgage interest deductions, benefit the middle class, as well as builders, mortgage bankers, and financiers.

Tax expenditures used to be called "tax loopholes." The term tax expenditure has come into vogue in recent decades as a less biased expression for the transfer of benefits through the tax code, but one that still emphasizes shifting money from the government to special groups. From the viewpoint of recipients, benefits received as tax expenditures are no less desirable or beneficial than benefits bestowed as transfer payments through budget expenditures.

A tax expenditure is a legal reduction in effective tax rates for certain classes of taxpayers, resulting in lower taxes. Tax expenditures create effective tax rates lower than nominal tax rates for beneficiaries, and differential effective rates for eligible taxpayers compared to noneligible taxpayers with similar incomes.

The tax expenditure budget has become an important tool for federal policy makers in judging the extent to which special exemptions have eroded the tax base. The 1974 Congressional Budget Act requires the president's budget to report tax expenditures for revenue plans contained in the federal budget.[49] In that legislation, tax expenditures are defined within the act as "revenue losses attributable to provisions of the federal tax laws which allow a special exclusion, exemption, or deduction from gross income or which provide a special credit, a preferential rate of tax, or a deferral of tax liability."

In addition to its redistributive impacts, policy makers have viewed tax expenditures as an alternative policy tool to budget expenditures, credit assistance, and regulatory instruments. At times, federal tax expenditures have encouraged such diverse activities as investment, housing, charities, municipal borrowing, and oil exploration.

Tax expenditure budgets outline the major legislative exemptions listed above, the beneficiary group, and the estimated revenue loss/size of benefit emanating from each legislative exception. While in practice full tax expenditure budgets have only been developed at the federal level, in theory they could be developed by state and local governments as well. While some fiscal notes developed for states have used some of the same analytic techniques, they have not been expanded into full tax expenditure budgets.

Initially, analyzing tax expenditures involved estimating revenue loss from provisions different from "normal tax structure." Analysts used the section of the president's budget message devoted to tax expenditures to guide them in identifying tax expenditures. Computing what the government does not collect from individuals and corporations proved difficult. Subsequently, tax expenditures have been estimated as outlay equivalents rather than as revenue losses, although revenue losses continue to be shown separately in the budget.[50]

A newer technique involves estimating tax expenditures as the outlays that would be required to provide beneficiaries with an equal after-tax income—a technique that results in higher numbers than the revenue loss procedure, since taxpayers would have to pay taxes on the higher income derived from direct budget outlays. Since both outlays and receipts are raised by the amount of the outlay equivalent, however, the federal deficit is not changed by the newer methodology.

A.   Current Federal Tax Expenditures

The 1986 Tax Reform Act lowered marginal tax rates considerably, from a maximum of 50% on individuals to a maximum of 33%. Simultaneously, the tax base was extended through the abolition of several tax expenditures. Among those removed from the tax code were interest on consumer debt, preferential treatment for capital gains, and deductions for state and local sales taxes. Tax-deductible contributions to individual retirement accounts (IRAs) were limited. Nonetheless, substantial tax expenditures remain.

Tax expenditures in 1988 were estimated at $361 billion, compared to an estimate of direct budget expenditures by the CBO of $1,069 billion. The estimated deficit for FY 1988 was $169 billion, so that tax expenditures exceeded the deficit by almost $200 billion. Put another way, eliminating tax expenditures would have eliminated the federal deficit, and additionally generated a surplus to apply toward debt reduction. Despite the drain of tax expenditures on federal revenues, the public and many politicians consider the abolition of tax expenditures to be a tax increase, rather than the elimination of some special privilege. Current tax expenditures may be categorized into three major groups.

- Personal deductions under the individual income tax, for such items as state and local income and property taxes, contributions to charity, medical expenses, and mortgage interest paid
- Exclusions from taxable income, such as interest on state and local government bonds, employee benefits, and transfer payments, including Social Security, veterans' benefits, and welfare
- Tax credits and accelerated depreciation for investment

B. Bush and Capital Gains

During his first term, President Bush pushed hard to get Congress to readopt a capital gains tax. A capital gains tax existed before it was abolished in the 1986 act. With capital gains, income gained from appreciation when capital is sold is taxed at a rate lower than ordinary income. In the past, this rate has been half of the normal income tax rate. Its reenactment would benefit corporations and affluent individuals with large capital holdings.

Proponents argued that such special treatment of capital gains was necessary to stimulate new capital investment. Opponents contended that a capital gains tax would predominantly encourage turnover among existing capital assets, and would cause large revenue losses to the Treasury, further driving up the federal deficit. By the end of Bush's presidency, opponents prevailed.

C. Income Class Preferences for Tax and Budget Expenditures

The use of tax expenditures is not class-neutral. More affluent income classes and corporations have been frequent recipients of government benefits granted through the tax code, whereas poorer income classes more commonly receive government benefits through transfer payments allocated by direct budget expenditures. Several reasons underlie this class preference as a method of receiving government benefits.

1. Low-income groups that do not pay tax do not benefit from tax expenditures. Lower-income classes do not pay much tax, since they are in lower marginal tax brackets. The lowest-income groups may fall below the income level that is a minimum for paying income tax. They are less likely to own property and benefit from mortgage interest deductions, a standard middle-class tax expenditure.
2. High-income groups have higher marginal tax rates, and therefore benefit more from exclusions and deductions than do moderate- or low-income groups. Under progressive tax systems, high-income groups receive more tax savings for every dollar shielded from taxes than do low-income groups. While the 1986 tax changes significantly reduced marginal rates on high-income groups, rates subsequently still ranged from 12% to 33%, making a tax expenditure worth almost three times as much to those in the highest bracket as to those in the lowest bracket.
3. Politically sophisticated groups prefer tax expenditures because they are less visible than direct budget expenditures and therefore are less subject to opposition. The visibility of direct budget expenditures sometimes causes them to become a target of political opposition. For example, welfare and social service expenditures are very visible, with recipients clearly identified along with the dollar amount individual beneficiaries receive, and total expenditures made for those purposes. By contrast, tax expenditures are much less visible to the public. Often identifying who and how many beneficiaries are receiving a particular tax expenditure is difficult, and may involve making assumptions about the economic behavior of recipient groups. Higher-income groups and corporations are considerably more sophisticated politically than are less educated low-income groups, and realize the advantages of low public visibility.
4. Tax codes, and the benefits transferred through them in the form of tax expenditures, continue indefinitely once enacted, since debate over existing tax expenditures is episodic and irregular. As discussed above, the tax and budget processes differ substantially in that the latter needs overt action to continue while the former continues unless there is overt action. Budget appropriations are debated annually, not only nationally, but in most states. Even states with biennial budget processes often have smaller stopgap supplemental appropriations bills in the off-budget years. Thus, every year recipients of direct expenditures must defend their budget base. Neither the federal nor state governments annually scrutinize their entire tax code in the same fashion. Tax codes and tax expenditures are scrutinized irregularly, with long periods sometimes existing between waves of tax reform. During the interim, few questions are directed toward the continued existence of tax expenditures.
5. Tax expenditures, as methods of achieving public purposes and goals, are not held to the same rigorous

standards of performance as direct budget expenditures. Direct budget expenditures are not only more visible, but are also often subject to performance evaluation studies by the executive agencies, federal departments, outside consultants, OMB, GAO, and CBO. Program failures become the object of political ridicule and public outcry. By contrast, tax expenditures are rarely subjected to rigorous evaluation studies of the same fashion applied to direct expenditures. Ineffective tax expenditures that do not achieve their stated public purpose but that do erode the tax base and lower the effective tax rate for beneficiary groups are allowed to continue with little criticism.

6.   Tax expenditures reduce overall funding for government, and hence coincide with conservative biases toward a small government with little redistribution between income classes. While some affluent taxpayers do not hold these biases, their prevalence among higher-income groups is quite common. The decided preference of high-income groups and corporations for tax expenditures over direct expenditures does not mean that the middle class never benefits from exclusions and deductions from the tax code. In particular, the middle class, as well as upper-income groups, has benefitted from the mortgage interest deduction and Social Security exclusion.

D.   The Difficulty of Measuring Who Benefits from Tax Expenditures

The difficulty of exactly measuring who benefits from tax expenditures allows them to continue, raising deficits through losses of Treasury revenues. When tax incidence or burden is not explicit, everyone feels they are personally paying too much and resists tax increases, even those on other income classes. Despite the acknowledged redistributive impacts of tax expenditures and progressive rate structures, the changes in the income distribution resulting from tax policy are harder to assess than are those of direct expenditure policy. Considerable disagreement exists about the appropriate way to measure tax structure incidence, and no single measurement comparable to the unemployment index or the consumer price index has been developed to aid politicians debating proposed tax changes. Two separate approaches have been used—deductive equilibrium analysis and empirically based inductive techniques.

1.   Equilibrium Analysis

Under this approach, supply and demand equations describing the economy are developed using an equilibrium model that assumes the economy is able to and should reach equilibrium, where supply equals demand under market competition. This model is widely accepted in economics and influences the advice economists provide policy makers. Analysts employing equilibrium analysis examine the impact of tax policy on commodity prices and equilibrium conditions. Tax incidence is measured in terms of relative changes in commodity prices for the factors of production (e.g., capital and labor). Although equilibrium analyses of tax policy are widespread and common among economists, they provide little assistance to national policy makers or the public when they try to analyze and understand the redistributive effects of proposed tax changes.

Equilibrium analyses rarely address the interesting questions that confront national policy makers. Congressmembers and their constituents might be concerned with the degree to which a proposed change in tax policy enhances horizontal equity, so that individuals with equal income are treated equally, or impacts vertical equity, so that individuals with unequal incomes are treated unequally. Is the unequal treatment progressive, so that higher-income groups pay a higher percentage of their incomes in taxes than low-income groups in accordance with the ability-to-pay principle and declining marginal utility, or is it regressive, so that low-income groups bear the greater proportionate tax burden? Are there trade-offs or incompatibilities between tax policies designed to promote the redistributive goal of greater equality and tax policies designed to promote the stabilization goals of reducing unemployment and inflation and promoting productivity and growth? Rarely do equilibrium analyses address these questions.

One reason for this failure to address questions of interest to national policy makers and their constituencies is the reluctance of economists to specify redistributive goals. While obtaining superficial agreement over the desirability of horizontal equity, consensus is by no means universal, nor is the definition. For instance, Feldstein and Musgrave have argued that the concept of horizontal equity should be reformulated in terms of utility, rather than ability to pay, or in terms of income, even though current difficulties in operationalizing utility (satisfaction) in a way that would allow meaningful interpersonal comparisons have not been resolved.[51] Phelps questioned the desirability of horizontal equity on efficiency grounds, arguing that an efficient tax system, whatever its tilt between rich and poor, would potentially want to discriminate between sources of income, depending on the ability of the sources to avoid tax incidence by shifting the burden elsewhere.[52]

Nor has the Pareto optimum evaluation criterion employed by economists in their optimal taxation literature been particularly helpful to national policy makers. This criterion specifies that any action that can increase overall satisfaction (income) without undercutting the satisfaction of a single person should be enacted. But actions that detract from a single individual's welfare either should not be enacted or should be politically negotiated. Pareto optimality implies a zero sum conflict situation in which no one person can be made better without making some other person worse off.

Despite being deeply embedded in economics, this criterion provides little practical guidance to the Congressmember who must daily confront lobbyists, special interests, political action committees, taxpayers, and corporations, each demanding special benefits in the arena of power politics. Nor does this criterion necessarily consider the desirability in terms of equity of the original distribution of income (utility), but only evaluates changes from that distribution. It implies any uncompensated individual loss in income is undesirable, without considering how wealthy the person was relative to others.

2. Empirical Estimation Techniques of Tax Incidence

Some economists have conducted empirical studies of tax incidence. These studies have also confronted problems and have been sensitive to the assumptions made. Several broad problems plaguing the empirical analyses of tax burden have been identified, including the following:

1. One difficulty is how to assess the impact of indirect taxes that are placed on things or transactions rather than on individuals, as are direct taxes. While it is reasonable to assume that the individual on whom the direct tax (such as an income or payroll tax) is placed bears the burden of paying it, who bears the burden of indirect taxes (corporate income taxes, gasoline taxes, excise and sales taxes, customs taxes, etc.) is less clear. Under certain conditions the tax burden can be shifted forward to consumers and renters, or backward to producers and suppliers so that the individual or corporation that initially pays the tax is not the unit that ultimately bears its burden. Accordingly, economists make assumptions about degrees of shifting and who bears these tax burdens, and the conclusions they make about the progressivity and regressivity of various taxes and proposed tax changes is highly dependent upon the assumptions they make.

2. A second difficulty is that tax changes do not occur in isolation, but typically are accompanied by changes in spending as well. Sorting out these two impacts is difficult when using a before and after income distribution comparison to assess tax incidence. Measures have been developed of income inequality across the distribution of income classes, especially the Gini index of inequality. Presumably a progressive tax change will result in a decrease in income inequality, while a regressive tax change will result in an increase in inequality. If there is no change in the degree of inequality, the tax change would be neutral. A common assumption employed in tax incidence studies using this approach is that governmental expenditures resulting from the tax change are distributionally neutral—a highly speculative assumption at best.[53] This assumption also ignores distortions in the labor-leisure trade-off that may be induced by the tax change, as well as tax-generated distortions in the willingness to take risks. By focusing only on the distribution of income in a particular year, this approach also ignores the life-cycle nature of income. Personal income usually increases from youth through middle age and then declines in old age; hence the distribution of population in various age cohorts may affect the before-tax and after-tax Gini coefficients, although the age-generated effect will be attributed to tax incidence. Finally, the after-tax inequality is a function of three quantities—the inequality of income before the tax, the average tax rate, and the tax progressivity. This approach fails to distinguish between reductions in inequality caused by the average tax rate and those caused by tax progressivity.[54]

3. Some economists have applied measures of inequality, such as the Gini index approach, directly to taxes paid by different income classes to measure tax burden more directly, rather than measuring tax incidence indirectly through shifts in income distribution. This approach also has several problems. The biggest is that the data on the actual taxes paid by various income groups can be collected only after a tax change has been implemented, and hence the method has limited utility when trying to assess the impact of proposed tax changes before they are implemented. While the potential taxes paid by an average taxpayer in a particular class can be calculated beforehand, such calculations do not capture how taxpayers will behave in response to the tax, and how many will alter behavior that affects taxes due

as a result of the tax change. Further, the analyst must still make assumptions about the degree to which indirect and nonpersonal taxes are shifted. Assuming competitive market conditions implies less shifting, while noncompetitive assumptions result in greater shifting. Finally, measures such as Suits's S, that apply the Gini coefficient directly to taxes, do a poor job of determining the incidence of taxes that vary in impact across different income ranges, so that the tax is progressive in some ranges and regressive or proportional in others.[55]

3. Indirect Measures of Tax Incidence

Despite the crucial role that the redistributive effects of taxes play in the development of tax changes and tax reform, easy measurement of the nature of the impact has eluded both economists and policy makers. One alternative economists have used is to measure a related concept—tax elasticity, or how fast tax revenues grow relative to the growth in the tax base, usually measured as income—as a substitute for a direct measure of tax progressivity. As discussed previously, progressive taxes are also elastic, while regressive taxes are inelastic. Employing this relationship, some economists have used measures of tax elasticity as substitute measures for tax incidence.

Yet this approach is also plagued by the difficulty of applying it to proposed tax changes before they are implemented. In the absence of better measures of redistribution, policy makers continue to respond to the pressures of special interests and constituents on an ad hoc basis when formulating and voting on tax legislation. The overall federal tax system remains only very mildly progressive. The politics of taxation often dictate that any abolition in tax expenditures, which broadens the tax base and theoretically could increase income equality, be accompanied by a diminution in average tax rates, which undercuts and neutralizes the redistributive impact of the tax system. The politics of the 1986 Tax Reform Act were played out with this trade-off.

IX. REFORMING THE TAX PROCESS

Tax revenues have been inadequate to finance government expenditures, resulting in large federal deficits. The tax process has been criticized for being long, irregular, and cumbersome. Critics contend that tax laws are unnecessarily detailed, complicated, and difficult to understand. Special interest groups and constituencies have a disproportionate impact at the expense of the general public, eroding the tax base and the revenues for government services by gaining special benefits. Tax expenditures riddle the tax code, reduce the tax base, and undermine equity.

Several reforms have been proposed to address some of these difficulties, including the following:

1. Require Congress to declare its intention with general tax policy, and allow the Treasury Department to work out the details. Only major conflicts would be brought back to the attention of the tax committees. Proponents argue that this procedure would contribute to the simplification of tax law. Critics argue that the Treasury Department is not elected, and would be just as subject to influence from special interest groups as Congress.
2. Organize commissions of experts periodically, perhaps every 5 years, to reexamine the tax code and report recommendations for legislation. Supporters contend greater use of special commissions would inject regular, detached examination of the tax code into the fiscal policy process. Critics contend that special commissions would not alter the tax legislative process within Congress or diminish the power of special interests there.
3. Reform the tax structure through sunset legislation. With sunset provisions, the tax code would expire unless reenacted much like appropriations within the budget process. In a modified form, only major tax expenditures would be subject to a time limit and expiration through sunset provisions unless reenacted. Supporters argue that this would force reevaluation and examination of revenues, relative to current needs. Critics contend it would create chaos.
4. Provide greater coordination of the taxing and spending committees within Congress. Supporters argue that this would increase accountability and diminish free spending. Critics contend that the federal programs with the greatest increases in spending—namely, Social Security and Medicare—have been within the jurisdiction of the taxing committees where responsibility for raising program revenues and approving program spending has been combined.

5.   Provide greater emphasis to the fiscal implications of tax policy. Various procedures have been suggested to accomplish this, including binding directives from the budget committees to the taxing committees. Procedural reforms, however, will not diminish the impact of special interests on tax legislation or require stabilization needs to take precedence over the distribution of benefits through the tax code.

X.   CONCLUSION

Persistent growing federal deficits have plagued economic policy makers in recent years. Critics of deficits argue that they drive up interest rates, absorb available capital from alternate uses in the private sector, and deeply mortgage future generations. Many pressures drive spending and deficits upward. The federal budget process is lengthy and complicated, reflecting fragmentation of power between Congress and the executive, as well as within Congress. In such an environment, the iron triangle consisting of various actors, all with incentives for increasing spending—congressional committees, bureaucrats administering programs, and program clienteles and beneficiaries—is alive and well. Process reforms have been instituted to try to lower deficits by making the budget process less incremental, more rational, and more efficient. While some gains have been achieved in rationalizing the complex budget process, including increasing the knowledge and expertise available to key budget actors, deficits have not been significantly lowered. Many of the pressures that force spending upward, including the potency of the iron triangle, have not changed.

Interest group politics also shape the outcomes of revenue and taxation policies, limiting their capacities to lower deficits. Public dislike of and discontent with taxes makes it very difficult for politicians to raise taxes. Strategies, such as earmarking and taxing the economically weak, may make political sense in that new needed revenues are realized that otherwise would not be available, but such strategies may run contrary to broader economic policy goals. Wide public resistance to new taxes has confounded deficit reduction efforts in recent years and contributed to mounting national debt, as well as increasing reliance on foreign capital to finance it.

Throughout the history of taxation in the United States, special interests have sought exemptions from taxes ordinarily due. Affluent individuals and businesses often benefit more from tax deductions, exemptions, and exclusions than do low-income individuals, making tax expenditures the method of choice by the wealthy for receiving public subsidies. Further, tax expenditures are reviewed episodically and infrequently, if at all, and their effectiveness is not scrutinized as stringently or as systematically as the effectiveness of program expenditures. Despite periodic reform efforts to eliminate certain tax expenditures, pressure mounts almost immediately to reinstall them into the tax code.

Tax levels and structure are deliberated in Congress with little formal required coordination with the appropriations and budget committees. Directives to the finance committees from the budget committee during reconciliation are nonbinding. Deficits are funded through greater borrowing, and debt ceilings are periodically raised to accommodate greater outstanding debt.

Various actors in the tax process contribute analyses, data, and other inputs into decision making about tax policy, but also increase decision fragmentation. In the absence of any meaningful and publicly recognizable measure of the redistributive impacts of taxes, decisions continue to be made on the basis of widely varying notions of fairness. Some aspects of the federal tax structure are countercyclical in nature, but tax policy remains an area in which interest group politics reigns, with the consequence of rising federal deficits.

NOTES

1.   U.S. Census Bureau (1993). *Statistical Abstract of the United States, 1993* Economics and Statistics Division, U.S. Department of Commerce, Washington, D.C., pp. 328, 330, 335.
2.   Ippolito, D. S. (1978). *The Budget and National Politics*, W. H. Freeman, San Francisco.
3.   Dye, T. R. (1984). *Understanding Public Policy*, Prentice-Hall, Englewood Cliffs, N.J.
4.   U.S. Census Bureau, p. 331.
5.   Rivlin, A. M., ed. (1984). *Economic Choices 1984*, the Brookings Institute, Washington, D.C.
6.   U.S. Census Bureau, p. 328.
7.   Browning, E. K. and Browning, J. M. (1983). *Public Finance and the Price System*, 2nd ed., MacMillian, New York; see also Dornbusch, R. and Fischer, S. (1981). *Macro-Economics*, 2nd ed., McGraw-Hill, New York.
8.   Mills, G. B. and Palmer, J. L., eds. (1984). *Federal Budget Policy in the 1980s*, The Urban Institute, Washington, D.C.

9. Wildavsky, A. (1984). *The Politics of the Budgetary Process*, 4th ed., Little Brown, Boston.
10. Lyden, F. J. and Lindenberg, M. (1983). *Public Budgeting in Theory and Practice*, Longman, New York.
11. LeLoup, L. T. (1977). *Budgetary Politics*, 2nd ed., King's Court Communications, Brunswick, Ohio.
12. Ippolito, D. S. (1981). *Congressional Spending*, Cornell University Press, Ithaca, N.Y.
13. Havemann, J. (1978). *Congress and the Budget*, Indiana University Press, Bloomington.
14. Wanat, J. (1978). *Introduction to Budgeting*, Duxbury Press, North Scituate, Mass.
15. Ott, D. J. and Ott, A. F. (1977). *Federal Budget Policy*, 3rd ed., the Brookings Institution, Washington, D.C.
16. Fenno, R. F. Jr. (1973). *Congressmen in Committees*, Little Brown, Boston.
17. Shuman, H. E. (1984). *Politics and the Budget: The Struggle Between the President and the Congress*, Prentice-Hall, Englewood Cliffs, N.J.,
18. Derthick, M. (1975). *Uncontrollable Spending for Social Services Grants*, the Brookings Institutions, Washington, D.C.
19. Wander, et al.
20. Musgrave, R. A. and Musgrave, P. B. (1984). *Public Finance in Theory and Practice*, 4th ed., McGraw-Hill, New York.
21. Weicher, J. C., ed. (1984). *Maintaining the Safety Net: Income Redistribution Programs in the Reagan Administration*, American Enterprise Institute, Washington, D.C.
22. Friedman, B. M. (1989). "A Deficit of Civic Courage," *N.Y. Rev.* (June 1): 23–26.
23. Schick, A. (1980). *Congress and Money: Budgeting, Spending, and Taxing*, the Urban Institute, Washington, D.C.
24. Shuman, H. E. (1988). *Politics and the Budget: The Struggle Between the President and the Congress*, 2nd ed., Prentice-Hall, Englewood Cliffs, N.J., pp. 274–301.
25. Mikesell, J. L. (1982). *Fiscal Administration: Analysis and Applications for the Public Sector*, Dorsey, Homewood, Ill.
26. Boskin, M. J. and Wildavsky, A., eds. (1982). *The Federal Budget: Economics and Politics*, Institute for Contemporary Studies, San Francisco.
27. Moore, W. S. and Penner, R. G., eds. (1980). *The Constitution and the Budget*, American Enterprise Institute, Washington, D.C.
28. Shuman, note 24, pp. 274–301.
29. Thomas, R. and Barry, J. (1990). "Bush Puts Congress in a Box by Turning Gramm-Rudman to His Advantage," *Newsweek* (Feb. 20): 20.
30. Shuman, H. E. (1992). *Politics and the Budget: The Struggle Between the President and the Congress*, 3rd ed., Prentice-Hall, Englewood Cliffs, N.J.
31. Pechman, J. A. (1987). *Federal Tax Policy*, 5th ed., the Brookings Institution, Washington, D.C.
32. U.S. Advisory Commission on Intergovernmental Relations (1988). *Significant Features of Fiscal Federalism: Volume II*, U.S. Government Printing Office, Washington, D.C., p. 64.
33. Pechman, note 31, p. 1.
34. Swanson, D. F. (1963). *The Origins of Hamilton's Fiscal Policies*, University of Florida Press, Gainesville.
35. Hansen, S. B. (1983). *The Politics of Taxation: Revenue Without Representation*, Praeger, New York.
36. Hansen, note 35, pp. 79–81.
37. Hansen, note 35, pp. 84–86.
38. Pechman, note 31, pp. 76–77.
39. Anderson, W., Wallace, M. S., and Warner, J. T. (1986). *South. Econ. J.*, *52*: 630–639.
40. Friedman, M. (1972). *An Economist's Protest*, Thomas Horton, N.J; see also Friedman (1978). *Policy Rev.* (summer): 7–14.
41. Buchanan, J. M. and Wagner, R. W. (1977). *Democracy in Deficit*, Academic Press, New York.
42. Musgrave, R. A. (1983). *Why Governments Grow: Measuring Public Sector Size*, (C. L. Taylor, ed.) Sage, Beverly Hills, Calif., pp. 50–58.
43. Barro, R. J. (1974). *J. Polit. Econ.*: 1095–1118.
44. Pechman, note 31, pp. 14–16.
45. Pechman, note 31, p. 18.
46. Rubin, I. S. (1990). *The Politics of Public Budgeting: Getting and Spending, Borrowing and Balancing*, Chatham House, Chatham, N.J., pp. 29–57.
47. Rubin, note 46.
48. Pechman, note 31, p. 45.
49. Mikesell, J. L. (1986). *Fiscal Administration: Analysis and Applications for the Public Sector*, 2nd ed., Dorsey Press, Chicago, pp. 363–365.
50. Pechman, note 31, p. 356.
51. Goetz, M. L. (1978). *South. Econ. J.*, *44*: 798–812.
52. Phelps, E. S. (1977). *Soc. Res.*, *44*: 657–667.
53. Browning, E. K. (1978). *J. Polit. Econ.*, *86*: August, 649–671; see also Bird, R. M. (1980). *Amer. Econ. Rev. Papers Proc.*, *70*: 77–81.
54. Kakwani, N. C. (1979). *Econ. J.*, *89*: 653–657.
55. Suits, D. B. (1977). *Amer. Econ. Rev.*, *67*: 747–752.

42

The Debt Burden: What You Don't See

John B. Carlson
Federal Reserve Bank of Cleveland, Cleveland, Ohio

A day doesn't pass without some public discussion of the federal deficit. Advocates of immediate deficit cutting use terms like *explosive* and *unstable* to describe the debt burden, suggesting imminent catastrophe. Others describe this as hysteria, pointing to the current performance of the economy as evidence that nothing serious is wrong. Neither view is quite right.

The deficit problem could more properly be characterized as an insidious danger, much like a slow leak in a car tire. A tire with inadequate air pressure wears much faster, but worse, it eventually becomes permanently damaged and potentially dangerous. Unfortunately, one cannot always tell whether or not a tire is damaged by looking at it from the outside. This makes it difficult to assess how soon a low tire will become dangerous; hence it's always prudent to treat the problem as urgent. One doesn't wait until an accident occurs to acquire insurance.

Similarly, the case for urgent action on the deficit is to ensure against the risk that government debt requirements will stifle private investment that is necessary for a healthy, growing economy. The current state of the economy, like the outside of the tire, doesn't reveal the problem. The unfortunate consequences of deficits will manifest themselves in the future. The insidious danger of large persistent deficits is that they are likely to reduce growth of output and to reduce our standard of living.

This chapter examines some potential problems that could be caused by large persistent deficits. It begins by identifying conditions that could lead to runaway debt. The real cost of deficits—a primary element of these conditions—is described in some detail.

Recent projections by the administration and by Congress suggest that while large deficits will persist, there is no evidence they are explosive. Nevertheless, the projected deficits will lead to a continued imbalance between domestic credit demands and private savings. The implications of this imbalance are discussed in the final section of this chapter.

I. THE POTENTIAL OF RUNAWAY DEBT

In some respects, the federal debt situation is like debt in personal finance. Early in adult life people typically build up debt for a sustained period as they purchase their first homes, furniture, appliances, and cars. During this stage, the change in a family's outstanding debt has two components: one is generated by interest payments on the past accumulation of debt—*debt service*—and the other is created by current overspending—the *primary deficit*.*

Debt service has a momentum of its own, a momentum determined by interest rates, and by the rate of

---

Adapted from *Economic Commentary* (May 1, 1985) by permission of the Federal Reserve Bank of Cleveland.

*Although debt service is sometimes defined to include repayment of principal, it is assumed here that principal due is refinanced.

increase in the individual's income. To illustrate, suppose an individual needs only to borrow an amount equal to the interest on his existing debt so that his primary deficit would be zero. If the market rate of interest were 10%, then his debt would grow 10% that year, even though his noninterest expenditures would not exceed his income. In this way, an initial level of debt would increase at a rate equal to the interest rate. The higher the interest rate, the faster the debt would accumulate and the greater would be the concern about default.

An increase in an individual's income, on the other hand, would reduce concern about his debt because it increases his ability to service the debt without further borrowing. Even if borrowing and debt service were to grow over a period, the momentum of debt service would not be problematic unless debt service were to increase persistently at a rate faster than income. An important distinction therefore is between the interest rate paid on the debt and the rate of growth in an individual's income.

This distinction is also relevant for government debt.* Much attention has been given to the issue of whether or not deficits are explosive; that is, whether or not the growth of debt service alone could overwhelm growth in the economy. The term explosive is misleading because it refers to long-term growth without limit that, like the tire with a slow leak, does not necessarily cause an immediate blowout.

The essence of the issue is simply that debt cannot grow relative to GNP without limit—and become runaway—because borrowing to finance debt service would ultimately absorb all current income in the economy. In the process, private incentives to invest would be overwhelmed by the ever-increasing credit needs of government. Conditions sufficient for runaway debt are that the level of the deficit exceed the level of interest payments and that the interest rate on government debt be greater than the growth rate of the economy.[†]

II. THE NET REAL COST OF DEBT

Most of us who have borrowed know that the nominal interest rate is not an accurate measure of the actual cost of our debts. The real cost is affected by our own marginal tax rates and by inflation. These same factors are also important in assessing the real burden of government debt.[‡] The appropriate measure of the cost of private or public debt is the interest rate adjusted for inflation and taxes.

A home mortgage provides a clear illustration of how the tax rate affects the effective interest rate an individual pays. Because an individual can write off mortgage interest as a deduction against taxable income, he offsets part of his interest payments through reduced taxes. For example, an individual in a 25% tax bracket will recoup 25% of his interest payments. The net interest rate he pays will be 25% less than the nominal interest rate on the mortgage.

Federal income taxes also reduce the effective rate that the government pays on its debt, but by a reverse process. Whereas the individual benefits by reducing his tax liability, the federal government benefits by increasing its revenues because the public pays taxes on some of the interest payments. The government recoups part of its interest payments through extra taxes that are paid on taxable interest income. A common estimate is that the marginal tax rate on government debt is about 25%. Thus, the after-tax nominal interest rate paid by government would be about 25% less than its average nominal yield.

Inflation also has an important effect on the burden of debt. To illustrate, consider someone seeking a loan in a market where the interest rate is 10%, while the expected rate of inflation is 5%. Ignoring tax advantages, the individual expects to pay a real interest rate of only 5%; that is, measured in terms of work effort or commodities sacrificed, 5% of the value of the debt will be paid in interest. If inflation actually turns out to be 7.5%, then the individual pays only 2.5% in real terms. An unanticipated increase in inflation favors the debtor over the creditor, but an unanticipated decrease in inflation favors the creditor.

---

*However, unlike the individual whose earning potential will ultimately end, government income (its revenues) can grow indefinitely at rates as fast as the economy will allow. Most estimates of potential growth of the economy exceed 2.5% annual rates. Population growth alone generally assures growth in advanced economies over long periods. Increasing productivity will account for additional gains. This seemingly endless potential for growth has made deficit spending politically attractive.

[†]These conditions are not necessary, however. Deficits could be explosive even if there is a primary surplus; that is, if the total deficit is less than interest payments. If the primary surplus were not great enough to cover growth in interest payments above trend growth in the economy, the deficit would still grow without limit relative to GNP.

[‡]The relevance of these and other factors for federal debt dynamics was presented in Tobin's discussion in *Savings and Government Policy*, Conference Series No. 25, sponsored by the Federal Reserve Bank of Boston, October 1982, pp. 126–37.

The same reasoning holds true for government debt. The nominal interest rate overstates the real cost of debt in an economy with inflation. This suggests an obvious way that a government might reduce the real cost of its debt; that is, by deliberately pursuing inflationary policies. This would only work, however, if the public could be fooled by continuous unanticipated inflation into accepting a low interest rate for government securities.

Although unanticipated increases in inflation sharply reduced the real value of federal debt in the 1970s, the government cannot count on surprises in inflation. Most economists today believe that policy makers have no advantage over the public in anticipating inflation and hence cannot adopt an inflationary strategy to reduce the real cost of debt.

Unlike individuals, the federal government has another important factor that reduces the real cost of its debt. This factor is seigniorage—the revenue earned by the government when it provides money for the economy. In early exchange economies, seigniorage was the profit taken from minting coins, usually the difference between the value of the bullion and the face value of the coin.[*]

In the modern U.S. economy, the revenue from money creation is earned by the Federal Reserve, which acquires government debt when it supplies bank reserves and Federal Reserve notes (currency)—base money. The revenue (minus relatively small and fixed expenses) is turned back to the U.S. Treasury. In effect, an increase in base money directly reduces the net cost of the federal government's outstanding debt. To obtain the net cost of government debt, one must exclude the effects of seigniorage by reducing the nominal interest rate by the proportion of government debt held by the Federal Reserve.

Taking account of all factors, the net real interest rate on government debt (r_{net}) is approximated by the following:

$$r_{net} = (1 - m)(1 - t)R - P$$

where

m = proportion of the debt monitized
t = average marginal tax rate
R = nominal interest rate
P = inflation rate

The relevant value of each factor is the equilibrium value, measured by its expected long-term average.[†]

III.   IS THE DEFICIT EXPLOSIVE?

Whether or not the deficit is explosive depends on the net real interest rate on government debt, r_{net}, and on the trend growth rate of the economy (g). If r_{net} is greater than g, and if the deficit exceeds interest payments, then, sooner or later, deficit financing required by debt service will exceed total income and output of the economy. The critical problem then is to estimate long-run average values of g and r_{net}, where determinants are all related to each other and to the real growth rate of the economy.

Although econometric forecasting models may provide reasonably reliable estimates of these variables in the short run, the models are not considered a reliable basis for long-term forecasting. Nevertheless, medium-term projections based on macroeconomic models, and on rules of thumb, may offer some indication about whether or not the deficit is on an explosive track.

Recently the Office of Management and Budget (OMB) and the Congressional Budget Office (CBO) each released a report that presented its projections of federal revenues and spending through 1990. While the

---

[*]Total revenue of government could be increased so long as the government could induce the public to hold additional coins without affecting the general price level. Stable prices, then as now, implied some constraint on seigniorage.

[†]Indexation of tax rates makes a difference here. The government recoups in tax revenues on the amount of taxes paid on the interest payments it makes on its own debt. The holders of debt report the *nominal* value of interest payments as income. Thus, the tax rates apply to the nominal yields. The real net return is approximated by factoring out the tax payments from the nominal return before subtracting inflation. Until recently, tax rates were not indexed. This meant that inflation, whether anticipated or not, pushed taxpayers into higher tax brackets. Thus, the average marginal tax rate grew relative to income. While indexation of tax rates will tend to stabilize marginal tax rates around current levels, rising real income level will still tend to raise the average marginal tax rate.

CBO projections assumed that current laws and policies would remain unchanged, the OMB based its projections on the assumption that Congress would pass the Reagan administration's current budget proposals. Neither projection indicates that the debt will become runaway. However, taken together, they indicate that a deficit reduction policy would reduce the probability of such an event.

Congressional Budget Office projections seem to suggest that the deficit borders on being *explosive,* at least over the 5-year horizon, even though output is projected to increase without interruption. Interest payments on debt rise relative to real output. However, the estimates of r_{net} tell a different story. Because r_{net} is less than g, interest payments will ultimately slow relative to GNP. Interest payments increase through 1990 only because the primary deficit adds to the stock of outstanding debt faster than the government can retire debt with its increasing revenues. Eventually, however, increases in output will be more than enough to cover interest payments on the accumulated debt. At this time, the total deficit would either stabilize or fall, relative to GNP, depending on whether or not the primary deficit were to stabilize or to fall.

The OMB deficit projections are more optimistic in that the total deficit falls relative to GNP. While the OMB published its interest payments projection only through 1988, it is apparent that a surplus would arise in the primary deficit for 1989 and beyond. Besides assuming passage of a deficit reduction policy, the OMB projections are based on an optimistic 4.0% growth trend for real GNP. This assumes a substantially faster growth in productivity than prevailed in the 1970s.

Although neither of the projections provides evidence of *explosive* deficits, both seem precariously dependent on optimistic recession-free outlooks. Such outlooks imply that future deficits would be almost exclusively structural—that is, unrelated to the business cycle. The OMB defends its trend growth assumption on historical grounds. It notes that from 1961 to 1969, the economy grew 4.6%. But this performance—the longest expansion on record—was also accompanied by accelerating inflation. Many analysts are skeptical that noninflationary economic growth can endure for so long. If a cyclical slowdown occurs in the next 3 years, it would be quite probable that the primary deficit would jump sharply, reflecting the additional spending on automatic stabilization programs and reduced revenues. The addition of such cyclical deficits would put increased pressure on credit markets, potentially leading to conditions consistent with runaway deficits.

IV. THE SHORTFALL IN DOMESTIC SAVINGS

Even if debt is not explosive, a persistent structural deficit in the neighborhood of 5% of GNP—as projected by the CBO—poses a serious threat to long-term economic growth. The danger stems from the current imbalance between domestic savings and credit demands—an imbalance that is likely to continue.

Historically, the private domestic savings rate has been stable, and impervious to the level of interest rates and credit demands of the federal government. In this situation, any large increase in federal credit demands must be met either by an increase in foreign savings (a net capital inflow) or by a decline in private credit demands.

The present concern is that federal demands will crowd out private credit demands and thereby stifle private investment. So far this has not happened because the shortfall in domestic savings has been met by a sharp increase in the net inflow of foreign savings. In the past year alone, this net inflow approached $100 billion, amounting to almost one-third of the net private domestic savings and to more than one-half the budget deficit.

Financing a large structural deficit with foreign savings is not without cost, either in the short run or in the long run. The immediate costs are clear. The net inflow of savings has encouraged a very strong dollar. The strong dollar, in turn, has made goods produced in the United States more expensive relative to goods produced abroad and thereby has contributed importantly to the record trade deficits. Thus, while the large budget deficit has not yet had a discernible adverse effect on domestic investment, it has crowded out exporters, farmers, and businesses that compete with imports.

This has put the current economic expansion in a precarious position. If the dollar were to strengthen significantly this year, the growing imbalances in the export sector could spill over into the general economy, leading to a slowdown in overall growth. What's more, the adverse impact on certain sectors of the economy would lead to additional political pressures for trade restrictions and economic relief which, in the long run, would only make the situation worse. Ironically, a slowdown in the economy would also worsen chances for substantially reducing the federal deficit.

Many analysts believe that a rapid decline in the dollar is a greater risk. This would be accompanied by a weakening in foreign savings that would put upward pressure on interest rates. At the same time, the falling dollar would also put upward pressure on the inflation rate.

The long-run costs of the deficit depend on how long the net inflow of foreign capital can be sustained. If it is to continue, holdings of U.S. assets by foreigners must grow at unprecedented rates. Most economists believe that foreign portfolios will eventually become saturated with dollar-denominated assets. The inflow of foreign savings would then cease, unless interest rates were to rise. In either case, federal credit demands would then begin to crowd out private investment. A slowdown in private investment reduces the rate at which new production techniques are adopted, thereby slowing productivity growth. This has the obvious effect of reducing potential growth and hence the standard of living relative to what it might be. A cessation of foreign savings would also lead to a fall in the dollar and to an increase in interest rates and inflation.

So far, the behavior of foreign savings has confounded forecasters throughout the recovery. Predicting when the inflow of foreign savings will cease, like predicting when an underinflated tire will become damaged, is virtually impossible. This is what makes the deficit so insidious and so dangerous.

43

Government Debt Management

Organization for Economic Cooperation and Development
Paris, France

I. INTRODUCTION

A. The Purpose of the Report and the Method of Work

The purpose of the present report has been defined in the detailed terms of reference which the Committee on Financial Markets formulated at its March 1979 meeting when—in the light of the large-scale financing problems with which many member governments were being faced—it decided to set up a temporary Ad Hoc Group of Experts on Technical Aspects of Debt Management. The Group was asked

i) to inquire into and report on characteristics of typical government debt instruments used in OECD Member countries and to compare and evaluate their advantages and disadvantages as regards borrowing costs, effects on market interest rates and related expectations of market participants, amounts which may be raised at a given moment or during a given period, maturities, principal categories of investors, degree of marketability and liquidity from the point of view of investors, and other criteria or technical features which may be of interest. Special emphasis should be given to Member countries' experiences with the introduction of new debt instruments;

ii) to inquire into and report on various techniques of selling government debt instruments and to compare and evaluate the advantages and disadvantages of these techniques as regards intermediation costs, effects on market interest rates and related expectations of market participants and amounts which can be raised at a given moment, or otherwise;

iii) to inquire into and report on Member countries' practices as regards the scheduling over time and the announcement of issues of government debt instruments other than those which are offered 'on tap' and to compare and evaluate the advantages and disadvantages of such practices as regards their impact on financial markets and on expectations of market participants.

When agreeing on the terms of reference it was understood that the mandate was flexible enough for the Group to cover other technical aspects not specifically mentioned, if the participants of the Group found this desirable.

In implementing its mandate the Group undertook as a first step a detailed fact-finding exercise on characteristics of government debt instruments utilized in OECD member countries, on techniques which these countries apply in selling such debt instruments, and on the practices regarding the timing and the announcement of individual government debt operations. In addition to this fact-finding exercise the Group's discussions were extended to review the objectives of debt management policy, the combination of debt instruments utilized and their respective roles, the main legal and institutional features affecting or constraining the use of particular debt instruments, and the ways in which debt management policy has been implemented in recent years. The reason for extending the discussions in this manner was that the Group found it necessary to receive information on the country context within which the use of particular debt

---

Adapted from *Government Debt Management*, vol. 1, "Objectives and Techniques," with the permission of OECD.

instruments and the application of particular practices regarding the selling of such instruments and the timing and announcement of debt operations had to be seen and judged. The Group considered that without such a country background material, a comparison of government borrowing and debt management practices would be misleading. An attempt will be made to present, in volume II of this report, most of this factual information in the form of synoptic tables, which are intended to facilitate the understanding of the common technical features of, and differences between, practices of OECD member countries in the field of government borrowing and debt management.

Because of the importance of the country context the Group found it difficult to deal with the second aspects of its terms of reference, namely to compare on a country-by-country basis, characteristics of debt instruments, selling techniques, and practices regarding the timing and the announcement of debt operations and to evaluate the advantages and disadvantages of these various practices from a variety of viewpoints as indicated in the terms of reference. The view was widely shared that country practices of government borrowing and debt management could only be evaluated in the context of a country taken as a whole, having due regard to debt management policy objectives pursued in the country concerned, to the legal and institutional framework within which the debt manager of each country operates and to other relevant features such as relations between the government and financial institutions and changes in the financial environment. It was understood that such comprehensive country reviews would fall outside the Group's mandate. The Group found it, on the other hand, desirable not to confine its activity to the compilation of descriptive material only, notwithstanding the usefulness of such a fact-finding exercise. It rather considered that the value of its report could be much enhanced if the information compiled in the fact-finding exercise could be amplified by exploring the technical features of some of the options available to debt managers in OECD member countries under present-day circumstances. Thus, the Group decided to discuss technical aspects of government debt management in the context of specific objectives. (See Section I.B.)

This approach to analyzing choices in the field of characteristics of debt instruments, methods of selling such instruments and practices regarding the announcement and the timing of government debt operations is in no way meant to arrive at suggested solutions to problems of debt management policies in concrete country cases. The Group considered that the formulation of recommendations in this field was not possible in a report of this nature because of the considerable differences which exist from country to country as regards objectives of debt management policy, the overall economic and financial situation, the state and the structure of financial markets, and the institutional and legal framework within which the debt manager and the other market participants operate. The analysis is more in the nature of an annotated checklist of technical points which are relevant to debt management techniques and policies. The Group hopes that a technical discussion of this kind will help to clarify the subjects for those who have an interest in an examination and evaluation of debt management policies.

In view of the Group's desire to make this report available to a wider public it was decided that the exploration of technical options should come first, in this volume, and that the results of the factual inquiry into practices of OECD member countries as regards characteristics of debt instruments, selling techniques, and the announcement and the timing of debt operations should be summarized in volume II.

The Group found it useful to set its discussions against the background of major factors which may have had an important impact on debt management techniques in recent years. On the one hand, such techniques may have been influenced by debt management policy objectives. The following section seeks to identify the main objectives which have been pursued in some, but not necessarily in all, OECD member countries in recent years and explains briefly the way in which these objectives are related to the section headings of this report. On the other hand, it appeared from the Group's discussions that changes in the financial environment have had a considerable bearing on the shaping of debt management techniques in recent years. Major features of these changes are briefly sketched out in Section C.

B.   Debt Management Policy Objectives

The Group decided to discuss technical aspects of government debt management under the following headings:

1.   Broadening the range and the distribution of government debt instruments
2.   Effective management of selling operations
3.   Efficient secondary markets for government securities

4. Minimizing borrowing costs
5. Achieving a balanced maturity structure
6. Coordination with conjunctural economic policy

In each section the following type of question will be discussed: If a country's debt manager wanted to achieve a particular objective of debt management policy, such as indicated in the section heading, which kinds of technical options in the field of characteristics of government debt instruments, selling techniques, or practices regarding the timing and the announcement of government debt operations could be considered as being relevant?

In choosing these section headings, each of which is intended to encompass a particular grouping of debt management objectives, the Group was guided by the intention to deal in an effective manner with the major objectives in this field which have played, or still play, a role in one or another member country and which have been mentioned in the Group's discussions. The purpose of this section is to comment on these objectives. It should be noted that there has been no intention to discuss in any way the question of the desirability of pursuing particular objectives or to suggest a desirable combination or hierarchy of objectives in the field of debt management. In practice, there are considerable differences from country to country as regards the number and the kinds of objectives and their ranking according to priorities which, moreover, may change in one and the same country over time with changing economic and financial conditions and related problems. It seemed to the Group that, because of such differences between countries as regards debt management policy objectives and also because of differences in the legal and institutional framework within which debt managers in different countries operate, it is only possible to produce a report of the general nature like the present one if the analysis is directed to the technical characteristics of the various aspects of debt management and if the various objectives are considered as given, though not all will play a role in all countries.

It should also be noted that in the context of this report, the term *debt management* does not only refer to a given amount of outstanding government debt; it covers also all operations which give rise to the creation of new government debt, irrespective of the purpose of such borrowing operations, whether they serve for example, to finance budget deficits, or to influence monetary conditions. Redemption techniques, which have also to do with the management of debt, are covered by the report as well. Considerations concerning the determination of the desirable size of government budget deficits are excluded from the scope of the present report. The Group decided that, because of its often complex nature the more fundamental question concerning the choice between external borrowing and domestic borrowing by the government should be excluded from the discussion in the report as well. This applies also to technical aspects of borrowing abroad because such operations take place in a totally different environment.

1. Broadening the Range and the Distribution of Government Debt Instruments

Under this heading can be grouped two basic and closely interrelated objectives of government debt management

- Covering the government's gross borrowing needs
- Ensuring continued government access, or broadening the government's access, to financial markets

These objectives are relevant particularly under conditions of very large, or sharply rising, borrowing needs when it may not be possible to cover the government's borrowing needs through recourse to traditional sources of funds for the government. The objective of covering the government's gross borrowing needs is a basic one, insofar as it is pursued by all debt managers as a matter of high priority. Gross borrowing needs may consist of requirements for financing a gap between expenditure and revenue in a given period and/or needs for refunding maturing debt. In circumstances in which, occasionally or systematically, debt management is conducted in support of monetary policy, gross borrowing needs may also include debt issues which are directed to the purpose of mopping up excess liquidity in the economy or of containing monetary expansion. In other circumstances government borrowing operations may contribute to strengthening the country's foreign exchange reserves or to financing external deficits. In yet other circumstances, government borrowing operations may serve the sole purpose of supplying institutional investors with investment outlets which are required by specific legislation. Thus, there may be considerable differences in the definition and the components of a government's gross borrowing needs. But in each case the debt manager has to pay attention to fulfilling the basic task of covering any such borrowing needs in a given period even if in the process some other objectives would have temporarily to be given less priority.

It is clear that the achievement of the objective of covering the government's gross borrowing needs requires that the debt manager strives to maintain investors' demand for government debt and thereby ensures continued or broader access to financial markets. In other words, another basic objective of debt management is the need to maintain the marketability of the government's debt instruments, or what comes to the same; to maintain the market's absorptive capacity for such instruments. The term *capacity* here refers to the continued willingness of investors in financial markets to absorb the government's paper. This consideration refers, of course, to situations where governments rely essentially on recourse to financial markets as opposed to making extensive use of mandatory investment regulations or of other financing facilities which make it possible for governments to avoid meeting the test of the market.

Broadening the range of government debt instruments may be an important requirement for achieving a number of other objectives. First of all, increasing the government's access to financial markets by broadening the distribution of government debt instruments taken as a whole may under particular circumstances only be possible by broadening the range of government debt instruments; i.e., by introducing new instruments which are specially designed to attract new investors into the market for government paper. A relatively wide range of debt instruments would, notably under conditions of relatively large borrowing requirements, also be useful or even necessary, if the debt manager wanted to take into account objectives such as minimizing borrowing costs, achieving a balanced maturity structure, minimizing an undesirable market impact of individual debt operations, maintaining orderly market conditions, or supporting the monetary authorities' interest rate policy. All these objectives just enumerated could be more easily achieved if the debt manager were flexible in the use of different types of instruments and in the timing of their issues. The most important aspect of the question of broadening the range of government debt instruments may however be that maintaining the momentum of sales of government debt to the market under changing conditions may be facilitated by a flexible use of instruments with different characteristics. As far as the Group's mandate is concerned, it should be noted that the section on broadening the range and the distribution of government debt instruments deals mainly with questions concerning characteristics of such instruments and thus covers an essential part of item *i)* of the Group's terms of reference.

2. *Effective Management of Selling Operations*

To sell government debt instruments in as an effective manner as possible is an important objective of debt management insofar as the techniques which are utilized for selling government debt and the skills with which such techniques are applied in individual debt operations may have an important bearing on the achievement of a number of other objectives of debt management. One important aspect of this complex question is that debt managers generally attempt, as a matter of continued effort, to reconcile as much as possible the following two objectives:

• To ensure the success of an issue operation in quantitative terms or to realize quantitative borrowing targets
• To obtain the lowest possible issue costs under given circumstances

When selling government debt the debt manager may also be concerned with the problem of minimizing, or avoiding altogether, any undesirable market impact, or he may want to achieve a particular desired market impact. This objective may often imply that government debt operations should not disrupt the smooth flow of funds from investors to the markets for government paper. The choice of selling techniques may, in a particular country context, also be influenced by the debt manager's longer-term objective to broaden the distribution of government debt instruments through increasing the sale of government paper to the household sector, for example. In some circumstances this latter objective may be closely related to the objective of containing monetary expansion by selling government debt to the non-bank sector.

In conducting selling operations, the debt manager may be expected to reconcile all, or several objectives mentioned, in a variety of combinations and priority settings. Thus, effective management of selling operations may mean different things in different countries or different things at different times in one and the same country. For this reason the Group considered it appropriate to discuss all aspects of selling techniques in one section instead of dealing with different aspects of these questions under different headings. This approach may be more practical and may be justified also by the experience that selling techniques cannot be changed as flexibly as certain characteristics of government debt instruments and that changes in this field require careful consideration of all relevant circumstances.

3.   Efficient Secondary Markets for Government Securities

Existence of broad and efficient secondary markets for government securities may be an important condition for facilitating the successful launching of new issues through the fixing of issue terms at adequate levels. Efficient secondary markets may be considered by the debt managers of some countries as an important condition for ensuring, also in the long run, both an effective management of selling operations and continued access by the government to financial markets. The achievement of some other objectives of debt management policy, such as smoothing bond price movements, minimizing the impact of redemption payments, or minimizing an undesirable impact on interest rates of debt operations, may also be facilitated if open market interventions can be conducted in broad and well-functioning secondary markets.

4.   Minimizing Borrowing Costs

This objective is, in comparison with the two basic objectives of covering the government's borrowing needs and ensuring continued access to financial markets, of a supplementary, or conditional, nature. There are three aspects which may receive a debt manager's attention at different degrees. Under present-day conditions the most important aspect is the debt manager's continued endeavor to obtain in each debt operation best possible issue terms under given circumstances. Since this problem arises in connection with selling operations, the Group decided to deal with this aspect of the cost question in Section III.

The second aspect is the minimization of borrowing costs in absolute terms. In countries in which interest payments on outstanding government debt have become an important item in the government's budget, this aspect may have received increasing attention. Nevertheless, it should be realized that with increased importance of other objectives, there may be less scope for the debt managers to pursue the objective of minimizing borrowing costs in absolute terms in a systematic manner. Moreover, it should be remembered that various measures which may produce optical, or short-run, cost advantages to the government may have negative effects on other borrowers, on fixed capital formation and on the effective allocation of financial and real resources so that the overall effect on the economy as a whole could be negative. Finally, there is the aspect of commissions and fees which debt managers may have to pay to financial institutions which are actively engaged in the distribution of government debt instruments to ultimate investors, or which may assist the government in the servicing of its debt.

5.   Achieving a Satisfactory Maturity Structure

This objective essentially means that a heavy bunching of maturing debt and of corresponding redemption payments and refunding operations in particular periods or on particular dates during the year should be avoided. It is clear that the greater the amount of outstanding debt and the faster its increase, the more attention the debt manager has to pay to this problem. The longer the average life of the total debt and the more balanced the distribution of maturity dates and the amounts of maturing debt, the smaller the refunding needs in a particular year, or in a particular month within each year. A balanced maturity structure could thus contribute to achieving other objectives, such as maintaining orderly market conditions and minimizing the market impact of government debt operations. It could also facilitate medium-term planning in the field of fiscal and debt management policies.

6.   Coordination with Conjunctural Economic Policy

Some countries may find it appropriate, and practical, to link, or to coordinate, debt management policy with conjunctural economic policies, notably monetary policy. Such links may be established by general guidelines according to which the debt manager, when conducting debt operations, should take into account respective objectives of conjunctural policy. In some situations such guidelines may require that the debt manager should support, or should not disturb, by his debt operations a certain interest rate policy, or debt management may be used as an instrument for influencing interest rates in a desired direction. Alternatively, the debt manager may under particular circumstances be requested to launch a major bond issue operation for the sole purpose of mopping up liquidity from the economy and sterilize it on central bank account. A still closer linkage may be obtained by arrangements under which debt management is used as a major instrument of monetary policy. Under such arrangements the debt manager's objective may be to sell sufficient amounts of government paper to domestic sectors other than the banking system in order to contain monetary expansion. In other situations it may be considered appropriate to separate responsibilities in different areas of conjunctural policy. Under such an arrangement, debt management could be required to remain as neutral as possible as regards its effects on the conjunctural situations.

7. Other Objectives of Debt Management Policy

There are a number of objectives of debt management policy which have been mentioned in the Group's discussions but which have not so far been commented upon in the present section. Some of these relate to the structure and the functioning—in the short and the longer run—of the financial system and financial markets. These are

- Broadening the bond market generally
- Improving the functioning and the efficiency of the financial system and financial markets as a whole
- Avoiding, or minimizing, disturbances in the bond market as a whole

Others are related more closely, though not necessarily solely, to social policy objectives. These are

- Promoting longer-term forms of private household savings
- Improving the distribution of income and private wealth

These five objectives are explained in detail in the following paragraphs.

8. Broadening the Bond Market Generally

This objective may be motivated by the authorities' desire to increase the supply of long-term funds in the economy generally as part of a broader policy toward promoting productive investment and growth. Alternatively, it may be interrelated with the objective of promoting longer-term forms of household savings, an objective which will be explained below. The debt manager could contribute to the achievement of this objective by broadening the market for his own bonds, a question which is dealt with in Section II.

9. Improving the Functioning and the Efficiency of the Financial System and the Financial Markets as a Whole

This objective may be viewed in the context of the aim to improve the allocation of financial resources within the economy. The debt manager could support the achievement of this objective by contributing to greater competition in the system through appropriate measures such as the introduction of new debt instruments and the application of effective selling techniques. Technical aspects of these questions are dealt with in Sections II and III.

10. Avoiding, or Minimizing, Disturbances in the Bond Market as a Whole

This objective usually implies that erratic fluctuations in bond prices which may lead to disruptions in the flow of funds from investors to the bond market, notably the new issue market, should be avoided as much as possible. This objective is sometimes formulated in terms of "maintaining orderly market conditions" or "ensuring the well-functioning of the bond market." The debt manager may be expected to contribute to the achievement of this broader objective of bond market policy by minimizing the market impact of his own debt operations or by appropriate interventions in the secondary markets for his own issues. Related technical aspects of these questions are discussed in Sections III and IV.

11. Promoting Longer-Term Forms of Private Household Savings

This objective may be motivated by the authorities' desire to increase the total supply of long-term capital in the economy. Alternatively, the objective may be related to anti-inflationary policies or to the need to contain monetary expansion. The objective may also be formulated in more general terms as promoting private household saving generally with a view to increasing total saving in the economy. The debt manager could contribute to the achievement of this objective by efforts to sell more government paper to the household sector. Technical aspects of this question are dealt with in Section II.

12. *Improving the Distribution of Income and Wealth*

This objective may be given higher priority under conditions of high inflation or when the yield curve is inverted for a prolonged period. The debt manager could contribute to the achievement of this objective by promoting the sale to small savers of debt instruments which give them an equal opportunity with larger investors of achieving returns in line with market conditions. It may also help to promote this objective if preferential tax treatment of income from such debt instruments, which generally favors savers in higher income brackets, is eliminated or limited. To attract small savers the debt manager would have to pay special attention to their preference for liquidity and capital certainty. Technical aspects of this objective are dealt with in Section II.

C. Changes in the Financial Environment

The Group found it useful to set its discussions on technical aspects of government debt management against the background of two major changes in the financial environment which have taken place over the last decade and which have had a considerable bearing on the conduct of government borrowing operations and debt management. A trend toward wider swings and greater volatility in interest rates has been observable in many countries since the late 1960s. And there have been marked shifts in the financial positions of, and the financial flows between, major sectors of the economies of many countries since the first half of the 1970s. The emergence of large government deficits is in many cases only one important feature of this latter development.

The Group had neither the time nor the mandate to study these changes and the factors behind them in any detail. The following comments are in the nature of impressions, particularly in respect of changes in investment behavior. The Group thought, nevertheless, that these points could usefully be made as they might help toward understanding of many of the problems discussed in the report and of the innovations which have taken place in debt management.

1. *Wider Swings and Greater Volatility in Interest Rates*

Wider swings and greater volatility in interest rates are probably the result of a number of interacting factors among which the more important ones may have been experiences with high inflation rates and floating exchange rates. These experiences have no doubt increased investors' and borrowers' sensitivity to changes in interest rates and inflation rates. As a result, many investors and borrowers may have become more flexible and more sophisticated in their asset and liability management. This trend may have been strongly supported by better information flows. This, in fact, may have reinforced the tendency toward wider swings and greater volatility in interest rates insofar as investor and borrower reactions to interest rate expectations often tend to enhance an underlying trend.

As far as investors are concerned, their more sophisticated investment behavior could perhaps be described as a general effort to obtain returns on financial assets which are higher than the inflation rate in the investor's home country. Often this may imply that in the short run investors try to avoid, or minimize, capital losses on fixed-interest securities in phases of rising interest rates and possibly making capital gains during periods of falling interest rates. Domestic investors who have access to international markets would, in addition, try to maximize total return including the effects of exchange rate changes.

In situations in which many investors are guided by such short-term objectives of avoiding, or minimizing, capital losses, or maximizing capital gains on fixed-interest securities, it could be expected that demand for long-term marketable bonds would be strong in phases of declining interest rates, a demand which would subside, or even turn into selling, when interest rates approach a cyclical low. During phases of uncertainty or of generally rising interest rates, investor demand would largely concentrate on short-term paper, floating rate instruments, or short-term deposits. In circumstances in which such investment behavior has become widespread, borrowers may have adjusted to the situation by becoming more flexible with regard to maturities or by introducing floating rate instruments.

Such developments toward greater volatility in interest rates have been enhanced, first, by a general trend in OECD member countries, since the mid-1960s, toward greater freedom of banks to fix interest rates on liability instruments and loans and credits; and second, by the emergence and rapid expansion of the international markets for short-, medium-, and long-term capital. These latter markets, which operate under conditions of full competition, have no doubt had an important impact on the competitive climate also on the domestic financial markets in many countries. Their existence, coupled with increased investment and borrowing opportunities in major national financial markets, and this moreover under conditions of floating exchange rates, has increased the scope for international capital flows, which at times can contribute strongly to greater volatility in interest rates.

2. Changes in Sector Financial Positions

Trends in sector financial positions in the economies of many countries since the first half of the 1970s have been generally characterized by increased imbalances which have given rise to increased financial flows between major sectors. A sharp deterioration in the government's net financial position has been a general feature of these trends. Reductions in government revenue resulting from worldwide recessionary developments after 1973, coupled with expansionary fiscal action, were a major contributing factor. Governments which in previous years had surplus, or balanced, positions turned into sizeable deficits. In other countries, already existing government deficits were largely increased. Because of generally weak economic activity in most recent years, this general situation of rather strained financial positions of governments has continued or has even been reinforced.

The financial consequences of these developments have been large increases in borrowing activities of governments, partly for financing large budget deficits but also for refunding increasing amounts of maturing debt. In some countries where the average maturity of the government's debt has become relatively short, such refunding needs, on an annual basis, have become huge indeed. Some other countries have, for the first time, become confronted with borrowing and debt management problems on a larger scale.

The generally sharp increase in the borrowing needs of governments has for a number of countries raised problems as regards the instruments which should be used and the sources which should be tapped for covering such increased financing requirements. Large-scale recourse to short-term financing was in many countries not found desirable because of fears that this could have an inflationary impact. On the other hand, the absorptive capacity of the traditional sources of long-term funds, notably of the bond markets, was often not found sufficient to meet increased financing demands from the government. Hence, the importance of the objective of many debt managers to broaden the distribution of government debt instruments partly by introducing new instruments and partly by broadening the bond markets. In some countries solutions to the increased financing problems were sought by having recourse to foreign financial markets or by diverting borrowing requirements of other sectors of the economy to such markets, thereby increasing the scope for government borrowing on the domestic financial markets. Sometimes some governments also succeeded in attracting foreign investor demand into domestically issued government debt instruments. Such financing strategies were in harmony with balance-of-payments policies in those countries which at the same time were faced with large external financing requirements, which was often the case in the period after 1973.

In countries which were able to maintain, or to quickly restore, balanced external positions, the financing task of the government was facilitated insofar as the deterioration of the government's financial position was matched by an improvement in the private sector's financial position. This could mean, depending on the country situation, any combination of increased demand for financial assets by the private sector, notably households, and reduced borrowing needs of the private sector, notably by the enterprises sector. However, even under conditions of a global matching of government deficits with private sector surpluses, financing and debt management problems may have arisen insofar as the demand for financial assets by the private sector may not fully correspond with the types of financial assets which a debt manager may prefer to offer. This problem of a mismatching of demand for, and supply of, different financial instruments may be particularly pronounced if demand for financial assets stems largely from private households, which often save to a large extent in forms which represent money and near-money. This particular feature would seem to explain why debt managers in several countries have made in recent years an increased effort to tap household sector savings directly by offering adequate instruments, a question which has received particular attention in this report.

Though the foregoing analysis is meant to be a generalization which is intended to provide some relevant background to the report which deals with technical aspects of debt management, it is thought that some features of these general trends have been observable in many countries in which government budget deficits and corresponding financing needs have become substantial in relation to the size of the economy and of the financial markets. It is obvious that debt management policies have had to adjust to such changes in the financial environment. Such adjustments have largely consisted of tailoring debt instruments more to the needs of particular investor groups. In several countries such innovations in the field of debt instruments have also been dictated by innovative behavior of other borrowers with which debt managers have had to compete in the financial markets. These various considerations concerning debt instruments should make it clear why the question of characteristics of government debt instruments has received so much attention as it does in this report.

II. BROADENING THE RANGE AND THE DISTRIBUTION OF GOVERNMENT DEBT INSTRUMENTS

A. General

The aim of broadening the range and the distribution of government debt instruments encompasses a number of important objectives of debt management policy. A government's present and future gross borrowing needs may be such that recourse to traditional sources of funds may no longer be sufficient for covering such needs and that therefore the attraction of new investor groups may have become an urgent task. The availability of a relatively wide range of different debt instruments would, moreover, increase a debt manager's scope for effectively pursuing objectives such as minimizing an undesirable market impact of debt operations, minimizing borrowing costs over the medium term, and supporting conjunctural economic policy. The achievement of these objectives could indeed be facilitated if a debt manager had at his disposal various short-, medium-, and long-term instruments which could be utilized flexibly with regard to both the amounts and the timing of issues. A wide distribution of government debt instruments, notably of marketable notes and bonds, may also be instrumental in pursuing the objective of developing broad and efficient secondary markets in such instruments. Achievement of the latter objective may be an important requirement for a successful sale of new issues, for ensuring marketability of government securities also in the long run, for maintaining orderly market conditions and a sustained supply of funds in the bond market as a whole.

The objective of broadening the distribution of government debt instruments could be approached from two angles: first, by general measures aimed at making already existing instruments more attractive to all, or several investor groups; second, by special measures aimed at increasing the government's recourse to particular investor groups. Such special measures could include the introduction of new instruments which were specially designed for particular investors and which could give the government access to sectors of the financial market which it had not tapped before. However, such a step could in a particular country context raise the more fundamental question of whether and to what extent the government should compete with other borrowers in particular segments of the financial market. Some countries may prefer a policy of limiting competition by allocating particular market segments to particular borrowing sectors. The first approach—the taking of general measures to attract all, or several, investor groups—is of particular interest in the context of the objective of broadening the distribution of marketable government notes and bonds. The technical aspects of this question will be discussed in the following Section II.B. The second approach—the taking of special measures aimed at increasing the government's recourse to particular investor groups—will be dealt with in Section II.C.

B. Broadening the Market for Government Bonds

This section deals with the question whether and to what extent particular characteristics of marketable government bonds and notes may be considered as being suitable for broadening the market for government bonds or for maintaining the momentum of sales of such paper during phases of difficult market situations. The technical aspects which will be examined concern essentially interest rates and their flexibility, maturities and related options of the issuer or the holder, redemption features and techniques, exchange features, tax features, and the use of government bonds under mandatory or prudential investment regulations. It should be noted that some of the technical questions concerning flexibility in interest rates and flexibility in maturities or maturity features, redemption features, and exchange features are closely interrelated and hence could be discussed under one or the other heading. An attempt has been made to avoid repetition as much as possible when these interrelated features are examined.

It should also be noted, in relation to the discussion of technical aspects of the question of broadening the market for government bonds, that some problems are dealt with in other sections of the report. This applies in particular to measures aimed at maintaining orderly market conditions, or aimed at developing, or maintaining, efficient secondary markets which are important from the point of view of liquidity features of government bonds. The question of using appropriate selling techniques is also discussed in another section.

Before starting the discussion of these various technical features, it may be worth noting that none of the characteristics to be examined could be considered as substitutes for an adequate yield which needs to be offered to investors if a debt manager aims at an effective broadening of the government bond market or at widening the distribution of government debt instruments generally. It seems obvious that the task of selling government bonds under conditions of rather volatile interest rates requires that the debt manager is sufficiently flexible in setting the yields of new issues so that they are attractive to investors. The question of how this could be done technically in different market situations and with due account being taken of interest rate expectations, will be discussed in Section III, which deals with selling techniques. The present section examines interest rate features in a more technical sense, and concentrates on the question of how interest rates could be made more flexible during the life of a bond issue.

1.   Flexibility in Interest Rates

Under conditions of increased volatility in interest rates, the debt manager could make an attempt to contribute to a broadening of the government bond market, or to promoting the sale of government bonds under difficult market conditions, or to forestalling a shortening in maturities, by making interest rates on medium- or long-term bond issues more flexible. In this way the scope for a decline in bond prices in phases of rising interest rates could be reduced, which in turn could make such bonds more attractive to investors than bonds with coupon rates which are fixed for the whole life of the issue. There are essentially two different ways of providing flexibility of interest rates on government bonds. In the first case, the interest rate is variable and may be tied to another interest rate or an interest rate index, or to another indicator such as a price index. In this case the development of the interest rate could not be known in advance. In the second case, some flexibility in interest rates would be obtained by fixing in advance different coupon rates for different phases of the whole life of a bond issue. As this technique is closely related to the question of flexibility in maturities it will be discussed under that heading. This section thus deals only with the first approach to rendering interest rates on government bonds flexible.

Interest rates on government bonds could be made flexible by linking the coupon rate of interest to other interest rates, such as a specific money market interest rate, the central bank discount rate, or a specific bond yield index, thereby introducing what is customarily called a "floating rate" of "variable rate" note or bond. This feature could improve the attraction of government bonds because this would enable investors to benefit to some extent from a rise in short-term interest rates with less exposure to book losses on the capital. However, much depends in this regard on the way in which the link with short-term interest rates is technically implemented, for example, whether the reference interest rate is calculated as an average over a specified period preceding the interest rate adjustment date, or whether actual market rates prevailing at the time of the adjustment serve as reference rates. Important also is the interval at which interest rates are adjustable. The longer these intervals the greater the scope for bond prices to deviate from par and the smaller the chance for the investor to benefit from rapid increases to short-term interest rates. Vis-à-vis competing short-term instruments a "floating rate" government bond or note could be made more attractive by applying a relatively high minimum rate of interest below which the coupon rate on a bond could not fall. However, such a feature could not prevent a variable rate instrument from becoming less attractive to investors in phases of falling interest rates when longer-term instruments with fixed interest rates provide a chance for capital gains.

Whether and to what extent a debt manager may want to make use of variable interest rate notes or bonds may depend on a number of other circumstances. If in a particular country context such instruments were particularly attractive to commercial banks the debt manager of that country could wish to make no, or only limited, use of them because a large-scale recourse by the government to the banking system may not be desirable from a monetary policy point of view. Another reason for not introducing this instrument may be the authorities' fear that its utilization on a larger scale could contribute to even greater volatility in interest rates. However, if a debt manager held the view that greater flexibility in interest rates could contribute to maintaining the momentum of sales of government bonds during phases of market difficulties he might want to have such an instrument at his disposal at least for occasional use. In such a case the use of floating-rate instruments would be an alternative to relying on short-term debt and might help to avoid the liquidity effects or the shortening of the average maturity of the public debt which would result from the latter.

2. Flexibility in Maturities

In a particular country context a debt manager may be faced with the situation that with an experience of greater volatility and wider swings in interest rates investor preferences regarding maturities of marketable bonds and notes change considerably over the interest rate cycle and that, in addition, there are considerable differences in this regard between different categories of investors. In pursuing the objective of broadening the market for government bonds or maintaining a relatively high level of sales of such paper under conditions of uncertainty the debt manager may wish to take into account such differences in maturity preferences over time or as between different types of investors. This could be done, technically speaking, in different ways, depending in part on the issuing technique which is being applied. If the technique of public offerings during a short subscription period were used the debt manager could offer a package of several maturities, for example, a short-term paper in the 1-to-3-year maturity range, a medium-term paper in the 4-to-8-year range and a long-term paper with maturities of over 10 or 15 years. If it were difficult to assess the market situation for each maturity class and fix the offering yields accordingly, an advantage may be seen in leaving the issue amounts open so that they could be determined by the market. If for one reason or another it were preferable to fix and announce to the market, the overall amount which the debt manager wanted to raise through a particular debt operation—the technique of firm underwriting would require this in any case—the distribution of the total among the different maturity tranches could nevertheless be determined by the market, a feature which could facilitate the placing of the overall issue amount.

Under conditions of changing market sentiment and corresponding shifts in maturity preferences a debt manager may find it suitable to meet changing demand for different maturities by offering a range of notes and bonds with different maturities for sale over a period and by adjusting their issue yields in the light of changes in secondary market conditions and in line with quantitative selling intentions. Another approach to satisfying the demand for different maturities under rapidly changing market conditions could be the organization of regular auctions at which offering amounts and the corresponding issue terms for different maturity types would be determined as a function of the bids received.

It could be argued that changing investor demand for different maturities could be more easily met through the existence of broad secondary markets in which a whole range of securities with different residual maturities may be traded. However, this condition could only be fulfilled if the amount of outstanding government debt were already substantial and if the total debt were sufficiently diversified as regards the maturity distribution.

Some flexibility in maturities could also be obtained by offering to the holder of a particular government bond issue certain options regarding final maturity. The debt manager may offer a bond issue with a relatively long maturity of, for example, 25 years. But the holder may be allowed to ask for early redemption after a shorter period of, for example, 5 or 10 years; or, after an initial period of say 5 years, on any subsequent interest payment date. Thus, the total life of a bond issue could be split up into two or more subperiods during which, moreover, coupon rates of interest could be different, which would provide also some flexibility to interest rates, as has already been mentioned in the previous section.

The debt manager could also issue a bond with a relatively short maturity of say, 5 years and could offer to the holder the option to extend the holding for another 5-year period; or—what would come to the same—to exchange the bond into a new bond with the same or another maturity. The exchange conditions would be fixed in advance. The bond to be acquired could be an entirely new issue, the terms of which were however fixed, and hence known by the holder, in advance, or, in order to enhance its marketability, it could, with regard to the coupon rate of interest and the final maturity, correspond to an issue which was already in the market. This former feature differs from an arrangement according to which a bond holder may be allowed to use a maturing bond as payment for a new issue which is being offered on, or near, the maturity date, but the conditions of which are not set until the time of exchange. (See Section II.B.4.)

Both types of option features regarding the final maturities could help to sell government bonds in an environment of uncertainty about future interest rate developments when borrowers and investors are likely to have conflicting objectives as regards maturities in which they want to borrow or invest. Investors have the option of early redemption if market rates on the option date are better than the rate they could earn if they extended their bond holding. If alternatively they extend their bond holdings, the debt manager's future financing task will be reduced. If the majority of investors opt in favor of extending their bond holdings the debt manager may find that such an extension turns out ex post to be more costly than a new issue at that time, but equally he may have sold the original bond, with the option to convert, more cheaply than he could have sold an equivalent bond at that time without the option. As far as investor attitudes are concerned, the exercising of their options may be made more difficult if the period of notice which they are required to give is relatively lengthy. In such a case investors cannot be entirely sure about the interest rate constellation prevailing at the moment when the early repayment, or the extension, becomes effective.

Options regarding final maturity which can be exercised by bondholders should be distinguished from those which enable only the issuer to redeem a bond before final maturity. Such early-call provisions would enable him to replace a high-coupon issue by one with a lower coupon several years before final maturity if market conditions made this desirable and possible. From the point of view of promoting the sale of government bonds in difficult market situations it would, however, not seem preferable to use such call clauses as they would increase the investors' uncertainty regarding the final maturity of the bond in question. If the debt manager wanted to make use of such clauses despite such investor aversion against them he might have to "sweeten" the issue by offering either a corresponding redemption premium or comparatively better issue terms.

3. Redemption Features

The question for discussion in this paragraph is whether particular investor groups have preferences regarding redemption techniques and hence whether particular redemption techniques are more suitable than others for promoting the sale of government bonds. For purposes of this discussion it may be sufficient to distinguish between the following redemption features. One criterion for distinction is the timing of the redemption payments whether the whole amount is repaid in a lump sum at the end of the maturity or whether redemption payments are spread over several years and are made in regular, or irregular, installments. Another criterion for distinction is the value at which an issue, or parts of it, are repaid, whether redemptions are made at par, or at some other predetermined price, or whether the debt manager repurchases an issue in the open market at the prevailing market price. Finally, it seems to be important whether and to what extent the market is informed of redemption payments if the debt manager operates an annual purchase fund for an issue.

It is conceivable that some investors have a preference for the spreading of redemption payments over the life of a bond issue because they may expect that such periodic repayments will have a support effect on bond prices in a depressed market situation. With a view to meeting such a preference the debt manager could make use of a provision according to which he would repurchase in the open market annually a relatively small percentage of an issue, for example, up to 5% of the total issue amount provided that the issue in question were quoted below par. In the case of lump sum redemptions at final maturity, such effects on bond prices could, of course, also be achieved if the debt manager made corresponding interventions which in principle would not consist of redemption payments. Some investors may have an interest in bonds which are redeemed by annual drawings at par value to the extent that such bonds may provide a chance for rather important and quick capital gains, which is the case if such bonds are traded in the secondary market substantially below par. In general, in determining redemption features the debt manager will need to have regard to the preferences of the investors to whom he is seeking to sell bonds and the established practice in the market. In addition, considerations concerning the administrative and technical handling of a large amount of debt and the planning of a balanced maturity structure may also be important, notably when borrowing needs are very high. From a purely administrative point of view lump sum redemptions at final maturity may be preferable to other redemption techniques though the administrative problems may be alleviated if a book entry system is in place. Similar administrative considerations may lead institutional investors to prefer lump sum redemptions.

4. Exchange Features

A provision according to which a bondholder has the option to ask for early redemption or to exchange a bond against another one on predetermined conditions thereby extending his holding, has already been discussed in the section on flexibility in maturities. The question for discussion here is whether investors would find an advantage in being entitled to use a maturing bond as payment for acquiring a newly offered bond, the terms of which are not known long before the opening of the issue. It is indeed conceivable that such an exchange feature would enhance the attraction of bonds because bondholders can be sure to receive a new bond if they so wish. This may be considered as an advantage in issues where the total amount is announced, notably in a situation when heavy oversubscription of a particular issue, and hence a sharply reduced allotment, is very likely. It is conceivable that under such conditions there is heavy trading in the maturing issue immediately before the opening of the new issue into which the old issue may be exchanged.

5.   Taxation Features

If the broadening of the market for government bonds and a corresponding promotion of the sale of such paper were an urgent task a debt manager could envisage making use of special tax features. The income from government bonds could be made tax-free, or could be taxed at preferential rates. A more powerful measure would be to permit the deduction from taxable income of—possibly limited—amounts which were invested in government bonds. In designing such measures a debt manager would, however, probably wish to take into account any implications which such a step could have for the bond market as a whole. He may also be concerned with the overall cost effects.

With the introduction of such measures the bond market would most likely be initially segmented in favor of government bonds. However, under conditions of well-functioning secondary markets, interest rates in the two segments of the market would probably adjust in such a way that after-tax yields would be more or less in line, which would mean that gross yields on nongovernment issues would be higher than otherwise. Whether such a development would entail some crowding out of issuers, other than the government, would depend on a number of other circumstances. In viewing this problem it should be taken into account that government borrowing could lead to some crowding out also if no use were made of special tax features, simply through aggressive bidding for funds. The effect of such tax features would essentially be to pass part of the cost of government borrowing on to other borrowers, whether or not financial crowding out can be said to take place. It is unlikely that such taxation features in themselves, would lead to crowding out; they would merely affect the manner in which crowding out occurs. As far as overall cost effects are concerned the debt manager would have to take into account that preferential tax treatment of income from government bonds would reduce government revenue which would have to be compared with any interest cost saving. If a debt manager wanted to limit any such undesirable effects which could result from a preferential tax treatment of government bonds he could consider to limit the tax privileges in a suitable way, for example, by limiting the annual amount of individual tax-free income from government bonds or by using relatively low rates of withholding taxes on such income.

6.   Mandatory Investment and Prudential Regulations

The sale of government bonds could be supported by the introduction of mandatory investment and/or prudential regulations which could be imposed on banks and other financial institutions. However, this would not necessarily result in a broadening of the "true" market for government bonds. Much would depend in this regard on the importance of the amounts held under such regulations in relation to the total size of the government bond market, and on the interest rates which would be applied. If the debt manager would use compulsory investment regulations with a view to raising funds at below-market interest rates there could result considerable distortions in the bond market as a whole. Interest rates in the markets for "noneligible" bonds would tend to be higher than they would be in the absence of such regulations, partly because institutional investors, which would be subject to compulsory investments at below-market rates, would attempt to obtain correspondingly higher returns on their "free" assets, partly because borrowers other than the government would tend to bid up interest rates in the "free" markets for funds. Such effects would be essentially similar to those arising out of using special tax features. Any such distorting effects could be reduced if the debt manager issued the bonds which were eligible under mandatory investment and/or prudential regulations in the open market at competitive interest rates. If there were to develop some differential between interest rates on eligible and noneligible paper, the debt manager could aim at reducing it by increasing the supply of government bonds considerably beyond the needs arising from such regulations.

C.   Increasing the Government's Recourse to Particular Investor Groups

1.   General

The preceding section dealt with measures designed to broaden the government bond market, without special reference to particular investor groups. Various characteristics of bonds were discussed from the point of view of the question whether and to what extent they could be suitable for attracting new investors of whatever category. The present section examines in more detail the question whether and to what extent the characteristics not only of bonds but also of other types of government debt instruments could be designed to meet special preferences of particular investor groups, notably of private households, but also of nonfinancial enterprises, nonbank financial institutions, and commercial banks. The question of attracting foreign investors has been excluded from the present report.

As far as policy objectives are concerned, which could be pursued by increasing the government's recourse to various sectors of the economy, it is recalled that many countries have been faced in recent years with the problem of covering large borrowing needs for budget deficit financing and refunding purposes and that under such conditions governments could be interested in exploring more systematically possibilities for broadening the distribution of government debt instruments within particular sectors of the economy by attempting to meet particular investor preferences with greater precision than before.

The question of increasing the recourse to household sector savings may deserve special attention in this context for several reasons. Savings from the household sector represent a most important pool of loanable funds; and in some countries they have increased in recent years quite substantially, not only in absolute, but also in relative terms, for example, as a ratio of gross domestic product. Under such circumstances the government, as a major borrower, may wish to secure an adequate share in direct access to the supply of funds from this sector instead of relying too heavily on those financial institutions which operate as intermediaries for household funds. A government may also be interested in increasing its recourse to household sector savings in the context of monetary policy in that it may attempt to contain monetary expansion by selling government paper to the household sector. Other objectives that may be pursued by promoting the sale of government debt instruments to the household sector may be the promotion of saving in the economy generally or promoting the formation of long-term capital for financing real investment. Sometimes the promotion of household saving may also be motivated by social policy considerations, such as favoring wealth formation or safeguarding the financial position of retired people.

The following section deals with the main technical points which have to be clarified if a debt manager intends to increase his direct recourse to household sector savings. Questions concerning characteristics of nonmarketable instruments receive special attention. The relatively long section on private households is followed by brief sections dealing with questions concerning the debt manager's recourse to nonfinancial enterprises, nonbank financial institutions, and commercial banks. It should be noted that the present section does not discuss questions relating to selling techniques though the method of selling government debt instruments may be of considerable importance in the context of the objective of broadening the distribution of such instruments. For more details of this aspect of the question, the reader is referred to Section III, which deals especially with selling techniques.

2. Increasing the Recourse to the Household Sector

a. General.   If a debt manager intended to attract additional funds from private households either by selling more government paper to those who hold already such paper, or by attracting new savers, he would have to offer instruments which can easily compete with instruments offered by other borrowers, notably banks, and which meet essential investment preferences of this particular investor group. Typically, savers in the household sector tend to be strongly risk-averse and thus attach importance to liquidity and capital certainty as well as to competitive after-tax yields. Investment preferences may vary considerably within this broad sector depending on the income level and the saving capacity of each household, and on the experience which savers may have gained in dealing with investment matters in an inflationary environment. Relatively inexperienced and uninformed savers would normally have a strong preference for instruments which combine a high degree of liquidity with no, or little, risk of capital losses and may be less sensitive to interest rate differentials vis-à-vis other savings instruments. However, under the influence of rising inflation rates and more volatile interest rates many savers may have become better informed, developed more sophisticated investment patterns, and become more interest rate sensitive. Such savers may also have become aware of opportunities for capital gains arising in connection with falling interest rates, and may, accordingly, also see more clearly the risks of capital losses which exist at times of uncertainty or of generally rising interest rates.

In designing new instruments for attracting additional funds from the household sector, the debt manager would have to take into account the degree of experience in investment matters exhibited by private savers in his country and would have to identify which segment of the household sector, in terms of sophistication, interest-rate sensitivity, and risk aversion, he was seeking to tap. Accordingly, he would have to take a first basic decision which concerns the choice between a nonmarketable and a marketable instrument. These two main options will be examined in the present section. Particular attention will be paid to characteristics of nonmarketable instruments. The discussion of marketable instruments will be kept relatively short, because some choices regarding characteristics of marketable instruments have already been examined in the preceding section, which deals with the problem of broadening the government bond market.

b.   *Nonmarketable Government Securities for Private Savers.*   Nonmarketable instruments are by definition instruments which cannot be traded on a secondary market and which can therefore not be subject to any capital losses which otherwise would arise in connection with rising interest rates. Thus, nonmarketable instruments appear to be particularly suitable for risk-averse investors. Nonmarketability, however, implies at the same time that the paper cannot be mobilized on a secondary market. If a debt manager wanted to meet special liquidity preferences of private savers, he could do so only by providing the holder with the right to return the paper to the issuer for redemption at any time, possibly after expiration of a specified initial waiting period. The provision of such particular liquidity features would not pose any problems for the debt manager if such paper were essentially held by savers who are not particularly interest-rate sensitive, or as long as interest rates on such instruments were to remain competitive.

The possibility for the saver to request premature redemption may, however, turn out to become a considerable drawback for the debt manager if substantial amounts of such paper were held by more interest-rate sensitive savers and if yields on such paper were to get out of line with yields obtainable on competing instruments. If this were to happen under conditions of rapidly increasing interest rates, the debt manager could indeed be faced with sizeable backflows of such paper just at a time when it is usually difficult to raise funds in financial markets. This raises not only the question of what the debt manager could do in order to forestall premature redemptions on a massive scale; a more important and more fundamental question in this context is whether a nonmarketable government debt instrument can be designed in such a way that it can be effectively used for attracting additional funds from private households also under conditions of volatile interest rates and of much increased interest-rate sensitivity on the part of private savers. The question of flexibility of interest rates on nonmarketable debt instruments which will be discussed in the following paragraphs, is of prime importance in this regard. Other characteristics which could also contribute to increasing the attraction of such paper for private savers and which could thus provide a disincentive against premature redemption, will be considered subsequently.

The question of greater flexibility of interest rates on nonmarketable government debt instruments concerns both new issues and outstanding amounts of earlier issues. At the new issue stage interest rates on nonmarketable paper could be made more flexible by changing the series of paper to be offered every time when a change in the market situation makes this desirable, so that issue terms could remain attractive vis-à-vis competing instruments. An essential condition for implementing such a flexible issuing policy is that the paper in question is issued "on tap" or at relatively short intervals and that the related decision-making processes and the administrative and technical procedures involved can be handled effectively so that the replacement of one series of nonmarketable paper by another can take place within a relatively short time. This may be difficult to achieve if the paper in question is being distributed to the general public through a wide network of banks and bank branches. However, the application of modern communication and computer techniques and the use of "book-entry" securities could greatly facilitate such an issuing practice. Difficulties in this regard may arise if a large number of private savers still insist on the delivery of definitive bonds.

However, achieving greater flexibility of interest rates on new issues of nonmarketable government paper would not solve the problem of discouraging holders of older series of such paper from requesting premature reimbursement if they felt that the yields earned on such paper were out of line with yields obtainable elsewhere. Thus, the question arises in which way interest rates on outstanding amounts of already issued nonmarketable paper could be made more flexible. Three solutions seem possible

- Holders of older series with inadequate yields could be permitted to exchange these holdings against new issues offering higher yields
- Holders of older series could receive special bonus payments
- Interest rates on new issues and older series are the same and could be changed simultaneously in line with market conditions

These three techniques are briefly considered in turn.

The first solution would have the drawback that it could become very costly because of the increased commissions which the debt manager would have to pay to banks and other financial institutions which operate as the debt manager's sales agents. Unless special arrangements were made, these sales agents would receive the same commission irrespective of the fact whether a newly issued paper were sold in exchange for paper from an older series or not. Under the second approach investors could receive every year, in addition to the original coupon rate of interest, a bonus payment which would bring total interest earnings in line with market yields. However, such a practice, if applying retroactively, could encounter difficulties if it were regarded as inequitable as compared with the treatment of holders of other government debt instruments. In addition, holders would not be flexible as regards the timing of eventual requests for early redemption unless they were prepared to forego the bonus payment for a particular year. A system under which such bonus payments are fixed in advance and are progressively increased is discussed further below.

The third solution-applying the same interest rates on new issues and older series simultaneously—would correspond to a principle which is often used for remunerating savings accounts. From an administrative point of view the problems would be the same as those with which banks which manage large numbers of savings accounts, are faced. Modern computer techniques could facilitate such a task. It could be argued against this solution that it could become very costly at times of strongly rising interest rates. However, by the same token it could be argued that, in phases of declining interest rates, total costs of borrowing would go down accordingly, unless it were politically difficult to reduce interest rates on such an instrument which were especially designed for small savers. In judging the borrowing cost question, a debt manager would have to have regard of possible alternatives and of the risk of massive return flows of older issues, which could take place if interest rates on older issues were getting out of line with market yields.

An index-linked nonmarketable government debt instrument would be a special form of such a variable interest rate paper described in the preceding paragraph. Instead of fixing the variable interest rate in line with other market rates, the return on index-linked government paper could consist of a relatively low coupon rate of interest to which a variable rate of interest which would correspond to the rate of inflation—measured in a suitable way—would be added. Whether such index features would attract large amounts of additional savings from private households would depend on yields obtainable on alternative savings instruments. It is conceivable that in particular market situations the expected real return from instruments which are not index-linked could be higher than the known real return offered by index-linked instruments. If a debt manager were reluctant to introduce index linking on a larger scale because of fear of the repercussions which such a step could have on the financial system, or because of problems of tax treatment, he could consider limiting its use by applying relatively low ceilings on individual holdings of such paper.

If the debt manager were reluctant to introduce flexible interest rates on both new issues and outstanding amounts of older series of nonmarketable paper he could consider to reduce the scope for premature redemptions of such paper by applying a relatively long initial waiting period during which early redemption were not possible. A disincentive against early redemption could also be provided by not paying interest during the first year, or first half-year, in the case of early redemption during such an initial period. This latter feature could be considered as a special form of a scheme of progressive interest rates; i.e., a scheme which provides that interest rates rise with each successive year of investment. Whether such a device would provide an incentive for a saver to hold the instrument until the yield reaches its final level depends very much on the way in which the scale of progressive interest rates fits with interest rates obtainable on competitive instruments. The yield after 3 years could, for example, be set close to interest rates paid on 3-year savings or time deposits if it were an aim to attract savers with such an investment horizon. The yield on say 5 years could be fixed slightly below yields obtainable on 5-year government bonds. The negative yield differential vis-à-vis the latter could be justified by the argument that a nonmarketable instrument is not exposed to the risk of a capital loss. On the other hand, it could of course also be argued that a nonmarketable instrument does not provide the chance of a capital gain in phases of declining interest rates, which would be an argument in favor of setting yields on nonmarketable instruments above yields of marketable instruments with similar maturities, at least in a situation when a decline in interest rates is likely.

Instead of offering relatively favorable interest rates on nonmarketable instruments in comparison to yields on instruments issued by other borrowers, the debt manager could try to attract household savings and forestall premature redemptions by providing favorable tax features, for example, by leaving the interest income from such instruments tax-free, or by applying lower than normal tax rates. The cost aspects of such features are discussed in Section V. Whether the debt manager would achieve his objective of attracting additional funds from the household sector would depend very much on the reactions of other borrowers as regards the fixing of yields on comparable instruments offered by them. It should also be taken into account that any such privileged tax treatment would tend to favor savers in higher income brackets. Small savers would benefit relatively less, or not at all, from such features. Any such distorting effects could be limited by applying ceilings to the amounts which individuals could invest in such paper overall, or on an annual basis.

Other characteristics which a debt manager may consider when designing nonmarketable instruments for sale to private savers concern the way in which interest should be paid and the choice of final maturities. As far as interest payments are concerned, there may be differences in investor preferences. Some savers who have an interest in receiving current investment income may prefer annual payments of interest. Other investors may find it particularly attractive to receive interest in cumulative form to be paid together with the invested capital amount at the moment of redemption. The debt manager could meet such preferences by offering two different types of paper which take account of these preferences. As far as final maturities are concerned, it is possible that such conditions of relatively volatile interest rates private savers have certain preference for medium-term rather than long-term paper. Much depends in this regard on tradition, on experiences in past years and on competing instruments offered by other borrowers. The fixing of maturities has little operational value for either the debt manager or the saver as long as the latter is entitled to return the paper to the issuer at any time. The maturity question may, nevertheless, be important in connection with the setting of offering terms if it were the debt manager's intention to fix the issue yield in relation to yields obtainable on competing instruments.

c. *Marketable Government Securities for Private Savers.*   In planning measures to increase his direct access to household savings the debt manager may also explore ways and means of making marketable securities more attractive to private savers or he may reconsider present market practices which may so far have prevented individuals from acquiring particular instruments. As far as longer-term bonds are concerned it is conceivable that some private individuals would be attracted by "deep discount" bonds; i.e., bonds with relatively low coupon rates of interest offered at a relatively low issue price. In this way, the overall issue yield would contain a relatively important capital gain element which the investor would receive at the moment of redemption. At the same time the current income element would be relatively low. The balance between current income and capital gain will vary significantly with the maturity of the bond. An extreme case of this technique would be a full discount paper, which would not provide any current interest income, a feature which has already been mentioned in the section which deals with nonmarketable government debt instruments. Some private savers may see an advantage in the accumulation of interest insofar as the problem of reinvesting earnings would not arise. "Deep" or "full" discount paper is probably most attractive if interest rates are perceived to be exceptionally high. Under particular taxation arrangements concerning the treatment of capital gains there may be an additional advantage for private savers in higher income brackets insofar as the after-tax yield on deep discount or full discount paper may be higher than on paper with higher coupon rates offering the same gross yield.

It is conceivable that some private investors would also be attracted by the issue of lottery, or premium, bonds. Such bonds would not earn regular interest. The interest amounts on the issue taken as a whole would be distributed annually in the form of prizes which were to be drawn by lottery. Such gambling features may appeal to some private savers, notably if the prizes to be gained were subject to some preferential tax treatment.

The debt manager could also consider the question whether he should make an attempt to attract household savings in liquid form through the issue of short-term paper with maturities of less than 1 year. It is conceivable that, notably in periods of relatively high and rising interest rates, such instruments would be rather attractive to individuals who would thus be enabled to benefit from money market interest rates which in periods of tight monetary conditions tend to be considerably higher than interest rates on more traditional savings instruments. Such a step would, however, raise the more fundamental question whether and to what extent the debt manager should compete with banks and other savings institutions in the field of collecting small and liquid savings. In considering this question the debt manager would have to take into account that for selling any type of securities to small savers he would have to use banks and other financial institutions as sales agents, a fact which could make it difficult, or costly, to arrive at satisfactory arrangements for selling short-term paper to a large number of savers. The debt manager may also be reluctant to attract liquid savings of households on a larger scale because this could increase the government's short-term debt to an extent which may be undesirable. Uncertainties regarding interest costs which are involved in rolling over a high volume of short-term debt could become unacceptably great.

It is obvious that the denomination size of individual government securities which can be acquired by investors is an important feature by which the debt manager can influence the demand for government securities as regards the participation of different types of investors. If the debt manager wants to deal only with institutional investors he will offer only paper with relatively large denominations. If he has an interest in a wide distribution of government paper among the general public including small savers the minimum denomination of individual debt instruments should be reduced to relatively small amounts.

3. Increasing the Recourse to Nonfinancial Enterprises

A debt manager who is faced with substantial financing problems may wish to consider possibilities for attracting funds from the corporate sector. The question for discussion here is whether corporate treasurers have special investment preferences from their cash management point of view which the debt manager would have to take into account if he wanted to have greater direct access to the financial resources of the corporate sector. It could be assumed that corporations have generally a relatively high liquidity preference and that they would be mainly interested in buying government paper with relatively short maturities. If such short-term government paper were eligible for secondary liquidity reserve requirements of commercial banks it could however turn out that interest rates on such instruments were not competitive with rates on other money market instruments. In order to make government paper more attractive to corporate treasurers under such conditions the debt manager might have to consider the introduction of similar instruments which were not eligible for secondary liquidity reserve purposes of banks. Or, the debt manager could attempt to raise interest rates to competitive levels by increasing the supply of such paper substantially beyond the needs of financial institutions.

It may, however, be more convenient for the debt manager to compete directly with the banking system and to offer to corporate treasurers instruments which correspond fully, or in essential parts, with time deposits or certificates of deposits. In this context it may be an important consideration that corporate treasurers may have a preference for investment facilities which they can use in a flexible manner depending on the particularities of their cash flow, which may show fairly irregular patterns except for payments of wages and salaries and taxes which are usually payable on predetermined dates. Such special liquidity needs may often be met by time deposits held with commercial banks which fall due on the specific dates when such large foreseeable payments have to be made. If the debt manager wanted to compete with the commercial banks in this field he would have to offer investment facilities which give corresponding freedom in the choice of maturity dates and which, moreover, could be extended to allow the investment of odd amounts. These facilities could take the form of regular issues of short-term paper or private placements. Alternatively, corporations could be offered the opportunity to hold deposit balances with the government, which, in addition, could be debited with any tax liabilities when they fall due. From a purely technical point of view it would not seem that the management of such accounts would raise more problems for the debt manager than the administration of a computerized book-entry system for government securities. The introduction of facilities of this nature would however raise the same basic question as has already been discussed in the section on increasing the recourse to the household sector, namely whether and to what extent the debt manager should compete with the banking system in the field of short-term investment opportunities.

4. Increasing the Recourse to Nonbank Financial Institutions

The question for discussion in this section is whether nonbank financial institutions, notably insurance companies and pension funds, which have typically long-term liabilities, have in recent years developed particular investment preferences which the debt manager would have to take into account if he wanted to increase his recourse to this sector of the financial system. It seems that, at least in some countries, these investors, like other investors, have also become more sensitive to greater volatility in interest rates and bond prices. This may have led these institutions to some extent to turn to a more active management of their liquidity reserves or of parts of their portfolios in an attempt to improve the overall return on their assets. In this connection some institutions may have also become more attracted by short- and medium-term securities. Related questions and problems have already been discussed in other parts of the report, notably in Section II.B.

The bulk of the investment demand of insurance companies and pension funds still seems to be concentrated on longer-term instruments because the liabilities of these institutions have remained of a long-term nature. What could have changed in some companies in recent years with the experience of greater volatility and wider swings in interest rates is the appearance of a certain aversion against marketable long-term government bonds as these could give rise to substantial capital losses. Thus, there could have developed some increased preference for nonmarketable instruments insofar as capital losses on such paper cannot be established by reference to changes in secondary market quotations. However, much would depend in this regard on accounting regulations and practices. If nonmarketable instruments such as direct loans would not be subject to valuation changes for accounting purposes, and if the institutions in question were allowed, under prudential regulations, to acquire relatively important amounts of nonmarketable instruments, the debt manager could indeed attempt to increase his recourse to these institutions by offering such instruments which would be more in the nature of loans rather than securities. Such private loans, or loans against promissory notes, could to some extent be tailored to the needs of the investors as far as maturity dates and redemption features are concerned. Placing procedures could also be simplified if the instruments in question were to be offered to a relatively limited number of large institutional investors, and issue terms could thus be determined by way of direct negotiation, which may, however, not necessarily be an advantage from the debt manager's point of view. More generally, it is conceivable that such close and direct contacts between the debt manager and single institutional investors were politically not acceptable. In such a case, the debt manager would have to find ways and means of inviting such investors to submit their bids under competitive conditions, possibly by applying an auction technique.

5. *Increasing the Recourse to the Banking System*

It is not the intention to deal in this section with all aspects of government borrowing from the banking system, the more so as some related questions have already been discussed in Section II.B. The question addressed here is a rather special one, namely whether a debt manager could increase his recourse to the banking system by offering instruments which are less liquid than marketable instruments and the acquisition of which would, therefore, not improve the liquid asset position of an individual bank in the same way as if a bank would acquire short-term marketable paper. It is indeed conceivable that the government could make use of ordinary bank loans in the same way as private enterprises. Banks might be interested in acquiring within certain limits medium-term claims on the government which, like ordinary bank loans, would not give rise to capital losses resulting from valuation changes, and which would offer an adequate return. The attraction of such instruments to banks could possibly be increased if such claims could be transferred once or twice to other banks or institutional investors, and if interest rates could be made flexible in the same way as in the case of "variable rate" notes. Increasing the government's recourse to the banking system in this way could require closer and more direct contacts between the debt manager and the banks than existed before. However, once such contacts were established it would seem possible for the debt manager to use this source of finance in a flexible way for raising large amounts at very short notice and without any cumbersome formalities and procedures.

III. EFFECTIVE MANAGEMENT OF SELLING OPERATIONS

A. Relations to Debt Management Policy Objectives

The techniques which are used for selling government debt instruments and the skills with which such techniques are applied in individual debt operations may have an important bearing on the achievement of a number of debt management policy objectives. When selling government debt instruments the debt manager may, first of all, be concerned with the problem of reconciling the two following objectives:

- To ensure the success of an issue operation in quantitative terms
- To obtain the lowest issue costs under given circumstances

One question for discussion in this section is how different selling techniques may be used for dealing with this problem of realizing specific quantitative borrowing targets, while at the same time obtaining lowest possible issue costs. It should be noted that this problem could, to some extent, be approached by flexibility in the use of different instruments and in the timing of corresponding issue operations. The scope for flexibility in this regard is, however, reduced if the government's financing requirements are substantial. The need for funds may be such that the debt manager has to issue debt instruments almost continuously or at relatively short intervals.

When selling government debt instruments, the debt manager may also be concerned with the problem of minimizing, or avoiding altogether, any undesirable market impact, or he may want to achieve a particular desired market impact. This objective could imply that government debt operations should not disrupt the smooth functioning of financial markets. Rapid and wide fluctuations in bond prices could have undesirable effects on the flow of funds from investors to the market for government paper or to the bond market generally. In an environment of uncertainty or of rising interest rates, sharp downward movements in bond prices could disrupt the supply of funds on the bond market, which in turn could reinforce the drop in bond prices. At times of sharp upward movements in bond prices there could be an undesirably strong rush into the bond market, which could unduly accelerate the decline in interest rates. This could eventually produce a setback in the market when those investors who operate on a relatively short investment horizon, turn to sizeable sales of government paper, or other bonds, in order to realize capital gains. The debt manager could be expected to contribute to avoiding such fluctuations through an appropriate choice of selling techniques, debt instruments, and timing of issues, or through appropriate secondary market interventions.

In this context, it should be noted that government debt operations may have an impact on interest rates and bond prices at three stages. The announcement of a borrowing program, or of an individual debt operation, may affect market expectations as regards future interest rate developments and may cause corresponding reactions on the part of investors. The opening of an issue, in those cases where the debt manager fixes the issue terms, or the setting of issue terms on "tap issues" may have certain signal, or surprise, effects on the market which may produce desirable, or undesirable, reactions on the part of the investors. Finally, the result of a particular government debt operation may have a desirable, or undesirable, impact on the behavior of investors and hence on interest rates and bond prices. Related commentary by the specialized press and other observers of the market are often an additional factor affecting market sentiment and investor behavior.

The question of the choice and use of selling techniques may also be relevant in the context of other objectives, such as broadening the distribution of government debt instruments, or supporting monetary policy. As far as the first objective is concerned, it could be argued that in some circumstances the institutional organization of a network of agents which are authorized to sell government debt instruments is also important in this context. Publicity is also an important factor by which the sale of government paper to a wide range of investors could be effectively promoted. As regards the objective of supporting monetary policy, some countries place emphasis on selling government debt outside the banking system as a means of controlling monetary aggregates, in which case monetary policy objectives may have an important influence on the choice of selling techniques. Other countries may place emphasis on interest rate objectives, but will equally be concerned to utilize appropriate selling techniques.

In conducting selling operations, the debt manager may be held to reconcile all, or several, objectives mentioned, in combinations and priority settings which may differ from country to country, or which may change over time in one and the same country. Thus, he may attempt, at the same time, to realize a particular quantitative borrowing target in a given period or with an individual borrowing operation, to obtain the lowest possible issue costs and to avoid an undesirable, or achieve a desirable, impact on interest rates.

B.   The Relevance of Market Conditions

Under favorble conditions, it may be possible to accomplish such a reconciliation of objectives to a considerable degree. This would, however, require—irrespective of the selling technique which were to be used—a realistic assessment of the market situation at the time when the debt operations were to take place. The debt manager could arrive at such an assessment through various forms of contacts with the market. Possibilities for such contacts may range widely from formal arrangements, such as regular meetings with an advisory committee on capital market issues to informal and personal contacts between the debt manager and bankers or security dealers. Such direct contacts and consultations could be an important factor contributing to an effective management of selling operations, in the sense of reaching a high degree of reconciliation of different objectives through a realistic assessment of the market situation. The debt manager's opportunities for being currently informed of market developments would be much enhanced if he, or an agent acting on his behalf, were present in the over-the-counter market or at the stock exchange.

Under conditions of uncertainty and volatile interest rates it is, however, difficult for the debt manager to arrive at a realistic assessment of the market situation and, moreover, to anticipate market movements and reactions at the moment when an issue is being offered. In the case of an unanticipated increase in interest rates, a given quantitative borrowing target may not be realized through sales in the market, if the issue yield is not changed in line with the market movements. If, in such a situation, the debt manager has to rely entirely on support from the market, he may opt for one of the two extremes unless he chooses to withdraw the issue; to leave the issue yield unchanged and accept a smaller than originally intended issue amount, or to leave the issue amount unchanged and accept a correspondingly higher issue yield. In practice he may most often attempt to steer a course between the two extremes just mentioned by adjusting both variables: amount and issue yield.

Under conditions of falling interest rates when it is easier to realize quantitative borrowing targets, the debt manager may be faced with a conflict between the objective of seeking lowest possible issue yields and the other objective of moderating the decline in interest rates. If there were an unanticipated further decline in interest rates at the moment when a new issue was being offered, an adjustment to the new market conditions could be made in several ways. The debt market could stick to the originally fixed issue yield and increase the issue amount. If he did not do this, he might have to ration the allotment of the issue, for example, on a pro rata basis, possibly giving special treatment to small investors. Alternatively, the debt manager could stick to the originally intended issue amount and lower the issue yield in line with the market movement. Finally, he could make adjustments to both amount and issue yield. If the aim of moderating the interest decline received priority, he would have to adopt the first solution, namely, to increase the issue amount. This would, however, be in conflict with the objective of obtaining lowest possible issue terms. If the latter objective received priority, the debt manager would in an extreme case wait with the launching of new issues until interest rates were approaching the lower turning point.

C. Other Factors Affecting the Choice of Selling Techniques

There may be some other factors which could affect a debt manager's choice regarding selling techniques which could differ from country to country, depending on a number of institutional and structural features of a country's financial system and financial markets. Thus, a debt manager may find it appropriate to apply different selling techniques to different instruments depending on the categories of investors who are the main buyers of the instrument in question, whether a given instrument is to be widely distributed among numerous small investors who tend to buy relatively small amounts, or whether the bulk of a given instrument is to be sold to a relatively small number of institutional investors. Another factor which may have a bearing on the debt manager's choice regarding selling techniques is the role of the banks in the functioning of the securities markets and the relationship between the debt manager and the banks or security dealer firms. If the debt manager depends largely on such institutions in selling government debt instruments, he will also depend on them as regards the use of particular selling techniques. Any changes in this field would require close cooperation with the banks and security dealer firms.

A final factor which could affect the choice regarding selling techniques is the size of the financing task which the debt manager may have to accomplish, whether gross financing needs are relatively small so that they could easily be covered by occasional issues of one or another instrument; or whether financing requirements are so large that the debt manager has to come to the market almost continuously or at relatively short intervals. In the discussion which follows in this chapter, it is generally assumed that the financing needs are relatively large and that, accordingly, the volume of new issues of government debt instruments is important. Most of the arguments used will refer to marketable government securities unless indicated otherwise. Before starting the discussion, it will be necessary to give some detail on the essential technical features of the main categories of selling techniques.

D. Main Features of Alternative Selling Techniques

With a view to simplifying the discussion, selling techniques will be grouped, and discussed, under the following broad headings:

- Selling government securities on a fixed-yield basis during a relatively short subscription period
- Selling government securities by an auction technique
- Selling government securities "on tap"; i.e., on a continuous basis

Any combinations and variants of these techniques will be mentioned under these headings as may be appropriate.

The main features of the three broad categories of selling techniques may be usefully described as follows:

1. New issues are sold on a fixed-yield basis during a relatively short subscription period.

a.   Issue conditions are negotiated with an issuing consortium which guarantees the placing of the issue (firm underwriting); the issue amount has to be announced.

b.   Issue conditions are fixed by the debt manager after consultations with banks and security dealers which act as sales agents; the placing of the issue is not guaranteed by the sales agents (no firm underwriting); the issue amount may, or may not, be announced.

2.   New issues are sold via an auction technique. New issue yields are determined on the basis of competitive bids from the participants in the auction who indicate the amounts they wish to acquire and the price they are prepared to pay at a given coupon rate of interest, or the yield they are prepared to accept, if no coupon rate is fixed.

On the basis of the bids thus received, the debt manager may either determine the amount he wants to raise and accepts passively the issue yield associated with this amount; or, he decides on the issue yield he is prepared to offer and accepts passively the amounts of the bids which are associated with that issue yield. As far as the determination of total issue costs is concerned, a distinction would have to be made between:

a.   The uniform price (yield) auction which is sometimes called the "Dutch" auction.

b.   The "conventional" auction; i.e., an auction technique which does not apply a uniform allotment price.

In the case of the uniform price auction all successful bidders pay the same price, the uniform auction price, which is the lowest price at which bids are accepted with a view to reaching the intended issue amount. This price is also called the "stop-out" price. In the "uniform yield auction" successful bidders pay the price which is associated with the highest yield at which bids are accepted.

In the case of a "conventional" acution, the competitive bidders—i.e., bidders which state a tender price or a tender yield—pay the price they bid (case of price auction), or they pay the price which is associated with the yield they bid (case of yield auction).

The choice between the uniform price (yield) auction and the conventional auction has implications for the treatment of noncompetitive bidders, as regards the price (yield) which applies to them. (Noncompetitive bidders are those who indicate only the amount of an issue they want to acquire; they do not tender a price or yield.) In the case of the uniform price (yield) auction, noncompetitive bidders pay the same uniform price as the other bidders. In the case of the conventional auction, noncompetitive bidders pay the weighted average price of all accepted competitive bids, which in fact corresponds to total issue costs as expressed in a single issue price and issue yield.

3.   New issues are sold on a continuous basis with or without specifying a relatively short initial subscription period (issue "on tap"). Issue conditions including the period in which the issue is available on tap are fixed by the debt manager and may be changed more or less flexibly in the light of changing market conditions. Offerings of different series of securities may be started, or suspended, at the discretion of the debt manager.

E. Selling Government Securities on a Fixed-yield Basis During a Relatively Short Subscription Period

The present section deals essentially with the method of selling government securities on a fixed-yield basis during a relatively short subscription period of several days; the debt manager fixes, and announces, the issue yield and often also the intended issue amount. The application of this method—as of any other method—does not pose any particular problems under conditions of stable interest rates and if, moreover, the debt manager is flexible in choosing a favorable moment for launching an issue. Under such conditions, it is relatively straightforward to arrive at a realistic assessment of the market situation and fix the issue amount and the issue yield simultaneously in line with these conditions so that a smooth selling is ensured. However, if the government's borrowing needs are high and if accordingly, borrowing operations have to take place at relatively short intervals the debt manager has much less scope for flexibility as regards the timing of debt operations. Moreover, under conditions of uncertainty and volatile interest rates a realistic assessment of the market situation tends to become more difficult and, more important, the market situation may change during the subscription period so that the originally fixed issue amount/issue yield combination gets out of line with market conditions. In the case of rising interest rates this may result in an undersubscription of the issue. In the case of falling interest rates, the issue may become oversubscribed, which would mean that the debt manager would have to cut down individual allotments of the issue unless he were able to increase the issue amount.

Undersubscription of an issue by market participants may be considered as undesirable, even if the issue were fully underwritten. Undersubscription may be interpreted by the market as a failure and may thus affect expectations in the direction of a further deterioration of market conditions. Such announcement effects, which may be caused not only by informing the market of the result of an issue, but which may already occur at the stage when the issue plans are announced, or at the stage of the opening of the issue, may be particularly strong in connection with selling government securities on a fixed-yield basis. Oversubscription on the other hand may also be undesirable, notably if it is substantial. The market and the debt manager may consider such a result as an indication that the issue yield has been set too high and that the lowest possible terms have not been obtained. Oversubscription, notably when it is heavy, may also be undesirable because the resulting cut-down of allotments of the issue to the subscribers if it were to happen repeatedly may make it more difficult to sell government debt in the future.

The debt manager, without changing the basic selling method, may deal with these problems in various ways. The risk that in the case of undersubscription he will not get the originally intended issue amount could be avoided by two different institutional selling arrangements. The first solution would be to apply the selling technique of firm underwriting which usually, not necessarily, implies that the debt manager cooperates with an issuing syndicate of banks and possibly also security dealer firms, which guarantee the placing of the issue. In the case of undersubscription by the general public, the underwriters would take on their own books any unsold amounts of the issue. For this placing guarantee the underwriters would receive a commission which may, or may not, be specified in the underwriting agreement. The second solution would be an arrangement according to which the central bank, or another official institution, would take up the unsold balance of a given issue with the intention to sell these amounts later in the market.

The choice between these approaches depends in the first place on the general relationships between the government and the banking system, which play an important role as regards institutional arrangements for selling government securities. But it depends also on other circumstances. The use of an issuing syndicate may generally be preferable in a market structure in which private individual investors, including small savers, play an important role as buyers of government paper and other bonds. The banks and security firms which are participants in the issue consortium may undertake particular efforts to achieve a wide distribution of newly issued securities. The higher the borrowing needs and the shorter the intervals between two issues, the greater such selling efforts because the consortium members have to get prepared to underwrite subsequent issues.

There may be less need for using the consortium technique in a market structure which is dominated by institutional investors or where investors, including numerous small savers, have relatively close relationship with the banking institutions as regards investment matters or have opportunities for direct subscription to new issues. With a view to making sure that he gets the originally planned issue amounts, even if the issue cannot be fully placed in the market, the debt manager may consider the use of individual underwriting by the more important banks or institutional investors, or he may use the second solution mentioned, namely, applying an arrangement according to which the central bank, or another offical institution, would take up any amount of a new issue which could not be sold in the market. The official institution in question would then try to sell these residual amounts later in the market. This latter solution may be preferred by the debt manager if he wanted also for some other reasons to combine essential features of the technique of selling government debt instruments on a fixed-yield basis with essential features of the tap issue techniques.

The question for discussion in this paragraph is how far the different solutions just mentioned are likely to achieve lowest possible issue costs in a given market situation. As far as fees and commissions are concerned, in the case of firm underwriting such fees, which are paid separately from any issue discount, the fees are higher because the underwriters receive a higher commission to compensate the risk they carry in guaranteeing the firm placement of the issue. This would suggest that because of this risk premium which the debt manager has to pay in addition to the ordinary sales commission the overall costs of this issuing technique have to be relatively high. However, depending on the strength of his bargaining position, the debt manager, in negotiating with the consortium, may be able to arrive at an issue yield which would be lower than the one he would have to offer if he could not count on a full underwriting guarantee. Nevertheless, an issuing consortium could not be forced repeatedly to accept issues that are too tightly priced. Similar considerations could also apply to the sales technique according to which the central bank, or another official institution, would take up any unsold amount. In this case the debt manager's ability to pare the issue terms in relation to secondary market yield levels still more finely, may be even greater since he does not have to negotiate with an issuing consortium. However, whether the debt manager is willing, or able, to do this depends on the circumstances. If the central bank were to take up a large part of an issue, the market could consider such an issue as having failed, a situation which the debt manager may wish to avoid as much as possible. On the other hand, the central bank may not be willing to take up repeatedly large amounts of successive issues as this would produce a concentration of government debt on its books, a situation which may be undesirable from a monetary policy point of view. This latter consideration would, of course, not apply in a case in which central bank participation in the underwriting of new issues for subsequent resale "on tap" is an essential feature of the selling arrangement.

The problem of avoiding a situation of undersubscription, and also of oversubscription, could also be approached by the following arrangements. The risk of a change in the market situation during the subscription period could be eliminated by an arrangement with the central bank, or some other official institution, according to which the market would be stabilized during the subscription period through appropriate open market operations. If markets were not too volatile, this could be a useful approach to ensuring an effective management of selling operations. However, from a monetary policy point of view, such an arrangement may not be acceptable, notably if government issues were being launched in rapid succession, since any action toward monetary tightening, or easing, as may be the case, would be inhibited during each subscription period. Another approach in dealing with the problem of avoiding formal under- or oversubscription of an issue by the market would be for the debt manager to leave the issue amount open. The debt manager would only fix, and announce, the issue yield, and the issue amount would be determined by the market. In some market structures the selling agents, before deciding their subscriptions, may however want to have an idea about the orders of magnitudes which are intended to be involved.

In the following paragraphs it will be discussed how the technique of selling government securities on a fixed-yield basis will be affected if the aim is to minimize, or to avoid altogether, an undesirable impact on the market and on investor expectations regarding future interest rates. A relevant aspect in this regard is the fact that because of the shortness of the subscription period, the whole sales effort is concentrated on a relatively short period of time. Also, the time between the announcement of the issue plans, the opening of the issue, and the information of the market about the issue result, whether the issue "went well" or "badly," is relatively short. This may mean that an issue sold in this way may receive particular attention by the market participants and market observers. The market will thus form its own views about whether the issue amount and the issue yield, and other characteristics have been adequate in comparison with the investor demand and market conditions and may on this basis draw conclusions about the future development of interest rates. This in turn may affect investor behavior.

These considerations suggest that a debt manager when applying this selling method should pay particular attention to getting a realistic picture of the market situation if he intends to fix both the issue amount and the issue yield in such a way so as to avoid an undesirable impact on interest rates and related expectations. The use of the consortium technique provides an advantage in this regard insofar as the negotiation of the issue amount and the issue yield which is involved, is usually based on an assessment of the market situation by the members of the consortium who are generally interested in a smooth selling of the issue. This negotiation procedure could imply that an adverse announcement effect on interest rates and bond prices, which otherwise could result, were reduced. However, it is conceivable that a negative announcement effect could already occur at the moment when the debt manager approaches the consortium. Already at this early stage some members of the consortium could make preparations for taking up a new issue by reducing their bond holdings, or by inviting clients to do so, before the negotiations start. A depressing effect on bond prices could result.

In using the consortium technique the debt manager could also consider reducing the market impact of an issue by stretching out the period between the first announcement of the rough issue plans and the final fixing of the issue amount. During this period the members of the consortium could explore with greater care than otherwise investor preferences regarding subscription amounts, issue yields, and other characteristics of the planned issue. In this way, it might be easier for the debt manager, and the consortium members, to form views about the market's absorptive capacity under the given circumstances and to fix issue conditions accordingly. This practice could, of course, not eliminate the risk that market conditions could deteriorate immediately after the final fixing of issue terms. In this case the consortium would have to take up any amount of the issue which the investor clientele were not prepared to absorb.

As a result of the effects of the underwriting guarantee, it may become less evident to the market if a government issue has not been fully placed with the banks' investor clientele. This may help to avoid, or minimize, an undesirable impact on interest rates which otherwise could result from an announcement that a government issue had become a failure. Much depends in this regard, however, on the behavior of the individual consortium members and the comments they are prepared to make on the issue in question. In addition, it should be taken into account that if underwriters had to take sizeable amounts of an issue on their own books, there is a considerable risk that after closure of the issue such unsold amounts would be "dumped" in the secondary market. This could eventually produce the undesirable downward pressure on bond prices which the debt manager attempts to avoid by applying the consortium technique. With a view to forestalling such dumping operations, the debt manager could apply effective price restrictions on the reselling of new issues which could form part of the underwriting agreement. Consortium members could, for example, be requested by the debt manager not to resell government paper lower than the original issue price during a specified period after the closure of the issue. It may at times, however, be difficult for the debt manager to maintain the price restrictions if some members panicked and tried to cut their losses. In any case, it is very likely that an experience by the consortium of taking up relatively large amounts of unsold new issues will have an impact on the negotiation of the conditions of a subsequent issue.

In the case of selling government securities on a fixed-yield basis without using an underwriter consortium, the debt manager could try to avoid, or minimize, an undesirable market impact by leaving the determination of the issue amount to the market. This practice may, however, not entirely exclude the possibility that the announcement of the final issue result has an undesirable impact on the market. Market participants would be in a position to compare the result of a new issue with previous issues and with estimated borrowing needs of the government, and might then draw conclusions about the likely future trend in interest rates.

F.   Selling Government Securities by an Auction Technique

The auction technique represents an alternative way in which the debt manager may approach the problems he faces in selling government securities. If the debt manager were, as a matter of priority, interested in raising a specific amount through an individual debt operation he could, by applying an auction technique without setting a minimum or maximum tender price, avoid the problem of fixing himself the issue yield in line with market conditions; a problem which is particularly difficult to approach under conditions of uncertainty and volatile interest rates. Instead, he would passively accept the issue yield which, via the auction mechanism, is associated with the amount in question. This results from the essence of the working of an auction mechanism. All competitive bidders, by submitting their bids, indicate simultaneously the amount of the issue they wish to receive and the yield they wish to obtain—or, what comes to the same, the price they are prepared to pay. Assuming that any noncompetitive bidders; i.e., bidders who indicate only the amount they wish to acquire but not the price they are prepared to pay, are allotted predetermined amounts, the debt manager would then rank all competitive bids received according to the prices (or yields) tendered and would draw the line after that tranche of the bidding scale which would provide together with all other bids ranging above this line, the amount he intended to raise.

The calculation of the yield for the issue taken as a whole depends on the technique which is being used. In the case of the uniform or Dutch auction the yield for the issue as a whole is identical with the yield of the last tranche of bids which are accepted. In the case of the conventional auction, in which each bidder pays the price he bids, or obtains the yield he bids, the yield of the issue taken as a whole corresponds to the weighted average of all bid prices (or yields) which have been accepted. These technical explanations show that the debt manager could also apply an auction technique if he wanted to obtain a specific issue yield for an issue as a whole. However, this would mean that he would accept passively the issue amount which would be associated with such a specific issue yield.

Applying an auction technique may be seen by some debt managers as an advantage insofar as, in preparing a new issue, the debt manager does not have to take a decision vis-à-vis the market on both the issue amount and the issue yield. Under conditions of great uncertainty when a realistic assessment of the market situation is difficult he could even abstain from announcing the intended issue amount and could confine himself to setting a coupon rate of interest. In such a case both the issue amount and the issue yield would be set by the market in the sense that the debt manager could on the basis of the bids received choose among various issue yield and issue amount combinations. In some market structures the participants in an auction may however prefer to have fairly clear ideas about the intended issue amount before submitting their bids.

An auction technique may also be seen as suitable for coping with the problem that the market situation may deteriorate during the period between the opening and the closure of an issue. In the case of a sale on a fixed-yield basis such a sudden change could easily result in a failure of an issue while in the case of an auction the deterioration of market conditions would be absorbed by the bids, which are usually submitted only very shortly before the closure of the auction. This does not mean, however, that the application of an auction technique would ensure in all cases that the debt manager would be able to receive the amount which he wanted to raise. Auction operations, as sales on a fixed-yield basis, may also fail to raise the amount intended though this is likely to happen only under particular circumstances. In a situation of extreme uncertainty when some investors expect for one reason or another that market conditions will deteriorate sharply after the closure of an issue and when others are uncertain about what will happen, a number of potential bidders may perfer to abstain from submitting their bids. It could be argued that they were free to anticipate sharp price declines by adjusting their bids accordingly. However, they may not wish to do so because of the risk of not bidding successfully. Thus, in extreme situations it could happen that the bids which the debt manager receives would not cover the announced, or intended, issue amount.

As the auction technique leaves the determination of the issue yield to the market, provided that the debt manager fixes the issue amount, it could be argued that this selling method is suitable for minimizing borrowing costs in the sense of obtaining in a given market situation the lowest possible issue yield. In addition, the debt manager could benefit from any interest rate decline which might occur in the period between the opening and the closure of an issue. Whether this will be the case depends on a number of circumstances. In order that the auction technique works properly in the way described and that the issue yields obtained reflect the true market situation, a number of conditions should be fulfilled. The participants in the auction should be largely professional and hence sophisticated investors who are able to form an adequate view of the market situation. Bidders should largely operate on a competitive basis; i.e., the market should not be dominated by a few very large investors, so that the risk of collusion is very small. The proportion of bids from noncompetitive bidders; i.e., from investors who are less able to judge the market situation properly, should remain relatively small.

Whether the debt manager would in a given market situation obtain best possible issue terms also seem to depend to some extent on the technique of price (or yield) determination which is applied; in other words whether the uniform price auction or the conventional auction is used. It might be expected that a conventional auction would encourage bidders to bid more sharply in relation to relevant secondary market conditions than a uniform auction, precisely because they have to pay the price they bid. The incentive for sharp bidding would be greater under selling arrangements which do not provide any commissions to be paid to the sales agents for placing government paper with their clients, although bidders would not want to set their bid prices too low because of the risk of falling outside that part of the bidding scale which is accepted. On the other hand, bidders may equally feel it necessary to bid sharply in a uniform price auction, because they will recognize that a high bid on their part, designed to secure full allocation, in the expectation that they will only pay the uniform price, may in fact raise the uniform price if all, or most, bidders follow the same tactic. These considerations suggest that the extent to which one or other form of auction will help the debt manager obtain the best possible issue terms will depend very much on the nature of his market and on the degree to which he receives, or wants to encourage, bids from nonprofessional investors. This question is discussed in the next paragraph.

This leads to the question of whether and to what extent an auction technique is suitable for, or can be adapted to, selling government paper to a widely spread investor clientele including numerous small savers, many of which may not be in a position to judge the market situation adequately and to submit bids accordingly. Some degree of protection against the risk of unrealistically high bids can be afforded to nonprofessional investors by using the uniform price auction technique as discussed above. Alternatively, two other broad types of arrangements seem practicable. Under the first type of arrangement the selling process would take place in two stages. Participation in the auction would be confined to banks and securities dealer firms; and these institutions would resell the newly issued paper to their investor clientele, possibly taking up orders from their clients before submitting bids. Under the second type of arrangement noncompetitive bidders would be allowed to participate in the auction; they would just indicate the amounts they wish to acquire without tendering a price (or yield). Certain arrangements could be made with a view to limiting the weight of any such noncompetitive bids. An overall quota of, for example, 25% could be applied. Noncompetitive bids exceeding this quota would be allotted on a pro rata basis. Alternatively, relatively low individual ceilings on such bids could be applied. It is conceivable that both techniques of price determination could be applied: the conventional auction as well as the uniform price auction. In the first case the noncompetitive bidders would pay the weighted average price of the issue; in the second case the uniform price would be applied.

In a particular country context the debt manager may be expected to allow the central bank or foreign investors to participate in auctions notably of shorter-term government paper; but at the same time the authorities may be interested in limiting the impact on interest rates which the participation in the auction from such sources could have. This problem could be approached by accepting from these types of bidders only noncompetitive bids and by increasing the originally planned issue amount accordingly.

A final question for discussion in this section is whether and to what extent an auction technique is suitable for minimizing, or avoiding altogether, an undesirable market impact of debt issue operations. The selling of a sizeable volume of government debt is bound to have an impact on the market in one way or another the more so if the selling effort is concentrated on one point in time, which is practically the case if an issue is sold by auction. If the government comes to the market with a sizeable issue, market participants and commentators may form their own views about how this amount compares with the expected absorptive capacity of the market. Depending on the outcome of such an assessment, there could be changes in expectations regarding future interest rate developments, which could be reflected in the bids which investors may submit in the auction process. In this way the announcement also of auction operations could result in an upward pressure on interest rates. It could also happen that market participants and commentators were surprised by the outcome of a given auction, which may also produce an adverse effect on investment behavior and hence on bond prices and interest rates.

In applying auction techniques to the sale of government securities, it could be an advantage from the point of view of minimizing an undesirable impact on interest rates if the use of this method were combined with a relatively high degree of routinization of issuing activity so that surprise effects which could result otherwise could be reduced. If the market were informed that the government intended to launch auction issues of similar orders of magnitude more frequently it would be less likely that the announcement of such issues would have a disturbing effect on the market. Surprise effects might nevertheless occur if the size of the auction, or the issue terms, deviated considerably from what major market participants or commentators expected. More generally, it could be argued that as far as the broad market impact is concerned, the auction technique is not much different from the method of selling securities on a fixed-yield basis during a short subscription period. In both cases the sales effort is concentrated more or less on one point in time, which means that the impact is practically instantaneous. This is a difference vis-à-vis the tap sale technique. It should be noted, however, that this difference between the latter technique and the two other techniques could be reduced considerably, if sales by auction, or on a fixed-yield basis, were to take place at short intervals and in relatively small amounts.

G.   Selling Government Securities on Tap

As far as issues of marketable debt are concerned the tap sale method may provide considerable scope for the debt manager to respond flexibly—though to different degrees in different institutional contexts—to the problems with which he may be faced if he wants to sell sizeable amounts of securities under conditions of uncertainty and volatile interest rates. Though securities are offered on a more or less continuing basis, it is possible for the debt manager to pursue quantitative borrowing objectives for periods of several weeks or so and to attempt to realize such objectives by adjusting his offering yields to reflect changing market conditions. Such tap sales may be made directly in the secondary market or on an over-the-counter basis through a network of sales agents. Even where the technique is not considered appropriate for sales of marketable debt, it may be a useful approach to selling nonmarketable savings instruments, though in this case it may, for administrative reasons, be more difficult to change new issue yields flexibly in line with changing market conditions. (See Section II.)

If shortly after the opening of an issue of marketable debt, sales were slowing down because issue yields were getting out of line with market conditions as a result of a general increase in interest rates, the debt manager has the opportunity to adjust the offering terms in response to changes in secondary market yields. In doing so, he will need to have regard to the impact that such adjustments may have on conditions in the market; and in the case of over-the-counter sales, he may need time to communicate any adjustment in offering yields to his sales agents. He may thus not be entirely free to make small successive adjustments in issue yields and may instead wait and make a large once-and-for-all adjustment once the market has established a new level of yields, in order to maintain thereafter a more continuous flow of sales. However, in comparing the tap sale technique with the other main categories of selling techniques—sale on a fixed-yield basis during a relatively short subscription period and sale by auction—it is obvious that the tap sale technique, at least when it takes the form of sales in the secondary market, is more flexible both with regard to the timing of the selling process and the scope for adjusting issue yields to reflect changing market conditions. Thus, the problem of a government issue being regarded as a failure if initial subscriptions do not cover it on issue does not arise in the case of tap sales, although the market may, of course, subsequently become aware if a debt manager operating tap sales is failing to achieve his quantitative borrowing objective over a period of time. In this sense the problems inherent in achieving quantitative borrowing objectives over an extended period of time seem likely to be much the same in principle, for given market conditions, whatever method of sale is adopted.

As far as the problem of obtaining the best possible issue terms is concerned, the tap sale technique offers similar flexibility, mainly because the timing of the selling process can be stretched out. In the case of the other two techniques, the selling process is concentrated on the issue period and the debt manager thus cannot benefit from any interest rate decline which may occur after that period. Conversely, however, the debt manager using these techniques is protected against any rise in interest rates following the issue period. In the case of a tap sale, the debt manager has flexibility to take advantage of favorable market conditions and to try to avoid the effects on borrowing costs of short phases of unfavorable conditions.

The tap sale technique offers similar flexibility in pursuing the aim of avoiding an undesirable impact on interest rates which could result from government debt operations, or of producing a desirable impact on interest rates. If the objective were not to accelerate an upward movement in interest rates in the market, the debt manager could, under most selling techniques, suspend the sale of issues. He would then run the risk of failing to meet his quantitative borrowing objectives. With the tap technique, the debt manager has the opportunity to resume new issuing activity with the minimum of delay if this were desirable from the point of view of reaching specific quantitative borrowing objectives within a certain period. Conversely, the tap sale technique would also enable the debt manager to contribute to a smooth dampening of an interest rate decline if this were desirable, by attracting investor demand into new issues through an appropriate setting of issue yields. This could be done at very short notice, while in the case of sale on a fixed-yield basis or sale by auction, a certain period of preparation of a new issue would be required during which period investor demand would be directed into the secondary market, with correspondingly sharper price movement effects.

These considerations suggest that the tap sale technique can also be used by a debt manager whose objective is to support the authorities' interest rate policy. Securities with different maturities could be simultaneously offered on tap, thereby enabling the debt manager to try to influence the shape of the yield curve if this were desirable. If the debt manager did not want to use the tap sale technique, the same effect could be achieved by open market operations by the central bank or some other official institution. The existence of broad secondary markets would, however, be an essential condition in such a case.

The major requirements for the tap sale technique to be operated in a flexible manner as described above would seem to be that the debt manager has available a broad, active, and integrated secondary market; that there be well-established market-makers capable of maintaining a two-way market; that he be in close contact with the market, for example, by participating in the daily stock exchange dealings and by having regard to daily market movements in fixing his offering terms. In this way the debt manager may be able to respond flexibly to the dilemma with which each debt manager is faced, irrespective of the selling technique he applies, namely, that in volatile markets he cannot achieve particular objectives regarding interest rates without being flexible, in the short run, in the selling of issue amounts, or that he cannot realize specific borrowing targets within a given period of several weeks or so without being flexible in the setting of issue yields. The technique of tap sales thus offers scope for flexibility in adjusting the balance between these objectives, though whatever selling technique is used the debt manager will necessarily be constrained, to different degrees at different times, by market conditions and by his need to meet particular operating objectives.

The question for discussion in this paragraph is, to what extent the tap sale technique could be considered as suitable for pursuing the objective of a wide distribution of government debt instruments. It could be argued, for example, that the consortium technique may be more suitable, because of the sales efforts which the consortium members usually undertake in order to make room for underwriting subsequent government issues, and that this driving force to sell government paper is not present in the case of tap sales. Against this, it could be held that an essential factor in this regard is the nature of the relationships between investors and the banks and other agents who are authorized to sell government paper to their clients. If the service departments of such institutions who give investment advice to their clientele are well developed and widely spread over the country and if, moreover, the government makes an effort to publicize its own security issues, it is conceivable that a wide distribution of new issues can be achieved irrespective of the sales technique which is being used. Tap sales made over the counter, through a network of agents, offer the additional advantage from the private individual investor's point of view that he can buy new issues at any moment. If tap sales are made in the secondary market, an opportunity can also be provided for private individual investors to purchase new issues at any time if they are offered for sale generally to the public for an initial period or continuously until the issue is terminated.

IV. EFFICIENT SECONDARY MARKETS FOR GOVERNMENT SECURITIES

Efficient and broad secondary markets for government securities are important for a number of reasons. First, their existence facilitates an effective selling of new government issues. Since the debt manager in fixing yields on new issues usually takes interest rates prevailing in the secondary market as a reference, it is important for the success of new issues that secondary market conditions reflect as correctly as possible the true capital demand and supply situation in the corresponding segment of the market. Second, efficient secondary markets are important for ensuring in the long run a successful marketing and a wide distribution of government securities, because it is through the existence of such markets that government securities can be endowed with adequate liquidity features which investors may require. Third, well-functioning and active secondary markets for government securities would also facilitate the achievement of some other objectives of debt management policy, such as avoiding erratic movements in bond prices, stabilizing the market during the subscription period for new issues, and smoothing the impact of large-scale redemption payments. Existence of such markets would provide increased scope for open market operations: flexible interventions for influencing the interest rate structure could be facilitated, or an undesirable interest rate effect of open market operations designed to influence the supply of central bank money could be minimized or avoided altogether.

Secondary markets for government securities are generally considered as efficient and as functioning well if such securities can be bought and sold at any time in sufficient quantities at market prices which are determined by market forces under conditions of free competition and which, moreover, can easily be known by all market participants. Under conditions of stable interest rate expectations, a relatively low degree of price sensitivity in relation to the volume of transaction could be considered as an additional criterion of efficiency in this context.

A first major condition for the development of efficient secondary markets for government securities is a sufficient volume of outstanding government debt. In addition, there should be a wide distribution of such debt. The larger the number of holders of government securities and the larger the amounts held, the greater the chances that at any time there will be buyers and sellers who operate in the secondary market. This, in turn, could contribute to reducing the price sensitivity of the market in relation to turnover because the chance that market participants have different views about future bond price developments is greater. Thus, a debt manager who intended to create conditions which are favorable to the development of broad secondary markets for government securities could consider to pursue systematically a policy of broadening the distribution of such securities.

A second major condition for an efficient functioning of secondary markets for government securities is the existence of private financial intermediaries who are prepared to quote to investors firm "bid" and "offer" prices for government securities and who are prepared to deal in agreed amounts at these prices. The intermediaries should also be prepared, and be able, to trade government securities in both rising and falling markets. Under conditions of a wide distribution of government debt instruments and sufficient interest on the part of investors to buy and sell such securities in the secondary market, it could be expected that there exist private financial institutions which find it attractive and profitable to provide a secondary market facility as described, notably if they were active as distributors of new government issues.

The authorities could encourage the development of private institutions which offer such secondary market facilities for government securities by providing an appropriate legal and regulatory framework within which such institutions can operate and maintain an adequate capital base. Two institutional and organizational aspects seem to be of particular importance in this context: the type of institutions which provide, or are allowed to provide, secondary market facilities and the trading mechanism which is used for determining secondary market prices and yields. As far as institutions are concerned, an important question is whether they set their "ask" and "bid" prices in such a way that the accumulation of sizeable inventories in government securities is avoided or whether, in unsettled markets, they are able and willing to assume relatively large positions. It is conceivable that in the former case price fluctuations in the secondary market are greater than in the case in which the intermediaries could act as buffers for absorbing important demand/supply imbalances. If private institutions were generally not prepared to provide the counterpart in the market in the event of heavy selling on the part of ultimate investors, there might be a need for an official institution to intervene, with a view to maintaining orderly market conditions. This task could be assigned to the central bank or to some other official institution, but stabilizing interventions of this nature could conflict with monetary policy objectives.

As far as the organization of the trading mechanism is concerned, two broad types could usefully be distinguished. Government securities could be traded in an "over-the-counter market" in which dealers communicate with each other over the telephone or telex and are prepared to quote quasi continuously ask and bid prices during the normal office hours. The other type is the concentration of all trading operations on a stock exchange where the price for a particular issue is quoted only once, or eventually also several times, during a stock-exchange session. Various combinations of essential features of the two systems seem possible. Each system, or combination of systems, may have its advantages and disadvantages from various points of view, which are relevant in the more general context of organizing securities markets. The over-the-counter market may offer more scope for flexible reactions of professional dealers and investors to changing market conditions, but the market process is less transparent to nonprofessional investors, including small savers. On a stock exchange, it may be possible to achieve a greater concentration of demand and supply for a particular security in a particular moment; the prices thus determined may be applied to buying and selling operations of the banks' and securities' dealers clients, an arrangement which may be desirable from a confidence and saver protection point of view. It is not possible within the scope of this report to discuss these organizational aspects of secondary markets for government securities in detail. It is conceivable that each existing system could be adapted in such a way so as to meet the requirements of efficiency, which inter alia implies that the quotations which are established should genuinely reflect supply and demand for a particular issue on the broadest possible basis.

V. MINIMIZING BORROWING COSTS

Whereas this section primarily deals with the minimization of borrowing costs in an accounting sense, it has to be remembered that these various measures which may produce optical or short-run cost advantages to the government may have negative effects on other borrowers, on fixed capital formation, and on the effective allocation of financial and real resources of the economy. The net effect on the national economy as a whole could be negative.

The objective of minimizing borrowing costs has essentially three aspects which may receive the debt manager's attention at different degrees, depending on the setting of priorities in the field of debt management. One important aspect, which has already been discussed in great detail in Section III, is the objective of obtaining best possible issue terms in a given market situation. Debt managers persistently attempt to achieve this objective in an endeavor to sell government securities in as effective a manner as possible.

Another aspect of the cost minimization question is the objective of minimizing interest cost in absolute terms. This aspect has received growing attention again in public debate insofar as interest payments have been accounting for a rapidly increasing share in total budget expenditure in many countries in recent years, as a result of a rapid growth in government debt and generally rising interest rates. However, to the extent that other debt management policy objectives receive priority, it is considered in many countries as unavoidable that the objective of minimizing interest costs in absolute terms should be regarded as a more long-term objective and should in cases of conflict with such other objectives play a secondary role. Within such constraints, debt managers generally attempt to achieve this objective over the medium term, i.e., by taking into account any cyclical movements in interest rates and changes in investment preferences.

A third aspect of the cost minimization question relates to commissions and fees which debt managers may have to pay to private institutions which are engaged in the distribution of government debt instruments or which handle the debt service payments. Since the question of minimizing borrowing costs in relative terms by obtaining best possible issue conditions in a given market situation has been dealt with in Section III, the present section will only briefly discuss the problem of minimizing interest costs in absolute terms and the question of commissions and fees.

If the debt manager wanted to minimize interest rate costs on government debt in the longer run, and this under conditions of competitive markets, he would need to have at his disposal a number of different instruments which he could flexibly use over the interest rate cycle. When interest rates are at their cyclical peak, he would have an interest in concentrating his borrowing efforts on short-term markets even if short-term rates were higher than long-term rates. Conversely, when interest rates are at or near their cyclical low, he would have an interest in concentrating his borrowing efforts on the long end of the market with a view to benefiting over the long run from low interest rates, even if under short-term considerations it would be cheaper to borrow in the market for short-term funds. As for any other borrower, the problem is the forecasting of interest rate movements and of corresponding changes in the yield curve; i.e., in the relationship between short-, medium-, and long-term interest rates. With increased volatility in inflation rates and interest rates, notably if synchronization of movements in these rates and cyclical swings in production and income is lacking, it has become more difficult to assess future interest rate developments and adjust borrowing policies accordingly with a view to minimizing interest rate costs over the longer run. In addition, borrowing requirements may be of such a size that the question of availability of funds becomes more urgent than any narrow calculation of relative borrowing costs. The scope for pursuing a policy of cost minimization could also be reduced by an urgent need to extend the average maturity of the public debt or by pursuing the objective of selling large amounts of longer-term government paper to the nonbank sector, with a view to containing monetary expansion.

Governments could consider achieving the objective of minimizing interest costs on pubic debt by making extensive use of "privileged circuits" either in the form of mandatory investment regulations or in the form of offering tax privileges on income from, or even on amounts invested in, government paper. As a result, interest rates in the unprivileged, or free, sectors of the financial markets would be higher than otherwise, while interest rates on government debt would be kept at a relatively low level. In this way, the government would shift a part of the borrowing cost burden onto the other borrowers. The result could be to provide short-term cost benefits to the government at the cost of longer-term efficiency losses for the economy as a whole and, hence, reduce economic growth and government revenue in a longer perspective. To what extent the use of any such "privileged circuits" will ultimately result in some net saving of government expenditure is not clear. By providing tax privileges on income from, or on funds invested in, government paper, the government will at the same time reduce its tax revenue. The application of mandatory investment regulations, insofar as they would produce below-market interest rates, would also adversely affect the government's tax revenue because taxable interest income from government paper would be lower than otherwise. These reductions in tax revenue will not necessarily be offset by higher tax revenue generated by higher interest rates on nongovernment debt. These considerations suggest that the use of privileged tax treatment of government debt instruments, or of mandatory investment regulations, may not be considered as an effective means of dealing with the cost minimization problem. However, the use of these techniques may be motivated by other considerations, such as broadening the distribution of government paper and promoting private household saving. (See Section II.)

Another aspect of the question of minimizing borrowing costs is the level of commissions and fees which the debt manager may have to pay to those financial institutions which are engaged in the distribution of government paper to ultimate investors. A general discussion of this question is complicated by the fact that the level of commissions and fees is subject to negotiation between the two parties involved and, hence, depends entirely on the relationships between the government and the banking and securities industry; relationships which are necessarily different from country to country for a number of reasons, among which established practices in the private as well as the public sector may play an important role. Furthermore, the level of commissions and fees will depend on the services rendered and it is not obvious that a reduction in such costs resulting from the government itself providing the debt manager with such services would entail any savings to the economy as a whole.

On the face of it, it seems possible to make a distinction between expensive and less expensive selling techniques as far as commissions are concerned. Thus, it may be possible for the debt manager to have government securities sold via an auction technique or via a tap sale technique without paying any commissions to sales agents who may participate in the auction or may function as intermediaries for tap sales of government paper. However, if the debt manager aimed at a wide distribution of government debt instruments and considered it necessary for this purpose to utilize a wide network of banking institutions and securities firms, he might have to offer an attractive commission to the sales agents involved irrespective of the selling method which was used.

The method of selling government securites via an underwriting consortium is generally the most expensive one as far as commissions are concerned insofar as the members of the consortium usually demand a special remuneration for assuming the risk that an issue cannot be fully placed in the market. However, judging the costs of selling solely according to the size of the commissions and fees involved may be misleading. It is indeed difficult to determine whether a selling method which involves the payment of relatively high commissions and fees is really more costly in terms of overall borrowing costs—including yield costs—than a selling method which involves lower commissions and fees. In other words, it is conceivable that in one and the same country in a given market situation overall borrowing costs of an issue would not differ very much if different selling methods were used. Applying, for example, an auction technique which does not involve the payment of a commission is, in terms of overall borrowing costs, not necessarily cheaper for the debt manager than selling new issues through an underwriter consortium, which involves optically high commission payments. Banks and security dealer/broker firms which have strong positions in the security issuing and trading business may, irrespective of the issuing method which is used, be able to secure a margin in buying and reselling new issues which they consider as adequate.

VI. ACHIEVING A BALANCED MATURITY STRUCTURE

The objective of achieving a balanced maturity structure of the central government debt receives particular attention by the debt manager if the amount of outstanding debt is substantial. It is obvious that the maturity structure; i.e., the maturity distribution of the outstanding debt over time—not only annually, but also throughout each year—determines the size and the timing of those future debt operations which serve the purpose of the renewal of maturing debt. The longer the average life of the total debt and the more balanced the distribution of maturity dates and the amounts of maturing debt, the smaller the refunding needs in a given fiscal year, or in a given month within each fiscal year.

Achievement of a balanced maturity structure essentially means avoiding a heavy bunching of maturing debt and of corresponding redemption payments and refunding operations in particular single years or on particular dates during a given fiscal year. In addition, a relatively balanced maturity profile over time and a relatively long average life of the total debt is desirable from the point of view of medium-term planning of fiscal and debt management policies. If the average life of the debt is very short and if, accordingly, the amount of short-term debt which needs renewal is very high, the debt manager and the monetary authorities will need to have regard to maintaining conditions which will facilitate rolling over the stock of debt or funding it on a longer-term basis.

As far as the distribution of maturity dates within a given fiscal year is concerned, the debt manager may, in the case of strong seasonal movements in the government's cash position, have an interest in setting maturity dates in such a way that they fall into a period of the year when the cash position is seasonally strong. He would however have to note that after a period of rapid increase in total debt such seasonal patterns may tend to be reduced as a result of debt operations and interest payments. If in a particular country context debt operations were used for controlling monetary expansion, the objective of achieving a balanced maturity structure could imply that monetary expansion should not be affected in an irregular fashion by a heavy bunching of redemption payments, though early repurchase of debt by the authorities in the market, for example during the last year before redemption, can substantially alleviate the problem.

A satisfactory maturity structure could, technically speaking, be easily achieved if decisions regarding the setting of maturities of new issues could exclusively be taken in the light of this objective. The use of a few instruments with standard maturities which would have to be issued at fairly regular intervals could greatly facilitate the building up of a balanced maturity structure. In this context it would be relevant to consider procedures of regularization and routinization of issuing activity; i.e., the application of particular offering cycles for particular standard maturities.

However, any such systematic attempts to construct a regular maturity profile of public debt is likely to conflict with other important objectives of debt management. In a situation in which a government's borrowing needs for both new financing and refunding purposes are substantial, the debt manager may be obliged to take decisions on maturities of new issues essentially in the light of investor preferences in order to ensure the success of his borrowing operations. The maturities thus chosen may not necessarily correspond to the objective of achieving a balanced maturity structure. If the debt manager were expected to support the monetary authorities' interest rate policy, notably as regards the relationship between short-, medium-, and long-term interest rates, he would have to set maturities of new issues in the light of that objective. This could also conflict with the objective of achieving a satisfactory maturity structure.

There could also be a conflict with the objective of minimizing borrowing costs in absolute terms. This could be notably the case in prolonged phases of high interest rates, when the debt manager, for cost reasons, may be reluctant to issue long-term instruments in large volumes, but when for reasons of avoiding the accumulation of large amounts of short-term debt, it would be desirable to issue at least some medium- and long-term debt instruments. In such a situation, a compromise might be found by issuing medium-term floating rate notes if there were sufficient interest among investors in such instruments. In phases of relatively low long-term interest rates the debt manager could undertake special efforts to lengthen the average maturity of the debt by concentrating his borrowing operations on the long end of the market. This would be in harmony with the objective of minimizing borrowing costs over the long run. But there could be a conflict with the objective of supporting interest rate policy if the latter aimed at bringing long-term interest rates down.

VII.   COORDINATION WITH CONJUNCTURAL ECONOMIC POLICY

A.   General

This section deals with some technical aspects of the role which debt management policy could play in coordination with general conjunctural policy, notably monetary policy. Actual arrangements concerning the relationship between debt management policy and other policy areas which may play a role in the management of an economy differ considerably from country to country and may depend on many factors and considerations. A detailed study of such arrangements would go beyond the scope of this report. It may be sufficient to distinguish, somewhat schematically, between the following cases:

1. The debt manager may be expected in fairly general terms to conduct his debt operations in accordance with the general objectives of economic policy and not to impede the achievement of intermediate objectives which may have been set in the monetary and financial field. Within this framework debt managment would be primarily directed to the financing of the budget deficit and management of the government's debt.
2. The debt manager may be expected to contribute actively to the achievement of objectives which may have been formulated as regards the level and the structure of interest rates and/or liquidity in the economy, or in particular sectors of it.
3. Debt management may be operated as an integral part of a monetary policy which is essentially monetary-aggregate oriented.
4. Debt management may be operated as an integral part of overall economic policy which uses in the financial field what might be termed an overall credit budget approach which may, or may not, cover both domestic credit expansion and capital imports.

Whatever policy arrangements may be made, the technical aspects of debt management which may be involved can be discussed under two headings: interest rate effects of debt operations, and liquidity effects of debt operations. Before examining these questions it should be noted that the starting point for the discussion is a given budget deficit which the debt manager has to finance in one way or another. This means that total credit demand by the government is also taken as given. In the context of this chapter there is thus no particular need, or scope, for discussing technical aspects of policy arrangements described under item 4 above. It should also be noted that questions concerning the interaction of fiscal policy and debt management as regards the determination of a desired size of a budget deficit—though this problem is important from an overall interest rate policy point of view—are not dealt with in this report.

B.   Interest Rate Effects of Debt Operations

The starting point for the discussion in this section is the assumption that the debt manager is expected to conduct his debt operations within a given overall financing task in such a way that undesirable effects on interest rates are avoided or that he contributes actively to the achievement of particular objectives as regards interest rates.

A distinction may be made between three problems: to influence the overall level of interest rates, to influence the level of long-term interest rates alone, and to influence the shape of the yield curve; i.e., the relationship between short, medium-, and long-term interest rates. In practice, these problems are closely interrelated; but they may be discussed as separate issues. The term *influence* refers to both avoiding undesirable effects and achieving desired effects. A major general technical condition for enabling the debt manager to exert an influence on interest rates is the existence of an adequate arsenal of government debt instruments and financing facilities and flexibility in their use.

If the objective were to influence the level of interest rates irrespective of the shape of the yield curve, and if the debt manager were requested to contribute to such a policy, he should be able to choose flexibly between borrowing from domestic or from foreign sources, or he should have at his disposal an adequate range of domestic financing and cash management facilities. As far as borrowing from foreign sources is concerned, a choice may be made between attracting foreign investors into domestic markets for government securities or issuing government securities on foreign markets. It is conceivable that in the latter case the reduced recourse to domestic capital sources could contribute to avoiding an undesirable increase or to achieving a desirable decline in domestic market rates.

If the objective were to avoid undesirable increases, or to support a desirable decline, in long-term interest rates and if the debt manager were requested to support such a policy—a task which is generally all the more difficult to accomplish, the higher the government's overall borrowing needs—he should be able, apart from being allowed to borrow abroad, to concentrate his borrowing efforts on the short end of the market while reducing issues of long-term debt instruments on the domestic market to a relatively low level. The timing of any such long-term issues would have to be decided in the light of the market situation because in a period of uncertainty regarding interest rate developments, already the announcement of a major bond issue operation—via its impact on expectations—could have an adverse impact on bond prices, and hence on long-term interest rates. Ways and means of minimizing, or avoiding altogether any such announcement effects are discussed in Section III, which deals with selling techniques.

If the debt manager were requested to contribute to a policy of influencing the shape of the yield curve, which, as well as in the case of a policy of influencing long-term interest rates, would require a certain degree of segmentation of the markets for government debt instruments, and which may be possible only in the short run, he should be able to choose flexibly between short-, medium-, and long-term instruments and affect, or avoid, the various market segments as may be appropriate. By the same token he should be able to decide flexibly on the timing of issues of marketable paper of various maturity types. A condition for sufficient flexibility in this regard would be the absence of any legislative provision which could limit the use of a particular instrument.

Comparing alternative techniques for implementing a specific interest rate policy it seems obvious that the scope for the debt manager to support such a policy is rather limited even if the range of debt instruments available to him were relatively broad. A policy toward influencing the shape of the yield curve—assuming that such a policy were feasible—could be more effectively implemented by appropriate open market operations which could be made both ways while the debt manager has largely only the choice between issuing and not issuing debt with different maturities. Limitations to implementing such a policy may also arise for the debt manager from conflicts with other objectives. For example, if it were desirable to spare the bond market as much as possible with a view to allowing long-term interest rates to decline, the debt manager might for cost reasons, or for reasons of extending the average maturity of the government debt, or reasons of favorable placing conditions, wish to issue rather large amounts of longer-term debt instruments. In addition—this has already been mentioned—it may be relatively difficult to use government debt operations for bringing down the interest rate level, if the government's financing needs are very high and if the government does not wish to have substantial recourse to foreign borrowing. The announcement of a large government budget deficit alone may sometimes suffice to create adverse interest rate expectations, which could make it difficult to produce the desired decline in interest rates without substantial monetary easing. On the other hand, under conditions of relatively modest gross borrowing needs, the government may not be in a position to affect interest rates sufficiently in line with policy intentions because the transaction volume may be too small in relation to the size of the markets. In this context, it should also be taken into account that for constitutional reasons it may be impossible, or at least difficult, for a debt manager to engage in debt operations which do not serve the purpose of budget deficit financing or of replacing maturing debt.

C.   Liquidity Effects of Debt Operations

The starting point for the discussion in this section is the assumption that the debt manager is expected to conduct his debt operations within a given overall financing task in such a way that specific liquidity effects are achieved or that undesirable liquidity effects are avoided. From a technical viewpoint it may be useful to distinguish between the following cases:

1. The debt manager may, under special economic circumstance, be requested to contribute to a restrictive monetary policy by conducting large-scale liquidity sterilization operations.
2. If it were an objective of monetary policy to control monetary expansion, the debt manager may be requested to contribute to the achievement of this objective by selling debt to the nonbank sector on a more regular basis.
3. If it were an objective of monetary policy to influence the growth of the central bank money stock the debt manager may be requested to contribute to such a policy through appropriate debt operations.
4. If it were an objective of monetary policy to influence the liquidity structure of the banks' assets the debt manager may be requested to contribute to such a policy by issuing appropriate debt instruments.

If the monetary authorities' objective were to mop up excess liquidity in the economy on a larger scale without any particular specification whether bank or nonbank liquidity should be reduced, the debt manager could be requested to issue substantial amounts of longer-term bonds the proceeds of which would be blocked on central bank account or would be used for redeeming government debt held by the central bank. An essential condition for conducting such operations would be that the government is authorized, under budgetary or constitutional legislation, to issue debt for other than budget financing or debt renewal purposes, at least temporarily.

If the objective were to influence monetary expansion in the economy as a whole on a more or less regular basis, the debt manager could be requested to contribute to such a policy by the sale to the nonbank sector of government debt instruments which do not represent money or near-money. The use of government debt operations for this purpose depends on a number of circumstances and conditions. The structure of the banking system is of crucial importance in this regard. In a system which is dominated by multipurpose banks and in which the liabilities of those banks vis-à-vis nonbanks consist of both short-term deposits (money and near-money) and longer-term liabilities such as bank bonds, there is not necessarily any difference between debt operations with banks and operations with nonbanks as far as the monetary effects of such operations are concerned. Consequently, the considerations developed in this and the following paragraph would only apply to countries in which bank liabilities vis-à-vis nonbanks essentially represent money and near-money. If, in such a case, the debt manager wanted to influence monetary expansion through debt operations he should have at his disposal adequate debt instruments which he could sell to the nonbank sector in sufficient volume. The characteristics of these instruments should be designed in such a way so as to meet the various preferences of major categories of nonbank investors (private households, nonbank institutional investors, industrial and commercial companies).

In market structures in which banks generally buy only short- and medium-term government paper, with longer-term government paper being essentially placed outside the banking system, the debt manager would have to concentrate his borrowing efforts on the issue of long-term or nonmarketable instruments. In other market structures in which banks do play a relatively important role as buyers and holders of longer-term government paper, the debt manager would have to make large-scale use of instruments which are especially designed for sale to private households, to nonbank financial institutions, and to industrial and commercial companies. As far as private households are concerned, the debt manager could consider making substantial use of nonmarketable instruments of a savings bond type, though attention would have to be paid to the problem of early redemption which holders may request at any moment, possibly after an initial waiting period. As far as nonbank institutional investors are concerned, the debt manager could make use of a substantial volume of direct placements of promissory notes which could not be transferred to banks. As far as industrial and commercial companies are concerned, the debt manager could consider making use of various short-term facilities including deposits which companies could utilize, for example, for meeting tax liabilities. (See Section II.C.)

If it were an objective of monetary policy to control and regulate the amount of central bank money which should be made available to the economy in a given period the debt manager could be requested to contribute to such a policy. The main technical condition for enabling the debt manager to support a policy of controlling the stock of central bank money is that he can flexibly influence the government's net position vis-à-vis the central bank in line with monetary policy intentions. In phases of tightening monetary policy, he should be able to increase a net creditor position, or to reduce a net debitor position, vis-à-vis the central bank. The opposite movement should take place if monetary policy aimed at increasing the supply of central bank money to the banking system. The debt manager's task in this regard could be facilitated if he were able to issue instruments for blocking the borrowing proceeds on central bank account or for withdrawing government debt from the central bank portfolio. This technical feature has already been mentioned in the context of special action to mop up excess liquidity. (See above.) In phases of monetary relaxation any such central bank balances of the government could be reduced, or the central bank's holdings of claims on the government could be increased again.

Flexibility in this regard could be enhanced if the government had at its disposal cash balances and current account credit facilities both at the central bank and with commerical banks. Such an institutional arrangement would facilitate the shifting of funds between commercial banks and the central bank. The existence of a broad and active market for short-term government securities which could be flexibly used for regulating the government's net position vis-à-vis the central bank would also be an advantage. The debt manager's task to influence the government's net position vis-à-vis the central bank in line with monetary policy intentions could be further facilitated if the flow of incoming and outgoing payments were smoothed as much as possible so that sharp fluctuations in the cash position could be avoided. As far as the inflow of the proceeds from large borrowing operations is concerned, some smoothing could be obtained by applying a system of partial subscription payments. In a similar way large-scale redemption payments on particular dates could be avoided by a smooth repurchase of a maturing issue prior to the redemption date.

If it were an objective of the monetary authorities to influence the liquidity structure of the banking system's asset position in line with particular policy intentions, the debt manager might be requested to support such a policy by appropriate debt operations. The main technical condition for implementing such a policy would be the existence of government debt instruments with different liquidity features which the debt manager could offer to the banks in accordance with the objectives of monetary policy. If the intention were to increase the holdings of liquid assets of the banking system, the debt manager could issue substantial amounts of short- and medium-term or even long-term paper, provided that such paper could be either rediscounted at the central bank or could be used as collateral for central bank credit. If longer-term government paper could not be used in this way, it would have to be considered as a less liquid paper though it could be sold on a secondary market. However, under conditions of falling bond prices, banks may not be willing to make use of this facility. If the debt manager intended to borrow from the banking system without improving the liquidity structure of the banks' asset position, he could consider making use of ordinary bank credit or of loans against promissory notes which cannot, or can hardly, be mobilized. A flexible use of such different instruments in support of monetary policy would also require an appropriate setting of interest rates on such instruments so that banks could be effectively induced to acquire them in sufficient volume.

44

An Essay on Principles of Debt Management

James Tobin
Yale University, New Haven, Connecticut

I. THE FEDERAL DEBT AND ITS COMPOSITION

A. The Relevant Concept of Federal Debt

Claims against the federal government held by individuals and institutions outside the federal government are of several kinds: (1) transferable demand obligations, (2) marketable short-term securities, (3) marketable long-term securities, (4) nonmarketable securities, and (5) other commitments. The first category (1) includes currency issued by the Treasury and Federal Reserve, and deposit obligations of the Federal Reserve. Between categories (2) and (3) there is, of course, no sharp line. Maturities at issue vary from 3 months to 40 years. In Table 1, the dividing line between short term and long term is taken to be 1 year. Savings bonds are the principal example of category (4), securities obtainable only from the Treasury and disposable only by redemption at the Treasury. These securities are redeemable at specified values on demand, though often with some delay and inconvenience of collection. Although they are demand obligations, they cannot be traded among private holders, and in this important respect they differ from category (1).

The last category, (5), comprises a vast array of statutory commitments difficult to calculate in amount and timing, expressed in ways other than unconditional obligations to pay fixed sums of money at specified future dates. Examples are social security benefits, veterans' pensions, grants-in-aid to state and local governments. Quite possibly these obligations are a more weighty burden on future budgets than the conventional national debt, which receives so much attention because it can be precisely calculated. The extent of these obligations is the result of congressional decisions of social policy. It cannot be altered by administrative decisions of the Treasury or the Federal Reserve. These agencies have administrative discretion to increase one of the first four categories at the expense of another. But they cannot substitute obligations of the first four types for obligations of type (5), or vice versa.

The "federal debt" for the purposes of this memorandum is the total of the first four kinds of obligations outstanding at any moment, the net cumulation of past federal "deficits" and "surpluses." Total debt grows over time when federal "outlays" exceed "receipts" and declines as "receipts" exceed "outlays." The course of the total over time depends, therefore, on budgetary policies that determine the balance of receipts and outlays. The distribution of the total, at any moment of time, among the various categories of debt can be altered by the Treasury and Federal Reserve. The size of the debt results from fiscal policies; its composition is the province of debt management and monetary policies.

The concepts of "debt," "surplus," "deficit," "receipts," and "outlays," must be mutually consistent,

Adapted from *Fiscal and Debt Management Policies: A Series of Research Studies Prepared for the Committee on Money and Credit*, Committee for Economic Development (1963): 143-218, with the permission of the Committee for Economic Development.

Table 1   Composition and Distribution of Federal Debt December 31, 1955 and 1959
(billions of dollars)

Category of debt	Total outside Treasury and Federal Reserve		Held by commercial banks		Held by others	
	1955	1959	1955	1959	1955	1959
Demand obligations (currency and Federal Reserve deposits)	$ 51	51	22	21	29	30
Short-term marketable securities (maturity under 1 year)	43	59	10	11	33	48
Long-term marketable securities (maturity more than 1 year)	113	96	52	41	61	55
Nonmarketable securities	59	49	—	—	50	49
Total	$266	255	84	73	173	182

and the definitions chosen should be relevant to the choices available to the makers of government stabilization policy. The set of concepts used in this paper differs in several important respects from the conventions of federal government accounting.

1. Since obligations of the fifth type are excluded from the "debt," as defined here, payments by the public which give rise to such obligations can be counted as "receipts" which, other things equal, reduce federal debt. Social security taxes are the principal example. Receipt of these taxes enables the Treasury to reduce its obligation, in the first four categories, to the public. Likewise, expenditures to discharge obligations in the fifth category must be counted as "outlays," which, other things equal, increase federal debt. To pay social security benefits, the Treasury must increase its financial "debt" to the public. In reckoning the relevant "surplus" or "deficit," receipts and outlays of this kind must be included, although they are not included in the conventional budget. Correspondingly, the relevant concept of debt does not include the intragovernmental debts of the Treasury to social security and other trust funds.

2. Unlike the usual concept, "debt" here includes noninterest-bearing demand obligations, category (1). Accordingly, in reckoning the current surplus or deficit, "outlays" must include purchases which, like those of gold and silver, are financed by printing or coining money. "Receipts" include proceeds of the sale of gold. This is not the practice in conventional federal budget accounting. When the Treasury acquires precious metals, it is permitted to pay for its purchases by printing money. These purchases are not counted as expenditures in the conventional federal budget, evidently on the theory that the government has acquired an asset of equal value. Other outlays of the federal government must be financed by taxes or by selling interest-bearing debt, and must be counted as current expenditures in federal budgeting.

3. In reckoning the composition of the federal debt, the artificial distinction between the Treasury and Federal Reserve in the conventions of federal accounting should be ignored. A debt of the Treasury to the Federal Reserve is a debt of the left hand to the right. It does not enlarge the public's claims. The holder of a claim of a given category does not care whether it is a Treasury or Federal Reserve obligation. Treasury currency and Federal Reserve notes circulate interchangeably. The monetary impact of the debt depends on the composition of the public's holdings, not on the composition of what the Treasury originally issued. The Treasury's debt by conventional reckoning might consist substantially of long-term bonds at high interest rates. But if those bonds are held by the Federal Reserve banks, which have in turn incurred demand obligations to the banks and the public, the debt that counts is a noninterest-bearing demand debt. What counts in assaying monetary impact also counts in calculating the net interest costs to the taxpayer. Interest payments from the Treasury to the Federal Reserve are not a net cost. The profits of the Federal Reserve banks, above a fixed payment on the stock member banks are compelled to subscribe, belong to the Treasury. In Table 1 the Treasury and Federal Reserve are consolidated, and the composition of claims against them on two sample dates is shown.

B.   Fiscal vs. Monetary Effects

Government debt has two kinds of impact on aggregate demand for goods and services. The first occurs when the debt is acquired, and only then. This is the direct fiscal effect of the budget, of government expenditures in excess of receipts from the public. As is well understood from multiplier theory, the higher expenditures are in relation to receipts, the greater is aggregate demand. (It is not true, however, that the budget's impact on aggregate demand can be gauged simply by knowing its balance, the net deficit or surplus. Increase in government expenditures is generally expansionary even if offset dollar for dollar by increase in revenues.) The fiscal effect depends much more on the rate at which the debt is changing than on the size of the debt itself. To gauge the fiscal effect it is much more important to know, along with the size of the budget, whether the budget shows a deficit of 14 billion or a surplus of 3 billion than to know whether the debt at the beginning of the year is 30 billion, 150 billion, or 300 billion. No doubt the initial size of the debt affects somewhat the size of the multipliers that determine how much a budget deficit is magnified by its repercussions on private income and spending. But this is a second-order effect compared to the magnitude of the deficit itself and of the income it generates.

The second type of impact with which this paper is concerned is the monetary effect of the debt. This is the effect on aggregate demand of private ownership of claims against the central government. It depends on the total magnitude of those claims, and on their nature. The monetary effect of debt outlasts the deficits that produced it and their temporary fiscal effects. It endures as long as the debt itself. Aggregate demand for goods and services throughout the postwar period would have been different without the 250-300 billion dollar federal debt inherited from the war, even if postwar federal budgets had been the same. The fiscal effect works through the influence of budget expenditures and receipts on private income. The monetary effect works through the impact of the debt on the size and composition of private wealth.

C.   Fiscal vs. Monetary Policy Decisions

Within the second type of impact, a distinction must be made between the monetary effect of a change in the size of the debt and the monetary effect of a change in the composition of a debt of given total size. The distinction is important because only the latter kind of change is within the powers of those government authorities, whether at the Federal Reserve or the Treasury, charged with responsibility for monetary policy and debt management. These authorities can make swaps with the public—one kind of government debt for another. If they wish, they can alter the composition of the outstanding federal debt drastically within a very short time—a day or a week or a month. They cannot, however, change the size of the debt. (Here "size of the debt" means the total amount the government received from the public for its outstanding obligations; i.e., the net cumulative total of past budget deficits less surpluses. The monetary and debt management authorities can to a limited degree affect the market value of the debt, which may at any moment be greater or smaller than "the size of the debt.")

Changes in the size of the debt require budget deficits or surpluses. They are a by-product of fiscal policy rather than of monetary policy. They result from decisions of Congress and the Executive regarding government expenditures and taxes. Changes in the size of the debt also require time. A budget running a deficit at a rate of 12 billion a year will add only 1 billion to the debt in a month. Indeed, it will take between 2 and 3 years to increase the outstanding debt by 10%. A change in the size of the debt will have a different monetary effect depending on what form it takes. If an addition to debt takes the form of long-term obligations, for example, its monetary effect will be less expansionary than if it takes the form of demand or even short-term obligations. The monetary and debt management authorities can decide that. Given the change in the debt willed by the fiscal powers-that-be, the monetary authorities can and must choose the composition of the change. That decision is of the same nature as their choice of the composition of a debt of given size, and does not require separate analysis.

To summarize, changes in the size of the debt are the province of fiscal policy. They have two effects on demand. One, the fiscal effect, is temporary. The other, the monetary effect, is permanent. The strength of the monetary effect depends on the composition of the change in debt. This is the province of the authorities in charge of monetary policy and debt management. Indeed, their province is wider. They are not confined to deciding the form of marginal changes of the debt. They can alter the composition of the whole debt whether it is changing in size or not.

D.   Monetary Control and Debt Management

How can the Treasury and the Federal Reserve affect the composition of the total debt? The Treasury can replace security issues when they come due—at which time they are virtually demand obligations—with time obligations. By "advance refunding" offers or conceivably by repurchasing its own debt, the Treasury can convert short-term debt before it matures into long-term debt, or vice versa. The Treasury can increase nonmarketable debt at the expense of other categories by offering more attractive terms on savings bonds. The Treasury can increase the public's holdings of federal demand obligations by drawing down its deposit balance in the Federal Reserve banks. Within limits the Treasury can issue new currency; i.e., literally print new money, to replace interest-bearing debt. Since 1933 the Treasury has generally owned a margin of unmonetized gold against which it could issue gold certificates.

The Federal Reserve also can change the composition of the debt, principally by its open market operations. By purchasing short-term securities, for example, the Federal Reserve at the same time increases the quantity of demand obligations outstanding and decreases by an equal amount the quantity of outstanding debt in the short-term marketable category. Federal Reserve sales of long-term securities diminish the outstanding demand debt and increase the outstanding long debt by an equal amount. By purchasing shorts and at the same time selling an equivalent quantity of longs the Federal Reserve could lengthen the marketable debt, leaving the demand debt unchanged. The Federal Reserve does not set the terms of nonmarketable securities kept on tap by the Treasury. But it may influence the demand for such securities indirectly by altering yields of marketable debt instruments.

There is no neat way to distinguish monetary policy from debt management, the province of the Federal Reserve from that of the Treasury. Both agencies are engaged in debt management in the broadest sense, and both have powers to influence the whole spectrum of debt. But monetary policy refers particularly to determination of the supply of demand debt, and debt management to determination of the amounts in the long and nonmarketable categories. In between, the quantity of short debt is determined as a residuum. From 1953 to 1961 this specialization was institutionalized in the United States. The Federal Reserve controlled the size of the demand debt independently of the Treasury. The Treasury decided the amount of long-term and nonmarketable debt; under its "bills only" policy, the Federal Reserve normally refrained from buying or selling long-term securities. Since February 1961, however, the Federal Reserve has operated in all maturities. Although variation of the quantity of demand debt outstanding through open market operations is perhaps the principal instrument of monetary policy, it is not the only one. The Federal Reserve sets the discount rate at which the banks can borrow reserves. Within limits set by Congress, the Federal Reserve sets required reserve-to-deposit ratios for commercial banks. Although these are purely monetary tools, how they are used has a great deal to do with both the economic impact and the net interest cost of a given federal debt structure.

Semantic distinctions and institutional specializations should not be permitted to obscure the essential indivisibility of the problem. The need for coordination in policy making, commensurate with the economic unity of the task of debt management, will be argued at length below. The monetary authorities at the Federal Reserve cannot make sensible decisions about demand debt, or about the other instruments they control, without taking into account the Treasury's actions regarding the supply of long debt. Neither can the Treasury, whatever its debt management objectives, pursue them intelligently without considering how much interest-bearing debt the Federal Reserve will leave outstanding.

II.   MONETARY EFFECTS OF CHANGES IN SIZE AND STRUCTURE OF DEBT

A.   Net Private Wealth and Its Composition

Suppose that at a given moment of time the net worth of every economic unit in the United States other than the federal government is calculated. Net private* wealth is the aggregate of these net worths. In the aggregation private debts wash out. They appear as assets on the balance sheets of some units, but in equal amount on the liability side of other balance sheets. What remains? There are three basic components of net private wealth: (1) claims against the federal government; i.e., the federal debt defined in Section I; (2) the

---

*The word *private* is not altogether appropriate, since among the economic units in the aggregate would be state and local governments. "Private" should be interpreted, in this context, as nonfederal.

value of the U.S. physical capital stock, other than capital owned by the federal government, and (3) net claims of U.S. economic units, again excepting the federal government, against the rest of the world. The first component grows with federal deficits or declines with federal surpluses, as explained in Section I. The second component grows with net investment in plant and equipment, residential construction, and stock of goods. It changes also with market valuations of existing capital goods and real estate. The third component grows when U.S. residents acquire claims against foreigners or invest in property and capital abroad; it declines when foreigners acquire claims against us or equity in property here.* In what follows, the third category will be ignored, or consolidated with the second. The net capital position of the United States vis-à-vis the rest of the world is an important topic in its own right, but it is not the subject here. It will not distort the analysis of debt management to assume a closed economy in order to focus attention on the relative magnitudes of the first two components of net private wealth.

B. Stabilization Policy and the Supply Price of Capital

Control of the course of aggregate economic activity—economic stabilization—is the principal purpose of monetary and debt management. What is the route by which management of money and public debt may affect economic activity? Ultimately its effectiveness depends on its ability to influence the terms on which investors will hold the existing stock of real capital and absorb new capital. If investors demand a higher rate of return on capital than the existing stock can yield, given the state of technology and the supplies of labor and other factors of production, investment will decline and the economic climate will be deflationary. If investors are willing and anxious to expand their holdings of capital at a rate of return lower than the marginal productivity of the capital stock, investment will tend to outrun saving and the outlook will be inflationary. The same point may be expressed in another way. If investors are content with a low rate of return on equity in real capital, relative to its marginal productivity, their bids for existing capital will cause its valuation to exceed its replacement cost; the difference will be an incentive to expand production of capital goods. But if investors require a relatively high rate of return on equity in real capital, the valuation of capital in place will be low relative to its replacement cost and will deter further production of investment goods. The course of economic activity, then, depends on the difference between two rates of return on ownership of capital. One is the anticipated marginal productivity of capital, determined by technology, factor supplies, and expectations about the economy. This cannot be controlled by the managers of money and public debt, except in the indirect sense that if they somehow successfully control the economy they control all economic magnitudes. The second rate of return on capital equity is that rate at which the public would be willing to hold the existing stock of capital, valued at current prices. It is this rate of return, the *supply price of capital*, which the monetary and debt authorities may hope to influence through changing the supplies and yields of assets and debts that compete with real capital for place in the portfolios and balance sheets of economic units.

Broadly speaking, the authorities can lower the supply price of capital by lowering the yields of competing assets. But it is important to remember that these yields—interest rates on national debt instruments, bank loan rates, mortgage rates, etc.—are means rather than ends. The target is the supply price of capital. This rate, although influenced by the yields of other assets, is not identical with any of them. It is a mistake to use the rate on long-term government or corporate bonds, for example, as an unerring gauge of the tightness of monetary control of the economy. The differential between a long-term bond interest rate and the rate of return investors require of equity is surely as variable as any differential in the whole gamut of the structure of interest rates. Lowering the long-term government bond rate is not expansionary if the premium above it required for investment in real capital is at the same time commensurately increased. Increasing the long-term bond rate is not deflationary if the means that increase it at the same time lower in equal degree the equity-bond differential.

What is the monetary effect of an increase in the public debt? Other things equal, what difference does the size of the debt make to the supply price of capital? Will a larger debt change the rate of return that the community of private investors requires in order to hold a given stock of capital? The answer of this section is that the monetary effect of an increase in the debt is to lower the required rate of return on capital, to make

---

*One implication of the concept of federal debt adopted in Section I should be noted. When the United States finances a balance of trade deficit by selling gold or by foreign acquisition of U.S. government securities, it is the federal debt component of private wealth that declines. When the same deficit is financed by U.S. banks' incurring deposit obligations to foreigners, it is the third component of private wealth that declines.

it easier to absorb a growing capital stock into portfolios and balance sheets. The magnitude of the effect depends on the form that the increase in debt takes. The expansionary effect is strongest, of course, if the increment of debt is "monetized"; i.e., if it takes the form of demand debt. The effect is weaker for short debt and still weaker for long debt. But, it is argued here, the direction of the effect is unambiguous. Given the present assortment of debt instruments, the enduring monetary effect of increase in government debt is expansionary. To have a neutral or restrictive effect on the demand for capital, an increase in debt would have to take unconventional form. This is a principal motivation for the proposal set forth in Section IV below for new debt instruments geared for the purchasing power of the dollar.

A $1 billion increase in public debt, while the value of the capital stock is given, means a $1 billion increase in net private wealth. At given rates of return on debt instruments and on equity in capital, owners of wealth would be unlikely to choose to concentrate the whole of a billion dollar increase in wealth on public debt. Rather, they would choose a balanced expansion of their holdings. Their new acquisitions would be divided between public debt and capital. Consequently, to induce the community to absorb the whole of an increase in wealth in the form of public debt, yields of public debt instruments must rise relative to the rate of return on capital. The differential of capital equity over public debt must fall. If the public debt were homogeneous and the yield on the uniform debt instrument were fixed, the result of debt expansion would be perfectly clear. The differential in favor of capital would have to fall; otherwise the public would not be content with portfolios in which capital forms a smaller proportion and government debt a larger proportion. Given a fixed yield of government debt, the differential could fall only if the supply price of capital were to fall.

In practice, the public debt is not homogeneous, and the yields on debt instruments are not absolutely fixed. However, there are certain fixed anchors to the structure of yields on public debt. First, the rate on the transferable demand debt of the government—currency for nonbank holders, reserve balances in Federal Reserve banks for banks—is zero. The rate on demand deposits is likewise legally set at zero; every dollar of public holding of deposits is indirectly a holding of a fraction of a dollar, the required reserve ratio, for government demand debt. Second, banks can obtain additional holdings of demand debt at the Federal Reserve discount rate. So long as it is maintained constant, the discount rate provides another fixed pivot for the structure of rates.

About a quarter of the marketable U.S. federal debt is demand debt, subject to legally or administratively fixed yield. The rest takes the form of instruments whose yields are determined in the market. Although they are market-determined, these yields cannot stray too far from the fixed yields of the demand debt. The time obligations of the government—the Treasury or the Federal Reserve—are more or less substitutable for its demand obligations, and an effective chain of substitution keeps the yields even of long maturities in line. Therefore, if yields on public debt must rise relative to the rate of return on capital, the main brunt of the adjustment falls on the latter. The inducement to increase the proportion of wealth held as public debt, decreasing the share held as capital equity, must be in substantial part a fall in the yield of equity.

To say that an increase in debt is expansionary, and likewise that debt retirement has a deflationary monetary effect, is not to say that neutralization of these effects is beyond the powers of the monetary and debt authorities. The assertion is merely that effects in the indicated direction will occur in the absence of deliberate action to offset them. The Federal Reserve may be able to neutralize the expansionary influence of an increase in debt by raising the discount rate. Or the effect of a change in the size of the debt may be counteracted by a change in the composition of the initial debt. For example, expansion of long-term debt might be neutralized by a tighter monetary policy, open market sales substituting short debt for demand debt. The effects of changes in the composition of debt of a given total size are discussed in Section II.G.

C.   Effects of Change in the Supply of Demand Debt

The expansionary effect of an increase in debt is clearest and strongest when it takes the form of demand debt. Suppose that federal demand debt is increased by $1 billion, while the quantities of short and long government debt outside the Treasury and the Federal Reserve are unchanged. Assume that the Federal Reserve discount rate remains unchanged. Take the money value of the stock of capital, and the prices of goods, as given also. (Of course, in fact the stock of capital is always changing both in real amount and in money value at the same time as the federal debt. The assumption of a fixed amount and value of capital is made for analytical purposes, because the gauge of the impact of change in debt is what it does to the rate of return investors require of a *given* quantity of capital. As is usual in comparative static analysis, the purpose is to describe the difference it makes whether a parameter—in this case demand debt—is smaller or larger.

The analysis is timeless, even though it would be impossibly puristic to try to explain it without chronological language.)

Private wealth increases by $1 billion, and interest rates must adjust so that owners of wealth are content to put the whole increment into demand debt, either directly or through banks and other intermediaries. Public currency holdings are quite inelastic; it will not strain fact too much to assume them constant. Then the whole of the billion dollars must find its home with the banks, either as required reserves or as free reserves. Initially the deposits of the public in the banks will increase by the same amount as the increment in private wealth, and the free reserves of the banks will increase by a large fraction—five-sixths if the required reserve ratio is one-sixth—of that amount. As banks try to convert these excessive holdings of free reserves into earning assets, they bid government and private debt away from the public. The nonbank holders of these assets are induced to sell them, and to hold bank deposits instead, by a fall in their yields. Banks are willing to acquire them in spite of their reduced yields because they are, within limits, more profitable than free reserves. How far this process of expansion of banks' deposits and assets goes depends on the banks' preferences for cash and for freedom from debt to the Federal Reserve, relative to the yields of less liquid assets. If the banks' equilibrium demand for free reserves is constant, deposits and earning assets will expand by the textbook multiples of the original accretion of reserves. For example, if the average required reserve ratio is one to six, deposits will expand by 6 billion and earning assets by 5 billion, from an increase in demand debt of 1 billion dollars. However, these classic multiples probably overstate the expansion. The expansion is inevitably accompanied by a fall in the yields of government and private debts. With the Federal Reserve discount rate unchanged, this fall diminishes the inducement to borrow from the Federal Reserve. It increases the attractiveness of excess reserve balances. As a result, banks' equilibrium demand for free reserves will be higher. A part of the increment in demand debt will serve to satisfy an enhanced appetite for free reserves; not all of the billion will go into higher required reserves.

What is the adjustment of the public outside the banks? Suppose, provisionally, that in the end the banks keep free reserves unchanged. In order to absorb as required bank reserves a billion dollar increase in demand debt, the public must absorb a multibillion dollar increase in bank deposits. At the assumed required reserve ratio, the public must increase deposits by six times the increase in its wealth. Here is the significance of fractional-reserve banking. A substantial change in yields is required to effect a drastic shift in portfolio composition. A part of the increase in public willingness to hold bank deposits will be induced by reduction in yields of interest-bearing government debt. Short debt, in particular, is regarded by many corporations and institutions as a close substitute for cash. But it is hardly likely that these yields can fall enough to make the public *reduce* its holdings of federal debt by anything like five or six times the increase in net private wealth. In the balance sheet of the public, most of the room for the multiple expansion of deposits must come from an increase in the debt of the public to the banks, in response to a reduction in interest rates on private loans. This adjustment is a shift by private lenders from direct lending or from lending through nonbank intermediaries, which become less profitable, to bank deposits; the banks acquire the loan business given up. But unless the rate of return on capital falls too, the reduction in loan rates will stimulate new borrowing to finance new capital investment. But in the hypothetical example the stock of capital is assumed constant. To prevent the demand for capital from exceeding the existing stock, the yield of capital must fall. Its fall is the measure of the expansionary effect of the increase in debt.

Even if banks increase their equilibrium free reserve holdings, deposits will in all probability expand by a multiple—though smaller than the reciprocal of the required reserve ratio—of the increment of demand debt. Substantial reduction in the yields of alternative assets, including capital equity, would be necessary to induce the public to make this shift in the composition of their balance sheets.

Is it conceivable that banks' demand for free reserves would be so elastic with respect to yields on earning assets that they would absorb as free reserves five-sixths of the increment of demand debt? If so, the expansion of deposits would be limited to the growth of private wealth. Even an expansion of deposits thus limited would require, in general, some reductions in yields on other assets. Without the inducement provided by lower yields elsewhere, the public would not wish to keep even as little as 100% of an increase in its net worth in deposits. Conceivably the reduction in yields that would accomplish this reallocation of assets by the public might be sufficient to persuade the banks to hold their initial gain idle in free reserves. Something like this happened in the 1930s, when yields on earning assets were low and the banks were saturated with reserve funds. In normal times, and in the usual range of interest rates, the banks' demand for free reserves is much more easily satisfied.

Table 2 is a hypothetical illustration of the change in bank and public balance sheets necessary to absorb

Table 2 Hypothetical Illustration of Assets (+) and Liabilities (−) of Banks and Public Before and After an Increment of Demand Debt and Private Wealth Equal to 1% of Wealth

	Banks			Public			Total		
	Before	After	Change	Before	After	Change	Before	After	Change
Currency	0	0	0	+30	+30	0			
Required reserves	+20	+27	+7						
Free reserves	0	+3	+3						
Demand debt total	+20	+30	+10	+30	+30	0	+50	+60	+10
Short debt	+20	+30	+10	+60	+50	−10	+80	+80	0
Long debt	+10	+15	+5	+60	+55	−5	+70	+70	0
Private debt	+80	+97	+17	+320 −400	+303 −400	−17	0	0	0
Deposits	−120	−162	−42	+120	+162	+42	0	0	0
Capital	−10	−10	0	+810	+810	0	+800	+800	0
Total	0	0	0	+1000	+1010	+10	+1000	+1010	+10

an increment of demand debt and private wealth equal to 1% of initial wealth. The table is meant to be indicative of behavior and circumstances between the extremes discussed above; that is, a multiple expansion of deposits occurs, but not the full textbook multiple. Free reserves also increase.

D.   Change in the Supply of Short Debt

Suppose that private wealth is increased by government deficit financed by short debt. Demand debt, long debt, and the capital stock remain constant in supply, and the Federal Reserve maintains a fixed discount rate.

An extreme assumption will provide a useful point of departure for analysis of this case. The assumption is that the banks do, and the public does not, regard bills and free reserves as perfect substitutes at the prevailing bill rate. (Not all short debt is in the form of Treasury bills, but since the differences among short debt instruments are not of great moment, it is not misleading to use "bills" as a convenient synonym for short debt.) In this case an increase in bank holdings of short debt would have the same consequences as an equal increase in bank holdings of demand debt. In the "after" column of the example of Table 3 banks have absorbed an extra 9 of short debt. Net free reserves have become -6; banks have to borrow to meet reserve requirements. But banks act the same as if their free reserves had been increased by 3(9-6). They expand loans and deposits. The public makes room for part of the expansion of deposits, which exceeds the increment in private wealth, by selling long debt to the banks, but for most of it by relinquishing private loan business to the banks. Reductions in the long rate, loan rate, and return on capital equity are necessary to achieve this reconstitution of bank and public balance sheets. Because of the assumed perfect substitutability of short debt for cash in bank portfolio, the short rate remains unchanged. For this reason, the public increases its holdings of shorts (+1) as well as of bank deposits.

The assumption behind Table 3 is far-fetched but it is instructive. Short debt is not a perfect substitute for demand debt in bank portfolios, but it is within limits a good substitute. A bank needs a defensive buffer between its commercial loans and its required reserves. The purpose of the buffer is to enable it to withstand a loss of deposits and reserves, on the one hand, or compelling demands for loan accommodation, on the other hand. In neither case does the bank wish the necessity of meeting the reserve requirement to force it to disappoint customers, many of whom have earned the right to loan accommodation by faithfulness as depositors. Excess reserve balances are the most obvious defensive asset. Overnight loans of such balances— federal funds—to other banks are another. Treasury bills fill the defensive function almost as well. They can be sold quickly in a well-organized market. Since they are of short maturity, they subject the bank to very little risk of capital loss. Indeed, by staggering maturities the bank can contrive to meet most reserve stringencies by letting bills "run off" and need worry very little about the chance that it would have to sell bills in a declining market. In any case bills can be used, like other government securities, as collateral for

Table 3 Hypothetical Illustration of Assets (+) and Liabilities (–) of Banks and Public Before and After an Increment of Short Debt and Private Wealth Equal to 1% of Wealth (assuming short debt to be a perfect substitute for free reserves)

	Banks			Public			Total		
	Before	After	Change	Before	After	Change	Before	After	Change
Currency	0	0	0	+30	+30	0			
Required reserves	+20	+26	+6						
Free reserves	0	–6	–6						
Demand debt	+20	+20	0	+30	+30	0	+50	+50	0
Short debt	+20	+29	+9	+60	+61	+1	+80	+90	+10
Long debt	+10	+16	+6	+60	+54	–6	+70	+70	0
Private debt	+80	+101	+21	+320	+299	–21	0	0	0
				–400	–400				
Deposits	–120	–156	–36	+120	+136	+36	0	0	0
Capital	–10	–10	0	+810	+810	0	+800	+800	0
Total	0	0	0	+1000	+1010	+10	+1000	+1010	+10

advances from the Federal Reserve. This further reduces the chance of capital loss involved in using them as secondary reserves; if the bill market is down when the bank needs reserves, the bank may find it advantageous not to sell bills but to borrow the needed reserves, repaying the loan when its bills mature or its reserve position is replenished.

These considerations suggest that for the banking system as a whole, short Treasury debt is a good though imperfect substitute for net free reserves. When the bill is very low, banks will prefer excess reserves in order to avoid the slight risks and transactions costs involved in using bills as secondary reserves. This preference will be very little affected by the discount rate. Even at a very low discount rate, banks would not find it profitable to borrow in order to acquire or to retain bills. But at higher rates, banks' demand for bills relative to net free reserves will be sensitive to the differential between the discount rate and the bill rate. When the bill rate is high relative to the discount rate, banks short of reserves will borrow rather than sell bills, and banks with free funds will buy bills rather than repaying debt or adding to excess reserves. When the bill rate is low relative to the discount rate, banks short of reserves will sell bills rather than incur debt to the Federal Reserve and banks with free funds will repay debt or hold cash rather than buy bills.

Table 4 is a hypothetical illustration of the absorption of an increase in the supply of short debt, on the assumption that bills are a good but imperfect substitute for free reserves in bank portfolios. Here the short rate must rise slightly to provide banks the incentive to reduce net free reserves. Banks add to their holdings of short debt by more than they lower their free reserves. With their overall defensive position thus strengthened, they expand private loans and deposits, lowering the loan rate. The rate on long government debt also falls; there may be some reallocation of long debt between banks and public, but none is assumed in Table 4. The fall in the rate on private debt induces the public to switch to deposits, surrendering loan business to the banks. As before, the rate of return on equity capital—the supply price of capital—must fall to prevent an increase in demand for capital, as against the fixed supply, resulting from the reduction in long and private loan rates and from the increment of wealth.

How great the expansionary effect of short debt is depends crucially on whether the banks regard short debt as a better substitute for cash than the public does, or vice versa. The reason is that substitution of short debt for bank reserves economizes "high-powered money," demand debt, while public substitution of short debt for deposits economizes "low-powered money." In one case a dollar of bills takes the place of a dollar of demand debt. In the other case a dollar of bills takes the place of one-sixth of a dollar of demand debt. To take an example that is in a sense the opposite to Table 3, suppose that the public will substitute bills for cash without a change in the bill rate but that the banks will not. Banks will have no incentive to reduce their net free reserve position, since public demand will keep the bill rate from rising. Deposits will not increase. The only reductions in other interest rates, including the supply price of capital, will be those that suffice to induce the public to concentrate the increase in their wealth on holdings of short debt.

Table 4 Hypothetical Illustration of Assets (+) and Liabilities (−) of Banks and Public Before and After an Increment of Short Debt and Private Wealth Equal to 1% of Wealth

	Banks			Public			Total		
	Before	After	Change	Before	After	Change	Before	After	Change
Currency	0	0	0	+30	+30	0			
Required reserves	+20	+23	+3						
Free reserves	0	−3	−3						
Demand debt	+20	+20	0	+30	+30	0	+50	+50	0
Short debt	+20	+27	+7	+60	+63	+3	+80	+90	+10
Long debt	+10	+10	0	+60	+60	0	+70	+70	0
Private debt	+80	+91	+11	+320	+309	−11	0	0	0
				−400	−400				
Deposits	−120	−138	−18	+120	+138	+18	0	0	0
Capital	−10	−10	0	+810	+810	0	+800	+800	0
Total	0	0	0	+1000	+1010	+10	+1000	+1010	+10

E. Change in the Supply of Long Debt

On the direction of the effects discussed in Sections II.C and II.D there is general agreement, although on their magnitudes there is of course great uncertainty and disagreeement. In respect to the monetary effect of a change in the supply of *long* debt, other things equal, there is not even general agreement as to direction. It is sometimes argued that the monetary effect of an increase in the supply of long-term debt is deflationary, the effect of retirement of long-term debt expansionary. After all, an increase in long debt will raise the long-term rate of interest, and retirement of long debt will lower it; many economists are accustomed to judge the direction of impact on aggregate demand of any monetary event by what happens to "the" rate of interest, approximated by the yield of long-term government bonds. However, the differential of the yield of equity over the long rate may not be constant but systematically variable. If an increase in long debt lowers this differential more than it raises the long rate, it lowers the supply price of capital and is expansionary.

The effects of an increase in the supply of long-term government securities, keeping the supplies of other components of public debt constant, depend on whether these securities are directly and indirectly a better substitute for demand and short debt, on the one hand, or for ownership of capital, on the other hand. The concept of "better substitute" can be given precision, and this is done below. The meaning can be conveyed by considering two extreme models: A, in which long-term securities are a perfect substitute for demand debt, and not for capital, and B, in which long-term securities are a perfect substitute for capital, and not for demand debt. In the case of either pair, the term *perfect substitute* means that the two yields are held in a certain relation to each other—not necessarily equal—by the fact that investors will make wholesale substitutions of one asset for the other in their portfolios if the yield differential deviates in the slightest degree from normal.

Model A amounts to the case discussed above (Section II.B), where the public debt is homogeneous, at a fixed rate. For even though there are a variety of debt instruments, the structure of yields is not affected by the relative supplies of the various kinds of debt. Long securities are such a good substitute for cash, either directly or through the substitution chain of intermediate and short-term securities, that the rate on long securities cannot be changed by altering their supply. In a given state of market expectations, with a given Federal Reserve discount rate, the long rate is as good as pegged. On the other hand, the expansion of debt means that the equity-bond differential must change in favor of debt; capital and long-term debt are not perfect substitutes, and capital has become relatively more abundant. In model A, therefore, the supply price of capital must fall.

In model B it is the differential between capital and long-term government bond yields which substitution maintains unchanged. Issue of long-term bonds is essentially an increase in the combined supply of capital and capital substitutes. Meanwhile the supply of assets, government short and demand debt, which are imperfect substitutes for capital and long-term bonds is maintained. Accordingly the yield differential of capital over demand debt must rise. The rates on demand debt being fixed, the supply price of capital must rise. Likewise the rate on long-term securities must rise.

Is the world better approximated by A or by B? There are good reasons for believing that A is the better approximation, that debt instruments of varying maturities are better substitutes for each other than for equity in physical capital. The argument will be presented below. Economics has, however, been dominated by the tradition of model B, and the trained intuition of economists faced with a problem such as analyzing the monetary effects of deficit financing by long-term debt is to apply that model. The tradition of model B is involved in the proposition, common to Keynesians and anti-Keynesians, that investment in capital will be carried to the point where the marginal efficiency (or productivity) of capital equals "the rate of interest." "The rate of interest" is identified with the rate on long-term government bonds. The equality need not be taken strictly; some premium for risk may be subtracted from the expected return on capital to obtain the rate that is to be equated to the bond yield. Nevertheless, implicitly or explicitly capital investment and bond holding are regarded as perfect substitutes for each other at the proper rate differential. The risk premium, whatever else it depends on, does not vary systematically with the relative supplies of capital and long securities. Just as it conforms to model B in regarding capital and long securites as perfect substitutes, so the prevailing theoretical tradition regards cash and long securities as quite imperfect substitutes. The theory of liquidity preference, and of the maturity structure of interest rates, explains the differential of long rates over the yield of short securities and demand debt. In this explanation the relative supplies of the various imperfect substitutes play a crucial role. In the simple Keynesian model "*the* rate of interest"—the very same one to which the marginal efficiency of capital must be equated—is wholly determined by the supply of cash relative to the supply of bonds. It is quite remarkable that Keynes devoted so much attention to the cash-bond yield differential and so little to the capital-bond differential, and that he failed to apply to the second the principle—that yield differentials depend on relative supplies—he developed for the first. It is perhaps even more surprising that the general theoretical tradition of economics has followed him in these regards so closely so long.

If model A is the better approximation, though an imperfect one, the consequences of issue of long-term government debt may be described as follows: The public and the banks together have greater overall net worth, with the same holdings of capital equity, short debt, and demand debt as before but larger holdings of long-term government debt. It is of course highly unlikely that the public will wish to absorb the increase in net worth entirely in an increase of holdings of long-term government securities unless there is some change in the structure of yields and asset prices. The saving corresponding to the government deficit would not automatically take the permanent form of investment in long-term government bonds. As the public attempts to maintain portfolio balance, with their larger net worth, they will try to sell long-term governments in order to buy equity, private debt, short-term government debt, and deposits. Yields of long-term securities will rise relative to those of competing assets; this process will continue until the change in structure of yields reconciles investors to the new structure of relative asset supplies. Since long securities are good substitutes for short debt, the short rate may be pulled up too. The improvement in yields of interest-bearing debt will induce the banks to diminish net free reserves and the public to hold more debt relative to deposits and currency. Banks, with an overall increase in their holdings of defensive assets, may expand loans and reduce the loan rate even though the yields on these assets are higher. In any case it takes a decrease in the rate of return on equity to induce the public to increase their holdings of liquid assets, deposits plus government debt, by more even than the increase in their wealth. What might happen to bank and public balance sheets is illustrated in Table 5.

In the end the long-term rate is higher absolutely, and higher relative to the yield on capital equity and to the rates on shorter-term government securities. However, the rise in the long rate is limited by the readiness with which many holders will substitute long debt for shorter securities or cash. The short-long differential will not have to change much to induce banks and other institutional investors to shorten the average maturity of their holdings. Short securities are in turn a close substitute for cash; for banks, government bills are a close substitute for excess reserves or for reduction of debt to the Federal Reserve. Consequently short rates are fairly firmly anchored to the Federal Reserve discount rate and to the zero rate on demand debt and on deposits. Given these basic rates, the yields of short-term government securities can be changed substantially only by considerable shift in the relative supplies of demand and short debt. Here these supplies are taken to be constant. The rise in the long rate is, for these reasons, limited. But the differential of equity yield—the supply price of capital—over the long rate must fall. Indeed this differential must fall more than the differential, positive or negative, of short rates over long. That is a consequence of the assumption of model

Table 5   Hypothetical Illustration of Assets (+) and Liabilities (–) of Banks and Public Before and After an Increment of Long Debt and Private Wealth Equal to 1% of Wealth

	Banks			Public			Total		
	Before	After	Change	Before	After	Change	Before	After	Change
Currency				+30	+30	0			
Required reserves	+20	+21	+1						
Free reserves	0	–1	–1						
Demand debt	+20	+20	0	+30	+30	0	+50	+50	0
Short debt	+20	+22	+2	+60	+58	–2	+80	+80	0
Long debt	+10	+12	+2	+60	+68	+8	+70	+80	+10
Private debt	+80	+82	+2	+320	+318	–2	0	0	0
				–400	–400				
Deposits	–120	–126	–6	+120	+126	+6	0	0	0
Capital	–10	–10	0	+180	+810	0	+800	+800	0
Total	0	0	0	+1000	+1010	+10	+1000	+1010	+10

B that long debt is a better substitute for other government debt than for capital. Accordingly the supply price of capital must fall.

Debt issue is on balance expansionary, in spite of the fact that the long-term rate rises. Instead of being an indication that the operation has deflationary results, the rise in the long-term rate is in large part a symptom of the expansionary impact of the transaction. It results mainly from the effort to restore portfolio balance between capital equity and government debt. Another result of the same effort is a decrease in the supply price of capital.

The argument applies in reverse, of course, for retirement of government debt. Other things equal, a decrease in government debt due to budget surplus has an enduring deflationary monetary effect, superimposed on its transient deflationary fiscal effect. This is true even if debt retirement is concentrated entirely on long-term bonds. Given the supplies outstanding of short debt and demand debt, and given the discount rate, retirement of long-term securities from budget surplus will raise the supply price of capital.

F.   Correlations of Risks Among Debt Instruments and Capital Equity

What are the reasons for believing that government debt instruments are better substitutes for each other than any of them, even those of long maturity, are for equity in physical capital?

In general, an asset which is a candidate for an investor's portfolio may be characterized by two attributes of his estimate of the probability distribution of gains and losses from holding the asset for a given period ahead. One is the expectation of return, the means of the distribution. The other is a measure of dispersion or risk, the standard deviation of returns. Considering a number of assets together, the investor may be imagined to estimate a joint probability distribution, with possible positive or negative correlations in the returns on any pair of assets.

In general two assets are good substitutes for each other to the extent that they share the same risks; i.e., to the extent that their future rates of return are positively correlated with each other. If the same future contingencies that would make asset X turn out more profitably than expected on average would also make asset Y exceptionally remunerative, then X and Y are good substitutes. If the correlation is perfect, holding both X and Y in a portfolio does not accomplish any spreading of risk or hedging, in comparison with concentrating the same total investment on either asset alone. Considering two assets with high positive correlation of returns, which asset the investor chooses to concentrate on, or the proportions in which he holds the two assets, will be very sensitive to the difference between his expectations of return on the two assets.

When two assets have uncorrelated rates of return, the investor can reduce his risk by dividing his investment between them. The worst may happen to one, but it will be very unlikely to happen to both at the same time. This is, of course, the basic reason for portfolio diversification. To reduce overall risk, a portfolio manager balances his holdings of assets by seeking independent risks. Some assets he holds have less expected return than others; the justification for their inclusion in the portfolio is reduction of risk. To maintain balance and diversification as wealth grows, an investor will expand the risk-independent components of his portfolio together in rough proportion. He will sacrifice risk spreading and diversification only under the inducement of a higher expected rate of return on the riskier assets. A larger expected return differential is required for two reasons. There is an increase in overall risk due to the simple fact that one asset is riskier than the other. Added to this, in the case where the risks are independent, is an increase in risk due to loss of risk pooling.

When two assets have returns with negative correlation—i.e., events that would make X a big loser would more or less surely make Y a big winner—then real hedging is possible to reduce risk.

What are the risks of holding government obligations? All categories of government debt are free of risk of default. All categories of government debt, including demand debt, share their principal risk, namely uncertainty about the purchasing power of the dollar. Presumably each investor assigns to cash and to other obligations fixed in units of currency a real rate of return based on his expectation of the change in the price level. If his mean expectation is inflation at a rate of 3% per annum, his expected real rate of return on cash is -3% per annum. Likewise he will subtract 3% from the expected money return on any other obligation of fixed money value, in order to arrive at its expected real rate of return. But no one is sure about the price level. It may rise more than the expected 3%, or it may rise less, even fall. This is a risk in holding any asset of this kind. It is shared equally by all government debt instruments. If inflation takes away 50% of the value of cash during the next decade, it will also take away 50% of the value of a 10-year bond. If deflation adds 20% to the value of cash, it will also add 20% to the value of a bond. An investor cannot defend himself against risks of this kind by spreading investments among different kinds or maturities of government obligations.

The second risk of government obligations is due to uncertainty about future interest rates. This risk affects differently obligations of different maturities. An investor interested in the money value of his asset 3 months from now can be perfectly sure of it by holding cash or an obligation with maturity of 3 months or less. If he holds a debt of longer maturity, the value of his investment in 3 months will depend on the vagaries of the market. If the interest rate rises, he will suffer a capital loss; if it falls, he will gain. The degree of this uncertainty depends on the length of maturity. A one point change in interest rate cannot alter very much the capital value of an obligation due in another 3 months or a year. It can alter considerably the capital value of a distant maturity. If interest rates for various maturities are expected most probably to move together, the prospects of short-period return on obligations of different maturities are positively correlated, with greater risks on greater maturities. For investors of short horizon, therefore, the risk associated with interest rate changes works in the same direction as the risk associated with price level changes. It makes government obligations of different maturities good substitutes for each other.

Some investors have long horizons; they are interested in their aggregate return over 10 or 20 or 30 years, or more. They anticipate little or no probability that they will need to consume their capital at an earlier date. Accordingly they attach little importance to the value of their investments at intervening dates but concentrate on their ultimate value. For long-horizon investors, so far as risks of interest rate change are concerned, the ranking of maturities with respect to risk is reversed. One can be more certain of the amount of money he will have in 20 years by buying a 20-year bond than by buying a 10-year bond and planning to reinvest in a second 10-year bond when the first one matures. Uncertainty about the level of interest rates 10 years from now affects the second strategy but not the first. Uncertainty about the future of interest rates adds even more to the risk of a shorter initial investment, a 5-year or 1-year maturity instead of a 10-year bond. If interest rates fall next month and stay down, the long-horizon investor with a 20-year bond will nevertheless earn the original higher rate over the 20-year period. If he has a 10-year bond, he will at least enjoy the higher interest over a 10-year period. With a 1-year obligation, he will be stuck with a low rate of return over the 19 subsequent years. Similarly the long-horizon investor will gain more from a rise in interest rates the shorter his initial investment.

Although the ranking of maturities with respect to risk is reversed for a long-horizon investor, the risks of the various maturities are positively correlated. As in the case of short-horizon investment, this positive correlation makes obligations of different maturities good substitutes for each other. Investors will be sensitive to the structure of yields in choosing among alternative ways of accumulating a sum of money for a target date 20 years in the future. If the current rate on 10-year bonds is enough higher than that on 20-year bonds, they will buy 10-year bonds and take their chances on the interest rate 10 years from now. After all the absolute worst that can happen is that they will hold cash at zero interest for the last 10 years.

There is a third situation, in which the target date is neither at the beginning nor at the end of the maturity spectrum. Maturities both longer and shorter than the horizon entail risk, the more risk the more they diverge from the target date. But longer and shorter maturities can be combined as an imperfect hedge; and in this situation they are complements, rather than substitutes. Suppose an investor is holding both, and a rise in interest rates occurs before the target date. He suffers a capital loss on the longer maturities, but makes this up by increased earnings of interest as he reinvests the proceeds of his shorter maturities. Similarly, if interest rates fall, he loses as he reinvests the proceeds of the short maturities but makes a capital gain on the longer maturities. *Hedging combinations* of short and long securities are, of course, a substitute for the simple matching of maturity with timing of obligation or need. Likewise there are various possible hedging combinations—very short and very long, moderately short with moderately long, etc. Which procedure is followed depends on which promises the highest yield. In this sense various maturities are again substitutes for each other.

Gains or losses from ownership of capital depend on quite a different set of events and contingencies. To begin with, capital ownership is specific. It requires betting on particular kinds of capital goods, particular industries, particular managements. The risks of a poor specific choice are of the same nature as the risks of default of private obligations of fixed money value. Government obligations are free of such risk. It is true that the specific risks of capital ownership can be reduced, though not wholly eliminated, by diversification. The rise of mutual funds and of agglomerate corporations tends to make diversified portfolios generally available, even to small investors. What diversification cannot begin to do, of course, is to eliminate the risks common to capital ownership of all kinds. Though there are tremendous variations in the fortunes of specific equities, they are variations on a common theme. To judge the prospects, either short-run or long-run, of a particular equity investment, one must guess not only its specific merits relative to other equities but also the course of "the market" in general.

The long-run prospects of capital ownership in general depend upon what happens to the relative prices of capital and consumption goods, rather than what happens to the absolute consumers' price level. In the short run there can, of course, be considerable discrepancy between the market's valuation of capital in place and the replacement cost of capital, even of the most up-to-date technological vintage. Market valuations fluctuate violently and erratically as investors speculate regarding the prospects of the economy and regarding each others' speculations. Whether in the stock market or in the markets for real capital goods, the terms of trade between capital ownership and consumption-goods may turn in favor of owners of capital or against them. But what happens to these terms of trade is quite independent of what happens to the terms of trade between consumption goods and money. The main sources of inflation or deflation cause both capital goods and consumption goods prices to rise. Ownership of capital is therefore a good though incomplete hedge against the risks of changes in the consumer price index. Ownership of government debt or its equivalent avoids the risks due to changes in the relative prices of investment goods, either as measured day to day in the stock market valuations of capital in place or as measured by the real cost of new capital equipment.

Another risk of capital ownership is due to uncertainty about the rate of technological obsolescence. All capital may be expected to decline in value in relation to its replacement cost as time and technological advance bring better ways of doing the same things. The anticipated rate of return on replacement cost that initially induces investors to acquire a capital item contains some allowance for the expected decline in value of the item due to obsolescence. If obsolescence is slower than anticipated, the net return on the item will be better than anticipated. But if obsolescence occurs faster than this guess, the return on the investment will be disappointing. Diversification of capital investments is a way of avoiding the consequences of miscalculation of obsolescence prospects in a particular line. But uncertainty about the rate of technological progress in the economy as a whole remains. Again, this is a risk that is not shared by government debt instruments nor correlated with their characteristic risks.

The conclusion is that there is substantial independence of risk between ownership of capital and ownership of government obligations. In contrast, there is considerable positive correlation of real rates of return within each of the two categories, among different kinds of government debt, on the one hand, and among different capital equities, on the other. The public will use government debt and capital equity to balance each other in diversified portfolios. They will shift the proportions of this balance only in response to changes in the differential real rates of return expected on the two categories. If, for example, the public must absorb a greater proportion of capital equity, the expected rate of return on capital equity must rise relatively to the expected rate on government debt. The rise must be sufficient to induce investors not only to assume more of the intrinsic risks of capital ownership but also to forego some of the defense against these risks afforded by a balanced holding of claims fixed in money value.

G. Changes in the Composition of a Given Debt

Previous sections have discussed the monetary effects of increasing the debt in each of three forms: demand, short, and long. If those sections are shifted into reverse gear, they describe the effects of reducing the debt outstanding in each of these forms. Most of the operations of the monetary and debt management authorities involve changes in the composition of a given debt; i.e., increasing the supply of one kind of debt and reducing the supply of another. The effects of such operations are already implicitly described in the previous sections. For example, the effects of open market purchases of bills can be inferred from Section II.C with the hypothetical example of Table 2, which describes an increase in the supply of demand debt, and from a reverse reading of Section II.D and the hypothetical example of Table 4, which would describe an equal decrease in short debt. The assumptions about substitutabilities among assets made in the preceding sections already imply: (1) substitution of demand debt for short debt is expansionary, (2) substitution of demand debt for long debt is even more expansionary, and (3) substitution of short debt for long debt is expansionary, but probably less so, dollar for dollar, than either of the other two operations. These conclusions all assume that no category of debt is a perfect substitute for another, either in bank portfolios or public balance sheets. If, contrary to this view, banks regarded bills as perfect sustitutes for free reserves, open market purchases and sales of bills would have little effect. Or, if the public, say, regarded short and long debt as perfect substitutes, it would not matter whether open market operations were conducted in the one kind of security or the other (operations 1 and 2 would have the same effect) and lengthening or shortening the interest-bearing debt (operation 3) would make no difference to the state of aggregate demand.

Tables 6, 7, and 8 provide hypothetical examples of each of the three shifts in debt composition mentioned. These examples are consistent with those of Tables 2, 4, and 5.

H. Gross vs. Net Federal Debt

The activities of the federal government as a financial intermediary and the activities of quasi-governmental agencies and institutions serving as financial intermediaries with obligations bearing government guarantee, have not been discussed so far. These activities do not add to the net debt of the government or to the net private wealth of the community. Nonetheless they may have very significant monetary effects. Even when no government subsidy is involved, they reduce the supply price of capital by accommodating private

Table 6 Hypothetical Illustration of Open Market Purchase of Bills—Assets (+) and Liabilities (–) of Banks and Public Before and After Increase in Demand Debt Offset by Equal Decrease in Short Debt

	Banks			Public			Total		
	Before	After	Change	Before	After	Change	Before	After	Change
Currency	0	0	0	+30	+30	0			
Required reserves	+20	+20	+4						
Free reserves	0	+6	+6	——	——	——			
Demand debt	+20	+30	+10	+30	+30	0	+50	+60	+10
Short debt	+20	+23	+3	+60	+47	–13	+80	+70	–10
Long debt	+10	+15	+5	+60	+55	–5	+70	+70	0
Private debt	+80	+86	+6	+320 −400	+314 −400	–6	0	0	0
Deposits	–120	–144	–24	+120	+144	+24	0	0	0
Capital	–10	–10	0	+810	+810	0	+800	+800	0
Total	0	0	0	+1000	+1000	0	+1000	+1000	0

Table 7 Hypothetical Illustration of Open Market Purchases of Long Securities—Assets (+) and Liabilities (–) of Banks and Public Before and After Increase in Demand Debt Offset by Equal Decrease in Long Debt

	Banks			Public			Total		
	Before	After	Change	Before	After	Change	Before	After	Change
Currency	0	0	0	+30	+30	0			
Required reserves	+20	+26	+6						
Free reserves	0	+4	+4						
Demand debt	+20	+30	+10	+30	+30	0	+50	+60	+10
Short debt	+20	+28	+8	+60	+52	–8	+80	+80	0
Long debt	+10	+13	+3	+60	+47	–13	+70	+60	–10
Private debt	+80	+95	+15	+320 / –400	+305 / –400	–15	0	0	0
Deposits	–120	–156	–36	+120	+156	+36	0	0	0
Capital	–10	–10	0	+810	+810	0	+800	+800	0
Total	0	0	0	+1000	+1000	0	+1000	+1000	0

borrowers at lower rates than they could otherwise obtain. This is accomplished by the substitution of the government's credit for the private borrowers' credit. The agency either obtains the funds by issuing Treasury obligations or the equivalent, or by guaranteeing the private obligation. In either event, the lenders will supply the funds at lower yield than if they were supplying them directly to the borrowers. Nor is the reduction of private loan rates confined to borrowers served by the government. Competition will reduce loan rates to borrowers served by private lenders as well. The availability of a larger gross supply of government obligations, which can serve as secondary reserves and as hedges in portfolios, will lower private loan rates and the supply price of capital. This will be true even though these intermediary activities tend to raise somewhat government rates themselves. The earlier analysis of Section II.B applies. Here again there is an increase in government debt relative to the other component of private wealth, the capital stock. Indeed, here it is virtually as if the capital stock that must be placed in private portfolios is decreased concurrently with the increase in

Table 8 Hypothetical Illustration of Shortening of Interest-bearing Debt—Assets (+) and Liabilities (–) of Banks and Public Before and After Increase in Short Debt Offset by Equal Decrease in Long Debt

	Banks			Public			Total		
	Before	After	Change	Before	After	Change	Before	After	Change
Currency	0	0	0	+30	+30	0			
Required reserves	+20	+22	+2						
Free reserves	0	–2	–2						
Demand debt	+20	+20	0	+30	+30	0	+50	+50	0
Short debt	+20	+25	+5	+60	+65	+5	+80	+90	+10
Long debt	+10	+8	–2	+60	+52	–8	+70	+60	–10
Private debt	+80	+89	+9	+320 / –400	+311 / –400	–9	0	0	0
Deposits	–120	–132	–12	+120	+132	+12	0	0	0
Capital	–10	–10	0	+810	+810	0	+800	+800	0
Total	0	0	0	+1000	+1000	0	+1000	+1000	0

government debt. Though capital is not actually bought by the government, it is acquired by borrowers served by the government. So much less, then, needs to be lodged in private hands through the normal channels and incentives of capital markets and private financial institutions.

The intermediary activities of the federal government have monetary effects but they are not under the control of the monetary authorities. On occasion these activities have expanded when monetary policy was restrictive, and vice versa. Conceivably government intermediaries could thwart monetary policy more than private financial intermediaries. Private institutions are held in rein by interest rates which are within reach of the Federal Reserve. The scope of governmental intermediary operations is determined not by profit opportunities but by legislative and executive decision.

Greater coordination of activities that give rise to federal debt, under the control of the monetary and debt management authorities, is desirable. This does not mean, of course, abandonment of the aims for which Congress has authorized selective interventions in the credit market, though some economists may regard these interventions as unwise. Government credit and intermediation can still be used to channel funds to categories of borrowers or kinds of capital formation that Congress desires to foster. Selectivity of this kind cannot be practiced by the Federal Reserve itself. So long as open market operations are confined to government securities, the monetary authorities have no way to exert direct influence over the structure of private interest rates; e.g., to lower mortgage rates relative to corporate bond yields, or to lower rates on loans to finance farm crops while raising rates for commercial construction.

Government financial intermediation is one way of practicing selective monetary control. Selective regulations applicable to private lenders are another way. The Federal Reserve administers regulations concerning stock market credit and at times has regulated consumer and residential mortgage lending. If security reserve requirements of some kind were imposed on private financial intermediaries other than banks, variation of these requirements would be a third type of selective control, perhaps more powerful than either of the other two. Whatever administrative discretion exists in selective credit control, through government financial intermediaries and by other means, should be coordinated and to some degree centralized. Otherwise it may be used counter to the prevailing overall objectives of monetary and debt management policy. And it may not even add up to a consistent policy with respect to the structure of private interest rates and credit availabilities. For example, it would not make sense to expand the federal government's open market operations in mortgages, via "Fanny Mae," at the same time the Federal Reserve is stiffening regulations about mortgage down payments and maturities.

Federal debt instruments serve so many purposes in the contemporary monetary and financial system that observers sometimes wonder what the sytem would do if the debt were eliminated by a miraculous series of budget surpluses. What would we do for a currency supply, for bank reserves, for the money market, for secondary reserves of all kinds, etc? One answer is that private obligations would adapt to fill the vacuum. Private obligations of the quality, design, and maturity appropriate for money market trans-actions and for secondary reserves would increase in supply. Banks would take advantage of Federal Reserve willingness to make advances on private collateral or to rediscount. Relieved of the competition of government bills for the attention of dealers and of the money market, bankers' acceptances might flourish, fulfilling an ancient Federal Reserve dream. Banks might operate to a much greater degree than at present on borrowed reserves; this was the practice in the 1920s in the United States and is the practice today in France and other countries. But even these adaptations would not be necessary. The net debt could vanish—the government might even acquire net claims against the private economy—while a gross debt still remains. Government debt instruments to serve the useful purposes they serve today could be issued to finance the lending activities of government financial intermediaries. If more demand debt were needed, for example, the Federal Reserve could monetize the obligations of government lending agencies. This would keep the Federal Reserve itself free of the difficulties that would attend direct open market dealings in private securities on any scale.

I. The Central Bank Discount Rate

In addition to its powers over the composition of the debt, the Federal Reserve has at its command cer-tain control instruments that do not alter the structure of the debt. The most important are the power to set the discount rate at which member banks can borrow reserves and the power to set required reserve ra-tios. Within broad limits, either or both of these tools may be substituted for open market operations in government securities. Whatever degree of monetary restraint the authorities desire, there are a variety of combinations of controls that can achieve it. Since these purely monetary instruments are close substitutes for debt management operations, they cannot be omitted from a consideration of debt management policy.

What are the monetary effects of lowering the discount rate, while the supplies of all categories of government debt and of capital remain unchanged? A word of caution is in order regarding interpretation of the phrase "lowering the discount rate." What is really to be analyzed is the difference it makes to equilibrium bank and public balance sheets and to the structure of interest rates whether the discount rate stands at one level rather than another, ceteris paribus. Among the other things to be taken as equal are the expectations of the market, its estimates of the future of the economy and of interest rates. The exercise is one of comparative statics. No attempt is made to trace the process of change from one level of discount rate to another, in particular the alterations in expectation generated by the central bank's announcement of a new discount rate. For many students of central bank policy the psychology of the announcement is the most important and perhaps the only important aspect of the discount rate. Unfortunately there is little of a systematic character that can be said about it. Will the public conclude from the announcement of a fall in the discount rate that predictions of recession are now confirmed by the expert economic intelligence of the central bank, and therefore regard the announcement as a deflationary portent? Or will the market judge that the authorities have thus indicated their resolute intention of preventing deflation, arresting and reversing the recession, and accordingly interpret the announcement as an inflationary sign? What do the authorities themselves regard as the likely psychological effects of their announcements? Clearly it is easy to become enmeshed in a game of infinite regress between the central bank and the market. A conclusive justification for separating the analysis of discount policy from expectational effects is that the central bank can, if it chooses, separate them in practice. The authorities can and do make announcements, with calculated psychological impact, *without* changing the discount rate. The distinctive thing about lowering the discount rate is that it reduces the cost of advances to the banks.

Reduction of the discount rate gives banks incentive to reduce their net free reserves by increasing their debt to the Federal Reserve, substituting secondary reserve assets, in particular short government debt, for free reserves. As bank demand for bills increases, in response to the improved differential of the bill rate over the discount rate, the bill rate falls. The fall in the bill rate leads the public to supply bills to the banks, substituting deposits. The lower bill rate also stimulates banks to bid long debt and private debt away from the public; lower yields on these assets induce the public to shift to deposits. All rates, including the supply price of capital, fall, although not in proportion to the initial fall in the discount rate. The new structure of rates provides banks incentive to decrease their net free reserves (increase their borrowing at the Federal Reserve) and at the same time provides the public inducement to expand their deposits by six times the reduction in banks' free reserves.

A rise in the discount rate has the opposite effects. Other rates rise, though not in proportion to the discount rate. Banks increase their free reserves, and the public diminishes its deposits by a multiple of the increase in banks' free reserves. The change in the rate structure must accomplish both of these portfolio shifts at the same time.

There are limits to discount policy at both ends. Banks may be so heavily indebted to the Federal Reserve that they will not respond to further incentive to borrow. Or the bill rate may be so low that it would not compensate banks for the trouble and risk of borrowing to hold bills, even at a zero discount rate. At the other extreme, the discount rate may be so high as to be "out of touch" with the money market. That is, banks are already free of debt to the Federal Reserve, or substantially so, and increasing the bill rate cannot make them reduce indebtedness further. The relevant basic money rate is then the conventional zero rate paid on excess reserves and currency rather than the discount rate charged on borrowed reserves.

J. Changes in Required Reserve Ratios

The second "purely monetary" instrument is prescription of required reserve ratios. Within specified limits, Congress has delegated this power to the Federal Reserve. Changes outside those limits would require congressional action.

Changing required reserve ratios is an extremely powerful tool. Compare it, for example, with open market operations in bills. The Federal Reserve can effect a given initial increase in free reserves, calculated against an unchanged volume of deposits, either by open market purchases of bills from the banks or by a reduction in required reserve ratios. The first method does not alter the banks' overall defensive position; their holdings of free reserves plus bills amount to the same fraction of their disposable assets (total assets less required reserves) as before. The second method, reduction of required reserve ratios, improves the banks' overall defensive position at the same time that it augments their free reserves. Banks' free reserves plus bill holdings become a larger share of their disposable assets. The second method, therefore, gives the banks the greater incentive to expand loans. In the case of open market operations, reduction of free reserves to desired levels entails a multiple deposit expansion based on established reserve ratios. In the case of a lowering of required reserve ratios, reduction of free reserves to desired levels entails deposit expansion by a higher multiple, based on the new reserve ratios.

In the example of Table 6 the increase of demand debt was 10. This could be regarded as the initial increase in free reserves, calculating reserve requirements against the original deposit volume, 120. A similar increase in free reserves could be provided by halving required reserve ratios, so that required reserves against deposits of 120 would be only 10 instead of 20. But this 10 in free reserves is more high-powered than the 10 in free reserves provided by open market operations. It could support a deposit expansion of 120 instead of 60. In neither case will the full potential deposit expansion eventuate. As banks expand loans and deposits, interest rates will fall; and this fall in rates will restrain banks from converting all their new free reserves into required reserves. Banks will push the expansion of deposits farther in the second case than in the first; they will be willing to do so, even though they encounter lower yields on earning assets, because they are better supplied with free reserves and other defensive assets. At the same time they will probably not push the expansion of deposits twice as far in the second case; yields on earning assets would be too low to induce banks to accept an expansion of that magnitude in less liquid assets relative to free and secondary reserves. Clearly the lowering of required reserve ratios will accomplish a bigger reduction in yields of long debt, private debt, and capital than open market purchases of equivalent initial magnitude. Table 9 provides a hypothetical illustration which may be compared with Table 6.

An implication of the foregoing comparison is that the Federal Reserve can have a net expansionary impact by simultaneously (1) reducing required reserve ratios so as to free 10 of reserves and (2) mopping up those freed reserves by open market sales of bills. The immediate consequence of these two moves is that banks have the same free reserves as before, but a larger supply of bills. As banks seek to swap bills with the public for long and private debt, the bill rate will rise and the yields on less liquid assets will fall. The rise in the bill rate will induce some reduction in banks' net free reserves, and each dollar reduction means a deposit expansion at the new higher multiple. This expansion is a further reason for reduction in the yields of private loans, and in the supply price of capital. The net result of the two operations is definitely expansionary. Likewise the Federal Reserve can have a net restrictive effect by raising reserve requirements and supplying the newly needed reserves by open market purchases.

Table 9 Hypothetical Illustration of Assets (+) and Liabilities (–) of Banks and Public Before and After a Reduction in Reserve Requirements Providing Initial Free Reserves Equal to 1% of Wealth

	Banks			Public			Total		
	Before	After	Change	Before	After	Change	Before	After	Change
Currency	0	0	0	+30	+30	0			
Required reserves	+20	+16	–4						
Free reserves	0	+4	+4						
Demand debt	+20	+20	0	+30	+30	0	+50	+50	0
Short debt	+20	+35	+15	+60	+45	–15	+80	+80	0
Long debt	+10	+17	+ 7	+60	+53	–7	+70	+70	0
Private debt	+80	+130	+50	+320	+270	–50	0	0	0
				–400	–400				
Deposits	–120	–192	–72	+120	+192	+72	0	0	0
Capital	–10	–10	0	+810	+810	0	+800	+800	0
Total	0	0	0	+1000	+1000	0	+1000	+1000	0

III. DEBT MANAGEMENT POLICY

A. Criterion for Optimal Policy: Minimum Cost for Required Economic Impact

The objective of government policies for economic stabilization is to maintain balance between aggregate supply and demand at a desired degree of full employment. Whether the target should be 2% unemployment, or 3%, or 5% is a matter of judgment, in which the advantages of greater production and employment must be weighed against their costs, in particular the hazards of faster secular increase in the price level. Whatever target is chosen, there are a variety of ways to pursue it. If aggregate demand threatens to become excessive, it can be restricted by fiscal means or by monetary means. Taxes can be increased to curtail private spending; which taxes are increased will determine whose spending and what kinds of spending are curtailed. Alternatively, demand may be restricted by higher interest rates and lower availability of credit. On what criteria shall these choices of stabilization tools be made? If a number of alternatives will have the same consequences so far as stabilization is concerned, the choice among them must depend on their other consequences.

The composition of national output is an important criterion. Depending on the choice of tools, the national output will be divided in different proportions between investment and consumption. If the government seeks a higher rate of growth, it may prefer a selection of stabilization tools that favors investment demand at the expense of consumption demand. For example, investment may be stimulated by low-interest, "easy" monetary and debt management policies, while consumption is restrained by taxes reducing the spendable incomes of households. Other criteria include equity in the distribution of income and wealth and efficiency in the allocation of resources to accord with the needs and preferences of the society. A stabilization policy which encourages saving by shifting income to higher-income groups might be regarded by some as inequitable, by others as equitable. A stabilization policy which works through curtailing the school construction programs of local governments might raise some objections on the score of efficiency.

One implication of the goal of efficiency is the desirability, other things equal, of minimizing taxes. Taxation by any known feasible method imposes some burden or "deadweight" loss, even if the proceeds are returned to the community of taxpayers rather than used to commandeer productive resources for governmental purposes. This burden is not simply the cost of administration and enforcement. Beyond that, the tax causes taxpayers to adjust their decisions between leisure and work, one job and another job, saving and consuming, risk taking and security, consumption of this and consumption of that, in directions that reduce their tax liability. These adjustments may alter the allocation of national resources and the consumption of national output in socially undesirable directions. Taxation does not always cause misallocation. A certain amount of taxation, skillfully designed, may improve resource allocation, correcting distortions that would otherwise occur. But the size of modern government gives ample scope for corrective taxation. The marginal amounts of taxation involved in decisions to rely more heavily on fiscal measures to restrict demand, and less heavily on other measures, will almost surely cause distorting rather than correcting adjustments in taxpayers' economic decisions. Against this consideration must be placed, of course, the objectives that can be served by relatively heavy reliance on fiscal measures, in particular the stimulation of saving, investment, and growth.

Here it may be assumed that the target of stabilization policy has been decided, and the broad choice between fiscal and monetary instruments has been made. These decisions have the effect of assigning to the monetary and debt management authorities a certain stabilization task. They must aim at a certain degree of monetary restraint, or stimulus, upon the economy. The required degree of monetary restraint will be smaller the more restrictive the fiscal policy; and it will be smaller, for given fiscal policy, the lower the chosen unemployment target.

In achieving their assigned stabilization task, in maintaining the desired degree of monetary restraint or stimulus, the central bank and the managers of the debt have, in their turn, alternative instruments and combinations of instruments. Which should be used? What are the criteria of choice? In the absence of more important criteria, preference could be given to methods of monetary control that minimize the long-run costs of the federal debt to the Treasury. For the reasons given above, taxation to pay interest on the debt has disadvantages on grounds of allocative efficiency. It is logical, therefore, to ask that the monetary and debt management authorities achieve their stabilization task with as little burden on the federal taxpayer as possible. It is worthwhile pursuing the implications of this mandate, even though the course of the pursuit will encounter some constraining criteria—equity, avoidance of controls, and regulations.

The problem of debt management, then, can be put in these terms: How are long-run interest costs on a given volume of federal debt to be minimized, given the contribution that debt management and monetary policy jointly make to economic stabilization? The proviso is, of course, crucial. It is easy to think of ways to minimize interest costs that do not meet it. Interest costs could be reduced to zero by monetizing the entire debt, but that would clearly not maintain intact the restraint that monetary policy and debt management now impose on aggregate demand. The trick is to reduce interest costs without impairing that restraint.

To state the criterion of debt management policy in this way is not to assign minimization of interest transfers a high priority among the goals of national economic policy. These transfers are in the main internal transfers from taxpayers to the Treasury's creditors. They are not a draft on the productive capacity of the country; unlike government purchases of goods and services, they do not require labor or capital equipment or natural resources that might be used for other purposes. This elementary fact was rightly stressed by advocates of "functional finance" who were urging deficit financing to combat unemployment and depression. Those who were ready to welcome increases in interest charged due to expansion of debt have in logic little license now to oppose increases in interest payments due to higher rates on the same total debt. In either case, we are still paying it to ourselves. Similarly the equanimity with which advocates of orthodox finance view increase in total interest burden today, when they result from higher rates, is scarcely consistent with the alarm they expressed over increases in the interest burden yesterday, when they resulted from expansion of debt.

How much taxation is necessary to cover a dollar expansion of interest payments? Enough to neutralize its effect on the demand for national output: if the recipients of a marginal dollar of interest transfer will spend 50 cents of this dollar increase in income, while taxpayers will reduce their spending by 75% of any increase in their tax payments, tax revenues need be increased only 66.7 cents (50/.75) for every dollar increase in interest transfers. It is probable that the marginal propensity to spend from interest transfers is in fact smaller than the marginal propensity to spend from reduction of federal taxes. Indeed, the fact that interest recipients are in general individuals of higher wealth and income than taxpayers is one of the stock objections to interest transfers. It is a valid objection, but its validity to some extent weakens the force of the efficiency objection, because the very regressivity of interest transfers makes less taxation necessary to neutralize them. The concept of fiscal neutrality is the relevant criterion. Balancing marginal revenues and outlays dollar for dollar has no economic logic, except as a rough approximation to fiscal neutrality. Usually it is a poor appoximation. In the particular case at hand it overstates the need for additional taxation. For expenditures on goods and services and transfer payments other than interest, it generally understates the need for additional taxation.

Maximum production, full employment, economic growth, equity in distribution of income and wealth, efficient allocation of resources, balance of payments equilibrium, stabilization of prices these are prime goals of economic policy. We should not sacrifice much in our pursuit of them just to lower the interest burden on the debt. But we probably do not have to. The tools available for monetary control and debt management are sufficient in number and in power to permit us to minimize interest costs, within limits, without impairing the contribution that monetary control and debt management can make to the achievement and reconciliation of the prime goals. Unfortunately this does not mean that the government possesses sufficient tools of economic policy in general to pursue simultaneously all the prime goals. These are some irreconcilable conflicts among them, and hard choices have to be made. The relative abundance of monetary and debt management tools cannot, unhappily, be used to eliminate these conflicts. It is because they can contribute little in that arena that these tools are free to be used for the secondary purpose of minimizing interest transfers. An exception to this statement is that outflows of funds abroad may be more sensitive to short-term interest rates than to long-term rates, at least in the short run. When interest-oriented outflows are a danger, it may be possible to prevent them or diminish them by monetary and debt management techniques which keep short rates relatively high without tightening the overall domestic impact of monetary policy. This objective may well take priority over minimization of interest cost to taxpayers.

A noneconomic reason for concern over the size of government interest payments may be found in the symbolic status that the government's conventional budget has achieved. The size of conventional budget expenditures in a fiscal year is the number that enters political debate, newspaper editorials, and popular discussion. The state of balance of the conventional budget, judged by the eternal knife-edge precepts of Mr. Micawber, is the badge of fiscal success of failure. From the economist's point of view, the focus of attention on the size and state of balance of the conventional budget is quite misplaced. Its size does not measure the government's draft on the productive resources of the economy. Its balance does not measure the effect of the government's transactions with the public on the overall economic balance between supply and demand. But given its symbolic status, the conventional budget is difficult to increase even when the increase is of no economic significance. And given the magical significance vested in the concept of balance of the conventional budget, it is difficult to substitute the criterion of fiscal neutrality. As a matter of political fact, therefore, an increase in interest payments on the national debt may well come at the expense of government outlays on programs of national importance —defense, or school construction, or urban renewal. For it will be argued that the nation cannot afford higher outlays, which would have to be covered dollar for dollar by higher taxes to preserve budget balance. So long as government uses of resources for national purposes are rationed by this set of attitudes—and not merely by collective judgment concerning the marginal utility of the alternative private uses—it makes sense to try to keep interest transfers from impinging on the conventional budget.

The interest entry in the conventional budget is already an exaggerated one, including interest payments from the Treasury to other agencies of the government, principally the social security funds and the Federal Reserve banks, as well as to the general public. It would be desirable to reduce the apparent size of these nominal transfers by creating a special instrument for intragovernmental debt—a simple memorandum of indebtedness without specific maturity, bearing no interest or a nominal interest rate of, say, 1%. A substantial part of the Federal Reserve's current holdings of government securities will almost certainly never be sold to the public. These could be converted into interagency debt, leaving the Federal Reserve with an ample working stock of marketable securities for possible open market sale. If the working stock later became depleted, contrary to initial expectation, the Federal Reserve would have the right to ask the Treasury for marketable securities of any specification desired, in exchange for nonmarketable interagency memoranda of debt.

B.   Reserve Requirements on Banks and Other Institutions

The debt management problem, as defined in Section III.A, may be examined either (1) assuming unchanged the existing institutional framework: existing legislation, financial institutions, markets, debt instruments, or (2) considering certain institutional changes that would contribute to the objective. The discussion is usually carried on solely in the first context, in which the problem reduces to the question how the total debt outstanding should be divided among the various maturities of conventional debt instruments. This question is discussed below, in Section III.C. Quite possibly, however, the potential contributions of optimal management of the maturity structure in the existing institutional framework are small compared to the savings of interest costs that institutional changes could accomplish. It is remarkable how sacrosanct prevailing institutions become even when they have emerged and survived by quite accidental and arbitrary processes.

One institutional change that would reduce interest costs is the introduction of bonds with purchasing power escalation, discussed in Section IV below. These bonds have other important advantages, and interest reduction is only a by-product. The introduction of such bonds might be economical to the Treasury because the general public would be willing to accept lower yields in order to avoid the risks of changes in the price level. The authorities could permit these lower yields to take effect, because they would not signify any reduction in the supply price of capital, any relaxation in the degree of monetary restraint. This is because the low yields on purchasing power bonds would reflect in part a shift out of capital equity, by investors who would prefer a safe hedge against inflation to the risky hedge of capital ownership. Indeed, this initial process of substitution of purchasing power bonds for capital equity would tend to raise the supply price of capital. In order to avoid this tightening of the degree of monetary restriction, the Federal Reserve would have to take expansionary measures, further reducing interest charges on the government debt.

The second major category of possible institutional change is to impose on financial institutions new requirements to hold government securities. These requirements would increase the captive market for government securities. That would leave a smaller quantity of government debt to be placed in the voluntary market, consequently it could be placed on better terms. The authorities could acquiesce in the resulting reduction of yields on government obligations, because the new reserve requirements would accomplish some of the restriction of private demand that now must be achieved by high interest rates. The more the job of restricting private borrowing from financial institutions is done by compelling the institutions to hold larger reserves of government debt, the less the job must be done by higher interest rates.

The principal captive market for government debt at present is, of course, the reserve requirement imposed on member commercial banks. This requirement makes it possible to place about $20 billion of federal debt, 7% of the total, as noninterest bearing demand debt. Within limits set by Congress, the Federal Reserve can raise or lower required reserve-deposit ratios. This is one of its instruments of monetary control, but of course the Federal Reserve has others. The board always has a choice among several combinations of instruments, all of which would achieve the same impact on the economy via the banking system. The Federal Reserve could increase reserve requirements, offsetting the restrictive effects of this action by open market purchases of government securities. (See Section II.G above.) Even if the net result was that market interest rates were maintained, the government would save interest by converting interest-bearing debt into noninterest-bearing demand debt. But the Federal Reserve would have to go even farther, and reduce interest rates, either by additional open market purchases or by lowering its discount rate, in order to neutralize the increase in reserve requirements. Unless interest rates on government securities fall, banks will absorb part of the increase of required reserves by restricting their lending to private borrowers and making the terms of such loans more severe. The fall in government debt interest rates not only encourages banks to maintain private lending relative to defensive holdings of government securities; it also induces the public to switch from government securities to bank deposits, providing securities for the Federal Reserve and the banks to buy. The necessary reduction in yields of government obligations adds to the savings of Treasury interest costs that can be accomplished by an increase in reserve requirements neutralized by expansionary manipulation of other monetary controls.

There is an economic limit to this process, probably well beyond the upper limits on required reserve ratios currently set by Congress. If reserve requirements of banks are increased enough, banks will be able to maintain their lending only by dispensing entirely with defensive holdings of government securities. This they would be unwilling to do even if short-term rates were pushed to zero. After the Federal Reserve has pushed short-term rates to their lower limit, it no longer has the power to neutralize increases in reserve requirements. Clearly the banking system is very far from this limit today.

The same argument can show that neutralized reductions of reserve requirements increase Treasury interest costs on two counts: they replace zero-interest debt with interest-bearing debt, and they involve an increase in interest rates on government securities. This has, in fact, been Federal Reserve policy over the last 8 years; reserve requirements have been relaxed when monetary ease was desired, but subsequent tightening has been accomplished by open market sales or increases of the discount rate.

Contrary to widely held assumptions of the strategic importance of fractional reserve requirements for monetary control, it would be possible to exercise monetary controls much as at present with zero reserve requirements. It would be possible, but expensive. It would be necessary merely to impose the same periodic reserve tests as at present, with the same penalties for deficiencies (overdrafts of the Federal Reserve), and the same facilities for borrowing. The government would lose a substantial captive market for its debt, and the Federal Reserve would have to make up for the absence of reserve requirement by a high discount rate and substantial open market sales of government securities. The extreme example will suffice to drive home the point that the Congress and the Federal Reserve, in deciding by what combination of reserve requirements and other instruments to exercise a given degree of monetary restraint, are helping to decide how much the debt costs the Treasury.

In the short run, what the taxpayers lose by such decisions the shareholders of existing commercial banks gain, and vice versa. How true this is in the long run depends on how well competitive mechanisms work in the banking industry. When reserve requirements are lower and interest rates on safe government securities are higher, the marginal dollar of deposits is worth more to the individual bank. Although banks are prevented from competing for deposits by offering interest, imperfect competition for deposits does occur, with ancillary services, promotional expenses, and preferential loan treatment for good depositor-customers taking the place of outright interest rate competition. Thus bank depositor-customers share with bank shareholders the gains of a policy of low reserve requirements neutralized by high interest rates. In the still longer run, higher bank profits may encourage entry into the industry, so that the Treasury's losses are spread among a wider group of shareholders, not concentrated on those of existing banks. Although some observers may find this less objectionable on grounds of equity, encouragement of new enterprises is not to be welcomed on grounds of efficiency in an industry which already seems to exhibit the wastes of monopolistic competition.

One obvious way to save the Treasury money, then, is to increase the required ratios of reserves, as presently defined, to commercial bank deposits. Under present legislation, the Federal Reserve has discretion to increase required reserves on the present volume of demand and time deposits by $5.7 billion, 2% of the outstanding federal debt. Further increases would depend on new legislation.

Additional reserve requirements on commercial banks do not have to take the same form as present requirements. Congress could authorize the Federal Reserve to impose a secondary requirement, for which not only primary reserve assets but also holdings of specified interest-bearing Treasury obligations would be eligible. The form of the requirement might be, for example, that total holdings of eligible assets must average

30% of average deposits of all kinds over the reserve test period, while at the same time holdings of reserve balances (plus "excess"currency) must meet the usual primary reserve requirements on demand and time deposits. This kind of required "liquid asset" ratio occurs in banking systems abroad, including England and Canada. If additional reserve requirements on banks take this form, the Treasury sacrifices the first of the two sources of economy of interest payments discussed above. The secondary requirement does not enlarge the captive market for interest-free demand debt. But the other source of interest saving remains. The supplementary requirement permits the Federal Reserve to let interest rates on government obligations fall, without diluting the restrictive impact of monetary policy. These interest rates would tend to fall of their own accord, as banks sought securities to meet the new requirement.

One of the greatest fallacies in discussions of proposals of this kind is the assertion that they will expand the banks' demand for the eligible assets only to the extent, if any, that the imposed requirement exceeds the voluntary practice of the banks. It is alleged, therefore, that if banks now find it prudent to carry 30% of their deposits as liquid assets, a compulsory 30% requirement would not affect bank portfolios but would merely formalize prevailing secondary reserve practices. This position is based on a misunderstanding of the role of voluntary secondary reserves. Banks hold certain quantities of excess reserves or of other assets that—from the point of view of a single bank—can be quickly and safely converted into the primary reserves, in order to be able to pass the *present* primary reserve tests. In case of unusual losses of deposits or demands of good customers for loans, they wish to be able to meet their reserve requirements without cost or loss or embarrassment. It is true that assets held to meet a compulsory secondary reserve requirement will still be available, as at present, to meet the primary cash requirement. But banks will also have to worry about meeting the overall 30% liquid asset requirement. The same contingencies—loss of deposits or extraordinary loan demands—would put them in danger of failing this test. To guard against this danger, they will have to hold additional voluntary secondary reserves, on top of the compulsory secondary reserves.

A simple numerical example will illustrate the point. Consider a bank subject to a 10% primary reserve requirement which, in the absence of any secondary requirement, finds it prudent to hold secondary reserves of 15%. The bank is protected against a 20% (15/75) increase in demands upon it for illiquid loans at its present volume of deposits, or against a 16.7% loss of deposits without the necessity for curtailing its lending. (Of the 16 2/3, 15 is covered by liquidation of secondary reserve and 1 2/3 by reduction of required reserves.) Suppose that the bank is now subject to a 25% overall liquid asset requirement. To retain the same protection as before, the bank would need an additional 12.5% voluntary holding of secondary reserves. This would take care of a 20% (12.5/62.5) increase in lending requirements or a 16.7% decline in deposits. (Of the 16 2/3, 12 1/2 is covered by liquidation of the voluntary secondary reserve and 4 1/6 by reduction of overall required reserves.) However, banks would in all likelihood be content with a somewhat weaker defensive position than before. Defensive assets would fall in yield relative to bank loans; as a result, banks would be content with somewhat less protection. To continue the simple numerical example, the loan-deposit ratio might fall only to 67.5% instead of to 62.5%; the bank has a defensive position of 7.5% of deposits instead of 15%. It would be protected against an 11% (7.5/67.5) increase in loans or a 10% loss of deposits (by 7.5 excess reserves and 2.5 reduction of reserve requirements).

A by-product of the reduction in government security yields that would result from imposition of additional reserve requirements on banks would be substitution by the public of bank deposits for government securities. Indeed, only by inducing such substitution could the banking system as a whole obtain the assets necessary to meet the new requirements, with the same margin of safety as before. The resulting expansion of bank deposits and the money supply would be an innocuous one, for which the central bank could safely provide the cash reserve. It would not signify an expansion of bank lending or an easing of terms to private borrowers. Without an increase in bank deposits, in fact, bank credit would contract and tighten. (In the numerical example above, the representative bank changes from a 75% loan-deposit ratio to a 67.5% loan-deposit ratio. If this change in ratio is to leave the absolute volume of bank lending unchanged, deposits must increase by 11%. If banks started out with liquid assets equal to 25% of initial deposits, public substitution of deposits for direct holdings of government securities enough to increase deposits 11% would give the banks reserve asset holdings of 32.5% of their new volume of deposits [36/111]. To enable banks to meet the cash requirement against the new deposits, the Federal Reserve would absorb 1/10 of the securities surrendered by the public.)

This expansion of bank deposits should not be forgotten in calculating the impact of additional required reserves on bank profits. As a first approximation to neutralizing a new requirement, the Federal Reserve can permit the volume of bank lending and the terms of bank credit to private borrowers to remain unchanged.

This means that the only change in the portfolio earnings of the banking system would be on account of bank holdings of government debt. These, in turn, can be divided into two categories; required reserves, and voluntary secondary reserves. Voluntary secondary reserve earnings will be smaller; for reasons given above, the yields of these assets will be lower and banks' holdings of excess secondary reserves smaller.

If the increase of reserve requirements takes the form of a simple increase in the required ratio of primary zero-interest reserves to deposits, earnings on required reserves are zero both before and after the change. Bank earnings as a whole unambiguously fall. The Treasury saves money partly on this account, and partly at the expense of the nonbank public. The public is induced by lower yields on government securities to substitute indirect holdings, via bank deposits at zero interest, for direct holdings; and the public receives lower yields on the direct holdings it retains.

If, however, the additional reserve requirements can be met by marketable interest-bearing government securities, the upshot for bank earnings is not so clear. Here there is an increase in earnings on the required reserve portion of banks' portfolios, which now consist of a primary reserve earning no interest and a secondary reserve earning interest. Conceivably this might do more than offset the decline in earnings on voluntary secondary reserves. In the numerical example above, reserve assets on which interest is earned (required and voluntary secondary reserves) increase from 15 to 25 (in percent of initial deposit level). If the yields of such assets fall less than 40%, the banks gain from the new requirement. The loss to the nonbank public is the same no matter what form the new requirement on the banks takes. To the extent that the government permits the banks to earn interest on reserves, the Treasury shares with the banks what can be gained from the public.

Reference to "losses" by the nonbank public does not mean, of course, that holders of unmatured government securities at the time the new reserve requirement is imposed will lose. They will in fact enjoy capital gains. The loss of the nonbank public, and the corresponding saving to the Treasury, is that as issues mature their holders will be able to replace them only at lower yields.

Commercial banks are not the only possible captive market for government securities. Congress might authorize the Federal Reserve to impose new reserve requirements, or increase existing ones, on other financial intermediaries—life insurance companies, pension funds, savings and loan associations, mutual savings banks. Analysis of the consequences of such requirements is much the same as in the case of commerical banks, and gives much the same results. Yields on government securities eligible for the requirements, and others closely substitutable for them, will tend to fall. The monetary authorities can permit them to fall without loosening the bite of monetary control. The Treasury will save interest payments, certainly at the expense of its ultimate creditors, and possibly also at the expense of the intermediary institutions.

There is one important difference, however, between banks and other intermediaries. Banks do not, except in indirect and imperfect ways, compete for deposits by offering interest. The other intermediaries compete for their creditors' funds via the interest or dividends they offer. The equilibrium of an intermediary industry or category other than banks is one in which the interest or dividend offered to creditors is adjusted to the additional earnings an enterprise in the industry can obtain by investing an extra dollar of funds. The word *adjusted* is used deliberately in place of *equated*, for these are not perfectly competitive industries, but ones in which each of the competing firms has distinctive appeal to certain savers and special opportunities for lending to a particular market of borrowers. This equilibrium condition does not apply in the case of banks. In that industry the total volume of assets and liabilities is controlled by adjusting the earnings from an additional dollar of loans not to the cost of an additional dollar of deposits, but to the cost and risk of holding a dollar less of net reserves.

If a reserve requirement, to be met by holding of government securities, is imposed on a nonbank financial intermediary, the investment value of the marginal dollar of its liabilities is reduced. Consequently these institutions will seek to meet the requirement partly by selling their private investments and curtailing their private loans, substituting government securities, and partly by lowering the inducements they offer their creditors, thereby contracting their liabilities. The public shifts out of government securities and out of the liabilities of intermediaries. Into what? Partly into the private securities and loans the intermediaries get rid of, or into the capital equities those debts were financing; partly, perhaps principally, into bank deposits. The authorities can—and indeed must, if they are going to neutralize the effects of the new controls and on balance keep private loan rates and the supply price of capital from rising—countenance this expansion of bank deposits and permit banks to fill the gap created by contraction of the lending of intermediaries. The banks and the Treasury gain, and the newly regulated intermediaries and their creditors lose. Borrowers specifically adjusted to the intermediaries lose, and borrowers in a position to profit from cheaper bank credit gain.

Clearly there is a ticklish question of equity involved in the present special treatment of banks, and no judgment on it will be essayed here. Competing financial intermediaries are not subject to the reserve requirements now imposed on banks. On the other hand, neither do they have the advantage of a government-enforced covenant to avoid price competition for funds. When banks chafe under the bit of the interest-barren reserves they are compelled to hold, they are inclined to forget the advantages of having industry equilibrium maintained where marginal asset earnings considerably exceed the interest paid on deposits. Banks would have a better case for asking that the burden of reserve requirements be spread more widely if they were willing at the same time to restore competitive determination of interest on demand and time deposits.

Economy to the Treasury and equity to banks are not the only possible reasons for advocating reserve requirements for other financial intermediaries. Another reason is to strengthen the effectiveness of monetary control and to make its impact more immediately felt. The unregulated activities of other financial interme-diaries provide the economy a partial escape from central bank control measures. When the availability of bank credit is restricted, borrowers denied credit or discouraged by stiffer terms can turn to other interme-diaries for accommodation. At the same time the intermediaries can attract additional funds—which in the absence of restrictive measures would take the form of bank deposits—without more than a slight sweetening of the terms offered their creditors. Private loan rates and the supply price of capital rise less, in response to a given restrictive action by the monetary authority, than if nonbank intermediaries were prevented from expanding. This does not mean that the existence of these intermediaries makes monetary policy impotent. But it does mean that central bank action must be more drastic—e.g., a larger volume of open market sales—in order to achieve a given effect, and that the lag between action and effect is longer. If nonbank intermediaries were subject to a security reserve requirement, any central bank action raising government security yields would tend to make them contract like banks. For one thing, the increase in yields might induce the intermediaries themselves to hold more excess reserves. More important, the increase in yields may cause the public to substitute direct ownership of government securities for holdings of intermediary liabilities. A dollar of such substitution means a multiple contraction in intermediary private lending. Unlike commercial banks, other intermediaries can counter this threat to their reserves by offering higher yields on their own liabilities. But this increase in the cost of funds will be reflected in harsher terms to private borrowers, and thus in a rise in the supply price of capital. Credit would be tighter, and the volume of lending smaller, at both banks and other intermediaries. The actions of the nonbank intermediaries would support rather than oppose the objectives of the central bank.

Is enlargement of the captive market for government securities to be abhorred as a violation of the principles of a free economy? Much official and private opposition to proposals for supplementary reserve requirements, either on banks or on other financial intermediaries, is expressly based on high ideological grounds. Interest rates, it is said, including those at which the government borrows, should be set in the free market, not by government fiat. The government should not rig the capital market in its own favor, discriminating against other claimants on the people's savings.

These expressions of ideological principle will not withstand careful analysis. Interest rates are already under government control. The market that determines them does so under the watchful eyes of the monetary authorities, and in an environment of their making. If the Federal Reserve and Treasury do not like the market's results they can and do intervene to change them. Without such interventions, the prospects of monetary stabilization would be very dim. There already exists a substantial captive market for government debt, indeed for zero-interest demand debt. Ideological consistency would require abolition of commercial bank reserve requirements. Matters of degree are poor material for invocation of "the basic principles of a free economy." There is no escape from the necessity to judge proposals for extension of reserve requirements on the more pragmatic grounds of the efficiency of stabilization policy, administrative possibility and inconvenience, and equity to various institutions, savers, borrowers, and taxpayers.

The kernel of truth in the ideological objections is that Congress and the president should to some extent be guided, in their decisions as to the scope of government investment programs and other public uses of resources, by the productivity of capital and other resources in the private sector of the economy. If a high interest rate on government securities is a signal that saving is in heavy demand for highly productive private investment projects, it is right that Congress and the president should be deterred from further borrowing and indeed encouraged to run a surplus. Similarly, a low interest rate on government securities, indicative that saving is not in great demand for private expansion of capital, should encourage the federal government to borrow for public investment. The signal, and the deterrent or incentive, provided by fluctuating interest rates on government securities should not be destroyed. Nor would they be. Extension of reserve requirements would mean a general lowering of the average over time of interest rates on government debt, but not a stabilization of rates. The rates would fluctuate as now, but around a lower mean. The timing signal that these fluctuations send to the government would not be lost. It is *not* proposed to vary reserve requirements in a countercyclical way so that monetary control could be exercised without variation of interest rates on government debt. The signal given by *changes* in rates would be retained, and more than that cannot be expected. The absolute level of interest rate on government debt is very far from measuring the opportunity cost of capital. The social productivity of private investment is not the same as its private productivity, and the latter is related to a government bond yield only through a complicated and variable system of risk premiums. The social productivity of public expenditure is even more difficult to quantify. The accounting procedures of the government are irrational; they probably work to restrict public investment unduly, since they force the Treasury to count the complete cost of highly durable assets as current expense. The fiscal balance of the government is necessarily the result of a complex of policy considerations and objectives. In its decisions on fiscal policy the central government should be above the economic deterrents and incentives that operate on other economic units. For all these reasons, the importance to the allocative efficiency of government investment decisions of the level of interest rates on government securities is quite small. It is, in any case, not a significant objection to new reserve requirements.

C. Management of the Maturity Structure of Debt

1. The Criterion.

The narrower problem of debt management is to arrange the maturity composition of the debt so as to obtain a given economic impact at minimal cost to the Treasury, without any change in reserve requirements, or in types of debt instruments.

A useful simplification, which still retains the essentials of the problem, is to consider only three categories of debt: demand debt, bearing zero interest rate; short debt, yielding r_s; and long debt, yielding η. Denote the Federal Reserve discount rate by r_d. The following are important identities:

Total debt, a constant = demand debt + short debt + long debt (1)

Net cost = (0 x demand debt) - (r_d x borrowed reserves) + (r_s x short debt) + (η x long debt) (2)

Demand debt = currency outside banks or vault cash not counted as bank reserves + required reserves + excess reserves - borrowed reserves (3)

(There is a certain asymmetry here, in that the discount rate is charged on borrowed reserves but not paid to banks on excess reserves.) The authorities have three instruments of control: fixing the magnitudes of any two of the three categories of debt, and setting the discount rate.

Which authorities? It is evident from the statement of the problem that debt management is not a task that is divisible into two provinces, monetary control on the one hand and management of the interest-bearing debt on the other. The problem is a unit, and it is anomalous to attempt, as we do in the United States, to split it into two administrative packages. The current division of labor and responsibility appears to assign to the Federal Reserve the fixing of the quantity of demand debt and of the discount rate, and to the Treasury determination of the amount of long debt.[*] Unless there is coordination and agreement between the two agencies, this division of the task cannot produce optimal, or even satisfactory results. Even if the two agencies concur in their diagnoses of current money and capital markets and business trends, and in their objectives, neither can make an intelligent use of the control instruments at its disposal without knowing what the other is doing. In analyzing the problem of debt management, we should not be imprisoned by current administrative arrangements or by conventional and artificial distinctions between monetary policy and debt management. It is best to attack the problem as a whole, as if there were a unified or coordinated authority to make and execute the three decisions. Some administrative recommendations consistent with the economics of the problem will be offered below.

Imagine the three decisions to be made for a certain planning period, the next quarter or the next year. What is the cost which the authorities should seek to minimize over that period, subject to the fulfillment of their responsibility for economic stabilization? The relevant cost—the cost to the government of owing its debt over the planning period—may be expressed as (4) Net cost = net interest outlays + increase in market value of the debt. In other words, the cost to the government of owing the debt over the period is simply the

---

[*]This division has been blurred by the Federal Reserve's decision in February 1961 to operate in all sectors of the government securities market.

negative of the gains to the public of owning the debt. Under this concept, what the creditors gain, the debtors loses, and vice versa.

Now why should the government concern itself with changes in the market value of its obligations, when they involve no actual outlays of cash? Suppose that market interest rates on long-term bonds are expected to fall over the period ahead from 4% to 3%. This expectation should, other things equal, deter the Treasury from new long-term borrowing—better to wait for the lower interest rate. In effect, the rate on new long-term borrowing over the period is more than 4%. It is 4% plus the capital gain associated with a fall in the rate to 3%; this gain depends on the exact maturity and coupon of the bonds. Say the effective rate is 4 1/2%. If the authorities can borrow the funds short for less than 4 1/2%, even for 4 1/4%, without compromising their stabilization responsibilities, they should do so. But if the attention of the authorities were confined to interest outlays, they would regard 4% on the new long-term borrowing as quite satisfactory. Including changes in market value of the debt in the criterion is the way to make the authorities pay proper attention to the timing of long-term borrowing.

But that is not all. If the expectation of a fall in long-term market yield from 4% to 3% were sufficient to deter the Treasury from issuing new long-term debt, it should also be a signal to the government to purchase outstanding long-term bonds from the public, selling the appropriate neutral quantity of shorts to replace them. From the taxpayer's point of view, it is better for the Federal Reserve to enjoy the capital gains on longs than for the public to receive them.

The definition of net cost in (4) is the same as in (2), provided that the yields r_s and η are correctly defined. The yield η on a long bond during a period is the interest accrual to which ownership of the bond entitles the holder plus the appreciation of the value of the bond over the period, expressed as percent of the initial market value of the bond, and converted to a per annum basis. This is the 4 1/2% rate in the example above. This—rather than coupon yield on face value or coupon yield on market value—is the relevant rate an investor considers. It is also the relevant rate for the borrower, even the government. A similar definition applies for short rates. However, here the simplification has been made that there is only one short security, and its maturity will be assumed not to exceed the planning period. Thus the government does not have to worry about capital gains and losses on its short obligations. In practice, of course, the distinction of long and short, in this as in other regards, is not so sharp. If the authorities minimize (2), with the rates thus defined, they will also minimize (4).

Another illustration will make clear the importance of attention to market yields rather than simply to coupons. Suppose 20-year 2 1/2's with 10 years to run are available at prices below par in the market, yielding their holders 4 1/2%. Suppose that, as in the previous example, 4 1/2% is too high a rate, considering prevailing short-term rates, at which to issue a new 10-year bond. Then by the same token it is to the government's advantage to buy back the old bonds now at 84 rather than 10 years from now at 100. This saving overshadows the economy of the 2 1/2% coupon.

The government does not, of course, borrow in a perfect market. As the government makes security transactions, it turns the market against itself. Government purchases of longs and sale of shorts to replace them will cause the long rate to fall and the short rate to rise. The rate differential that made the switch advantageous to the government will tend to vanish as the authorities exploit it. This does not mean that it is fruitless to take advantage of favorable opportunities. They should be exploited until they are exhausted, and no farther. It does mean that pursuit of the suggested criterion (4) involves less drastic and frequent reshuffling of the debt structure than might at first appear.

Even so, the minimization objective is not to be regarded as something to be precisely and continuously achieved. It indicates the direction in which adjustments of the debt structure should be sought. The authorities may well wish to sacrifice some apparent economy of interest cost in order to avoid too frequent and drastic interventions in the market. Nevertheless, present administrative arrangements probably keep the debt structure too rigid and too unresponsive to the requirements of debt management.

One component of the relevant long-term yield is observable in the market; the other, the capital gain or loss, will be known for certain only after the event. The authorities are in a somewhat better position than the public to guess at it, but their best guess is subject to considerable uncertainty. So also is the response of the yield to the government's own operations. What effect should this uncertainty have on the government's behavior? The answer is none. The government should act on the basis of the statistical expectations of the values of the uncertain variables, ignoring the degree of uncertainty. If anyone is in the position to be his own insurer, clearly it is the secretary of the Treasury. It would be inappropriate for him to pay the public in order to avoid risks. Indeed, the contrary should be the case. The government should gain for the taxpayer the amounts that owners of the debt will pay, through sacrifices of yields, in order to reduce private risks.

When the appropriate yields are considered, and when the maturity structure of the debt is sufficiently flexible, the authorities can make their decisions for the period immediately ahead without considering more distant periods. Suppose, for example, that the long-term rate is now 3%, is expected to rise to 4% next period, and then after several more periods to fall to 2%. Assume an alternative short-term financing cost of 4%. Should the government wait until the long-term rate reaches 2% before borrowing long? In the period immediately ahead, the government should borrow long provided a rate in the neighborhood of 2 1/2% (3% less the expected capital loss) is highly satisfactory in the light of the prevailing short rate. At the time when the fall from 4% to 2% is expected, the long-term yield will be higher than 4%, and the authorities should seek to replace longs with shorts temporarily, borrowing long again to take advantage of the 2% rate. Applying the criterion successively in each period leads to the correct long-run strategy. It fails to do so only when the authorities attribute some cost to going in and out of the market. In that case, they may prefer to reduce the number of transactions by waiting until the rate reaches 2%, even though waiting adds to the government's interest costs.

Are the interest rates that determine how expensive the debt is to the government the same interest rates that determine the monetary impact of the debt on the economy? This is the assumption of the argument concerning optimal debt management. The yields relevant to the government, it was argued above, are market yields corrected for expectation of capital gain or loss. Thus if the long-term interest rate is expected to rise, the relevant long yield is smaller than the prevailing market yield. This is as true for the managers of private portfolios and balance sheets as it is for the Treasury's debt managers. The attractiveness of long bonds, relative to other investments, is clearly lessened by expectation of capital loss and enhanced by anticipation of capital gain. The market yield must be thus corrected, whether bonds are being compared in investment worth with cash and short-term securities or with physical capital.

Discussions of monetary theory and policy contain some confusion on this point. Although it is generally assumed, following Keynes, that expectations of capital gain or loss on bonds influences the demand for bonds relative to more liquid alternatives, it seems also to be generally assumed, again following Keynes, that the market yield of bonds *un*corrected for such expectations is the "interest rate" against which "the marginal efficiency of capital" must be tested. But if capital losses are expected on bonds, is this not as good reason to prefer equities as to prefer cash? Is not a private borrower encouraged to borrow long for investment purposes when long-term interest rates are temporarily low? If this principle is symmetrically and consistently applied, it appears that long-term rates are by no means as sticky over the trade cycle as they appear to be. Relevant long rates fluctuate a good deal more than observed market rates. At the bottom of recession, long-term rates are lower than they seem, because market yields are expected to rise. In high prosperity long-term rates are higher than they seem because market yields are expected to fall. On the other hand, in incipient recession apparent reductions in the long-term rate may be nullified by expectations of further declines in market yields. The effective rate contains allowance for capital gains and is still high. Similarly if a rise in rates generates expectations of a further rise, the relevant interest rate may not have increased at all. The authorities will do better, for this reason, to move with decisively large steps rather than to feel their way in gradual and small moves that lead the public to expect further steps in the same direction.

Generally speaking, then, the same concept of the interest rate is relevant both for governmental decision and for private decision. But of course expectations are not concrete and observable, like market yields. The government may not agree with the "market." Indeed the participants in the market do not agree with each other, and most of them are uncertain of their own best guesses. Moreover, private investors and borrowers may differ widely from each other, and from the government, in the length and timing of investment planning periods. It is these uncertainties and differences of opinion and circumstances that prevent widely held expectations from realizing themselves immediately.

The government must take into account its disagreements with the market. Cost depends on the government's view, provided of course it is the government experts who are right. Monetary restraint depends on the market's view. Suppose, for example, the market decides that long-term interest rates are going to rise, while the government does not think so. This means that the government can no longer purchase the same degree of monetary restraint at the same expected cost. To offset the expansionary effect of the market's anticipations, the authorities will have to take restrictive measures. In other instances divergence of public expectations from government predictions may enable the government to purchase the required degree of restraint more cheaply. To some degree market expectations are self-fulfilling, because the actions the authorities have to take to offset their monetary effects tend to move interest rates in the direction the market expects.

2. Administration

If the expected long rate η is too high, the amount of long debt should be reduced. How can this be done? The mere passage of time is constantly transferring some debt from the long category to the short. But this reduction of the long portion of the debt may at times be much too small for optimal debt management. Refundings at maturity, of course, can never reduce the quantity of long debt. At the time of refunding, maturing issues are by definition short. The only way to effect a significant reduction in long debt in the short run is for the government to buy back its own long securities, or refund them in advance with short debt. The obvious instrument for such purchases is the Federal Reserve Open Market Committee. It would have to undertake open market operations in the interests of Treasury costs as well as in the interests of stabilization. In the present example, open market purchases of longs would be compensated, for stabilization purposes, by open market sales of shorts, very likely in an amount exceeding the purchases. At other times, the appropriate long rate may signal that the amount of long debt should be increased. This is easier for the Treasury to do, simply by issuing longs in place of maturing shorts. The Federal Reserve can move easily in either direction.

The cleanest administrative solution, if the problem of debt management is to be taken seriously, is to concentrate all security dealings with the public in a single agency, responsible for issue of new securities to the public, redemption of maturing issues, and purchases and sales of old securities. Refundings and new issues would be integrated with open market operations. The agency would be in complete command of the maturity distribution of the debt at all times. Its mandate would be to minimize long-run interest costs to the government; i.e., to minimize net cost as defined above, subject to the achievement of the stabilization (and balance of payments) objectives that are the task of monetary control. With its mandate thus broadened, the Federal Reserve would be the logical repository of this responsiblity. The arrangement would have many incidental advantages, among them providing the government with an underwriting service that, alone among major borrowers, it now lacks through a perverse sense of self-denial.

Under the proposed arrangement, increases in debt to meet fiscal deficit would be accomplished in the first instance by replenishing the Treasury's cash balance in Federal Reserve banks. The Federal Reserve would receive in return Treasury securities, with maturities and other terms designed to Federal Reserve specifications. The Federal Reserve would sell these or other securities from its portfolio to the public in amounts and at times of its own discretion, in pursuit of its joint mission of debt management and stabilization. Similarly, when budget surplus augments the Treasury balance, the Treasury may use the excess over its working balance to reclaim some securities from the Federal Reserve stock.

3. Discount Policy

Federal Reserve discount rate policy is a purely monetary matter, if anything is. But since the discount rate affects both the net costs of government debt and the degree of monetary restraint upon the economy, its level is a part of the problem of debt management. To a considerable degree, moreover, it can be considered separately from the problem of optimal proportions of shorts and longs.

The Federal Reserve generally has a choice between maintaining a given degree of monetary restraint by (1) a low discount rate, a low volume of demand debt, negative net free reserves, with bank borrowing at the discount window encouraged by a favorable differential between yields on government securities and the discount rate, or (2) a high discount rate, a high volume of demand debt, positive net free reserves, with bank borrowing discouraged by an unprofitable differential between market yields on bills and other securities and the discount rate. Of course there are many more than two alternatives. The two contrasting possibilities are stated in order to dramatize the decision problem involved. In other words, it is generally possible to preserve the existing levels of deposits and bank loans either by lowering the discount rate and simultaneously making open market sales, or by raising the discount rates and simultaneously making open market purchases. There are limits to these possibilities, at both ends, as described in Section II.I.

What is the optimal combination of discount policy and open market operations? It is evidently of type (1), close to the second of the two extremes just outlined. The reasoning is as follows. Starting from some arbitrary combination of discount rate and demand debt, consider the change in net cost due to a dollar of open market purchases neutralized by an increase in the discount rate. The dollar of open market purchases will save the government r_s, the rate on short-term securities, which is to remain unchanged. On the other hand, borrowed reserves will be reduced, but by less than a dollar. Net free reserves will be increased by a dollar, but a part of this increase will be in excess reserves, and only a fraction, say, k, in reduction of debt.

When the discount rate is higher, some banks, even some which rarely if ever borrow, will hold more excess reserves in order to diminish the probability that they will need to borrow in case of loss of deposits or heavy demand for customer loans. Let $\delta \, r_d$ be the increase in discount rate necessary to bring about a reduction of k in borrowed reserves accompanied by an increase in 1 - k in excess reserves. The increase in revenue of the Federal Reserve is $\delta \, r_d$ (B - k) - r_dk where B is the original volume of borrowing. In order for the change to be worthwhile, the total saving must be positive.

$$r_s + \delta \, r_d \, B - (r_d + \delta \, r_d) \, k > 0$$

Clearly changes in this direction are profitable so long as the discount rate is lower than r_s/k, and even longer if allowance is made for some residual bank borrowing (B), inelastic to interest differential, on which the Federal Reserve can profit.

As in the case of reserve requirement policy, the optimal policy for the government is to convert as much debt into noninterest-bearing demand debt as the Federal Reserve can neutralize. Here the instrument of neutralization is a high discount rate, which has the incidental advantage of bringing in more revenue from insensitive borrowers. If this kind of policy is followed, the Federal Reserve will keep the discount rate *above* market short-term rates, and keep the banking system operating with positive net free reserves. The more the banks can be induced to carry as defensive assets noninterest-bearing government debt rather than interest-bearing debt, the cheaper it is for the government.

4.   *Optimal Debt Composition*

The strategy for determining the optimal proportions of shorts and longs can be described in general and formal terms. But it is not so easy to derive concrete conclusions concerning the optimal structure of maturities or of interest rates. Concrete conclusions depend on empirical estimates of the behavior relationships involved.

Suppose that a given degree of monetary restraint is to be maintained. Starting from an arbitrary composition of debt that accomplishes this task, consider an addition of 1 billion to short debt. Between them, demand debt and long debt must be diminished by 1 billion. How must this reduction be divided between these two categories? To concentrate the entire reduction on demand debt would certainly be deflationary, and to concentrate it all on long debt would generally be inflationary. To neutralize the addition to short debt, a fraction of it must replace demand debt and the remainder long debt. The fraction is a variable one, dependent on many circumstances. Among other things, it depends on the initial proportions of short and long debt. Suppose short debt is already abundant relative to demand debt and long debt. To increase short debt further will not be giving the public a very good substitute for cash, and substitution of short debt for long will not be very expansionary. Therefore the fraction of demand debt replaced by short debt must be small if deflation is to be avoided. But if short debt is relatively scarce to begin with, its expansion will have to be offset mainly by reduction of demand debt, and only to a small extent by reduction of long debt.

Figure 1 shows combinations of short debt (horizontal axis) and long debt (vertical axis) that produce a given degree of monetary tightness; i.e., a given supply price of capital. The combinations lie along the curve L_1S_1. The curve applies, of course, only for a given total debt T_1, shown on both axes. The sum L + S, implied by the curve L_1S_1 is shown as the vertical distance below the curve L_1I_1. This is the total interest-bearing debt, and the vertical difference between it and T_1 is the amount of demand debt. As the figure shows, demand debt and long debt increase together, as the amount of short debt is reduced. A greater degree of monetary restraint; i.e., a higher supply price of capital, would be indicated by a curve of the same general shape as L_1S_1 but above and to the right. Corresponding to each point on L_1S_1 are the interest rates, short and long, required to induce the public, including the banks, to hold the indicated quantities of short and long debt. At L_1 the long rate is high relative to the short rate; this differential declines as the quantity of short debt is increased, toward S_1. As the differential between the two rates declines, their general level increases, reflecting the fall in the quantity of demand debt.

In similar manner, loci of constant cost to the government can be constructed, without regard for the degree of monetary restraint. L_2S_2 is an example of such a locus. All combinations of short and long debt on this curve represent the same cost to the government; they do not all, of course, represent the same degree of monetary restraint. The total interest-bearing debt corresponding to L_2S_2 is shown as L_2I_2. The assumption made in Fig. 1 is that more interest-bearing debt can be placed in the hands of the banks and the public at given cost when it is a mixture of short and long debt than when it is concentrated heavily in either category.

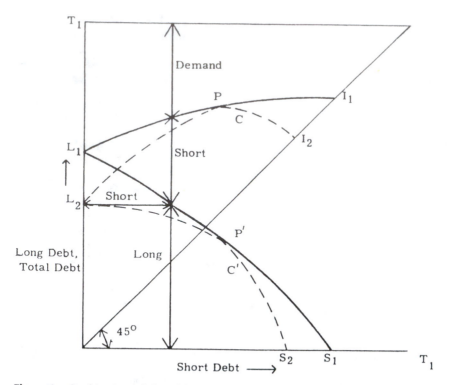

Figure 1   Combinations of short debt and long debt that produce a given degree of monetary tightness.

Some investors and institutions have special needs for longs, and others have special needs for shorts. It is economical for the government to cater to these special needs. Otherwise the government will have to pay the holders of its debt to take securities less well tailored to their needs and preferences, or attract other holders by higher yields. The maximum interest-bearing debt that can be placed at the cost represented by L_2S_2 is at point C, with a distribution between short and long as indicated by point C'. But C And C'do not accomplish the degree of monetary restriction represented by L_1S_1. As the figure is drawn, that is the maximum degree of monetary restraint that can be purchased at the cost corresponding to L_1S_1. It can be purchased by a total interest-bearing debt of P, somewhat smaller than C, divided between short and long as indicated by P', with less short and more long than at C'.

    The two kinds of loci—constant monetary restraint, and constant interest cost—are not independent of each other. The same asset preferences and interest rate sensitivities that determine the shape of one determine the shape of the other. This may be illustrated by some examples of extreme assumptions about asset preferences, some of which are the foundation, implicit or explicit, for current views about monetary policy and debt management.

    1. One extreme view is that only the quantity of demand debt matters, whatever may be the distribution of interest-bearing debt as between short and long. The locus of constant restraint L_1S_1 is then a line with unit slope, and the corresponding curve of total interest-bearing debt L_1I_1 is horizontal. The rate changes necessary to induce substitution of a dollar of short debt for a dollar of long would, on this view, have no net effect on the willingness of the community to hold capital at a given yield. To put the same point another way, it is the quantity of cash provided or absorbed in open market operations that matters, not what is bought or sold. This will be recognized as the core of "bills only" doctrine; bank reserves can be controlled as well by buying and selling bills as by dealing in other securities, and there are various technical advantages to confining operations to bills. Buying a dollar of shorts and selling a dollar of longs will affect to some degree the short-long rate differential, but that is all it will affect. On this view, once the requisite amount of demand debt is provided, the task is simply to find the cheapest way to place the remainder of the debt at interest. Point C coincides with P in the figure, and Point C' with P'. (See Fig. 2a.) This is a consistent point of view,

although its assumptions about the behavior of banks and other investors seem implausible. What is not consistent is to couple bills only with stress on the urgency of lengthening the interest-bearing debt. If bills only is correct then the Treasury can safely turn its attention to minimizing the cost of placing at interest the quantity of debt which the Federal Reserve does not monetize. If this requires substitution of 100 million of "more liquid" shorts for 100 million of "less liquid" longs, the authorities can rest secure in the knowledge that the increase in the short rate necessary to induce the substitution will automatically render the shorts as innocuous and as firmly held as the longs they replace. Neither is it consistent to berate at the same time the Treasury for wishing to lengthen the debt and the Federal Reserve for its adherence to bills only. If the Treasury should stick to the job of minimizing the cost of the interest-bearing debt, if it is indeed safe to ignore stabilization consequences of changing the maturity structure of the debt, it must be because the Federal Reserve can do what is needed for stabilization just by fixing the amount of demand debt.

A variant of this view has it that short and long securities are perfect substitutes for each other. Again, the degree of monetary restraint depends on the total quantity of a given debt represented by short debt and long debt combined, not on the split between them. But in addition, the interest rates on the two kinds of securities do not depend on their relative supplies. Whether the differential of longs over shorts is positive, zero, or negative may depend on the economic circumstances at the time. But it is not to be affected by changing the relative amounts of the two categories of debt. This may be referred to as the "arbitrage" variant of bills only doctrine. Although open market operations take place in shorts and affect the short rate in the first instance, arbitrage quickly spreads the effect throughout the range in maturities, restoring the appropriate structure of rates. In diagrammatic terms, the iso-cost curve is a straight line. In Fig. 2b the long rate is lower,

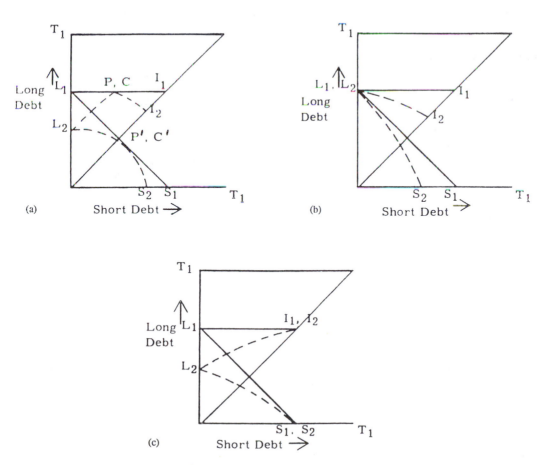

Figure 2

and optimal debt management would place the entire interest-bearing debt in longs. In Fig. 2c, the opposite is the case. If the appropriate structure of rate happens to be equality, then the maturity distribution of the debt does not matter.

2. Another common extreme view is associated with the tradition of aggregative economic theory, strongly reinforced by Keynes, that long-term government debt and private capital ownership are perfect substitutes for each other. "The marginal efficiency of capital must equal the rate of interest." (Some misleading implications of this tradition have been discussed elsewhere in this chapter.) Here this means that along a locus of constant monetary restraint the long rate is constant, in the appropriate relation to the constant supply price of capital. At these constant rates, the more long debt the community is asked to absorb, the lower must be the yield on short debt, and the greater the volume of demand debt. An interesting implication of this view is that optimal debt management requires a short rate below the long rate. This may be shown as follows: The cost of adding a dollar of long debt, while maintaining the degree of monetary restraint, is

$$r_l + S \cdot \frac{\delta r_s}{\delta L} + r_s \cdot \frac{\delta S}{\delta L}$$

where S is the quantity of short debt, L the quantity of long debt, r_l the constant long rate, and r_s the short rate. Long debt should not be increased, but decreased if this cost is positive; i.e., if

$$r_l > r_s \left(-\frac{\delta S}{\delta L} \right) + S \left(-\frac{\delta r_s}{\delta L} \right)$$

long debt should be increased if the inequality is the other way. Now both derivatives are negative, and $\delta S/\delta L$ exceeds one in absolute value. Thus if the short rate is as high as the long rate, or higher, the quantity of long debt is insufficient. In interpreting this result, it is important to remember the definitions of yields relevant to the debt management problem. They include a correction of market yields for expected capital gains or losses due to interest rate changes.

3. A third possible simple and extreme view is, in a sense, the opposite of the first. It is that short debt and demand debt are perfect substitutes for each other, at a given rate differential between them. The degree of monetary restraint then depends wholly on the *quantity* of long debt—not as in (b), on the long *rate*. As shown in Fig. 3, the constant-restraint locus is a horizontal line. Clearly the cheapest way to achieve such restraint is to have no short debt whatever, but to convert it all into demand debt. Given the current division of labor between the Treasury and Federal Reserve, this view would assign the whole responsibility of monetary restraint to the Treasury, which decides the outstanding quantity of long debt, and leave the Federal Reserve with the task of cost minimization. Extreme emphasis on the importance of lengthening the federal debt sometimes approximates this view.

The beliefs about bank and public behavior underlying this essay, as expounded and illustrated in Section II, lead to none of these special views, but to the general picture described in Fig. 1.

IV. BONDS WITH PURCHASING POWER ESCALATION

A. Improving the Effectiveness of Monetary Control

The power of the monetary and debt authorities to control the economy would be enhanced if they could deal in equities themselves or at least in debt instruments that are closer substitutes for equities than conventional government obligations. At present the authorities try to affect the supply price of capital by exchanging with the public one kind of government debt for another—demand debt for short debt, demand debt for long debt, short debt for long debt. These exchanges do not, of course, affect the overall size of the debt relative to the stock of capital. They do affect the composition of the debt and its rate structure. But the effects upon the rate structure are limited to the degree necessary to induce the public to make the exchanges. If investors regard one kind of debt as a good substitute for another, they will require little movement in rates. Accordingly they will require little change in the rate of return they receive on capital ownership. In contrast, imagine that the authorities could exchange government debt for equities. Then open market and debt management operations would alter the relative supplies of government debt and capital outstanding, and the supply price of capital would change. Open market and debt management operations would be a tremendously powerful

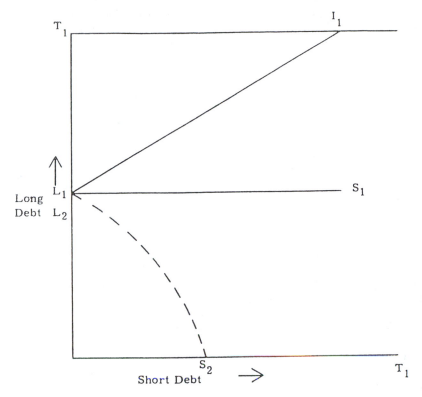

Figure 3

tool of economic stabilization. Clearly Federal Reserve and Treasury dealings in equities are out of the question. The choice of specific issues to buy or sell, with private fortunes riding on every arbitrary choice, would be political dynamite. From a strictly economic point of view, it would involve unintended and arbitrary distortion of the allocative mechanism of the capital markets. What the authorities need is a way to intervene in the market in a general way, affecting the overall rate of return investors require of capital equity without distorting the relative positions of specific equities. No private security can fill this role. What is required is a new government debt instrument, which is a better substitute for capital equity than conventional instruments and a worse substitute for other species of government debt. Exchanges with the public involving the new instrument would effect substantial changes in its rate of return; and the supply price of capital would tend to move with the rate of return on an instrument closely substitutable for equity.

This is where a marketable bond expressed in terms of purchasing power comes in. A substantial part of the independence of risk between current debt instruments and capital equity arises from their difference in status with respect to uncertainties of the future purchasing power of money. A purchasing power bond would share the role of capital equity as a hedge against changes in the price level. It would therefore be a much better substitute than existing debt instruments for ownership of capital. There would remain, of course, the additional risks of capital ownership, for which capital would command a premium over the rate of return on purchasing power bonds. This premium would vary with, among other things, the relative supplies of purchasing power bonds and real capital. For its part, the marketable purchasing power bond would involve risks of interest rate change, in the same manner as conventional bonds. But there would be less reason to expect its interest rate to move together with other government debt interest rates. The purchasing power bond would be substantially independent of other debt instruments in risk. It would be a much poorer substitute for other government obligations than long-term bonds are at present for short-term obligations and cash.

The most appropriate index for escalation of bond principal and interest is, all things considered, the Consumer Price Index (CPI). In principle, escalation to a capital goods price index, or even to an index of equity share prices, would provide a more effective medium of control. But such an index is too slippery conceptually and too difficult practically to provide a basis of escalation in which everyone would have confidence. The CPI is solidly entrenched in public confidence, and there are precedents for its use as an escalator. Moreover, there are compelling reasons, quite apart from improvement of techniques of economic control, for adding to the menu of financial assets available to the public government bonds with purchasing power guarantees.

B. Improving the Financial Menu

The menu is seriously deficient. It does not provide the variety of asset choices necessary to match the variety of needs, tastes, financial knowledge, and circumstances of American households.

We take pride in the subtlety and articulation of our financial institutions and markets, which tailor instruments and contracts to meet an enormous variety of needs, tastes, expectations, and circumstances, both on the borrowing side and on the lending side. But these institutions and markets do not provide, at any price, a riskless way of accumulating purchasing power for the future, whether for old age or for college educations or for heirs. They cannot do so without government help. Meanwhile we force savers to take risk, even if they would gladly pay for the privilege of avoiding it. What is worse, the government lends its own prestige to perpetuating via advertising and other public appeal the falsehood, or at best half-truth, that its own obligations are free of risk.

If the price level were certain to remain stable, various riskless investments would be available. These would include demand obligations of the government, both currency and savings bonds, and the obligations of banks and other savings institutions guaranteed by government insurance programs. The marketable time obligations of the Treasury would be riskless if held to maturity, though subject to the risks of interest rate fluctuation in the intervening period. Many private contractual obligations would be virtually riskless, carrying only negligible possibility of default. These would include many corporate bonds, for example, and most life insurance contracts. At the same time there would be ample opportunity for taking risk, even without the possibility of making bets on the course of the price level. An investor would be able to mix riskless and risky investments in proportions suitable to his need, taste, and temperament. In a world dominated by risk averters, no doubt willingness to assume risk would be rewarded by a higher average expectation of return.

This is presumably the theory of our financial system, if indeed a congeries of institutions that have emerged without conscious comprehensive plan can be said to have a theory. But in practice we do not have a system like this, and we never have had. No government, whatever may be its intentions and financial scruples, is able to guarantee the constancy of the price level even for its own tenure of office, much less for all time. No government has ever been able to do so, and none ever will be. It is just beyond the power of government in a free and decentralized economy with a democratic political order. It is sufficient to recall that war and its aftermath are the main generators of changes in the price level. No one, alas, can guarantee perpetual peace.

In the present circumstances the only way to avoid the risk of price level change is to accept another set of risks, those inherent in ownership of capital. In spite of the growth of mutual funds, it is still costly—in terms of brokerage and management costs and other transactions charges—for a small and intermittent saver to obtain the protection of diversification in equity investment. Even this protection leaves the irreducible *general* risks of equity investment. The stock market may happen to be low relative to consumer prices just when the investor needs his money.

Present institutions virtually compel the participant in a contributory retirement program and the life insurance policyholder to accept the risk of change in the purchasing power of the dollar. In both these cases saving is combined with actuarial provision; there is ample reason supported by experience why joint packages of this kind are economical both for buyer and seller. But it is most unfortunate that the saving part of this package should be confined to acquisition of claims fixed in money amounts. In recent history, of course, yields of such claims did not contain adequate allowance for the increase in the price level; the war and postwar inflations were not anticipated. Even now it is surprising how large a part of the population fail to realize the vulnerability to inflation of investment fixed in money value. Many who do realize it still make such investments, precisely because they come as an inseparable part of the joint packages of retirement and life insurance. In this way the inadequacies of our financial institutions help to perpetuate their own injustices—a principal reason that yields on bonds and other fixed-money-value investments fail to reflect adequately the expected rate of inflation is that these assets command a captive investment demand so long as retirement programs and life insurance companies are limited to the conventional contract. But even if the yields were high enough to offset the average expected rate of decline of purchasing power of money, present retirement and insurance contracts would still be deficient. There is a difference between providing sufficient yield on the average and providing it in every concrete case. Yields may be adjusted to the rate of inflation anticipated in advance by the market. There is a difference between the rate of inflation as now anticipated, and the rate of inflation that is actually realized over the lifetimes of a policyholder and his beneficiaries. With conventional contracts the saver necessarily takes a risk; the yield of his savings through retirement and insurance programs may overcompensate him for the actual change in the cost of living, or it may undercompensate him.

The variable annuity is a long overdue reform. One effect of it will be to help to correct the systematic bias of conventional contracts by liberating some of the captive demands for contracts with benefits fixed in money value and the corresponding captive demand of the insurance companies and retirement programs for bonds, mortgages, and other investments of fixed money value. The saving component of retirement and insurance packages can instead be equity investment. This option will benefit, through higher average returns, not only those who choose it but also those who stick with contracts of conventional type. The diversion of customers will cause the yields of conventional contracts to rise. But the variable annuity will not make it possible to choose a riskless retirement or insurance program. The beneficiaries cannot escape the irreducible risks of diversified equity investment.

No private institution can fill this gap. No insurance company or pension fund could assume the risk of offering purchasing power escalation to its creditors, without similarly escalated securities in which to invest at least part of their funds. Only the federal government is in a position to issue such securities. Once they are available, private financial institutions could offer the corresponding insurance and retirement policies. These should be available alongside conventional contracts, and contracts involving equity investment. In time, presumably, contracts with purchasing power guarantee would yield less than the other two, since they would involve less risk.

Nonmarketable savings bonds are also an important vehicle of long-run saving by small savers. To meet their preferences for a risk-free asset, the government should offer savings bonds with purchasing power escalation.

If purchasing power escalation were available in these forms of savings, what would happen to other saving institutions, the savings departments of commercial banks, mutual savings banks, and savings and loan associations? One possibility would be to leave them unchanged. The important thing is to enable small savers to eliminate the risk from long-run saving, where changes in the purchasing power of money can make a substantial difference. A savings deposit or savings and loan association share can be used to accumulate money for next summer's vacation or next April's taxes without great risk of loss of purchasing power. To keep the longer-run savings of informed conservative households, these institutions would have to offer higher interest and dividends to their depositors and shareowners. To some extent they would be enabled to do so by the rise in yields of fixed-money-value bonds and mortgages, which would accompany the introduction of purchasing power bonds and variable annuities. But this rise would not be sufficient to avoid some loss of business of these institutions, relative to the channels of saving that offer purchasing power escalation.

A second possibility would be to permit these institutions to offer to the public escalated deposits or shares. These liabilities would be backed by holdings of marketable purchasing power bonds, the same issues that would be used by insurance companies and retirement funds. The institutions would serve as middlemen, overcoming for the small savers the obstacles to direct ownership of bonds: indivisibilities, transaction costs, and interest rate risks. In this regard the institutions would serve many of the same functions that the Treasury's own savings bonds serve. But this would be no change from the current situation; these channels of saving are already competitors. Some savers prefer the divisibility and reversibility of savings deposits and saving and loan shares, and some prefer the long-run assurance of interest earnings given by a savings bond. At the savings institution one can add or subtract any amount at any time. One can withdraw a sum today, and redeposit it tomorrow, with no penalty except loss of interest from the previous crediting date; and even that loss can be avoided by a passbook loan. In contrast, if one cashes in a 9-year-old government savings bond today, he cannot buy it back tomorrow. He can buy only a brand-new bond, with 10 years to maturity instead of one. But savings bonds have the advantage of guaranteeing a schedule of interest accumulation over a long period in advance. The savings institutions cannot give a forward guarantee. These differentia would continue to exist under the proposal, even if the savings institutions would be serving only as middlemen between the government and the saver in the field of escalated savings.

The third possibility would be to introduce escalated private mortgage contracts with FHA insurance, and to let them serve along with government purchasing power bonds as the basis for escalated savings deposits and shares. This innovation would permit these savings institutions to compete in the field of escalated savings without abandoning their traditional role in housing finance. An escalated mortgage does not appear to be any less appropriate obligation for an average homeowner to assume than a conventional mortgage. Both house values and wages are probably more stable in terms of the CPI than in terms of the dollar. In any event, both options would be available. It would even be possible to arrange mixtures to suit the circumstances and tastes of the mortgager.

As it works out, our present financial system is an anachronism, appropriate perhaps to a small country dependent on external trade and finance but not to a great nation with a vast internal market, financing economic growth with its own savings. Our present arrangements can assure a saver, if he so desires, of a claim to a certain weight of gold. The claim is a highly theoretical one, and the gold is of no use anyway. If the United States were a small and undeveloped country, and if the gold represented a stable claim on the amenities of civilization elsewhere, a risk-free method of accumulating gold might be of some importance. In the United States today, provision of a risk-free method of accumulating claims to domestically produced consumer goods is much more pertinent.

C. Objections Considered

The principle argument against providing saving media with purchasing power escalation is that they would promote inflation.

Inflation is not an intrinsic evil, like famine or unemployment or juvenile delinquency. If it is an evil, that is because its consequences are evil. What are the evil consequences? Serious lists are rare. Economists, editorial writers, financiers, and politicians are better at denouncing inflation than in providing a rational account of its damage to the body economic, politic, and social. However, the principal damage almost always boils down to this: inflation causes erratic, unanticipated, and inequitable changes in the distribution of income and wealth. Those who have saved in fixed-money-value media lose. Those whose incomes directly or indirectly depend on investments in fixed-money-value assets lose. Those who borrow money from these unfortunate investors and acquire equity in goods gain. The purpose of purchasing power bonds and related opportunities for escalated saving is precisely to avoid the redistribution of wealth and income that are the principal objection to inflation in a closed economy.

A single country in a world economy linked by fixed exchange rates can of course incur balance-of-payments difficulties if its price level rises relative to the price levels of other countries. This consideration applies with force to the United States today. Avoidance of relative inflation is necessarily a prime objective of U.S. economic policy.

Nevertheless, it is far from clear that a regime with purchasing power bonds would actually be more susceptible to inflation than the present financial regime. In the first place, purchasing power bonds would strengthen the controls over the economy possessed by the monetary and debt management authorities. In the second place, the availability of a more satisfactory menu of assets might well increase noninflationary saving, encouraging the saving appetites of individuals and households of modest incomes. The experience of the last 20 years might discourage saving in the liquid media now available; better to consume a dollar's worth now than 50 cents worth 20 years from now. Or at any rate, better to save in the form of durable goods and houses rather than in liquid form. The opponents of purchasing power bonds always point out that they weaken the natural or built-in defense the economy now puts up against inflation. These defenses are the reductions in consumption spending by individuals and households who suffer capital losses, in real terms, when a rise in the price level impairs the purchasing power of their fixed-money-value assets. (The ethical logic of this argument is rather strange. The main evil of inflation turns out to be a principal built-in brake upon it. Don't remove the evil or you will destroy the brake.) What this observation neglects is the possibility that prospective savers may anticipate the contingency that they will have to serve involuntarily as a brake upon inflation, and save less—at least in liquid form—in the first place. If inflation is more likely because of the absence of suitable saving media, it is small consolation to know that the inequities that constitute the built-in brakes upon inflation are intact.

The political argument is more difficult to assess. The allegation is that escalation will vitiate the strength of political forces opposed to inflation. Presumably these forces now consist of people who stand to lose from inflation. If no one stands to lose, who will oppose it? The advent of purchasing power bonds will not mean that no one stands to lose from inflation. As at present, it will still be possible to bet that the accumulation of interest on fixed-money-value assets will outrun the price level. Those who take that side of the bet will favor anti-inflationary governmental policies. But in any case economists are probably inclined to exaggerate the degree to which positions on government economic policy reflect calculated self-interest with respect to inflation or deflation. To a large degree they seem to reflect ideological and moral attitudes, primitive economic reasoning, and entrenched political positions.

A frequent objection to purchasing power bonds is that they saddle upon the government an incalculable and possibly enormous furture burden in terms of dollars. But the burden of the present debt is incalculable in terms of purchasing power and in terms of tax base of the federal government. These are much more relevant benchmarks for measuring the debt than the nominal dollar, and in terms of these benchmarks a purchasing power debt would be more calculable rather than less. Moreover, at the present time the federal government has undertaken many incalculable future obligations, outside the tidy little package formed by the conventional debt. Who can say what is the present value of the federal government's commitments under the Old Age and Survivor's Insurance program, for example? As for the possible size of the burden of a purchasing power debt, if it grows in dollars the tax base will grow with it. It is true that the federal government will, to the extent that it uses purchasing power obligations, forego the possibility of attrition of the real burden of its debt via inflation. (Should not the removal of this temptation strengthen rather than weaken political defenses against inflation?) But there will be countervailing gains. The Treasury should be able to borrow more cheaply with purchasing power bonds, since the public will pay the Treasury for assuming a risk which the government, and the government alone thanks to its taxing power, can assume without cost. Indeed in the long run exclusion of purchasing power bonds from the repertoire of debt instruments will cause greater debt costs to the Treasury, unless the public remains deceived concerning the possibilities of inflation. Should we follow a policy of debt management by which the Treasury gains only to extent that the public is deceived?

Evidently for many people the clinching argument against purchasing power bonds is that their introduction would be a signal that the government had given up its battle to control the price level. Similarly, unemployment insurance might be interpreted as a signal that the government had given up the battle to prevent unemployment. Civil defense might be regarded as an indication that the government no longer believed it possible to keep the peace or to defend the country from hydrogen bombing. To take precautions to protect people from unfortunate events does not mean that the government regards the events as inevitable, or even that the government intends to slacken its own efforts to prevent them. The public can understand that. The situation would be different were it easy or even possible to guarantee the price level. This is a guarantee a democratic government cannot give in our kind of economy and in the present state of the world. Debt policy should not be based on the myth that the government can guarantee the price level if it only musters the political will to do so.

V.   SUMMARY AND CONCLUDING REMARKS

Monetary control and debt management are jointly concerned with the composition of the net claims of the economy against the federal government. The total of these claims is the province of congressional and presidential fiscal policy; net federal debt grows with budget deficit and declines with budget surplus. The composition of the total, and of changes in the total, is for the Federal Reserve and the Treasury's debt managers to decide.

The *monetary effect* of changes in federal debt must be distinguished from the *fiscal effect*. The monetary effect is permanent and depends upon the size of the debt. The fiscal effect is temporary and depends upon the rate at which deficit or surplus is changing the size of the debt. The monetary effect may be measured by the supply price of capital, the rate of return at which the community is willing to hold in its portfolios and balance sheets the existing stock of privately owned productive physical capital. Events and policy measures that lower the supply price of capital are expansionary; events and measures that raise it are deflationary.

On this criterion, increases in federal debt—whether as demand debt or as interest-bearing debt of short or long maturity—are expansionary. Likewise, substitution of demand debt for short or long debt, and substitution of shorter debt for longer debt, are expansionary. Altering the composition of the debt in one of these ways, or in reverse if contraction of aggregate demand is desired, is the principal tool of monetary control. In addition, the monetary authorities have the power to vary the discount rate and required reserve ratios.

The extent of the task of economic stabilization that falls on monetary control and debt management depends on how much of the job is assigned to taxation and other fiscal measures. The balance among instruments of stabilization must be decided with a view to the composition of output, economic growth, the distribution of wealth and income, and economic efficiency. Once the share of monetary measures in the control of aggregate demand is defined, the authorities have a wide choice of means. What criterion of choice should guide them? In the absence of more compelling criteria, minimization of net long-run interest cost to the Treasury is a sensible goal.

Optimal debt management, then, consists in accomplishing the task of monetary stabilization at the least cost to the Treasury. Some of the implications of this criterion are

1.   In achieving a given monetary effect, the Federal Reserve should give preference to measures that require or induce banks to increase their holdings of noninterest-bearing debt. The government saves money when monetary restriction is achieved by raising reserve requirements, or by raising the discount rate, rather than by open market sales of bills.

2.   Costs could be lowered, without sacrifice of monetary effect, by enlarging the captive market for government debt through a secondary reserve requirement on banks, and through reserve requirements on other financial intermediaries. These requirements would also improve the efficiency of monetary control. Against them must be weighed considerations of equity to the owners and customers of banks and other financial intermediaries.

3.   The government—comprising both the Federal Reserve and the Treasury—should continuously adjust the maturity structure of the debt, seeking to minimize its net cost while achieving the required restriction of aggregate demand. For this purpose, net cost to the government includes not only interest outlays but also increases in the market value of the outstanding debt. If this concept is used as the guide, the relevant interest rate on each maturity is the quoted market rate plus the capital gain (or minus the expected loss) due to interest rate changes anticipated in the immediate future. The Treasury should not borrow long if long rates are about to fall. On the contrary, at such times the government should repurchase or refund in advance its long obligations, replacing them with short maturities. To maintain monetary restriction intact, it is generally necessary to contract demand debt whenever the interest-bearing debt is shortened, and to expand demand debt whenever the interest-bearing debt is lengthened. That is, a dollar change either way in long debt must be accompanied by more than a dollar change in the opposite direction in short debt. Allowance must be made for this necessity in calculating the advantage to the government of lengthening or shortening the debt.

4.   The present administrative division of debt management responsibilities, even under the modus vivendi of bills only policy, is inadequate to the economic unity of the problem. The Federal Reserve cannot make rational decisions of monetary policy without knowing what kind of debt the Treasury intends to issue. The Treasury cannot rationally determine the maturity structure of the interest-bearing debt without knowing how much debt the Federal Reserve intends to monetize. Serious pursuit of the optimum in debt management would require more centralization of government security purchases and sales than now exists. The suggestion is to assign the entire task of debt management to the Federal Reserve, with the mandate to minimize cost to the extent consistent with stabilization objectives. There would no longer be any distinction between Federal Reserve open market operations and security issues or redemptions. The Federal Reserve would be provided with a varied inventory of securities and would sell them or buy them back from the public, as their mandate required. The Treasury would provide the Federal Reserve with new securities when its working balance needs to be augmented because of budget deficit or "redeem" securities held by the Federal Reserve from budget surplus. (A basic core of securities now held by the Federal Reserve represents a permanent monetization of federal debt, and it may be convenient to convert these into an intragovernmental memorandum of debt at zero or nominal interest.) Under this arrangement the Federal Reserve would be, like the Bank of England, the government's underwriter.

The government should issue marketable and nonmarketable bonds with purchasing power escalation, principal, and interest geared to the CPI. Marketable bonds of this type would generally improve the effectiveness of monetary control. The Federal Reserve, by buying or selling these securities, would be dealing in assets much closer to equity capital than conventional public debt instruments. The monetary authorities would thereby gain a much greater leverage over the supply price of capital. At the same time, purchasing power bonds would fill, either directly or through the intermediation of insurance companies and other institutions, a shameful gap in the available menu of financial assets. Savers of limited means and knowledge should not be forced to gamble either on the price level or on the stock market. Since investors will pay the government to avoid such risks, purchasing power bonds would save the taxpayer interest outlays. Various objections to purchasing power bonds are considered and refuted in Section IV.3.

Except under the stress of obvious and serious malfunction, society seldom takes the trouble to examine with real detachment the logic and utility of institutions ordinarily taken for granted. The fresh look at the nation's monetary and financial system undertaken by the Commission on Money and Credit is an exception, offering both an opportunity for constructive social engineering and a temptation to ratify the status quo. Existing arrangements are not necessarily inevitable or optimal or unique, but they are likely to seem so to people deeply involved in operating or observing them. Traditions and customs and commitments arise in remarkably short time. What seems natural and obvious procedure today was novel and revolutionary 50 or 20 or 10 years ago. By the same token, changes that appear radical today will be defended by vested champions of the status quo tomorrow. The commission should not be too tender of existing institutions. They are expendable if they fail to accomplish their functions—the functions they ought to perform today, which are generally quite different from the functions they were designed to perform. There are many respects in which our present arrangements for monetary control and debt management are irrational and anachronistic. They were not designed for a public debt that is so large a part of aggregate private wealth, so strategic a factor in monetary control, and so important a burden on the federal budget. They were not designed for a world in which economic stabilization has such a high priority on the agenda of government, and in which monetary control bears so large a responsibility for stabilization. They were not even designed for a system in which general economic stabilization—rather than prevention of panic and reponsiveness to "needs of trade"—is the principal goal of the central bank. They were not designed for an era in which inevitable uncertainty about the price level makes gambles of fixed money value assets, traditionally regarded as perfectly safe. Sooner or later, slowly or rapidly, our institutions will evolve so that they more adequately meet the needs of the day. The Commission on Money and Credit has the opportunity to speed, to smooth, and to guide that evolution.

APPENDIX

The analysis in the text is based on a model that can be explicitly stated in formal terms.

1. Defintiions of variables and parameters

   M_1 Amount of demand debt outside the Federal Reserve and Treasury
   M_2 Amount of short debt outside the Federal Reserve and Treasury
   M_3 Amount of long debt outside the Federal Reserve and Treasury
   C   Value of the privately owned capital stock, at current prices
   L   Net indebtedness of private borrowers to banks
   D   Bank deposits
   k   Required ratio of bank reserve to deposits
   E   Shareowners' equity in banks
   M_{ib} Amount of debt of category i held by banks (i = 1, 2, 3)
   M_{ip} Amount of debt of category i held by nonbank public (i = 1, 2, 3)
   M_{1b} Banks' net free reserves
   W   Net private wealth
   r_1 Federal Reserve discount rate
   r_2 Rate on short-term government securities
   r_3 Rate on long-term government securities
   r_4 Rate on private loans
   r_5 Supply price of capital

2. Accounting identities and definitions

   $$M_1 + M_2 + M_3 + C = W \qquad\qquad\qquad\qquad\qquad\qquad\qquad\qquad\qquad (A1)$$

   Net private wealth is equal to claims against the government plus the value of the privately owned capital stock.

$$M_{1p} + M_{2p} + M_{3p} + D-L + C + E = W \tag{A2}$$

The sum of assets held by the nonbank public, less its indebtedness, is equal to net private wealth.

$$M_{ib} + M_{ip} = M_i \ (i = 1, 2, 3) \tag{A3}$$

Outstanding debt, in each form, is divided between bank holdings and nonbank public holdings.

$$M_{1b} + M_{2b} + M_{3b} + L-D-E = 0 \tag{A4}$$

Bank liabilities plus shareowner's equity equal bank assets. This can be derived, from (1), (2), and (3).

$$M_{1b} = kD + M'_{1b} \tag{A5}$$

Bank holding of demand debt is equal to required reserves plus net free reserves.

3. Behavioral relations

3.1   Banks

$$M'_{1b} = m_{1b} \ (r_1, r_2, r_3, r_4) \ (1-k)D \tag{B1}$$

The proportion (positive, zero, or negative) or bank disposable assets held as net free reserves depends directly on the discount rate and inversely on the interest rate on the three types of earning assets in banks' portfolios. The most important determinants are r_1 and r_2. Banks have incentive to borrow reserves when the differential between r_2 and r_1 is favorable. At the same time, with a given differential, the demand for net free reserves will diminish when these two rates are higher.

$$M_{2b} = m_{2b} \ (r_1, r_2, r_3, r_4) \ (1-k)D \tag{B2}$$
$$M_{3b} = m_{3b} \ (r_1, r_2, r_3, r_4) \ (1-k)D \tag{B3}$$
$$L = l_b \ (r_1, r_2, r_3, r_4) \ (1-k)D + E \tag{B4}$$

These three equations, together with the first, say that the proportions in which banks divide their disposable assets among the four categories depend on the four interest rates. Shareowners' eqwuity is assumed to take entirely the form of private loans. In each case demand for an asset is assumed positively related to its own rate, negatively to the other rates. The discount rate might be omitted from the last three equations, following the same logic that would omit r_3 and r_4 from (B1). In any case, only three of these euqations are independent. The fourth may be derived from the other three with the help of the identities (A4), (A5), (A6).

3.2   Nonbank public

$$M_{2p} = m_{2p} \ (r_2, r_3, r_4, r_5) \ W \tag{P2}$$
$$M_{3p} = m_{3p} \ (r_2, r_3, r_4, r_5) \ W \tag{P3}$$

Direct holdings of short government debt, as a propotion of private wealth, depend directly on the short rate and inversely on the rates that compete for place in public portfolios. A similar relationship holds for long debt.

$$L = l_p \ (r_2, r_3, r_4, r_5) \ W \tag{P4}$$

L, net public borrowing from banks, is a negative number and becomes smaller algebraically, larger absolutely, when r_4, the loan rate, declines and when the other rates rise. These reactions are due both to the direct lending behavior of the public and to its borrowing behavior. When the loan rate declines and other rates rise, the lending sector of the public will prefer other assets to private loans. When the loan rate declines and other rates rise, particularly r_5, the borrowing sector of the public will wish to increase its debt. On both counts, there will be more demand for bank loans.

$$D = d_p \ (r_2, r_3, r_4, r_5) \ W \tag{P5}$$

Public demand for deposits is negatively related to all the rates and is probably especially sensitive to the short rate r_2.

$$C = c_p \, (r_2, \, r_3, \, r_4, \, r_5) \, W \tag{P6}$$

Public demand for capital is higher the greater is r_5, and the lower are the other rates. Since much capital holding is financed by borrowing, the private loan rate r_4 is especially important.

Public equity in bank enterprises, E, may be taken as a constant. The six equations for the public balance sheet are not all independent. Using (A2) one of them can be derived from the other five.

4. Balance equations

Demand debt, from (A5), (B1), (P1), and (P5)

$$kd_p \, (\ ) \, W + m_{1b} \, (\ ) \, (1{-}k) \, d_p \, (\ ) \, W + m_{1p} \, W = M_1 \tag{1}$$

Short debt, from (B2) and (P2)

$$m_{2b} \, (\ ) \, (1{-}k) \, d_p \, (\ ) \, W + m_{2p} \, (\ ) \, W = M_2 \tag{2}$$

Long debt, from (B3) and (P3)

$$m_{3b} \, (\ ) \, (1{-}k) \, d_p \, (\ ) \, W + m_{2p} \, (\ ) \, W = M_3 \tag{3}$$

Loans, from (B4) and (P4)

$$l_b \, (\ ) \, (1{-}k) \, d_p \, (\ ) \, W + E{-}l_p \, (\ ) \, W = O \tag{4}$$

Capital, from (P6)

$$c_p \, (\ ) \, W = C \tag{5}$$

Where parentheses follow a symbol, e.g., c_p ( ), a function is indicated, with the arguments, interest rates, as previously noted.

Since one of the bank portfolio equations can be derived from the other bank equations, and one of the public asset demand equations from the other public equations, the five blaance equations are not independent. One can be eliminated, for example Eq. 4. Then Eqs. 1, 2, 3, 5 determine simultaneously the four market interest rates r_2, r_3, r_4, r_5, given M_1, M_2, M_3, K, and therefore given W, their sum; given the discount rate r_1; and given the required reserve ration k. The monetary effect of an increase in debt of a given category, say M_1, can be ound by differentiating the system of equations partially with respect to M_1, remembering that $\frac{\partial w}{\partial M_1} = 1$, and solving for $\frac{\partial r_5}{\partial M_1}$. The monetary effect of open market purchases of short debt would be $\frac{\partial r_5}{\partial M_1} - \frac{\partial r_5}{\partial M_2}$; of open market purchases of long debt, $\frac{\partial r_5}{\partial M_1} - \frac{\partial r_5}{\partial M_3}$; of substitution of short debt for long debt $\frac{\partial r_5}{\partial M_2} - \frac{\partial r_5}{\partial M_3}$. In a similar manner, $\frac{\partial r_5}{\partial r_1}$ and $\frac{\partial r_5}{\partial k}$ can be found (remembering that $\frac{\partial W}{\partial r_1}$ and $\frac{\partial W}{\partial k}$ are zero). The effects of a parameter change on any item in a bank or public balance sheet may be found by using the solutions of the four differentiated equations and behavior equations of Section 3. For example, the effects of a change in reserve requirements on bank deposits would be using (P5)

$$\frac{\partial D}{\partial k} = W \left(\frac{\partial d_p}{\partial r_2} \frac{\partial r_2}{\partial k} + \frac{\partial d_p}{\partial r_3} \frac{\partial r_3}{\partial k} + \frac{\partial d_p}{\partial r_4} \frac{\partial r_4}{\partial k} + \frac{\partial d_p}{\partial r_5} \frac{\partial r_5}{\partial k} \right)$$

To find debt combinations that give equivalent restraint on demand, r_5 can be held constant in Eq 1, 2, 3, 5. Holding W and K constant also, the four equations can then be regarded as giving r_2, r_3, r_4, and M_3 as functions of M_2. In particular $\frac{\partial M_3}{\partial M_2}$ gives the quantity by which long debt must be changed to offset the effect on r_5 of a dollar change in outstanding short debt. Since total debt is fixed, M_1 can be found as a residual.

In similar manner debt combinations of equal cost (where cost is $r_2 M_2 + r_3 M_3$) can be determined from the same system of equations.

45

Principles of Debt Management

Earl R. Rolph
University of California at Berkeley, Berkeley, California

The offering of gratuitous advice to finance ministers is an honorable and ancient role of economists. There has been no shortage of pronouncements about how a national debt should be managed.* Clear statements of principles are not so plentiful. It is the purpose of this chapter to offer a principle appropriate for national debt management.

National debt management shall be taken to refer to any official action, by central banks as well as treasuries, designed to alter the quantity and kinds of a national government's debt obligations outstanding in private domestic hands. Foreign-held national debts and the debts of subsidiary government units are excluded from the inquiry. No attempt is made to distinguish sharply monetary and fiscal policy as usually conceived.

The principle to be elucidated is an efficiency rule; it extends an old idea in economics to another area. An outstanding national debt is looked upon as providing a utility to a government. Different debt combinations may provide the same utility but at different costs to the government. The composition and size of an outstanding national debt is optimal when the marginal utility of each kind of debt instrument is made proportional to its marginal cost.

A national debt is said to have a utility (or, alternatively, a social function) when a government has a preference for some pattern of monetary stability and when an outstanding debt affects expenditures for current output. A national debt of any size as given by past financial practices may be reduced to any figure at all by the simple expedient of substituting created money for debt. A national government has the option of purchasing its outstanding liabilities. An experimental reduction of a national debt by official purchase is objectionable provided that the changes thereby induced in private expenditures are objectionable. The utility of an outstanding debt is its effectiveness in preventing as high a level of private expenditures as would occur if the debt were reduced to zero, when such a high level of private expenditures is contrary to official stabilization objectives.

The marginal utility of an outstanding debt is normally positive, but, like that of whiskey, it can on occasion be negative. Its marginal utility is negative when private expenditures are too low judged in terms of a stabilization goal. Then the debt should be reduced (i.e., money should be substituted for debt) until total private expenditures reach a level consistent with official stabilization policies. The utility of an outstanding debt therefore rises during upswings and falls during downswings of business activity.

The concept of cost of a national debt is troublesome. There are the administrative expenses involved in the issuance and reissuance of particular kinds of debt instruments, the honoring of coupons, and the

---

Adapted from *American Economic Review*, XLVII (June 1957): 302–320 by permission of American Economic Association.
*See, for example, the symposium "How to Manage the National Debt," by S. E. Harris, L. H. Seltzer, C. C. Abbott, R. A. Musgrave, and A. H. Hansen, *Rev. Econ. Stat.*, Feb. 1949, XXVI, 15–32, and any textbook on public finance or money and banking.

keeping of records. The main expense is, of course, the interest commitment of the government. An efficiency principle calls for making these costs a minimum for any given utility of a debt combination.

In discussions of economy in government, only rarely is attention directed toward means of curtailing these expenses. Yet the interest expense of many national governments is a substantial item in their budgets, and historically it has often been the largest single item.* The lack of concern cannot be attributed to the insignificance of the amount of the costs of an outstanding debt. Nor is it explained simply by the fact that the interest expenditures are classified as transfer payments. The interest expense is usually looked upon as a fixed charge, not subject to control by legislative or administrative decision.

Even though the main cost of an outstanding debt is a type of transfer payment, there are reasons to economize on the amount. A transfer program of a government increases the spending potential of private groups. Devices are needed to offset the inflationary effects of transfers as well as those of government expenditures for current output. Of the offset devices available, taxes are easily the most important. As a practical matter, tax devices are subject to diminishing returns since the greater become the revenue requirements of a government the more it must resort to inferior tax devices.† Such considerations as fairness, equity, and economic efficiency in taxation are given less weight as the revenue pressure increases. If, somehow, the substantial transfer payments made by national governments could be eliminated, a revised tax program could be an improved one simply because less stress would need to be placed upon the selection of tax devices primarily for their revenue potential. This consideration alone suggests the importance of avoiding unnecessary costs in connection with a national debt. Interest costs are subject to the test of economy just as other transfer payments are and for the same reasons.

The precept that a government should attempt to minimize the cost of its outstanding debt in a manner compatible with the social objective of debt management rests then upon two fundamental value judgments: (1) that some level and some changes in the level of private expenditures are from a social point of view superior to others, and (2) that the expense to government for its outstanding debt should be minimized for any given stabilization goal. These value judgments are reasonable in the sense that their denial would conflict with well-entrenched beliefs about the responsibilities of national governments in the contemporary scene.

I.   THE CONCEPT OF A NATIONAL DEBT

Certain views about debt management and governmental fiscal operations have already been violated by the suggestion that an outstanding debt has a utility to a government. Anyone whose ideas have been framed by the current textbook literature, and, I am afraid, the technical literature as well, "knows" that government borrowing is a stimulating and debt retirement a deflationary policy. The impression has been created that rising national debts are necessary if government finance is to exert a stimulating influence in growing societies.‡ Just what is meant by statements that government borrowing is inflationary or that debt retirement is deflationary? Taken literally, such statements are patently untrue. Official sales of government debt, for example, induce higher rates of interest. Would anyone claim that official measures that raise rates of interest are inflationary? Nothing so crude as this can be intended. What is presumably meant is that a government deficit of a given size plus government borrowing of an equal amount together raise the level of national income.§ The validity of this proposition need not for the moment concern us. What does matter is the idea that the change in a government's

---

*J. S. Mill observed that the interest on the British national debt amounted to about one-half of the government revenues in his day. See *Principles of Political Economy* (Ashley ed.), Book V, Ch. 7, par. 3, p. 879.

†A similar point is made by Roy Blough, *The Federal Taxing Process* (New York, 1952), p. 234.

‡See, for example, S. E. Harris, *The National Debt and the New Economics* (New York, 1947).

§There are difficulties with this proposition. One is the implicit theory that the combined effects of government expenditures, transfer formulae and tax formulae can somehow be reduced to the effects of a budget deficit and surplus. In some fiscal theories, this view is repudiated. Another is the assumption that the stimulating effect of a deficit, granted that this method of statement makes sense, is greater than the deflationary effect of the sale of an equal amount of debt. Systematic demonstrations of this position are surprisingly rare. William Fellner, who has pursued the question, poses the issue in terms of the comparative effect of a given marginal increase in government expenditures for goods and services and an equal dollar increase in the sale of government securities. His results vary from an increase in gross national product equal to the increase in government expenditures at one limit to a contraction of unspecified amount at the other. See his *Monetary Policies and Full Employment*, 2nd ed. (University of California Press, 1947), pp. 174–185; also Hugo Hegeland, *The Quantity Theory of Money* (Goteborg, Sweden, 1951), pp. 228–240.

debt depends rigidly upon the size of its budget surplus or deficit. Those who look forward to persistent increases in public debts presumably do so, not out of love of large public debts, but because they view this development as a necessary by-product of a stimulating tax-expenditure policy.*

Yet there is no economic requirement that a national government allow the budget facts to dictate the change in its outstanding debt. Indeed, any budgeting unit has greater freedom than this because deficits or surpluses may be covered by release or absorption of cash. Persistent surpluses can be tolerated indefinitely; anyone is free to hold more cash. A person or a business, however, experiencing persistent deficits runs up against the combined constraints of his dwindling assets and impaired borrowing power. But a national government is not subject to these constraints in dealing with its own people. A sovereign government can obtain whatever amounts of cash it wishes. A central bank has become the standard instrument to provide national governments with unlimited funds.

To obtain a concept of a national debt that reflects this choice open to debt officials, we need to restrict the definition of a national debt to those obligations of a government that are held outside official agencies including, especially, a central bank. The *net debt* or the *outstanding debt* of a national government may therefore be defined as those contractual obligations of a national government and its agencies.† Agencies include all government corporations as well as the central bank. The change in the size of the outstanding net national debt is an independent variable subject to the control of official groups. We are not bound to suppose that a national government must either sell debt or tax in order to finance itself.

II. EFFECT OF DEBT OPERATIONS UPON PRIVATE EXPENDITURES

Our first main proposition is that an increase in the size of the net debt of a national government, given the debt composition, has the effect of *decreasing*, and a decrease in the net debt has the effect of *increasing*, GNP expenditures. It is elementary that the sale of government securities by a central bank is a deflationary policy. We simply generalize this observation to sales of government debt by any official agency.

The defense of this proposition is identical with the defense of monetary policy. It would be inappropriate to attempt a full-dress defense of that position here.‡ Happily skepticism about the efficacy of monetary policy appears to have dwindled in professional circles.§

There are, however, a number of ways to explain the effect of government debt operations on private expenditures. One way relates debt change to the rate of interest and the rate of interest to national income through an investment schedule. This method is denied us because it presupposes that the pattern of rates

---

*This appears to be A. H. Hansen's position. After observing that future expansion of the economy will require large increases in the quantity of money, he writes: "It is not probable that this could happen without a substantial increase in the public debt." *Monetary Theory and Fiscal Policy* (New York, 1949), p. 195.

†This concept of a national debt is, I suggest, the relevant one for economic analysis. An exchange of assets between a Treasury department and a government corporation or between a Treasury department and the central bank is a bookkeeping arrangement. What matters is the increase or decrease in the government's debt in private hands. We have long become accustomed to view the quantity of currency as consisting of currency outside the hands of official agencies. For the same reason, the stacks of national debt held by the government and its central bank should not be counted as debt that matters.

‡Of the various systems of the determinants of aggregate expenditures, the neo-Keynesian position, as employed for example to demonstrate the balanced-budget theorem, would presumably imply that debt operations are without effect. Government expenditures and private investment are treated as autonomous, i.e., unexplained, and consumption is treated exclusively as a function of current income after taxes. There is nothing left for interest rates and hence for government debt policy to influence. For a clear exposition of this point of view, see P. A. Samuelson, "The Simple Mathematics of Income Determination," in L. A. Metzler et al.; *Income, Employment and Public Policy, Essays in Honor of Alvin H. Hansen* (New York, 1948), pp. 133–155.

The original Keynesian position, at least as expounded by Keynes, implies that debt sales are deflationary except when "the" rate of interest has reached its floor, since investment is treated as a (negative) function of rates of interest.

The-quantity-of money approach and the cash-balance doctrine give similar results because official debt sales decrease and debt purchases increase the quantity of privately owned money, and expenditures are treated as functionally related to the money supply.

The asset position, which the present writer finds congenial, makes both private consumption and investment expenditures depend upon the capital values of assets and hence upon their yields, and debt operations are functionally related to capital values. See Rolph, *The Theory of Fiscal Economics* (Berkeley, 1954), Ch. 5.

§Skepticism does continue to survive; witness the views of W. L. Smith ("On the Effectiveness of Monetary Policy," *Am. Econ. Rev.*, Sept. 1956, XLVI, 588–606). Like others before him, Smith somewhat spoils the purity of his position by allowing that monetary policy may work too well (ibid., p. 599, bottom).

of interest can be reduced to a unique rate, whereas the analysis to follow requires that the pattern of rates be a variable.* A related approach, but one that does not require the assumption of a single rate of interest, examines the effects of debt operations through their influence upon the money demands for goods and services. This approach is used here.

A change in the outstanding debt, say an increase, means that official agencies succeed in persuading people and organizations to hold public debt instead of holding other things. The necessary and sufficient condition for getting any good, including government debt, out of government hands and into private hands through a market mechanism is a reduction in the price of the good as compared to what it would be if the government offer to sell were not made. It is sufficient for this conclusion that the amount demanded of anything be a negative function of price.

If the other things that debt buyers are persuaded not to hold consist entirely of money, the government obtains cash that by definition would not have been used to finance anything else. In this limiting case, the sale of more debt has a zero direct deflationary effect on private expenditures. But the necessary condition for this limiting case is that government debt and money be treated as perfect substitutes by each debt buyer. Ordinary observation suggests however that government debt and cash are not generally so treated. People do not shift altogether out of holding cash and into holding debt as the result of a slight reduction in the prices of debt. Rather they are found to hold both debt and cash in the face of large variations in the prices of debt. Thus an increase in the outstanding debt is accomplished by inducing people to give up the holding of cash and other assets. This behavior means that the money demand schedules for these other assets are pushed downward by a positive debt operation. Similarly a reduction in the outstanding debt increases money demands for other things, except in the limiting case when people and organizations who hold debt treat it as a perfect substitute for money.

III. EFFECT OF A CHANGING COMPOSITION OF PUBLIC DEBT

The second main proposition is that different kinds of national debt instruments may have different utilities per dollar to a government. In order to show that this is possible, it is first necessary to demonstrate that public debt instruments are not generally treated as perfect substitutes. If they were so treated, some investors should be found holding all of one form; or if found holding more than one, they should be prepared to make all-or-none choices among debt forms. An investor found holding bonds and bills should in the event of a slight rise in the yield of bonds part with all of his bills. We know that holders of government debt commonly hold various public debt forms and continue to do so in the face of variations of yields. Various debt forms are different, although related, commodities.[†]

Granted that various forms are not a homogeneous commodity, the hypothesis may be advanced that the utility of various public debt forms is positively correlated with their maturity. A shift in the composition of an outstanding public debt of given size that reduces its average maturity increases private expenditures, and vice versa for increases in its average maturity. Like any empirical generalization, this proposition does not hold for all circumstances.

The conditions necessary for the hypothesis are twofold: (1) of various public debt forms, the shorter their life expectancy, the more they must possess the characteristics here called "moneyness," and (2) the marginal utility of the moneyness of assets must be positive. By the moneyness of an asset we mean that its realizable price is predetermined and known for any future date.[‡] Thus an asset other than cash—demand

---

*There are other serious difficulties with this approach. A fundamental one is the justification of a negatively sloped investment schedule. In this connection, see A. P. Lerner, "On the Marginal Product of Capital and the Marginal Efficiency of Investment," *J. Pol. Econ.*, Feb. 1953, LXI, 1–14; and J. A. Stockfisch, "The Relationships between Money Cost, Investment, and the Rate of Return," *Q. J. Econ.*, May 1956, LXX, 295–302.

[†]This observation should not be interpreted to imply that markets for government securities are necessarily imperfect or, in deference to E. H. Chamberlin, characterized as imbued with monopolistic elements. The market for U.S. Treasury bills may be perfectly competitive and so may the market for 30-year bonds without implying that bills and bonds are the same commodity.

[‡]F. Modigliani objects to a similar concept employed by J. R. Hicks on the following grounds: "Whatever one's definition of liquidity, to say that a government bond, a speculative share, a house, are money in different degrees, can at best generate unnecessary confusion. It is true that money and securities are close substitutes, but this connection is to be found elsewhere than in degrees of moneyness." ("Liquidity Preference and the Theory of Interest and Money," *Econometrica*, Jan. 1944, XII, 45–88, reprinted in *Readings in Monetary Theory*, p. 235.) Yet his claim that securities and money are closer substitutes than are money and real assets presupposes that there is something special about securities that makes them substitutes for cash. I suggest that this something needs a name, and "moneyness" seems as good as any.

deposits and currency—has a maximum of moneyness when it is exactly like cash except in not being spendable as such. Savings deposits ordinarily fill this requirement precisely. So do many demand forms of government debt such as U.S. savings bonds. Short-term government debt does not fulfill this requirement exactly because some variation can occur in the price of the instrument during its life that cannot always be confidently predicted in advance. Yet the description of such holdings as "liquid" or "protective" assets among financial practitioners is based on the fact that the prices of such instruments can vary only within narrow limits during relevant periods. By contrast, the longest maturity conceivable—a perpetuity—exposes its holder to the possibility of large gains or losses; it is unlike money. It was this observation that led Henry Simons to describe government-issued perpetuities as "pure" debt.*

For long-term public debt forms to be more effective in curtailing private expenditures per dollar outstanding than short-term, it is also necessary that the marginal utility of the moneyness of assets be positive. For if it were to be zero, investors would look only to the income in holding or acquiring assets, and the perfect substitution assumption, so often found in theoretical discussions, would come back into its own.† Since it may be assumed that the marginal utility of future income is always positive—this is a necessary condition for the functioning of a money-price system—the condition that the marginal utility of the moneyness of assets be positive implies that the subjective or computed yields of securities vary inversely with their degree of moneyness.‡

The condition that the marginal utility of the moneyness of debts must be positive applies, but in the negative sense, to debtors as well. If yields were positively correlated with maturity, and if debtors were completely indifferent about the maturities of their obligations, they could always gain by concentrating their debt in the shortest form. Consequently only short-term private securities would be left outstanding or the yields of securities of different maturity would become equal. In the latter event, the marginal utility of the extra moneyness of short-term securities would become zero.

If our twin conditions are satisfied, namely that shorter-term obligations possess stronger money characteristics than long-term public debt and that the marginal utility of the moneyness of assets is generally positive, an official debt operation designed to shorten the average maturity of the public debt becomes an inflationary measure.

To establish this result, let us examine a case least favorable for it, namely one in which public debts have no moneyness features not shared by private debts. Suppose that private debts are treated, maturity for maturity, as perfect substitutes of public debts. In addition, suppose that borrowers can sell debts of any maturity they please and can do so under competitive conditions. Consider, then, the position of a representative borrower. To satisfy the condition that the marginal utility of the moneyness of assets is positive for him, he will be in equilibrium with respect to a distribution of maturities of his outstanding obligations only when the market yields of his debts increase with the remoteness of their maturity. In the absence of objective constraints, other than differences in yields, on the maturity distribution of his debts, a representative borrower would prefer longer to shorter obligations at the same yields because of the correspondingly reduced necessity for maintaining a liquid position.§ A cental bank or treasury operation designed to shorten the average maturity of public debt calls for the purchase in the market of long-term bonds and the sale of an equal amount

---

*See Henry Simons, "On Debt Policy," *J. Pol. Econ.*, Dec. 1944, LII, 356–61. Simons viewed short-term instruments as partly money.

†If the only relevant dimension of debts is the yield, they become homogeneous commodities because future dollar income is inherently homogeneous.

‡Subjective yields may differ from market yields to maturity for many reasons, such as tax considerations or anticipations of changes in the capital value of the asset. However, the point of view here adopted is inconsistent with the type of expectation theory to explain differences among market yields to maturity presented, for example, by F. H. Lutz and J. R. Hicks. That position makes the strong requirement that any one investor should select securities only on the basis of income. If he is found holding 1-year maturities yielding 4% and 2-year maturities yielding 5%, he is assumed to expect that the yield on 1-year maturities will a year hence rise to approximately 6%. This requirement means that all debt forms when classified by maturity must be perfect substitutes. See F. H. Lutz, "The Structure of Interest Rates," *Q. J. Econ.*, Nov. 1940, LV, 36–63, reprinted in *Readings on the Theory of Income Distribution*, pp. 512–520; and J. R. Hicks, *Value and Capital* (Oxford, 1939), pp. 144–152. Hicks, unlike Lutz, tries to have it both ways holding that interest is to be explained by the degree of departure of an asset from being like money—degrees of illiquidity—and that income is the only relevant dimension of debts. This inconsistency is alluded to by Lutz, op. cit., p. 528.

§The assumed conditions rule out credit rationing such that lenders discriminate against particular borrowers. They do not rule out consideration by lenders of the risk position of a borrower.

of short-term bills, thus lowering the yields of bonds and raising those of bills. This altered pattern of yields induces our representative borrower, granted no change in his preferences, to shift his debts toward the longer maturities. Since he prefers longer-term to shorter-term obligations at the same yields, he now finds that it costs relatively less to satisfy this preference. Thus his adjustment may appear simply to offset the official maneuver.

However, from his point of view his entire position now entails less of something he dislikes, namely risk—the negative of moneyness; and the marginal disutility of risk increases with increasing risk.* People will bet small sums when they will not bet large sums at the same odds. Applied to a borrower's asset position, our theory means that he now will be willing to take more risk than he would have before because his liability position entails less risk. But taking more risk is another way of saying that he will be inclined to hold less cash since cash is the safest possible asset to hold. In other words, he is induced to acquire more real assets.

This conclusion is not upset if creditors refuse to regard private debts as providing the moneyness features associated with public debts. In fact, a large segment of private debt contracts are entailed assets. The creditor is expected to hold them for the life of the contract. In such circumstances, short-term private debts are not good substitutes for short-term public debts; they are closer substitutes for those public obligations held mainly for income purposes; that is, public bonds. An official operation designed to shorten the average life expectancy of the public debt remains stimulating because the addition of bills to the market induces investors to hold less cash while not affecting their inclination to hold short-term private debts, and at the same time the subtraction of long-term debt induces creditors to offer more attractive terms to private borrowers at all maturities.

The above argument may be unnecessary for those to whom it is intuitively obvious that long-term public debt is less like money than short-term. However, our twin conditions do help in making judgments about the circumstances under which the hypothesis will not hold. In countries, for example, where the local population has limited trust in the obligations of their governments, all public debt obligations may be treated as unlike money. The assumption of investors in Western countries that the obligations of their governments are free of default risk is not shared by the people of some of the less developed countries, and often for good reasons. What is more important, however, is the failure of the condition that the marginal utility of the moneyness of assets is generally positive. In many countries, the experience of persistent inflation appears to have undermined a taste for domestic money and moneylike assets.

For Western countries, at least for the period since 1930, the twin conditions appear to have been generally satisifed. Individuals as well as organizations have exhibited a positive liking for assets because of their moneyness features. The success of governments in pouring out huge quantities of demand forms of government debt as well as short-term debts at yields less than, and often much less than, the yields on long-term debts strongly suggests, but of course does not prove, that the marginal utility of the moneyness of assets has generally been positive. People have indicated a willingness to pay something in foregone income to possess securities for their moneylike features. Whether this set of tastes can be expected to endure is of course a speculation.[†]

IV. OPTIMUM SIZE AND COMPOSITION OF PUBLIC DEBT

Our two basic propositions may now be represented graphically. Let government debt be grouped into two classes, say, 90-day bills and 30-year bonds. In Fig. 1, along the vertical axis measure the amount of 90-day bills, and along the horizontal axis, units of 30-year bonds. In both cases, the unit is the maturity value in dollars. Suppose that the amounts of debt inherited from the past are those shown by point Q. Then the 45° line VM is a constant-debt line. The curves G_4, G_3, G_2, and G_1, are (private) GNP isoquants. A GNP isoquant shows the combinations of short-term and long-term debt that leave private expenditures upon current output

---

*For a good defense of this view, see E. D. Domar and R. A. Musgrave, "Proportional Taxation and Risk-Taking," *Q. J. Econ.*, May 1944, LVIII, 388–422.

[†]Prior to 1914, short-term rates were commonly above long- term rates—a fact that seriously damages a liquidity or moneyness approach to explain differences in yields. The authoritative empirical study of this experience is the work of F. R. Macaulay, *Some Theoretical Problems Suggested by the Movement of Interest Rates, Bond Yields and Stock Prices in the United States since 1856* (New York, 1938).

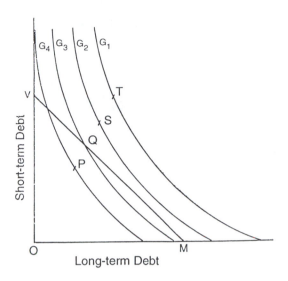

Figure 1

unchanged, given the public debt inherited from the past and given all remaining government financial policies.*

The relations among the isoquants are as follows. Consider the point Q, the quantity of debt inherited from the past. Let official agencies decrease the debt without altering the composition, giving the combination shown as P on the isoquant G_4. Then G_4 shows all combinations of short- and long-term government debt that provide the same level of GNP expenditures as found for point P. The G_4 curve also indicates a higher level of private expenditures upon current output than that given by the curve G_3. Similarly, points S and T on curves G_2 and G_1 represent combinations of outstanding debt resulting in successively more deflation, i.e., lower levels of private expenditures upon current output. The economic justification of this representation is our first fundamental proposition: a decrease in the outstanding government debt with composition unchanged, increases private expenditures and an increase in debt decreases private expenditures.

The slopes of the G curves follow from the proposition that short-term debt has less utility per dollar (maturity value) than has long-term debt. This condition means that the isoquants cut the VM line from above (the negative slope of any one G curve is greater than that of the VM line). Let us suppose, for example, that government policy is intended to make the outstanding debt have the same effect upon private expenditures as that given by the amount of debt inherited from the past; the objective is to remain on the G_3 curve. If it is also desired to increase the proportion of long-term debt there must be a reduction in the total debt; otherwise the objective of leaving private expenditures unchanged would be defeated. To offset the deflationary effect of the increase in the proportion of long-term debt, the government should simultaneously increase the quantity of money.†

The most efficient method of managing the debt is found when the utility of debt, the realization of some

---

*In the realm of fiscal measures other than debt measures, the conditions mean that government expenditures are treated as given, and its subsidy and tax formulae (not their yields) are also treated as given. In the realm of monetary measures, other than debt measures, the customary or legal reserve requirements of banks are to be treated as invariant, and any access to central bank funds except by open-market operations is excluded. These ceteris paribus conditions are necessary to avoid mixing the effects of the debt operations with the effects of other fiscal and monetary policies. Once the effects of each class of policies have been determined, integrated analysis of the combined effects of any combination of official monetary, debt, and fiscal acts becomes possible.

†The G curves must be convex to the origin because, as successive substitutions of short-term for long-term debt are made, total debt increases and the money supply decreases. But the successive substitutions of short-term debt, *per unit* of long-term debt withdrawn, must necessarily increase because short-term debt becomes an increasingly poor substitute for money as the supply of money decreases. A similar analysis will show that the curves must also be convex for decreases in short-term and increases in long-term debt.

level of private expenditures upon current output, is obtained at the minimum expense. The main cost, annual interest expense, depends mainly upon the size of the debt, its composition, and the price or yield of the securities.*

The interest cost of various debt combinations is shown graphically in Fig. 2. Let the axes have the same meaning as in Fig. 1, and let Q also be the amount of debt inherited from the past. At prevailing interest rates, say 2% on short-term and 4% on long-term, the interest cost to the government of all debt combinations that result in the same interest cost as the Q combination is shown by the line LM. The selection of a lower rate of interest for short-term securities reflects the condition that moneyness of assets has a positive utility—yields on short-term securities are lower than on long-term. The linear relation shown by LM could hold, however, only if variations in the proportion of government debt could be accomplished without any change in rates of interest. But this would be to treat short- and long-term securities as one commodity, and their relative yields as invariant.

A more appropriate way to reflect these facts is by the iso-interest curves C_1, C_2, and C_3. A curve such as C_2 is defined as all combinations of long-term and short-term debt that result in the same interest commitment of the government as the interest cost at point Q. Iso-interest curves may be expected to be

---

*Theoretically, since interest on government debt is a form of transfer income, the expense to the government should be measured by the interest paid to private groups minus the tax liability occasioned by the interest. This factor is of importance for our topic only if there is a significant difference between the tax liability per dollar of interest paid on short-term and on long-term government debt. Tax treatment of interest on government debt varies widely among countries; it is still common to exempt such income altogether under income tax laws. Furthermore, even in countries that appear to subject interest income from government debt to the same tax treatment as other income, the channeling of this income through financial intermediaries such as insurance companies serves to dissipate the amount that becomes reportable income to individuals, especially when, as in the United States, the accrued interest on life insurance policies is tax-exempt. Whether, on balance, these and other considerations result in differences in the effective rate of income taxation of the interest on different classes of federal government securities in the United States is a nice question to which no definite answer can as yet be given.

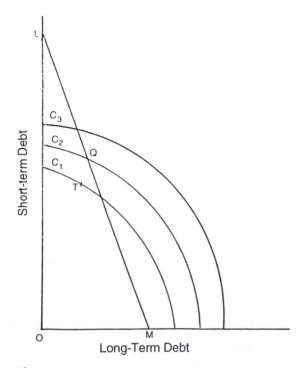

Figure 2

concave. For example, at point Q, \$1 of bonds carries the same interest expense as \$2 of bills. As bills are added and bonds subtracted from the market, the yields on bills will rise and those on bonds will fall. Then, moving from the combination given by Q, increasingly smaller amounts of bills must be substituted for a given amount of bonds if total interest costs are to be held constant. Thus the C curves are concave or linear. They are linear in the limiting case when bills and bonds are generally treated as perfect substitutes. A lower curve such as C_1 is defined as the combination of debt that results in the same expense as the combination shown by T. The interest cost is lower for C_1 than for C_2 because the debt has been reduced and the rates of interest on both short- and long-term securities are lower.

When the C curves of Fig. 2 are placed together with the G curves of Fig. 1, the optimum solution emerges as shown in Fig. 3. With the initial amount of debt at Q, the interest expense is that indicated by the iso-interest curve C_2. If the policy is to obtain the level of private expenditures indicated by G_2, the debt is too large and the proportion of short-term debt is also too great. To obtain the optimum solution, the composition should be changed by increasing the proportion of long-term debt and the entire debt should be reduced. This result is given by the tangency solution shown as point S. There is a saving in interest expense indicated by the difference between the interest cost for C_2 combinations and that for C_1 combinations. This saving will be mainly at the expense of those organizations and persons in the economy who like to hold large amounts of short-term government securities.

Our solution remains subject to two restrictions: the assumptions that a national debt consists of two classes of securities only and that current rates of interest accurately measure the cost to the government of an outstanding debt. Only the former will be considered in detail.*

---

*The use of current yields to measure the interest cost of an outstanding debt ignores the possible capital gains or losses a government may experience in debt management. Since even an abbreviated analysis of this aspect of the topic is rather involved and has not resulted in any important revision of the basic point of view, the question will be passed over.

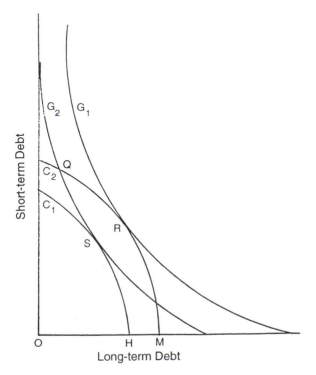

Figure 3

Instead of two classes of securities, let the kinds of government debt outstanding vary from some minimum maturity, say 1 day, to some maximum, say a perpetuity. The market-yield curve Y_m in Fig. 4 shows the yield-maturity relation observed at any date. Y_m is positively sloped to reflect the fact that actual market-yield curves have exhibited this characteristic for many years.* From this market-yield curve, we may construct what may be called an economic-yield curve, shown as Y_e. An economic-yield curve is derived from two functional relations, the market-yield curve as shown and a variable multiplier. The variable multiplier refers to the number of units of government debt measured in par values required to make a given change in private expenditures upon current output. Suppose, for example, that the sale of $1.00 of debt of 25-year maturity or greater would reduce private expenditures by $1.00. Then if the sale of some shorter maturity, say 20 years, reduces private expenditures by less than $1.00, more than $1.00 of 20-year maturity debt is required to have the same GNP effect as $1.00 of 25-year maturity debt. As the maturity approaches zero, government debt approaches being money and the multiplier approaches a maximum. If empirical information on the variable multiplier can be secured, any point on the Y_e curve may be derived. Select, say, point S on curve Y_e. The distance RM is the market yield of a unit of debt of that maturity, say, 3%. Let one and one-half units of debt of this maturity have the same GNP effect as $1.00 of debt of 25-year maturity. Therefore the distance SM is obtained by multiplying the distance RM by one and one-half. The effectiveness of debt—the size of the multiplier—is a decreasing function of the maturity of the debt up to some point.

Economical debt management calls ideally for making the Y_e curve a straight horizontal line. The interest on a national debt is a minimum when the interest cost of each type of debt instrument per dollar of "product" (i.e., change in private expenditures) is equal. Then if at any given time the composition of a government debt is such that its economic-yield curve is negatively sloped, the short-term end of the economic-yield curve should be lowered and the long-term end raised. This result is accomplished by retiring short-term maturities and selling long-term, and, if an unchanged level of GNP expenditures is desired, by reducing the total debt. In the process of doing this, the market-yield curve will twist, with the lower end shifting down and upper end shifting up, somewhat as shown by the dotted line Y'_m. As this shift occurs, the economic yield curve tends to flatten out and if the job is done perfectly, it becomes a straight line.†

---

*Yield-maturity curves for U.S. federal securities have exhibited positive slopes since about 1933. In earlier years, flat curves and even negatively sloped curves are sometimes found.

†If debts of all maturities have the same effect upon private expenditures, the multiplier is invariant, and the economic-yield curve coincides with the market-yield curve. In this event, a government should behave just as if it were a private operator in the market and look only to keeping its interest expense a minimum. The debt should be concentrated in the shortest maturity that is practicable in view of administrative costs, unless the market-yield curve becomes flat before all of the debt can be shifted.

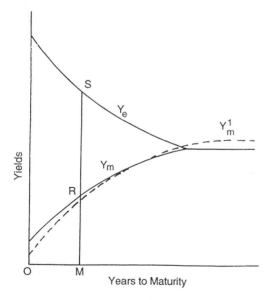

Figure 4

V. DEBT POLICY AND COMMERCIAL BANKS

An outstanding public debt will have a utility to a government regardless of the kind of commercial banking system, provided that banks operate under financial constraints. As already observed (see Section II), sale of debt by official agencies is a deflationary operation except in the limiting case when buyers treat government debt as a perfect substitute for cash. A strong government can, for example, decree that government debt of certain types shall constitute legal reserves for banks and make its debt a kind of money for banks. Alternatively, a central bank may announce that the prices of each kind of government debt will be fixed and, provided the announcement is accepted in good faith, make the debt a kind of income-yielding money. The crucial aspect of these and many other schemes is the inducement made to banks to treat government debt as a perfect substitute for cash. To the extent that such schemes are successful, and in recent wartime financing they were successful, the government persuades banks to create money for government account without imposing any restrictions upon their power to create money for private account.

But if banks are subject to effective reserve requirements, whether set by law, custom, or prudent practice, the acquisition of any earning asset including government debt is subject to constraints. If any one bank is induced to hold more government debt, it must forego the acquisition of other assets. The position of a bank in this connection does not differ in principle from that of an individual or an insurance company. All have limited means; all must make competing choices with respect to asset holdings. Thus a government's sale of debt which happens to be purchased by banks reduces the demands of the latter for other assets.

A banking system of money does influence the utility of an outstanding debt and also affects the comparative utility of different debt forms. The peculiarities of a banking system of money arise from the fact that liabilities of a particular kind of private organization are money and that these organizations can change the quantity of this money by their own operations. It is the latter fact that has special relevance for the present topic. If reserve requirements were 100%, a banking system of money would differ only in inconsequential details from a pure government currency system. Banks would have lost their power to create and destroy money—a main reason advocates of a 100% reserve system urge its adoption. We may analyze the role of fractional reserve systems with respect to debt management by comparing such systems with a 100% reserve system.*

The lower the reserve requirements of banks, however established, the greater, ceteris paribus, is the utility of an outstanding debt to a government. An experimental reduction of an outstanding debt by the substitution of central-bank-created money for debt permits banks as a group to multiply their holdings of earning assets. The multiplier is of course the reciprocal of the reserve ratio. Thus the lower reserve requirements are, the greater will be the inflationary effect of debt reduction and hence the greater is the utility of an outstanding debt to a government. This observation is simply another facet of the well-established theory that fractional reserves provide a more sensitive financial structure than do 100% reserve systems.[†]

Fractional reserve systems also tend to reduce the utility of short-term relative to long-term government debt. With fractional reserves, banks need to hold some of their assets in forms that they regard as similar to cash to provide for contingencies such as large adverse clearing drains. By contrast, with 100% reserves, or more generally, higher as opposed to lower reserve ratios, the needs of banks for cashlike assets are satisfied more by the reserves themselves. The marginal utility of the moneyness of assets may be expected to diminish. In addition, larger as opposed to smaller reserve ratios result in a smaller income from banking, and the marginal utility of income may be expected to be greater on this account. This factor would operate in the direction of inducing banks to sacrifice liquidity to obtain more income and hence hold more of their assets in long-term government bonds. An experimental shift in the composition of an outstanding public debt in the direction of lowering its average maturity may, therefore, be expected to be more expansionary under a lower as compared with a higher set of reserve ratios.[‡] The institution of a fractional reserve system of banking does not upset the principle that debt management is conducted most efficiently when the marginal utility of each public debt form is made proportional to its marginal cost.

---

*There is no intent here to argue in favor of or against the 100% reserve plan.

[†]See J. G. Gurley and E. S. Shaw, "Financial Aspects of Economic Development," *Am. Econ. Rev.*, Sept. 1955, XLV, p. 536.

[‡]This suggests that the spread in yields of public securities classified by maturity is a function of reserve ratios.

VI. CONCLUDING REMARKS

There remains untouched the crucial question of how to implement the suggested principle. Such a task would be far from simple; in fact no government could expect to achieve the precise size and composition of debt forms called for by the rule. Yet it is not an objection to a principle that it may be difficult to implement. Its role is to give direction to policy, to permit students and others to agree upon what constitutes relevant information, and to indicate types of financial administration most appropriate for the realization of rational decisions. As such, the principle is offered as a guide for debt management (including open-market operations) in the same spirit that the principle of marginal cost pricing has been offered as a guide for the regulation of public utility prices, and indeed for analogous reasons.

46

How to Manage the National Debt: A Symposium

Seymour E. Harris[†]

Few problems of public policy arouse as much heat and disagreement as that of the management of the national debt. The contributors to this symposium are in substantial agreement that the problems are difficult and that the management of the national debt interferes with the adjustment of the supply of money to the amount required for a well functioning economy. As Seltzer shows, the monetary authority does not dare allow the price of government securities to be determined by free market forces; instead, it seeks a balance between (1) protection against a cumulative decline and (2) a long-run stability in the price of long-term issues which would result in a wholesale desertion of short-term low-yielding issues for the more lucrative long-term issues.

Monetary expansion related to the support of the government bond market is the crucial problem. With a debt of $250 billion, with the danger of war confronting this country, with a market primarily in the financial institutions which may dump large amounts in short periods (Seltzer), with a decline resolving itself into a possible chain reaction (Musgrave), the government cannot afford to allow market governors to control. As Musgrave well shows, monetary control is not a precise weapon: it would be very helpful if monetary restraint might be introduced, the effects of which could be mapped out at the outset. Unfortunately, a change in the short-term rate involves repercussions on the long-term rate and attendant effects long after the initial cause has ceased to operate (Seltzer).

Few would be willing to unpeg the price of government securities. Surely the experience since June 1947 is not one that would support the destabilizers. Few would deny that the rate of interest has an important function to perform, though recent developments in monetary theory suggest its role is not so great as was assumed at the outset of the depression. Moreover, it is possible, as Seltzer has shown more than once, and as the board of governors of the Federal Reserve System suggested, largely to stabilize the market on government securities and yet allow the rates elsewhere to respond substantially to market forces. By immobilizing a large part of the outstanding issues as reserves of commercial banks, the authorities could stabilize rates on public securities with some effectiveness. Furthermore, as Musgrave proposes (and Seltzer seconds), it would be possible to contribute generally toward stabilization by substituting nonmarketable for marketable long-term securities. With demand artificially stimulated and fluctuations in supply reduced, in the manner suggested above, a greater approach to stabilization would be achieved.

Obviously, the monetary authority is powerless even with a prerogative to increase reserve requirements so long as a decline of reserves or an increase in reserve requirements can be matched by sales of government securities to the Reserve Banks. Thus, a recent rise of reserve requirements of several billion dollars was matched by a roughly equal increase of holdings of earning assets by the Reserve Banks, and an inflow of gold. This impasse is the unfortunate result of the need of supporting the bond market.

Adapted from the Introduction to "How to Manage the National Debt: A Symposium," *Review of Economics and Statistics, 31* (1949): 15–34, by permission of Elsevier Science: Amsterdam Publishing Division and by Richard A. Musgrave.
[†]Deceased.

But if anti-inflationary policy is weak on the monetary front, it need not be equally impotent elsewhere. In fiscal policy, for example, two tax reduction acts were especially unfortunate. It now appears that the federal government's contribution to the anti-inflation fight will be 11 billion dollars less in fiscal 1949 than in the first 6 months of 1948; and a reduction of tax receipts accounts for 5 billion of the total.[a] The authorities could also do a much more effective job of qualitative control—and that means consumer and housing credit, both in relation to banks and nonbanking lenders. If the objective of public policy is to provide an adequate housing program, a rearmament program, an ERP, all on top of the high level of consumption in relation to income, and in an economy surfeited with liquid assets not easily controlled, then the government also will have to strengthen certain controls, the most important of which are allocation controls. It is possible to provide a high level of consumption (inclusive of adequate education, social security, and housing) and of defense, but not if free competition for scarce factors is tolerated.

A large national debt raises other issues of transcendent significance. Abbott, for example, discusses the competition of unproductive, deadweight public securities, with the productive assets of industry, and many other serious problems confronting the private economy as a result of the large public debt.

It might be helpful in these days when the headaches of managing our national debt are uppermost in our minds not to lose perspective. With the growth of national debt, the country has accumulated liquid assets which create a problem in inflationary periods but serve as a buffer against excessive declines in depression. Professor Abbott may be correct in referring to the national debt as unproductive, at least, insofar as its origin is war, though here again one might consider winning the war a productive achievement. It is not equally easy to identify the debt accumulated in peace as unproductive. In fact, in one very important sense the national debt accumulated in both war and peace has been uniquely productive: who would say that this country would have experienced even the modest incomes of the 1930s or the unprecedented incomes of the 1940s without this accumulation of debt? The net rise of income over the years 1933–1948 resulting from debt accumulation may well have been several times that of the additions to debt. For example, against a rise of public debt of 209 billion dollars in 1940–1945, gross income in these 6 years rose by 450 billion (over six times the average for 1930–1939), and in 1941–1945 by 294 billion dollars over the 1939 level.[b] Of course, it would have been much better if we could have attained these high levels without war and growth of public debt; but it is well to weigh the costs and annoyances of the growth in debt against the gains from reduced wastage of resources.

The appearance of the volume *The National Debt and the National Welfare* by the *Committee on Public Debt Policy* suggests a few additional points. This committee has made many wise statements about our national debt; but only too often its results have been marred by an *excessive* concern over free markets, over the importance of the rate of interest, over the inadequacy of savings, over repayment of debt. In its final volume, the committee repeats many of its earlier mistakes.

Indeed, more savings are required in the present economy in order to strengthen inflationary forces; but this is far from saying that the country needs higher rates of interest to elicit more savings.[c] In fact, as is generally known, higher interest rates may well, through income effects, reduce savings. Again, the Committee seems to favor a long-run plan for repaying the national debt.[d] Nothing could be further from a wise policy than a long-term program which would involve repayment irrespective of economic conditions.[e] Should depression come in 1951, say, would the committee suggest debt reduction? If it would, then it has learned little from the economics of the 1930s and the 1940s. In Vol. 4 of the series, Professor Ratchford even proposes a 50-year debt retirement program which would entail total interest and principal payments of about 10 billion dollars yearly; or a 100-year minimum program involving annual outlays of 7.5 billion dollars.[f]

Despite its concern for the repayment of debt—and surely 1945–1948 were years to repay debt—the committee is strangely silent about the tax reduction program, and in fact urges further cuts in taxes.[g] As might be expected, the committee urges economy in government. Few would disagree on general grounds; and surely we want the greatest value for every dollar spent. But when the committee insists that education is the responsibility of local government, it is in fact saying that the country is doomed to an inadequate

[a]*Survey of Current Business*, October 1948, p. 8. The 1948 figures are at an annual rate.
[b]S. E. Harris, *The National Debt and the New Economics* (New York, 1947), pp. 27, 173.
[c]*The National Debt and the National Welfare*, p. 21.
[d]Ibid., p. 19.
[e]Cf. S. E. Harris, op. cit., Chap. XXIII.
[f]*The National Debt and the Budget*, p. 10.
[g]*The National Debt and the National Welfare*, pp. 10–11.

educational system; for the general property tax which finances 90% of the country's local governments pays the bill for education; and its yield in a 200 billion dollar economy is little more than that in a 40 billion dollar economy.[a]

Finally, it is no adequate answer to the economist that it is no use pushing for correct fiscal policies (e.g., spend more and tax less in depression), because politicians insist on spending more also in prosperity. It is our task, then, to educate the politicians, not to abandon correct principles.[b] Nor can we subscribe to the refutation of modern fiscal theories presented by Professor Ratchford, who, despite all the outpourings of the last 15 years, still thinks that the compensatory theory is merely a matter of pumping out *more money*.[c]

A great many of the fears of a rising public debt which have circulated since 1932 have been dissipated by the history of the last 15 years. Against the inflationary pressures associated in part with the growth of debt—and this is a serious problem—we should take into account the rise of income from 40 billion dollars in 1932–1933 to around 220 billion in 1948 (a growth of 200% in dollars of 1932–1933 purchasing power). With this rise of 180 billion dollars in income, the increase in the interest charge has been less than 5 billion dollars. Surely, the debt charge is not out of line with the growth of income to which the rising debt has greatly contributed. With sound management we may increase our national income another 50 to 100 billion dollars in the next generation. If we can do so without a large growth of debt, so much the better; but if with further debt growth the ratio of the debt charge to income does not increase greatly over the next generation and income remains between 200 and 300 billion dollars, we shall have succeeded in using fiscal and monetary policy for the general welfare of the nation. It is, however, important to manage our debt well and to control the inflationary forces so that any harmful effects may be contained.

It is also well to recall the great fears expressed in 1945. Yet our debt, which reached a peak of 278 billion dollars in February 1948, was but 252 billion in the middle of 1948. The liquidation was largely in securities held by the banks. (The reader should compare the contributions of Abbott, Musgrave, and Hansen on the net effects of these repayments.) Individual investors actually increased their holdings from February 1946 to July 1948, which was contrary to expectations; but the decline of 7.2 billion dollars (or about one quarter of their holdings in February 1946) by corporations and associations was small in view of the large investment demands stimulated by prosperity and rising prices. Their sales were largely offset by increased investments of the U.S. government.[d] As Seltzer shows, insurance companies alone seemed to have displayed a rather dubious spirit of cooperation in the last year.

---

[a]See S. E. Harris, *How Shall We Pay for Education?* (New York, 1948), Chaps. 5 and 6.

[b]Ibid., p. 10.

[c]Op. cit., p. 14: "The compensatory theory rests upon an extremely simple and mechanical view of our economy—pour in more money and get one, and only one, result. It is naive and superficial to assume that all the ills of our economy can be cured by the panacea of more and ever more money."

[d]*Treasury Bulletin*, Oct. 1948, p. 30.

47

Notes on Managing the Public Debt

Lawrence H. Seltzer[†]

I see no single simple solution to the problems of managing the public debt. The various legitimate objectives of debt management are bound to compete among themselves at various times and to compete also with other purposes of public policy. A different compromise may well be indicated at one time than at another.

The immediate situation recently confronting the authorities richly illustrates some of these conflicts. In a period of full employment, inflationary advances in prices, and still-rising bank credit, how long should they continue to create additional money for the purpose of supporting the prices of long-term government securities? Besides causing a severalfold increase in the lending power of the commercial banks, they knew that the new money was being used in the first instance by the principal sellers of long-term governments to swell the monetary demand for current output through loans for new construction and for fixed and working capital of business enterprises. The authorities had shown by their statements, their recommendations to Congress, and such actions as raising the required reserve percentages, that they feared further inflation and wished to restrain the expansion of bank credit.

The case for continuing the support of the government bond market in the face of these conditions was impressively summarized by Allan Sproul, president of the Federal Reserve Bank of New York, in the following words:

> Without our support, under present conditions, almost any sale of Government bonds, undertaken for whatever purpose (laudable or otherwise) would be likely to find an almost 'bottomless market' on the first day support was withdrawn. A rapid descent in prices going far beyond any question of the Government's credit (which is high) or relative interest rates would be most likely. Uncertainty would almost surely persist for a considerable time after such a development, the Government's necessary refunding operations would be made very difficult, and private security markets would be seriously affected. In such circumstances, there could easily be a flight of 'cash' out of both markets, and price changes so erratic as to make new financing almost impossible for some time, with what ramifications I do not like to contemplate. In the face of a Federal debt of over 250 billion dollars, in all sorts of forms held by all sorts of holders, and with a high consumption high employment economy, in which there are already severe stresses and strains, we can't treat the Government security market as we might a $50 million issue of the XYZ corporation. I am not a believer in more and more Government controls, certainly, but this is one control which I would not want to try to let go, voluntarily, under present circumstances.[*]

Many persons who shared Mr. Sproul's views in greater or lesser degree nevertheless favored (and still favor) having the authorities permit a "moderate" decline in bond prices and moderate rise in interest rates

---

Adapted from Part 2 of "How to Manage the National Debt: A Symposium," *Review of Economics and Statistics*, 31 (1949): 15–34 by permission of Elsevier Science: Amsterdam Publishing Division and by Richard A. Musgrave.
[†]Deceased.
[*]Address before the New York Bankers Association, January 26, 1948.

on the grounds that this would halt the dumping of government securities and attract adequate private investment support without creating great disturbance.* But those who confidently argued to this effect, contending that a drop in the supporting price levels to a few points below par would automatically inhibit selling by many institutional holders, tended to ignore the real risk that such action might set off two or three times as much selling by others. The market's confidence in the intention and ability of the authorities to continue their support was badly impaired when the Federal Reserve System suddenly lowered support levels on Christmas Eve of 1947. Since then numerous reassuring statements have been issued, and the Reserve System has unfalteringly maintained the new prices in the face of extremely heavy selling pressure. If the Reserve Banks were now to retreat again it is probable, in my opinion, that they would have to absorb a greater volume of offerings, and so create more member bank reserves, than if they continued the present supports.

Since the history of credit restriction amply demonstrates that it is rarely possible to use the traditional instruments to achieve carefully delimited results, the authorities must question whether the latter part of a long boom, when long-accumulated stresses are already restraining the expansionist tempo of our economy, is a good time in which to use methods capable of bringing about a violent reversal. And in the state of actual or incipient warfare in which our country and most others now live—the political philosophers term it "a state of nature"—the authorities have special reason for moving with rare caution.

In the meantime, the authorities have been able in fact to offset most of the new reserves created by their purchases of long-term bonds by open market sales of short-term securities, by raising the required reserve proportions, and by persuading the Treasury Department to use the excess of its cash receipts over cash expenditures to retire securities held by the Reserve and member banks. The existing amount of excess reserves is probably no greater than is needed for working purposes. While the member banks are in a position at any time to add to their reserves by selling some of their huge holdings of governments to the Reserve Banks, moral suasion may perhaps go far to discourage them from doing so. It is to be noted that bank lending to business, consumers, and purchasers of real estate was roughly stationary or declining in the aggregate in the last quarter of 1948 as contrasted with the sharp expansion that took place in this period in 1947. A number of factors contributed to this result, among them the large loans made by nonbank lenders, principally life insurance companies, but a more restrictive attitude on the part of banks was doubtless one of these. Since October, moreover, the heavy liquidation of long-term government bonds by insurance companies and other institutional investors, which had forced the Reserve Banks to buy some $4 billion of them in the preceding 12 months to maintain the established market prices, has slackened notably, and prices have risen somewhat above the support levels. Consequently the situation has become much less acute.

Nevertheless, the longer the present support levels are maintained, the greater are the implied or expressed commitments to continue them, and the harder it becomes to give them up. But an assured continuance of rigid prices for long-term government bonds would, of course, remove the effective distinction between long- and short-term securities, and indeed between the longest term bonds and money itself. No restraint would exist on the ability of holders of governments to turn them into money at will, and to this extent to influence the supply of money and the volume of spending without regard to the policies of the monetary authorities. To meet this dilemma, the authorities are compelled to walk a tightrope, promising the holders of long-term governments enough price support, in combination with yield, to overcome their fears of declining bond prices, but not enough to make it safe, as well as profitable, for banks and all other investors to exchange short-term obligations and cash for long-terms under a guarantee that they can get their cash again at any time without loss.

Similar conflicts complicate the longer-run management of the debt. The power to vary the supply and cost of credit is the heart of central banking. Occasionally this power is used with invaluable results to expand credit to meet emergency situations. But its most common use since the 1920s has been directed at moderating cyclical fluctuations in business. Flexible interest rates would appear to be essential to the exercise of this power. Even if the authorities became convinced, as many students have, that neither the demand for credit nor the volume of saving is highly responsive to ordinary changes in interest rates, and decided to seek no changes in them deliberately as an ordinary instrument of policy, they could hardly keep the rates stable if they made significant changes in the availability of credit.

A serious complication of changes in interest rates is the tendency of their effects to outrange and to outlast the conditions that occasion them. A rise in short-term rates cannot easily be prevented from spreading

*E.g., Robert C. Leffingwell, "How to Control Inflation," *Fortune*, Oct. 1948.

to long-term rates. When this happens, not only are new long-term debt contracts directly affected for many years to come, but the market values of all existing capital assets tend to be lowered. Because of the immense growth in the proportion of private wealth represented by marketable securities, alterations in the market values of capital assets exert a much wider and deeper influence than formerly on the temper of investors and of those who lead business enterprises. Moreover, the effects of changes in interest rates upon market values, and the effects of the latter changes, are slow to become fully consummated, with the result that they tend to persist after the short-term conditions that occasioned them have passed. These are reasons why monetary policies involving significant changes in interest rates are not so readily adapted, as many believe, to short-term objectives. The hope of the authorities in this connection is that they will be able in one way or another to maintain a fair degree of stability in the long-term markets while exercising a significant measure of flexible power over short-term rates.

Essential to this purpose is a great diminution in the sensitiveness of the government bond market. The coercive influence of this market upon monetary policy, and the burden of managing it, can be eased only by radically reducing the principal sources of large-scale open market liquidation. The authorities will be able to maintain a high degree of marketability in long-term government securities—meaning a quick, close market—without making their credit policy subordinate to this purpose, only if relatively small amounts of long-term governments are bought or sold in any short period. Good marketability is possible for any security only under such conditions. Even for the most widely known and most popular stocks on the New York Stock Exchange, brokers nowadays find it necessary to organize a selling group and to make other special efforts to obtain adequate distribution whenever a sizable block of stock, perhaps from an estate, must be sold. Today, about 70% of all marketable government securities not held by government agencies or the Reserve Banks is concentrated in the hands of commercial banks, insurance companies, and mutual savings banks. Except to the extent that they sell to one another, and perhaps even then, large scale liquidation by these institutions is bound to create disorders in the market, unless the central banking authorities come to the rescue. No other members of the public commonly possess large amounts of liquid funds available for investment purchases. More fundamentally, the rate of current saving of the public cannot be expected to adjust itself to such selling. Even these three classes of institutional investors do not ordinarily carry large idle balances and are not usually in a position to put into the market more than their recent receipts from premiums, interest, dividends, rents, saving deposits, etc. The net liquidation of 1,174 million dollars of government securities by member banks in 1937 was made possible without more than a moderate tightening of interest rates and without more than modest aid from the Reserve Banks (134 million dollars) only because the insurance companies and mutual savings banks added to their holdings nearly as much as the banks sold.*

To a very large degree, the recent heavy liquidation of long-term governments, and the related difficulties of the authorities, must be attributed to the lending and portfolio policies of certain institutional investors. notably some large insurance companies that were conspicuously in conflict with the declared objectives of the Reserve System. During the Treasury financing of the depression and war periods, representatives of such institutions repeatedly urged upon the Treasury that adequate provision be made to satisfy their needs for long term, relatively high-yielding bonds. They argued that they were characteristically long-term investors who had little use for short-term obligations. Nevertheless, in recent months, with full knowledge that the banking authorities were attempting to restrain the expansion of credit by restricting consumer credit, raising reserve requirements, recommending new legislation, and otherwise inducing the commercial banks to adopt conservative lending policies, some of the insurance companies took advantage of the Reserve System's need to support the government market to dump their holdings on the market and to lend the proceeds for business and construction spending.

Little is possible to improve this situation in the short run other than moral suasion. In the long run, I would like to see a gradual displacement of a large part of the long-term marketable securities held by insurance companies and mutual savings banks by a nonmarketable but redeemable security of the type of the G savings bond. With this type of security, the holder does not receive the average overall rate of interest unless he holds to maturity; earlier redemption is discouraged by a discount representing the difference between the average rate of interest that has been previously paid and the lower effective yield actually offered

---

*Nonbank investors absorbed the whole of the 1,168 million dollars increase that year in the privately held interest-bearing public debt, but much of this took place through the organized sale of discount bonds to persons who do not ordinarily purchase government securities.

for the elapsed period of holding. Conceivably, a somewhat higher average overall rate of interest might be necessary on such a security at first because of its novelty for institutional investors and because of the certain penalty incurred for redemption in advance of maturity.

Partly for similar reasons, but also for others that I have outlined elsewhere,* I would like to have the commercial banks ultimately exchange the bulk of their government securities either for interest-earning reserve deposits or for a new Treasury obligation, redeemable on demand, but required to be held as a part of their statutory reserves. A variant of this proposal was recommended to Congress by the Board of Governors of the Federal Reserve System in its annual report for 1947. Such a measure would not only help to reduce the sensitiveness of the bond market but would make the commercial banks invulnerable to price declines in their holdings of government securities, reinforce the margin of safety now provided by their extremely thin capital ratios, and, most important, restore to the Federal Reserve authorities effective control over the volume of bank credit.

I would maintain a large volume of short-term marketable securities for their great value to the money market and central banking authorities, and their low cost to the Treasury.

I have no illusions, however, that these concrete measures by themselves, even if they could be adopted at once, would eliminate those problems of managing the public debt that I have chosen to discuss here. Some of the measures would raise problems of their own that I cannot discuss now because of limitations of space. They need to be supplemented by the enlightened cooperation of the big institutional holders of government securities with the monetary authorities. The large insurance companies and banks, in their own interests, must look behind the letter of their bond contracts. They must each recognize that they are not insignificant members of a vast market, but highly important parts of an interdependent financial community to which, for their common safety, they owe a responsibility.

---

*"The Problem of Our Excessive Banking Reserves," *Journal of the American Statistical Association*, vol. 35, no. 209 (March 1940), and "The Changed Environment of Monetary Banking Policy," *American Economic Review, Proceedings*, Vol. XXXVI, No. 2 (May, 1946).

48

Government Debt and Private Investment Policy

Charles C. Abbott[†]

Much of the recent literature concerning the federal debt and the problems of debt management has been primarily concerned with broad issues of public policy. To a considerable extent the discussion has proceeded in a frame of reference whose chief points were fiscal policy, the possibility of so managing the debt as to mitigate fluctuations in the business cycle, the level of interest rates, the differentials separating the yields of short-, intermediate-, and long-term government paper, the interest burden, and the relations between Federal Reserve and Treasury policies. All these elements must of course be brought under scrutiny if problems inherent in the debt and in debt management are to be seen in their entirety. Certainly some, if not all, of these topics have possessed an importance of the first order during the 3 years that have elapsed since V-J Day.

Yet the very emphasis that has been given to these broad aspects of the debt problem has tended to obscure other facets that in the long run may prove to be of equal or even greater moment. Relatively little attention, at least in academic circles, has as yet been given to the effects produced on investment decisions and procedures by the fact that the country now has a 250 billion dollar government debt. The considerations stemming from the existence of this enormous debt, which individual investors, portfolio managers, trustees, and corporate financial officers must now weigh, and the alternative courses of action which the presence of the debt opens to them, seem not to have received all the study that they merit. Such aspects of the debt problem are significant, not only because of their own intrinsic importance, but also because of their repercussions on the larger issues of debt policy. For in the last analysis the actions of individual persons circumscribe the area within which public debt policy must be planned and carried out. It is the purpose of this chapter to outline some of the questions which the fact of the debt has posed to private financial management and to indicate some of the ways in which these questions impinge upon the larger issues of public policy and upon matters usually considered as strictly within the orbit of economic theory.

The appearance in the economy of a very large federal debt has introduced a new element into the field of property management and has furnished private financial management with a new vehicle. In substance, the creation of the debt has given a most important medium of investment to officers of both financial and nonfinancial corporations, as well as to individual investors, that they did not formerly possess. It may be doubted whether either the practical or the theoretical effects of this circumstance are as yet fully understood.

Since the end of the war something like half of the assets of private financial institutions have been held in the form of Treasury securities, and private individuals, trust funds, and nonfinancial business corporations have owned some 42 to 50 billion dollars of marketable government paper. Furthermore, the numerous issues of Treasury securities available, when considered in relation to their characteristics—namely, maturity, yield,

Adapted from Part 3 of "How to Manage the National Debt: A Symposium," *Review of Economics and Statistics, 31* (1949): 15–34 by permission of Elsevier Science: Amsterdam Publishing Division and by Richard A. Musgrave.
[†]Deceased.

stability, marketability, bank eligibility, etc.—have provided a wide range of choice. Such a situation has furnished portfolio managers of financial institutions, treasurers of nonfinancial corporations, trustees, and individual investors with alternatives in the management of their affairs that hardly existed during the 1920s or 1930s. Moreover, so long as the market for Treasury securities is supported, either at fixed points or within a relatively narrow range, as has been the case since early in the war, the risk attaching to some of the possible courses of action has been much reduced. Such reductions of risk have of course served to widen the range of feasible investment procedures, particularly for fiduciary institutions.

This situation—the growth of the debt, the increase in the kinds of federal debt, and the widespread ownership of the debt—has posed two general questions to a very large number of financial officers and individual investors. The two problems may be phrased as follows: (1) What proportion of an individual's or a business concern's total assets shall be held in the form of Treasury securities? (2) What particular issues of Treasury securities shall be held? The collective answers given by private investors to these questions in turn form the basis, the very essence, of many of the problems of debt management faced by fiscal authority. It will be convenient to deal with these two questions separately, in the order indicated.

During the war the range of choice for the size of the government portfolio in the case of many financial institutions was in considerable measure determined by factors external to the institution itself and its investment policies. Since the end of the war, however, the degree of latitude has steadily grown, and the scope within which policies of individual institutions may operate has widened.

Although many of the numerous influences that govern the volume of Treasury securities owned at a particular time by an individual institution or investor must be omitted from this discussion because of lack of space, two are immediately pertinent, namely, the respective sizes of the cash account and the holdings of Treasury paper and, in the case of financial institutions, the respective magnitudes of the government portfolio and the portfolio of other types of earning assets.

Let us first consider the relationship of the government portfolio to the cash account. The existence of a large volume of government securities, particularly of redeemable and short-dated paper, together with a pegged market for the latter type, has made Treasury securities for many purposes the equivalent of cash. Financial managers have found it possible to convert with comparative safety unused cash balances and cash reserves into government securities. Here we may recall the investment in government debt of the large excess reserves of commercial banks that existed at the beginning of the war, and the employment during and since the war of unexpended reserves in the government market by nonfinancial corporations. In short, the government portfolio—or a part thereof—has tended to become a second cash account, and the financial manager's choice has in considerable measure been one of deciding whether to hold more (or fewer) government securities and less (or more) cash.

At least three significant results have followed from this situation. First, from the point of view of the individual business institution, it has been possible safely to convert cash—ordinarily a nonearning asset—into an earning asset. Second, from the point of view of authorities concerned with credit control, the easy access to funds provided by the widespread ownership of government paper and the pegged market for such securities has made unusually difficult the adjustment of available credit to the needs of the economy. Third, from the point of view of persons interested in capital formation, the conversion by business concerns of government securities into cash and the employment of such cash in the construction of plant and equipment or the creation of inventories has made more than ordinarily elusive the connection between savings and investment.

Under present circumstances financial institutions may, within very wide limits, make use either of government securities as earning assets or of credit instruments originating in the private segment of the economy, such as commercial and industrial loans, mortgages, and corporate securities. The manner in which institutions allocate their earning assets between these two types of outlets for funds is influenced by a wide variety of considerations, such as liquidity needs, rates of return, the demand by private borrows for funds, the business outlook, etc. The overall allocation of assets made by financial institutions as between earning assets created by the government and earning assets created by private borrowers bears directly on the operations of the fiscal authorities: The greater the volume of government credit which private investors wish to hold, the lower—other things being equal—can Treasury interest rates be, the easier will it be to maintain the market for government securities, and the simpler will be the Treasury's "refunding problem." Conversely, the smaller the amount of government paper that is acceptable to private investors, the more acute these aspects of debt management become.

The fact that a very large amount of an investment medium—i.e., government debt—exists which can be used either as a substitute for cash or as a substitute for earning assets has provided private financial management with a range of investment choices that for the most part did not exist 20 years ago. One element in the situation is of especial interest both to men of affairs and to economic theorists. Private financial institutions can now in substance withdraw from the private investment field if they so desire without suffering the loss of earnings that used to be the penalty of converting earning assets into cash. They can, if they wish, convert all earning assets into government debt and still earn a modest return. Under some circumstances this may be an attractive policy. Yet the situation raises immediately the following questions, which it leaves unanswered: What is the proper function of a financial institution in a private enterprise economy? What are the considerations that ought to determine whether such an institution invests its assets in deadweight, unproductive government debt or in productive industry, the source of the tax base that gives value to Treasury paper? How should private wealth weigh its respective responsibilities as a repository for nonproductive government debt and as a source of financing for the production and distribution of goods and services? Although the relative rates of return and estimated risks attaching to public and private securities provide practical answers to this question, such considerations do not yield a solution that is entirely satisfactory in an overall social sense. The general problem remains a fit subject of speculation for those concerned with a proper functioning of the economy.

Discussion of the factors that bear on the selection of particular Treasury issues for the government portfolio is best initiated by reminding the reader that different types of Treasury issues are typically used for different purposes. Long-term issues tend to be held by financial institutions for income purposes, short-term issues for liquidity purposes. Nonfinancial corporations find government debt a useful repository of reserve funds, both short- and long-term reserves. Other purposes or uses of government paper could readily be pointed out. The selection of the issues best suited to the purposes of the particular person or institution is perhaps the essence of portfolio management. As conditions change, as liquidity becomes of more importance to a particular institution than income, as individual investment policies shift, as the demand for money rises or falls, the portfolio manager must shift his holdings so as to meet the new prospect.

Yet adaptation of the portfolio to the needs of the individual investor or investing institution is not the whole story. Particular issues of Treasury securities are, within limits, alternative, competitive outlets for funds, just as the different investment instruments originating in the private economy compete with each other and with Treasury securities for the investor's dollar. As the interest structure changes, as differentials separating short-, intermediate-, and long-term rates alter, investment funds tend to flow from one issue of government debt to another, even in the absence of other changes in the situation of a particular investor or in general monetary conditions. For example, a slight fall in the return on 8-year paper compared with the (lower) return on 4-year paper may make the longer-term investment relatively less attractive. In that case funds will tend to flow from one investment medium to the other, even if no other changes in the money market take place and even if the needs of portfolio managers remain constant.

If space permitted, it would be profitable to explore various implications of this condition of "quasi-competing markets" that exists within the government securities market and between the government market and other investment markets. One aspect of the situation, however, must be noted here. Shifts in the government portfolio of private investors can and do take place for at least three distinct kinds of reasons: (1) because the needs of particular investors, and the purposes served by their government holdings, change; (2) because government securities as a class become more or less attractive as compared with other types of securities; (3) because particular issues of Treasury securities become more or less desirable relative to other Treasury issues. Commonly, of course, shifts in government portfolios are made because of a combination of reasons.

The general significance of these considerations seems to be as follows: Irrespective of which particular causes induce changes in private holdings of government securities, the changes themselves induce or magnify problems of debt management. No matter what the reasons—whether "frivolous" or fundamental—that lead to changes in the government portfolio of private holders, fiscal authority must reckon with them and with their consequences.

We are now in a position to sum up the import of the preceding discussion.

In a very large measure the actions of individual investors and portfolio managers in adapting their holdings of governments to their shifting needs create the major problems that fiscal authorities face in managing the debt. Particularly is this the case when one of the purposes of public policy is to hold prices of individual Treasury issues at stated levels or within a given range. This circumstance may be illustrated by two extreme examples. These examples are not realistic; they are introduced merely to indicate some of the inherent logics of debt management.

If over a period of time all holders of government debt found their holdings ideally suited to their needs, so that there was no motive to alter the proportions of cash and governments owned or to convert Treasury paper into other types of earning assets (or vice versa), the volume of transactions in the government market would fall to very low levels. It is even possible to imagine a situation in which no transactions took place, and price quotations were nominal. Under such circumstances the market would be stabilized, not by pegging operations on the part of fiscal authority, but because government security holders were entirely satisfied with the size and character of their holdings, in view of their appraisal of the economic prospect. Under such conditions fiscal authority would find that many problems inherent in stabilizing the government market had virtually disappeared. Furthermore, such variations as took place under these conditions in the volume of commercial bank or central bank credit outstanding would, presumably, be attributable to fluctuations in demand for funds and the changing needs of the economy. If this appears to be too extreme a statement, one may at least assume that under the given conditions variations in the volume of outstanding bank credit would not be traceable to debt management.

On the other hand, if during some period private holders of government securities endeavored to liquidate all—or a major portion—of their portfolios, and fiscal authorities were the only buyers, the volume of bank credit would expand rapidly. Such an expansion would not, in all probability, have any direct connection with the legitimate needs of the economy, and extremely powerful inflationary forces would be generated. In fact, if for some considerable time fiscal authorities were the only purchasers it is quite conceivable that their market stabilizing operations would have to be abandoned, with all the results that a forced cessation of stabilizing operations entails.

We reach, then, this general conclusion: The more closely the size and structure of the debt accommodates the collective needs of all private holders, so that transactions in the government market are at a minimum, the simpler will be many problems of debt management and the more attention fiscal authority will be able to devote to the stabilization of the economy as a whole, without regard to debt management. The general truth of this contention seems quite compatible with the admitted fact that the collective needs of private holders of government securities continually vary as time passes and business conditions change. On the other hand, should the size or character of the debt become radically out of touch with the collective needs of private holders, either because of a shift in the economic outlook, of investor sentiment, or for any other reason, not only would debt management in the present sense of the term become virtually impossible but so would maintenance of a reasonably stable and healthy economy.

It thus appears that one of the fundamental policies of debt management must be to keep the size and character of the debt in accord with the needs of the debt holders. By character of the debt is meant the number and types of issues, the maturity pattern, rates of return, bank eligibility, marketability, etc. Insofar as this end is accomplished many special problems, such as price stabilization, maintenance of a firm market for refunding issues, and the separation of debt management and credit control will be commensurately simplified. Insofar as this goal is not reached, these problems will be made commensurately difficult of solution.

The type of debt structure that is, or will be, best suited to the needs of the debt holders, in view of the situations in which they find themselves, is too large a subject to be explored here. But it is a matter that merits the most careful continuing study. Even if there were no other reasons for undertaking such analyses, the future course of events will in all probability necessitate that a growing amount of attention be given to this topic, to appraisal of the kind of structure best suited to the needs of actual or potential owners of Treasury securities.

49

Debt Management and Inflation

Richard A. Musgrave*

The present discussion will be focused on the contribution of debt policy to economic stability and, in particular, to checking inflation. While not the only consideration, this is the most difficult and probably the most important aspect of the problem.[†]

In simplified form, the basic nexus may be stated as follows: Suppose the public holds a given total of claims, partly in money, partly in public debt, and partly in private obligations. As long as claims are held in public debt, they are not shifted into money with a possible subsequent transfer into private investment. During inflation this is helpful. Authorities will want investors to continue their debt holdings or to exchange money for additional debt; and as an inducement, the return on debt holding will have to be raised. During deflation, authorities will want investors to move in the other direction, to reduce their debt holdings, exchange debt for additional money, and place such funds into private investment. As an inducement, the reward for debt holding will have to be lowered.

Two complications should be added to obtain a more complete picture. First, the problem is not only one of shifts between debt and money, but also between debt obligations of varying degrees of liquidity. The rate issue, similarly, is one of pattern as well as level. Second, the significance of swaps between debt and money is greatly increased by the peculiarity of fractional reserve banking. In a loaned-up system, such swaps lead to multiple changes in credit supply; in fact, they are the major instrument of controlling the credit base. Not only do debt and credit policy act upon the same determinant of economic activity (the availability of claims in more or less liquid form); they also share open market operations (by Federal Reserve and/or Treasury) as the most important technique of control.

Expansionary credit and debt policy called for under conditions of deflation is relatively simple but not very effective. In the absence of restored profit expectations, increased availability of funds will add to unused balances (excess reserves) rather than capital formation. Restrictive credit and debt policy called for under conditions of inflation is potentially powerful but difficult to apply. Not that there is any doubt in theory about the proper prescription; the objective is to compete funds away from private investment, to restrict credit expansion (or force contraction), and to pay the price required in terms of rising yield on public debt. If carried sufficiently far, there is no doubt that such a policy *can* exert a powerful check to inflation. The problem is, rather, whether it can be administered in the proper doses and without prohibitive interference with other objectives.

Numerous objections have been advanced to this course of action. Some have little merit, including the

Adapted from Part 4 of "How to Manage the National Debt: A Symposium," *Review of Economics and Statistics, 31* (1949): 15–34 by permission of Elsevier Science: Amsterdam Publishing Division and by Richard A. Musgrave.

*Formerly of Harvard University, Cambridge, Massachusetts.

[†]For a fuller discussion see my paper "Credit Controls, Interest Rates and Management of Public Debt" in *Income, Employment and Public Policy, Essays in Honor of Alvin Hansen* (New York), 1948.

notions that higher interest rates on public debt are intolerable at a time "when economy in government expenditures is called for"; that rising cost of borrowing reflects upon the Treasury's credit standing; and that to permit a fall in security values is to betray the confidence of the bondholder.* Somewhat more valid is the objection that higher rates may have undesirable effects on the distribution of incomes and there is foundation for the concern that vested interests created by a current rate increase may make a reversal of rate policy difficult at a later date.† These defects must be balanced against the advantages to be gained from a restrictive policy, but they establish no a priori case against rate increases.

The crucial point, however, is the unpredictability of restrictive measures. With the large war debt and an investor psychology lulled by a long period of rising or stable bond prices, a sharp upward adjustment in yields (including those on medium- and longer-term issues) may well send the security market into a tailspin. This might be the signal for excessive contraction rather than an orderly check to inflation. Unless public authorities are prepared to take the risk, they may have to step in and purchase more debt than would have been necessary had stability been maintained in the first place.‡ To some extent this contingency might be met by proceeding in gradual steps, but gradual adjustment (the essence of which is that investors consider each move to be the last) is a game which cannot be played for long.

Is it not better then to relay on more controllable checks to inflation such as higher taxes or direct price-wage controls, and to discard the liquidity approach? Unfortunately this is a rhetorical question. The fact is that we have shown little ability to restrain inflation along these other lines and the politics of the case promise little improvement. Every effort should be made, therefore, in an inflationary situation to provide checks from the liquidity side, wherever this can be done short of inviting excessive contraction.

The most obvious move is to place greater reliance upon selective controls of the consumer credit and margin type, including the more vigorous use of existing, and the development of new, measures. By imposing eligibility rules on would-be borrowers, the demand for funds is curtailed through such controls. Thereby credit is restricted without forcing up rates. Perhaps as much as one-half of the postwar loan expansion has been in areas susceptible to the application of selective controls and (asuming coordination of public lending policies) a good part of the credit problem might have been solved in this fashion and without destabilizing effects on the security market.

Selective measures, however, cannot be applied in all areas and do not obviate the need for a higher degree of general credit control. Here the major requirement is for restraints upon the ability of commercial banks to turn debt holdings into excess reserves by sale to the Federal Reserve.§ The most direct step is to impose substantially higher reserve requirements (which will force banks to exchange security holdings against required reserves), supplemented if necessary by interest payments on reserve balances. A less extreme measure is the Board of Governor's 1947 plan for adding addition reserve requirements in the form

---

*Economy in interest payment does not mean that interest payments should be low absolutely, but that they should purchase illiquidity in the most efficient fashion. This is quite a different matter.

Low interest rates carry no necessary implication of good Treasury management. The government is not a corporation that may pride itself in getting money cheap. The level of demand for government securities is largely of the government's own making (i.e., a result of monetary policy), and the criterion is provision of the proper degree of liquidity, not low interest cost.

The dictum that bond prices must not fall below par is logically untenable. The goverment's commitment is to pay interest and to redeem at par at maturity, not to pay long-term rates on what (in a pegged market) comes close to being a demand balance.

†Stabilization objectives of debt management may conflict with income distribution objectives, which may call for special treatment of various investor groups. As far as banks are concerned, this conflict should be met head on. A possible prospect of excessive bank earnings should not be permitted to speak against a policy of restriction (involving higher rates) if such a policy is called for on general grounds. If earnings are excessive, this should be handled through appropriate tax measures. Similarly, the possibility of inadequate bank earnings should not be permitted to check policy moves in the opposite direction, if they are called for on general grounds. The profit motive of banks is no automatic regulator of the proper money supply; but by regulating the money supply, authorities cannot but exert far-reaching control over bank profits.

‡It is recognized that the additional money, supplied in this process, will not be reflected at once in higher capital outlays. Rather, the uncertainty created in the course of rate adjustment will result in greatly increased liquidity preference. However, this is exactly why the danger of excessive contraction arises.

§Such restrains should have been applied long ago. By now a good part of the damage is done; the liquidity of banks has been substantially reduced through the debt retirement program and sales to the Federal Reserve, but bank holdings of short-term issues are still substantial.

of short-term U.S. security holdings. After the secondary reserve position of commercial banks is reduced in this fashion, control over bank reserves will be more effective and involve less pressure on security prices.

Debt holdings by nonbank investors present a more difficult problem. Sales by nonbank holders to the Federal Reserve not only give them cash but also add to bank reserves, just as do direct sales by commercial banks. Since the effects of yield changes on security prices are greater the longer the maturity of the issue, and since long-term issues are held largely by nonbank investors, this is where the major problem of stability arises. To some extent the situation might be relieved by applying a "hundred per cent ceiling reserve requirement" under which old deposits would be subject to the present fractional reserves while deposit increments would require 100% reserves. This would sterilize the reserve effects of open market purchases made in support of debt prices.

However, the bondholder would still be free to obtain cash on a one-to-one basis and the only way to prevent this is to formulate debt contracts so that investors are restrained from withdrawing their commitments under inflation conditions. The old problem of funded vs. unfunded debt must be reconsidered in this perspective. Given the condition that the security market cannot be permitted to fluctuate widely, the technicality of long-term maturity does not protect the government against having to pay whenever the investor is sufficiently eager to terminate his commitment. In fact, short-term debt is superior in this case. It involves less fluctuation in value and danger of cumulated instability and it leaves more freedom for flexible policy adjustments.

Accordingly, the rigidities and (under most conditions) higher costs of a longer commitment are worthwhile for the government only if there is assurance on the investor's part that his investment *will stick*; i.e., that he will retain his illiquidity when economic stability thus requires. *This is the real meaning of funding.* It involves a longer-term debt contract (although I doubt whether much can be gained in this respect by extending it beyond, say, 7 to 10 years), but also suggests that such debt should be nonmarketable and noncashable on demand, or at least, that its terms should impose effective restraints against cashing at the wrong time. The nonmarketability and the accelerated interest features of the savings bond are a first step in the right direction, but more effective techniques need be developed.* To be sure, this may not be a simple task, but unless the nonbank-held debt can be funded in this proper sense of the term (and funded at rates which are not prohibitive from the point of view of distributional considerations) it should be replaced eventually by short-term issues.

But this will take time. The immediate problem is what to do in the present setting, over and above increased reliance on selective credit controls. First with regard to the long rate. While inflation conditions continue, the upward pressure on the long rate which broke through in the closing months of 1947 is likely to continue as well, forcing further open-market support and supply of reserve funds. If the long rate were unpegged, the resulting desire for liquidity on the part of lenders (rather than the reduced demand for funds due to the increase in interest as a cost item!) might at once impose a powerful check to investment, but this result would rest on the condition that no new peg was established in an effective fashion. Merely a somewhat higher level of pegged rates would hardly be of much value. Yet, it is precisely the absence of an immediate

---

*Henry Simons' solution ("On Debt Policy," *Journal of Political Economy*, December 1944), to restrict liquid assets to two forms, consoles or money, is ruled out by our condition of reasonable market stability. But even if the market is permitted to fluctuate, I see no merit in this extreme approach; different investors have legitimate preferences regarding the time periods for which they wish to commit themselves. There is no reason why these should not be satisfied and why the government should not save interest cost by adapting its offerings to the preferences of various investor groups.

There is a question at what price investors will wish to commit themselves to an investment which freezes their position for set periods or at times when speculative shifts might be profitable. As far as small individual investors are concerned, a clause might be included, permitting immediate cashing in case of emergency, such as for payment of hospital bills. As far as institutional investors go, I see no obligation on the government's part to provide a speculative medium. If they are unwilling to purchase "funded" debt at reasonable rates, let them invest in private or short-term government issues. To be sure, the placing of "funded" debt will cost the government more, but at least it will receive an illiquidity commitment in return, which is not the case under present arrangements. Where the price of funding becomes excessive from the point of view of distributional considerations, supplementary tax measures have to be relied upon.

Notwithstanding the longer-term commitments involved, the proposed funding policy still permits cyclical adaptation in the long rate. In inflation, new funded debt can be issued at more attractive terms, while the old funded debt remains largely frozen. In depression, no new funded debt will be offered. Some difficulty arises because claims lodged in the old funded debt cannot be dislodged and pushed toward private investment, but this is not too serious. Additional funds may be provided in other ways and part of the problem might be met by extending the call feature in the debt contract.

peg that would create the danger of chain reaction and force the prompt imposition of a new support level. In short, it does not seem likely that much can be accomplished along this line until the long-term debt structure has been made over.

Operations on the short end of the rate structure are more feasible and restriction of bank credit might be achieved, perhaps, at the cost of rising short rates only. With higher rates on short-term government securities, commercial banks will be less likely to shift into commercial loans and other assets and expand credit in the process. But what if commercial loan rates show a similar rise? For the rise in short rates to be effective, it must then be either that the demand for commercial loans is fairly elastic to rising interest cost, or that commercial banks are adjusting their portfolios so as to meet a set earnings goal. Of the two, the latter factor is likely to carry more weight. However, there is the announcement effect of rising rates which will induce banks to be cautious while the adjustment occurs. As a partial offset to what may be accomplished in this fashion, rising short rates will also reflect upon the long rate and hence require larger purchases of long issues. This will cause a considerable leakage, and some rise in the long rate might have to be taken into account; but even though larger purchases in the long market may be required, this policy has the redeeming feature of speeding up the withdrawal of marketable long-term issues and opening the way for replacing them later with "funded" debt.* Permitting short rates to rise, in all, appears to be the least risky approach under given conditions.

The outlook is dimmed somewhat by the shrinkage and prospective disappearance of a current budget surplus. The debt retirement program, undoubtedly, has been helpful in exerting such pressures on bank reserves as have been applied since the end of the war. But though the beneficial effects of the retirement program have been underrated by some, their importance may also be overstated.[†] The main contribution of the retirement program was in its dampening effect on the current income flow, rather than in its bearing upon the level of reserves. Withholding of surplus tax receipts on Federal Reserve balance (or, which is the same, its use for debt retirement) was a convenient way of exerting reserve pressure, and so was the uncertainty introduced into the position of banks through the shifting of large surplus funds. However, with or without budget surplus, and even with some deficit, Federal Reserve and Treasury authorities can exert great pressure on reserves (through open-market sales or appropriate refunding operations) if they so desire. The fundamental difficulty is that the risk of exerting such pressure is too great in the present setting—not that we lack the means by which pressure may be exerted. An upward adjustment in short rates might help somewhat in retarding credit expansion, but no really effective check to inflation should be expected from credit and debt policy until the setting is provided in which these tools can be used more safely.

---

*Under current law, open-market operations are handicapped by the incongruous situation where expansionary policy is not subject to any qualitative restriction (the Federal Reserve can purchase whatever issues it pleases) whereas restrictive policies are strictly limited to the sale of issues which happen to be in the Federal Reserve portfolio and—a recent innovation!—in Treasury trust accounts. The lack of longer-term issues in the Federal Reserve portfolio, which presented a problem in checking downward pressures on yields in 1946 and the first part of 1947, has been filled in somewhat by purchases since December 1947. However, to provide a more thorough remedy, consider whether the Federal Reserve and Treasury should not be given the authority to turn debt bought in the open market into such issues as would be most helpful in implementing a policy of open-market sales when called for.

[†]It goes without saying that a surplus policy is most deflationary where (case 1) the current excess of tax receipts is retained on Treasury balance with the Federal Reserve, or used to retire Federal Reserve-held debt. If this is done, the net effect of the operations is to leave the taxpayer with that much less disposable income to spend and in addition to put pressure on banks to contract credit to a multiple of this amount. If, instead, the surplus receipts are returned to the public, this return flow provides an inflationary offset to the initial deflationary effect of the withdrawal. What then is the net effect of both transactions?

Where the payment is in redemption of debt held by nonbank investors (case 2) there is no effect on the volume of bank credit or reserves. However, it is quite likely that the net effect of the transaction is deflationary because there is a strong presumption that the taxpayer's expenditures will be reduced more than the expenditures of the investor (who receives the redemption payments) will be increased.

Where the payment is in redemption of commercial bank-held debt (case 3), note that the resulting reduction in deposits also frees required reserves, thus creating an expansion potential. Now distinguish two cases. First (case 3a) assume that the commercial banks expand by making additional commercial loans which otherwise would not have been made and that deposits are restored in this fashion. Thus, the monetary effect is neutral, as in case 2. However, the presumption as to income effects is reverse; the borrowers most likely will want to expend all their newly obtained funds and the net result of the transaction is probably inflationary. Then consider a second possibility (case 3b), where it is assumed that the Federal Reserve steps in and absorbs the newly created excess reserves through open-market sales of short issues. (The case is the same whether the commercial banks purchase from the Federal Reserve directly, or indirectly through nonbank investors.) If this is done, the surplus funds are not restored to the market. While the net result is not as deflationary as in case 1—there is no multiple contraction in this instance—it is clearly deflationary, and more so than in case 2.

In order to resolve the recent controversy (See O. C. Hardy, *American Economic Review*, *Proceedings*, May 1948, p. 395, and *Credit Policies*, Hearings before the Joint Committee on the Economic Report, Eightieth Congress, Second Session, April 13–May 27, 1948, pp. 5 and 6) whether the net effect of raising a surplus and applying the same to the retirement of bank-held debt has been deflationary, we must decide whether the typical situation was as under 3a or 3b. I suggest that case 3b is clearly the more proper interpretation; i.e., that the net effect of the whole transaction was deflationary.

This follows quite simply from the fact that after the process of taxing and paying off bank-held debt, the commercial banks were left with the option to restore themselves to exactly the same position in which they found themselves before the transaction began. They did have this option because this was a period in which the prices of short-term issues were rigidly fixed, so that any such issues lost through retirement could be replaced by purchases in the open market (or, in a period of selling, by correspondingly reduced sales to the Federal Reserve). But if the taxing-redemption process left unchanged the relevant data (i.e., total reserve balances, the return at which short-term issues could be secured and their profitability relative to private paper), and if we grant a reasonable degree of alertness in bank management, it also follows that this process could not have induced a shift into private paper which would not have occurred otherwise.

This reasoning may not apply with equal force where the retired issues were long term and could not be replaced readily at equal yield, but the bulk of the reduction in bank-held debt was in certificate form.

50

Comments on the Symposium

Alvin H. Hansen[†]

The huge volume of liquid assets created by the war financing offers an opportunity for econometric research on the impact of these assets on the consumption function and the inducement to invest. About this we know as yet relatively little. In the postwar period, how much of the spending, whether for consumption or investment, can be attributed to the fact that individuals and corporations have been in possession of large amounts of deposits and U.S. securities? The answer is certainly not so easy as might appear on the surface.

Nevertheless, it will probably be generally agreed that the high volume of liquid assets has added to the inflationary pressures. If this be so, the reduction in the volume of liquid assets would help to check the inflationary boom. In view of the magnitude of these assets, however, nothing much could be achieved (apart from drastic measures such as blocking, capital levies, etc.) in the short run. A budget surplus cannot be large enough to cut down the liquid assets appreciably in 1 or 2 years.

Fortunately, however, a budget surplus has influences in various directions. These are (1) the *income* effect, (2) the *asset* effect (referred to above), and (3) the *monetary* effect.

Most important of all is the *income* effect. This *directly* influences the total outlay on goods and services. Funds are drawn, via the tax surplus, from the income stream, leaving a smaller disposable income to spend.* The income effect is unmistakable and decisive quite apart from the question as to what the monetary authorities do with the cash surplus. Even though the cash surplus were used to retire bonds held by nonbanking investors, that would not per se enlarge the *income* stream. It would only force the former holders of the retired securities to find some other financial investment outlet. If, in fact, the availability of these funds served to stimulate outlays on new plant and equipment which would not otherwise have been made, then indeed the return on the cash would feed back into the income stream. But under liquidity conditions such as those obtaining currently in the United States, it is hardly probable that decisions to expand plant and equipment would have been significantly different with or without retirement of bonds held by the public. On the other hand, there can be no doubt that a large tax surplus does leave a smaller disposable income to spend on goods and services. The income effect is *direct* and certain. Consumption expenditures will be cut, and this in turn may more or less affect investment outlays.

I have discounted in what is said about the *asset* effect of a budget surplus, but I do not want to overstate the case. A budget surplus does mean that people are somewhat poorer than they would otherwise have been in terms of liquid assets holdings. On top of the fact that the current income *after taxes* of corporations and individuals is reduced, is the further fact that assets holdings are also cut down. In consequence, dividend payments may not be increased and individuals may feel less free to spend, than they habitually would, out

Adapted from Part 5 of "How to Manage the National Debt: A Symposium," *Review of Economics and Statistics, 31* (1949): 15–34 by permission of Elsevier Science: Amsterdam Publishing Division and by Richard A. Musgrave.
[†] Deceased.

*Here it is the *cash* budget, not the conventional budget, that is relevant.

of a given income after taxes. More or less the consumption function may fall. Thus the *asset* effect may in some measure reinforce the *income* effect of a budget surplus.

Third, a Treasury cash surplus* may be used to decrease the money supply. This is the *monetary* effect. If the cash surplus is held idle in the Treasury account with the Federal Reserve Banks, or is used to retire securities owned by the Reserve Banks, the effect is to reduce not only the volume of deposits but also the member bank reserve balances. But the restraint on credit expansion is likely to be a mild transitional restraint. Reserves can always be restored so long as the commercial banks have U.S. securities which they can sell and which the Reserve Banks find it necessary to buy in order to support the market. Under these circumstances the money supply cannot be effectively controlled by the monetary authorities. Control of the money supply becomes rather a question of bringing "investment" into line with "current savings." This may require, in addition to fiscal measures, direct controls at strategic points in the economy, including not only control of consumer credit but also control of capital expenditures and capital issues.

Some continuous restraint can be imposed if the monetary authorities counter their purchases of long terms (whether from bank or nonbank investors) by selling short terms,† thereby maintaining a continued pressure on bank reserves. The effect would be to raise the short-term rate in relation to the (protected) long-term rate. While there are certainly limits to this process, banks might become content to hold higher yield short terms instead of striving to build up reserves in order to make loans to business or consumers or buy private issues. And nonbank institutional investors, notably the life insurance companies, might be induced (though this is probably not very promising unless implemented by new legislation) to take savings-type bonds in exchange for the marketable issues now held, thereby reducing the monetization of the debt held by nonbank investors. Such measures would strengthen the effectiveness with which a cash surplus could be used to provide a mild but persistent monetary restraint. And this is all that ought to be done. A reasonably high level of liquidity is essential for the smooth functioning of a modern market economy. Any attempt to control inflation by a drastic cutting down of liquidity would turn the economy into a nosedive.

A cash surplus can be used to "damp down" monetary expansion. But this cannot be the major restraining factor. In a depression, however, the large deficit should be financed heavily by means of monetary expansion and not by borrowing from the public. On these lines—a mild monetary restraint in the boom and a strong monetary expansion in the depression—the money supply would tend to rise secularly. This is as it should be. A continued rise in the national real income calls for a more or less commensurate increase in the money supply. This aspect of the problem constitutes an important part of long-run debt management. Liquidity and debt management are, under modern conditions, inseparable. And the optimum degree of liquidity (neither too much nor too little) should over the years be a major concern of debt management.

Finally, I should like to comment briefly on a few points raised by Professor Abbott in his interesting paper with much of which I heartily agree. He says: "Financial managers have found it possible to convert with comparative safety unused cash balances and cash reserves into government securities." If nonbank investors collectively have unwanted cash, the purchase of securities from the banks reduces the money supply. This is as it should be, and I see nothing here to worry about. The reverse operation in an inflationary period is, however, a matter of concern, and this problem is canvased from various angles in this symposium.

Professor Abbott raises the question whether the very existence of a large debt will not dry up funds for private investment. Should financial institutions in a private enterprise economy not invest their funds in productive industry? The implication seems to be that because of the creation of large liquid assets (through the war financing) less funds are available for productive industry. I do not see how this could be so, and the postwar experience suggests, indeed, quite the opposite. If indeed the fund of wealth claims were somehow more that is put into government securities, the less is available for private issues. But this is not the case. War financing *created* new deposits and new issues on top of the private wealth claims already held.

Possibly, however, the matter under consideration relates to the investment of savings from *current income*. If there are strong investment outlets, as in the current boom, the existence of a large public debt offers no obstacle to funds moving into private investment. Indeed the danger is quite the opposite as we are

---

*With respect to the *income* and *monetary* effects, it is the cash receipts and expenditures that count; the conventional budget, on the other hand, is decisive for changes in total liquid assets (money and U.S. securities) outstanding.

†This operation on a large scale would require that the monetary authorities be permitted, as Professor Musgrave suggests, to replace any bonds held in their portfolios with issues of any desired maturities. In view of the fact that the Federal Reserve Banks already have half of their holdings in securities other than bills and certificates, this matter is assuming some importance.

currently witnessing with respect to life insurance companies. If, on the other hand, prospective rates of return in private investment are not good, current savings may indeed flow into government securities instead of being hoarded in idle balances. If this happens, that is all to the good, since this would tend to lower the rate of interest—a condition favorable for expansion.

In general, the relative interest rate structure of private and public securities does provide a satisfactory guidance for flow of savings into investment channels. Wide-awake financial institutions are not likely to forego the more attractive rates offered by private industry. There is indeed the problem of a rentier class. But widespread holdings of U.S. securities by socially useful institutions, including savings banks, insurance companies, and government trust funds, presents no problem of this sort. Any rich society with a large volume of fixed interest-bearing claims, private or public, offers to be sure a haven for a rentier class in part represented by private trust funds managing inactive accumulated wealth. The modern progressive income and inheritance tax structure affords, however, an effective safeguard. Nowadays we hear relatively little about the "bloated bondholder." And with respect to active financial and business institutions, their dynamic role in the economy can be performed all the more effectively if they hold an adequate reserve of liquid assets—a point made long ago by Alexander Hamilton in his *First Report on the Public Credit*.

Professor Abbott is concerned about the inflationary forces which might be generated if private holders of governments endeavored to liquidate on a huge scale. But it is not quite clear what it is he fears. If there were a *liquidation panic*, the consequences would be deflationary, not inflationary, as Professor Musgrave shows. If the movement represents a continued shift from government security holdings into private investment outlets (as in the case of recent sale of governments by life insurance companies) then, of course, the effect is inflationary. In a boom period, a large outstanding volume of marketable U.S. securities does indeed create a problem for the monetary authorities, a problem discussed in an illuminating way by both Professor Musgrave and Professor Seltzer in this symposium.

51

Managing the Public Debt

D. Keith Sill
Federal Reserve Bank of Philadelphia, Philadelphia, Pennsylvania

As the Clinton administration and Congress wrestle with government spending and deficit reduction, the size of the public debt and interest payments on it are much in the news. The administration, in its 1993 budget plan "A Vision of Change for America," claimed that the government could save about $11.5 billion over the next 4 years if it issued less long-term debt and more short-term debt to finance deficits, because short-term debt generally has a lower interest rate than long-term debt. In May 1993, the Treasury Department announced that it would begin reducing the amount of long-term debt that it issued. As a result, the Treasury now offers 30-year bonds semiannually (instead of quarterly) and has eliminated issues of 7-year notes. The Treasury is moving toward borrowing primarily at maturities of less than 3 years.

By altering the average maturity of the debt the government hopes to save money on interest payments. Does the average maturity of the debt really matter? Should governments issue short-term debt or long-term debt or maintain a balance between the two? Are there other considerations besides interest costs that are important to consider in choosing an average maturity of the debt?

I. THE PUBLIC DEBT IN THE UNITED STATES

The deficit, or the excess of government expenditures over its revenues, is the amount of new borrowing the government must undertake in a year; the debt is the accumulation of all past deficits. At the end of 1993, the interest-bearing portion of federal government debt held by the public stood at slightly over $2.9 trillion. The federal government ran a deficit of $254.7 billion in 1993, a number much smaller than the size of the public debt. If the government persistently runs deficits, the public debt accumulates. If the government runs budget surpluses, the public debt declines.

Most of the government debt is in the form of Treasury securities such as Treasury bills, Treasury notes, and Treasury bonds. In 1992, for example, such securities accounted for about 86% of private sector holdings of interest-bearing public debt. The remaining 14% was composed of private sector holdings of savings bonds and holdings of certain types of securities issued by agencies of the U.S. government such as the Federal Housing Administration and the Federal Deposit Insurance Corporation.

The size of the public debt relative to the size of the U.S. economy has shown fairly dramatic movement

Adapted from *Business Review* (July-August 1994) by permission of Federal Reserve, Bank of Philadelphia.

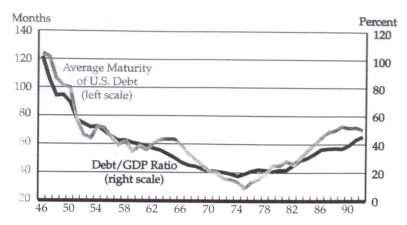

Figure 1   Debt/GDP ratio and average maturity of debt. *Note*: The public debt used in computing debt/GDP ratio is the total interest-bearing public securities held by private investors. *Source*: *Treasury Bulletin*, various issues, Department of the Treasury.

since World War II. If we look at the public debt relative to gross domestic product (GDP), the ratio has varied from less than 20% to over 100% (Fig. 1).

The maturity of a security is defined as the length of time until payments from the security expire. The average maturity of the public debt has varied a great deal in the postwar period, ranging from a high of 124 months in 1946 to a low of 29 months in 1975 (Fig. 1). Also, during this period the average maturity of the debt declined when the debt-to-GDP ratio declined and rose when the debt-to-GDP ratio rose. In 1992 average maturity was about 70 months. The Treasury's recent changes will shorten the average maturity of the debt some 12 months (to 58 months) by 1998. So, even though the Treasury is reducing the average maturity of the debt, it will still be about twice as high as the postwar low in 1975.

II. DOES DEBT MATURITY MATTER?

How does a change in the average maturity of the public debt affect the economy? Economic theory says that under certain circumstances the average maturity of the debt is irrelevant for economic welfare. In this case debt management policy is neutral with respect to the economy.

This debt neutrality proposition depends on whether households and investors can trade in securities in such a way as to completely offset any actions that the government takes regarding the mix of debt and taxes that it uses to finance its expenditures. If households can trade in securities so as to undo the financing mix put in place by the government, any particular financing mix will be irrelevant in the sense that household consumption and savings decisions are unaffected by how the government finances its spending. (See *A Case of Debt Neutrality* for an example of this neutrality proposition.)

However, this strong neutrality result relies primarily on three assumptions, some of which clearly do not hold in reality: (1) households correctly recognize the link between the government budget constraint and household budget constraints as well as the relationship between current debt and future taxes, (2) tax rates do not affect the relative prices that households face (such taxes are called nondistortionary), and (3) the set of investment portfolio choices available to households is unaffected by the government action.

A Case of Debt Neutrality

Assume that the three assumptions for debt neutrality hold. Suppose the government issues debt in the form of one-year and two-year discount bonds, each of which pays $1 at maturity. Assume further that the current price of the one-year bonds is $0.95 and the current price of two-year bonds is $0.90. For simplicity we will allow fractions of a bond to be bought and sold. If the government issues one additional one-year bond and uses the proceeds ($0.95) to buy back 1.055 units of two-year bonds (since $0.90 times 1.055 is $0.95), there is now more one-year debt and less two-year debt, and government spending and taxes are unchanged.

Households, in aggregate, have purchased one additional unit of one-year debt for $0.90 and financed that purchase by selling back to the government 1.055 units of two-year debt (which raises the $0.90 needed to buy the one-year debt). Aggregate consumption by the households is unchanged initially. At the end of the first year, the government has to raise $1 in taxes to pay off the new one-year debt that it issued. But households can use the proceeds ($1) of their purchase of one-year debt to pay the higher taxes. Hence, at the end of the first year households can maintain the same level of consumption as before the average maturity of government debt was shortened. At the end of the second year, households have $1.055 less coming in because of their sale of two-year bonds back to the government. But government liabilities have fallen by $1.055 because less two-year debt is outstanding. The government could thus lower taxes by $1.055, and again, household consumption at the end of the second year would be no different than it was prior to the government action.

Since households are able to undo the change in government financing, any particular mix of debt and taxes the government uses to finance its spending will not affect household consumption and savings decisions. Households will merely readjust their portfolios in response to the government action. In this situation the debt structure is neutral; it has no real effects.

If these assumptions are violated, a change in the way government spending is financed will change relative prices in the economy and hence redirect resources. In this case the financing mix is not neutral, and a change in the average maturity of the debt can affect the economy. Nonetheless, the neutrality proposition is a useful starting point from which to consider debt maturity policies. The extent to which departures from neutrality occur is an empirical matter.*

III. INTEREST RATES AND DEBT MATURITY

Bearing in mind the debt neutrality proposition, why might the government try to lower the interest costs of its debt? If taxes distort economic activity, lower interest costs mean less distortion, since tax revenues are used in part to pay interest on the debt. The interest rate that the government must pay on its bonds often changes with the time to maturity of the bonds. If the government's objective in managing the public debt is to minimize interest costs, perhaps altering the average maturity of the debt can achieve it.

---

*The empirical results on the effects of debt management policies are mixed. Two representative studies are presented in the 1992 volume by Agell, Persson, and Friedman. The study by Agell and Persson finds the debt management policies have little consequence for relative asset yields. The study by Friedman finds a much more significant impact of debt management on asset yields.

A. Term Structure of Interest Rates

The yield curve conveniently summarizes the relationship between the term to maturity of government debt and the interest rate (Fig. 2). This relationship between yield and maturity is called the term structure of interest rates. The horizontal axis shows the time to maturity of the security, and the vertical axis shows the interest rate, which is measured by yield to maturity.* Notice that the relationship between yields and maturities changes over time. For one thing, when comparing the yields for 1954, 1965, and 1980, we see that the yield curves shifted up over time, reflecting a general trend of rising interest rates. Next, we see that the slope of the yield curve changes over time. In 1954 and 1990 the yield curve had an upward slope, indicating that the interest rate on long-term debt exceeded that on short-term debt. In 1965 the yield curve was approximately flat; long-term debt paid about the same interest rate as short-term debt. In 1980 the yield curve was downward sloping, indicating that the interest rate on long-term debt was lower than that on short-term debt.

   Is there a "normal" shape, or slope, to the yield curve? If we compare short-term and long-term interest rates over time, we see that generally long-term rates exceed short-term rates, suggesting that the normal shape of the yield curve is upward sloping. The steepness of the yield curve, which is measured by the gap between the two lines in Fig. 3, varies quite a bit, but there are few episodes in which the yield on short-term government bonds exceed that on long-term government bonds.

B. A Theory of the Term Structure

Economists have developed and tested several theories to explain why the term structure of interest rates behaves as it does over time.[†] One such theory is called the expectations theory of the term structure, which states that the yield to maturity on a long-term bond is equal to a weighted average of expected future short-term interest rates plus a risk premium. It seems reasonable to suppose that the yield on long-term bonds is related to expected future short-term interest rates. Suppose investors know that the interest rate on 1-year bonds will average 5% a year over the next 10 years. In this case the risk premium would be zero, and investors will buy and sell 10-year bonds until their yield to maturity equals the average of those expected 1-year rates, or 5%. Absent a risk premium, the same conclusion follows if investors expect the yield on

---

*Yield to maturity is defined as the interest rate that answers the following question: if an investor were to buy a bond and hold it until it matured, what average annualized return would he get over the life of the bond? For example, if an investor were to pay $100 for a bond that pays $121 in 2 years, the yield to maturity would be 10%. This follows from the fact that $100 × 1.10 × 1.10 = $121.

[†]An excellent survey of theories of the term structure is the 1990 article by Robert Shiller.

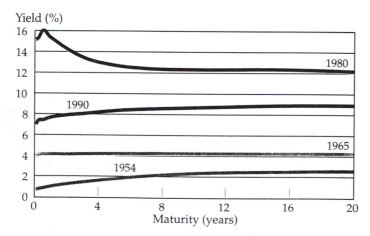

Figure 2   Treasury yield curves *Source*: J. H. McCulloch and Heon-Chul Kwon, "U.S. Term Structure Data, 1947–1991," Ohio State University Working Paper 93-6.

Yield (%)

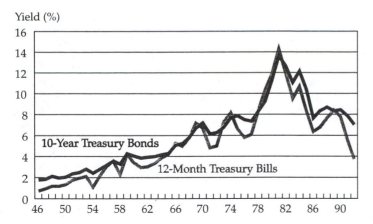

Figure 3   Interest rates of theUnited States (1946–1992) *Source*: J. H. McCulloch and Heon-Chul Kwon, "U.S. Term Structure Data, 1947–1991," Ohio State University Working Paper 93-6, and the Federal Reserve System.

1-year bonds to average 5% per year, but don't know for sure. If investors know that 1-year interest rates will rise above 5% per year in the future, the yield to maturity on the 10-year bond should be above 5%. Absent a risk premium, an upward-sloping yield curve means that investors believe future short-term interest rates will rise, while a downward-sloping yield curve suggests that traders believe future short-term interest rates will fall.

The risk premium can arise because investors typically do not like bearing risk. Long-term bonds are risky because future interest rates are uncertain and because uncertainty about future interest rates translates into uncertainty about future bond prices. That uncertainty could work in investors' favor, or it could work against them.

The manner in which long-term bonds act as a hedge against future income uncertainty determines whether the risk premium is positive or negative. For example, suppose investors could hold a bond whose price is high when income is unexpectedly low and whose price is low when income is unexpectedly high. Investors would be willing to pay a premium for such a bond because if offers them some insurance against their uncertain income: in a year when income is low, the investor could cash in the bond and receive a capital gain (since the price at which he sells the bond is higher than the price at which the bond was purchased), helping him to maintain his level of consumption. Such a bond would have a negative risk premium. A bond with a positive risk premium would be one whose price is low when income is unexpectedly low. In this case, when the investor receives low income and cashes in the bond, he will take a capital loss. Thus, an investor would have to receive some compensation, in the form of a higher return, for investing in such a security. In this case the risk premium would be positive.*

Although theory suggests that the risk premium on long-term bonds can be either positive or negative, the normal, upward-sloping shape of the yield curve suggests that the premium is positive.[†]

---

*An alternative theory about why the yield to maturity on a long-term bond may differ from the average of expected 1-year interest rates is called the preferred habitat theory. This theory, which was developed by Franco Modigliani and Robert Sutch (1966), states that investors have preferred maturities that correspond to their investment horizons. For example, if you were investing for a child's college education, you may choose to invest in a long-term bond rather than a series of short-term bonds. The premium (negative or positive) associated with a particular maturity then depends on the supply and demand for funds at that maturity. Suppose that lenders prefer to lend with a short-term commitment and borrowers want to borrow long term. Then there would need to be a positive premium on long-term debt to get lenders to loan funds for a longer period than they would otherwise want to.

[†]In the absence of a risk premium, the usual upward slope of the yield curve suggests that short-term interest rates are expected to rise. In actual practice, short-term interest rates are usually just as likely to rise as to fall. If the risk premium were indeed zero, this suggests that bond-market traders are making persistent errors in forecasting interest rates, which seems unlikely. On the other hand, if the risk premium is positive, the yield curve would tend to have a normal upward slope, and persistent errors in forecasting future interest rates need not occur.

C. Minimizing Interest Costs

If the yield curve is upward sloping, should the government borrow long or short to minimize interest costs? First, suppose there's no uncertainty about future short-term interest rates (which implies that the risk premium will be zero). The expectations theory implies that future short-term interest rates will be higher than current short-term interest rates. In this case, even though short-term rates will be higher in the future, it does not matter whether the government borrows short or long—the interest cost will be the same.

A simple example will help to make this clear. Suppose the 1-year interest rate today is 5%, and the 1-year interest rate 1 year from today will be 10%. The government decides to borrow $1000 and repay the borrowing at the end of the second year. If the government borrows using 1-year debt, at the end of the year it must repay $1050. If the government rolls over the debt, at the end of the second year it will have to pay interest on the $1050, so that total interest and principal due at the end of the second year is $1155.

What would the government's cost be if it used 2-year debt instead. Since there is no risk, investors would demand the same return on the 2-year bond as on the sequence of 1-year bonds. Using the expectations theory, the yield to maturity on the 2- year bond is the average of the 1-year interest rates, which is 7.5%. At the end of 2 years, the total cost of borrowing for 2 years is the same ($1155), regardless of whether the government borrows short or long.*

If we introduce uncertainty, the picture becomes more complicated. Now bond-market traders form expectations of future interest rates. Further, the introduction of uncertainty brings the risk premium into the picture. If the risk premium is positive, on average the government will have a lower interest cost by borrowing short term. But the lower average interest cost comes at the price of higher uncertainty concerning the final payment.

Suppose again that the government borrows $1000 today. The 1-year interest rate today is known to be 5%, but the 1-year interest rate 1 year from today is not known. Suppose bond traders believe that there's a 25% chance that the interest rate next year will be 8%, a 50% chance that it will be 10%, and a 25% chance that it will be 12%.

Consider first the strategy of borrowing short term. At the end of the first year the government will owe $1050 with certainty. If it rolls over the debt, at the end of the second year, there's a 25% chance that the government will owe $1134, a 50% chance that it will owe $1155, and a 25% chance that it will owe $1176. On average, the government will owe $1155.

Now suppose the government decides to borrow using 2-year debt. What will its cost be in this case? If we assume that the expectations hypothesis is true and that there's a positive risk premium, the yield to maturity on a 2-year bond will be the average of today's 1-year interest rate and the expected 1-year interest rate in the second year, plus the risk premium. The average of the short-term rates is 7.5% (the average of 5% and the expected 10%). Thus, the yield to maturity on the 2-year bond is 7.5% plus the risk premium. Let's assume the risk premium is 0.2%, so the yield to maturity is 7.7%. Then, the interest and principal that has to be repaid at the end of 2 years is $1159.93 ($1000 ×) (1.077) ×) (1.077)) = $1159.93).

Should the government borrow long term or short term? In the example, the expected interest cost to the government of borrowing short term is $155. If the government borrows using 2-year debt, the interest cost will exceed $155. This result seems to favor short-term borrowing. However, by borrowing short term the government faces a risky outcome. In the example, there's a 25% chance that borrowing short term will cost $176, which exceeds the cost of borrowing using 2-year debt. On average, the cost of borrowing short term will be lower than the cost of borrowing long term, but the lower interest cost comes at the price of a risky outcome.[†]

---

*The exact formula for the 2-year rate gives an interest rate slightly lower than 7.5% because of the effects of compounding interest. In an environment with no risk the formula for the implied 2-year rate is given by $(1+i_{2yr})^2 = (1+.05)(1+.10)$.

[†]We have neglected to mention transactions costs. By having a shorter average maturity of debt, the government rolls over the debt more frequently and thus pays more in transaction costs. For example, if the government borrowed for 10 years, it could make one transaction by issuing one 10-year bond, or it could make 10 transactions by issuing ten 1-year bonds. The higher transactions costs must also be considered in assessing the extent to which the government saves money by issuing short-term debt.

IV. BENEFITS OF LONG-TERM DEBT

We have seen that if the government tries to manage the public debt to minimize interest costs, it can lower its interest cost, on average, by borrowing short term rather than long term, but at the price of bearing greater risk. Aside from this interest rate minimization issue, are there other factors that the government should consider when planning the average maturity of its debt?

A. Debt Maturity and Insuring Against Risk

Economic theory suggests that debt of different maturities may offer investors different opportunities to insure against economic uncertainty. We will frame this discussion in terms of a simple economic model in which consumers live for two periods.* We can think of the first period of life as the working years and the second period of life as retirement. In the first period, consumers work and invest in an asset that is risky in the sense that the return is unknown to investors at the time of investment.

Investing in the risky asset is like buying corporate stocks to save for retirement. However, in any period only one of the two generations alive at that date bears the risk of the investing, namely the retirees. Everyone would be happier if some of the asset risk could be transferred from the retirees to the workers.

This intergenerational risk sharing can be accomplished by introducing government debt into the economy. Suppose the government introduces one-period debt into the economy. This debt offers young investors a safe asset to invest in. Since investing in public debt carries no risk, it allows the young to attain, with certainty, some amount of consumption when they retire. If investors don't like risk, they may be better off if they have the opportunity to guarantee some amount of consumption when they retire, compared with investing all of their savings in the risky asset.

By issuing one-period bonds, the government allows intergenerational risk-sharing in the following sense. Buying a one-period government bond is like buying a claim on the next generation. When the young buy bonds, they hold them until they retire; the bonds are then paid off by the government. But the government pays off the bonds by transferring resources from the new young generation of workers to the retirees. Thus, by transferring resources from the young to the old, the debt serves to guarantee retirees some level of consumption.

Debt of maturity longer than one period would be more risky for these investors because of capital gains and losses that can occur when economywide rates of return change. But under certain circumstances this riskiness of long-term debt could be advantageous to investors even if one-period debt is not. Suppose that investors observe that the return to the risky asset is high, and further, they expect the return on risky assets to be high next period. In this situation the current price of a two-period bond will be low.† Similarly, if the return to the risky asset is currently low, the price of two-period bonds will be high. However, if the price of bonds is high when the return to investment is low, the two-period debt is a better hedge against the risky investment.

Why is this so? The argument is much the same as that in our discussion of the risk premium. Take the case of investors who purchased both two-period bonds and the risky asset to save for their retirement. At retirement, these investors will want to sell their bonds (which have become one-period maturity bonds) to the new young generation. If the return on the asset turns out to have been low, new investors, seeing that the return to the asset was low, expect a low return to their investment in the asset (remember that we are assuming a positive correlation in investment returns). Therefore, the new investors will want to buy bonds from the retirees, bidding up the price of those bonds. These retirees get a capital gain (an appreciation in the bond price) that in part compensates them for the low return on the risky asset. No such capital gain would be realized if the retirees had purchased one-period debt instead of two-period debt.

This argument is not limited to two-period bonds. Thus, the economy could be better off if investors had

---

*This argument is based on an article by Douglas Gale.

†Returns on bonds and returns on the risky asset will be linked by investors' demand for the two alternatives. If the expected return to the asset rises, while the uncertainty associated with the asset return remains unchanged, then investors have an incentive to shift their investment funds toward the risk asset and away from bonds. As investors shift funds out of bonds, the price of bonds falls and the return on bonds rises.

the opportunity to invest in long-term debt securities because long-term debt might provide better insurance against the uncertainty associated with risky assets.*

B. Confidence Crises

Another argument in favor of governments' issuing long-term debt can be made. Long-term debt can raise investors' confidence that the government will be able to meet its obligations in the event of a crisis. A 1990 paper by Alberto Alesina, Alessandro Prati, and Guido Tabellini develops this argument using a case study of the public debt in Italy. The Italian debt-to-GDP ratio is close to 100%, and the Italian government has to pay a steep premium to borrow long term. Alesina and associates show issuing long-term debt may be beneficial to the government, even though it is more costly than short-term debt, because long-term debt can help to avoid confidence crises.

A confidence crisis could occur if government bondholders thought that the government might have difficulty making payments on the debt. Suppose the government finances its borrowing by issuing only 1-year debt. In that case, a large quantity of the debt comes due each year, and the government must borrow a large quantity each year, both to finance any current deficit and to roll over the existing debt. If investors thought the government might have difficulty repaying its debt obligations, they could all demand repayment of their debt holdings. The government would find itself unable to borrow to roll over existing debt. The government would have to either raise taxes substantially to pay off debt holders or default on the debt.[†]

On the other hand, if the government issued long-term debt and had an evenly concentrated amount of debt coming due each year, it could diminish the likelihood of a confidence crisis. By issuing long-term debt to finance deficits, the government has a smaller quantity of debt that comes due each year. Therefore, this strategy may raise investor confidence in the government's ability to meet its obligations, and runs on the government debt may become less likely. In the case of the Italian debt, Alesina and associates note that by using long-term debt and reducing the risk of a debt crisis, the government could lower the risk premium on the entire maturity structure of the debt and, therefore, lower debt-servicing costs.[‡]

V. DEBT POLICY AND FISCAL INCENTIVES

We have examined several different theories that point out some of the costs and benefits of both short-term and long-term debt. An optimal debt maturity structure takes these factors into account, as well as the incentives that current government policy places on the policies of future governments.

A. Time-Consistent Policy

Economists have considered how the maturity of the public debt can be used as part of a strategy to implement a fiscal policy that is optimal *over time*. In a dynamic environment, fiscal policy takes the form of a plan for both the present and the future. If today's government forms a fiscal plan, that plan has implications for future tax rates, future government spending, and future borrowing. But can we guarantee that some future government will find it optimal to stick to the plan that we develop today? In general, the answer is no, so we say that the plans are not time-consistent.

The issue of time-consistent plans is discussed in more detail in a 1985 article by Herbert Taylor in his *Business Review*. For our purposes a simple example will help clarify the idea. The United States incurred a large debt when it fought the war for its independence. The government was able to borrow because it promised to repay the debt after the war. However, once the war was over, many Americans advocated defaulting on the debt because repaying creditors would require an increase in taxation; thus, the government had an incentive to deviate from the policy implemented earlier. Alexander Hamilton, the first secretary of the Treasury, argued against this time-inconsistency, realizing that in the future the new government would likely

---

*Referring to the discussion of debt neutrality, the reason that debt maturity matters in the example just given is that trading in government securities offers investors opportunities that they otherwise would not have and so assumption 3 is violated.

[†]If taxes are distortionary, economic theory suggests that government should try to smooth taxes over time. Distortionary taxes and tax smoothing are the reason that the maturity structure of the government debt matters in this model.

[‡]The confidence crisis story is less applicable to the United States than to countries such as Italy. In the United States the default premium on government debt is considered to be virtually zero.

need to borrow again. Had the government defaulted on the war debt, borrowing in the future would have been more difficult and costly.

B. Debt Maturity and Optimal Fiscal Policy

In general, successor governments will have an incentive to deviate from an optimal fiscal policy put in place by today's government. But economic theory suggests that the maturity structure of the public debt can help provide incentives for future governments to stick to a fiscal plan developed today. This happens because a government that inherits a public debt has reduced flexibility; it must pay interest on the inherited debt and either pay off debt coming due or roll it over.* If a government inherits a large quantity of public debt that comes due during its time in office, its incentive, say, with respect to taxation, may be different than if the inherited debt is long term and thus not all coming due during the government's tenure.

Suppose today's government believes higher taxes and higher inflation reduce economic welfare. The government might then form a fiscal plan that tries to set current and future taxes and inflation in a way that increases society's well-being. A strategy for the public debt could be a key part of this calculation, since debt allows governments to smooth taxes over time and to reduce the temptation for future governments to deviate from the fiscal plan.

The maturity of the public debt can be used to lessen the government's incentive to try to use inflation to reduce the value of its debt.† Consider the case of a government that inherits a stock of long-term, fixed-rate debt. The government recognizes that since the debt was issued in the past, the interest payments on that debt are fixed in dollar terms. This gives the government an incentive to increase the rate of inflation so that it can pay off its inherited debt in cheaper dollars. This inflation acts like a tax, and the nominal debt comprises part of the tax base. The real value of the payments that investors receive from their bond holdings declines when the price level rises.‡

By reducing the average maturity of the debt, current governments can reduce successor governments' incentives to increase inflation. A government that inherits short-term debt will gain little by increasing the inflation rate. When the debt is short term, it is rolled over frequently, giving the government little opportunity to pay off the debt in cheaper dollars. In addition, any attempt to raise inflation will be quickly reflected in higher interest rates on short-term debt; investors will demand to be compensated for higher anticipated inflation. In effect, a greater quantity of short-term debt lowers the inflation tax base available to the government and, therefore, lessens the incentive to use inflation to raise revenue.

VI. CONCLUSION

Deciding on a preferred maturity structure of the public debt involves many considerations. On the one hand, the maturity structure of the debt may be largely irrelevant for the economy if departures from the neutrality proposition are small. On the other hand, if the departures from neutrality are significant, then the choice of a debt maturity structure may be guided by factors such as interest cost minimization, risk-sharing arrangements, confidence crises, and reinforcing incentives for future policy makers. Economists have not yet reached agreement on the questions of whether there is an optimal maturity of the debt and, if so, what factors are involved.

The U.S. Treasury is engaging in a strategy to reduce the average maturity of the public debt. Our analysis suggests that on average, this strategy should reduce the costs of borrowing, but the government also takes on more risk, since future interest rates are uncertain. The shorter average maturity may also weaken the incentives future governments have to use inflation to raise tax revenue.

---

*We are assuming that the costs of defaulting on the debt are so high that future governments do not consider defaulting as a policy option.
†This discussion is based on the work of Guillermo Calvo and Pablo Guidotti.
‡This argument applies to debt with a fixed nominal face value, which is the predominant form of debt issued by governments. The government has an incentive to raise inflation even if the gains from doing so are illusory in the sense that bondholders, at the time they purchased the bonds, demanded an inflation premium in the form of a higher interest rate.

REFERENCES

Agell, J., Persson, M., and Friedman, B. M. (1992). *Does Debt Management Matter?* Oxford University Press, Oxford, U.K.

Alesina, A., Prati, A., and Tabellini, G. (1990). "Public Confidence and Debt Management: A Model and a Case Study of Italy," in *Public Debt Management: Theory and History* (R. Dornbusch and M. Draghi, eds.), Cambridge University Press, Cambridge, U.K.

Calvo, G. A., and Guidotti, P. E. (1990). "Credibility and Nominal Debt," *IMF Staff Papers*, 37 (Sept.), pp. 612–35.

Gale, D. (1990). "The Efficient Design of Public Debt," in *Public Debt Management: Theory and History* (R. Dornbusch and M. Draghi, eds.), Cambridge University Press, Cambridge, U.K.

Modigliani, F., and Sutch, R. (1966). "Innovations in Interest Rate Policy," *American Economic Review*, 56 (May), pp. 178–97.

Shiller, R. J. (1990). "The Term Structure of Interest Rates," in *Handbook of Monetary Economics*, vol. *I* (B. M. Friedman and F. H. Hahn, eds.), Elsevier, Amsterdam.

Taylor, H. E. (1985). "Time-Inconsistency: A Potential Problem for Policymakers," *Business Review* (March/April).

Tobin, J. A. "An Essay on the Principles of Debt Management," in *Fiscal and Debt Management Policies*, Prentice-Hall, Englewood Cliffs, N.J., pp. 143–218. (an early, excellent reference on managing the public debt).

52

Indexed Bonds as an Aid to Economic Policy

Robert L. Hetzel

Federal Reserve Bank of Richmond, Richmond, Virginia

Contracts requiring payment of dollars in the future for future delivery of goods and services are a regular part of economic life. Workers enter into contracts, formal and informal, for a dollar wage for the next year. Colleges set tuition payments once a year. Rents for apartments are set annually and homeowners contract for mortgage payments in dollars. The purchasing power represented by these dollar payments, however, depends upon the rate of inflation realized after the contracts are signed. People must forecast inflation in order to estimate the purchasing power of future dollar payments.

This article argues that it would be helpful to the Federal Reserve System to have a measure of the public's inflation forecast. The Fed, through its control of the money stock, controls the long-run rate of inflation. There is, however, always considerable short-run uncertainty regarding the way in which changes in its policy instrument (reserves or the federal funds rate) will ultimately affect money growth and inflation. A measure of the inflation forecast by the public would offer the Fed a useful "outside" assessment of the inflationary consequences thought likely to follow from its policy actions. This inflation forecast could be inferred from the yield gap between the interest rates paid on conventional bonds and on bonds indexed to the price level.[1] Unfortunately, indexed bonds are not now traded in the United States. This chapter proposes that the U.S. Treasury issue indexed bonds to create a measure of the public's inflation forecast.

I. THE PROPOSAL

A measure of the inflation expected by the public could be created by legislation requiring the Treasury to issue zero-coupon bonds with maturities of 1 year, 2 years, and so on out to 20 years. A zero-coupon bond is a promise to make a future one-time payment. Zero-coupon bonds sell at a discount and yield a return through capital appreciation. Under the proposal, half the bonds issued would be conventional (nonindexed) zero-coupon bonds that would offer a principal payment of a given dollar amount. The other half would offer a principal payment in dollars of constant purchasing power achieved by indexing the principal payment to the price level. For example, if the principal payment of the conventional zero-coupon bond were $100 and the price level were to rise by 5% in the year after the sale of the bonds, an indexed bond with a maturity of 1 year would pay $105.[2]

Holders of indexed bonds do not have to worry about the depreciation of the dollars in which they are paid. For a zero-coupon bond sold in, say, 1992, both the amount bid and the purchasing power afforded by the principal payment are measured in 1992 dollars. The discount on the bond, therefore, is a measure of the real yield (real capital appreciation) offered by the bond over its life. The yield on indexed bonds would offer

Adapted from *Economic Review*, 78: (Jan.-Feb.) 1992: 13–23 by permission of the Federal Reserve Bank of Richmond.

a direct measure of the real (inflation-adjusted) rate of interest. Furthermore, the existence of indexed bonds of different maturities would provide a measure of the term structure of real rates of interest.[3]

Because holders of the indexed bonds are guaranteed payment representing a known amount of purchasing power, they do not have to forecast inflation. In contrast, holders of the nonindexed bonds *would* have to forecast future changes in the value of the dollar. Consequently, the yield on the nonindexed bonds would incorporate an inflation premium to compensate for the expected depreciation in the purchasing power of the dollar, and the difference in yields between the nonindexed and indexed bonds, therefore, would measure the inflation expected by investors over the life of the bond. The existence of bonds of different maturities would offer a term structure of the expected future inflation. Given the current price level, this term structure would yield a time profile of the future price level expected by the public.

Figure 1 illustrates a hypothetical example in which the public expects future inflation to remain steady at 4% a year. (The contemporaneous price level is also taken to be 138, the current value of the CPI.) If nonindexed and indexed zero-coupon bonds are issued at maturities ranging from 1 year to 20 years, the yield gap on successive issues would permit inference of a term structure of future inflation. These yearly expected inflation rates, when applied to the current price level, would allow construction of the time profile of the future price level expected by the public shown in Fig. 1.

Consider an indexed 1-year-maturity zero-coupon bond that is a promise to pay $100 in 1 year, with the $100 indexed to the consumer price index. If the real rate of interest were 3%, the bond would sell for $97. If the public believed that the 1-year inflation rate would be 4%, a comparable nonindexed bond would sell for $93, returning 4% in compensation for the expected inflation and a 3% expected real yield. The interest rate on the nonindexed bond would then be 7%, with a 3% real interest rate on the indexed bond. The "yield gap" between these two rates is the 4% inflation rate expected by the market.

II. THE YIELD GAP AS AN INDICATOR OF MONETARY POLICY

In order to achieve its inflation objective, the Fed could, in principle, change its policy instrument in response to discrepancies between the actual price level and a target path for the price level. Because individual policy actions affect prices only with long lags, however, such a straightforward strategy could be destabilizing. In practice, the Fed monitors indicator variables to determine whether the changes in its policy instrument are consistent with the inflation rate it considers acceptable.

Some economists have suggested that the Fed change its policy instrument in response to movements in the prices of actively traded commodities. These prices *do* move freely in response to changes in expenditure

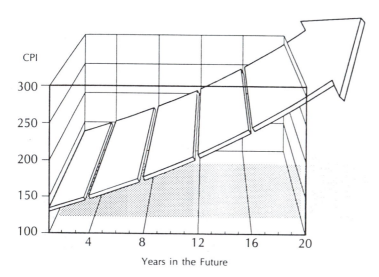

Figure 1   Time profile of expected future price level. Hypothetical observations are based on assumed 4% rate of inflation.

produced by monetary policy actions; however, the often move in response to market-specific disturbances. At such times, commodity prices might give misleading signals about the thrust of monetary policy.

Milton Friedman has long advocated a low, stable rate of growth of M2 as the guide to monetary policy. M2 has maintained a reliable relationship to the public's dollar expenditure over long periods of time. In fact, the ratio of dollar GNP to M2, known as M2 velocity, is currently about 1.63, little changed from its value in 1914 when the Federal Reserve was founded. Over periods of time as long as several years, however, M2 velocity fluctuates significantly. Many economists also fear that future financial innovation could alter the long-run relationship between M2 and GNP. It is possible that a consensus will never emerge that a particular monetary aggregate is a reliable indicator of the stance of monetary policy.

In contrast to these alternatives, the yield gap between nonindexed and indexed bonds would offer a direct measure of expected inflation. This measure would offer useful information to monetary policy makers because it would be formed by market participants who have a direct financial interest in forecasting inflation.

III.   AVOIDING INFLATION AND DISINFLATION

The lag between changes in the Federal Reserve's policy instrument and changes in prices means that it is difficult to associate particular policy actions with inflation. This difficulty lowers the cost of exerting political pressure for an inflationary policy; moreover, the quicker impact of stimulative monetary policy on output than on prices generates political pressure to trade off immediate output gains against a delayed rise in inflation. Indexed bonds of the sort proposed here would balance these pressures by threatening an immediate rise in the yield gap between indexed and nonindexed bonds. The Fed would have a clear and more immediate justification for resisting inflationary pressures.

Further, with indexed bonds, public pressure for an inflationary monetary policy that was associated with a rise in the yield gap in itself would produce countervailing pressure. Holders of nonindexed bonds would suffer a capital loss when the yield gap rose. All creditors receiving payment in nonindexed dollars in the future would feel worse off. The yield gap would restrain pressure for inflationary policy by offering an immediate and continuous market assessment of the potential impact of such a policy.

Surprise inflation acts like a capital levy imposed on money and government securities. The essentially fiscal transfer that arises from surprise inflation does not have to be legislated explicitly. Federal Reserve independence is designed to prevent monetary policy from becoming the handmaiden of fiscal policy. Institutional arrangements, like the federal structure of the Fed with its regional bank presidents and long terms for members of the Board of Governors, give substance to central bank independence. The continuous market assessment of the level of future inflation offered by the yield gap between nonindexed and indexed bonds would constitute an additional safeguard against surprise inflation.

IV.   POSSIBLE DISTORTIONS IN THE YIELD GAP

The information on expected inflation offered by the yield gap between nonindexed and indexed bonds of equal maturities would be diminished if the gap fluctuated in response to tax and/or risk premium factors. These possibilities are considered in turn.

A.   Tax Distortions

Ideally, for both the nonindexed bond and the indexed bond, income subject to taxation would be indexed for inflation; that is, holders of both types of bonds would pay taxes only on the increase in purchasing power gained from holding the bonds, rather than on any increase in the dollar value of the bond that only compensates for inflation.

In order to illustrate this point, consider the following hypothetical example. Suppose that, for both the indexed and nonindexed bonds, only the return that represents a gain in purchasing power is taxed. As before, if the real rate of return is 3%, an indexed bond that promises to pay $100 of constant purchasing power next year would sell for $97 in the current year. If, subsequently, inflation turns out to be 4%, the holder of the indexed bond will receive $104. In this case, taxable income would be calculated as the $7 in total income minus the $4 inflation adjustment, which is a capital depreciation allowance to maintain the purchasing power of the investor's capital. The holder of the *nonindexed* bond also would be taxed only on the real portion of the bond's yield.[4]

If, alternatively, taxable income were not indexed for inflation, an increase in the inflation rate would increase the taxes paid by the holders of indexed bonds, which would reduce the real after-tax yield on the bonds even if there had been no reduction in the real before-tax yield. Unless the tax code were indexed, the yield on the indexed bond would rise as inflation rose to compensate for the increase in taxes imposed by higher inflation. The yield on the indexed bond would then offer a distorted measure of the economywide real rate of interest. With the relatively moderate levels of inflation experienced in the 1980s, however, the distortions caused by the present absence of inflation indexing in the tax code would not greatly impair the usefulness of the indexed bond as a measure of the real rate of interest. Moreover, if the tax treatment for the nonindexed and indexed bond were the same, information about expected inflation contained in the yield gap between the nonindexed and indexed bond would not be distorted by changes in the rate of inflation.

B.   Possible Risk Premium Distortion

Because the public might be willing to pay something to hold an asset whose value is not arbitrarily affected by unanticipated inflation, it is possible that a risk premium might bias the yield gap upward. The yield gap would then overstate expected inflation. Also, the risk premium could vary so that the yield gap would change even with no change in expected inflation. (Note that if the yield gap incorporated a risk premium, the Treasury would have to compensate investors for the inflation risk entailed by holding its nonindexed bonds. Indexed bonds would not carry this cost.)

Whether a risk premium would, in fact, be incorporated in the yield gap is of course an empirical question. Woodward (1990) examined the behavior of the yield gap between nonindexed and indexed British bonds and concluded that any risk premium must have been very small.[5] If the risk premium had been significant, the yield gap between conventional and indexed bonds would have implied implausibly low estimates of expected inflation for Britain for the 1980s. Furthermore, Woodward's measure of real yields (adjusted for preferential tax treatment of indexed bonds) produces surprisingly high values. Because real yields averaged around 5.5%, it is implausible that holders of indexed bonds were foregoing much yield as protection against surprise inflation. (See Fig. 2.)

The magnitude of a possible risk premium also would depend upon monetary policy. Suppose that the central bank had made a credible commitment to price stability. With such a policy, random shocks would still cause the central bank to miss its price level target, but these misses subsequently would be offset. Consequently, the price level would fluctuate around a fixed value, and the magnitude of any discrepancy between yields of nonindexed and indexed bonds due to a risk premium would decline as maturities lengthened.

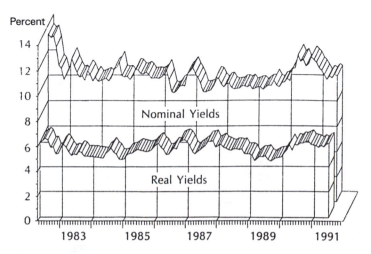

Figure 2   Yields on indexed and nonindexed bonds. Monthly observations of yields on indexed bonds issued in April 1982 and maturing in August 2011 and of yields on conventional bonds maturing in August 2011. Data were furnished by G. Thomas Woodward.

Alternatively, suppose that the central bank allowed contemporaneous price level shocks to be incorporated permanently in the future price level target. Consequently, the price level would wander randomly over time. (The central bank could allow this kind of price-level drift even if it did not introduce a systematic bias in favor of inflation.) The difficulty in predicting the real purchasing power of a promise to pay a fixed dollar amount in the future would increase as the time horizon lengthened. With this policy, the magnitude of any discrepancy between yields of nonindexed and indexed bonds due to a risk premium would not decline as maturities lengthened.

Even if the yield gap between nonindexed and indexed bonds were to incorporate a risk premium, changes in the yield gap would still convey important information to the central bank. Increases in the yield gap would be of concern to the central bank even if they were caused by an increase in the risk premium, rather than by an increase in expected inflation. A central bank must assure markets that its independence is a safeguard against surprise inflation. An increase in the size of the risk premium caused by increased concern for surprise future inflation would indicate to the central bank a need to reinforce the credibility of its commitment to monetary stability.

V. ISSUES FOR DEBT MANAGEMENT

The idea of indexed bonds has been advanced numerous times in the past. The Treasury possesses the authority to issue indexed bonds, but has always resisted doing so. In congressional hearings on indexed bonds (U.S. Congress, 1985), Francis Cavanaugh, the director of the Office of Government Finance and Market Analysis of the Treasury, detailed the reasons.

Mr. Cavanaugh argued that the Treasury did not know whether anyone would buy indexed bonds.[6] If there were no demand for them, their issuance would increase the Treasury's cost of funding the government's debt.

> we have yet to see any strong evidence of potential demand for such an indexed bond in this country . . . An indexed bond, because of its novel features, would not realize the full benefits of the liquidity of the conventional Treasury market, and its relative lack of liquidity would be reflected in the bid price received by the Treasury in an indexed bond auction . . . Thus a requirement that the U.S. Treasury issue indexed bonds, especially fixed amounts each year, could lead to significant increases in the cost of financing the public debt (U.S. Congress, pp. 17 and 20).[7]

According to this argument, there is uncertainty over whether anyone would value the inflation protection offered by indexing. Because inaccurate inflation forecasts are costly, however, it seems implausible that no savers would be interested in protecting against such risk. Consider, for example, the experience of someone who bought and held a 30-year government bond 30 years ago. In 1961, the long-term government bond yield was 3.9%. On average, over the 3 years 1959, 1960, and 1961, CPI inflation averaged 1.1%. Assuming, given this experience, that in 1961 investors believed that the long-term rate of inflation would be 1.1%, a purchaser of a 30-year bond would have anticipated a yearly gain in real terms of 2.8% (3.9% minus 1.1%). In fact, over the 30-year period from 1961 to 1991, CPI inflation averaged 5.2%. The investor lost 1.3% of his capital each year (3.9% minus 5.2%) because of inflation (not counting taxes paid on coupon payments). Instead of a 30% gain in capital from holding the bond for 30 years, the investor lost 30% of his capital. Munnell and Grolnic (1986) make a persuasive case that, at a minimum, pension funds and holders of IRAs would be interested in indexed bonds.[8]

VI. BRITISH EXPERIENCE

A. British Indexed Gilts

Britain has issued indexed bonds (gilts) since 1981. Unfortunately, indexing in Britain is poorly designed for measuring expected inflation. British bonds are indexed to the retail price index (RPI), which is a poor measure of inflation because it includes the cost of mortgage interest payments. Also, coupon and principal payments are indexed with an 8-month lag.[9] This 8-month lag makes real yields on indexed bonds with a maturity even as long as 5 years sensitive to variations in inflation. The difference between yields on nonindexed and indexed bonds, therefore, cannot reliably be used to measure expected inflation over periods as short as a few years.

The practice of issuing only long-term indexed bonds compounds the difficulty of measuring the public's expected inflation over periods as short as a few years. In order to observe a yield gap on bonds of short maturity, it is necessary to wait until the passage of time reduces the maturity of the long-term bonds. Even though indexed bonds were first issued in 1981, there is still a paucity of indexed bonds with a short period to maturity. As of the end of 1990, the average maturity of indexed bonds outstanding was 18.9 years. There were only £1.05 billion of indexed securities outstanding with maturities of 5 years or less. Also, for short-term maturities, the absence of nonindexed bonds with exactly the same maturity as indexed bonds becomes more of a problem.

In a personal communication with the author, Alan Walters noted that in Britain the exchequer varied the relative supplies of nonindexed short-term debt and long-term indexed bonds in response to changes in the yield gap between the two kinds of debt. In order to ensure that the yield gap reflects expectations of inflation rather than relative supplies, he recommended that in the future indexed and nonindexed debt be issued in fixed proportions.[10]

B.   British Monetary Policy

The usefulness of a yield gap between nonindexed and indexed bonds as a measure of expected inflation has been questioned on the basis of the British experience. In an article in the *Financial Times* (April 29, 1991), Anthony Harris stated that the "gap has tracked current inflation faithfully, but has no forecasting value at all. The market forecasts the way a picnicker does—by looking out of the window." Therefore, he concludes, the nonindexed-indexed bond gap cannot "give a valuable steer on monetary policy." Presumably, Mr. Harris has in mind the failure of the yield gap to predict the increase in inflation that occurred in 1988. A brief review of British monetary policy in the latter 1980s proves to be helpful in understanding Mr. Harris' contention that bond markets are not forward-looking.

In Britain, inflation fell from 20% in 1980 to an average of about 3.5% in 1986 and 1987. (Figures for inflation are for the RPI excluding mortgage interest payments.) Until 1988, actual inflation moved fairly closely with long-term expected inflation, inferred from the yield gap between the indexed bond issued in 1982 and maturing in 2006 and a conventional bond with approximately the same maturity.[11] (See Fig. 3.) Over 1986 and 1987, in particular, the yield gap averaged about 3.5%. Actual inflation began to rise in early 1988 and peaked in 1990 somewhat above 9%. The yield-gap measure of expected inflation did rise steadily with actual inflation in early 1988, but reached a peak of only about 6% in early 1990.

Annual Percentage Change

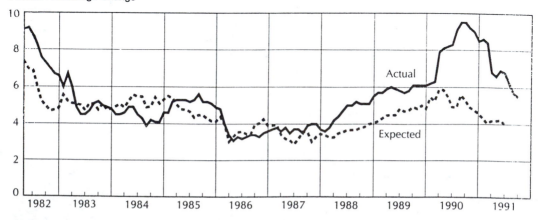

Figure 3   Actual and expected inflation in the United Kingdom. Actual inflation is the annual percentage change in the RPI excluding mortgage interest payments over the preceding 12-month period. Expected inflation is inferred from the yield gap between an indexed bond maturing in 2006 and a conventional bond with approximately the same maturity. The yield gap was adjusted for different tax treatment in the two bonds. The expected inflation series was supplied by G. Thomas Woodward.

What caused the sharp rise in inflation, which was understated by the yield gap? After the Louvre Accord on February 3, 1987, Nigel Lawson, chancellor of the exchequer, began to peg the DM/£ exchange rate informally at 3 to 1. At the same time, the real terms of trade began to appreciate steadily in Britain's favor; that is, British physical assets and commodities became more attractive. This appreciation was prompted by three factors. First, the Conservative electoral victory in 1987 made Britain appear to be a safe haven for foreign capital. Second, the rise in the price of oil after its 1986 trough and a large oil discovery announced on March 8, 1988, raised the value of British exports. Finally, the reduction in marginal tax rates, announced March 15, 1988, increased the attractiveness of investment in Britain and reduced capital outflows.

With a pegged exchange rate, the appreciation in the real terms of trade appeared as a rise in British prices, which was accommodated by high money growth. Growth in the monetary base went from about 4% in the middle of 1987 to more than 10% toward the end of 1988. In the spring of 1988, Mr. Lawson allowed the DM/£ exchange rate to rise, but only grudgingly. To retard the pound's appreciation, he lowered the U.K. bank base lending rate to a low of 7.5% in May 1988, from a high of 11% in early 1987. In June 1988, in response to the sustained rise in inflation that began in early 1988, Mr. Lawson reversed course and began to raise the base rate, which reached 15% in October 1989.

In light of this experience, were the holders of British bonds making forward-looking predictions of inflation? In 1987, the holders of bonds maturing in 2006 were predicting inflation of somewhat less than 4% over the next 19 years. Can this prediction be defended as forward-looking in light of the increase in British inflation from somewhat less than 4% in 1988 to almost 10% in 1990? With the pound pegged to the mark, British inflation must equal German inflation plus whatever appreciation (or minus whatever depreciation) occurs in the terms of trade. Historically, German inflation has varied around 3 to 4%. If changes in the terms of trade are inherently unpredictable, then a prediction of inflation of 3 to 4% was a reasonable estimate.[12]

Ex post, predicted inflation in the 3 to 4% range now appears to have been reasonable. Since Britain's formal entry into the EMS in the autumn of 1990, the DM/£ exchange rate has stayed very close to 3 to 1. With the cessation in the appreciation in the British terms of trade, British inflation had to fall to the German level. By autumn 1991, it had been brought roughly into line with German inflation of about 4%.[13] In short, there is nothing in British experience to indicate that bondholders are not forward-looking.

C.   Can Bond Markets Predict Inflation?

On the basis of an examination of the British experience, Gabriel de Kock (1991) concludes that using a yield gap to measure expected inflation as proposed here would not be useful to the Fed. Based on the British experience, he makes two assertions. First, he asserts that the yield on the indexed bond does not offer a measure of the economy's real yield. Second, he claims that the yield gap between nonindexed and indexed bonds possesses no predictive power for future inflation beyond what is furnished by recent, actual inflation. The empirical tests De Kock conducts, however, are not capable of proving or disproving these assertions.[14]

De Kock tests whether the yield gap predicts subsequent inflation rates over 12-, 24-, and 36-month periods, respectively. Apparently, he chooses these rates because they are of "primary concern to policymakers." They were not, however, what bondholders were trying to predict. The author derives his measure of expected inflation from comparing the yield on nonindexed bonds with the yield of indexed bonds of roughly the same maturity issued in March 1982 and maturing in July 1996. For example, the first observation used by the author is dated March 1982. The yield gap between nonindexed and indexed bonds then reflects the market's expectation of inflation from March 1982 to July 1996. The author compares this expectation of inflation with actual inflation over the much shorter periods beginning in March 1982 and ending in March 1983, March 1984, and March 1984. In order to perform the kind of ex post test of predictive power the author wishes to conduct, it will be necessary to wait until 1996 (or close to that date).[15]

Despite the inability of De Kock's tests to bring evidence to bear on the ex post predictive accuracy of the yield gap as a measure of expected inflation, his work does raise the interesting question of how to interpret evidence on ex post predictive accuracy. Would evidence that investors predict inflation poorly affect the value to the central bank of a yield-gap measure of expected inflation? The answer would appear to be no. What matters in determining the real rate of interest is what inflation rate financial markets expect, not whether ex post they predicted inflation accurately. Moreover, evidence from a yield-gap measure of expected inflation demonstrating that the public in practice predicts inflation poorly would provide an incentive to the central bank to alter monetary policy to ensure that at least in the long term the price level would be easy to predict.

VII. SUMMARY AND CONCLUDING COMMENTS

The yield-gap proposal advanced here differs from earlier proposals for indexed bonds in its recommendation that (1) equal amounts of nonindexed and indexed bonds of the same maturity be issued and (2) the resulting yield gap be used as an indicator of whether particular monetary policy actions are consistent with the Federal Reserve's inflation objective.[16]

The Federal Reserve determines the long-term rate of inflation. The measure of expected inflation proposed here would allow the Fed to observe whether there was a discrepancy between the rate of inflation expected by the public and the rate of inflation it seeks to achieve. Monetary policy makers would then be in a better position to make policy in a way that avoids discrepancies between expected and subsequently realized inflation. The yield-gap measure of expected inflation would allow monetary policy to be evaluated on whether or not it provides a stable monetary environment characterized by moderate fluctuations in expected inflation and the absence of inflationary and disinflationary surprises.

APPENDIX: USING INDEXED BONDS IN MAKING MONETARY POLICY—AN ILLUSTRATION

At present, the Fed must infer how its actions affect the public's perception of the inflation rate that it, the Fed, considers acceptable. The Fed becomes concerned when financial markets appear to interpret a policy action as signaling a willingness on its part to tolerate a higher inflation rate. A yield gap indicator would allow the Fed to observe directly how it is influencing the public's expectation of inflation. The example below illustrates this point.

Figure 4 displays hypothetical time profiles of the public's expectation of the future price level as inferred from the yield gap between nonindexed and indexed bonds of successively longer maturity. To simplify the discussion, I assume initially that the public believes the Fed will maintain the rate of inflation at 0% on average. Line A in Fig. 4 (the solid line) reflects the assumption of expected long-term price stability. (The yield gap between nonindexed and indexed bonds is zero. The current value of the price index is taken to be 100.) Figure 5 displays the term structure of real yields inferred from indexed bond yields of successively longer maturity. Initially, I assume that the yields on indexed bonds indicate that the public believes real yields will remain at 3%. Line 1 in Fig. 5 (the solid line) reflects this assumption.

Finally, I assume that the rate of growth of real GNP has declined relative to what the Fed considers a sustainable rate. In response, the Fed has over time gradually worked the funds rate down (by lowering its borrowed reserves target or by reducing the discount rate). At some point, a rise in long-term bond rates follows a reduction in the funds rate. The Fed then must decide whether this rise should deter future funds rate reductions. The Fed will be concerned that the rise in bond rates signals the market's belief that it is willing to tolerate a higher inflation rate. In this situation, a yield gap indicator would help the Fed understand the cause of the rise in bond rates. Consider the following possibilities:

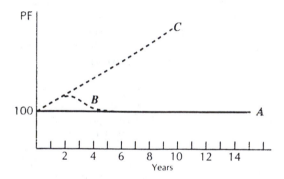

Figure 4   Time profile of the future price level expected by the public (PF) inferred from the yield gap between nonindexed and indexed bonds of successively longer maturities.

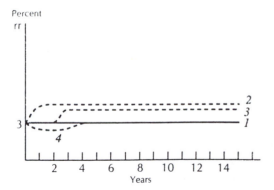

Figure 5   Term structure of the real rate of interest (rr) inferred from yields on indexed bonds of successively longer maturities.

1. The measure of the public's expectation of inflation remains unchanged; that is, line A in Fig. 4 continues to measure the future profile of the price level expected by the public. Bond yields have risen because real yields have risen.

    a. Line 2 in Fig. 5 shows a first possible case. It shows real yields rising at all but the very shortest maturities. (Yields on the shortest maturities are tied down by the current value of the funds rate.) This evidence suggests that the economy has begun to strengthen. It favors prompt action to reverse the recent reduction in the funds rate.

    b. Line 3 in Fig. 2 shows a second case. It shows real yields rising only in the future. This evidence suggests that market participants expect a rise in real rates in the future, perhaps because of an optimistic assessment of prospects for a future revival of economic activity. This evidence suggests ceasing actions that lower the funds rate, but delaying actions to raise it. In this latter case, the delayed rise in the real rate could also reflect the market's belief that the Fed will be reluctant initially to let short-term market rates rise in response to stronger economic activity. Such a belief, however, would appear unlikely because of the assumption of an unchanged expectation of inflation (an absence of movement in line A in Fig. 4).

2. A second possibility is that bond yields have risen because the public now expects positive inflation to replace price stability.

    a. In the first case considered, line A changes to line B in Fig. 4. As depicted by line B, the public now believes that the Fed will maintain an unchanged price level in the long term, but that the near-term inflation rate will be positive. If real yields have remained unchanged (line 1 is unchanged in Fig. 5), then it is likely that market participants expect some transitory increase in inflation unrelated to monetary policy. In this case, the Fed is likely to postpone further policy actions that would reduce the funds rate.

    b. In the second case, the rise in bonds rates is accompanied by a change in the expected future price profile from line A to line C in Fig. 4. If, at the same time, real yields rise (line 1 in Fig. 5 changes to line 2), it is likely that the market believes that Fed easing has gone too far. It believes that the cumulative reduction in the funds rate will not only stimulate economic activity, but also will create inflation. This information is likely to induce the Fed to reverse its most recent action reducing the funds rate.

    c. A third case is illustrated by the combination of movement to line C in Fig. 4 and line 4 in Fig. 5. This combination suggests that market participants have become concerned that monetary policy will become inflationary in the future, but real rates are falling in the climate of weakness in economic activity. This information suggests that the Fed should continue to reduce the funds rate, but reaffirm its commitment to maintaining price stability. For example, the Fed could communicate to the public the level of future inflation it considers acceptable by specifying an explicit target path for the future price level.

NOTES

1. See Hetzel (1990 and 1991) and *Bondweek* (1991). The idea of indexed bonds is an old one. In his *Review* article, "The Concept of Indexation in the History of Economic Thought," Humphrey (1974) lists a number of early economists who advocated indexed bonds: John Maynard Keynes in 1924; George Bach and Richard Musgrave in 1941; and Milton Friedman in 1951. Humphrey also notes two early examples of indexed bonds. During the American Revolution, the Massachusetts legislature issued bonds with interest and principal tied to an index of the prices of staple commodities. In 1925 the Rand Kardex Co., at the urging of Irving Fisher, issues a 30-year bond indexed to the wholesale price index. In 1985, Senators Quayle and Trible introduced a bill to index government bonds (S. 1088, the "Price Indexed Bonds Act of 1985") and Representative Lungren introduced a similar bill in the House (H. R. 1773, "The Price Indexed Bonds Act of 1985"). See the U.S. Congress (1985) Hearings, "Inflation Indexing of Government Securities."

2. The bonds would be issued and retired just after the middle of the month, when the CPI is announced for the preceding month. The dollar principal payment on an indexed bond would then be increased by the percentage increase in the CPI from the month preceding its issue to the month preceding its redemption. Zero-coupon bonds avoid problems of how to index partially accrued coupon payments when a bond is traded before maturity.

3. Forward rates for individual years would be inferred under the assumption that the yield over the life of the bond is a geometric average of the yields over the successive individual years.

4. The issue of how to tax capital gains is perennially contentious. There is a consensus among economists, however, that taxing capital gains representing only paper gains that compensate for inflation distorts investment and savings decisions undesirably.

5. Woodward has published a series on the real yield on indexed bonds and on the implied expected inflation rate. A key feature of his series is an adjustment for different tax treatment of nonindexed and indexed gilts. In Britain, holders of indexed bonds do not pay taxes on that part of the income due to capital appreciation, while holders of nonindexed bonds pay taxes on the inflation premium built into interest payments. This difference in tax treatment increases the size of the yield gap between the two kinds of bonds beyond bondholders' expectation of inflation. Woodward reduces the gap by the estimated amount due to this tax effect. Subtracting this reduced difference from the yield on nonindexed bonds gives a tax-adjusted real yield series; that is, it provides a measure of the real yield that holders of indexed bonds would receive in the absence of favorable tax treatment.

6. Treasury opposition to the issue of indexed bonds also appears to reflect a general hesitation to innovate in debt management techniques. "A poorly received Treasury issue, because of faulty design or a misreading of a new potential market, could adversely affect Treasury's credibility in the market. So we approach innovation with great care" (U.S. Congress, 1985, p. 20).

7. Mr. Cavanaugh actually expressed both the concern that there would be no demand for indexed bonds and that there would be too much demand. In the latter case, their issue would be a problem because they would compete with S&Ls for funds (U.S. Congress, p. 23). It is hard to know what to make of the assertion that the market for indexed bonds would be illiquid. If dealers in government securities find it profitable to sell conventional debt, why would they not find it profitable also to sell indexed debt?

8. Munnell and Grolnic (1986, pp. 4,5) note, "Anyone saving for a specific goal, such as purchasing a house or sending children to college, should welcome the opportunity to ensure that such savings will not be eroded by inflation . . . Moreover, in the United States there may well be a niche for index bonds that has not been adequately explored—namely, the financing of fully indexed annuities for retirees. These annuities could play an important role in protecting elderly people against the erosion of their pension income during their retirement years." Munnell and Grolic then document that pension plans have not historically adjusted payments to beneficiaries to compensate fully for inflation.

     They also note that there are no financial instruments that can satisfactorily protect purchasing power against inflation. "Common stocks . . . seem to be a particularly unsuitable investment for producing a stable real income. While over the past 30 years stocks have provided a high average real return, this return has been so volatile that investors have experienced significant periods of negative real earnings. Long-term bonds have fared even less well: their average real return has been near zero and in recent years the variability has been almost as great as that for common stocks. Treasury bills do appear to offer a stable real positive return, but this return is very low and these instruments are a less than perfect hedge against inflation" (Munnell and Grolnic, 1986, p. 18).

9. An 8-month lag was adopted to simplify calculation of accrued interest on bonds with semiannual coupon payments. With the 8-month lag, immediately after a coupon payment, assuming the most recently available price index is for 2 months in the past, one can calculate the indexed value of the coupon payment 6 months in the future.

10. The Bank of England supplied the author with data on outstanding debt by maturity for both nonindexed and indexed debt. The yield gap between nonindexed and indexed debt did indeed influence relative supplies of the two kinds of debt. Relative supplies, however, did not appear to influence the subsequent yield gap.

11. Data for expected inflation were supplied by Thomas Woodward. They are derived from the yield gap between conventional and indexed bonds after an adjustment for the favorable tax treatment of indexed bonds. See note 5 and Woodward (1990).

12. In 1990, expected inflation measured by the yield gap rose to about 6%, which was higher than the trend rate of German inflation. Investors in British bonds may have believed that Britain would abandon the 3-to-1 DM/£ exchange

rate to avoid the costs of a severe disinflation. They may also have believed that the trend rate of German inflation would rise because of fiscal pressures from German reunification.

13. The DM/£ exchange rate began to fall in 1989. This fall indicated that the terms of trade were no longer appreciating in Britain's favor. A pegged exchange rate then required a convergence of British and German rates of inflation. This convergence in inflation rates required a drastic monetary deceleration in Britain. In 1989 and the first part of 1990, growth in the broad monetary aggregate M4 was around 20%, while growth in the monetary base M0 was around 8%. By autumn 1991, M4 growth had fallen to around 8% and M0 growth had fallen to around 2%.

14. See De Kock (1991). De Kock supports the first assertion by pointing to the absence of a negative relationship between the yield on indexed bonds and future changes in economic activity. Economic theory, however, does not predict a negative (or any predictable) relationship between these two variables. In fact, in any macroeconomic model, the sign of the correlation between the real rate of interest and future economic activity depends upon the kind of shock impinging upon the economy. In a standard IS-LM model, for example, a positive real sector shock (rightward shift in the IS schedule) will lead to a *higher* real rate of interest and a *higher* level of real GNP.

   The author's rationale for his test appears to rely on the assumption that a rise in interest rates necessarily reflects a tightening of monetary policy, and conversely. For example, he argues that the yield gap could not have been an adequate measure of inflation expectations in Britain in the period from early 1988 through mid-1990. Over this period, long-term market rates rose (monetary policy was tightened according to De Kock) and expected inflation (measured by the yield gap) rose, rather than fell. Measured by growth of the monetary aggregates, however, monetary policy was expansionary. Growth in the monetary aggregates M0 and M4 was quite rapid. Monetary deceleration did not begin until mid-1990. Market rates could have risen because expected inflation rose.

15. The favorable tax treatment accorded indexed bonds widens the size of the yield gap. Because the author fails to correct for this tax effect, he concludes that the yield gap is a biased measure of inflation; that is, he finds that the yield gap, which includes a tax effect, consistently overpredicts inflation. Also, the author uses a theoretically unsatisfactory measure of inflation. He uses the retail price index that includes mortgage interest payments. It would have been better to use the retail price index that excludes these payments.

16. In a personal communication to the author, Milton Friedman argued for using the yield gap as a *target*. He would instruct the Federal Reserve to eliminate the gap over time.

REFERENCES

Bondweek (1991). "Treasury to Get Proposal for Inflation-Indexed Bonds." Nov. 11.

De Kock, G. (1991). "Expected Inflation and Real Interest Rates Based on Index-linked Bond Prices: The U.K. Experience," Federal Reserve Bank of New York, *Quarterly Review* (autumn): 47–60.

Hetzel, R. L. (1990). "Maintaining Price Stability: A Proposal," Federal Reserve Bank of Richmond, *Economic Review*, 76 (March/April): 53–55.

Hetzel, R. L. (1991). "A Better Way to Fight Inflation," *Wall Street Journal*, April 25.

Humphrey, T. M. (1974). "The Concept of Indexation in the History of Economic Thought," Federal Reserve Bank of Richmond, *Economic Review*, 60 (Nov./Dec.): 3–16.

Munnell, A. H. and Crolnic, J. B. (1986). "Should the U.S. Government Issue Index Bonds?" Federal Reserve Bank of Boston, *New England Economic Review* (Sept./Oct.): 3–21.

U.S. Congress. (1985). "Inflation Indexing of Government Securities," hearing before the Subcommittee on Trade, Productivity, and Economic Growth of the Joint Economic Committee, 99th Cong., 1st sess., May 14.

Woodward, G. T. (1987). "Should the Treasury Issue Indexed Bonds?" Congressional Research Service Report for Congress, December 31.

Woodward, G. T. (1990). "The Real Thing: A Dynamic Profile of the Term Structure of Real Interest Rate and Inflation Expectations in the United Kingdom, 1982–89," *Journal of Business*, 63 (July): 373–98.

Woodward, G. T. "Evidence of the Fisher Effect from U.K. Indexed Bonds," Forthcoming *Review of Economics and Statistics*.

53

Treasury Auction Issues

United States Department of the Treasury, United States Securities and Exchange Commission, and Board of Governors of the Federal Reserve System
Washington, D.C.

I. AUCTION TECHNIQUE

This chapter examines simple descriptions of auction organization and discusses in more detail two specific proposals for reform of the auction process. While much of this discussion is in theoretical terms, it should be understood that market specifics make it difficult to translate theory into practice, with the goal of assessing the efficacy of any auction reform.

For example, unlike most of the simple theoretical constructs that appear in the economics literature, the Treasury offers *multiple* units of the auctioned security, with open trading in those securities preceding (in the when-issued market) and following (in the secondary market) the issuance of securities. Another deviation from common theoretical assumptions is that investors can adjust their behavior in many ways, such as by varying the amount of information collected, by altering the volume of bids, or by placing bids indirectly through dealer intermediaries. These considerations are important in the policy context, and this chapter attempts to address them as well as presenting a basic theoretical framework for assessing auction methods.

A. Auction Methods

There have been many important contributions to the academic literature on auctions, including early efforts by William Vickrey and Milton Friedman, as well as significant later work by Paul Milgrom, among others.[*]
This research has classified the types of auctions, modeled the bidding strategies rigorously, and ranked the outcomes by various criteria. A number of similarities among auctions have emerged, as well as equivalence propositions concerning the revenue to the seller. Unfortunately, members of the financial and academic communities describe auction formats by a variety of names, some overlapping and others conflicting. To reduce confusion, this section will use explicit, if somewhat unwieldy, names for each auction type.

William Vickrey originated the standard auction taxonomy, classifying auction types based on the order in which prices were quoted, as well as the auction forum. First, awards can be made at prices that are progressively lowered (or, equivalently, at yields that are raised) until all of the goods or securities are sold;

Adapted from the *Joint Report of the Government Securities Market* (January 1992), Appendix B: B17–B63.

[*]The early references include William Vickrey, "Counterspeculation, auctions, and competitive sealed tenders," *Journal of Finance*, vol. 16 (March 1961), pp. 8–37, and Milton Friedman, "Comment on 'Collusion in the auction market for Treasury bills,'" *Journal of Political Economy*, vol. 72 (Oct. 1964), pp. 513–514. Recent work is summarized and reviewed in R. Preston McAfee and John McMillan, "Auctions and bidding," *Journal of Economic Literature*, vol. 25 (June 1987), 669–738; Paul Milgrom, "Auctions and bidders: a primer," *Journal of Economic Perspectives*, vol. 3 (summer 1989), pp. 3–22; and Paul Milgrom and Robert J. Weber, "A theory of auctions and competitive bidding," *Econometrica*, vol. 50 (Sept. 1982), pp. 1089–1122. A less rigorous overview with applications to Treasury securities is provided by Loretta J. Mester, "Going, going, gone: setting prices with auctions," *Federal Reserve Bank of Philadelphia Business Review*, (March/April 1988), pp. 3–13.

alternatively, the bids can be arranged in ascending order by their price and a single price determined that just places the total issue. Second, the auction can be conducted with sealed bids entered any time up to a deadline and subsequently opened by the auctioneer; on the other hand, the auction can be conducted with open bids put forth by participants in an open gathering or some other means of direct communication with the auctioneer (such as by telephone). This two-by-two classification scheme yields four auction types, described below.

Beyond these categories, models can be stratified further by the assumption concerning bidders' information about the value of the auctioned object. In the "private-values" case, bidders make subjective decisions as to the value of the object on the auction block, independent of each other. In the "common-values" case, each participant attempts to measure the item's value by the same objective yardstick. The auction of a unique piece of art is the prototypical private-values example, while a Treasury auction—with each bidder guessing at the security's resale value—matches the common-values assumption.

1. Multiple-Price, Sealed-Bid Auction

The Treasury's current auction methodology falls into this category, which in the financial community is termed an English auction (except by the English, who call it an American auction). Bidders spell out their intentions on tender forms that must be turned in before an established deadline. An individual sealed bid, known only to the tenderer and to the auctioneer, reports the quantity and price for the auctioned security that the bidder is willing to pay.* The auctioneer than ranks those bids by tendered price (or equivalent yield) and makes awards at the highest prices covering the total auction size. Thus, participants pay differing prices reflecting the strength of their bids, with the surest winner the one furthest above the market consensus. This type of auction is called a "first-price" auction when a single unit is for sale because it is the first, or highest, price that is accepted.

In this case, winning is losing, as entering the highest bid signals that the bidder's valuation exceeds that of all other interested parties. Because all participants, in effect, are guessing about the same common value—the price at which the security will trade after the auction—a high bid signals a heightened probability of subsequent loss for that bidder. This is the "winner's curse" and gives bidders an incentive to rein in their enthusiasm. The optimal strategy is to shade a bid toward the perceived market consensus.†

The risk of the winner's curse puts a premium on market information entering the auction, and this incentive shapes bidders' behavior before and at the auction in three major ways. First, when-issued trading before the auction allows a market consensus about auction pricing to coalesce. Second, a core of bidders at the auction routinely exchanges information about probable market conditions. Third, participants who are unable or unwilling to commit the resources needed to collect market information pool their bids, as a group of investors is more likely to have a clearer view of the market consensus and is less likely to place off-market bids. The pooling of bids is one service provided by primary dealers, who collect customer business and place large-scale orders.

2. Uniform-Price, Sealed-Bid Auction

In this type of auction, the auctioneer collects sealed bids, arranges them by price, and makes awards at the single price that just places the entire issue. This type of auction is called a "second-price" action when a single unit is sold because the price charged would be that of the highest failed bid, or the second-best price. It is often called a "Dutch" auction in the financial press and has recently gained some prominence as a potential substitute for current Treasury practice. Aggressive bidders receive sure awards but pay a price closer to the market consensus. As a result, there should be less of the shading of bids that marks the response to the winner's curse. With the threat of awards above the consensus reduced, there is less of a need for large bidders to compare notes before the auction and customers might be more willing to place their business directly by bidding at the auction rather than going through a primary dealer.

---

*A bidder's intention will be measured here in terms of the price he or she is willing to pay for the security rather than the equivalent yield he or she is willing to earn on the security.
†This strategy is explained in James L. Smith, "Non- aggressive bidding behavior and the 'winner's curse'," *Economic Inquiry*, vol. 19 (July 1981), pp. 380–88.

3. Descending-Price, Open-Outcry Auction

This procedure has been used to auction flowers in the Netherlands; hence, academics refer to it as a Dutch auction. Bidders congregate in one room, or its electronic equivalent, and the auctioneer calls out a sequence of decreasing prices. In an auction of one unit of a good or security, the auction stops when one bidder is willing to pay the price called out. For multiple units, the eager bidder would be awarded the security and the auction would continue, selling the remaining securities at progressively lower prices. In fact, the strategic decision is identical to that of the multiple-price, sealed-bid auction; the optimal bidder does not want to be too aggressive and stop the auction well above the likely market consensus, but rather, will shade his or her bid to avoid the winner's curse.* As a result, investors have the same incentive to trade information and to pool bids by placing customer orders at primary dealers.

4. Ascending-Price, Open-Outcry Auction

The auctioneer could announce an ascending sequence of prices to a group of bidders, who would submit their bids at each price. The auction would stop when just enough bids were received to sell the total issue of securities or total units of the good for sale. One form of this auction category is the method commonly used to sell, for example, works of art, when a single unit is on the block.†

In selling multiple units of securities, the auction would begin as a price was called out and all interested parties submitted their quantities demanded. The volume of bids at that price would be announced and, in successive rounds, the price would be raised until the volume demanded was smaller than the size of the issue. When that point was reached, the auctioneer would know that the price previously called was the highest price consistent with selling the entire issue. In other words, the second highest price clears the auction market. Bidders who bid above that market-clearing price plus some fraction of the bidders at the market-clearing price would receive awards. Those partial awards to the bidders that had not moved up to the highest price either could be based on a common fraction of the bids of all members of that group or could be allotted to those who were electronically timed as having placed their bids soonest at the market-clearing price.

From the viewpoint of an investor, this increasing sequence of prices lessens the possibility of the winner's curse, as the public announcement of bids provides information about the security's common value. That is, the presence of other bidders provides support that a bidder is not alone in valuing the security highly. Even if an investor truly valued the security far above his or her competitors, the bidding would cease before the price moved very far from the consensus.

B. Potential Changes to the Treasury Auction Method

1. Milton Friedman's Proposal

Recent events have kindled enthusiasm for reform of the auction process. In a recent contribution, Milton Friedman has repeated a proposal he advanced in 1959 concerning the auction of Treasury securities.‡ Essentially, Friedman argues for a uniform-price, sealed-bid auction, commonly called a Dutch auction. In the one alteration to current practice, the Treasury would no longer award securities at the price equivalent to the yield bid but instead charge a uniform price (award a uniform yield) to winning bidders.

Friedman asserts that the switch would end cornering attempts by eliminating the profit potential in market manipulation. And, perhaps paradoxically, he also argues that total revenue to the Treasury would be higher by surrendering the ability to "price-discriminate" or charge bidders different prices based on their bids.

Friedman argues that the current Treasury technique reduces demand at auctions, as well as making it more price sensitive relative to the demand of the ultimate buy-and-hold investor. As explained above, this is the rational response to multiple-price awards; the investor is reluctant to expose his or her true valuation to a seller (the Treasury) whose stated intention is to garner the highest price possible. But with this induced difference in demands in the primary and secondary markets, a potential market cornerer can buy at the auction just above the market consensus and sell in the secondary market to a larger group of investors.

Moving to a uniform-price award method permits bidding at the auction to reflect the true nature of

---

*This strategic equivalence was first noted by Vickrey, op. cit.

†Academics term this an English auction. Indeed, in the private-values model (which is not analyzed here), another equivalence proposition holds: what has been popularly referred to as a Dutch auction is strategically identical to what academics refer to as an English auction. When there is a time limit on bidding, it is called a Scotch auction.

‡Milton Friedman, "How to sell government securities," *Wall Street Journal* (Aug. 28, 1991).

investor preferences. This should allow investors to bypass the dealer intermediaries and bid directly in the auctions. In the case envisioned by Friedman, uniform-price awards would make the auction demand curve identical to the secondary market demand curve. This integration of the auction and secondary markets would eliminate the incentive to corner an issue, because any cornerer who bids securities away from investors at an auction would not find buyers willing to pay a higher price in the secondary market. Thus, under Friedman's assumptions, the cornering motivation would be eliminated by removing the potential for profit.

This result requires that the switch in auction technique completely unifies the primary and secondary markets. In other words, Friedman assumes that dealers exist solely to bear the bidding risk because of the Treasury's discriminatory pricing. However, even after the adoption of uniform-price awards, presence at auctions may still be limited to a segment of the investor populace, perhaps to those who are more price sensitive. Participants at an auction face uncertain outcomes, since they may not be awarded securities if they have not appropriately cast their bids. Those particularly averse to this quantity risk well may delay purchase to secondary trading. Those who sell the auctioned securities short in the when-issued market may prefer to cover their positions quickly at the auction. Furthermore, direct bidding requires incurring the costs of arranging for the placement of bids and the payment of awards—the prospects for which depend on the pace of automation and changes in the regulatory environment. As a result, the infrequent purchaser may remain in the secondary market. In general, if dealers provide any service in the distribution of securities, then a wedge will remain between the auction and secondary-market demand schedules. A sufficiently large wedge provides an opportunity for market manipulation.

With demand at the auctions still differing somewhat from that in secondary trading and with the Treasury continuing to solicit sealed bids, Friedman's proposal would not discourage attempts to corner the market. For example, under Friedman's "Dutch" auction regime, a market manipulator could place bids for a substantial fraction of an issue well above the market consensus price, ensuring significant awards, but would pay only that price required to allocate the remaining portion of securities to unsuspecting competitors. However, even if the threat of manipulation remains, the lessened importance of bidding near the market consensus should reduce the desire to share information and the associated pre-auction discussion and pooling of bids that could provide cover for market manipulation.

With regard to revenue, Friedman would have the Treasury surrender part of the revenue from its current auction practice—that earned from charging winners the price that they bid rather than a common price—in the expectation that added investor demand and more aggressive bidding would more than replace that loss. This assertion can be spelled out using Henry Goldstein's 1962 analysis.* As Fig. 1 shows, part of the Treasury's total revenue owes to its charging winners the price that they bid, which for the current practice is measured by the area under the demand schedule labeled "multiple-price." That price discrimination, however, discourages some demand, as investors shade their bids for fear of the winner's curse. Adopting Friedman's uniform-price system turns part of that surplus back to the bidders, thus shifting out the demand schedule to that labeled uniform-price. Under a multiple-price scheme, the Treasury works its way down the inner demand schedule, awarding securities at lower prices to place the total issue (marked by the vertical dashed line). Under the uniform- price scheme, one price, depicted by the horizontal line, would exhaust the issue. The consequences for revenue depend on whether the area of the first triangle, the loss from the inability to price discriminate, outweighs the area of the second triangle, the gain from added demand.

The Friedman proposal has some support in the economics literature, as analysts working with explicit models of bidder behavior in a Treasury-like regime, rather than simple demand schedules, generally find that a uniform-price scheme does produce higher revenue for the seller.[†] Friedman himself, in 1962, made a persuasive argument that revenue would increase.[‡]

*Henry Goldstein, "The Friedman proposal for auctioning Treasury bills," *Journal of Political Economy*, vol. 70 (Aug. 1962), pp. 386–392.

[†]Early support for Friedman's contention can be found in Vernon L. Smith, "Bidding theory and the Treasury bill auction: does price discrimination increase bill prices?" *Review of Economics and Statistics*, vol. 48 (1966), pp. 141–146. Exact conditions under which revenue increases in a model closer to current practice are given in Sushil Bikhchandari and Chi-Fu Huang, "Auctions with resale markets: an exploratory model of Treasury bill markets," *The Review of Financial Studies*, vol. 2 (1989), pp. 311–339. Also see theorem 4 in Robert J. Weber, "Multiple-object auctions," in Richard Englebrecht-Wiggans, Martin Shubik, and Robert M. Stark, eds., *Auctions, Bidding, and Contracting: Uses and Theory*, New York: New York University Press, (1983), pp. 165–191.

[‡]Correspondence quoted in Goldstein, op. cit.

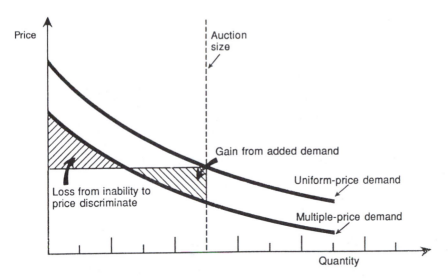

Figure 1 Proposed auctioning of Treasury bills.

Dealers devote considerable energies to the auction only to sell those securities almost immediately to customers—and most profit from doing so. Part of those resources devoted to that distribution could accrue to the Treasury if it could directly deal with those customers. A uniform-price auction, since it is less penalizing to the uninformed, may be the best vehicle to attract those people. Nonetheless, the little empirical evidence available is considerably more ambiguous than this theorizing would suggest. In the few instances in which organizations have run the two types of auctions virtually side by side, neither has come out as clearly resulting in higher revenue to the seller. Friedman's proposal may mark an improvement on current Treasury practice. However, it might not deter manipulative bidders from profiting from the inherently closed nature of sealed bids, which does not give other participants a chance to react.

2. Open-Outcry, Ascending-Price Auction

In contrast to the sealed-bid framework, applying an open-outcry bidding system would let participants react to surprise bids during the auction. If the Treasury were to conduct an open-outcry, ascending-price auction, registered dealers and other financial institutions would connect by phone (with appropriately designed security) to a central computer. Those not preregistered could appear at their local Federal Reserve bank with sufficient documentation to be included as bidders. These gathered bidders would state their demands as the auctioneer announced an increasing sequence of prices.* Prices called out at the auction would climb to the point where total demand was just below the issue size. At that point, the previously announced price would mark the single, market-clearing price that placed the entire issue.

A bidder (or bidders) attempting to corner this type of auction would effectively disclose its intentions to its competitors, as it would continually bid in size as the Treasury auctioneer raises the price. This allows those not party to the attempted market manipulation—particularly those short the security in the when-issued market—to bid along with the manipulators. Hence, the bidders may fail in cornering the security or, at the least, would find it a more expensive proposition.

In a sealed-bid auction, by contrast, the bulk of the increase in price comes at the announcement of surprising awards—when other bidders realize that they have not been awarded securities as expected and react by bidding up the price in the secondary market. In a real-time auction, that reaction occurs when the bidding is still open, and thus the Treasury garners part of the profits of the attempted corner. Indeed, auction theory suggests that, in general, Treasury revenue would not suffer and indeed might increase in the switch

---

*Announcing an ascending sequence of prices would bolster demand at the auction. Recalling Vickrey's result discussed earlier, starting high and progressively lowering the price (a descending-price, open-outcry auction) raises the specter of the winner's curse that results in bid shading.

to an open-outcry, ascending-price system. Since awards are made at a single price and a bidder is aware of the strength of the competition, the possibility of a winner's curse is eliminated.

Of course, a real-time auction may pose a daunting technical challenge and, unlike Friedman's uniform-price, sealed-bid auction, would require a substantial development cost. The goal of equal access to the Treasury auction requires that every effort be made to decentralize the system: anyone willing to pay the fixed expense of a properly configured terminal for bidding should be allowed to participate in the auctions. At the same time, each bidder would need to be screened to ensure payment if their bid were to be successful. If the fixed cost of entry were too large, then participation at the auction would be limited, perhaps perpetuating a two-tiered distribution system for the securities and all the attendant risks. If access were too open, then the physical demands of directing a large volume of electronic messages in a narrow span of time could prove prohibitively expensive. The private sector provides some precedents, but those efforts are small relative to what is required to automate the Treasury auction.

II. INTERNATIONAL COMPARISON

A. Methods of Sale of Government Securities: OECD Countries

Central government debt managers in the countries that belong to the Organization for Economic Cooperation and Development (OECD) largely have been moving toward selling government securities domestically in auctions since the early 1980s. Prior to that time, government debt managers had relied heavily on selling bonds through underwriting syndicates, private placements, and sales to financial institutions on a fixed-price subscription basis. The increased financing requirements of the governments in the OECD countries in the 1980s and the more competitive capital markets generally contributed to the movement toward competitive market pricing of securities.

Methods of sale of central government securities in the OECD countries are summarized below and presented in more detail in the country-by-country descriptions following this summary. Several of the OECD central governments borrow in foreign currencies abroad for balance of payments reasons. These borrowings, which largely are done through underwriting syndicates and private placements, are not discussed in this chapter. Table 1 presents data on the size of the central government surplus or deficit for the most recent fiscal year, the size of the central government debt held by the public (excluding holdings of central banks and government accounts, such as social security trust funds), debt as a share of gross domestic product or

Table 1 OECD Country Debt Statistics in U.S. Dollar Equivalents

Country	Surplus or deficit FY 1991 (billions)	Privately held government debt, 12-31-90 (billions)	Debt to GNP/GDP (percent)	Turnover rate (1991)
Australia	−8.4	37.4	12.8%	390 mil./day
Belgium	−12.7	233.0	109.6	1.4 bil./day
Canada	−26.3	265.5	45.9	173.6 bil./month
Denmark	−6.5	83.8	60.0	21.4 bil./month
France	−18.4	350.1	27.5	9.8 bil./day[a]
Germany	−40.0	381.3	22.0	n.a.
Italy	−128.4	1,168.6	99.2	3.8 bil./day
Japan	−22.5	765.2	24.0	82.5 bil./day
Netherlands	−12.6	196.4	70.0	9.8 bil./month
New Zealand	−2.2	73.7	63.5	5.0 bil./month
Switzerland	−1.2	11.1	4.3	n.a.
United Kingdom	+1.0	314.0	28.9	8.8 bil./day
United States	−268.7	2,492.0	43.9	122.5 bil./day

[a]Medium- and long-term (original issue) OAT bonds only.
Source: Data for each country from respective government.

gross national product, and market trading volume statistics for a recent period in 1991. These data are indicators of the magnitude of the government's financing in absolute terms and relative to the size of the country's economy and the liquidity of the domestic bond markets.

A number of countries have used sales of marketable U.S. Treasury debt securities by multiple-price/yield, sealed-bid auctions as a model. Currently, such auctions are used exclusively in Australia, France, and New Zealand to sell marketable securities.

Other central governments that use multiple-price/yield auctions to sell portions of their marketable debt are: Belgium, for securities issued to institutional investors; Canada, for all marketables, except about one-quarter of long-term bonds which are sold by fixed-price subscription (the rest of these bonds are sold at multiple-yield auctions); Germany, for medium-term notes since July 1991 and for a portion of longer-term bonds since July 1990; Italy, for short-term bills denominated in lire; Japan, for short-term bills and longer-term notes and bonds, including 60% of 10-year bonds, which account for a major proportion of Japanese government borrowing; and the United Kingdom, for bills and longer-term debt (gilts). The Netherlands used multiple-price auctions for long-term bonds but changed in 1991 to selling long-term bonds on tap.

Several of the governments use sealed-bid, uniform-price auctions, in which all securities are awarded at the highest yield (lowest price) of accepted tenders, to sell portions of their debt. OECD countries using uniform price auctions are: Denmark, for short-term bills; Italy, for bills denominated in European Currency Units and bonds maturing in 2 to 10 years (longest sold); and Switzerland, for bills, notes, and bonds. The United Kingdom uses the minimum price tender method of selling gilts, a modified form of uniform price auction. Uniform-price auctions have been used only seldom in the Netherlands in recent years.

Trading on a when-issued basis before an auction of securities occurs in Canada, France, Germany, Italy, and the United Kingdom. In the Netherlands, where tap issues remain open for a relatively short period of 1 or 2 weeks, when-issued trading may occur before a tap issue is closed.

Tap issues are used by a number of OECD countries to sell nonmarketable savings instruments to small investors. In a tap issue, the government announces the interest rate and maturity of the security, sets the price, and allows the market to subscribe. Tap issues may remain open for short or long periods of time, depending upon the government's financing needs and market conditions.

Marketable securities are sold on tap by: Australia, to sell marketable government securities in small amounts to small investors; Denmark, for notes and bonds—the most important instruments sold domestically; Germany, for the portion of long-term bonds that is not sold by competitive price auction or underwriting syndicates and for sales of 5-year special notes to individuals and charitable organizations; the Netherlands, for most long-term issues; and the United Kingdom, to sell the portion of gilts that remain unsold from minimum price tender sales or to sell additional amounts of existing issues placed with the Bank of England.

Sales of central government securities are conducted domestically through underwriting syndicates and private placements in several of the OECD countries. In an underwriting syndicate sale, the country negotiates with the syndicate with regard to volume and price of the security, as well as timing. Negotiations of private placements are similar, but they usually are brought to a government debt manager by an intermediary that does not act as principal in the transaction, and securities are distributed to fewer investors. It is standard procedure for the government to pay fees in syndicate and private placement sales.

Underwriting syndicates are used by: Germany, to sell the portions of long-term bonds that are not sold by multiple-price auction or on tap; Japan, to sell the 40% portion of 10-year bonds that is not sold at auction and to sell small amounts of 5-year bonds; and Switzerland, to sell securities maturing in 3 to 10 years. In the case of Japan, the price for the syndicated underwriting is the price that results from the auction of the 10-year bonds, which immediately precedes the placement of the underwritten portion of an issue.

Several OECD countries sell marketable securities in several tranches to increase the overall size of issues for the purposes of enhancing market liquidity and preventing price distortions. The sales may be through reopenings of securities that are auctioned or through issues that remain on tap. This technique is used by Australia, Belgium, Denmark, France, the Netherlands, New Zealand, Switzerland, and the United Kingdom.

In many of the OECD countries, the central banks have arrangements with the equivalents of U.S. primary dealers, through which they conduct monetary policy. These same dealers usually are the major market makers for government securities, although that is not necessarily the case. In some other countries, the Ministry of Finance/Treasury selects primary dealers specifically to distribute government securities. Firms in OECD countries generally, however, must have a primary dealer designation, be approved by the central bank, or belong to a stock exchange to bid without a deposit in government security auctions.

There are no primary dealers in Denmark, Germany, Japan, the Netherlands, or New Zealand. In Japan, central bank open market operations are conducted through several money market brokers, who are not part of the underwriting syndicate. In New Zealand, open market operations are conducted through entities that register with the Reserve Bank of New Zealand to bid in auctions of government securities. Australia, Belgium, Canada, France, Italy, and the United Kingdom have primary dealers.

There is no uniformity of structures for regulation of the government securities markets among the OECD countries. In Canada, Germany, and Switzerland, there is central government prudential regulation of depository institutions and provincial or state supervision of securities trading. The Bank of England provides prudential regulation of depository institutions, while the Securities and Investments Board supervises the protection of investors. In Australia and New Zealand, the central banks provide prudential regulation of depository institutions, but there is no specific regulation of the government securities market. The Japanese Ministry of Finance and the Danish Supervisory Authority for Financial Affairs provide centralized regulation of the government securities markets in their respective countries, while the Amsterdam Stock Exchange provides centralized regulation of the government securities market in the Netherlands.

III. AUCTION AUTOMATION

A. The Current Auction Process

1. Submission of Tenders

Bidders in Treasury auctions can submit tenders through the Federal Reserve banks and branches or directly to the Treasury's Bureau of the Public Debt. Competitive tenders must be received by the closing time for each auction, which is typically 1:00 P.M. eastern time on the day of the auction. Noncompetitive tenders must be submitted by 12:00 P.M. eastern time on the day of the auction or can be submitted by mail provided they are postmarked no later than midnight of the day prior to the auction and the tender is received on or before the issue date.

Procedures for submitting tenders currently vary among Federal Reserve districts. Bidders can send a facsimile message containing all required tender information (in a few districts), by sending an administrative message over the Federal Reserve's communications network containing all required tender information (in a few districts), or by sending representatives to the lobby of a Federal Reserve bank or branch to submit paper tenders (in all districts).

Some Federal Reserve banks with large competitive bidders in their district provide access for use by the bidders' representatives to establish communications with the bidders' trading desks. Typically, these representatives first enter all the information required on the tender form except for the par amounts and yields (or discount rates in the case of Treasury bills) to be bid. In the closing moments of the auction, following instructions from their trading desks, the representatives enter the par amounts and yields and submit the tender form to the Federal Reserve bank.

2. Processing of Tenders

Competitive and noncompetitive tenders are manually processed by Federal Reserve bank staff upon their receipt. This includes checking to ensure that each tender has been signed by an authorized official and that those submitting tenders for customers are duly authorized and are depository institutions or registered broker-dealers. Payment arrangements are also verified at this stage; if full payment does not accompany the tender, auction staff check that an autocharge agreement or a guarantee from a commercial bank or primary dealer of 5% of the par amount tendered is on file for the bidder if it is not a depository institution with a funds account.

At each Federal Reserve bank, competitive tenders are manually sorted by rates or yields. The tenders are checked to ensure that those received at one rate/yield from any one bidder do not exceed 35% of the public offering. Bidders who have tendered for over 35% of the public offering at one yield have these bid amounts cut back to the 35% maximum. Bidders that have indicated a net long position greater than $200 million in the auctioned security are noted at this stage. Noncompetitive tenders are totaled, and an initial check is made to ensure that noncompetitive bids would not exceed the award limits for a single bidder. A second, more thorough check for compliance with the Treasury's single bidder guidelines is made after the noncompetitive totals have been transmitted to the Treasury in the interest of timely auction processing.

OECD Countries: Techniques to Sell Central Government Debt Internally

General comments	Auction	Other sale methods
Australia		
The treasury is responsible for government debt management and the Reserve Bank of Australia is its fiscal agent. There is no permanent lending by the RBA to the government although a short-term overdraft facility at market-related interest rates is available. Australia had surpluses in FYs 1988–91 (ended 6/30/91). This year the economy has been in recession, and a deficit of U.S. $8.4 billion equivalent is estimated in the 1991–92 budget.	All government securities have been sold through *multiple-yield auctions* since 1982. Bids are accepted from parties registered for this purpose with RBA. Any potential bidder that can establish its financial capability can bid without deposit. The minimum competitive bid is U.S. $77,800 equivalent.	Australian government savings bonds were issued on tap until 1987. The government no longer issues bonds targeted specifically at household savings.
		The RBA stands ready to fill small orders for marketable government securities (U.S. $780 to U.S. $39,000 equivalent) from its own portfolio at a price prevailing in the market, plus a small service charge. Small amounts can be sold to the RBA under the same terms.
The types of debt instruments issued are: short-term notes (5-, 13-, and 26-week maturities) sold weekly, and short- (1 to 3 years), medium- (3 to 5 years), and long-term (over 5 years) bonds. Australian government securities are in book-entry form.	No limit is set on awards to one entity, nor is there any restriction on the number of bids any entity can submit. Usually reopen outstanding issues rather than issuing new ones. Bids usually amount to 3 to 4 times the amount offered. There is no when-issued trading.	From time to time the government, through RBA, has repurchased outstanding bonds for cancellation or has exchanged current issues for older bonds to improve the overall liquidity of the market.
There are two groups of authorized dealers, with which RBA conducts open market operations. First, 8 "authorized short-term money-market dealers" have a contractual relationship with RBA to provide liquidity to the government securities market. RBA conducts most open market operations through short-term market makers. Second, there are 18 "reporting bond dealers" through which RBA conducts OMO in bonds. The reporting bond dealers have no privileges or obligations regarding issuance of government debt. The government securities market is informally regulated by the RBA		

OECD Countries (*continued*)

General comments	Auction	Other sale methods
Belgium The Ministry of Finance is responsible for public debt management, and the National Bank of Belgium is its fiscal agent. The government may borrow up to U.S. $485 million equivalent for day-to-day cash management from NBB. In FY 1990 (ended 12/31/90) the budget deficit totaled U.S. $12.69 billion equivalent. The types of debt instruments issued are: short-term bills (3-, 6-, and 12-month), long-term public subscription bonds and "linear" bonds maturing in 3 to 15 years. The bills and linear bonds are issued in book-entry form to institutional investors and dealers. Public subscription bonds are in paper form. Most trading is on stock exchanges. The MOF has selected 14 primary dealers to bid in auctions and make secondary markets in short-term bills and linear bonds. Immediately after an auction, they have the sole right to purchase, on a noncompetitive basis at the auction average, additional amounts of the securities. Primary dealers and other intermediaries may be used by NBB to conduct open market operations. The Securities Regulation Fund, established under the authority of the MOF and the NBB, regulates participants in the government securities market.	Short-term certificates and "linear" bonds have been sold by *multiple-yield auctions* since January 1991. Linear bonds are issued monthly as reopenings of bonds with the same maturity, interest rate, and identifying number. Bids are accepted without deposit from parties registered for this purpose with the NBB. No limit is placed on awards to any one entity, nor is there a limit on the number of bids that can be submitted. The minimum bid is for U.S. $322,000 equivalent for bills and U.S. $1.6 million equivalent for linear bonds. There is no when-issued trading prior to the auction.	Long-term public subscription bonds are sold 3 or 4 times per year. The coupon and maturity are set by the MOF and subscriptions are taken for about 2 weeks. The bonds are targeted to smaller investors. The minimum purchase amount is U.S. $322 equivalent. MOF pays banks a commission for selling them to the public.

Canada

The Department of Finance is responsible for debt management, and works closely with its fiscal agent, the Bank of Canada, to develop policy. The budget deficit has been stable at about U.S. $26 billion equivalent for the last 5 years

Bonds are bullet maturities with fixed rates and are redeemable at maturity. Bonds mature in 2 to 30 years. Canada auctions each week 3- and 6-month bills and year bills. About 90% of bonds are in book-entry form in the Canadian Depository for Securities. Bills are in bearer paper form.

Marketable government bonds are sold only to a group of primary distributors, including commercial banks (5) and investment dealers (55). Primary distributors and all Canadian banks can bid for bills. The Bank of Canada conducts open market operations through 10 jobbers, a subset of the primary distributors. Most trading is over the counter, although some is done through securities exchanges.

Bank dealers in government securities are regulated by the Canadian federal banking regulator. Other government securities dealers are regulated by provincial securities commissions, the key one of which is the Securities Commission of Ontario.

Canada began selling index-linked bonds in November 1991.

About 3/4 of marketable bonds and all short-term bills are sold in *multiple-yield auctions*. Awards, including awards for customers, are limited to 20% of amount offered of bonds and one-third of the amount offered of bills. When-issued trading begins when an issue is announced for auction. No commissions are paid for bonds and bills sold by auction. Canada is moving toward using auctions to sell all marketable securities.

Fixed-price subscription offerings are used for about 1/4 of marketable bonds; the coupon and price are announced 1 1/2 days before the deadline for subscriptions. The Bank of Canada buys any portion of an issue that the primary distributors do not buy. A commission is paid on bonds sold via the syndicate.

Canadian savings bonds are sold and the outstanding stock is also repriced each October. They are puttable at any time with accrued interest. Fees are paid for sale and processing of Canada Savings Bonds.

OECD Countries (*continued*)

General comments	Auction	Other sale methods
Denmark		
Debt management is the responsibility of the Ministry of Finance, with the central bank as fiscal agent. The budget deficit has widened in recent years, and is estimated at U.S. $6.5 billion equivalent in 1991. The government has a cash account with the central bank, which makes it possible for government borrowing to lead or lag the government's borrowing needs.	Domestically, bills are sold through *uniform-price auction* quarterly. Also, the central bank purchases them and sells them on tap. Banks and nonbank dealers that are connected to the Danish Securities Center, a private nonprofit depository clearance and settlement system, can submit bids in auctions. There is no limit on awards to a single bidder. Trading is not permitted prior to the auction.	Treasury notes and bonds are sold on tap. New issues are sold by the central bank through the Stock Exchange. Banks and security brokers accept applications which are passed on to the Stock Exchange like orders for secondary market purchases. The National Bank, acting on behalf of the Treasury, may set new issue yield at its discretion during Stock Exchange sessions. A new note issue is usually sold on tap for 9 months after original issue. There are no regulations as to the length of the tap period for bonds. There is a tax-related minimum interest rate rule, which may require closing a tap issue if market yields rise.
Main types of securities issued to the public are: fixed and floating rate bonds (5–10 years); notes (1.1 to 2.2 years); and bills (3 and 6 months). Government securities are in book-entry form.		
In the domestic market there are no primary dealers or private underwriters for government bonds. Trading is over the counter and through the Copenhagen Stock Exchange. The government borrows in foreign currencies abroad for exchange stabilization purposes and uses underwriting syndicates to place the securities. Foreign investors participate in the domestic market.		
The central bank conducts open market operations through the Copenhagen Stock Exchange. Participants in the government securities market are regulated by the Supervisory Authority of Financial Affairs.		

France

The Ministry of the Economy and Finance is responsible for debt management, and the Bank of France is its fiscal agent. Budget deficits widened in the 1980s, and the deficit amounted to U.S. $18.4 billion equivalent in 1990. The Bank of France does not lend directly to the government.

The Treasury has selected 15 primary dealers (SVTs) that are responsible for bidding in auctions, making markets, and providing screen quotations to the public. There are also 2 reporting dealers (CVTs). The primary dealers established an interdealer broker in 1987; only SVTs and CVTs have access to it. The Bank of France executes open market operations through a group of 26 interbank market agents that are selected separately by the Bank.

All marketable securities are in book-entry form. Participants in Treasury auctions must have an account at the Bank of France or bid through an institution that has an account at the Bank of France. Secondary market trading is over the counter. The government does not pay commissions to purchasers of marketable securities. Bank participants in the government securities market are regulated by the Banking Commission. The Stock Exchange Operations Commission supervises other participants in the government securities market.

Multiple-price auctions are used to sell coupon securities which pay interest annually and principal at maturity. The "fungible" OAT bond, which is the most important security from the standpoints of new issues and trading, matures in 4–30 years and is reopened in new tranches to increase the size of each issue and enhance liquidity. Until mid-day the day after an auction, each SVT is permitted to submit noncompetitive bids for the most recently auctioned OAT bond at the auction average price in an amount up to 30% of its average awards in the previous 3 OAT bond auctions. The minimum purchase in the auction is U.S. $9.8 million equivalent. The Treasury also auctions 2-year and 5-year fixed rate bonds in a minimum of U.S. $196,000 equivalent.

Multiple-rate auctions are used to sell short-term bills (maturing in 13, 26, and 52 weeks) issued at a discount. The minimum purchase amount in the auction is U.S. $196,000 equivalent.

When-issued trading begins when a security is announced.

There are U.S. $5.9 billion equivalent of 5-year nonmarketable savings bonds outstanding. No effort is made to promote sales of savings bonds.

OECD Countries (*continued*)

General comments	Auction	Other sale methods
Germany Ministry of Finance is the issuer and Bundesbank is its fiscal agent. German budget deficits have been widening in recent years, and in FY 1991 is estimated at U.S. $40.0 billion equivalent. Temporary cash advances of up to U.S. $4 billion equivalent are regularly made from the Bundesbank to the government.	Medium-term notes, mostly with 4 years to maturity, have been sold in *multiple-price auctions* since May 1991. A portion of each sale of Bunds has been auctioned since 1990. When-issued trading begins with the announcement of an auction. There is no limit on awards to any one entity. There is no commission paid to entities that are awarded securities in an auction.	Bunds usually have 10 years to maturity. Since July 1990, Bunds have been sold in 3-part sales: (1) negotiated through syndicate, 32%; (2) *multiple-price auctions*, 39%; and (3) Bundesbank market-tending portion, 29%, distributed when the price is favorable to the government. Syndicate allocations have been based on auction awards since October 1991. Commissions are paid to the syndicate for the underwritten portion of securities and those sold on tap.
The most important debt instruments are longer-term bonds, called Bunds, and 5-year special notes. Very little financing is done in short-term maturities under 1 year. All new public debt is in book-entry form.		5-year special notes are issued on tap only to individuals and charitable organizations; when an issue is completed, it is traded in the secondary market.
A 110-member consortium of banks (including 49 affiliated with foreign banks) comprise the syndicate for negotiated placements and the eligible bidders in auctions. Consortium members are selected by the Bundesbank, acting as MOF's agent. The consortium members are also used by the Bundesbank to execute open market operations and to sell government securities on tap. Noncompetitive bidding is through consortium members.		Private placements of short-term paper have been used in the past, but were not done in 1991.
Public debt securities are traded on stock exchanges. The Federal Banking Supervisory Office licenses all entities that trade securities for the accounts of third parties. The eight regional stock exchanges, which are under the supervision of the state (Laender) governments, are SROs and have broad authority to regulate market participants and trading.		

Italy

The Treasury Ministry is responsible for debt management and the Bank of Italy is its fiscal agent. Italian budget deficits widened in the 1980s, and the deficit was the equivalent of U.S. $128.4 billion in 1990. The government may borrow directly from the Bank of Italy. Only 4% of the public debt is foreign-owned.

The government issues: short-term Treasury bills in lire and in ECU; medium- and long-term variable and fixed-rate bonds in lire and ECU. Short-term bills and longer-term bonds indexed to short-term rates account for over 70% of the public debt. The longest maturity is 10 years. More than 90% of marketable government securities are in book-entry form through the Central Depository System run by the Bank of Italy.

Most trading is on a wholesale screen-based market, whose participants are regulated by the Bank of Italy. There are 23 primary dealers selected by the Bank of Italy, which uses them together with other market participants to execute open market operations.

Membership in the screen-based market is voluntary. There are entities acting as dealers that are not subject to any regulatory regime.

Short-term bills denominated in lire are auctioned in *multiple-price auctions*. The Treasury sets no minimum acceptable price for *multiple-price auctions*. The Treasury sets no minimum acceptable price for *multiple-price auctions*. A set amount is reserved for noncompetitive awards. Treasury bills denominated in ECU are sold in *uniform-yield auctions*. Treasury bonds in lire and ECU maturing in 5 to 10 years are sold in *uniform-price auctions*. The government sets the maximum acceptable yield (minimum price) in *uniform yield/price auctions*.

Trading begins when new security issues are announced by the Treasury. Minimum competitive bids in all auctions are U.S. $88,550 equivalent of lire or U.S. $73,350 equivalent ECU. While there is no cap on the value of awards, no entity may submit more than 5 bids per auction. Noncompetitive bids are not accepted in uniform price/yield auctions. Participation in the auction is limited to banks, credit institutions, insurance and financial companies, and stockbrokers.

About 9% of the public debt is in the form of small investor savings certificates and deposits in the Post Office System. Once a significant contributor to public financing, this system has declined in importance in recent years.

OECD Countries (*continued*)

General comments	Auction	Other sale methods
Japan The Ministry of Finance is responsible for debt management and the Bank of Japan is its fiscal agent. Budget deficits have been declining since the mid-1980s. The 1990 deficit was U.S. $22.5 billion equivalent. The Japanese government bond market is the second largest in the world. Most trading is in an OTC market, though some transactions are on the eight stock exchanges. About one-third of OTC trading volume is done through one brokers' broker, which is owned by its members. MOF sells short-term bills and intermediate- and long-term bonds. Monthly sales of 10-year bonds account for 80% of government debt outstanding and are the most actively traded issues in the secondary market. All marketable Japanese bonds are in book-entry form. There are no firms designated as primary dealers, although the market and the underwriting group are dominated by several large participants. The Bank of Japan uses several brokers, which are not part of the underwriting syndicate, as intermediaries to execute open market operations. The government securities market is regulated by the Ministry of Finance.	*Multiple-price auctions* are used for securities maturing in 2, 3, and 6 months and 2, 3, 4, and 20 years. When-issued trading is illegal at any price prior to the auction and is illegal at a discount in the immediate postauction period. For 10-year bonds, 60% are awarded in *multiple-price auctions* and 40% are distributed through an 833-member syndicate (includes 675 banks and 158 securities firms). Awards are limited to 30% of amount auctioned; thus, 18% of the total of a 10-year. The government pays commissions to purchases in the auction and to the underwriting syndicate.	The remaining 40% of each 10-year bond is sold through the syndicate, which obtains the bonds at the average of accepted competitive tenders. 5-year bonds are placed fully through the underwriting syndicate, but comprise only a small proportion of total issues. Government compensation bonds to war-surviving families. Such nonmarketable bonds account for only about 1% of government bonds outstanding.

Netherlands

The Ministry of Finance is responsible for debt management and the central bank is its fiscal agent. Budget deficits have been declining since the mid-1980s. The deficit amounted to U.S. $12.8 billion equivalent in FY 1991. The central bank may lend temporarily directly to the government in limited amounts. It also purchases government securities through open market operations. The MOF often purchases and sells government bonds to stabilize prices.

Bonds maturing in 10 years accounted for 75% of MOF borrowing in 1990/91. Short-term bills were not sold in 1990/91. Subscriptions on original issue are limited exclusively to members of the Amsterdam Stock Exchange (banks and securities broker/dealers). Foreign investors hold 23% of Netherlands government securities. MOF emphasizes debt lengthening and does not borrow in foreign currencies or sell indexed or variable rate securities.

Government securities are available in bearer definitive and registered forms.

There are no primary dealers. The market for government securities is regulated by the Amsterdam Stock Exchange.

During the late 1980s through early 1991, MOF sold bonds in *multiple-yield auctions*. Since March 1991, however, government bonds have been sold on tap exclusively.

Bonds are all sold on tap. An issue stays open for 1 or 2 weeks. There may be when-issued trading before the issue is closed. The government may change the price during the tap period. No fees are paid by MOF to subscribers to tap issues. The minimum purchase amount is U.S. $1.5 million equivalent.

Private placements of long-term bonds account for most of the rest of government borrowing. Intermediaries in private placements receive fees from the MOF.

Nonmarketable savings bonds are not offered by the government.

OECD Countries (*continued*)

General comments	Auction	Other sale methods
New Zealand The Treasury is responsible for debt management and the Reserve Bank of New Zealand is its fiscal agent for internal borrowing. New Zealand had surpluses in FYs 1988–90 and a surplus of U.S. $1.0 billion equivalent in 1991. Nearly half of the debt is owned by foreign investors. The government may borrow from RBNZ.	All marketable securities are sold in *multiple-yield auctions*. There is no limit on the proportion of an auction that can be purchased by any bidder. When-issued trading begins when a security is announced. No commissions are paid by the Treasury to purchasers in auctions. The government does not set a maximum acceptable yield.	Nonmarketable Kiwi bonds are sold to retail investors on tap. They are puttable at a discount, and the minimum purchase is U.S. $600 equivalent. Fees are paid to institutions that handle Kiwi bond transactions. Kiwi bonds account for 3% of internal public debt.
Securities include short-term bills (32% of internal public debt) and government stock maturing in up to 10 years (57% of internal public debt). Outstanding issues are reopened to foster market liquidity.		
All bidders in auctions must be registered with the RBNZ or bid through an entity that is registered. The RBNZ conducts open market operations, including issuing 63-day RBNZ bills, through dealers that are registered with RBNZ as counterparties for open market operations. There are no primary dealers. All marketable debt is in book-entry form. Tenders in auctions are in paper form.		
There is no specific regulation of the government securities market. The RBNZ provides prudential regulation of banks.		

Switzerland

The Federal Department of Finance is responsible for debt management and Swiss National Bank is its fiscal agent. The Swiss central government borrows little and the public debt is small. Most governmental activity is carried out by the cantons, or states. Foreign participation in the government securities market is unknown, because all securities are in bearer form.

There are no primary dealers. The Swiss central bank rarely conducts open market operations.

The government issues a variety of securities, including 3- and 6-month bills, medium-term notes, and long-term bonds.

Trading is over the counter and through regional stock exchanges. There is no comprehensive government securities regulation. Banks are subject to the supervision of the Federal Banking Commission. The cantons regulate the regional stock exchanges. The cantons of Zurich and Basel, where the most important financial centers are located, license over-the-counter market participants as well as exchange participants.

Swiss Debt Register Claims maturing in 3 and 6 months are issued every 2 weeks through *uniform-price auctions*. Long-term bonds, which account for the majority of the debt, are sold from time to time through *uniform-price auctions*. No tender price limits are applied. The government gives a rough indication of the desired issue amount.

All categories of investors are authorized to participate in auctions. There are no limits on the amount that can be awarded to any bidder in an auction. When-issued trading is permitted prior to the auction. Noncompetitive bids are accepted, and usually are small relative to the size of auctions.

Bills usually with maturities of 3 to 24 months are sold on a discount basis only to commercial banks. The price is set by the central bank and banks subscribe for a fixed overall amount.

Government notes with maturities of 3 to 10 years are sold through private placements on a commission basis.

OECD Countries (*continued*)

General comments	Auction	Other sale methods
United Kingdom The Treasury works closely with the Bank of England (fiscal agent) to develop debt management policy. The budget has been in surplus in recent years, with the surplus in 1991 U.S. $960 million equivalent. The government borrows directly from the Bank of England.	*Multiple-price auctions* are used for bills and longer-term debt (gilts). When-issued trading is allowed, beginning with the announcement of auction details. Bank of England has discretion not to allot more than 25% of the amount offered to an individual bidder if to do so would be likely to lead to market price distortion. The Bank of England does not set a minimum price, but securities may not be allotted if the price is unacceptably low.	Bank of England buys gilts that remain unsold from minimum price tender sales; these are subsequently sold on tap to the GEMMs. Guiding principle is that the bank refrains from selling gilts into a falling market. There usually is a "fallow period" following an auction during which additional amounts are not sold on tap.
Bidding in gilt auctions is open to all investors, either on a competitive basis (minimum of U.S. $960,000 equivalent) or noncompetitive basis (bids from U.S. $1,920 to $960,000 equivalent). The bulk of bids are submitted by primary dealers (18 gilt-edged market makers) either on behalf of customers or for their own account. The GEMMs ensure the liquidity of the secondary market by quoting continuous two-way prices in all gilts in all trading conditions; they have a direct dealing relationship with the Bank of England and exclusive access to interdealer brokers and gilt borrowing facilities.	*Minimum price tender* sales are used to sell gilts; bidding is open to all investors. The minimum price is set in advance for fixed-rate gilts. Gilts are allotted at a common price, either minimum price or price at which all gilts offered are sold (if higher). Tenders for index-linked stocks normally have no minimum price, but authorities do not usually allot at a price that they perceive to be below market. Any unsold gilts are bought by the Bank of England for sale on tap to GEMMs.	Gilts can be issued and placed directly with the Bank of England for sale to the GEMMs, in exactly the same way as above. Usually, in the form of *tranchettes* (small additional amounts of existing stocks), but sometimes in larger amounts. Nonmarketable savings instruments are sold to individual investors through post offices.
Participants in the gilt-edged market are subject to prudential supervision of the Bank of England. The Securities Investment Board, which is under the Department of Trade and Industry, oversees protection of investors.		

Competitive bid totals are posted by yield to an auction summary report, together with the noncompetitive total.* While specific bids are generally not reported separately in the summaries, the tenders of bidders with net long positions greater than $200 million are recorded on the auction summary report if the tenders suggest that the entity might receive 35% of the auction after including the pre-auction position and noncompetitive bids.† The tenders of bidders who have tendered for an aggregate total of more than 35% of the public offering are noted on the report. In addition, any tenders for more than 35% of the public offering at one yield from a single bidder (that have been reduced to the allowable bidding limit) are noted.

At each Federal Reserve bank, the auction summary report is signed by an authorized employee and transmitted by facsimile to the Treasury Department's Bureau of the Public Debt. At the Bureau of the Public Debt, the auction summary information is manually entered into an automated auction program, which computes the range of accepted bids based on the yields tendered by competitive bidders and the total amount of noncompetitive awards. The weighted average accepted yield for competitive tenders and any proration necessary at the stop-out (or highest accepted) yield, as well as supplementary auction statistics, are also computed. Two computers are used for verification purposes, both of which independently compute the auction statistics from the summary data. Manual backup procedures are also provided for additional flexibility. The appropriate Federal Reserve banks are contacted if the summaries are incomplete or if there are questions about particular tenders. Any questions regarding the 35% award limitation to a single bidder or the noncompetitive award limitations are also resolved before finalizing the auction results.

After reviewing the auction results, the Bureau of the Public Debt prepares the press release containing the information on the range of accepted bids, proration at the stop-out yield, and other pertinent auction statistics. This press release is transmitted to the Treasury press room and released to the public at approximately 2:00 P.M. on the day of the auction.

Between the auction date and the settlement date (usually about 5 days) the tender and award information necessary for issuing securities to successful bidders is manually entered into a computer system that processes securities issued in the commercial book-entry system and in the TREASURY DIRECT system. On the settlement date, the securities are issued against payment.

B. The Automation Project

1. Strategy and Project Scope

The strategy for automating the auction process is first to automate the current auction process in order to move auction participants and administrators from the current manual process to an electronic, automated environment. The system-development phase of this effort is currently being conducted at two Federal Reserve banks, as fiscal agents of the Treasury. The Federal Reserve Bank of Kansas City is nearing completion on one phase of the project, described below. The core of the project is a centralized tender receiving and processing computer system called the Treasury Automated Auction Processing System (TAAPS), which is under development at the Federal Reserve Bank of New York.

The first two phases are scheduled to be completed by the end of 1992. At that time, a telecommunications infrastructure will be in place, all participants will have the necessary terminal and communications equipment to submit tenders electronically, and the Federal Reserve banks and the Treasury will have the capability to process electronic tenders. Once this is accomplished, it will be possible to implement the open, iterative, ascending-price auction process described elsewhere in this report by modifying the operation of the existing system. The design requirements for this new auction process are still being formulated.

The automation project can be thought of as having four phases, as outlined below. The elements of each phase are described in more detail later in this section.

Phase 1: The electronic acceptance and processing of bids submitted nationwide by smaller bidders and depository institutions
Phase 2: The electronic acceptance and processing of bids submitted nationwide by large aggressive bidders
Phase 3: The automation of the Treasury's auction procedures on the centralized processing system

---

*Additional noncompetitive tenders may arrive by mail after this time.
†With this report, the Treasury is announcing that bidders may not submit both competitive and noncompetitive tenders in one auction.

Phase 4: Automation and centralization of issuance of securities to successful bidders through the commercial book-entry system

2. Electronic Bidding Systems

Completion of Phases I and II will allow bidders to submit tenders from a "Standard FedLine" connection, a "FaST FedLine" connection, or computer interface (CI) connections that meet the Federal Reserve System's Computer Interface Protocol Specifications standards.

The Standard FedLine is a software and communication application project that is ongoing at the Federal Reserve Bank of Kansas City. This system will provide a capability principally for smaller bidders and depository institutions to submit electronic tenders using a standard Federal Reserve System terminal for securities to be held in both the commercial book-entry and TREASURY DIRECT systems. This project is scheduled for completion by mid-1992.

The FaST FedLine is a software and communications application being developed at the FRBNY, as part of TAAPS, that is designed for use by large competitive bidders. Large competitive bidders require the capability to submit bids quickly in the last seconds before an auction closes on their own behalf and on behalf of their customers. The FaST FedLine software application, which will run on a personal computer, is being developed to meet these specialized requirements.

FaST FedLine terminals will be linked by telephone to the central TAAPS computer. When the Treasury announces an issue, a broadcast message will be sent to all FedLine terminals announcing the auction, and a description of the security, including issue date and maturity date, will be downloaded to the FaST FedLine terminals. At any time prior to the auction closing time, a bidder will complete an electronic copy of a tender form for the particular auction containing empty "fields" for security description, clearing bank information, and customer information. The bidder will be able to quickly fill in the FaST FedLine fields using "pop-up" menus linked to the bidder's database. The bidder will also be required to fill in a net long position field if necessary. The bidder will then be able to transmit the tender to the central computer at the FRBNY within seconds.

3. Tender Acceptance

The central TAAPS host computer application will receive and process electronic tenders from the Standard FedLine, the FaST FedLine, and CI connections. It will also provide a mechanism for inputting data from paper tenders submitted to Federal Reserve banks over the counter and via mail. Though processing will be centralized, Federal Reserve districts will continue to serve their current customer base and maintain primary control of tenders submitted by their customers. Districts will continue to be responsible for reviewing their tenders and oversight of original issue processing for their district; the centralized system will be a vehicle for supporting these operations.

While Fast FedLine terminals will have direct communications connections with the TAAPS host computer at the FRBNY, Standard FedLine tenders will be routed through the Federal Reserve banks. All tenders and customer lists from submitting institutions will be printed upon receipt at the Federal Reserve bank and stored in a machine-readable format. Additionally, submitting institutions will receive an acknowledgment indicating the tender was received. Once TAAPS is operational, a "tender-forwarding" capability will be implemented to transmit all Standard FedLine tenders through the Federal Reserve's communication network to the TAAPS computer for centralized processing.

Once transmitted to the FRBNY, the electronic tenders will be stored at the primary computer and also at the contingency processing site at the East Rutherford Operations Center (EROC). Should there be a failure at the FRBNY computer, or communications failure of any kind, the FaST FedLine users will reestablish a communications connection with the EROC and continue transmitting tenders. It is expected that this recovery could be accomplished in less than 5 minutes. If FRBNY's primary centralized processing system fails, Standard FedLine users will have their electronic tender submission capability restored by establishing communications between the local Federal Reserve bank's computer and the contingency site at the EROC. This recovery is expected to take 30 to 45 minutes. If the local Federal Reserve bank's computer fails, Standard FedLine users will use manual backup procedures to submit their bids. To support contingency processing, the system's operators will be able to reassign a district's processing responsibilities to another district. For example, if Minneapolis were unable to process its tenders, Chicago could be reassigned to perform this function.

4. Tender Processing

As tenders are transmitted to the central computer, a series of checks will automatically be performed on them. As a result, each tender will be added to one of two tender databases. The tenders that successfully pass all checks will be added to the "good" database; tenders that fail one or more checks will be added to the "questionable" database. TAAPS will send a message to each bidder's terminal advising the bidder that the tender has been received and stored and informing the bidder which checks, if any, the tender failed.

Some of these checks will simply involve examining the tender to determine whether all required information has been included in the tender and that tenders were received before the designated closing time. Some of the checks will require TAAPS to search its database of bidder information to determine that, for example, bids submitted on behalf of customers have been authorized and payment arrangements have been made. TAAPS will also flag any tenders that may require auction rule enforcement. This would include bids for more than 35% of the public offering at one yield, bids from related entities, and tenders submitted by one entity through multiple broker-dealers or depository institutions.

In order to screen bids for obvious data-entry errors, the TAAPS system will flag tenders that exceed a par amount that is a predetermined percentage above an amount based upon the bidder's prior submissions, and bids at a rate or yield that exceeds a predetermined band on either side of the when-issued market for that security. This type of monitoring should catch errors such as a bid for a yield of 7.08% instead of 8.08%, or for $5 billion instead of $5 million.

All flagged bids will be reviewed by Federal Reserve bank staff. After consultation with the bidder and with the Treasury in these cases, the auction staff will have the ability—with the Treasury's approval—to correct obvious keying errors (or allow the bidders to submit corrected tenders), reject questionable bids, or return them to the good database. Any tender that is changed must be reviewed and approved by the appropriate officials before being included in the auction, and complete documentation of these changes will be maintained.

After the process of reviewing tenders and resolving any questions is complete, the Treasury will be notified that district-level processing of tenders is complete. The Treasury auction staff will then execute a program that will use the information in the good tender database, aggregated by yield, to calculate the range of accepted bids and all relevant auction statistics. The Treasury will review the results, and then broadcast the auction results to all FedLine users and simultaneously issue a public press release.

Successful bidders in the auction will be notified of their awards via a message to their FedLine terminals. The TAAPS system will instruct the commercial book-entry system to issue the securities against payment to the successful bidders on the issue's settlement date. TAAPS will also be able to accommodate the requirements of the new commercial book-entry system being implemented in the next few years.

C. Automation Benefits

1. Speed and Productivity Improvements

The current process is labor intensive at all stages of the auction for the Treasury, the Federal Reserve banks, and the bidders. Automation should allow fewer people to conduct the auctions faster, as it will reduce significantly the amount of time devoted to manually entering data from tender forms, both for auction processing and for original issue of the securities. Bidders will be afforded the ease and convenience of electronic bidding, and savings will result for some bidders from eliminating the need to send messengers to submit tenders.

Electronic bidding should also reduce bidding errors. Bids communicated over a telephone and hastily transcribed by a messenger at the last moment may be inaccurate, illegible, or difficult to interpret. Bids entered at a terminal will not have these problems. While different types of errors, such as keying errors, may be introduced, the automatic screening procedures described above should mitigate these problems.

2. Wider Participation in the Auctions

Over 9,000 depository institutions have FedLine terminals connected to their local Federal Reserve banks. Upon completion of the project for electronic bidding by depository institutions, all of these institutions will have the capability of electronically submitting competitive and noncompetitive bids for securities to be held in either the commercial book-entry or TREASURY DIRECT systems. Registered brokers and dealers and other large bidders will have the opportunity to install computer terminals for auction bidding purposes.

Depository institutions with FedLine terminals—particularly those in remote locations—may find it easier and more convenient to submit electronic bids on behalf of TREASURY DIRECT participants than it is with current procedures.

3.   More Efficient Monitoring of the Auction Rules

TAAPS will be able to collect, organize, and present information quickly about potential or actual rule violations to Federal Reserve bank and Treasury staff reviewing bids. For example, the computer will be able to sort tenders and customer lists by name independently of the dealer or depository institution through which the bids were submitted. This will make it easier to aggregate bids of related entities or of customers that bid through several dealers or depository institutions, which will facilitate enforcement of the 35% bid and award limitations and the noncompetitive award limitations.

4.   Standardized Auction Procedures

With standard Federal Reserve terminals, standard FedLine applications, and centralized processing, all bidders and districts will have the same screens and procedures for submitting and processing tenders. Use of standard Federal Reserve terminals and communications facilities allows the use of existing mechanisms for distributing and supporting terminals, and the use of existing and planned Federal Reserve backup sites, systems, and arrangements.

IV.   AUCTION RULE ENFORCEMENT

The Treasury's longstanding policies of encouraging widespread ownership of Treasury securities and limiting concentration of awards at auctions have led to the two primary auction rules, or policies: the 35% limitation of overall awards to a single bidder and the total dollar limitations on noncompetitive bidding.

Recent events, as well as the Treasury's examination of auction activity in light of disclosures by Salomon Brothers Inc. ("Salomon"), have resulted in certain abuses and enforcement problems being uncovered regarding each of these rules. This section discusses the enforcement of current Treasury auction rules, including identified problems, possible causes, and potential solutions. Further discussion of policies that might address these issues, such as changes to auction rules and techniques, is contained in other sections of this chapter.

A.   The 35% Limitation

The 35% limitation on awards to single bidders in an auction is designed to prevent excessive concentration of ownership of a particular Treasury security as a result of an auction. A limitation of this kind has been in effect since 1962. Since July 1990, an additional Treasury rule has been in effect that limits the amount Treasury will recognize as bid by a single bidder at a single yield to 35% of the public offering.*

Contrary to what is commonly suggested, the Treasury does not prohibit tenders for more than 35% of a particular auction amount or require bidders to certify that they have not done so.† The Treasury has, however, stated that bids at one yield for more than 35% of the public offering amount at any auction from a single bidder will be recognized only up to the 35% limit, and that the Treasury will not award more than 35% of the public offering amount to a single entity. While this policy encourages bidders to limit their bids voluntarily, it places a substantial degree of enforcement responsibility on the Treasury and the Federal Reserve banks that act as the Treasury's fiscal agents in conducting the auctions and referring any potential problems to the Treasury.

In addition, the Treasury requires bidders to certify on the auction tender form that the bidder's or customer's net long position in the securities auctioned does not exceed $200 million or to report on the form

---

*This rule was a response to a strategy in which bidders would attempt to increase their prorated awards at the highest accepted yield in an auction. Large bidders would place bids well in excess of 35% of the public offering amount at what they guessed to be the highest accepted yield, assuming that they would be awarded some fraction of this account. This strategy disadvantaged other bidders who could not risk being awarded much more of the securities than they intended to purchase.

†In fact, for Treasury bills, it is possible for bidders to know precisely what the public offering amount will be prior to the announcement of the auction results.

any net long position of more than $200 million as of 12:30 P.M. on the day of the auction, one-half hour before the closing time for receipt of competitive tenders.* This requirement was designed to aid in the administration of the 35% limitation, allowing the Treasury to aggregate bidders' existing net long positions with potential auction awards in determining the maximum securities awarded to a particular entity. In recent years, the Treasury has reduced awards based on bidder's long positions in a number of auctions, although such action has not often been necessary.

1. Problems and Abuses

The Treasury's enforcement of the 35% limitation on auction awards has generally been effective. The unauthorized customer bids submitted by Salomon that allowed it to purchase more than 35% in several Treasury auctions are the only instances of which the Treasury is aware since the 35% limitation has been in place in which a single bidder was awarded more than 35% of the publicly offered auction amount.

In the widely publicized Salomon case, several of the unauthorized bids submitted for customers by Salomon resulted in awards to Salomon in excess of 35% of the public offering amount. These include the February 21, 1991 5-year note auction, in which Salomon bought 57% of the notes through a bid for itself and two unauthorized bids in customer names, and the May 22, 1991 2-year note auction, in which Salomon effectively purchased 38% of the auctioned notes. Salomon has also admitted that it failed to report a sizeable long when-issued position in the May 1991 2-year note auction.[†] Had the position been duly reported, the amount awarded would have been reduced by the amount of the long position.

B. The Noncompetitive Award Limitation

Securities awarded noncompetitively earn a yield equal to the weighted average yield of accepted competitive bids. Bidding noncompetitively assures an investor of receiving a desired amount of securities, with a market-based yield determined by the auction results. The noncompetitive award process was designed for smaller investors that do not have the resources or information to bid competitively. Noncompetitive bidding was never intended to serve as a substitute for competitive bidding by sophisticated and large bidders who have the resources, knowledge, and expertise to bid competitively. For this reason, and because the Treasury desires a predominantly competitive pricing system for its securities, noncompetitive awards to each bidder are limited. The noncompetitive award limits have changed over time and are currently $1 million for bills and $5 million for notes and bonds.

Every auction tender form states that noncompetitive tenders are not to exceed the specified amount allowable for a single bidder. In addition, the tender form indicates that a noncompetitive bidder may not have entered into an agreement with respect to noncompetitive awards prior to the closing time for receipt of tenders. This rule is intended to prevent an investor from obtaining more than the specified amount of securities at the average yield by arranging to acquire them from other investors who plan to bid non-competitively.

1. Problems and Abuses

There have been several instances of investors using noncompetitive awards for what appear to be arbitrage purposes. Market participants have discerned a tendency of prices of Treasury securities to be slightly higher than the average auction price immediately following the announcement of the auction results. This means that securities purchased noncompetitively at the average yield can be resold immediately after the announcement of the auction results in the when-issued market, often for a profit.

The pattern is similar in most of these cases that the Treasury has uncovered. An investment or trading firm submits bids for the maximum noncompetitive award in the names of a list of employees or customers. The bids are either pooled through a primary dealer, or spread throughout a number of different dealers. The securities are then resold immediately after the auction and before payment is acquired. Only if the securities

---

*With this report, Treasury is announcing that in order to reduce the reporting burden, it will not require bidders to report their net long positions at the time of the auction unless the total of the bidder's net long position plus its bid is greater than a significant amount of the auctioned issue.

[†]See *Statement of Salomon Inc.* submitted in conjunction with the testimony of Deryck C. Maughan, Chief Operating Offer of Salomon Brothers Inc. and Robert E. Denham, General Counsel of Salomon Inc. before the Subcommittee on Oversight, Committee on Ways and Means, United States House of Representatives, September 24, 1991.

are sold at a loss does the bidding entity require any payment from participants. However, in some cases, it may be that pool participants were actually required to put up a certain amount of margin toward the positions. Often the same list of participants is used repeatedly in different auctions.

The Treasury has investigated these schemes, and, in some cases, referred them to the SEC. Participants have maintained that they are not violating any specific auction rule, as they claim that all bids are properly authorized and that they have not made any pre-auction agreements regarding the securities. While the Treasury has not taken the position of prohibiting resale of noncompetitively awarded securities immediately following the auction, these activities do appear to have gone against the spirit of the noncompetitive award system, and, in some cases, may have violated the prohibition on pre-auction agreements.

In several other instances, related entities, such as multiple bank subsidiaries are branches within a single bank holding company, have submitted bids, either through the same dealer or through other dealers, that combined exceed the noncompetitive bidding limits. In most of these cases, the entities do not appear to have been acting in concert to garner a larger share of noncompetitive awards, but rather were probably unaware of their affiliates' auction activities. In several of these instances, the potential problem was detected by the Federal Reserve and Treasury auction staff, and auction awards were appropriately reduced to conform to the single-bidder limitations. However, there have also been a few instances in which Federal Reserve bank and Treasury staff were not aware of the multiple bids and therefore did not limit the combined awards as would be appropriate.

Another potential problem is that primary dealers often submit auction tenders for the maximum noncompetitive amount for their own accounts. Treasury has not rejected noncompetitive bids in these cases, even though primary dealers also bid competitively and often take pre-auction positions in the securities being auctioned.

C. Underlying Causes and Potential Solutions

Changes to the underlying auction technique or policies toward market "squeezes" could alleviate the problems discussed above because such changes would likely remove the benefits to evading either the 35% limitation or the noncompetitive limitation.* The major contributing factors to the enforcement problems and abuses under the current auction framework are discussed below.

1. Bidding by Related Entities

Despite the much-publicized Warburg/Mercury case, in which Salomon submitted an unauthorized bid in the name of an S. G. Warburg affiliate, the problem of bids from related entities has mainly arisen in the noncompetitive bidding area due to the thousands of noncompetitive bids that are submitted at each auction.

The wide array of corporate and partnership affiliations makes it difficult to determine which entities should be considered together as a single bidder for purposes of the 35% auction award and bidding limitations and the noncompetitive award limitation. A bank holding company, for example, may have numerous subsidiaries throughout the country that may not communicate with one another on a regular basis, and may submit bids through different Federal Reserve districts. Partnerships with essentially identical memberships and different family members are also considered to be a single bidder under the Treasury's guidelines.

To date, most single-bidder issues have been handled on a case-by-case basis, usually after the auction has taken place. More systematic enforcement of the single-bidder guidelines would require the Treasury and the Federal Reserve banks to maintain a comprehensive database of corporate affiliations that could be used as a ready reference tool.

2. Bidder Certifications

As mentioned previously, auction tender forms currently include several statements regarding noncompetitive purchases and a certification with respect to net long positions of bidders and their customers.

---

*Under a uniform-price auction method, for example, the Treasury would probably maintain the noncompetitive bidding mechanism, as would allow small investors to be assured of receiving the desired amount of securities. However, since all investors would receive the same yield, the incentives for noncompetitive relative to competitive bidding would be greatly reduced.

Treasury currently has no satisfactory way of independently verifying the position certifications. The prohibition against pre-auction agreements regarding noncompetitive awards has also required some clarification.

The Treasury is clarifying these issues in the new offering circular, which also should eliminate any current ambiguity as to the appropriate usage of noncompetitive awards. While the Treasury has traditionally maintained that covering short when- issued positions with noncompetitive awards violates the auction rules, the auction rules will further disallow noncompetitive awards to bidders who also bid competitively in a particular auction and who hold when-issued, futures, or forward positions in the security being auctioned. This policy change should ensure that the noncompetitive bidding privilege is not misused by sophisticated traders and dealers rather than smaller, less sophisticated investors.

3. Lack of Centralized Surveillance System

The auction bidding system is very decentralized, with tenders being submitted at many locations around the country. Much of the enforcement of the auction award limitations is administered at the Federal Reserve banks. There is currently no automated surveillance system in place that would capture all tender information and perform a timely and comprehensive check that any multiple bids by the same or related entities do not exceed the bidding and award limitations in the short span of time available between submission of tenders and announcement of results. As a result, surveillance and enforcement of bidding limitations is currently very labor and time intensive.

As discussed elsewhere in this report, electronic bidding and automation of the auction process will alleviate many of the operational problems in auction rule enforcement. Automation would allow nationwide policing of any single-bidder problems and verification of customer bids and would facilitate a rapid response to such problems by auction administrators.

In the meantime, the Treasury and the FRBNY have already implemented a policy of spot-checking large customer bids for authenticity. Because of the verification policies in place or currently being developed, it is less likely that circumvention of the 35% limit through unauthorized bidding will be a problem in the future. The Treasury and Federal Reserve staff have also strengthened the routine policing of any potential noncompetitive award problems.

V. CONCENTRATION OF AUCTION AWARDS

The Treasury has pursued policies over the years to make Treasury marketable securities available to a broad range of investors and to diminish the likelihood that ownership of the securities will be heavily concentrated as a result of Treasury auction awards. Treasury actions to broaden distribution of Treasury securities in the auction include limiting awards to any one bidder to 35% of the amount offered to the public and making marketable Treasury securities available on a noncompetitive basis. The Treasury offers securities across the maturity spectrum in order to appeal to a wide range of types of investors and to balance the maturity structure of the outstanding debt.

It is advantageous for the Treasury to distribute new marketable securities to a number of auction participants, rather than to allow any entity, even through competitive bidding, to obtain all or nearly all of a Treasury security. If there were a market perception that awards in Treasury auctions may be to only one or a few entities, over the longer term, other potential participants in Treasury auctions may be discouraged from submitting tenders and Treasury borrowing costs could rise. The ability of any investor to purchase Treasury securities on original issue, directly from the Treasury or through a government securities dealer, ensures that sales of Treasury securities are perceived as fair by market participants. Distribution of securities to a number of market participants also has the advantage that the securities may be sold to a broader customer base than would be the case if auction awards were more concentrated.

A. Statistical Evaluation of Concentration of Auction Awards

The primary dealers, as a group, purchase large proportions of Treasury securities in auctions. This is not surprising, since the primary dealers are the major market makers for Treasury securities and they focus their capital and expertise on trading government securities. The primary dealers are expected by the FRBNY to be "consistent and meaningful participant[s] in Treasury auctions of new securities."* This section of the study presents data on competitive awards to primary dealers, their customers, and other competitive and noncompetitive bidders for the period of January 1990 through the end of September 1991, using tenders submitted in Treasury auctions as the source of data. The data have been adjusted to count as awards to a primary dealer the awards on unauthorized bids submitted by Salomon.†

Primary dealers bidding for their own accounts were awarded about 72% of Treasury bills, notes, and bonds awarded to private investors during the January 1990 through September 1991 period.‡ (See Tables 2 and 3.) Auction awards to customers of primary dealers accounted for about 5% of private awards of Treasury bills and about 15% of notes and bonds. Noncompetitive awards accounted for 20% of Treasury bill auction awards to private investors on average but less than 9% of note and bond auction awards.

Awards in each auction were ranked as to amounts awarded to primary dealer firms and their customers. The top 10 firms and their customers combined took 50% of total private awards in bill auctions and 66% in note and bond auctions during the January 1990 through September 1991 period. (See Tables 4 and 5.)

One primary dealer and its customer were awarded 35% or more of the total offered to the public in 17 out of a total of 66 Treasury note and bond auctions. The 35% maximum was purchased by one primary dealer for its own account in 6 of the 66 auctions. Awards to the top three bidders (a primary dealer for its own account or another entity, not combined) averaged nearly 41% of total private awards in note and bond auctions between January 1990 and September 1991. (See Table 6.)

The figures on awards to primary dealers for their own accounts overstate the concentration of ownership of Treasury securities as a result of the auction, because primary dealers in the aggregate usually have large

---

*Federal Reserve Bank of New York, *Primary Dealers: Criteria and Procedures Applied to Firms Interested in Becoming and Remaining Primary Dealers*, 1988.
†See *Statement of Salomon Inc.* submitted in conjunction with the testimony of Warren E. Buffet, Chairman and Chief Executive Officer of Salomon Inc. before the Securities Subcommittee of the Senate Committee on Banking, Housing, and Urban Affairs, September 10, 1991.
‡Awards to private investors include awards on competitive and noncompetitive tenders and exclude noncompetitive awards to the Federal Reserve banks for the system open market account and official foreign custody accounts. Awards to foreign accounts held outside the Federal Reserve are included with awards to private investors.

Table 2 Awards in Treasury Bill Auctions, January 1990 Through September 1991 (millions of dollars)

| | Competitive | | | | | | |
	Primary dealer	P. dealer customer	Total	Other direct	Total comp.	Private noncomp.[a]	Total private
13-week	$428,186	$32,509	$460,695	$26,868	$487,563	$145,559	$633,122
26-week	417,449	24,998	442,447	14,421	456,868	114,895	571,763
52-week	154,753	11,008	165,761	7,895	173,656	19,789	193,445
Total	$1,000,388	$68,515	$1,068,903	$49,184	$1,118,087	$280,243	$1,398,330

Percent of Private Awards

| | Competitive | | | | | | |
	Primary dealer	P. dealer customer	Total	Other direct	Total comp.	Private noncomp.[a]	Total private
13-week	67.6%	5.1%	72.8%	4.2%	77.0%	23.0%	100.0%
26-week	73.0	4.4	77.4	2.5	79.9	20.1	100.0
52-week	80.0	5.7	85.7	4.1	89.9	10.2	100.0
Total	71.5%	4.9%	76.4%	3.5%	80.0%	20.0%	100.0%

Note: Based on auction date, not issue date. Excludes cash management bills.
[a]Excludes awards to foreign custody accounts and to the Federal Reserve for its own account.
Source: U.S. Treasury Department

Table 3 Awards in Treasury Note and Bond Auctions, January 1990 Through September 1991 (millions of dollars)

| | Competitive | | | | | | |
	Primary dealer	P. dealer customer	Total	Other direct	Total comp.	Private noncomp.[a]	Total private
2-year	$174,133	$32,769	$206,902	$20,406	$227,308	$29,389	$256,697
3-year	61,731	12,786	74,517	1,947	76,464	9,176	85,640
4-year	23,362	4,989	28,351	1,180	29,531	3,384	32,915
5-year	87,058	18,540	105,598	2,384	107,982	8,594	116,576
7-year	46,654	5,985	52,639	1,807	54,446	3,387	57,833
10-year	53,453	17,566	71,019	1,536	72,555	4,183	76,738
30-year	59,226	12,047	71,273	1,966	73,239	2,577	75,816
Total	$505,617	$104,682	$610,299	$31,226	$641,525	$60,690	$702,215

Percent of Private Awards

| | Competitive | | | | | | |
	Primary dealer	P. dealer customer	Total	Other direct	Total comp.	Private non-comp[a]	Total private
2-year	67.8%	12.8%	80.6%	7.9%	88.6%	11.4%	100.0%
3-year	72.1	14.9	87.0	2.3	89.3	10.7	100.0
4-year	71.0	15.2	86.1	3.6	89.7	10.3	100.0
5-year	74.7	15.9	90.6	2.0	92.6	7.4	100.0
7-year	80.7	10.3	91.0	3.1	94.1	5.9	100.0
10-year	69.7	22.9	92.5	2.0	94.5	5.5	100.0
30-year	78.1	15.9	94.0	2.6	96.6	3.4	100.0
Total	72.0%	14.9%	86.9%	4.4%	91.4%	8.6%	100.0%

Note: Based on auction date, not issue date.
[a]Excludes awards to foreign custody accounts and to the Federal Reserve for its own account.
Source: U.S. Treasury Department.

net short positions going into the auctions. Part of the primary dealers' market-making function is to distribute Treasury securities in the when-issued market prior to the auction. Primary dealers in the aggregate had net short positions prior to every auction of notes and bonds in the January 1990 through September 1991 period. Net short positions averaged nearly 40% of auction awards to primary dealers for their own accounts during that period. (See Table 7.)

B. Potential Ways to Lessen Concentration

The squeeze in the May 2-year note, following the auction on May 22, 1991, point up the need to review ways to lessen the potential for concentration of auction awards. In that auction Salomon and its customers were awarded 87% of the total amount offered. This highly concentrated auction result, while not unprecedented, was followed by unusual distortions in the cash and repo markets for that note. With these distortions in mind, the Treasury began a review of auction procedures following the May 1991 2-year note auction and has made changes to lessen the potential for a repeat of the experience.

1. Steps that Have Been Taken

1. The Treasury has changed auction rules since May 1991 by increasing the maximum amount of notes and bonds that can be purchased by a single bidder through noncompetitive tenders from $1 million to $5 million, effective with the 3-year note auction on November 5, 1991.

Table 4 Awards to Top Ten Primary Dealers and Customers in Treasury Bill Auctions, January 1990 Through September 1991 (millions of dollars)

| | Competitive | | | | | | |
	Primary dealer	P. dealer customer	Total	Other direct	Total comp.	Private noncomp.[a]	Total private
13-week	$280,313	$27,389	$307,702	$179,861	$487,563	$145,559	$633,122
26-week	260,695	21,307	282,002	174,866	456,868	114,895	571,763
52-week	103,058	10,090	113,148	60,508	173,656	19,789	193,445
Total	$644,066	$58,786	$702,852	$415,235	$1,118,087	$280,243	$1,398,330

Percent of Private Awards

| | Competitive | | | | | | |
	Primary dealer	P. dealer customer	Total	Other direct	Total comp.	Private noncomp.[a]	Total private
13-week	44.3%	4.3%	48.6%	28.4%	77.0%	23.0%	100.0%
26-week	45.6	3.7	49.3	30.6	79.9	20.1	100.0
52-week	53.3	5.2	58.5	31.3	89.8	10.2	100.0
Total	46.1%	4.2%	50.3%	29.7%	80.0%	20.0%	100.0%

Note: Based on auction date, not issue date. Excludes cash management bills.
[a]Excludes awards to foreign custody accounts and to the Federal Reserve for its own account.
Source: U.S. Treasury Department.

In the auction of the 3-year notes on November 5, 1991, the Treasury awarded $852 million of noncompetitive tenders to the public, compared with the average of $1.311 billion in the 3-year note auctions between January 1990 and September 1991. In the 10-year note auction on November 6, $614 million of noncompetitive tenders were awarded to the public, compared with the $597 million average in January 1990 through September 1991, and $937 million of 30-year bonds were awarded to the public on a noncompetitive basis in the auction on November 7, compared with an average of $368 million. Thus, total noncompetitive awards to the public in November 1991 were slightly higher than average. The distribution of awards among the three securities in November appears to reflect an investor preference for the relatively higher yields on longer-term securities at the time of the November auctions.

2. Also effective with the November 3-year note auction, the Treasury allows all registered and noticed government securities brokers and dealers to bid for customer accounts, a privilege that previously had been granted only to primary dealers and depository institutions.

2. Possible Further Measures

1. The Treasury could require than an auction participant who bids for more than a specific amount of a bill, note, or bond (for example 10 or 15% of the amount offered to the public) bid directly at a Federal Reserve bank rather than submit its tender(s) through a dealer(s). The advantages of direct bidding are that it would: (1) eliminate the information advantage of a dealer who bids in large size for customers; (2) make it more difficult for dealers and customers to act in concert in an auction and in the secondary market immediately after the auction; and (3) make the auction more competitive and therefore attract potential bidders who may be discouraged from taking the risks involved in participating in an auction if awards can be expected to be concentrated.

The disadvantages would be that: (1) it would force a dealer that was planning to submit a large bid for its own account, or that had a large volume of customer bids, to advise its customers to take their business elsewhere or face a cutback in the amount the customer wants to buy; (2) it would deny a customer the advice and other services of a dealer firm that the customer prefers; (3) in the current manual data processing environment, bidders would have to arrange to submit tenders physically to a Federal Reserve bank; (4)

Table 5 Awards to Top Ten Primary Dealers and Customers in Treasury Note and Bond Auctions, January 1990 Through September 1991, (millions of dollars)

	Competitive					Private noncomp.[a]	Total private
	Primary dealer	P. dealer customer	Total	Other direct	Total comp.		
2-year	$113,315	$29,781	$143,096	$84,212	$227,308	$29,389	$256,697
3-year	46,408	10,867	57,275	19,189	76,464	9,176	85,640
4-year	19,700	4,855	24,555	4,976	29,531	3,384	32,915
5-year	66,992	17,466	84,458	23,524	107,982	8,594	116,576
7-year	33,590	5,286	38,876	15,570	54,446	3,387	57,833
10-year	40,747	16,388	57,135	15,420	72,555	4,183	76,738
30-year	44,828	10,566	55,394	17,845	73,239	2,577	75,816
Total	$365,580	$95,209	$460,789	$180,736	$641,525	$60,690	$702,215

Percent of Private Awards

	Competitive					Private noncomp.[a]	Total private
	Primary dealer	P. dealer customer	Total	Other direct	Total comp.		
2-year	44.1%	11.6%	55.7%	32.8%	88.6%	11.4%	100.0%
3-year	54.2	12.7	66.9	22.4	89.3	10.7	100.0
4-year	59.9	14.8	74.6	15.1	89.7	10.3	100.0
5-year	57.5	15.0	72.4	20.2	92.6	7.4	100.0
7-year	58.1	9.1	67.2	26.9	94.1	5.9	100.0
10-year	53.1	21.4	74.5	20.1	94.5	5.5	100.0
30-year	59.1	13.9	73.1	23.5	96.6	3.4	100.0
Total	52.1%	13.6%	65.6%	25.7%	91.4%	8.6%	100.0%

Note: Based on auction date, not issue date.
[a]Excludes awards to foreign custody accounts and to the Federal Reserve for its own account.
Source: U.S. Treasury Department.

Table 6 Awards to Top Three Bidders in Treasury Note and Bond Auctions, January 1990 Through September 1991 (millions of dollars)

	Awards to top 3 bidders[a]	Percent of		Awards to top 3 dealers and customers[b]	Percent of	
		Comp. awards	Pvt. awards		Comp. awards	Pvt. awards
2-year	$92,223	40.6%	35.9%	$102,689	46.2%	40.0%
3-year	39,103	51.1	45.7	42,454	55.5	49.6
4-year	18,439	62.4	56.0	21,108	71.5	64.1
5-year	55,160	51.1	47.3	64,661	60.0	55.5
7-year	21,312	39.1	36.9	26,020	47.8	45.0
10-year	32,289	44.5	42.1	42,868	59.1	55.9
30-year	28,548	39.0	37.7	36,657	51.4	49.7
Total	$287,074	44.7%	40.9%	$337,461	52.6%	48.1%

Note: Based on auction date, not issue date.
[a]Bidder may be a primary dealer or a customer of a primary dealer.
[b]Primary dealer plus customer of the primary dealer.
Source: U.S. Treasury Department.

Table 7 Primary Dealer Net Position Before Auctions, as a Percent of
Account Awards to Primary Dealers, January 1990 Through September 1991
(millions of dollars)

	Primary account competitive awards	Primary dealer net position before auction[a]	Net position as percent of awards
2-year	$173,633	−$80,637	−46.4%
3-year	61,731	−22,194	−36.0
4-year	22,852	−5,338	−23.4
5-year	83,058	−39,890	−48.0
7-year	46,654	−11,221	−24.1
10-year	53,453	−14,262	−26.7
30-year	58,356	−17,387	−29.8
Total	$499,737	−$190,929	−38.2%

Note: Based on auction date, not issue date.
[a]Aggregate primary dealer net position as of 3:30 p.m. the day before the auction.
Source: U.S. Treasury Department and Federal Reserve Bank of New York.

bidders would have to arrange for a payment mechanism with a depository institution; and (5) bidders might not have sufficient information on current market conditions to be able to bid competitively.

The Treasury has decided to facilitate direct bidding, rather than to require it. Requiring large bidders to tender directly might not achieve the desired end, but could instead provide impetus for retail accounts to purchase securities from dealers in when-issued trading and circumvent the auction entirely.

The FRBNY and the Treasury are working to automate Treasury auctions. When the automated bidding system becomes operational late in 1992, depository institutions and government securities brokers and dealers will be able to submit tenders electronically. In addition, the Treasury and the FRBNY plan to extend electronic bidding capability to other large bidders, who could arrange to pay for their securities through autocharge agreements. It is likely that large bidders would have existing banking relationships that could be expanded to include autocharge agreements. In addition, the agencies are working on ways to encourage the expansion of coverage information on prices and trading volume in the government securities market and to extend the availability of on-line, real-time interdealer broker information systems. The greater availability of information that is expected to result from the efforts should promote an increase in direct bidding.

2. The Treasury could lower the 35% award maximum. The 35% maximum award ensures that awards will be made to at least three competitive bidders, after taking into account noncompetitive awards. Lowering the maximum to 25 or 30% of the amount offered has been proposed and could result in distributing awards to a larger number of market participants, which potentially would encourage more entities to participate in the auction. A disadvantage of a lower maximum award limit would be that it could discourage aggressive bidding, which could tend to reduce demand for the securities and increase the cost of financing the debt.

3. The Treasury could increase the noncompetitive award limit further. As indicated above, the Treasury is reviewing the results of the recent increase in the noncompetitive award limit. It is too early to assess whether the change will result in a change in bidding behavior. An advantage of a higher limit might be that bidders would be willing to submit larger noncompetitive tenders, which could result in larger amounts being awarded to entities other than government securities brokers and dealers, thus potentially reducing the concentration of auction awards. A disadvantage could be a reduction in the size of the competitive pool that might impair efficient pricing in the auction.

54

How the U.S. Treasury Should Auction Its Debt

V. V. Chari

Federal Reserve Bank of Minneapolis, Minneapolis, Minnesota, and J. L. Kellogg Graduate School of Management, Northwestern University, Chicago, Illinois

Robert J. Weber

J. L. Kellogg Graduate School of Management, Northwestern University, Chicago, Illinois

Auctions have been around for more than 2,000 years. The Babylonians arranged marriages by auction. The Roman legions sold booty at auction, and on one notable occasion, the Praetorian Guard killed the emperor and put up the whole empire for auction. Today, members of the general public sell at auction such diverse things as tobacco, fish, cut flowers, works of art, thoroughbred horses, and used cars. The U.S. government sells natural resources by auction and may soon take bids on radio airwaves and pollution rights. And in the largest auctions in recorded human history, the U.S. Treasury each year sells roughly $2.5 trillion worth of debt. With such large amounts at stake, even small improvements in the Treasury's auction procedure can lead to large gains for taxpayers. In this chapter, we review what economic theory tells us about ways to improve this procedure.

The Treasury's current procedure is what is known as a *multiple-price, sealed-bid* auction. Roughly a week before each of its more than 150 annual auctions, the Treasury announces the amount of debt it plans to sell. Eligible dealers and brokers submit competitive sealed bids which specify the price they are willing to pay for a particular quantity of debt. Investors may also submit so-called noncompetitive bids up to a fairly low quantity ceiling without specifying a price if they are willing to accept whatever will turn out to be the average accepted-bid price. Once all bids are in, the Treasury first adds up the quantity of noncompetitive bids and subtracts that from the total debt it plans to sell. Then, starting at the highest price bid and moving down, the Treasury adds up the competitive quantities bid until it hits its total. Each competitive bidder who has won (or, in the Treasury's jargon, has been "awarded" the bid) pays the price stated in his or her sealed bid; thus, each winning bidder may pay a different price. Noncompetitive bidders, again, pay the average of the awarded competitive bids.

This multiple-price, sealed-bid procedure, of course, is not the only way to design an auction. Indeed, most economists agree that it is not the best one for the Treasury. We argue here, based on economic theory, that the Treasury should switch to a *uniform-price, sealed-bid* auction. Under this procedure, with bids ordered by price, from the highest to the lowest, the Treasury would still accept quantities up to the amount it planned to sell, but the price winning bidders paid wouldn't vary. Instead, all bidders would pay the same price, that of the highest bid not accepted—the price that just clears the market.

The main reason to make this change is that the current auction procedure provides incentives for bidders to acquire more information than is socially desirable. In the current procedure, again, bidders pay the amount

Adapted from *Quarterly Review* (Fall 1992): 3-12 by permission of the Federal Reserve, Bank of Minneapolis.

of their bids if they win. Therefore, bidders have an incentive to shade their bids below the maximum amount they are willing to pay in order to try to obtain the securities at a lower price. But bid-shading carries with it the risk that the bid is so low that the bidder is not awarded any securities. In selecting a bid price, therefore, bidders want to balance the gain from a lower winning bid against the risk of not winning. Thus, they have incentives to learn what others plan to bid.

In a uniform-price auction, by contrast, the price paid by a winning bidder does not depend on that bidder's bid. Therefore, bid-shading is less extreme than in multiple-price auctions, and the incentives to acquire information about what others plan to bid is smaller. Information about how bidders plan to bid is of no value to society as a whole since such information merely ends up redistributing payments from uninformed to informed bidders. But acquiring this information is costly. The loser from the resources expended in information acquisition is the Treasury (and, of course, ultimately, the taxpayers). A uniform-price, sealed-bid auction will therefore yield more revenue to the Treasury.

Uniform-price auctions are also likely to be less susceptible to market manipulation. In 1990, Salomon Brothers Inc. violated Treasury rules designed to protect against market manipulation, and in 1991 the market was allegedly manipulated twice more. We argue that episodes of this kind are less likely under a uniform-price auction.

The Treasury did, in fact, experiment with such an auction briefly in the 1970s, but abandoned the experiment as largely inconclusive. As will become obvious, we think the experiment was abandoned too hastily. In any event, more recently, the Treasury embarked on a review of its auction procedures in collaboration with the Securities and Exchange Commission and the Board of Governors of the Federal Reserve System. (See U.S. Department of the Treasury et al., 1992.) Therefore, a review of what economic theory tells us about Treasury auctions seems particularly desirable. (For recent reviews of auctions in general, see McAfee and McMillan, 1987; Mester, 1988; and Milgrom, 1989.)

The plan for our review is as follows. We begin by laying out a general framework for analyzing bidder behavior in auctions. We apply this framework to two models in which only one unit of an object is being sold at auction: a simple model called the *independent private-values* model and an extension called the *correlated-values* model. We then discuss more complicated auctions like the Treasury's, auctions in which more than one unit is sold. We argue that the incentives to acquire information are smaller with uniform-price auctions than with multiple-price auctions and that uniform-price auctions are less susceptible to manipulation.

I.   THE GENERAL FRAMEWORK: GAME THEORY

Let's start by describing how economists generally think about bidder behavior under any type of auction procedure. The framework we use is *game theory*. This is a way to analyze how rational decisions are made by competitors in uncertain conditions. In auctions, of course, the competitors are primarily the bidders.

A seller faced with the problem of choosing among auction procedures must predict how bidders will act. Each bidder in a given auction, in turn, must predict how order bidders will act. These actions depend both on how much the bidder values the object being sold and on guesses about how others will bid on it. Each bidder's valuation of the object depends on his or her information about the object. For example, a bidder on an oil tract may know something about oil or neighboring tracts. Or in an art auction, bidders may know how valuable a painting will be to them. Successful bidding at an auction, therefore, involves successful guesses about other bidders' information and successful guesses about how these others will guess about each other's information.

This is an apparently intractable problem, but the language of noncooperative game theory offers a neat way around it. The way is to shift attention from bids to *bidding strategies*. Formally, a (pure) *strategy* for a bidder is a description of the relationship between what is known—the information of the bidder and the history of the auction—and what should occur—for each bidder's information and each stage of the auction, the appropriate decision for the bidder to make. Of course, in practice, bidders simply choose their bids rather than their strategies. A strategy for a particular bidder is simply a way of describing how other bidders imagine the particular bidder will act under various circumstances. A *Nash equilibrium* is a collection of strategies, one for each bidder, such that given the strategies of the other bidders, no one prefers to change his or her own strategy.

II.   SINGLE-OBJECT AUCTIONS

From this perspective, the nature of the information possessed by each bidder is critical in determining the outcome of a given auction procedure. The seller's problem is simply to compare equilibrium outcomes across auction procedures and pick the one that does best for him or her. (Of course, the chosen auction procedure may alter bidders' incentives to acquire information. We return to this theme later.) Here we consider two models of the information possessed by bidders: the independent private-values model and the correlated-values model. In both, we assume only one object is being sold.

A.   The Independent Private-Values Model

Suppose a painting is being auctioned. Each buyer knows how valuable this painting is to him- or herself but is uncertain about its value to other bidders. The seller is also uncertain about its value to the bidders. No bidder plans to resell the painting. This assumption of no resale means that each bidder cares about the value of the painting to others only insofar as it affects how others will bid. Put differently, even if bidders knew each other's values, no bidder would change the maximum amount he or she would be willing to pay. In this model, that is, bidders have *independent private values*.

Assume the model has N bidders. Let v_i denote the value of the painting to bidder i; that is, v_i is the maximum amount bidder i is willing to pay for the painting. We model the uncertainty about other bidders' values by assuming that bidder i's value is a random variable drawn from a distribution $F_i(\cdot)$ on $[0,V]$. We assume that bidders are risk-neutral, so that a bidder who pays m and receives the painting has a payoff of $(v_i - m)$. The seller is also risk-neutral. Bidders and the seller care about expected payoffs.

Each auction procedure can be described as a set of rules for bidders, describing at each stage what bidders can do as a function of the history of the auction. Given these rules, a *strategy* for a bidder prescribes what the bidder should do at each stage of the auction as a function of the history up to that stage and as a function of that bidder's private valuation v_i. A collection of such strategies for each of the bidders together with the rules of the auction procedure determines the outcome of the auction. This outcome should be thought of as who gets the object and how much each bidder pays. This outcome determines the *payoffs* of each bidder. Again, a *Nash equilibrium* is a collection of such prescriptions or strategies, such that given the strategies of the other bidders, none strictly prefers to change his or her strategy.

Now, this may sound numbingly complex, and it is. Fortunately, an insight due to Myerson (1979) and Harris and Townsend (1981) allows us to simplify the problem considerably.

Consider replacing a complicated auction procedure by the following mechanism. All bidders, privately and confidentially, report their valuation, v_i, to an impartial computer. The computer is programmed with the equilibrium strategies of the complicated auction and uses them by, in effect, running through the entire auction, doing what the bidders would have done, and producing an outcome. This outcome, of course, depends on the valuations of all the bidders. With this computerized mechanism, the decision problem of an individual is simply what value to enter into the computer. This mechanism is called a *revelation mechanism* since each individual reveals his or her private information to the computer.

The remarkable result, due to Myerson (1979) and Harris and Townsend (1981), is that the equilibrium outcome of any auction procedure can be reproduced as a truth-telling equilibrium of the revelation mechanism. The reason is simple. Since the original strategies constituted an equilibrium and the computer is going to play those strategies anyway, no bidder could do better by reporting a different value than the true one; all that a different report would do is make the computer choose a different—and, hence, less desirable—course of action.

From the perspective of bidder i, the revelation mechanism induces three outcome functions. Each of these is a function of the report, $\hat{v}_i$, of bidder i. These functions are the probability of winning the object, $p_i(\cdot)$; the expected payment conditional on winning the object, $w_i(\cdot)$; and the expected payment conditional on losing the object, $l_i(\cdot)$.

The payoff to a bidder who reports a value $\hat{v}_i$ and whose true valuation is v_i is, then, given by

$$\pi_i(v_i,\hat{v}_i) = p_i(\hat{v}_i)[v_i - w_i(\hat{v}_i)] - [1 - p_i(\hat{v}_i)]l_i(\hat{v}_i) \tag{1}$$

At a truth-telling equilibrium, we have, for all i

$$\pi_i(v_i,v_i) \geq \pi_i(v_i,\hat{v}_i) \tag{2}$$

Alternatively, if the expected payoff is differentiable in $\hat{v}_i$, we have

$$\partial\pi_i(v_i, v_i)/\partial\hat{v}_i = 0 \tag{3}$$

828 HOW THE U.S. TREASURY SHOULD AUCTION ITS DEBT

Condition (2) or (3) can be used with some additional assumptions to establish a remarkable result known as the *revenue equivalence theorem*. This theorem requires that we specialize the model further. Assume that the bidders' valuations are symmetric; that is, the distribution functions are the same for all bidders. Denote this common distribution function by F. We will say that an auction procedure is *efficient* if it allocates the object to the bidder with the highest value. Assume also that the lowest valuation bidders receive zero expected payoff. The theorem asserts that all auction procedures with these properties have the same expected payoff to the seller. Formally, we have this

Proposition (revenue equivalence theorem): *Every efficient auction with symmetric, risk-neutral, independent private-values bidders which assigns zero expected payoffs to bidders with the lowest values yields the same expected revenues to the seller.*

Proof. Note that, with symmetric bidders, the expected payoff functions of all bidders are the same. Denote these common expected payoffs at the truth-telling equilibrium by $\pi^*(v_i)$. Using the envelope theorem in (3), we have

$$\pi^{*\prime}(v_i) = p_i(v_i) \tag{4}$$

Integrating (4) and using the hypothesis that $\pi^*(0) = 0$, we have

$$\pi^*(v_i) = \int_0^{v_i} p_i(x)\,dx$$

For an efficient auction, $p_i(x)$ is simply the probability that the highest bidder's valuation is x. Thus, the expected payoffs of bidders are entirely determined from the distribution function $F(\cdot)$. Therefore, all auction procedures satisfying the hypotheses of the proposition yield the same expected payoffs to bidders. Since all auctions generate the same total surplus, the expected payoff of the seller is the same. Q.E.D.

To understand the relevance of this result, consider some examples of specific types of auctions when only one object is being sold. In *sealed-bid* auctions, each bidder silently submits a bid. In a *first-price*, sealed-bid auction, each bidder submits a bid and the object is awarded to the highest bidder at that bidder's price. In a *second-price*, sealed-bid auction, each bidder submits a bid and the object is awarded to the highest bidder at the price bid by the next-highest bidder. In *open-outcry* auctions, an auctioneer calls out prices to all bidders. In a *descending-price*, open-outcry auction (also called a *Dutch* auction since it was used in Holland to sell tulips), the auctioneer starts the price high and lowers it until some bidder claims the object. In an *ascending-price*, open-outcry auction (also called an *English* auction), the auctioneer starts the price low and raises it, stopping when only one bidder remains. With symmetry, all of these auctions are efficient and give zero payoffs to the lowest bidder. Thus, they all yield the same expected revenue.

Now, on the surface, these auctions seem quite different. In a second-price auction, for example, the best a bidder can do is submit his or her true valuation. Obviously, bidding higher than the true valuation would mean running the risk of paying more than the object is worth. Might a bidder want to bid less than the value of the object to that bidder? No, because all that such a strategy would do is reduce the chances of winning. It would have no effect on the price paid if the bidder wins. Thus, bidding one's valuation regardless of the actions of others is a *dominant strategy*. The seller's revenues are given by the value of the object to the second-highest bidder.

How could such an auction yield the same revenue as a first-price, sealed-bid auction? The result, due to Vickrey (1961), comes from the following reasoning. In a first-price auction, bidders shade their bids below their valuations. By doing so, they risk losing the object but pay less when they win. In equilibrium, each bidder's strategy is an increasing function of value. Thus, the object is assigned to the bidder with the highest valuation. The revenue equivalence theorem tells us that the bid-shading in the first-price auction results in exactly the same revenue as the second-price auction yielded. One can apply similar reasoning to other auctions (as Milgrom and Weber, 1982, have done).

B. The Correlated-Values Model

The revenue equivalence theorem tells us that which type of auction the seller chooses doesn't matter much. But, of course, the theorem follows from assumptions which may or may not be relevant in actual applications. For the example of an auction for Treasury debt, one assumption is very questionable. Treasury securities are easy to resell in the active secondary market. Thus, the value of a particular Treasury security to a bidder depends on how much others are willing to pay for it. Thus, the assumption of independent private values seems very unlikely to hold here. We turn, therefore, to a model with correlated values.

Consider again the example of the painting being sold, but now assume that the painting can be bought and then sold to others. In this situation, a bidder's willingness to pay is affected both by the bidder's own valuation and by what the painting would fetch if it were resold in the secondary market. The price in the resale market, in turn, depends on the willingness to pay of others; that is, in determining a bid, each bidder must take into account all the bidders' values—bidder values are *correlated*. In the example of the painting, suppose that the winning bidder plans to keep the painting for some time and then to sell it. A bidder's willingness to pay now depends both on how much the painting is worth to that bidder while the bidder owns it and on how much it will fetch when sold. We will use the term *value estimate* to describe a bidder's maximum willingness to pay given that bidder's information.

In this situation, a phenomenon known as the *winner's curse* can emerge. Consider, for example, a first-price, sealed-bid auction for our well-worn painting. Imagine that you have submitted a bid and have just been called and told "Congratulations, you have won." Along with the thrill of winning comes a frightening thought. By winning, you have found out that your bid was higher than anybody else's; thus, others probably value the painting less than you do. Therefore, if you wanted to resell it, you would probably lose money. As a winner, you are cursed.

On more careful inspection, though, this phenomenon does not imply that winners should vow never again to attend an auction. Instead, it implies that bidders will optimally shade their bids, recognizing that, if they win, their bid was the highest.

The revenue equivalence theorem now does not necessarily hold. Milgrom and Weber (1982) have shown that the expected revenues of someone selling a single object in four different types of auctions can be ranked this way, from highest to lowest revenues:

1. The ascending-price, open-outcry (English) auction
2. The second-price, sealed-bid auction
3. Tied: The first-price, sealed-bid auction and the descending-price, open-outcry (Dutch) auction

Rather than repeat Milgrom and Weber's (1982) formal results here, we provide some intuition. Recall that when values are correlated, the winner's curse causes bid-shading. A first-price auction awards the object to the highest bidder at the bid price. If other bidders value the object much less than the highest bidder does, then the object is worth much less than the bid price if the winner wants to resell it. Thus, all bidders fearing this kind of event end up shading their bids well below their own estimates. In contrast, in a second-price auction, the winner pays the price bid by the next-highest bidder. Thus, bidders are induced to raise their bids above their first-price auction bids by the knowledge that they will not lose if other bidders estimate the value of the object to be very low. In fact, the equilibrium bidding strategies in a second-price auction turn out to be fairly simple. Each bidder tries to answer the following question: "If I knew that my estimate was the highest and that the second-highest estimate was just marginally below mine, what would I then revise my estimate to be?" The equilibrium strategy is to bid the revised estimate. So, while the equilibrium strategy is not quite as simple as it was in the independent private-values environment, it is still relatively easy.

In an ascending-price, open-outcry (English) auction, revenues are even higher than in the second-price auction. The reason is that, as this auction proceeds, it reveals information about the value estimates of other bidders. As the auctioneer raises prices, some bidders drop out. Other bidders gain information about the value estimates of the dropouts and thus are able to revise their own estimates. The availability of this information reduces the winner's curse and causes bidders to bid more aggressively. That raises the seller's revenues.

One simple way of thinking about this English auction (as in Milgrom and Weber 1982) is to consider a situation with only two bidders. Each bidder's strategy is described by a single number which specifies at what price that bidder will drop out. The price paid by the winning bidder is marginally higher than the dropout price of the losing bidder. From a strategic point of view, of course, this is the same as a second-price auction. Thus, the seller's revenues are the same in both types of auctions.

Now consider an auction which initially had N bidders but $N-2$ have dropped out. The remaining two bidders know the prices at which the others have dropped out and have revised their value estimates accordingly. These two bidders now engage in a second-price auction with appropriately revised estimates.

Why does this revelation of information during the auction cause bidders to bid more aggressively during the auction?

One way to think about the reasoning is as follows. Recall that in a second-price auction, the equilibrium strategy is to assume that one's own value estimate is the highest and that the next-highest bid is just slightly lower. Assume that three bidders are engaged in a second-price auction. Label these bidders *1, 2,* and *3.* Consider informing bidder 1, just before that bidder is to submit a bid, that his or her value estimate is the highest. Would this change bidder 1's strategy? The answer is that it would not since the bidder has effectively already assumed that his or her estimate is the highest. Suppose now that you informed bidder 1 of the opposite: that his or her estimate is the lowest. Clearly, this information would cause the bidder to bid more aggressively. In effect, the English auction reveals this information to bidder 1 as it proceeds. Thus, it leads to higher revenues for the seller.

One implication of the theory is that auctions should be conducted as ascending-price, open-outcry auctions. Indeed, most auctions are of this type. To maximize the seller's revenue, most others should use the second-price, sealed-bid procedure. Yet auctions often use the first-price, sealed-bid procedure. Why are some auctions of this apparently inferior type?

In some situations, sealed-bid auctions are simply more practical than open-outcry auctions. Obviously, open-outcry auctions require bidders or their trusted agents to be present during the auction, and that is not always possible. Now, in theory, bidders could effectively duplicate the ascending-price, open-outcry auctions by submitting written or electronic bid schedules, telling the auctioneer how they would bid as a function of the prices at which other bidders drop out. But such bid schedules would have to be so incredibly long and complicated that they are just not feasible.

The next-best procedure should be the second-price, sealed-bid auction. But this has a serious problem too—one it shares, in fact, with the open-outcry auction. Both of these procedures require that the auctioneer be completely trustworthy, a somewhat unrealistic condition in the private sector. Consider what happens, for example, in a second-price, sealed-bid auction if the auctioneer is not trustworthy. Once the bids are opened, the auctioneer has a great incentive to cheat: to insert bids just below the winning bid in order to extract higher revenue. Bidders, of course, recognize that fact before they bid and respond by treating second-price auctions as first-price auctions. In the private sector, therefore, the lower-revenue first-price auctions are common.

When a government agency is the auctioneer, however, cheating seems much less liekly. Thus, unlike private sellers, the U.S. Treasury could use the higher-revenue second-price auction procedure.

III.   COMPLICATIONS

While the theory developed thus far has dealt with single-object auctions, the results generalize relatively straightforwardly to more complicated situations, like auctions with more than one object for sale. The results do not generalize quite so straightforwardly if bidders are risk-averse or if they collude. However, we will argue that risk-neutrality and competitive behavior are reasonable assumptions for Treasury auctions.

Consider first a situation with N bidders, each of whom wishes to buy one unit, and where $M < N$ units are offered for sale. The multiple-price analog of a first-price auction is a *discriminatory* auction, where the M highest bidders are awarded the items at their bid prices. The analog of a second-price auction is a *uniform-price* auction, where each bidder pays the price bid by the highest rejected bidder. The theory can be extended to cover these situations, and the results are the same: the uniform-price (second-price) auction dominates the discriminatory (first-price) auction.

Matters are more complicated when bidders have demand schedules expressing the number of units they are willing to buy at various prices. While the theory has not been completely developed for that situation, the economic logic of the arguments for the single-object environment seem likely to carry over.

Thus far, we have assumed that bidders are risk-neutral. Now let's see what happens if they're risk-averse.

If bidders are risk-averse in the independent private-values context, then the seller's expected revenues are higher in a first-price (discriminatory) auction than in a second-price (uniform-price) auction. The reason is that submitting one's true valuation remains a dominant strategy in the second- (or uniform-) price auction. Risk-aversion implies a willingness to pay an actuarially unfair premium to avoid large losses. Thus, in a first-price (discriminatory) auction, risk-averse bidders are willing to pay more than risk-neutral bidders to avoid the large loss from failing to win the object. (See Matthews, 1983, for an analysis of auctions with risk-averse bidders.)

If value estimates are correlated, however, the comparison for seller revenues across auction types becomes ambiguous. The theory, therefore, does not have much to say about the consequences for the Treasury if bidders are risk-averse. If risk-aversion is a major concern, the Treasury should not switch to a uniform-price auction. But we think risk-aversion should not be a major concern; no single Treasury auction is large relative to the wealth of actual and potential market participants, and it is not clear whether the Treasury does, or should have, attitudes toward risk that are substantially different from those of the participants. We thus think risk-aversion issues may be reasonably ignored for Treasury auctions.

The theory is also ambiguous if bidder valuations are drawn from different distributions (See Milgrom, 1989, for a nice example.) As a practical matter, market participants acquire information about eventual market prices in roughly the same way. Therefore, this issue too may be safely ignored.

What about collusive behavior among bidders? Let's answer that first for single-object auctions. In the independent private-values context, second-price auctions are more susceptible to collusive behavior than first-price auctions are. To see this, suppose a second-price auction has only two bidders, and they agree to tell each other their valuations and to adopt a strategy where the one with the lower value bids zero and the one with the higher value bids that value. For a promised side-payment, the lower-value bidder agrees to this arrangement and has an incentive to abide by it. Consider now what happens with a first-price auction. The only way the higher-value bidder can gain over the outcome without collusion is to bid less than the lower-value bidder's valuation. (Recall the revenue equivalence theorem.) But now the lower-value bidder has an incentive to defect.

In situations with multiple objects, recall the analog of a second-price auction is a uniform-price auction and the analog of a first-price auction is a discriminatory auction. Thus, considerations of collusive behavior seem to suggest that discriminatory auctions should be factored for Treasury debt. However, two considerations militate against accepting this conclusion too quickly. First, the Treasury's current system has 39 primary dealers. Setting up, and enforcing, collusive arrangements among this large a group would be a formidable task. Second, as we shall see in the next section, uniform-price auctions stimulate entry into bidding, which is anticollusive.

IV.   BENEFITS OF UNIFORM-PRICE AUCTIONS

If the Treasury switched its auctions to the more-feasible of the two auction types that yield the highest revenue—the uniform-price auction—then the general public welfare would be improved in at least two ways.

A.   Less Information Acquisition

The current system for auctioning Treasury debt creates large incentives to acquire information about other bidders' actions as well as the eventual state of market demand. These incentives would be much smaller under the uniform-price auction system.

To see this, consider a situation where one of the bidders—say, bidder 1—incurs a cost and acquires the estimated values of all other bidders. Acquiring these estimates will cause bidder 1's estimate to be revised; but if the original estimate was unbiased, then the expected value of the revised estimate will be the same as the original estimate. For now, therefore, assume that acquiring this information causes no change in the estimated value for bidder 1. Assume for now also that other bidders do not change their strategies.

We want to focus on how bidder 1's bidding strategy changes after acquiring the information. Recall that bids are increasing in the estimated values. When bidder 1 does not have the information of other bidders' estimates, the bidder wins whenever his or her estimate is the highest.

Consider, first, the situation when the bidder's estimate, before the information was acquired, was the highest. In a second- or uniform-price auction, such a situation would not change the amount paid by the bidder (since we have assumed no change in the behavior of other bidders). In contrast, in a first-price or discriminatory auction, bidder 1 now shades his or her bid further down to just above the bid of the next-highest bidder. Thus, whenever the bidder would have won, a first-price or discriminatory auction yields a gain to information and a second- or uniform-price auction does not.

In situations where the bidder would have lost, matters are more complicated. Once bidder 1 acquires the information, that bidder is willing to pay any amount up to the estimate. Two possibilities must be considered. Either some bidders' bids are more than bidder 1's estimate, or some bidders' bids are less than bidder 1's estimate but more than bidder 1's bid without the information.

If some bidders are willing to pay more than bidder 1's estimate, the bidder drops out of the auction. Now, recall that bid-shading is more extreme with first-price (or discriminatory) auctions than with second- (or uniform-) price auctions. In both types of auctions, bidder 1 would have lost without the information and is happy to do so with the information. Since bid-shading is more extreme with first-price (discriminatory) auctions, the probability that some bidders will bid higher than bidder 1's estimate is smaller in those auctions than in second- (or uniform-) price auctions. The potential gains to changing the strategy are therefore higher.

Next, consider the case when some bidders' bids are between bidder 1's estimate and bidder 1's bid without the information. In this situation, the theory is ambiguous about which auction provides greater incentives to acquire information. However, given the gains in the other two situations, the overall effect is likely to enhance the incentives to acquire information.

Of course, if other bidders recognize that bidder 1 has acquired information, they will modify their strategies as well. One way of modeling the change in other bidders' behavior is to assume that, by incurring a cost, bidder 1 is informed, with some small probability, of the valuations of other bidders. The other bidders do not know whether or not bidder 1 has acquired this information. If the probability of acquiring the information is sufficiently small, then the change in the bidding strategies of the other bidders will be small, and the analysis above applies. If this probability is 1, it can be shown that the expected payoff to the less-informed bidders is zero under both types of auctions. Thus, in this case, the incentives to acquire information are the same under both types. Therefore, we argue that the incentives to acquire information are generally higher with first-price (or discriminatory) auctions.

From this result comes the conclusion that first-price (discriminatory) auctions yield lower revenues to the Treasury and lead to larger amounts of resources devoted to gathering information than do second-price (uniform-price) auctions. Is this information gathering a socially valuable activity? To the extent that it involves gathering information about how much other bidders are willing to pay, it merely redistributes payments from uninformed to informed bidders. This information has no value to society as a whole. Even worse, the existence of informed bidders drives relatively uninformed bidders away from the auction. Thus, auction procedures which provide large incentives to acquire information lead to fewer active uninformed bidders. This reduction in the number of bidders tends to reduce revenues to the Treasury.

We want to emphasize here that the true social cost of the current auction procedures is the excessive resources devoted to gathering information about potential bidders. Channeling these resources to other activities is likely to enhance welfare.

B. Less Market Manipulation

A switch to a uniform-price auction procedure would improve welfare in at least one other way. The Treasury's recent review of its auction procedures was spurred, in part, from violations of Treasury rules by Salomon Brothers in 1990 and from two instances of so-called short squeezes in 1991. These sorts of attempts to manipulate the market for Treasury securities should be less likely under a uniform-price auction procedure.

Let's briefly review the current structure of the market for Treasury securities. Approximately a week to 10 days before a Treasury auction, dealers and investors actively participate in a *when-issued market*. This is a market in forward contracts. Participants agree to deliver and accept delivery of specified quantities of a Treasury security when it is issued at a currently agreed-on price. Those who agree to deliver soon after the security is issued are known as the *shorts*; those who agree to wait for delivery, the *longs*. The market performs a *price-discovery* role; that is, it provides information to bidders about the likely state of market demand for the Treasury security when it is issued. This information benefits auction bidders who face uncertainty about the prices at which they will be able to resell Treasury securities.

To see the possibilities for market manipulation, consider the following scenario. A trader or group of traders commits to a forward contract for a large amount of a Treasury security, on the long side of the contract; they agree to accept delivery of the security when it is issued. The same person or group then purchases a large amount of the Treasury security at the auction. Now, those who have committed to deliver the security (the *shorts*) must acquire the security in the marketplace. But they find that most of the securities are held by those on the long side of the forward contract. Since the forward contract specifies delivery of that particular security, the shorts are squeezed. (See Sundaresan, 1992, for a proposal to replace the when-issued market by a cash-settled futures market.) This possibility tends to reduce the volume of trade in the when-issued market and thus raise the costs of price discovery. The risks imposed on bidders are then passed on to the Treasury as lower revenues.

The Treasury recognizes this problem and is also sensitive to general concerns that particular traders may seek to corner a market. It therefore imposes limits on the amount that bidders can bid at the auction. These are the rules that traders at Salomon Brothers tried to circumvent in 1990 by submitting fraudulent bids in customers' names.

What are the likely consequences of our proposed reform on the when-issued market and on the prospect for short squeezes? First, a switch to a uniform-price auction procedure would reduce the role of the when-issued market. With uniform pricing, bidders would have less of an incentive to acquire information about other bidders' willingness to pay. We have already argued that this reduction is socially desirable. Second, to the extent that short traders fear the prospect of a squeeze, a uniform-price auction procedure would let these traders purchase the security at the auction more cheaply than they can under the current system. The reason is that, under the current system, a short trader must submit a bid at a high price and be willing to pay that price to guarantee not being squeezed. Under a uniform-price auction, short traders are unlikely to substantially affect the price they pay for the security by submitting a high price. Therefore, they can protect themselves better, and the prospects of market manipulation are reduced.

V. CONCLUDING REMARKS

A switch to either an ascending-price, open-outcry auction or a uniform-price auction for U.S. Treasury debt is likely to raise Treasury revenues and reduce excessive resources devoted to information gathering. The ascending-price auction has the disadvantage of requiring physical presence at the auction. (Of course, this type of auction could be conducted with remote electronic terminals.) To the extent that such presence is costly, it raises entry barriers to the auction and is wasteful. Furthermore, it is more burdensome to bidders since the strategic calculations involved are more complicated. The uniform-price auction is strategically much less complicated. This feature also tends to reduce entry barriers.

Ultimately, the issue is relatively simple. The current organization of the Treasury market has primary dealers who purchase at the auction and resell to the public at large. With so many close substitutes and an efficient Treasury market, no reforms of the auction procedure will change prices to the ultimate holders very much, if at all. Entry is possible into the dealer/broker arena, and the market is competitive enough that, as a first approximation, such dealers make no more than the normal return on their investments. The only questions that remain are whether those investments are affected by the Treasury's auction procedure and whether they are at the socially optimal level.

The investments of Treasury dealer/brokers are in the form of a network of people who have learned to work with each other, ultimate buyers, and the Treasury. An important part of their activity is to acquire information about the behavior of actual and potential bidders. The when-issued market serves this role. We have argued that, given the auction procedure, this information is privately valuable and that market participants will rationally invest to acquire it. We have also argued that this information has dubious social value. with our proposed change in the auction procedure, the incentives to acquire this information would be lower, and over time, these investments would not be replaced. Thus, over time, the returns going to these investments would accrue to the Treasury.

These arguments suggest that changes in the auction procedure will take time to yield gains in Treasury revenue. No experiment conducted over any period as short as even a year is likely to generate significant changes in Treasury revenue. Patience appears to be a must.

Another implication of our arguments is that if the reforms are implemented, the when-issued market will likely shrink. This market currently serves a variety of purposes, one of which is price discovery; the market lets participants learn about each other's willingness to pay for Treasury securities. This role is extremely important for participants who want to reduce the risks of the Treasury auction. But the risks are largely due to the current form of the auction. The talents and resources now involved in the when-issued market are a rational response to the current auction procedure. With a uniform-price auction, some of these talents and resources could go to more socially productive activities.

We are certainly not the first to advocate a change in the Treasury auction procedure, or even this specific change. Milton Friedman advocated a uniform-price auction in testimony to the Joint Economic Committee in 1959 (excerpted in Friedman, 1991). More recently, other economists have advocated this proposal—for example, Merton Miller in Henriques, 1991. We think a large majority of economists support the proposal (which, admittedly, may be a popular argument against it). In this chapter, we have tried to argue that everything we know from economic theory tends to support it.

REFERENCES

Friedman, M. (1991). How to sell government securities. *Wall Street Journal* (Aug. 28): A8.

Harris, M. and Townsend, R. M. (1981). Resource allocation under asymmetric information. *Econometrica, 49* (Jan.): 33–64.

Henriques, D. B. (1991). Treasury's troubled auctions. *New York Times* (Sept. 15): 13.

Matthews, S. A. (1983). Selling to risk averse buyers with unobservable tastes. *Journal of Economic Theory, 30* (Aug.): 370–400.

McAfee, R. P. and McMillan, J. (1987). Auctions and bidding. *Journal of Economic Literature, 25* (June): 699–738.

Mester, L. J. (1988). Going, going, gone: Setting prices with auctions. *Federal Reserve Bank of Philadelphia Business Review* (March/April): 3–13.

Milgrom, P. R. (1989). Auctions and bidding: A primer. *Journal of Economic Perspectives, 3* (summer): 3–22.

Milgrom, P. R. and Weber, R. J. (1982). A theory of auctions and competitive bidding. *Econometrica, 50* (Sept.): 1089–1122.

Myerson, R. B. (1979). Incentive compatibility and the bargaining problem. *Econometrica, 47* (Jan.): 61–73.

Sundaresan, S. (1992). Pre-auction markets and post-auction efficiency: The case for cash settled futures on on-the-run Treasures. manuscript, Columbia University.

U.S. Department of the Treasury, Securities and Exchange Commission, and Board of Governors of the Federal Reserve System (1992). *Joint report on the government securities market*, U.S. Government Printing Office, Washington, D.C.

Vickrey, W. (1961). Counterspeculation, auctions, and competitive sealed tenders. *Journal of Finance, 16* (March): 8–37.

55

An Analysis of Potential Treasury Auction Techniques

Vincent R. Reinhart
Board of Governors of the Federal Reserve, Washington, D.C.

Last summer's revelation of abuses of the rules governing the primary market for government securities spurred a comprehensive review of all aspects of market activity. Some of that work appeared in the *Joint Report on the Government Securities Market*, which the U.S. Department of the Treasury, the U.S. Securities and Exchange Commission, and the Board of Governors of the Federal Reserve System transmitted to the Congress in January 1992. While the *Joint Report* addressed many issues, its advocacy of experimentation with alternative auction designs for selling Treasury securities in particular attracted considerable attention. This attention likely owed to the sizable stakes. With the outstanding federal debt totaling $2.8 trillion and mounting with each year's fiscal deficit, the gain to the Treasury from even a modest improvement in selling technique could be substantial. In fiscal year 1991, for example, gross issuance by the federal government exceeded $1.7 trillion. Given that scale of borrowing, a reduction of one basis point in the average annual issuing rate at Treasury auctions would trim more than $200 million from the federal deficit each year. At the same time, the Treasury must maintain the integrity of the auction process by ensuring that no illicit activity is hidden by the sheer volume of transactions. A concern by investors that the market was not open and fair would be translated into lessened demands for Treasury debt and higher costs of borrowing.

By reviewing the academic literature on auctions, this article puts current Treasury practice and a popular proposal for reform in critical perspective. It also examines the alternative scheme embraced in the *Joint Report* that uses technology to give better protection against certain kinds of manipulative behavior and that has a potential for lowering borrowing costs.

I. BACKGROUND ON BIDDING

There is a large academic literature on auctions, with important early contributions by William Vickrey and Milton Friedman and significant later work by Paul Milgrom, among others. (See the references at the end of the chapter.) This research has classified the types of auctions, rigorously modeled the bidding strategies, and ranked auctions by various criteria regarding efficiency. Unfortunately, this literature has a language all its own that differs from the terms that the financial press uses. To avoid confusion, this chapter will use explicit, if somewhat unwieldy, names for each auction.

William Vickrey established the basic taxonomy of auctions by classifying them based on the order in which prices are quoted and the way in which bids are entered.* First, securities can be awarded at prices that are progressively lowered until the entire issue is sold; alternatively, the auctioneer can arrange the bids in ascending order by their price and decide on a single price that places the total issue. By the second

Adapted from *Federal Reserve Bulletin* (June 1992): 403–413.
*Vickrey (1961).

measure, the auction can be a private affair with sealed bids opened by the auctioneer, or it can be conducted in real time, with participants in a single room or connected by phone bidding in public. This two-by-two classification yields four auction types: the first-price sealed-bid auction, the second-price sealed-bid auction, the descending-price open-outcry auction, and the ascending-price open-outcry auction.

Complicating matters, researchers after Vickrey further classified models by an assumption about the information that bidders have regarding the value of the auctioned object. One such model is the private-values case, in which bidders' valuations are subjective decisions, independent of each other. Another is the common-values case, in which each participant attempts to measure the value of the item by the same objective yardstick. The auction of a unique work of art not for resale is the prototypical private-values model, whereas a Treasury auction—with each bidder guessing at the security's value at the end of the day—is an example of a common-values model. This chapter concentrates on the common-values case, which is applicable to the sale of Treasury securities, and also assumes that agents care only about maximizing profit.

In general terms, the expected profit from winning an auction for bidder 1, π_1, depends on the expected value of the security in secondary market trading, v_1, less the awarded price, b_1, times the probability of winning the auction, $Pr\{\cdot\}$. In more formal terms and using i as an index to represent the bidders in the auction,

$$\pi_1 = (v_1 - b_1) \cdot Pr\{b_1 > b_1, \text{for all other } i\}.$$

The format of the auction determines how the bid price affects the probability of winning and the profit from acquiring the security, as well as what information is revealed about the security's value through the auction process.

A.   First-Price Sealed-Bid Auction

The current practice of auctioning government securities falls into the first-price sealed-bid category, which in the financial community is termed an English auction (except by the English, who call it an American auction). Bidding takes place in private and, as Fig. 1 shows, awards are made at the highest priced bids covering the total auction size. It is termed a first-price auction because in the sale of one unit of good or security the award is made at the highest bid. In the figure, the horizontal bars measure the cumulative amount of bids at the given price or higher.* Thus, participants pay differing prices reflecting the strength of their bids.

In terms of the expected return from winning the auction, a high bid lowers the profit from victory and raises the probability of winning. The strategic bidder trades between the two; he or she lowers the bid relative to valuation in order to profit more from winning and accepts the risk of lowering the probability of winning. The optimal strategy is to shade a bid toward the perceived market consensus; the more certain that consensus is (in terms of lower variability), the more the strategic investor will shade his or her bid.[†]

---

*Treasury auctions are actually conducted in terms of yields; for convenience, I discuss them in terms of price.
[†]Smith (1981.)

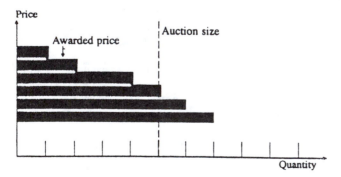

Figure 1   First-price sealed-bid auction.

Another factor comes into play in the common-values case: Since all participants guess about the price—where the security will trade after the auction—a high bid signals a heightened probability of subsequent loss of profit for that bidder. In that sense, winning is losing, as entering the highest bid signals that one's valuation exceeds that of all other interested parties. This is the "winner's curse" and gives aggressive bidders an additional reason to rein in their enthusiasm. Avoiding the winner's curse may lead to the pooling of bids, as a group of investors is more likely to have a clearer view of the market consensus and is less likely to be in the far end of the bid-price distribution. The pooling of bids is a service provided by dealers, who collect customer business and place large-scale orders.

B. Second-Price Sealed-Bid Auction

The Treasury could collect sealed bids, arrange them by price, and award all the securities at a single price that just places the entire issue (Fig. 2). This auction is termed second-price because, when a single unit is on the block, the price charged would be that of the highest bid below the price that places the issue, or the second-best price. The second-price auction, called a Dutch auction in the financial press, has been proposed as a simple alternative to current Treasury practice that would prevent the type of abuses witnessed last year while lowering average borrowing costs.*

A second-price auction, in which the winner pays, not his or her bid, but only the second-best bid, severs the gain in winning from the probability of winning. An aggressive bidder can receive a sure award but pay a price closer to the market consensus. As a result, less of the shading that marks the response to the winner's curse should occur. Accordingly, customers may be more willing to place their business directly by bidding at the auction than to go through a dealer.

C. Descending-Price Open-Outcry Auction

This procedure is used to auction flowers in the Netherlands, hence it is referred to by academics as a Dutch auction. Bidders congregate in one room, or plug into its electronic equivalent, and wait as the auctioneer calls out a sequence of decreasing prices. In an auction of one unit of a good or security (Fig. 3), the auction stops when one bidder is willing to pay the price called out. For multiple units, the eager bidder is awarded the security, and the auction continues, with the auctioneer selling the remaining securities at progressively lower prices. The strategic decision is identical to that of the first-price sealed-bid auction; the optimal bidder does not want to be too aggressive and stop the auction well above the likely market consensus, but will shade his or her bid to avoid the winner's curse. In other words, what market participants refer to as an English auction is strategically identical to what academics refer to as a Dutch auction. As a result, investors have the same incentive to pool bids and place customer orders at dealers.

---

*Friedman (1991). Merton Miller also has embraced this reform, as quoted in Henrique (1991).

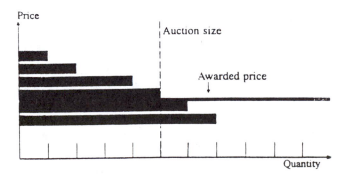

Figure 2   Second-price sealed-bid auction.

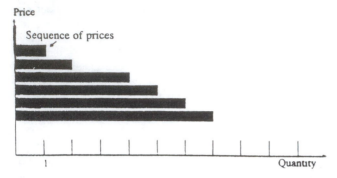

Figure 3   Descending-price open-outcry auction.

D.   Ascending-Price Open-Outcry Auction

The auctioneer can just as well cry out an ascending sequence of prices to the gathered bidders, stopping the auction when enough are willing to take down the total issue. Such a price sequence is plotted in Fig. 4 for the auction of a single good or security. In keeping with the mirror imaging, academics term this an English auction.*

The auction of multiple units of a security begins as a price is called out and all interested parties submit their quantities demanded. The volume of bids at that price is announced and, in successive rounds, the price is raised until the volume demanded is smaller than the issue. When that point is reached, the seller knows that the price just previously called out is the highest price consistent with placing the entire issue—that is, it clears the primary market. Everyone who bids at the top price and some fraction of the bidders at the previous price not in the top group receive awards at that lower price.[†] As the auctioneer calls out an increasing price list, bidders receive news that participants prize the security more highly than those low quotes. In effect, the auctioneer's initial announcements rule out low-price outcomes, revealing that the true market value is probably higher. This increasing sequence of prices lessens the winner's curse. Besides, if an investor is truly alone in valuing the security highly, the auction stops before the price is pushed too far up when the other bidders drop out.

In 1961, Vickrey established that the four major auction formats provide equal proceeds to the seller when individual valuations are independent. Obviously, the Treasury market violates this assumption, as the value that bidders place on the security reflects an imperfect estimate of the price in subsequent market trading—that is, bidders in a Treasury auction care about the common value of the security. In the common-values case, as later researchers showed, an ascending-price open-outcry delivers the greatest proceeds to the seller under many circumstances.[‡] Essentially, in such an auction, bidders condition their behavior on the highest expected value of the security and shade their bids the least relative to the other formats.

II.   THE POTENTIAL FOR PROFIT IN AUCTIONS

The current auction format elicits one form of strategic behavior; because awards are priced at the bid, the participants have incentives to shade their bids to avoid the winner's curse. As a result, customers have an incentive to pool their bids with dealers so that a combination of bids can, by a law of large numbers, be appropriately cast. The auction format may encourage two other types of strategic behavior as well. First, a dealer may combine with a customer to corner a significant portion of one auction—70% under the current

---

*Indeed, in the private-values model (which we do not analyze), another equivalence proposition holds. What market participants refer to as a Dutch auction is strategically identical to what academics refer to as an English auction—unless there is a time limit on the bidding, in which case it is called a Scotch auction.

[†]Those partial awards might go to those who were electronically timed as placing the earliest bids or to all bidders on a pro rata basis.

[‡]This was shown formally by Milgrom and Weber (1982), theorem 11.

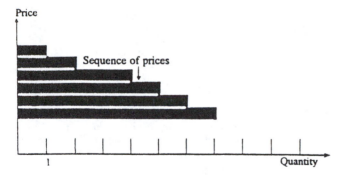

Figure 4   Ascending-price open-outcry auction.

rules. This strategy is called single-dealer cornering. Second, a group of dealers can conspire to accomplish the same end; this strategy is called collusive combining. In a sealed-bid auction, to garner the lion's share of awards, the single strategist or the group need make only a slightly more aggressive bid than the other participants expect. Indeed, the second-price auction, a popular candidate to replace the current format, may make these strategies less expensive for the purchasers than they would be under current practice. The strategic purchaser could corner the issue by bidding substantially more than the market consensus but pay a price closer to the mass of the distribution that marks the other bids.

Clearly, single-dealer cornering and collusive combining are similar. However, the informational requirements and incentives for these two types of strategic behavior vary across auction type, and actions taken to combat one might make the other more likely. To analyze the collusive potential in auctions, one must first understand the incentive behind cornering an auction—or the way in which one variety of squeeze can work.

A.   How a Corner Works

The potential for profit in a corner, or squeeze, lies in the interaction of the three main trading forums for Treasury securities: the when-issued market, the Treasury auction, and the secondary market. Those markets are represented by the three panels of Fig. 5, arrayed by time—before, at, and after the auction. As the right panel shows, the price of a Treasury security must satisfy the ultimate holders of securities (pension funds, insurance companies, mutual funds, and the general investing public), seen as the intersection of their downwardly sloped demand schedule with the vertical Treasury supply schedule.

Current auction procedures, however, get securities to those holders indirectly, through the intermediation of dealers. As the middle panel shows, the demand derived from current and anticipated customer orders produces a flatter and more inward schedule at the auction as a result of the shading of bids in the attempt to avoid the winner's curse.

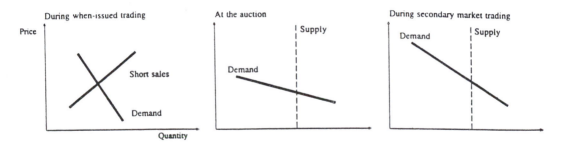

Figure 5   The main markets for Treasury securities, according to time of trading.

An investor can purchase the security before the auction, as long as he or she can find someone willing to sell it short. The when-issued market, shown in the left panel, matches those parties. Those seeking secure ownership rights trace a downwardly sloped demand schedule, while those willing to sell what they do not yet have make up the short-sale schedule. Selling a security before the auction involves a risk, as short sellers may not win awards at the auction to cover their open positions and so will have to borrow or buy the security after the auction settles to make delivery. Accordingly, the when-issued price should clear above the expected auction price.

The cornering of an auction is depicted in Fig. 6. Short sales are made at a price just enough above the anticipated auction price to pay the sellers for exposing themselves to the likely risk at the auction. Those sellers, however, turn out to be wrong about the auction for, while the market consensus coalesces around bids consistent with the Demand schedule in the middle panel, one party comes in with bids that shift the actual schedule to Demand'. The cornerer exploits the sealed-bid nature of the auction; by bettering the market consensus, the schemer wins the bulk of the awards (measured by the horizontal distance between the two demand schedules).*

Since other parties cannot react, the Treasury receives only a modestly higher price for its auctioned securities, but the major price action awaits secondary market trading. The cornerer restricts the supply of the security in the secondary market (seen as the inward shift in the vertical supply schedule in the right panel), so that the price that clears that market is well above the auction price. From there, the cornerer slowly unwinds that position, expanding market supply to sell at prices above the ultimate level determined by the final owners of Treasuries. In effect, the cornerer acts as a discriminating monopolist, carefully regulating secondary market sales to earn all the revenue given by the area under the demand schedule. The cornerer's cost is given by the unshaded rectangle, leading to the profit given by the shaded area.

Indeed, the profit from a market squeeze may come by other means. While the issue remains in the cornerer's control during secondary trading, short sellers must borrow the security to make delivery. That transaction is one side of a repurchase agreement in which the owner of the desirable security—the cornerer—lends it to a short seller in return for cash at a preferential borrowing rate. In effect, by creating a demand for the issue, the cornerer can finance his or her position at a below-market borrowing rate.

The when-issued market plays two important roles in cornering strategy. First, early trading allows the market consensus to coalesce quickly and thus provides a usually accurate forecast of the auction price. By aiding in the "price discovery" of the appropriate price on the security to be auctioned, the when-issued market serves in tightening the spread of bids; thus, the cornerer needs to bid only slightly higher than that consensus to be assured awards. Second, a group of thwarted bidders—those who shorted in the when-issued market—are forced to the secondary market to close their positions. Their surprising presence makes the demand schedule less price sensitive, as no substitute exists for the security that they promised to deliver. As a result, as long as they keep their positions open, short sellers will need to borrow the desirable security and thus provide the cornerer favorable financing in the repurchase market.

----

*A manipulator could bypass the auction by amassing a controlling position in either when-issued or secondary market trading. To effect that strategy, purchase orders would have to be spread across many sellers in an effort to hide the intent to corner from the general market.

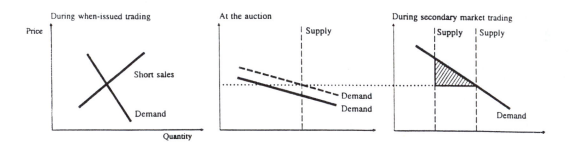

Figure 6   How a corner works.

The successful cornerer makes use of three elements of the current practice

- When-issued trading creates a core of reliable demanders for the auctioned security (those who sold short).
- The first-price method of allocating awards reduces demand at the auction and makes that demand more price sensitive.
- Sealed bids allow a cornerer to place bids only marginally better than the consensus to win all the awards.

These characteristics of current procedures promise profit in successfully cornering a Treasury auction, although such trades are not without considerable risk. Even slight shifts in the prevailing level of interest rates could more than wipe out the profit from controlling a significant portion of an outstanding issue.

B.   The Potential for Collusion

One dealer with adequate capital and the willingness to be exposed to substantial risk can possibly take advantage in the current market. A harder problem to assess is whether or not an auction's design may entice a group of dealers to conspire in an attempt to corner. The theoretical analysis of the incentives for collusion in auctions proceeds as follows.

Let us suppose that a few dealers, intent on extracting profit from those not in the ring, willfully plan together to purchase all that is sold at an auction. They agree on a price just above the market consensus that is sure to win all the awards. A sealed-bid auction, however, tempts each of the conspirators to move just above the agreed-upon price and to steal awards; as a result, the cartel likely will not hold.* Hence, on the one hand, incentives in the classic first-price sealed-bid auction are structured so as to make collusion unlikely. On the other hand, in an ascending-price open-outcry auction, such a conniver among conspirators has to show his or her hand, making such manipulation less likely. Even if bidding is secret, the other members of the cartel will know by the price movement that someone has cheated. The cartel will hold.

By this theoretical argument, one might surmise that the current first-price sealed-bid auction protects, at least, against the willful joining of dealers to exploit the Treasury and other dealers. Unfortunately, a gap exists between models and reality, as the rule limiting awards to 35% of the issue paradoxically turns incentives back toward collusion. If a conniver plays within the lines of the 35% rule, he or she will not win enough securities at the auction to control the secondary market. Consequently, tough enforcement of quantity limits more strongly binds conspirators together.

More to the point, theoretical analyses of collusion assume that a small number of colluding parties share information, an assumption that ignores the multiple arenas in which dealers compete. Dealers will not cooperate in auctions if such cooperation jeopardizes their trading in the secondary market. Given the large number of participants and the apparent mistrust among dealers, auction format is unlikely to bring them together.† Thus, from the standpoint of public policy, the chief risk seems to lie in the manipulative actions of a single dealer, the rogue with capital, which threaten the integrity of the market.

III.   A CLOSER LOOK AT A POPULAR PROPOSAL FOR REFORM

The abuses of the auction rules last summer rekindled enthusiasm for a simple alternative, the second-price sealed-bid auction, to the current discriminatory pricing practice. Proponents argue that awarding securities at a uniform price rather than at the bid prices would end cornering attempts by eliminating the profit potential in market manipulation. And in a way that sounds contradictory, they argue that total revenue would increase by the surrender of the ability to discriminate across bids.

A.   The Consequences for Revenue

The algebra required to calculate an optimal bidding plan in a multiple-unit auction quickly becomes intractable. No analyst yet has worked through the strategic implications of a large core of bidders carving

---

*This outcome also holds for a descending-price open-outcry auction. The first one to leave the pool stops the auction before the others can react.

†The existence of interdealer brokers is one sign of the level of mistrust among dealers. These intermediaries provide anonymity to dealers in transactions between dealers, who are reluctant to phone their competition directly and to show which side of the market they are on.

up a block of securities. The logic of the single-unit case, however, suggests that the extent of bid shading can be extreme. In a first-price auction of multiple units, a strategic bidder does not have to beat the participant with the next highest valuation to win but must better only the middle of the pack of bidders.

If one steps away from the explicit modeling of bidder behavior, the implications for revenue can be spelled out in terms of shifts in the demand schedule for the auctioned security.* As shown in Fig. 7 (which repeats the middle panel of the three-figured determination of market prices), part of the Treasury's total revenue results from its charging winners the price that they bid, which for its current practice is measured by the area under the demand schedule labeled "First price." That price discrimination, however, discourages some demand, as investors shade their bids for fear of the winner's curse. Adopting a second-price system turns part of that surplus back to the bidders, shifting out the demand schedule to the position labeled "Second price." Under a first-price scheme, the Treasury would have to work down the left demand schedule and award securities at lower prices to place the total issue (marked by the vertical dashed line). Under the second-price scheme, one price, depicted by the horizontal line drawn to intersect the right demand schedule at the issuance size, exhausts the issue. The consequences for revenue depend on whether or not the loss from the inability to price discriminate (left triangle) is greater than the gain from added demand (right triangle).

Support for the second-price scheme is stronger than the balancing of these welfare triangles would suggest. Those analysts working with explicit models of bidder behavior in a Treasury-like format, rather than with reduced-form demand schedules, typically find that a second-price scheme does produce higher revenue for the seller. Further, in 1962 Milton Friedman made a persuasive argument that revenue would increase.[†] Dealers devote considerable energy to the auction only to sell those securities almost immediately to customers—and most profit from doing so. Part of the resources devoted to that distribution could be appropriated by the Treasury if it could directly deal with those customers. A second-price auction, because it is less penalizing to the aggressive or the uninformed, may be the best vehicle to attract those people.

B.   The Consequences for Cornering

As seen previously, the current format reduces demand at auctions and makes it more sensitive to price in relation to the demand determined by the buy-and-hold ownership of the long-time investor. This reduction is the rational response to the Treasury's discriminating pricing; the investor shows less of his true consumer surplus to a seller whose stated intention is to seize it.

Moving to a common-price format permits demand at the auction to reflect the true nature of investor preference. With no friction, investors can bypass the dealer intermediaries and bid directly, sharing the resulting savings with the Treasury. Viewed in terms of the three-figured determination of Treasury prices, second-price awards would make the auction demand curve identical to the secondary market demand curve

---

*For details, see Goldstein (1962).
[†]From correspondence quoted in Goldstein (1962).

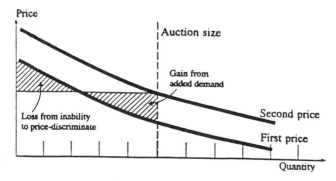

Figure 7   The effect of second-price awards on revenue.

(Fig. 8). Against this backdrop, the cornerer of an auction would place surprising bids that shift the demand schedule from Demand to Demand'. The horizontal distance of that shift represents the cornerer's awards, or the extent to which secondary market supply can be restricted. As seen in the right panel of the figure, however, the investors who are unwilling to pay the auction price will be unwilling to pay the secondary market price. Now the cornerer acting as a discriminating monopolist, rather than maximizing profit, minimizes loss (the shaded triangle). Clearly, one cannot profit from cornering a market with invariant demand, because one ultimately must sell the security to those from whom it was bid away. In this simple world, cornering would be eliminated by the removal of the potential for profit.

This result, however, requires that the switch in auction technique completely unify the primary and secondary markets. Even after the adoption of common-price awards, presence at auctions may still be limited to a segment of the investor populace, perhaps to those who are more sensitive to price. Those who sold short in the when-issued market want quickly to cover their positions at the auction. Also, participants at an auction face uncertain outcomes, since they may not be awarded securities if they have not cast their bids appropriately. Those particularly averse to this quantity risk may well delay purchase to secondary trading. Most important, direct bidding requires incurring the fixed costs of ensuring payment and arranging for the placement of bids—the prospects for which depend on the pace of automation and the nature of regulation. As a result, the infrequent purchaser may remain in the secondary market. In other words, advocates of this format assume that dealers exist solely to shade bids because of the Treasury's discriminatory pricing. If, however, dealers provide any other service in the distribution of securities, then a gap remains between the demand schedules of the auction and the secondary market. A sufficiently large gap represents an opportunity for manipulation. Indeed, second-price awards might encourage strategems should differences between primary and secondary markets remain. A would-be manipulator could place bids for a substantial fraction of an issue well above the market consensus, and thus ensure awards, but pay only that price required to allocate the remaining portion of securities to his or her unsuspecting competitors.

IV. AN ALTERNATIVE PROPOSAL

On balance, the switch to single-price awards likely represents an improvement on current Treasury practice; however, the *Joint Report* recommended the study of a more radical change. Collusive behavior relies on the closed nature of sealed bids—whether in the current first-price procedure or in the second-price alternative. A schemer needs only to beat the market's best guess formed moments before bidding closes in order to leave his or her competitors no chance to react.

An open-outcry system lets other market participants react to any surprise. Technologically, pieces of paper are not needed for the expression of the intent to purchase Treasury securities. As an alternative, registered dealers could connect by phone (with appropriately designed security) to a central computer; those not preregistered could appear at their local Reserve Bank with sufficient documentation to be included as a serious bidder. The scenario might unfold as follows. The auction begins as the Treasury calls out a price and all interested parties submit their quantity demanded. With quick tabulation, the volume of bids at that price is announced and, in successive rounds, the price is raised until the volume demanded is smaller than the size of the issuance. The next-to-last price called out clears the auction market because it is the highest

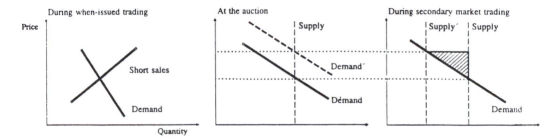

Figure 8 The effect of second-price awards on cornering.

price consistent with selling the entire issue. Everyone who bid at the top price would be guaranteed awards at the lower, market-clearing price. Those who bid at the next-to-last price but who did not move up into the top group receive the remaining securities at that lower price. Since bids from that group would exceed the remaining securities, some scheme for partial awards would be required.

Strategically, a dealer attempting to corner this auction must show his or her hand to the competition as the Treasury auctioneer raises the price. But the public exposure of the manipulator's addition to the volume of bids warns other participants—particularly those short the when-issued security—that they must raise their own bids if they want to receive awards. That opportunity for others to react should narrow the potential for profit in a corner attempt. To the extent that the average issuing price is raised in the attempt, the Treasury garners part of the profits. In contrast, in a sealed-bid auction, the bulk of the price action comes at the announcement of surprising awards, when other dealers realize that they are short and then react. In a real-time auction, that reaction occurs during the bidding. Also, the positive information revealed by the ascending-price nature of this auction format, on average, should benefit Treasury revenue.

A real-time auction may pose a daunting technical challenge. The goal of equal access requires that every effort be made to decentralize the system; anyone willing to pay the fixed cost of a properly configured terminal should be allowed to enter. At the same time, all bidders must be screened to ensure payment if their bids are successful. If the fixed cost of entry is too large, participation at the auction will be limited and a two-tiered distribution of securities and all the attendant risks may be perpetuated. If access is too free, the physical demands of directing a large volume of messages in a narrow span of time may prove taxing to any computer network. The private sector provides some precedent, but those efforts are small relative to the scale of operation required to sell Treasury securities.

Opening the auction might create new opportunities for large traders to move prices. For example, the surprising presence of a large trader elevating demand during the early stages of an auction might lead to a groundswell of enthusiasm that would push up the market-clearing price.* Similarly, the sudden dropping out by a large trader at a low price might dampen spirits enough to lower the market-clearing price. Either action might present the potential for profit. Also, as long as the three trading forums in Treasury securities are imperfectly integrated, the possibility of a market squeeze remains. At the least, an open-outcry auction does not abet a squeeze attempt by facilitating the bidding away of securities by surprise, as both types of sealed-bid auctions do. Thus, the Treasury would be less likely to be the counterparty from which a manipulator amassed a controlling position. Further, with easy entry, large traders would be pitted against each other in their pursuit of trading profits, as an open-outcry system turns market forces against market manipulation. As an added benefit, the technical sophistication required to conduct an automated open-outcry system could also be made available for surveillance regarding compliance with the auction rules.

V. CONCLUSION

While the academic literature suggests that the current Treasury procedure has drawbacks, it does not readily identify the best way to auction government securities. Individual elements of the problem are addressed, but other considerations do not fit nicely into the theoretical models. The Treasury is obliged to provide easy entry into the auctions, broadening, where possible, the ownership of the public debt; and it must adhere closely to a crowded schedule of borrowing. Also, while the Treasury may not always get top dollar for its issues, the present auction system may ease the conduct of monetary policy and ensure a deep and active secondary market in government obligations.

The shift to single-price awards may mark an improvement over the current technique, but it may not avoid the repetition of recent experience. No matter how rigidly rules are enforced, the incentive to manipulate the market remains.

This reading of the literature suggests that the optimal Treasury auction would have the following attributes (in order of decreasing importance):

- *Second price.* If all securities are awarded at the lowest price of an accepted bid, investors wary of the winner's curse may enter the auction directly. Such entrance raises total demand because bidders no

---

*See the description of the "herd effect" provided by Gastineau and Jarrow (1991).

longer feel the need to shade their bids. Also, by making direct bidding more attractive, individual dealers will no longer have as much access to customer business in attempts to swing the market.

- *Real time.* Auctions involving many participants that are conducted on an open-outcry basis are less susceptible to corners, which rely on surprise. In a sealed-bid auction, such surprise requires only stepping above the market consensus. That surprise is lost if market participants can react during the bidding.
- *Ascending price.* If the auctioneer calls out an ascending list of prices until the issue sold, the surprise of a cornering attempt is further eroded. Simply, other participants remain in the bidding. Also, an ascending-price auction produces the highest expected revenue to the seller.

In this regard, the open outcry of bids is a form of insurance against threats to the integrity of trading; an auction in real time makes active manipulation more difficult. As a side benefit, an open-outcry auction returns some of the potential profit from collusion to the Treasury in the form of higher prices.

There are no guarantees that any system will prevent manipulation. Any new system, however, should be flexible enough to permit experimentation with auction design. Planning for an open-outcry system may provide the requisite flexibility.

A transition to a new auction system has potential problems, as any reform is likely to be designed to entice investors to bid directly. Investors, however, may be hesitant at first to step in, preferring to observe before acting, especially if bidding has a substantial fixed cost. In the interim between the change in format and direct participation by investors, the auction would rely on dealers for their usual role—buying a large share of issuance—even though the reforms would ultimately erode their customer base and lessen their market power. If dealers left the market before final investors appeared, experimentation with alternative auction techniques might prove expensive. However, if access to the auction were kept as open as possible, scores of price-sensitive investors in the Treasury market might step in should auction prices differ markedly from those in secondary trading. Indeed, the threat of entry in itself might be sufficient to lessen the risk of an adverse reaction.

REFERENCES

Bikhchandani, S. and Chi-fu Huang (1989). "Auctions with Resale Markets: An Exploratory Model of Treasury Bill Markets," *Review of Financial Studies*, vol. 2 pp. 311–339.

Eatwell, J., Milgate, M., and Newman, P., eds. (1987). *The New Palgrave: A Dictionary of Economics*, Macmillan Press, New York.

Friedman, M. (1964). "Comment on 'Collusion in the Auction Market for Treasury Bills.' " *Journal of Political. Economy, 72* (Oct.): 513–514.

Friedman, M. (1991). "How to Sell Government Securities." *Wall Street Journal*, Aug. 28.

Gastineau, G. L. and Jarrow, R. A. (1991). "Large-Trader Impact and Market Regulation." *Financial Analysts Journal* (July/Aug.): 40–51.

Goldstein, H. (1962). "The Friedman Proposal for Auctioning Treasury Bills." *Journal of Political Economy, 70* (Aug.): 386–392.

Graham, D. A. and Marshall, R. C. (1987). "Collusive Bidder Behavior at Single-Object Second-Price and English Auctions." *Journal of Political Economy, 95* (Dec.): 1217–1239.

Henriques, D. B. (1991). "Treasury's Troubled Auctions." *New York Times*, Sept. 15.

McAfee, R. P., and McMillan, J. (1987). "Auctions and Bidding." *Journal of Economic Literature, 25* (June): 699–738.

Mester, L. J. (1988). "Going, Going, Gone: Setting Prices with Auctions." *Federal Reserve Bank of Philadelphia Business Review* (March/April): 3–13.

Milgrom, P. (1989). "Auctions and Bidders: A Primer." *Journal of Economic Perspectives, 3*(summer): 3–22.

Milgrom, P., and Weber, R. J., (1982). "A Theory of Auctions and Competitive Bidding." *Econometrica, 50* (Sept.): 1089–1122.

Robinson, M. S. (1985). "Collusion and the Choice of Auction." *The Rand Journal of Economics, 16* (spring): 141–145.

Smith, J. L. (1981). "Non-Aggressive Bidding Behavior and the 'Winner's Curse.' " *Economic Inquiry, 19* (July): 380–88.

Smith, V. L. (1966). "Bidding Theory and the Treasury Bill Auction: Does Price Discrimination Increase Bill Prices?" *Review of Economics and Statistics, 48* (May): 141–146.

U.S. Department of the Treasury, U.S. Securities and Exchange Commission, and Board of Governors of the Federal Reserve System (1992). *Joint Report on the Government Securities Market*, Government Printing Office, Washington, D.C.

Vickrey, W. (1961). "Counterspeculation, Auctions, and Competitive Sealed Tenders." *Journal of Finance, 16* (March): 8–37.

Weber, R. J. (1983). "Multiple-Object Auctions," *Auctions, Bidding, and Contracting: Uses and Theory* (R. Englebrecht-Wiggans, M. Shubik, and R. M. Stark, eds.) New York University Press, New York; pp. 165–191.

56

Auctioning Treasury Securities

E. J. Stevens and Diana Dumitru
Federal Reserve Bank of Cleveland, Cleveland, Ohio

The U.S. Treasury expects to sell about a trillion dollars of new securities this fiscal year to finance a projected $400 billion budget deficit and to refinance maturing debt. Most of the securities will be issued through public auctions, where competition among bidders might be expected to minimize interest payments on the debt.

The competitiveness of Treasury auctions was called into question last August, however, when Salomon Brothers, a large securities dealer, admitted to having placed unauthorized bids in the names of customers during eight auctions. For example, in the May 22, 1991 note auction, the firm controlled more than 90% of the issue, far exceeding the 35% limit set by the Treasury. Rumors of a market "squeeze" had surfaced even before the notes were issued on May 31.[1] Disappointed bidders, with contracts to deliver the security after it was issued, had to pay an unexpectedly high price for the issue in the secondary market, where Salomon controlled most of the supply.

Two causes for concern emerge from this incident. First, of course, is simply that the market is not fair when auction rules are broken. Some investors might shun the Treasury securities market rather than be exposed to losses resulting from market manipulation. Thus, any short-term gain to the Treasury from an artificially high price at a single auction could be outweighed by lower demand and prices in all auctions. Second, as suggested here, is the possibility that the auction process itself may be at fault. Perhaps a different system of selling new issues of Treasury debt would reduce incentives for manipulation.

Following Salomon's admissions and other reported irregularities, the Treasury Department, the Board of Governors of the Federal Reserve System, and the Securities and Exchange Commission conducted a study in 1991 leading to a joint report on the government securities market. The report reaffirms that public auctions are the best means of issuing new Treasury debt and recommends some minor adjustments that have already been adopted to ensure public access to the existing auction process. It also recommends a more thorough exploration of alternative methods of conducting public auctions. This *Economic Commentary* examines the rationales for adopting a different system for determining the price paid by a winning bidder and a new technology for bidding.[2] Both of these changes could make public auctions of Treasury securities less susceptible to manipulation.

I. TODAY'S AUCTIONS: MULTIPLE-PRICE, SEALED-BID

The Treasury maintains a regular schedule of auctions in which it sells bonds, notes, and bills. Bonds and notes are sold in $1,000 denominations and pay interest every 6 months until maturity, which ranges from

Adapted from *Economic Commentary* (June 15, 1992) by permission of the Federal Reserve Bank of Cleveland.

10 to 30 years for bonds and from 1 to 10 years for notes. The recent schedule has included monthly auctions of 2- and 5-year notes and quarterly auctions of 3-, 7-, and 10-year notes and 30-year bonds.

Treasury bills, in $10,000 denominations, have no coupon. An investor's return comes from the difference between the maturity value and the price paid—the "discount." Bills maturing in 13 weeks and 26 weeks are auctioned every Monday. Bills maturing in 52 weeks are offered every 4 weeks.

About a week before each auction, the Treasury announces the auction day, size, maturity, and the settlement day when successful bidders must make payment. From this announcement until settlement, the impending security actually trades in the market on a "when-issued" basis, with the promise of delivery on settlement day. When-issued trading thus may provide potential bidders with information about the likely price in the auction.

By 1:00 p.m. on auction day, bidders must submit tenders (written, sealed bids) at Federal Reserve Banks or their branches. Two kinds of tenders can be used. Competitive tenders state the amount of securities desired (as much as several billion dollars) and either a yield bid (for bonds and notes) in one-basis-point increments or a price bid (for bills) on the basis of 100 (for example, 98.995). Noncompetitive tenders can be placed only for smaller amounts (up to $5 million for notes and bonds, or $1 million for bills), with the yield or price determined by the average of awards in competitive bidding.

At 1:00 p.m. on the day of an auction, bids are tabulated and transmitted to the Treasury. Securities are awarded to all noncompetitive bidders; the remainder of the issue is awarded to competitive bidders in descending order of price bid (increasing yield bid).[3] A bidder may submit tenders up to a maximum of 35% of the amount being auctioned, with bids at various prices. The exception is that if too many bids are received at the lowest accepted "stop-out" price, these awards are made in proportion to the total of all bids received at that price.

The process can be summarized as a sealed-bid auction, open to anyone, with awards at multiple prices. Modifications already adopted address the openness of the process, to ensure that any financially responsible party can participate in a Treasury auction. Some drawbacks are nevertheless associated with multiple prices and sealed bidding.

II. THE WINNER'S CURSE

Making auction awards at multiple prices means that the highest bidders must follow through, actually paying the prices they offered even though others are paying less for the identical security. This may seem only fair. After all, if the high bidders didn't think the securities were worth so much, they shouldn't have bid so much. This view assumes that the item's value to the winner may be largely independent of the lower value placed on the item by unsuccessful bidders.

In the case of Treasury auctions, however, the value of a security is not independent of the market. A dealer wants the security being auctioned only in order to sell it, but must compete with other dealers who may have paid less in the auction; an investor wants the securities for portfolio purposes and could wait to buy in the postauction market. No matter how fair it may seem, paying a high price for an award of securities that other have bought more cheaply truly involves a "winner's curse."

The winner's curse has serious implications for Treasury auctions. While a high bid will increase the chances of an award, it also raises the possibility of paying more than the postauction market value of the security. The auction process might reveal something about that value, but only the smallest-volume bidders can benefit by submitting noncompetitive tenders; competitive bidders cannot take advantage of the information revealed in the auction. The winner's curse dampens the aggressiveness of their bidding, resulting in a lower auction price received by the Treasury. Bids may be lowered to cover the costs of gathering information about what others are likely to bid. Alternatively, customers may submit their bids through a small number of well-informed dealers, where bidding might tend to become concentrated. Thus, a winner's curse may dampen all competitive bidding and lower multiple auction prices relative to market values.

Sealed bidding, on the other hand, when coupled with multiple prices, enables a single bidder to corner the postauction market, transforming the auction-winner's curse into a postauction blessing. A well-informed and well-financed bidder or group of bidders could deliberately submit a high bid to ensure receiving a dominant share of auction awards. Because of the substantial volume of when-issued trading, controlling the postauction supply of a Treasury security places the high bidder in a position to squeeze unsuccessful bidders who had contracted to deliver the security after the auction. While not a necessary outcome, the current auction setup does contain the seeds of market manipulation that can discourage demand. The winner's curse places a premium on discovering how others will bid, creating the basis for a bid that will corner an auction and squeeze the postauction market.

III. SAFEGUARDS AGAINST MANIPULATION

Treasury auctions contain an important safeguard against cornering the supply of a new issue; a single bidder is prohibited from acquiring more than 35% of an issue. As the Salomon example attests, enforcing this rule is not easy. For example, winning bidders must be contacted to ensure that customers' names are not used improperly by a dealer trying to control more than his share of an issue. Moreover, 35% is an arbitrary limit that may restrict demand and unnecessarily lower auction prices when there is no threat of manipulation.

One alternative to this rule is to reopen the issue whose supply has been cornered. Augmenting supply would drive down an artificially high price and eliminate profits expected by the perpetrators of the squeeze. Knowing that the Treasury would respond in this way would eliminate the incentive to manipulate the market. Of course, this approach is simply the price equivalent of the 35% rule, reducing the high bidder's market share by increasing total supply. It would involve an equally arbitrary judgment about the permissible range within which the postauction price could vary without triggering a reopening, as well as arbitrary judgments about whether prices reflected manipulation or a change in market fundamentals.

IV. A SINGLE-PRICE AUCTION

Changing to a single-price auction has been proposed as an alternative to enforcing arbitrary rules on the current auction process.[4] This procedure would be identical to the current one, except that all competitive awards would be made at the stop-out price, which is the price that clears the market. The winner's curse would disappear because winning bidders would receive their awards at the stop-out, even if they bid higher.

Resistance to a single-price auction centers around its implication for the cost of servicing government debt. With a single-price auction, the Treasury would forgo revenue now received from the difference between successful price bids and the stop-out price. Actually, however, Treasury auction revenues might increase, although auction theory is ambivalent on this matter.[5] Revenue forgone by shifting from a multiple- to a single-price auction might be more than offset by an increase in demand as participants bid more aggressively in the absence of a winner's curse, as illustrated in Fig. 1. Whether the gain would actually exceed forgone

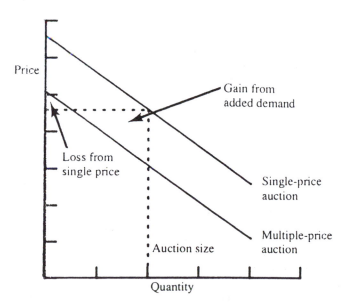

Figure 1   Single-price auctions: gains and losses.

revenues, though, depends in part in the *size* of the increase in demand. It could be slight if most participants are already so averse to the risk of not getting an award that they bid aggressively in multiple-price auctions, despite the winner's curse. So, a single-price auction will increase demand, but might not reduce the interest cost of financing the debt.

More to the point, a single-price auction also might or might not produce a less fertile environment for market manipulation. A high bid could garner a dominant market position without requiring the successful bidder to pay any more than the stop-out price. But other incentives to corner the market might be weaker, because bidders would no longer conduct as intensive a pre-auction search for information about others' bids. Thus, a bidder would have to make special efforts to gather information; cornering the market would become more costly. Chances of pre-auction detection by other bidders, who might raise their own bids by enough to defeat an attempted corner, would also increase.

V. AN AUCTION BY OPEN OUTCRY

Perhaps the most intriguing alternative presented in the joint report is that of conducting Treasury auctions by open outcry, rather than by sealed bid. The disadvantage of sealed bidding is that participants cannot be certain of the distribution of all other bids. In the multiple-price auction, winning with a bid higher than the stop-out implies that your estimate was too high, and the risk of this winner's curse leads to conservative bidding. In a single-price auction, your winning bid is lowered to the stop-out, based on the auctioneer's information about the actual distribution of bids, all of which will be less conservative than in a multiple-price auction. In an open-outcry auction, which is typically used to sell antiques or works of art, information about the distribution of bids is revealed gradually to all bidders before the auction closes. As the auction process drives the bidding higher and higher, low prices become irrelevant.

An attempt to gain a dominant share of Treasury auction awards seems unlikely to succeed with this system, because the auction process reveals more information about the actual distribution of bids. If the distribution of bids initially contains an unusually large bid at a high price, the ascending price reveals that a large number of bidders underestimated the value of the security and therefore can raise their bids. While the final auction price may be unusually high, the individual who attempted to corner will not gain a large share of awards.

In the past, formidable obstacles have stood in the way of conducting Treasury auctions by open outcry, obstacles mostly absent from the typical auction of a unique art object. At one time, it might have been difficult even to assemble all bidding in a single place, but today, open communication lines to Federal Reserve offices and to individual bidders could overcome that geographic problem, just as telephone bidding does in major art auctions.

More difficult, and unlike an auction a single work of art, bidders must cry out not just a price, but a *quantity* at each price. Bidding must ascend from low prices, where the demand for securities exceeds the supply, to the market-clearing price, where demand exactly equals supply. As envisioned in the joint report, bidding would have to proceed in discreet "rounds," starting from a low price and rising by small increments. As the results of each round were announced, participants could drop out, resubmit the same quantity, or adjust the quantity in light of information gained from the previous round.

Auctioning Treasury securities by open outcry would consume too much time to be feasible with current auction technology. Each round of bidding probably would take more than an hour using today's paper tenders, manual tabulation, verification of payment status, transmission to the Treasury, and final compilation. Each open-outcry auction might consume most of a day during which unfolding world events might be moving market fundamentals enough to change bidding decisions, to prevent the process from moving smoothly toward an equilibrium market-clearing price.

The Treasury expects to automate the current sealed-bid, multiple-price auction process this year, allowing telecommunication of tenders and computerized compilation of bids. Going any further toward auctions by electronic open outcry would require substantial investments, both in hardware and software, and, before that, in design. One critical design question would involve the information feedback provided at the end of each round of bidding. Simply announcing the amount of excess demand might not be sufficient for bidders to detect an aggressive effort to dominate the awards. On the other hand, a complete (anonymous) list of all bid quantities received might prove too cumbersome for rapid rounds of bidding. Another design question involves the computer and telecommunications capacity required to receive large numbers of bids virtually simultaneously. Too little is known at this time, but automation could conceivably reduce the turnaround time between successive rounds of bidding to a matter of minutes, with an entire auction lasting perhaps less than an hour.[6] Given the information benefits of open outcry, serious further exploration seems warranted.

VI. CONCLUSION

The U.S. Treasury securities market is the largest and most efficient market in the world today. Nonetheless, the events of 1991 demonstrated that concerted strong bidding in the primary market for an issue could result in a squeeze in the secondary market. More aggressive policing of the current rule against control of more than 35% of a new issue promises to reduce chances of similar episodes in the future.

Embedded in the current sealed-bid, multiple-price auction process are both incentives and opportunities for a bidder to seek a dominant share of awards. New methods of conducting auctions are worth serious consideration if they would reduce the need for arbitrary policing of the market. A single-price, sealed-bid auction would reduce the current incentive of each bidder to discover the price at which other bidders will make tenders. With less of their activity focused on discovering one another's intentions, bidders would have less opportunity and incentive to corner an issue. Perhaps more promising would be to enlist telecommunications and computer technology in conducting auctions by electronic open outcry, relying on competition among the bidders themselves to limit the share of auction awards controlled by any single bidder.

NOTES

1. A squeeze occurs when there is an unexpected restriction of supply relative to demand for a particular security, manifested by an unusually high price of that security relative to prices of comparable securities.
2. See *Joint Report on the Government Securities Market.* Washington, D.C.: Department of the Treasury, Securities and Exchange Commission, and Board of Governors of the Federal Reserve System, Jan. 1992. A somewhat more technical examination of these matters appeared recently in Vincent Reinhart, "Theory and Evidence on Reform of the Treasury's Auction Procedures," Federal Reserve Board, Finance and Economics Discussion Series no. 190, March 1992.
3. Federal Reserve Bank and government tenders are also awarded in full at the price established for noncompetitive bidders, but the amount of these awards is added to the amount being auctioned.
4. Milton Friedman has been a long-time proponent of this procedure. For references, see *Joint Report on the Government Securities Market*, p. B-22.
5. See Robert J. Weber, "Multiple-Object Auctions," in Richard Engelbrecht-Wiggins, Martin Shubik, and Robert M. Stark, eds., *Auctions, Bidding, and Contracting: Uses and Theory.* New York: New York University Press, 1983.
6. An alternative to rounds of bidding might be to conduct auctions on an interactive, open-screen basis. Qualified bidders would have access directly (or at a Federal Reserve Bank) to a telecommunications terminal. Beginning hours (or days) before the close of an auction, a screen would display an instantaneously updated list of all (anonymous) bids received and their implied auction stop-out price. Bidders would have the right to alter their bids up until the close of the auction, when the final stop-out price would be determined, with awards made to all who bid at or above that price.

57

Can the Government Roll Over Its Debt Forever?

Andrew B. Abel

The Wharton School, University of Pennsylvania, Philadelphia, Pennsylvania

In the past dozen years, the federal government has regularly run large deficits, usually well in excess of $100 billion per year. The amount of federal government debt outstanding has quadrupled during this time, from a value of $908 billion at the end of fiscal year 1980 to a value of $3,665 billion at the end of fiscal year 1991. Even after correcting for inflation, the amount of government debt has grown by a factor of 2.5 over this period. This apparent explosion in the amount of government debt has led to spirited and protracted public debate about federal tax policy and federal expenditures. Despite the widely professed desire to reduce the federal deficit and to limit the growth of federal government debt, a consensus about how to achieve these alleged goals has not yet emerged. Faced with continuing deficits, the government has resorted to rolling over its debt—that is, issuing new debt to pay the interest on existing debt and to pay off holders of maturing debt.

Is rolling over the debt the solution that we have been looking for? Can the government simply roll over its debt forever without having to take the politically costly steps of raising taxes or cutting expenditures in the future? This article discusses the feasibility of rolling over government debt forever. As we will see, this question is related to another important question about the future of the economy: Is the economy as a whole saving an appropriate amount for the future? In addition, both of these questions are related to the question of whether an entity can run a Ponzi game.

I. THE SIMPLE ARITHMETIC OF GOVERNMENT DEBT ACCUMULATION

To address the question of whether the government can roll over its debt forever, we need to quantify the factors that contribute to the growth of government debt over time. We begin by specifying the relationship between government deficits and the growth rate of government debt. Then we examine whether the public would be willing to hold ever-increasing amounts of government debt, thereby permitting the government to roll over its debt forever.

A. Primary and Total Deficits

Although it is tempting to think of both "debt" and "deficits" as representing the "D word," there is an important distinction between debt and deficits. Government debt is the liability of the government owed to holders of government bonds at any particular moment; it is measured in dollars as of a particular date, such as $3,665 billion as of September 30, 1991. A government deficit is the excess of government expenditures over government receipts during a particular period. The government deficit equals the increase in the amount

Adapted from *Business Review* (Nov.–Dec. 1992): 3–18 by permission of the Federal Reserve Bank of Philadelphia.

of government debt during a particular interval; it is measured in terms of dollars per unit of time, such as $320.9 billion per year during fiscal year 1991 (October 1, 1990–September 30, 1991). In terms of familiar accounting concepts, government debt is a balance sheet concept, whereas the government deficit is an income statement concept.

Although the definition of the government deficit as the excess of government expenditures over government receipts during a particular period seems fairly unambiguous, actually two different deficit concepts are widely used. The difference between these two deficit concepts lies in whether interest payments on government debt are included as part of government expenditure. One deficit concept, known as the primary deficit, does not include interest payments on the government debt as part of government expenditure. Thus, the primary government deficit is calculated as all noninterest expenditure by the government minus government receipts. The primary government deficit was "only" $34.9 billion in fiscal 1991 (Table 1).

The other deficit concept, known as the total deficit or simply the deficit, includes interest payments by the government as part of government expenditure. Thus the total deficit equals total government expenditure, including interest payments, minus government receipts. In fiscal 1991, interest payments by the government amounted to $286.0 billion, so that the total government deficit of $320.9 billion exceeded the primary government deficit by $286.0 billion.

Why are there two different deficit concepts? The reason economists and policy makers look at both of these deficit concepts is that each concept provides the answer to a different question. Specifically, the primary deficit answers the question: Are current taxes sufficient to pay for spending on current government programs? More precisely, the primary deficit measures the extent to which spending on current programs exceeds the taxes currently collected. The total deficit answers a different question: How much will the government have to borrow to pay for its expenditures? The total deficit during a year measures the increase in government debt during that year.

B. The Debt-GNP Ratio

How do we gauge whether a government's debt is too large? One way to gauge the size of a government's debt is by the government's ability to repay the debt. Governments that have access to larger tax bases would be able to support larger amounts of debt than governments with smaller tax bases. For the federal government, we can gauge the size of the tax base by some measure of national income, such as gross national product (GNP) or gross domestic product (GDP). In this article, we will use GNP as the measure of national income, and thus we will use the ratio of government debt to GNP—known as the debt-GNP ratio—to gauge the size of government debt.

The historical behavior of the debt-GNP ratio over the last century in the United States is shown in Fig. 1. Notice that the debt-GNP ratio rose sharply during World War I and World War II, and then fell gradually after these wars (and also fell gradually for about a half century after the Civil War). In addition to the increases in the debt-GNP ratio during wars, the debt–GNP ratio also rose sharply during the Great Depression of the 1930s and during the 1980s.

Table 1   Government Deficit, Fiscal Year 1991 (Oct. 1, 1990–Sept. 30, 1991)

Government expenditures	
Noninterest expenditures[a]	$795.3 billion
Interest payments by government[b]	$286.0 billion
Total expenditures[c]	$1,081.3 billion
Government receipts[c]	$760.4 billion

Primary deficit = $795.3 billion − $760.4 billion = $34.9 billion
Total deficit = $1,081.3 billion − $760.4 billion = $320.9 billion

[a]*Source*: calculated as total expenditures minus interest payments by government.
[b]*Source*: Treasury Bulletin, March 1992.
[c]*Source*: Economic Report of the President, 1992, Table B-75.

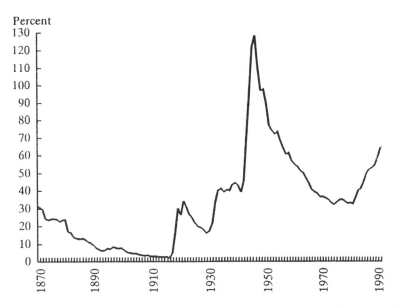

Percent

Figure 1 Debt-GNP ratio. *Sources*: Ratio of government debt to GNP. Source of government debt (end of fiscal year): 1869–1839 from *Historical Statistics of the United States*, series y338; 1940–1969 from *Banking and Monetary Statistics, 1941–1970*, Table 13.1, C; 1970–1979 from *Federal Reserve Board Annual Statistical Digest, 1970–1979*, Table 27; 1980–1989 from *Federal Reserve Board Annual Statistical Digest, 1980–1989*, Table 26; 1990–1991 from *Treasury Bulletin*, March 1992, Table FD-1. Source of GNP: 1869–1958, Balke, N. S. and Gordon, R. J., Appendix B: Historical Data, in *The American Business Cycle: Continuity and Change*, R. J. Gordon (ed.), Chicago and London: University of Chicago Press, 1986; 1959–1991 from Data Resources Incorporated (1960 GNP is 2% higher in DRI than in Balke and Gordon).

What causes the debt-GNP ratio to increase from one year to the next? Just as a matter of simple arithmetic, the debt-GNP ratio will rise whenever the growth rate of the numerator, i.e., the growth rate of government debt, is higher than the growth rate of the denominator, i.e., the growth rate of GNP. As we have discussed earlier, the increase in government debt during a year equals the total deficit, which in turn equals the primary deficit plus interest payments by the government. Thus, the debt-GNP ratio tends to increase when (1) the primary government deficit is large; (2) interest payments by the government are large; and (3) the growth rate of GNP is small. The following equation, which is an approximation derived in Appendix A, captures the simple arithmetic of government debt accumulation:

Growth rate of debt-GNP ratio = primary deficit/debt + interest rate − growth rate of GNP   (1)

Note that when the growth rate of the debt–GNP ratio is positive, this ratio is growing, and when the growth rate of the debt-GNP ratio is negative, the debt-GNP ratio is falling.

The three components of the growth rate of the debt-GNP ratio on the right-hand side of Eq. (1) explain, in an arithmetic sense at least, the historical behavior of the debt-GNP ratio shown in Fig. 1. The sharp increase in the debt-GNP ratio during both world wars resulted from sharp increases in the primary deficit (Fig. 2). Of course, the increase in the primary deficit reflects the large increase in military expenditure during wartime. The rise in the debt-GNP ratio during the Great Depression resulted from large declines in GNP during the early 1930s and from large primary deficits beginning in 1932. The decline in the debt-GNP ratio during the three-and-a-half decades following World War II resulted from a combination of factors: (1) a small—indeed usually negative—primary deficit; and (2) an interest rate that was usually smaller than the growth rate of GNP. However, during the 1980s the debt-GNP ratio departed from its typical pattern of peacetime behavior and began to rise. Arithmetically, the positive growth rate of the debt-GNP ratio was accounted for by a relatively large ratio of the primary deficit to government debt in the early 1980s and by the fact that the interest rate exceeded the growth rate of GNP for most of the 1980s.

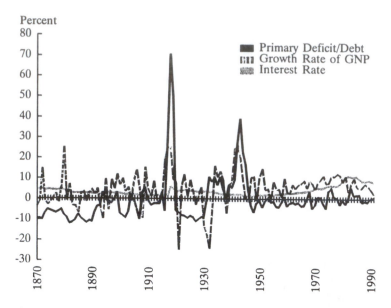

Figure 2   Components of debt-GNP growth rate. *Sources:* Primary deficit calculated as total deficit minus interest payments by the government. Source of total deficit: 1869–1939 from *Historical Statistics of the United States,* series y337; 1940–1991 from *Economic Report of the President,* Feb. 1992, Table B-74, on-budget. Source of interest payments: 1869–1969: from *Historical Statistics of the United States,* series y461; 1970–1991 from *Treasury Bulletin,* various issues, Table FFO-3. Interest rate calculated as interest payments in current fiscal year divided by government debt at end of previous fiscal year (see note to Fig. 1 for source of data on government debt). Growth rate of GNP calculated from GNP data described in note to Fig. 1.

C. Rolling Over Government Debt

Our discussion of the debt-GNP ratio was motivated by the desire to gauge the size of government debt relative to the government's ability to repay that debt. What problems might be associated with a high value of the debt-GNP ratio? If the debt-GNP ratio were to become too large, the public might begin to suspect that one day the government would default on its debt, and this suspicion might make the public unwilling to buy additional government debt. There are many ways the government could default on its debt. The government could simply renounce its liabilities and refuse to pay holders of government bonds. Alternatively, the government could heavily tax the principal and/or interest on government bonds, effectively defaulting on at least a fraction of its liabilities. More subtly, the government could print money and create inflation, which reduces the real purchasing power of its dollar liabilities represented by government bonds. Another problem with a very high debt-GNP ratio is that the interest payments on government debt become a very large fraction of GNP. If the debt–GNP ratio becomes extremely large, the increase in government debt needed to pay the interest on the outstanding government debt could become larger than all of GNP* and the public would not be able to buy this debt.

The willingness or unwillingness of the public to buy additional government debt when the debt-GNP ratio gets large determines whether the government can roll over its debt forever. If a policy of rolling over government debt forever would cause the debt-GNP ratio to grow forever without bound, the public would become unwilling to buy the government debt offered for sale and the rollover policy would have to terminate. However, if the debt-GNP ratio falls forever when the government is pursuing a rollover policy, it would be possible to roll over government debt forever.

But how could the debt-GNP ratio fall forever while the government is rolling over its debt? To answer

---

*If the debt-GNP ratio exceeds the reciprocal of the interest rate on government bonds, interest payments on government debt would exceed GNP.

this question, we will first precisely define a policy or rolling over the debt in terms of the primary deficit, and then we will use Eq. (1) to see how the debt-GNP ratio changes over time under a policy of debt rollover.

Quite simply, a government is rolling over its debt if its primary deficit is zero, so that its total deficit equals its interest payments on government debt. In this case, the government sells additional government bonds (debt) to pay the interest on government debt and to pay off holders of maturing government debt. If the government can run a zero primary deficit forever, selling bonds to cover the total deficit, then it can roll over its debt forever. Whether the government is able to run a zero primary deficit forever depends on whether the debt–GNP ratio eventually becomes too large when the government runs a zero primary deficit year after year.

To see if a government can run a zero primary deficit forever, we simply set the primary deficit in Eq. (1) equal to zero and observe that in this case the growth rate of the debt-GNP ratio equals the interest rate minus the growth rate of GNP. If the interest rate is higher than the growth rate, the debt-GNP ratio grows forever without bound, and eventually the government would lose its ability to roll over its debt. However, if the interest rate is smaller than the growth rate of GNP, the growth rate of the debt-GNP ratio would be negative, and the government could roll over its debt forever. For instance, if the interest rate is 3% per year and the growth rate of GNP is 4% per year, interest payments amount to 3% of government debt. If the government sells new bonds to pay these interest payments, the supply of government debt will increase by 3% per year, which is less than the 4% annual growth rate of GNP. Thus, the debt–GNP ratio would decline.

For most of the last century in the United States, the interest rate on government debt has been lower than the growth rate of GNP (Fig. 2). In fact, the average interest rate on government debt was 4.12% per year, and the average growth rate of GNP was 5.86% per year over the period 1869–1991. If this pattern with the average interest rate below the average growth rate were to continue to hold forever, it would appear that the U.S. government could roll over its debt forever.

II.   What Happens When The Interest Rate Is Less Than The Growth Rate of GNP?

We have seen that over the last century the average interest rate on government debt was lower than the average growth rate of GNP. One important implication of having an interest rate lower than the growth rate of GNP is that the government can roll over its debt forever. In this section, we discuss two other important—and surprising—implications of having an interest rate lower than the economy's growth rate.

A.   The Economy Has Too Much Capital

The most important factor determining the standard of living of future generations is the long-run rate of economic growth. One of the primary ways that an economy can help promote economic growth is to save for the future by increasing the capital stock of productive equipment and structures. This process of capital accumulation combines a present sacrifice in the form of reduced present consumption with a future benefit in the form of increased future output and consumption. At various times in recent history, policy makers have made the judgment that the future gain is worth the present sacrifice, and national economic policy focused directly on stimulating capital formation by providing tax incentives in the form of accelerated depreciation allowances and the investment tax credit.

Is it possible for an economy to overdo it? More precisely, is it possible for an economy to accumulate and maintain a level of capital that is unambiguously too high? Surprisingly, the answer is yes. An economy can accumulate so much capital that the current sacrifice associated with current investment actually leads to a future sacrifice in the form of reduced future consumption. In this situation, the present sacrifice associated with capital formation is clearly not worth undertaking. An interest rate smaller than the growth rate of the economy signals that such a situation exists.

To see how it would be possible to have too much capital, suppose a piece of capital requires $5 worth of resources every year to maintain it in working order, but the capital contributes additional output worth only $4 per year. The economy would be suffering a net loss of $1 per year and would be better off without the capital.* At the level of the national economy, we can say that an economy has too much capital if in

---

*In this numerical example, net investment is zero, but the same principle applies when there is positive net investment. For example, consider a firm that operates a factory with a work force that grows by 2% per year. If the firm maintains a constant ratio of capital to labor, the firm's capital stock would grow by 2% per year. However, if the contribution to total output of each unit of capital is only 1% of the value of the capital stock, then the firm would be pouring more resources into the factory than it gets out of the factory, and it would be better off closing that factory.

every year the amount of resources devoted to creating new capital and maintaining old capital is greater than the contribution to total output of the total capital stock. To put this condition in the language of national income accounting, an economy has too much capital if in every year gross investment (the amount of resources devoted to new capital formation and replacement of depreciated capital) exceeds gross capital income (which measures the contribution of capital to total output). We write this condition as

Too much capital if: gross investment > gross capital income in every year   (2)

Now we can relate the condition for too much capital to the relationship between the interest rate and the growth rate. This relationship is clearest for an economy growing at a constant rate year after year, so let's suppose that the economy is growing at constant rate g every year. Thus, for example, GNP is growing at the rate g and the total capital stock, K, is also growing at the rate g. With the capital stock growing at the rate g per year, the amount of net capital formation during a year is gK. In addition, some resources are devoted to replacing capital that depreciates during the year. Letting d be the fraction of the capital stock that depreciates during a year, the total amount of depreciation during a year that must be offset by capital formation is dK. Gross investment is the sum of net capital formation and depreciation

$$\text{Gross investment} = gK + dK = (g + d)K \qquad (3)$$

The contribution of capital to total output is measured by gross capital income. Letting R denote the gross rate of return on capital, we have

$$\text{Gross capital income} = RK \qquad (4)$$

Comparing gross investment in Eq. (3) with gross capital income in Eq. (4), we see that the economy has too much capital if $(g + d)K > R K$ in every year, or equivalently

Too much capital if: $g + d > R$ in every year   (5)

To see the role of the interest rate in this condition, we observe that in an economy in which there is no uncertainty, the interest rate r would equal the net rate of return on capital, which is the gross rate of return R minus the rate of depreciation. In symbols we have

$$\begin{array}{cc} r & = & R - d \\ \text{(interest rate)} & \text{(net rate of return on capital)} \end{array} \qquad (6)$$

Finally, we obtain the condition for too much capital in terms of the interest rate and the growth rate by subtracting the depreciation rate d from both sides of Eq. (5) and using the fact that $r = R - d$ to obtain

Too much capital if: $g > r$ in every year.   (7)

Thus, we can see that in the absence of uncertainty, an economy growing at a constant rate has too much capital if the interest rate is less than the growth rate. An economy in this situation could realize both a present gain and a future gain by permanently reducing the amount of investment. Present consumption would increase as the economy's current resources shifted from investment to consumption. Future consumption would increase as fewer resources were, on net, poured into the formation and maintenance of capital. As a result of the reduction in investment, the capital stock would fall, and as capital became less abundant, the rate of return on capital would increase. When the rate of investment has fallen enough, the net rate of return on capital and the interest rate will rise above the growth rate of the economy, so that the symptom of too much capital will disappear.

Recall that during the period 1869–1991 the average interest rate in the United States was smaller than the average growth rate. Thus, Eq. (7) would seem to suggest that the United States has too much capital. We will take another look at this provocative implication later in this article.

B. Ponzi Games

In the early twentieth century, Charles Ponzi promised investors the opportunity to double their money in 90 days by investing in international postal coupons. Over the course of 8 months, Ponzi acquired about $150,000,000 from 40,000 investors. Not surprisingly, Ponzi's promises proved to be too good to be true, and

Ponzi was arrested in August 1920.* Economists now use the term "Ponzi game" to describe a situation in which an entity (a person, business, or government) sells securities to investors and never uses any of its own money to pay dividends or interest or to repay the principal. Any subsequent payments (such as dividends, interest, or return of principal) to holders of these securities are financed by selling additional securities. Our discussion will focus on rational Ponzi games, which are Ponzi games in which there is no fraud or deceit on the part of the seller of securities and no lack of understanding or foresight on the part of buyers of these securities.

As a simple example of a rational Ponzi game, consider an entity that sells $100 million of long-term bonds, promising to pay an interest rate of 4% per year. At the end of 1 year, when it is time to pay investors $4 million in interest, the entity sells an additional $4 million of bonds to investors, bringing total bonds outstanding to $104 million. Then at the end of 2 years, when $4.16 million of interest (4% of $104 million) is due, the entity sells an additional $4.16 million of bonds, and so on. The amount of bonds outstanding grows at the rate of interest, which is 4% per year in this example. For this Ponzi game to be feasible, the public must be willing to hold the ever-increasing amount of bonds issued. If investors' wealth is growing at, say, 5% per year, there would be sufficient demand by the public for newly issued bonds, and thus the entity would be able to sell additional bonds to pay the interest on its debt without having to use any of its own resources.

In the Ponzi game described above, suppose that the entity selling the bonds is the government. Then the Ponzi game amounts to rolling over government debt forever. The Ponzi game will be feasible, that is, the government will be able to roll over its debt forever, provided that the growth rate of aggregate wealth exceeds the interest rate. The growth rate of aggregate wealth is not readily measured, but in the absence of a trend in the ratio of wealth to GNP, the growth rate of aggregate wealth can be proxied by the growth rate of GNP. Thus, the government will be able to roll over its debt forever if the growth rate of GNP exceeds the interest rate.[†]

To summarize, if the interest rate is lower than the growth rate of GNP, (1) the economy has too much capital; (2) entities can run rational Ponzi games; and (3) in particular, the government can roll over its debt forever. As we have seen, over the last century in the United States, the average interest rate has been lower than the average growth rate of GNP. Thus, it might seem that the United States has too much capital, that entities can run rational Ponzi games, and that the government can roll over its debt forever. However, these three results do not strike most observers as plausible descriptions of the U.S. economy. The implausibility of these results stimulated new research into these questions in the past several years. A point of departure for much of this research is the fact that the results presented above were derived under the assumption of a constant interest rate and a constant growth rate, but, as is evident in Fig. 2, the interest rate, and especially the growth rate, have displayed substantial variability in the United States. Recent research has focused on uncertainty as the source of variation in the interest rate and the growth rate and has found that the results summarized above need to be substantially altered when uncertainty is incorporated into the analysis.

III. THE IMPORTANCE OF UNCERTAINTY

Recent research into the questions of whether an economy has too much capital and whether a government can roll over its debt forever has shown that simply comparing the average interest rate and the average growth rate of the economy can produce misleading answers to these questions. Much of this research is ongoing and many important questions remain unanswered, but this research has yielded some important insights.

---

*See O'Connell and Zeldes (1992).

[†]The discussion in this article ignores distortions arising from taxes or from externalities. In a recent paper, Ian King (1992) has argued that with endogenous growth arising from externalities in the stock of knowledge, it is possible for Ponzi games to be feasible even though the economy does not suffer from overaccumulation of capital. This result arises because the private and social returns to capital differ in the presence of externalities. Capital overaccumulation occurs if the social rate of return to capital is lower than the growth rate of the economy, and Ponzi games are feasible if the private rate of return to capital is lower than the growth rate of the economy. In King's model, the social rate of return can be higher than the growth rate, which can be higher than the private rate of return.

A.   Another Look at Whether an Economy Has Too Much Capital

In a world without uncertainty, we can compare the interest rate and the growth rate of the economy to determine whether the economy has too much capital. In deriving Eq. (7) we used the fact [Eq. (6)] that in the absence of uncertainty, the net rate of return on capital, $R - d$, equals the interest rate, r, on government debt. However, in the presence of uncertainty, the rates of return on different assets, in particular the rates of return on capital and on government bonds, can in general differ. Thus, the comparison of the interest rate and the growth rate in Eq. (7) is no longer appropriate for assessing whether an economy has too much capital.

In the presence of uncertainty, the appropriate criterion for determining whether an economy has too much capital is Eq. (2); if gross investment exceeds gross capital income in every year, the economy has too much capital. If gross investment is less than gross capital income in every year, we conclude that the economy is not plagued by too much capital. A recent study* has examined gross investment and gross capital income in the United States for the period 1929–1985 and found that in every year, including the Great Depression of the 1930s, gross investment was less than gross capital income. Thus, despite the fact that the average interest rate was less than the average growth rate of the economy, we can conclude that the United States was not afflicted with too much capital.[†] This study also examined six other countries, including Japan, which is often cited as a country with high rates of saving and investment. For all of these countries, including high-investing Japan, gross investment was always less than gross capital income, and hence, none of these countries had too much capital.

B.   Debt Rollover When the Average Interest Rate Is Lower Than the Average Growth Rate

We have just seen that the introduction of uncertainty invalidates the comparison of the average interest rate and the average growth rate for the purpose of determining whether an economy has too much capital. Now we will see that the introduction of uncertainty also invalidates the comparison of the average interest rate and the average growth rate for the purpose of determining whether a Ponzi game is feasible. We focus this discussion on a particular Ponzi game, namely rolling over government debt forever. This section presents a numerical example with the following surprising feature: despite the fact that the interest rate on government debt is lower than the average growth rate of GNP, the expected value of the debt-GNP ratio grows without bound. Eventually, the government would become unable to roll over its debt.

Before presenting this example it is useful to calculate an exact expression for the growth rate of the debt-GNP ratio when the government is following a rollover policy [Eq. (1) is an approximate expression.] Remember that a rollover policy means that the primary deficit is zero in every year. If the current amount of government debt is B and if the government has a zero primary deficit, its total deficit is rB, where r is the interest rate. Thus, the government must sell an additional rB bonds, and the amount of bonds next year rises to $(1 + r)B$. If the current level of GNP is Y and if the growth rate of GNP over the next year is g, the level of GNP next year is $(1 + g)Y$. Thus, the value of the debt-GNP ratio next year is $[(1 + r)/(1 + g)][B/Y]$, which is $(1 + r)/(1 + g)$ times as large as the current debt-GNP ratio, B/Y. Thus, if r is larger than g, so that $(1 + r)/(1 + g)$ is larger than one, the debt-GNP ratio grows between this year and next year. Alternatively, if r is smaller than g, so that $(1 + r)/(1 + g)$ is smaller than one, the debt-GNP ratio falls between this year and next year. These results are consistent with the approximation in Eq. (1).[‡]

Now we can discuss the numerical example presented in Table 2, which has the following features: the interest rate r is constant and is smaller than the average value of g, the growth rate of GNP. However, g varies in such a way that the average value of $(1 + r)/(1 + g)$ is greater than 1, so that the expected value of the debt-GNP ratio in the next period is always greater than the current value of the debt-GNP ratio. In this example, the uncertainty comes from the fact that GNP growth is unpredictable from one period to the next. To make the example simple, suppose that GNP growth is determined by the flip of a fair coin each period. If the coin comes up heads, GNP grows by 60% during the next period, and if the

---

*Abel et al. (1989).

[†]This conclusion is based on the implicit assumption that the fact that gross investment has always been smaller than gross capital income will continue forever.

[‡]The approximation involved in Eq. (1) is that the growth rate of a ratio is approximately equal to the growth rate of the numerator minus the growth rate of the denominator. (See Appendix A: Derivation of the Growth Rate of the Debt-GNP Ratio.)

Table 2   A Growing Debt-GNP Ratio with the Interest Rate Below the
Average Growth Rate

period	1	2	3
debt	$100	$104.70	$109.62

GNP tree:

```
GNP    $1000
                        $600              $360
                        (50%)            (25%)
                                          $960
                                         (25%)
                        $1600             $960
                        (50%)            (25%)
                                          $2560
                                         (25%)
```

expected GNP	$1000	$1100	$1210

debt/GNP tree:

```
debt/GNP    0.10
                        0.1745           0.3045
                        (50%)            (25%)
                                          0.1142
                                         (25%)
                        0.0654           0.1142
                        (50%)            (25%)
                                          0.0428
                                         (25%)
```

expected debt/GNP	0.1000	0.1200	0.1439

coin comes up tails, GNP falls by 40%.* Thus, if GNP is currently $1000, there is a 50% chance that next period's GNP will be $1600 and a 50% chance that next period's GNP will be $600. Thus, the average, or expected, value of next period's GNP is $1100 (($1600 + $600)/2), which represents a 10% expected growth rate.

Now suppose that the interest rate on government debt is always 4.7% per period, which is less than the average growth rate of the economy, and let's see how the debt-GNP ratio behaves in this economy. Suppose that in period 1 the amount of government debt is $100. Thus, the debt-GNP ratio is $100/$1000 = 0.10.

The first panel of numbers in Table 2 shows the evolution of government debt over time. With a 4.7%

---

*These large changes in GNP in this example were chosen to make the effects very apparent. To make the example seem more realistic, think of a period as being a decade rather than a year. Notice that between 1929 and 1933 in the United States real GNP fell by 30% and nominal GNP fell by 46%, so a 40% drop in GNP during a decade is not inconceivable. However, the probability of such a bad decade is almost surely much less than the value of 50% assumed in this example.

interest rate, the amount of government debt grows at the rate of 4.7% per period. Thus, government debt equals $104.70 in period 2 and $109.62 in period 3.

The second panel of numbers in Table 2, which shows GNP, requires a little additional explanation. As shown in the first column, GNP is $1000 in period 1. The second column shows that there is a 50% chance that GNP in period 2 will be $600 and a 50% chance that GNP in period 2 will be $1600, so that the expected value of GNP in period 2 is ($600 + $1600)/2 = $1100. The third column of numbers shows the possible values of GNP in period 3. If GNP in period 2 is $600, there is a 50% chance it will fall by 40%, to $360, in period 3, and a 50% chance it will rise by 60%, to $960, in period 3. Alternatively, if GNP in period 2 is $1600, there is a 50% chance it will fall by 40%, to $960, in period 3, and a 50% chance it will rise by 60%, to $2560, in period 3. Taking account of all of these possibilities for the value of GNP in period 3, there is a 25% chance it will be $360, a 50% chance it will be $960, and a 25% chance it will be $2560. The average, or expected, value of GNP in period 3 is $1210.

The third panel of numbers in Table 2 shows the possible values of the debt-GNP in each of the three periods. These numbers are calculated by dividing the value of debt in the first panel by the value of GNP in the second panel. For example, in period 2, debt will equal $104.70. There is a 50% chance GNP will equal $600, in which case the debt/GNP ratio will be $104.70/$600 = 0.1745, as reported in the third panel; there is a 50% chance GNP will equal $1600, in which case the debt/GNP ratio will be $104.70/$1600 = 0.0654. The average, or expected, value of the debt-GNP ratio in period 2 is (0.1745 + 0.0654)/2 = 0.1200, which is higher than the debt-GNP ratio in period 1. Despite the fact that the interest rate is smaller than the average growth rate of GNP, the risk of a sharp drop in GNP makes the expected value of the debt-GNP ratio in period 2 higher than the value of the debt-GNP ratio in period 1. As shown in the third column, the expected value of the debt-GNP ratio in period 3 is 0.1439. In fact, the expected value of the debt-GNP ratio will grow at a rate of approximately 20% per period forever. Eventually, the expected value of the debt-GNP ratio would become so large that the government would be unable to roll over its debt despite the fact that the interest rate on government debt is lower than the average growth rate of the economy.

IV. WHAT CAN WE CONCLUDE ABOUT U.S. FISCAL POLICY?

We have shown that in the presence of uncertainty it may be impossible for the government to roll over its debt forever, even though the average interest rate is lower than the average growth rate of GNP. So, how then do we empirically assess whether the government can roll over its debt forever? This question is at the frontier of economic research and has not yet been fully resolved. Nevertheless, recent research has yielded some insights and some speculation about future findings.

One important insight is that if an economy has too much capital, Ponzi games are possible and the government can roll over its debt forever. However, a recent study cited earlier* found that none of the countries studied, including the United States, is afflicted by too much capital.

Does the finding that an economy does not have too much capital imply that Ponzi games are not possible and, in particular, that the government cannot roll over its debt forever? In a world without uncertainty, the answer to this question would be "yes," as we illustrated earlier. Unfortunately, the answer is ambiguous in the presence of uncertainty; in some economies that do not have too much capital, it is possible for the government to roll over its debt forever, while in other economies that do not have too much capital, it is impossible for the government to roll over its debt forever.[†]

The current state of economic research suggests that the crucial issue for determining whether a government can roll over its debt forever is whether there is a rich enough set of existing securities in the economy. If the set of existing securities is not rich enough in the relevant sense, government debt might be such a sufficiently different and attractive security that investors would welcome the opportunity to hold it in their portfolios and would allow the government to roll over its debt forever. However, if the set of existing securities is sufficiently rich, government debt may not be sufficiently different or attractive for investors to

---

*Abel et al. (1989).

[†]Technically, under certainty, capital overaccumulation is a necessary and sufficient condition for Ponzi games and for rolling over government debt forever. Under uncertainty, capital overaccumulation is a sufficient, but not necessary, condition for Ponzi games and for rolling over government debt forever.

allow the government to roll its debt over forever.* Unfortunately, the current state of economic research does not allow a convincing empirical test to distinguish between these two cases, so we cannot yet test whether an actual government can roll over its debt forever.[†]

Although we cannot yet empirically test whether an economy can roll over its debt forever, we are not left entirely in the dark about the future course of U.S. fiscal policy. Recently, Henning Bohn (1991a) has developed and implemented a test of whether a government is following a sustainable policy. This is not a test of whether a zero primary deficit accompanied by rolling over the debt is permanently sustainable. Rather it is a test of whether the historical tax and expenditure policies of the government can be permanently maintained without a major shift in the conduct of policy. Applying this test to data on U.S. fiscal policy, Bohn finds that this policy is sustainable. An important component of this conclusion is the finding that, on average, U.S. fiscal policy produces a smaller primary deficit (or a larger primary surplus) when the debt-GNP ratio becomes larger. This tendency of the government to run smaller (or even negative) primary deficits as the debt-GNP ratio gets larger is a means of keeping the debt-GNP ratio from growing too large.

While Bohn's result that U.S. fiscal policy is sustainable may appear comforting, this finding focuses attention on potentially painful choices. If the United States is to follow its historical pattern of reducing primary deficits when the debt-GNP ratio rises, the increase in the debt-GNP ratio over the past dozen years would seem to require a reduction in the primary deficit. Such a reduction in the primary deficit would require an increase in tax revenues and/or a cut in government expenditure, neither of which will be universally popular.

APPENDIX A: DERIVATION OF THE GROWTH RATE OF THE DEBT-GNP RATIO

Let B be the amount of government bonds outstanding, and let Y be the measure of national income, such as GNP. Thus the debt-GNP ratio is B/Y. The growth rate of any ratio is approximately equal to the growth rate of the numerator minus the growth rate of the denominator so that

$$\frac{\Delta(B/Y)}{B/Y} = \frac{\Delta B}{B} - \frac{\Delta Y}{Y} \tag{A1}$$

where the symbol Δ denotes the change from one period to the next. The change in government bonds, ΔB, equals the total deficit, which equals the primary deficit plus interest payments

$$\Delta B = \text{primary deficit} + rB \tag{A2}$$

where r is the interest rate on government bonds, so that rB is the amount of interest payments by the government. Now divide both sides of (A2) by the amount of government bonds B to obtain

$$\Delta B/B = \text{primary deficit}/B + r \tag{A3}$$

Now let g denote the growth rate of income so that

$$\Delta Y/Y = g \tag{A4}$$

Substituting (A3) and (A4) into (A1) yields

$$\frac{\Delta(B/Y)}{B/Y} = \text{primary deficit }/B + r - g \tag{A5}$$

which is Eq. (1) in the text.

---

*Blanchard and Weil (1992) present examples of economies that do not have too much capital. In some of these examples, the set of securities is not sufficiently rich, and the government can roll over its debt forever. In other examples, the set of securities is sufficiently rich, and the government cannot roll over its debt forever.
[†]A related—and also unresolved—question is why the average interest rate on government debt is so much lower than the average rate of return on capital. One potential explanation is that there is a very rich set of securities available but investors are very risk averse and essentially pay a large premium for the opportunity to hold safe government debt. In this case, the government would not be able to roll over its debt forever. Another potential explanation is that the set of securities is not sufficiently rich and that investors find government debt sufficiently different and attractive that they willingly hold it at a low interest rate. In this case, the government might be able to roll over its debt forever. See Bohn (1991b).

APPENDIX B: AN ECONOMIC MODEL OF THE INTEREST RATE AND THE GROWTH RATE

This appendix presents a general equilibrium model underlying the example presented in Table 2. Suppose that consumption equals output in every period as in the widely used Lucas (1978) asset pricing model. The standard condition determining the riskless interest rate r in a representative consumer economy is

$$(1 + r)\beta E_t\{u'(c_{t+1})/u'(c_t)\} = 1 \tag{B1}$$

where $E_t\{\}$ is the expectation conditional on information at time t, c_t is consumption per capita at time t, $u'(c_t)$ is the marginal utility of consumption at time t, and $\beta > 0$ is the time preference discount factor (so that $\beta^{-1}-1$ is the rate of time preference). Assume that the utility function is logarithmic so that $u'(c_t) = 1/c_t$. In this case, Eq. (B1) becomes

$$1 + r = [\beta E_t\{(c_t/c_{t+1})\}]^{-1} \tag{B2}$$

Now let $g_{t+1} = (c_{t+1}/c_t) - 1$ be the growth rate of consumption and output between time t and time t + 1, and assume that g_{t+1} is i.i.d. over time. Under this assumption we have

$$1 + r = [\beta E\{1/(1 + g_{t+1})\}]^{-1} \tag{B3}$$

The ratio of the debt-GNP ratio in period t + 1 to the debt-GNP ratio in period t is $(1 + r)/(1 + g_{t+1})$ and the expected value of this ratio is

$$E\{(1 + r)/(1 + g_{t+1})\} = E\{1/(1 + g_{t+1})\} [\beta E\{1/(1 + g_{t+1})\}]^{-1} = 1/\beta \tag{B4}$$

Notice that if $\beta < 1$, then $1/\beta > 1$ and the expected value of the debt-GNP ratio grows over time. The example in Table 2 is based on the following assumptions: $\beta = 0.8333$; and $Pr\{1 + g_{t+1} = 0.6\} = Pr\{1 + g_{t+1} = 1.6\} = 0.5$. These assumptions imply that $1 + r = 1.0473$, $E\{1 + g_{t+1}\} = 1.1$, and $E\{(1 + r)/(1 + g_{t+1})\} = 1/\beta = 1.2$.

ACKNOWLEDGMENTS

The author thanks Thomas Stark for extremely capable research assistance. He also thanks Henning Bohn, Satyajit Chatterjee, Dean Croushore, Jamie McAndrews, Steve Meyer, and Stephen Zeldes for helpful discussions, and Sally Burke for valuable editorial advice.

REFERENCES

Abel, A B., Mankow N. G., Summers, L. H., and Zeckhauser, R. J. (1989). "Assessing Dynamic Efficiency: Theory and Evidence," *Review of Economic Studies*, 56 (Jan.): 1–20.

Blanchard, O. J. and Weil, P. (1992). "Dynamic Efficiency, the Riskless Rate and Debt Ponzi Games Under Uncertainty," National Bureau of Economic Research Working Paper no. 3992, Feb.

Bohn, H. (1991a). "On Testing the Sustainability of Government Deficits in a Stochastic Environment," Rodney L. White Center for Financial Research Working Paper no. 19–91, Aug.

Bohn, H. (1991b). "Fiscal Policy and the Mehra-Prescott Puzzle: On the Welfare Implications of High Budget Deficits with Low Interest Rates," Wharton School of the University of Pennsylvania, April.

King, I. (1992). "Ponzi Games, Dynamic Efficiency and Endogenous Growth," Department of Economics, University of Victoria, British Columbia, mimeo.

Lucas, R. E. Jr. (1978). "Asset Prices in an Exchange Economy," *Econometrica*, 46(Nov.): 1429–45.

O'Connell, S. A. and Zeldes S. P. (1992). "Ponzi Games," in *The New Palgrave Dictionary of Money and Finance*.

APPENDIX I

Study Outline: Municipal Securities Representative Qualification Examination

Municipal Securities Rulemaking Board
Washington, D.C.

I. INTRODUCTION

A. Study Outline

This study outline lists the topics covered by the Municipal Securities Representative Qualification Examination (Test Series 52), and as such serves as a guide to the subject matter tested by the examination. Reference materials, discussing in a substantive way the topics set out in sections of this outline, are listed at the end of the outline.

The sample questions at the end of the appendix are similar to the types of multiple-choice questions that will appear in the examination.

B. The Examination

The Municipal Securities Representative Qualification Examination is designed to measure a candidate's qualification and competency to engage in the municipal securities business. The examination includes questions not only on municipal securities and the municipal markets but also on U.S. government, federal agency, and other financial instruments, economic activity, government policy, the behavior of interest rates, and applicable federal securities laws and regulations. The percentages assigned to each of these topics on the examination are as follows:

Municipal securities	60%
U.S. government, federal agencies, and other financial instruments	10%
Economic activity, government policy, and the behavior of interest rates	10%
Federal legal considerations	20%

The examination consists of 100 multiple-choice questions that test the topics specified in this outline. Each multiple-choice question is worth one point, and the passing grade set by the board is 70%. It is in a candidate's best interest to answer all questions because an unanswered question is considered an incorrect answer. Candidates are allowed 3 hours to complete the examination.*

Adopted from a work in the public domain.

*The examination is administered by the NASD on the PLATO system. For further information on application and administration procedures for MSRB examinations, please refer to the board's *Professional Qualification Handbook* or contact the NASD at (301) 590-6500.

The questions used in the examination are reviewed and updated on a regular basis and reflect current market practices and securities. Questions which test new board rules or amendments will be included in the examination after the effective data of the rule or rule change. Existing questions on rules or portions of rules, which have been amended or deleted, will be removed from the examination prior to the effective date of the amendment.

Because the examination is a closed-book test, candidates are not permitted any reference materials during the test administration. Electronic calculators may be used during the examination provided that they are simple, handheld devices having an independent power source and no tape print mechanisms. Calculator/computers capable of capturing alphanumeric data may not be used during the examination.

C. Confidentiality

In order to ensure that its examinations constitute valid tests of the qualifications of persons who take them, the board has instituted various procedures, in the question writing as well as the administration phases, which are designed to preserve the confidentiality of the examinations. On several occasions, the board has found it necessary to take legal action, alleging copyright violations, against securities training schools that had used in their training material questions and answers that appeared to have been taken from questions contained in board qualification examinations. In addition, candidates are advised that the practice of "debriefing" persons who have taken a qualification examination may not only give rise to an infringement of the board's copyright but would be a violation of board rules for the candidate. Rule G-3(g)* "Confidentiality of Qualification Requirements" states that

No associated person of a municipal securities broker or municipal securities dealer shall

1. In the course of taking a qualification examination required by this rule receive or give assistance of any nature
2. Disclose to any person questions, or answers to any questions, on any qualification examination required by this rule
3. Engage in any activity inconsistent with the confidential nature of any qualification examination required by this rule, or with its purpose as a test of the qualification of persons taking such examinations
4. Knowingly sign a false certification concerning any such qualification examination

II. PART I: MUNICIPAL SECURITIES (60%)

I. Types of municipal securities
  A. General obligation bonds
    1. Source of payment: generally payable from taxes
      a) Limited tax
      b) Unlimited tax
    2. Limitations on issuance
      a) Voter approval
      b) Statutory or constitutional
  B. Revenue bonds
    1. Source of payment: generally payable from project revenues
    2. Limitations on issuance
      a) Usually not subject to statutory debt limitations
      b) May be issued by any authorized political entity
    3. Purposes
      a) Utility revenue (e.g., water, sewer, electric)
      b) Housing revenue (e.g., single-family, multifamily)
      c) Transportation (e.g., airport revenue, toll road)
      d) Education (e.g., dormitory, student loan)
      e) Health (e.g., hospital, life care)

*Amendments have been filed with the SEC that revise the organization of rule G-3 to clarify its requirements. When approved, the provisions currently found in rule G-3(g) will become rule G-3(e), "Confidentiality of Qualification Examinations."

          f)   Industrial (e.g., industrial development, pollution control)

C. Special type bonds
1. New/Public Housing Authority (NHA/PHA)
2. Special tax
3. Special assessment
4. Moral obligation
5. Enhanced security (e.g., advance refunded, insured, letter of credit)
6. Double-barrelled
7. Lease rental
8. Certificates of participation
9. Variable rate securities

D. Short-term obligations
1. Notes
    a) Tax anticipation notes (TANs)
    b) Bond anticipation notes (BANs)
    c) Revenue anticipation notes (RANs)
    d) Construction loan notes (CLNs)
    e) Variable-rate demand notes
    f) Grant anticipation notes (GANs)
2. Tax-exempt commercial paper

II. Characteristics
A. Basic characteristics
1. Method of quotations
    a) Yield/basis price
    b) Dollar price
2. Form of ownership
    a) Bearer
    b) Registered as to principal only
    c) Fully registered
        (1) Interchangeable with bearer
        (2) Noninterchangeable
    d) Book-entry only
3. Depository eligibility
4. Delivery procedures
    a) Cash (same day)
    b) Regular way
    c) Delayed delivery
    d) When-as-and-if-issued (WI)
    e) As mutually agreed upon
5. Legal opinion
6. Interest
    a) Rates
        (1) Fixed
        (2) Variable/floating
        (3) Zero
        (4) Convertible
    b) Payment periods
7. Maturity
    a) Term
    b) Serial
8. Denominations
9. Early redemption
    a) Types
        (1) Optional
        (2) Sinking fund

    (3) Extraordinary
    (4) Mandatory
   b) Bond-refunding methods
    (1) Direct exchange versus sale of new issue
    (2) Refunding at call date
    (3) Escrowed to maturity (ETM)
    (4) Crossover refundings
   c) Procedures
    (1) Tender
    (2) Call
    (3) Puts
    (4) Open-market purchase
   d) Advantages and disadvantages
    (1) To issuer
    (2) To investor
 B. Tax considerations
  1. Interest
   a) Federal income tax status
    (1) Tax-exempt
    (2) Taxable
    (3) Alternative minimum tax (AMT)
    (4) Bank qualified bonds
   b) State and local income tax status
   c) Value of tax exemption
    (1) To investor
    (2) To issuer
  2. Principal
   a) Premiums and discounts
    (1) Amortization of premiums
    (2) Accretion of discounts
    (3) Tax consequences for different types of investors
   b) Capital gains/losses
    (1) Cost basis
    (2) Rates
    (3) Wash sales
    (4) Offsets
    (5) Tax swaps
  3. Original issue discount
  4. Compound accreted value
 C. Factors affecting marketability and liquidity
  1. Quality
  2. Ratings
  3. Maturity
  4. Call feature
  5. Coupon
  6. Block size
  7. Issue size
  8. Dollar price
  9. Issuer name, local or national
  10. Sinking fund
  11. Registered, bearer or book-entry only form
  12. Blue sky laws
III. The market for municipal securities
 A. Primary market
  1. Methods of primary financing

       a) Competitive sale
       b) Negotiated sale
           (1) Public offering
           (2) Private placement
2.   Information sources
       a) Notice of Sale (see Attachment A)
       b) Official statement
           (1) Preliminary
           (2) Final (see Attachment B)
       c) Direct mail from issuers or financial advisors
       d) *The Bond Buyer*
       e) Munifacts
       f) Dalnet
       g) Newspapers and publications
       h) *Bond Buyer* new issue worksheets
       i) Moody's bond survey
3.   Underwriting procedures
       a) Account formation procedures
           (1) Determining members and participation
           (2) Underwriting account agreement
               (a) Documents
                   (i) Syndicate letter (competitive)
                   (ii) Agreement among underwriters (negotiated)
               (b) Types of accounts
                   (i) Undivided (eastern account)
                   (ii) Divided (western account)
               (c) Roles of underwriters
                   i) Responsibilities of manager
                   ii) Responsibilities of members
           (3) Formation of selling groups
       b) Determination of syndicate bid
           (1) Components
               (a) Scale
               (b) Spread
               (c) Interest rates
           (2) Computation of bid
               (a) Production
               (b) Bid price
               (c) Bid form
               (d) Basis for award
                   i) Net interest cost
                   ii) True interest cost (Canadian method)
           (3) Factors relevant to the member's participation in the bid
               (a) Presale orders
               (b) Determination of liability
               (c) Scale and spread
               (d) Ability to sell this issue
       c) Syndicate operational procedures
           (1) Establish offering terms
               (a) Order period
               (b) Concessions and takedowns
               (c) Retention bonds
               (d) Priority provisions
                   i) Group orders
                   ii) Designated orders

            iii) Member orders
- (2) Settlement terms
  - (a) When-as-and-if-issued
  - (b) Establishment of delivery dates
  - (c) Final accounting and settlement
4. Functions of a bond attorney
   - a) Determine authority for bond issuance
   - b) Render an opinion concerning tax status
   - c) Issue a legal opinion
5. Role of financial advisor

B. Secondary market
1. Characteristics
   - a) Negotiated versus auction
   - b) Over-the-counter (OTC)
2. Information sources
   - a) *The Blue List*
   - b) *The Bond buyer*
   - c) Munifacts
   - d) Dealers' offering sheets
   - e) Brokers' brokers communications
   - f) Interdealer communications
3. Market participants
   - a) Institutional
   - b) Retail
   - c) Interdealer
   - d) Brokers' brokers
4. Secondary market procedures
   - a) Kinds of transactions
     - (1) Principal
     - (2) Agency
   - b) Trading terms
     - (1) Quote
     - (2) Firm bid
     - (3) Firm offering
     - (4) List
     - (5) Down bid
     - (6) Workable indications
     - (7) Evaluation
     - (8) All or none (AON)
     - (9) "Multiples of"
     - (10) "Out firm"
     - (11) "Fill-or-kill"
5. Functions of municipal bond trader
   - a) Make markets
   - b) Position trading
   - c) Joint accounts
   - d) Appraisals and evaluations
   - e) Hedging

C. Market indicators
1. *The Blue List* total
2. *The Bond Buyer*
   - a) Placement ratio
   - b) Indices
     - (1) Twenty GO bonds index
     - (2) Eleven GO bonds index

              (3)   Twenty-five revenue bonds index
              (4)   Municipal bond index (40 bond)
          c) Visible supply
      3.   Other market-level indicators
          a) New-issue scales
          b) Secondary market activity
          c) Dollar bond market activity
          d) Market activity in other securities
          e) Current economic factors
          f) Financial futures
   D. Customer suitability considerations
      1.   Financial profile
      2.   Tax status
      3.   Investment objectives
          a) Safety of principal
          b) Income requirements
          c) Liquidity requirements
          d) Diversification
              (1)   Geographical
              (2)   Maturity
              (3)   Purpose of issue
              (4)   Security
              (5)   Quality
          e) Kinds of investment risks
              (1)   Financial (credit risk)
              (2)   Market (interest rate risk)
              (3)   Put and call features
              (4)   Legislative changes
              (5)   Inflationary
              (6)   Reinvestment
IV. Analyzing municipal credit
   A. General obligation securities
      1.   Demographic considerations
          a) Tax base
          b) Diversification of economic activity
          c) Population trends
          c) Geography
      2.   Nature of the issuer's debt
          a) Present and past attitudes toward debt
          b) Debt trend
          c) Schedule of debt service requirements
          d) Contemplated financing
          e) Relation of debt to the life of improvement
      3.   Factors affecting ability to pay
          a) Budgetary practices
          b) Current financial condition
          c) Unfunded liabilities (pension funds, etc.)
          d) Tax limitations
          e) Tax rates, trends, and comparisons
          f) Tax collection record
          g) Trends in assessed valuation
          h) Nontax revenues
          i) Overlapping debt
          j) Litigation
      4.   Municipal debt ratios

        a) Net overall (direct and overlapping) debt to assessed valuation
        b) Net overall (direct and overlapping) debt to estimated real valuation
        c) Per capita net debt
        d) Debt service to annual revenues
  B. Revenue bonds
      1. Feasibility study
         a) Need for project
         b) Existing or potential competitive facilities
         c) Engineering reports
         d) Economic viability
      2. Sources of revenue
         a) User charges
         b) Concessions and fees
         c) Special taxes
         d) Rental or lease payments
            (1) Public agencies
            (2) Private agencies
         e) Legislative appropriation
      3. Security
         a) Bond indenture
            (1) Rate covenant
            (2) Insurance covenant
            (3) Operation and maintenance covenant
            (4) Nondiscrimination covenant
            (5) Requirement for financial reports and outside audits
            (6) Restrictions on issuance of additional bonds
               (*a*) Open-end indenture
               (*b*) Closed-end indenture
               (*c*) Project completion
         b) Flow of funds
            (1) Types of funds
               (*a*) Revenue fund
               (*b*) Operation and maintenance fund
               (*c*) Sinking fund or debt service fund
               (*d*) Debt service reserve fund
               (*e*) Reserve maintenance fund
               (*f*) Renewal and replacement (depreciation) fund
               (*g*) Surplus fund
            (2) Application of revenue
               (*a*) Net revenue pledge
               (*b*) Gross revenue pledge
         c) Debt service coverage
  C. Sources of credit information
      1. The issuer
      2. Advisory councils and services of certain states
      3. Commercial research services
      4. Industry and general publications
  D. Rating services
  E. Credit enhancements
V. Mathematical calculations and methods
  A. Yields
      1. Yield to maturity
      2. Yield to early redemption
         a) Put
         b) Call

        c) Par option
- 3. Current yield
- 4. After-tax yield
- 5. Taxable equivalent yield
- B. Relationship of bond prices to changes
  - 1. In maturity
  - 2. In coupon
  - 3. In yield
- C. Basis points
- D. Dollar value of points and fractions
- E. Use of basis book
  - 1. To determine dollar price
  - 2. To determine yield
- F. Accrued interest
  - 1. Regular coupon
  - 2. Odd first coupon
- G. Level debt service
- H. Underwriting computations
  - 1. Bond years
  - 2. Production
  - 3. Spread
  - 4. Net interest cost
  - 5. True interest cost
- I. Capital gains
- J. Amortization of premium
- K. Accretion of discount
- L. Day-count basis of computations of dollar price and accrued interest
  - 1. Notes (variable)
  - 2. Bonds (30/360)
- M. Flat

III. PART II: U.S. GOVERNMENT, FEDERAL AGENCY, AND OTHER FINANCIAL INSTRUMENTS (10%)

I. Types
- A. Obligations of the U.S. Treasury
  - 1. Bills
  - 2. Notes
  - 3. Bonds
  - 4. STRIPS
  - 5. SLGS
- B. Obligations of federal agencies
  - 1. Federal Farm Credit Banks
  - 2. Federal Home Loan Bank (FHLB)
  - 3. Federal Home Loan Mortgage Corporation (FHLMC or Freddie Mac)
  - 4. Federal National Mortgage Association (FNMA or Fannie Mae)
  - 5. Government National Mortgage Association (FNMA or Ginnie Mae)
    - *a)* Mortgage-backed bonds
    - *b)* Pass-through securities
    - *c)* Student Loan Marketing Association (SLMA or Salle Mae)
- C. Money market and other financial instruments
  - 1. Bankers acceptances
  - 2. Certificates of deposit
  - 3. Commercial paper

        4.   Federal funds
        5.   Repurchase and reverse repurchase agreements
        6.   Money market mutual funds
        7.   Asset-backed securities
        8.   Collateralized mortgage obligations (CMOs)

II.   Characteristics of various U.S. government, federal agency, and other financial instuments
    A. Marketability
        1.   Liquidity
        2.   Price volatility
    B. Federal and state tax treatment
        1.   Interest income
        2.   Amortization of premium
        3.   Accretion of discount
        4.   Capital gains/loss
        5.   Flower bonds
    C. Trading
        1.   Discount basis
        2.   Bond equivalent yield
        3.   Yield quotation
        4.   Dollar price quotation and fractions (1/32)
    D. Settlement
        1.   Cash
        2.   Regular way
    E. Delivery
        1.   Book-entry only
        2.   Bearer
        3.   Registered

III. The market for U.S. government, federal agency, and other financial instruments
    A. New-issue marketing methods
        1.   Auction
            a)   Competitive tenders
            b)   Noncompetitive tenders
        2.   Agency selling group
        3.   Dealer market
    B. Secondary market
        1.   Broker
        2.   Dealer
    C. Federal Reserve's open-market participation in the market for each security, where applicable

IV. Credit features
    A. Definition of each investment sccurity and comparative credit strength for all U.S. government, federal agency, and money market instruments
    B. Treasury guaranties (direct, secondary, or implied where applicable)

IV. PART III: ECONOMIC ACTIVITY, GOVERNMENT POLICY, AND THE BEHAVIOR OF INTEREST RATES (10%)

I.   Monetary Policy
    A. Objectives of Federal Reserve monetary policy
        1.   Price stability
        2.   Long-term economic growth
        3.   Stable foreign exchange markets
    B. Operating tools of the Federal Reserve
        1.   Open market operations
        2.   Discount rate

         3.   Reserve requirements
         4.   Margin requirements
    C. Operations of the Federal Reserve
         1.   Policy role of the Federal Open Market Committee
         2.   Market role of the Open Market Trading Desk
    D. Major factors influencing Federal Reserve policy
         1.   Monetary aggregates
         2.   Economic indices
         3.   Commodity prices
         4.   Foreign exchange rates

II. Fiscal Policy
    A. U.S. Treasury debt management practices—impact of short-term and long-term financings
    B. Federal budgetary practices and their impact on the money and capital markets
         1.   Deficits and surpluses
         2.   Taxation and spending

III. Behavior of Interest Rates
    A. Supply and demand for credit relative to the economic cycle
    B. The effect of inflation and investor expectations on interest rate levels
    C. Yield curve analysis
         1.   Financial and economic characteristics of a positive/negative (inverted) sloped yield curve
         2.   Uses and implications
    D. Yield spread differentials between credit quality groups
         1.   Impact of economic and financial conditions
         2.   During periods of high/low interest rate levels
    E. Changes in commodity and currency prices

V. PART IV: FEDERAL LEGAL CONSIDERATIONS (20%)

I. Legislation affecting municipal securities
    A. Securities Act of 1933
         1.   Municipal securities exempt from registration requirements
         2.   Antifraud provisions applicable to municipal issuers as well as brokers and dealers
    B. Securities Exchange Act of 1934
         1.   Municipal issuers exempt from reporting requirements
         2.   Antifraud provisions applicable to municipal issuers as well as brokers and dealers
         3.   Amendments of 1975
             a) Registration of municipal brokers, dealers, and bank dealers with the SEC
             b) Regulators
                 (1) Rule making
                     (*a*) Municipal Securities Rulemaking Board (MSRB)
                     (*b*) Securities and Exchange Commission (SEC)
                 (2) Enforcement
                     (*a*) SEC
                     (*b*) National Association of Securities Dealers
                     (*c*) Federal Reserve Board
                     (*d*) Comptroller of the Currency
                     (*e*) Federal Deposit Insurance Corporation
    C. Securities Investor Protection Act of 1970
         1.   Purpose of Securities Investor Protection Corporation (SIPC)
         2.   Inapplicable to bank dealers
         3.   Coverage limitations

II. Regulation of municipal market professionals
    A. Applicable SEC rules
         1.   SEC financial responsibility rules (inapplicable to banks)

  2. SEC antifraud rules
  3. SEC rule 15c2-12 on municipal securities disclosure
 B. MSRB rules
  1. Professional Qualifications (G-2 through G-7)
  2. Recordkeeping (G-8)
  3. Investor Brochure (G-10)
  4. Sales During the Underwriting Period (G-11)
  5. Uniform Practice (G-12)
  6. Quotations and Sales Reports (G-13 and G-14)
  7. Confirmation, Clearance, and Settlement of Transactions with Customers (G-15)
  8. Conduct of Municipal Securities Business (G-17)
  9. Execution of Transactions (G-18)
  10. Suitability of Recommendations and Transactions (G-19)
  11. Gifts and Gratuities (G-20)
  12. Advertising (G-21)
   a) Relating to professional services
   b) Relating to municipal securities products
   c) Relating to new-issue municipal securities
  13. Disclosure of Control Relationships (G-22)
  14. Activities of Financial Advisors (G-23)
  15. Use of Ownership Information Obtained in a Fiduciary Capacity (G-24)
  16. Improper Use of Assets (G-25)
  17. Customer Account Transfers (G-26)
  18. Supervision (G-27)
  19. Transactions with Employees of Other Professionals (G-28)
  20. Availability of Board Rules (G-29)
  21. Prices and Commissions (G-30)
  22. Reciprocal Dealings with Municipal Securities Investment Companies (G-31)
  23. Disclosures in Connection with New Issues (G-23)
  24. CUSIP Numbers and Dissemination of Initial Trade Date Information (G-34)
  25. Arbitration (general knowledge) (G-35)
   a) Matters subject to arbitration
   b) Persons subject to arbitration
   c) Customers' small claims
  26. Delivery of Official Statements, Advance Refunding Documents, and Forms G-36 (OS) and G-36 (ARD) to Board or Its Designee (G-36)

VI. ATTACHMENT A: CONTENTS OF A TYPICAL NOTICE OF BOND SALE

1. Date, time, and place of sale
2. Name and description of issuer
3. Type of bond
4. Bidding restrictions
5. Interest payment dates
6. Dated date, interest accrual date, first coupon payment date
7. Maturity structure
8. Call provisions
9. Denominations and registration provisions
10. Expenses to be borne by purchaser or issuer
11. Amount of good faith deposit
12. Paying agent and/or trustee
13. Name of attorney providing legal opinion
14. Details of delivery
15. Right of rejection
16. Criteria for award

VII. ATTACHMENT B: OUTLINE OF A TYPICAL OFFICIAL STATEMENT

1. Offering terms
2. Summary statement
3. Purpose of issue
4. Authorization of bonds
5. Security of bonds
6. Description of bonds
7. Description of issuer
   a. Organization and management
   b. Area economy
   c. Financial summary
8. Construction program
9. Project feasibility
10. Regulatory matters
11. Specific provisions of indenture and/or resolution
    a. Funds and accounts
    b. Investment of funds
    c. Additional bonds
    d. Insurance
    e. Events of default
12. Legal proceedings
13. Tax status
14. Appendix
    a. Various consultant reports
    b. Legal opinion
    c. Financial statements

VIII. REFERENCE MATERIAL

The following list of reference materials is presented here for convenience but is not intended to be all-inclusive.

A. Primary Reference Material on the Functioning of the Municipal, Government, and Money Markets

Darst, D. M. (1975). *The Complete Bond Book*, McGraw-Hill, New York.

Fabozzi, F. J., Feldstein, S. G., Pollack, I. M., and Zarb, F. G., eds. (1983). *The Municipal Bond Handbook*, 2 vols., Dow Jones-Irwin, Homewood, Ill.

Federal Reserve Bank of Richmond (1988). *Instruments of the Money Market*, 6th ed.

The First Boston Corporation (1990). *Handbook of Securities of the United States Government and Federal Agencies.*

Lamb, R. and Rappaport, S. P. (1987). *Municipal Bonds*, 2nd ed, McGraw-Hill, New York.

Municipal Securities Rulemaking Board (1985). *Glossary of Municipal Securities Terms*, MSRB, Washington, D.C.

Municipal Securities Rulemaking Board *MSRB Manual*, Commerce Clearing House, Chicago.

Public Securities Association (1990). *Fundamentals of Municipal Bonds*, 4th ed., PSA, New York.

Securities Investor Protection Corporation (1988). *How SIPC Protects You*, SIPC, Washington, D.C.

Stigum, M. (1983). *The Money Market*, rev. ed., Dow Jones-Irwin, Homewood, Ill.

White, W. (1985). *The Municipal Bond Market*, the Financial Press, Jersey City, N. J.

B. Additional Reference Material on Municipal Finance and Investments

The Board of Governors of the Federal Reserve System (1985). *The Federal Reserve System—Purposes and Functions*, Washington, D.C.

Darst, D. M. (1981). *The Handbook of the Bond and Money Markets*, McGraw-Hill, New York.

Fabozzi, F. J., Fabozzi, T. D., and Pollack, I. M., eds. (1991). *The Handbook of Fixed Income Securities*, 3rd ed. Dow Jones-Irwin, Homewood, Ill.

Fabozzi, F. J. and Zarb, F. G., eds. (1986). *Handbook of Financial Markets—Securities, Options, Futures*, 2nd ed., Dow Jones-Irwin, Homewood, Ill.

Government Finance Officers Association (1988). *Disclosure Guidelines for State and Local Government Securities*, GFOA, Chicago.

Homer, S. and Leibowitz, M. L. (1973). *Inside the Yield Book*, Prentice-Hall, Englewood Cliffs, N.J.

Miller, G. (1982). *A Public Investors Guide to Money Market Instruments*, Municipal Finance Officers Association, Chicago.

Moak, L. L. (1976). *Administration of Local Government Debt*, Municipal Finance Officers Association, Chicago.

Smith, W. S. (1979). *The Appraisal of Municipal Credit Risk*, Moody's Investors Service, New York.

Stigum, M. and Mann, J. (1988). *Money Market Calculations: Yields, Break-Evens, and Arbitrage*, 2nd ed., Dow Jones-Irwin, Homewood, Ill.

Zarb, F. G. and Kerekes, G. T. (1970) *The Stock Market Handbook*, Dow Jones-Irwin, Homewood, Ill.

IX. SAMPLE QUESTIONS

The following questions are similar in format and content to questions on the examination. The sample questions, however, are not intended to parallel either the level of difficulty or the subject coverage of the examination. The sample questions are intended to assist candidates in preparing for the types of multiple-choice questions that will appear on the examination.

1. A municipal securities trade occurs on July 14. Assuming there are no intervening holidays, regular way settlement would occur on
   (A) July 15
   (B) July 19
   (C) July 21
   (D) July 25

2. An investor in the 28% tax bracket purchases a 5.60% municipal bond at par. To realize the same net return from a taxable investment purchased at par, the investor would have to purchase a taxable bond with which of the following yields?
   (A) 5.60%
   (B) 7.78%
   (C) 11.20%
   (D) 20.00%

3. A municipal bond that is offered at a yield-to-maturity higher than its coupon rate is recognized as trading
   (A) at a discount
   (B) at a premium
   (C) flat
   (D) at par

4. The MSRB has been authorized by Congress to regulate the municipal securities activities of all the following EXCEPT
   (A) securities firms who sell to retail accounts
   (B) bank dealers who underwrite general obligation bonds
   (C) broker/dealers who sell to institutional accounts
   (D) state political entities selling new-issue municipal securities

Questions 5–7 are based on the exhibit:

In the opinion of Co-Bond Counsel, under existing laws, interest on the Bonds is exempt from federal income tax and interest on the Bonds and the gain on the sale thereof are exempt from taxation in the State of New Jersey under the New Jersey Gross Income Tax Act as enacted and construed on the date hereof.

NEW ISSUE

$16,000,000
New Jersey Health Care Facilities
Financing Authority
Revenue Bonds
City Hospital Association of Portsmouth Issue,
Series A

Dated: March 1, 1992   Due: July 1, as shown below

Principal and semi-annual interest (payable July 1, 1992 and each January 1 and July 1 thereafter) are payable at the principal corporate trust office of First National Bank, Portsmouth, New Jersey, the Trustee, or at the option of the holder at the principal corporate trust office of Chemical Bank, New York, New York, Co-Paying Agent. The Bonds are issuable in the form of coupon Bonds in denominations of $5,000 registrable as to principal only, or as to both principal and interest, at the principal corporate trust office of the Trustee. The Bonds are subject to redemption prior to maturity as described in the Official Statement.

The Bonds will be special obligations of the Authority and not a debt of the State of New Jersey or any political subdivision thereof other than the Authority. The Bonds will be equally and ratably payable from certain revenues of the Authority received from City Hospital Association of Portsmouth pursuant to the Loan and Security Agreement and Mortgage and will be secured thereunder and under the provisions of the Resolution (as both are defined in the Official Statement). The Authority has no taxing power.

Amount	Due	Interest Rate	Price	Amount	Due	Interest Rate	Price	Amount	Due	Interest Rate	Price
$ 85,000	1996	8 ½%	100%	$105,000	1998	9 %	100	$145,000	2001	9 ¼%	100%
95,000	1997	8 ¾	100	115,000	1999	9 ¼	100	160,000	2002	10	100
				130,000	2000	9 ½	100				

$1,000,000   11   % Term Bonds due July 1, 2007 @ 100   %
$8,000,000   11 ⅝ % Term Bonds due July 1, 2021 @ 100   %
$6,165,000   10   % Term Bonds due July 1, 2025 @   87 ¼ %

(Accrued Interest to be added.)

5. These bonds are BEST described as
   (A) revenue bonds
   (B) limited tax bonds
   (C) general obligation bonds
   (D) special assessment bonds
6. An investor who purchased $5M July 1, 2000 bonds during the underwriting period would have received what amount of interest on the first coupon payment date?
   (A) $47.50
   (B) $95.00
   (C) $158.33
   (D) $237.50
7. If the bonds maturing in 2007 are called at a premium in 2002, an investor who purchased the bonds at par would have an effective yield of
   (A) exactly 10%
   (B) exactly 11%
   (C) less than 11% but not 10%
   (D) more than 11%
8. Under MSRB rules, which of the following does NOT have to be included on a dealer confirmation?
   (A) Amount of concession
   (B) Name of paying agent
   (C) An indication if the securities are callable

    (D)   Par value
9. All of the following statements concerning Treasury bills are true EXCEPT:
    (A)   They are issued at a discount.
    (B)   They must be held to maturity.
    (C)   They are obligations of the U.S. government.
    (D)   They are available in book-entry form.
10. Which two of the following are of significance when evaluating the credit risk of a new issue of general obligation bonds?
    I.   Debt service coverage
    II.   Per capita debt service requirements
    III.   Present prices of the issuer's outstanding securities
    IV.   Tax rates, trends, and comparison
        (A)   I and III
        (B)   I and IV
        (C)   II and III
        (D)   II and IV

Answers

1. C   6. C
2. B   7. D
3. A   8. B
4. D   9. B
5. A   10. D

APPENDIX II

Study Outline: Municipal Securities Principal Qualification Examination

Municipal Securities Rulemaking Board
Washington, D.C.

I. INTRODUCTION

MSRB rules require a dealer to supervise the municipal securities activities of its associated persons and the conduct of its business, and require that one or more municipal securities principals must be designated to carry out this supervisory responsibility. The board has urged the enforcement agencies to look to a dealer's supervisors to ensure that compliance procedures are established and enforced. Moreover, the board has taken the position that violations of board rules, particularly those that indicate a lack of effective supervisory controls, also may constitute a "failure to supervise" on the part of the designated principal and the dealer.

A. The Municipal Securities Principal

The municipal securities principal bears primary responsibility for overseeing the municipal securities activities of a securities firm or bank dealer. In this capacity, a municipal securities principal *manages*, *directs*, or *supervises* one or more of the following activities:

- Underwriting municipal securities
- Trading municipal securities
- Buying or selling municipal securities from or to customers
- Rendering financial advisory or consultant services to issuers of municipal securities
- Communicating with customers about any of the above activities
- Maintaining records on the above activities
- Processing, clearing, and (in the case of securities firms) safekeeping municipal securities
- Training principals or representatives

B. The Examination

The Municipal Securities Principal Qualification Examination is designed to determine whether an individual meets the board's qualification standards for municipal securities principals. To do this, the examination measures a candidate's knowledge of the board's rules, rule interpretations, and federal statutory provisions applicable to the activities listed above. It also measures the candidate's ability to apply these rules and interpretations to given fact situations.

Adapted from a work in the public domain.

The examination consists of 100 multiple-choice questions assigned at the six areas of the examination as follows:

Federal regulations   5%
General supervision   24%
Sales supervision   22%
Origination and syndication   23%
Trading   8%
Operations   18%

These questions are further distributed among the various subtopics in a manner that reflects the distribution of subject matter in the study outline. Each question is worth one point, and the passing grade is 70%. Candidates are allowed 3 hours to complete the examination. During the administration of the examination, candidates are not permitted to use reference materials.*

The questions used in the examination are reviewed and updated on a regular basis. Questions that test a new rule or a new rule amendment will be included in the examination after the effective date of the rule or rule change. Existing questions on rules or portions of rules that have been amended or deleted will be removed from the examination prior to the effective date of the amendment.

C. Confidentiality

In order to ensure that its examinations constitute valid tests of the qualifications of persons who take them, the board has instituted various procedures, in the question writing as well as the administration phases, that are designed to preserve the confidentiality of the examinations. On several occasions, the board has found it necessary to take legal action, alleging copyright violations, against securities training schools that had used in their training material questions and answers that appeared to have been taken from questions contained in board qualification examinations. In addition, candidates are advised that the practice of "debriefing" persons who have taken a qualification examination may not only give rise to an infringement of the board's copyright but would be a violation of board rules for the candidate.[†]

D. The Study Outline

This study outline serves as a guide to the subject matter tested by the Municipal Securities Principal Qualification Examination (Test Series 53). It lists the topics covered by the examination, discusses reference materials, and provides sample questions similar to the type used in the examination.

The arrangement of the subject matter in the study outline reflects the various aspects of municipal securities activity within a securities firm or bank dealer and the tasks of a municipal securities principal in supervising such activities. Reference is made to the appropriate MSRB rule or federal regulation that governs each task.[†] Not only are questions in the examination based on these federal regulations and board rules, but also are based on the interpretations that follow each board rule.

II. PART I: FEDERAL REGULATIONS (5%)

A. Securities Exchange Act of 1934

* Antifraud provisions applicable to all per-   '34 act, sect. 10 (b) and sect. 15 (c)
  sons, including municipal issuers, brokers,
  dealers, and municipal securities dealers

---

*The examination is administered by the NASD on the PROCTOR system. For further information on application and administration procedures for MSRB examinations, please refer to the board's *Professional Qualification Handbook* or contact the NASD at (301) 590–6500.

Rule G-3(e), "Confidentiality of Qualification Examinations," states that "No associated person of a broker, dealer, or municipal securities dealer shall: (i) in the course of taking a qualification examination required by this rule receive or give assistance of any nature; (ii) disclose to any person questions, or answers to any questions, on any qualification examination required by this rule; (iii) engage in any activity inconsistent with the confidential nature of any qualification examination required by this rule, or with its purpose as a test of the qualification of persons taking such examinations; or (iv) knowingly sign a false certification concerning any such qualification examination."

[†]Referenced MSRB rules and federal regulations are found in the *MSRB Manual*.

- Regulatory framework for the municipal
  securities industry
  —Rule-making process   MSRB manual, par. 104
  —Enforcement of MSRB rules:
  Enforcement agencies   '34 act, sect. 15B(c)(5); sect. 15A(b)(2); and sect.
  3(a)(34)(A)

  Compliance examinations   '34 act, sect. 15B(c)(7)(A); and G-16*

B. Rules of the Securities and Exchange Commission

- Employment of manipulative and
  deceptive devices
  —By brokers, dealers, or municipal
  securities dealers   SEC rule 10b-3
  —By any person, including municipal   SEC rule 10b-5
  issuers, brokers, dealers, and municipal
  securities dealers
- Fraud and misrepresentations by brokers,   SEC rule 15c1-2
  dealers, and municipal securities dealers

C. Securities Investor Protection Corporation (SIPC)

- Purpose of SIPC   SIPA[†] sect. 5 and sect. 9
- Coverage limitations

III.   PART II: GENERAL SUPERVISION (24%)

A. Definitional Rules

- "Bank dealer"   D-8
- "Customer"   SEC rule 15c1-1; D-9
- "Discretionary account"   D-10
- "Associated person"   D-11

B. Qualification and Registration

- Broker/dealer
  —SEC registration requirements   '34 act, sects. 15 (a) and 15B (a)
  —Registration with the MSRB and payment   A-12
  of initial fee
  —MSRB annual fee   A-14
  —Notification to the MSRB of change in   A-15
  status
  —Separately identifiable department or   G-1
  division of a bank (definition of municipal
  securities dealer activities)
  —Standards of professional qualification   G-2
  —Minimum requirements to have a certain   G-3 (b) (iii); and G-3 (d) (iii)
  number of principals

---

[*]All rule references in the study outline, unless otherwise noted, are to MSRB rules (e.g., A-12, D-8, or G-16).

[†]Securities Investor Protection Act of 1970—a recommended source of information on these subjects is the SIPC brochure entitled *How SIPC Protects You*, which may be obtained by calling SIPC.

- Associated persons
  - —Definition of associated person   G-7 (a)
  - —Information to be compiled on each as-   G-7 (b)
    sociated person
  - —Verification, maintenance, and filing of   G-7 (c) through G-7 (h)
    such information
  - —Definitions and qualification requirements:
  Municipal securities representatives   G-3 (a) (i) and (ii)
  Municipal securities principals   G-3 (b) (i) and (ii)
  Municipal securities sales principals   G-3 (c)
  Financial and operations principals   G-3 (d) (i) and (ii)
  - —Confidentiality of qualification exam-   G-3 (e)
    inations
  - —Retaking of qualification examinations   G-3 (f)
  - —Waiver of qualification requirements   G-3 (g)
  - —Apprenticeship requirement   G-3 (a) (iii)*
- Disqualification
- —Statutory disqualifications   G-4
- —Disciplinary actions by appropriate regula-   G-5 (a)
  tory agencies
- —Remedial notices by registered securities as-   G-5 (b)
  sociations

C. Supervisory Responsibilities

- Dealer's obligation to supervise   G-27 (a)
- Designation of principals
  - —Responsible for municipal securities bus-   G-27 (b) (i)
    iness and activities of associated persons
  - —Written record of designations   G-27 (b) (ii) G-8 (a) (xiv)
  - —Appropriate principal   G-27 (b) (iii)
- Written supervisory procedures†   G-27 (c)
- Duty to update and review written procedures   G-27 (d)
- Gifts and gratuities   G-20
- Availability of board rules   G-29

D. Conduct of Business

- Fair dealing
  - —"Fair dealing" rule   G-17
  - —Use of ownership information obtained in   G-24
    a fiduciary or agency capacity
  - —Improper use of assets   G-25 (a)
- Prices and commissions
  - —Principal transactions   G-30 (a)
  - —Agency transactions   G-30 (b)
- Control relationships
  - —Definition   G-22 (a)

---

*Restrictions concerning apprentices communicating with customers are found in Part III.

†Requirements for *specific* supervisory procedures are found under the appropriate topics, i.e., "opening customer accounts" (Sec. III. A) and "communications with customers" (Sec. III. B); also "discretionary accounts" (Sec. III. E) and "customer complaints" (Sec. III.F).

IV.   PART III: SALES SUPERVISION (22%)

A.   Opening Customer Accounts

B.   Communications with Customers

C.   Suitability

D.   Improper Activities

E.   Discretionary Accounts

F.   Customer Complaints

V. PART IV: ORIGINATION AND SYNDICATION (23%)

A. Financial Advisors

- Purpose of financial advisory rule and
  applicability of state or local law   G-23 (a), (f)
- Financial advisory relationship   G-23 (b)
- Basis of compensation   G-23 (c)
- Underwriting activities   G-23 (d)
- Disclosures to customers   G-23 (e)
- Responsibility to make official statement
  available   G-32 (b) (ii)

B. Practices Relating to New Issue Underwritings

- Obligations of municipal underwriters under
  SEC rules
  —"Reasonable basis" interpretation   SEC release no. 34-26100, part III
  —Availability and review of official state-   SEC rule 15c2-12
    ments
- Sales of new issue municipal securities dur-
  ing the underwriting period
  —Definitions   G-11 (a)
  —Disclosure of capacity   G-11 (b)
  —Confirmations of sale   G-11 (c)
  —Disclosure of group orders   G-11 (d)
  —Priority provisions   G-11 (e)
  —Communications relating to priority pro-   G-11 (f)
    visions and order period
  —Disclosure of allocation of securities   G-11 (g)
  —Disclosure of syndicate expenses and   G-11 (h)
    other information
- Disclosures in connection with new issues
  —Disclosure requirements   G-32 (a)
  —Responsibility of managing underwriters   G-32 (b) (i)
    and sole underwriters
  —Definitions   G-32 (c)
- CUSIP numbers and dissemination of initial
  trade date information
  —New issue securities   G-34 (a)
  —Dissemination of initial trade date in-   G-34 (c)
    formation
  —Eligibility   G-34 (d)
- New issue advertisements   G-21 (d)
- Syndicate administration
  —Underwriting assessment   A-13
  —Delivery of official statements, advance
    refunding documents and forms G-36 (OS)   G-36
    and G-36 (ARD) to the board or its
    designee
  —Records of syndicate transactions   G-8 (a) (viii)
  —Records concerning deliveries of official   G-8 (a) (xiii)
    statements

B. Books and Records

- Books and records required to be made*
  —Records of original entry   G-8 (a) (i)
  —Account records   G-8 (a) (ii)
  —Securities records   G-8 (a) (iii)
  —Subsidiary records   G-8 (a) (iv)
  —Records of put options and repurchase   G-8 (a) (v)
    agreements
  —Copies of confirmations and certain other   G-8 (a) (ix)
    notices to customers
  —Financial records specified by SEC rules   G-8 (a) (x)
- Manner in which books and records are to   G-8 (b)
  be maintained
- Nonclearing brokers and dealers   G-8 (c)
- Introducing brokers and dealers   G-8 (d)
- Definition of customer   G-8 (e)
- Compliance with SEC rules
  —Records to be made   G-8 (f)
  —Preservation of records maintained under   G-9 (g)
    SEC rules
- Preservation of records
  —Period of time records must be preserved   G-9 (a) through G-9 (c)
  —Accessibility and availability   G-9 (d)
  —Method of record retention   G-9 (e)
  —Effect of lapse in dealer's registration   G-9 (f)

C. Customer Account Transfers   G-26

D. Lost and Stolen Securities   '34 act, sect. 17 (f) (1); SEC rule 17f-1

E. Calculations (General Knowledge)   G-33

VIII. SAMPLE QUESTIONS

The following questions are similar in format and content to questions on the examination. The sample questions, however, are not intended to parallel either the level of difficulty or the subject coverage of the examination. The sample questions are only intended to assist candidates in preparing for the types of multiple-choice questions that will appear on the examination.

1. A municipal securities dealer must send a copy of the final official statement to a customer who purchased new-issue securities during the underwriting period only if
   A) the issuer provides an official statement on the new issue
   B) the issue is a refunding issue
   C) the securities are rated at less than investment grade by the rating agencies
   D) the SEC has denied registration of the new issue for any reason
2. Reclamation of municipal securities is permitted for one business day following delivery for which of the following reasons?
   A) If there is a disagreement as to the purchase price
   B) If a coupon is discovered to be mutilated
   C) If the CUSIP number is not imprinted on the certificates
   D) If the securities go into default

*Other required books and records are listed under specific topics.

3. In disclosing account expenses to members of a syndicate formed to negotiate the sale of a new issue of municipal securities, the manager is required to furnish which of the following information to the account?
    I.   All printing and legal fees
    II.   The amount of clearance fees
    III. The amount of the management fee
    IV.   Each miscellaneous expense
        A) III only
        B) I and IV only
        C) I, II, and III only
        D) I, II, III, and IV

4. Managing underwriters of municipal securities syndicates must maintain, for each syndicate account, books and records that show all of the following information EXCEPT
    A) the terms and conditions governing operation of the syndicate account
    B) a reconciliation of the profits and expenses of the syndicate
    C) all allotments of those securities to syndicate members and the price at which sold
    D) the names and addresses of each customer purchasing securities from a syndicate member

Answers

1. A   3. C
2. B   4. D

APPENDIX III

Glossary of Municipal Securities Terms

Municipal Securities Rulemaking Board
Washington, D.C.

ACCEPTANCE RATIO—See: PLACEMENT RATIO.

ACCRETION OF A DISCOUNT—An accounting process by which the book value of a security purchased at a discount from par is increased during the security's holding period. The accretion reflects the increase in the security's holding value as it approaches the redemption date. Under a "straight line" accretion method, the amount of the yearly accretion is the same for all years, and is equal to the product of the total amount of the discount divided by the number of years to redemption. Under a "scientific" (or "constant interest") accretion method, the amount of the yearly accretion increases as the redemption date approaches, and for any semi-annual period is equal to (a) the original semi-annual yield to maturity multiplied by the current book value less (b) the current interest payment. Compare: AMORTIZATION OF A PREMIUM.

ACCRUED INTEREST—On a transaction in a security, the dollar amount of interest, based upon the stated rate or rates of interest, which has accumulated on a security from (and including) the most recent interest payment date (or, in certain circumstances, the dated date or other stated date), up to but not including the date of settlement of the transaction. Accrued interest is paid to the seller by the purchaser. Accrued interest is usually calculated on the basis of a 360-day year (assuming that each month has 30 days), but alternative day counting methods are used for certain types of securities (*e.g.*, some municipal notes and some bonds that bear interest at a variable rate). The formula for computing accrued interest is as follows:

$$\text{Accrued Interest} = \text{Interest Rate} \times \text{Par Value} \times \frac{\text{Number of Days}}{360}$$

EXAMPLES:

(1) City Y sold a $10,000,000 new issue of municipal bonds on August 15. The bonds were dated June 1 and delivered on September 15. The interest rate bid on the bonds was 7%.

Adapted by permission of State of Florida, Department of State, Jim Smith, Secretary of State,. and by the Municipal Securities Rulemaking Board.

On delivery date

$$\text{Accrued Interest} = .07 \times \$10{,}000{,}000 \times \frac{104}{360} = \$202{,}222.22$$

paid by underwriter

(2) Ms. Smith bought $100,000 of municipal bonds in the secondary market. The bonds were dated June 1, had a 7% coupon rate and paid interest semi-annually on December 1 and June 1. Settlement date was April 12.

On settlement date

$$\text{Accrued Interest} = .07 \times \$100{,}000 \times \frac{131}{360} = \$2{,}547.22$$

payable by Ms. Smith

ACCUMULATION ACCOUNT—An account established by the sponsor of a unit investment trust into which securities purchased for the portfolio of the trust are placed until they are formally deposited into the trust and the trust is formally created. See: BOND FUND.

ADDITIONAL BONDS TEST—The earnings test which must be satisfied under the provisions of a revenue bond contract before bonds of an additional issue having the same lien on a pledged revenue source can be issued. Typically, the test would require that historical revenues plus future estimated revenues (in some cases) exceed projected debt service requirements for both the existing issue and the proposed issue by a certain ratio. See: COVENANTS.

ADJUSTED TRADE—An offsetting pair of transactions, effected in violation of SEC and MSRB rules, in which a dealer purchases a security held in an investor's portfolio at a price above its market value, and the investor purchases a different security from the dealer at an adjusted price which exceeds that security's market value by at least the same amount. An institutional investor which is permitted to hold investment assets on its books at cost can fraudulently inflate the book value of its holdings through adjusted trades, since such trades permit it to liquidate portfolio holdings without reflecting losses on its books (although the losses are, of course, built into the new positions acquired as a result of the adjusted trade). This practice violates MSRB pricing rules, general SEC anti-fraud rules, and, if the institutional investor is a bank, applicable banking laws.

AD VALOREM TAX—A direct tax calculated "according to value" of property. Such tax is based on an assigned valuation (market or assessed) of real property and, in certain cases, on a valuation of tangible or intangible personal property. In virtually all jurisdictions the tax is a lien on the property enforceable by seizure and sale of the property. An ad valorem tax is normally the one substantial tax which may be raised or lowered by a local governing body without the sanction of superior levels of government (although general restrictions (e.g., rate limitations) may exist on the exercise of this right); hence, ad valorem taxes often function as the balancing element in local budgets. See: MILLAGE.

ADVANCE REFUNDING—A procedure whereby outstanding securities are refinanced by the proceeds of a new issue of securities prior to the date on which the outstanding securities become due or are callable. Accordingly, for a period of time, both the issue being refunded and the refunding issue are outstanding. The proceeds of the refunding securities are generally invested in U.S. Government or federal agency securities (although other instruments such as bank certificates of deposit are occasionally used), with principal and interest from these securities being used to pay principal and interest on the refunded securities (or, in some cases, interest on the refunding securities and subsequently principal on the refunded securities). Securities are "escrowed to maturity" when the proceeds of the refunding securities are deposited in escrow for investment in an amount sufficient to pay the principal of and interest on the issue being refunded on the original interest payment and maturity dates. Securities are considered "prerefunded" when the refunding issue's proceeds are escrowed only until a call date or dates on the refunded issue, with the refunded issue redeemed at that time. The Internal Revenue Code and regulations thereunder restrict the yield which may be earned on investment of the proceeds of refunding bonds. There are several methods of advance refunding:

Net Cash Refunding—A method of advance refunding in which the refunding issue constitutes a principal amount which, together with interest earnings thereon, will produce sufficient funds to pay debt service on the refunded obligations.

Full Cash or Gross Refunding—A method of advance refunding in which the refunding issue constitutes a principal amount which itself is sufficient to pay debt service on the refunded obligations. Such a refunding issue generally consists of two series of securities: the refunding securities, which pay debt service on the refunded issue; and "special obligation securities," which pay a portion of the debt service on the refunding securities. The special obligation securities are paid from the interest earnings on the invested refunding security proceeds. Thus, even though a larger total amount of principal may be outstanding as a result of this type of refunding, the issuer's total annual debt service requirements may be reduced because the special obligation securities are secured by the earnings on the refunding series. See: I.R.C. §103 and regulations promulgated thereunder.

investors. Under the terms of the agreement the transaction, which is subject to various consents and regulatory approvals, is expected to be consummated by March 31, 1985. Bonds insured by AMBAC are currently granted a Standard & Poor's rating of AAA. The name "AMBAC" is an acronym for "American Municipal Bond Assurance Corporation," the original name of the corporation.

AMORTIZATION OF A PREMIUM—An accounting process by which the book value of a security purchased at a premium above par is decreased during the security's holding period. The amortization reflects the decrease in the security's holding value as it approaches the redemption date. Under a "straight line" amortization method, the amount of the yearly amortization is the same for all years, and is equal to the product of the total amount of the premium divided by the number of years to redemption. Under a "scientific" (or "constant interest") amortization method, the amount of the yearly amortization decreases as the redemption date approaches, and for any semi-annual period is equal to (a) the current interest payment less (b) the original semi-annual yield to maturity multiplied by the current book value. Compare: ACCRETION OF A DISCOUNT.

AMORTIZATION OF DEBT—The process of paying the principal amount of an issue of securities by periodic payments either directly to securityholders or to a sinking fund for the benefit of securityholders. See: DEBT SERVICE; DEBT SERVICE SCHEDULE.

AMORTIZATION SCHEDULE—A table showing the gradual repayment of an amount of indebtedness, such as a mortgage or bond, over a period of time. This table is often set up to show interest payments in addition to principal repayments. See: DEBT SERVICE SCHEDULE.

ANY-INTEREST-DATE CALL—A call feature under which the issuer may redeem outstanding securities (at par or at a premium) on any date (after a specified commencement date) on which there is an interest payment due.

APPROVING OPINION—See: LEGAL OPINION.

ARBITRAGE—(1) Generally, transactions by which securities are bought and sold in different markets at the same time for the sake of the profit arising from a difference in prices in the two markets.

(2) With respect to the issuance of municipal securities, arbitrage usually refers to the difference between the interest paid on the tax-exempt securities and the interest earned by investing the security proceeds in higher-yielding taxable securities. Internal Revenue Service regulations govern arbitrage on the proceeds from issuance of municipal securities. Reference: I.R.S. Reg. 1.103-13 through 1.103-15.

Crossover Refunding—In a crossover refunding the revenue stream originally pledged to secure the securities being refunded continues to be used to pay debt service on the refunded securities until they mature or are called. At that time the pledged revenues "cross over" to pay debt service on the refunding securities. During the period when both the refunded and the refunding securities are outstanding, interest expense on the refunding securities is paid from interest earnings on the invested proceeds of the refunding issue.

See: ARBITRAGE; DEFEASANCE; REFUNDING; SLGS.

AFFIRMATION—An acknowledgment transmitted by an institutional customer or its agent through the facilities of an automated confirmation system indicating that the customer agrees with the details of a transaction previously confirmed through the system by the dealer on the other side of the transaction. See: NATIONAL INSTITUTIONAL DELIVERY SYSTEM.

AGENCIES—A colloquial term for securities issued by one of the federal agencies (*e.g.*, the Federal National Mortgage Association or the Government National Mortgage Association).

AGENCY CROSS—An offsetting purchase and sale transaction in which a municipal securities broker or dealer purchases securities from one of its customers and sells the securities to another of its customers while acting as agent for both customers. See: "AS AGENT" TRADE.

AGREEMENT AMONG UNDERWRITERS—The contract among the members of an underwriting syndicate establishing the rights, duties and commitments of each with respect to the new issue of municipal securities being underwritten. See: SYNDICATE.

A.I.D. CALL—See: ANY-INTEREST-DATE CALL.

ALL OR NONE or **AON**—A type of offering in which a party interested in purchasing the securities is required to buy (or bid for) all of the securities being offered if it wishes to buy any.

AMBAC INDEMNITY CORPORATION or **AMBAC**—A wholly owned subsidiary of MGIC Investment Corporation which offers noncancellable insurance contracts by which it agrees to pay a securityholder all, or any part, of scheduled principal and interest payments on the securities as they become due and payable, in the event that the issuer is unable to pay. Under an agreement entered into in January 1985, the municipal bond insurance business of AMBAC has been purchased by an investor group consisting of the management of AMBAC, Johnson & Higgins, Stephens Inc., Xerox Corporation, Citicorp, and other major

ARBITRAGE BONDS—Bonds which are deemed by the Internal Revenue Service to violate federal arbitrage regulations. If the Internal Revenue Service finds that bonds are "arbitrage bonds," "the interest becomes taxable and therefore must be included in each bondholder's gross income for federal income tax purposes. Reference: I.R.S. Reg. 1.103-13 through 1.103-15.

ARBITRATION—A system offered under MSRB rules for resolving disputes, under which two parties who have a disagreement involving a municipal securities transaction may submit the disagreement to an impartial panel for resolution. Municipal securities dealers may be compelled to arbitrate disputes; customers cannot be compelled to arbitrate disputes involving securities law claims, although they can be forced to resolve general contractual disputes through arbitration if a valid arbitration agreement had been previously executed. Decisions of an arbitration panel are binding on the parties to the claim. Other arbitration facilities, for disputes involving other types of securities, are made available by the securities exchanges and the NASD. Reference: MSRB Rule G-35.

"AS AGENT" TRADE—A securities transaction executed by a dealer on behalf of and under the instruction of another party. The dealer does not act in a principal capacity and may be compensated by a commission or fee (which must be disclosed to the party for whom it is acting) rather than by a mark-up. To function as a customer's agent a dealer must disclose or express willingness to disclose the identity of the other side of the transaction. Compare: PRINCIPAL TRADE.

A.S.C.A.—An abbreviation for "all subsequent coupons attached," generally found in the description of a coupon-bearing bond. The alternative abbreviation "S.C.A." (for "subsequent coupons attached") is also used.

EXAMPLE:

$5,000 State of Florida Full Faith & Credit Pollution Control Bond, Series A, dated 7-1-80, 10.80%, due 7-1-97, number 4006, with coupon number 3 and A.S.C.A. (or "and S.C.A.")

ASSESSED VALUATION—The appraised worth of property as set by a taxing authority for purposes of ad valorem taxation. It is important to note that the method of establishing assessed valuation varies from state to state, with the method generally specified by state law. For example, in certain jurisdictions the assessed valuation is equal to the full or market value of the property; in other jurisdictions the assessed valuation is equal to a set percentage of full or market value.

ASSIGNMENT—The form imprinted on a registered securities certificate which, when completed and signed by the registered owner, authorizes the transfer of the security into the name of a new owner (designated on the form as the "assignee"). The assignment also usually provides for the granting by the registered owner of power of attorney to another person (usually the new owner or someone acting on his or her behalf) to accomplish the transfer. Assignments are often executed by the registered owner "in blank," with the name of the assignee and the person granted power of attorney filled in subsequently. See: REGISTERED BOND; TRANSFER.

ASSOCIATED PERSON—Any partner, officer, director or other employee of a broker or dealer other than persons whose functions are solely clerical or administrative; in the case of a bank dealer, the term refers only to persons who are involved in the bank's dealer activities (or have some control over them). Associated persons are most often (but not always) qualified in one of the four qualification categories specified in MSRB rules. See: FINANCIAL AND OPERATIONS PRINCIPAL; MUNICIPAL SECURITIES PRINCIPAL; MUNICIPAL SECURITIES REPRESENTATIVE; MUNICIPAL SECURITIES SALES PRINCIPAL.

AUCTION MARKET—A market for securities, typically found on a national securities exchange, in which trading in a particular security is conducted at a specific location with all qualified persons at that post able to bid or offer securities against orders via outcry. Very few municipal securities are traded in an auction market system. Compare: OVER-THE-COUNTER MARKET.

AUDITED STATEMENT—A financial statement which has been examined by an auditor and upon which the auditor has expressed or disclaimed an opinion.

AUDITOR'S REPORT—The written report of an independent auditor upon completion of the audit. The auditor's report describes the scope of the auditor's examination and gives or disclaims an opinion as to the fairness of the financial statements. It accompanies the financial statements as a part of the audit report.

AUDIT REPORT—The report prepared by an auditor following his audit or investigation of an entity's financial position and results of operations for a given period of time. As a general rule, the report should include: (a) a statement of the scope of the audit; (b) explanatory comments concerning exceptions from generally accepted accounting principles and auditing standards; (c) expression or disclaimer of opinions; (d) explanatory comments concerning verification procedures; (e) financial

(1) Years	(2) Principal	(3) Number of Bonds	(4) Bond Years (1 × 3)
1	$ 1,740,000	1,740	1,740
2	1,860,000	1,860	3,720
3	1,990,000	1,990	5,970
4	2,130,000	2,130	8,520
5	2,280,000	2,280	11,400
Total	$10,000,000	10,000	31,350

$$\frac{31,350}{10,000} = 3.135 \text{ years average life}$$

See: BOND YEAR.

AWARD—Acceptance by the issuer of a bid by an underwriter to purchase a new issue of municipal securities. The date of the award is generally considered the "sale date" of an issue. Compare: BID. See: BOND PURCHASE AGREEMENT.

statements and schedules; and (f) statistical tables, supplementary comments and recommendations. The auditor's signature follows item (c) or (d).

AUTHORITY—A unit or agency of government established to perform specialized functions, usually financed by service charges, fees or tolls, although it may also have taxing powers. In many cases authorities have the power to issue debt which is secured by the lease rental payments made by a governmental unit using the facilities constructed with bond proceeds. An authority may function independently of other governmental units, or it may depend upon other units for its creation, funding or administrative oversight. Examples of authorities include health facilities authorities, industrial development authorities and housing authorities.

AUTHORIZING RESOLUTION or ORDINANCE—With respect to an issue of municipal securities the document adopted by the issuer which implements its power to issue the securities. The legal grant of such authority may be found in the enabling provisions of the constitution, statutes, charters and ordinances applicable to the issuer. Adoption of an authorizing resolution or ordinance by the issuer's governing body is a condition precedent to the issuance of the proposed securities. See: BOND RESOLUTION.

AVERAGE LIFE or AVERAGE MATURITY—The number of years to the point at which half of an issue will have been redeemed. The average life is a reflection of the rapidity with which the principal of an issue is expected to be paid. Under one commonly used calculation method, it is equal to the total bond years divided by the total number of bonds (1 bond equals $1,000 par amount, regardless of actual certificate denomination); note that this computation method does not take into account the time value of the principal amounts. The formula for this computation is:

$$\text{Average Life} = \frac{\text{Total Bond Years}}{\text{Number of Bonds}}$$

EXAMPLE:

Issue size:	$10,000,000
Interest rate:	7%
Maturity of issue:	5 years
1 bond	= $1,000

B

BALANCE ORDER—A document generated by a registered clearing agency operating a system for the comparison and netting of inter-dealer transactions which reflects an obligation to deliver securities to (a "deliver balance order" or "DBO"), or receive securities from (a "receive balance order" or "RBO"), another dealer. See: NETTING.

BALLOON MATURITY—A maturity within a serial issue of securities (usually a later maturity) which contains a disproportionately large percentage of the principal amount of the original issue. A balloon maturity is generally distinguished from a term bond by the presence of serial maturities in the years immediately preceding the balloon maturity. Compare: TERM BONDS.

BALLOON PAYMENT—A principal payment on a balloon maturity.

BANK DEALER—See: DEALER BANK.

BANs—See: NOTE.

BASIS BOOK—A book of mathematical tables used to convert yields to equivalent dollar prices and vice versa. The factors contained in the book are time to redemption, interest rate, yield (or basis) and dollar price. The basis book is used to find the dollar price when yield is known for a given interest rate and time, or to find the yield for a given dollar price when interest rate and time are known.

BASIS POINT—1/100 of 1 percent of yield. If a yield increases from 8.25% to 8.50%, the difference is referred to as a 25 basis point increase. Compare: POINT.

BASIS PRICE—A price of a security expressed in terms of the yield to be realized by the purchaser. Compare: DOLLAR PRICE.

BEARER BOND—A bond which is presumed to be owned by the person who holds it. The Internal Revenue Code imposes penalties on the issuance of securities in bearer form after June 30, 1983, with the exception of obligations maturing in one year or less or obligations of a type not generally offered to the public. Compare: REGISTERED BOND. Reference: I.R.C. §103(j).

BELL-SHAPED YIELD CURVE—See: YIELD CURVE.

BENEFICIAL OWNER—The person to whom the benefits of ownership of given securities accrue, even though the securities might be held by, or in the name of, another person or held in an account over which another person has investment discretion. For example, a securities firm might hold securities in "street name" in its vaults or at a securities depository, with the beneficial owners of the securities only designated on the firm's records.

BID—A proposal to purchase securities at a specified price. With respect to a new issue of municipal securities, the bid specifies the interest rate(s) for each maturity and the purchase price. The purchase price is usually stated in terms of par, par plus a premium or par minus a discount. Compare: OFFER; QUALIFIED BID. See: AWARD.

BIDDING LIMITATIONS—The restrictions (if any) stated by the issuer in the notice of sale on the terms of bids submitted by prospective underwriters. Such restrictions might include, for example, indications of the maximum range of permissible interest rates, the number of different interest rates permitted, whether a particular interest rate structure is required (or prohibited), and whether a discount bid is allowable.

BIDDING SYNDICATE—Two or more underwriters that act together to submit a proposal to underwrite a new issue of municipal securities. See: MANAGER; SYNDICATE; UNDERWRITER.

BID FORM—A document, generally included with the notice of sale, to be completed by underwriters interested in submitting a bid on a new issue of municipal securities to be sold at a competitive sale. A bidding underwriter will state on the bid form its proposed interest rate(s) on the issue and the price it would be willing to pay for the new issue (subject to any conditions stated by the issuer in the notice of sale), and may be asked to propose a structure for the issue. See: BIDDING LIMITATIONS; COMPETITIVE BID.

BID WANTED—A listing of securities on which the listing dealer does not show a price but rather solicits bids from other dealers interested in purchasing the securities.

BIGI—See: BOND INVESTORS GUARANTY INSURANCE COMPANY.

BLUE LIST, THE—A daily publication (*The Blue List of Current Municipal Offerings*) listing municipal bonds and notes being offered by dealers in the inter-dealer market. The par value, issuer, interest rate, maturity date, price or yield and offering dealer are indicated for each security offered.

BLUE LIST TOTAL—The total of the par values of all municipal securities offered for sale in *The Blue List*. The *Blue List* Total, as a measure of the supply of municipal securities available for purchase, is considered to be an indicator of the status of the secondary market for municipal securities.

BLUE-SKY LAWS—A colloquial term for state securities laws, derived from a statement that such laws were directed at unethical promoters who "would sell building lots in the blue sky." Although these laws vary from state to state, most contain provisions concerning (a) prohibitions against fraud, (b) regulation of brokers and dealers doing business in the state, and (c) registration of securities. In many states certain of these requirements have been integrated with the federal securities laws, so that separate actions need not be taken to comply with them. Issues of municipal securities are generally exempt from state securities registration requirements, although brokers and dealers selling them are subject to many states' registration and regulatory requirements.

BOND—Evidence of the issuer's obligation to repay a specified principal amount on a date certain (maturity date), together with interest at a stated rate, or according to a formula for determining that rate. Bonds are distinguishable from notes, which usually mature in a much shorter period of time. Bonds may be classified according to maturity structure (serial vs. term), source of payment (general obligation vs. revenue), method of transfer (bearer vs. registered), issuer (state vs. municipality vs. special district) or price (discount vs. premium). Compare: NOTE.

BOND AMORTIZATION FUND—See: MANDATORY REDEMPTION ACCOUNT.

BOND AND INTEREST RECORD—The record maintained for each bond issue by the issuer or its agent. Information recorded may include the dated date, original principal amount issued, paying agent, certificate numbers, coupon numbers (if any), maturity schedule for life of the issue, amounts and dates of principal and interest payments made, and outstanding balances of principal and interest. Compare: BOND REGISTER.

BOND ANTICIPATION NOTE—See: NOTE.

BOND ATTORNEY, BOND APPROVING ATTORNEY, or BOND APPROVING COUNSEL—See: BOND COUNSEL.

BOND BUYER, THE—A trade paper of the municipal securities industry published each business day, which contains advertisements for offerings of new issues of municipal securities, notices of bond redemptions, statistical analyses of market activity, results of previous bond sales, and articles relating to financial markets and public finance. A second publication, *Credit Markets*, provides similar information on a weekly basis.

BOND BUYER INDEXES—Indicators published on a periodic basis by *The Bond Buyer* showing the price levels for various groups of municipal securities. Three of the indexes represent weekly averages, based upon estimates from municipal securities underwriters, of the yields which would be offered to investors if an issuer were to bring certain types of securities to market at par on a given day. These indexes are named after the number of issuers used in each index (the same issuers are used each week):

  11 Bond Index—An estimation of the yield which would be offered on 20-year general obligation bonds with a composite rating of approximately "Aa" or "AA." The 11 issuers which comprise this index are also included in the 20 Bond Index.

  20 Bond Index—An estimation of the yield which would be offered on 20-year general obligation bonds with a composite rating of approximately "A."

  25 Bond Index or Revdex—An estimation of the yield which would be offered on 30-year revenue bonds. The 25 issuers used for this index cover a broad range of types of issues (transportation, housing, hospitals, water and sewer, pollution control, etc.) and vary in ratings from Moody's Baa1 to Aaa and Standard and Poor's A to AAA, for a composite rating of Moody's A1 or Standard and Poor's A+.

The fourth index, the *Bond Buyer Municipal Bond Index*, represents an average of the prices, adjusted to an 8.00 yield basis, of 40 recently issued securities, based on quotations obtained from five municipal securities broker's brokers. The 40 component issues are selected according to defined criteria and are replaced by newer issues on a periodic basis. This index is published daily and serves as the basis of a proposed futures contract.

BOND CONTRACT—An agreement which the issuer is obligated to perform by virtue of issuing its bonds. The terms of the agreement may be determined by reference to specified documents associated with the bond issue. Typically, the bond resolution or ordinance, trust indenture and security agreements constitute parts of the contract, as do those laws in force at the time of issuance. The documents which form the bond contract vary according to the terms of each issue. See: BOND RESOLUTION.

BOND COUNSEL—An attorney (or firm of attorneys) retained by the issuer to give a legal opinion that the issuer is authorized to issue proposed securities, the issuer has met all legal requirements necessary for issuance, and interest on the proposed securities will be exempt from federal income taxation and, where applicable, from state and local taxation. Typically, bond counsel may prepare, or review and advise the issuer regarding authorizing resolutions or ordinances, trust indentures, official statements, validation proceedings and litigation. The bond counsel may also be referred to as the "bond attorney," the "bond approving attorney" or the "bond approving counsel." Compare: UNDERWRITER'S COUNSEL.

BOND COVENANT—See: COVENANTS.

BONDED DEBT—The portion of an issuer's total indebtedness represented by outstanding bonds:

  Direct Debt or Gross Bonded Debt—The sum of the total bonded debt and any short-term debt of the issuer. Direct debt may be incurred in the issuer's own name or assumed through the annexation of territory or consolidation with another governmental unit.

  Net Direct Debt or Net Bonded Debt—Direct debt less sinking fund accumulations and all self-supporting debt.

  Total Overall Debt or Total Direct and Overlapping Debt—Total direct debt plus the issuer's applicable share of the total debt of all overlapping jurisdictions.

  Net Overall Debt or Net Direct and Overlapping Debt—Net direct debt plus the issuer's applicable share of the net debt of all overlapping jurisdictions.

  Overlapping Debt—The issuer's proportionate share of the debt of other local governmental units which either overlap it (the issuer is located either wholly or partly within the geographic limits of the other units) or underlie it (the other units are located within the geographic limits of the issuer). The debt is generally apportioned based upon relative assessed values.

See: DEBT RATIOS.

BOND ELECTION or BOND REFERENDUM—A process whereby the voters of a governmental unit are given the opportunity to approve or disapprove a proposed issue of municipal securities. An election is most commonly required in connection with general obligation bonds. Requirements for voter approval may be imposed by constitution, statute or local ordinance.

BOND EQUIVALENT YIELD or COUPON EQUIVALENT YIELD—The return on a discounted security figured on a basis which permits comparison with interest-bearing securities. On a short-term (under six months) discounted security the bond equivalent yield is an annualized rate of return; on a longer term discounted security the bond equivalent yield is determined by a computation which adjusts for the absence of periodic payments over the life of the security.

BOND FISCAL YEAR—The twelve-month accounting period, established under some bond contracts, used in connection with an issue of municipal securities. Principal and interest payments are scheduled in accordance with the bond fiscal year. The bond fiscal year may not necessarily coincide with the issuing agency's own fiscal year, and may be established in order to take full advantage of the scheduled cash flow of projected pledged revenues. See: FISCAL YEAR.

BOND FUND—A colloquial term for a municipal securities investment company. The investment company holds a diversified portfolio of municipal securities, and units or shares in the investment company are sold to investors. There are two basic types of bond funds:

Unit Investment Trust or U.I.T.—A fixed portfolio of municipal securities sold to investors in trust "units," which represent fractional undivided ownership interests in the portfolio. The same securities are held in the portfolio until maturity or redemption. A U.I.T. is a "closed end" fund, i.e., with a fixed number of units available to investors.

Managed Fund—A fund, similar to a corporate securities mutual fund, in which investors own "shares" of a portfolio of municipal securities. An investment advisor actively manages the portfolio in line with the set investment policy; managed funds are also "open end" funds (i.e., they offer new shares to the public continuously). Managed funds may maintain portfolios of specialized types of municipal securities (e.g., short-term securities, or higher yielding long-term securities).

BONDHOLDER—The owner of a municipal bond. The owner of a bearer bond is the person having possession of it, while the owner of a registered bond is the person whose name is noted on the bond register.

BOND INVESTORS GUARANTY INSURANCE COMPANY or BIGI—An insurance program formed by its shareholders and equal partners: American International Group, Inc.; Bankers Trust New York Corp.; Geico; Phibro-Salomon, Inc.; and Xerox Credit Corp. BIGI insurance guarantees the timely payment of principal and interest of municipal bonds and notes. BIGI also issues insurance in the secondary market, including unit investment trusts, mutual funds, bond portfolios and secondary market blocks. The BIGI program is still in its formative stages and does not expect to receive official ratings until early Spring 1985.

BOND ISSUE—See: ISSUE OF BONDS.

BOND ORDINANCE—See: BOND RESOLUTION.

BOND POWER—A separate document attached to a registered securities certificate which is used in lieu of an assignment form to authorize the transfer of the securities. A completed bond power includes a description of the securities to be transferred, in addition to the information generally provided on the assignment form. Bond powers are typically used when no assignment form is imprinted on the securities, or when the securities must be transmitted through the mails (in which case the completed bond powers are often mailed separately). As is the case with an assignment, bond powers are often executed by the registered owner "in blank." Compare: ASSIGNMENT. See: REGISTERED BOND; TRANSFER.

BOND PROCEEDS—The money paid to the issuer by the purchaser or underwriter of a new issue of municipal securities. These moneys are used to finance the project or purpose for which the securities were issued and to pay certain costs of issuance as may be provided in the bond contract.

BOND PURCHASE AGREEMENT—The contract between the underwriter and the issuer setting forth the final terms, prices and conditions upon which the underwriter purchases a new issue of municipal securities.

BOND REFERENDUM—See: BOND ELECTION.

BOND REGISTER—A record, kept by a transfer agent or registrar on behalf of the issuer, which lists the names and addresses of the owners of registered bonds. See: REGISTERED BOND; REGISTRAR.

BOND RESOLUTION or ORDINANCE—The document or documents in which the issuer authorizes the issuance and sale of municipal securities. Issuance of the securities is usually approved in the authorizing resolution or ordinance, and sale is usually authorized in a separate document known as the "sale" or "award" resolution. All such resolutions, read together, constitute the bond resolution, which describes the nature of the obligation and the issuer's duties to the bondholders. State law or local ordinances may prescribe whether a bond issue may be authorized by resolution, or whether the more formal procedure of adopting an ordinance is required. See: AUTHORIZING RESOLUTION; BOND CONTRACT; MASTER RESOLUTION.

BOND SERVICE FUND—See: SINKING FUND.

BOND SINKING FUND—See: SINKING FUND.

BOND TRANSCRIPT—All legal documents, including minutes of appropriate meetings of the issuer, associated with the offering of a new issue of municipal securities. Bond counsel's opinion is given after a review of the transcript and becomes a part thereof.

BOND YEAR—$1000 of debt outstanding for one year. The number of "bond years" in an issue is equal to the product of the number of bonds (1 bond equals $1,000 regardless of actual certificate denomination) and the number of years from the dated date (or other stated date) to the stated maturity. The total number of bond years is used in calculating the average life of an issue and its net interest cost. Computations are often made of bond years for each maturity or for each coupon rate, as well as total bond years for an entire issue. See: AVERAGE LIFE for an example.

BOOK-ENTRY CLEARANCE—A system for the transfer of ownership of securities through entries on the records of a centralized agency. The centralized agency holds securities on behalf of their owners; when the securities are sold ownership is transferred by bookkeeping entry from the seller to the purchaser. In the case of certain U.S. Government securities, securities certificates are not issued, and ownership of the securities is evidenced in computer records maintained by the Federal Reserve system. For other types of securities book-entry clearance is made available through linked or interfaced systems maintained by four securities depositories, which hold securities and act on behalf of their participants. Transactions cleared by means of the depositories' book-entry clearance systems may involve either immobilized securities or book-entry form securities. See: BOOK-ENTRY SECURITY; IMMOBILIZATION; IMMOBILIZED SECURITY.

BOOK-ENTRY SECURITY or BOOK-ENTRY FORM SECURITY—A security which is not available to purchasers in physical form. Such a security may be held either as a computer entry on the records of a central holder (as is the case with certain U.S. Government securities) or in the form of a single, global certificate. Compare: IMMOBILIZED SECURITY. See: GLOBAL CERTIFICATE.

BOOK VALUE—The value at which a security is carried on the inventory lists or other financial records of an investor. This value may be the original cost of acquisition of the security, or original cost adjusted by amortization of a premium or accretion of a discount. The book value may differ significantly from the security's current value in the market. Compare: MARKET VALUE.

BROKER or MUNICIPAL SECURITIES BROKER—A person or firm which acts as an intermediary by purchasing and selling securities (in the case of a "municipal securities broker," municipal securities) for others rather than for its own account. For purposes of the Securities Exchange Act of 1934 the term does not include a dealer bank. The term is also colloquially used to refer to a municipal securities broker's broker. Compare: BROKER'S BROKER; DEALER.

BROKER/DEALER—A general term for a securities firm which is engaged in both buying and selling securities on behalf of customers and also buying and selling on behalf of its own account. The term would not be used to refer to a dealer bank or a municipal securities broker's broker. See: BROKER; DEALER.

BROKER'S BROKER or MUNICIPAL SECURITIES BROKER'S BROKER—A broker that deals exclusively with other municipal securities brokers and dealers and not with public investors. The services of a broker's broker are available, generally at a standard fee established by each broker's broker, only to certain municipal securities professionals that are selected by the broker's broker. Broker's brokers do not take inventory positions in municipal issues.

BUDGET—A plan of financial operation embodying an estimate of proposed expenditures for a given period and the proposed means of financing them. Used without any modifier, the term usually indicates a financial plan for a single fiscal year. In actual practice the term "budget" has two connotations: the financial plan presented to the appropriating body for adoption; and the plan finally approved by that body. It is usually necessary to specify whether the budget under consideration is proposed or whether it has been approved by the appropriating body.

BUY-IN—See: CLOSE-OUT.

CAB—See: CAPITAL APPRECIATION BOND.

CALAMITY CALL—See: REDEMPTION PROVISIONS.

CALL—See: REDEMPTION.

CALLABLE BOND—A bond which the issuer is permitted or required to redeem before the stated maturity date at a specified price, usually at or above par, by giving notice of redemption in a manner specified in the bond contract. Compare: NON-CALLABLE BOND; PUT BOND. See: REDEMPTION; REDEMPTION PROVISIONS.

CALL FEATURES—See: REDEMPTION PROVISIONS.

CALL PRICE—The price, as established in the bond contract, at which securities will be redeemed, if called. The call price is generally at or above par (although it may be at or above the ''compound accreted value'' on certain types of securities) and is stated as a percentage of the principal amount called.

CALL PROTECTION—The aspects of the redemption provisions of an issue of callable securities which partially protect an investor against an issuer's call of the securities or act as a disincentive to the issuer's exercise of its call privileges. These features include restrictions on an issuer's right to call securities for a period of time after issuance (for example, an issue that cannot be called for ten years after its issuance is said to have ''ten years 'call protection' ''), or requirements that an issuer pay a premium redemption price for securities called within a certain period of time after issuance. The term may also be used to refer to market factors which would discourage an issuer from calling the securities (for example, a security callable at par which has a current trading market value of 70 is said to have ''30 points of call protection''). See: REDEMPTION PROVISIONS.

CANADIAN INTEREST COST or C.I.C.—See: TRUE INTEREST COST.

CAPITAL APPRECIATION BOND or CAB—A long-term municipal security on which the investment return on an initial principal amount is assumed to be reinvested at a stated compounded rate until maturity, at which time the investor receives a single payment (the "maturity value") representing both the initial principal amount and the total investment return. Several different types of capital appreciation bonds are issued, including compound interest bonds and multiplier bonds. Capital appreciation bonds are distinct from traditional zero coupon bonds because the investment return is considered to be in the form of compounded interest, rather than accreted original issue discount; for this reason only the initial principal amount of a capital appreciation bond would be counted against a municipal issuer's statutory debt limit, rather than the total par value, as in the case of a traditional zero coupon bond. Compare: ZERO COUPON BOND. See: COMPOUND INTEREST BOND; MULTIPLIER.

CAPITALIZED INTEREST or FUNDED INTEREST—A portion of the proceeds of an issue which is set aside to pay interest on the securities for a specified period of time. Interest is commonly capitalized for the construction period of a revenue-producing project. In an accounting sense capitalized interest is the interest expense paid during the construction period (net of income earned on construction funds) which is added to the book value of the asset being built.

CAPITAL MARKET—The market for equity securities (stocks) and debt obligations with maturities in excess of one year.

CARRYING COST—The interest expense incurred in financing an inventory of securities. It is considered "negative carry" when the cost incurred in borrowing to finance the holding of securities exceeds the income from the securities, and "positive carry" when the yield of the securities is in excess of the interest cost of the funds borrowed to finance the holding of the securities.

CASH TRADE—A securities transaction in which the settlement date is the same as the trade date. Compare: "REGULAR WAY" TRADE.

CATASTROPHE CALL—See: REDEMPTION PROVISIONS.

C.A.V.—See: COMPOUND ACCRETED VALUE.

CERTIFICATE—The physical document representing a security. The certificate is typically an engraved paper setting forth certain information concerning the issuer of the securities and details of the specific issue. The American National Standards Institute publishes guidelines for the format of registered municipal securities certificates. Compare: BOOK-ENTRY SECURITY.

CERTIFICATED SECURITY—A security whose ownership may be represented by a physical document. Such a security is also described as being available in "definitive form." Compare: BOOK-ENTRY SECURITY.

CHURNING—A practice, in violation of MSRB and SEC rules, in which a salesperson effects a series of transactions in a customer's account which are excessive in size and/or frequency in relation to the size and investment objectives of the account. A salesperson churning an account is normally seeking to maximize the income (in commissions, sales credits or mark-ups) derived from the account. MSRB rule G-19 on suitability expressly prohibits churning of accounts. Reference: MSRB rule G-19(e).

C.I.C.—See: TRUE INTEREST COST.

CLEARING AGENT—A firm or bank who handles the clearance and settlement of securities transactions on behalf of its clients. The term generally is not used to refer to one of the registered clearing agencies. See: REGISTERED CLEARING AGENCY.

CLEARING CORPORATION—An organization registered as a clearing agency with the Securities and Exchange Commission which provides specialized comparison, clearance and settlement services for its members, but which does not safekeep securities on their behalf. Clearing corporations typically offer services such as envelope delivery systems, automated comparison systems, and transaction netting systems. The four registered clearing corporations are the Midwest Clearing Corporation (Chicago), the National Securities Clearing Corporation (New York), the Pacific Clearing Corporation (Los Angeles/San Francisco), and the Stock Clearing Corporation of Philadelphia. Compare: DEPOSITORY. See: REGISTERED CLEARING AGENCY.

CLEARING HOUSE FUNDS—Funds drawn on one commercial bank which are deposited in another commercial bank. It may take one or more days after the date of deposit for payments presented in this form to be credited and available to the recipient. Compare: FEDERAL FUNDS.

CLNs—See: NOTE.

CLOSED END FUND—See: BOND FUND.

CLOSED LIEN or CLOSED END LIEN—A general characterization of the security provisions on a revenue bond where these provisions preclude the issuer from issuing any additional bonds which have an equal claim on the pledged revenues. Compare: OPEN END LIEN.

CLOSE-OUT—A procedure provided under MSRB rules which permits a broker, dealer or dealer bank which has purchased securities from another broker, dealer or dealer bank but has not yet received them (or which, as a seller of securities, has tendered a good delivery of the securities but has had such delivery improperly rejected) to take action to complete the transaction. After following specified notice requirements the dealer may act to "execute" the close-out in one of several specified ways. A purchasing dealer seeking to close out a transaction may acquire the securities from another party and charge the original seller any additional costs incurred (this is known as a "buy-in"), negotiate a substitution of comparable securities, or force the seller to repurchase the securities; a selling dealer seeking to close out a transaction can sell the securities in the open market and charge the dealer who had improperly rejected the delivery for any losses or costs incurred (this is known as a "sell-out"). Reference: MSRB Rule G-12(h).

CLOSING—The meeting of concerned parties on the date of delivery of a new issue of municipal securities for the issuer to make physical delivery of the signed securities (or other evidences of indebtedness) and the requisite legal documents in exchange for the purchase price. The parties attending the closing usually include representatives of the issuer, bond counsel and the purchasers (underwriters). Sometimes a pre-closing meeting is held on the day before delivery to review the adequacy of the closing procedures and documents. See: DELIVERY DATE.

CNS—See: NETTING.

CO-MANAGER—See: MANAGER; SYNDICATE.

COMMERCIAL PAPER (TAX-EXEMPT)—Very short-term, unsecured promissory notes issued in either registered or bearer form, and usually backed by a line of credit with a bank.

COMMISSION—A form of remuneration received by a broker, dealer or dealer bank purchasing or selling securities when acting as agent for a customer. The commission is typically a charge to the customer of a set fee per security, although many dealers accept the concession as the sole form of remuneration on this type of trade. The commission (or any other remuneration received) must be disclosed to the customer as a separate item on the confirmation of an "as agent" transaction. Compare: CONCESSION; MARK-DOWN; MARK-UP.

COMPARISON—(1) The process of matching the data concerning an inter-dealer transaction specified by each party to the transaction in order to determine that both parties are agreed on the details of the transaction. Discrepancies or other problems discovered in the comparison process

are resolved or otherwise disposed of in accordance with procedures set forth in MSRB rule G-12(d) or the rules of an automated comparison system.

(2) A term used to refer to an inter-dealer confirmation. See: CONFIRMATION.

COMPETITIVE BID or COMPETITIVE BIDDING—A method of submitting proposals for the purchase of a new issue of municipal securities by which the securities are awarded to the underwriting syndicate presenting the best bid according to stipulated criteria set forth in the notice of sale. The underwriting of securities in this manner is also referred to as a competitive or public sale. Compare: NEGOTIATED SALE. See: BID; NET INTEREST COST; TRUE INTEREST COST.

COMPOUND ACCRETED VALUE or C.A.V.—The nominal value, from time to time, of a security such as a zero coupon, multiplier or interest-paying original issue discount bond on which all or a portion of the investment return is received in the form of an accretion from an initial principal amount to a maturity or redemption value. The compound accreted value as of a given time is equal to the initial principal amount plus the accretion (figured on the scientific method) to that date. A security's compound accreted value may, of course, differ from its market value depending on the current state of interest rates. Typically a schedule of compound accreted values at six month intervals is included in the official statement and on the certificate. See: ACCRETION OF A DISCOUNT.

COMPOUND ACCRETED VALUE CALL or C.A.V. CALL—A redemption provision in which the price to be paid to the holder in the event of a call is based on the compound accreted value of the security as of the call date. Such call features are typically found on zero coupon, multiplier and some interest-paying original issue discount bonds. See: REDEMPTION PROVISIONS.

COMPOUND INTEREST BOND—A long-term security in which the semi-annual "interest" on the security is assumed to be reinvested at a stated rate, with the investor receiving all investment return (*i.e.*, the compounded interest payments) at maturity. A compound interest bond is usually distinguished from the otherwise similar multiplier bond by the fact that the initial principal amount at which the compound interest bond is sold is typically an amount in even $100's or $1,000's, with the maturity value often an odd amount. Compare: MULTIPLIER; ZERO COUPON BOND. See: CAPITAL APPRECIATION BOND.

CONCESSION or DEALER'S ALLOWANCE—(1) In the sale of a new issue of municipal securities, the amount of reduction from the public

COSTS OF ISSUANCE—The expenses associated with the sale of a new issue of municipal securities, including such items as printing, legal and rating agency fees, and others. In certain cases, the underwriter's spread may be considered one of the costs of issuance.

COUPON—(1) A detachable part of a bond which evidences interest due. The coupon specifies the date, place and dollar amount of interest payable, among other matters. Coupons may be redeemed (usually semi-annually) by detaching them from bonds and presenting them to the issuer's paying agent for payment or to a bank for collection. See: COUPON BOND.

(2) The term is also used colloquially to refer to a security's interest rate.

COUPON BOND—A bearer bond, or a bond registered as to principal only, carrying coupons as evidence of future interest payments. Prior to June 30, 1983, most municipal bonds were issued in coupon form. However, I.R.C. §103(j) essentially provides that, subsequent to that date, all long term municipal bonds must be issued in registered form. Compare: REGISTERED BOND. See: BEARER BOND.

COUPON EQUIVALENT YIELD—See: BOND EQUIVALENT YIELD.

COUPON RATE—The annual rate of interest payable on a coupon security expressed as a percentage of the principal amount. See: NOMINAL INTEREST RATE.

COVENANTS or BOND COVENANTS—The issuer's enforceable promise to perform or refrain from performing certain actions. With respect to municipal securities, covenants are generally stated in the bond contract. Covenants commonly made in connection with a bond issue include covenants to charge fees sufficient to provide required pledged revenues (called a "rate covenant"); to maintain casualty insurance on the project; to complete, maintain and operate the project; not to sell or encumber the project; not to issue parity bonds unless certain earnings tests are met (called an "additional bonds covenant"); and not to take actions which would cause the bonds to be arbitrage bonds. See: NEGATIVE COVENANTS; PROTECTIVE COVENANTS.

COVER—The difference between the winning bid on a new issue or secondary market item and the next best bid. The cover on a new issue is most often expressed in terms of the difference in the interest cost (in either basis point or gross dollar terms); on secondary market items it may be expressed in terms of basis points or dollars per bond. The next best bid is called the "cover bid," although it is sometimes also referred to as the "cover."

offering price a syndicate grants to a dealer not a member of the syndicate, expressed as a percentage of par value. See: SPREAD.

(2) In the secondary market, bonds are usually offered to other dealers "less a concession," that is, at a price expressed in terms of a net offering price (in basis or dollar price terms) minus a differential (in points or dollars per security) granted between professionals; this differential is called the "concession." Compare: NET OFFERING.

CONDUIT FINANCING—The issuance of securities by a governmental unit to finance a project to be used primarily by a third party, usually a corporation engaged in private enterprise. The security for this type of issue is the credit of the private user rather than the governmental issuer. Usually such securities do not constitute general obligations of the issuer because the corporate obligor is liable for generating the pledged revenues. Industrial development bonds are a common type of conduit financing.

CONFIRMATION—A written summary of a transaction involving the purchase or sale of municipal securities, which a broker or dealer provides to the contra-party. The confirmation must contain certain information describing the securities and the parties to the transaction. The minimum requirements for the confirmation sent to customers are prescribed by MSRB Rule G-15(a); the minimum requirements for the inter-dealer confirmation are prescribed by MSRB Rule G-12(c).

CONSTRUCTION LOAN NOTE—See: NOTE.

CONSULTING ENGINEER—An expert who assists in the preparation of feasibility studies for proposed construction projects. These studies forecast construction costs and may include a rate analysis to provide substantiation that debt service can be met from pledged revenues.

CONTINUOUS NET SETTLEMENT—See: NETTING.

CONTRACT CLAUSE—Federal and state constitutional provisions prohibiting state governments from enacting any law which impairs the obligation of contracts. The question of contract impairment commonly arises with respect to municipal securities when action is taken or proposed which has the effect of reducing revenues pledged for payment of the securities. Such action would be invalid as an unconstitutional impairment of the bondholders' contract with the issuer or obligor unless provision is made for adequate substitute funding. Reference: Article I, 10(1), U.S. Constitution.

CONTRA-PARTY or CONTRA-SIDE—The municipal securities professional or customer to whom a person has sold municipal securities or from whom a person has purchased municipal securities.

COVERAGE or DEBT SERVICE COVERAGE—The ratio of pledged revenues available annually to pay debt service to the annual debt service requirement. Pledged revenues are usually calculated as net income before the deduction of interest, depreciation and amortization expenses. This ratio is one indication of the margin of safety for payment of debt service. The formula for determining coverage is as follows:

$$\text{Coverage} = \frac{\text{Pledged Revenues}}{\text{Debt Service Requirement}}$$

EXAMPLE:

$$\text{Coverage} = \frac{\$2,000,000}{\$1,200,000} = 1.66$$

See: PLEDGED REVENUES.

CREDIT RATING—See: RATINGS.

CROSSOVER REFUNDING—See: ADVANCE REFUNDING.

CURRENT COUPON—An interest rate which is in line with interest rates on new issues of securities being sold at the current time. A bond with a "current coupon" would be trading at a price close to par and would have a yield to maturity approximately equal to its interest rate.

CURRENT YIELD—The ratio of the annual dollar amount of interest paid on a security to the purchase price or market price of the security, stated as a percentage. For example, a $1,000 bond purchased at par with an 8% coupon pays $80 per year, or a current yield of 8%. The same bond, if purchased at a discount price of $800, would have a current yield of 10%. Compare: YIELD TO CALL; YIELD TO MATURITY.

CUSIP NUMBER (COMMITTEE ON UNIFORM SECURITIES IDENTIFICATION PROCEDURES)—An identification number assigned to each maturity of an issue, which is usually printed on the face of each individual certificate of the issue. The CUSIP numbers are intended to help facilitate the identification and clearance of municipal securities.

DATED DATE—The date of an issue, printed on each security, from which interest on the issue usually starts to accrue, even though the issue may actually be delivered at some later date.

DBA—See: DEALER BANK ASSOCIATION.

DEALER or MUNICIPAL SECURITIES DEALER—A person or organization which engages in the business of underwriting, trading and selling securities (in the case of a "municipal securities dealer," municipal securities). For purposes of the Securities Exchange Act of 1934 the term "dealer" does not include a bank; under the Act, however, the term "municipal securities dealer" expressly does include a bank, or a separately identifiable department of a bank, which is engaged in underwriting, trading and selling municipal securities. In colloquial usage both terms are used to refer to both securities firms and dealer banks. Compare: BROKER.

DEALER BANK—A bank which is engaged in the business of buying and selling government securities, municipal securities and/or certain money market instruments for its own account.

DEALER BANK ASSOCIATION or DBA—A non-profit organization of commercial banks which underwrite, deal or trade in public securities.

DEALER BOOK—A semi-annual publication by *The Bond Buyer* which lists municipal bond dealers, municipal finance consultants and bond attorneys in the United States. Although the book is actually titled *Directory of Municipal Bond Dealers of the United States*, it is commonly referred to as the "red book" due to the color of its cover. Standard & Poor's Corporation publishes *Securities Dealers of North America* (which also has a red cover), a similar directory which lists all of the dealers in securities (municipals and/or others) in the United States and Canada.

DEALER'S ALLOWANCE—See: CONCESSION.

DEBT LIMIT—The maximum amount of debt which an issuer of municipal securities is permitted to incur under constitutional, statutory or charter provisions. The debt limit is usually expressed as a percentage of assessed valuation.

DEBT RATIOS—Comparative statistics showing the relationship between the issuer's outstanding debt and such factors as its tax base, income or population. Such ratios are often used in the process of determining credit quality of an issue, primarily on general obligation bonds. Some of the more commonly used ratios are (a) net overall debt to assessed valuation, (b) net overall debt to estimated full valuation, and (c) net overall debt per capita. See: BONDED DEBT.

DEBT SERVICE—The amount of money necessary to pay interest on an outstanding debt, the principal of maturing serial bonds and the required contributions to a sinking fund for term bonds. Debt service on bonds may be calculated on a calendar year, fiscal year, or bond fiscal year basis.

DEBT SERVICE COVERAGE—See: COVERAGE.

DEBT SERVICE FUND—See: SINKING FUND.

DEBT SERVICE RESERVE FUND—The fund in which moneys are placed which may be used to pay debt service if pledged revenues are insufficient to satisfy the debt service requirements. The debt service reserve fund may be entirely funded with bond proceeds, or it may only be partly funded at the time of issuance and allowed to reach its full funding requirement over time, due to the accumulation of pledged revenues. If the debt service reserve fund is used in whole or part to pay debt service, the issuer usually is required to replenish the funds from the first available funds or revenues. A typical reserve requirement might be the maximum aggregate annual debt service requirement for any year remaining until the bonds reach maturity. The size and investment of the reserve may be subject to arbitrage regulations. Under a typical revenue pledge this fund is the third to be funded out of the revenue fund. See: FLOW OF FUNDS.

DEBT SERVICE SCHEDULE—A table listing the periodic payments necessary to meet debt service requirements over the period of time the securities are to be outstanding. See: AMORTIZATION SCHEDULE.

DEFAULT—Breach of some covenant, promise or duty imposed by the bond contract. The most serious default occurs when the issuer fails to pay principal, interest, or both, when due. Other, "technical" defaults result when specifically defined events of default occur, such as failure to perform covenants. Technical defaults may include failing to charge

rates sufficient to meet rate covenants or failing to maintain insurance on the project. If the issuer defaults in the payment of principal, interest, or both, or if a technical default is not cured within a specified period of time, the bondholders or trustee may exercise legally available rights and remedies for enforcement of the bond contract.

DEFEASANCE—Termination of the rights and interests of the bondholders and of their lien on the pledged revenues in accordance with the terms of the bond contract for an issue of securities. Defeasance usually occurs in connection with the refunding of an outstanding issue after provision has been made for future payment through funds provided by the issuance of a new series of bonds. See: ADVANCE REFUNDING; REFUNDING.

DEFINITIVE FORM—See: CERTIFICATED SECURITY.

DELAYED DELIVERY TRADE—A securities transaction in which the settlement date is more than the standard five business days after the trade date. Compare: "REGULAR WAY" TRADE.

DELIVERY DATE—The date on which securities are delivered in exchange for the payment of the purchase price. In the case of new issues, the delivery date, not the dated date, is considered the date of issuance. Compare: SETTLEMENT DATE. See: ISSUANCE. Reference: I.R.S. Reg. 1.103-13(b)(6).

DELIVERY VS. PAYMENT or DVP—A method of settling transactions whereby payment on the transaction is made when the securities involved in the transaction are delivered and accepted. The term is often used to refer specifically to a transaction settled in this manner where a customer (typically an institutional investor) has purchased securities from a dealer. The term is also used generally to refer to all types of transactions settled in this way. Compare: RECEIPT VS. PAYMENT.

DEMAND BOND or DEMAND NOTE—A long-term-maturity security which is subject to a frequently available put option or tender option feature under which the holder may put the security back to the issuer or its agent at a predetermined price (generally par) after giving specified notice. The put option or tender option right is typically available to the investor on a weekly or monthly basis, although on some demand securities the investor has a daily right to exercise the put option. Many of these securities are floating or variable rate securities, with the put option exercisable on dates on which the floating rate changes. These latter securities are often called "variable rate demand notes," or, colloquially, "lower floaters." See: FLOATING RATE.

DENOMINATION—The par value amount represented by a particular securities certificate. Bearer bonds are typically issued in denominations

establish several requirements specifically applicable to discretionary accounts. Reference: MSRB Rules G-19, G-27.

DIVERSIFICATION—The practice of including in a portfolio different types of assets (*e.g.*, securities which differ by location or type of issuer, maturity, or credit quality) in order to minimize risks or improve overall portfolio performance. Diversifying a securities portfolio by location or type of issuer, for example, might protect the portfolio against adverse conditions in a particular industry or region of the country; diversifying by credit quality might permit the acquisition of lower-rated, higher-yielding securities while protecting most of the portfolio's capital in higher quality securities.

DIVIDED ACCOUNT—See: SYNDICATE.

DK—A designation (derived from an abbreviation of the words "don't know") indicating that a party does not have a record of a transaction another party is confirming to him or has no instructions or records indicating that he should accept a delivery being tendered to him.

DOLLAR BOND—A colloquial term for a bond which is usually quoted and traded in terms of dollar price rather than yield. Dollar bonds are generally more actively traded securities from larger, term issues rather than securities from serial issues.

DOLLAR PRICE—A quoted price of a security, expressed in terms of dollars per $100 par value. The dollar price may be the transaction price, or may be derived from the yield price (basis price) of the transaction. The dollar price is equal to the sum of the present values of the redemption price of the security and the interest payments. Compare: BASIS PRICE.

DOUBLE-BARRELED BOND—A bond secured by both a defined source of revenue (other than property taxes) plus the full faith and credit of an issuer which has taxing powers. The term is occasionally, although erroneously, used in reference to bonds secured by any two sources of pledged revenue.

DOUBLE EXEMPT or DOUBLE EXEMPTION—See: TAX-EXEMPT BOND.

DOWNGRADE—The lowering of a bond rating by a rating service. Compare: UPGRADE. See: RATINGS.

DRAWDOWN SCHEDULE—An estimated schedule of payments on a construction project, which shows the periodic payments, or "draws," to which the contractor is entitled at progressive stages of completion.

of $1,000 or (more commonly) $5,000 par value per certificate. Registered bonds are typically issued in variable denominations, multiples of $1,000 up to $100,000 or more per certificate (although denominations of larger than $100,000 are not acceptable for delivery purposes between dealers unless specifically identified as such at the time of trade). Notes are typically issued in denominations of $25,000 or more per certificate.

DEPOSITORY—A clearing agency registered with the Securities and Exchange Commission which provides immobilization, safekeeping and book-entry settlement services to its participants. The four registered depositories are The Depository Trust Company (New York), the Midwest Securities Trust Company (Chicago), the Pacific Securities Depository Trust Company (San Francisco), and the Philadelphia Depository Trust Company. Compare: CLEARING CORPORATION. See: REGISTERED CLEARING AGENCY.

DESIGNATED ORDER—An order for securities held in a syndicate which is submitted by an account member on behalf of a buyer on which all or a portion of the takedown is to be credited to certain members of the syndicate. The buyer directs who will receive the designation and what percentage of the total designation each member will receive. Generally two or more syndicate members will be designated to receive a portion of the credit. See: PRIORITY PROVISIONS.

DIRECT DEBT—See: BONDED DEBT.

DISCLOSURE—See: FULL DISCLOSURE.

DISCOUNT—The amount by which the par value of a security exceeds the price paid for the security. Compare: PREMIUM. See: ORIGINAL ISSUE DISCOUNT.

DISCOUNTED SECURITY—A security which is sold on the basis of a bank rate of discount, with the investment return realized solely from the accretion of this discounted amount to the security's maturity value. The most common type of discounted security is the U.S. Treasury bill; some municipal notes are issued on a discounted basis.

DISCOUNT SECURITY—A security which can be purchased for less than the par value. Compare: PREMIUM SECURITY.

DISCRETIONARY ACCOUNT—A customer account in which the customer has given to the broker or dealer carrying the account full authority to determine what securities to purchase or sell for the account, when to do so and at what prices. This authority must be granted in writing (in a document referred to as a "discretionary account authorization"), and the customer often specifies certain investment objectives or criteria limiting the dealer's exercise of its discretion. MSRB rules

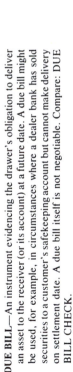

DUE BILL—An instrument evidencing the drawer's obligation to deliver an asset to the receiver (or its account) at a future date. A due bill might be used, for example, in circumstances where a dealer bank has sold securities to a customer's safekeeping account but cannot make delivery on settlement date. A due bill itself is not negotiable. Compare: DUE BILL CHECK.

DUE BILL CHECK—An instrument evidencing the drawer's obligation to make a payment to the receiver at a specified future date. The receiver can negotiate the due bill check on that date (*e.g.*, deposit it in its bank). Compare: DUE BILL.

DUE DILIGENCE—The process of thorough investigation of a bond issue, usually by underwriter's counsel. Such inquiry is made to assure that all material facts are fully disclosed to potential investors and that there have been no material omissions or misstatements of fact. The issuer, covenants of the bonds, and the true obligor in a conduit financing are investigated. Further inquiry may be required if the investigation reveals facts which are incomplete, suspect or inconsistent, either on their face or in light of other facts known to counsel. See: DUE DILIGENCE OPINION; FULL DISCLOSURE; RULE l0b-5.

DUE DILIGENCE OPINION—The written legal conclusion, based upon a thorough investigation of all material facts, that no material omissions or misstatements of relevant facts have been made in connection with a proposed bond issue. A due diligence opinion may or may not be issued, depending on the nature and complexities of the new issue of municipal securities. See: DUE DILIGENCE; FULL DISCLOSURE; RULE 10b-5.

DURATION—A measure of the timing of the cash flows (*i.e.*, the interest payments and the principal repayment) to be received from a given fixed income security. The duration of the security is equal to (a) the sum of the present values of each of the cash flows weighted by the time to receipt of each cash flow divided by (b) the total of the present values of the cash flows. The duration of a security is a useful indicator of its price volatility for given changes in interest rates. Duration is also a useful concept in assessing the reinvestment risk associated with a given portfolio or the interest rate risk associated with matching particular interest-rate-sensitive assets and liabilities.

EASTERN ACCOUNT—See: SYNDICATE.

EFFECTIVE INTEREST COST—The rate at which the total debt service payable on a new issue of bonds would be discounted to provide a present value equal to the amount bid on the new issue.

EFFECTIVE INTEREST RATE—The actual rate of interest earned by the investor on securities, which takes into account the amortization of any premium or the accretion of any discount over the period of the investment. See: YIELD TO MATURITY.

ENTERPRISE ACTIVITY—A revenue-generating project or business which provides funds necessary to pay debt service on securities issued to finance the facility. The debts of such projects are self-liquidating when the projects earn sufficient moneys to cover all debt service and other requirements imposed under the bond contract. Common examples include water and sewer plants, electric supply facilities and private business projects financed with industrial development bonds.

ENVELOPE SYSTEM—A system for the delivery and receipt of securities in which special envelopes containing securities are brought by each delivering party to a central location and sorted by recipient. Each recipient's envelopes are then placed in a receptacle maintained by the recipient and subsequently picked up by its employees. These systems are provided by each of the registered clearing corporations for their participants.

ESCROW ACCOUNT—A fund established to hold moneys pledged and to be used to pay debt service on an outstanding issue. See: ADVANCE REFUNDING.

ESCROWED TO MATURITY—See: ADVANCE REFUNDING.

EXCISE TAX—An indirect tax levied upon the manufacture, sale or consumption of commodities or upon the license to pursue certain occupations or upon corporate privileges within a taxing jurisdiction. Examples of such taxes include sales and use taxes and taxes on alcohol and cigarettes.

EXEMPT SECURITIES or EXEMPTED SECURITIES—Issues not subject to registration requirements of the Securities Act of 1933 or the reporting requirements of the Securities Exchange Act of 1934. In general, obligations of the United States Government, federal agencies, states, municipalities or other political subdivisions are exempted from such requirements. Reference: 15 United States Code §77(c)(2).

EX-LEGAL—A term which refers to the absence of a legal opinion. An "ex-legal" delivery is a delivery of municipal securities in the secondary market without a copy of the legal opinion being provided. See: GOOD DELIVERY.

EXPIRATION DATE—See: PUT OPTION.

EXTRAORDINARY MANDATORY REDEMPTION—See: REDEMPTION PROVISIONS.

EXTRAORDINARY OPTIONAL REDEMPTION—See: REDEMPTION PROVISIONS.

FACE AMOUNT—See: PAR VALUE.

FAIL—A transaction between two municipal securities brokers or dealers on which delivery does not take place on the settlement date. A transaction in which a dealer has yet to deliver securities is referred to as a "fail to deliver;" a transaction in which a dealer has not yet received securities is referred to as a "fail to receive."

FANNIE MAE—See: FEDERAL NATIONAL MORTGAGE ASSOCIATION.

FARMERS HOME ADMINISTRATION or FmHA—An agency of the federal Department of Agriculture empowered to make loans to farm owners or tenants primarily to finance the acquisition and improvement of farm properties. FmHA also makes loans to qualified municipal issuers for certain community facilities. The agency funds its loans through the issuance of Certificates of Beneficial Ownership (CBOs), most of which are purchased by the Federal Financing Bank.

FEASIBILITY STUDY—A report detailing the economic practicality and the need for a proposed capital program. The feasibility study may include estimates of revenues that will be generated and details of the physical, operating, economic or engineering aspects of the proposed project.

FEDERAL FUNDS—Immediately available funds representing non-interest-bearing deposits at Federal Reserve banks. Federal funds are actively traded among commercial bank members of the Federal Reserve system. Federal funds are often used to pay for new issues of municipal securities and for secondary market transactions in certain types of securities. Compare: CLEARING HOUSE FUNDS.

FEDERAL HOME LOAN MORTGAGE CORPORATION or FHLMC or FREDDIE MAC—A federally created corporation established to facilitate the financing of single-family residential housing by creating and maintaining an active secondary market for conventional home mortgages. The Corporation finances its mortgage purchases through the issuance of two types of securities: guaranteed mortgage certificates (GMCs), which represent undivided interests in mortgages underwritten by the Corporation, and which pay interest semi-annually and return principal amounts annually; and mortgage participation certificates (PCs), which are pass-through instruments, guaranteed by the Corporation, under which a pro-rata share of principal and interest collections are paid monthly to each holder.

FEDERAL NATIONAL MORTGAGE ASSOCIATION or FNMA or FANNIE MAE—A government-sponsored private corporation authorized to purchase and sell mortgages and to otherwise facilitate the orderly operation of a secondary market for home mortgages. The purchase of mortgages by FNMA is financed by the sale of its corporate debentures and notes. Sellers of mortgages may be required to purchase FNMA stock in connection with some transactions. Compare: GOVERNMENT NATIONAL MORTGAGE ASSOCIATION.

FGIC—See: FINANCIAL GUARANTY INSURANCE COMPANY.

FHLMC—See: FEDERAL HOME LOAN MORTGAGE CORPORATION.

FILL OR KILL—See: FIRM.

FINAL OFFICIAL STATEMENT—See: OFFICIAL STATEMENT.

FINANCIAL ADVISOR—With respect to a new issue of municipal securities, a consultant who advises the issuer on matters pertinent to the issue, such as structure, timing, marketing, fairness of pricing, terms and bond ratings. A financial advisor may also be employed to provide advice on subjects unrelated to a new issue of municipal securities, such as advising on cash flow and investment matters. The financial advisor is sometimes referred to as a "fiscal consultant" or "fiscal agent." MSRB Rule G-23 provides that a firm or bank which has acted in a financial advisory capacity with respect to a new issue of municipal securities (pursuant to a written contract) may underwrite the new issue (a) on a negotiated basis after making certain disclosures, obtaining the consent of the issuer and terminating the financial advisory relationship; or (b) on a competitive basis if the issuer gives written consent before the financial advisor's bid is submitted.

FINANCIAL AND OPERATIONS PRINCIPAL (FINOP)—A person associated with a securities firm who has supervisory responsibility for the firm's compliance with recordkeeping, net capital, customer protection

and financial reporting rules. Such persons must qualify by means of an examination. Reference: MSRB Rule G-3.

FINANCIAL GUARANTY INSURANCE COMPANY or FGIC—A wholly owned subsidiary of FGIC Corporation which offers non-cancellable insurance guarantying the full and timely payment of principal and interest due on securities on stated maturity, mandatory sinking fund, and interest payment dates. FGIC writes insurance on (a) new issue tax-exempt securities which may be insured partially or entirely and (b) unit investment trusts. In the case of unit investment trusts, individual issues may be insured for their entire life or until an issue is sold out of the trust. FGIC Corporation, the parent company, is owned by six shareholder companies: General Electric Credit Corporation; General Re Corporation; J. P. Morgan & Co. Incorporated; Lumbermen's Mutual Casualty Company; Merrill Lynch & Co., Inc.; and Shearson Lehman Brothers Inc. Bonds insured by FGIC are currently rated AAA by Standard & Poor's and Aaa by Moody's Investors Service, Inc.

FINS NUMBER—An identification number assigned to each financial institution (bank, broker/dealer or investor) active in the securities markets. The term is derived from the acronym for "Financial Industry Numbering Standard" number.

FIRM or FIRM PRICE—A designation that a quotation (a bid or an offering price) will not be changed for a specified period of time and will be the price of any transaction executed with the party to whom the quotation is given during that period; the dealer giving a firm quotation also commits itself not to effect a transaction in the securities with any other party during that period. For example, a dealer may give another dealer an offering price on specified securities that is "firm for one hour;" if the second dealer wishes to purchase those securities at that price, it would contact the first dealer during that time period and execute the transaction. Firm quotations may sometimes be subject to a "recall," either immediately upon notice or after a specified period. For example, a dealer may give another dealer an offering price that is "firm for one hour with a five-minute recall," in this case the quoting dealer has the right to contact the second dealer and inform it that the offering price will no longer be valid if the second dealer does not execute a transaction against the price within five minutes. Alternatively, the quotation might be "firm, fill or kill," in which case the quoting dealer has the right to contact the second dealer and inform it that it must execute a transaction against the offering price immediately or the quotation will be withdrawn.

FISCAL AGENT—See: FINANCIAL ADVISOR.

ing including a balance sheet and income statement) is filed quarterly and annually. The term is derived from the acronym for "Financial and Operational Combined Uniform Single" report.

FOUR-R FUND (4-R FUND)—A "reasonably required reserve or replacement" fund. The designation of the amount held in a reserve or replacement fund as being "reasonably required" has significance for Treasury arbitrage restrictions. Reference: I.R.S. Reg. 1.103-14(d).

FREDDIE MAC—See: FEDERAL HOME LOAN MORTGAGE CORPORATION.

FULL CASH REFUNDING—See: ADVANCE REFUNDING.

FULL DISCLOSURE—The principle that accurate and complete information material to a securities transaction which a potential investor would be likely to consider important in making investment decisions must be made available to purchasers or prospective purchasers. Material facts may include descriptions of the issuer and the true obligor in a conduit financing, as well as the structure of a bond issue and the security therefor. Full disclosure enables the investor to evaluate the credit quality of an issue. The material facts pertinent to a new issue of municipal securities are generally disclosed in the official statement, which also states that there have been no material misstatements or omissions by the issuer with respect to the issue, and that no facts have become known which would render false or misleading any statement which was made. Unlike full disclosure requirements in connection with corporate debt and equity securities, filing, registration and reporting to the Securities and Exchange Commission are not required with respect to municipal securities. See: RULE 10b-5. Reference: GFOA publication, "Disclosure Guidelines for Offerings of Securities by State and Local Governments."

FULL FAITH AND CREDIT BOND—See: GENERAL OBLIGATION BOND.

FULLY REGISTERED—A security which has been registered as to both principal and interest. Such securities are payable only to the owner, or to order of the owner, whose name is noted on records of the issuer or its agent. Compare: BEARER BOND. See: BOND REGISTER; REGISTERED BOND; REGISTRAR.

FUNDED INTEREST—See: CAPITALIZED INTEREST.

FUNGIBILITY—The inherent characteristic of existing in many separate units, each of which is the same as, and can be used in place of any other unit. Municipal securities are considered generally to lack fungibility because, given the large number of issues and the relatively small

FISCAL CONSULTANT—See: FINANCIAL ADVISOR.

FISCAL YEAR—A twelve-month period at the end of which financial position and results of operations are determined. Financial reporting, budgeting and accounting periods are determined on the basis of the applicable fiscal year.

FITCH INVESTORS SERVICE—An independent service company based in New York City which provides ratings for municipal securities and other financial information to investors. See: RATINGS.

FLAT—A designation that a particular transaction has been effected on terms that do not include accrued interest. A bond typically trades flat twice a year, when the settlement date on a transaction is the interest payment date, but might be traded flat at other times by agreement between the parties. Securities in default as to payments of interest are also generally traded flat.

FLAT YIELD CURVE—See: YIELD CURVE.

FLOATER—A colloquial term for a security with a floating or variable interest rate. See: FLOATING RATE.

FLOATING RATE or VARIABLE RATE—An interest rate on a security which changes at intervals according to an index or a formula or other standard of measurement as stated in the bond contract. One common method is to calculate the interest rate as a percentage of the rate paid on selected issues of Treasury securities on specified dates.

FLOW OF FUNDS—The order and priority of handling, depositing and disbursing pledged revenues, as set forth in the bond contract. Generally, the revenues are deposited, as received, into a general collection account or revenue fund for disbursement into the other accounts established by the bond contract. Such other accounts generally provide for payment of the costs of debt service, debt service reserve deposits, operation and maintenance costs, redemption, renewal and replacement and other requirements. See: REVENUE FUND; OPERATIONS AND MAINTENANCE FUND; SINKING FUND; DEBT SERVICE RESERVE FUND; RESERVE MAINTENANCE FUND; RENEWAL AND REPLACEMENT FUND; SURPLUS FUND.

FmHA—See: FARMERS HOME ADMINISTRATION.

FNMA—See: FEDERAL NATIONAL MORTGAGE ASSOCIATION.

FOCUS REPORT—A document summarizing information concerning a broker/dealer's financial and operational status that is provided to the firm's regulatory authority on a periodic basis. Part I (an abbreviated listing of essential data) is filed monthly; Part II (a more detailed report-

principal amount outstanding on most issues, a person seeking to replace securities of a specific issue (*e.g.*, in order to make delivery on a transaction) often finds it difficult to locate identical securities elsewhere in the market. The features of securities which must be identical in order for them to be considered fungible for delivery purposes are specified in MSRB Rules G-12(e) and G-15(c).

GANs—See: NOTE.

GASB—See: GOVERNMENTAL ACCOUNTING STANDARDS BOARD.

GENERAL OBLIGATION BOND or G.O. BOND—A bond which is secured by the full faith and credit of an issuer with taxing power. General obligation bonds issued by local units of government are typically secured by a pledge of the issuer's ad valorem taxing power; general obligation bonds issued by states are generally based upon appropriations made by the state legislature for the purposes specified. Ad valorem taxes necessary to pay debt service on general obligation bonds are often not subject to the constitutional property tax millage limits. Such bonds constitute debts of the issuer and normally require approval by election prior to issuance. In the event of default, the holders of general obligation bonds have the right to compel a tax levy or legislative appropriation, by mandamus or injunction, in order to satisfy the issuer's obligation on the defaulted bonds. Compare: LIMITED TAX BOND; REVENUE BOND; SPECIAL ASSESSMENT BOND; SPECIAL OBLIGATION BONDS; UNLIMITED TAX BOND.

GFOA—See: GOVERNMENT FINANCE OFFICERS ASSOCIATION.

GINNIE MAE—See: GOVERNMENT NATIONAL MORTGAGE ASSOCIATION.

GLASS-STEAGALL ACT OF 1933—A federal law which, in part, separated commercial banking from investment banking and which generally precludes commercial banks from underwriting certain types of municipal revenue bonds. Reference: 12 United States Code §378.

GLOBAL CERTIFICATE—A single certificate, in either bearer or registered form, representing the whole of an issue of securities. Such certificates are often used in book-entry systems in cases where the issuer is obliged under state law to issue its securities in certificated form. In these cases, the issuer issues a global certificate which is then lodged in the facilities of a securities depository or other book-entry agent and safekept by the agent until maturity. The securities are available to purchasers only in book-entry form, and no definitive certificates can be obtained. See: BOOK-ENTRY SECURITY.

GNMA—See: GOVERNMENT NATIONAL MORTGAGE ASSOCIATION.

GOING AWAY—An indication that an order for securities (usually new issue securities) is from an investor, rather than from a dealer seeking to purchase the securities for trading inventory.

GOOD DELIVERY—The presentation by a seller of securities previously sold to a purchaser which are in acceptable form for delivery purposes as defined in MSRB Rules G-12(e) (with respect to inter-dealer deliveries) and G-15(c) (with respect to deliveries to customers). The delivery standards specified in those rules cover such matters as the criteria for fungibility of securities; denominations; the attachment of legal opinions and other required documents; the presentation of interest payment checks in certain circumstances; and other similar matters. See: EX-LEGAL; SETTLEMENT.

GOOD FAITH DEPOSIT—A sum of money provided to an issuer of a new issue of municipal securities sold at competitive bid by an underwriter or underwriting syndicate as an assurance of performance on its bid. The good faith deposit is usually in an amount from 1% to 5% of the par value of the issue, and generally is provided in the form of a certified or cashier's check. The check is returned to the bidder if its bid is not accepted, but the check of the successful bidder is retained by the issuer until the issue is delivered. In the event the winning bidder fails to pay for the new issue on the delivery date the check is usually retained by the issuer as full or partial liquidated damages.

GOVERNMENTAL ACCOUNTING STANDARDS BOARD—A standard-setting body, associated with the Financial Accounting Foundation and comparable to the Financial Accounting Standards Board, which prescribes standard accounting practices for governmental units in maintaining their financial records and releasing financial data to the public.

GOVERNMENT FINANCE OFFICERS ASSOCIATION or GFOA—An organization of state and local government finance officers formed to improve professional standards of government fiscal and debt administration. The organization was formerly named the Municipal Finance Officers Association (MFOA).

GOVERNMENT NATIONAL MORTGAGE ASSOCIATION or GNMA or GINNIE MAE—An agency of the federal Department of Housing and Urban Development empowered to provide special assistance in financing home mortgages which is responsible for management and liquidation of federally owned mortgage portfolios. GNMA's special assistance functions are carried out by issuing two types of securities pledging the full faith and credit of the United States Government: pass-through securities by which principal and interest payments on mortgages in specified pools are passed on to the holders of such certificates; and mortgage-backed bonds. Its liquidation functions involve the issuance of participation certificates (PCs) representing beneficial interests in future payments on a pool of mortgages. Compare: FEDERAL NATIONAL MORTGAGE ASSOCIATION.

GRANT ANTICIPATION NOTE—See: NOTE.

GROSS BONDED DEBT—See: BONDED DEBT.

GROSS PLEDGE or GROSS REVENUE PLEDGE—See: PLEDGED REVENUES.

GROSS REFUNDING—See: ADVANCE REFUNDING.

GROSS SPREAD or GROSS UNDERWRITING SPREAD—See: SPREAD.

GROUP NET ORDER—An order submitted to an underwriting syndicate for a new municipal issue which, if allocated, is allocated at the public offering price without deducting the concession or takedown. A group net order benefits all members of the syndicate according to their percentage participation in the account, and consequently is normally accorded the highest priority of all orders received during the order period. See: PRIORITY PROVISIONS.

HAIRCUT—In the computation of net capital for purposes of SEC rules, the amount which a broker/dealer must deduct from its net worth in connection with each net long or net short inventory position it maintains in securities. For example, with respect to an inventory position in municipal securities maturing in twenty years, a broker/dealer must deduct from its net worth a haircut equal to 7% of the current market value of the securities. The haircut may be considered a reserve against loss due to a subsequent decline in the market value of the securities. See: NET CAPITAL RULE.

HEALTH INDUSTRY BOND INSURANCE or HIBI—An insurance program sponsored by Industrial Indemnity Company (a Crum and Forster insurance company) and American Health Capital HIBI Management, Inc., to provide insurance for the timely payment of principal and interest to qualifying not-for-profit and for-profit health care institutions including hospitals, health care systems and health maintenance organizations. The program supports taxable and tax-exempt debt for new construction, renovation, acquisition, equipment and refunding. Bonds insured by HIBI are currently rated AAA by Standard & Poor's.

HOUSING REVENUE BOND—A bond which is secured by revenues derived from rentals from financed housing projects or house mortgages. There are two major types of housing revenue securities:

Single-Family Mortgage Revenue Bonds—Bonds issued to finance mortgages on single-family homes, either directly by purchasing newly originated or existing mortgage loans or indirectly by allowing lenders to purchase mortgage loans using bond proceeds. Repayment of the mortgages may be guaranteed under federal programs or through private mortgage insurance. The issuance of single-family mortgage revenue bonds is subject to stringent requirements under Section 103A of the Internal Revenue Code.

Multi-Family Housing Revenue Bonds—Bonds issued to finance construction of multi-family housing projects, typically for the elderly or for moderate- and low-income families. These securities also

I

may provide financing either directly or through a loans-to-lenders program, and may be secured, in whole or in part, by federal guarantees or subsidies.

HUMPBACKED YIELD CURVE—See: YIELD CURVE.

IDB—See: INDUSTRIAL DEVELOPMENT BOND.

IDBI MANAGERS, INC. or IDBI—A wholly owned subsidiary of Corroon & Black Corporation which offers insurance contracts on the payment of principal and interest on issues of industrial development bonds. Policies offered by IDBI are written by Firemen's Insurance Company of Newark, a subsidiary of the Continental Insurance Companies. IDBI has insured new issues financing both industrial and commercial development projects; most of these issues have been privately placed by the underwriters. Bonds insured by IDBI are currently granted a Standard & Poor's rating of AAA. The name ''IDBI'' is derived from the acronym for ''Industrial Development Bond Insurance.''

IDR—See: INDUSTRIAL DEVELOPMENT BOND.

I.D. SYSTEM—See: NATIONAL INSTITUTIONAL DELIVERY SYSTEM.

IMMOBILIZATION—A procedure to eliminate actual physical movement of securities. Delivery of securities is effected by changes in the record of ownership rather than by delivery of engraved certificates. See: BOOK-ENTRY CLEARANCE.

IMMOBILIZED SECURITY—A physical security which is held in a central depository for the account of its beneficial owner but which may be withdrawn from the depository in physical form. Immobilized securities may be transferred when sold by entries on the records of the depository or by withdrawal of the actual certificates. Compare: BOOK-ENTRY SECURITY.

INDENTURE—See: TRUST INDENTURE.

INDICATION—See: NOMINAL QUOTATION.

INDUCEMENT RESOLUTION—The first ''official action'' indicating a local issuer's intent to issue industrial development bonds (IDBs). Because

INTEREST CLAIM—A request that a person who received an interest payment on a security but was not entitled to it forward the proceeds of the payment to the rightful recipient (or a person acting on such person's behalf). An interest claim would typically be sent if registered securities were sold prior to an interest payment date but could not be transferred before the record date. In this circumstance the interest payment would be sent to the person who had sold the securities; an interest claim would then be filed on behalf of the person who had purchased them, to whom the interest payment was due. See: RECORD DATE.

INTEREST RATE—The annual rate, expressed as a percentage of principal, payable for use of borrowed money.

INTERIM PERIOD FINANCIAL STATEMENTS—Unaudited financial statements covering the interim period since the governmental entity's most recent audited financial statement. Compare: AUDITED STATEMENT.

INTERMEDIATE RANGE—A designation given to the maturities of a serial issue between the short-term maturities and the long-term maturities. Typically the intermediate range maturities are from six to fifteen years from issuance.

INVESTED SINKING FUND or INVESTED SINKER—A sinking fund for a term bond in which the required periodic deposits of money to be used to redeem the term bonds are invested to maturity, usually in U.S. Treasury obligations, rather than being used each year to call securities. The bond contract on an invested sinking fund issue usually provides that through the operation of the invested sinking fund the term bonds will be fully secured by Treasury securities several years prior to maturity. Amendments to the Treasury arbitrage rules adopted in 1979 effectively precluded issuers from using the invested sinking fund technique on subsequent issues. The term "invested sinker" may also be used to refer to an issue with an invested sinking fund feature. See: SINKING FUND.

INVESTMENT GRADE—The broad credit designation given bonds which have a high probability of being paid and minor, if any, speculative features. Bonds rated BBB or higher by Standard and Poor's Corporation or Baa or higher by Moody's Investors Service, Inc., are deemed by those agencies to be "investment grade." Banking law requires that certain types of securities acquired by bank portfolios must be both marketable and "investment grade"; it should be noted that the presence (or absence) of a rating deemed "investment grade" by the rating agencies is not necessarily indicative of a security's status for purposes of banking law. See: RATINGS.

the proceeds of IDBs generally may be used only to finance capital costs incurred after "official action" has been taken toward issuing the bonds, the inducement resolution determines the point after which the user of the project being financed can be reimbursed for capital costs paid or incurred in connection with the acquisition and construction of the project.

INDUSTRIAL DEVELOPMENT BOND or IDB—In general, securities issued by a state, a local government or development agency to finance the construction or purchase of industrial, commercial or manufacturing facilities to be purchased by or leased to a private user. IDBs are backed by the credit of the private user and generally are not considered liabilities of the governmental issuer (although in some jurisdictions they may also be backed by an issuer with taxing power). While the authorization to issue IDBs is provided by a state statute, the tax-exempt status of these bonds is derived from federal law (I.R.C. §103(b)(2)). IDBs are also referred to as industrial revenue bonds (IRBs). See: CONDUIT FINANCING.

INDUSTRIAL REVENUE BOND—See: INDUSTRIAL DEVELOPMENT BOND.

INSIDER TRADING—The act, in violation of SEC Rule 10b-5, of purchasing or selling securities (or derivative instruments based on those securities) based on information known to the party purchasing or selling the securities in his capacity as an insider (e.g., as an employee of the issuer of the securities) or as a result of information illicitly provided to him by an insider. Extensive case law exists concerning the varieties of acts which may be considered to be insider trading or the circumstances in which a person may be considered to be an insider or to be trading illegally on the basis of inside information. There do not appear to be any cases illustrating the application of the insider trading prohibitions under Rule 10b-5 to the municipal securities market; the concept, however, is applicable to participants in the municipal market. See: RULE 10b-5.

INSTITUTIONAL DELIVERY SYSTEM—See: NATIONAL INSTITUTIONAL DELIVERY SYSTEM.

INSTITUTIONAL SALES—Sales of securities to banks, financial institutions, bond funds, insurance companies or other business organizations (institutional investors) which possess or control considerable assets for large scale investing. Compare: RETAIL SALES.

INTEREST—The amount paid by a borrower as compensation for the use of borrowed money. This amount is generally an annual percentage of the principal amount. See: ACCRUED INTEREST; INTEREST RATE.

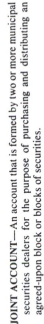

IRB—See: INDUSTRIAL DEVELOPMENT BOND.

ISSUANCE—Authorization, sale and delivery of a new issue of municipal securities. See: DELIVERY DATE. Reference: I.R.S. Reg. 1.103-13(b)(6).

ISSUE OF BONDS or ISSUE OF SECURITIES—Bonds or securities sold in one or more series which are authorized under the same resolution or indenture and have the same dated date.

ISSUER—A state, political subdivision, agency or authority that borrows money through the sale of bonds or notes.

JOINT ACCOUNT—An account that is formed by two or more municipal securities dealers for the purpose of purchasing and distributing an agreed-upon block or blocks of securities.

JOINT AND SEVERAL OBLIGATION—A form of contract in which each signing party is obligated both for the amount of liability designated to it under the contract and also for the total amount of the contract if other signing parties default on their obligations. Compare: SEVERAL OBLIGATION.

JOINT MANAGER—See: MANAGER; SYNDICATE.

JUMBO CERTIFICATE—A certificate for a registered security which is in an unusually large denomination. Persons who hold large amounts of securities (*e.g.*, securities depositories, large institutional investors) often keep most of their holdings in jumbo certificate form, to minimize the need for vault space.

JUNIOR LIEN BONDS—Bonds which have a subordinate claim against pledged revenues. Compare: PARITY BONDS; SENIOR LIEN BONDS.

nee'' which serves as the registered owner for securities which they own. Compare: ''STREET'' NAME. See: NOMINEE.

LEGAL OPINION or LEGAL or APPROVING OPINION—The written conclusions of bond counsel that the issuance of municipal securities and the proceedings taken in connection therewith comply with applicable laws, and that interest on the securities will be exempt from federal income taxation and, where applicable, from state and local taxation. The legal opinion is generally printed on the securities. Compare: DUE DILIGENCE OPINION. See: BOND COUNSEL; QUALIFIED LEGAL OPINION.

LETTER OF CREDIT or LC or L.O.C.—A commitment, usually made by a commercial bank, to honor demands for payment of a debt upon compliance with conditions and/or the occurrence of certain events specified under the terms of the commitment. In municipal financings, bank letters of credit are sometimes used as additional sources of security for issues of municipal notes, commercial paper or bonds, with the bank issuing the letter of credit committing to pay principal and interest on the securities in the event that the issuer is unable to do so. A letter of credit may also be used to provide liquidity for the retirement of commercial paper or put bonds. See: COMMERCIAL PAPER (TAX-EXEMPT); PUT BONDS.

LEVEL DEBT SERVICE—A maturity schedule in which the combined annual amount of principal and interest payments remains relatively constant over the life of the issue.

EXAMPLE:

Level Debt Service Assumptions:
Size of issue: $10,000,000
Interest rate: 7%
Maturity of issue: 5 years

Debt Schedule

Years	Principal	Interest	Total*
1	$ 1,740,000	$ 700,000	$ 2,440,000
2	1,860,000	578,200	2,438,200
3	1,990,000	448,000	2,438,000
4	2,130,000	308,700	2,438,700
5	2,280,000	159,600	2,439,600
Total	$10,000,000	$2,194,500	$12,194,500

*Total of principal and interest remains substantially level throughout life of issue.

LIMITED TAX BOND—A general obligation bond secured by the pledge of a specified tax (usually the property tax) or category of taxes which is limited as to rate or amount. Compare: GENERAL OBLIGATION BOND; REVENUE BOND; UNLIMITED TAX BOND.

LIQUIDITY—The quality of being readily convertible into cash without substantial transaction costs; the liquidity of a particular investment would also be affected by any discrepancy between the investment's acquisition cost and its current market value. A municipal security's liquidity is a function of both maturity and marketability; a ''liquid'' municipal security is generally both short-term and highly marketable. Compare: MARKETABILITY.

L.O.C.—See: LETTER OF CREDIT.

LOCKED MARKET—A trading situation in which the prices shown for a particular issue of securities by the dealer posting the highest bid and the dealer showing the lowest offering are the same. Locked markets can only exist on issues for which several dealers are making competitive markets, and generally last only for a short period of time.

LONG COUPON—See: ODD COUPON.

LOWER FLOATER—A colloquial term for a security with a variable or floating interest rate which also has a put option feature permitting the holder to put the securities back to an agent of the issuer on demand or on short notice. The put option feature has the practical effect of making the securities short-term; the variable interest rate on the securities, therefore, tends to fluctuate in the ''lower'' range of interest rates appropriate for short-term securities. See: DEMAND BOND; FLOATING RATE.

LT—See: LIMITED TAX BOND.

M—A designation indicating that a number is to be read in thousands. For example, a transaction for "250M bonds" would involve securities having a par value of $250,000. Numbers in millions are often indicated by the designation "MM."

MANAGED FUND—See: BOND FUND.

MANAGER—The member (or members) of an underwriting syndicate charged with primary responsibility for conducting the affairs of the syndicate. The manager generally takes the largest underwriting commitment.

Lead Manager or Senior Manager—The underwriter serving as head of the syndicate. The lead manager generally handles negotiations in a negotiated underwriting of a new issue of municipal securities or directs the processes by which a bid is determined for a competitive underwriting. The lead manager also is charged with allocating securities among the members of the syndicate according to the terms of the syndicate agreement and the orders received.

Joint Manager or Co-Manager—Any member of the management group (although the term is often used to refer to a member other than the lead manager).

See: SYNDICATE.

MANAGING UNDERWRITER—See: MANAGER; SYNDICATE.

MANDATORY REDEMPTION—See: REDEMPTION PROVISIONS.

MANDATORY REDEMPTION ACCOUNT—A separate account in the sinking fund into which the issuer makes periodic deposits of moneys to be used to purchase bonds in the open market or to pay the costs of calling bonds in accordance with the mandatory redemption schedule in the bond contract. Such an account may also be known as a bond amortization fund. See: CALLABLE BOND; REDEMPTION PROVISIONS.

MARK-DOWN—(1) The difference between the cost at which securities were acquired and their current offering price, in cases in which the market value of the securities has declined since their acquisition.

(2) For regulatory purposes, the remuneration received by a dealer or dealer bank selling securities as principal on behalf of a customer to a third party. The remuneration consists of the differential between the price of the sale to the third party and the (lower) price paid to the customer by the dealer. Compare: COMMISSION; MARK-UP.

MARKETABILITY—The ease or difficulty with which securities can be sold in the market. An issue's marketability depends upon many factors, including its interest rate, security provisions, maturity and credit quality, plus (in the case of the sale of a new issue) the size of the issue, the timing of its issuance, and the volume of comparable issues being sold. Compare: LIQUIDITY.

MARKET MAKER—A dealer or dealer bank which holds itself out as willing to make a bid or offer at any time on a particular security or type of security. The term is also used loosely to describe dealers who are active participants in the market for certain types of issues (*e.g.*, all general obligation securities of a state issuer), even though they might not maintain continuous markets in specific securities. The use of the term in the municipal market is therefore less precise than its sense in the corporate securities markets, where market makers are specifically designated as such by a regulatory authority, have defined responsibilities and are typically obliged to effect transactions at published quotations.

MARKET VALUE—The price at which a security can be currently traded in the market. Compare: BOOK VALUE.

MARK-TO-MARKET—A process whereby the value of an inventory position of securities is adjusted on a dealer's records to its current market value. Certain regulatory requirements mandate that dealers and dealer banks carry trading inventory at prices no higher than current market values.

MARK-UP—(1) The difference between the cost at which securities were acquired and their current offering price, in cases in which the market value of the securities has risen since their acquisition.

(2) With respect to a security purchased by a dealer at a net offering price less a concession, any remuneration in addition to the concession received by the dealer as a result of increasing the offering price on the securities.

(3) For regulatory purposes, a form of remuneration received by a dealer or dealer bank when selling securities as principal to a customer.

The fairness of a mark-up may be evaluated by matching the sale price against the prices of other contemporaneous sale transactions, against the price of the offsetting purchase or other contemporaneous purchase of the securities, or against the prevailing inter-dealer offering price for the securities. Compare: COMMISSION; MARK-DOWN.

MASTER RESOLUTION or MASTER INDENTURE—The document stating the general terms and conditions under which an issuer can offer more than one series of bonds. Among the terms which generally must be satisfied in order for a new series of bonds to be issued are the "additional bonds" covenants. See: AUTHORIZING RESOLUTION; BOND RESOLUTION.

MATURITY or MATURITY DATE—The date upon which the principal of a municipal security becomes due and payable to the securityholder.

MATURITY VALUE—The amount (other than a periodic interest payment) that will be received at the time a security is redeemed at its maturity. On most securities the maturity value equals the par value; on zero coupon, compound interest and multiplier bonds, however, the maturity value will equal the principal amount of the security at issuance plus the accumulated investment return on the security.

MBIA—See: MUNICIPAL BOND INSURANCE ASSOCIATION.

MEMBER ORDER—An order for new issue municipal securities placed with a syndicate by a member of the syndicate, where the securities would be confirmed to that member at syndicate terms (*i.e.*, less the total takedown). See: PRIORITY PROVISIONS.

MFOA—See: GOVERNMENT FINANCE OFFICERS ASSOCIATION.

MIG—The designation used by Moody's Investors Service in rating municipal notes. The term is an acronym for "Moody's Investment Grade" and, in specific ratings, is followed by the number 1, 2, 3, or 4, denoting successively lower levels of quality.

MILL—One-tenth (0.1) of one cent or .001 of one dollar. Rates of taxation of assessed valuation are often expressed in mills. See: MILLAGE.

MILLAGE—The rate used in calculating taxes based upon the value of property, expressed in mills per dollar of property value. See: AD VALOREM TAX; MILL.

MONEY MARKET INSTRUMENTS—Obligations which are commonly traded in the money market. Money market instruments are generally short term and highly liquid. In addition to certain U.S. Government securities, the following are commonly traded in the money market:

Bankers Acceptance or B.A.—A draft or bill of exchange, most commonly generated in import or export transactions, representing moneys due at a future date in connection with the transaction, the payment of which has been guaranteed by the "accepting" bank. BAs are typically sold on a discounted basis in a wide variety of denominations. Many BAs are eligible for discounting at the Federal Reserve.

Certificate of Deposit or CD—A negotiable instrument representing a large time deposit at a commercial bank. Most CDs are interest-bearing (typically paying interest at maturity), but some discounted CDs are issued. CDs are typically sold in denominations of from $100,000 to $1,000,000 principal amount.

Eurodollar Deposit—A time deposit of Eurodollars. Eurodollars are U.S. dollars on deposit at a branch of a U.S. bank or a foreign bank located outside of the United States.

Repurchase Agreement or RP or Repo—An agreement consisting of two simultaneous transactions whereby one party purchases securities from a second party, and the second party agrees to repurchase the securities on a certain future date at a price which produces an agreed-upon rate of return (the "repo rate").

Reverse Repurchase Agreement or Reverse Repo or Reverse—An agreement consisting of two simultaneous transactions whereby one party purchases securities from a second party and agrees to resell them to the second party on a certain future date at a price which produces an agreed-upon rate of return.

See: TREASURY SECURITIES.

MONEY SUPPLY—The amount of money in circulation. The money supply measures currently (1985) used by the Federal Reserve System are:

M1—Currency in circulation + demand deposits + other check-type deposits.

M2—M1 + savings and small denomination time deposits + overnight repurchase agreements at commercial banks + overnight Eurodollars + money market mutual fund shares.

M3—M2 + large-denomination time deposits + term repurchase agreements.

L—M3 + other liquid assets (such as term Eurodollars, bankers acceptances, commercial paper, Treasury securities and U.S. Savings Bonds).

MOODY'S INVESTORS SERVICE, INC.—An independent service subsidiary of Dun & Bradstreet Corp. which provides ratings for municipal securities and other financial information to investors. See: RATINGS.

MORAL OBLIGATION BOND—A bond, typically issued by a state agency or authority, which is secured by the revenues from the financed project and, additionally, by a non-binding undertaking that any deficiency in pledged revenues will be reported to the state legislature which may apportion state moneys to make up the shortfall. Legislation authorizing the issuance of moral obligation securities typically grants the state legislature the authority to apportion money to support the debt service payments on any such securities, but does not legally oblige the legislature to do so. Compare: GENERAL OBLIGATION BOND.

MSRB—See: MUNICIPAL SECURITIES RULEMAKING BOARD.

MULTIPLIER or MULTIPLIER BOND—A long-term municipal security on which the investment return accretes at a stated compounded rate to maturity, at which time the investor receives a lump-sum payment comprising the initial principal amount plus the total investment return. The multiplier bond is usually distinguished from the otherwise similar compound interest bond by the fact that the maturity value of the multiplier bond is typically an amount in even $100's or $1,000's. Multiplier bonds have been issued by different underwriters under a variety of trade names. Compare: COMPOUND INTEREST BOND; ZERO COUPON BOND. See: CAPITAL APPRECIATION BOND.

MUNICIPAL BOND INSURANCE ASSOCIATION or MBIA—An association of five insurance companies (The Aetna Casualty & Surety Co., Fireman's Fund Insurance Companies, The Travelers Indemnity Company, CIGNA Corporation, and The Continental Insurance Company) which offers insurance policies on qualified municipal issues under which the payment of principal and interest when due is guaranteed, in the event of issuer default. Such insurance may be acquired in the process of structuring a new issue of municipal securities; in such cases MBIA premiums are paid in full and the policy is issued at the time of issuance with coverage existing throughout the life of the issue. MBIA also makes available similar insurance with respect to parts of an issue which may be purchased by certain types of securityholders after issuance. The two principal rating agencies assign their highest ratings to all municipal issues insured by MBIA.

MUNICIPAL BONDS—See: BOND; MUNICIPAL SECURITIES; TAX-EXEMPT BOND.

MUNICIPAL FINANCE OFFICERS ASSOCIATION—See: GOVERNMENT FINANCE OFFICERS ASSOCIATION.

MUNICIPAL NOTES—See: MUNICIPAL SECURITIES; NOTE.

MUNICIPAL SECURITIES—A general term referring to securities issued by local governmental subdivisions such as cities, towns, villages, counties, or special districts, as well as securities issued by states and political subdivisions or agencies of states. A prime feature of these securities is that interest on them is generally exempt from federal income taxation. See: BOND; NOTE; TAX-EXEMPT BOND.

MUNICIPAL SECURITIES BROKER—See: BROKER.

MUNICIPAL SECURITIES BROKER'S BROKER—See: BROKER'S BROKER.

MUNICIPAL SECURITIES DEALER—See: DEALER.

MUNICIPAL SECURITIES PRINCIPAL—A person associated with a municipal securities broker or dealer who is responsible for the supervision of municipal securities representative activities (*e.g.*, underwriting, trading, sales, financial advisory services, etc.) or the training of municipal securities representatives or principals. Such persons must qualify by means of an examination. Reference: MSRB Rule G-3.

MUNICIPAL SECURITIES REPRESENTATIVE—A person associated with a municipal securities broker or dealer who is engaged in the underwriting, trading or sales of municipal securities; the provision of financial advice to municipal issuers; or the provision of research or investment advice regarding municipal securities. Such persons must qualify by means of an examination. Reference: MSRB Rule G-3.

MUNICIPAL SECURITIES RULEMAKING BOARD or MSRB—An independent self-regulatory organization established by the Securities Acts Amendments of 1975, which is charged with primary rulemaking authority over dealers, dealer banks and brokers in municipal securities. Its 15 members represent three categories—securities firms, bank dealers and the public—each category having equal representation on the Board.

MUNICIPAL SECURITIES SALES PRINCIPAL—A person associated with a securities firm whose supervisory functions are limited to the supervision of those activities associated with customer sales and purchases of securities (most typically someone who functions as a branch office manager for a full service broker/dealer). Such persons must qualify by means of an examination. Reference: MSRB Rule G-3.

MUNIFACTS—A private wire communication system originating in the New York editorial offices of *The Bond Buyer*. Munifacts transmits current bond market information which is printed out on terminals located in the offices of its subscribers.

MUTILATED CERTIFICATE (NOTE or BOND)—A certificate which has been torn, defaced or otherwise damaged to such an extent that information needed at the time of its redemption or to assure its validity is no longer ascertainable. A mutilated certificate cannot be used in a delivery until the certificate has been validated. The standards used in evaluating whether a certificate is mutilated are set forth in MSRB rule G-12(e)(ix). Compare: MUTILATED COUPON. See: VALIDATION.

MUTILATED COUPON—A coupon which has been torn, defaced or otherwise damaged to such an extent that information needed at the time of its redemption or to assure its validity is no longer ascertainable. A security to which a mutilated coupon is attached cannot be used in a delivery until the coupon has been validated. The standards used in evaluating whether a coupon is mutilated are set forth in MSRB rule G-12(e)(vii). Compare: MUTILATED CERTIFICATE. See: VALIDATION.

NATIONAL ASSOCIATION OF BOND LAWYERS or NABL—A professional society of bond counsel organized to improve the law and solve common legal problems relating to municipal securities.

NATIONAL ASSOCIATION OF SECURITIES DEALERS, INC. or NASD—A self-regulatory organization of broker/dealers active in the securities markets. The NASD was established as a "registered securities association" pursuant to Section 15A of the Securities Exchange Act of 1934, and has authority to adopt rules governing the conduct of its members and to inspect its members for compliance with applicable rules; with respect to municipal securities, however, the NASD has very limited rulewriting authority and is primarily responsible for enforcing members' compliance with MSRB rules. All securities firms (other than those dealing solely in government and federal agency securities) must be NASD members.

NATIONAL INSTITUTIONAL DELIVERY SYSTEM or NIDS—A system offered by the four depositories for the automated transmission of a confirmation from a dealer to an institutional investor, the transmission of an affirmation of that confirmation by the investor, and the automatic book-entry settlement of the transaction. The system is also known as the "Institutional Delivery" or "I.D." system, or under other specific names used by the individual depositories. MSRB rules require that NIDS be used on certain transactions between dealers and customers.

NEGATIVE CARRY—See: CARRYING COST.

NEGATIVE COVENANTS—Promises contained in the bond contract, whereby the issuer obligates itself to refrain from performing certain actions. One common example of a negative covenant is a promise not to sell or encumber the project. Compare: PROTECTIVE COVENANTS. See: COVENANTS.

NEGATIVE YIELD CURVE—See: YIELD CURVE.

NEGOTIATED SALE—The sale of a new issue of municipal securities by an issuer through an exclusive agreement with an underwriter or underwriting syndicate selected by the issuer. A negotiated sale should be distinguished from a competitive sale, which requires public bidding by the underwriters. The primary points of negotiation for an issuer are the interest rate and purchase price on the issue. The sale of a new issue of securities in this manner is also known as a negotiated underwriting. Compare: COMPETITIVE BID.

NET BONDED DEBT—See: BONDED DEBT.

NET CAPITAL RULE—An SEC regulation which requires broker/dealers to maintain "net capital" (net worth adjusted by certain deductions for illiquid assets and reserves against possible market losses on securities positions) equal to or greater than a specified percentage of certain liabilities incurred by the dealer (its "aggregate indebtedness") or a specified percentage of the aggregate of transactional moneys owed to the dealer by customers (its "aggregate debit items"). Broker/dealers are required to suspend or terminate their securities activities if they are unable to meet this test. Reference: SEC Rule 15c3-1.

NET CASH REFUNDING—See: ADVANCE REFUNDING.

NET DIRECT DEBT—See: BONDED DEBT.

NET INTEREST COST or NIC—A common method of computing the interest expense to the issuer of issuing bonds, which usually serves as the basis of award in a competitive sale. NIC takes into account any premium and discount paid on the issue. NIC represents the dollar amount of coupon interest payable over the life of a serial issue, without taking into account the time value of money (as would be done in other calculation methods, such as the "true interest cost" method). While the term "net interest cost" actually refers to the dollar amount of the issuer's interest cost, it is also used to refer to the overall rate of interest to be paid by the issuer over the life of the bonds. The formula for calculating the NIC rate is:

$$\frac{\text{Total Coupon Interest Payments} + \text{Discount (or } - \text{ Premium)}}{\text{Bond Years}}$$

EXAMPLE: (assumes issuer is paid par)

(1) Years to Maturity	(2) Principal Maturing	(3) Interest Rate	(4) Bond Years (1 × 2)	(5) Coupon Payment (3 × 4)
1	1,000	8%	1,000	80
2	2,000	8.75%	4,000	350
3	2,000	9%	6,000	540
Total			11,000	970

$$\frac{970 + 0}{11,000} \text{ (no discount or premium)} = 8.81818\% \text{ NIC rate}$$

Compare: TRUE INTEREST COST.

NET OFFERING—An offering made at a net price. See: NET PRICE.

NET OVERALL DEBT—See: BONDED DEBT.

NET PLEDGE or NET REVENUE PLEDGE— See: PLEDGED REVENUES.

NET PRICE—The price at which a security is offered to the general public. The price of a transaction between municipal securities professionals is generally the net price less a concession or dealer's allowance.

NET REVENUES—The amount of money available after subtracting from gross revenues such costs and expenses as may be provided for in the bond contract. The costs and expenses most often deducted are operations and maintenance expenses.

NETTING—A process used in an automated system made available by the clearing corporations whereby sequences of transactions in a single issue of securities are consolidated into a reduced number of delivery obligations. Persons in the transaction sequence who purchase and subsequently resell the same securities are "netted out," so that deliveries are generally made from the initial sellers of the securities to the ultimate buyers. (For example, if a single block of $100,000 par value securities were sold by dealer A to dealer B, who subsequently resold them to dealer C, netting of the transaction would result in a single delivery obligation of $100,000 par value securities from A to C.) If the transactions are to be cleared by the physical delivery of securities, only transactions which are for the same settlement date will be netted, and balance orders will be produced which are used as instructions for the deliveries. If the transactions will be cleared by book-entry, the more sophisticated "continuous net settlement" or "CNS" system is used, which permits the netting of transactions for a given settlement date

cution or delivery of the bonds issued; the existence or boundaries of the issuing entity (on general obligation bonds); or the validity or legality of provisions authorizing the payment of principal and interest on the bonds. The non-litigation certificate may also affirm the incumbency of specified officers, or this may be done in a separate document.

NORMAL YIELD CURVE—See: YIELD CURVE.

NOTE—A written, short-term promise of an issuer to repay a specified principal amount on a date certain, together with interest at a stated rate, payable from a defined source of anticipated revenue. Notes usually mature in one year or less, although notes of longer maturities are also issued. The following types of notes are common in the municipal market:

  Bond Anticipation Notes (BANs)—Notes issued by a governmental unit, usually for capital projects, which are paid from the proceeds of the issuance of long term bonds.

  Construction Loan Notes (CLNs)—Notes issued to fund construction of housing projects. CLNs are repaid by the permanent financing, which may be provided from bond proceeds or some pre-arranged commitment, such as a GNMA takeout.

  Grant Anticipation Notes (GANs)—Notes issued on the expectation of receiving grant moneys, usually from the federal government. The notes are payable from the grant funds, when received.

  Project Notes (PNs)—Notes issued under a program of the United States Department of Housing and Urban Development to fund local housing or urban renewal projects. Project notes are secured by revenues from those projects and are guaranteed by the United States Government. Reference: 42 Op. Att'y Gen. U.S. 305 (Nov. 2, 1965); 41 Op. Att'y Gen. U.S. 138 (May 15, 1953).

  Revenue Anticipation Notes (RANs)—Notes issued in anticipation of receiving revenues at a future date.

  Tax Anticipation Notes (TANs)—Notes issued in anticipation of future tax receipts, such as receipts of ad valorem taxes which are due and payable at a set time of the year.

GANs, RANs and TANs may be issued to finance capital projects or to alleviate cash flow problems of the issuer. Compare: BOND.

NOTICE FOR TENDERS or REQUEST FOR TENDERS—An invitation by the issuer of bonds, or by its representative, which is made to bondholders to sell bonds back either at a predetermined price or at a price which the bondholder will accept. The notice for tenders usually allows the issuer to reject tender offers in whole or in part. Compare: TENDER OFFER.

against all open positions from prior settlement dates and provides for the automated transmission of instructions for the book-entry delivery.

NEW HOUSING AUTHORITY BOND or NHA BOND—A bond issued by a local housing authority to finance public housing, the payment on which is guaranteed by the federal Department of Housing and Urban Development. The bond is secured in the first instance by revenues from the financed project, with the federal guarantee available to cover any deficiency. These are also called "public housing authority bonds" or "PHA bonds."

NEW ISSUE—An issue of securities which is purchased from the issuer and offered to investors, usually on a "when issued" basis, for the first time.

NIC—See: NET INTEREST COST.

NOMINAL INTEREST RATE—The annual rate of interest payable on a security expressed as a percentage of the principal amount. The nominal interest rate does not take into account any discount (or premium) in the purchase price of the security. Compare: CURRENT YIELD; EFFECTIVE INTEREST RATE; YIELD TO MATURITY.

NOMINAL QUOTATION—An indication of the approximate market value of a security, provided for informational purposes only. A nominal quotation does not represent an actual bid for or offer of securities. A nominal quotation may also be referred to as an "indication." Compare: WORKABLE.

NOMINEE—A partnership established by a bank, securities firm or other corporation to be used as the holder of record for registered securities owned by the bank, securities firm or corporation. These entities register securities in the name of a nominee to avoid the difficulties of registering and transferring securities in a corporate name; additionally, this form of registration is satisfactory for purposes of delivery on inter-dealer transactions. The name of a corporation's nominee is generally registered with the American Society of Corporate Secretaries, which publishes a directory of nominees. Compare: "STREET" NAME. See: LEGAL ITEM.

NON-CALLABLE BOND—A bond that cannot be redeemed at the issuer's option before its stated maturity date. Compare: CALLABLE BOND.

NON-LITIGATION CERTIFICATE—A document executed prior to delivery of a new bond issue by an issuer of municipal bonds certifying that there is no litigation known to the issuer to be currently pending, threatened, or contemplated that would affect in any materially adverse manner the validity or security of the bonds issued; the issuance, exe-

O

NOTICE OF REDEMPTION—A publication announcing the issuer's intention to call outstanding bonds prior to their stated maturity dates. See: CALLABLE BOND; REDEMPTION; REDEMPTION PROVISIONS.

NOTICE OF SALE—A publication by an issuer describing the terms of sale of an anticipated new offering of municipal securities. It generally contains the date, time and place of sale, amount of issue, type of security, amount of good faith deposit, basis of award, name of bond counsel, maturity schedule, method of delivery, time and place of delivery, and bid form.

ODD COUPON—An interest payment for a period other than the standard six months. A payment for a period of less than six months is a "short" coupon; a payment for a period of more than six months is a "long" coupon. Usually only the first interest payment on an issue would be an odd coupon, but some issues have an odd last coupon. The term might also be used to refer to an initial interest payment period of other than six months on a registered security.

ODD LOT—A principal amount of securities which is smaller than that which is considered a normal trading unit and which would typically be traded at a price that would include a differential attributable to the size of the lot (*e.g.*, a dealer would typically bid lower for an odd lot than for a larger block). There is disagreement in the industry as to what constitutes an odd lot of municipal securities, with some dealers viewing any lot smaller than $25,000 as an odd lot but others viewing any lot smaller than $100,000 as an odd lot. Compare: ROUND LOT.

OFFER—A proposal to sell securities at a stated price or yield. Compare: BID. See: OFFERING PRICE.

OFFERING CIRCULAR—A document generally prepared by the underwriters about an issue of securities expected to be offered in the primary market. The document discloses to the investor basic information regarding the securities to be offered and is used as an advertisement for the sale of the securities. The term is also used to refer to a document prepared and used by dealers when selling large blocks of previously issued securities in the secondary market.

OFFERING PRICE—The price or yield at which dealers or members of an underwriting syndicate will offer securities to investors. See: REOFFERING SCALE.

OFFICIAL STATEMENT or FINAL OFFICIAL STATEMENT or O.S.— A document published by the issuer which generally discloses material information on a new issue of municipal securities including the purposes of the issue, how the securities will be repaid, and the financial, economic and social characteristics of the issuing government. Investors may use this information to evaluate the credit quality of the securities. Compare: PRELIMINARY OFFICIAL STATEMENT.

O.I.D.—See: ORIGINAL ISSUE DISCOUNT.

OPEN END FUND—See: BOND FUND.

OPEN END LIEN—A general characterization of the security provisions on a revenue bond where these provisions permit the issuer to issue additional securities which have an equal claim on the pledged revenues under certain circumstances (typically upon satisfaction of an "additional bonds test"). Compare: CLOSED LIEN.

OPERATIONS AND MAINTENANCE FUND—A fund established by the bond contract of a revenue bond issue into which moneys to be used for the purpose of meeting the costs of operating and maintaining the financed project are deposited. Under a typical revenue pledge, this fund is the first (under a net revenue pledge) or the second (under a gross revenue pledge) to be funded out of the revenue fund. See: FLOW OF FUNDS.

OPTION—See: PAR OPTION.

ORDER PERIOD—The period of time following the competitive sale of a new issue during which non-priority orders submitted by account members are allocated without consideration of time of submission. The length of the order period is usually determined by the manager. In a negotiated sale the order period is the period of time established by the manager during which orders are accepted from account members. The order period generally precedes the sale by the issuer. At times order periods are established at subsequent points in the life of a syndicate. Such order periods occur when securities are repriced or market conditions improve dramatically.

ORIGINAL ISSUE DISCOUNT or O.I.D.—An amount by which the par value of a security exceeds its public offering price at the time it was originally offered to an investor. The original issue discount is amortized over the life of the security and, on a municipal security, is generally treated as tax-exempt interest. When the investor sells the security before maturity, any profit realized on such sale is figured (for tax purposes) on the adjusted cost basis, which is calculated for each year the security is outstanding by adding the accretion value to the original offering price. The amount of the accretion value (and the existence and total amount of original issue discount) is determined in accordance with

the provisions of the Internal Revenue Code and the rules and regulations of the Internal Revenue Service.

O.S.—See: OFFICIAL STATEMENT.

OVERLAPPING DEBT—See: BONDED DEBT.

OVER-THE-COUNTER MARKET—A market for securities which are traded other than on a national securities exchange. The over-the-counter (or "OTC") market is characterized most particularly by a system of dealer market-making rather than the auction market system common on the securities exchanges. Almost all municipal securities are traded exclusively in the OTC market. Compare: AUCTION MARKET.

P

PAR—100% of face value of a security.

PAR BOND—A bond selling at its face value.

PARI PASSU BONDS—See: PARITY BONDS.

PARITY BONDS—Two or more issues of bonds which have the same priority of claim or lien against pledged revenues. Parity bonds are also referred to as "pari passu bonds." Compare: JUNIOR LIEN BONDS; SENIOR LIEN BONDS.

PARKING—A practice, in violation of SEC and MSRB rules, consisting of selling securities to a customer and, at the same time, repurchasing the securities in an unbooked transaction (with the transaction later booked as an ostensibly unrelated trade) in an attempt to create an appearance of market activity in the issue or to avoid applicable charges under the SEC's net capital rule.

PAR OPTION—A redemption provision which permits the issuer to call securities at par. Compare: PREMIUM CALL. See: REDEMPTION PROVISIONS.

PARTIAL DELIVERY—A delivery on a transaction of less than the total par value amount of securities involved in the transaction. Dealers are not obliged to accept partial deliveries under MSRB rules.

PARTICIPANT—An organization which has access to and uses the facilities of a registered clearing agency for the confirmation, clearance and/or settlement of securities transactions. An organization which is itself a member of a registered clearing agency is referred to as a "direct participant"; one which is not a member but which uses a clearing agent which is a member is considered an "indirect participant."

PAR VALUE—The amount of principal which must be paid at maturity. The par value is also referred to as the face amount of a security.

operations, e.g., whether the account should be extended or terminated, how bids for bonds at other than listed offering prices should be handled, etc. Members' votes are usually weighted by their percentage participation in the underwriting.

POLLUTION CONTROL REVENUE BOND or PCR—An industrial development revenue bond issued by a state or local authority and used to finance the acquisition of pollution control equipment by a corporation. The security for a pollution control revenue bond is the payments from the corporation under an agreement for leasing or installment purchase of the equipment.

P.O.S.—See: PRELIMINARY OFFICIAL STATEMENT.

POSITION TRADING—A type of trading activity in which a dealer purchases securities and holds them ("positions" them) in its trading inventory, based on the expectation that the value of the securities will rise due to a decline in interest rates or credit considerations about the security itself.

POSITIVE CARRY—See: CARRYING COST.

POWER OF ATTORNEY RELEASE—With respect to a delivery of registered securities, a document provided by a person previously granted power of attorney to transfer the securities. This document grants power of attorney to the recipient of the delivery to transfer the securities. The power of attorney release permits the recipient the right to grant the power of attorney to another person. The release may also be executed "in blank," with the name of the person to be granted authority to transfer the securities to be filled in subsequently. See: ASSIGNMENT.

PRELIMINARY OFFICIAL STATEMENT or RED HERRING or P.O.S.—A preliminary version of the official statement which is used by an issuer or underwriters to describe the proposed issue of municipal securities prior to the determination of the interest rate(s) and offering price(s). The preliminary official statement may be used by issuers to gauge underwriters' interest in an issue and is often relied upon by potential purchasers in making their investment decisions. Normally, offers for the sale of or acceptance of securities are not made on the basis of the preliminary official statement, and a statement to that effect appears on the face of the document generally in red print, which gives the document its nickname, "red herring." The preliminary official statement is technically a draft. Compare: OFFICIAL STATEMENT.

PREMIUM—The amount by which the price paid for a security exceeds the security's par value. Compare: DISCOUNT.

PAYING AGENT—The entity responsible for transmitting payments of interest and principal from an issuer of municipal securities to the securityholders. The paying agent is usually a bank or trust company, but may be the treasurer or some other officer of the issuer. The paying agent may also provide other services for the issuer such as reconciliation of the securities and coupons paid, destruction of paid securities and coupons, and similar services.

PAYMENT DATE—The date on which interest, or principal and interest, is payable on a municipal security. Interest payment dates usually occur semi-annually for bonds.

PCR—See: POLLUTION CONTROL REVENUE BOND.

PER CAPITA DEBT—The amount of an issuing municipality's debt outstanding divided by the population residing in the municipality. This is often used as an indication of the issuer's credit position since it can be used to compare the proportion of debt borne per resident with that borne by the residents of other municipalities. See: DEBT RATIOS.

PHA BOND—See: NEW HOUSING AUTHORITY BOND.

PLACEMENT RATIO—The amount of bonds sold by underwriting syndicates each week as a percentage of the amount issued that week by issuers selling $1,000,000 par value or more of securities. The placement ratio is compiled weekly and is published in *The Bond Buyer*.

PLEDGED REVENUES—The moneys obligated for the payment of debt service and other deposits required by the bond contract.

Gross Pledge or Gross Revenue Pledge—A pledge that all revenues received will be used for debt service prior to deductions for any costs or expenses.

Net Pledge or Net Revenue Pledge—A pledge that all funds remaining after certain operational and maintenance costs and expenses are paid will be used for payment of debt service. See: FLOW OF FUNDS.

PNs—See: NOTE.

POINT—One percent of par value. Because municipal dollar prices are quoted in terms of a percentage of $1,000, a point is worth $10 regardless of the actual denomination of a security. A security discounted 2 1/2 points, or $25, is quoted at "97 1/2" (97 1/2 percent of its value), or $975 per $1,000. Compare: BASIS POINT.

POLLING THE ACCOUNT—The practice by the lead manager of a syndicate of contacting and seeking the vote of members of a syndicate in connection with various questions that might arise concerning syndicate

PREMIUM CALL—A redemption provision which permits the issuer to call securities at a price above par (or, in the case of certain original issue discount or multiplier securities, above the compound accreted value). Compare: PAR OPTION.

PREMIUM CALL PRICE—The price in excess of par value (or compound accreted value, in the case of certain original issue discount or multiplier securities), expressed as a percentage of par (or compound accreted value), which the issuer agrees to pay upon redemption of its outstanding bonds prior to the stated maturity date. The amount of premium to be paid often declines as the possible redemption date approaches the maturity date. See: REDEMPTION PROVISIONS.

PREMIUM SECURITY—A security which can be purchased at a price in excess of par value. Compare: DISCOUNT SECURITY.

PREREFUNDED BOND or PREREFUNDING—See: ADVANCE REFUNDING.

PRE-SALE ORDER—An order given to the syndicate manager prior to the purchase of securities from the issuer, which indicates a prospective investor's intention to purchase the securities at a predetermined price level. Pre-sale orders are normally afforded top priority in allocation of securities from the syndicate. See: PRIORITY PROVISIONS.

PRESENT VALUE—The value at the current time of a cash payment which is expected to be received in the future, allowing for the fact that an amount received today could be invested to earn interest for the period to the future date.

PRESENT VALUE INTEREST COST—See: TRUE INTEREST COST.

PRIMARY MARKET—The market for new issues of municipal securities. Compare: SECONDARY MARKET.

PRINCIPAL—The face amount or par value of a security payable on the maturity date. Compare: INTEREST. See: PAR VALUE.

PRINCIPAL TRADE—A transaction in which the dealer or dealer bank effecting the trade takes ownership of the securities. Compare: "AS AGENT" TRADE.

PRIOR ISSUE—An outstanding issue of municipal bonds. The term is usually used in the context of refunding to denote the obligations being refinanced, sometimes called "refunded bonds." It is also used with respect to previous bond issues which normally possess a first or senior lien on pledged revenues. Compare: JUNIOR LIEN BONDS.

PRIORITY PROVISIONS—The rules adopted by an underwriting syndicate specifying the priority to be given different types of orders received by the syndicate. The most common priority provision gives pre-sale orders top priority, followed by group net orders, designated orders, and member orders. MSRB rules require syndicates to adopt priority provisions in writing, and to make them available to all interested parties. See: DESIGNATED ORDER; GROUP NET ORDER; MEMBER ORDER; PRE-SALE ORDER.

PRIVATE PLACEMENT—With respect to municipal securities, a negotiated sale in which the new issue securities are sold directly to institutional or private investors rather than through a public offering. Issuers often require investors purchasing privately placed securities to agree to restrictions as to resale; the investor may provide a signed agreement to abide by those restrictions.

PRODUCTION—The total amount of proceeds which would be received by an underwriting syndicate if all securities held by the syndicate were sold at the prices listed in the reoffering scale.

PROJECT NOTE—See: NOTE.

PRO-RATA SHARE—The percentage of the total liability of an undivided underwriting account for which a particular account member bears liability. This is equal to the original percentage participation accepted by the member, and is used to determine, for example, the member's portion of syndicate profits or losses. See: SYNDICATE.

PROTECTIVE COVENANTS—Agreements in the bond contract which impose duties upon the issuer, in order to protect the interests of the bondholders. Typical protective covenants relate to such items as maintenance of rates adequate to cover debt service, segregation of funds, proper project maintenance, insurance, maintenance of specified books and records, and tests for the issuance of additional parity bonds. Compare: NEGATIVE COVENANTS. See: COVENANTS.

PROVISIONAL RATING—An indication of what the credit quality of an issue is expected to be a construction or interim period is concluded. The provisional rating does not, however, represent a judgment of what might happen if problems are experienced during the construction or interim period. An investor must exercise his own judgment with respect to such potential risk. Provisional ratings are typically assigned when the debt service on an issue is secured solely by revenues to be derived from a project whose construction is financed by the issue; the rating remains provisional until the construction is completed and the project has begun to generate the revenues.

PUBLIC HOUSING AUTHORITY BOND—See: NEW HOUSING AUTHORITY BOND.

PUBLIC SECURITIES ASSOCIATION or PSA—A national trade organization of dealers and dealer banks that underwrite, trade and sell municipal securities, United States Government and federal agency securities, and certain securitized mortgage obligations.

PURCHASE CONTRACT—See: BOND CONTRACT; BOND PURCHASE AGREEMENT; BOND RESOLUTION.

PUT BOND or TENDER OPTION BOND—Obligations which grant the bondholder the right to require the issuer or a specified third party acting as agent for the issuer to purchase the bonds, usually at par, at a certain time or times prior to maturity or upon the occurrence of specified events or conditions. Compare: CALLABLE BOND.

PUT OPTION or TENDER OPTION—(1) A provision in a bond contract under which the investor has the right, on specified dates after required notification, to return the securities to the issuer (or someone acting on the issuer's behalf) at a predetermined price (usually par).

(2) An instrument issued by a financial institution which permits the purchaser to sell, after giving required notice, a specified amount of securities from a specified issue to the financial institution on a predetermined future date or dates (the "expiration date(s)") at a predetermined price (the "strike price"). Put options are generally backed by a bank letter of credit or line of credit. The put option is often originally sold as an attachment to the security, and may be subsequently transferred with that security. In many cases, however, the put option may be sold separately from that security, or sold attached to other securities from the same issue.

(3) An agreement concluded by the parties to a particular transaction under which the purchaser has the right to return the securities to the seller at a specified price on a specified future date or dates. This arrangement is distinguished from (2) above in that this put option right is not transferrable and is rarely reflected in a separate instrument, but rather is typically described only on, or as a attachment to, the transaction confirmation.

QUALIFIED BID—A bid in the secondary market entered to purchase bonds subject to conditions set forth by either party to the transaction. For example, the purchaser might stipulate that a legal opinion acceptable to it must be available on the security, or that the bid is only valid if the seller can guarantee delivery by a certain date; similarly, the seller might impose certain requirements, such as delivery in a certain city.

QUALIFIED LEGAL OPINION—Conditional affirmation of the legality of securities, before or after they are sold. An unqualified or "clean" legal opinion, on the other hand, is an unconditional affirmation of the legality of securities. See: LEGAL OPINION.

R

RANs—See: NOTE.

RATING AGENCIES—The organizations which provide publicly available ratings of the credit quality of securities issuers. The term is most often used to refer to the two nationally recognized agencies, Moody's Investors Service, Inc., and Standard & Poor's Corporation. See: MOODY'S INVESTORS SERVICE, INC.; STANDARD & POOR'S CORPORATION.

RATINGS—Evaluations of the credit quality of notes and bonds usually made by independent rating services. Ratings are intended to measure the probability of the timely repayment of principal of and interest on municipal securities. Ratings are initially made before issuance and are periodically reviewed and may be amended to reflect changes in the issuer's credit position. The information required by the rating agencies varies with each issue, but generally includes information regarding the issuer's demographics, debt burden, economic base, finances and management structure. Many financial institutions also assign their own individual ratings to securities. See: DOWNGRADE; UPGRADE.

REALIZED COMPOUND YIELD—A yield measure reflecting, in addition to the direct return on a periodic-interest fixed income security, the return to be received from reinvestment of the periodic interest payments received at an assumed reinvestment rate (or rates). Compare: YIELD TO MATURITY.

RECALL—See: FIRM.

RECEIPT VS. PAYMENT or RVP—A method of settling transactions whereby payment on the transaction is made when a delivery of the securities involved in the transaction has been received and accepted. The term is used to refer to a transaction settled in this manner where a customer (typically an institutional investor) has sold securities to a dealer. Compare: DELIVERY VS. PAYMENT.

RECIPROCAL IMMUNITY DOCTRINE—The principle that neither the states nor the federal government may tax income received from securities issued by the other (states may, however, tax the interest on obligations of other states). The doctrine provides the original, constitutional basis for the federal income tax exemption on interest paid on municipal securities. Reference: *Pollock v. Farmers' Loan and Trust Co.*, 157 U.S. 429 (1895); *National Life Insurance Co. v. United States*, 277 U.S. 508 (1928).

RECLAMATION—The return of securities previously accepted on a delivery due to the discovery that some deficiency exists with respect to the securities which would have caused the rejection of the original delivery had it been discovered at that time. The payment tendered at the time of the original delivery is returned to the reclaiming dealer and the transaction (or the reclaimed portion of the transaction) is reopened as if the original delivery had not taken place. Compare: REJECTION. Reference: MSRB Rule G-12(g).

RECORD DATE—A fixed date prior to the interest payment date on an issue of registered securities which is used to determine to whom the next interest payment should be made. Persons who are listed as the registered owners of the security on the record date will be sent the interest payment. The registrar for the issue prepares a list of all persons who are registered as the owners of the security on the record date. The registrar provides this list to the paying agent on the issue, who disburses the interest payment checks to the registered owners on the interest payment date. The record date on an issue paying interest on the first of a month is typically the 15th of the preceding month (or the last business day before it); the record date on an issue paying interest on the 15th of a month is typically the last business day of the preceding month.

RED BOOK—See: DEALER BOOK.

REDEMPTION—A transaction in which the issuer returns the principal amount represented by an outstanding security (plus, in certain cases, an additional amount). Redemption can be made under several different circumstances: at maturity of the security, as a result of the issuer's call of the securities, or (in rare cases) as a result of the securityholder's election to exercise a put or tender option privilege. See: PUT OPTION; REDEMPTION PROVISIONS.

REDEMPTION PROVISIONS or CALL FEATURES—The terms of the bond contract giving the issuer the right or requiring the issuer to redeem or "call" all or a portion of an outstanding issue of bonds prior to their stated dates of maturity at a specified price, usually at or above par. Common types of redemption provisions include:

Optional Redemption—The issuer has the right to redeem bonds, usually after a stated date and at a premium, but is not required to do so.

Mandatory Redemption—The issuer is required to call outstanding bonds based on a predetermined schedule or as otherwise provided in the bond contract. Frequently, the issuer is allowed to make open market purchases in lieu of calling the bonds. See: MANDATORY REDEMPTION ACCOUNT.

Extraordinary Optional Redemption—The issuer has the right to call or redeem an issue of bonds upon the occurrence of certain events. For example, the right to extraordinary optional redemption of an issue of bonds may be exercised when mortgages are prepaid in connection with a housing revenue bond issue.

Extraordinary Mandatory Redemption—The issuer is required to call or redeem all or part of an issue of bonds upon the occurrence of certain events. For example, the issuer may be required to call or redeem bonds when proceeds of an issue are not expended for the purpose of the issue as of a given time; when excess bond proceeds exist after completion of a project; or when the facility has been substantially destroyed during construction due to an accident. The latter situation is also known as a "calamity call" or "catastrophe call."

RED HERRING—See: PRELIMINARY OFFICIAL STATEMENT.

REFUNDING—A procedure whereby an issuer refinances an outstanding bond issue by issuing new bonds. There are generally two major reasons for refunding: to reduce the issuer's interest costs or to remove a burdensome or restrictive covenant imposed by the terms of the bonds being refinanced. The proceeds of the new bonds are either deposited in escrow to pay the debt service on the outstanding obligations, when due (in which case the financing is known as an "advance refunding"), or used to immediately retire the outstanding obligations. The new obligations are referred to as the "refunding bonds," and the outstanding obligations being refinanced are referred to as the "refunded bonds" or the "prior issue." For accounting purposes, refunded obligations are not considered a part of the issuer's debt because the lien of the holders of the refunded bonds, in the first instance, is on the escrowed funds, not on the originally pledged source of revenues. The refunded bonds, however, will continue to hold a lien on the originally pledged source of revenues unless provisions have been made in the bond contract on the refunded bonds for defeasance of the bonds prior to redemption. See: ADVANCE REFUNDING; DEFEASANCE; SLGS.

REGISTERED BOND—A bond whose owner is designated on records maintained for this purpose by a registrar, the ownership of which cannot be transferred without the registrar recording the transfer on these records. The principal and interest on "fully registered" bonds is paid directly by check (or other funds transfer) to the registered owner. Bonds issued prior to July 1983 may sometimes be "registered as to principal only"; in this form coupons reflecting the interest payments due remain attached to the bonds and must be detached and redeemed in order to receive the interest due. Most municipal securities issued after June 1983 are in "fully registered" form due to provisions of the Internal Revenue Code which deny tax-exemption to interest paid on issues (other than those exempt from this provision) which are not in registered form. Compare: BEARER BOND.

REGISTERED CLEARING AGENCY—An organization, registered with the Securities and Exchange Commission pursuant to Section 17A of the Securities Exchange Act of 1934, which provides specialized systems for the confirmation, comparison, clearance and settlement of securities transactions. The four clearing corporations and the four depositories are all registered clearing agencies. See: CLEARING CORPORATION; DEPOSITORY.

REGISTRAR—The person or entity responsible for maintaining records on behalf of the issuer for the purpose of noting the owners of registered bonds. Compare: TRANSFER AGENT.

"REGULAR WAY" TRADE—A securities transaction in which the settlement date is the fifth business day following the trade date. "Regular way" trades are the standard for settlement in the municipal securities industry. Compare: CASH TRADE; DELAYED DELIVERY TRADE.

REINVESTMENT RISK—The risk that a purchaser of a fixed income security incurs that interest rates will be lower when the purchaser seeks to reinvest income received from the security.

REJECTION—A refusal by a dealer to accept a delivery tendered to him by another dealer. Compare: RECLAMATION.

RELATED PORTFOLIO—A portfolio investing in municipal securities which is operated by or associated in some way with a municipal securities dealer (e.g., a dealer bank's portfolio). Certain disclosure requirements under MSRB rules are applicable to orders for new issue municipal securities from related portfolios. Reference: MSRB Rule G-11.

RENEWAL AND REPLACEMENT FUND—A fund established by the bond contract of a revenue bond issue into which moneys are deposited to cover anticipated expenses for major repairs of the project or its equipment or for replacement of equipment. Under a typical revenue pledge this fund is the fifth to be funded out of the revenue fund. See: FLOW OF FUNDS.

REOFFERING SCALE—The prices and/or yields, listed by maturity, at which securities are offered to the public by the underwriters.

REPURCHASE AGREEMENT or REPO—See: MONEY MARKET INSTRUMENTS.

REQUEST FOR TENDERS—See: NOTICE FOR TENDERS.

RESERVE FUND—See: DEBT SERVICE RESERVE FUND.

RESERVE MAINTENANCE FUND—A fund established by the bond contract of a revenue bond issue into which moneys set aside for extraordinary maintenance or repair expenses are deposited. The fund is intended to protect the bondholders by ensuring against interruptions of operation of the financed project due to unavailability of moneys to pay for repairs of unexpected damage or breakdown. Under a typical revenue pledge this fund is the fourth to be funded out of the revenue fund. See: FLOW OF FUNDS.

RETAIL SALES—Sales of securities to individual investors and small institutions. Compare: INSTITUTIONAL SALES.

REVENUE ANTICIPATION NOTE—See: NOTE.

REVENUE BOND—A bond which is payable from a specific source of revenue and to which the full faith and credit of an issuer with taxing power is not pledged. Revenue bonds are payable from identified sources of revenue, and do not permit the bondholders to compel taxation or legislative appropriation of funds not pledged for payment of debt service. Pledged revenues may be derived from operation of the financed project, grants and excise or other specified non-ad-valorem taxes. Generally, no voter approval is required prior to issuance of such obligations. Compare: GENERAL OBLIGATION BOND.

REVENUE FUND—A fund established by the bond contract of a revenue bond issue into which all gross revenues from the financed project are initially placed and from which the moneys for all other funds are drawn. See: FLOW OF FUNDS.

REVERSE REPURCHASE AGREEMENT or REVERSE or REVERSE REPO—See: MONEY MARKET INSTRUMENTS.

ROUND LOT—The increment in which securities can be traded without addition or deduction of a price differential due to the size of the block. There is disagreement in the industry as to what constitutes a round lot of municipal securities, with $25,000, $100,000, and $250,000 par value lots each considered the minimum round lot size by some industry members. Compare: ODD LOT.

RP—See: MONEY MARKET INSTRUMENTS.

RULE 10b-5—A regulation of the Securities and Exchange Commission, adopted pursuant to the Securities Exchange Act of 1934, which makes it unlawful for any person to employ any device, scheme, or artifice to defraud; to make any untrue statement of a material fact or to omit to state a material fact necessary in order to make the statements made, in the light of the circumstances under which they were made, not misleading; or to engage in any act, practice, or course of business which operates or would operate as a fraud or deceit upon any person, in connection with the purchase or sale of any security. See: DUE DILIGENCE; FULL DISCLOSURE; INSIDER TRADING. Reference: *Shores v. Sklar*, 647 F.2d 462 (5th Cir. 1981).

SALLIE MAE—See: STUDENT LOAN MARKETING ASSOCIATION.

S.C.A.—See: A.S.C.A.

SCALE—See: REOFFERING SCALE.

S.E.C.—See: SECURITIES AND EXCHANGE COMMISSION.

SECONDARY MARKET—The market for securities previously offered and sold. Compare: PRIMARY MARKET.

SECURITIES AND EXCHANGE COMMISSION or S.E.C.—The federal agency responsible for supervising and regulating the securities industry. Generally, municipal securities are exempt from the SEC's registration and reporting requirements. Brokers and dealers in municipal securities, however, are subject to SEC regulation and oversight. The SEC also has responsibility for the approval of MSRB rules, and has jurisdiction, pursuant to SEC Rule 10b-5, over fraud in the sale of municipal securities. Reference: 15 United States Code §78(d).

SECURITIES INDUSTRY ASSOCIATION or S.I.A.—An organization representing the interests of investment banking and securities brokerage firms.

SECURITIES INVESTOR PROTECTION CORPORATION or SIPC—A non-profit corporation created by the Securities Investor Protection Act of 1970 under which investors are partially insured against the possibility of loss resulting from the insolvency of a broker/dealer. In the event of failure of a firm, SIPC appoints a trustee to conclude the affairs of the firm. The trustee typically would return identifiable property (*e.g.*, securities registered in a particular customer's name) to customers, and handle customer claims for other securities or funds due them. SIPC maintains a trust fund for the protection of customers into which broker/dealers make quarterly contributions, and may pay customer claims out of this fund, up to certain specified limits.

SETTLEMENT DATE—The date on which settlement of a transaction is presumed to occur. This date is used in price and interest computations, and is usually the date of delivery. Compare: TRADE DATE. See: DELIVERY DATE; SETTLEMENT. Reference: MSRB Rule G-12.

SEVERAL OBLIGATION—A form of contract in which each signing party is obligated only to the amount of liability originally designated to it under the contract. Compare: JOINT AND SEVERAL OBLIGATION.

SHORT COUPON—See: ODD COUPON.

SHORT POSITION—A trading inventory position reflecting a sale by a dealer of securities which it did not own at the time of sale.

SHORT SALE—A sale of securities which the selling dealer does not own. The selling dealer is obliged to go into the market and subsequently purchase the securities from a third party in order to make delivery on this transaction.

S.I.A.—See: SECURITIES INDUSTRY ASSOCIATION.

SIGNATURE GUARANTEE—A written representation placed by an authorized person on the assignment or bond power attached to a registered security affirming that the person who signed the assignment or bond power is the person in whose name the securities are registered or is authorized to act on behalf of such person, and that the signature is genuine. The signature guarantee provides assurance to the transfer agent that the transfer is proper and can be completed. Although the authority of different classes of persons to guarantee signatures may differ depending on the transfer agent, signature guarantees provided by exchange-member broker/dealers and commercial banks are generally considered valid. See: ASSIGNMENT.

SINKING FUND—(1) A fund established by the bond contract of an issue into which the issuer makes periodic deposits to assure the timely availability of sufficient moneys for the payment of debt service requirements. The amounts of the revenues to be deposited into the sinking fund and the payments therefrom are determined by the terms of the bond contract. Under a typical revenue pledge this fund is the first (under a gross revenue pledge) or the second (under a net revenue pledge) to be funded out of the revenue fund. This fund is sometimes referred to as the "Debt Service Fund." See: FLOW OF FUNDS.

(2) A separate account in the overall sinking fund into which moneys are placed to be used to redeem securities, by open-market purchase, request for tenders or call, in accordance with a redemption schedule in the bond contract.

SECURITY—Generally, an instrument evidencing debt of or equity in a common enterprise in which a person invests on the expectation of financial gain. The term includes notes, stocks, bonds, debentures or other forms of negotiable and non-negotiable evidences of indebtedness or ownership. Reference: 15 United States Code §77b(1) (Securities Act of 1933); 15 United States Code §78c(a)(10) (Securities Exchange Act of 1934).

SECURITY FOR THE BONDS or SECURITY—The specific revenue sources or assets of an issuer which are pledged for payment of debt service on a series of bonds, as well as the covenants or other legal provisions protecting the bondholders.

SELF-SUPPORTING DEBT or SELF-LIQUIDATING DEBT—Debt which is to be repaid from proceeds exclusively generated by the enterprise activity for which the debt was issued.

SELLING GROUP—A group of municipal securities brokers and dealers that assists in the distribution of a new issue of securities. Selling group members are able to acquire new issue securities from the underwriting syndicate at syndicate terms (*i.e.*, less the total takedown) but do not participate in residual syndicate profits nor share any liability for any unsold balance. Compare: SYNDICATE.

SELL-OUT—See: CLOSE-OUT.

SENIOR LIEN BONDS—Bonds having a prior claim on pledged revenues. Compare: JUNIOR LIEN BONDS; PARITY BONDS.

SENIOR MANAGER—See: MANAGER; SYNDICATE.

SERIAL BONDS—Bonds of an issue in which some bonds mature in successive years without interruption. Compare: TERM BONDS.

SERIAL ISSUE—An issue of bonds having maturities scheduled over several years, thereby allowing the issuer to amortize principal over a period of years. Maturity schedules for serial bonds often provide for level debt service or level principal payments. Compare: TERM ISSUE.

SETTLEMENT—Delivery of and payment for a security. In the case of a new issue of municipal securities, settlement usually occurs within 30 days after the securities are awarded to the underwriters, which allows for printing of the securities and the completion of certain legal matters. In the case of the purchase of a security in the secondary market, settlement occurs upon delivery of and payment for the security, usually five business days after purchase. See: DELIVERY DATE; GOOD DELIVERY. Reference: MSRB Rule G-12.

SIPC—See: SECURITIES INVESTOR PROTECTION CORPORATION.

SLGS—An acronym (pronounced "slugs") for "State and Local Government Series." SLGS are special United States Government securities sold by the Treasury to states, municipalities and other local government bodies through individual subscription agreements. The interest rates and maturities of SLGS are arranged to comply with arbitrage restrictions imposed under Section 103 of the Internal Revenue Code. SLGS are most commonly used for deposit in escrow in connection with the issuance of refunding bonds. See: ADVANCE REFUNDING; REFUNDING.

SLMA—See: STUDENT LOAN MARKETING ASSOCIATION.

SPECIAL ASSESSMENT—A charge imposed against property in a particular locality because that property receives a special benefit by virtue of some public improvement, separate and apart from the general benefit accruing to the value of the benefit received, rather than the cost of the improvement, and may not exceed the value of such benefit or the cost of the improvement, whichever is less. Compare: TAX.

SPECIAL ASSESSMENT BOND—An obligation payable from special assessment revenues. See: SPECIAL ASSESSMENT.

SPECIAL DISTRICTS—Single-purpose or limited-purpose units of government formed under state enabling legislation to meet certain local needs not satisfied by existing general purpose governments in a given geographical area. In some states, special districts (such as school districts) may be granted taxing powers.

SPECIAL OBLIGATION BONDS—(1) That portion of a full cash refunding bond issue which is secured by the interest earnings on U.S. Government securities purchased with the proceeds of the refunding bonds. See: ADVANCE REFUNDING.

(2) In several states, the term may also be used to refer to bonds secured by a limited revenue source.

SPECIAL TAX BOND—A bond secured by one or more designated taxes other than ad valorem taxes. For example, bonds for a particular purpose might be supported by sales, cigarette, fuel or business license taxes; however, the designated tax does not have to be directly related to the project purpose. Such bonds are not considered "self-supporting" debt.

SPLIT RATINGS—An assignment of materially different ratings on an issue of municipal securities by the two nationally recognized rating services.

SPREAD—(1) With respect to new issue municipal securities, the differential between the price paid to the issuer for the new issue and the prices at which the securities are initially offered to the investing public; this is also termed the "gross spread" or "gross underwriting spread." To the extent that the initial offering prices are subsequently lowered by the syndicate, the full amount of the spread may not be realized by the syndicate. The spread is usually expressed in points or fractions thereof. The spread generally has four components:

(a) *Expenses*—The costs of operating the syndicate for which the lead manager may be reimbursed.

(b) *Management Fee*—The amount paid to the lead manager for handling the affairs of the syndicate.

(c) *Takedown*—Normally the largest component of the spread, similar to a commission, which represents the income derived from the sale of the securities. If bonds are sold by a member of the syndicate, the seller is entitled to the full takedown (also called the "total takedown"); if bonds are sold by a dealer which is not a member of the syndicate, such seller receives only that portion of the takedown known as the concession or dealer's allowance, with the balance (often termed the "additional takedown") retained by the syndicate.

(d) *Risk or Residual*—The amount of profit or spread left in a syndicate account after meeting all other expenses or deductions. A portion of the residual is paid to each underwriter within a syndicate on a pro rata basis according to the number of bonds each dealer has committed to sell without regard to the actual sales by each member.

The concept of "spread" used for purposes of Treasury arbitrage regulations is somewhat different. See: CONCESSION; SYNDICATE.

(2) With respect to securities trading in the secondary market, the differential between the bid price and the offering price in a two-sided market quotation.

(3) The difference in yields, expressed in basis points, between two securities or groups of securities (*e.g.*, credit rating categories).

STABILIZATION—A practice used in connection with certain sales of new issues of municipal securities, in which an underwriter posts an open bid for securities of the new issue at a stated price, or purchases securities of the issue offered in the secondary market if the offering price declines below a certain level. Stabilization is intended to maintain an orderly market for the securities during the underwriting, and to prevent sharp fluctuations in the market for the securities due simply to supply factors. Stabilization conducted outside of the new issue context for any fraudulent or manipulative purpose is a violation of SEC and MSRB rules.

STANDARD & POOR'S CORPORATION or S&P—An independent financial service company, a subsidiary of McGraw-Hill Company, which provides ratings for municipal securities and other financial information to investors. See: RATINGS.

STEPPED COUPON BONDS—A serial issue of bonds on which the interest rate periodically changes (generally by increasing) over the life of the issue for all bonds remaining outstanding. The use of this financing technique may result in interest cost savings by structuring the issue with a high percentage of the principal maturing in the early years; the issuer would then be required to pay interest at high rates in the later years on less principal. Redemption premiums may be higher than on conventional bonds, in order to assure the bondholder that the yield to call would not be less than his expected yield to maturity.

STICKERING—The act of amending or supplementing the information provided in an official statement on a new issue. The amendment typically provides current information regarding new developments affecting the issuer or the issue, or updated information regarding matters already discussed in the official statement. The new information is often printed on paper with adhesive backing, so that it can be glued to the appropriate pages of the official statement; this is the origin of the name.

"STREET" NAME—The name of a broker/dealer. Securities registered in the name of a broker/dealer are described as being "registered in 'street' name." These securities generally can be transferred more easily than securities with other forms of registration, and are considered to be in "good delivery" form for purposes of inter-dealer transactions. Compare: LEGAL ITEM; NOMINEE.

STRIKE PRICE—See: PUT OPTION.

STRIP CALL—Redemption of municipal bonds by calling a portion of each outstanding maturity or selected maturities as provided in the bond contract. A strip call may be proportional, by redeeming in each maturity the proportion which the maturity bears to the total amount of principal outstanding, or it may be a level debt service reduction, whereby an amount is redeemed in each maturity so that annual debt service payments remain constant.

STRIP ORDER—An order for bonds in successive maturities of a serial issue.

STRUCTURING AN ISSUE—The process of formulating an issue within the issuer's legal and financial constraints so that the security is marketable. In structuring a new issue of municipal securities the issuer must determine the maturities, the method of repayment, redemption provisions, application of proceeds, security provisions and covenants.

STUB PERIOD FINANCIALS or STUB PERIOD AUDIT—See: INTERIM PERIOD FINANCIAL STATEMENTS.

STUDENT LOAN MARKETING ASSOCIATION or SLMA or SALLIE MAE—A private, for-profit corporation formed under the Guaranteed Student Loan Program to provide liquidity for insured student loans. The corporation is empowered to issue common and preferred voting stock, and may warehouse, service, sell and otherwise deal, in student loans.

SUITABILITY—The appropriateness of a particular security as an investment for a particular investor, taking into account the investor's financial capabilities and sophistication, tax status, investment objectives and other relevant considerations. A security which seems appropriate for the investor in light of these factors is said to be "suitable," whereas one which does not seem appropriate (one which entails undue credit risk, for example, or matures significantly before or after a time when the investor expects to need the money) would be "unsuitable." Municipal securities representatives are required under MSRB rules to reach certain determinations about suitability before recommending particular investments or investment strategies to customers. Reference: MSRB Rule G-19.

SUPER SINKER—A term maturity, usually from a single family mortgage revenue issue with several term maturities, which will be the first to be called from a sinking fund into which all proceeds from prepayments of mortgages financed by the issue are deposited. The maturity's priority status under the call provisions means that it is likely to be redeemed in its entirety well before the stated maturity date. Therefore the super sinker maturity is considered attractive to investors because it offers long-term interest rates on what is effectively a short-term security.

SUPPLEMENTAL COUPONS—Additional interest coupons attached to a new issue security which reflect an issuer's commitment to pay additional interest, above the stated interest rate on the issue, for a short period of time following issuance of the securities. Supplemental coupons are used as a means of providing compensation to the underwriters of the new issue, who detach the coupons and either sell them on a discounted basis or hold them until redemption at their stated maturity. Supplemental coupons have fallen out of use in the municipal industry.

SURPLUS FUND—A fund established by the bond contract of a revenue bond issue into which moneys are deposited which remain after oper-

SWAP—A sale of a security and the simultaneous purchase of another security, for purposes of enhancing the investor's holdings. The swap may be used to achieve desired tax results, to gain income or principal, or to alter various features of a bond portfolio, including call protection, diversification or consolidation, and marketability of holdings. Compare: TAX SWAP.

SYNDICATE—A group of underwriters formed to purchase (underwrite) a new issue of municipal securities from the issuer and offer it for resale to the general public. The syndicate is organized for the purposes of sharing the risks of underwriting the issue, obtaining sufficient capital to purchase an issue and for broader distribution of the issue to the investing public. One of the underwriting firms will be designated as the syndicate manager or lead manager to administer the operations of the syndicate. There are two major types of syndication agreements:

Divided or Western Account—A method for determining liability stated in the agreement among underwriters in which each member of an underwriting syndicate is liable only for the amount of its participation in the issue, and not for any unsold portion of the participation amounts allocated to the other underwriters.

Undivided or Eastern Account—A method for determining liability stated in the underwriting agreement in which each member of the underwriting syndicate is liable for any unsold portion of the issue according to each member's percentage participation in the syndicate.

See: MANAGER.

SYNDICATE ACCOUNT LETTER—A document sent by the syndicate manager on a competitive new issue to the members which defines the terms of operation of the syndicate. This document designates the syndicate manager and identifies the account, the priority of allocating securities and the members' participations, among other matters. Members typically signify their acceptance of the terms by signing and returning the letter to the manager.

SYNDICATE MANAGER—See: MANAGER; SYNDICATE.

ations and maintenance, sinking fund, debt service reserve and other mandated distributions have been satisfied. Moneys in this fund may be used for any lawful purposes of the enterprise. See: FLOW OF FUNDS.

TAKEDOWN—See: SPREAD.

TAKE OR PAY CONTRACT—A sales agreement which requires the purchaser to pay the seller whether or not goods or services are available and, if available, whether or not the purchaser uses them. This type of requirement is often used in electric power sales contracts which stipulate that payments will be made by the purchasers to the electricity wholesaler whether or not the power supply projects are complete or operational. Such payments are not conditioned upon the performance of the wholesaler, the completion or operation of the power project or the use of the goods or services.

TAKE OUT—A permanent loan commitment where the proceeds of the permanent loan are used to pay or "take out" the interim loan.

TANs—See: NOTE.

TAX or TAXES—Compulsory charges levied by a governmental unit for the purpose of raising revenue. Taxes should be distinguished from special assessments, which are levied according to the actual benefits derived, and from fees, which must bear a reasonable relation to the costs of administration or regulation, and are imposed under a government's police power. Tax revenues are used to pay for services or improvements provided for the general public benefit. Compare: SPECIAL ASSESSMENT. See: AD VALOREM TAX; EXCISE TAX.

TAXABLE EQUIVALENT YIELD or TAXABLE YIELD EQUIVALENT—The interest rate which must be received on a taxable security to provide the holder the same after-tax return as that earned on a tax-exempt security. Because interest earned on municipal securities is not subject to federal income taxation, a tax-exempt security does not have to yield to a holder as much as a taxable security to produce an equivalent after-tax yield; this differential is attributable to the effect of the tax liability incurred by the holder if it held a taxable security. The taxable equivalent yield varies according to the holder's marginal federal income tax bracket, and, where applicable, any state or local tax liability as well. The formula for determining the taxable equivalent yield is:

$$\frac{\text{Tax-Exempt Yield}}{100\% - \text{Marginal Tax Bracket}} = \text{Taxable Equivalent Yield}$$

TAX ANTICIPATION NOTE—See: NOTE.

TAX BASE—The total property and resources available to a governmental entity for taxation.

TAX-EXEMPT BOND—Another term for a municipal bond. Interest on municipal securities is exempt from federal income taxation pursuant to Section 103 of the Internal Revenue Code, and may or may not be exempt from state income or personal property taxation in the jurisdiction where issued. If the bond is exempt from state income tax, it possesses "double exemption" status. "Triple exemption" bonds are exempt from municipal or local income taxes, as well as from federal and state income tax.

TAX RATE—The amount of tax stated in terms of a unit of the tax base; for example, 10 mills per dollar of assessed valuation of taxable property.

TAX RATE LIMIT—The maximum rate or millage of tax which a local government may levy. This limit may apply to taxes raised for a particular purpose or for all purposes; to a single government, or class of governments; or to all governments operating in a particular area. See: AD VALOREM TAX; MILL; MILLAGE; TAX RATE.

TAX ROLL—The official list showing the amount of taxes levied against each taxpayer or parcel of property, prepared and authenticated in proper form to warrant the collecting officers to proceed with administering the tax.

TAX SWAP—The sale of a security at a loss and the simultaneous purchase of another similar security. By creating a loss, the tax swap reduces the investor's current tax liability. The tax swap may also serve purposes similar to those of other types of swaps. See: SWAP.

TENDER OFFER—A proposal by the bondholder to sell his bond to the issuer or the issuer's representative for a stated price. Compare: NOTICE FOR TENDERS.

TENDER OPTION—See: PUT OPTION.

TENDER OPTION BOND—See: PUT BOND.

TERM BONDS—Bonds comprising a large part or all of a particular issue which come due in a single maturity. The issuer usually agrees to make periodic payments into a sinking fund for mandatory redemption of term bonds before maturity or for payment at maturity. Compare: SERIAL BONDS.

TERM ISSUE—An issue of municipal securities that has a single stated maturity. Compare: SERIAL ISSUE.

30-DAY VISIBLE or 30-DAY VISIBLE SUPPLY—See: VISIBLE SUPPLY

TIC—See: TRUE INTEREST COST.

TOMBSTONE—An advertisement placed by underwriters announcing the terms of a new municipal offering setting forth some or all of the following information: the name of the issuer, maturities, interest rate, reoffering scale, ratings and members of the underwriting syndicate. Compare: NOTICE OF SALE.

TOTAL OVERALL DEBT—See: BONDED DEBT.

TRADE DATE—The date on which two parties agree to effect a transaction in certain securities at an agreed upon price. Compare: SETTLEMENT DATE.

TRANSCRIPT OF PROCEEDINGS—See: BOND TRANSCRIPT.

TRANSFER—The process of effecting a change in the ownership of a registered security by (a) updating the list of registered holders of an issue and (b) issuing a new securities certificate (or, in some cases, reissuing the old certificate) with the new registered owner's name imprinted on it. Both of these functions are most typically performed by the same entity, although in certain cases different entities may be used to perform each function. See: REGISTRAR; REGISTERED BOND; TRANSFER AGENT.

TRANSFER AGENT—The person or entity who performs the transfer function for an issue of registered municipal securities. This person or entity may be the issuer or an official of the issuer, or an outside organization employed by the issuer to act as its agent. In certain cases the transfer agent performs only that part of the transfer function involving the issuance or reissuance of securities certificates in the name of the new registered owner, with the function of maintaining the list of registered owners performed by a separate entity (known as the "registrar"). The entity performing the transfer function may also act in other capacities (e.g., as paying agent) on the issue. See: REGISTRAR; REGISTERED BOND; TRANSFER.

TREASURY SECURITIES—Debt obligations of the United States Government sold by the Treasury Department in the form of Bills, Notes, and Bonds:

Bills—Short-term obligations which mature in 1 year or less and are sold on the basis of a rate of discount.

Notes—Obligations which mature between 1 year and 10 years.

Bonds—Long-term obligations which generally mature in 10 years or more.

TRIPLE EXEMPT or TRIPLE EXEMPTION—See: TAX-EXEMPT BOND.

TRUE INTEREST COST or TIC—Also known as "Canadian Interest Cost." Under this method of computing the borrowing issuer's cost, interest cost is defined as the rate, compounded semi-annually, necessary to discount the amounts payable on the respective principal and interest payment dates to the purchase price received for the new issue securities. TIC computations produce a figure slightly different from the net interest cost ("NIC") method since TIC considers the time value of money while NIC does not. Compare: NET INTEREST COST.

TRUE INTEREST COST BID—An underwriter's bid which takes into account both the total dollar of interest payments and the timing of the interest and principal payments. See: TRUE INTEREST COST.

TRUSTEE—A financial institution with trust powers which acts in a fiduciary capacity for the benefit of the bondholders in enforcing the terms of the bond contract.

TRUST INDENTURE—A contract between the issuer of municipal securities and a trustee, for the benefit of the bondholders. The trustee administers the funds or property specified in the indenture in a fiduciary capacity on behalf of the bondholders. The trust indenture, which is generally a part of the bond contract, establishes the rights, duties, responsibilities and remedies of the issuer and trustee and determines the exact nature of the security for the bonds. The trustee is generally empowered to enforce the bond contract on behalf of the bondholders. See: BOND CONTRACT; TRUSTEE.

TWO-SIDED MARKET—A statement of the bid and offer prices at which a dealer would be willing to effect a transaction in a security. Due to the lack of fungibility of municipal securities, professionals are generally unwilling to make two-sided markets in most issues, since they would be unwilling to sell securities that they did not own and might be unable to find in the market. Some dealers make two-sided markets on larger, term bond issues.

U.I.T.—See: BOND FUND.

UNDERWRITE or UNDERWRITING—The process of purchasing all or any part of a new issue of municipal securities from the issuer, and offering such securities for sale to investors. See: SYNDICATE; UNDERWRITER.

UNDERWRITER—A dealer which purchases a new issue of municipal securities for resale. The underwriter may acquire the securities either by negotiation with the issuer or by award on the basis of competitive bidding. See: COMPETITIVE BID; NEGOTIATED SALE; SYNDICATE.

UNDERWRITER'S COUNSEL—An attorney or law firm retained to represent the interests of the underwriters in connection with the purchase of a new issue of municipal securities. The duties of underwriter's counsel may include review of the issuer's bond resolution or ordinance and documentation on behalf of the underwriter; review of the official statement to determine the adequacy of disclosure; negotiation of the agreement among underwriters; and preparation of the due diligence opinion. Compare: BOND COUNSEL. See: DUE DILIGENCE; DUE DILIGENCE OPINION.

UNDERWRITING AGREEMENT—See: AGREEMENT AMONG UNDERWRITERS.

UNDERWRITING PERIOD—The period of time during which the underwriting process is considered to be continuing and during which certain requirements of MSRB rules are applicable. MSRB rules define the "underwriting period" as commencing at the time of the first submission to the underwriter(s) of an order for the new issue securities or the purchase of the new issue from the issuer, whichever occurs first, and ending at the time of the delivery of the securities to the underwriter(s) by the issuer or the sale of the last of the securities by the underwriter(s), whichever occurs last.

UNDERWRITING SYNDICATE—See: SYNDICATE.

UNDIVIDED ACCOUNT—See: SYNDICATE.

UNEXPENDED FUNDS CALL or UNEXPENDED PROCEEDS CALL—An extraordinary mandatory redemption feature under which securities must be called if all or a portion of the proceeds of the original issue are not expended on the intended purpose of the issue by a certain date. This type of call is often found in housing revenue issues or similar types of issues. See: REDEMPTION PROVISIONS.

UNIT INVESTMENT TRUST—See: BOND FUND.

UNLIMITED TAX BOND—A general obligation bond secured by a pledge of taxes that are not limited in rate or amount. Compare: LIMITED TAX BOND. See: GENERAL OBLIGATION BOND.

UPGRADE—The raising of a rating by a rating service due to the improved credit quality of the issue or issuer. The term also refers to the replacing of a security in an investment portfolio with one of a higher quality. Compare: DOWNGRADE. See: RATINGS.

U.T.—See: UNLIMITED TAX BOND.

VALIDATION—(1) A procedure whereby a certificate or coupon which has been torn or otherwise damaged ("mutilated") is endorsed as being a valid or binding obligation of the issuer. Validation of damaged certificates is normally done by the issuer or its agent (*e.g.*, the paying agent, trustee, registrar or transfer agent); validation of damaged coupons can also be done by a commercial bank.

(2) A procedure followed in certain states whereby the legality of a proposed issue of securities may be determined in advance of its issuance.

VARIABLE RATE—See: FLOATING RATE.

VARIABLE RATE DEMAND NOTE—See: DEMAND BOND.

VISIBLE SUPPLY—The total dollar volume of securities expected to be offered over the next 30 days. The visible supply, which is compiled and published by *The Bond Buyer*, indicates the near-term activity in the municipal market.

WARRANT—A security, generally sold attached to another security of the same issuer, which gives the owner the right to purchase a third security of the same issuer, described on the warrant, within a stated period of time at a stated price. The warrant generally is detachable and tradable separately from the security with which it was originally sold. Warrants have occasionally been used in the municipal market by a few larger issuers.

WASH SALE—A transaction in which securities are sold for the purpose of establishing a tax loss but are reacquired (or a "substantially identical" security is reacquired) within 30 days prior to or 30 days after the date of the sale. Under such circumstances the deduction of the loss for tax purposes would be disallowed.

WESTERN ACCOUNT—See: SYNDICATE.

"WHEN, AS AND IF ISSUED"—A phrase used to describe the time period in the life of an issue of securities from the original date of the sale by the issuer to the delivery of the securities to, and payment by, the underwriter. Sales made during the "when, as and if issued" period (also called the "when-issued" period") are subject to receipt of the securities from the issuer by the underwriter in good form. The abbreviation "WAII" (or "WI" for "when issued") is also commonly used.

WOODEN TICKET—A confirmation, sent in violation of MSRB and SEC rules, "confirming" the terms of a transaction with a customer which, in fact, did not take place. An unscrupulous dealer might send these fraudulent confirmations to unsophisticated investors on the chance that some investors might mistakenly honor the transactions. The practice of sending wooden tickets is a violation of MSRB fair dealing and SEC anti-fraud rules.

WORKABLE—A bid price at which a dealer states its willingness to purchase securities from another dealer. A dealer soliciting a "workable" often is working to satisfy a customer's order to sell the securities, and will advise the customer of the workable so that the customer can determine whether it wishes to sell the securities. A dealer giving a workable is free to revise its bid for the securities if market conditions change; the workable does represent an indication of willingness to effect a transaction at the stated price, however, and hence is different from a nominal quotation. Compare: NOMINAL QUOTATION; FIRM.

YIELD CURVE—A graph which plots market yields on securities of equivalent quality but different maturities, at a given point in time. The vertical axis represents the yields, while the horizontal axis depicts time to maturity. The term structure of interest rates, as reflected by the yield curve, will vary according to market conditions, resulting in a variety of yield curve configurations, as follows:

Normal or Positive Yield Curve—Indicates that short-term securities have a lower interest rate than long-term securities.

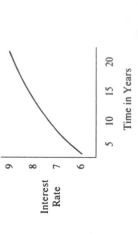

Inverted or Negative Yield Curve—Reflects the situation of short-term rates exceeding long-term rates.

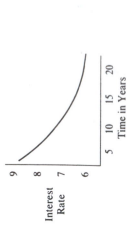

Flat Yield Curve—Reflects the situation when short- and long-term rates are approximately the same.

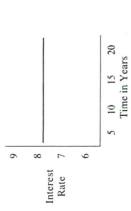

Humpbacked or Bell-Shaped Yield Curve—An unusual shape, indicating that rates are low in the early years, peak in the middle years and decline in later years.

YIELD PRICE—See: BASIS PRICE.

YIELD TO CALL—The rate of return to the investor earned from payments of principal and interest, with interest compounded semi-annually at the stated yield, presuming that the security is redeemed prior to its stated maturity date (if the security is redeemed at a premium call price, the amount of the premium is also reflected in the yield). Compare: YIELD TO MATURITY.

YIELD TO MATURITY—The rate of return to the investor earned from payments of principal and interest, with interest compounded semi-annually at the stated yield, presuming that the security remains outstanding until the maturity date. Yield to maturity takes into account the amount of the premium or discount, if any, and the time value of the investment. Compare: CURRENT YIELD; YIELD TO CALL.

YIELD TO OPTION—A yield to a call at par. Compare: YIELD TO MATURITY. See: YIELD TO CALL.

YIELD TO PUT OPTION—The rate of return to the investor, presuming that the security is put back to the issuer or its agent (or a third party) on a specified date in accordance with the terms of a put option granted by the issuer (or the third party). The investment return reflected in the yield consists of the return of the principal (or the portion of the principal amount payable upon the exercise of the put) and payment of the interest (with the interest compounded semi-annually) to the put date. Compare: YIELD TO CALL.

Z

ZERO COUPON BOND—An original issue discount bond on which no periodic interest payments are made, but which is issued at a deep discount from par, accreting (at the rate represented by the offering yield at issuance) to its full value at maturity. Compare: CAPITAL APPRECIATION BOND. See: ORIGINAL ISSUE DISCOUNT.

Index

About the Editor

GERALD J. MILLER is Associate Professor of Public Administration at Rutgers—The State University of New Jersey in Newark. The author of over 50 research articles, his work has been published in numerous journals in the United States and abroad, including the *Public Administration Review*, the *Policy Studies Journal*, *Public Productivity and Management Review*, the *International Journal of Public Administration*, and the *Public Administration Quarterly*. Having published over 20 books, he is the author of *Government Financial Management*, coeditor of the *Handbook of Strategic Management* and the *Handbook of Public Administration* (both with Jack Rabin and W. Bartley Hildreth), and coeditor of the *Handbook of Public Personnel Administration and Labor Relations*, the *Handbook of Public Sector Labor Relations*, and the *Handbook of Public Personnel Administration* (all with Jack Rabin, Thomas Vocino, and W. Bartley Hildreth [all titles, Marcel Dekker, Inc.]). In addition, he is coauthor of the *Public Budgeting Laboratory* (with Jack Rabin and W. Bartley Hildreth) and coeditor of *Managerial Behavior and Organization Demands* (with Robert T. Golembiewski and Frank K. Gibson) and *Budget Management* and *Budgeting: Formulation and Execution* (both with Jack Rabin and W. Bartley Hildreth). He is an editorial board member of the *International Journal of Public Administration* (Marcel Dekker, Inc.), the *Municipal Finance Journal*, *Public Productivity and Management Review*, the *Journal of Public Management*, and the *Journal of Health and Human Resources Administration*. He also serves as a book review editor for the *Public Administration Quarterly*. As a former investment banker with the firm of Rauscher, Pierce, Refsnes, Inc., Phoenix, Arizona, Dr. Miller continues an active consulting practice in the United States, Canada, and Western Europe with clients including national, state, and local government organizations in legislative, executive, and judicial branches of government, as well as private business and business and public sector associations. His research seeks understanding and asserts the dominance of resource allocation in the control of public organizations; his work has received continuous and substantial support from government and private donors in the United States, Canada, England, Wales, and the European Union. Dr. Miller received the B.S. degree in economics and the M.P.A. degree from Auburn University, Alabama, and the Ph.D. degree in political science from the University of Georgia, Athens.